BUSINESS ETHICS

D1540731

Readings and Cases in Corporate Morality

FOURTH EDITION

W. Michael Hoffman

Bentley College
Center for Business Ethics

Robert E. Frederick

Bentley College
Center for Business Ethics

Mark S. Schwartz

York University
Schulich School of Business
and
University of Pennsylvania
The Wharton School

Boston   Burr Ridge, IL   Dubuque, IA   Madison, WI   New York   San Francisco   St. Louis
Bangkok   Bogotá   Caracas   Lisbon   London   Madrid
Mexico City   Milan   New Delhi   Seoul   Singapore   Sydney   Taipei   Toronto

McGraw-Hill Higher Education

A Division of The **McGraw-Hill** *Companies*

BUSINESS ETHICS: READINGS AND CASES IN CORPORATE MORALITY
FOURTH EDITION

Published by McGraw-Hill, an imprint of The McGraw-Hill Companies, Inc., 1221 Avenue of the Americas, New York, NY 10020. Copyright © 2001, 1995, 1990, 1984 by The McGraw-Hill Companies, Inc. All rights reserved. No part of this publication may be reproduced or distributed in any form or by any means, or stored in a database or retrieval system, without the prior written consent of The McGraw-Hill Companies, Inc., including, but not limited to, in any network or other electronic storage or transmission, or broadcast for distance learning.

Some ancillaries, including electronic and print components, may not be available to customers outside the United States.

This book is printed on acid-free paper.

1 2 3 4 5 6 7 8 9 0 DOC/DOC 0 9 8 7 6 5 4 3 2 1 0

ISBN 0–07–229724–7

Vice president and editor-in-chief: *Thalia Dorwick*
Editorial director: *Jane E. Vaicunas*
Sponsoring editor: *Monica Eckman*
Editorial coordinator: *Hannah Glover*
Senior marketing manager: *Daniel M. Loch*
Project manager: *Mary Lee Harms*
Production supervisor: *Laura Fuller*
Coordinator of freelance design: *David W. Hash*
Cover designer: *Joshua Van Drake*
Cover illustration: © *Tim Lewis/Laughing Stock*
Compositor: *Shepherd, Inc.*
Typeface: *10/11.5 Times Roman*
Printer: *R. R. Donnelley & Sons Company/Crawfordsville, IN*

Library of Congress Cataloging-in-Publication Data

Business ethics: readings and cases in corporate morality / [edited by] W. Michael Hoffman, Robert E. Frederick, Mark S. Schwartz. — 4th ed.
    p. cm.
  ISBN 0–07–229724–7
  1. Business ethics.   2. Business ethics—Case studies.   I. Hoffman, W. Michael.
II. Frederick, Robert E.   III. Schwartz, Mark S.

HF5387 .B873   2001
174'.4—dc21
                                      00–036131
                                        CIP

www.mhhe.com

ABOUT THE AUTHORS

W. MICHAEL HOFFMAN is founder and executive director of the Center for Business Ethics at Bentley College in Waltham, Massachusetts, a 25-year-old research and consulting institute and educational forum for the exchange of ideas and information in business ethics. Dr. Hoffman received his Ph.D. in philosophy at the University of Massachusetts in 1972 and is professor of philosophy at Bentley College. Dr. Hoffman has authored or edited sixteen books and has published over sixty articles. He also serves as a consultant on business ethics for corporations and institutions of higher learning and as an expert witness on business ethics in litigation. Dr. Hoffman is a past National Endowment for the Humanities Fellow and consultant, a lecturer at universities and conferences, and a member of many journal editorial boards. He was a founder and president of the Society for Business Ethics, served on the advisory board of the U.S. Sentencing Commission, and is frequently sought out globally for professional lectures and media interviews.

ROBERT E. FREDERICK is associate professor and chair of the department of philosophy at Bentley College and research scholar at the Center for Business Ethics. In the past he served as assistant director of the Center. Dr. Frederick received his Ph.D. in philosophy from Brown University. He has published articles in business and environmental ethics and in other fields of philosophy. He is the editor of the journal *Business and Society Review,* and he sits on the editorial board of several other journals.

MARK S. SCHWARTZ is lecturer of business ethics at the Wharton School of the University of Pennsylvania. Previously, he was co-director of the Joint M.B.A./LL.B. Program, coordinator of business law, and lecturer of business law and business ethics at the Schulich School of Business, York University (Toronto,

Canada). He is a lawyer in the Province of Ontario and graduated from the Joint M.B.A./LL.B. Program at Osgoode Hall Law School and the Schulich School of Business in 1991. He received his Ph.D. from the Schulich School of Business in 1999, focusing on the subject of business ethics. He is a research fellow for the Center for Business Ethics, Bentley College, and has consulted for a number of companies on business ethics-related matters.

CONTENTS

PREFACE

The preface to the first edition of *Business Ethics: Readings and Cases in Corporate Morality* began with advice from Cicero's *De Officiis*: "To everyone who proposes to have a good career, moral philosophy is indispensable." Cicero's words are as true and as timely as ever, and the fourth edition of this text represents our continuing commitment to the union of ethics and business.

The field of business ethics has grown tremendously since 1984, when the first edition was released. At that time, business ethics had just begun to gain momentum. Today it is a mature field. In a 1988 report, the Business Roundtable referred to corporate ethics as "a prime business asset," and corporations have begun to take significant steps toward integrating ethical values into their corporate cultures. In fact, the Center for Business Ethics at Bentley College was the facilitating institution for a newly formed organization made up of practicing ethics officers of major corporations. The American Assembly of Collegiate Schools of Business has strengthened its call for grounding in ethics as one of the essential elements of sound business education. Literature in business ethics continues to grow and deepen.

In the fourth edition of *Business Ethics*, we have attempted to include both the best new thinking on ethical issues in business and the first, second, and third edition's time-tested favorites. The goals of the text remain the same. We have tried to be comprehensive. In our coverage of the issues, we have selected what we believe to be the most important currently debated moral concerns in the field. We have retained many of the topics from the third edition and have added new material on issues such as workplace snooping and women in the workplace. All of the chapters have been revised to some extent. We have added a completely new chapter addressing emerging ethical issues in business, including such topics as the individual investor, accounting fraud, the ethics of the information age, and competitive intelligence. The final section of the moral corporation has been extensively revised and now includes material on the ethics of caring as well as moral leadership. Many cases from the third edition remain, but we have included timely new cases such as those on Texaco's discrimination lawsuit, Aaron Feuerstein and Malden Mills, and Magnum Industries, a gun manufacturer. We have also added a new feature to the fourth edition, a series of mini-cases, two for each of the five parts. The mini-cases add another means for readers to consider and discuss ethical issues faced by individuals in business.

As with earlier editions, we have tried to be impartial. The format of the text, wherever appropriate, is point/counterpoint, and we have included the strongest statements we could find of different perspectives on the issues. We have made an effort to include articles by thinkers from a wide range of constituencies—not just academics, but representatives from a variety of other professions.

Finally, we have tried to be systematic. We have retained the basic organization of earlier editions. We begin with theoretical, structural, or more widely focused issues such as economic justice, the justice of economic systems, and the nature and responsibility of business. These give a framework for discussion and understanding of more specific, concrete issues such as employee rights, the ethics of marketing and consumer protection, environmental ethics, and multinational issues. We conclude with a chapter on the development of the moral corporation of the future. Of course, the book may be used in many different ways. Some instructors may prefer to save the more abstract topics for the end of their course. We believe that the book lends itself readily to organizational variations.

The fourth edition continues to include an introduction to each part that sets out the major themes of the articles and places them in context. This new edition also includes brief introductions to the mini-cases and cases, and point out which articles might be most directly relevant to them. A set of discussion questions follows each chapter. These can be used as a focus for student discussion, review, tests, quizzes, or student assignments.

Hoffman and Frederick are delighted to have Mark Schwartz from the Schulich School of Business, York University (Toronto, Canada) and a Fellow of the Center for Business Ethics at Bentley College join us in the preparation of this edition of *Business Ethics.*

We would like to express our appreciation to Bentley College for its support of this and other projects in business ethics. From the Center for Business Ethics at Bentley College, thanks go to Mary Chiasson, administrative coordinator, Patricia Aucoin, administrative secretary, Neil Moir, research assistant, and Mollie Painter-Morland, research assistant. Thanks also go to Donna Coveney, secretary of the Bentley College Department of Philosophy.

Finally, we are grateful to the following scholars for their reviews of earlier versions of this book: William C. Gentry, Henderson State University; Charles T. Hughes, Chapman University; William L. Langenfus, John Carroll University; Christopher P. Mooney, Nassau Community College; Jon W. Nelson, University of Nebraska at Kearney; and Richard Srb, Middlesex Community Technical College. We also gratefully acknowledge the reviewers of this edition: Chris Pines, University of Rio Grande; Michael W. Martin, Chapman University; William Pamerleau, University of Pittsburgh at Greensburg; Mitchell Gabhart, Auburn University; Glenn A. Moots, Northwood University; John Rowan, Purdue University-Calumet; WB Griffith, George Washington University; John DuFour, College of Santa Fe; and Denis Arnold, Pacific Lutheran University.

W. Michael Hoffman, Robert E. Frederick, Mark S. Schwartz

INTRODUCTION

THE NATURE OF BUSINESS ETHICS

Business is a complex web of human relationships—relationships between manufacturers and consumers, employers and employees, managers and stockholders, members of corporations and members of communities in which those corporations operate. These are economic relationships, created by the exchange of goods and services; but they are also moral relationships. Questions concerning profit, growth, and technological advance have ethical dimensions. These include the effects of pollution and depletion of natural resources on society at large, the quality and character of the work environment, and the safety of consumers. As an anthology in business ethics, this text proposes to explore the moral dimension of business.

Ethics may be defined as the study of what is good or right for human beings. It asks what goals people ought to pursue and what actions they ought to perform. Business ethics is a branch of applied ethics; it studies the relationship of what is good and right to business.[1]

But how do we know what is right or wrong or good or bad for business? Before discussing in more detail the content of the various ethical principles, it might be helpful to clarify what ethics is not.

Ethics and Etiquette: For some, ethics or morality is confused with the notion of etiquette. In most cases etiquette refers to behavior that is considered socially acceptable, as opposed to morally right or wrong. Concepts such as politeness, manners, one's dress, or rules of conduct might be associated with etiquette. For example, etiquette might require one to use a handkerchief upon sneezing or to shake the hand of a person one is meeting for the first time. There may be cases, though, when proper etiquette can cross over the line into the domain of morality. For example, in some countries acceptance of gifts might be considered proper etiquette, although arguments can be raised that such activity is unethical.

Ethics and the Law: Typically, the law tends to reflect or embody the moral norms of society, and on this basis it can be suggested that what is legal is also ethical. Although ethics and the law often overlap, this may not always be the case. Some laws could be considered amoral, such as driving on the right-hand or left-hand side of the road. Many acts that are legal might still be considered to be unethical, however, such as receiving gifts from suppliers, conducting personal business on company time, or invading one's privacy. Still, in other cases, laws themselves may be determined to be unethical, such as the previous apartheid laws in South Africa, or the previous racial discrimination laws in the United States. For this reason, it is important to realized that the law does not always equal ethics, and in most cases merely sets out the minimum standards of expected behavior.

Ethics and Religion: In a number of respects, ethics and religion are related to each other. Many of our ethical prescriptions, such as don't kill or steal, derive from religious doctrine. The "golden rule," or "Do unto others as you would want done to yourself," can be found expressed in some form across most religions. Although ethics and religion often overlap, this is also not always the case. Certain religious prescriptions have been considered by others to be immoral or unethical, such as religious decrees prohibiting abortion or euthanasia. Certain religious prescriptions regarding the role of women in society have also been considered by others as being immoral or unethical. One must therefore be careful before necessarily accepting that ethics and religion are one and the same.

It is sometimes said that business and ethics don't mix. In business, some argue, profit takes precedence. Business has its own rules and objectives, so ethical concepts, standards, and judgments are inappropriate in the context of business. But this view is fundamentally mistaken. Business is an economic institution, but like our economy as a whole, it has a moral foundation. The free market system reflects our convictions about the nature of the good life and the good society, about the fair distribution of goods and services, and about what kinds of goods and services to distribute. It is true that the goal of business has been profit, but profit making is not a morally neutral activity. Traditionally, we have encouraged business to pursue profits because we believed—rightly or wrongly—that profit seeking violates no rights and is best for society as a whole. This conviction has been the source of business' legitimacy, our belief in its right to exist. In the past two decades, however, the belief that business makes an entirely positive contribution to the general welfare has been challenged. For many, business' connection with the moral foundation that justified it no longer seems clear. Distrust of business has increased; recent polls, for example, indicate that Americans believe the ethical standards of business are lower than those of society as a whole. Many thinkers contend that business faces a crisis of legitimacy. In such a climate, an investigation of business values, of the moral dimension of business, and of the role of business in society becomes urgent. To undertake such an investigation is the task of business ethics. This anthology approaches this task on four levels:

1. An ethical investigation of the context in which American business is conducted—that is, capitalism or the free market system. Does the system truly contribute to a good society and reflect our most important social values? In particular, is it a just system, one that reflects our beliefs about the fair distribution of goods and services? The selections included in Part One of this text explore the meaning of justice in a modern economy, and the question of whether capitalism embodies that ideal. It also suggests some specific ways in which ethical values have operated or should operate in business decision making.
2. An inquiry, within this broad economic context, into the nature and role of business organizations. Is the function of business activity simply to make a profit? Do busi-

nesses have other obligations because of their vast power or relationship to other elements of society? How might corporate structures best reflect the nature and responsibilities of corporations? Such questions are taken up in Part Two of this text.

3. An examination of particular ethical issues that arise in the course of business activity, such as employee rights and duties, relationships in working life, hiring practices, advertising and product safety, obligations to the environment, and operating in foreign countries. A range of such issues is covered in Parts Three and Four.

4. An examination and ethical assessment of the values that reside implicitly in business organizations and business activity in general, such as freedom of opportunity, economic growth, and material well-being. We pursue this endeavor throughout the text, and in Part Five we examine several emerging ethical issues and reflect on the future of the moral corporation.

Engaging in ethical reflection on business at each of these levels requires using ethical concepts, theories, and standards of judgment. The remainder of this introduction presents some of the most important principles of ethical theory. To provide a context for discussion of these principles, we begin with a brief history of the field of business ethics. We then discuss the types of business decisions we can make.

BRIEF HISTORY OF BUSINESS ETHICS

How has the field of business ethics developed over time? Is it merely a passing management fad? This hardly appears to be the case. Certainly ethics in business has been an issue since the very first business transaction. For example, the Code of Hammurabi, created nearly four thousand years ago, records that Mesopotamian rulers attempted to create honest prices. During the fourth century B.C., Aristotle discusses the vices and virtues of tradesmen and merchants. The Old Testament and the Jewish Talmud discuss the proper way to conduct business, including topics such as fraud, theft, proper weights and measures, competition and free entry, misleading advertising, just prices, and environment issues. The New Testament and the Islamic Koran also discuss business ethics as it relates to poverty and wealth. Throughout the history of commerce, these codes have had an impact on business dealings. During the nineteenth century, the creation of monopolies and the use of slavery were important business ethics issues, which continue to be debated up until today.

In recent times, business ethics has moved through several stages of development. Prior to the 1960s, business was primarily considered to be an amoral activity; concepts like ethics and social responsibility were rarely mentioned. During the 1960s, a number of social issues in business began to emerge, including civil rights, the environment, safety in the workplace, and consumer issues. During the 1970s, the field of business ethics took hold in academia, with most U.S. schools offering a course in business ethics by 1980. From 1980 to 1985 the business ethics field continued to consolidate, with journals, research centres, and conferences taking place. From 1985 to 1995 business ethics became integrated into large corporations, with the development of codes of ethics, ethics training, ethics hotlines, and ethics officers. Since 1995, issues related to international business activity have come to the forefront, including issues of bribery and corruption, and the use of child and slave labor abroad.

Let's now look at an example of the kind of ethical decision individuals sometimes face in business.

TYPES OF BUSINESS DECISIONS

The Amalgamated Machinery Dilemma

Ted Brown is worried. A salesman for Amalgamated Machinery, he is in charge of negotiating an important sale of construction equipment to the government of a small but rapidly developing nation. Deeply in debt, Amalgamated has staked its future on penetrating foreign markets. And Ted's potential contract not only is a very large one, it also could open the door to even bigger sales in the future. If he lands the contract, Ted's future in the firm is bright—and he was convinced he would get the contract until he spoke with a powerful government official who is involved in the negotiations. Ted's bid, the official explained, is regarded very favorably. In fact, it is the lowest. All that is needed to clinch the deal is a $100,000 "commission fee" payable in cash to the official. If Ted does not pay the fee, the official regrets that the contract will go to a competitor.

Ted knows that the sale is crucial for his company. He believes that his customers would get the best possible deal by buying Amalgamated's equipment. And he knows that $100,000 is a relatively small sum compared with the potential profits represented by the contract. Yet, although he is aware that such payments are not unusual in many countries, he has always felt that they were wrong, and has never before used them to secure a deal.

Ted Brown's dilemma is fictitious, but it is not farfetched. It illustrates a problem business people often face: Should the interests of the firm override personal convictions about the right thing to do, or should one always act on one's personal convictions despite the consequences for the firm? Clearly, Ted's decision will not be easy. How should he go about deciding what to do? And if Ted were to ask you for advice, what would you say?

One thing you might point out is that Ted needs to understand the kind of decision he is making. Although he can only do one of two things—either pay the $100,000 or not—he can formulate his decision from at least three distinct perspectives or points of view.

1. Which is the better decision from a *business* point of view?
2. Which is the better decision from a *legal* point of view?
3. Which is the better decision from a *moral* point of view?

A second point is that in most (but not all) cases, when someone decides to do something that he or she regards as important, the decision to act comes at the end of a process of deliberation. And to deliberate about an action is (roughly) to weigh the reasons for doing it according to some standard or principle. Such standards or principles have two important features. First, they are supposed to apply to all decisions of a certain kind regardless of who makes the decision. Second, they purport to differentiate between better and worse decisions of that kind. For example, if Ted were to decide from a business point of view he would weigh the reasons for paying or not paying according to a principle that differentiates between better and worse business decisions. Often that principle is assumed to be this: In every business undertaking, one ought to do whatever maximizes long-term profits. So if Ted believes that the decision should be made from a business point of view, and if he were to judge that paying the bribe would maximize long-term profits, he would pay up.

Suppose, however, Ted believes that the decision should be made from a legal point of view. Now the principle might be this: For any action to which the law applies, one ought not do that act if it is illegal. As anyone familiar with the law knows, determining whether a specific act is legal or not can be difficult. But assume Ted decides that it is illegal to make the payment. Then the principle instructs him not to pay. On the other hand, suppose he decides it is legal. Should he pay? Not necessarily. The standard only says "If something is illegal, don't do it." It doesn't say "If it is legal, do it." So, in a sense the legal principle is incomplete. Once Ted decides that the act is legal, it has nothing further to tell him about what is best to do.

The third way that Ted could make his decision—the one we will be most concerned with in this introduction—is from a moral point of view. What is it to decide from a moral point of view? If we follow the model just presented, it is to evaluate the reasons, to deliberate, about doing one thing rather than another according to some moral standard or principle that differentiates between better and worse moral decisions. So to decide from a moral point of view we need, first, to know what kind of moral principles there are; second, what kind of reasons are relevant to moral action; and third, how to evaluate those reasons in light of the principle. For example, suppose the moral principle Ted accepts is this: One always ought to do what is in one's own self-interest. Then he would consider the reasons for believing that paying the bribe, or not paying, is in his best interest. Suppose, for example, that after analyzing the business aspects of paying the bribe he finds that paying would maximize profit. This could be to his advantage since a firm that places a high value on profit is also likely to place high value on employees who contribute to profit. However, if the bribe is illegal, and if it is discovered that Ted paid the bribe, he would be in trouble. The authorities would probably impose a heavy fine on the firm, and this would not endear Ted to upper management. Furthermore, Ted might face legal sanctions himself. It seems, then, that if Ted wants to do what is in his own best interest, he has a lot of thinking to do. Making the correct decision from a moral point of view will not be easy.

In fact, it is characteristic of moral decisions that they are not easy. There are three main reasons for this. First, much more often than not, moral decisions are important. They affect our lives and the lives of others in significant ways. Second, moral decisions are complex. Frequently no obvious or easy solution presents itself, and it is not unusual for there to be several alternatives that seem equally reasonable. Finally, there is often deep disagreement about which moral principle should be applied to the decision. Different people may have very different ideas about which standard is appropriate. To take a (slightly modified) famous example, suppose someone, call him Paul, faces the problem of either leaving home and joining the forces defending his country from invasion by an evil empire, or staying home and comforting his mother through the last stages of a debilitating and fatal illness. Should he go or stay?

Suppose Paul accepts Ted's moral standard: One always ought to do what is in one's own best interest. And suppose Paul decides that it is in his best interest, all things considered, to avoid the problem altogether. So he decides to relieve his mother of what small savings she has accumulated and purchase a ticket on the next plane leaving for a more peaceful and prosperous kingdom. Surely, he reasons, this would be better for him than risking his life in a war or dawdling about waiting for an old woman to die.

Most people would probably be outraged by Paul's decision. Some might argue that he has duties to his mother that override his self-interest. Others might say that he should promote the common good of his fellow citizens by defending his homeland. And still others would say that his decision shows character flaws such as cowardice and ingratitude. Each of these responses makes implicit appeal to a different ethical viewpoint—a different way of understanding what Paul ought to do. In the pages to come we will discuss each of these viewpoints. But before we do so we will return briefly to the three different ways that Ted can understand his decision.

THE PROBLEM OF CONFLICTING DECISION-MAKING RULES

We said that Ted can understand his decision from a business, legal, or ethical point of view. The question naturally arises: Which should he choose? The question would not be hard to answer were there never any possibility of conflict between them, that is, if the best business decision were always and at the same time the best legal and ethical decision. But there is a possibility of conflict. For example, it might maximize profits to pay the bribe even if it is illegal and immoral. And bribery might be immoral even if not illegal. So the best thing to do from a moral point of view need not be the best thing to do from a business or legal point of view. On the other hand, conflict is not always present. In many cases, perhaps in most cases, the best business decision will also be legally and morally acceptable. In addition, a growing body of empirical evidence has emerged suggesting that "Good ethics is good business," or at least that "Bad ethics is bad business."[2] But when conflict is present, we need some way to decide what to do. For example, companies which base their decision making on what is the best business decision, will inevitably engage in unethical activity when it is profitable to do so.

To resolve potential conflicts, consider the following rules:

1. Whenever there is a conflict between ethics and the law, one ought always do what the law requires.
2. Whenever there is a conflict between ethics and business principles, one ought always do what business principles require.

These rules tell us what to do in situations in which ethical and legal or business principles give different instructions. Thus, they resolve cases of conflict between ethics and law, and ethics and business. But should we follow them? Might there be circumstances in which it would be wrong to follow them?

There are many examples that seem to show that ethical obligations can outweigh legal obligations, and that in certain circumstances it is permissible to break the law. For instance, in the American civil rights movement, laws were deliberately broken when it appeared that no other alternative was available to change an intolerable situation. These laws, such as laws preventing blacks from voting, were clearly unjust. They perpetuated and enforced social arrangements that were deliberately intended to deprive blacks and other minorities of the opportunity to participate meaningfully in the economic, educational, and political system. Since many legislatures were controlled by persons unwilling to change the laws, civil disobedience was, in our view, both justified and necessary.

Two things follow from this example. First, in some circumstances breaking the law is justified. Such circumstances may be rare, but they do occur. Second, the justification for such acts derives from ethical principles, for example, principles of justice. Thus rule number 1 is not acceptable as a general rule for resolving conflicts between the law and ethics. Sometimes we ought to follow ethical principles even though what we do is against the law.

There are also many cases, a number of them in this book, which seem to show that ethical principles sometimes take precedence over the business principle of maximizing profit. For instance, suppose a paper company were to move to a country that has few laws protecting the environment. To minimize costs, and thus enhance profits, the company legally dumps the toxic waste it produces into a nearby river. Eventually this causes health problems for the local inhabitants. The company's actions may be both legal and warranted by considerations of profit. In our view, however, they are ethically unacceptable. Corporate profit does not justify causing harm to persons, particularly when such harm is both foreseeable and preventable.

If this is correct, then profit maximization in business is not always justified. And on occasion the justification for not doing so derives from ethical principles, for example, the principle that one should not cause preventable harm. Thus, rule number 2 is not acceptable as a general principle for resolving conflicts between ethical and business principles. Sometimes one should follow ethical principles even when profit suffers.

The preceding examples show that legal and business principles do not always take precedence over ethical principles. But the examples do not show that ethics always comes first. That is, they do not show that

3. Whenever there is a conflict between ethical principles and business or legal principles, one ought always do what ethical principles require.

Should we accept rule number 3? If someone were to do so, then for that person obeying the law and maximizing profits would always be secondary to ethics. As we will see, many philosophers have defended ethical principles that imply rule number 3 or something very close to it. The content of these principles, and the arguments for them, is our next topic.

ETHICAL SUBJECTIVISM

Understanding Subjectivism

Ethical subjectivism is a viewpoint that is sometimes expressed as "What is right for me may not be right for you." This statement is open to various interpretations. For instance, it could mean the following: Given our different circumstances, it would be morally right for me to do X, but it would not be morally right for you to do X. Suppose, for example, that Smith is very wealthy and Brown is very poor. Then it might be morally right for Smith annually to donate a considerable sum to charity, but wrong for Brown to do so because it would deprive her children of basic necessities. Understood this way, the statement highlights an important truth, namely, that the morally correct decision often depends on the circumstances of the person making it. If the circumstances of different persons are very different, then the right decision for them may be different even though they accept the same moral standards.

The statement might also mean this: What I think is right may not be what you think is right. Once again this expresses a truth, for, as the debate over abortion abundantly shows, there are many disagreements about what is ethically right.

Neither of the interpretations mentioned so far is objectionable. But there is a third interpretation that is much more controversial. It is this: The correct ethical principle for me may not be the correct ethical principle for you. Unlike the other two interpretations, this one is not obviously true. One reason it is not true, many people would argue, is that ethical principles such as "Do unto others as you would have them do unto you" apply to everyone. Whether all ethical principles apply to everyone is a difficult issue that we will discuss briefly later. However, we will try to show that subjectivism is not an acceptable account of ethics even if ethical principles do not apply universally. To explain why, we must examine it in more detail. We begin with a basic statement of the subjectivist position:

> Ethical Subjectivism: What is ethically right or wrong is strictly a matter for individuals to decide based on ethical principles they have chosen. This is because (1) each individual is the sole judge of whether the principle he or she has chosen is the right one for him or her, and (2) each individual is the sole judge of whether his or her action is ethically permissible according to his or her principle.

If ethical subjectivism is true, then what is ethically right or wrong is entirely a personal matter. Each person is the single source and only authority concerning the selection and applicability of his or her own moral standards. There are no valid public standards of moral accountability—no standards that apply to more than one person, except insofar as different people choose the same principle by chance. For example, suppose Green and Robinson are thinking about whether some action X is morally permissible. Based on standards he has chosen, Green decides it is permissible and does X. Based on standards she has chosen, Robinson decides X is not morally permissible and does not do it. If Robinson accepts the argument just given, she is in no position to say to Green "What you did is ethically wrong." Since she acknowledges that each person is sovereign in his or her choice of ethical principles, and that each person is the exclusive judge of whether his or her action conforms to the principle, the best she can do is say "What you did is wrong according to my standards." But this is simply a statement of fact. It makes no moral evaluation of Green's action.

Subjectivism has great appeal in our diverse society where all persons are expected to think seriously about ethical issues and to come to their own conclusions. Furthermore, within limits they have a right to express and to act on those conclusions. We expect that even when citizens very seriously disagree with each other, each will treat the other with respect. Ethical subjectivism seems to capture this attitude of tolerance and respect for diversity.

First Objection to Subjectivism

An objection to ethical subjectivism is that it has unacceptable consequences. For example, in the Smith and Brown example given above, it was said to be ethically permissible for Smith to give a large sum to charity, but not ethically permissible for Brown because it would deprive her children of basic necessities. This judgment rests on the ethical standard "It is wrong for parents voluntarily to deprive their children of basic necessities." But suppose Brown is an ethical subjectivist and that she accepts quite a different standard, one such as "I should give to charity regardless of how it affects the welfare of my relations." Then from her point of view it would be ethically right for her to give to charity; indeed, it would be wrong of her to choose not to give on the grounds that her children would suffer.

One would think that Brown should have moral commitments to the welfare of her children that place reasonable restrictions on her choice of other ethical principles. She should accept principles that confirm those commitments and reject those that ignore them. However, since Brown is an ethical subjectivist, there are in principle no constraints on her choice of ethical principles other than the ones she accepts. If she chooses principles compatible with the welfare of her children, well and good. If not, then, if one is an ethical subjectivist, there is no moral reason to complain of her choice.

The main point of the Brown example is this. Ethical subjectivism places no limitations on the *content* of the principles individuals choose. It is consistent with subjectivism that individuals choose principles that license behavior detrimental to the interests and welfare of people, that ignore their rights, and that abjure personal responsibility. So Brown can choose to ignore the welfare of her children, or accept other principles such as "It is permissible for me to lie when I want to" and violate no stricture of ethical subjectivism. In short, as far as subjectivism is concerned, *any* behavior by an individual is ethically permissible as long as the behavior is permitted by a principle that individual has chosen.

But this cannot be correct. It is an unacceptable consequence of subjectivism that it places no restrictions on the kind of ethical principle an individual might select. Principles of the sort just mentioned for example, ones that permit harm to others, are not ethical principles; rather, they are anti-ethical principles. They are the antithesis of ethics. It may be true that the ethical principles a person lives by are ultimately chosen by that individual, but it does not follow from this that any principle an individual might choose is rendered ethically acceptable by the mere fact that it was chosen. Persons can choose principles of evil as well as good. Since ethical subjectivism does not distinguish between such choices, it is not an acceptable account of ethics.

Second Objection to Subjectivism

Suppose a subjectivist were to respond to our argument as follows: You may be right that choosing evil principles is compatible with subjectivism, but that has nothing to do with me. My principles are good, not evil, so your argument is not relevant to the choices I have made. I have no qualms about being a subjectivist. It is those other people that you need to worry about.

This response points to a second and equally important reason to reject subjectivism. To see what it is, suppose we were to ask Brown why she follows a principle that obligates her to give to charity at the expense of her children's welfare. She could give one of two answers. The first is that the choice was arbitrary. There is no reason why she chose that principle instead of another one. Since her choice is arbitrary, tomorrow she might decide, again for no reason, to select a different principle. Arbitrary choices imply no commitment. Since they are made for no reason, there is no reason not to change them on a whim.

People who make arbitrary choices that affect their interests and welfare, or the interests and welfare of other people, are not rational. Since one can never tell what they might do from one minute to the next, the best policy for the rest of us would be to avoid them whenever possible so that we are not harmed by their unpredictable actions. A subjectivist who arbitrarily chooses principles that guide his or her behavior would be a dangerous person. And he or she would not be someone who takes the importance and complexity of moral decisions seriously.

A subjectivist might reply that *of course* the choice was not made arbitrarily. It is based on reasons, which is the second of the two possible answers mentioned previously. And the reasons cannot be arbitrary. Otherwise they could be changed on a whim, and the same problem would occur. They must be good reasons. But what is a good reason?

A complete answer would take us far beyond the bounds of this introduction. At least we know, however, that a good reason is not an arbitrary reason. So it would help if we knew more about the difference between good reasons and arbitrary reasons. Let us try this. The mark of a good reason—one that is not arbitrary—is that it withstands scrutiny and criticism by other reasonable people. Put another way, the goodness, so to speak, of a good reason is public in the sense that it is open to inspection and evaluation by more than one person. Thus, if a subjectivist offers good reasons for choosing an ethical principle, those reasons are available for other people to judge. If they judge that the reasons offered are not good, then a subjectivist can do one of three things. First, she might try to convince people that the reasons are good after all. Second, she might try to find different reasons that support her choice and are judged good. Finally, she might abandon her choice of ethical principles. What she cannot do, and still maintain that her choice is based on good reasons, is refuse to defend or modify her position. Were she to do so she would be deciding arbitrarily, which is something she is committed not to do.

Is engaging in a public process of evaluating reasons for choosing ethical standards compatible with ethical subjectivism? The answer is clearly "no." For subjectivists the choice of ethical standards is supposed to be entirely personal. No person, other than the one making the choice, has any legitimate say in the matter. But subjectivists are committed to giving good reasons for their choice. Since good reasons are public, not private, other people do have a role in judging the worth of reasons. If the reasons offered are not good, subjectivists cannot refuse to modify their position without violating their own intellectual commitments. Hence, the choice is not entirely private. Other people are involved in the process.

This is the second problem with subjectivism. It is unacceptable because it is inconsistent. On the one hand, subjectivists claim that the choice of ethical standards is completely personal. On the other, if they claim that their choice of principles is based on good reasons, they acknowledge that other people have a role to play in the choice. They cannot have it both ways; at least, not if they claim that subjectivism is a rational ethical viewpoint.

There are two ways that subjectivists could try to avoid this conclusion. The first is to say that the choice of principles is arbitrary, and not based on good reasons. But, as we argued earlier, this position is also irrational. The second is to provide a plausible account of good reasons that does not make the reasons for choosing ethical principles open to public evaluation. No subjectivist has attempted this, nor, we suggest, would a subjectivist be likely to succeed were he or she to try. We conclude, then, that subjectivism is not a defensible ethical view.

Recall for a moment the subjectivist's complaint that she has chosen good principles, so the argument that subjectivism has unacceptable consequences does not apply to her. We can now see where her complaint goes wrong. A good ethical principle, whatever else it might be, is one that is acceptable for good reasons. And what counts as a good reason is in large part determined by public standards. The public nature of ethics is inescapable. It cannot be, as subjectivists would have it, an entirely private matter.

CHARACTERISTICS OF DISCUSSIONS ABOUT ETHICS

Let us stop for a moment and review the discussion of ethical subjectivism. We began by trying to give a clear statement of subjectivism. We then tried to show that subjectivism has implausible consequences. To avoid these consequences we attempted to modify the original statement of subjectivism. But this failed because the modification led to an inconsistency: the inconsistency that for a subjectivist the choice of ethical principles both is and is not an entirely personal matter. Thus, we claimed, subjectivism should be rejected.

In the pages to come, the general pattern of this discussion will be repeated, sometimes with slight alterations, in the analysis of other ethical principles and viewpoints. The reason is that underlying the pattern are several common assumptions and shared ideas about how to judge the validity and adequacy of ethical principles or viewpoints. These assumptions and ideas provide a context for the debate about ethics. They are the "rules of the game" that prevent it from degenerating into a pointless shouting match. It is important to know something about them for two reasons. First, it is much easier to follow the debate when one understands the rules. In the context of the rules the pattern of the discussion makes sense. And it makes sense of why some points for or against a certain ethical principle are thought to be more telling than others. Second, not all persons who try to be a part of the discussion accept all the rules. They are playing a different game, which explains why the things they say about ethics may seem so peculiar.

We have divided the assumptions and ideas into three categories. The first category is essential for any discussion, regardless of the topic.

1. All parties to the debate are rational in the minimal sense that (a) they believe it is relevant and appropriate to give reasons for what one believes, (b) if given good reasons for believing something, reasons that withstand public scrutiny, then, *ceteris paribus,* they will believe it, and (c) they are able to see that statements have logical consequences—they recognize that if some statements are true (or false), other statements are true (or false).

2. No logically inconsistent position is rationally acceptable. To have a logically inconsistent belief amounts to believing that some statement both is and is not true. Logically inconsistent ethical beliefs are not rationally acceptable because they will entail, for every action, both that it is ethically right or good and that it is not ethically right or good.

The second category relates more directly to ethics. It has to do with the nature of ethical judgments, and with the kinds of reasons relevant to ethical judgments.

3. Ethical judgments apply primarily to the actions of moral agents. The paradigm example of a moral agent is a person who is rational and who has enough intelligence and background information about the world to recognize that (a) persons have interests and welfare that can be enhanced or harmed, and (b) certain actions are likely to have consequences affecting the interests and welfare of persons. If someone, for example, a child, does not fit this characterization of a moral agent, then his or her actions are not properly subject to ethical judgments.

4. Ethical judgments are a part of a public system for evaluating actions of moral agents that affect themselves or other persons. Actions are evaluated as ethically right or wrong, good or bad, or praiseworthy or blameworthy. These evaluations are made according to reasons and principles subject to public appraisal. Thus, whether an evaluation is fitting or not is also open to public inspection and appraisal. Just as one's choice of ethical principles is an appropriate topic of public debate, so one's evaluation of an act is an appropriate topic of public debate.

5. Since ethical judgments are about actions of moral agents that affect the interests and welfare of persons, statements that describe the interests and welfare of persons, or describe or anticipate the effects of acts on interests and welfare, are relevant to ethical

judgments. These statements (if true) are morally relevant facts. In conjunction with ethical principles, these facts give us reasons for acting one way rather than another. In addition, statements describing the intentions, motives, and character of moral agents are relevant to ethical judgments. Such statements are vital for understanding the reasons for an action, and understanding the reasons for an action is germane to making ethical judgments about it. Since intentions, motives, and character are in part the cause or source of action, they are also subject to moral evaluation.

The third set of ideas and assumptions directly relates to methods for evaluating ethical principles.

6. Ethical principles are impartial in the sense that they do not allow special exceptions that benefit or harm a specific person or group. This does not necessarily imply that ethical principles are invariably neutral between the interests and welfare of persons. It may be morally permissible, for instance, to be partial to the interests and welfare of one's children. However, an ethical principle that allows partiality of this kind must allow each person to be partial to the interests of his or her children. It must not allow, say, Jones to be partial to his children, but prohibit Smith from being partial to hers.

7. Ethical principles (a) are rules for deciding between alternative courses of action involving the interests and welfare of moral agents; (b) do not require conflicting acts; (c) prescribe no act or course of action that in considered belief systematically worsens the long-term welfare of persons, or is clearly detrimental to reasonable individual or group interests.

The third provision of the last assumption requires some comment. It is unavoidable, in our opinion, that one test of an ethical principle is how well it fits with considered beliefs about what is right and wrong. It cannot help but count against an ethical principle if it prescribes acts that seem plainly wrong. But one must be cautious here, for even the most carefully considered beliefs about right and wrong are not always reliable. Prejudice and bias are common human failings, as is the ability to rationalize unacceptable behavior or simply to refuse to see that a moral issue is at stake. Given all of this, often it is our judgments that need to be changed, not the principle in question. Still, there comes a time when argument, criticism, and evaluation come to an end. That time may be put off as long as possible, but eventually a choice of principles must be made.

ETHICAL RELATIVISM

Relativism Explained

The next ethical viewpoint we will discuss is ethical relativism. This is the position that there is no universal ethical principle or set of principles by which to judge the morality of an action. Instead, each society or social group has its own set of moral rules. Furthermore, since a particular society's rules are justified by internal procedures and standards specific to and distinctive of that society, it is inappropriate, relativists argue, to evaluate one society's rules using the procedures and standards of other societies. Thus, relativists claim, ethics cannot be reduced to some master list of rules applicable to everyone. There are no ethical principles that everyone should follow. There are only local ethical principles that apply locally.

Ethical relativism, if true, implies that no culture's ethical code has the special status of being "better" or "truer" than another. Each culture's code is on a par with every other culture's code. For example, in Ted's situation a colleague that is an ethical relativist might argue that although bribery is immoral in the United States, it is an acceptable practice in the country in which he is trying to sell machinery. Different countries have different ethical principles, and different ways in which those principles are justified and agreed upon. Since Ted is not a member of the culture in which he is trying to do business, he is in no position to pass judgment, either favorable or unfavorable, on their ethical views.

In the bribery example the relativist's argument may seem reasonable. After all, if the members of a certain society believe bribery is ethically permissible, who are we to tell them otherwise? But in other cases this attitude of "ethical neutrality" is much less plausible. For instance, if a culture were to practice slavery, then, if ethical relativism is correct, it would be inappropriate for us to say "What you are doing is ethically wrong" because we would be applying our standards to the practices of a culture with a different ethical code. The best we could do is say "What you are doing is wrong according to our standards." This is not an ethical judgment, but a statement of fact. In this respect ethical subjectivists and ethical relativists are similar. Just as subjectivists cannot legitimately make ethical judgment about the practices of other individuals, so ethical relativists cannot legitimately make ethical judgments about the practices of other cultures.

This is a disturbing consequence of relativism. Although we may be reluctant to make judgments about things like bribery, most of us are convinced that slavery and other acts that unjustifiably harm people are plainly wrong regardless of where they occur or who does them. And most of us feel that we are justified in condemning such practices when they occur. Since ethical relativism seems to prevent us from making judgments about these practices in other cultures, there need to be powerful reasons for us to put aside our convictions and accept relativism. Are there such reasons?

The Evidence for Relativism

It is undeniable that different societies have different ethical practices: Acts permissible in some societies are impermissible in others. And in many cases differences in practice seem to derive from differences in ethical principles. This is often taken to be conclusive evidence in favor of ethical relativism. However, the evidence is not unequivocal. Differences in ethical practices may turn not on differences in ethical principles, but on a variety of other things such as different physical environments, levels of social wealth, or beliefs about morally relevant facts. In one society, for instance, the practice was to kill one's parents as they began to grow old. This was morally permissible because it was thought that one would spend the afterlife in the physical state in which one died. If one were to die in a body racked by pain and disability, one would suffer torment for eternity. It was a kindness, a mark of concern for the welfare of one's parents, to ensure that they did not live to experience the infirmities of old age. Thus, despite very different practices in that culture and ours, there are underlying similarities of principle, for example, the principle that one ought to honor one's parents. We can understand and appreciate the motives for these acts while at the same time we may disagree about the facts of existence in the hereafter, assuming there is a hereafter.

Let us suppose, however, that a society S_1 has an ethical standard prohibiting acts of type A, society S_2 has an ethical standard prohibiting acts of type A, and the difference cannot be explained by differences in environment, wealth, or beliefs about morally relevant facts. Does this show that ethical relativism is true?

Not unless several other possibilities can be eliminated. One of them is that neither S_1 nor S_2 has made an error in logic. For example, suppose the members of S_1 falsely believe that a statement logically entails (or does not entail) some other statement, and that this belief plays an important role in their justification of the principle permitting the acts in question. If they were to find or be convinced that they were wrong about the entailment, they might also abandon the principle since it no longer is justified for them. In this case the difference between S_1 and S_2 is more a matter of logic than ethics.

Another possibility is that the error is epistemic rather than logical. For instance, suppose that according to their own canons of evidence the members of S_1 have incorrectly evaluated their reasons for holding the principle. They have made a mistake in judging the weight of the various reasons or omitted reasons that should have been taken into account or included in the justification reasons that should not have been included. The error here is one which, by S_1's own standards, they would admit were they to become aware of it.

A third possibility is that they are not aware that certain practices should be ethically evaluated. For example, in the recent past many societies, our own among them, were not concerned with environmental problems caused by pollution, disposal of toxic wastes, and so on. It was not that they had carefully thought about these issues and decided that they were unimportant, but rather that they had not thought about them at all. It was only when they became aware that ethical issues were involved that they began to see environmental practices from an ethical point of view.

A final possibility is that S_1 and S_2 attach different meanings to ethical words we might try to translate as "good," "justice," or "rights." If they do not realize that they are using these or similar words in different senses, then what may look like a difference in ethical principles could turn out to be a difference in the use of key ethical words. The possibility of misunderstanding or miscommunication should never be overlooked. Subtle differences in meaning can have important consequences for how one culture interprets the principles and justifications another culture gives for its ethical practices.

If any of these possibilities is realized, the fundamental disagreement is not about ethical principles. There is a prior point of contention or confusion—logical, epistemic or semantic—that needs to be resolved before the discussion about ethics can begin. If it cannot be resolved, then the ethical differences are a consequence of disagreement about a nonethical matter. If it can be resolved, then S_1 and S_2 might come to agree about the basic principles of ethics.

Relativism and the Possibility of Error

Some ethical relativists claim that if members of a society *believe* that acts of a certain type are ethically correct, then they *are* correct for that society. Thus, in ethics unlike, say, science, there is no difference between what is believed to be true and what is true. However, this claim is not convincing because it overlooks the possibility that social groups, like individuals, can make errors. A social group might have incorrect factual beliefs, make invalid inferences, mistakenly weigh evidence, or make some other error. In their own discussions about ethics or in conversation with other groups, they may come to realize that their ethical beliefs are unacceptable on their own standards of logic and evidence. Were this to happen it is likely that their ethical beliefs would change. People certainly have the capacity to make errors. Happily, they also have the capacity to recognize their errors and eliminate them by changing their beliefs.

It is not hard to find examples of this. At one time, for instance, blatant racial and sexual discrimination were common in this country. Much of this discrimination, though not all of it, was based on the false belief that blacks and women are intellectually inferior to white men. As these false beliefs are replaced by true ones we can reasonably hope and expect that discrimination will gradually disappear, for once this belief is gone, a major obstacle to living up to our own ideal of equal opportunity for all will be gone as well.

Ethical relativists who deny or ignore the possibility that social groups can make errors also counsel us to be tolerant of the beliefs of other societies. This is good advice. Our experience with discrimination shows that our society is as vulnerable to error as any other. It is a mistake to assume that our way of doing things is the only ethically acceptable way. But the reason relativists advise us to be tolerant is that they believe there is little basis for rational discussion between societies with different ethical viewpoints. After all, if a society cannot be mistaken about what it believes, there is no reason for it to subject its beliefs to critical evaluation by outsiders. Thus, relativists seem to think, since rational discussion is impossible, the only alternative modes of ethical interaction available, given the close proximity of different societies in the modern world, are tolerance and conflict. Since tolerance is much the better of the two choices, we should be tolerant. For the reasons given earlier, however, the fact that different societies have different ethical beliefs does not show that there is no basis for rational discussion between them. Nor does tolerance warrant indifference or inattention to the practices of other societies. If there is good reason to believe that an ethical practice is based on false beliefs about the facts, incorrect reasoning, and so on, we may have a duty to speak out, or even take action in extreme cases, regardless of where the practice occurs. As history amply shows, the consequences of not doing so can be horrendous.

Bedrock Ethical Differences

But what if, after all the possible nonethical areas of disagreement are eliminated, S_1 and S_2 still have different ethical principles? Now should we accept ethical relativism?

As far as we know, there are no noncontroversial examples of this kind of disagreement. But let us imagine that S_1 and S_2 have completely different principles. Every principle S_1 accepts is rejected by S_2 and vice versa. And suppose S_2 is a culture very much like our own, with ethical values and principles we can understand and appreciate. What would S_1 be like?

In S_1 lying, cheating, and random violence would be the norm. There would be no strictures against murder, robbery, rape, or other acts of violence. In business there could be no contracts since there would be no trust or expectation of fair dealing. There would be little or no family life since no one would be committed to the welfare of others. There would be no religion, law, or social institutions of any kind, for if such institutions are to work, people must have basic respect for themselves and others. Nor could S_1 have traditions, shared ideals, social organization, or even a history that is anything other than a series of random events. In short, S_1 would not be a human culture at all. It would not have, and could not sustain, the minimum social structure needed to support a viable culture.

We mentioned earlier that relativists cite diversity of ethical practice as evidence for diversity of ethical standards. However, if the preceding argument is correct, there could not be a complete diversity of principles. And, as it turns out, it does seem that all societies have certain ethical rules in common, for example, rules that promote reciprocity and fair play, and prohibit wanton violence. The reason is that were there no such rules, there would be no human societies. Many rules that societies have in common are essential for cultural survival. They establish the necessary conditions that make social life possible. Thus, there could not be a human society that has ethical rules completely different from our own.

If this is correct, then the more radical claims made on behalf of ethical relativism are implausible. The main evidence cited in favor of ethical relativism—that different societies have different ethical practices—does not support the claim that there is a radical and unbridgeable gap between the ethics of different societies. For one thing, all functioning societies have rules intended to help preserve social order. The evidence suggests that these rules are similar in different societies, which is not surprising since people have the same basic needs regardless of where they live. Furthermore, for all the reasons listed earlier, a difference in practice need not amount to a difference in principle. In fact, we suggest that a genuine difference in ethical principles not attributable to a different understanding of facts, different circumstances, errors of logic and evidence, and so on, is likely to be rare.[3]

There still remains the possibility that different societies have different principles not attributable to any of the sources mentioned earlier. It may be very difficult to decide in any particular instance whether an apparent difference is a genuine one, but they might occur. What should we say about such differences, assuming one could be found?

Since such a difference would be a bedrock ethical difference not attributable to any nonethical source, it might seem as if a modified relativism must be true. Maybe not all rules can differ, a relativist might say, but some can, and about these rules and the practices they permit no rational intercultural discussion can take place, and no intercultural judgments can be made. Every society, at least potentially, differs ethically in some respect from other societies. This difference signifies a kind of ethical autonomy, an area of ethical freedom, into which it would be disrespectful for other societies to intrude.

Although there is some truth to this argument, it is important to see what it does and does not establish. It does not show that there are genuine differences in ethical principles, but only that there might be. It does not show that apparent differences are genuine. And it does not show that different practices are grounded in different principles. Moreover, if genuine differences are to be found, rational discussion between societies must take place. Arguments must be evaluated, circumstances assessed, mistakes discovered and corrected, and agreements reached about what is and is not a real difference. But this, of course, is a paradigm of rational ethical debate and analysis. It is precisely the process by which we discuss and analyze ethical practices in our own culture as well as others. Thus, far from showing that ethical discussion between societies is impossible, ethical relativism, if true, would seem to require that it take place. Only in this way can genuine differences be found if they are present.

Finally, note that respect for the ethical autonomy of other cultures is proposed as a universal value, one that does not have merely local application. All of us, the relativist would say, should respect the views of other societies, and one way to do this is to be tolerant of differences when we find them. But there are other ways to be respectful of ethical autonomy. One of them, even more important than tolerance in our judgment, is to respect the rationality of others. We should not assume that apparent ethical differences are irrational or founded in reasons that we cannot comprehend. If we suppose that our society has good reasons for accepting certain ethical values, principles, and judgments, then it would be impertinent and contemptuous not to attribute the same to other societies. Tolerance, unless grounded in respect for rationality, is no more than a mean spirited paternalism. It is an attitude taken toward those inferior in intellect and ability, those with whom it is fruitless to engage in meaningful debate. If relativists are to avoid this highly unattractive attitude, if they are to grant others the full measure of respect they are due, they cannot in good conscience advise us simply to be tolerant of diversity. They must instead concede that diversity marks the beginning of rational debate about ethics, not the end.

We hope by now to have shown that ethical relativism is a fairly innocuous ethical viewpoint. It cannot support the more radical claims sometimes made on its behalf. At best it shows that some diversity of ethical principles is possible. It does not show that differences are necessary, nor that they are extensive, nor even that when real diversity is found it cannot be rationally discussed. Relativism can serve as a reminder of the complexity of ethical views, and of how arduous it may be to understand and appreciate ethical differences. But beyond this its implications for ethical theory and practice are minimal.

The Question of Relevance

In our discussion thus far there is a question, or series of questions, that we have not addressed but that some readers may have wondered about. Suppose someone responded to our analysis of ethical relativism as follows: You may be right that ethical relativism does not imply that one should not make ethical judgments about practices in other cultures, nor does it imply that rational discussion about ethics cannot take place between different societies. But nothing in your argument shows that I should make such judgments. Why should I care about what happens in other cultures? Granted that brutality, corruption, aggression, and injustice are common in the world, what does that have to do with me? Why should I be concerned?

In one sense these questions are unanswerable. If some persons have no concern about the fate of anyone other than themselves, if they resolutely refuse to consider the possibility that they have ethical obligations that extend beyond the circle of their immediate acquaintance, then little we can say will change their mind. Argument is futile with those who will not listen. In another sense, however, there is an answer. To see what it is, we need to suppose that the questions implicitly contain an argument of the following sort: I should only be concerned about those things that affect my self-interest. What happens to people in distant lands has little or no effect on my self-interest. Hence, I need not be concerned about them.

The second premise of this argument is highly questionable. It is no longer true, if it ever was, that what happens in the rest of the world is of little consequence to individuals in the United States. The global economy has effectively put an end to economic and political isolationism, and with it an end to the idea that distant events are irrelevant to individual self-interest. Thus, the argument as given does not justify lack of concern about those in distant lands.

A response to the objection is that one should be concerned about distant events only to the extent that one's self-interest is involved. If there is no reasonable connection between a particular individual's self-interest and the lives of those in other lands, then that individual need not be concerned with them.

This response brings us to the first premise, the thesis that self-interest is all that matters. As we will see in the next section, this view comes in several different guises. So we can better respond to it, and better give our final answer to the argument that one need not be concerned with the fate of others, we will first place it in the context of what are usually called consequentialist ethical theories.

CONSEQUENTIALISM

Essentials of Consequentialism

Consequentialism is a family of ethical viewpoints based on two central ideas. The first is a claim about what is of value for human beings. The second is that whether an act is ethically permissible or not is solely a matter of whether the act maximizes the value. For example, suppose the value is happiness. Then an act is ethically permissible if and only if it maximizes happiness—if and only if it is a consequence of the act that it produces at least as much happiness as any other act. Acts that do not maximize happiness are not ethically permissible. For example, suppose the only acts available to Jones are A, B and C, and that she can do exactly one of A, B or C. And suppose A and B both maximize happiness, and C does not. Then it is ethically permissible for Jones to do A or to do B, and impermissible for her to do C. Since no acts are available to her except A, B and C, and since no acts are ethically permissible for her except A and B, she is ethically obligated to do either A or B. No other ethically permissible choices are available to her.

Consequentialist theories can be subdivided according to (1) for whom the value is to be maximized, and (2) the kind of value to be maximized. For instance, the version of consequentialism called *ethical egoism* claims that an act is morally permissible for a person P if and only if the act maximizes the value for P. Nonegoistic versions of consequentialism say that an act is morally permissible for P if and only if the value is maximized for some larger group of people that includes P. To distinguish this theory from ethical egoism, it is commonly called *utilitarianism*.

Values to be maximized include both intrinsic and instrumental goods. Intrinsic goods are valuable in themselves, and not valuable merely as means to something else. Examples might be truth, beauty, love, friendship, pleasure and happiness. Instrumental goods are not valuable in themselves, but are valuable because they are means to some other end. An example of an instrumental good is money. In this introduction we have space to discuss only one of these possible intrinsic goods. We will give examples of how egoism and utilitarianism propose that this good be maximized, and we will review some of the objections that have been raised against these versions of consequentialism. But before we do this there is another position that needs discussion. It is an empirical relation of ethical egoism called *psychological egoism*. Since modern business and economic theory rely heavily on psychological egoism, we will examine it in some detail.

Psychological Egoism Explained

There is an important difference between what *is* and what *ought to be*. For example, through no fault of their own many people suffer from hunger and malnutrition. This is a fact about the world, a report of what is. But this fact about the world does not imply that things ought to be this way. Were the world a more accommodating place, there would be no hunger. No one would suffer from malnutrition. That is the way the world ought to be.

Psychological egoists make a claim about what is. It is a fact about human beings, they say, that individual humans act only to advance their self-interest. It is not merely that humans act from self-interest in limited but extreme circumstances, for example, when their lives are at stake, or that humans act from self-interest in certain social conditions, for example, in capitalist economies, but rather that each person acts from self-interest in every situation. Self-interest is and can be the only human motivation. That is the way humans are. Thus, it is useless to suggest that persons should be concerned about the welfare of others. People are incapable of concern for others except insofar as it enhances their own interests.

If psychological egoism is true, then ethics is pointless. Nothing is to be gained by exhorting people to do what they are incapable of doing, nor can they be blamed for failing to take the interests and welfare of others into account. So, for example, it would be pointless to argue that Ted Brown should consider the effects bribery would have on anyone other than himself, or to blame him for failing to do so. According to psychological egoists, it is a psychological fact that he cannot be concerned with the interests of others unless their interests are directly related to his.

Problems with Psychological Egoism

An immediate problem with psychological egoism is that apparent counterexamples are easy to find. We all know or have heard of cases in which people have sacrificed their fortunes or even their lives for the sake of others. And it is likely that many of us, when we reflect on our own experience, can recall occasions when we acted primarily from concern for others. Yet if psychological egoism is true, such acts are impossible. How do egoists explain this?[4]

One explanation egoists give is that acts apparently motivated by concern for others are, if examined closely, really motivated by self-interest. This explanation may be true in many cases. Acts that appear altruistic, that is, motivated by concern for others, may be consciously or unconsciously self-interested. However, the fact that *some* apparently altruistic acts are self-interested does not show, as psychological egoism requires, that *all* apparently altruistic acts are really self-interested. To show that, egoists need to provide a lot more detail about why they think their view is true.

One argument egoists sometimes use is that people invariably do what they most want to do, assuming their action is voluntary.[5] The idea here is that people act to satisfy their desires. If they desire several things, they always pick the one that, *ceteris paribus,* they most desire. Furthermore, people always most desire to do what is in their self-interest. Thus, if one person intentionally acts in a way that benefits another person, it is because that act is what the person most wanted to do, and he or she most wanted to do it because benefitting the other person contributes to his or her self-interest.

There are three difficulties with this argument. We will mention the first two and discuss the third in more detail. The first is that it is not clear that people always do what they most desire. Sometimes they do things they would very much prefer not to, like pay taxes or keep a promise. Second, it certainly seems as if people often desire things and do things they know are not in their self-interest. For instance, many people smoke even though they acknowledge that smoking is not in their self-interest. Finally, it could be that what someone most desires to do is intended solely to benefit someone else. For instance, in war, soldiers sometimes sacrifice their lives to save their comrades. Doesn't this show that psychological egoism is false?

Psychological egoists would claim it does not. People cannot most desire to act solely for the benefit of someone other than themselves. It is not psychologically possible. If A acts to benefit B, it must be because A believes, consciously or unconsciously, that the benefit to B helps A in some way. Otherwise A would not act to benefit B. Thus, when soldiers give their lives to save their comrades, they must (somehow) believe that it is to their benefit. For example, they might believe that to witness their friends die would be a worse fate than their own death.

However, this response begs the question—it assumes the very point at issue. The alleged reason that one person cannot act solely for the benefit of another is because psychological egoism is true. But the argument is supposed to show that psychological egoism is true, and nothing is accomplished if one must assume something is true to show that it is true. So we are still left with the question: Exactly why isn't it possible for one person to act solely for the benefit of another?

The Argument from Self-Satisfaction

There are two kinds of benefits one person can derive from helping another. The first is what we might call an external benefit. For example, Jones saves Smith from the burning building to ensure that Smith is around to repay the considerable sum he owes Jones. But another kind of benefit is internal. People never act solely for the benefit of others, egoists argue, because they always get an internal feeling of self-satisfaction from helping others. Indeed, if the purpose of helping others is not to assure some external gain, then the only reason people try to benefit others is to get this feeling of self-satisfaction. And since feeling good about ourselves is pleasurable, and feeling pleasure is in a person's self-interest, psychological egoism is true after all.

This argument is not persuasive for two reasons. The first is that self-satisfaction is not the same as self-interest. Things in our self-interest may not give us self-satisfaction, and things that give us self-satisfaction may not be in our self-interest. For example, it might be very much in Smith's self-interest to pay his debt to his bookie even though he gets no self-satisfaction from it. And many people get self-satisfaction from donating supplies to victims of natural disasters even though it is not remotely in their self-interest to help. Self-interested behavior and behavior that gives self-satisfaction are just not the same.

The second problem with the argument is that it assumes that if, say, Jones, helps another person, then her *reason* for helping must be to feel good about herself. Yet suppose Jones were to say "Although it is true that I feel good as a result of helping others, that is not the reason I do it. I help others because I am ethically obligated to do so, and I would continue to help them even if I stopped getting self-satisfaction from it." How might psychological egoists respond?

The only response they could make is that Jones is mistaken about her motivation. She thinks she is motivated by ethical obligation, they would say, but were we to analyze her act carefully we would find that she is actually motivated by self-interest. The reason we can be assured she is so motivated is that psychological egoism is true. People are motivated only by self-interest. Moreover, despite what Jones says, if she were to stop getting satisfaction from helping others, she would stop helping them. The reason is the same—psychological egoism is true. But by now this type of response should be familiar. It assumes the point at issue and thus begs the question.

Psychological Egoism: A Proposal

At this point, it might be helpful to review the discussion. We have posed a series of counterexamples to psychological egoism in which an individual reports that he or she performs an act for the benefit of someone else. Benefit to the other person is alleged to be the reason the act was performed, not external or internal benefit to the person performing the act. Psychological egoists then claim that the report must be mistaken because all behavior is self-interested. However, they offer no evidence that the act was self-interested other than appeal to the theory of psychological egoism.

But this is unacceptable because it begs the question. Is there any way for egoists to avoid this problem?

The only way is for egoists to *show* that the acts are self-interested, and not *assert* they are because psychological egoism is true. To do this they must insist that showing that an act has a certain *effect* does not automatically show that it has a certain *motivation*. Otherwise acts clearly detrimental to a person's self-interest would immediately prove that psychological egoism is false. But then by parity of reasoning, egoists cannot claim that acts beneficial to the person performing them provide strong evidence for egoism, for such benefits could be incidental rather than intentional. Thus, the effect of acts is relatively weak evidence either for or against egoism. What egoists need is psychological evidence, that is, truthful reports of motivation from the person performing the act. And since many people report altruistic motivation, egoists must show that these reports are mistaken. Furthermore, egoists cannot take reports of self-interested motivation at face value. If they claim that reports of altruism can be mistaken, they must allow that reports of self-interest can be mistaken. If they do not, if they assert that reports of self-interested motivation cannot be wrong, they again run the risk of begging the question.

If all of this is correct, psychological egoists have an enormous research project ahead of them. To make a case for egoism they must conduct an in-depth psychological examination of individual persons to uncover or confirm the genuine motivation of particular acts done on specific occasions. Since the theoretical and practical obstacles to this project are immense, at best it will be difficult to complete, and it may be impossible. It is not surprising, then, that it remains largely undone, and that the evidence to date is not encouraging for egoism.[6]

The question remains of what to do until empirical research settles the issue. We suggest that in the meantime it is reasonable to believe that some acts are genuinely altruistic. There simply is no good evidence that psychological egoism is true, nor are there any convincing philosophical arguments in its favor. Moreover, there is a great deal of evidence, both anecdotal and experimental, in favor of altruism, and psychological egoists have given no compelling reason to think that this evidence is wrong. Until that happens, altruism remains a possibility, and, in our opinion, a strong probability. If this is right, then psychological egoism poses no significant threat for ethics.

Ethical Egoism

Unlike psychological egoists, ethical egoists make a claim about what ought to be. They argue that each person ought to maximize his or her own self-interest. The principle they advocate is this:

> Ethical Egoism: An act A is ethically permissible for a person P if and only if A maximizes P's self-interest. Acts that do not maximize P's self-interest are not ethically permissible for P.

Ethical egoism is the ethical principle Ted Brown tried to follow when deciding whether he should offer a bribe. In our discussion of Ted's dilemma we pointed out that his decision is not easy because it is often difficult to anticipate the consequences of one's actions. But we said little about what Ted believes his self-interest to be, nor were we very precise about self-interest in our discussion of psychological egoism. However, to examine ethical egoism we need to be more precise about self-interest. Note that any analysis of self-interest we might give is constrained by ethical egoism's requirement that self-interest be maximized. Since to maximize something comparisons of more and less must be made, to apply the principle of ethical egoism it must be possible to make comparisons of self-interest. So what is this comparative concept of self-interest?

An answer favored by many people is to equate self-interest with happiness. Surely, they claim, it is in our self-interest to be happy. Furthermore, we often compare present states of happiness with those of the past and future, for example, "I'm much happier now than I used to be and I expect to be happier still in the future." And there is a rough intuitive sense to the notion that happiness can be maximized. On the other hand, the concept of happiness may not be precise enough to give clear guidance for all choices that fall under the principle of ethical egoism. Consider, for example, an ethical egoist contemplating how he should lead his life. Assuming happiness is the same as self-interest, the principle of ethical egoism instructs him to do what will make him happiest. But we can imagine him asking "Exactly what will make me happiest? Is it fame, fortune, knowledge, reputation? How can I know in advance what will maximize my happiness? And if I cannot know, how can I make an ethical choice?"

Hedonistic Egoism

These are not easy questions. It looks as if the only way an individual could answer them is to have complete knowledge of his or her future. But this is impossible. And since individuals cannot be ethically required to do what is impossible, ethical egoism is unacceptable unless there is some way to show that it imposes no such requirement. But how might it be shown?

One method sometimes attempted is to further analyze the concept of happiness. Granted that we all want to be happy, just what is it to be happy anyway? A traditional answer is that people are happy when they experience pleasure, and unhappy when they experience pain. That is all there is to it. Happiness just is experiencing pleasure and avoiding pain. The nineteenth century philosopher John Stuart Mill puts it like this:

> The ultimate end, with reference to and for the sake of which all other things are desirable (whether we are considering our own good or that of other people), is an existence exempt as far as possible from pain, and as rich as possible in enjoyments.

Mill is here advocating a view sometimes called *hedonism*—that the only thing of intrinsic value for humans is pleasure and the avoidance of pain. Everything else is and ought to be a means to that end.

Ethical egoists who accept Mill's outlook equate maximizing self-interest with maximizing pleasure and minimizing pain. This view, which we will call *hedonistic egoism,* requires that *all* acts available to a person be evaluated solely on their potential to cause pleasure or pain to that specific person. Acts that maximize pleasure or minimize pain are ethically permissible. Otherwise they are ethically impermissible. For example, suppose Jones can do only A or B but not both, and suppose both A and B are pleasurable for Jones but A is more pleasurable. Then, hedonistic egoists argue, Jones should do A. If A and B cause the same amount of pleasure, then it does not matter which Jones does. If A is pleasurable for Jones and B is not, then Jones should do A. Finally, if both A and B cause Jones pain but A causes less pain than B, then Jones should do A. If A and B cause the same amount of pain, then it does not matter which Jones does. Let us say that acts that conform to these examples "create the greatest balance of pleasure over pain." Now we can give a more exact statement of hedonistic egoism:

> Hedonistic Egoism: An act A is ethically permissible for a person P if and only if A creates the greatest balance of pleasure over pain for P. Acts that do not create the greatest balance of pleasure over pain for P are not ethically permissible for P.

The advantage of using pleasure and pain as a measure of self-interest instead of happiness is that pleasure and pain seem much more concrete and immediate than vague feelings of happiness. Moreover, it is easier to figure out what will cause pleasure and pain than what will lead to happiness, and easier to compare degrees of pain and pleasure than degrees of happiness. Perhaps the reason for this is that pleasure and pain have a basis in human physiology that happiness seems not to have, or not to have to the same degree. However, there are two misconceptions about hedonism that should be cleared up before we consider the arguments for hedonistic egoism. First, the hedonist's concept of pleasure should not be narrowly understood. In addition to ordinary physical pleasure, it can include a variety of other things such as intellectual and aesthetic pleasure, and the pleasures of friendship. Second, it is sometimes thought that hedonists care only about immediate pleasure and give no thought to the possibility that what causes them great pleasure now may lead to even greater pain in the future. But this need not be true. Rational hedonists will strive to create the greatest balance of pleasure over pain for themselves over the long term. Thus, they will forego a short-term pleasure that leads to long-term pain, and will undergo short-term pain to gain long-term pleasure. A more serious objection to hedonism is this: Happiness is too complex an idea to be captured by something as one dimensional as experiencing pleasure and avoiding pain, even if pleasure and pain are understood in the broadest sense. There is more to happiness than hedonists admit. It is possible that a life filled with little pleasure be happy for other reasons. Or that a life of great pleasure be ethically repugnant. Consider, for example, a powerful dictator who receives great pleasure from tormenting others. Consequently, it is a serious error to think that happiness can be understood solely in terms of pleasure and pain.

The Case for Hedonistic Egoism

We will not speculate about how hedonistic egoists might respond to the above objection. Instead, we will suppose for the present that hedonism gives an adequate account of happiness, and that self-interest is best understood in terms of happiness. The next task is to examine the arguments for hedonistic egoism. It is important to see that hedonistic egoists believe that everyone should always follow the principle of hedonistic egoism. Thus, they are unlike ethical subjectivists and ethical relativists, and unlike those who believe that business or legal principles should sometimes take precedence over ethics. But since hedonistic egoists believe that everyone should accept their position, they need to give good reasons for it. Are there such reasons?

Here is one argument. Suppose there is a God who rewards each person with the pleasures of heaven or the pains of hell based on how well the person lives up to some set of God's commands while living on this earth. The pleasures of heaven and pains of hell are both intense and everlasting, so it maximizes long-term pleasure to attain heaven and avoid hell. Thus, it is in each person's interests to follow the commands while he or she is alive. And since persons are judged as individuals, each person is well advised to look after his or her own interests. Given the existence of such a God, ethical egoism is the only reasonable ethical viewpoint.

There are two main problems with this argument. First, it works only if there is a God who metes out rewards and punishments as described. Not everyone is convinced of this. However, granting there is such a God, say, the God of the New Testament, the second problem concerns the commands God issues. One of them is to "love thy neighbor as thyself." This in part implies that one should place the interests and welfare of one's neighbors on a par with one's own. And, furthermore, that one should be motivated by genuine altruism, and not see protecting the interests of one's neighbors merely as a means of gaining a reward in heaven. But this is inconsistent with hedonistic egoism since it dictates that persons should be concerned only with their own interests. Thus, the argument does not give good reasons for everyone to be a hedonistic egoist. If anything, it shows that hedonistic egoism is an unacceptable ethical viewpoint.

A second argument is that individuals best know their own interests and are best able to look after their interests. Intervening in the lives of others usually causes more problems than it solves. In addition, many people do not want anyone meddling in their affairs, even when well intended. They think of it as an invasion of privacy. Thus, were we all to look out only for ourselves, it is likely we would all be better off in the long term.

The main idea in the second argument is that one should be a hedonistic egoist because it enhances the common good—everyone would be better off. But if so, then enhancing the common good is the ultimate goal of ethical action. Hedonistic egoism is no more than the (alleged) best means to that end. This puts hedonistic egoists in a very bad position for two reasons. The first is that if the generalization is false and hedonistic egoism is not in fact the best means to the common good, then hedonistic egoists would be obliged to abandon their position and search for a better means. And there are grounds for thinking it false. People are often helped rather than hurt by intervention in their lives. No doubt such intervention sometimes goes awry, but it does not follow from this that were it to cease entirely, everyone would be better off. The second reason is that the notion of valuing the common good is quite foreign to hedonistic egoism. The main point of the theory is that, ethically speaking, it is the good of the individual that counts, not the good of the group. So for hedonistic egoists to appeal to the common good to justify their position is peculiar to say the least. If hedonistic egoists are to persuade others to accept their view, they must find better reasons than the ones we have examined so far.

Hedonistic Egoism Reconsidered

So far the arguments for hedonistic egoism are not very convincing. And there are some reasons to reject it altogether. Here is one of them. Recall that if Jones has a choice of doing A or B, and if A and B cause her the same amount of pleasure (or pain), then from the point of view of hedonistic egoism it does not matter which she does. But suppose Jones knows that if she does A, then Smith will suffer a great deal of unprovoked and unnecessary harm. Yet if Jones does B, Smith will experience harmless pleasure. Can it be correct, as hedonistic egoism implies, that it is ethically indifferent which Jones does? It certainly seems not. Smith's well-being must count for something. If Jones's actions can either harm or benefit Smith at no cost to Jones, then it would seem an ethical imperative that she choose to benefit Jones. To be indifferent to Smith's well-being is ethically reprehensible. Since hedonistic egoism implies that it is not reprehensible but a matter of indifference, hedonistic egoism is unacceptable.

Another reason to reject hedonistic egoism is this. Suppose Jones and Smith are suffering from a disease that is rapidly fatal if left untreated. There is a pill that will cure the disease, but only one. According to hedonistic egoism, Jones is ethically required to take the pill, and so is Smith. Thus, if Jones tries to take it, Smith is ethically bound to prevent her. And if Smith tries to take it, Jones is ethically bound to prevent him. Thus Jones can act ethically only by preventing Smith from doing so, and vice versa. But can any ethical viewpoint be acceptable that implies that on some occasions one person can act ethically only by *preventing* another person from acting ethically?

Let us make the case a little more concrete. Suppose Jones and Smith are siblings, and Jones knows that even if she takes the pill she will die within a few months from some other painless but fatal ailment. If Smith takes the pill, however, he will be completely restored to health and will likely lead a long and happy life. Now suppose Jones decides to let Smith take the pill. How should Jones's action be evaluated? Most of us would probably think that she made the right decision, and that she should be praised and respected. At the very least she should not be condemned for acting unethically. But, if hedonistic egoism is true, it is possible that Jones acts unethically. It does not matter that she has only a few months to live as long as taking the pill will maximize benefit to her. If it does, hedonistic egoism requires that she take it. Not to do so is ethically impermissible.

In our judgment these consequences of hedonistic egoism show that it is an unacceptable ethical viewpoint. They illustrate two deep flaws. The first is that hedonistic egoism has no method of resolving ethical conflict. When it appears that one person can act ethically only by preventing another person from doing so, the conflict between them needs to be resolved in an ethically acceptable manner. But hedonistic egoism provides no such mechanism. The second flaw is that hedonistic egoism censures acts of self-sacrifice. Sometimes it is wrong to sacrifice one's interests for the sake of others, but it is not, as hedonistic egoism implies, *always* ethically impermissible. Were it so, the world would be a poor place indeed.

Although the case for hedonistic egoism is weak and the reasons for rejecting it are compelling, we concede that it has an intuitive appeal that is hard to dismiss. We suggest that its appeal is grounded in two insights that any realistic ethical viewpoint needs to capture. The first is that mature and competent persons generally best know their own interests, and are best able to look out after them. The conviction that this is true is one reason most people find paternalism so unattractive. Moreover, there is no need to appeal to the common good to justify persons looking out for their own interests. The fact that something is beneficial to someone is *prima facie* justification enough for him or her to do it. The second reason is that as a practical matter it is extremely difficult or even impossible for most persons consistently to renounce their interests for the sake of others. But if ethics is to be relevant to our lives, it must be compatible with what it is possible for humans to do. It cannot constantly require of individuals that they heroically sacrifice their own interests.

Hedonistic egoism incorporates these insights, but it omits others that are equally important. The main one is that ethics is about relationships between people, relationships in which the interests of all parties must be considered. For hedonistic egoists only self-interest matters, and this is a fatal flaw.

Utilitarianism

In its traditional forms utilitarianism does not permit an individual to place special weight on his or her self-interest. Instead, the interests of all persons affected by an individual's action are given the same weight. So, for example, if Jones performs an action that affects the interests of Smith and Brown, then if she is a utilitarian she will give the interests of Smith and Brown the same weight she gives her own. For utilitarians, no one deserves or is granted special consideration. Everyone is treated alike.

But in what respect do utilitarians believe that everyone be treated alike? To understand this, we need to make some assumptions. The first is that self-interest is equivalent to experiencing pleasure and avoiding pain. In this utilitarians are like hedonistic egoists. The second is that the pleasures and pains of any one person are similar to those of any other person. Thus, Jones's pleasures and pains are like Smith's and Brown's. The third is that the duration and intensity of pleasure and pains can be quantified and measured. So, for example, it can be determined in any particular case whether Jones is experiencing more or less pleasure than Smith or Brown, and how much more or less. Finally, utilitarians assume that individuals are able to canvass the acts available to them and make reliable judgments about the amount of pleasure and pain distinct acts will cause each individual affected by the act. Given these assumptions, Jeremy Bentham, who founded modern utilitarianism in the eighteenth century, writes that we should:

> Sum up all the values of all the pleasures on the one side, and those of all the pains on the other. The balance if it be on the side of pleasure, will give the *good* tendency of the act . . . , with respect to the interests of that *individual* person; if on the side of pain, the bad tendency. . . . [then] Take an account of the *number* of persons whose interests appear to be concerned; and repeat the above process with respect to each. . . . Take the *balance;* which, if on the side of *pleasure,* will give the general *good tendency* of the act, with respect to the total number of the community of individuals concerned; if on the side of pain, the general *evil tendency,* with respect to the same community.

Bentham's idea is to take the balance of pleasure over pain for each individual affected by an act and add them all up. Acts are then ranked according to how much total pleasure or pain they cause. Bentham then supposes that the act that causes the greatest total amount of pleasure, or the least amount of pain, is the morally best act. Let us say that an act that causes the greatest total amount of pleasure for everyone affected by the act, or the least amount of pain, *maximizes utility.* This gives us the following utilitarian principle:

> Hedonistic Utilitarianism: An act is ethically permissible if and only if it maximizes utility. Acts that do not maximize utility are not ethically permissible.

For example, suppose Jones can do either A or B but not both, and that Jones, Smith, and Brown are the only people affected by A and B. To make calculation of utility easier, also suppose pleasure is measured in positive units and pain in negative units. Now, to decide which act maximizes utility, Jones first estimates the units of pleasure A causes Smith and adds the units of pain. For instance, suppose A causes Smith six units of pleasure and two units of pain, for a sum of four units of pleasure. She does the same thing for Brown and finds that A causes her, say, five units of pleasure. Finally, she anticipates the amount of pleasure and pain A will cause herself. Assume it is one unit of pain. Then she adds all three together and determines that A causes a total of eight units of pleasure. She repeats the same process for B and calculates that B causes a total of seven units of pleasure. Since the amount of total pleasure A causes is greater than the amount B causes, A maximizes utility.

Utilitarianism: For and Against

All forms of consequentialism claim that the morally right thing to do is to promote the good of persons. This view has great appeal. Surely it is right to do good for people. No ethical view that denied this would be remotely plausible. In addition, consequentialism has the virtue of simplicity—all actions are ethically measured against the single standard of promoting good. And consequentialism is compatible with common sense ideas about the kinds of acts that ought to be praised or condemned. Everyone agrees that promoting the good of persons deserves praise, and inhibiting it deserves condemnation. For these reasons consequentialism is a powerful ethical view, one that cannot be dismissed lightly.

Consequentialism begins to lose its attractions, however, when we start to think about how to implement it. For instance, particular versions of consequentialism, for example, hedonistic utilitarianism, are only as plausible as the theory of human good that they advocate. So hedonistic utilitarianism is only as good as the hedonistic psychology on which it rests. And hedonism is neither a very convincing theory of actual human motivation, nor of what human motivation ought to be.

But leaving that problem aside, there remain practical difficulties that may be insurmountable. For example, hedonistic utilitarianism supposes that individuals can compare their own pleasures and pains; for example, Jones can say with certainty that this act causes her twice as much pleasure as that act, or that the pleasure of this is three times as much as the pain of that. But can we make such comparisons? You may like chocolate ice cream more than vanilla, but can you say that it gives you exactly twice as much pleasure? Or that eating chocolate causes you three times more pleasure than getting a paper cut causes you pain? No doubt some pleasures are greater than others, as are some pains, but it seems unlikely that we can say exactly how much greater. And it is not clear that pleasures can at all be quantitatively compared with pains. Furthermore, how can the pleasures and pains of one individual be compared with those of another? How can one person determine that his pleasure from eating chocolate is more, less, or the same as another person's? The only way, it would seem, is for the first person to experience the pleasure of the second and compare it with his own. But this is impossible. One person cannot experience the pleasures and pains of another. And if a person cannot know exactly how much pleasure or pain an act will cause others, there is no way to calculate utility. So there is no way to decide which act is ethically permissible. And nothing could be more useless than an ethical view that exhorts one to act ethically and at the same time is so constructed as to assure that one never knows whether one is acting ethically or not.

To implement hedonistic utilitarianism, persons must make calculations that cannot be made. Thus, as it stands, hedonistic egoism is not acceptable. Nor can it be made acceptable by substituting an alternative account of human good as long as the good for human is tied to subjective experience. For example, one might try, as Mill did, to distinguish between the kinds of pleasures that persons experience. Some pleasures, Mill argued, are qualitatively better than others; for example, intellectual pleasures are better than the pleasure one gets from food. He proposed that "competent judges", who had experienced a variety of pleasures, establish a hierarchy of different kinds of pleasure. Then, when making utilitarian calculations, "better" pleasures would count more heavily than "worse" pleasures. However, what standard of measurement do these judges use to decide that some pleasures are *better* than others instead of just *different* than others? Why should their standard be used instead of some other? And how do they know that what they experience as "better" is not experienced as "worse" by some other person? Mill has no convincing answer to these questions. Regardless of the kind or quality of the subjective experience said to constitute the good for persons, it seems impossible to establish an objective measure of that experience that can be used to calculate utility.[7]

Hedonistic utilitarians could respond to these objections by pointing out that, despite the difficulties mentioned, judgments about the relative amount of pain and pleasure an act will cause are often made. For example, think of the judgments made by parents, teachers, judges, and government officials. Making judgments about the subjective experience an act will cause is an inescapable part of the responsible exercise of legal and administrative power. And it is not as chancy an enterprise as the objection portrays. Mature and thoughtful people generally have a good idea of what will cause others pleasure and pain, and of how much it will cause. So there is no need to abandon hedonistic utilitarianism so quickly. Perhaps measurement of pains and pleasures cannot be precise, but it can be good enough to permit reliable judgments about the relative ethical worth of actions.

Hedonistic utilitarians who make this reply are advocating an important revision in the theory. They are abandoning the idea that *maximizing* utility is the sole criterion of the ethical worth of an action, and are substituting in its place the criterion of "*doing the best one can*" to maximize utility. For example, suppose Jones can do either A or B but not both. She estimates as best she can the amount of utility A will cause and the amount B will cause. She decides that A will cause more utility and so does A. As things turn out, her estimate is wrong and A causes less utility than B would have. According to the original principle of hedonistic utilitarianism, Jones's act is ethically impermissible. But since she did the best she could to estimate the utilities of A and B, on the revised theory it can no longer be said that what she did was wrong.

How can one judge whether an act is permissible or not according to the new criterion? Formerly it was alleged to be a relatively objective matter. If an act maximized utility it was ethically permissible; otherwise, it was not. Judgments about the intentions and abilities of the person performing the act were not relevant. But now such judgments are relevant because one must decide whether a person really did do the best he or she could. One must decide, for example, whether the person diligently looked for all the available data and made a rational judgment based on the data. The outcome of the act—the utility it causes—becomes less important than the effort and skill the person put into deciding what to do. Consequences become subordinate to good faith effort by individuals. Thus, it is the ethical worth of individuals, not actions, that is of primary importance.

This change has far reaching implications for hedonistic utilitarianism. So much so that it is questionable whether it is accurate to continue to classify the theory as consequentialist. But we will leave this issue and discuss another problem with implementing hedonistic utilitarianism.

Suppose Jones can do either A or B but not both, and that A and B affect only Jones, Smith, and Brown. Jones determines that A causes twelve units of pleasure for Smith, and one unit of pain each for Jones and Brown. Thus A causes a total of ten units of pleasure. B causes three units of pleasure each for Jones, Smith, and Brown, for a total of nine units of pleasure. The principle of hedonistic utilitarianism instructs Jones to maximize utility, so she should do A. But suppose she does B instead. Has she acted unethically?

Imagine Jones defends her action as follows: I know that A maximizes utility but I choose to do B because A *unfairly distributes* pain and pleasure. Smith gets all the pleasure and Brown and I get all the pain. B, on the other hand, gives each of us some pleasure and no one suffers pain. That seems much more fair. After all, why should Brown and I agree to suffer pain just so Smith can get all that pleasure? Why should we bear all the burdens and he get all the benefits?

Jones's defense highlights what many consider the most serious defect in hedonistic utilitarianism. It is completely insensitive to the distribution of pain and pleasure. It does not matter who gets how much pain or how much pleasure as long as utility is maximized. This makes it easy to construct examples in which hedonistic utilitarianism requires action that seems clearly wrong. For instance, suppose utility is maximized in the United States by ensuring that an ethnic minority gets all the pain and the white majority gets all the pleasure. That is unfair, but nothing in hedonistic utilitarianism prohibits it. Thus, if one believes that some distributions are more fair or just than others, and that being fair or just takes precedence over maximizing utility, then one will reject hedonistic utilitarianism.

One might suppose that utilitarianism can be repaired by adding some principle of distribution to the theory. And many attempts have been made to do this.[8] Some have argued, for instance, that individuals are justified in attaching greater weight to their own utility, thus enabling them to avoid sacrificing their personal good for the sake of the community except in rare circumstances. Others have argued that some distributions are unacceptable because they violate individual rights. These strategies assume that there is something about persons that insulates them from certain kinds of treatment, that makes it unfair or unjust to treat them in certain ways. We will discuss several of these views in the pages to come. But before we do we would like to emphasize again the importance and appeal of utilitarianism. Although many objections can be raised against it, in our opinion there is something undeniably right about utilitarianism. The basic idea—that it is morally right to contribute to the common welfare—is intuitively unassailable. The problem is to figure out exactly what one is obligated to contribute under different conditions. Sophisticated forms of utilitarianism make valiant efforts to address this problem, and not without success. Unfortunately we are unable to discuss these theories in this introduction, but we commend them to you. Some of them are listed in the suggested readings.

DEONTOLOGICAL ETHICS

Kant and the Good Will

The ethical view developed by the eighteenth-century philosopher Immanuel Kant stands in sharp contrast to consequentialism, relativism, and subjectivism. Kant's ethics does not depend on some prior concept of human good, it does not judge the ethical worth of actions based on their consequences, and it does not appeal to the desires of individuals or the common opinion of groups as a basis for ethical rules. Instead, Kant attempts to derive certain special ethical rules from the concept of reason. And because Kant believed that all mature persons have the capacity to reason, he thought that these rules applied to everyone. His arguments are subtle and complex. They are also among the most important and influential ethical arguments ever devised.

One place to begin Kant's ethics is to ask the following: What gives an action moral worth? What is it about a morally praiseworthy action that makes it praiseworthy? Consequentialists think that morally praiseworthy acts are those that have the best overall consequences. Results are what count; nothing else is relevant. Kant disagrees. He argues that we cannot judge the ethical worth of an action by its consequences because we cannot guarantee that what we intend to do actually occurs. Things can, and often do, go wrong. We may will to do good and inadvertently cause evil, or will to do evil and cause good. So the moral worth of an action cannot be defined by its consequences. Rather, Kant argues, it is defined by the act of willing itself. To see how this happens we need to make two preliminary points.

The first is that, according to Kant, the will is an internal faculty common to all persons. The will issues commands such as "let me now do X." But it only issues commands at the end of a process of reasoning. Hence, to will to do something is to rationally choose to do that thing. Kant says that the commands issued by the will can be formulated in statements he calls *maxims*. He believes that every act of will is associated with a maxim that expresses the intention of the agent. For example, if Jones wills to pay money she owes, the maxim that expresses her intention is "Let me now pay my debt."

The second point is that Kant thinks of morality as the performance of duty. To perform a moral duty, for Kant, is to fulfill a requirement that is binding on all persons. We determine our duties by using a special rule of ethics that Kant calls the moral law. But there are at least two motivations for following a law. One is because we desire something, for example, to gain the approval of our peers or to avoid a fine or other penalty. The other is respect for the law itself. One can choose to obey the law, not from desire or fear or calculated self-interest, but solely because one honors the law, because following the law is the right thing to do. When a person respects the moral law, and does what is right because it is right and for no other reason, Kant says that he or she is acting from a *good will.*

Kant believes that a good will is good without qualification. It is the only good thing that cannot be put to a bad use. When we act from a good will—when we do our duty out of respect for the moral law—then and only then do our actions have moral worth. Thus, we have Kant's answer to the question asked previously—an action has moral worth just in case it is done from a good will. However, it leads naturally to another question, namely, what is the moral law?

Kant and the Categorical Imperative

To answer the second question it is helpful to understand Kant's ethical view as an attempt to find a rule for sorting maxims into those that are ethically acceptable and those that are not. For example, suppose Jones borrowed $5 from Smith and promised to pay it back the next day. When Jones sees Smith she could choose the maxim "Let me now pay my debt" or "Let me now avoid paying my debt." Kant believes that the former maxim is ethically correct and the latter is not. What he wants to do is find an ethical rule that always directs us to choose the former. It is this rule that he calls the moral law.

Kant argues that the rule, or moral law, will be expressed in the form of a command or imperative. He points out that there are two kinds of imperatives: hypothetical imperatives, which have the form "If you desire A, do B"; and categorical imperatives, which have the form "Do A." However, the imperative Kant is looking for cannot be hypothetical. The reason is that the moral law is both *universal* and *necessary.* It is universal in that it applies to all persons, and necessary in that it does not depend on human sense experience; for example, it does not refer to desires. But hypothetical imperatives make reference to our desires. Desires are discovered in sense experience; they are neither universal nor necessary. Thus, hypothetical imperatives are neither universal nor necessary. Thus, the rule for choosing maxims is a categorical imperative.

A categorical imperative, Kant argues, derives strictly from human reason. It makes no reference to consequences and is independent of desire. And since it arises from reason, it is acceptable to and binding upon all rational agents simply in virtue of their rationality.

It is important to see that a command like "Shut the door!" is not a categorical imperative, even though it seems to have the form "Do A." The reason is that it makes implicit reference to desire, the desire to have the door shut. A true categorical imperative makes neither explicit nor implicit reference to desire. It applies to persons regardless of their desires.

To summarize thus far, Kant argues that the moral law is a categorical imperative. This imperative has the following characteristics: (1) it applies to all persons, (2) it makes no reference to desire, (3) it is a product of human reason, and (4) it can be used to sort maxims into those that are morally acceptable and those that are not. After many pages of complex argument, Kant proposes the following as the categorical imperative:

> First Categorical Imperative: Act only according to that maxim whereby you can at the same time will that it should become a universal law.

This is the moral law. It meets all of Kant's requirements. It is a categorical imperative. It is expressed in a universal form that applies to everyone. It makes no reference to desire or consequences. And, Kant tries to show, it arises from pure reason. This is why it is appropriate to call it a law. It is a law, not in the sense that it is passed by a legislature, but because it is a product of our own reason. Since each person has the faculty of reason, each person is (or could be) the author of the moral law. So in a sense we legislate the law to ourselves. We are not bound to obey it by some external force; rather, we are motivated to follow it by respect for ourselves and our own rationality. We follow the moral law because doing so expresses our nature as rational beings. To refuse to follow it is, therefore, irrational and against our nature.

How is one supposed to use the moral law to choose maxims? The idea is something like this. When a person is faced with a moral choice he or she formulates the maxim of his or her choice as a categorical "Do this." Then the person asks whether the maxim can be *universalized* that is, whether it can be willed that everyone, in similar circumstances, choose the same maxim and follow it. If it can be willed as a universal law, one that everyone should always follow, let us say it is *compatible with* the moral law. Maxims that are compatible with the moral law are morally acceptable. If a maxim is not compatible with the moral law, it is not morally acceptable.

But why does compatibility matter? What difference does it make whether a maxim is compatible with the moral law or not? One reason it matters, Kant says, is because the moral law is a principle of reason, and maxims incompatible with the moral law are rationally inconsistent. They require us both to will a certain act at a certain time and not to will the same act at the same time. But we cannot rationally consent both to do something and not to do it, and anything to which we cannot rationally consent cannot imply moral duties. Thus, maxims incompatible with the moral law are not ethically acceptable guides for action.

An example of how this is supposed to work might help. Recall Ted Brown's dilemma about whether or not to pay a bribe to get a big contract. To offer a bribe is to try to ensure that one secretly receives special treatment, treatment that puts others at a clear disadvantage. Can Ted consistently will that everyone in his circumstances pay the bribe? He cannot, for if it were to be a universal law that everyone offered a bribe to get a big contract, Ted would no longer be able to use bribery to get special treatment. Everyone would know about it, and his advantage would disappear. Thus, Ted cannot universalize his action. His maxim is not compatible with the moral law and so is not morally acceptable.

Here is another example. Suppose Jones promises Smith to do something although she has no intention of keeping her promise. The maxim of her act is "Make promises when it is to your advantage even when you have no intention of keeping them." Can this be universalized? No, because if everyone were to do this the practice of promising would be undermined. No one would accept a promise at face value. As Kant says "no one would believe what was promised to him but would only laugh at any such assertion as vain pretense." Since the maxim cannot be universalized, it is incompatible with the moral law and is not morally acceptable.

Criticisms of Kant

One of the main features of universalizable maxims is that they prevent persons who follow them from regarding themselves as special cases deserving of treatment that others are denied. That is one of the strength of Kant's theory. It is not ethically acceptable to make exceptions for oneself. As it turns out, however, the feature of allowing no exceptions can be turned against Kant. Here is one of Kant's own examples.

Suppose Brown, who is innocent of any wrongdoing, is fleeing from someone who intends to murder him. Brown sees you and tells you where he is going to hide. Then the murderer comes along and asks you where Brown went. Should you tell the truth?

Since a general policy of lying is incompatible with the moral law, Kant argues that you should. As he puts it, "To be truthful in all deliberations, therefore, is a sacred and absolutely commanding decree of reason, limited by no expediency." Thus, Kant seems to believe there can be no exceptions to telling the truth.

But this cannot be the whole story. It cannot be right that one's only duty is to tell the truth. Surely one also has a duty to protect Brown. However, Kant permits no exceptions for Brown. What has gone wrong?

The main problem is that in the circumstances in which you find yourself, it is unclear which maxim you should universalize. One possibility is "Always lie when asked a question." This is obviously incompatible with the moral law and should be rejected. But Kant seems to assume that rejecting this maxim implies accepting "Never lie when asked a question," which he believes is compatible with the moral law. However, there are other maxims one might follow, for example, "Lie when no other alternative is available to protect the innocent from serious harm." This seems compatible with the moral law. If it were universalized, murderers would no longer ask for directions, but that is no loss. Yet both maxims, the one Kant accepts and the one about protecting the innocent, apply in the present situation. How do you decide which to follow? And does it make a *moral* difference which decision you make?

The root of the difficulty is this: any action can be described in a number of ways. These descriptions can be formulated into maxims, some of which will be universalizable and some not. However, Kant provides no method to decide which of the universalizable maxims should be chosen. Without this method his theory cannot be used to make an exact determination of our moral duty. Thus, Kant's theory is incomplete. It does not give clear-cut guidance in situations in which moral choices must be made.

Someone (not Kant) might respond that it makes no moral difference which maxim one chooses as long as it is universalizable and one acts from respect for the moral law. But this is wrong. It does make a difference. Based on the maxim you choose, Brown either lives or dies. And that is certainly a moral difference. Universalizability is not sufficient to tell us our moral duty. Something else is needed, something that tells us which universalizable maxim to follow.

If universalizability is not a sufficient test for moral duty, then perhaps universalizable maxims give us only *prima facie* duties, that is, duties that hold unless overridden by other moral considerations. For example, the duty not to lie may be overridden by our obligation to protect the innocent. So to know our moral duty, we need to know when one obligation is overridden by another. Since Kant believes that duties are absolute rather than *prima facie,* he has nothing to say about this. However, here is a suggestion that might work: A duty D_1 is overridden by another duty D_2 in circumstances C just in case there is a reason for doing D_2 rather than D_1 in C that every rational person would accept.

The danger here is that there may be no such reason—no reason for doing one thing rather than another that everyone would accept. If so, then there will be cases of conflict of duty that cannot be resolved. No matter what one does, one acts immorally. That would be a moral tragedy.

The Second Version of the Categorical Imperative

Kant gives a second version of the categorical imperative that he (rather mysteriously) claims is equivalent to the first.

> Second Categorical Imperative: Act so that you treat humanity, whether in your own person or that of another, always as an end and never as a means only.

This imperative includes two of the main ideas of ethics in the western tradition. The first is that persons should be treated as ends in themselves, that is, as beings that are intrinsically valuable in themselves. The reason, for Kant, is that persons are centers of moral goodness. He believes that moral goodness can exist in the world only in beings that can apprehend the moral law and freely choose to act from a sense of duty. The second idea is that persons are never to be treated merely as means to an end. Although we often use people as a means to gain something we want, we should at the same time acknowledge that they have value independent of their usefulness to us. They are not to be manipulated or exploited and then cast aside as one would a broken tool. For example, in relationships between teachers and students, doctors and patients, parents and children, and legislators and citizens, each party uses the other as a means to some end. But, Kant argues, each party should also regard the other as ends in themselves, and should treat them with the dignity and respect they deserve. Surely he is right about this.

Although the second imperative undeniably captures an important part of our ethical intuitions, it suffers from the same defect as the first. It does not give specific guidance in situations involving a moral choice. For example, suppose Ted Brown tries to follow the second imperative when deciding whether to offer a bribe. Does bribery treat others as ends in themselves or merely as means to an end? On one hand, it might be said that bribery does use others as mere means since it is a deceptive attempt to gain an unfair advantage. On the other, exactly which "others" are being so used? The other people who submitted a bid on the contract? But these people presumably did not submit the bid for themselves; rather, they were acting for a corporation. Corporations are not the sorts of things that apprehend the moral law and act from a sense of duty; that is something that only people can do. Thus, corporations are not intrinsically valuable in themselves. Thus, there is nothing wrong with using them as mere means.

In many business situations relations between persons, corporations, governments, unions, public interest groups, and so on, are very complex. What does it mean, what could it mean, to treat persons as ends in themselves in these circumstances? Without doubt, the sentiment is admirable, but sentiment is next to useless when one needs to know *precisely* what to do *now*. About this, the second imperative has nothing to say.

In response it could be argued that the objection raised against the second imperative is unfair. Kant never envisioned Ted Brown's dilemma, nor would he claim that the second imperative gives specific instructions in all circumstances. It is most useful in personal relationships in which people know each other and can judge more accurately when a specific behavior inappropriately uses others as means. That is its real application, and it is an important one.

We concede the point. The second imperative does not comfortably fit cases like Ted Brown's, so in a sense the objection is unfair. However, even in more personal relationships it does not do much better. For example, if you tell Brown's murderer where Brown is hidden, are you treating Brown with respect as an end in himself? Or if you lie to his murderer, are you treating the murderer as a mere means? The answers are not clear; arguments could be given either way. So the second imperative, like the first, needs something else, something that permits more precise answers to the questions raised.

One possible way to supplement Kant's theory is with the idea that people have moral rights that proscribe or compel certain behaviors. We will discuss rights in the next section. But before we do, recall that at the end of the section on relativism, the question was posed: Why should I care about the interests of others as long as my interests are not involved? Kant's answer, and it is a good one, is that individuals should care about other people because they are centers of moral goodness and bearers of intrinsic value. Therefore, all people deserve to be treated with respect and dignity. To ignore the interests of other people, to shrug off the value they possess and pretend they do not matter, is to deny them what they are due. Furthermore, unless one is willing to be treated with disrespect and contempt oneself, it is to universalize a maxim that is plainly incompatible with the moral law. It is to say "I need not consider the interests of others provided they cannot harm or help me, but when I cannot harm or help them, I want them to consider my interests nevertheless." In other words, one makes an exception for oneself for no good reason, indeed, for no reason at all other than "That is what I want."

Before we leave this section on Kant we should emphasize that we have given only the briefest introduction to many important facets of Kant's ethical philosophy, and we have left others out entirely. At best we have provided in interpretation of Kant's ethics, one that we think fairly represents some of the things he had to say, but no doubt one that some scholars will disagree with. We encourage everyone interested in ethical questions to read Kant and make up his or her mind about what he has to say. Kant's works are sometimes difficult, but they are invariably rewarding.

RIGHTS

The Nature of Rights

Over the last several centuries the language of rights has become commonplace in moral discourse. The conviction that people have rights has motivated the writing of documents from the U.S. Declaration of Independence and the Bill of Rights to the United Nations' Universal Declaration of Human Rights. Everyone thinks he or she has rights, and everyone thinks rights are important. Among these rights are said to be rights to freedom of speech and assembly, property rights, rights to equal treatment, rights to equal pay for equal work, rights to education and basic medical care, rights to privacy, a right to know, and even a right to periodic vacation with pay. It is standard practice to invoke these and other rights in a throng of heated disputes about social and legal issues, for example, abortion, affirmative action, workplace privacy, the treatment of children, and environmental protection. But what are rights? Which rights do we have? And how important are they?

In many cases to say that someone has a right is to say that he or she has a justified claim against some person or group of persons. Rights of this kind are called *claim rights*. If a person has a claim right, then he or she is justly due something from others, something that can be demanded without appealing to their kindness, gratitude, pity, or good will. No favor, permission, or grant is needed to exact anything that one has as a matter of right. A person can insist that his or her rights be respected regardless of the wishes or inclinations of others, and, should those rights be denied without sufficient justification, properly raise indignant complaint. Thus, to have a claim right to something puts it beyond the reach of others to deny or withhold except in the most extreme circumstances. It is to have the most compelling and powerful claim of all.

One reason claim rights are so powerful is because they are correlative with duties—with what is due the holder of the right. If someone has a claim right of a certain kind, others have duties toward that person. These duties require either that other people not behave in certain ways toward the person or that he or she be provided with certain goods or benefits. For example, if someone has a right not to be tortured, then others have a duty not to torture him or her; if he or she has a right to medical care, then others are required to provide him or her with medical care. Let us say that claim rights of the former kind are *barrier rights*. If someone has a barrier right, then others are barred from acting in certain ways toward that person. Claim rights of the latter kind are *welfare rights*. If someone has a welfare right, then others are required to provide the person with some good or make the good available to the person.

Although claim rights are an important class of rights, not all rights are claim rights because not all rights imply that other people have specific duties. For example, in the United States a woman has a right to get an abortion, but no individual has a duty to perform abortions. In business, companies have a right to compete for market share, but no one has a duty to see to it that they succeed. We will not discuss these other rights in this introduction. However, several detailed analyses of rights are listed in the suggested readings.

Legal and Moral Rights

Claim rights ("rights" for brevity) can be further classified as either legal or moral rights. In the United States legal rights derive from the Constitution, laws passed by legislatures and common law. Moral rights differ from legal rights in three important ways. First, they do not originate in nor are they justified by the actions of judges or legislative bodies. Second, they are held equally by all persons at all places and times. Third, unless they are codified in law, moral rights are not legally enforceable. To assert one's moral rights is to make a moral rather than a legal claim.[9] But all of this presents a puzzle. If moral rights are had by everyone but do not derive from legislative or judicial action, then evidently one does not have to do anything to possess them. Where, then, do they come from? In virtue of what do persons possess them? And if in many cases they cannot be legally enforced, why value them? In fact, why suppose there are moral rights at all?[10]

A Case for Rights

One reason to think there are moral rights is that they seem to be both the source of many legal rights and the ground or basis from which legitimate criticisms can be made of legal rights. For example, the authors of the Declaration of Independence appealed to "unalienable rights" as a basis from which to criticize the rule of Great Britain and declare it invalid. These rights, for instance, the "Right of the People" to form a new government with new laws, were not legal rights. Indeed, they were used to justify actions that were decidedly illegal.

Moral rights can also be used to justify maintaining as well as changing law. For example, suppose that, using legal means provided for in the Constitution, an attempt is made to repeal the Bill of Rights. If you believe that this is not only a bad idea but also that persons would be wronged unless government is prevented from taking actions prohibited in the Bill of Rights, then you are assuming and appealing to moral rights that are independent of the law.[11]

There are many other examples of moral rights being used to criticize the law or as a justification for passing laws. Social movements, such as the civil rights movement, have been organized to gain rights not codified in law. Wars have been fought to maintain them, and revolutions begun to achieve them. This reiterates a point made earlier: Most people have the concept of a moral right and believe it has meaningful application in human affairs. Perhaps this pragmatic justification of moral rights is all that is needed. However, in our view there is another and more compelling justification. To see what it is, we need to return to Kant.

Kant argues that persons are intrinsically valuable. By this he means, in part, that they have value that is independent of their being valued. Thus, persons have value independent of their value as means to some end. As Kant says, they are ends in themselves. Moreover, all persons have value regardless of whether it is acknowledged or recognized. And all persons have the same degree of intrinsic value. Individuals differ in ability, achievement, and moral and personal virtue, but their intrinsic value is the same.

Now, to say that something is intrinsically valuable or valuable in itself sometimes implies that it is *worth seeking* for itself, and not only worth seeking because it is useful. Pleasure and happiness are intrinsically valuable in this sense. But pleasure and happiness are *psychological states.* They are experiences worth seeking for themselves, and seeking to experience such states is how humans acknowledge their value. But humans are not experiences; they are things that have experiences. Thus, they are not worth seeking in the sense that pleasure and happiness are worth seeking. Thus, to acknowledge the value of persons is not to seek a certain kind of experience. If we are to acknowledge the value of persons, if we are to see them as things that are worthwhile in themselves, something else must be done. But what?

To begin with, note that Kant and the utilitarians share an important belief, which is, roughly, that persons have a moral obligation to promote, protect, or enhance whatever is intrinsically valuable. For utilitarians intrinsic value is located, so to speak, in experience, for example, the experience of pleasure. So utilitarians take it to be their moral obligation to maximize experiences of pleasure. Kant, on the other hand, locates intrinsic value in persons, and only derivatively in human experience. Thus, he believes there is a moral obligation to promote, protect, or enhance persons *qua* persons. This he proposes to do by treating persons as ends in themselves. But exactly how should we acknowledge the intrinsic value that all persons equally possess?

Here is a possibility. All normal persons have the capacity to exercise free choice in service of their interests. We suggest, then, that one way to promote, protect, and enhance the intrinsic value of persons is to grant that they have a valid claim, a *right,* to use this capacity. To respect this right is one way to acknowledge the value of persons. It is to grant that, in an important sense, to freely choose for oneself what one will do, believe, or become, is part of what it means to be a human. It need not be the only way that human value is acknowledged, but is the only way that gives persons the "moral space" to fashion their own lives according to their own rights. It is one way to respect our common humanity, to grant us our due as beings who can apprehend the moral law and freely choose to follow it.

Barrier Rights and Welfare Rights

So far we have argued that everyone has a right to exercise free choice in service of his or her interests. This right can be used to discover other rights. For example, if one has a right to free choice, then it seems reasonable that one has a right to whatever is needed to exercise free choice, for without these other rights the right to free choice would be empty. Among the things needed to exercise free choice is physical security. If the security of one's person or property can be denied or abridged without penalty by arbitrary government edicts or the caprice of individuals, then free choice means little. The right to physical security in turn implies that persons have a right not to be unjustifiably harmed, for example, the right not to be murdered or tortured. These are what we earlier called barrier rights.

A number of other barrier rights have been proposed. Whether these can be derived from the right to free choice is controversial. However, it is generally supposed that barrier rights of all kinds protect vital human interests. Two important examples are the interests persons have in participating in the life of the community, and having a reasonable expectation of accomplishing personal goals. Barrier rights that protect the first interest might be, for example, rights to free speech and assembly, a right to equal treatment under law, and the right to vote and seek political office.

Barrier rights also protect the second interest. Without physical security, for example, no one could have reasonable expectations about the future. A number of people have argued, however, that barrier rights are not enough to protect the second interest. Welfare rights are needed as well. Rights to basic education, health care, and a guaranteed minimum standard of living are all needed, it has been argued, if one is to have any prospects for the future or any hope of undertaking a life plan. Whether there are welfare rights, and if there are, what specific obligations they impose, are issues we will not try to settle. We only note that if persons have a vital interest in living a fulfilling life, then it is difficult to see how one could not claim, as a matter of right, the basic goods needed to make a fulfilling life possible.[12]

Conflict of Rights

In political, social and personal interactions there are many cases in which rights seem to conflict. For example, one person's right to free speech may conflict with another's right to privacy, or one person's right to nondiscriminatory treatment may conflict with another's right to associate with whomever he or she pleases. These cases can be handled in one of two ways. First, a conflict of rights is often only apparent and not actual. Frequently rights are stated in simple and unqualified language that encourages bold assertions based on modest reasons. Unless properly qualified, one person's "I have a right to say what I please" will inevitably conflict with another's "I have a right not to be offended by language I find distasteful." In these cases the specific content of the right and the circumstances under which it holds need to be carefully analyzed. Not all rights hold in all situations without exception. An assertion of right should always be given due consideration, but it does not entitle one to shout "Fire!" in a crowded theater, nor to censor works of art, literature, or political expression.

Sometimes, however, the conflict is real. It then should be recognized that rights, like duties, are *prima facie:* One right can be overridden by another in special cases. For example, the right to peaceful enjoyment of one's property may be overridden by concerns for public safety. The general rule is that, since rights protect interests, when one person's interests are stronger or more compelling than another's, then rights to the latter can be justifiably overridden by rights to the former. Some interests are so strong, however, that it is difficult to imagine cases in which rights protecting those interests can be justifiably overridden. An example is the right not to be tortured.

Although rights can be overridden, the reasons for doing so must be very strong. One person's rights cannot be overridden by the whims of others or by marginal gains for the good of the community. Recognizing rights demonstrates our belief in the value and dignity of persons. To override a right for less than overwhelming reasons belittles the value of persons and denies their dignity. It is not something to be undertaken lightly.

THE ETHICS OF VIRTUE

The Issue of Character

At the beginning of this introduction we defined ethics as the study of what is good or right for persons, of the goals they ought to pursue, and the actions they ought to perform. We understood this definition to imply that the main task of ethics is to discover what responsible moral agents should do when confronted with decisions about right and wrong. One way to approach this task is to carefully formulate ethical or moral principles that distinguish between ethically permissible and ethically impermissible behavior. The principles are then used as guides for making ethical decisions. Utilitarianism and Kantianism are rival accounts of what those principles should be.

There is, however, quite a different way to understand the main task of ethics. Instead of focusing on moral principles, which are used to help answer the question "What should I do," it focuses primarily on moral character and asks "What kind of person should I be or become?" This approach to ethics is based on the concept of *virtue*. It emphasizes moral education and the development of moral character rather than a strict adherence to moral principles. The advantage of this approach, its proponents believe, is that it gives a much more complete and useful account of human life as it is actually lived by real persons in the historical and cultural circumstances in which they find themselves. It does not suppose that persons are, as one writer put it, "faceless ethical agents" striving to follow some abstract utilitarian or Kantian principle. Rather, it tries to describe and understand the traits that enable a person to lead a full and satisfying ethical life.

Virtues are traits of character that both help individuals achieve their goals and are beneficial to the larger community. Examples of virtues are courage, temperance, compassion, generosity, kindness, honesty, and concern for justice. Virtues should be distinguished from other personal traits, such as good health or innate intelligence, because virtues are components of one's character that engage the will. Virtuous acts do not happen by chance. They are chosen by someone who is fully aware of what he or she is doing. And they are chosen because they are virtuous, not because they satisfy self-interest or are pleasurable. However, the Greek philosopher Aristotle, whose analysis of virtue is justly famous and influential, claimed that if one were trained or trained oneself to be, say, charitable, then charitable acts would become pleasurable and miserly acts painful. The charitable person does not begrudge giving money, nor does he or she resent those who receive it. For the charitable person, giving is enjoyable. But, once again, the reason one gives is not because it is enjoyable, but because it is virtuous.

The value of virtues for the individual and the community seems evident. Persons without some measure of the virtues just mentioned are not widely admired, nor, despite certain media images to the contrary, do they generally succeed in life. And a community composed of persons with few virtues is not likely to do well in the long run. Liars, cheats, cowards, and scofflaws are not valuable citizens. An important question, then, is how do persons become virtuous? According to Aristotle, it begins with moral education. Through education one learns the appropriate way to act in different circumstances. One acquires the virtue of honesty, for example, by being taught to act honestly and acting honestly in a variety of situations. Eventually these acts are chosen for their own sake, and honesty becomes a part of one's character. Other virtues are acquired in the same way.

Can one teach oneself to be virtuous? For example, can one teach oneself to be courageous? It would seem so provided three conditions are met. First, one needs a model to follow, someone who actually is courageous. Second, one needs the willpower to act as that person would act if he or she were in a situation that calls for courage. Third, one needs real opportunities to act courageously. Courage (and all other virtues) is a behavior that is learned by doing. For instance, suppose you are a soldier about to enter a battle. You know you are not particularly courageous, but your friend Jones is. When you are in danger, you could ask yourself, "What would Jones do now?" Since Jones is courageous, she would act courageously as a matter of course. If you model your behavior after what she would do, then eventually you will become courageous as well.

If one becomes virtuous by being taught to be virtuous or modeling one's behavior after virtuous persons, then moral education is of the highest importance for a society that values virtuous people. To coin a phrase, virtuous people are made, not born. The social structure in which people live—family, religion, school, and other legal and social institutions—is of central importance in teaching virtue and making it possible for the virtues to be taught. If, through failure of will or lack of conviction, society does not ensure that people have the opportunity to learn to be virtuous, then it should come as no surprise when they are not. This does not imply that people should be brainwashed or indoctrinated with the beliefs of the cultural elite. But it does imply that stands must be taken about the kinds of behaviors that are and are not socially acceptable. Tolerance of the behavior of others is a virtue, but tolerance can be taken to extremes. To tolerate all behavior is to abandon any hope that personal and social relations can be useful, satisfying, or conducive to the general good.

Virtues and Ethical Principles

Philosophers have discussed many issues about virtues that we will be unable to cover in this introduction. They have wondered, for example, whether all virtues have something in common, whether one can have some but not all of the virtues, whether one can be virtuous some but not all of the time, and whether one can exemplify virtues in the service of evil goals. There is, however, one issue we will mention briefly. It is the issue of the relation between virtue ethics and ethical principles of the kind advocated by utilitarians and Kantians. Some virtue theorists claim that one can dispense with ethical principles altogether and construct a complete ethical viewpoint based solely on virtue. Is this possible?

We believe that ethical principles must play an important role in any ethical viewpoint. For example, consider the virtue of honesty in the context of Kant's example of the man fleeing the murderer. Suppose you are an honest person. When the murderer asks you where the man went, what is the honest thing to do? Do you tell the murderer or not?

In this case simply being honest is of no use unless you know which act is honest. And knowing which act is honest depends in part on which ethical principles you hold. For example, suppose you believe that the man fleeing the murderer has a right to life, and that this right cannot be overridden by the murderer's request. Then you would not tell the murderer where the man went. On the other hand, suppose you are a member of a slave owning society, and that in your society a slave owner can do with his slaves as he will. And suppose that the man fleeing is a slave owned by the murderer. Do you tell the murderer where he went? Yes, because you believe that it is the honest thing to do. The rights of the slave are not a consideration, either because you believe that slaves have no rights or because you believe that property rights override the slave's right to life.[13]

The difference between these two societies is not that one has honest men and women and the other does not. The difference is that they hold very different principles about the rights of persons. The slave owning society has the wrong ethical principles. This society may be honest, but it is honesty tainted by service to a mistaken ethical viewpoint.

If our argument is correct, then a complete ethical viewpoint cannot be based solely on virtue. Ethical principles also have an important part to play. However, the role of the virtues should not be underestimated. If we were to ignore them in our account of ethics, then we would omit any understanding of what it means to be a person who actually leads an ethical life. And if we were to ignore them in our practice, then we would lack the continuity, coherence, and content that give our lives meaning. To modify one of Kant's famous phrases, virtuous people who lack ethical principles are ethically blind, but ethical principles without virtuous people are empty.

CONCLUSION

Those first beginning the study of ethics often find it confusing and even disheartening. There seem to be so many different ethical views, each apparently vulnerable to criticism, that it is very difficult to sort it all out and discover a reasonable ethical position that is applicable to everyday concerns. One might be tempted to thow up one's hands and say "When they have it all figured out, then I will listen. Until then, I will just muddle through somehow."

But there is no need to give up so easily. Things are not as bad as they may seem. What follows is a suggestion about how one might proceed.

Suppose we try to combine some of the insights of utilitarianism and Kantianism. Suppose, for example, that we take as basic principles the two parts of Kant's second version of the categorical imperative. In other words, we adopt as a basic principle, first, that no one be treated as a means, and second, that as far as possible, all persons be treated as an end in themselves. And suppose we take the first to imply that persons have, at a minimum, barrier rights that can justifiably be overridden only in extreme circumstances. And we take the second to imply that we should enhance the well being of others—their happiness—to the extent we are able. Thus, by accepting barrier rights we ensure that persons are not treated as means, and by promoting happiness we treat them as ends in themselves.

This gives us two practical principles of ethics—respect the rights of others, and promote their happiness. However, it is possible that enhancing the happiness of some unjustifiably violates the rights of others. So we need to state our "Kantian utilitarian" principle as follows:

An act is ethically permissible if and only if (1) it does not unjustifiably violate any barrier rights, and (2) it brings about as much overall happiness as is consistent with (1). Acts that do not meet conditions (1) and (2) are not ethically permissible.

This principle clearly needs elaboration, analysis, and defense. For instance, it might be said that welfare rights should be included in addition to barrier rights. The number and strength of barrier rights needs to be discussed, as do the conditions under which those rights can be overriden. There remain problems about measuring the amount of happiness that one's actions bring about, and even about whether happiness is the appropriate value to use. And one could object that the principle is too stringent, that it requires too much of persons for them to use it in their ordinary lives. Still, it is, we suggest, a plausible and defensible step in the right direction. It attempts to combine the Kantian insight that it is ethically unacceptable to treat people in certain ways with the utilitarian insight that one should contribute to the general welfare. Whether it proves successful from both a philosophical and practical viewpoint is something that, for the present, we must leave for others to judge.[14]

In this introduction, lengthy though it is, we have omitted many topics in ethics and barely touched on others. This is not because they are unimportant or unworthy of extended comment, but only because choices had to be made. For good or ill, the choices we made reflect what we believe to be the minimum necessary for understanding ethical issues in the world of business. We hope that we have given the reader some of the flavor of ethics, a taste of its richness and complexity. And we hope that the reader will be motivated to continue the study of ethics. Some things, we have tried to argue, are not only useful, they are worthwhile in themselves. We believe the study of ethics is one of them.

NOTES

1. In this introduction we will use the words *moral* and *ethical* interchangeably.
2. See several meta-studies conducted, including Moses L. Pava and Joshua Krausz (March 1996), "The Association Between Corporate Social-Responsibility and Financial Performance: The Paradox of Social Cost," *Journal of Business Ethics* 15(3), 321–358; Jeff Frooman (1997), "Socially Irresponsible and Illegal Behaviour and Shareholder Wealth," *Business & Society* 36(3), 221–249; and Ronald M. Roman, Sefa Hayibor, and Bradley R. Agle (March 1999), "The Relationship Between Social and Financial Performance," *Business & Society* 38(1), 109–125.
3. Someone might object here that even assuming all societies have a common set of ethical rules does not show that those rules are ethically acceptable. It might be that all societies make a similar error about the rules or that they simply follow a rule that is ethically unacceptable.
4. We will sometimes use "egoist" as an abbreviation for "psychological egoist." It is important to see that an egoist, as we will use the term, is an advocate of a theory of human motivation, not someone who has the personality trait of being self-centered.
5. By "act," we mean to include both acts and omissions.
6. For an excellent discussion of this issue, see Amitai Etzioni, *The Moral Dimension: Toward a New Economics* (New York: Free Press, 1988), and Robert H. Frank, *Passions Within Reason: The Strategic Role of the Emotions* (New York: Norton, 1988).
7. Contemporary theories try to avoid this problem by using the notion of preference instead of pleasure. What is maximized is not pleasure, but the choices available to someone. Note that distribution problems could still occur. It might happen that total preferences for a group be maximized by severely restricting the choices available to a minority.
8. Bentham made such an attempt by using the notion of "extent" in his analysis of pleasure.

9. Many moral rights are codified in law. An example is the right to not be murdered. Other moral rights are not a part of law. For instance, a legal right that many people say is not a moral right is the right to an abortion. And an example of what some allege to be a moral right that is not a legal right in the United States is the right to be guaranteed a job.

10. See Jeremy Bentham, "Anarchial Fallacies," in A. I. Melden, ed., *Human Rights* (Belmont, Calif.: Wadsworth, 1970): 28–39.

11. This example is taken from David Lyon's introduction to *Rights* (Belmont, Calif.: Wadsworth, 1979): 3–4.

12. For a defense of welfare rights, see James Sterba, "The Welfare Rights of Distant Peoples and Future Generations: Moral Side Constraints on Social Policy," Social Theory and Practice 7 (Spring 1981).

13. For an excellent discussion of slave societies of this kind, and of many other issues concerning slavery, see Orlando Patterson, *Slavery and Social Death* (Cambridge, Mass.: Harvard University Press, 1982): 190–193.

14. This argument is taken from James W. Cornman and Keith Lehrer, *Philosophical Problems and Arguments: An Introduction* (New York: The Macmillan Company, 1968): 432–434.

SUGGESTED READINGS

There are many fine books on ethics and ethical theory. We include only a very brief selection of those that the reader may find of use should he or she wish to continue the study of ethics.

Utilitarianism

The classic source for utilitarian ethics is John Stuart Mill's *Utilitarianism,* which is in many editions. An excellent collection that includes Mill's work is *Mill: Utilitarianism,* ed. Samuel Gorovitz (Indianapolis: Bobbs-Merrill, 1971). Also see J. J. C. Smart and Bernard Williams, *Utilitarianism: For and Against* (Cambridge: Cambridge University Press, 1980), and Samuel Scheffler, *The Rejection of Consequentialism* (Oxford: Oxford University Press, 1984). A sophisticated utilitarian theory is developed by Richard B. Brandt in his *A Theory of the Good and Right* (Oxford: Clarendon Press, 1979).

Deontological Ethics

Immanuel Kant's writings about ethics extend over several volumes. Perhaps the best place to begin is his *Groundwork of the Metaphysic of Morals,* many editions. An excellent secondary source is Bruce Aune's *Kant's Theory of Morals* (Princeton: Princeton University Press, 1979).

Rights

Among the many books on rights are Ronald Dworkin, *Taking Rights Seriously* (Cambridge: Harvard University Press, 1977), James W. Nickel, *Making Sense of Human Rights* (Berkeley: University of California Press, 1987), Henry Shue, *Basic Rights* (Princeton: Princeton University Press, 1980). For a view of rights that has consequentialist underpinnings, see L. W. Sumner, *The Moral Foundation of Rights* (Oxford: Clarendon Press, 1989).

Virtue

Any investigation of the virtues should probably begin with Aristotle's *Nicomachean Ethics,* many editions. For a contemporary view see Alasdair MacIntyre, *After Virtue* (Notre Dame: University of Notre Dame Press, 1981), and *Whose Justice? Which Rationality?* (Notre Dame: University of Notre Dame Press, 1988). An anthology that has many useful readings on virtue is Christina Sommers and Fred Sommers, eds., *Vice and Virtue in Everyday Life* (New York: Harcourt Brace, 1993).

Ethics and Economics

In addition to the volumes by Etzioni and Frank listed in the endnotes to the introduction, an excellent book about ethics and its relation to economics is Allen Buchanan's *Ethics, Efficiency and the Market* (Totowa, NJ: Rowman and Allanheld, 1985). Also see David Gauthier's *Morals by Agreement* (Oxford: Clarendon Press, 1986) for his insightful development of a theory of morals as a part of the theory of rational choice.

Ethical Skepticism

Finally, for a skeptical view of ethics, nothing is better than J. L. Mackie's book, *Ethics: Inventing Right and Wrong* (New York: Penguin Books, 1977), and Bernard William's *Ethics and the Limits of Philosophy* (Cambridge: Harvard University Press, 1985).

PART ONE

ETHICS AND BUSINESS: FROM THEORY TO PRACTICE

In exploring the ethical dimensions business activity, it is not always enough to focus attention on specific ethical problems. Such issues as rights and duties of employees, product liability, and the responsibility of business to the environment arise in the context of a comprehensive economic system that deeply influences our values and structures the range of choices available to us. Often we will find that the most important ethical question is not "What is right or wrong in this particular situation?" but rather "What is the ethical status of a situation that forces such a choice on the agent?" or "How can it be restructured to provide a more satisfactory climate for ethical decision making?" Some ethical problems are not isolated but systemic; for this reason Chapter 1 of this part examines the free market system itself from an ethical perspective. What we seek when we evaluate economic system ethically, at least in part, is a framework for business transactions and decisions, a set of procedures that, if followed, will generally bring about just results. Justice of this kind—called procedural justice—can be illustrated by the familiar method of dividing a piece of cake between two children: Assuming that the two should receive equal slices, if one child cuts the cake and the other chooses the first slice, justice should be served. Not all just procedures result as just as this one does. But in choosing an economic system we look for one that provides as much justice as possible. Traditionally, it has been held in America that capitalism is such a system; critics challenge this claim. An examination of this controversy requires a clear conception of what justice is, and the first three articles in Chapter 1 provide the groundwork for such a conception by presenting important theories of economic justice.

Even if the free market system is just, it may not mean every event that occurs according to the rules of the system is just. Just procedures are not always sufficient to ensure just results. Suppose, for example, that a person owns one of the five waterholes on an island and that the other four unexpectedly dry up, leaving the owner with a monopoly over the water supply and the opportunity to charge exorbitantly high prices for water. It might be argued that even if the owner of the waterhole acquired it legally, did not conspire to monopolize, and allowed his prices to be determined by the fluctuations of the market, this situation is unjust. Although procedural justice may be necessary to bring about ethical outcomes, it may not be sufficient by itself to do so. Thus, although a just economic system is essential for an ethical business climate, we may also find it necessary to examine the relationships and transactions that take place within the system and to make ethical reasoning a part of business decision making at a more specific, less general level. Chapter 2 suggests some ways in which this might be done.

DISTRIBUTIVE JUSTICE

Questions of economic justice arise when people find themselves in competition for scarce resources—wealth, income, jobs, food, housing. If there are not enough of society's benefits—and too many of society's burdens—to satisfy everyone, we must ask how to distribute these benefits and burdens fairly. One of the most important problems of economic justice, then, is that of the fair distribution of limited commodities.

What does it mean to distribute things justly or fairly? To do justice is to give each person what he or she deserves or is owed. If those who have the most in a society deserved the most and those who have the least deserve the least, that society is a just one. If not, it is unjust. But what makes one person more, another less, deserving?

Philosophers have offered a wide range of criteria for determining who deserves what. One suggestion is that every one deserves an equal share. Others hold that benefits and burdens should be distributed on the basis of need, merit, effort or hard work, or contribution to society. John Rawls, Robert Nozick, and J. J. C. Smart each emphasize one or more of these criteria in constructing a theory of economic justice.

The theory of economic justice underlying American capitalism has tended to emphasize contribution to society, along with merit and hard work, as the basis of distribution. We do not expect everyone to end up with an equal share of benefits and burdens under a capitalist system. But supporters of capitalism hold that those who receive more do so because of their greater contribution, and that for this reason the inequalities are just. Recalling the Kantian ethical principles examined in the general introduction to the text, however, it might be argued that rewarding people on the basis of what they contribute to the general welfare implies treating them as means to an end rather than as ends in themselves and overlooks the intrinsic value of persons. Each person's contribution, furthermore, depends largely on inborn skills and qualities and circumstances that permit the development of these traits. Ought people to be rewarded in proportion to accidents of birth over which they have no control? Some philosophers, like John Rawls, think not.

As an egalitarian, Rawls believes that there are no characteristics that make one person more deserving than another, there are no differences between people that justify inequalities in the distribution of social benefits and burdens. Everyone deserves an equal share. That this is true does not mean that Rawls finds all inequalities unjust; but his theory permits only inequalities that benefit everyone and to which everyone has equal opportunity.

Rawls's principles of distribution are just, he claims, because they are the principles that would be chosen by a group of rational persons designing a society—providing they are ignorant of their own abilities, preferences, and eventual social position. We ought to choose our principles of justice, Rawls argues, from behind a "veil of ignorance," a position strikingly similar to that of the child who cuts the cake evenly, unsure of which piece he or she will eventually have. Although all those in Rawls's hypothetical situation seek to protect their own interest, they are prevented from choosing a principle of distribution that will benefit themselves at the expense of others. Thus they are likely to reject a utilitarian principles of justice under which the happiness of a few might be sacrificed to maximize total well-being or a notion of justice in which distribution depends in part upon luck, skill, natural endowments, or social position. Rawls believes that they would select egalitarian principles.

Some critics have challenged Rawls's claim that rational persons acting from behind a veil of ignorance would choose egalitarian principles of justice. Rawls assumes that all people are egoists, and he fails to take account of the gamblers among us. Others ask whether the choice of egalitarian principles by uninformed egoists is really enough to justify them ethically. A possible defense of Rawls' argument involves an appeal to the Kantian ethical principle examined in the introduction to the text. Kant held that one test of the ethical acceptability of a principle is whether it can be made into a universal law without contradiction. By placing us behind a hypothetical veil of ignorance, Rawls asks us to choose principles of justice that apply to ourselves and all others equally. As a universal law, Rawls seems to be saying, only the egalitarian theory of justice is fully consistent.

Because he gives everyone a voice in what the principle of justice is to be, and because equal treatment seems to recognize every person's intrinsic worth, Rawls's theory of justice also seems to satisfy the second Kantian test, the treatment of all people as ends in themselves. It is not clear, however, that the egalitarian way is the only way to treat people as ends in themselves. Robert Nozick's libertarianism, which emphasizes individual rights instead of equal distribution, might also be susceptible to a Kantian defense.

Unlike Rawls, Nozick focuses his attention not on what each person ends up with, but on how each person acquired what he or she has. Justice for Nozick is historical, it resides in the process of acquisition. A theory of justice thus consists of setting forth rules for just acquisition, and something that has been justly acquired justly belongs to its owner even if this means that some people will receive a far greater share of benefits or burdens than others.

Nozick objects to the attempt to bring about justice by imposing a preconceived pattern of distribution, such as the egalitarian one, because he believes that no such pattern can be realized without violating people's rights. As the word "libertarian" suggests, the right most heavily emphasized by Nozick is a barrier right, the right of freedom, or noninterference. Interference, he holds, is permitted only when the rights of other's are being violated. Second is the right to property that has been justly acquired. Under a libertarian theory of justice, taxation to redistribute and equalize wealth is a violation of human rights, an appropriation of the fruit of other people's freedom akin to forced labor. One might also look upon it as the treatment of others as means. The only way to treat people as ends in themselves, a libertarian might argue, is to grant them freedom from coercion. The only just pattern of distribution, libertarians claim, is not a pattern at all, but the product of a multitude of free, individual choices.

Critics of the libertarian theory generally attack what they view as its truncated conception of human rights. It may be true, they say, that persons have rights of noninterference. But surely there are other human rights more positive in nature. If persons have a right to life, for example, it could be argued that they also have welfare rights to certain things they need in order to live: food, clothing, shelter, and so on. If this is true, their right to these things might sometimes override someone else's right to noninterference.

For example, Nozick himself admits that it is unjust for one person to appropriate the entire supply of something necessary for life, as in the example of the waterhole mentioned earlier. If it is correct that there are welfare rights that supersede the right to noninterference, libertarianism needs reexamining.

J. J. C. Smart's utilitarian theory of justice differs from both Nozick's and Rawls's in that it neither attempts to make distribution conform to a specific pattern nor focuses on the process by which distribution takes place. As a utilitarian, Smart is concerned with the maximization of happiness or pleasure, and approves of any distribution of goods that accomplishes this goal. Thus, utilitarian justice could be compatible with either an equal or an unequal distribution of goods, depending on which of the two is shown to provide the greatest total happiness. Although in general Smart believes that an egalitarian distribution of benefits and burdens is most likely to maximize happiness, he is in no way committed to equality as a principle of distribution. On the contrary, if he were to find that extreme inequalities maximize happiness, he would be committed to these strategies. Utilitarianism, in short, is interested in the maximization of happiness and not in its distribution.

Some thinkers find utilitarianism's stress on the sum total of happiness to be incompatible with the very idea of justice, and Smart admits that justice is only a subordinate interest for utilitarians. Under utilitarianism, people may be denied what they deserve because that denial increases total happiness.

JUSTICE AND ECONOMIC SYSTEMS

Rawls, Nozick and Smart offer three different theories of economic justice. They have made no claims, however, about how their principles of justice might best be embodied in an economic system. Rawls, for example, might assert that his theory is compatible with both capitalism and socialism. In articles by James Q. Wilson and Kai Nielsen, we examine the concepts of morality and justice underlying two quite different economic systems. James Q. Wilson offers a qualified defense of the morality of capitalism, whereas Kai Nielsen presents a moral case for socialism.

Perhaps the two most important features of capitalism are (1) private ownership of the means of production (as opposed to common or government ownership), and (2) a market system in which prices and wages are not controlled by the government or an elite group, but fluctuate according to supply and demand. Essential to the system is economic freedom—the freedom of workers to move from job to job, the freedom of businesses to produce goods and provide services, and the freedom of everyone to participate in the market. Given these freedoms, James Q. Wilson argues, there is no question that capitalism can produce a greater abundance of material goods, at a lower cost, for a greater number of people, than economic systems such as socialism where economic freedom is restricted. In economic terms, them, capitalism is clearly preferable to other economic arrangements. Thus, if it is subject to criticism, Wilson says, it cannot be because it is an inferior economic system. The criticism must be on other grounds. What might those grounds be?

According to Wilson, they are primarily moral. It may be true that capitalism produces material abundance, but, the critics allege, it does so at too high a price. The costs in social injustice, environmental degradation, and human suffering caused by economic dislocation, are much too high. Thus, we would all be better off were we to accept a lower standard of living, in economic terms, if we could thereby preserve and enhance other things that we value, such as social justice.

Wilson concedes that capitalism has its moral costs—but so does any large scale human activity. Thus, the real question, he says, is whether there are other, workable, economic arrangements that have fewer moral costs. In a wide ranging essay that draws on a number of sources, Wilson tries to show that there is no alternative to capitalism that is both economically feasible and morally superior. Capitalism, he says, is not irrelevant to morality. Like all economic systems, it requires and encourages certain moral dispositions, and threatens others. For example, he argues that capitalism is necessary, if not sufficient, for political democracy, and that is fosters virtues such as trustworthiness, self-command, and cosmopolitanism. Consequently, he concludes, considered as a whole, capitalism poses no greater moral hazard to individuals than other economic systems that might be proposed.

However, this does not imply that capitalism does not have moral problems. The genuine danger, Wilson argues, is not systemic, that is, is not a consequence of the capitalist system, but occurs at the level of individual firms. If individual firms ignore the fact that their activities can and should be judged in moral as well as economic terms, if they neglect their moral obligations and act in ways that the public finds morally unacceptable, then they endanger the system itself. The public need not be expected to tolerate repeated corporate moral failings, nor should it have to bear the burden of corrupt corporate practices. And since the only certain way to eliminate or reduce such immoral practices is through political action, action that could well severely restrict corporate and personal economic freedom, individual firms that act immorally threaten the system itself. Hence, Wilson argues, serious corporate executives must recognize the moral dimensions of corporate activity, and work toward making corporations full and responsible participants in the moral life of the community.

In contrast to Wilson, Kai Nielsen argues that a very different economic system—socialism—should be undertaken in the interest of social justice. In large part, it is because capitalism is supposedly inconsistent with social justice that socialists like Nielsen reject it.

According to Nielsen, capitalism should be rejected because it is consistent with a high degree of inequality. Placing ownership in private hands, socialists believe, creates a class system in which wealth is concentrated in the hands of a few, and the rich get richer at the expense of the poor. These economic inequalities lead to inequalities in liberty and power as well. According to socialists, a capitalist society can never be truly democratic, even in a democratic political system, because the wealthy few are far more free and powerful than others.

These problems can be solved, socialists claim, by public ownership of the means of production and careful, systematic planning. Public ownership would eliminate the need for private profit, decrease prices, and allow enterprises to better serve the public. Planning would direct the economy for the public interest, rather than allow it to be controlled randomly by the self-interest actions of a few. Socialists do not believe that planning will interfere with individual liberty and democracy, Nielsen explains. Rather, socialists are committed to democratic planning in which the people vote to determine economic goals and directions. If fact, socialism, as Nielsen presents it, sees itself as more democratic than capitalism because it involves the extension of democracy from the political into the economic arena.

Neilsen's argument is specifically a *moral* argument for socialism. He believes that moral principles should take precedence over the demand for profit. The rationale for production in capitalism is profit and capital accumulation. But in socialism, Neilsen argues, the rationale is to meet human needs. Moreover, he claims that democratic socialism will produce greater autonomy, more nearly equal life chances, and a greater equality of opportunity. Thus, in his view, an economy based on democratic socialism would be a more humane and just system than capitalism.

FROM THEORY TO PRACTICE

In Chapter 2 we turn from an examination of the justice of economic systems to an investigation of ethical business decision making within the system at a concrete, specific level. Some of the issues and difficulties business persons face when making ethical business decisions are illustrated in the cases at the end of Part One. For example, in "Why Should My Conscience Bother Me?" Kermit Vandivier's discussion of his own part in the B. F. Goodrich aircraft brake scandal highlights the importance of ethics in business decision making. Striking in Goodrich's decision to market a defective brake are the lack of clarity concerning corporate values, the evasion of responsibility, and the refusal or inability of managers to engage in ethical reflection. Although Vandivier and his associates recognized that they were trapped in an ethical dilemma, they lacked the conceptual and analytic tools to state the dilemma clearly and to make their concerns impact upon corporate policy in an effective way.

These tools are discussed in detail in the articles by Michael Josephson, and Craig Dreilinger and Dan Rice. These articles examine what is required for ethical decisions on a personal level, and describe a decision-making process managers can use when confronted with an ethical decision. Josephson defines a series of essential terms that he uses in his discussion of ethical values and principles. He also analyses some of the more common misconceptions about ethics, and goes over excuses and rationalizations for acting unethically. He concludes that using principled ethical decision-making procedures helps accomplish two important things. The first is to distinguish ethical from unethical responses. All too often business people do not consider the ethical dimensions of their choices, or they assume that business or legal principles take precedence over ethics. This leads them to accept unethical choices, or even to fail to acknowledge that ethics is a factor in the decision. The second thing using principled ethical decision making accomplishes is to help rank acceptable ethical alternatives. For a variety of reasons, for example, crucial facts about the consequences of a certain decision are unknown or ambiguous, some of the alternatives may be better than others.

Craig Dreilinger and Dan Rice discuss a systematic model for analyzing ethical decisions. The components of the model include identifying desired outcomes; defining the problem; examining obstacles; developing alternatives; selecting the best solution; delineating specific steps; and identifying reactions. As a part of their discussion they describe three conditions under which it is impossible to resolve ethical issues. These are conditions that preclude obtaining the required knowledge, that preclude exercising freedom of choice, and conditions under which a manager lacks the power to influence the outcome. These three conditions in effect describe circumstances that excuse inaction and block moral blame from attaching to managers. Not all moral problems that one knows about are something that one can do something about.

It should be emphasized that the procedure Dreilinger and Rice propose is not intended to be a deterministic algorithm that invariably generates an acceptable solution to ethical issues. It is instead a heuristic that, for its proper application, makes great demands on the judgment, discernment and sensitivity of the persons who use it. But that is not surprising, given the complexity of most ethical problems.

In the next article James Waters and Frederick Bird provide a way of conceptualizing the kinds of ethical decisions managers make. They propose a four part typology of morally questionable managerial acts: non-role against the firm; role failure against the firm; role distortion for the firm; and role assertion for the firm. According to this typology, the acts that Vandivier and his associates engaged in were role distortion for the firm. As Waters and Bird point out, acts that fall in this particular category receive less managerial attention than, for example, role failure acts against the firm. They argue that such acts should receive more attention because they occur more often in the corporate life of typical managers.

In the final two articles in Chapter 2, a popular method of evaluating business decisions is discussed in articles by Steven Kelman, and Herman Leonard and Richard Zeckhauser. Kelman sees in this widely used technique for business decision making—cost-benefit analysis—a close resemblance to the utilitarian principle examined in the general introduction. He uses theoretical ethics to illuminate cost-benefit analysis and to argue for his claim that it should not be used as the primary tool in making ethical decisions. Commitment to cost-benefit analysis, as Kelman describes it, implies that costs and benefits should be totaled and weighed against each other in making a decision, that an act should not be undertaken unless its benefits exceed its costs, and that benefits and costs must be assigned dollar values so that they can be compared on a common scale.

We have already encountered the primary objections to utilitarianism in the introduction to the text. Kelman reiterates some of these. Utilitarianism identified what is right with what maximizes benefits and minimizes costs, Kelman explains. But he argues that there are instances—those that involve the breaking of a promise, for example, or the violation of a human right—in which an act may be wrong even if its benefits outweigh its costs. Kelman cites examples to illustrate his claim that the utilitarian principle permits or even requires some actions that we are inclined to feel are morally repugnant.

Kelman also challenges the possibility of placing dollar values on nonmarket items such as clean air, health and safety, and human life. And even if it were possible to determine prices for these goods that truly reflect their value to society, he holds, it would not be advisable to do so. Certain items like life and health are "priceless," and the very act of placing a price on them may distort their perceived value in society. Kelman fears that placing a price on these things declares that they are for sale; thus, a worker's health may be traded because its dollar value is less than that of the equipment required to protect it. Cost-benefit analysis is particularly inappropriate, Kelman argues, when such "specially valued things" are at stake.

Leonard and Zeckhauser attempt to rebut several of the objections Kelman raises against cost-benefit analysis. They argue cost-benefit analysis is an appropriate tool for making decisions affecting the public interest. They concede that not everything of value can be represented within the framework of cost-benefit analysis, but point out that this does not diminish its usefulness. It may be true that more is at stake than can be measured in terms of costs and benefits, but that does not mean that they are unimportant. Finally, they note that cost-benefit analysis is particularly valuable in decisions involving the imposition of risk. They say it is the most practical of the ethically defensible decision-making methods available. It is not without flaws, but it is better than the alternatives.

MINI-CASES AND CASES IN PART ONE

The two mini-cases in Part One involve individuals facing ethical dilemmas at the workplace. In the mini-case "Tina Wilson," an employee must address a conflict of interest situation, whereas the mini-case "Tony Benson" involves an employee confronting the fact he may have just disclosed important confidential information. The articles in Chapter 2 involving ethical decision making can be instructive in helping to resolve the dilemmas.

The cases included in Part One involve issues of economic justice as well as ethical decision making. Consider the "Parable of the Sadhu." The case involves a series of ethical issues related to the decision by a Wall Street executive to leave behind an Indian holy man in the Himalayan mountains. Did the executive act appropriately in the circumstances? The case "Dorrence Corporation Trade-Offs" involves critical budgetary decisions faced by the company's CEO. Some of the budget issues regard matters such as research and development expenditures, capital investment, employee health insurance costs, and plant closures. What items should take priority? On what basis? The article "Less Cost, More Risk" asks the reader to balance the cost savings obtained by flying discount airlines such as ValuJet versus the increased safety risks. The case asks the question "How much do you think your life is worth?" Both of these cases entail important issues of justice and cost-benefit analysis. In "Why Should My Conscience Bother Me?" Kermit Vandivier must decide whether to disclose inappropriate testing methods used to qualify B. F. Goodrich's aircraft brakes. Why did Vandivier make the decision to go along with those around him? How did he end up getting caught in his ethical trap? One potential means by which employees such as Vandivier could use to make ethical decisions is provided in a "Framework for Ethical Decision-Making," used by PricewaterhouseCoopers.

CHAPTER 1

Theories of Economic Justice

Justice as Fairness

John Rawls
James Bryant Conant University
Professor,Emeritus, Harvard University

THE MAIN IDEA OF THE THEORY OF JUSTICE

My aim is to present a conception of justice which generalizes and carries to a higher level of abstraction the familiar theory of the social contract as found, say, in Locke, Rousseau, and Kant. In order to do this we are not to think of the original contract as one to enter a particular society or to set up a particular form of government. Rather, the guiding idea is that the principles of justice for the basic structure of society are the object of the original agreement. They are the principles that free and rational persons concerned to further their own interests would accept in an initial position of equality as defining the fundamental terms of their association. These princi-

ples are to regulate all further agreements: they specify the kinds of social cooperation that can be entered into and the forms of government that can be established. This way of regarding the principles of justice I shall call justice as fairness.

Thus we are to imagine that those who engage in social cooperation choose together, in one joint act, the principles which are to assign basic rights and duties and to determine the division of social benefits. Men are to decide in advance how they are to regulate their claims against one another and what is to be the foundation charter of their society. Just as each person must decide by rational reflection what constitutes his good, that is, the system of ends which it is rational for him to pursue, so a group of persons must decide once and for all what is to count among them as just and unjust. The choice which rational men would make in this hypothetical situation of equal liberty, assuming for the present that this choice problem has a solution, determines the principles of justice.

In justice as fairness the original position of equality corresponds to the state of nature in the traditional theory of the social contract. This original position is not, of course, thought of as an actual historical state of affairs, much less as a primitive condition of culture. It is understood as a purely hypothetical situation characterized so as to lead to a certain conception of justice. Among the essential features of this situation is that no one knows his place in society, his class position or social status, nor does any one know his fortune in the distribution of natural assets and abilities, his intelligence, strength, and the like. I shall even assume that the parties do not know their conceptions of the good or their special psychological propensities. The principles of justice are chosen behind a veil of ignorance. This ensures that no one is advantaged or disadvantaged in the choice of principles by the outcome of natural chance or the contingency of social circumstances. Since all are similarly situated and no one is able to design principles to favor his particular condition, the principles of justice are the result of a fair agreement or bargain. For given the circumstances of the original position, the symmetry of everyone's relations to each other, this initial situation is fair between individuals as moral persons, that is, as rational beings with their own ends and capable, I shall assume, of a sense of justice. The original position is, one might say, the appropriate initial status quo, and thus the fundamental agreements reached in it are fair. This explains the propriety of the name "justice as fairness": it conveys the idea that the principles of justice are agreed to in an initial situation that is fair. The name does not mean that the concepts of justice and fairness are the same, any more than the phrase "poetry as metaphor" means that the concepts of poetry and metaphor are the same.

Justice as fairness begins, as I have said, with one of the most general of all choices which persons might make together, namely, with the choice of the first principles of a conception of justice which is to regulate all subsequent criticism and reform of institutions. Then, having chosen a conception of justice, we can suppose that they are to choose a constitution and a legislature to enact laws, and so on, all in accordance with the principles of justice initially agreed upon. Our social situation is just if it is such that by this sequence of hypothetical agreements we would have contracted into the general system of rules which defines it.

It maybe observed that once the principles of justice are thought of as arising from an original agreement in a situation of equality, it is an open question whether the principle of utility would be acknowledged. Offhand it hardly seems likely that persons who view themselves as equals, entitled to press their claims upon one another, would agree to a principle which may require lesser life prospects for some simply for the sake of a greater sum of advantages enjoyed by others. Since each desires to protect his interests, his capacity to advance his conception of the good, no one has a reason to acquiesce in an enduring loss for himself in order to bring about a greater net balance of satisfaction. In the absence of strong and lasting benevolent impulses, a rational man would not accept a basic structure merely because it maximized the algebraic sum of advantages irrespective of its permanent effects on his own basic rights and interests. Thus it seems that the principle of utility is incompatible with the conception of social cooperation among equals for mutual advantage. It appears to be inconsistent with the idea of reciprocity implicit in the notion of a well-ordered society. Or, at any rate, so I shall argue.

I shall maintain instead that the persons in the initial situation would choose two rather different principles: the first requires equality in the assignment of basic rights and duties, while the second holds that social and economic inequalities, for example inequalities of wealth and authority, are just only if they result in compensating benefits for everyone, and in particular for the least advantaged members of society. These principles rule out justifying institutions on the grounds that the hardships of some are offset by a greater good in the aggregate. It may be expedient but it is not just that some should have less in order that others may prosper. But there is no injustice in the greater benefits earned by a few provided that the situation of persons not so fortunate is thereby improved. The intuitive idea is that since everyone's well-being depends upon a scheme of cooperation without which no one could have a satisfactory life, the division of advantages should be such as to draw forth the willing cooperation of everyone taking part in it, including those less well situated. Yet this can be expected only if reasonable terms are proposed. The two principles mentioned seem to be a fair agreement on the basis of which those better endowed, or more fortunate in their social position, neither of which we can be said to deserve, could expect the willing cooperation of others when some workable scheme is a necessary condition of the welfare of all.[1] Once we decide to look for a conception of justice that nullifies the accidents of natural endowment and the contingencies of social circumstance as counters in quest for political and economic advantage, we are led to these principles. They express the result of leaving aside those aspects of the social world that seem arbitrary from a moral point of view.

The idea of the original position is to set up a fair procedure so that any principles agreed to will be just. Some how we must nullify the effects of specific contingencies which put men at odds and tempt them to exploit social and natural circumstances to their own advantage. Now in order to do this I assume that the parties are situated behind a veil of ignorance. They do not know how the various alternatives will affect their own particular case and they are obliged to evaluate principles solely on the basis of general considerations.[2] The veil of ignorance enables us to make vivid to ourselves the restrictions that it seems reasonable to impose on arguments for principles of justice, and therefore on these principles themselves. Thus it seems reasonable and generally acceptable that no one should be advantaged or disadvantaged by natural fortune or social circumstances in the choice of principles. It also seems widely agreed that it should be impossible to tailor principles to the circumstances of one's own case. We should insure further that particular inclinations and aspirations, and persons' conceptions of their good do not affect the principles adopted. The aim is to rule out those principles that it would be rational to propose for acceptance, however little the chance of success, only if one knew certain things that are irrelevant from the stand point of justice. For example, if a man knew that he was wealthy, he might find it rational to advance the principle that various taxes for welfare measures be counted unjust; if he knew that he was poor, he would most likely propose the contrary principle. To represent the desired restrictions one imagines a situation in which everyone is deprived of this sort of information. One excludes the knowledge of those contingencies which sets men at odds and allows them to be guided by their prejudices.

It is assumed, then, that the parties do not know certain kinds of particular facts. First of all, no one knows his place in society, his class position or social status; nor does he know his fortune in the distribution of natural assets and abilities, his intelligence and strength, and the like. Nor, again, does anyone know his conception of the good, the particulars of his rational plan of life, or even the special features of his psychology such as his aversion to risk or liability to optimism or pessimism. More than this, I assume that the parties do not know the particular circumstances of their own society. That is, they do not know its economic or political situation, or the level of civilization and culture it has been able to achieve. The persons in the original position have no information as to which generation they belong. These broader restrictions on knowledge are appropriate in part because questions of social justice arise between generations as well as within them, for example, the question of the appropriate rate of capital saving and of the conservation of natural resources and the environment of nature. There is also, theoretically anyway, the question of a reasonable genetic policy. In these cases too, in order to carry through the idea of the original position, the parties must not know the contingencies that set them in opposition. They must choose principles the consequences of which they are prepared to live with whatever generation they turn out to belong to. As far as possible, then, the only particular facts which the parties know is that their society is subject to the circumstances of justice and whatever this implies.

The restrictions on particular information in the original position are of fundamental importance. The veil of ignorance makes possible a unanimous choice of a particular conception of justice. Without these limitations on knowledge the bargaining problem of the original position would be hopelessly complicated. Even if theoretically a solution were to exist, we would not, at present anyway, be able to determine it.

The Rationality of the Parties

I have assumed throughout that the persons in the original position are rational. In choosing between principles each tries as best he can to advance his interests. But I have also assumed that the parties do not know their conception of the good. This means that while they know that they have some rational plan of life, they do not know the details of this plan, the particular ends and interests which it is calculated to promote. How, then, can they decide which conceptions of justice are most to their advantage? Or must we suppose that they are reduced to mere guessing? To meet this difficulty, I postulate that they would prefer more primary social goods rather than less (i.e., rights and liberties, powers and opportunities, income and wealth and self-respect). Of course, it may turn out, once the veil of ignorance is removed, that some of them for religious or other reasons may not, in fact, want more of these goods. But from the standpoint of the original position, it is rational for the parties to suppose that they do want a larger share, since in any case they are not compelled to accept more if they do not wish to nor does a person suffer from a greater liberty. Thus even though the parties are deprived of information about their particular ends, they have enough knowledge to rank the alternatives. They know that in general they must try to protect their liberties, widen their opportunities, and enlarge their means for promoting their aims whatever these are. Guided by the theory of the good and the general facts of moral psychology, their deliberations are no longer guesswork. They can make a rational decision in the ordinary sense.

The assumption of mutually disinterested rationality, then, comes to this: the persons in the original position try to acknowledge principles which advance their system of ends as far as possible. They do this by attempting to win for themselves the highest index of primary social goods, since this enables them to promote their conception of the good most effectively whatever it turns out to be. The parties do not seek to confer benefits or to impose injuries on one another; they are not moved by affection or rancor. Nor do they try to gain relative to each other; they are not envious or vain. Put in terms of a game, we might say: they strive for as high an absolutes core as possible. They do not wish a high or a low score for their opponents, nor do they seek to maximize or minimize the difference between their successes and those of others. The idea of a game does not really apply, since the parties are not concerned to win but to get as many points as possible judged by their own system of ends.

I shall now state in a provisional form the two principles of justice that I believe would be chosen in the original position. The first statement of the two principles reads as follows.

- First: each person is to have an equal right to the most extensive basic liberty compatible with a similar liberty for others.
- Second: social and economic inequalities are to be arranged so that they are both (a) reasonably expected to be to everyone's advantage, and (b) attached to positions and offices open to all.

By way of general comment, these principles primarily apply, as I have said, to the basic structure of society. They are to govern the assignment of rights and duties and to regulate the distribution of social and economic advantages. As their formulation suggests, these principles presuppose that the social structure can be divided into two more or less distinct parts, the first principle applying to the one, the second to the other. They distinguish between those aspects of the social system that define and secure the equal liberties of citizenship and those that specify and establish social and economic inequalities. The basic liberties of citizens are, roughly speaking, political liberty (the right to vote and to be eligible for public office) together with freedom of speech and assembly; liberty of conscience and freedom of thought; freedom of the person along with the right to hold (personal) property; and freedom from arbitrary arrest and seizure as defined by the concept of the rule of law. These liberties are all required to be equal by the first principle, since citizens of a just society are to have the same basic rights.

The second principle applies, in the first approximation, to the distribution of income and wealth and to the design of organizations that make use of differences in authority and responsibility, or chains of command. While the distribution of wealth and income need not be equal, it must be to everyone's advantage, and at the same time, positions of authority and offices of command must be accessible to all. One applies the second principle by holding positions open, and then, subject to this constraint, arranges social and economic inequalities so that everyone benefits.

These principles are to be arranged in a serial order with the first principle prior to the second. This ordering means that a departure from the institutions of equal liberty required by the first principle cannot be justified by, or compensated for, by greater social and economic advantages. The distribution of wealth and income, and the hierarchies of authority, must be consistent with both the liberties of equal citizenship and equality of opportunity.

It is clear that these principles are rather specific in their content, and their acceptance rests on certain assumptions that I must eventually try to explain and justify. For the present, it should be observed that the two principles (and this holds for all formulations) are a special case of a more general conception of justice that can be expressed as follows.

> All social values—liberty and opportunity, income and wealth, and the bases of self-respect—are to be distributed equally unless an unequal distribution of any, or all, of these values is to everyone's advantage.

Injustice, then, is simply inequalities that are not to the benefit of all. Of course, this conception is extremely vague and requires interpretation.

As a first step, suppose that the basic structure of society distributes certain primary goods, that is, things that every rational man is presumed to want. These goods normally have a use whatever a person's rational plan of life. For simplicity, assume that the chief primary goods at the disposition of society are rights and liberties, powers and opportunities, income and wealth. These are the social primary goods. Other primary goods such as health and vigor, intelligence and imagination, are natural goods; although their possession is influenced by the basic structure, they are not so directly under its control. Imagine, then, a hypothetical initial arrangement in which all the social primary goods are equally distributed: everyone has similar rights and duties, and income and wealth are evenly shared. This state of affairs pro-vides a benchmark for judging improvements. If certain inequalities of wealth and organizational powers would make everyone better off than in this hypothetical starting situation, then they accord with the general conception.

Now it is possible, at least theoretically, that by giving up some of their fundamental liberties men are sufficiently compensated by the resulting social and economic gains. The general conception of justice imposes no restrictions on what sort of inequalities are permissible; it only requires that everyone's position be improved.

The second principle insists that each person benefit from permissible inequalities in the basic structure. This means that it must be reasonable for each relevant representative man defined by this structure, when he views it as a going concern, to prefer his prospects with the inequality to his prospects without it. One is not allowed to justify differences in income or organizational powers on the ground that the disadvantages of those in one position are outweighed by the greater advantages of those in another. Much less can infringements of liberty be counterbalanced in this way. Applied to the basic structure, the principle of utility would have us maximize the sum of expectations of representative men (weighted by the number of persons they represent, on the classical view); and this would permit us to compensate for the losses of some by the gains of others. Instead, the two principles require that everyone benefit from economic and social inequalities.

The Tendency to Equality

I wish to conclude this discussion of the two principles by explaining the sense in which they express an egalitarian conception of justice. Also I should like to forestall the objection to the principle of fair opportunity that it leads to a callous meritocratic society. In order to prepare the way for doing this, I note several aspects of the conception of justice that I have set out.

First we may observe that the difference principle gives some weight to the considerations singled out by the principle of redress. This is the principle that undeserved inequalities call for redress; and since inequalities of birth and natural endowment are undeserved, these inequalities are to be somehow compensated for.[3] Thus the principle holds that in order to treat all persons equally, to provide genuine equality of opportunity, society must give more attention to those with fewer native assets and to those born into the less favorable social positions. The idea is to redress the bias of contingencies in the direction of equality. In pursuit of this principle greater resources might be spent on the education of the less rather than the more intelligent, at least over a certain time of life, say the earlier years of school.

Now the principle of redress has not to my knowledge been proposed as the sole criterion of justice, as the single aim of the social order. It is plausible as most such principles are only as a *prima facie* principle, one that is to be weighed in the balance with others. For example, we are to weigh it against the principle to improve the average standard of life, or to advance the common good. But whatever other principles we hold, the claims of redress are to be taken into account. It is thought to represent one of the elements in our conception of justice. Now the difference principle is not of course the principle of redress. It does not require society to try to even out handicaps as if all were expected to compete on a fair basis in the same race. But the difference principle would allocate resources in education, say, so as to improve the long-term expectation of the least favored. If this end is attained by giving more attention to the better endowed, it is permissible; otherwise not. And in making this decision, the value of education should not be assessed only in terms of economic efficiency and social welfare. Equally if not more important is the role of education in enabling a person to enjoy the culture of his society and to take part in its affairs, and in this way to provide for each individual a secure sense of his own worth.

Thus although the difference principle is not the same as that of redress, it does achieve some of the intent of the latter principle. It transforms the aims of the basic structure so that the total scheme of institutions no longer emphasizes social efficiency and technocratic values. We see then that the difference principle represents, in effect, an agreement to regard the distribution of natural talents as a common asset and to share in the benefits of this distribution whatever it turns out to be. Those who have been favored by nature, whoever they are, may gain from their good fortune only on terms that improve the situation of those who have lost out. The naturally advantaged are not to gain merely because they are more gifted, but only to cover the costs of training and education and for using their endowments in ways that help the less fortunate as well. No one deserves his greater natural capacity nor merits a more favorable starting place in society. But it does not follow that one should eliminate these distinctions. There is another way to deal with them. The basic structure can be arranged so that these contingencies work for the good of the least fortunate. Thus we are led to the difference principle if we wish to set up the social system so that no one gains or loses from his arbitrary place in the distribution of natural assets or his initial position in society without giving or receiving compensating advantages in return.

The natural distribution of talents is neither just nor unjust; nor is it unjust that men are born into society at some particular position. These are simply natural facts. What is just and unjust is the way that institutions deal with these facts. Aristocratic and caste societies are unjust because they make these contingencies the ascriptive basis for belonging to more or less enclosed and privileged social classes. The basic structure of these societies incorporates the arbitrariness found in nature. But there is no necessity for men to resign themselves to these contingencies. The social system is not an unchangeable order beyond human control but a pattern of human action. In justice as fairness men agree to share one another's fate. In designing institutions they undertake to avail themselves of the accidents of nature and social circumstance only when doing so is for the common benefit. The two principles are a fair way of meeting the arbitrariness of fortune; and while no doubt imperfect in other ways, the institutions which satisfy these principles are just.

There is a natural inclination to object that those better situated deserve their greater advantages whether or not they are to the benefit of others. At this point it is necessary to be clear about the notion of desert. It is perfectly true that given a just system of cooperation as a scheme of public rules and the expectations set up by it, those who, with the prospect of improving their condition, have done what the system announces that it will reward are entitled to their advantages. In this sense the more fortunate have a claim to their better situation; their claims are legitimate expectations established by social institutions, and the community is obligated to meet them. But this sense of desert presupposes the existence of the cooperative scheme; it is irrelevant to the question whether in the first place the scheme is to be designed in accordance with the difference principle or some other criterion.

Perhaps some will think that the person with greater natural endowments deserves those assets and the superior character that made their development possible. Because he is more worthy in this sense, he deserves the greater advantages that he could achieve with them. This view, however, is surely incorrect. It seems to be one of the fixed points of our considered judgments that no one deserves his place in the distribution of native endowments, any more than one deserves one's initial starting place in society. The assertion that a man deserves the superior character that enables him to make the effort to cultivate his abilities is equally problematic; for his character depends in large part upon fortunate family and social circumstances for which he can claim no credit. The notion of desert seems not to apply to these cases. Thus the more advantaged representative man cannot say that he deserves and therefore has a right to a scheme of cooperation in which he is permitted to acquire benefits in ways that do not contribute to the welfare of others. There is no basis for his making this claim. From the standpoint of common sense, then, the difference principle appears to be acceptable both to the more advantaged and to the less advantaged individual.

NOTES

1. For the formulation of this intuitive idea I am indebted to Allan Gibbard.
2. The veil of ignorance is so natural a condition that something like it must have occurred to many. The closest express statement of it known to me is found in J. C. Harsanyi, "Cardinal Utility in Welfare Economics and in the Theory of Risk-Taking." *Journal of Political Economy,* vol. 61 (1953). Harsanyi uses it to develop a utilitarian theory.
3. See Herbert Spiegelberg, "A Defense of Human Equality," *Philosophical Review,* vol. 53 (1944), pp. 101, 113–123; and D. D. Raphael, "Justice and Liberty," *Proceedings of the Aristotelian Society,* vol. 51 (1950–1951), p. 187f.

Distributive Justice

Robert Nozick
Pellegrino University Professor, Harvard University

The minimal state is the most extensive state that can be justified. Any state more extensive violates people's rights. Yet many persons have put forth reasons purporting to justify a more extensive state. It is impossible within the compass of this book to examine all the reasons that have been put forth. Therefore, I shall focus upon those generally acknowledged to be most weighty and influential, to see precisely wherein they fail. In this paper we consider the claim that a more extensive state is justified, because necessary (or the best instrument) to achieve distributive justice.

The term "distributive justice" is not a neutral one. Hearing the term "distribution," most people presume that some thing or mechanism uses some principle or criterion to give out a supply of things. Into this process of distributing shares some error may have crept. So it is an open question, at least, whether *re*distribution should take place; whether we should do again what has already been done once, though poorly. However, we are not in the position of children who have been given portions of pie by someone who now makes last minute adjustments to rectify careless cutting. There is no *central* distribution, no person or group entitled to control all the resources, jointly deciding how they are to be doled out. What each person gets, he gets from others who give to him in exchange for something, or as a gift. In a free society, diverse persons control different resources, and new holdings arise out of the voluntary exchanges and actions of persons. There is no more a distributing or distribution of shares than there is a distributing of mates in a society in which persons choose whom they shall marry. The total result is the product of many individual decisions which the different individuals involved are entitled to make.

THE ENTITLEMENT THEORY

The subject of justice in holdings consists of three major topics. The first is the *original acquisition of holdings,* the appropriation of unheld things. This includes the issues of how unheld things may come to be held, the process, or processes, by which unheld things may come to be held, the things that may come to be held by these processes, the extent of what comes to be held by a particular process, and so on. We shall refer to the complicated truth about this topic, which we shall not formulate here, as the principle of justice in acquisition. The second topic concerns the *transfer of holdings* from one person to another. By what processes may a person transfer holdings to another? How may a person acquire a holding from another who holds it? Under this topic come general descriptions of voluntary exchange, and gift and (on the other hand) fraud, as well as reference to particular conventional details fixed upon in a given society. The complicated truth about this subject (with placeholders for conventional details) we shall call the principle of justice in transfer. (And we shall suppose it also includes principles governing how a person may divest himself of a holding, passing it into an unheld state.)

If the world were wholly just, the following inductive definition would exhaustively cover the subject of justice in holdings.

1. A person who acquires a holding in accordance with the principle of justice in acquisition is entitled to that holding.

2. A person who acquires a holding in accordance with the principle of justice in transfer, from someone else entitled to the holding, is entitled to the holding.

3. No one is entitled to a holding except by (repeated) applications of 1 and 2.

The complete principle of distributive justice would say simply that a distribution is just if everyone is entitled to the holdings they possess under the distribution.

A distribution is just if it arises from another just distribution by legitimate means. The legitimate means of moving from one distribution to another are specified by the principle of justice in transfer. The legitimate first "moves" are specified by the principle of justice in acquisition. Whatever arises from a just situation by just steps is itself just. The means of change specified by the principle of justice is transfer preserve justice. As correct rules of inference are truth-preserving, and any conclusion deduced via repeated application of such rules from only true premises is itself true, so the means of transition from one situation to another specified by the principle of justice in transfer are justice-preserving, and any situation actually arising from repeated transitions in accordance with the principle from a just situation is itself just. The parallel between justice-preserving transformations and truth-preserving transformations illuminates where it fails as well as where it holds. That a conclusion could have been deduced by truth-preserving means from premises that are true suffices to show its truth. That from a just situation a situation *could* have arisen via justice-preserving means does *not* suffice to show its justice. The fact that a thief's victims voluntarily *could* have presented him with gifts does not entitle the thief to his ill-gotten gains. Justice in holdings is historical; it depends upon what actually has happened. We shall return to this point later.

Not all actual situations are generated in accordance with the two principles of justice in holdings: the principle of justice in acquisition and the principle of justice in transfer. Some people steal from others, or defraud them, or enslave them, seizing their product and preventing them from living as they choose, or forcibly exclude others from competing in exchanges. None of these are permissible modes of transition from one situation to another. And some persons acquire holdings by means not sanctioned by the principle of justice in acquisition. The existence of past injustice (previous violations of the first two principles of justice in holdings) raises the third major topic under justice in holdings: the rectification of injustice in holdings. If past injustice has shaped present holdings in various ways, some identifiable and some not, what now, if anything, ought to be done to rectify these injustices? What obligations do the performers of injustice have toward those whose position is worse than it would have been had the injustice not been done? Or, that it would have been had compensation been paid promptly? How, if at all, do things change if the beneficiaries and those made worse off are not the direct parties in the act of injustice, but, for example, their descendants? Is an injustice done to someone whose holding was itself based upon an unrectified injustice? How far back must one go in wiping clean the historical slate of injustices? What may victims of injustice permissibly do in order to rectify the injustices being done to them, including the many injustices done by persons acting through their government? I do not know of a thorough or theoretically sophisticated treatment of such issues. Idealizing greatly, let us suppose theoretical investigation will produce a principle of rectification. This principle uses historical information about previous situations and injustices done in them (as defined by the first two principles of justice and rights against interference), and information about the actual course of events that flowed from these injustices, until the present, and it yields a description (or descriptions) of holdings in the society. The principle of rectification presumably will make use of its best estimate of subjunctive information about what would have occurred (or a probability distribution over what might have occurred, using the expected value) if the injustice had not taken place. If the actual description of holdings turns out not to be one of the descriptions yielded by the princi-

ple, then one of the descriptions yielded must be realized.

The general outlines of the theory of justice in holdings are that the holdings of a person are just if he is entitled to them by the principles of justice in acquisition and transfer, or by the principle of rectification of injustice (as specified by the first two principles). If each person's holdings are just, then the total set (distribution) of holdings is just. To turn these general outlines into a specific theory we would have to specify the details of each of the three principles of justice in holdings: the principle of acquisition of holdings, the principle of transfer of holdings, and the principle of rectification of violations of the first two principles. I shall not attempt that task here. (Locke's principle of justice in acquisition is discussed below.)

HISTORICAL PRINCIPLES AND END-RESULT PRINCIPLES

The general outlines of the entitlement theory illuminate the nature and defects of other conceptions of distributive justice. The entitlement theory of justice in distribution is *historical;* whether a distribution is just depends upon how it came about. In contrast, *current time-slice principles* of justice hold that the justice of a distribution is determined by how things are distributed (who has what) as judged by some *structural* principle(s) of just distribution. A utilitarian who judges between any two distributions by seeing which has the greater sum of utility and, if the sums tie, applies some fixed equality criterion to choose the more equal distribution, would hold a current time-slice principle of justice. As would someone who had a fixed schedule of trade-offs between the sum of happiness and equality. According to a current time-slice principle, all that needs to be looked at, in judging the justice of a distribution, is who ends up with what; in comparing any two distributions one need look only at the matrix presenting the distributions. No further information need be fed into a principle of justice. It is a consequence of such principles of justice that any two structurally identical distributions are equally just. (Two distributions are structurally identical if they present the same profile, but perhaps have different persons occupying the particular slots. My having ten and your having five, and my having five and your having ten are structurally identical distributions.) Welfare economics is the theory of current time-slice principles of justice. The subject is conceived as operating on matrices representing only current information about distribution. This, as well as some of the usual conditions (for example, the choice of distribution is invariant under relabeling of columns), guarantees that welfare economics will be a current time-slice theory, with all of its inadequacies.

Most persons do not accept current time-slice principles as constituting the whole story about distributive shares. They think it relevant in assessing the justice of a situation to consider not only the distribution it embodies, but also how that distribution came about. If some persons are in prison for murder or war crimes, we do not say that to assess the justice of the distribution in the society we must look only at what this person has, and that person has, and that person has, . . . at the current time. We think it relevant to ask whether someone did something so that he *deserved* to be punished, deserved to have a lower share.

PATTERNING

The entitlement principles of justice in holdings that we have sketched are historical principles of justice. To better understand their precise character, we shall distinguish them from another subclass of the historical principles. Consider, as an example, the principle of distribution according to moral merit. This principle requires that total distributive shares vary directly with moral merit; no person should have a greater share than anyone whose moral merit is greater. Or consider the principle that results by substituting "usefulness to society" for "moral merit" in the previous principle. Or instead of "distribute according to moral merit," or "distribute according to usefulness to society," we might consider "distribute according to the weighted sum of moral merit, usefulness to society, and need," with the weights of the different dimensions equal. Let us call a principle of distribution

patterned if it specifies that a distribution is to vary along with some natural dimension, weighted sum of natural dimensions, or lexicographic ordering of natural dimensions. And let us say a distribution is patterned if it accords with some patterned principle. The principle of distribution in accordance with moral merit is a patterned historical principle, which specifies a patterned distribution. "Distribute according to I.Q." is a patterned principle that looks to information not contained in distributional matrices. It is not historical, however, in that it does not look to any past actions creating differential entitlements to evaluate a distribution; it requires only distributional matrices whose columns are labeled by I.Q. scores. The distribution in a society, however, may be composed of such simple patterned distributions, without itself being simply patterned. Different sectors may operate different patterns, or some combination of patterns may operate in different proportions across a society. A distribution composed in this manner, from a small number of patterned distributions, we also shall term "patterned." And we extend the use of "pattern" to include the overall designs put forth by combinations of end-state principles.

Almost every suggested principle of distributive justice is patterned: to each according to his moral merit, or needs, or marginal product, or how hard he tries, or the weighted sum of the foregoing, and so on. The principle of entitlement we have sketched is *not* patterned. There is no one natural dimension or weighted sum or combination of a small number of natural dimensions that yields the distributions generated in accordance with the principle of entitlement. The set of holdings that results when some persons receive their marginal products, others win at gambling, others receive a share of their mate's income, others receive gifts from foundations, others receive interest on loans, others receive gifts from admirers, others receive returns on investment, others make for themselves much of what they have, others find things, and so on, will not be patterned.

To think that the task of a theory of distributive justice is to fill in the blank in "to each according to his ___" is to be predisposed to search for a pattern; and the separate treatment of "from each according to his ___" treats production and distribution as two separate and independent issues. On an entitlement view these are *not* two separate questions. Whoever makes something, having bought or contracted for all other held resources used in the process (transferring some of his holdings for these cooperating factors), is entitled to it. The situation is *not* one of something's getting made, and there being an open question of who is to get it. Things come into the world already attached to people having entitlements over them. From the point of view of the historical entitlement conception of justice in holdings, those who start afresh to complete "to each according to his ___" treat objects as if they appeared from nowhere, out of nothing. A complete theory of justice might cover this limited case as well; perhaps here is a use for the usual conceptions of distributive justice.

So entrenched are maxims of the usual form that perhaps we should present the entitlement conception as a competitor. Ignoring acquisition and rectification, we might say:

> From each according to what he chooses to do, to each according to what he makes for himself (perhaps with the contracted aid of others) and what others choose to do for him and choose to give him of what they've been given previously (under this maxim) and haven't yet expended or transferred.

This, the discerning reader will have noticed, has its defects as a slogan. So as a summary and great simplification (and not as a maxim with any independent meaning) we have:

> From each as they choose, to each as they are chosen.

HOW LIBERTY UPSETS PATTERNS

It is not clear how those holding alternative conceptions of distributive justice can reject the entitlement conception of justice in holdings. For suppose a distribution favored by one of these non-entitlement conceptions is realized. Let us suppose it is your favorite one and let us call this distribution D_1; perhaps everyone has an equal share, perhaps shares vary in accordance with some dimension you treasure. Now suppose that Wilt Chamberlain is greatly in demand by basketball teams, being a great gate attraction. (Also suppose contracts run only for a year, with players being free agents.) He signs the following sort of contract with a team: In each home game, twenty-five cents from the price of each ticket of admission goes to him. (We ignore the question of whether he is "gouging" the owners, letting them look out for themselves.) The season starts, and people cheerfully attend his team's games; they buy their tickets, each time dropping a separate twenty-five cents of their admission price into a special box with Chamberlain's name on it. They are excited about seeing him play; it is worth the total admission price to them. Let us suppose that in one season one million persons attend his home games, and Wilt Chamberlain winds up with $250,000, a much larger sum than the average income and larger even than anyone else has. Is he entitled to this income? Is this new distribution D_2 unjust? If so, why? There is *no* question about whether each of the people was entitled to the control over the resources they held in D_1; because that was the distribution (your favorite) that (for the purposes of argument) we assumed was acceptable. Each of these persons *chose* to give twenty-five cents of their money to Chamberlain. They could have spent it on going to the movies, or on candy bars, or on copies of *Dissent* magazine, or of *Monthly Review*. But they all, at least one million of them, converged on giving it to Wilt Chamberlain in exchange for watching him play basketball. If D_1 was a just distribution, and people voluntarily moved from it to D_2, transferring parts of their shares they were given under D_1 (what was it for if not to do something with?), isn't D_2 also just? If the people were entitled to dispose of the resources to which they were entitled (under D_1), didn't this include their being entitled to give it to, or exchange it with, Wilt Chamberlain? Can anyone else complain on grounds of justice? Each other person already has his legitimate share under D_1. Under D_1, there is nothing that anyone has that anyone else has a claim of justice against. After someone transfers something to Wilt Chamberlain, third parties *still* have their legitimate shares; *their* shares are not changed. By what process could such a transfer among two persons give rise to a legitimate claim of distributive justice on a portion of what was transferred, by a third party who had no claim of justice on any holding of the others *before* the transfer? To cut off objections irrelevant here, we might imagine the exchanges occurring in a socialist society, after hours. After playing whatever basketball he does in his daily work, or doing whatever other daily work he does, Wilt Chamberlain decides to put in *overtime* to earn additional money. (First his work quota is set; he works time over that.) Or imagine it is a skilled juggler people like to see, who puts on shows after hours.

The general point illustrated by the Wilt Chamberlain example and the example of the entrepreneur in a socialist society is that no end-state principle or distributional patterned principle of justice can be continuously realized without continuous interference with people's lives. Any favored pattern would be transformed into one unfavored by the principle, by people choosing to act in various ways; for example, by people exchanging goods and services with other people, or giving things to other people, things the transferrers are entitled to under the favored distributional pattern. To maintain a pattern one must either continually interfere to stop people from transferring resources as they wish to, or continually (or periodically) interfere to take from some persons resources that others for some reason chose to transfer to them.

Patterned principles of distributive justice necessitate *re*distributive activities. The likelihood is small that any actual freely-arrived-at set of holdings fit a given pattern; and the likelihood is nil that it will continue to fit the pattern as people exchange and give. From the point of view of an entitlement theory, redistribution is a serious matter indeed, involving, as it does, the violation of people's rights. (An exception is those takings that fall under the principle of the rectification of injustices.) From other points of view, also, it is serious.

Taxation of earnings from labor is on a par with forced labor. Some persons find this claim obviously true: taking the earnings of *n* hours labor is like taking *n* hours from the person; it is like forcing the person to work *n* hours for another's purpose. Others find the claim absurd. But even these, *if* they object to forced labor, would oppose forc-

ing unemployed hippies to work for the benefit of the needy. And they would also object to forcing each person to work five extra hours each week for the benefit of the needy. But a system that takes five hours' wages in taxes does not seem to them like one that forces someone to work five hours, since it offers the person forced a wider range of choice in activities than does taxation in kind with the particular labor specified.

Whether it is done through taxation on wages or on wages over a certain amount, or through seizure of profits, or through there being a big *social pot* so that it's not clear what's coming from where and what's going where, patterned principles of distributive justice involve appropriating the actions of other persons. Seizing the results of someone's labor is equivalent to seizing hours from him and directing him to carry on various activities. If people force you to do certain work, or unrewarded work, for a certain period of time, they decide what you are to do and what purposes your work is to serve apart from your decisions. This process whereby they take this decision from you makes them a *part-owner* of you; it gives them a property right in you. Just as having such partial control and power of decision, by right, over an animal or inanimate object would be to have a property right in it.

LOCKE'S THEORY OF ACQUISITION

We must introduce an additional bit of complexity into the structure of the entitlement theory. This is best approached by considering Locke's attempt to specify a principle of justice in acquisition. Locke views property rights in an unowned object as originating through someone's mixing his labor with it. This gives rise to many questions. What are the boundaries of what labor is mixed with? If a private astronaut clears a place on Mars, has he mixed his labor with (so that he comes to own) the whole planet, the whole uninhabited universe, or just a particular plot? Which plot does an act bring under ownership?

Locke's proviso that there be "enough and as good left in common for others" is meant to ensure that the situation of others is not worsened. I assume that any adequate theory of justice in acquisition will contain a proviso similar to Locke's. A process normally giving rise to a permanent bequeathable property right in a previously unowned thing will not do so if the position of others no longer at liberty to use the thing is thereby worsened. It is important to specify *this* particular mode of worsening the situation of others, for the proviso does not encompass other modes. It does not include the worsening due to more limited opportunities to appropriate, and it does not include how I "worsen" a seller's position if I appropriate materials to make some of what he is selling, and then enter into competition with him. Someone whose appropriation otherwise would violate the proviso still may appropriate provided he compensates the others so that their situation is not thereby worsened; unless he does compensate these others, his appropriation will violate the proviso of the principle of justice in acquisition and will be an illegitimate one. A theory of appropriation incorporating this Lockean proviso will handle correctly the cases (objections to the theory lacking the proviso) where someone appropriates the total supply of something necessary for life.

A theory which includes this proviso in its principle of justice in acquisition must also contain a more complex principle of justice in transfer. Some reflection of the proviso about appropriation constrains later actions. If my appropriating all of a certain substance violates the Lockean proviso, then so does my appropriating some and purchasing all the rest from others who obtained it without otherwise violating the Lockean proviso. If the proviso excludes someone's appropriating all the drinkable water in the world, it also excludes his purchasing it all. (More weakly, and messily, it may exclude his charging certain prices for some of his supply.) This proviso (almost?) never will come into effect; the more someone acquires of a scarce substance which others want, the higher the price of the rest will go, and the more difficult it will become for him to acquire it all. But still, we can imagine, at least, that something like this occurs: someone makes simultaneous secret bids to the separate owners of a substance, each of whom sells assuming he can easily purchase more from

the other owners; or some natural catastrophe destroys all of the supply of something except that in one person's possession. The total supply could not be permissibly appropriated by one person at the beginning. His later acquisition of it all does not show that the original appropriation violated the proviso. Rather, it is the combination of the original appropriation *plus* all the later transfers and actions that violates the Lockean proviso.

Each owner's title to his holding includes the historical shadow of the Lockean proviso on appropriation. This excludes his transferring it into an agglomeration that does violate the Lockean proviso and excludes his using it in a way, in coordination with others or independently of them, so as to violate the proviso by making the situation of others worse than their baseline situation. Once it is known that someone's ownership runs afoul of the Lockean proviso, there are stringent limits on what he may do with (what it is difficult any longer unreservedly to call) "his property." Thus a person may not appropriate the only water hole in a desert and charge what he will. Nor may he charge what he will if he possesses one, and unfortunately it happens that all the water holes in the desert dry up, except for his. This unfortunate circumstance, admittedly no fault of his, brings into operation the Lockean proviso and limits his property rights. Similarly, an owner's property right in the only island in an area does not allow him to order a castaway from a shipwreck off his island as a trespasser, for this would violate the Lockean proviso.

Notice that the theory does not say that owners do not have these rights, but that the rights are overridden to avoid some catastrophe. (Overridden rights do not disappear; they leave a trace of a sort absent in the cases under discussion.) There is no such external (and *ad hoc?*) overriding. Considerations internal to the theory of property itself, to its theory of acquisition and appropriation, provide the means for handling such cases.

I believe that the free operation of a market system will not actually run afoul of the Lockean proviso. If this is correct, the proviso will not provide a significant opportunity for future state action.

Distributive Justice and Utilitarianism

J. J. C. Smart
Center for Information Science Research,
The Australian National University

INTRODUCTION

In this paper I shall not be concerned with the defense of utilitarianism against other types of ethical theory. Indeed I hold that questions of ultimate ethical principle are not susceptible of proof, though something can be done to render them more acceptable by presenting them in a clear light and by clearing up certain confusions which (for some people) may get in the way of their acceptance. Ultimately the utilitarian appeals to the sentiment of generalized benevolence, and speaks to others who feel this sentiment too and for whom it is an over-riding feeling.[1] (This does not mean that he will always act from this over-riding feeling. There can be backsliding and action may result from more particular feelings, just as an egoist may go against his own interests, and may regret this.) I shall be concerned here merely to investigate certain consequences of utilitarianism, as they relate to questions of distributive justice. The type of utilitarianism with which I am concerned is act utilitarianism.

THE PLACE OF JUSTICE IN UTILITARIAN THEORY

The concept of justice as a fundamental ethical concept is really quite foreign to utilitarianism. A utilitarian would compromise his utilitarianism if he allowed principles of justice which might conflict with the maximization of happiness (or more generally of goodness, should he be an "ideal" utilitarian). He is concerned with the maximiza-

tion of happiness[2] and not with the distribution of it. Nevertheless he may well deduce from his ethical principle that certain ways of distributing the means to happiness (e.g., money, food, housing) are more conducive to the general good than are others. He will be interested in justice in so far as it is a political or legal or quasi-legal concept. He will consider whether the legal institutions and customary sanctions which operate in particular societies are more or less conducive to the utilitarian end than are other possible institutions and customs. Even if the society consisted entirely of utilitarians (and of course no actual societies have thus consisted) it might still be important to have legal and customary sanctions relating to distribution of goods, because utilitarians might be tempted to backslide and favour non-optimistic distributions, perhaps because of bias in their own favour. They might be helped to act in a more nearly utilitarian way because of the presence of these sanctions.

As a utilitarian, therefore, I do not allow the concept of justice as a fundamental moral concept, but I am nevertheless interested in justice in a subordinate way, as a means to the utilitarian end. Thus even though I hold that it does not matter in what way happiness is distributed among different persons, provided that the total amount of happiness is maximized, I do of course hold that it can be of vital importance that the means to happiness should be distributed in some ways and not in others. Suppose that I have the choice of two alternative actions as follows: I can either give $500 to each of two needy men, Smith and Campbell, or else give $1000 to Smith and nothing to Campbell. It is of course likely to produce the greatest happiness if I divide the money equally. For this reason utilitarianism can often emerge as a theory with egalitarian consequences. If it does so this is because of the empirical situation, and not because of any moral commitment to egalitarianism as such. Consider, for example, another empirical situation in which the $500 was replaced by a half-dose of a life saving drug, in which case the utilitarian would advocate giving two half-doses to Smith or Campbell and none to the other. Indeed if Smith and Campbell each possessed a half-dose it

Excerpted from "Distributive Justice and Utilitarianism," published in *Justice and Economic Distribution*, edited by John Arthur and William H. Shaw, Englewood Cliffs, N.J.: Prentice Hall, 1978. Reprinted by permission of the author.

would be right to take one of the half-doses and give it to the other. (I am assuming that a whole dose would preserve life and that a half-dose would not. I am also assuming a simplified situation: in some possible situations, especially in a society of nonutilitarians, the wide social ramifications of taking a half-dose from Smith and giving it to Campbell might conceivably outweigh the good results of saving Campbell's life.) However, it is probable that in most situations the equal distribution of the means to happiness will be the right utilitarian action, even though the utilitarian has no ultimate moral commitment to egalitarianism. If a utilitarian is given the choice of two actions, one of which will give 2 units of happiness to Smith and 2 to Campbell, and the other of which will give 1 unit of happiness to Smith and 9 to Campbell, he will choose the latter course.[3] It may also be that I have the choice between two alternative actions, one of which gives −1 unit of happiness to Smith and +9 units to Campbell, and the other of which gives +2 to Smith and +2 to Campbell. As a utilitarian I will choose the former course, and here I will be in conflict with John Rawls' theory, whose maximin principle would rule out making Smith worse off.

UTILITARIANISM AND RAWLS' THEORY

Rawls deduces his ethical principles from the contract which would be made by a group of rational egoists in an 'original position' in which they thought behind a 'veil of ignorance,' so that they would not know who they were or even what generation they belonged to.[4] Reasoning behind this veil of ignorance, they would apply the maximin principle. John Harsanyi earlier used the notion of a contract in such a position of ignorance, but used not the maximin principle but the principle of maximizing expected utility.[5] Harsanyi's method leads to a form of rule utilitarianism. I see no great merit in this roundabout approach to ethics *via* a contrary to fact supposition, which involves the tricky notion of a social contract and which thus appears already to presuppose a moral position. The approach seems also too Hobbesian: it is anthropologically incorrect to suppose that we are all

originally little egoists. I prefer to base ethics on a principle of generalized benevolence, to which some of those with whom I discuss ethics may immediately respond. Possibly it might show something interesting about our common moral notions if it could be proved that they follow from what would be contracted by rational egoists in an 'original position,' but as a utilitarian I am more concerned to advocate a normative theory which might replace our common moral notions than I am to explain these notions. Though some form of utilitarianism might be deducible (as by Harsanyi) from a contract or original position theory, I do not think that it either ought to be or need be defended in this sort of way.

Be that as it may, it is clear that utilitarian views about distribution of happiness do differ from Rawls' view. I have made a distinction between justice as a moral concept and justice as a legal or quasi-legal concept. The utilitarian has no room for the former, but he can have strong views about the latter, though *what* these views are will depend on empirical considerations. Thus whether he will prefer a political theory which advocates a completely socialist state, or whether he will prefer one which advocates a minimal state (as Robert Nozick's book does[6]), or whether again he will advocate something between the two, is something which depends on the facts of economics, sociology, and so on. As someone not expert in these fields I have no desire to dogmatize on these empirical matters. (My own private non-expert opinion is that probably neither extreme leads to maximization of happiness, though I have a liking for rather more socialism than exists in Australia or U.S.A. at present.) As a utilitarian my approach to political theory has to be tentative and empirical. Not believing in moral rights as such I can not deduce theories about the best political arrangements by making deductions (as Nozick does) from propositions which purport to be about such basic rights.

Rawls deduces two principles of justice.[7] The first of these is that 'each person is to have an equal right to the most extensive basic liberty compatible with a similar liberty for others,' and the second one is that 'social and economic inequalities are to be arranged so that they are both (a) reasonably expected to be to everyone's advantage, and (b) attached to positions and offices open to all.' Though a utilitarian could (on empirical grounds) be very much in sympathy with both of these principles, he could not accept them as universal rules. Suppose that a society which had no danger of nuclear war could be achieved only by reducing the liberty of one percent of the world's population. Might it not be right to bring about such a state of affairs if it were in one's power? Indeed might it not be right greatly to reduce the liberty of 100% of the world's population if such a desirable outcome could be achieved? Perhaps the present generation would be pretty miserable and would hanker for their lost liberties. However we must also think about the countless future generations which might exist and be happy provided that mankind can avoid exterminating itself, and we must also think of all the pain, misery and genetic damage which would be brought about by nuclear war even if this did not lead to the total extermination of mankind.

Suppose that this loss of freedom prevented a war so devastating that the whole process of evolution on this planet would come to an end. At the cost of the loss of freedom, instead of the war and the end of evolution there might occur an evolutionary process which was not only long lived but also beneficial: in millions of years there might be creatures descended from *homo sapiens* which had vastly increased talents and capacity for happiness. At least such considerations show that Rawls' first principle is far from obvious to the utilitarian, though in certain mundane contexts he might accede to it as a useful approximation. Indeed I do not believe that restriction of liberty, in our present society, could have beneficial results in helping to prevent nuclear war, though a case could be made for certain restrictions on the liberty of all present members of society so as to enable the government to prevent nuclear blackmail by gangs of terrorists.

Perhaps in the past considerable restrictions on the personal liberties of a large proportion of citizens may have been justifiable on utilitarian grounds. In view of the glories of Athens and its contributions to civilization it is possible that the Athenian slave society was justifiable. In one part of his paper, 'Nature and Soundness of the Contract and Coherence Arguments,'[8] David Lyons has judiciously discussed the question of whether in certain circumstances a utilitarian would condone slavery. He says that it would be unlikely that a utilitarian could condone slavery as it has existed in modern times. However, he considers the possibility that less objectionable forms of slavery or near slavery have existed. The less objectionable these may have been, the more likely it is that utilitarianism would have condoned them. Lyons remarks that our judgments about the relative advantages of different societies must be very tentative because we do not know enough about human history to say what were the social alternatives at any juncture.[9]

Similar reflections naturally occur in connection with Rawls' second principle. Oligarchic societies, such as that of eighteenth century Britain, may well have been in fact better governed than they would have been if posts of responsibility had been available to all. Certainly to resolve this question we should have to go deeply into empirical investigations of the historical facts. (To prevent misunderstanding, I do think that in our present society utilitarianism would imply adherence to Rawls' second principle as a general rule.)

A utilitarian is concerned with maximizing total happiness (or goodness, if he is an ideal utilitarian). Rawls largely concerns himself with certain 'primary goods,' as he calls them. These include 'rights and liberties, powers and opportunities, income and wealth.'[10] A utilitarian would regard these as mere means to the ultimate good. Nevertheless if he is proposing new laws or changes to social institutions the utilitarian will have to concern himself in practice with the distribution of these 'primary goods' (as Bentham did).[11] But if as an approximation we neglect this distinction, which may be justifiable to the extent that there is a correlation between happiness and the level of these 'primary goods,' we may say that according to Rawls an action is right only if it is to the benefit of the least advantaged person. A utilitarian will hold that a redistribution of the means to happiness is right if it maximizes the general happiness, even though some persons, even the least advantaged ones, are made worse off. A position which is intermediate between the utilitarian position and

Rawls' position would be one which held that one ought to maximize some sort of trade-off between total happiness and distribution of happiness. Such a position would imply that sometimes we should redistribute in such a way as to make some persons, even the least advantaged ones, worse off, but this would happen less often than it would according to the classical utilitarian theory.

UTILITARIANISM AND NOZICK'S THEORY

General adherence to Robert Nozick's theory (in his *Anarchy, State and Utopia*)[12] would be compatible with the existence of very great inequality indeed. This is because the whole theory is based quite explicitly on the notion of *rights:* in the very first sentence of the preface of his book we read 'Individuals have rights. . . .' The utilitarian would demur here. A utilitarian legislator might tax the rich in order to give aid to the poor, but a Nozickian legislator would not do so. A utilitarian legislator might impose a heavy tax on inherited wealth, whereas Nozick would allow the relatively fortunate to become even more fortunate, provided that they did not infringe the *rights* of the less fortunate. The utilitarian legislator would hope to increase the total happiness by equalizing things a bit. How far he should go in this direction would depend on empirical considerations. He would not want to equalize things too much if this led to too much weakening of the incentive to work, for example. Of course according to Nozick's system there would be no reason why members of society should not set up a utilitarian utopia, and voluntarily equalize their wealth, and also give wealth to poorer communities outside. However, it is questionable whether such isolated utopias could survive in a modern environment, but if they did survive, the conformity of the behaviour of their members to utilitarian theory, rather than the conformity to Nozick's theory, would be what would commend their societies to me.

SUMMARY

In this article I have explained that the notion of justice is not a fundamental notion in utilitarianism, but that utilitarians will characteristically have certain views about such things as the distribution of wealth, savings for the benefit of future generations and for the third world countries and other practical matters. Utilitarianism differs from John Rawls' theory in that it is ready to contemplate some sacrifice to certain individuals (or classes of individuals) for the sake of the greater good of all, and in particular may allow certain limitations of personal freedom which would be ruled out by Rawls' theory. *In practice,* however, the general tendency of utilitarianism may well be towards an egalitarian form of society.

NOTES

1. In hoping that utilitarianism can be rendered acceptable to some people by presenting it in a clear light, I do not deny the possibility of the reverse happening. Thus I confess to a bit of a pull the other way when I consider Nozick's example of an 'experience machine.' See Robert Nozick, *Anarchy, State and Utopia* (Oxford: Blackwell, 1975), pp. 42–45, though I am at least partially reassured by Peter Singer's remarks towards the end of his review of Nozick, *New York Review of Books,* March 6, 1975. Nozick's example of an experience machine is more worrying than the more familiar one of a pleasure inducing machine, because it seems to apply to ideal as well as to hedonistic utilitarianism.

2. In this paper I shall assume a hedonistic utilitarianism, though most of what I have to say will be applicable to ideal utilitarianism too.

3. There are of course difficult problems about the assignment of cardinal utilities to states of mind, but for the purposes of this paper I am assuming that we can intelligibly talk, as utilitarians do, about units of happiness.

4. John Rawls, *A Theory of Justice* (Cambridge, Mass: Harvard University Press, 1971).

5. John C. Harsanyi, 'Cardinal Utility in Welfare Economics and the Theory of Risk-Taking,' *Journal of Political Economy,* **61** (1953), 434–435, and 'Cardinal Welfare, Individualistic Ethics, and Interpersonal Comparisons of Utility,' *ibid.,* **63** (1955), 309–321. Harsanyi has discussed Rawls' use of the maximin principle and has defended the principle of maximizing expected utility instead, in a paper 'Can the Maximin Principle Serve as a Basis for Morality? A Critique of John Rawls' Theory.' *The American Political Science Review,* **69** (1975), 594–606.

These articles have been reprinted in John C. Harsanyi, *Essays on Ethics, Social Behavior, and Scientific Explanation* (Dordrecht, Holland: D. Reidel, 1976).

6. Robert Nozick, *Anarchy, State and Utopia.* (See note 1 above.)
7. Rawls, *A Theory of Justice*, p. 60.
8. In Norman Daniels (ed.), *Reading Rawls* (Oxford: Blackwell, 1975), pp. 141–167. See pp. 148–149.
9. Lyons, *op. cit.,* p. 149, near top.
10. Rawls, *op. cit.,* p. 62.
11. On this point see Brian Barry, *The Liberal Theory of Justice* (London: Oxford University Press, 1973), p. 55.
12. See note 1.

Capitalism and Morality

James Q. Wilson
Professor of Strategy and Organization and James A. Collins Chair in Management, UCLA; former Shattuck Professor of Government, Harvard University

Twenty-five years ago, the two founding editors of this magazine published important essays on the cultural and moral status of capitalism. Irving Kristol worried that the most intelligent contemporary defenders of capitalism were now mostly libertarians who praised the market because it produced material benefits and enhanced human freedom but who denied that markets had anything to do with morality. Friedrich Hayek, for example, had written that "in a free society it is neither desirable nor practicable that material rewards should be made generally to correspond to what men recognize as merit." It is not practicable because no one can supply a non-arbitrary definition of merit (or justice); it is not desirable because any attempt to impose such a definition would create a despotism. Kristol worried that people would not support any economic order in which "the will to success and privilege was severed from its moral moorings."

Reprinted with permission of the author from *The Public Interest,* No. 121 (Fall 1995), pp. 52–71. © 1995 by National Affairs, Inc.

Capitalism could not survive it, quoting George Fitzhugh, "none but the selfish virtues are in repute" because in such a society "virtue loses all her loveliness" and social order becomes impossible.

In the same issue, Daniel Bell published his famous essay on "The Cultural Contradictions of Capitalism" in which he suggested that the bourgeois culture—rational, pragmatic, and moral—that had created capitalism was now being destroyed by the success of capitalism. As capitalism replaced feudal stagnation with material success, it replaced tradition with materialism; as privation was supplanted by abundance, prudence was displaced by prodigality. Capitalism created both a parvenu class of rich plutocrats and corporate climbers and a counterculture of critical intellectuals and disaffected youth. The latter began to have a field day exposing what they took to be the greed, hypocrisy, and Philistinism of the former.

CAPITALISM'S GREAT TEST

Both Kristol and Bell were amplifying on a theme first developed by Joseph Schumpeter: Contrary to what Marx had taught, capitalism would be destroyed not by its failures but by its successes. Their views did not go unchallenged; a decade later George Gilder, in *Wealth and Poverty,* launched a frontal attack on the Schumpeterian theory (and its development by Kristol and Bell) by arguing that capitalism was, in fact, a highly moral enterprise because it "begins with giving" and requires "faith."

However one judges that debate, it is striking that in 1970—at a time when socialism still had many defenders, when certain American economists (and the CIA!) were suggesting that the Soviet economy was growing faster than the American, when books were being written explaining how Fidel Castro could achieve by the use of "moral incentives" what other nations achieved by employing material ones—Kristol and Bell saw that the great test of capitalism would not be economic but moral. Time has proved them right. Except for a handful of American professors, everyone here and abroad now recognizes that capitalism produces greater material abundance for more people than any other economic system ever invented. The evidence is not in dispute.

A series of natural experiments were conducted on a scale that every social scientist must envy: Several nations—China, Germany, Korea, and Vietnam—were sawed in two, and capitalism was installed in one part and "socialism" in the other. In every case, the capitalist part out-produced, by a vast margin, the non-capitalist one.

Moreover, it has become clear during the last half century that democratic regimes only flourish in capitalist societies. Not every nation with something approximating capitalism is democratic, but every nation that is democratic is, to some significant degree, capitalist. (By "capitalist," I mean that production is chiefly organized on the basis of privately owned enterprises, and exchange takes place primarily through voluntary markets.)

If capitalism is an economic success and the necessary (but not sufficient) precondition for democracy, it only remains vulnerable on cultural and moral grounds. That is, of course, why today's radical intellectuals have embraced the more extreme forms of multiculturalism and postmodernism. These doctrines are an attack on the hegemony of bourgeois society and the legitimacy of bourgeois values. The attack takes various forms—denying the existence of any foundation for morality, asserting the incommensurability of cultural forms, rejecting the possibility of textual meaning, or elevating the claims of non-Western (or non-white or non-Anglo) traditions. By whatever route it travels, contemporary radicalism ends with a rejection of the moral claims of capitalism: Because morality is meaningless, because capitalism is mere power, or because markets and corporations destroy culture, capitalism is arbitrary, oppressive, or corrupting.

Most critics of capitalism, of course, are not radicals. Liberal critics recognize, as postmodernists pretend not to, that, if you are going to offer a moral criticism of capitalism, you had better believe that moral judgments are possible and can be made persuasive. To liberals, the failure of capitalism lies in its production of unjustifiable inequalities of wealth and its reckless destruction of the natural environment. Capitalism may produce material abundance, the argument goes, but at too high a price in human suffering and social injustice.

I do not deny that capitalism has costs; every human activity has them. (It was a defender of capitalism, after all, who reminded us that there is no such thing as a free lunch). For people worried about inequality of environmental degradation, the question is not whether capitalism has consequences but whether its consequences are better or worse than those of some feasible economic alternative. (I stress "feasible" because I tire of hearing critics compare capitalist reality to socialist—or communitarian or cooperative—ideals. When ideals are converted into reality, they tend not to look so ideal.) And, in evaluating consequences, one must reckon up not simply the costs but the costs set against the benefits. In addition, one must count as benefits the tendency of an economic system to produce beliefs and actions that support a prudent concern for mitigating the unreasonable costs of the system.

CAPITALISM AND PUBLIC POLICY

By these tests, practical alternatives to capitalism do not seem very appealing. Inequality is a feature of every modern society; Adam Smith expected that it would be a particular feature of what we call capitalism. Indeed, he began *The Wealth of Nations* by setting forth a puzzle that he hoped to solve. It was this: in "the savage nations of hunters and fishers" (what we later learned to call euphemistically "native cultures" or "less-developed nations"), everyone works and almost everyone acquires the essentials of human sustenance, but they tend to be "so miserable poor" that they are reduced, on occasion, to killing babies and abandoning the elderly and the infirm. Among prosperous nations, by contrast, many people do not work at all and many more live lives of great luxury, yet the general level of prosperity is so high that even the poorest people are better off than the richest person in a primitive society. His book was an effort to explain why "the system of natural liberty" would produce both prosperity and inequality and to defend as tolerable the inequality that was the inevitable (and perhaps necessary) corollary of prosperity.

Smith certainly succeeded in the first task but was less successful in the second, at least to judge by the number of people who believe that inequality can be eliminated without sacrificing prosperity. Many nations have claimed to eliminate market-based inequalities, but they have done so only by creating non-market inequalities—a Soviet nomenklatura, a ruling military elite, an elaborate black market, or a set of non-cash perks. Between unconstrained market inequality and the lesser inequality achieved by some redistribution, there is much to discuss and decide, and so the welfare-state debate proceeds. Participants in this debate sometimes forget that the only societies in which such a debate can have much meaning are those that have produced wealth that can be redistributed and that have acquired a government that will do so democratically—in short, capitalist societies.

Similarly with respect to the environment: Only rich (that is, capitalist) nations can afford to worry much about the environment, and only democratic (that is, capitalist) nations have governments that will listen to environmentalists. As with inequality, environmental policies in capitalist systems will vary greatly—from the inconsequential through the prudent to the loony—but they will scarcely exist in non-capitalist ones. If anyone doubted this, they were surely convinced when the Iron Curtain was torn down in 1989, giving the West its first real look at what had been hidden behind the Berlin Wall. Eastern Europe had been turned into a vast toxic waste dump. Vaclav Havel explained why: A government that commands the economy will inevitably command the polity; given a commanding position, a government will distort or destroy the former and corrupt or oppress the latter.

To compel people engaged in production and exchange to internalize all of the costs of production and exchange without destroying production and exchange, one must be able to make proposals to people who do not want to hear such proposals, induce action among people who do not want to act, and monitor performance by people who do not like monitors, and do all of this only to the extent that the gains in human welfare are purchased at acceptable costs. No regime will make this result certain, but only democratic capitalist regimes make it at all possible.

Capitalism creates what are often called "post-material values" that lead some private parties to make environment-protecting proposals. Capitalism, because it requires private property, sustains a distinction between the public and the private sphere and thereby provides a protected place for people to stand who wish to make controversial proposals. And capitalism permits (but does not require) the emergence of democratic institutions that can (but may not) respond to such proposals. Or to put it simply: environmental action arises out of the demands of journalists, professors, foundation executives, and private-sector activists who, for the most part, would not exist in a non-capitalist regime.

CAPITALISM AND THE GOOD LIFE

Many readers may accept the view that capitalism permits, or possibly even facilitates, the making of desirable public policies but reject the idea that this is because there is anything moral about it. At best, it is amoral, a tool for the achievement of human wants that is neither good nor bad. At worst, it is an immoral system that glorifies greed but, by happy accident, occasionally makes possible popular government and pays the bills of some public-interest lobbies that can get on with the business of doing good. Hardly anyone regards it as moral.

People with these views can find much support in *The Wealth of Nations*. They will recall the famous passage in which Smith points out that it is from the "interest," not the "benevolence," of the butcher, the brewer, or the baker that we expect our dinner. An "invisible hand" leads him to promote the public good, though this is "no part of his intention." Should they study the book more carefully, they will come across passages predicting the degradation of the human spirit that is likely to occur from the division of labor, the incessant seeking after monopoly benefits and political privilege that will follow from the expansion of manufacturing, and the "low profligacy and vice" that will attend upon the growth of large cities. The average worker employed in repetitive tasks will become "stupid and ignorant," the successful merchant living in a big city will become personally licentious and politically advantaged.

Karl Marx, a close student of Smith's writings, had these passages in mind (and, indeed, referred to them) when he drew his picture of the alienation man would suffer as a consequence of private property and capitalism, But Marx (and, in some careless passages, even Smith) had made an error. They had confused the consequences of modernization (that is, of industrialization and urbanization) with the consequences of capitalism. The division of labor can be furthered and large industrial enterprises created by statist regimes as well as by free ones; people will flock to cities to seek opportunities conferred by socialist as well as capitalist economies; a profligate and self-serving elite will spring up to seize the benefits supplied by aristocratic or socialist or authoritarian or free-market systems. Show people the road to wealth, status, or power, and they will rush down that road; many will do some rather unattractive things along the way,

Among the feasible systems of political economy, capitalism offers the best possibility for checking some, but not all, of these tendencies toward degradation and depravity. When Smith suggested that the increased division of labor would turn most workers into unhappy copies of Charlie Chaplin in *Modern Times,* he thought that only public education could provide a remedy. Because he wrote long before the advent of modern technology, he can be forgiven for not having foreseen the tendency of free markets to substitute capital for labor in ways that relieve many workers of precisely those mindlessly repetitive tasks that Smith supposed would destroy the human spirit.

Urbanization is the result of modernity—that is, of the weakening of village ties, the advent of large-scale enterprise, the rise of mass markets, and an improvement in transportation—and modernity may have non-capitalist as well as capitalist sources. Mexico City, Sao Paulo, Rio de Janeiro, and Moscow have long been among the dozen largest cities in the world, but, until quite recently (and still quite uncertainly), none of these was located in a nation that could be fairly described as capitalist. They were state-dominated economies, either socialist or mercantilist, and Smith would have had no use for any of them.

And, being non-capitalist, most of these states were barely democratic (the USSR not at all). Lacking either a truly private sector or a truly democratic regime, reformist and meliorist tendencies designed to counteract the adverse consequences of massive urbanization were not much in evidence. Americans who rightly think that high rates of crime are characteristic of big cities, but wrongly suppose that this is especially true of capitalist cities, need to spend some time in Moscow, Rio, and Mexico City.

Capitalism creates privilege; socialism creates privilege; mercantilism creates privilege; primitivism creates privilege. Men and women everywhere will seek advantage, grasp power, and create hierarchies. But to the extent that a society is capitalist, it is more likely than its alternatives to sustain challenges to privilege. These arise from economic rivals, privately financed voluntary associations, and democratically elected power-holders; they operate through market competition, government regulation, legal action, and moral suasion. But they operate clumsily and imperfectly, and, in the routine aspects of ordinary morality, they may not operate well enough.

CAPITALISM AND THE MORALITY OF EVERYDAY LIFE

By this point, I may have persuaded a few readers that a system of rival interests has some beneficial moral effects, at least in comparison to statist economies in which the playing field is tilted by one set of greedy actors having decisive power over another. But nothing I have said is inconsistent with the view that capitalism rests on greed and therefore with the view that, at best, capitalism is amoral.

This was not, I think, the view of either Smith or many of other earlier defenders of capitalism. In *The Wealth of Nations,* he certainly gives an unflinchingly honest account of how self-interest drives economic decisions. But, as Albert Hirschman has suggested, eighteenth-century thinkers did not divide human motives into reason and interests, they divided them into reason, passions, and interests. Having seen the failures of unaided reason and the perils of unguided passions, they hoped that calm interests would inform reason and temper passion.

This was the argument about the beneficial effects of doux commerce—sweet (or gentle) commerce—and it was implicitly taken up by the American Founders when they made their case for a commercial republic. It has been repeated of late by the British anthropologist and philosopher Ernest Gellner who, in reflecting on the failure of European communism, observes that no society can avoid finding a way to channel the desire men have to advance themselves. In traditional and in statist societies, the way to attain wealth is first to attain power, usually by force. But, in market societies, "production becomes a better path to wealth than domination."

Critics of capitalism argue that wealth confers power, and indeed it does, up to a point. But this is not a decisive criticism unless one supposes, fancifully, that there is some way to arrange human affairs so that the desire for wealth vanishes. The real choice is between becoming wealthy by first acquiring political or military power or by getting money directly without bothering with conquest or domination. Max Weber put it this way: All economic systems rest on greed, but capitalism, because it depends on profit, is the one that disciplines greed.

In the process of imposing that discipline, capitalism contributes to self-discipline. It encourages civility, trust, self-command, the cosmopolitanism by first making these traits useful and then making them habitual.

Smith alluded to this when he observed that "commerce and manufactures gradually introduced order and good government, and with them, the liberty and security of individuals . . . who had before lived almost in a continual state of war with their neighbours and of servile dependency upon their superiors." Lest Smith be interpreted as arguing in favor of central government, he makes clear in other places that the beneficial effects of free and orderly commerce operate chiefly on the character of individuals, especially would-be lords and conquerors now converted into merchants. Nor is he, in the passage quoted above, contradicting his account of the baleful effects on ordinary

people of an extreme division of labor; capitalism may bring liberty and security, but it also brings temerity, narrowness, and profligacy. To Smith, sweet commerce was sweet-and-sour.

Smith's ambivalence reflected his analysis of the class structure of society. Commerce would create a middle class whose new members would mostly be decent people. "In the middling and inferior stations of life," he wrote, the "the road to virtue and that to fortune . . . are, happily, very nearly the same." Among people engaged in middle-class occupations, "real and solid professional abilities, joined to prudent, just, firm, and temperate conduct, can very seldom fail of success." In this circumstance, the proverb that "honesty is the best policy" proves true. But matters are very different in "the superior stations of life," in part, because the rich and well-born live in a self-constructed world of privilege that isolates them from the effective judgment of ordinary (and ordinarily decent) men, and, in part, because merchants and manufacturers will move to cities where they will have countless opportunities to acquire political privileges—monopolies, loopholes, and subsidies—that insulate them from fair market judgments about their products, services, and practices.

Smith's worries, so often quoted, about the affluent few detract, I think, from the much more important impact of capitalism on the not-so-affluent many. An economic system that provides many alternative suppliers for any desired product or service creates an incentive for each supplier to act as if he or she cared about the interests of the customer. Everyone has heard enough stories about surly waiters in Soviet restaurants to acknowledge that communist managers never took customers as seriously as they took commissars, but perhaps this was simply the extreme result of doing business in a pathological society. I doubt that. There has been comparable evidence available in the United States for many years. Until recently, most big airports supplied food to travelers by giving an exclusive franchise to a single vendor. Of late, many airports are giving franchises to several rival vendors—McDonald's, Burger King, Taco Bell, and the like—to offer food competitively in airports. Without question, the quality of food and service has gone up.

A skeptic will rejoin that competition merely requires suppliers to act as if they cared about the customer. But, as any economist will note, a firm's reputation has a capital value (it is sometimes measured on the balance sheet as good will) and so business executives who wish to maximize that value will devote a great deal of effort to inculcating a service ethic in their employees. One cannot do that cynically. "If you can fake sincerity, you've got it made," someone once said. That may be true for a few individuals, but organizing such fakery on a large scale is impossible—the teaching will be unconvincing, and the lesson will be ignored.

But acting as if one cared has more than economic significance. Our characters are formed, as Aristotle observed, by the process of habituation. Any process that makes a personal disposition habitual is character forming. Parents know this, which is why they teach good manners to their children by means of constant small reminders and an insistence on routine observances. Though I am aware of no evidence bearing on it, there is little reason to suppose that habituation ends with adulthood or cannot occur outside the family. Are young people who have worked for three years at McDonald's and been taught to parrot learned phrases ("How may I serve you?" "Will that be all?" "Thank you.") more likely on leaving for better jobs to be civil than are similar youngsters who worked in a company that attached no value to civility? I don't know, but I think so.

When Smith wrote that the "understandings of the greater part of men are necessarily formed by their ordinary employments," he was worrying about the harmful effect on the mind of dull and exhausting labor. But the shortened work day and the use of machinery have made this effect much less likely than it was in the eighteenth century. Today, it may be that it is the manners of people that are formed in part by their daily employment.

CAPITALIST VIRTUES

Capitalism requires some measure of trust. In any economic system, buying and selling occurs, but voluntary buying and selling on a large scale among strangers requires confidence in fair dealing that cannot depend on one party having much detailed knowledge about the other. Routinized exchanges present some of the same problems as a "Prisoner's Dilemma" in which both participants have an incentive to cheat if they assume they will only play the game—or engage in the exchange—once. The solution to the dilemma lies in repeating the game in conformity with this rule: do to the other party what he has just done to you ("tit for tat," in political scientist Robert Axelrod's phrase), but make your first move a "nice" one in order to encourage the other party to do the same. In some societies, mainly Western ones, this rule is enforced by contract law; in others, notably Eastern ones, by group affiliations. Capitalism takes advantage of this rule in order to create large, permanent markets among strangers that can operate without incessant recourse to retribution. In so doing, it strengthens conformity to the premise on which it depends: some minimum level of trust. This is a moralizing activity even though every customer knows that another rule—*caveat emptor*—also operates.

In a recent paper, John Mueller of the University of Rochester has observed that price haggling—once a common feature of most markets and still characteristic of some—has been abandoned even though it conferred short-term advantages on the seller. (This was true because sellers, knowing more about their wares than customers, had an advantage over most casual shoppers.) But some sellers discovered that, in the long run, they did more business by setting attractive, fixed prices. This practice lowered transaction costs for customers, thereby enlarging the number of customers.[1] Mueller notes that, as early as 1727, businessman-turned-novelist Daniel Defoe argued against haggling because it encouraged both

---

[1]Why, then, does price haggling still occur in the sale of automobiles? In part, it is because the purchaser, as well as the dealer, has something to sell. The purchaser usually has a used car to trade in and has little incentive to set a fixed price for it. He bargains over what the trade-in is worth and so the dealer must bargain over what the new car is worth. Even here, however, some dealers are experimenting with fixed-price sales.

parties to lie. The rise of fixed-price dealing has shifted misrepresentation from price to quality (or at least to advertising about quality).

Another premise on which capitalism depends is self-command. Smith understood that investment was required for capital to be accumulated and that investment, in turn, required that some people be willing to postpone immediate gratification for later (and larger) benefits. Smith did not explain why we should assume that the number of savers will be sufficient to produce the necessary investment. He observed that "prodigality," the result of a "passion for present enjoyment," will diminish the capital available for economic growth, and so it will be necessary for the "frugal man" to save enough to spare the rest of us from the consequences of our own prodigality. But will this occur? Smith predicts that "the profusion or imprudence of some" will be "always more than compensated for by the frugality and good conduct of others." Why? Well, the desire to save comes from an innate desire to better our condition. But, since only a few save a lot, the desire must be limited to a few. Will they be too few?

People differ in their degree of self-command but are alike in the high regard in which they hold people who display self-command (provided the display is not excessive, as it is with personalities that are miserly or rigid). Self-command is, in short, regarded (up to a point) as a virtue, one that is essential to capitalism and that capitalism strengthens to the extent that it induces more and more people to think about the future. (Indeed, economic growth requires that people have a concept of a secular future, a notion that may well have been absent or meaningless in feudal Europe.) The recent decline in the rate of American private savings corresponds to a period in which self-indulgence has been conspicuous. I have no idea what to make of this parallel except to suggest that complete understanding will almost surely require a cultural, as well as economic, analysis. If all that mattered were net yields on savings, the Japanese would not be saving anything. Their banks pay very low interest rates, yet their customers save at world-record rates.

Finally, capitalism contributes to cosmopolitanism. This remark will be laughable to any reader who, when hearing the word "capitalist," conjures up an image of George Babbitt or Henry Ford. Capitalism, having been linked by artists to bourgeois culture, has forever been linked to narrow Philistinism. But, long ago, Gary Becker explained why markets are the enemy of racial or ethnic discrimination. Prejudice is costly: It cuts a supplier off from potential customers and an employer off from potential workers, thus reducing sales and raising factor costs.

Embedded in a thoroughly racist community, capitalism can easily exist side by side with prejudice because there are no competitive disadvantages to acting on the basis of prejudice: Since white workers and customers will not mingle with black workers and customers, all employers are on the same footing. But let a crack develop in the unanimity of racist sentiment; let some workers and some customers become indifferent to the racial identity of their colleagues; let nationwide enterprises discover that some customers dislike racism and will make their purchasing decisions on that basis; let this happen, and market pressures will swiftly penalize employers who think that they can, without cost, cater to prejudice.

None of this is to deny the important role played by law, court order, and the example of desegregated government agencies. But imagine rapid desegregation occurring if only law, order, and example were operating. It would be slow, uneven, and painful. Public schools desegregated more slowly than hotels and restaurants not only because white parents cared more about who their children went to school with than about who was in the next hotel room or at the next cafe table but also because school authorities lacked any market incentive to admit more or different pupils. Indeed, a statist economy would not only resist desegregation, it would allocate economic benefits—franchises, licenses, credit—precisely on the basis of political, class, ethnic, or racial status.

CAPITALISM AGAINST SLAVERY

In a remarkable essay, historian Thomas L. Haskell of Rice University has connected capitalism to the attack on slavery in a bold and new way. The conventional view among historians of the social-control school has been that reform efforts, including the attack on slavery, were intended to further the hegemonic interests of the bourgeoisie. When abolishing slavery was the most rational way to insure the docility of the workers and enhance the legitimacy of the bourgeoisie, slavery was abolished.

This argument is not crudely Marxist; sophisticated control theorists do not necessarily say that businessmen stood to benefit immediately and materially from an end to slavery. They are even prepared to concede that the business classes deceived themselves about what they were doing. But, what they insist upon is that the bourgeoisie could not really have acted out of altruistic motives. And it does seem strange to think that they might have done so. After all, British capitalists were practicing profitable large-scale agriculture in the West Indies. They had many allies, including customers, in London. Then, all of a sudden, slavery was ended after a public debate that rested almost entirely, as far as I can tell, on humanitarian principles. Control theorists suggest that it came about because the capitalists wanted to enhance their legitimacy by abolishing slave labor so that labor for slave wages would not be suspect. As David Brion Davis put it, the abolitionist movement "helped clear an ideological path for British industrialists" that, by exaggerating the harshness of slavery, "gave sanction to less barbarous modes of social discipline."

Haskell finds this a somewhat tortured argument. Can capitalist opponents of slavery, notably the successful Quaker businessmen of the late eighteenth century, really have thought that their "ideological hegemony" (whatever they thought that might be) would be enhanced by attacking the slave system, and that this was more important to them than what they repeatedly and eloquently said was their motive—namely, the horror they felt toward involuntary servitude?

In place of the social-control theory, Haskell suggests that capitalism supported, and was wholly consistent with, the religious convictions of the Quaker abolitionists. As capitalism spread, it carried with it a universalistic message. An important part was the new, high value attached to keeping promises and the concordant development and enforcement of contract law. As commerce spread, promise keeping and contract writing were increasingly carried on with strangers and foreigners, including Jews, heathens, and Levantines. Capitalism sharpened one's sense of, and commitment to, the future, and it equipped its more skillful practitioners with experience in dealing with contingencies. Successful capitalists learned to deal fairly with distant strangers and thus learned to attach greater importance to individual reliability than to group membership.

Commerce across cultures can be profitable, but it is risky. In coping with the risks, capitalists learned ways of dealing with remote circumstances. They acquired, in Haskell's phrase, "recipes for intervention," or what a social scientist would call a sense of efficacy. By this route, some came to believe that is was possible, as well as desirable, to challenge slavery. Haskell does not argue that capitalism was inherently a moral argument against slavery, only that it was a cultural, as well as economic, movement that contained within its assumptions and practices certain preconditions—beliefs, experiences, recipes—for expanding the humanitarian sensibility to strangers. This cultural change made possible, in about the length of one man's life, the abolition of a practice supported by custom, profits, argument, and property rights.

CAPITALISM AND BUREAUCRACY

Capitalism is a system of action, but it is also one in which large-scale institutions operate. Like politics, economics creates bureaucracies, and bureaucracies have a logic different from that of either markets or politics. A large enterprise, whether private or public, tends to generate commitments to co-workers and subunits rather than to the enterprise as a whole, to separate employees from the customers or citizens affected by employee actions, and to operate on the basis of standard operating procedures that seem instrumentally rational even when they are substantively irrational. In short, bureaucracy diffuses or displaces the sense of personal responsibility. Firms differ from government agencies in many important respects, but this does not mean that they are free from the vices attendant on large-scale organization. There may be economic returns to scale, but not moral ones.

With all the talk about white-collar crime, we have remarkably little information about what kinds of organizational arrangements stimulate or impede misconduct. Big firms probably are more likely than smaller ones to obey certain laws and regulations because they have a more visible reputation to protect and the financial resources to hire specialists to do the protecting (for example, by discovering and complying with government rules). But big firms may be less inclined to right conduct of a different sort—that is, fair play in the most general sense.

One meaning of fairness is the Golden Rule: Treat customers, workers, and suppliers as you would wish to be treated under the same circumstances. That rule, however, will operate differently when the other party is dealt with at second or third hand, invisibly and impersonally, than when he is confronted personally. Even when we deal with a person face to face, we often find it quite easy to invent rationales for discounting their interests or rejecting their claims: "This guy is (take your pick) different, insincere, or unworthy." But it is much easier to conceive of other people as convenient abstractions when they are known only by labels, words, or numbers, as is likely the case when we are members of a large organization.

Fairness can also be defined as receiving rewards proportional to effort. In face-to-face transactions, effort is the product delivered or the service rendered, and rewards are the cash received or the thanks expressed. In impersonal transactions, effort may be the skill displayed at currying favor from one's superiors and rewards the promotions and preferment that result from successful currying. Bureaucratization not only insulates some parts of a firm from market forces but also isolates them from human forces. Bureaucratization involves specialization that often implies encapsulation, reducing the proportion of workers who deal intimately and regularly with other specialists. (In sociological jargon, there is a decline in boundary-spanning roles.)

Bureaucratization also requires measures of employee achievement that are poor proxies for market success. In a firm, a successful accountant, lawyer, or personnel officer is rarely the one who has increased profits or sales for the enterprise (managers rarely can know whether these people have materially helped or hurt profits); it is the person who has best conformed with higher-level expectations as to how an accountant, lawyer, or personnel officer is supposed to behave (and these may be reasonable, unreasonable, or self-serving expectations).

Robert Jackall, in his book *Moral Mazes,* explores how managers in two large corporations define the rules, and thus implicitly the moral requirements, of their jobs. In both firms, he found struggles for status and dominance, perceived gaps between reward and merit, and a preoccupation with the maintenance of good public relations over sound policy. Managers seeking advancement had to keep their eye out for "the main chance," and that, in turn, meant, among other things, "unrelenting attentiveness to the social intricacies of one's organization." The tone of Jackall's book suggests that he is no friend of corporations, but his detailed observations cannot for that reason be ignored.

Corporate executives are aware that they live at a time when great attention is paid to "corporate responsibility" and "business ethics." Observers who are well-disposed toward capitalism and suspicious of elite fads may dismiss these preoccupations as mere catering to a hostile media. That would be a mistake. Though much of this talk may be fatuous or superficial, the problem of imbuing large-scale enterprise with a decent moral life is fundamental. Chester Barnard made this clear nearly 60 years ago in *The Functions of the Executive.* However ready people are to comply with the self-regarding demands of a group and conform to the narrow culture of an organization, most people know the difference between doing things they are proud to tell their children about and things they hope their children never find out about.

Serious executives know this and worry about it. The emergence of codes of corporate ethics and the emphasis on fashioning a defensible corporate culture are not, I think, merely public relations (though they are sometimes just that). They are, at their best, a recognition that people want to believe that they live and work in a reasonably just and decent world. Americans are gloomy about the decency of their culture and the justice of their politics; it may be one of the supreme ironies of our time that they are often more satisfied with their employer than with their community. If true, Marx has been stood squarely on his head: Life has become more alienating then work.

As Michael Novak has observed, the corporation is an important mediating structure that stands, like the family and the church, between the individual and the state. It constitutes not simply a utilitarian arrangement but a community of sorts that shapes human conduct. People, of course, know the difference between a profit-making firm, on the one hand, and a child-rearing family or a soul-comforting church, on the other. They have different expectations from each. But no economist should suppose that since firms are about profits, that is all they are about, anymore than he should imagine that because families are about sex, that is all they are about. Corporations are not vehicles for realizing the ideal society; one of their good features, as Paul Johnson has noted, is that they attach little value to Utopian causes. But they are systems of human action that cannot for long command the loyalty of their members if their standards of collective action are materially lower than those of their individual members.

Capitalism is not irrelevant to morality: It assumes the existence of certain moral dispositions, strengthens some of these, and threatens still others. The problem for capitalists is to recognize that, while free markets will ruthlessly eliminate inefficient firms, the moral sentiments of man will only gradually and uncertainly penalize immoral ones. But, while the quick destruction of inefficient corporations threatens only individual firms, the slow anger at immoral ones threatens capitalism—and thus freedom—itself.

A Moral Case for Socialism

Kai Nielsen
Emeritus Professor of Philosophy, University of Calgary, and Adjunct Professor of Philosophy, Concordia University

I.

In North America socialism gets a bad press. It is under criticism for its alleged economic inefficiency and for its moral and human inadequacy. I want here to address the latter issue.[1] Looking at capitalism and socialism, I want to consider, against the grain of our culture, what kind of moral case can be made for socialism.

The first thing to do, given the extensive, and, I would add, inexcusably extensive, confusions about this, is to say what socialism and capitalism are. That done I will then, appealing to a cluster of values which are basic in our culture, concerning which there is a considerable and indeed a reflective consensus, examine how capitalism and socialism fare with respect to these values.[2] Given that people generally, at least in Western societies, would want it to be the case that these values have a stable exemplification in our social lives, it is appropriate to ask the question: which of these social systems is more likely stably to exemplify them? I shall argue, facing the gamut of a careful comparison in the light of these values, that, everything considered, socialism comes out better than capitalism. And this, if right, would give us good reason for believing that socialism is preferable—indeed morally preferable—to capitalism if it also turns out to be a feasible socio-economic system.

What, then, are socialism and capitalism? Put most succinctly, capitalism requires the existence of private *productive* property (private ownership of the means of production) while socialism works toward its abolition. What is essential for socialism is public ownership and control of the means of production and public ownership means just what

From *Critical Review,* Vol. 3, Nos. 3 & 4 (Summer/Fall, 1989), pp. 542–553. Reprinted by permission of *Critical Review,* 275 W. Park Ave., New Haven, CT 06511.

it says: *ownership by the public.* Under capitalism there is a domain of private property rights in the means of production which are not subject to political determination. That is, even where the political domain is a democratic one, they are not subject to determination by the public; only an individual or a set of individuals who own that property can make the final determination of what is to be done with that property.[3] These individuals make that determination and not citizens at large, as under socialism. In fully developed socialism, by contrast, there is, with respect to productive property, no domain which is not subject to political determination by the public, namely by the citizenry at large. Thus, where this public ownership and control is genuine, and not a mask for control by an elite of state bureaucrats, it will mean genuine popular and democratic control over productive property. What socialism is *not* is *state* ownership in the absence of, at the very least, popular sovereignty, i.e., genuine popular control over the state apparatus including any economic functions it might have.

The property that is owned in common under socialism is the means of existence—the productive property in the society. Socialism does not proscribe the ownership of private personal property, such as houses, cars, television sets and the like. It only proscribes the private ownership of the means of production.

The above characterizations catch the minimal core of socialism and capitalism, what used to be called the essence of those concepts.[4] But beyond these core features, it is well, in helping us to make our comparison, to see some other important features which characteristically go with capitalism and socialism. Minimally, capitalism is private ownership of the means of production but it is also, at least characteristically, a social system in which a class of capitalists owns and controls the means of production and hires workers who, owning little or no means of production, sell their labor-power to some capitalist or other for a wage. This means that a capitalist society will a be a class society in which there will be two principal classes: capitalists and workers. Socialism by contrast is a social system in which every able-bodied person is, was or will be a worker. These workers

commonly own and control the means of production (this is the characteristic form of public ownership).[5] Thus in socialism we have, in a perfectly literal sense, a classless society for there is no division between human beings along class lines.[6]

There are both pure and impure forms of capitalism and socialism.[7] The pure form of capitalism is competitive capitalism, the capitalism that Milton Friedman would tell us is the real capitalism while, he would add, the impure form is monopoly or corporate capitalism. Similarly the pure form of socialism is democratic socialism, with firm workers' control of the means of production and an industrial as well as a political democracy, while the impure form is state bureaucratic socialism.

Now it is a noteworthy fact that, to understate it, actually existing capitalisms and actually existing socialisms tend to be the impure forms. Many partisans of capitalism lament the fact that the actually existing capitalisms overwhelmingly tend to be forms of corporate capitalism where the state massively intervenes in the running of the economy. It is unclear whether anything like a fully competitive capitalism actually exists—perhaps Hong Kong approximates it—and it is also unclear whether many of the actual players in the major capitalist societies (the existing capitalists and their managers) want or even expect that it is possible to have laissez-faire capitalism again (if indeed we ever had it). Some capitalist societies are further down the corporate road than other societies, but they are all forms of corporate, perhaps in some instances even monopoly, capitalism. Competitive capitalism seems to be more of a libertarian dream than a sociological reality or even something desired by many informed and tough-minded members of the capitalist class. Socialism has had a similar fate. Its historical exemplifications tend to be of the impure forms, namely the bureaucratic state socialisms.[8] Yugoslavia is perhaps to socialism what Hong Kong is to capitalism. It is a candidate for what might count as an exemplification, or at least a near approximation, of the pure form.

This paucity of exemplifications of pure forms of either capitalism or socialism raises the question of whether the pure forms are at best unstable social systems and at worse merely utopian ideals.

I shall not try directly to settle that issue here. What I shall do instead is to compare *models* with *models*. In asking about the moral case for socialism, I shall compare forms that a not inconsiderable number of the theoretical protagonists of each take to be pure forms but which are still, they believe, historically feasible. But I will also be concerned to ask whether these models—these pure forms—can reasonably be expected to come to have a home. If they are not historically feasible models, then, even if we can make a good theoretical moral case for them, we will have hardly provided a good moral case for socialism or capitalism. To avoid bad utopianism we must be talking about forms which could be on the historical agenda. (I plainly here do not take "bad utopianism" to be pleonastic.)

II.

Setting aside for the time being the feasibility question, let us compare the pure forms of capitalism and socialism—that is to say, competitive capitalism and democratic socialism—as to how they stand with respect to sustaining and furthering the values of freedom and autonomy, equality, justice, rights and democracy. My argument shall be that socialism comes out better with respect to those values.

Let us first look at freedom and autonomy. An autonomous person is a person who is able to set her ends for herself and in optimal circumstances is able to pursue those ends. But freedom does not only mean being autonomous; it also means the absence of unjustified political and social interference in the pursuit of one's ends. Some might even say that it is just the absence of interference with one's ends. Still it is self-direction—autonomy—not non-interference which is *intrinsically* desirable. Non-interference is only valuable where it is an aid to our being able to do what we want and where we are sufficiently autonomous to have some control over our wants.

How do capitalism and socialism fare in providing the social conditions which will help or impede the flourishing of autonomy? Which model society would make for the greater flourishing of auton-

omy? My argument is (a) that democratic socialism makes it possible for more people to be more fully autonomous than would be autonomous under capitalism; and (b) that democratic socialism also interferes less in people's exercise of their autonomy than any form of capitalism. All societies limit liberty by interfering with people doing what they want to do in some ways, but the restrictions are more extensive, deeper and more undermining of autonomy in capitalism than in democratic socialism. Where there is private ownership of productive property, which, remember, is private ownership of the means of life, it cannot help but be the case that a few (the owning and controlling capitalist class) will have, along with the managers beholden to them, except in periods of revolutionary turmoil, a firm control, indeed a domination, over the vast majority of people in the society. The capitalist class with the help of their managers determines whether workers (taken now as individuals) can work, how they work, on what they work, the conditions under which they work and what is done with what they produce (where they are producers) and what use is made of their skills and the like.[9] As we move to welfare state capitalism—a compromise still favoring capital which emerged out of long and bitter class struggles—the state places some restrictions on some of these powers of capital. Hours, working conditions and the like are controlled in certain ways. Yet whether workers work and continue to work, how they work and on what, what is done with what they produce, and the rationale for their work are not determined by the workers themselves but by the owners of capital and their managers; this means a very considerable limitation on the autonomy and freedom of workers. Since workers are the great majority, such socio-economic relations place a very considerable limitation on human freedom and indeed on the very most important freedom that people have, namely their being able to live in a self-directed manner, when compared with the industrial democracy of democratic socialism. Under capitalist arrangements it simply cannot fail to be the case that a very large number of people will lose control over a very central set of facets of their lives, namely central aspects of their work and indeed in many instances, over their very chance to be able to work.

Socialism would indeed prohibit capitalist acts between consenting adults; the capitalist class would lose its freedom to buy and sell and to control the labor market. There should be no blinking at the fact that socialist social relations would impose some limitations on freedom, for there is, and indeed can be, no society without norms and some sanctions. In any society you like there will be some things you are at liberty to do and some things that you may not do.[10] However, democratic socialism must bring with it an industrial democracy where workers by various democratic procedures would determine how they are to work, on what they are to work, the hours of their work, under what conditions they are to work (insofar as this is alterable by human effort at all), what they will produce and how much, and what is to be done with what they produce. Since, instead of there being "private ownership of the means of production," there is in a genuinely socialist society "public ownership of the means of production," the means of life are owned by everyone and thus each person has a *right* to work: she has, that is, a right to the means of life. It is no longer the private preserve of an individual owner of capital but it is owned in common by us all. This means that each of us has an equal right to the means of life. Members of the capitalist class would have a few of their liberties restricted, but these are linked with owning and controlling capital and are not the important civil and political liberties that we all rightly cherish. Moreover, the limitation of the capitalist liberties to buy and sell and the like would make for a more extensive liberty for many, many more people.

One cannot respond to the above by saying that workers are free to leave the working class and become capitalists or at least petty bourgeoisie. They may indeed all in theory, taken *individually,* be free to leave the working class, but if many in fact try to leave the exits will very quickly become blocked.[11] Individuals are only free on the condition that the great mass of people, taken collectively, are not. We could not have capitalism without a working class and the working class is not free within the

capitalist system to cease being wage laborers. We cannot all be capitalists. A people's capitalism is nonsense. Though a petty commodity production system (the family farm writ large) is a logical possibility, it is hardly a stable empirical possibility and, what is most important for the present discussion, such a system would not be a capitalist system. Under capitalism, most of us, if we are to find any work at all, will just have to sell (or *perhaps* "rent" is the better word) our labor-power as a commodity. Whether you sell or rent your labor power or, where it is provided, you go on welfare, you will not have much control over areas very crucial to your life. If these are the only feasible alternatives facing the working class, working class autonomy is very limited indeed. But these are the only alternatives under capitalism.

Capitalist acts between consenting adults, if they become sufficiently widespread, lead to severe imbalances in power. These imbalances in power tend to undermine autonomy by creating differentials in wealth and control between workers and capitalists. Such imbalances are the name of the game for capitalism. Even if we (perversely I believe) call a system of petty commodity production capitalism, we still must say that such a socio-economic system is inherently unstable. Certain individuals would win out in this exchanging of commodities and in fairly quick order it would lead to a class system and the imbalances of power—the domination of the many by the few—that I take to be definitive of capitalism. By abolishing capitalist acts between consenting adults, then (but leaving personal property and civil and political liberties untouched), socialism protects more extensive freedoms for more people and in far more important areas of their lives.

III.

So democratic socialism does better regarding the value that epitomizes capitalist pride (*hubris,* would, I think, be a better term), namely autonomy. It also does better, I shall now argue, than capitalism with respect to another of our basic values, namely democracy. Since this is almost a corollary of what I have said about autonomy I can afford to be briefer. In capitalist societies, democracy must simply be *political* democracy. There can in the nature of the case be no genuine or thorough workplace democracy. When we enter the sphere of production, capitalists and not workers own, and therefore at least ultimately control, the means of production. While capitalism, as in some workplaces in West Germany and Sweden, sometimes can be pressured into allowing an ameliorative measure of worker control, once ownership rights are given up, we no longer have private productive property but public productive property (and in that way social ownership): capitalism is given up and we have socialism. However, where worker control is restricted to a few firms, we do not yet have socialism. What makes a system socialist or capitalist depends on what happens across the whole society, not just in isolated firms.[12] Moreover, managers can become very important within capitalist firms, but as long as ownership, including the ability to close the place down and liquidate the business, rests in the hands of capitalists we can have no genuine workplace democracy. Socialism, in its pure form, carries with it, in a way capitalism in any form cannot, workplace democracy. (That some of the existing socialisms are anything but pure does not belie this.)[13]

Similarly, whatever may be said of existing socialisms or at least of some existing socialisms, it is not the case that there is anything in the very idea of socialism that militates against political as well as industrial democracy. Socialists are indeed justly suspicious of some of the tricks played by parliamentary democracy in bourgeois countries, aware of its not infrequent hypocrisy and the limitations of its stress on purely legal and formal political rights and liberties. Socialists are also, without at all wishing to throw the baby out with the bath water, rightly suspicious of any simple reliance on majority rule, unsupplemented by other democratic procedures and safeguards.[14] But there is nothing in socialist theory that would set it against political democracy and the protection of political and civil rights; indeed there is much in socialism that favors them, namely its stress on both autonomy and equality.

The fact that political democracy came into being and achieved stability within capitalist societies may prove something about conditions necessary for its coming into being, but it says nothing about capitalism being necessary for sustaining it. In Chile, South Africa and Nazi Germany, indeed, capitalism has flourished without the protection of civil and political rights or anything like a respect for the democratic tradition. There is nothing structural in socialism that would prevent it from continuing those democratic traditions or cherishing those political and civil rights. That something came about under certain conditions does not establish that these conditions are necessary for its continued existence. That men initially took an interest in chess does not establish that women cannot quite naturally take an interest in it as well. When capitalist societies with long-flourishing democratic traditions move to socialism there is no reason at all to believe that they will not continue to be democratic. (Where societies previously had no democratic tradition or only a very weak one, matters are more problematic.)

IV.

I now want to turn to a third basic value, equality. In societies across the political spectrum, *moral* equality (the belief that everyone's life matters equally) is an accepted value.[15] Or, to be somewhat cynical about the matter, at least lip service is paid to it. But even this lip service is the compliment that vice pays to virtue. That is to say, such a belief is a deeply held considered conviction in modernized societies, though it has not been at all times and is not today a value held in all societies. This is most evident concerning moral equality.

While this value is genuinely held by the vast majority of people in capitalist societies, it can hardly be an effective or functional working norm where there is such a diminishment of autonomy as we have seen obtains unavoidably in such societies. Self-respect is deeply threatened where so many people lack effective control over their own lives, where there are structures of domination, where there is alienated labor, where great power differentials and differences in wealth make for very different (and often very bleak) life chances. For not inconsiderable numbers, in fact, it is difficult to maintain self-respect under such conditions unless they are actively struggling against the system. And, given present conditions, fighting the system, particularly in societies such as the United States, may well be felt to be a hopeless task. Under such conditions any real equality of opportunity is out of the question. And the circumstances are such, in spite of what is often said about these states, that equality of condition is an even more remote possibility. But without at least some of these things moral equality cannot even be approximated. Indeed, even to speak of it sounds like an obscene joke given the social realities of our lives.

Although under welfare-state capitalism some of the worst inequalities of capitalism are ameliorated, workers still lack effective control over their work, with repercussions in political and public life as well. Differentials of wealth cannot but give rise to differentials in power and control in politics, in the media, in education, in the direction of social life and in what options get seriously debated. The life chances of workers and those not even lucky enough to be workers (whose ranks are growing and will continue to grow under capitalism) are impoverished compared to the life chances of members of the capitalist class and its docile professional support stratum.

None of these equality-undermining features would obtain under democratic socialism. Such societies would, for starters, be classless, eliminating the power and control differentials that go with the class system of capitalism. In addition to political democracy, industrial democracy and all the egalitarian and participatory control that goes with that would, in turn, reinforce moral equality. Indeed it would make it possible where before it was impossible. There would be a commitment under democratic socialism to attaining or at least approximating, as far as it is feasible, equality of condition; and this, where approximated, would help make for real equality of opportunity, making equal life chances something less utopian than it must be under capitalism.

In fine, the very things, as we have seen, that make for greater autonomy under socialism than

under capitalism, would, in being more equally distributed, make for greater equality of condition, greater equality of opportunity and greater moral equality in a democratic socialist society than in a capitalist one. These values are values commonly shared by both capitalistically inclined people and those who are socialistically inclined. What the former do not see is that in modern industrial societies, democratic socialism can better deliver these goods than even progressive capitalism.

There is, without doubt, legitimate worry about bureaucratic control under socialism.[16] But that is a worry under any historically feasible capitalism as well, and it is anything but clear that state bureaucracies are worse than great corporate bureaucracies. Indeed, if socialist bureaucrats were, as the socialist system requires, really committed to production for needs and to achieving equality of condition, they might, bad as they are, be the lesser of two evils. But in any event democratic socialism is not bureaucratic state socialism, and there is no structural reason to believe that it must—if it arises in a society with skilled workers committed to democracy—give rise to bureaucratic state socialism. There will, inescapably, be some bureaucracy, but in a democratic socialist society it must and indeed will be controlled. This is not merely a matter of optimism about the will of socialists, for there are more mechanisms for democratic control of bureaucracy within a democratic socialism that is both a political and an industrial democracy, than there can be under even the most benign capitalist democracies—democracies which for structural reasons can never be industrial democracies. If, all that notwithstanding, bureaucratic creepage is inescapable in modern societies, then that is just as much a problem for capitalism as for socialism.

The underlying rationale for production under capitalism is profit and capital accumulation. Capitalism is indeed a marvelous engine for building up the productive forces (though clearly at the expense of considerations of equality and autonomy). We might look on it, going back to earlier historical times, as something like a forced march to develop the productive forces. But now that the productive forces in advanced capitalist societies are wondrously developed, we are in a position to direct them to far more humane and more equitable uses under a socio-economic system whose rationale for production is to meet human needs (the needs of everyone as far as this is possible). This egalitarian thrust, together with the socialists' commitment to attaining, as far as that is possible, equality of condition, makes it clear that socialism will produce more equality than capitalism.

V.

In talking about autonomy, democracy and equality, we have, in effect, already been talking about justice. A society or set of institutions that does better in these respects than another society will be a more just society than the other society.[17]

Fairness is a less fancy name for justice. If we compare two societies and the first is more democratic than the second; there is more autonomy in the first society than in the second; there are more nearly equal life chances in the first society than in the second and thus greater equality of opportunity; if, without sacrifice of autonomy, there is more equality of condition in the first society than in the second; and if there is more moral equality in the first society than in the second, then we cannot but conclude that the first society is a society with more fairness than the second and, thus, that it is the more just society. But this is exactly how socialism comes out vis-à-vis even the best form of capitalism.[18]

A society which undermines autonomy, heels in democracy (where democracy is not violating rights), makes equality impossible to achieve and violates rights cannot be a just society. If, as I contend, that is what capitalism does, and cannot help doing, then a capitalist society cannot be a just society. Democratic socialism, by contrast, does not need to do any of those things, and we can predict that it would not, for there are no structural imperatives in democratic socialism to do so and there are deep sentiments in that tradition urging us not to do so. I do not for a moment deny that there are similar sentiments for autonomy and democracy in capitalist societies, but the logic of capitalism, the underlying structures of capitalist societies—even the best of capitalist societies—frustrate the real-

ization of the states of affairs at which those sympathies aim.[19] A radical democrat with a commitment to human rights, to human autonomy and moral equality and fair equality of opportunity ought to be a democratic socialist and a firm opponent of capitalism—even a capitalism with a human face.

NOTES

1. For arguments about efficiency see David Schweickart, *Capitalism or Worker Control?* (New York: Praeger, 1980) and Samuel Bowles, David M. Gordon and Thomas E. Weisskopf, *Beyond the Wasteland: A Democratic Alternative to Economic Decline* (New York: Anchor Doubleday, 1983).
2. Andrew Levine's work is very important here and my own account has been extensively influenced by his. See Andrew Levine, *Arguing for Socialism* (London: Routledge & Kegan Paul, 1984); Andrew Levine, "On Arguing for Socialism—Theoretical Considerations," *Socialism and Democracy* (Spring/Summer 1968): 19–28; and Andrew Levine, *The Withering Away of the State* (London: Verso, 1987).
3. That this is a system which is distinctive of capitalism and to which there are many working alternatives is shown by A. M. Honoré, "Property, Title and Redistribution" in Virginia Held, ed., *Property, Profits and Economic Justice* (Belmont, Calif.: Wadsworth Publishing, 1980), 84–92.
4. This is carefully argued for by Andrew Levine. See the references in my second note.
5. Kai Nielsen, "Capitalism, Socialism and Justice" in Tom Regan and Donald Van De Veere, eds., *And Justice for All* (Totowa, N.J.: Rowman and Littlefield, 1982), 264–96.
6. G. A. Cohen, "The Structure of Proletarian Unfreedom," *Philosophy and Public Affairs* 12, no. 1 (Winter 1983): 2–33 and John Exdell, "Liberty, Equality and Capitalism," *Canadian Journal of Philosophy* II, no. 3 (September 1981): 457–72.
7. Nielsen, "Capitalism, Socialism and Justice," 264–69.
8. Ferenc Fehér, Agnes Heller, György Markus, *Dictatorship over Needs: An Analysis of Soviet Societies* (Oxford: Basil Blackwell, 1983).
9. Cohen, "The Structure of Proletarian Unfreedom."
10. G. A. Cohen, "Freedom, Justice and Capitalism," *New Left Review* no. 26 (March/April 1981) and his

"Illusions About Private Property and Freedom," *Issues in Marxist Philosophy,* vol. IV, ed. John Mepham and David-Hillel Ruben (Sussex: Harvester Press, 1981), 223–39.

11. G. A. Cohen, *Karl Marx's Theory of History* (Oxford: Clarendon Press, 1978), 73–7.
12. Levine, *Arguing for Socialism,* 1–11.
13. How far they are from that is shown by Fehér, Heller and Markus, *Dictatorship over Needs.*
14. Claus Offe, *Disorganized Capitalism* (Cambridge, Mass.: MIT Press, 1985), 259–99.
15. Thomas Nagel, *Mortal Questions* (Cambridge: Cambridge University Press, 1979), 106–27.
16. Fehér, Heller and Markus, *Dictatorship over Needs.*
17. John Rawls, *A Theory of Justice* (Cambridge, Mass.: Harvard University Press, 1971); Kai Nielsen, *Equality and Liberty: A Defense of Radical Egalitarianism* (Totowa, N.J.: Rowman and Allanheld, 1985); and Samuel Bowles and Herbert Gintis, *Democracy and Capitalism* (New York: Basic Books, 1986).
18. Levine citations in note 2 above and Nielsen, *Equality and Liberty.*
19. See Richard C. Edwards, Michael Reich and Thomas E. Weisekopf, eds., *The Capitalist System,* 3rd ed. (Englewood Cliffs, N.J.: Prentice Hall, 1986), and Samuel Bowles and Richard Edwards, *Understanding Capitalism* (New York: Harper and Row, 1985).

QUESTIONS FOR DISCUSSION

1. You have been asked to distribute a sum of money *justly* among the following people. Think of your funds as a pie to be divided into six pieces, and rank the six people listed below from highest (the one to whom you should give the most money) to lowest. You may assign one or more of the candidates an equal rank. Defend your distribution, explaining *why* you think it is just. How would your distribution be assessed by Rawls, Norick, and Smart?
   a. A man who lives off the interest on his inherited wealth
   b. An unemployed man from the inner city
   c. A single mother or five who works as a rest room attendant during the day and moonlights as a prostitute
   d. A blue-collar worker on an automobile plant assembly line
   e. A high-level manager of a consumer products company, male, married
   f. A married woman who holds an exactly comparable position in a similar consumer products company
2. Rawls argues that just principles are those that would be chosen by rational, self-interested people, if they have placed behind a "veil of ignorance." What is the purpose of Rawls's "veil of ignorance"? Do you think that people placed behind such a veil really would choose the principles Rawls claims they would choose?
3. Nozick rejects a system that tries to ensure equality among persons, because he believes such a system would inevitably interfere with people's liberty. Would people be equally free under a Nozickian system of justice? If not, can we call Nozick's theory of justice a truly "libertarian" one?
4. Why does Smart believe that the general tendency of utilitarianism is toward equality? What would be the exceptions to this tendency? What might Rawls and Nozick have to say about Smart's theory of justice?
5. Nielsen claims that socialism is a more just system than capitalism, but he has little to say about which system is more efficient. Is capitalism a more efficient system? Must it be? Assuming it is, and assuming that socialism is more just, which should we accept: economic efficiency at the cost of justice, or justice at the cost of economic efficiency? How might the decision be made? What would Wilson's position appear to be?

CHAPTER 2

Ethics and Business Decision Making

Teaching Ethical Decision Making and Principled Reasoning

Michael Josephson
President, Josephson Institute for the Advancement of Ethics

The ethical quality of our society is determined by the separate actions of public officials and their staffs, employers and their employees, parents and their children, teachers and their students, professionals and their clients, individuals and their friends. Each of us is almost always in one or more of these roles and our decisions are important. They are important on an individual level because they establish and define our ethical character. They are important on a social level because they produce significant direct consequences and, indirectly, help to set the moral tone of all social interactions.

Every day we face situations which test our ethical consciousness and commitment. Sometimes, the ethical implications of our decisions are apparent. Our consciences are awake and active, warning us to be good. In such cases, we know we will be held accountable for our conduct and we do not tell big lies, steal or break important promises.

Most of our decisions, however, are more mundane. They deal with our basic personal and occupational relationships and activities and there are no sirens causing us to view the choice as an ethical one. We rely heavily on habits, common sense and our perceptions of custom (i.e., what we think is generally considered acceptable by those engaged in similar activities). The dominant consideration is expediency—accomplishing our tasks, getting what we want, with as little hassle as possible.

Most of us do pretty well in dealing with the big and obvious ethical decisions. We tend to judge ourselves, and would like others to judge us by, these self-conscious choices which usually display our virtue. Unfortunately, we are more likely to be judged, and tripped up, by the way we handle the hundreds of ethical "sleepers" that cumulatively shape our reputations.

In recent years we have witnessed a growing concern about the way people are behaving. In fact, the proliferation of well-publicized examples of dishonesty, hypocrisy, cheating and greed has created some alarm about the state of personal ethics. If these incidents are indicative of a trend, there is much reason for concern because they reflect a level of selfishness, shortsightedness and insensitivity that could undermine the moral fabric of our society.

Excerpted from *Ethics: Easier Said Than Done* (Winter 1988). Reprinted by permission of the Josephson Institute for the Advancement of Ethics.

ETHICS EDUCATION

In response to this new awareness, there has been a revived interest in ethics education. The pendulum of social conscience seems to be swinging the other way and there is a call for a return to traditional moral values and value-centered education. It has become clear to many that "value clarification," "situational ethics," and "ethical relativism" do not provide the inspiration, motivation or training to generate either the good will or discipline that are essential to moral conduct. Moreover, most academic courses which teach *about* ethics do not seem to engage students on a level that is likely to affect their behavior. The goal of the reformers is to find a way to increase ethical conduct.

We know that ethics are "learned" or "developed," yet many are not sure if ethics can be "taught." We do know that attitudes and character traits are not conveyed in the same way we convey other forms of knowledge (i.e., ethics is not something that can be taught like history or geography). Basic moral education occurs during the process of growing up. We learn from parents, teachers, religious leaders, coaches, employers, friends and others and, as a result, most of us reach adulthood with our character essentially formed and with a basic understanding of, and fundamental respect for, ethical values.

But, the presumptive values adopted in our youth are not immutably etched in our character. We know that values are constantly shuffled and prioritized, for better and for worse, in response to life experiences. Thus, youthful idealism is tested as we are emancipated into a world where important and binding decisions must be made. Only then do we discover what we are really willing to do to get and hold a job and be successful in a competitive society. By the same process, the blind competitiveness and materialism of young adulthood will later be challenged by life-changing experiences (e.g., illness, parenthood, divorce, death of a loved one) or the simple fact of maturation, causing one to reflect on the meaning of life (sometimes inducing a "mid-life crisis").

The point, and it has enormous significance for ethics educators, is that the formation, refinement and modification of a person's operational value system—the attitudes and beliefs that motivate conduct—are an ongoing process which continues throughout one's adult life. It is never too late.

APPROACHES TO ETHICS EDUCATION

One approach to conduct-oriented ethics education deals directly with the development of character and the inculcation and reinforcement of basic moral values such as honesty, caring, fairness and accountability. This approach has potential in the education of children and adolescents, but it is not likely to be effective in dealing with young adults and mature professionals.

The second approach focuses on the development of qualities beyond character—qualities that can be developed or enhanced even in adults. Ethical behavior is the result of ethical decisions, and ethical decision making requires: 1) *ethical commitment*—the personal resolve to act ethically, to do the right thing; 2) *ethical consciousness*—the ability to perceive the ethical implications of a situation; 3) *ethical competency*—the ability to engage in sound moral reasoning and develop practical problem solving strategies.

The purpose of this article is to present a theory of ethics education and to describe a framework for analyzing ethical problems which can be taught in college, postgraduate professional courses, and ethical decision making workshops.

SETTING REASONABLE GOALS

I am only one, but still I am one. I cannot do everything, but I can do something. And, because I cannot do everything, I will not refuse to do what I can.

—Edwin Hale

Those who believe they can do something are probably right, and so are those who believe they can't.

—Unknown

It is important to recognize the limitations of ethics education. Many people will simply not respond to appeals to conscience or moral principle. Many people are unwilling, or at a particular point in their lives, unready, to examine the ethical quality of their conduct and change their priorities.

Thus, the most appropriate target for ethics programs is not bad and selfish people who knowingly do wrong, but the vast majority of decent people who are already disposed to act with propriety but who, because of lack of insight, rigorous moral reasoning or practical problem solving ability, lose sight of their ethical aspirations and make wrong decisions.

The importance and value of ethics education does not depend on the eradication of all misconduct. If just some of the people act more ethically just some of the time, the effort is worthwhile.

DEFINING TERMS

In order to avoid the semantic quicksand that often engulfs discussions about ethics, it is necessary to define the essential terms and concepts involved.

Ethics refers to a system or code of conduct based on moral duties and obligations which indicate how we should behave; it deals with the ability to distinguish right from wrong and the commitment to do what is right.

Morals refers to what is good and right in character and conduct. The term is essentially interchangeable with ethics, though in common usage, "morality" often implies particular dogmatic views of propriety, especially as to sexual and religious matters. Since the term "ethics" does not carry these same connotations, it is more neutral.

Personal ethics refers to an individual's operational code of ethics based on personal values and beliefs as to what is right or good.

Values are core beliefs which guide or motivate attitudes and actions. Many values have nothing to do with ethics.

Ethical values are beliefs (e.g., honesty and fairness) which are inherently concerned with what is intrinsically good or right and the way one should act.

Nonethical values are ethically neutral values (e.g., wealth, security, comfort, prestige and approval). They are not necessarily inconsistent with ethical values, but often there is a conflict.

Ethical principles are standards or rules describing the kind of behavior an ethical person should and should not engage in. For example, the value of honesty translates into principles demanding truthfulness and candor and forbidding deception and cheating.

ETHICAL NORMS

What is morality in any given time or place? It is what the majority then and there happen to like and immorality is what they dislike

—Alfred North Whitehead

The so-called new morality is too often the old immorality condoned.

—Lord Shawcross

In matters of principle stand like a rock; in matters of taste swim with the current.

—Thomas Jefferson

It is critical to effective ethics education to overcome the cynicism of ethical relativism—the view that ethics is just a matter of opinion and personal belief as in politics or religion. Though debatable beliefs regarding sexual matters and religion often do travel under the passport of morality, there are ethical norms that transcend cultures and time.

While ethics educators must be aware that sermonizing and moralizing about particular ethical principles are not generally effective—after all, "No one likes to be 'should' upon" (a wonderful phrase from *How Can I Help?* by Ram Dass and Paul Gorman, Knopf 1985)—it is not constructive to be so value neutral that everyone is allowed to think that ethics is simply a matter of personal opinion and that one person's answer is necessarily as good as that of another's.

In fact, the study of history, philosophy and religion reveal a strong consensus as to certain universal and timeless values essential to the ethical life: 1) *Honesty,* 2) *Integrity,* 3) *Promise-keeping,* 4) *Fidelity,* 5) *Fairness,* 6) *Caring for Others,* 7) *Respect for Others,* 8) *Responsible Citizenship,* 9) *Pursuit of Excellence,* and 10) *Accountability.*

These ten core values yield a series of *principles,* do's and don'ts, which delineate right and wrong in general terms and, therefore, provide a guide to behavior. Individuals may want to edit or augment the list, but we have found it to be a valuable tool in examining the ethical implications of a situation and providing solid reference points for ethical problem solving.

Ethical Principles

Honesty Be truthful, sincere, forthright, straight-forward, frank, candid; do not cheat, steal, lie, deceive, or act deviously.

Integrity Be principled, honorable, upright, courageous and act on convictions; do not be two-faced, or unscrupulous or adopt an end-justifies-the-means philosophy that ignores principle.

Promise-Keeping Be worthy of trust, keep promises, fulfill commitments, abide by the spirit as well as the letter of an agreement; do not interpret agreements in a technical or legalistic manner in order to rationalize noncompliance or create excuses for breaking commitments.

Fidelity Be faithful and loyal to family, friends, employers, and country; do not use or disclose information learned in confidence; in a professional context, safeguard the ability to make independent professional judgments by scrupulously avoiding undue influences and conflicts of interest.

Fairness Be fair and open-minded, be willing to admit error and, where appropriate, change positions and beliefs, demonstrate a commitment to justice, the equal treatment of individuals, and tolerance for diversity; do not overreach or take undue advantage of another's mistakes or adversities.

Caring for Others Be caring, kind and compassionate; share, be giving, serve others; help those in need and avoid harming others.

Respect for Others Demonstrate respect for human dignity, privacy, and the right to self-determination of all people; be courteous, prompt, and decent; provide others with the information they need to make informed decisions about their own lives; do not patronize, embarrass or demean.

Responsible Citizenship Obey just laws (if a law is unjust, openly protest it); exercise all democratic rights and privileges responsibly by participation (voting and expressing informed views), social consciousness and public service; when in a position of leadership or authority, openly respect and honor democratic processes of decision making, avoid unnecessary secrecy or concealment of information, and assure that others have the information needed to make intelligent choices and exercise their rights.

Pursuit of Excellence Pursue excellence in all matters; in meeting personal and professional responsibilities, be diligent, reliable, industrious, and committed; perform all tasks to the best of your ability, develop and maintain a high degree of competence, be well informed and well prepared; do not be content with mediocrity but do not seek to win "at any cost."

Accountability Be accountable, accept responsibility for decisions and the foreseeable consequences of actions and inactions, and for setting an example for others. Parents, teachers, employers, many professionals and public officials have a special obligation to lead by example, to safeguard and advance the integrity and reputation of their families, companies, professions and the government; avoid even the appearance of impropriety and take whatever actions are necessary to correct or prevent inappropriate conduct of others.

The first question in ethical decision making is: "Which ethical principles are involved in the decision?" Considering the above list is an excellent way to isolate the relevant issues involved.

ETHICAL THEORIES

Though we run the risk of alienating many philosophy-oriented ethicists, in the Institute's programs we have not found it particularly useful to dwell on ethical theories. Our time with audiences is limited and most want to get immediately to the heart of ethical problem solving.

In fact, we present a variation of philosopher W. D. Ross' notion that there are certain *prima facie obligations* which impose ethical duties that can be avoided only in order to perform superior ethical duties—a kind of compromise between Kant's strict duty theory and John Stuart Mill's utilitarianism. Thus, implicit in our analysis of practical decision making situations is the principle that ethical duties are real, important and binding, and that they can be overborne only by other ethical duties.

The Golden Rule   On the other hand, we have found it helpful to emphasize the Golden Rule: "Do unto others as you would have them do unto you; and love thy neighbor as thyself." Most of the ethical principles listed above can be derived from these simple statements.

This approach to ethical decision making is surprisingly effective. In many cases, simply by asking, "How would I want to be treated in this situation?" the ethical response becomes clear. We do not want to be lied to or deceived, so we should not lie to or deceive others. We want people to keep their promises and treat us fairly, so we should keep our promises and treat others fairly.

The major problem with the Golden Rule is that in complex cases, where a decision is likely to affect different people in different ways, a more sophisticated method of sorting out ethical responsibilities is necessary.

Stakeholder Analysis   To deal with these complex situations, we advocate an analytical tool developed in the corporate responsibility literature. Since decision is often likely to affect an entire network of people with differing interests, it is necessary to carefully sort out the interests by determining, in a systematic way, which people have a stake in the decision. Thus, a threshold question in analyzing a problem is: "Who are the stakeholders and how is the decision likely to affect them?" This method does not solve the problem, but it helps the decision maker see all the ethical implications of conduct and reduces the likelihood of inadvertent harm.

ETHICAL BEHAVIOR

> Would the boy you were be proud of the man you are?
>
> —Laurence Peter

> The trouble with the rat race is that even if you win, you're still a rat.
>
> —Lily Tomlin

Ethics education works best when it builds upon our positive inclinations. Most people want to be ethical; they want to be worthy of the respect and admiration of others and they want to be proud of themselves and what they do for a living. Self-esteem and self-respect depend on the private assessment of our own character. Very few people can accept the fact that they are less ethical than others. In fact, most people believe that they are more ethical.

Because of the importance of this positive self-image, many people will alter their conduct if they discover it is inconsistent with their espoused values. Thus, it is important to discuss candidly the common misconceptions and normal excuses, rationalization, and temptations which impede ethical conduct. Although some level of confrontation may be necessary to cut through natural defenses, it is critical to avoid an adversary atmosphere which will merely produce resistance. The most successful methods present participants with the opportunity to discuss pertinent and specific problems with peers and help them to clarify their ethical aspirations, engage in moral reflection, and enhance their ethical issue-spotting, reasoning and problem-solving abilities.

Common Misconceptions

Ethics Are Only Concerned with Misconduct
Most discussions about ethics focus on misconduct and improprieties—the negative dimension of ethics. But, as is apparent from our list of ethical principles, an equally important dimension of ethics focuses on positive actions, doing the right thing, on producing good, helping and caring, rather than on avoiding wrongdoing. Under this affirmative perspective, ethical principles are not merely burdens and limitations; they are also guidelines for the constructive role a person of virtue can play in society.

If It's Legal, It's Ethical   Law abidingness is an aspect of responsible citizenship and an ethical principle especially important in a democracy. We should not, however, confuse ethics with legality. Laws and written codes of ethics are minimalist in nature—they only establish the lines of consensus impropriety.

Ethics requires more of a person than technical compliance with rules. Everything that is lawful is not, *ipso facto,* ethical. Thus, the fact that certain conduct escapes the label of illegality, including the fact that a person has been formally acquitted of a criminal charge, does not, in itself, provide moral exoneration.

People we regard as ethical do not measure their conduct in terms of minimal standards of virtue. They do not walk the line, nor consistently resort to legalistic rationales to circumvent legitimate standards of behavior or the spirit of their agreements. Ethical persons consciously advance ethical principles by choosing to do more than they have to and less than they have a right to do.

The ethical person may, however, occasionally choose to openly violate a law believed to be unjust. The ethical value of lawfulness can be overborne by other conscience driven values. Thus, civil disobedience, the open and deliberate refusal to abide by certain laws, has a long and honorable history. The thing that makes such lawbreaking ethically justifiable is the integrity of the violator and the courage of convictions shown by the willingness to publicly challenge the law and bear the consequences. On the other hand, it is not ethical to break a law one disagrees with in the hope of not being found out. The kind of covert lawlessness that characterized the darker side of the Iran-Contra scandal does not qualify as civil disobedience.

There Is a Single Right Answer   An ethical decision maker does not proceed on the assumption that there is a single "right" answer to all ethical dilemmas. In most situations, there are a number of ethical responses. The first task is to distinguish ethical from unethical responses; the second, is to choose the best response from the ethically appropriate ones. Although there may be several ethical responses to a situation, all are not equal. Some are more ethical than others, and some are more consistent with an individual's personal goals and value system than others.

Excuses, Rationalizations and Temptations

It is important to try to understand why people tend to act unethically. An easy answer is that they are just plain bad. This is simply not so. The truth is that a great deal of improper conduct is committed by fundamentally decent people who believe in and are committed to ethical values. There are three major reasons that ethically concerned persons fail to conform to their own moral principles: 1) *unawareness and insensitivity,* 2) *selfishness,* consisting of self-indulgence, self-protection, and self-righteousness, and 3) *defective reasoning.*

Unawareness and Insensitivity   At the turn of the century, a Russian noblewoman attended an opera and wept out of compassion at the death of a poor peasant. She was still weeping when she left the opera house and found that her footman had frozen to death while waiting for her as he was instructed to do. She became angry, cursing his ignorance and her inconvenience, making no connection between her compassion and her conduct.

Moral blindness, the failure to perceive all the ethical implications of conduct, is a major source of impropriety. In some cases, this blindness results from the operation of subconscious defense mechanisms which protect the psyche from having to cope with the fact that many of the things we do and want to do are not consistent with our ethical beliefs. Elaborate and internally persuasive excuses and rationalizations are used to fool our consciences. Among the most potent are:

- Everyone does it.
- To get along, go along.
- They don't understand.
- I can't do anyone any good if I lose my job.
- I have no time for ethical subtleties.
- Ethics is a luxury I can't afford right now.
- Its not my job/worry/problem.

> You can't learn too soon that the most useful thing about principle is that it can always be sacrificed to expediency.
>
> —Somerset Maugham

> Senators who go down in defeat in defense of a single principle will not be on hand to fight for that or any other principle in the future.
>
> —John F. Kennedy

A common context for this ethical self-deception is occupational behavior. Most occupations develop the "insider syndrome" which rationalizes ethically dubious conduct and immunizes the occupation from the criticism of outsiders on the grounds that the critics simply don't understand the necessities and values that insiders take for granted.

Insider rationales are particularly effective at making expediency a new ethical principle which overrides integrity, honesty and accountability in order to achieve the "greater good" (i.e., the end justifies the means). For example, politicians are viewed as frequently relying on insider rationales to justify various forms of deception, the leaking of confidential information, and cynical manipulation of campaign financing and outside income rules. Journalists are thought to justify the use of stolen documents, invasions of privacy, and arrogant and offensive interviewing behavior—all based upon vague notions of the public's right to know, though the public regularly denounces such press tactics.

Selfishness   Implicit in all ethical theories is the notion of caring for and respecting others. In many cases, this requires us to forego personal benefits or bear personal burdens; some level of self-sacrifice is essential to consistent ethical conduct. Thus, selfishness continually assaults the conscience with temptations and rationalizations.

The natural inclination to selfishness has been amplified by certain self-actualizing philosophies coming out of the 1960's and 1970's which either advocated or were misinterpreted to condone selfishness. In the 1980's these philosophies seemed to spawn a generation of greedy people whose dominant values stress materialism.

Although there are many who proudly proclaim their individualistic "everyone for himself/herself" creed, most do not. Most still believe in the primacy of traditional values such as integrity, loyalty, giving, and sharing, but they are influenced by their environment and the ample supply of excuses and justifications developed to defend the new faith. Selfishness comes in three major forms: 1) self-indulgence, 2) self-protection, and 3) self-righteousness.

Self-Indulgence   Perhaps the most common and easily identifiable source of unethical conduct is self-indulgence. Although few people are as open as Ivan Boesky was when he publicly asserted that

"greed is good," many people lie, break commitments, violate or evade laws, and fail to demonstrate caring, compassion and charity in order to advance narrow personal interests. They often cover-up the selfish motive with noble sounding sentiments, e.g., "I'm doing it for my family"; "I'm creating (or protecting) jobs"; "If the business doesn't survive it will be worse for everyone"; "It's in the interests of all the shareholders (or the public)"; and, "My constituency needs me."

Self-Protection   The instinct for self-protection often generates lying, deception and cover-ups, including big and little lies (e.g., "I knew nothing about this"; "The check is in the mail"; "Tell him I'm not in"), concealment, blameshifting, and even document destruction. These actions frequently result from a fear of, or unwillingness to accept, the consequences of prior behavior. The temptation to sacrifice ethical principles is particularly great when it is believed that the consequences will be unfair or disproportionate—an easy thing to believe when you are the one to suffer the consequences.

Self-Righteousness   A particularly troublesome type of selfishness results from a form of arrogance arising from self-righteousness. For example, Colonel Oliver North demonstrated a type of integrity when he decided to "go above the law" by shredding documents, lying and deceiving, and withholding vital information to advance his strong personal convictions. The ethical problem arises, however, from the fact that he knew that his beliefs were at variance with honest good faith beliefs of others who had at least an equal right to participate in the decision making process. His conduct denied these people the ability to exercise personal autonomy and deprived them of the ability to carry out their constitutional responsibilities. He did not openly disagree with the Congressional mandates and statutes; instead, he sought to privately nullify them by ignoring them. To accomplish his goals he violated ethical principles of honesty, promise-keeping, respect for others, and responsible democratic citizenship.

Defective Reasoning In addition to sorting out the various values involved and those stakeholders affected, a substantial amount of factual analysis and prediction of consequences is necessary to ethical decision making. This requires sophisticated reasoning skills; defects in reasoning or mistakes in evaluation can result in decisions which are inconsistent with ethical principles. We find two common errors: people consistently overestimate the costs of doing the right thing, and underestimate the cost of failing to do the right thing.

Principled reasoning directs the decision maker to recognize where information is incomplete, uncertain or ambiguous, and to make reasonable efforts to get additional information and clarify the ambiguities! After evaluating the facts, the next step is to predict, with as much certainty as is reasonably possible, the likely consequences of contemplated conduct on all those affected by a decision (i.e., stakeholders).

Another defective reasoning problem, related to the selfishness issues, emanates from the fact that unethical conduct normally yields short-run benefits which, when looked at through the distorted lens of self-interest, seem to outweigh the *possibility* of long-range harms which may flow from unethical conduct. Often, it is easier to lie, deceive, conceal or disregard commitments than to confront a problem head on and accept the costs inherent in honesty and integrity.

The fact is that an ethical person must often sacrifice short-term benefits to achieve long-term advantages. He or she must also be prepared to sacrifice physical or material gains for abstract intangibles such as self-esteem, the respect of others, reputation and a clear conscience. An ethical person must be able to distinguish between short-term and long-term benefits and costs.

ETHICAL DECISION MAKING

Ethical decision making refers to a process of choosing (i.e., principled reasoning) which systematically considers and evaluates alternate courses of conduct in terms of the list of ethical principles. It does not proceed on the assumption that there is a single "right" answer to most problems. To the contrary, it recognizes that though some responses would be unethical, in most situations there are a number of ethical ways of dealing with a situation.

The first task of ethical decision making is to distinguish ethical from unethical responses; the second is to choose the best response from the ethically appropriate ones. Although there may be several ethical responses to a situation, all are not equal.

Making the distinctions necessary is much more difficult and complex than is normally thought because, in so many real world situations, there are a multitude of competing interests and values, and crucial facts are unknown or ambiguous. Since our actions are likely to benefit some at the expense of others, ethical decision makers also attempt to foresee the likely consequences of their actions.

We cannot solve all problems by resorting to some mechanistic formula, but we can be more effective if we have a structure. A process which systematically takes into account the ethical principles involved in a decision tends to prevent inadvertent unethical conduct and allows us to consciously choose which values to advance—to determine whom to aid and whom to harm.

When one is in the trenches, it is difficult, if not impossible, to analyze problems fully and objectively. While most people do not want more rules telling them what to do, they do want assistance in perceiving the ethical implications of their decisions and in developing realistic, morally-centered approaches for resolving ethical dilemmas. . . .

In the "real world" there are many shades of gray, even in routine decision making. Most of these decisions are made in the context of economic, professional, and social pressures which compete with ethical goals and conceal or confuse the moral issues. We must, therefore, be ever vigilant to use principled reasoning in the pursuit of ethical decision making. The essential skills *can* be taught to adults; their subsequent behavior *can* be more ethical. It may not always be simple to do, but, then again, ethics truly are "easier said than done."

Ethical Decision Making in Business

Craig Dreilinger
President, The Dreiford Group, and Executive Fellow, Center for Business Ethics, Bentley College

Dan Rice
Senior Consultant, The Dreiford Group

In essence, an ethical issue is a problem where some of the components suggest that values or moral judgments may come into conflict. Therefore, it makes eminent sense to approach such an issue by using a systematic problem-solving model to clarify the elements and issues involved in the problem, to generate possible solutions to the problem, and to provide a framework for choosing among those solutions. Because it provides a deliberate and considered approach, we have found that the problem-solving model presented here is of especial benefit in assisting one to resolve ethically related problems.

The first (of seven) steps in this problem-solving model requires that the decision maker *identify the desired outcome for the entire situation.* What, exactly, are you attempting to accomplish in dealing with the problem? In addition to the problem having been solved, what else should or should not occur when you have achieved the desired result? What is the ideal outcome? What outcome(s) might you be willing to "settle for"—i.e., are there "less-than-ideal" outcomes that are acceptable if the ideal outcome proves impossible or impractical to attain?

---

1. Identify Desired Outcome
2. Define the Problem
3. Examine Difficulties and Obstacles
4. Develop Alternative Solutions
5. Select Best Solution
6. Delineate Specific Steps
7. Identify Reactions/Rewards

Written for this text. Printed by permission of The Dreiford Group.

Once you feel assured that you thoroughly understand your desired outcome, you should then *define the problem* by asking yourself questions about its antecedents and about the environment in which it is occurring. What, precisely, created or is causing this situation? Is the problem you have recognized the "real" concern, or is it actually symptomatic of a more basic, underlying problem? Who, exactly, is involved in generating or exacerbating this problem? Who, specifically, is it affecting?

When and where does this problem occur? Is this a short-term problem which is likely to be resolved with a reasonable degree of immediacy, or is it a long-term problem requiring a sustained effort to resolve? The more questions you find to ask regarding the problem, the more successful you will be in defining and comprehending the issues with which you are struggling.

After you have defined the problem as thoroughly as possible, you then need to *examine the difficulties involved in solving the problem.* In order to further clarify the solutions that may be available to you, you need to be aware of the specific difficulties that have prevented or may prevent the problem from being solved. Are there reasons that you have avoided or would like to avoid dealing with for solving the problem? Are there reasons that you or others have perpetuated the problem or allowed it to occur or persist? Why has this problem not been solved previously, or by others? What are the costs (not just financially, but also in terms of such factors as harm to others, or damage to the organization's image or ability to function, etc.) of not solving the problem? What costs are associated with solving it? Is it more costly to solve the problem or more costly to allow it to continue?

When examining the difficulties involved in solving the problem, you also need to be aware that obstacles or conditions may exist which will make it arduous or impossible to do so.

Obstacles which make it *arduous* to resolve ethical issues are those which *can* be overcome by the decision maker involved. These obstacles suggest areas of responsibility to which you will need to attend in order to ensure that decisions are properly made. The following obstacles make it arduous to resolve ethical issues:

The true facts of the situation are unclear or incomplete Any decision must be made on the basis of the facts available. The ramifications or consequences of decisions involving ethical issues are often unclear or obscured by other considerations. Therefore, it is especially important that you expend every effort to uncover all the data available in regard to ethical considerations when making such decisions.

However, you should not ignore hunches just because you do not yet have all the facts to support them. Often, a sense of discomfort is an important clue in identifying ethical issues; likewise, a feeling that the resolution to a problem lies in a certain direction may be an indication as to where to begin in searching for further information about the situation.

Words used to describe the issue are "loaded" Ethical issues are often described in terms of "fairness," "justice," or "doing right." Such words or phrases mean different things to different people and may make it onerous for them to agree upon the facts concerned. Such words also carry an emotional content which may create an unwarranted bias towards selecting one of a possible number of alternatives. Whenever possible, avoid using "loaded" words in defining or describing ethical issues.

Subjectivity and personal perceptions create barriers to objectivity It is important that decisions involving ethical issues be made rationally and objectively. They must be supported by the facts of the situation. Examine your personal viewpoints on the matter to determine whether or not your feelings may be preventing you from impartially considering the facts or otherwise assessing the issue. Again, however, your instincts (or those of others) may provide you with information about the situation and should be examined rather than ignored.

Emotions get in the way of logic This especially occurs when ethical issues are being discussed with others. Even when you have attempted to rationally and impersonally analyze the facts of the matter, you may find that pertinent discussions become so emotionally charged that logic and clear-sightedness are unable to prevail. When you find yourself in such a situation, attempt to diffuse its intensity before allowing yourself or others to commit to adamant positions. When logic seems to conflict with your values or those of others, that may indicate a need to further explore the situation.

Obstacles which make it *impossible* to resolve ethical issues are those which impede such issues from being fully considered. The best choice for a decision maker under these conditions is to refuse to take action at all, if possible. These are situations to avoid, or if inescapable, they are situations in which no responsibility can be reasonably assigned. Often, the culture of an organization may be responsible for creating the conditions which lead to these impossible obstacles. These fall into three categories (DeGeorge, 1982).[1]

Conditions preclude obtaining the required knowledge These conditions make it impossible for you to acquire the knowledge necessary to make the decision or to anticipate its outcome. The first of these conditions is "excusable ignorance," where you have made every effort to gather the facts about the situation, but could not have been reasonably expected to recognize, understand, or acquire all the relevant facts. The second of these conditions is "invincible ignorance," where it is impossible for you to know about or understand all of the facts involved. If you suspect that important data about a situation lies beyond your grasp, you should either avoid making a decision regarding the ethical issue until such time as you can gather or understand further data, or you should pass the decision on to those better equipped to make it, if at all feasible.

Conditions preclude exercising the required freedom These conditions make it impossible to employ the freedom of choice. They include the absence of alternatives, a lack of the control or power to influence the decision, or overwhelming coercion. Under these circumstances it is best not to take action at all. If that is not an option, you cannot be expected to assume responsibility for the consequences of decisions into which you were forced.

Conditions preclude the possibility of action These conditions apply most often to situations in which harm or, less likely, benefit to others is anticipated if you fail to act. Ethically-related actions may be impossible to perform, or you may not have the ability or opportunity to perform them (e.g., "I know that X may occur and may cause harm to others, but there is nothing *I* can do to prevent X from occurring"). In such instances, your best alternative may be to alert those who might have the ability to take the action or take control of the circumstances.

Awareness of the obstacles to resolving ethical issues can assist you to take steps to overcome them, or may warn you away from involvement or decision making in those instances where overcoming the obstacles is impossible.

Having identified desirable outcomes, defined the problem, and examined the difficulties and obstacles involved in solving it, you should be in a position to *develop alternative solutions to the problem.* By their very nature, problems have alternative solutions. If there is only one possible solution, the difficulty you face is not in solving the problem, but rather in acting upon the solution. In such a case, you need to change your focus from problem-solving to determining why the solution has not been implemented.

Use brainstorming or similar techniques to generate as many alternative solutions to the problem as possible. Avoid rejecting any solution until you have examined it carefully.

Developing alternative solutions often proves easier than selecting the best of those solutions. The following two "frameworks" are designed to be applied at this stage of problem solving. Each provides a systematic approach for screening alternative solutions and selecting the one best suited to resolving the issue you are faced with. There is no "better" framework; you might select one based on its practicality or theoretical appeal, or you may wish to use both of them, choosing the one that seems to best fit the situation at hand.

THE FOUR FACTOR PROCESS

Henderson (1982)[2] noted that there are four factors related to business which can serve as checkpoints when ethical issues arise: goals, methods, motives, and consequences. Examining the com-

ponents of each of these factors results in a process that facilitates decision making.

The *goals* of an organization can be examined from three perspectives, the first of which is *goal multiplicity.* In any given situation, the organization may be pursuing more than one goal. For example, a corporation may wish to reduce pollution for a number of reasons: to comply with laws, to improve the corporate image, in accordance with a genuine commitment to cleaner air, etc. Additionally, an organization has a number of stakeholders whose goals must be taken into account. You need to clearly identify and set priorities for the various goals that may play a part in making the decision.

Next, you need to determine *stakeholder priorities,* and which stakeholders' priorities take precedence. There may be times when goal priorities and stakeholder priorities come into conflict. This circumstance can direct your attention to further considerations that need to be made in deciding which goals are to be paramount in resolving the issue.

Finally, a check should be made to ensure *goal compatibility,* that is, that the goals decided upon are not mutually exclusive or in conflict. If this proves to be the case, further priorities need to be determined.

Once you have decided upon the goals that need to be achieved in the given situation, you then need to settle on the *methods* for accomplishing them. First, *stakeholder acceptability* needs to be determined. This involves once again examining the stakeholders and ascertaining whether proposed methods will be acceptable to them, or whether these methods will violate the values they hold.

Then, you need to think about whether to select *methods that satisfy or maximize goals.* Should you choose methods that simply accommodate the goals in question or should you pick those which attempt to achieve the maximum potential possible? For example, should you just comply with the minimum acceptable standards for decreasing air pollution, or should you attempt to reduce pollution as much as you possibly can?

Finally, you should determine whether the methods you are contemplating are *essential, incidental, or extraneous.* Are they essential for achieving goals? Are they incidental, in that they might work and so might be worth attempting? Or are they extraneous and based mainly on personal whims or predilections? Weeding out incidental and extraneous methods diminishes the possibility that the methodology selected will miscarry or have unforeseen consequences.

The *motivation* behind the goals or methods embraced can have an effect on outcomes or on others' perceptions of decisions. Are your motives *hidden or evident?* Concealed motives often cause others to become suspicious of or misinterpret decision makers' intentions. At the very least, you should be aware of your own motives and those of others involved, and should know when to reveal them.

Are motives *shared or selfish?* Decision makers need to determine whether their motives are self-centered or are shared by others. Mutually held motives imply that there is a consensus regarding the decision to be made, which enhances its chances for success.

What is the *value orientation* regarding your approach to the situation? Do the motives underlying goals and methods reflect both your own and the organization's values?

As a last step, you should review the goals, methods, and motives you have identified as being relevant to the ethical issue to be resolved. You need to examine the possible *consequences* of the alternatives under consideration on the stakeholders and others, and need to determine whether or not that impact will be affected by time or by possible outside influences. Consider all the imaginable repercussions of the course of action you are contemplating. Once you have done so, you are ready to select the alternative that is most likely to achieve the desired results.

THE THREE APPROACHES METHOD

In an article prepared for the Harvard Business School, Kenneth Goodpaster[3] proposed a process for resolving ethical issues which entails examining three different approaches to ethical problems. This method is helpful for both generating and selecting alternative solutions. Goodpaster suggests that decision makers first determine the answers to two questions:

1. Who are my stakeholders and what, precisely, are the ethical issues that must be resolved in regard to each stakeholder?
2. What are the critical ethical values and assumptions pertaining to or held by each of these stakeholders?

Once the answers to these questions have been satisfactorily determined, Goodpaster recommends that they be re-examined in light of three different approaches:

Approach 1: What are the actions I can take that give each stakeholder the greatest cost/benefit ratio? What facts support these conclusions?

Approach 2: What are the actions I can take that best respect the rights of each stakeholder and ensure that they are treated fairly? What facts support these conclusions?

Approach 3: Given my duties and obligations to each stakeholder, which take priority? Why?

Having approached the situation from these three viewpoints, you are now in position to answer a final set of questions which should enable you to choose a best solution to the problem:

3. Do the three approaches examined above converge on a particular course of action, or do they suggest divergent actions?
4. If they suggest divergent courses of action, which should take precedence over the others?
5. Are there other ethically relevant considerations which have not been covered by the three approaches? What are they?
6. What is my decision or plan for action?

Having developed alternative solutions, and applied and reviewed appropriate frameworks, you should now be able to make your selection of the best alternative solution.

At this point, you need to carefully *delineate the specific steps that will be required* to put the solution you have selected into action. For each step, you need to define the indicators that will enable you to determine whether that step is succeeding or failing. Decide how and when you should alter your proposed solution-steps if they do not appear to be working. Develop criteria that you can use to decide whether to continue with the effort to carry out your selected solution, or when and whether you should abandon it and attempt a new solution.

Finally, you need to *identify likely reactions to and rewards for your solution.* Remain aware of your own and others' reactions to your solution as it is being carried out. Are there things you or others are doing, either consciously or otherwise, to sabotage the solution in order to "keep the problem"? What recompense do you and others need in order to make the steps towards your solution work? Are these rewards forthcoming? Once the problem has been initially resolved to your satisfaction, you also need to ensure that those involved (including yourself) are sufficiently repaid for your efforts, to guarantee that the endeavor to implement the solution will continue.

Many other problem-solving methodologies than the one we have outlined above exist, and you may find another that you feel will work better for you. Whatever the technique you choose to use, however, we suggest that when you are faced with resolving problems with *ethically related* components, it is highly important that you first have the clearest possible understanding of the problem, that you recognize the need to be aware of obstacles to resolving the problem, and that you employ a means that will serve you as a filter for selecting among alternatives the solution that will best enable you to resolve the ethical issue you have identified.

NOTES

1. DeGeorge, Richard T. *Business Ethics.* New York. Macmillan, 1982.
2. Henderson, Verne E. "The Ethical Side of Enterprise." *Sloan Management Review.* Vol. 23, No. 3, 1982.
3. Goodpaster, Kenneth E. "Some Avenues for Ethical Analysis in General Management." Harvard Business School case 9-383-007.

Attending to Ethics in Management

James A. Waters
Former Graduate Dean, William Carroll
Graduate School of Management, Boston College

Frederick Bird
Former Professor of Theology, Concordia University

Consider the following examples of morally questionable managerial acts:

- cheating on an expense report
- conducting a superficial performance appraisal
- bribing a purchasing agent in order to make a sale
- closing a plant in a region of high unemployment

In a very broad sense, these are all examples of ethical issues that may arise in a managerial context and require management attention. At the same time, however, it is obvious that these examples differ from one another in important ways. Given these differences among such issues, it may be very difficult to understand what is meant if a CEO or other senior executive states simply that he or she is concerned about ethical issues in an organization. Talking about ethical issues at a global level of abstraction or aggregation can be at best uninformative and at worst misleading because important distinctions among the various types of such issues are obscured. A finer grained language with respect to ethical conduct and ethical questions can help senior managers to clarify and communicate their concerns more effectively. One purpose of this article then is to present a typology of morally questionable managerial acts which managers can use to develop and communicate a more differentiated appreciation of the variety of ethical issues that can arise in their own organizations. The typology was derived from analysis of the results of interviews we conducted with a wide variety of managers about the ethical questions that arise in their work lives (Waters, et al., 1986).

Found in *Journal of Business Ethics,* vol. 8, no. 6 (1989), pp. 493–497. Copyright © 1989 Kluwer Academic Publishers. Reprinted by permission of Kluwer Academic Publishers.

A second purpose of this article is to draw attention to the fact that the different types of morally questionable managerial acts typically receive very different amounts of attention from senior managers. We will suggest that, ironically, the kinds of issues that receive the most attention are those that are the least problematic for most managers; and that the issues which are the most troublesome for most managers are relatively ignored in most organizations. Appreciation of this typically unbalanced attention to ethical issues has implications for how senior managers act on their concerns in this area of organizational life.

TYPES OF MORALLY QUESTIONABLE ACTS

The phrase "ethical issues" is frequently used to refer to questions or dilemmas which involve moral judgement. In that popular usage of the phrase, relatively unambiguous actions like expense account cheating are excluded. To avoid this slipperiness in the usage of the phrase "ethical issues" and to ensure that the entire range of behavior for which ethical judgement is salient receives attention, the discussion builds on the idea of morally questionable acts.

A four part typology of morally questionable managerial acts is proposed for use, distinguishing among the acts on the basis in which the managerial role is used or observed. The typology is summarized in Figure 1.

Non-role acts are those in which the actor is acting outside his or her role as manager, they are managerial primarily in the sense that they take place in organizations and frequently involve people who may also be managers. Examples might include embezzlement of company funds, stealing supplies, cheating on expense reports, making false claims for sick leave, utilizing suppliers in which one has a financial interest, insider trading, directing the company's maintenance department to paint one's private residence and the like. In all these examples, the costs are borne directly by the organization and the payoffs are gained directly by the individual. These are morally questionable acts committed against the organization; in the short-

FIGURE 1

Types of morally questionable managerial acts

Type	Direct Effect	Examples
1. Non-role	against-the-firm	• expense account cheating • embezzlement • stealing supplies
2. Role-failure	against-the-firm	• superficial performance appraisal • not confronting expense account cheating • palming off a poor performer with inflated praise
3. Role-distortion	for-the-firm	• bribery • price fixing • manipulation of suppliers
4. Role-assertion	for-the-firm	• invest in South Africa • utilize nuclear technology for energy generation • do not withdraw product line in face of initial allegations of inadequate safety

form notation used in Figure 1, the direct effect of such acts is "against-the-firm."

The second category, also with against-the-firm direct effect, concerns what we term *role-failure acts*. In contrast to non-role, these activities essentially involve a failure to perform the managerial role. Thus, managers may fail to conduct candid performance appraisals or fail to confront a subordinate cheating on his/her expense report in order to avoid the personal stress of such confrontations. They may deny promotion or training opportunities to high-performers in order to keep such subordinates in their own department, or they "palm off" a poor performer to another department with inflated words of praise. They may undercut their bosses behind the scenes or slant proposals or withhold information to suit their own emotional commitments. Though the element of financial gain is not part of these examples, there is still the theme of direct personal gain at the expense of the organization (and, in many of these cases, at the expense of some other person's best interests).

In contrast to non-role and role-failure acts, the direct effects of the next two types of morally questionable acts are described as for, "for-the-firm," i.e., they are committed on behalf of the organization of which the actor is a member. From the vantage point of the long-run welfare of a given firm and the industry and society in which it is embedded, all illegal and unethical acts may be considered as committed against the best interests of the firm. Similarly, in a kind of economic calculus of human behaviour, all actions may be said to be taken to further the self-interest, however conceived, of the individual focal actor. However, in terms of how morally questionable acts are experienced by the focal actor and those affected by the act, the distinction between against-the-firm and for-the-firm direct effect is reasonably clear in the short run. In contrast to the former, acts in the latter category involve direct gain for the organization and only indirectly benefit the individual actor; direct costs are borne largely by parties outside the organization.

Role-distortion acts are those in which the actor is pursuing his or her role mandate (e.g. increase sales, reduce costs, etc.) but is distorting that mandate in the sense that widely accepted moral standards, implicitly part of the role mandate, are not being observed. Examples of role-distortion acts might include bribery, price-fixing, unjustified differential pricing, padding insurance claims, falsifying product safety test results, manipulating suppliers and the like. Though such acts would, if they were widely known, be regarded with disapproval in most organizations, their direct effect is gain for the organization at the expense of outside parties such as customers, suppliers and competitors.

In contrast to role-distortion acts which involve failure to observe generally accepted moral principles, *role-assertion acts* involve situations which have something of a one-of-a-kind quality where little authoritative direction from law, precedent or customary practice exists. In the absence of generally accepted moral principles, the corporate position must be more or less asserted in public debate (Waters, 1980). Role-assertion acts typically are morally defensible. They are often controversial because cogent moral arguments can be and are invoked to argue for competing alternative responses to a given question. Examples in this category might include withdrawing investment in South Africa, utilizing nuclear energy for power generation, investing in weapons manufacturing, failure to cooperate openly with regulatory agencies, production of dangerous chemicals, selling non-union picked produce, closing a plant in an area of high unemployment and the like.

Implicit in the examples cited above is the image that role-assertion acts involve major questions with potentially great impact on the character of the organization, and that they are highly visible in terms of media attention, senior management involvement and public announcements of decisions. These attributes will often characterize role-acts, but they are not definitive. In our interview research, we identified a small number of examples where mid-level managers unobtrusively asserted moral positions on smaller scope questions. Thus, for example, lower-level managers may "bend the rules" in their treatment of employees caught stealing or suffering from alcoholism, or in making arrangements for severance benefits for discharged employees. What is definitive in identifying role-assertion acts is that moral arguments are involved to justify actions as morally acceptable or at least morally neutral, and these arguments are used to counter the positions of others who would or do judge those actions to be morally unacceptable.

In summary then, we are suggesting that all morally questionable managerial acts can be classified in one of four categories depending on how the managerial role is used (role-assertion), abused (role-failure and role-distortion) or ignored (non-role). The value of such a typology rests on the extent to which it directs attention to differences among the categories which are important to management and management research. It is to that question we now turn.

THE TYPICAL FOCUS OF MANAGEMENT ATTENTION

Given the four different types of morally questionable managerial acts, how much management attention does each typically receive in large organizations? It has been observed that conventional accounting and control systems are almost exclusively concerned with against-the-firm acts of the non-role type (Waters and Chant, 1982). There is some evidence also that these non-role type acts are the primary focus of corporate codes of ethics. In a preliminary report on a review of corporate codes of ethics of a large sample of Fortune 500 firms, Mathews (1986) reports that it was rare to find proscriptions dealing with for-the-firm type acts, and that the most prominent theme in these codes was protection of the firm against what we are labelling here as non-role acts. A survey conducted in 1979 for the Ethics Resource Center found that of those firms having formal codes of ethics, 94% prohibited conflict of interest activities, and 97% specifically prohibited the taking of bribes or favors to influence decisions. Also, 62% of the firms reported that their codes specifically prohibited the abuse of expense accounts, special allowances and perquisites (Opinion Research Corporation, 1979; also see Taylor, 1980).

Thus, we can say with some confidence that non-role acts receive a great deal of attention in many large organizations. What then of the other three categories? Role-assertion acts frequently receive a great deal of attention because, as noted, these often are high-stakes public issues in which the most senior managers are directly involved. The very nature of such acts, involving questions for which generally accepted societal positions have not crystallized and where competing moral arguments are publicly invoked (witness, for example, debate about nuclear energy or compulsory airbags in automobiles), make them popular targets of interest for managers, media representatives, so-

cial critics, and case teachers in business schools. In some organizations, this attention has given rise to the formation of staff groups specifically concerned with so-called social issues in management.

In contrast to the managerial attention directed at non-role acts and role-assertion acts, that directed at role-failure acts and role-distortion acts appears quite minimal. We make that assertion based on our own experiences in different organizations, informal conversations over the years with many managers, and interviews with a variety of managers about the ethical questions they face (Waters et al., 1986). The picture that emerges from all these sources is that role-distortion and role-failure acts seldom receive systematic attention in most organizations and they certainly receive less attention than is given to the other two categories.

The irony of this unbalanced attention to the different kinds of morally questionable acts is that the kinds of acts that are most salient and indeed troublesome for most managers on a day to day basis are the kinds that receive the least attention in terms of proactive management and control. When managers are asked to describe the ethical questions that come up in their own professional lives and in their organizations, their responses are predominantly in the role-failure and role-distortion categories (Waters et al., 1986).[1]

This idea that the "high-attention" categories are least problematic for most managers is readily understandable when one considers their nature. Little ambiguity and few competing standards surround conduct that we have labelled non-role. There is no subtlety to fraud, embezzlement or cheating on expense reports and the overwhelmingly majority of managers do not engage in such activities and view them with repugnance. Managers rarely are placed in a moral dilemma regarding how they ought to respond to this type of conduct.

The other "high-attention" category, role-assertion acts, also tends to be non-problematic for most managers, but for different reasons. Here, a great deal of ambiguity and many competing principles surround the issues and, as noted earlier, reasonable people can disagree on the best course of action. More to the point though, these issues most typically are unique, arise infrequently, and are the province of the most senior managers and directors. While these kinds of issues may attract the most attention from philosophers and journalists, they are simply a less critical aspect of most managers consciousness with respect to everyday ethical concerns in management.

These observations are not made in order to denigrate the importance of these issues or suggest that they should receive less attention in management circles. Rather, it is to suggest that the two neglected categories, the two which in fact are most salient for most managers, should receive more attention. Widely shared standards exist to guide managers in developing their own responses to situations which can lead to role-failure and role-distortion acts (e.g., honesty in communication, fair treatment, fair competition, etc.) (Bird and Waters, 1986). However, these standards are inherently abstract and frequently in conflict and as a result are typically not experienced by managers as being very helpful in providing concrete direction in specific situations. When does legitimate entertainment become bribery? At what point does legitimate concealment of a basic position in negotiating with an employee or supplier become dishonesty? These are the types of difficult questions with which managers must grapple on an everyday basis. Such questions resist easy generalizations; trade-offs and compromises will often be required in response to particular conditions and situations. Given the very overt pressure for performance in most organizations, a failure on the part of senior managers to devote systematic attention to the potential problems of role-failure and role-distortion acts puts a great deal of stress on the members of their organizations. It is only through increased conscious attention on the part of organization leaders to such problems that the moral instincts of all organizational members can be supported and reinforced in the face of competitive pressures.

We have made suggestions elsewhere about how that increased attention might be shaped and acted upon. These include encouragement of dialogue and debate (Waters, 1978), internal control mechanisms to monitor the attention given to such issues (Waters and Chant, 1982) and systematic

management of "the moral dimension of organizational culture" (Waters and Bird, 1986). Our intention here has been to highlight the lack of balanced attention to the full range of morally questionable acts in most organizations. Awareness of the different types of morally questionable acts and of the relative neglect of role-failure and role-distortion acts can help managers to see ethical issues more clearly and to attend more effectively to their own moral concerns.

NOTE

1. More specifically, of 122 examples which directly referenced morally questionable acts, 57 percent concerned role-distortion acts, 23 percent concerned role-failure acts, 17 percent concerned role-assertion acts and 3 percent concerned non-role acts.

REFERENCES

Bird, Frederick and James A. Waters: 1987, 'The nature of managerial moral standards,.' *Journal of Business Ethics* 6. No. 1, 1–3.

Mathew, M. Cash: August 1986, 'Self-regulation: The effect of codes of ethics on corporate illegalities,' paper presented at Academy of Management.

Opinion Research Corporation: June 1979, 'Codes of ethics in corporations and trade associations and the teaching of ethics in graduate business schools,' a survey conducted for Ethics Resource Center, ORC Study No. 65302.

Taylor, Mark L: 1980, *A Study of Corporate Ethical Policy Statements* (Dallas: The Foundation of the Southwestern Graduate Schools of Banking).

Waters, James A: Winter 1980, 'Of saints, sinners and socially responsible executives,' *Business and Society* 19–2 and 20–1.

Waters, James A: Spring 1978. 'Catch 20.5: Corporate morality as an organizational phenomenon,' *Organizational Dynamics*.

Waters, James A. and Frederick Bird: 1987, 'The moral dimension of organizational culture,' *Journal of Business Ethics* 6, No. 1, 15–22.

Waters, James A., Frederick Bird, and Peter D. Chant: 1986. 'Everyday moral issues experienced by managers,' *Journal of Business Ethics* 5, No. 5, 373–384.

Waters, James A. and Peter D. Chant: Spring 1982, 'Internal control of management integrity: Beyond accounting systems,' *California Management Review*.

Cost-Benefit Analysis: An Ethical Critique

Steven Kelman
Weatherhead Professor of Public Management, Kennedy School of Government, Harvard University

At the broadest and vaguest level, cost-benefit analysis may be regarded simply as systematic thinking about decision-making. Who can oppose, economists sometimes ask, efforts to think in a systematic way about the consequences of different courses of action? The alternative, it would appear, is unexamined decision-making. But defining cost-benefit analysis so simply leaves it with few implications for actual regulatory decision-making. Presumably, therefore, those who urge regulators to make greater use of the technique have a more extensive prescription in mind. I assume here that their prescription includes the following views:

1. There exists a strong presumption that an act should not be undertaken unless its benefits outweigh its costs.
2. In order to determine whether benefits outweigh costs, it is desirable to attempt to express all benefits and costs in a common scale or denominator, so that they can be compared with each other, even when some benefits and costs are not traded on markets and hence have no established dollar values.
3. Getting decision-makers to make more use of cost-benefit techniques is important enough to warrant both the expense required to gather the data for improved cost-benefit estimation and the political efforts needed to give the activity higher priority compared to other activities, also valuable in and of themselves.

My focus is on cost-benefit analysis as applied to environmental, safety, and health regulation. In

that context, I examine each of the above propositions from the perspective of formal ethical theory, that is, the study of what actions it is morally right to undertake. My conclusions are:

1. In areas of environmental, safety, and health regulation, there may be many instances where a certain decision might be right even though its benefits do not outweigh its costs.
2. There are good reasons to oppose efforts to put dollar values on non-marketed benefits and costs.
3. Given the relative frequency of occasions in the areas of environmental, safety, and health regulation where one would not wish to use a benefits-outweigh-costs test as a decision rule, and given the reasons to oppose the monetizing of non-marketed benefits or costs that is a prerequisite for cost-benefit analysis, it is not justifiable to devote major resources to the generation of data for cost-benefit calculations or to undertake efforts to "spread the gospel" of cost-benefit analysis further.

I

How do we decide whether a given action is morally right or wrong and hence, assuming the desire to act morally, why it should be undertaken or refrained from? Like the Molière character who spoke prose without knowing it, economists who advocate use of cost-benefit analysis for public decisions are philosophers without knowing it: the answer given by cost-benefit analysis, that actions should be undertaken so as to maximize net benefits, represents one of the classic answers given by moral philosophers—that given by utilitarians. To determine whether an action is right or wrong, utilitarians tote up all the positive consequences of the action in terms of human satisfaction. The act that maximizes attainment of satisfaction under the circumstances is the right act. That the economists' answer is also the answer of one school of philosophers should not be surprising. Early on, economics was a branch of moral philosophy, and only later did it become an independent discipline.

Before proceeding further, the subtlety of the utilitarian position should be noted. The positive

Excerpted from "Cost-Benefit Analysis: An Ethical Critique," *Regulation,* January–February 1981. Reprinted by permission of the publisher.

and negative consequences of an act for satisfaction may go beyond the act's immediate consequences. A facile version of utilitarianism would give moral sanction to a lie, for instance, if the satisfaction of an individual attained by telling the lie was greater than the suffering imposed on the lie's victim. Few utilitarians would agree. Most of them would add to the list of negative consequences the effect of the one lie on the tendency of the person who lies to tell other lies, even in instances when the lying produced less satisfaction for him than dissatisfaction for others. They would also add the negative effects of the lie on the general level of social regard for truth-telling, which has many consequences for future utility. A further consequence may be added as well. It is sometimes said that we should include in a utilitarian calculation the feelings of dissatisfaction produced in the liar (and perhaps in others) because, by telling a lie, one has "done the wrong thing." Correspondingly, in this view, among the positive consequences to be weighed into a utilitarian calculation of truth-telling is satisfaction arising from "doing the right thing." This view rests on an error, however, because it *assumes* what it is the purpose of the calculation to *determine*—that telling the truth in the instance in question is indeed the right thing to do. Economists are likely to object to this point, arguing that no feeling ought "arbitrarily" to be excluded from a complete cost-benefit calculation, including a feeling of dissatisfaction at doing the wrong thing. Indeed, the economists' cost-benefit calculations would, at least ideally, include such feelings. Note the difference between the economist's and the philosopher's cost-benefit calculations, however. The economist may choose to include feelings of dissatisfaction in his cost-benefit calculation, but what happens if somebody asks the economist, "Why is it right to evaluate an action on the basis of a cost-benefit test?" If an answer is to be given to that question (which does not normally preoccupy economists but which does concern both philosophers and the rest of us who need to be persuaded that cost-benefit analysis is right), then the circularity problem reemerges. And there is also another difficulty with counting feelings of dissatisfaction at doing

the wrong thing in a cost-benefit calculation. It leads to the perverse result that under certain circumstances a lie, for example, might be morally right if the individual contemplating the lie felt no compunction about lying and morally wrong only if the individual felt such a compunction!

This error is revealing, however, because it begins to suggest a critique of utilitarianism. Utilitarianism is an important and powerful moral doctrine. But it is probably a minority position among contemporary moral philosophers. It is amazing that economists can proceed in unanimous endorsement of cost-benefit analysis as if unaware that their conceptual framework is highly controversial in the discipline from which it arose—moral philosophy.

Let us explore the critique of utilitarianism. The logical error discussed before appears to suggest that we have a notion of certain things being right or wrong that *predates* our calculation of costs and benefits. Imagine the case of an old man in Nazi Germany who is hostile to the regime. He is wondering whether he should speak out against Hitler. If he speaks out, he will lose his pension. And his action will have done nothing to increase the chances that the Nazi regime will be overthrown: he is regarded as somewhat eccentric by those around him, and nobody has ever consulted his views on political questions. Recall that one cannot add to the benefits of speaking out any satisfaction from doing "the right thing," because the purpose of the exercise is to determine whether speaking out *is* the right thing. How would the utilitarian calculation go? The benefits of the old man's speaking out would, as the example is presented, be nil, while the costs would be his loss of his pension. So the costs of the action would outweigh the benefits. By the utilitarians' cost-benefit calculation, it would be *morally wrong* for the man to speak out.

To those who believe that it would not be morally wrong for the old man to speak out in Nazi Germany, utilitarianism is insufficient as a moral view. We believe that some acts whose costs are greater than their benefits may be morally right and, contrariwise, some acts whose benefits are greater than their costs may be morally wrong.

This does not mean that the question whether benefits are greater than costs is morally irrelevant. Few would claim such. Indeed, for a broad range of individual and social decisions, whether an act's benefits outweigh its costs is a sufficient question to ask. But not for all such decisions. These may involve situations where certain duties—duties not to lie, break promises, or kill, for example—make an act wrong, even if it would result in an excess of benefits over costs. Or they may involve instances where people's rights are at stake. We would not permit rape even if it could be demonstrated that the rapist derived enormous happiness from his act, while the victim experienced only minor displeasure. We do not do cost-benefit analyses of freedom of speech or trial by jury. The Bill of Rights was not RARGed.*

As the United Steelworkers noted in a comment on the Occupational Safety and Health Administration's economic analysis of its proposed rule to reduce worker exposure to carcinogenic coke-oven emissions, the Emancipation Proclamation was not subjected to an inflationary impact statement. The notion of human rights involves the idea that people may make certain claims to be allowed to act in certain ways or to be treated in certain ways, even if the sum of benefits achieved thereby does not outweigh the sum of costs. It is this view that underlies the statement that "workers have a right to a safe and healthy work place" and the expectation that OSHA's decisions will reflect that judgment.

In the most convincing versions of nonutilitarian ethics, various duties or rights are not absolute. But each has a *prima facie* moral validity so that, if duties or rights do not conflict, the morally right act is the act that reflects a duty or respects a right. If duties or rights do conflict, a moral judgment, based on conscious deliberation, must be made. Since one of the duties non-utilitarian philosophers enumerate is the duty of beneficence (the duty to maximize happiness), which in effect incorporates all of utilitarianism by reference, a non-utilitarian who is faced with conflicts between the results of cost-benefit analysis and non-utility-based considerations will need to undertake such deliberation. But in that deliberation, additional elements, which cannot be reduced to a question of whether benefits outweigh costs, have been introduced. Indeed, depending on the moral importance we attach to the right or duty involved, cost-benefit questions may, within wide ranges, become irrelevant to the outcome of the moral judgment.

In addition to questions involving duties and rights, there is a final sort of question where, in my view, the issue of whether benefits outweigh costs should not govern moral judgment. I noted earlier that, for the common run of questions facing individuals and societies, it is possible to begin and end our judgment simply by finding out if the benefits of the contemplated act outweigh the costs. This very fact means that one way to show the great importance, or value, attached to an area is to say that decisions involving the area should not be determined by cost-benefit calculations. This applies, I think, to the view many environmentalists have of decisions involving our natural environment. When officials are deciding what level of pollution will harm certain vulnerable people—such as asthmatics or the elderly—while not harming others, one issue involved may be the right of those people not to be sacrificed on the altar of somewhat higher living standards for the rest of us. But more broadly than this, many environmentalists fear that subjecting decisions about clean air or water to the cost-benefit tests that determine the general run of decisions removes those matters from the realm of specially valued things.

II

In order for cost-benefit calculations to be performed the way they are supposed to be, all costs and benefits must be expressed in a common measure, typically dollars, including things not normally bought and sold on markets, and to which dollar prices are therefore not attached. The most dramatic example of such things is human life itself; but many of the other benefits achieved or preserved by environmental policy—such as peace and quiet, fresh-smelling air, swimmable rivers, spectacular vistas—are not traded on markets either.

Economists who do cost-benefit analysis regard the quest after dollar values for non-market things as a difficult challenge—but one to be met with relish. They have tried to develop methods for imputing a person's "willingness to pay" for such things, their approach generally involving a search for bundled goods that *are* traded on markets and that vary as to whether they include a feature that is, *by itself,* not marketed. Thus, fresh air is not marketed, but houses in different parts of Los Angeles that are similar except for the degree of smog are. Peace and quiet is not marketed, but similar houses inside and outside airport flight paths are. The risk of death is not marketed, but similar jobs that have different levels of risk are. Economists have produced many often ingenious efforts to impute dollar prices to non-marketed things by observing the premiums accorded homes in clean air areas over similar homes in dirty areas or the premiums paid for risky jobs over similar nonrisky jobs.

These ingenious efforts are subject to criticism on a number of technical grounds. It may be difficult to control for all the dimensions of quality other than the presence or absence of the non-marketed thing. More important, in a world where people have different preferences and are subject to different constraints as they make their choices, the dollar value imputed to the nonmarket things that most people would wish to avoid will be lower than otherwise, because people with unusually weak aversion to those things or unusually strong constraints on their choices will be willing to take the bundled good in question at less of a discount than the average person. Thus, to use the property value discount of homes near airports as a measure of people's willingness to pay for quiet means to accept as a proxy for the rest of us the behavior of those least sensitive to noise, of airport employees (who value the convenience of a near-airport location) or of others who are susceptible to an agent's assurances that "it's not so bad." To use the wage premiums accorded hazardous work as a measure of the value of life means to accept as proxies for the rest of us the choices of people who do not have many choices or who are exceptional risk-seekers.

A second problem is that the attempts of economists to measure people's willingness to pay for non-marketed things assume that there is no difference between the price a person would require for *giving up* something to which he has a preexisting right and the price he would pay to *gain* something to which he enjoys no right. Thus, the analysis assumes no difference between how much a home-owner would need to be paid in order to give up an unobstructed mountain view that he already enjoys and how much he would be willing to pay to get an obstruction moved once it is already in place. Available evidence suggests that most people would insist on being paid far more to assent to a worsening of their situation than they would be willing to pay to improve their situation. The difference arises from such factors as being accustomed to and psychologically attached to that which one believes one enjoys by right. But this creates a circularity problem for any attempt to use cost-benefit analysis to determine *whether* to assign to, say, the homeowner the right to an unobstructed mountain view. For willingness to pay will be different depending on whether the right is assigned initially or not. The value judgment about whether to assign the right must thus be made first. (In order to set an upper bound on the value of the benefit, one might hypothetically assign the right to the person and determine how much he would need to be paid to give it up.)

Third, the efforts of economists to impute willingness to pay invariably involve bundled goods exchanged in *private* transactions. Those who use figures garnered from such analysis to provide guidance for *public* decisions assume no difference between how people value certain things in private individual transactions and how they would wish those same things to be valued in public collective decisions. In making such assumptions, economists insidiously slip into their analysis an important and controversial value judgment, growing naturally out of the highly individualistic microeconomic tradition—namely, the view that there should be no difference between private behavior and the behavior we display in public social life. An alternative view—one that enjoys, I would suggest, wide resonance among citizens—would be that public, social decisions provide an opportunity to give certain things a higher valuation than we choose, for one reason or another, to give them in our private activities.

Thus, opponents of stricter regulation of health risks often argue that we show by our daily risk-taking behavior that we do not value life infinitely, and therefore our public decisions should not reflect the high value of life that proponents of strict regulation propose. However, an alternative view is equally plausible. Precisely because we fail, for whatever reasons, to give lifesaving the value in everyday personal decisions that we in some general terms believe we should give it, we may wish our social decisions to provide us the occasion to display the reverence for life that we espouse but do not always show. By this view, people do not have fixed unambiguous "preferences" to which they give expression through private activities and which therefore should be given expression in public decisions. Rather, they may have what they themselves regard as "higher" and "lower" preferences. The latter may come to the fore in private decisions, but people may want the former to come to the fore in public decisions. They may sometimes display racial prejudice, but support antidiscrimination laws. They may buy a certain product after seeing a seductive ad, but be skeptical enough of advertising to want the government to keep a close eye on it. In such cases, the use of private behavior to impute the values that should be entered for public decisions, as is done by using willingness to pay in private transactions, commits grievous offense against a view of the behavior of the citizen that is deeply engrained in our democratic tradition. It is a view that denudes politics of any independent role in society, reducing it to a mechanistic, mimicking recalculation based on private behavior.

Finally, one may oppose the effort to place prices on a non-market thing and hence in effect incorporate it into the market system out of a fear that the very act of doing so will reduce the thing's perceived value. To place a price on the benefit may, in other words, reduce the value of that benefit. Cost-benefit analysis thus may be like the thermometer that, when placed in a liquid to be measured, itself changes the liquid's temperature.

Examples of the perceived cheapening of a thing's value by the very act of buying and selling it abound in everyday life and language. The disgust that accompanies the idea of buying and selling human beings is based on the sense that this would dramatically diminish human worth. Epithets such as "he prostituted himself," applied as linguistic analogies to people who have sold something, reflect the view that certain things should not be sold because doing so diminishes their value. Praise that is bought is worth little, even to the person buying it. A true anecdote is told of an economist who retired to another university community and complained that he was having difficulty making friends. The laconic response of a critical colleague—"If you want a friend why don't you buy yourself one"—illustrates in a pithy way the intuition that, for some things, the very act of placing a price on them reduces their perceived value.

The first reason that pricing something decreases its perceived value is that, in many circumstances, non-market exchange is associated with the production of certain values not associated with market exchange. These may include spontaneity and various other feelings that come from personal relationships. If a good becomes less associated with the production of positively valued feelings because of market exchange, the perceived value of the good declines to the extent that those feelings are valued. This can be seen clearly in instances where a thing may be transferred both by market and by non-market mechanisms. The willingness to pay for sex bought from a prostitute is less than the perceived value of the sex consummating love. (Imagine the reaction if a practitioner of cost-benefit analysis computed the benefits of sex based on the price of prostitute services.)

Furthermore, if one values in a general sense the existence of a non-market sector because of its connection with the production of certain valued feelings, then one ascribes added value to any non-marketed good simply as a repository of values represented by the non-sector one wishes to preserve. This seems certainly to be the case for things in nature, such as pristine streams or undisturbed forests: for many people who value them, part of their value comes from their position as repositories of values the non-market sector represents.

The second way in which placing a market price on a thing decreases its perceived value is by removing the possibility of proclaiming that the thing is "not for sale," since things on the market by definition are for sale. The very statement that something is not for sale affirms, enhances, and protects a thing's value in a number of ways. To begin with, the statement is a way of showing that a thing is valued for its own sake, whereas selling a thing for money demonstrates that it was valued only instrumentally. Furthermore, to say that something cannot be transferred in that way places it in the exceptional category—which requires the person interested in obtaining that thing to be able to offer something else that is exceptional, rather than allowing him the easier alternative of obtaining the thing for money that could have been obtained in an infinity of ways. This enhances its value. If I am willing to say "You're a really kind person" to whoever pays me to do so, my praise loses the value that attaches to it from being exchangeable only for an act of kindness.

In addition, if we have already decided we value something highly, one way of stamping it with a cachet affirming its high value is to announce that it is "not for sale." Such an announcement does more, however, than just reflect a preexisting high valuation. It signals a thing's distinctive value to others and helps us persuade them to value the thing more highly than they otherwise might. It also expresses our resolution to safeguard that distinctive value. To state that something is not for sale is thus also a source of value for that thing, since if a thing's value is easy to affirm or protect, it will be worth more than an otherwise similar thing without such attributes.

If we proclaim that something is not for sale, we make a once-and-for-all-judgment of its special value. When something is priced, the issue of its perceived value is constantly coming up, as a

standing invitation to reconsider that original judgment. Were people constantly faced with questions such as "how much money could get you to give up your freedom of speech?" or "how much would you sell your vote for if you could?", the perceived value of the freedom to speak or the right to vote would soon become devastated as, in moments of weakness, people started saying "maybe it's not worth *so much* after all." Better not to be faced with the constant questioning in the first place. Something similar did in fact occur when the slogan "better red than dead" was launched by some pacifists during the Cold War. Critics pointed out that the very posing of this stark choice—in effect, "would you *really* be willing to give up your life in exchange for not living under communism?"—reduced the value people attached to freedom and thus diminished resistance to attacks on freedom.

Finally, of some things valued very highly it is stated that they are "priceless" or that they have "infinite value." Such expressions are reserved for a subset of things not for sale, such as life or health. Economists tend to scoff at talk of pricelessness. For them, saying that something is priceless is to state a willingness to trade off an infinite quantity of all other goods for one unit of the priceless good, a situation that empirically appears highly unlikely. For most people, however, the word priceless is pregnant with meaning. Its value-affirming and value-protecting functions cannot be bestowed on expressions that merely denote a determinate, albeit high, valuation. John Kennedy in his inaugural address proclaimed that the nation was ready to "pay any price [and] bear any burden . . . to assure the survival and the success of liberty." Had he said instead that we were willing to "pay a high price" or "bear a large burden" for liberty, the statement would have rung hollow.

III

An objection that advocates of cost-benefit analysis might well make to the preceding argument should be considered. I noted earlier that, in cases where various non-utility-based duties or rights conflict with the maximization of utility, it is necessary to make a deliberative judgment about what act is finally right. I also argued earlier that the search for commensurability might not always be a desirable one, that the attempt to go beyond expressing benefits in terms of (say) lives saved and costs in terms of dollars is not something devoutly to be wished.

In situations involving things that are not expressed in a common measure, advocates of cost-benefit analysis argue that people making judgments "in effect" perform cost-benefit calculations anyway. If government regulators promulgate a regulation that saves 100 lives at a cost of $1 billion, they are "in effect" valuing a life at (a minimum of) $10 million, whether or not they say that they are willing to place a dollar value on a human life. Since, in this view, cost-analysis "in effect" is inevitable, it might as well be made specific.

This argument misconstrues the real difference in the reasoning processes involved. In cost-benefit analysis, equivalencies are established *in advance* as one of the raw materials for the calculation. One determines costs and benefits, one determines equivalencies (to be able to put various costs and benefits into a common measure), and then one sets to toting things up—waiting, as it were, with bated breath for the results of the calculation to come out. The outcome is determined by the arithmetic; if the outcome is a close call or if one is not good at long division, one does not know how it will turn out until the calculation is finished. In the kind of deliberative judgment that is performed without a common measure, no establishment of equivalencies occurs in advance. Equivalencies are not aids to the decision process. In fact, the decision-maker might not even be aware of what the "in effect" equivalencies were, at least before they are revealed to him afterwards by someone pointing out what he had "in effect" done. The decision-maker would see himself as simply having made a deliberative judgment; the "in effect" equivalency number did not play a causal role in the decision but at most merely reflects it. Given this, the argument against making the process explicit is the one discussed earlier in the discussion of problems with putting specific values on things that are not normally quantified– that the very act of doing so may serve to reduce the value of those things.

My own judgment is that modest efforts to assess levels of benefits and costs are justified, although I do not believe that government agencies ought to sponsor efforts to put dollar prices on non-market things. I also do not believe that the cry for more cost-benefit analysis in regulation is, on the whole, justified. If regulatory officials were so insensitive about regulatory costs that they did not provide acceptable raw material for deliberative judgments (even if not of a strictly cost-benefit nature), my conclusion might be different. But a good deal of research into costs and benefits already occurs—actually, far more in the U.S. regulatory process than in that of any other industrial society. The danger now would seem to come more from the other side.

Cost-Benefit Analysis Defended

Herman B. Leonard
Academic Dean, Kennedy School of Government,
Harvard University

Richard J. Zeckhauser
Ramsey Professor of Political Economy,
Kennedy School of Government, Harvard University

Cost-benefit analysis, particularly as applied to public decisions involving risks to life and health, has not been notably popular. A number of setbacks— Three Mile Island is perhaps the most memorable— have called into question the reliability of analytic approaches to risk issues. We believe that the current low reputation of cost-analysis is unjustified, and that a close examination of the objections most frequently raised against the method will show that it deserves wider public support.

Society does not and indeed could not require the explicit consent of every affected individual in order to implement public decisions that impose

From *The Report from The Institute for Philosophy and Public Policy,* Vol. 3, No. 3 (Summer 1983). Reprinted by permission of The Institute for Philosophy and Public Policy, University of Maryland at College Park, College Park, MD 20742.

costs or risks. The transactions costs of assembling unanimous consent would be prohibitive, leading to paralysis in the status quo. Moreover, any system that required unanimous consent would create incentives for individuals to misrepresent their beliefs so as to secure compensation or to prevent the imposition of relatively small costs on them even if the benefits to others might be great.

If actual individual consent is an impractically strong standard to require of centralized decisions, how should such decisions be made? Our test for a proposed public decision is whether the net benefits of the action are positive. The same criterion is frequently phrased: Will those favored by the decision gain enough that they would have a net benefit even if they fully compensated those hurt by the decision? Applying this criterion to all possible actions, we discover that the chosen alternative should be the one for which benefits most exceed costs. We believe that the benefit-cost criterion is a useful way of defining "hypothetical consent" for centralized decisions affecting individuals with widely divergent interests: hypothetically, if compensation could be paid, all would agree to the decision offering the highest net benefits. We turn now to objections commonly raised against this approach.

COMPENSATION AND HYPOTHETICAL CONSENT

An immediate problem with the pure cost-benefit criterion is that it does not require the actual payment of compensation to those on whom a given decision imposes net costs. Our standard for public decision-making does not require that losers be compensated, but only that they *could* be if a perfect system of transfers existed. But unless those harmed by a decision are *actually* compensated, they will get little solace from the fact that someone is reaping a surplus in which they could have shared.

To this we make two replies. First, it is typically infeasible to design a compensation system that ensures that all individuals will be net winners. The transactions costs involved in such a system would often be so high as to make the proj-

ect as a whole a net loss. But it may not even be desirable to construct full compensation systems, since losers will generally have an incentive under such systems to overstate their anticipated losses in order to secure greater compensation.

Second, the problem of compensation is probably smaller in practice than in principle. Society tends to compensate large losses where possible or to avoid imposing large losses when adequate compensation is not practical. Moreover, compensation is sometimes overpaid; having made allowances *ex ante* for imposing risks, society still chooses sometimes to pay additional compensation *ex post* to those who actually suffer losses.

Libertarians raise one additional argument about the ethical basis of a system that does not require full compensation to losers. They argue that a public decision process that imposes uncompensated losses constitutes an illegal taking of property by the state and should not be tolerated. This objection, however strongly grounded ethically, would lead to an untenable position for society by unduly constraining public decisions to rest with the status quo.

ATTENTION TO DISTRIBUTION

Two distinct types of distributional issue are relevant in cost-benefit analysis. First, we can be concerned about the losers in a particular decision, whoever they may be. Second, we can be concerned with the transfers between income classes (or other defined groups) engendered by a given project. If costs are imposed differentially on groups that are generally disadvantaged, should the decision criterion include special consideration of their interests? This question is closely intertwined with the issue of compensation, because it is often alleged that the uncompensated costs of projects evaluated by cost-benefit criteria frequently fall on those who are disadvantaged to start with.

These objections have little to do with cost-benefit analysis as a method. We see no reason why any widely agreed upon notion of equity, or weighting of different individual's interests, cannot in principle be built into the cost-benefit decision framework. It is merely a matter of defining carefully what is meant by a benefit or a cost. If, in society's view, benefits (or costs) to some individuals are more valuable (costly) than those to others, this can be reflected in the construction of the decision criterion.

But although distribution concerns could be systematically included in cost-benefit analyses, it is not always—or even generally—a good idea to do so. Taxes and direct expenditures represent a far more efficient means of effecting redistribution than virtually any other public program; we would strongly prefer to rely on one consistent comprehensive tax and expenditure package for redistribution than on attempts to redistribute within every project.

First, if distributional issues are considered everywhere, they will probably not be adequately, carefully, and correctly treated anywhere. Many critics of cost-benefit analysis believe that project-based distributional analysis would create a net addition to society's total redistributive effort; we suggest that is likely, instead, to be only an inefficient substitution.

Second, treating distributional concerns within each project can only lead to transfers within the group affected by a project, often only a small subset of the community. For example, unisex rating of auto insurance redistributes only among drivers. Cross-subsidization of medical costs affects only those who need medical services. Why should not the larger society share the burden of redistribution?

Third, the view that distributional considerations should be treated project-by-project reflects a presumption that on average they do not balance out—that is, that some groups systematically lose more often than others. If it were found that some groups were severely and systematically disadvantaged by the application of cost-benefit analyses that ignore distributional concerns, we would favor redressing the balance. We do not believe this is generally the case.

SENSITIVE SOCIAL VALUES

Cost-benefit analysis, it is frequently alleged, does a disservice to society because it cannot treat important social values with appropriate sensitivity. We believe that this view does a disservice to society by unduly constraining the use of a reasonable and helpful method for organizing the debate about public decisions. We are not claiming that every important social value can be represented effectively within the confines of cost-benefit analysis. Some values will never fit in a cost-benefit framework and will have to be treated as "additional considerations" in coming to a final decision. Some, such as the inviolability of human life, may simply be binding constraints that cannot be traded off to obtain other gains. Nor can we carry out a cost-benefit analysis to decide which values should be included and which treated separately—this decision will always have to be made in some other manner.

These considerations do not invalidate cost-benefit analysis, but merely illustrate that more is at stake than just dollar measures of costs and benefits. We would, however, make two observations. First, we must be very careful that only genuinely important and relevant social values be permitted to outweigh the findings of an analysis. Second, social values that frequently stand in the way of important efficiency gains have a way of breaking down and being replaced over time, so that in the long run society manages to accommodate itself to some form of cost-benefit criterion. If nuclear power were 1000 times more dangerous for its employees but 10 times less expensive than it is, we might feel that ethical considerations were respected and the national interest well served if we had rotating cadres of nuclear power employees serving short terms in high-risk positions, much as members of the armed services do. In like fashion, we have fire-fighters risk their lives; universal sprinkler systems would be less dangerous, but more costly. Such policies reflect an accommodation to the costs as a recognition of the benefits.

MEASURABILITY

Another objection frequently raised against cost-benefit analysis is that some costs and benefits tend to be ignored because they are much more difficult to measure than others. The long-term environmental impacts of large projects are frequently cited as an example. Cost-benefit analysis is charged with being systematically biased toward consideration of the quantifiable aspects of decisions.

This is unquestionably true: cost-benefit analysis is *designed* as a method of quantification, so it surely is better able to deal with more quantifiable aspects of the issues it confronts. But this limitation is in itself ethically neutral unless it can be shown that the quantifiable considerations systematically push decisions in a particular direction. Its detractors must show that the errors of cost-benefit analysis are systematically unjust or inefficient—for example, that it frequently helps the rich at the expense of the poor, or despoils the environment to the benefit of industry, or vice versa. We have not seen any carefully researched evidence to support such assertions.

We take some comfort in the fact that cost-benefit analysis is sometimes accused of being biased toward development projects and sometimes of being biased against them. Cost-benefit analyses have foiled conservation efforts in national forests—perhaps they systematically weight the future too little. But they have also squelched clearly silly projects designed to bring "economic development" to Alaska—and the developers argued that the analysis gave insufficient weight to the "unquantifiable" value of future industrialization.

In our experience, cost-benefit analysis is often a tool of the "outs"—those not currently in control of the political process. Those who have the political power to back the projects they support often have little need of analyses. By contrast, analysis can be an effective tool for those who are otherwise not strongly empowered politically.

ANALYZING RISKS

Even those who accept the ethical propriety of cost-benefit analysis of decisions involving transfers of money or other tangible economic costs and benefits sometimes feel that the principles do not extend to analyzing decisions involving the imposition of risks. We believe that such applications constitute a *particularly* important area in which cost-benefit analysis can be of value. The

very difficulties of reaching appropriate decisions where risks are involved make it all the more vital to employ the soundest methods available, both ethically and practically.

Historically, cost-benefit analysis has been applied widely to the imposition and regulation of risks, in particular to risks of health loss or bodily harm. The cost-benefit approach is particularly valuable here, for several reasons. Few health risks can be exchanged on a voluntary basis. Their magnitude is difficult to measure. Even if they could be accurately measured, individuals have difficulty interpreting probabilities or gauging how they would feel should the harm eventuate. Compounding these problems of valuation are difficulties in contract, since risks are rarely conveyed singly between one individual and another.

The problem of risks conveyed in the absence of contractual approval has been addressed for centuries through the law of torts, which is designed to provide compensation after a harm has been received. If only a low-probability risk is involved, it is often efficient to wait to see whether a harm occurs, for in the overwhelming majority of circumstances transactions costs will be avoided. This approach also limits debate over the magnitude of a potential harm that has not yet eventuated. The creator of the risk has the incentive to gauge accurately, for he is the one who must pay if harm does occur.

While in principle it provides efficient results, the torts approach encounters at least four difficulties when applied to many of the risks that are encountered in a modern technological society. The option of declaring bankruptcy allows the responsible party to avoid paying and so to impose risks that it should not impose. Causality is often difficult to assign for misfortunes that may have alternative or multiple (and synergistically related) causes. Did the individual contract lung cancer from air pollution or from his own smoking, or both? Furthermore, the traditional torts requirement that individuals be made whole cannot be met in many instances (death, loss of a limb). Finally, paying compensation after the fact may also produce inappropriate incentives, and hence be inefficient. Workers who can be more or less careful around dangerous machinery, for example, are likely to be more careful if they will not be compensated for losing an appendage.

Our normal market and legal system tends to break down when substantial health risks are imposed on a relatively large population. These are, therefore, precisely the situations in which the cost-benefit approach is and should be called into play. Cost-benefit analysis is typically used in just those situations where our normal risk decision processes run into difficulty. We should therefore not expect it to lead to outcomes that are as satisfactory as those that evolve when ordinary market and private contractual trade are employed. But we should be able to expect better outcomes than we would achieve by muddling through unsystematically.

We have defended cost-benefit analysis as the most practical of ethically defensible methods and the most ethical of practically usable methods for conducting public decision-making. It cannot substitute for—nor can it adequately encompass, analyze, or consider—the sensitive application of social values. Thus it cannot be made the final arbiter of public decisions. But it does add a useful structure to public debate, and it does enable us to quantify some of the quantifiable aspects of public decisions. Our defense parallels Winston Churchill's argument for democracy: it is not perfect, but it is better than the alternatives.

QUESTIONS FOR DISCUSSION

1. Use the guidelines developed by Michael Josephson, or those developed by Craig Dreilinger and Dan Rice, to discuss the case "Why Should My Conscience Bother Me?"
2. Waters and Bird argue that certain categories of unethical acts receive less attention from management than they should. What are they? Do you agree with Waters and Bird that management should direct more attention toward these acts? If so, how should management focus more attention to these kinds of acts? If not, why not?
3. In "Dorrence Corporation Trade-offs" the firm faces a number of difficult decisions that have both economic and ethical consequences. Analyze and discuss those decisions using the techniques developed in the articles in this chapter. Compare and contrast the methods used by Josephson, for example, and cost-benefit analysis.
4. Turn to the cost-benefit analysis performed by the Ford Motor Company in Part Four. How might Kelman respond to this example? How might Leonard and Zeckhauser reply?

Tina Wilson

Tina Wilson is a secretary for one of the Assurance and Business Advisory Services partners. This morning, while she was talking with the partner about priorities for the day, her meeting was interrupted by one of the managers. Among other things, the manager asked whether one of the other secretaries—a good friend of hers—had been told that she was being let go.

Noting Wilson's shock, the partner explained that the secretary's work was way below standard and that the situation was getting worse by the day. He admonished Wilson not to say anything to the secretary, observing, "I know this is hard for you because she is a friend. We'll be talking with her at the end of the week."

Later that day, the secretary rushed over to Wilson at lunch. "You'll never guess what has happened. The Ford dealer just called and accepted my offer on the car I want. It'll be a stretch, but it'll be worth the hardship. I'll be eating peanut butter and jelly for awhile. Anyway, I'm going over tonight to pick the car up."

Wilson feels terrible. What should she do?

DISCUSSION QUESTIONS

- Are the firm's interests and personal interests in this situation in conflict?
- What alternatives does the secretary have for resolving this situation?
- If the secretary elects to tell her friend about the impending termination, what obligations does she then have to the firm (if any)?

Tony Benson

Tony Benson enjoys working in the print shop at PricewaterhouseCoopers. He takes pride in what he does, and he feels that he makes a contribution to the various products that go out the door representing the firm.

Every once in a while, Benson catches a problem, which gives him a sense of real satisfaction. For example, last week he noticed a typo on the cover of a report he was given to copy. It was an assessment of a potential merger between two major companies in the financial services area. Benson felt that he had saved the firm considerable embarrassment—if not more—by catching the mistake.

The problem is that Benson is the one who is embarrassed now. Over a drink after work with some non-PricewaterhouseCoopers friends, Benson reported his good deed, mentioning the names of the two high-profile financial firms being assessed. One of the people in the group, someone he did not know well, seemed particularly interested. When he asked a question about the content of the report, Benson began to feel uneasy and quickly changed the conversation.

This morning, the front page of the newspaper carried a brief story about the potential merger. It cited a confidential source. Benson is afraid that it might have been him.

What should Benson do?

DISCUSSION QUESTIONS

- How do we want people to handle situations where they have made a mistake?
- What obligation is there to report this potential breach of confidentiality?
- What should be done with someone who makes a mistake like this?
- Does the fact that the person is an administrative staff member affect the situation?

After encountering a dying pilgrim on a climbing trip in the Himalayas, a businessman ponders the differences between individual and corporate ethics.

The Parable of the Sadhu

Bowen H. McCoy

Former Managing Partner at Morgan Stanley; now real estate and business counselor, teacher, and philanthropist

Last year, as the first participant in the new six-month sabbatical program that Morgan Stanley has adopted, I enjoyed a rare opportunity to collect my thoughts as well as do some traveling. I spent the first three months in Nepal, walking 600 miles through 200 villages in the Himalayas and climbing some 120,000 vertical feet. My sole Western companion on the trip was an anthropologist who shed light on the cultural patterns of the villages that we passed through.

During the Nepal hike, something occurred that has had a powerful impact on my thinking about corporate ethics. Although some might argue that the experience has no relevance to business, it was a situation in which a basic ethical dilemma suddenly intruded into the lives of a group of individuals. How the group responded holds a lesson for all organizations, no matter how defined.

THE SADHU

The Nepal experience was more rugged than I had anticipated. Most commercial treks last two or three weeks and cover a quarter of the distance we traveled.

My friend Stephen, the anthropologist, and I were halfway through the 60-day Himalayan part of the trip when we reached the high point, an 18,000-foot pass over a crest that we'd have to traverse to reach the village of Muklinath, an ancient holy place for pilgrims.

Six years earlier, I had suffered pulmonary edema, an acute form of altitude sickness, at 16,500 feet in the vicinity of Everest base camp—so we were understandably concerned about what would happen at 18,000 feet. Moreover, the Himalayas were having their wettest spring in 20 years; hip-deep powder and ice had already driven us off one ridge. If we failed to cross the pass, I feared that the last half of our once-in-a-lifetime trip would be ruined.

The night before we would try the pass, we camped in a hut at 14,500 feet. In the photos taken at that camp, my face appears wan. The last village we'd passed through was a sturdy two-day walk below us, and I was tired.

During the late afternoon, four backpackers from New Zealand joined us, and we spent most of the night awake, anticipating the climb. Below, we could see the fires of two other parties, which turned out to be two Swiss couples and a Japanese hiking club.

To get over the steep part of the climb before the sun melted the steps cut in the ice, we departed at 3:30 A.M. The New Zealanders left first, followed by Stephen and myself, our porters and Sherpas, and then the Swiss. The Japanese lingered in their camp. The sky was clear, and we were confident that no spring storm would erupt that day to close the pass.

At 15,500 feet, it looked to me as if Stephen were shuffling and staggering a bit, which are symptoms of altitude sickness. (The initial stage of altitude sickness brings a headache and nausea. As the condition worsens, a climber may encounter difficult breathing, disorientation, aphasia, and paralysis.) I felt strong—my adrenaline was flowing—but I was very concerned about my ultimate ability to get across. A couple of our porters were also suffering from the height, and Pasang, our Sherpa sirdar (leader), was worried.

Just after daybreak, while we rested at 15,500 feet, one of the New Zealanders, who had gone ahead, came staggering down toward us with a body slung across his shoulders. He dumped the almost naked, barefoot body of an Indian holy man—a sadhu—at my feet. He had found the pilgrim lying on the ice, shivering and suffering from hypothermia. I cradled the sadhu's head and laid him out on the rocks. The New Zealander was angry. He wanted to get across the pass before the bright sun melted the snow. He said, "Look, I've done what I can. You have porters and Sherpa guides. You care for him. We're going on!" He turned and went back up the mountain to join his friends.

I took a carotid pulse and found that the sadhu was still alive. We figured he had probably visited the holy shrines at Muklinath and was on his way home. It was fruitless to question why he had chosen this desperately high route instead of the safe, heavily traveled caravan route through the Kali Gandaki gorge. Or why he was shoeless and almost naked, or how he had been lying in the pass. The answers weren't going to solve our problem.

Stephen and the four Swiss began stripping off their outer clothing and opening their packs. The sadhu was soon clothed from head to foot. He was not able to walk, but he was very much alive. I looked down the mountain and spotted the Japanese climbers, marching up with a horse.

Without a great deal of thought, I told Stephen and Pasang that I was concerned about withstanding the heights to come and wanted to get over the pass. I took off after several of our porters who had gone ahead.

On the steep part of the ascent where, if the ice steps had given way, I would have slid down about 3,000 feet, I felt vertigo. I stopped for a breather, allowing the Swiss to catch up with me. I inquired about the sadhu and Stephen. They said that the sadhu was fine and that Stephen was just behind them. I set off again for the summit.

Stephen arrived at the summit an hour after I did. Still exhilarated by victory, I ran down the slope to congratulate him. He was suffering from altitude sickness—walking 15 steps, then stopping, walking 15 steps, then stopping. Pasang accompanied him all the way up. When I reached them, Stephen glared at me and said: "How do you feel about contributing to the death of a fellow man?"

I did not completely comprehend what he meant. "Is the sadhu dead?" I inquired.

"No," replied Stephen, "but he surely will be!"

After I had gone, followed not long after by the Swiss, Stephen had remained with the sadhu. When the Japanese had arrived, Stephen had asked to use their horse to transport the sadhu down to the hut. They had refused. He had then asked Pasang to have a group of our porters carry the sadhu. Pasang had resisted the idea, saying that the porters would have to exert all their energy to get themselves over the pass. He believed they could not carry a man down 1,000 feet to the hut, reclimb the slope, and get across safely before the snow melted. Pasang had pressed Stephen not to delay any longer.

The Sherpas had carried the sadhu down to a rock in the sun at about 15,000 feet and pointed out the hut another 500 feet below. The Japanese had given him food and drink. When they had last seen him, he was listlessly throwing rocks at the Japanese party's dog, which had frightened him.

We do not know if the sadhu lived or died.

For many of the following days and evenings, Stephen and I discussed and debated our behavior toward the sadhu. Stephen is a committed Quaker with deep moral vision. He said, "I feel that what happened with the sadhu is a good example of the breakdown between the individual ethic and the corporate ethic. No one person was willing to assume ultimate responsibility for the sadhu. Each was willing to do his bit just so long as it was not too inconvenient. When it got to be a bother, everyone just passed the buck to someone else and took off. Jesus was relevant to a more individualistic stage of society, but how do we interpret his teaching today in a world filled with large, impersonal organizations and groups?"

I defended the larger group, saying, "Look, we all cared. We all gave aid and comfort. Everyone did his bit. The New Zealander carried him down below the snow line. I took his pulse and suggested we treat him for hypothermia. You and the Swiss gave him clothing and got him warmed up. The Japanese gave him food and water. The Sherpas carried him down to the sun and pointed out the easy trail toward the hut. He was well enough to throw rocks at a dog. What more could we do?"

"You have just described the typical affluent Westerner's response to a problem. Throwing money—in this case, food and sweaters—at it, but not solving the fundamentals!" Stephen retorted.

"What would satisfy you?" I said. "Here we are, a group of New Zealanders, Swiss, Americans, and Japanese who have never met before and who are at the apex of one of the most powerful experiences of our lives. Some years the pass is so bad no one gets over it. What right does an almost naked pilgrim who chooses the wrong trail have to disrupt our lives? Even the Sherpas had no interest in risking the trip to help him beyond a certain point."

Stephen calmly rebutted, "I wonder what the Sherpas would have done if the sadhu had been a well-dressed Nepali, or what the Japanese would have done if the sadhu had been a well-dressed Asian, or what you would have done, Buzz, if the sadhu had been a well-dressed Western woman?"

"Where, in your opinion," I asked, "is the limit of our responsibility in a situation like this? We had our own well-being to worry about. Our Sherpa guides were unwilling to jeopardize us or the porters for the sadhu. No one else on the mountain was willing to commit himself beyond certain self-imposed limits."

Stephen said, "As individual Christians or people with a Western ethical tradition, we can fulfill our obligations in such a situation only if one, the sadhu dies in our care; two, the sadhu demonstrates to us that he can undertake the two-day walk down to the village; or three, we carry the sadhu for two days down to the village and persuade someone there to care for him."

"Leaving the sadhu in the sun with food and clothing—where he demonstrated hand-eye coordination by throwing a rock at a dog—comes close to fulfilling items one and two," I answered. "And it wouldn't have made sense to take him to the village where the people appeared to be far less caring than the Sherpas, so the third condition is impractical. Are you really saying that, no matter what the implications, we should, at the drop of a hat, have changed our entire plan?"

THE INDIVIDUAL VERSUS THE GROUP ETHIC

Despite my arguments, I felt and continue to feel guilt about the sadhu. I had literally walked through a classic moral dilemma without fully thinking through the consequences. My excuses for my actions include a high adrenaline flow, a superordinate goal, and a once-in-a-lifetime opportunity—common factors in corporate situations, especially stressful ones.

Real moral dilemmas are ambiguous, and many of us hike right through them, unaware that they exist. When, usually after the fact, someone makes an issue of one, we tend to resent his or her bringing it up. Often, when the full import of what we have done (or not done) hits us, we dig into a defensive position from which it is very difficult to emerge. In rare circumstances, we may contemplate what we have done from inside a prison.

Had we mountaineers been free of stress caused by the effort and the high altitude, we might have treated the sadhu differently. Yet isn't stress the real test of personal and corporate values? The instant decisions that executives make under pressure reveal the most about personal and corporate character.

Among the many questions that occur to me when I ponder my experience with the sadhu are: What are the practical limits of moral imagination and vision? Is there a collective or institutional ethic that differs from the ethics of the individual? At what level of effort or commitment can one discharge one's ethical responsibilities?

Not every ethical dilemma has a right solution. Reasonable people often disagree; otherwise there would be no dilemma. In a business context, however, it is essential that managers agree on a process for dealing with dilemmas.

Our experience with the sadhu offers an interesting parallel to business situations. An immediate response was mandatory. Failure to act was a decision in itself. Up on the mountain we could not resign and submit our résumés to a headhunter. In contrast to philosophy, business involves action and implementation—getting things done. Managers must come up with answers based on what they see and what they allow to influence their decision-making processes. On the mountain, none of us but Stephen realized the true dimensions of the situation we were facing.

One of our problems was that as a group we had no process for developing a consensus. We had no sense of purpose or plan. The difficulties of dealing with the sadhu were so complex that no one person could handle them. Because the group did not have a set of preconditions that could guide its action to an acceptable resolution, we reacted instinctively as individuals. The cross-cultural nature of the group added a further layer of complexity. We had no leader with whom we could all identify and in whose purpose we believed. Only Stephen was willing to take charge, but he could not gain adequate support from the group to care for the sadhu.

Some organizations do have values that transcend the personal values of their managers. Such values, which go beyond profitability, are usually revealed when the organization is under stress.

People throughout the organization generally accept its values, which, because they are not presented as a rigid list of commandments, may be somewhat ambiguous. The stories people tell, rather than printed materials, transmit the organization's conceptions of what is proper behavior.

For 20 years, I have been exposed at senior levels to a variety of corporations and organizations. It is amazing how quickly an outsider can sense the tone and style of an organization and, with that, the degree of tolerated openness and freedom to challenge management.

Organizations that do not have a heritage of mutually accepted, shared values tend to become unhinged during stress, with each individual bailing out for himself or herself. In the great takeover battles we have witnessed during past years, companies that had strong cultures drew the wagons around them and fought it out, while other companies saw executives—supported by golden parachutes—bail out of the struggles.

Because corporations and their members are interdependent, for the corporation to be strong the members need to share a preconceived notion of correct behavior, a "business ethic," and think of it as a positive force, not a constraint.

As an investment banker, I am continually warned by well-meaning lawyers, clients, and associates to be wary of conflicts of interest. Yet if I were to run away from every difficult situation, I wouldn't be an effective investment banker. I have to feel my way through conflicts. An effective manager can't run from risk either; he or she has to confront risk. To feel "safe" in doing that, managers need the guidelines of an agreed-upon process and set of values within the organization.

After my three months in Nepal, I spent three months as an executive-in-residence at both the Stanford Business School and the University of California at Berkeley's Center for Ethics and Social Policy of the Graduate Theological Union. Those six months away from my job gave me time to assimilate 20 years of business experience. My thoughts turned often to the meaning of the leadership role in any large organization. Students at the seminary thought of themselves as antibusiness. But when I questioned them, they agreed that they distrusted all large organizations, including the church. They perceived all large organizations as impersonal and opposed to individual values and needs. Yet we all know of organizations in which people's values and beliefs are respected and their expressions encouraged. What makes the difference? Can we identify the difference and, as a result, manage more effectively?

The word *ethics* turns off many and confuses more. Yet the notions of shared values and an agreed-upon process for dealing with adversity and change—what many people mean when they talk about corporate culture—seem to be at the heart of the ethical issue. People who are in touch with their own core beliefs and the beliefs of others and who are sustained by them can be more comfortable living on the cutting edge. At times, taking a tough line or a decisive stand in a muddle of ambiguity is the only ethical thing to do. If a manager is indecisive about a problem and spends time trying to figure out the "good" thing to do, the enterprise may be lost.

Business ethics, then, has to do with the authenticity and integrity of the enterprise. To be ethical is to follow the business as well as the cultural goals of the corporation, its owners, its employees, and its customers. Those who cannot serve the corporate vision are not authentic businesspeople and, therefore, are not ethical in the business sense.

At this stage of my own business experience, I have a strong interest in organizational behavior. Sociologists are keenly studying what they call corporate stories, legends, and heroes as a way organizations have of transmitting value systems. Corporations such as Arco have even hired consultants to perform an audit of their corporate culture. In a company, a leader is a person who understands, interprets, and manages the corporate value system. Effective managers, therefore, are action-oriented people who resolve conflict, are tolerant of ambiguity, stress, and change, and have a strong sense of purpose for themselves and their organizations.

If all this is true, I wonder about the role of the professional manager who moves from company to company. How can he or she quickly absorb the values and culture of different organizations? Or is there, indeed, an art of management that is totally transportable? Assuming that such fungible managers do exist, is it proper for them to manipulate the values of others?

What would have happened had Stephen and I carried the sadhu for two days back to the village and become involved with the villagers in his care? In four trips to Nepal, my most interesting experience occurred in 1975 when I lived in a Sherpa home in the Khumbu for five days while recovering from altitude sickness. The high point of Stephen's trip was an invitation to participate in a family funeral ceremony in Manang. Neither experience had to do with climbing the high passes of the Himalayas. Why were we so reluctant to try the lower path, the ambiguous trail? Perhaps because we did not have a leader who could reveal the greater purpose of the trip to us.

Why didn't Stephen, with his moral vision, opt to take the sadhu under his personal care? The answer is partly because Stephen was hard-stressed physically himself and partly because, without some support system that encompassed our involuntary and episodic community on the mountain, it was beyond his individual capacity to do so.

I see the current interest in corporate culture and corporate value systems as a positive response to pessimism such as Stephen's about the decline of the role of the individual in large organizations. Individuals who operate from a thoughtful set of personal values provide the foundation for a corporate culture. A corporate tradition that encourages freedom of inquiry, supports personal values, and reinforces a focused sense of direction can fulfill the need to combine individuality with the prosperity and success of the group. Without such corporate support, the individual is lost.

That is the lesson of the sadhu. In a complex corporate situation, the individual requires and deserves the support of the group. When people cannot find such support in their organizations, they don't know how to act. If such support is forthcoming, a person has a stake in the success of the group and can add much to the process of establishing and maintaining a corporate culture. Management's challenge is to be sensitive to individual needs, to shape them, and to direct and focus them for the benefit of the group as a whole.

For each of us the sadhu lives. Should we stop what we are doing and comfort him; or should we keep trudging up toward the high pass? Should I pause to help the derelict I pass on the street each night as I walk by the Yale Club en route to Grand Central Station? Am I his brother? What is the nature of our responsibility if we consider ourselves to be ethical persons? Perhaps it is to change the values of the group so that it can, with all its resources, take the other road.

WHEN DO WE TAKE A STAND?

I wrote about my experiences purposely to present an ambiguous situation. I never found out if the sadhu lived or died. I can attest, though, that the sadhu lives on in his story. He lives in the ethics classes I teach each year at business schools and churches. He lives in the classrooms of numerous business schools, where professors have taught the case to tens of thousands of students. He lives in several casebooks on ethics and on an educational video. And he lives in organizations such as the American Red Cross and AT&T, which use his story in their ethics training.

As I reflect on the sadhu now, 15 years after the fact, I first have to wonder, What actually happened on that Himalayan slope? When I first wrote about the event, I reported the experience in as much detail as I could remember, but I shaped it to the needs of a good classroom discussion. After years of reading my story, viewing it on video, and hearing others discuss it, I'm not sure I myself know what actually occurred on the mountainside that day!

I've also heard a wide variety of responses to the story. The sadhu, for example, may not have wanted our help at all—he may have been intentionally bringing on his own death as a way to holiness. Why had he taken the dangerous way over the pass instead of the caravan route through the gorge? Hindu businesspeople have told me that in trying to assist the sadhu, we were being typically arrogant Westerners imposing our cultural values on the world.

I've learned that each year along the pass, a few Nepali porters are left to freeze to death outside the tents of the unthinking tourists who hired them. A few years ago, a French group even left one of their own, a young French woman, to die there. The difficult pass seems to demonstrate a perverse version of Gresham's law of currency: The bad practices of previous travelers have driven out the values that new travelers might have followed if they were at home. Perhaps that helps to explain why our porters behaved as they did and why it was so difficult for Stephen or anyone else to establish a different approach on the spot.

Our Sherpa sirdar, Pasang, was focused on his responsibility for bringing us up the mountain safe and sound. (His livelihood and status in the Sherpa ethnic group depended on our safe return.) We were weak, our party was split, the porters were well on their way to the top with all our gear and food, and a storm would have separated us irrevocably from our logistical base.

The fact was, we had no plan for dealing with the contingency of the sadhu. There was nothing we could do to unite our multicultural group in the little time we had. An ethical dilemma had come upon us unexpectedly, an element of drama that may explain why the sadhu's story has continued to attract students.

I am often asked for help in teaching the story. I usually advise keeping the details as ambiguous as possible. A true ethical dilemma requires a decision between two hard choices. In the case of the sadhu, we had to decide how much to sacrifice ourselves to take care of a stranger. And given the constraints of our trek, we had to make a group decision, not an individual one. If a large majority of students in a class ends up thinking I'm a bad person because of my decision on the mountain, the instructor may not have given the case its due. The same is true if the majority sees no problem with the choices we made.

Any class's response depends on its setting, whether it's a business school, a church, or a corporation. I've found that younger students are more likely to see the issue as black-and-white, whereas older ones tend to see shades of gray. Some have seen a conflict between the different ethical approaches that we followed at the time. Stephen felt he had to do everything he could to save the sadhu's life, in accordance with his Christian ethic of compassion. I had a utilitarian response: do the greatest good for the greatest number. Give a burst of aid to minimize the sadhu's exposure, then continue on our way.

The basic question of the case remains, When do we take a stand? When do we allow a "sadhu" to intrude into our daily lives? Few of us can afford the time or effort to take care of every needy person we encounter. How much must we give of ourselves? And how do we prepare our organizations and institutions so they will respond appropriately in a crisis? How do we influence them if we do not agree with their points of view?

We cannot quit our jobs over every ethical dilemma, but if we continually ignore our sense of values, who do we become? As a journalist asked at a recent conference on ethics, "Which ditch are we willing to die in?" For each of us, the answer is a bit different. How we act in response to that question defines better than anything else who we are, just as, in a collective sense, our acts define our institutions. In effect, the sadhu is always there, ready to remind us of the tensions between our own goals and the claims of strangers.

Dorrence Corporation* Trade-offs

Hans A. Wolf
Former Vice Chairman and Chief Administrative Officer,
Syntax Co.

Arthur Cunningham, chief executive officer of the Dorrence Corporation, was reflecting on the presentations by the various divisions of the company

---

*Name of company and all data related to it have been disguised.
An Alling Foundation for Ethics Award case. Copyright © 1990 by Columbia University. Printed by permission of The Graduate School of Business, Columbia University.

of their operating plans and financial budgets for the next three years, which he had heard during the past several days. A number of critical decisions would have to be made at tomorrow's meeting of the nine senior executives who formed Dorrence's Corporate Operating Committee. Although the company's tradition was one of consensus management, Cunningham knew that he was expected to exercise leadership and would have the final word on, as well as the ultimate responsibility, for subsequent performance.

Dorrence, a large U.S.-based pharmaceutical company with sales and operations throughout the world, had achieved an outstanding long-term record of growth in sales and profits. It had not incurred a loss in any year since 1957 and profits had increased over the prior year in 28 out of the past 32 years. During the past 10 years, sales had grown at an average compound rate of 12 percent per year and profits had increased at a 15 percent average annual rate. Profits as a percent of sales was considerably higher than that of the average U.S. industrial concern. (See Exhibit 1).

The growth had produced a huge increase in the value of the company's stock. There are approximately 30,000 shareholders, with a small number of owners—pension and mutual funds, university endowments, and insurance companies—holding about 65 percent of the total. Dorrence grants stock options to its executives and permits employees in the U.S. and several other countries to purchase Dorrence stock through the company's savings plan. Executives own about two percent of the company's shares and all other employees about one percent. Thus, directly and indirectly, Dorrence is owned by many people, throughout the country, and perhaps around the world; all are affected to some degree by the policies and operations of the company, particularly as they affect the earnings and market price of Dorrence shares.

Dorrence's fine record of growth had also brought benefits to its customers, employees and the communities in which it had operations. It has steadily expanded its research expenditures at a greater rate than its sales growth and has developed important new products that improved the quality of life—or extended life—for hundreds of thousands of people. Because of its profitability, the company has been able to pay higher than average compensation to its employees, including sizeable incentive awards to middle and upper management and profit-related bonuses to all employees. Dorrence's growth has also provided unusual opportunities for employees' career development. Its managers have prided themselves on the company as a good citizen in the communities in which its laboratories and factories are located. It regularly contributes to local charities and encourages its employees to work constructively in community organizations.

Cunningham found that 1989 earnings were, however, very disappointing. The company fell short of the goals established for the year. Growth in sales and profits was far below the rate of recent years and, what hurt the most, below the levels achieved by several of Dorrence's competitors in the pharmaceutical industry. Management incentive awards and employee bonuses were, therefore, about 5 percent smaller than those distributed for 1988. The value of Dorrence stock had lost about a fifth of its value since its recent high.

Cunningham considered it important that Dorrence commit itself to achieving at least a 13 percent profit growth in 1990, and higher rates in the two following years. He recognized that such an achievement would not be easy. Not only would it demand the best efforts of the entire organization, but it would also require some tough managerial decisions.

The 1990 budgets proposed by the divisions added up to a growth rate of only 8 percent in profit-after-taxes, five percentage points below what Cunningham considered a minimum acceptable level. As a rough rule of thumb each percentage point increase in profit growth rate would require about $8 million additional profit-before-taxes. Thus, each percentage point improvement could be achieved in a number of ways: $13 million additional sales volume accompanied by normal incremental costs, $8 million additional revenue from price increases, $8 million of additional interest income on the company's invested cash, or an $8 million reduction in expenditures. During the course of a three-day division-by-division presentation, he had identified several possibilities for such improvements. In his notes he had summarized them as follows:

1. **Size of the research budget:** Dorrence's total expenditures for research and developmental (R&D) had climbed annually, not only in absolute dollars but also as a percent of sales. During the current year they totaled about 17 percent of sales, one of the higher levels in the industry.

   The proposed budget included a further increase for R&D, and Cunningham knew that many promising projects required additional funding if the company were to demonstrate the safety and efficacy of important new drugs in a timely manner. He also knew that pharmaceutical R&D are very risky activities. The failure rate was high, with many years elapsing before managers knew if an effort was either a success or a failure. Typically, it took seven to 10 years from the identification of a potential new drug to Food & Drug Administration (FDA) approval for market sales. Approval also had to be sought from similar regulatory agencies in foreign countries, if the company was to sell the product abroad. On average, a pharmaceutical company brought to market only one new drug or product for each $100 million of R&D expenditures.

   Clearly, there was a trade-off between investing for future growth and achieving acceptable profits in the short run. On Cunningham's list of possible changes in the proposed 1990 budget was a $10 million reduction in the amount of money requested for R&D.

2. **Export sales:** The International Division had presented an opportunity for a $4 million sale of Savolene to the Philippine government, not included in the 1990 budget because of lack of product availability. It was a new Dorrence-developed injectable drug for the treatment of serious viral infections, including measles. The drug was difficult and expensive to manufacture and had been in very short supply since its introduction.

   A large lot, costing about $1 million, had been rejected for the U.S. market on the basis of a new, very sensitive test for endotoxin recently required by the FDA, in addition to a standard test that had been used for many years. The new test had shown a very low level of endotoxin on this batch of Savolene, even though no endotoxin has been revealed by the older test.

Cunningham had asked whether this ruled out shipping the batch to the Philippines. The company's chief medical safety officer had answered:

Officially the Philippines and a lot of other countries still rely only on the old test. It always takes them a while to follow U.S. practice, and sometimes they never do. Endotoxin might cause high fever when injected into patients, but I can't tell you that the level in this batch is high enough to cause trouble. But how can we have a double standard, one for the U.S. and one for the Third World countries?

However, when Cunningham asked Dorrence's export vice president the same question, she said:

It's not our job to over-protect other countries. The health authorities in the Philippines know what they're doing. Our FDA always takes an extreme position. Measles is a serious illness. Last year in the Philippines half the kids who had measles died. It's not only good business but also good ethics to send them the only batch of Savolene we have available.

3. **Capital investments:** Among the capital investments that had been included in the proposed budgets was a $200 million plant-automation program for Dorrence's Haitian chemical plant. The purpose of the investment was to permit a dramatic reduction in the cost of Libam, Dorrence's principal product whose U.S. patent would expire in a couple of years. Patent protection had already ended in most other countries and chemical manufacturers in Italy, Hungary and India were selling Libam's active ingredient at very low prices. Once there was no longer patent protection in the U.S., companies based abroad and those in the U.S. could capture a large share of Dorrence's existing sales unless Dorrence were able to match their low prices. Automating the Haitian plant was essential to achieving such a match. Successful implementation of the new technology would enable the plant to achieve the required output with far fewer people than currently employed in the domestic plant. If U.S. plants were closed, the company would have to contend with longtime employees thrown out of work. He did not know whether many of them or if any could be transferred to other plants.

Dorrence was currently earning about 9 percent interest on its cash funds. The proposed automation project would use up $200 million of them and thus reduce interest income. Spending funds on the project would have reduced interest income for 1990 by about $9 million. If the automation program were stretched out over a longer period, almost half of that "loss" of income would be postponed a year, thus adding $4 million to 1990 profits. The down-side was that a slowdown in constructing the automated plant would mean delays in its production, needed to meet the expected competition.

4. **Employee health insurance costs:** Like all U.S. companies Dorrence was experiencing rapid escalation in the cost of its employee health insurance program. Dorrence paid 100 percent of the premium for its employees and 80 percent of the premiums for their dependents. After meeting certain deductibles, employees were reimbursed 80 percent to 90 percent of their medical and dental costs. The company's cost of maintaining the plan was budgeted to increase 22 percent, or $12 million in 1990. An important issue, therefore, was whether the plan should be changed to shift all or a portion of that cost increase to the employees through reducing the company's share of premiums, increasing deductibles, reducing reimbursements, or some combination of these changes.

5. **Closing Dorrence's plant in Argentina:** Dorrence had purchased a small pharmaceutical company in Argentina in the early 1950s when prospects for growth in the local market seemed excellent. However, in most years since then Argentina has been plagued by hyperinflation. With rapidly rising wage rates and other costs on the one hand, and strictly controlled drug prices, on the other,

Dorrence's Argentine subsidiary had consistently lost money. The 1990 budget projected a loss of $4 million.

For the past year the company had tried to find a buyer for the subsidiary—a buyer who would retain the present sales force of 120 and continue to operate the Buenos Aires plant with its 250 employees. No such buyer had been found, but recently a local company had offered to purchase the rights to Dorrence's product line. It would manufacture them in its own under-utilized plant, distributing them through its own sales force. If Dorrence accepted this offer, the 370 company employees in Argentina would be laid off. Dorrence had already created a financial reserve for the government-mandated severance payments. Thus if he recommended ending the operations in Argentina, corporate profits would improve by $4 million in 1990.

6. **Price increase on principal product sold in the U.S.:** The budget proposed by Dorrence's U.S. pharmaceutical division already assumed a five percent price increase on all its current products at the end of the first quarter of the year, producing a $40 million increase in sales revenues. A substantially higher price increase on Libam, its largest selling product, could probably be implemented without adversely affecting sales to volume. For example, if the budgeted price increase were 10 percent instead of five percent, an additional $12 million would be generated. Alternately, if two five-percent price increases were implemented six months apart, Dorrence would earn $4 million above the proposed budget. Libam is used by chronically ill patients, many of them elderly.

In most countries pharmaceutical prices are controlled by the government. The United States is one of the few countries in which pharmaceutical companies are free to decide what prices to charge for their drugs. Physicians generally prescribe the drug which they feel will be most beneficial to their patients regardless of price. Unless the patent on a drug has expired and a generic equivalent is available, the demand for a prescription drug is not very sensitive to its price. Consequently, drug prices in the United States are substantially higher than in most other countries.

Cunningham was very conscious, however, of the growing public concern about health care costs. Although drugs constitute only a small fraction of the nation's total health care bill, drug prices are an easily identified target and drug companies were becoming increasingly under attack for their price increases.

7. **New Costa Rican manufacturing plant:** $10 million in sales of a new life-saving drug developed by Dorrence had been removed from the budget because of an unexpected problem at the new plant, which had been expected to be in operation this year, supplying the drug.

Three years earlier Dorrence had built the plant in a small Costa Rican town after evaluating various possible sites. The town had won the company's choice because it offered inexpensive land, relatively low wages, certain tax concessions, and a promise by the local government to build a new municipal waste treatment facility by the time the plant would be completed. In addition, Dorrence managers felt they would be fulfilling the company's social responsibilities by creating jobs in an area of high unemployment.

A few days before Dorrence's budget meeting the company had learned that completion of the municipal waste treatment plant was delayed at least a year. Although Costa Rica's environmental regulations are less stringent than those of industrialized countries, local law prohibits the discharge of untreated factory waste water into streams. Without a means of disposing of its waste water, the Dorrence plant could not operate.

A message from the Dorrence plant manager received yesterday seemed to solve the problem. The city sanitation commissioner had given Dorrence a special exemption that would allow it to discharge its waste water into a stream behind the plant until the city's waste treatment facility was completed. Cunningham had immediately asked for a fuller report on the situation. The plant manager had sent the following additional details:

The stream is used to irrigate sugar-cane fields and small vegetable plots on which people in this area depend. There is, therefore, a chance that substances in the waste water would be absorbed by the crops that people are going to eat. I wonder if that is acceptable? On the other hand, I fear that all the good we have accomplished here will go down the drain if we don't begin manufacturing operations. Construction of the plant was completed on schedule three months ago. Building our own waste treatment facility now would add $5 million to the cost of the plant and would take at least 12 months. I've already hired over 100 workers and have given them extensive training. We obviously can't pay the workers for a year to sit around in an idle plant. Losing their jobs would be devastating to them and the whole community. Besides, there is no other Dorrence facility or plant of another company that could accomplish the synthesis required for this product. Lots of people in the United States are anxiously waiting for this new drug.

8. **Pricing of an important new product:** Finally, there was the issue of what price to charge for another new Dorrence drug, Miracule, which was expected to be introduced later in the year. In most cases patients for whom Miracule was prescribed would require the drug for the rest of their lives, unless an even more effective drug became available. The budget had assumed a price that would result in a daily cost of $1.75 (including wholesaler and drug store markups) for the average patient. A price of $2.50 would yield an additional $8 million profit to Dorrence during 1990 and far greater sums in subsequent years.

Despite the difficulties surrounding each of the issues Cunningham had identified, he felt it was critical that the 1990 budget be improved to aim for 13 percent profit growth over 1989. He believed that a second year in a row of below average profit growth would be viewed very negatively by the investment community, be demoralizing to the company's managers, and could result in a substantial drop in the value of the company's stock as investors switched to pharmaceutical companies with

---

EXHIBIT 1

DORRENCE CORPORATION

Financial & Other Data

	1979	1980	1981	1982	1983	1984
SALES—$MILLIONS	826	1,074	1,181	1,259	1,333	1,453
PROFIT*—$MILLIONS	132	164	175	204	224	222
PROFIT* AS % OF SALES	16.0	15.3	14.8	16.2	16.8	15.3
EMPLOYEES	12,500	12,900	13,500	13,600	13,800	14,000
STOCKHOLDERS OF RECORD	26,500	25,000	23,900	23,300	22,300	21,700

	1985	1986	1987	1988	1989
SALES—$MILLIONS	1,466	1,703	2,063	2,493	2,572
PROFIT*—$MILLIONS	241	312	413	524	558
PROFIT* AS % OF SALES	16.4	18.3	20.0	21.8	21.7
EMPLOYEES	13,300	13,100	13,500	13,900	14,700
STOCKHOLDERS OF RECORD	20,300	21,200	24,500	28,900	29,800

*After taxes.

better 1990 results. He also recognized that large institutional investors, such as pension funds, were taking a more active role in demanding better performance from the managements of the companies in which they invested the funds entrusted to them. He worried that another year of disappointing growth might make them supportive of a take-over of the Dorrence Corporation.

Framework for Ethical Decision Making

PricewaterhouseCoopers

As a guide in deciding on a course of action, follow these steps:

1. *Recognize the Event, Decision or Issue* • You are asked to do something that you think might be wrong • You are aware of potentially illegal or unethical conduct on the part of others at PwC or a client • You are trying to make a decision and are not sure about the ethical course of action	**ETHICS QUESTIONS TO CONSIDER** • *Is it legal?* • *Does it feel right?*
2. *Think Before You Act* • Summarize and clarify your issue • Ask yourself, why the dilemma? • Consider the options and consequences • Consider who may be affected • Consult with others	• *How would it look in the newspapers?* • *Will it reflect negatively on you or the firm?* • *Who else could be impacted by this (others in the firm, clients, you, etc.)?*
3. *Decide On a Course of Action* • Determine your responsibility • Review all the relevant facts and information • Refer to applicable firm policies or professional standards • Assess the risks and how you could reduce them • Comtemplate the best course of action • Consult with others—if you are uncomfortable or uncertain who to talk to, call the Ethics Helpline at 1-888-4-ETHICS or write the Ethics Mailbox at Box 411, 167 Milk Street, Boston, MA 02109-4315	• *Would you be embarrassed if others knew you took this course of action?* • *Is there an alternative action that does not pose an ethical conflict?* • *Is it against firm or professional standards?*
4. *Test Your Decision* • Review the "Ethics Questions to Consider" again • Apply the Firm's values to your decisison • Make sure you have considered Firm policies, laws and professional standards • Consult with others—enlist their opinion of your planned action	• *What would a reasonable person think?* • *Can you sleep at night?*
5. *Proceed With Confidence*	

Source: From PricewaterhouseCoopers' Code of Conduct, *The Way We Do Business.* © 1999 PricewaterhouseCoopers. PricewaterhouseCoopers refers to the individual member firms of the worldwide PricewaterhouseCoopers organization. All rights reserved.

Why Should My Conscience Bother Me?

Kermit Vandivier
Retired writer and Sunday editor, *Troy Daily News,* Troy, OH

The B.F. Goodrich Co. is what business magazines like to speak of as "a major American corporation." It has operations in a dozen states and as many foreign countries, and of these far-flung facilities, the Goodrich plant at Troy, Ohio, is not the most imposing. It is a small, one-story building, once used to manufacture airplanes. Set in the grassy flatlands of west-central Ohio, it employs only about six hundred people. Nevertheless, it is one of the three largest manufacturers of aircraft wheels and brakes, a leader in a most profitable industry. Goodrich wheels and brakes support such well-known planes as the F111, the C5A, the Boeing 727, the XB70 and many others. Its customers include almost every aircraft manufacturer in the world.

Contracts for aircraft wheels and brakes often run into millions of dollars, and ordinarily a contract with a total value of less than $70,000, though welcome, would not create any special stir of joy in the hearts of Goodrich sales personnel. But purchase order P-23718, issued on June 18, 1967, by the LTV Aerospace Corporation, and ordering 202 brake assemblies for a new Air Force plane at a total price of $69,417, was received by Goodrich with considerable glee. And there was good reason. Some ten years previously, Goodrich had built a brake for LTV that was, to say the least, considerably less than a rousing success. The brake had not lived up to Goodrich's promises, and after experiencing considerable difficulty, LTV had written off Goodrich as a source of brakes. Since that time, Goodrich salesmen had been unable to sell so much as a shot of brake

fluid to LTV. So in 1967, when LTV requested bids on wheels and brakes for the new A7D light attack aircraft it proposed to build for the Air Force, Goodrich submitted a bid that was absurdly low, so low that LTV could not, in all prudence, turn it down.

Goodrich had, in industry parlance, "bought into the business." Not only did the company not expect to make a profit on the deal; it was prepared, if necessary, to lose money. For aircraft brakes are not something that can be ordered off the shelf. They are designed for a particular aircraft, and once an aircraft manufacturer buys a brake, he is forced to purchase all replacement parts from the brake manufacturer. The $70,000 that Goodrich would get for making the brake would be a drop in the bucket when compared with the cost of the linings and other parts the Air Force would have to buy from Goodrich during the lifetime of the aircraft. Furthermore, the company which manufactures brakes for one particular model of an aircraft quite naturally has the inside track to supply other brakes when the planes are updated and improved.

Thus, that first contract, regardless of the money involved, is very important, and Goodrich, when it learned that it had been awarded the A7D contract, was determined that while it may have slammed the door on its own foot ten years before, this time, the second time around, things would be different. The word was soon circulated throughout the plant: "We can't bungle it this time. We've got to give them a good brake, regardless of the cost."

There was another factor which had undoubtedly influenced LTV. All aircraft brakes made today are of the disk type, and the bid submitted by Goodrich called for a relatively small brake, one containing four disks and weighing only 106 pounds. The weight of any aircraft part is extremely important. The lighter a part is, the heavier the plane's payload can be. The four-rotor, 106-pound brake promised by Goodrich was about as light as could be expected, and this undoubtedly had helped move LTV to award the contract to Goodrich.

The brake was designed by one of Goodrich's most capable engineers, John Warren. A tall,

Excerpted from "Why Should My Conscience Bother Me?" by Kermit Vandivier, from *In The Name of Profit* by Robert Heilbroner. Copyright © 1972 by Doubleday, a division of Bantam Doubleday Dell Publishing Group, Inc. Used by permission of Doubleday, a division of Random House, Inc.

lanky blond and a graduate of Purdue, Warren had come from the Chrysler Corporation seven years before and had become adept at aircraft brake design. The happy-go-lucky manner he usually maintained belied a temper which exploded whenever anyone ventured to offer any criticism of his work, no matter how small. On these occasions, Warren would turn red in the face, often throwing or slamming something and then stalking from the scene. As his coworkers learned the consequences of criticizing him, they did so less and less readily, and when he submitted his preliminary design for the A7D brake, it was accepted without question.

Warren was named project engineer for the A7D, and he, in turn, assigned the task of producing the final production design to a newcomer to the Goodrich engineering stable, Searle Lawson. Just turned twenty-six, Lawson had been out of the Northrup Institute of Technology only one year when he came to Goodrich in January 1967. Like Warren, he had worked for a while in the automotive industry, but his engineering degree was in aeronautical and astronautical sciences, and when the opportunity came to enter his special field, via Goodrich, he took it. At the Troy plant, Lawson had been assigned to various "paper projects" to break him in, and after several months spent reviewing statistics and old brake designs, he was beginning to fret at the lack of challenge. When told he was being assigned to his first "real" project, he was elated and immediately plunged into his work.

The major portion of the design had already been completed by Warren, and major assemblies for the brake had already been ordered from Goodrich suppliers. Naturally, however, before Goodrich could start making the brakes on a production basis, much testing would have to be done. Lawson would 'have to determine the best materials to use for the linings and discover what minor adjustments in the design would have to be made.'

Then, after the preliminary testing and after the brake was judged ready for production, one whole brake assembly would undergo a series of grueling, simulated braking stops and other severe trials called qualification tests. These tests are required by the military, which gives very detailed specifi-

cations on how they are to be conducted, the criteria for failure, and so on. They are performed in the Goodrich plant's test laboratory, where huge machines called dynamometers can simulate the weight and speed of almost any aircraft. After the brakes pass the laboratory tests, they are approved for production, but before the brakes are accepted for use in military service, they must undergo further extensive flight tests.

Searle Lawson was well aware that much work had to be done before the A7D brake could go into production, and he knew that LTV had set the last two weeks in June, 1968, as the starting dates for flight tests. So he decided to begin testing immediately. Goodrich's suppliers had not yet delivered the brake housing and other parts, but the brake disks had arrived, and using the housing from a brake similar in size and weight to the A7D brake, Lawson built a prototype. The prototype was installed in a test wheel and placed on one of the big dynamometers in the plant's test laboratory. The dynamometer was adjusted to simulate the weight of the A7D and Lawson began a series of tests, "landing" the wheel and brake at the A7D's landing speed, and braking it to a stop. The main purpose of these preliminary tests was to learn what temperatures would develop within the brake during the simulated stops and to evaluate the lining materials tentatively selected for use.

During a normal aircraft landing the temperatures inside the brake may reach 1000 degrees, and occasionally a bit higher. During Lawson's first simulated landings, the temperature of his prototype brake reached 1500 degrees. The brake glowed a bright cherry-red and threw off incandescent particles of metal and lining material as the temperature reached its peak. After a few such stops, the brake was dismantled and the linings were found to be almost completely disintegrated. Lawson chalked this first failure up to chance and, ordering new lining materials, tried again.

The second attempt was a repeat of the first. The brake became extremely hot, causing the lining materials to crumble into dust.

After the third such failure, Lawson, inexperienced though he was, knew that the fault lay not in defective parts or unsuitable lining material but in the basic design of the brake itself. Ignoring Warren's original computations, Lawson made his own, and it didn't take him long to discover where the trouble lay—the brake was too small. There simply was not enough surface area on the disks to stop the aircraft without generating the excessive heat that caused the linings to fail.

The answer to the problem was obvious but far from simple—the four-disk brake would have to be scrapped, and a new design, using five disks, would have to be developed. The implications were not lost on Lawson. Such a step would require the junking of all the four-disk-brake subassemblies, many of which had now begun to arrive from the various suppliers. It would also mean several weeks of preliminary design and testing and many more weeks of waiting while the suppliers made and delivered the new subassemblies.

Yet, several weeks had already gone by since LTV's order had arrived, and the date for delivery of the first production brakes for flight testing was only a few months away.

Although project engineer John Warren had more or less turned the A7D over to Lawson, he knew of the difficulties Lawson had been experiencing. He had assured the young engineer that the problem revolved around getting the right kind of lining material. Once that was found, he said, the difficulties would end.

Despite the evidence of the abortive tests and Lawson's careful computations, Warren rejected the suggestion that the four-disk brake was too light for the job. Warren knew that his superior had already told LTV, in rather glowing terms, that the preliminary tests on the A7D brake were very successful. Indeed, Warren's superiors weren't aware at this time of the troubles on the brake. It would have been difficult for Warren to admit not only that he had made a serious error in his calculations and original design but that his mistakes had been caught by a green kid, barely out of college.

Warren's reaction to a five-disk brake was not unexpected by Lawson, and, seeing that the four-disk brake was not to be abandoned so easily, he took his calculations and dismal test results one step up the corporate ladder.

At Goodrich, the man who supervises the engineers working on projects slated for production is called, predictably, the projects manager. The job was held by a short, chubby and bald man named Robert Sink. A man truly devoted to his work, Sink was as likely to be found at his desk at ten o'clock on Sunday night as ten o'clock on Monday morning. His outside interests consisted mainly of tinkering on a Model-A Ford and an occasional game of golf. Some fifteen years before, Sink had begun working at Goodrich as a lowly draftsman. Slowly, he worked his way up. Despite his geniality, Sink was neither respected nor liked by the majority of the engineers, and his appointment as their supervisor did not improve their feelings about him. They thought he had only gone to high school. It quite naturally rankled those who had gone through years of college and acquired impressive specialties such as thermodynamics and astronautics to be commanded by a man whom they considered their intellectual inferior. But, though Sink had no college training, he had something even more useful: a fine working knowledge of company politics.

Puffing upon a Meerschaum pipe, Sink listened gravely as young Lawson confided his fears about the four-disk brake. Then he examined Lawson's calculations and the results of the abortive tests. Despite the fact that he was not a qualified engineer, in the strictest sense of the word, it must certainly have been obvious to Sink that Lawson's calculations were correct and that a four-disk brake would never have worked on the A7D.

But other things of equal importance were also obvious. First, to concede that Lawson's calculations were correct would also mean conceding that Warren's calculations were incorrect. As projects manager, he not only was responsible for Warren's activities, but, in admitting that Warren had erred, he would have to admit that he had erred in trusting Warren's judgment. It also meant that, as projects manager, it would be he who would have to explain the whole messy situation to the Goodrich hierarchy, not only at Troy but possibly on the corporate level at Goodrich's Akron offices. And, having taken Warren's judgment of the four-disk brake at face value (he was forced to do this since, not being an engineer, he was unable to exercise any engineering judgment of his own), he had assured LTV, not once but several times, that about all there was left to do on the brake was pack it in a crate and ship it out the back door.

There's really no problem at all, he told Lawson. After all, Warren was an experienced engineer, and if he said the brake would work, it would work. Just keep on testing and probably, maybe even on the very next try, it'll work out just fine.

Lawson was far from convinced, but without the support of his superiors there was little he could do except keep on testing. By now, housings for the four-disk brake had begun to arrive at the plant, and Lawson was able to build up a production model of the brake and begin the formal qualification tests demanded by the military.

The first qualification attempts went exactly as the tests on the prototype had. Terrific heat developed within the brakes and, after a few, short, simulated stops, the linings crumbled. A new type of lining material was ordered and once again an attempt to qualify the brake was made. Again, failure.

On April 11, the day the thirteenth test was completed. I became personally involved in the A7D situation.

I had worked in the Goodrich test laboratory for five years, starting first as an instrumentation engineer, then later becoming a data analyst and technical writer. As part of my duties, I analyzed the reams and reams of instrumentation data that came from the many testing machines in the laboratory, then transcribed it to a more usable form for the engineering department. And when a new-type brake had successfully completed the required qualification tests, I would issue a formal qualification report.

Qualification reports were an accumulation of all the data and test logs compiled by the test technicians during the qualification tests, and were documentary proof that a brake had met all the requirements established by the military specifications and was therefore presumed safe for flight testing. Before actual flight tests were conducted on a brake, qualification reports had to be delivered to the customer and to various government officials.

On April 11, I was looking over the data from the latest A7D test, and I noticed that many irregularities in testing methods had been noted on the test logs.

Technically, of course, there was nothing wrong with conducting tests in any manner desired, so long as the test was for research purposes only. But qualification test methods are clearly delineated by the military, and I knew that this test had been a formal qualification attempt. One particular notation on the test logs caught my eye. For some of the stops, the instrument which recorded the brake pressure had been deliberately miscalibrated so that, while the brake pressure used during the stops was recorded as 1000 psi (the maximum pressure that would be available on the A7D aircraft), the pressure had actually been 1100 psi!

I showed the test logs to the test lab supervisor, Ralph Gretzinger, who said he had learned from the technician who had miscalibrated the instrument that he had been asked to do so by Lawson. Lawson, said Gretzinger, readily admitted asking for the miscalibration, saying he had been told to do so by Sink.

I asked Gretzinger why anyone would want to miscalibrate the data-recording instruments.

"Why? I'll tell you why," he snorted. "That brake is a failure. It's way too small for the job, and they're not ever going to get it to work. They're getting desperate, and instead of scrapping the damned thing and starting over, they figure they can horse around down here in the lab and qualify it that way."

An expert engineer, Gretzinger had been responsible for several innovations in brake design. It was he who had invented the unique brake system used on the famous XB70. A graduate of Georgia Tech, he was a stickler for detail and he had some very firm ideas about honesty and ethics. "If you want to find out what's going on," said Gretzinger, "ask Lawson, he'll tell you."

Curious, I did ask Lawson the next time he came into the lab. He seemed eager to discuss the A7D and gave me the history of his months of frustrating efforts to get Warren and Sink to change the brake design. "I just can't believe this is really happening," said Lawson, shaking his head slowly. "This isn't engineering, at least not what I thought it would be. Back in school, I thought that when you were an engineer, you tried to do your best, no matter what it cost. But this is something else."

He sat across the desk from me, his chin propped in his hand. "Just wait," he warned. "You'll get a chance to see what I'm talking about. You're going to get in the act, too, because I've already had the word that we're going to make one more attempt to qualify the brake, and that's it. Win or lose, we're going to issue a qualification report!"

I reminded him that a qualification report could only be issued after a brake had successfully met all military requirements, and therefore, unless the next qualification attempt was a success, no report would be issued.

"You'll find out," retorted Lawson. "I was already told that regardless of what the brake does on test, it's going to be qualified." He said he had been told in those exact words at a conference with Sink and Russell Van Horn.

This was the first indication that Sink had brought his boss, Van Horn, into the mess. Although Van Horn, as manager of the design engineering section, was responsible for the entire department, he was not necessarily familiar with all phases of every project, and it was not uncommon for those under him to exercise the what-he-doesn't-know-won't-hurt-him philosophy. If he was aware of the full extent of the A7D situation, it meant that matters had truly reached a desperate stage—that Sink had decided not only to call for help but was looking toward that moment when blame must be borne and, if possible, shared.

Also, if Van Horn had said, "regardless what the brake does on test, it's going to be qualified," then it could only mean that, if necessary, a false qualification report would be issued! I discussed this possibility with Gretzinger, and he assured me that under no circumstances would such a report ever be issued.

"If they want a qualification report, we'll write them one, but we'll tell it just like it is," he declared emphatically. "No false data or false reports are going to come out of this lab."

On May 2, 1968, the fourteenth and final attempt to qualify the brake was begun. Although the same improper methods used to nurse the brake through the previous tests were employed, it soon became obvious that this too would end in failure.

When the tests were about half completed, Lawson asked if I would start preparing the various engineering curves and graphic displays which were normally incorporated in a qualification report. "It looks as though you'll be writing a qualification report shortly," he said.

I flatly refused to have anything to do with the matter and immediately told Gretzinger what I had been asked to do. He was furious and repeated his previous declaration that under no circumstances would any false data or other matter be issued from the lab.

"I'm going to get this settled right now, once and for all," he declared. "I'm going to see Line [Russell Line, manager of the Goodrich Technical Services Section, of which the test lab was a part] and find out just how far this thing is going to go!" He stormed out of the room.

In about an hour, he returned and called me to his desk. He sat silently for a few moments, then muttered, half to himself, "I wonder what the hell they'd do if I just quit?" I didn't answer and I didn't ask him what he meant. I knew. He had been beaten down. He had reached the point when the decision had to be made. Defy them now while there was still time—or knuckle under, sell out.

"You know," he went on uncertainly, looking down at his desk, "I've been an engineer for a long time, and I've always believed that ethics and integrity were every bit as important as theorems and formulas, and never once has anything happened to change my beliefs. Now this. . . . Hell, I've got two sons I've got to put through school and I just. . . ." His voice trailed off.

He sat for a few more minutes, then, looking over the top of his glasses, said hoarsely, "Well, it looks like we're licked. The way it stands now, we're to go ahead and prepare the data and other things for the graphic presentation in the report, and when we're finished, someone upstairs will actually write the report.

"After all," he continued, "we're just drawing some curves, and what happens to them after they leave here, well, we're not responsible for that."

He was trying to persuade himself that as long as we were concerned with only one part of the puzzle and didn't see the completed picture, we really weren't doing anything wrong. He didn't believe what he was saying, and he knew I didn't believe it either. It was an embarrassing and shameful moment for both of us.

I wasn't at all satisfied with the situation and decided that I too would discuss the matter with Russell Line, the senior executive in our section.

Tall, powerfully built, his teeth flashing white, his face tanned to a coffee-brown by a daily stint with a sun lamp, Line looked and acted every inch the executive. He was a crossword-puzzle enthusiast and an ardent golfer, and though he had lived in Troy only a short time, he had been accepted into the Troy Country Club and made an official of the golf committee. He commanded great respect and had come to be well liked by those of us who worked under him.

He listened sympathetically while I explained how I felt about the A7D situation, and when I had finished, he asked me what I wanted him to do about it. I said that as employees of the Goodrich Company we had a responsibility to protect the company and its reputation if at all possible. I said I was certain that officers on the corporate level would never knowingly allow such tactics as had been employed on the A7D.

"I agree with you," he remarked, "but I still want to know what you want me to do about it."

I suggested that in all probability the chief engineer at the Troy plant, H. C. "Bud" Sunderman, was unaware of the A7D problem and that he, Line, should tell him what was going on.

Line laughed, good-humoredly. "Sure, I could, but I'm not going to, Bud probably already knows about this thing anyway, and if he doesn't, I'm sure not going to be the one to tell him."

"But why?"

"Because it's none of my business, and it's none of yours. I learned a long time ago not to worry about things over which I had no control, I have no control over this."

I wasn't satisfied with this answer, and I asked him if his conscience wouldn't bother him if, say, during flight tests on the brake, something should happen resulting in death or injury to the test pilot.

"Look," he said, becoming somewhat exasperated, "I just told you I have no control over this thing. Why should my conscience bother me?"

His voice took on a quiet, soothing tone as he continued. "You're just getting all upset over this thing for nothing. I just do as I'm told, and I'd advise you to do the same."

He had made his decision, and now I had to make mine.

I made no attempt to rationalize what I had been asked to do. It made no difference who would falsify which part of the report or whether the actual falsification would be by misleading numbers or misleading words. Whether by acts of commission or omission, all of us who contributed to the fraud would be guilty. The only question left for me to decide was whether or not I would become a party to the fraud.

Before coming to Goodrich in 1963, I had held a variety of jobs, each a little more pleasant, a little more rewarding than the last. At forty-two, with seven children, I had decided that the Goodrich Company would probably be my "home" for the rest of my working life. The job paid well, it was pleasant and challenging, and the future looked reasonably bright. My wife and I had bought a home and we were ready to settle down into a comfortable, middle-age, middle-class rut. If I refused to take part in the A7D fraud, I would have to either resign or be fired. The report would be written by someone anyway, but I would have the satisfaction of knowing I had had no part in the matter. But bills aren't paid with personal satisfaction, nor house payments with ethical principles. I made my decision. The next morning, I telephoned Lawson and told him I was ready to begin on the qualification report.

In a few minutes, he was at my desk, ready to begin. Before we started, I asked him, "Do you realize what we are going to do?"

"Yeah," he replied bitterly, "we're going to screw LTV. And speaking of screwing," he continued, "I know now how a whore feels, because that's exactly what I've become, an engineering whore. I've sold myself. It's all I can do to look at myself in the mirror when I shave. I make me sick."

I was surprised at his vehemence. It was obvious that he too had done his share of soul-searching and didn't like what he had found. Somehow, though, the air seemed clearer after his outburst, and we began working on the report.

I had written dozens of qualification reports, and I knew what a "good" one looked like. Resorting to the actual test data only on occasion, Lawson and I proceeded to prepare page after page of elaborate, detailed engineering curves, charts, and test logs, which purported to show what had happened during the formal qualification tests. Where temperatures were too high, we deliberately chopped them down a few hundred degrees, and where they were too low, we raised them to a value that would appear reasonable to the LTV and military engineers. Brake pressure, torque values, distances, times—everything of consequence was tailored to fit the occasion.

Occasionally, we would find that some test either hadn't been performed at all or had been conducted improperly. On those occasions, we "conducted" the test—successfully, of course—on paper.

For nearly a month we worked on the graphic presentation that would be a part of the report. Meanwhile, the fourteenth and final qualification attempt had been completed, and the brake, not unexpectedly, had failed again.

During that month, Lawson and I talked of little else except the enormity of what we were doing. The more involved we became in our work, the more apparent became our own culpability. We discussed such things as the Nuremberg trials and how they related to our guilt and complicity in the A7D situation. Lawson often expressed his opinion that the brake was downright dangerous and that, once on flight tests, "anything is liable to happen."

I saw his boss, John Warren, at least twice during that month and needled him about what we were doing. He didn't take the jibes too kindly but managed to laugh the situation off as "one of those things." One day I remarked that what we were doing amounted to fraud, and he pulled out an en-

gineering handbook and turned to a section on laws as they related to the engineering profession.

He read the definition of fraud aloud, then said, "Well, technically I don't think what we're doing can be called fraud. I'll admit it's not right, but it's just one of those things. We're just kinda caught in the middle. About all I can tell you is, do like I'm doing. Make copies of everything and put them in your SYA file."

"What's an 'SYA' file?" I asked.

"That's a 'save your ass' file." He laughed.

On June 5, 1968, the report was officially published and copies were delivered in person to the Air Force and LTV. Within a week, flight tests were begun at Edwards Air Force Base in California. Searle Lawson was sent to California as Goodrich's representative. Within approximately two weeks, he returned because some rather unusual incidents during the tests had caused them to be canceled.

His face was grim as he related stories of several near crashes during landings—caused by brake troubles. He told me about one incident in which, upon landing, one brake was literally welded together by the intense heat developed during the test stop. The wheel locked, and the plane skidded for nearly 1500 feet before coming to a halt. The plane was jacked up and the wheel removed. The fused parts within the brake had to be pried apart.

Lawson had returned to Troy from California that same day, and that evening, he and others of the Goodrich engineering department left for Dallas for a high-level conference with LTV.

That evening I left work early and went to see my attorney. After I told him the story, he advised that, while I was probably not actually guilty of fraud, I was certainly part of a conspiracy to defraud. He advised me to go to the Federal Bureau of Investigation and offered to arrange an appointment. The following week he took me to the Dayton office of the FBI, and after I had been warned that I would not be immune from prosecution, I disclosed the A7D matter to one of the agents. The agent told me to say nothing about the episode to anyone and to report any further incident to him. He said he would forward the story to his superiors in Washington.

A few days later, Lawson returned from the conference in Dallas and said that the Air Force, which had previously approved the qualification report, had suddenly rescinded that approval and was demanding to see some of the raw test data taken during the tests. I gathered that the FBI had passed the word.

Finally, early in October 1968, Lawson submitted his resignation, to take effect on October 25. On October 18, I submitted my own resignation, to take effect on November 1. In my resignation, addressed to Russell Line, I cited the A7D report and stated: "As you are aware, this report contained numerous deliberate and willful misrepresentations which, according to legal counsel, constitute fraud and expose both myself and others to criminal charges of conspiracy to defraud. . . . The events of the past seven months have created an atmosphere of deceit and distrust in which it is impossible to work. . . ."

On October 25, I received a sharp summons to the office of Bud Sunderman. As chief engineer at the Troy plant, Sunderman was responsible for the entire engineering division. Tall and graying, impeccably dressed at all times, he was capable of producing a dazzling smile or a hearty chuckle or immobilizing his face into marble hardness, as the occasion required.

I faced the marble hardness when I reached his office. He motioned me to a chair. "I have your resignation here," he snapped, "and I must say you have made some rather shocking, I might even say irresponsible, charges. This is very serious."

Before I could reply, he was demanding an explanation. "I want to know exactly what the fraud is in connection with the A7D and how you can dare accuse this company of such a thing!"

I started to tell some of the things that had happened during the testing. but he shut me off saying, "There's nothing wrong with anything we've done here. You aren't aware of all the things that have been going on behind the scenes. If you had known the true situation, you would never have made these charges." He said that in view of my apparent "disloyalty" he had decided to accept my resignation "right now," and said it would be better for all concerned if I left the plant immediately.

As I got up to leave he asked me if I intended to "carry this thing further."

I answered simply, "Yes," to which he replied, "Suit yourself." Within twenty minutes, I had cleaned out my desk and left. Forty-eight hours later, the B. F. Goodrich Company recalled the qualification report and the four-disk brake, announcing that it would replace the brake with a new, improved, five-disk brake at no cost to LTV.

Ten months later, on August 13, 1969, I was the chief government witness at a hearing conducted before Senator William Proxmire's Economy in Government Subcommittee of the Congress's Joint Economic Committee. I related the A7D story to the committee, and my testimony was supported by Searle Lawson, who followed me to the witness stand. Air Force officers also testified, as well as a four-man team from the General Accounting Office, which had conducted an investigation of the A7D brake at the request of Senator Proxmire. Both Air Force and GAO investigators declared that the brake was dangerous and had not been tested properly.

Testifying for Goodrich was R. G. Jeter, vice-president and general counsel of the company, from the Akron headquarters. Representing the Troy plant was Robert Sink. These two denied any wrongdoing on the part of the Goodrich Company, despite expert testimony to the contrary by Air Force and GAO officials. Sink was quick to deny any connection with the writing of the report or of directing any falsifications, claiming to be on the West Coast at the time. John Warren was the man who supervised its writing, said Sink.

As for me, I was dismissed as a high-school graduate with no technical training, while Sink testified that Lawson was a young, inexperienced engineer. "We tried to give him guidance," Sink testified, "but he preferred to have his own convictions."

About changing the data and figures in the report. Sink said: "When you take data from several different sources, you have to rationalize among those data what is the true story. This is part of your engineering know-how." He admitted that changes had been made in the data, "but only to make them more consistent with the overall picture of the data that is available."

Jeter pooh-poohed the suggestion that anything improper occurred, saying "We have thirty-odd engineers at this plant . . . and I say to you that it is incredible that these men would stand idly by and see reports changed or falsified. . . . I mean you just do not have to do that working for anybody. . . . Just nobody does that."

The four-hour hearing adjourned with no real conclusion reached by the committee. But, the following day the Department of Defense made sweeping changes in its inspection, testing and reporting procedures. A spokesman for the DOD said the changes were a result of the Goodrich episode.

The A7D is now in service, sporting a Goodrich-made five-disk brake, a brake that works very well, I'm told. Business at the Goodrich plant is good. Lawson is now an engineer for LTV and has been assigned to the A7D project. And I am now a newspaper reporter.

At this writing, those remaining at Goodrich are still secure in the same positions, all except Russell Line and Robert Sink. Line has been rewarded with a promotion to production superintendent, a large step upward on the corporate ladder. As for Sink, he moved up into Line's old job.

Less Cost, More Risk

Michael Kinsley

Editor, *Slate*, an interactive magazine published by Microsoft

The Federal Aviation Administration disclosed last week that ValuJet has applied to resume flying. You can be pretty sure the FAA is not going to approve this application casually. Regulators shut down the discount airline after the May 11 crash in Florida that killed 110 people. The past

two months have seen a festival of recriminations about sloppy practices at both ValuJet and the FAA. A *Washington Post* editorial declared, "The public needs evidence that the government is insisting on the highest safety standards possible."

A seemingly unobjectionable sentiment—but there are two problems with it. The first is that the highest safety standards possible are too high. You can always make flying—or any other economic activity—safer by making it more expensive (increasing the minimum distance between aircraft, or the time between takeoffs, requiring wider aisles and so on). The inevitable trade-off between safety and cost, plus the law of diminishing returns, dictates that you stop well short of the highest possible standards.

Second, there is no reason every airline should meet the same level of safety. In fact, it makes perfect sense for discount airlines to be less safe than traditional full-price carriers. This is no excuse for negligence and rule breaking. But if the rules don't recognize that some people, quite rationally, will wish to buy less safety for less money, they are doing the flying public a disservice.

Try some rough math on the back of an envelope. According to Transportation Secretary Federico Peña, discount airlines have lowered ticket prices, on routes where they compete, by an average of $54 (or $70 to or from an airline "hub"). The standard statistic on airline safety is that you could fly once a day, every day, for 21,000 years before dying in an airplane crash. So suppose that flying discount made it 10 times more likely that you would die in a crash. Now the odds on a fatal crash are 1 in 2,100 years. Is it worth it—just to save $54? Well, by my calculation (checked with folks whose grounding in mathematics is sturdier and more recent), you're increasing your chance of a fatal crash by about 1 in 855,000. Looked at the other way, paying the extra $54 to avoid the added risk (and leaving aside other advantages of grownup airlines, such as the delicious meals, roomy seats, punctual departures, onboard golf courses, etc.) puts an implicit value on your life of about $46 million.

Now, you may think your life is worth $46 million, but unless you've got $46 million to spend on it, that's a hollow boast. Every day you make decisions—probably including the decision to step outside your house and risk being torn apart by hounds as you pick up the morning paper (you could, after all, hire someone to bring the paper inside for you every day, just to be safe)—that implicitly value your own life at less than $46 million. Of course Freedom of Neuroses is one of the basic American liberties we celebrated last week on Independence Day, and people should be free to spend $54 to avoid a 1-in-855,000 risk if they so desire. But society should not force them to do so. And society, in setting its rules, cannot possibly value each person's life at $46 million without grinding to a halt.

In recent years the FAA has been struggling with the question of whether to require small children to fly in safety seats. The rule has long been that kids less than two years old may sit in a parent's lap—and therefore, usually, fly for free. Flight attendants and other supporters of safety seats make a good argument that it's a bit odd for the government to require that coffee pots, and adults, be strapped down, but not little children. An FAA-commissioned study, however, determined that requiring safety seats would actually cost lives. How? By leading families to drive instead of fly. The study figured that ending the small-children-fly-free policy would raise the average fare for affected families by $185, causing one-fifth of them to use a car instead. Whereas the safety seats would save an average of one child's life per decade, the extra driving (far more dangerous than flying) would cost nine lives. Or so the study figured. Critics objected to the calculations, but the principle of thinking about safety in this way survives any quibbling about the numbers.

You could think about the discount-airline question the same way. Discounters carried some 47 million passengers last year. What fraction of that number chose to fly instead of drive because of the cheap fare, and how many of those would have died in traffic accidents if they'd driven? Even in the trade-off of lives for lives, let alone the less appealing trade-off of lives for dollars, making airlines too safe may be a bad deal.

The discount airlines deny vehemently that they are less safe than the majors, and the statistics show no clear connection between price and safety. But if there isn't a connection, that's too bad. Flying at a discount should be more dangerous. Otherwise, you're overpaying.

THE NATURE OF THE CORPORATION

In Part One we examined the ethical dimensions of the economic system in which business operates. Here, we turn attention to the nature and role of the corporation within that system. Reflection on the nature of the corporation is important, in part because our understanding of the corporation shapes our beliefs about the corporation's responsibilities. If we hold that a corporation is a privately owned enterprise designed to make a profit, for example, we are likely to have a narrower view of corporate responsibility than if we hold it to be a quasi-public institution. Chapter 3 begins to explore the debate by asking the initial question regarding the agency and legitimacy of the corporate entity. From there, the problem of the nature of the corporation is approached from the perspective of the corporate social responsibility debate.

Finally, we investigate the nature of the corporation from the perspective of its internal structure and governance. In the first three articles in Chapter 4, we focus on the corporate board of directors. Who should sit on the board? What is and what should be the relationship among the board, management, and stockholders? How far should the board's power extend? In the final article in Chapter 4, we investigate the use of the U.S. Federal Sentencing Guidelines as a means to encourage corporate self-regulation.

THE CORPORATE SOCIAL RESPONSIBILITY DEBATE

Before discussing the corporate social responsibility debate, it is important to clarify the meaning of two concepts that are often confused: "business ethics" and "corporate social responsibility." Some use the concepts interchangeably, while others believe that they are distinct. In some cases, business ethics is considered part of corporate social responsibility, whereas in other cases corporate social responsibility is thought to be just one aspect of business ethics. For the purpose of this text, the latter approach is taken. Business ethics, as the study of the relationship of what is good and right for business, also examines the specific issue of corporate social responsibility, that is, the proper role or obligations of corporations within society.

Now before discussing whether corporations have social responsibilities and what these might be, one might ask a more fundamental question regarding the nature of corporations. Are corporations capable of having responsibilities at all? Normally we associate moral responsibility with individual persons. But corporations are not individual persons. They are collections of individuals who work together to establish corporate policy, make corporate decisions, and execute corporate actions. Can such collections of individuals be morally responsible?

For example, what does it mean to say that the Ford Motor Company or Levi Strauss is responsible for a particular action? Who is to blame for an immoral corporate action? Does it make sense to look at the corporation as a moral agent, analogous to a person? And if not, does this mean that we cannot judge corporate actions according to ethical standards?

Kenneth Goodpaster and John Matthews in their article "Can a Corporation Have a Conscience?" argue that there is an analogy between individual and organizational behavior, and that for this reason corporate conduct can be evaluated in moral terms. Some thinkers have claimed that only persons are capable of moral responsibility in the full sense, because such responsibility presupposes the ability to reason, to have intentions, and to make autonomous choices. But although the corporation is not a person in a literal sense, Goodpaster and Matthews respond, it is made up of persons. For this reason, we can project many of the attributes of individual human beings to the corporate level. We already speak of corporations having goals, values, interests, strategies. Why, ask Goodpaster and Matthews, shouldn't we also speak of the corporate conscience?

Thinkers who assume that corporations cannot exercise moral responsibility advocate trust in the "invisible hand" of the market system to "moralize" the actions of corporations. Others feel that the "hand of government" is required to ensure moral corporate behavior. Both of these views, however, fail to locate the source of responsible corporate action in the corporation itself. Both rely upon systems and forces external to the corporation. Goodpaster and Matthews argue for a third alternative: endowing the corporation with a conscience analogous to that of an individual, recognizing the ability of corporations to exercise independent moral judgment, and locating the responsibility for corporate behavior in the hands of corporate managers. This "hand of management" alternative, they admit, is not without its problems—and it requires more thorough analysis on both the conceptual and practical levels. But Goodpaster and Matthews believe that it is the best alternative because it provides a framework for an inventory of corporate responsibilities and accepts corporations as legitimate members of the moral community.

Presuming that corporations are capable of being morally responsible, what should the extent of those responsibilities be? Traditionally it has been held that the major responsibility of business in American society is to produce goods and services and to sell them for a profit. This conception of business' role has been one of the cornerstones of its legitimacy—of society's belief in the right of business to exist. Recently, however, the traditional view has been questioned. Increasingly, business is being asked not only to refrain from harming society, but to contribute actively and directly to public well-being. Business firms are expected not only to obey a multitude of legal requirements, but also to go beyond the demands of the law and exercise moral judgment in making decisions. What are the reasons for this changing conception of corporate social responsibility?

In the context of the traditional view, businesses are understood as private property, instruments of their owners designed primarily to make money. Because the pressure of an "invisible hand" ensures that each entrepreneur's pursuit of his or her own profit will result in the good of the whole, and because businesses are the property of their owners to do with as they please, business has no other responsibility than to perform efficiently its economic function. As economist Milton Friedman, one of the most forceful exponents of the traditional ideology, puts it, "the social responsibility of business is to increase its profits."

Why has the old view begun to erode and a new one begun to take its place? One answer is that today's giant corporations no longer seem to fit the old model. Usually we associate ownership with control, but the modern corporation is owned by stockholders who have little or no psychological or operational involvement in it. Some thinkers have argued that corporations can no longer accurately be viewed as private property. As ownership separates from control, corporations seem less like instruments of their owners and more like autonomous entities capable of their own goals and decisions.

The tremendous impact on and power over our society exerted by corporations also cast doubt on their private character. Many thinkers argue that social power inevitably implies social responsibility, and they suggest that those who fail to exercise a responsibility commensurate with their power should lose that power. As the power of business has grown, we have become increasingly aware of the external costs—pollution, hazardous products, job dissatisfaction—corporations have passed on to society at large. These costs in turn call into question a basic assumption of the old view: the identity of individual and social well-being.

The corporation's evolution away from the kind of enterprise described in the traditional view leaves us with at least two alternatives. We can explicitly acknowledge the new idea that corporations have extensive social responsibilities, or we can attempt to make reality fit the old view once again. Some, such as Edward Freeman, take the first option, arguing that corporations are no longer merely economic institutions, but sociological institutions as well. Milton Friedman opts for the second alternative.

Friedman holds fast to the traditional values of a free market system and rejects the idea of corporate social responsibility because he feels it is "fundamentally subversive" of these values. For Friedman, the sole social responsibility of business is to increase its profits while staying within the legal and moral "rules of the game."

It is important to realize that Friedman is not claiming that the corporation has no responsibilities or obligations. Rather, he is arguing that corporations are directly responsible only to one set of people—their stockholders. Regardless of the actual relationship between ownership and control in the modern corporation, Friedman believes they ought not to be separate. Because the stockholders own the corporation and hire managers to run it for them, Friedman argues, managers are "fiduciaries" of the stockholders. They have an obligation to act in the best interests of the stockholders, which means, according to Friedman, that they should maximize profit. To demand that corporate managers exercise responsibility to society at large is to ask them to violate their obligations to stockholders.

Managers who assume "social responsibility," Friedman argues, are actually using stockholders' money to solve social problems without their permission. They are in effect "taxing" stockholders, but because they are private employees rather than publicly elected officials, their actions lack authority and legitimacy. Behind Friedman's arguments lies a conviction that each social institution exists to perform a particular function. The legitimacy of corporate activity depends on executives confining themselves to the role of agents serving the interests of those who own stock in the corporation. "Social re-sponsibility" is the job of government, not business.

In contrast to Friedman's view that the modern corporation should be managed solely for the benefit of stockholders, in "Stakeholder Theory of the Modern Corpora-tion," Edward Freeman argues that the corporation should be managed for the benefit of stakeholders, which are those groups and individuals who benefit from or are harmed by, and whose rights are violated or respected by, corporate actions. After dis-cussing several stakeholder groups, including owners, employees, suppliers, customers, and the local community, Freeman goes on to suggest that the ethical challenge for management is to meet the claims made by each of these groups. Sometimes one of these groups may benefit at the expense of others, but management's job is to keep the balance between them as best it can, coordinating and maximizing their joint interests. Freeman concludes by outlining a set of ground rules or principles to govern corporate relations with stakeholders.

As Freeman is careful to point out, his proposal essentially redefines the purpose of the corporation. Some possible difficulties with this redefinition are explored by George Brenkert in his article "Private Corporations and Public Welfare." Brenkert considers an objection to the idea that corporations have social responsibility. The objection is that re-quiring corporations to engage in creating public welfare involves illegitimate interfer-ence by private organizations into public interests. He notes that corporations may be in-flexible and insensitive to real community needs, that the programs of social responsibility they develop may be ill conceived or even harmful, and that corporations may deal paternalistically with stakeholders who have no real voice in corporate deci-sions. Given the potential for harm that corporate social programs have, Brenkert consid-ers whether large corporations should be made more fully public, in effect converting them into public instruments of social policy. He points out that this is something op-posed by many, and thus that we remain at a crossroads between one view of corpora-tions as a private competitive enterprise and another view of corporations as quasi-public institutions. He concludes that if one rejects the idea that corporations should become more fully public institutions, then one should also reject the idea that corporations have responsibilities for public welfare.

In the final article in Chapter 3, Norman Bowie takes a more balanced view, namely that corporations should pursue profit while respecting a moral minimum below which it is unacceptable to operate. Part of what it means to be a corporation is to cooperate with other corporations and government agencies to help solve social problems.

Bowie's basic argument is that profit should not be the goal of the firm; rather, profit is a byproduct of other goals, such as providing meaningful work for employees. By act-ing altruistically, he believes, corporations can create a "moral community" in which the moral commitments between the corporation and its various stakeholders are reciprocal—just as the corporation is committed to treat all stakeholders fairly, so stakeholders are committed to the welfare of the corporation.

If we accept Bowie's argument that profit should be a byproduct of other corporate goals, and that ethical relations between the corporation and its stakeholders impose du-ties on each of them, then we must abandon the traditional idea of the corporation as purely economic institution. Corporations, on this view, are as much instruments of social policy and change as they are centers for producing and distributing economic goods. If this is the future of the corporation, or if it ought to be, then ethics and the implications of ethics for corporate actions will play as central a role in business in the years to come as profit has played in the past.

CORPORATE ACCOUNTABILITY AND THE BOARD OF DIRECTORS

Central to the issue of corporate agency, legitimacy, and responsibility taken up in Chapter 3 is the issue of corporate accountability. To whom ought corporations be accountable? How can such accountability be implemented? The first three articles in Chapter 4 look not to regulations imposed on the corporation from outside, but on the corporate internal structure itself for answers to these questions. Because historically the board of directors has been an important locus of corporate accountability and because suggestions for changes in the role, election, and staffing of boards have been at the heart of several important proposals for reform, it is appropriate that they focus their attention on the nature, role, and composition of corporate boards.

Traditionally, corporate governance has been conceived on a rough analogy with the American political system. As the owners of the corporation, stockholders elect representatives—the board of directors—to establish broad objectives and direct corporate activities. The directors in turn select corporate officers to execute their policies. Management is thus accountable to the board of directors, and the board to stockholders.

But it is increasingly unclear that this picture represents the reality of corporate governance. Such writers as Ralph Nader, Mark Green, and Joel Seligman hold that management really controls the election of board members through its power over the machinery of proxy voting. The board, they claim, does not provide a check on the power of management; it does not really make policies or select executive officers, but routinely rubberstamps the decisions of management.

Furthermore, as a 1978 press release from the Senate Committee on Governmental Affairs indicates, corporate boards are so tightly interlocked that what power they do have is concentrated in the hands of a small elite. The overwhelming potential for conflicts of interest further impedes the ability of boards to check management power.

Nader, Green, and Seligman see an urgent need for a truly effective board that will make accountable the unbridled power of management. Their suggestions for achieving this goal include a revamping of the shareholder electoral system; the institutionalizing of a new profession, that of the professional director who devotes full time to supervising the activities of the corporation; and the prohibition of interlocking directorates.

Still other issues of corporate governance are raised by the vast power of the corporation in modern society. The traditional model of corporate governance assumes that the most important constituency of the corporation is its stockholders, and that it is primarily to stockholders that the corporation ought to be accountable. But perhaps this is not so. The view that the crucial form of corporate accountability is accountability to stockholders is based on the assumption that the corporation is a piece of private property; the stockholders are the owners of the corporation and therefore the corporation is answerable only to them. But we have already noted that this assumption has been challenged. Brenkert pointed out that social responsibility seems to require that the corporation not be thought of as private, but as a public institution. If this is true, presumably there ought to be some way to represent all relevant constituencies of the corporation in its internal structure. Milton Friedman has argued that to ask corporations to exercise "social" power is to make them into miniature governments; but Nader, Green, and Seligman claim that corporations do in fact exert such power and that they are governments in a sense for this reason. To ask corporations to be accountable only to stockholders is to permit governments to exist without the consent of the governed, an idea that is fundamentally at odds with the political philosophy of the United States. The election of "public interest directors," each of whom is placed in charge of overseeing such areas as consumer protection, employee welfare, and stockholder rights, may be one way to ensure corporate accountability to those whom it affects. And Nader, Green, and Seligman propose that the board should be made up only of "outside" directors—persons who have no other relationship to the corporation.

The interpretation of the corporation as a public institution is precisely what Irving Shapiro objects to in his essay on corporate governance. Corporations are not analogous to governments, he argues. They are private enterprises formed to execute the essential task of providing goods and services—a task, Shapiro suggests, government could not perform efficiently. The corporation has an important external locus of accountability government does not: the competition engendered by the free market system. For these reasons Shapiro defends the rationale behind the present system of corporate governance. He does not believe that a radical overhaul is required.

Shapiro does not look favorably on proposals that the board contain more "outside" directors representative of various interest groups. Although independence of judgment is crucial in a corporate director, he fears that outside directors may lack the depth of understanding of an industry's problems necessary for informed decision making. Such directors might find themselves dependent on the explanations of the chief executive officer, and thus unable to exert adequate control over management activities. And although the presence of public interest directors on the board could generate a healthy tension, it might also lead to conflicts of interest and to paralysis. A clear division of labor between boards of directors and management and a conscientious execution of their respective tasks, Shapiro concludes, are all that is necessary to produce an effective system of corporate governance that ensures accountability.

In "Who Should Control the Corporation?" Henry Mintzberg hopes to clarify the debate about who should control the corporation. He argues that the answer we eventually accept will determine what kind of society we and our children will live in. He identifies a number of different possibilities for controlling the corporation, such as nationalize it, regulate it, trust it, and ignore it. He considers the implications of the various alternatives, and concludes that the one thing we cannot do is hope for the best and ignore the power and influence of corporations. They are much too influential a force in our lives. The challenge, he concludes, is to find ways to direct and channel the power of corporations in ways that ensure that they remain responsive to our interests.

One way in which the United States government has tried to channel that power toward being responsive is through the enactment of the U.S. Federal Sentencing Guidelines in 1991. In the final article in Chapter 4 entitled "What Can We Learn From the U.S. Federal Sentencing Guidelines for Organizational Ethics?" Mark Schwartz, Dove Izraeli, and Joseph Murphy examine the U.S. Federal Sentencing Guidelines for Organizations. Essentially, the Guidelines use a "carrot and stick" approach to create incentives for corporate self-regulation. The Guidelines consist of a manual for judges to apply when determining the appropriate sentence for corporations convicted of a federal crime.

According to the Guidelines, judges are required to consider whether the convicted corporation had established an "effective compliance program" prior to the violation taking place, in other words, whether the corporation had taken appropriate steps to prevent and detect violations of the law. The authors explore the impact the Guidelines have had on corporate America and their effectiveness as a means of self-regulation. They also consider whether the Guidelines can be used as a model or framework by other countries. They conclude that despite the limitations of the Guidelines, they could potentially serve as a useful model for other jurisdictions to follow.

MINI-CASES AND CASES IN PART TWO

The two mini-cases in Part Two, "Stuart Howser" and "Deborah Wilson," focus on the social responsibilities of corporations. The articles on agency, legitimacy, and responsibility in Chapter 3 can be used as background for resolving the dilemmas faced by Stuart and Deborah.

We also include in Part Two a number of cases related to the nature of a corporation. In "Not a Fool, Not a Saint," the case of Aaron Feuerstein, CEO of Malden Mills, is discussed. Mr. Feuerstein made several significant decisions following the near complete destruction of his textile firm's factories caused by a fire. One of those decisions was to rebuild his factories in the same location as opposed to relocating where labor costs were cheaper. He also decided to continue paying his employees their wages despite no legal obligation to do so. The article asks, "Were these in fact socially responsible decisions? Or were they simply good business decisions?" In "Tennessee Coal & Iron," the division of United States Steel Corporation must address social responsibility issues such as its obligations related to improving racial integration as well as its obligations to the community. The case represents the classic tension facing companies in deciding between their obligations to their stockholders and those of other stakeholders. How broad should corporate obligations be? These two cases provide a practical context for discussing the social responsibility articles by Goodpaster and Matthews, Friedman, Freeman, Brenkert, and Bowie. In the "Report of the Compensation Committee of the Board of Directors" from General Electric Company, the issue is raised of what exactly is appropriate executive compensation. Finally, in "Words of Warning: Ruling Makes Directors Accountable for Compliance," boards of directors are put on notice as to their potential personal legal liability for ensuring their companies have effective compliance programs in place following the legal case *Caremark International.* The judge's decision in the case involves a direct consideration of the U.S. Federal Sentencing Guidelines, as discussed in the article "What Can We Learn From the U.S. Federal Sentencing Guidelines for Organizational Ethics?" by Schwartz, Izraeli, and Murphy.

CHAPTER 3

Agency, Legitimacy, and Responsibility

Can a Corporation Have a Conscience?

Kenneth E. Goodpaster
Professor and Koch Endowed Chair in Business Ethics,
The University of St. Thomas

John B. Matthews, Jr.
Former Wilson Professor of Business Administration, Emeritus,
Harvard University

During the severe racial tensions of the 1960s, Southern Steel Company (actual case, disguised name) faced considerable pressure from government and the press to explain and modify its policies regarding discrimination both within its plants and in the major city where it was located. SSC was the largest employer in the area (it had nearly 15,000 workers, one-third of whom were black) and had made great strides toward removing barriers to equal job opportunity in its several plants. In addition, its top executives (especially

its chief executive officer, James Weston) had distinguished themselves as private citizens for years in community programs for black housing, education, and small business as well as in attempts at desegregating all-white police and local government organizations.

SSC drew the line, however, at using its substantial economic influence in the local area to advance the cause of the civil rights movement by pressuring banks, suppliers, and the local government:

> As individuals we can exercise what influence we may have as citizens," James Weston said, "but for a corporation to attempt to exert any kind of economic compulsion to achieve a particular end in a social area seems to me to be quite beyond what a corporation should do and quite beyond what a corporation can do. I believe that while government may seek to compel social reforms, any attempt by a private organization like SSC to impose its views, its beliefs, and its will upon the community would be repugnant to our American constitutional concepts and that appropriate steps to correct this abuse of corporate power would be universally demanded by public opinion.

Weston could have been speaking in the early 1980s on any issue that corporations around the United States now face. Instead of social justice, his theme might be environmental protection, product safety, marketing practice, or international bribery. His statement for SSC raises the important issue of corporate responsibility. Can a corporation have a conscience?

Weston apparently felt comfortable saying it need not. The responsibilities of ordinary persons and of "artificial persons" like corporations are, in his view, separate. Persons' responsibilities go beyond those of corporations. Persons, he seems to have believed, ought to care not only about themselves but also about the dignity and well-being of those around them—ought not only to care but also to act. Organizations, he evidently thought, are creatures of, and to a degree prisoners of, the systems of economic incentive and political sanction that give them reality and therefore should not be expected to display the same moral attributes that we expect of persons.

Others inside business as well as outside share Weston's perception. One influential philosopher—John Ladd—carries Weston's view a step further:

"It is improper to expect organizational conduct to conform to the ordinary principles of morality," he says. "We cannot and must not expect formal organizations, or their representatives acting in their official capacities, to be honest, courageous, considerate, sympathetic, or to have any kind of moral integrity. Such concepts are not in the vocabulary, so to speak, of the organizational language game."[1]

In our opinion, this line of thought represents a tremendous barrier to the development of business ethics both as a field of inquiry and as a practical force in managerial decision making. This is a matter about which executives must be philosophical and philosophers must be practical. A corporation can and should have a conscience. The language of ethics does have a place in the vocabulary of an organization. There need not be and there should not be a disjunction of the sort attributed to SSC's James Weston. Organizational agents such as corporations should be no more and no less morally responsible (rational, self-interested, altruistic) than ordinary persons.

We take this position because we think an analogy holds between the individual and the corporation. If we analyze the concept of moral responsibility as it applies to persons, we find that projecting it to corporations as agents in society is possible.

DEFINING THE RESPONSIBILITY OF PERSONS

When we speak of the responsibility of individuals, philosophers say that we mean three things: someone is to blame, something has to be done, or some kind of trustworthiness can be expected.

We apply the first meaning, what we shall call the *causal* sense, primarily to legal and moral contexts where what is at issue is praise or blame for a past action. We say of a person that he or she was responsible for what happened, is to blame for it, should be held accountable. In this sense of the word, *responsibility* has to do with tracing the causes of actions and events, of finding out who is answerable in a given situation. Our aim is to determine someone's intention, free will, degree of participation, and appropriate reward or punishment.

We apply the second meaning of *responsibility* to rule following, to contexts where individuals are subject to externally imposed norms often associated with some social role that people play. We speak of the responsibilities of parents to children, of doctors to patients, of lawyers to clients, of citizens to the law. What is socially expected and what the party involved is to answer for are at issue here.

We use the third meaning of *responsibility* for decision making. With this meaning of the term, we say that individuals are responsible if they are trustworthy and reliable, if they allow appropriate factors to affect their judgment; we refer primarily to a person's independent thought processes and decision making, processes that justify an attitude of trust from those who interact with him or her as a responsible individual.

The distinguishing characteristic of moral responsibility, it seems to us, lies in this third sense of the term. Here the focus is on the intellectual and emotional processes in the individual's moral reasoning. Philosophers call this "taking a moral point of view" and contrast it with such other processes as being financially prudent and attending to legal obligations.

To be sure, characterizing a person as "morally responsible" may seem rather vague. But vagueness is a contextual notion. Everything depends on how we fill in the blank in "vague for _____ purposes."

In some contexts the term "six o'clockish" is vague, while in others it is useful and informative. As a response to a space-shuttle pilot who wants to know when to fire the reentry rockets, it will not do, but it might do in response to a spouse who wants to know when one will arrive home at the end of the workday.

We maintain that the processes underlying moral responsibility can be defined and are not themselves vague, even though gaining consensus on specific moral norms and decisions is not always easy.

What, then, characterizes the processes underlying the judgment of a person we call morally responsible? Philosopher William K. Frankena offers the following answer:

"A morality is a normative system in which judgments are made, more or less consciously, [out of a] consideration of the effects of actions . . . on the lives of persons . . . including the lives of others besides the person acting. . . . David Hume took a similar position when he argued that what speaks in a moral judgment is a kind of sympathy. . . . A little later, . . . Kant put the matter somewhat better by characterizing morality as the business of respecting persons as ends and not as means or as things. . . ."[2]

Frankena is pointing to two traits, both rooted in a long and diverse philosophical tradition:

1. *Rationality.* Taking a moral point of view includes the features we usually attribute to rational decision making, that is, lack of impulsiveness, care in mapping out alternatives and consequences, clarity about goals and purposes, attention to details of implementation.
2. *Respect.* The moral point of view also includes a special awareness of and concern for the effects of one's decisions and policies on others, special in the sense that it goes beyond the kind of awareness and concern that would ordinarily be part of rationality, that is, beyond seeing others merely as instrumental to accomplishing one's own purposes. This is respect for the lives of others and involves taking their needs and interests seriously, not simply as resources in one's own decision making but as limiting conditions which change the very definition of

one's habitat from a self-centered to a shared environment. It is what philosopher Immanuel Kant meant by the "categorical imperative" to treat others as valuable in and for themselves.

It is this feature that permits us to trust the morally responsible person. We know that such a person takes our point of view into account not merely as a useful precaution (as in "honesty is the best policy") but as important in its own right.

These components of moral responsibility are not too vague to be useful. Rationality and respect affect the manner in which a person approaches practical decision making: they affect the way in which the individual processes information and makes choices. A rational but not respectful Bill Jones will not lie to his friends *unless* he is reasonably sure he will not be found out. A rational but not respectful Mary Smith will defend an unjustly treated party *unless* she thinks it may be too costly to herself. A rational *and* respectful decision maker, however, notices—and cares—whether the consequences of his or her conduct lead to injuries or indignities to others.

Two individuals who take "the moral point of view" will not of course always agree on ethical matters, but they do at least have a basis for dialogue.

PROJECTING RESPONSIBILITY TO CORPORATIONS

Now that we have removed some of the vagueness from the notion of moral responsibility as it applies to persons, we can search for a frame of reference in which, by analogy with Bill Jones and Mary Smith, we can meaningfully and appropriately say that corporations are morally responsible. This is the issue reflected in the SSC case.

To deal with it, we must ask two questions: Is it meaningful to apply moral concepts to actors who are not persons but who are instead made up of persons? And even if meaningful, is it advisable to do so?

If a group can act like a person in some ways, then we can expect it to behave like a person in other ways. For one thing, we know that people organized into a group can act as a unit. As business people well know, legally a corporation is considered a unit. To approach unity, a group usually has some sort of internal decision structure, a system of rules that spell out authority relationships and specify the conditions under which certain individuals' actions become official actions of the group.[3]

If we can say that persons act responsibly only if they gather information about the impact of their actions on others and use it in making decisions, we can reasonably do the same for organizations. Our proposed frame of reference for thinking about and implementing corporate responsibility aims at spelling out the processes associated with the moral responsibility of individuals and projecting them to the level of organizations. This is similar to, though an inversion of, Plato's famous method in the *Republic,* in which justice in the community is used as a model for justice in the individual.

Hence, corporations that monitor their employment practices and the effects of their production processes and products on the environment and human health show the same kind of rationality and respect that morally responsible individuals do. Thus, attributing actions, strategies, decisions, and moral responsibilities to corporations as entities distinguishable from those who hold offices in them poses no problem.

And when we look about us, we can readily see differences in moral responsibility among corporations in much the same way that we see differences among persons. Some corporations have built features into their management incentive systems, board structures, internal control systems, and research agendas that in a person we would call self-control, integrity, and conscientiousness. Some have institutionalized awareness and concern for consumers, employees, and the rest of the public in ways that others clearly have not.

As a matter of course, some corporations attend to the human impact of their operations and policies and reject operations and policies that are questionable. Whether the issue be the health effects of sugared cereal or cigarettes, the safety of tires or tampons, civil liberties in the corporation or the community, an organization reveals its character as surely as a person does.

Indeed, the parallel may be even more dramatic. For just as the moral responsibility displayed by an individual develops over time from infancy to adulthood,[4] so too we may expect to find stages of development in organizational character that show significant patterns.

EVALUATING THE IDEA OF MORAL PROJECTION

Concepts like moral responsibility not only make sense when applied to organizations but also provide touchstones for designing more effective models than we have for guiding corporate policy.

Now we can understand what it means to invite SSC as a corporation to be morally responsible both in-house and in its community, but *should* we issue the invitation? Here we turn to the question of advisability. Should we require the organizational agents in our society to have the same moral attributes we require of ourselves?

Our proposal to spell out the processes associated with moral responsibility for individuals and then to project them to their organizational counterparts takes on added meaning when we examine alternative frames of reference for corporate responsibility.

Two frames of reference that compete for the allegiance of people who ponder the question of corporate responsibility are emphatically opposed to this principle of moral projection—what we might refer to as the "invisible hand" view and the "hand of government" view.

The Invisible Hand

The most eloquent spokesman of the first view is Milton Friedman (echoing many philosophers and economists since Adam Smith). According to this pattern of thought, the true and only social responsibilities of business organizations are to make profits and obey the laws. The workings of the free and competitive marketplace will "moralize" corporate behavior quite independently of any attempts to expand or transform decision making via moral projection.

A deliberate amorality in the executive suite is encouraged in the name of systemic morality: the common good is best served when each of us and our economic institutions pursue not the common good or moral purpose, advocates say, but competitive advantage. Morality, responsibility, and conscience reside in the invisible hand of the free market system, not in the hands of the organizations within the system, much less the managers within the organizations.

To be sure, people of this opinion admit, there is a sense in which social or ethical issues can and should enter the corporate mind, but the filtering of such issues is thorough: they go through the screens of custom, public opinion, public relations, and the law. And, in any case, self-interest maintains primacy as an objective and a guiding star.

The reaction from this frame of reference to the suggestion that moral judgment be integrated with corporate strategy is clearly negative. Such an integration is seen as inefficient and arrogant, and in the end both an illegitimate use of corporate power and an abuse of the manager's fiduciary role. With respect to our SSC case, advocates of the invisible hand model would vigorously resist efforts, beyond legal requirements, to make SSC right the wrongs of racial injustice. SSC's responsibility would be to make steel of high quality at least cost, to deliver it on time, and to satisfy its customers and stockholders. Justice would not be part of SSC's corporate mandate.

The Hand of Government

Advocates of the second dissenting frame of reference abound, but John Kenneth Galbraith's work has counterpointed Milton Friedman's with insight and style. Under this view of corporate responsibility, corporations are to pursue objectives that are rational and purely economic. The regulatory hands of the law and the political process rather than the invisible hand of the marketplace turns these objectives to the common good.

Again, in this view, it is a system that provides the moral direction for corporate decision making—a system, though, that is guided by political managers, the custodians of the public purpose. In the case of SSC, proponents of this view would look to the state for moral direction and responsible management, both within SSC and in the community. The corporation would have no moral responsibility beyond political and legal obedience.

What is striking is not so much the radical difference between the economic and social philosophies that underlie these two views of the source of corporate responsibility but the conceptual similarities. Both views locate morality, ethics, responsibility, and conscience in the systems of rules and incentives in which the modern corporation finds itself embedded. Both views reject the exercise of independent moral judgment by corporations as actors in society.

Neither view trusts corporate leaders with stewardship over what are often called noneconomic values. Both require corporate responsibility to march to the beat of drums outside. In the jargon of moral philosophy, both views press for a rule-centered or a system-centered ethics instead of an agent-centered ethics. These frames of reference countenance corporate rule-following responsibility for corporations but not corporate decision-making responsibility.

The Hand of Management

To be sure, the two views under discussion differ in that one looks to an invisible moral force in the market while the other looks to a visible moral force in government. But both would advise against a principle of moral projection that permits or encourages corporations to exercise independent, noneconomic judgment over matters that face them in their short- and long-term plans and operations.

Accordingly, both would reject a third view of corporate responsibility that seeks to affect the thought processes of the organization itself—a sort of "hand of management" view—since neither seems willing or able to see the engines of profit regulate themselves to the degree that would be implied by taking the principle of moral projection seriously. Cries of inefficiency and moral imperialism from the right would be matched by cries of insensitivity and illegitimacy from the left, all in the name of preserving us from corporations and managers run morally amok.

Better, critics would say, that moral philosophy be left to philosophers, philanthropists, and politicians than to business leaders. Better that corporate morality be kept to glossy annual reports, where it is safely insulated from policy and performance.

The two conventional frames of reference locate moral restraint in forces external to the person and the corporation. They deny moral reasoning and intent to the corporation in the name of either market competition or society's system of explicit legal constraints and presume that these have a better moral effect than that of rationality and respect.

Although the principle of moral projection, which underwrites the idea of a corporate conscience and patterns it on the thought and feeling processes of the person, is in our view compelling, we must acknowledge that it is neither part of the received wisdom, nor is its advisability beyond question or objection. Indeed, attributing the role of conscience to the corporation seems to carry with it new and disturbing implications for our usual ways of thinking about ethics and business.

Perhaps the best way to clarify and defend this frame of reference is to address the objections to the principle found in the last pages of this article. There we see a summary of the criticisms and counterarguments we have heard during hours of discussion with business executives and business school students. We believe that the replies to the objections about a corporation having a conscience are convincing.

LEAVING THE DOUBLE STANDARD BEHIND

We have come some distance from our opening reflection on Southern Steel Company and its role in its community. Our proposal—clarified, we hope, through these objections and replies—suggests that it is not sufficient to draw a sharp line between individuals' private ideas and efforts and a corporation's institutional efforts but that the latter can and should be built upon the former.

Does this frame of reference give us an unequivocal prescription for the behavior of SSC in its circumstances? No, it does not. Persuasive arguments might be made now and might have been made then that SSC should not have used its considerable economic clout to threaten the community into desegregation. A careful analysis of the realities of the environment might have disclosed that such a course would have been counterproductive, leading to more injustice than it would have alleviated.

The point is that some of the arguments and some of the analyses are or would have been moral arguments, and thereby the ultimate decision that of an ethically responsible organization. The significance of this point can hardly be overstated, for it represents the adoption of a new perspective on corporate policy and a new way of thinking about business ethics. We agree with one authority, who writes that "the business firm, as an organic entity intricately affected by and affecting its environment, is as appropriately adaptive . . . to demands for responsible behavior as for economic service."[5]

The frame of reference here developed does not offer a decision procedure for corporate managers. That has not been our purpose. It does, however, shed light on the conceptual foundations of business ethics by training attention on the corporation as a moral agent in society. Legal systems of rules and incentives are insufficient, even though they may be necessary, as frameworks for corporate responsibility. Taking conceptual cues from the features of moral responsibility normally expected of the person in our opinion deserves practicing managers' serious consideration.

The lack of congruence that James Weston saw between individual and corporate moral responsibility can be, and we think should be, overcome. In the process, what a number of writers have characterized as a double standard—a discrepancy between our personal lives and our lives in organizational settings—might be dampened. The principle of moral projection not only helps us to conceptualize the kinds of demands that we might make of corporations and other organizations but also offers the prospect of harmonizing those demands with the demands that we make of ourselves.

IS A CORPORATION A MORALLY RESPONSIBLE "PERSON"?

Objection 1 to the Analogy

Corporations are not persons. They are artificial legal constructions, machines for mobilizing economic investments toward the efficient production of goods and services. We cannot hold a corporation responsible. We can only hold individuals responsible.

Reply

Our frame of reference does not imply that corporations are persons in a literal sense. It simply means that in certain respects concepts and functions normally attributed to persons can also be attributed to organizations made up of persons. Goals, economic values, strategies, and other such personal attributes are often usefully projected to the corporate level by managers and researchers. Why should we not project the functions of conscience in the same way? As for holding corporations responsible, recent criminal prosecutions such as the case of Ford Motor Company and its Pinto gas tanks suggest that society finds the idea both intelligible and useful.

Objection 2

A corporation cannot be held responsible at the sacrifice of profit. Profitability and financial health have always been and should continue to be the "categorical imperatives" of a business operation.

Reply

We must of course acknowledge the imperatives of survival, stability, and growth when we discuss corporations, as indeed we must acknowledge them when we discuss the life of an individual. Self-sacrifice has been identified with moral responsibility in only the most extreme cases. The pursuit of profit and self-interest need not be pitted against the demands of moral responsibility. Moral demands are best viewed as containments— not replacements—for self-interest.

This is not to say that profit maximization never conflicts with morality. But profit maximization conflicts with other managerial values as well. The point is to coordinate imperatives, not deny their validity.

Objection 3

Corporate executives are not elected representatives of the people, nor are they anointed or appointed as social guardians. They therefore lack the social mandate that a democratic society rightly demands of those who would pursue ethically or socially motivated policies. By keeping corporate policies confined to economic motiva-tions, we keep the power of corporate executives in its proper place.

Reply

The objection betrays an oversimplified view of the relationship between the public and the private sector. Neither private individuals nor private corporations that guide their conduct by ethical or social values beyond the demands of law should be constrained merely because they are not elected to do so. The demands of moral responsibility are independent of the demands of political legitimacy and are in fact presupposed by them.

To be sure, the state and the political process will and must remain the primary mechanisms for protecting the public interest, but one might be forgiven the hope that the political process will not substitute for the moral judgment of the citizenry or other components of society such as corporations.

Objection 4

Our system of law carefully defines the role of agent or fiduciary and makes corporate managers accountable to shareholders and investors for the use of their assets. Management cannot, in the name of corporate moral responsibility, arrogate to itself the right to manage those assets by partially noneconomic criteria.

Reply

First, it is not so clear that investors insist on purely economic criteria in the management of their assets, especially if some of the shareholders' resolutions and board reforms of the last decade are any indication. For instance, companies doing buisness in South Africa have had stockholders question their activities, other companies have instituted audit committees for their boards before such auditing was mandated, and mutual funds for which "socially responsible behavior" is a major investment criterion now exist.

Second, the categories of "shareholder" and "investor" connote wider time spans than do immediate or short-term returns. As a practical matter, considerations of stability and long-term return on investment enlarge the class of principals to which managers bear a fiduciary relationship.

Third, the trust that managers hold does not and never has extended to "any means available" to advance the interests of the principals. Both legal and moral constraints must be understood to qualify that trust—even, perhaps, in the name of a larger trust and a more basic fiduciary relationship to the members of society at large.

Objection 5

The power, size, and scale of the modern corporation—domestic as well as international—are awesome. To unleash, even partially, such power from the discipline of the marketplace and the narrow or possibly nonexistent moral purpose implicit in that discipline would be socially dangerous. Had SSC acted in the community to further racial justice, its purposes might have been admirable, but those purposes could have led to a kind of moral imperialism or worse. Suppose SSC had thrown its power behind the Ku Klux Klan.

Reply

This is a very real and important objection. What seems not to be appreciated is the fact that power affects when it is used as well as when it is not used. A decision by SSC not to exercise its economic influence according to "noneconomic" criteria is inevitably a moral decision and just as inevitably affects the community. The issue in the end is not whether corporations (and other organizations) should be "unleashed" to exert moral force in our society but rather how critically and self-consciously they should choose to do so.

The degree of influence enjoyed by an agent, whether a person or an organization, is not so much a factor recommending moral disengagement as a factor demanding a high level of moral awareness. Imperialism is more to be feared when moral reasoning is absent than when it is present. Nor do we suggest that the "discipline of the marketplace" be diluted; rather, we call for it to be supplemented with the discipline of moral reflection.

Objection 6

The idea of moral projection is a useful device for structuring corporate responsibility only if our understanding of moral responsibility at the level of the person is in some sense richer than our understanding of moral responsibility on the level of the organization as a whole. If we are not clear about individual responsibility, the projection is fruitless.

Reply

The objection is well taken. The challenge offered by the idea of moral projection lies in our capacity to articulate criteria or frameworks of reasoning for the morally responsible person. And though such a challenge is formidable, it is not clear that it cannot be met, at least with sufficient consensus to be useful.

For centuries, the study and criticism of frameworks have gone on, carried forward by many disciplines, including psychology, the social sciences, and philosophy. And though it would be a mistake to suggest that any single framework (much less a decision mechanism) has emerged as the right one, it is true that recurrent patterns are discernible and well enough defined to structure moral discussion.

In the body of the article, we spoke of rationality and respect as components of individual responsibility. Further analysis of these components would translate them into social costs and benefits, justice in the distribution of goods and services, basic rights and duties, and fidelity to contracts. The view that pluralism in our society has undercut all possibility of moral agreement is anything but self-evident. Sincere moral disagreement is, of course, inevitable and not clearly lamentable. But a process and a vocabulary for articulating such values as we share is no small step forward when compared with the alternatives. Perhaps in our exploration of the moral projection we might make some surprising and even reassuring discoveries about ourselves.

Objection 7

Why is it necessary to project moral responsibility to the level of the organization? Isn't the task of defining corporate responsibility and business ethics sufficiently discharged if we clarify the responsibilities of men and women in business as individuals? Doesn't ethics finally rest on the honesty and integrity of the individual in the business world?

Reply

Yes and no. Yes, in the sense that the control of large organizations does finally rest in the hands of managers, of men and women. No, in the sense that what is being controlled is a cooperative system for a cooperative purpose. The projection of responsibility to the organization is simply an acknowledgment of the fact that the whole is more than the sum of its parts. Many intelligent people do not an intelligent organization make. Intelligence needs to be structured, organized, divided, and recombined in complex processes for complex purposes.

Studies of management have long shown that the attributes, successes, and failures of organizations are phenomena that emerge from the coordination of persons' attributes and that explanations of such phenomena require categories of analysis and description beyond the level of the individual. Moral responsibility is an attribute that can manifest itself in organizations as surely as competence or efficiency.

Objection 8

Is the frame of reference here proposed intended to replace or undercut the relevance of the "invisible hand" and the "government hand" views, which depend on external controls?

Reply

No. Just as regulation and economic competition are not substitutes for corporate responsibility, so corporate responsibility is not a substitute for law and the market. The imperatives of ethics cannot be relied on—nor have they ever been relied on— without a context of external sanctions. And this is true as much for individuals as for organizations.

This frame of reference takes us beneath, but not beyond, the realm of external systems of rules and incentives and into the thought processes that interpret and respond to the corporation's environment. Morality is more than merely part of that environment. It aims at the projection of conscience, not the enthronement of it in either the state or the competitive process.

The rise of the modern large corporation and the concomitant rise of the professional manager demand a conceptual framework in which these phenomena can be accommodated to moral thought. The principal of moral projection furthers such accommodation by recognizing a new level of agency in society and thus a new level of responsibility.

Objection 9

Corporations have always taken the interests of those outside the corporation into account in the sense that customer relations and public relations generally are an integral part of rational economic decision making. Market signals and social signals that filter through the market mechanism inevitably represent the interests of parties affected by the behavior of the company. What, then, is the point of adding respect to rationality?

Reply

Representing the affected parties solely as economic variables in the environment of the company is treating them as means or resources and not as ends in themselves. It implies that the only voice which affected parties should have in organizational decision making is that of potential buyers, sellers, regulators, or boycotters. Besides, many affected parties may not occupy such roles, and those who do may not be able to signal the organization with messages that effectively represent their stakes in its actions.

To be sure, classical economic theory would have us believe that perfect competition in free markets (with modest adjustments from the state) will result in all relevant signals being "heard," but the abstractions from reality implicit in such theory make it insufficient as a frame of reference for moral responsibility. In a world in which strict self-interest was congruent with the common good, moral responsibility might be unnecessary. We do not, alas, live in such a world.

The element of respect in our analysis of responsibility plays an essential role in ensuring the recognition of unrepresented or underrepresented voices in the decision making of organizations as agents. Showing respect for persons as ends and not mere means to organizational purposes is central to the concept of corporate moral responsibility.

NOTES

1. See John Ladd, "Morality and the Ideal of Rationality in Formal Organizations," *The Monist,* October 1970, p. 499.
2. See William K. Frankena, *Thinking About Morality* (Ann Arbor: University of Michigan Press, 1980), p. 26.
3. See Peter French, "The Corporation as a Moral Person," *American Philosophical Quarterly,* July 1979, p. 207.
4. A process that psychological researchers from Jean Piaget to Lawrence Kohlberg have examined carefully; see Jean Piaget, *The Moral Judgement of the Child* (New York: Free Press, 1965) and Lawrence Kohlberg, *The Philosophy of Moral Development* (New York: Harper & Row, 1981).
5. See Kenneth R. Andrews, *The Concept of Corporate Strategy,* revised edition (Homewood, Ill.: Dow Jones–Irwin, 1980), p. 99.

The Social Responsibility of Business Is to Increase Its Profits

Milton Friedman
Senior Research Fellow, Hoover Institution, Stanford University, and Nobel Prize-winning economist

When I hear businessmen speak eloquently about the "social responsibilities of business in a free-enterprise system," I am reminded of the wonderful line about the Frenchman who discovered at the age of 70 that he had been speaking prose all his life. The businessmen believe that they are defending free enterprise when they declaim that business is not concerned "merely" with profit but also with promoting desirable "social" ends; that business has a "social conscience" and takes seriously its responsibilities for providing employment, eliminating discrimination, avoiding pollution and whatever else may be the catchwords of

the contemporary crop of reformers. In fact they are—or would be if they or anyone else took them seriously—preaching pure and unadulterated socialism. Businessmen who talk this way are unwitting puppets of the intellectual forces that have been undermining the basis of a free society these past decades.

The discussions of the "social responsibilities of business" are notable for their analytical looseness and lack of rigor. What does it mean to say that "business" has responsibilities? Only people can have responsibilities. A corporation is an artificial person and in this sense may have artificial responsibilities, but "business" as a whole cannot be said to have responsibilities, even in this vague sense. The first step toward clarity in examining the doctrine of the social responsibility of business is to ask precisely what it implies for whom.

Presumably, the individuals who are to be responsible are businessmen, which means individual proprietors or corporate executives. Most of the discussion of social responsibility is directed at corporations, so in what follows I shall mostly neglect the individual proprietors and speak of corporate executives.

In a free-enterprise, private-property system, a corporate executive is an employee of the owners of the business. He has direct responsibility to his employers. That responsibility is to conduct the business in accordance with their desires, which generally will be to make as much money as possible while conforming to the basic rules of the society, both those embodied in law and those embodied in ethical custom. Of course, in some cases his employers may have a different objective. A group of persons might establish a corporation for an eleemosynary purpose—for example, a hospital or a school. The manager of such a corporation will not have money profit as his objectives but the rendering of certain services.

In either case, the key point is that, in his capacity as a corporate executive, the manager is the agent of the individuals who own the corporation or establish the eleemosynary institution, and his primary responsibility is to them.

Needless to say, this does not mean that it is easy to judge how well he is performing his task.

But at least the criterion of performance is straightforward, and the persons among whom a voluntary contractual arrangement exists are clearly defined.

Of course, the corporate executive is also a person in his own right. As a person, he may have many other responsibilities that he recognizes or assumes voluntarily—to his family, his conscience, his feelings of charity, his church, his clubs, his city, his country. He may feel impelled by these responsibilities to devote part of his income to causes he regards as worthy, to refuse to work for particular corporations, even to leave his job, for example, to join his country's armed forces. If we wish, we may refer to some of these responsibilities as "social responsibilities." But in these respects he is acting as a principal, not as an agent; he is spending his own money or time or energy, not the money of his employers or the time or energy he has contracted to devote to their purposes. If these are "social responsibilities," they are the social responsibilities of individuals, not of business.

What does it mean to say that the corporate executive has a "social responsibility" in his capacity as businessman? If this statement is not pure rhetoric, it must mean that he is to act in some way that is not in the interest of his employers. For example, that he is to refrain from increasing the price of the product in order to contribute to the social objective of preventing inflation, even though a price increase would be in the best interests of the corporation. Or that he is to make expenditures on reducing pollution beyond the amount that is in the best interests of the corporation or that is required by law in order to contribute to the social objective of improving the environment. Or that, at the expense of corporate profits, he is to hire "hard-core" unemployed instead of better qualified available workmen to contribute to the social objective of reducing poverty.

In each of these cases, the corporate executive would be spending someone else's money for a general social interest. Insofar as his actions in accord with his "social responsibility" reduce returns to stockholders, he is spending their money. Insofar as his actions raise the price to customers, he is spending the customers' money. Insofar as his actions lower the wages of some employees, he is spending their money.

The stockholders or the customers or the employees could separately spend their own money on the particular action if they wished to do so. The executive is exercising a distinct "social responsibility," rather than serving as an agent of the stockholders or the customers or the employees, only if he spends the money in a different way than they would have spent it.

But if he does this, he is in effect imposing taxes, on the one hand, and deciding how the tax proceeds shall be spent, on the other.

This process raises political questions on two levels: principle and consequences. On the level of political principle, the imposition of taxes and the expenditure of tax proceeds are governmental functions. We have established elaborate constitutional, parliamentary and judicial provisions to control these functions, to assure that taxes are imposed so far as possible in accordance with the preferences and desires of the public—after all, "taxation without representation" was one of the battle cries of the American Revolution. We have a system of checks and balances to separate the legislative function of imposing taxes and enacting expenditures from the executive function of collecting taxes and administering expenditure programs and from the judicial function of mediating disputes and interpreting the law.

Here the businessman—self-selected or appointed directly or indirectly by stockholders—is to be simultaneously legislator, executive and jurist. He is to decide whom to tax by how much and for what purpose, and he is to spend the proceeds—all this guided only by general exhortations from on high to restrain inflation, improve the environment, fight poverty and so on and on.

The whole justification for permitting the corporate executive to be selected by the stockholders is that the executive is an agent serving the interests of his principal. This justification disappears when the corporate executive imposes taxes and spends the proceeds for "social" purposes. He becomes in effect a public employee, a civil servant, even though he remains in name an employee of a private enterprise. On grounds of political principle, it is intolerable that such civil servants—insofar as their actions in the name of social responsibility are real and not just window-dressing—should be selected as they are now. If they are to be civil servants, then they must be elected through a political process. If they are to impose taxes and make expenditures to foster "social" objectives, then political machinery must be set up to make the assessment of taxes and to determine through a political process the objectives to be served.

This is the basic reason why the doctrine of "social responsibility" involves the acceptance of the socialist view that political mechanisms, not market mechanisms, are the appropriate way to determine the allocation of scarce resources to alternative uses.

On the grounds of consequences, can the corporate executive in fact discharge his alleged "social responsibilities"? On the other hand, suppose he could get away with spending the stockholders' or customers' or employees' money. How is he to know how to spend it? He is told that he must contribute to fighting inflation. How is he to know what action of his will contribute to that end? He is presumably an expert in running his company—in producing a product or selling it or financing it. But nothing about his selection makes him an expert on inflation. Will his holding down the price of his product reduce inflationary pressure? Or, by leaving more spending power in the hands of his customers, simply divert it elsewhere? Or, by forcing him to produce less because of the lower price, will it simply contribute to shortages? Even if he could answer these questions, how much cost is he justified in imposing on his stockholders, customers and employees for this social purpose? What is his appropriate share and what is the appropriate share of others?

And, whether he wants to or not, can he get away with spending his stockholders', customers' or employees' money? Will not the stockholders fire him? (Either the present ones or those who take over when his actions in the name of social responsibility have reduced the corporation's profits and the price of its stock.) His customers and his employees can desert him for other producers and employers less scrupulous in exercising their social responsibilities.

This facet of "social responsibility" doctrine is brought into sharp relief when the doctrine is used to justify wage restraint by trade unions. The conflict of interest is naked and clear when union officials are asked to subordinate the interest of their members to some more general purpose. If the union officials try to enforce wage restraint, the consequence is likely to be wildcat strikes, rank-and-file revolts and the emergence of strong competitors for their jobs. We thus have the ironic phenomenon that union leaders—at least in the U.S.—have objected to Government interference with the market far more consistently and courageously than have business leaders.

The difficulty of exercising "social responsibility" illustrates, of course, the great virtue of private competitive enterprise—it forces people to be responsible for their own actions and makes it difficult for them to "exploit" other people for either selfish or unselfish purposes. They can do good—but only at their own expense.

Many a reader who has followed the argument this far may be tempted to remonstrate that it is all well and good to speak of Government's having the responsibility to impose taxes and determine expenditures for such "social" purposes as controlling pollution or training the hard-core unemployed, but that the problems are too urgent to wait on the slow course of political processes, that the exercise of social responsibility by businessmen is a quicker and surer way to solve pressing current problems.

Aside from the question of fact—I share Adam Smith's skepticism about the benefits that can be expected from "those who affected to trade for the public good"—this argument must be rejected on grounds of principle. What it amounts to is an assertion that those who favor the taxes and expenditures in question have failed to persuade a majority of their fellow citizens to be of like mind and that they are seeking to attain by undemocratic procedures what they cannot attain by democratic procedures. In a free society, it is hard for "evil" people to do "evil," especially since one man's good is another's evil.

I have, for simplicity, concentrated on the special case of the corporate executive, except only for the brief digression on trade unions. But precisely the same argument applies to the newer phenomenon of calling upon stockholders to require corporations to exercise social responsibility (the recent G. M. crusade for example). In most of these cases, what is in effect involved is some stockholders trying to get other stockholders (or customers or employees) to contribute against their will to "social" causes favored by the activists. Insofar as they succeed, they are again imposing taxes and spending the proceeds.

The situation of the individual proprietor is somewhat different. If he acts to reduce the returns of his enterprise in order to exercise his "social responsibility," he is spending his own money, not someone else's. If he wishes to spend his money on such purposes, that is his right, and I cannot see that there is any objection to his doing so. In the process, he, too, may impose costs on employees and customers. However, because he is far less likely than a large corporation or union to have monopolistic power, any such side effects will tend to be minor.

Of course, in practice the doctrine of social responsibility is frequently a cloak for actions that are justified on other grounds rather than a reason for those actions.

To illustrate, it may well be in the long-run interest of a corporation that is a major employer in a small community to devote resources to providing amenities to that community or to improving its government. That may make it easier to attract desirable employees, it may reduce the wage bill or lessen losses from pilferage and sabotage or have other worthwhile effects. Or it may be that, given the laws about the deductibility of corporate charitable contributions, the stockholders can contribute more to charities they favor by having the corporation make the gift than by doing it themselves, since they can in that way contribute an amount that would otherwise have been paid as corporate taxes.

In each of these—and many similar—cases, there is a strong temptation to rationalize these actions as an exercise of "social responsibility." In the present climate of opinion, with its widespread aversion to "capitalism," "profits," the "soulless corporation" and so on, this is one way for a corporation to generate goodwill as a by-product of expenditures that are entirely justified in its own self-interest.

It would be inconsistent of me to call on corporate executives to refrain from this hypocritical window-dressing because it harms the foundations of a free society. That would be to call on them to exercise a "social responsibility"! If our institutions, and the attitudes of the public make it in their self-interest to cloak their actions in this way, I cannot summon much indignation to denounce them. At the same time, I can express admiration for those individual proprietors or owners of closely held corporations or stockholders of more broadly held corporations who disdain such tactics as approaching fraud.

Whether blameworthy or not, the use of the cloak of social responsibility, and the nonsense spoken in its name by influential and prestigious businessmen, does clearly harm the foundations of a free society. I have been impressed time and again by the schizophrenic character of many businessmen. They are capable of being extremely farsighted and clear-headed in matters that are internal to their businesses. They are incredibly short-sighted and muddle-headed in matters that are outside their businesses but affect the possible survival of business in general. This short-sightedness is strikingly exemplified in the calls from many businessmen for wage and price guidelines or controls or income policies. There is nothing that could do more in a brief period to destroy a market system and replace it by a centrally controlled system than effective governmental control of prices and wages.

The short-sightedness is also exemplified in speeches by businessmen on social responsibility. This may gain them kudos in the short run. But it helps to strengthen the already too prevalent view that the pursuit of profits is wicked and immoral and must be curbed and controlled by external forces. Once this view is adopted, the external forces that curb the market will not be the social consciences, however highly developed, of the pontificating executives; it will be the iron fist of government bureaucrats. Here, as with price and wage controls, businessmen seem to me to reveal a suicidal impulse.

The political principle that underlies the market mechanism is unanimity. In an ideal free market resting on private property, no individual can coerce any other, all cooperation is voluntary, all parties to such cooperation benefit or they need not participate. There are no values, no "social" responsibilities in any sense other than the shared values and responsibilities of individuals. Society is a collection of individuals and of the various groups they voluntarily form.

The political principle that underlies the political mechanism is conformity. The individual must serve a more general social interest—whether that be determined by a church or a dictator or a majority. The individual may have a vote and say in what is to be done, but if he is overruled, he must conform. It is appropriate for some to require others to contribute to a general social purpose whether they wish to or not.

Unfortunately, unanimity is not always feasible. There are some respects in which conformity appears unavoidable, so I do not see how one can avoid the use of the political mechanism altogether.

But the doctrine of "social responsibility" taken seriously would extend the scope of the political mechanism to every human activity. It does not differ in philosophy from the most explicitly collectivist doctrine. It differs only by professing to believe that collectivist ends can be attained without collectivist means. That is why, in my book "Capitalism and Freedom," I have called it a "fundamentally subversive doctrine" in a free society, and have said that in such a society, "there is one and only one social responsibility of business—to use its resources and engage in activities designed to increase its profits so long as it stays within the rules of the game, which is to say, engages in open and free competition without deception or fraud."

Stakeholder Theory of the Modern Corporation

R. Edward Freeman
Signe Olsson Professor of Business Administration, Olsson Center for Applied Ethics, The Darden School, University of Virginia

INTRODUCTION

> Corporations have ceased to be merely legal devices through which the private business transactions of individuals may be carried on. Though still much used for this purpose, the corporate form has acquired a larger significance. The corporation has, in fact, become both a method of property tenure and a means of organizing economic life. Grown to tremendous proportions, there may be said to have evolved a "corporate system"—which has attracted to itself a combination of attributes and powers, and has attained a degree of prominence entitling it to be dealt with as a major social institution.[1]

Despite these prophetic words of Berle and Means (1932), scholars and managers alike continue to hold sacred the view that managers bear a special relationship to the stockholders in the firm. Since stockholders own shares in the firm, they have certain rights and privileges, which must be granted to them by management, as well as by others. . . . Sanctions, in the form of "the law of corporations," and other protective mechanisms in the form of social custom, accepted management practice, myth, and ritual, are thought to reinforce the assumption of the primacy of the stockholder.

The purpose of this chapter is to pose several challenges to this assumption, from within the framework of managerial capitalism, and to suggest the bare bones of an alternative theory, *a stakeholder theory of the modern corporation.* I do not seek the demise of the modern corporation, either intellectually or in fact. Rather, I seek its transformation. In the words of Neurath, we shall

---

"Stakeholder Theory of the Modern Corporation." Reprinted by permission of the author.

attempt to "rebuild the ship, plank by plank, while it remains afloat."[2]

My thesis is that we can revitalize the concept of managerial capitalism by replacing the notion that managers have a duty to stockholders with the concept that managers bear a fiduciary relationship to stakeholders. Stakeholders are those groups who have a stake in or claim on the firm. Specifically I include suppliers, customers, employees, stockholders, and the local community, as well as management in its role as agent for these groups. I argue that the legal, economic, political, and moral challenges to the currently received theory of the firm, as a nexus of contracts among the owners of the factors of production and customers, require us to revise this concept. That is, each of these stakeholder groups has a right not to be treated as a means to some end, and therefore must participate in determining the future direction of the firm in which they have a stake.

The crux of my argument is that we must reconceptualize the firm around the following question: For whose benefit and at whose expense should the firm be managed? I shall set forth such a reconceptualization in the form of a *stakeholder theory of the firm*. I shall then critically examine the stakeholder view and its implications for the future of the capitalist system.

THE ATTACK ON MANAGERIAL CAPITALISM

The Legal Argument

The basic idea of managerial capitalism is that in return for controlling the firm, management vigorously pursues the interests of stockholders. Central to the managerial view of the firm is the idea that management can pursue market transactions with suppliers and customers in an unconstrained manner.

The law of corporations gives a less clear-cut answer to the question: In whose interest and for whose benefit should the modern corporation be governed? While it says that the corporations should be run primarily in the interests of the stockholders in the firm, it says further that the corporation exists "in contemplation of the law" and has personality as a "legal person," limited liability for its actions, and immortality, since its existence transcends that of its members. Therefore, directors and other officers of the firm have a fiduciary obligation to stockholders in the sense that the "affairs of the corporation" must be conducted in the interest of the stockholders. And stockholders can theoretically bring suit against those directors and managers for doing otherwise. But since the corporation is a legal person, existing in contemplation of the law, managers of the corporation are constrained by law.

Until recently, this was no constraint at all. In this century, however, the law has evolved to effectively constrain the pursuit of stockholder interests at the expense of other claimants on the firm. It has, in effect, required that the claims of customers, suppliers, local communities, and employees be taken into consideration, though in general they are subordinated to the claims of stockholders.

For instance, the doctrine of "privity of contract," as articulated in *Winterbottom v. Wright* in 1842, has been eroded by recent developments in products liability law. Indeed, *Greenman v. Yuba Power* gives the manufacturer strict liability for damage caused by its products, even though the seller has exercised all possible care in the preparation and sale of the product and the consumer has not bought the product from nor entered into any contractual arrangement with the manufacturer. Caveat emptor has been replaced, in large part, with caveat venditor.[3] The Consumer Product Safety Commission has the power to enact product recalls, and in 1980 one U.S. automobile company recalled more cars than it built. Some industries are required to provide information to customers about a product's ingredients, whether or not the customers want and are willing to pay for this information.[4]

The same argument is applicable to management's dealings with employees. The National Labor Relations Act gave employees the right to unionize and to bargain in good faith. It set up the National Labor Relations Board to enforce these rights with management. The Equal Pay Act of 1963 and Title VII of the Civil Rights Act of 1964 constrain management from discrimination in hiring practices; these have been followed with the

Age Discrimination in Employment Act of 1967.[5] The emergence of a body of administrative case law arising from labor-management disputes and the historic settling of discrimination claims with large employers such as AT&T have caused the emergence of a body of practice in the corporation that is consistent with the legal guarantee of the rights of the employees. The law has protected the due process rights of those employees who enter into collective bargaining agreements with management. As of the present, however, only 30 percent of the labor force are participating in such agreements; this has prompted one labor law scholar to propose a statutory law prohibiting dismissals of the 70 percent of the work force not protected.[6]

The law has also protected the interests of local communities. The Clean Air Act and Clean Water Act have constrained management from "spoiling the commons." In an historic case, *Marsh v. Alabama,* the Supreme Court ruled that a company-owned town was subject to the provisions of the U.S. Constitution, thereby guaranteeing the rights of local citizens and negating the "property rights" of the firm. Some states and municipalities have gone further and passed laws preventing firms from moving plants or limiting when and how plants can be closed. In sum, there is much current legal activity in this area to constrain management's pursuit of stockholders' interests at the expense of the local communities in which the firm operates.

I have argued that the result of such changes in the legal system can be viewed as giving some rights to those groups that have a claim on the firm, for example, customers, suppliers, employees, local communities, stockholders, and management. It raises the question, at the core of a theory of the firm: In whose interest and for whose benefit should the firm be managed? The answer proposed by managerial capitalism is clearly "the stockholders," but I have argued that the law has been progressively circumscribing this answer.

The Economic Argument

In its pure ideological form managerial capitalism seeks to maximize the interests of stockholders. In its perennial criticism of government regulation, management espouses the "invisible hand" doctrine. It contends that it creates the greatest good for the greatest number, and therefore government need not intervene. However, we know that externalities, moral hazards, and monopoly power exist in fact, whether or not they exist in theory. Further, some of the legal apparatus mentioned above has evolved to deal with just these issues.

The problem of the "tragedy of the commons" or the free-rider problem pervades the concept of public goods such as water and air. No one has an incentive to incur the cost of clean-up or the cost of nonpollution, since the marginal gain of one firm's action is small. Every firm reasons this way, and the result is pollution of water and air. Since the industrial revolution, firms have sought to internalize the benefits and externalize the costs of their actions. The cost must be borne by all, through taxation and regulation; hence we have the emergence of the environmental regulations of the 1970s.

Similarly, moral hazards arise when the purchaser of a good or service can pass along the cost of that good. There is no incentive to economize, on the part of either the producer or the consumer, and there is excessive use of the resources involved. The institutionalized practice of third-party payment in health care is a prime example.

Finally, we see the avoidance of competitive behavior on the part of firms, each seeking to monopolize a small portion of the market and not compete with one another. In a number of industries, oligopolies have emerged, and while there is questionable evidence that oligopolies are not the most efficient corporate form in some industries, suffice it to say that the potential for abuse of market power has again led to regulation of managerial activity. In the classic case, AT&T, arguably one of the great technological and managerial achievements of the century, was broken up into eight separate companies to prevent its abuse of monopoly power.

Externalities, moral hazards, and monopoly power have led to more external control on managerial capitalism. There are de facto constraints, due to these economic facts of life, on the ability of management to act in the interests of stockholders.

A STAKEHOLDER THEORY OF THE FIRM

The Stakeholder Concept

Corporations have stakeholders, that is, groups and individuals who benefit from or are harmed by, and whose rights are violated or respected by, corporate actions. The concept of stakeholders is a generalization of the notion of stockholders, who themselves have some special claim on the firm. Just as stockholders have a right to demand certain actions by management, so do other stakeholders have a right to make claims. The exact nature of these claims is a difficult question that I shall address, but the logic is identical to that of the stockholder theory. Stakes require action of a certain sort, and conflicting stakes require methods of resolution.

Freeman and Reed (1983)[7] distinguish two senses of *stakeholder*. The "narrow definition" includes those groups who are vital to the survival and success of the corporation. The "wide-definition" includes any group or individual who can affect or is affected by the corporation. I shall begin with a modest aim: to articulate a stakeholder theory using the narrow definition.

Stakeholders in the Modern Corporation

Figure 1 depicts the stakeholder in a typical large corporation. The stakes of each are reciprocal, since each can affect the other in terms of harms and benefits as well as rights and duties. The stakes of each are not univocal and would vary by particular cor-

poration. We merely set forth some general notions that seem to be common to many large firms.

Owners have financial stake in the corporation in the form of stocks, bonds, and so on, and they expect some kind of financial return from them. Either they have given money directly to the firm, or they have some historical claim made through a series of morally justified exchanges. The firm affects their livelihood or, if a substantial portion of their retirement income is in stocks or bonds, their ability to care for themselves when they can no longer work. Of course, the stakes of owners will differ by type of owner, preferences for money, moral preferences, and so on, as well as by type of firm. The owners of AT&T are quite different from the owners of Ford Motor Company, with stock of the former company being widely dispersed among 3 million stockholders and that of the latter being held by a small family group as well as by a large group of public stockholders.

Employees have their jobs and usually their livelihood at stake; they often have specialized skills for which there is usually no perfectly elastic market. In return for their labor, they expect security, wages, benefits, and meaningful work. In return for their loyalty, the corporation is expected to provide for them and carry them through difficult times. Employees are expected to follow the instructions of management most of the time, to speak favorably about the company, and to be responsible citizens in the local communities in which the company operates. Where they are used

FIGURE 1
A Stakeholder Model of the Corporation.

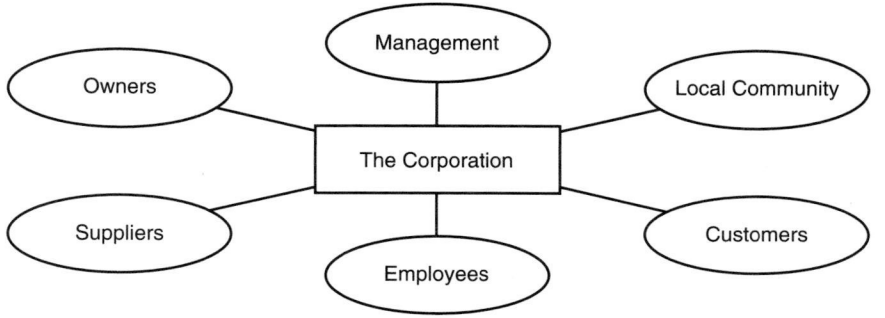

as means to an end, they must participate in decisions affecting such use. The evidence that such policies and values as described here lead to productive company-employee relationships is compelling. It is equally compelling to realize that the opportunities for "bad faith" on the part of both management and employees are enormous. "Mock participation" in quality circles, singing the company song, and wearing the company uniform solely to please management all lead to distrust and unproductive work.

Suppliers, interpreted in a stakeholder sense, are vital to the success of the firm, for raw materials will determine the final product's quality and price. In turn the firm is a customer of the supplier and is therefore vital to the success and survival of the supplier. When the firm treats the supplier as a valued member of the stakeholder network, rather than simply as a source of materials, the supplier will respond when the firm is in need. Chrysler traditionally had very close ties to its suppliers, even to the extent that led some to suspect the transfer of illegal payments. And when Chrysler was on the brink of disaster, the suppliers responded with price cuts, accepting late payments, financing, and so on. Supplier and company can rise and fall together. Of course, again, the particular supplier relationships will depend on a number of variables such as the number of suppliers and whether the supplies are finished goods or raw materials.

Customers exchange resources for the products of the firm and in return receive the benefits of the products. Customers provide the lifeblood of the firm in the form of revenue. Given the level of reinvestment of earnings in large corporations, customers indirectly pay for the development of new products and services. Peters and Waterman (1982)[8] have argued that being close to the customer leads to success with other stakeholders and that a distinguishing characteristic of some companies that have performed well is their emphasis on the customer. By paying attention to customers' needs, management automatically addresses the needs of suppliers and owners. Moreover, it seems that the ethic of customer service carries over to the community. Almost without fail the "excellent companies" in Peters and Waterman's study have

good reputations in the community. I would argue that Peters and Waterman have found multiple applications of Kant's dictum, "Treat persons as ends unto themselves," and it should come as no surprise that persons respond to such respectful treatment, be they customers, suppliers, owners, employees, or members of the local community. The real surprise is the novelty of the application of Kant's rule in a theory of good management practice.

The local community grants the firm the right to build facilities and, in turn, it benefits from the tax base and economic and social contributions of the firm. In return for the provision of local services, the firm is expected to be a good citizen, as is any person, either "natural or artificial." The firm cannot expose the community to unreasonable hazards in the form of pollution, toxic waste, and so on. If for some reason the firm must leave a community, it is expected to work with local leaders to make the transition as smoothly as possible. Of course, the firm does not have perfect knowledge, but when it discovers some danger or runs afoul of new competition, it is expected to inform the local community and to work with the community to overcome any problem. When the firm mismanages its relationship with the local community, it is in the same position as a citizen who commits a crime. It has violated the implicit social contract with the community and should expect to be distrusted and ostracized. It should not be surprised when punitive measures are invoked.

I have not included "competitors" as stakeholders in the narrow sense, since strictly speaking they are not necessary for the survival and success of the firm; the stakeholder theory works equally well in monopoly contexts. However, competitors and government would be the first to be included in an extension of this basic theory. It is simply not true that the interests of competitors in an industry are always in conflict. There is no reason why trade associations and other multi-organizational groups cannot band together to solve common problems that have little to do with how to restrain trade. Implementation of stakeholder management principles, in the long run, mitigates the need for industrial policy and an increasing role for government intervention and regulation.

The Role of Management

Management plays a special role, for it too has a stake in the modern corporation. On the one hand, management's stake is like that of employees, with some kind of explicit or implicit employment contract. But, on the other hand, management has a duty of safeguarding the welfare of the abstract entity that is the corporation. In short, management, especially top management, must look after the health of the corporation, and this involves balancing the multiple claims of conflicting stakeholders. Owners want higher financial returns, while customers want more money spent on research and development. Employees want higher wages and better benefits, while the local community wants better parks and day-care facilities.

The task of management in today's corporation is akin to that of King Solomon. The stakeholder theory does not give primacy to one stakeholder group over another, though there will surely be times when one group will benefit at the expense of others. In general, however, management must keep the relationships among stakeholders in balance. When these relationships become imbalanced, the survival of the firm is in jeopardy.

When wages are too high and product quality is too low, customers leave, suppliers suffer, and owners sell their stocks and bonds, depressing the stock price and making it difficult to raise new capital at favorable rates. Note, however, that the reason for paying returns to owners is not that they "own" the firm, but that their support is necessary for the survival of the firm, and that they have a legitimate claim on the firm. Similar reasoning applies in turn to each stakeholder group.

A stakeholder theory of the firm must redefine the purpose of the firm. The stockholder theory claims that the purpose of the firm is to maximize the welfare of the stockholders, perhaps subject to some moral or social constraints, either because such maximization leads to the greatest good or because of property rights. The purpose of the firm is quite different in my view.

"The stakeholder theory" can be unpacked into a number of stakeholder theories, each of which has a "normative core," inextricably linked to the way that corporations should be governed and the way that managers should act. So, attempts to more fully define, or more carefully define, a stakeholder theory are misguided. Following Donaldson and Preston, I want to insist that the normative, descriptive, instrumental, and metaphorical (my addition to their framework) uses of 'stakeholder' are tied together in particular political constructions to yield a number of possible "stakeholder theories." "Stakeholder theory" is thus a genre of stories about how we could live. Let me be more specific.

A "normative core" of a theory is a set of sentences that includes among others, sentences like:

1. Corporations ought to be governed . . .
2. Managers ought to act to . . . .

where we need arguments or further narratives which include business and moral terms to fill in the blanks. This normative core is not always reducible to a fundamental ground like the theory of property, but certain normative cores are consistent with modern understandings of property. Certain elaborations of the theory of private property plus the other institutions of political liberalism give rise to particular normative cores. But there are other institutions, other political conceptions of how society ought to be structured, so that there are different possible normative cores.

So, one normative core of a stakeholder theory might be a feminist standpoint one, rethinking how we would restructure "value-creating activity" along principles of caring and connection.[9] Another would be an ecological (or several ecological) normative cores. Mark Starik has argued that the very idea of a stakeholder theory of the *firm* ignores certain ecological necessities.[10] Exhibit 1 is suggestive of how these theories could be developed.

In the next section I shall sketch the normative core based on pragmatic liberalism. But, any normative core must address the questions in columns A or B, or explain why these questions may be irrelevant, as in the ecological view. In addition, each "theory," and I use the word hesitantly, must place the normative core within a more full-fledged

EXHIBIT 1

A REASONABLE PLURALISM

	A. Corporations ought to be governed . . .	B. Managers ought to act . . .	C. The background disciplines of "value creations" are . . .
Doctrine of Fair Contracts	. . . in accordance with the six principles.	. . . in the interests of stakeholders.	—business theories —theories that explain stakeholder behavior
Feminist Standpoint Theory	. . . in accordance with the principles of caring/connection and relationships.	. . . to maintain and care for relationships and networks of stakeholders.	—business theories —feminist theory —social science understanding of networks
Ecological Principles	. . . in accordance with the principle of caring for the earth.	. . . to care for the earth.	—business theories —ecology —other

account of how we could understand value-creating activity differently (column C). The only way to get on with this task is to see the stakeholder idea as a metaphor. The attempt to prescribe one and only one "normative core" and construct "a stakeholder theory is at best a disguised attempt to smuggle a normative core past the unsophisticated noses of other unsuspecting academics who are just happy to see the end of the stockholder orthodoxy.

If we begin with the view that we can understand value-creation activity as a contractual process among those parties affected, and if for simplicity's sake we initially designate those parties as financiers, customers, suppliers, employees, and communities, then we can construct a normative core that reflects the liberal notions of autonomy, solidarity, and fairness as articulated by John Rawls, Richard Rorty, and others.[11] Notice that building these moral notions into the foundations of how we understand value creation and contracting requires that we eschew separating the "business" part of the process from the "ethical" part, and that we start with the presumption of equality among the contractors, rather than the presumption in favor of financier rights.

The normative core for this redesigned contractual theory will capture the liberal idea of fairness if it ensures a basic equality among stakeholders in terms of their moral rights as these are realized in the firm, and if it recognizes that inequalities among stakeholders are justified if they raise the level of the least well-off stakeholder. The liberal ideal of autonomy is captured by the realization that each stakeholder must be free to enter agreements that create value for themselves, and solidarity is realized by the recognition of the mutuality of stakeholder interests.

One way to understand fairness in this context is to claim *à la* Rawls that a contract is fair if parties to the contract would agree to it in ignorance of their actual stakes. Thus, a contract is like a fair bet, if each party is willing to turn the tables and accept the other side. What would a fair contract among corporate stakeholders look like? If we can articulate this ideal, a sort of corporate constitution, we could then ask whether actual corporations measure up to this standard, and we also begin to design corporate structures which are consistent with this Doctrine of Fair Contracts.

Imagine if you will, representative stakeholders trying to decide on "the rules of the game." Each is rational in a straightforward sense, looking out for its own self-interest. At least *ex ante,* stakeholders are the relevant parties since they will be materially affected. Stakeholders know how economic activity is organized and could be organized. They know general facts about the way the corporate world works. They know that in the real world there are or could be transaction costs, externalities, and positive costs of contracting. Suppose they are uncertain about what other social institutions exist, but they know the range of those institutions. They do not know if government exists to pick up the tab for any externalities, or if they will exist in the nightwatchman state of libertarian theory. They know success and failure stories of businesses around the world. In short, they are behind a Rawls-like veil of ignorance, and they do not know what stake each will have when the veil is lifted. What groundrules would they choose to guide them?

The first groundrule is "The Principle of Entry and Exit." Any contract that is the corporation must have clearly defined entry, exit, and renegotiation conditions, or at least it must have methods or processes for so defining these conditions. The logic is straightforward: each stakeholder must be able to determine when an agreement exists and has a chance of fulfillment. This is not to imply that contracts cannot contain contingent claims or other methods for resolving uncertainty, but rather that it must contain methods for determining whether or not it is valid.

The second groundrule I shall call "The Principle of Governance," and it says that the procedure for changing the rules of the game must be agreed upon by unanimous consent. Think about the consequences of a majority of stakeholders systematically "selling out" a minority. Each stakeholder, in ignorance of its actual role, would seek to avoid such a situation. In reality this principle translates into each stakeholder never giving up its right to participate in the governance of the corporation, or perhaps into the existence of stakeholder governing boards.

The third groundrule I shall call "The Principle of Externalities," and it says that if a contract between A and B imposes a cost on C, then C has the option to become a party to the contract, and the terms are renegotiated. Once again the rationality of this condition is clear. Each stakeholder will want insurance that it does not become C.

The fourth groundrule is "The Principle of Contracting Costs," and it says that all parties to the contract must share in the cost of contracting. Once again the logic is straightforward. Any one stakeholder can get stuck.

A fifth groundrule is "The Agency Principle" that says that any agent must serve the interests of all stakeholders. It must adjudicate conflicts within the bounds of the other principals. Once again the logic is clear. Agents for any one group would have a privileged place.

A sixth and final groundrule we might call, "The Principle of Limited Immortality." The corporation shall be managed as if it can continue to serve the interests of stakeholders through time. Stakeholders are uncertain about the future but, subject to exit conditions, they realize that the continued existence of the corporation is in their interest. Therefore, it would be rational to hire managers who are fiduciaries to their interest and the interest of the collective. If it turns out the "collective interest" is the empty set, then this principle simply collapses into the Agency Principle.

Thus, the Doctrine of Fair Contracts consists of these six groundrules or principles:

1. The Principle of Entry and Exit
2. The Principle of Governance
3. The Principle of Externalities
4. The Principle of Contracting Costs
5. The Agency Principle
6. The Principle of Limited Immortality

Think of these groundrules as a doctrine which would guide actual stakeholders in devising a corporate constitution or charter. Think of management as having the duty to act in accordance with some specific constitution or charter.

Obviously, if the Doctrine of Fair Contracts and its accompanying background narratives are to effect real change, there must be requisite changes in the enabling laws of the land. I propose the following three principles to serve as constitutive elements of attempts to reform the law of corporations.

The Stakeholder Enabling Principle

Corporations shall be managed in the interests of their stakeholders, defined as employees, financiers, customers, employees, and communities.

The Principle of Director Responsibility

Directors of the corporation shall have a duty of care to use reasonable judgment to define and direct the affairs of the corporation in accordance with the Stakeholder Enabling Principle.

The Principle of Stakeholder Recourse

Stakeholders may bring an action against the directors for failure to perform the required duty of care.

Obviously, there is more work to be done to spell out these principles in terms of model legislation. As they stand, they try to capture the intuitions that drive the liberal ideals. It is equally plain that corporate constitutions which meet a test like the doctrine of fair contracts are meant to enable directors and executives to manage the corporation in conjunction with these same liberal ideals.

NOTES

1. Cf. A. Berle and G. Means, *The Modern Corporation and Private Property* (New York; Commerce Clearing House, 1932), 1. For a reassessment of Berle and Means' argument after 50 years, see *Journal of Law and Economics* 26 (June 1983), especially G. Stigler and C. Friedland, "The Literature of Economics: The Case of Berle and Means," 257–68; D. North, "Comment on Stigler and Friedland," 269–72; and G. Means, "Corporate Power in the Marketplace," 467–85.

2. The metaphor of rebuilding the ship while afloat is attributed to Neurath by W. Quine, *Word and Object* (Cambridge: Harvard University Press, 1960), and W. Quine and J. Ullian, *The Web of Belief* (New York: Random House, 1978). The point is that to keep the ship afloat during repairs we must replace a plank with one that will do a better job. Our argument is that stakeholder capitalism can so replace the current version of managerial capitalism.

3. See R. Charan and E. Freeman, "Planning for the Business Environment of the 1980s," *The Journal of Business Strategy* 1 (1980): 9–19, especially p. 15 for a brief account of the major developments in products liability law.

4. See S. Breyer, *Regulation and Its Reform* (Cambridge: Harvard University Press, 1983), 133, for an analysis of food additives.

5. See I. Millstein and S. Katsh, *The Limits of Corporate Power* (New York: Macmillan, 1981), Chapter 4.

6. Cf. C. Summers, "Protecting All Employees Against Unjust Dismissal," *Harvard Business Review* 58 (1980): 136, for a careful statement of the argument.

7. See E. Freeman and D. Reed, "Stockholders and Stakeholders: A New Perspective on Corporate Governance," in C. Huizinga, ed., *Corporate Governance: A Definitive Exploration of the Issues* (Los Angeles: UCLA Extension Press, 1983).

8. See T. Peters and R. Waterman, *In Search of Excellence* (New York: Harper and Row, 1982).

9. See, for instance, A. Wicks, D. Gilbert, and E. Freeman, "A Feminist Reinterpretation of the Stakeholder Concept," *Business Ethics Quarterly*, Vol. 4, No. 4, October 1994; and E. Freeman and J. Liedtka, "Corporate Social Responsibility: A Critical Approach," *Business Horizons*, Vol. 34, No. 4, July–August 1991, pp. 92–98.

10. At the Toronto workshop Mark Starik sketched how a theory would look if we took the environment to be a stakeholder. This fruitful line of work is one example of my main point about pluralism.

11. J. Rawls, *Political Liberalism,* New York: Columbia University Press, 1993; and R. Rorty, "The Priority of Democracy to Philosophy" in *Reading Rorty: Critical Responses to Philosophy and the Mirror of Nature (and Beyond),* ed. Alan R. Malachowski, Cambridge, MA: Blackwell, 1990.

Private Corporations and Public Welfare

George G. Brenkert
Professor and Director, Connelly Program in Business Ethics, McDonough School of Business, Georgetown University

I

The doctrine of corporate social responsibility comes in many varieties.[1] Its most developed version demands that corporations help alleviate "public welfare deficiencies," by which is understood problems of the inner city, drug problems, poverty, crime, illiteracy, lack of sufficient funding for educational institutions, inadequate health care delivery systems, chronic unemployment, etc.

In short, social responsibility, it is contended, requires that corporations assume part of the responsibility for the basic prerequisites of individ-

From *Public Affairs Quarterly,* Vol. 6, Issue 2 (April 1992), pp. 155–168. Reprinted by permission of *Public Affairs Quarterly.*

ual and social life within a community or society. Social responsibility demands this even though, it is claimed, corporations are not causally responsible for these conditions and doing so may not enhance their profits.

In response, corporations today provide job training for the hardcore unemployed, help renovate parks, sponsor clean-up programs, establish manufacturing plants in ghetto areas, offer seminars to high school students on how effectively to seek employment, support minority business adventures, provide educational films as well as additional instructors and tutors to public schools (i.e. "adopt" schools), etc.[2]

Such projects have, seemingly, met with a great deal of approval. Indeed, during a time when the welfare of many is deficient, one wonders how anyone could object to such activities. It might seem that any objections to such corporate behavior would stem not from their participating in these activities, but from their not participating even more.

Nevertheless, a number of objections to corporations engaging in such activities have been raised and are well-known. Many of these criticisms are not very good and will not be reviewed here. There is, however, one objection that is much more interesting, even if it is rarely developed. The essence of this objection is that corporate social responsibility to produce directly the public welfare involves the illegitimate encroachment of private organizations into the public realm. There is much greater merit to it than might appear at first glance.

II

This objection takes various forms. Theodore Levitt, for example, claims that the essence of free enterprise is the production of high-level profits. Private business corporations tend to impose this narrowly materialistic view on whatever they touch. Accordingly, corporate responsibility for welfare threatens to reduce pluralism and to create a monolithic society.[3] George C. Lodge similarly maintains that "the demand that business apply itself to problems which government is finding it increasingly difficult to com-

prehend or affect . . . is . . . absurd. Corporations, whatever else they may be, are not purveyors of social assistance."[4] Unelected businessmen, he claims, have "neither the right nor the competence" to define or establish the goals and the criteria by which society should repair or remake itself.[5] Finally, Richard DeGeorge claims that

> there is great danger in expecting corporations to take upon themselves the production of public welfare, because they already have enormous power and are not answerable for its use to the general public. Politicians are elected by the public and are expected to have the common good as their end. We should not expect corporations to do what they are neither competent nor organized to do . . .[6]

These criticisms question the right as well as the competence of corporations to contribute directly to the public welfare. Further, they challenge the influence which corporations in so acting may gain over society. Both increased corporate power and a decrease of social pluralism are feared results.[7]

Unfortunately, these criticisms are, more often than not, simply noted, rather than elaborated upon. In particular, the suggestion implicit within them that the provision of public welfare by private corporations runs afoul of an important distinction between what is public and what is private has not been discussed in recent literature. It is this point which requires greater attention.

The argument offered here is that corporate responsibility for public welfare threatens to reduce, transform, and in some cases eliminate important public dimensions of social life. For this reason we must be wary of it and reluctant to accept it in its present forms. Several characteristics of this argument should be noted at the outset. First, it does not pretend to show that all corporate measures that address public welfare deficiencies are (by themselves or individually) wrong, mischievous, or mistaken. Still, we must not be overly impressed by particular instances and thereby miss the systematic and general implications that are thereby promoted. It is not uncommon for individually rational actions to lead to collectively irrational or morally problematic results.

Second, this argument does not address corporate social responsibilities with regard to damages that corporations may themselves directly cause to the environment, employees, members of society, etc. For all these harms it is reasonable to believe that corporations do have responsibilities. The question this paper addresses concerns the implications of demanding that corporations go beyond correcting the damages they have brought about and assume responsibility for public welfare deficiencies for which they are not causally responsible.

Finally, if we could identify the harms that corporations directly *and* indirectly cause, then the arena of responsibilities that corporations have to society might significantly increase and the deficiencies in public welfare (assuming corporations fulfilled their responsibilities) might correspondingly decrease. This paper presupposes that, even in such a situation, there would remain public welfare deficiencies for which corporations are said to be socially responsible and for which they are neither directly nor indirectly causally responsible.[8]

The present argument has four parts. To begin with, it is important to highlight the different relation that exists between an individual (or group) who is aided by a private corporation, and the relation between such an individual (or group) and public attempts to aid their welfare. The differences in these relations will, in practice, often be insignificant—especially when things go well. However, when problems arise theoretical and practical differences can be important. Surely cases could be identified in which corporations have successfully enhanced the public welfare. However, it is not to be expected that corporations will always act so successfully or so clearly in accord with public needs.

The point here is not that corporations may act in misguided ways so much as what happens in those instances where there are problems. Obviously appeals and complaints can be made to the corporation. However, the fact remains that appeals to the corporation tend to be appeals from external constituencies. Inasmuch as those aided by the corporation are not members of the corporation, they have no standing, as it were, within the corporation other than the one the corporation decides to give them. They have no "constitutional" rights against corporations as they do against public endeavors. They are not "citizens" of the corporation. Thus, they have, in principle, no internal access to the corporation's decision-making processes. They are part of that process only if the corporation allows it. Those who make the decisions to undertake various programs cannot be voted out of office—there is no political, and little legal control, over them. Accordingly, to advocate corporate provision of, and responsibility for, public welfare is to advocate that the basic requisites for human well being are to be provided by institutions whose deliberations, at least at present, do not in principle include representation of those whose interests are affected. Those deficient in welfare lack formal control or power over those agencies from whom they obtain their welfare. Further, since those deficient in welfare tend to be those who are (in general) powerless, the advocacy of corporate responsibility for welfare tends to continue their powerlessness. Corporate social responsibility, in excluding any formal relation between those who are recipients of corporate aid and the corporation, maintains a division between the powerless and the powerful. A democratic society, one would suppose, would seek to moderate, rather than increase, the inequality presupposed in this division.

This situation contrasts with the state or other public bodies which provide, as part of their nature, various forms of administrative, legal and political redress.[9] The state's activities on behalf of its citizenry are hemmed in (at least in principle) by safeguards and guarantees (voting, representation, public hearings, sunshine laws, etc.) which are not imposed on corporations. Indeed, such public forms of access and standing are generally said to be contrary to the corporation's private status. Accordingly, whenever people outside the private corporation are granted such access it is simply due to the benevolence of the corporation.

Now this different relation between individuals and the agencies (private or public) which provide support for them is particularly crucial when that support concerns their basic welfare, i.e. items to which one might reasonably claim a right: e.g., minimal health care, educational opportunities, physical security, shelter, and food. Surely various private institutions such as corporations, churches, etc. may appropriately give aid to those who are deficient in such welfare, when this occurs on an occasional or special basis. Accordingly, private institutions may aid the welfare of their members (those who have access and voice within the organization) as well as non-members (those who do not have such access and voice).

However, those who advocate that this become the normal situation are (implicitly at least) also advocating a condition that places the recipients in a tenuous position vis-à-vis the granting agencies. Though recipients may receive various goods and/or services they need from private corporations, not only are such individuals dependent on those agencies for the aid they receive, but they also lose any formal or "constitutional" voice in the agency which purports to aid them. In effect, any right they have to such welfare is degraded to an act of benevolence on the part of the contributing organization. They can no longer insist or demand that they be treated in various ways, but must play the role of supplicants.

It is in this kind of situation that the view attributed to Andrew Carnegie can arise unchecked by formal mechanisms to control it: "In the exercise of his trust he was responsible only to his own conscience and judgment of what was best for the community."[10] Recipients of such aid lack means of redress which, in matters of basic importance such as welfare, are terribly significant.

Furthermore, when the institutions (i.e. large business corporations) involved in providing welfare are not themselves dedicated to the welfare of others but primarily focused on their own self-interested economic ends, and when these organizations are extremely large and powerful, then we must reflect on the implications of the lack of membership, and hence the lack of redress and voice, within those organizations. Specifically, we need to consider whether these needs ought not to be met by organizations which will grant those receiving such aid the voice and access which has traditionally protected people who are dependent upon others.

In short, when corporations are asked to undertake public welfare on an ongoing basis, the welfare they give is privatized in a manner that eliminates an important relation for those receiving such welfare. To the extent that it formalizes a relation between the powerful and the powerless, it exposes the recipients of such aid to abuses of power. At the same time, the equality that democracy implies is also jeopardized.[11]

Second, a variation on the preceding point concerns the standards by which decisions on the nature and means of implementing corporate welfare measures are made. Again, this might not appear to be a significant problem with regard to the construction or reconstruction of an inner-city park, a neighborhood clean-up campaign, or reading tutors in the schools.[12] Surely corporations will, by and large, consult with the people involved to get their ideas and approval. On other occasions, the people involved will seek out a corporation to aid them. But this does not lay the issue to rest since the standards the corporation seeks to follow may be primarily private in nature, rather than public or general.[13]

Suppose, for instance, that the welfare measures which the corporation seeks to provide (and to which their recipients agree) are of questionable constitutionality. They agree, perhaps, on educational films with a religious or a racist message for the public schools. Or, suppose they agree on an educational program but the corporation liberally sprinkles the presentation with its corporate logo, mascot, jingo, and the like. Suppose that in training of the hard-core unemployed they aim at white, rather than black or Hispanic, populations. The point at issue concerns the legitimacy of these decisions.

The standards according to which the public welfare is fulfilled must be a matter for the public (through its representatives) to determine, not the private corporation.[14] Two reasons lie behind this claim. Such welfare concerns what is common among the citizens, what holds the members of a society together, and what is the nature of their basic prerequisites. It constitutes a statement about how we, as a community or society, believe that we should live. Fulfillment of welfare deficiencies for some that manifests prejudice against other groups, or works to their disadvantage, requires special justification and close public scrutiny, if it is allowed to stand.

In addition, to the extent that corporate contributions to public welfare are tax deductible, the foregone tax revenues constitute a public contribution to itself, through the agency of the corporation. Since public monies are committed through such contributions, the public has a right to assure itself that the standards according to which such monies are expended meet its (minimal) standards.[15]

Accordingly, the legitimacy of the decisions the private corporation makes regarding public welfare cannot be judged simply according to its own private standards. Thus, if the corporation tries to impose its own view and standards, it is crossing an important line between the private and the public. It is naive, then, simply to argue that people's welfare is the responsibility of corporations, without providing for social determination and direction of the activities which corporations undertake.[16]

In those instances in which corporate contributions are of a charitable (or prudential) nature *and* the objects of their actions are wholly private, it would seem that corporations might legitimately give to those individuals or organizations which promote their own values and ideas. In this way, their gifts may reflect their own idiosyncratic standards. Accordingly, some object to business giving to private universities whose faculty advocate ideas opposed to capitalism.[17] However, in contrast, the direction and satisfaction of public welfare according to private standards is not appropriate, since the public welfare is not to be determined simply by this or that individual corporation's ideas and values, but by a political process and, ideally a community dialogue, on what those values should be.[18]

Finally, if corporations are said to be responsible for remedying certain deficient levels of public welfare, but are not given control (both in terms of applicable standards and practical direction) over how such remedies are to be emplaced, then when these measures fail the corporation can hardly be held accountable. Nevertheless, since they will be associated with such efforts, they will often be faulted for their lack of success. Hence, if corporations are required to engage in social responsibility efforts, there will be an understandable tendency for them to seek control over the situations in which they participate. This means, however, supplanting (or reducing) public control and substituting their own judgments and standards for those of the public. Consequently, the demand for corporate social responsibility is a demand that encourages the substitution of private standards, authority and control for those of the public.

III

Third, the demand for corporate social responsibility arises, it has been assumed, due to deficient public welfare, which stems, at least in part, from inadequate public funding. Corporate opposition to higher taxes has played a contributing role to this situation, since taxes are viewed as coercive takings of corporate property.[19] The lower the taxes the greater the return on investment corporations make and the greater the flexibility corporations have to use their resources as they choose. Part of the appeal of corporate social responsibility for public welfare is that the aid that is given is voluntary. Provision of such aid heads off higher taxes, government regulation and hence coercion, In short, behind the demand for corporate social responsibility is a view that holds that the public realm and the state constitute a sphere of coercion, while the private realm and the actions it takes are voluntary.[20]

This is illustrated in Friedman's comment that "the political principle that underlies the political mechanism is conformity. . . . It is appropriate for some to require others to contribute to a general social purpose whether they wish to or not."[21] Corporate social responsibility, then, explicitly seeks to reduce the realm of the public, by reducing the area within which coercion and force might be used.

Now if the public were simply a realm of coercion, such a view would seem unexceptionable. On the contrary, however, such a view arguably distorts the realm of the public. Corporate social responsibility implies that the public is simply an area within which individual prudential interests are worked out and coercion imposed by the state. Both eliminate an important sense of the public.

The public is also the area within which general and common interests are articulated. It is what binds people together, in contrast to the private realm within which people are separated from each other and view each other as limitations upon their freedom.[22] Accordingly, it is the realm of the "we," rather than the "you" or "I." It is what is done in all our names, and not just yours or mine. It is the area, some have even held, within which freedom is only possible.[23] There is (or can be) a different sense of accomplishment when the community builds or creates something rather than simply this or that private organization. Conversely, there is a different sense of loss when a public figure, a President or Prime Minister dies, rather than the head of a private corporation.

Now charity is an extension of the private into this public realm. It is personal, self-given, and can't be demanded in particular cases. It need not be based on political discussion or compromise so much as on one's own willingness to aid others. Those who receive do not have grounds upon which they can demand or negotiate beyond which the charitable organization allows. Charity does not necessarily involve any political or public process by which recipient and contributor are bound together. Thus, Hannah Arendt comments, "The bond of charity between people . . . is incapable of founding a public realm of its own . . ."[24] In short, charity cannot be the basis of a public or political dimension between people.

As such, corporate social responsibility drives out the political and the public. The appeal to corporate responsibility is a confession that the public or political realm has broken (or is breaking) down. It is an unwitting manifestation of liberal individualism extending the realm of the private to encompass the public.

Consequently, Friedman is quite wrong when he complains that the doctrine of social responsibility "taken serious would extend the scope of the political mechanism to every human activity."[25]

This is plausible only in that case when the corporation and its executives both engage in social responsibility activities *and,* as a result, become subject to political election procedures since they are viewed as "civil servants."[26] On the other hand, if this does not happen (and there is little present evidence that it will), then the doctrine of social responsibility extends the nature of private activities to many activities in the public or political realm. In short, quite the opposite of what Friedman contends, it extends the scope of the private "to every human activity."

The problem with this approach is that it is implausible to treat society as simply an example of an ideal market situation. This is implied by the above comments on the nature of the public. Not all public (or private) values can be produced or sustained by market exchanges. Friedman slips from discussion of market activities to talk of society without argument. Thus, after he portrays the voluntary nature of the ideal free market, he immediately goes on (without argument) to equate such exchanges with society itself.[27] However, it does not follow (and it is not plausible) to think of society as itself simply an ideal free market. Once again, then, corporate social responsibility involves views and demands which question legitimate distinctions between the private and the public.

IV

Finally, though the relation of the public and the private is a shifting relation, we must guard against collapsing one—either one—term of this relation into the other. The view that the public is simply the arena in which individual actions affect others without their voluntary approval impoverishes the notion of the public.[28] As noted above, the public is more and different than this. The public is what binds a people together and relates them to each other.[29] It is what is done in their common name; it is what makes them a people, rather than simply a random collection of individuals. It embodies the values, norms and ideals we strive towards even if we fail fully to achieve them. It is the responsibility of public agencies (the state or its government) to foster (at least) the minimal conditions under which the public may exist. To be a citizen is to owe allegiance to the government as it works to realize these principles and values.

Now suppose that the government does not fulfill its responsibilities to individuals for basic welfare. The demand that private corporations—rather than the government—dispense public welfare is a step in the privatization of the public realm. The benefits that individuals receive from the government have long been thought to play an important role in their obligations to the state and, hence, their citizenship within the state.[30] If these benefits come from private groups, rather than the state, then one would expect loyalties and obligations to be modified accordingly.

Consequently, if a corporation provides training for the hard-core unemployed, renovates the local park, or provides the house which shelters the sick, it is to the corporation that those aided will be grateful and indebted, not to the community or society of which they are members.[31] It is the corporation to which one's loyalties will be turned, and not to the city or state of which one is a citizen. Indeed, the very notion of citizenship thereby becomes impoverished. The grounds upon which the state has been said to acquire the obligations of its citizenry have been narrowed. In its place develop isolated (groups of) individuals beholden to private institutions of which they are not members (or citizens) and over which they have no formal control.

Surely in these days of popular advertising, the corporation may seem more personal, less abstract, than the community or the state. Through logos, jingoes and mascots corporations seek to get people to identify with them and their products. And through corporate measures to aid their welfare, individuals would have concrete reason to be indebted to them, even if not members or citizens of them. But to accept or promote this situation, and the view of the individual's relations to private and public institutions which it involves, merely reveals the state of poverty to which our notions of the public and citizenship have come. Such corporations encourage us to seek a common identity, rather than to foster our common (public) interests.[32] We are invited to replace the realm of

the public which unavoidably involves impersonality with a personal and privatized realm. We transform a realm laden with political meanings into a private and psychologized realm.[33]

However, the danger here does not simply stem from the implications of the altered identifications and loyalties that characterize citizens. The increasing privatization of the public realm that we see in shopping malls, corporate housing developments, the suburban environment, and corporate attempts to establish their own identity and role models within the schools carry other consequences to which we must be keenly sensitive. For example, in private shopping malls people may be prevented from political speech; in corporate housing developments, they may be prohibited from having children and remaining in their home; and cultural exhibits may be skewed to suit corporate purposes.[34] Rights which all citizens share may be, wittingly or unwittingly, foregone through private efforts uninformed by public reflection and participation. In short, the public values and interests of a society can be threatened not simply by an authoritarian government but also by self-interested, though well-meaning, private groups and institutions which lack a sense of the significance of the public realm and the meaning of citizenship.

V

In conclusion, several comments are appropriate. First, it may be allowed that many objections which can be brought against corporate attempts to secure public welfare can also be brought against government or public attempts. Thus, both government and corporations may be inflexible, insensitive, impersonal, non-innovative, as well as hard to move or get through to. They may produce programs which are misconceived, uncoordinated, and/or precipitously stopped, leaving people in the lurch. The production of such programs may increase their power, size and influence; they may also deal paternalistically with those they seek to aid. One would be tempted to abandon all attempts to aid those deficient in welfare were it not for the fact that many people continue to suffer grievously from inadequate welfare. Thus, the question is a complex and messy one. There is no easy and neat answer.

Second, large corporations, however, will continue to be part of our social and political landscape. Their significant economic and political power are obvious. In this situation, the thrust of the public/private argument is two-sided. It can be taken to urge the separation of private corporations and public institutions. This is fraught with all the problems of bureaucratization, distant government, powerful but indifferent corporations, and failed efforts to satisfy public welfare needs. This is not to say that these problems could not be overcome within a fairly strict separation of the private and the public.[35] Still, this would involve a recommitment (and rediscovery!) of the public realm that might be difficult in countries such as the U.S.

On the other hand, the above argument can also be taken to recommend that we require such large corporations be made more fully public, social organizations. Indeed, many argue that large corporations are no longer simply private organizations. George C. Lodge, for example, comments that "it is now obvious that our large public corporations are not private property at all . . . The best we can say," he continues, "is that the corporation is a sort of collective, floating in philosophic limbo, dangerously vulnerable to the charge of illegitimacy and to the charge that it is not amenable to community control."[36] Thus, that corporations increasingly are called to participate in the production of public welfare is not so surprising given their present, quasi-public nature. The further claim that has been made is that this quasi-public nature needs to be institutionalized so as to make it amenable to greater public control and direction. This direction, however, is one that others violently oppose.

Thus, we stand at a crossroads. This juncture is part and parcel of that "tension between self-reliant competitive enterprise and a sense of public solidarity espoused by civic republicans" that some have identified as "the most important unresolved problem in American history."[37] If one rejects the view that corporations must more fully

take on the character of public institutions, then demands for corporate social responsibility for public welfare should be seriously curtailed.

The preceding arguments do not show conclusively that corporations ought never to aid public welfare. They are one set of considerations which might, in some circumstances, be overridden. However, they do indicate important reasons why we should be more reluctant to proceed down the path that many have been encouraging us to take. When we are repeatedly told that the sight of corporate social responsibility is so lovely, and that the prospects of corporate responsibility for public welfare are so rosy, one may rightfully come to suspect that we are being led down the garden path.[38]

NOTES

1. "Private corporation" will be used to refer exclusively to private corporations engaged in the production of goods and services for profit.
2. Sandra L. Holmes reports in a study of how executives perceive social responsibility that 78% of the executives surveyed either strongly agreed or agreed more than they disagreed with the statement that "Business possesses the ability and means to be a *major* force in the alleviation of social problems" (pp. 39–40). It is clear from the context that by "social problems" is meant the kinds of problems listed in the text under "public welfare." Cf. Sandra L. Holmes, "Executive Perceptions of Corporate Social Responsibility," *Business Horizons* (June, 1976).
3. Theodore Levitt, "The Dangers of Social Responsibility." *Harvard Business Review,* vol. 36 (September–October, 1958), pp. 44–47.
4. George C. Lodge, *The New American Ideology* (New York: Alfred A. Knopf, 1975), p. 189.
5. *Ibid.,* p. 190. Cf., also p. 218.
6. DeGeorge, *Business Ethics,* 3rd ed. (New York: Macmillan Publishing Co., 1986), p. 171.
7. Cf. Levitt, "The Dangers of Social Responsibility."
8. The importance of indirect causal factors and the resulting responsibility of corporations has been defended by Larry May in his comments, "Corporate Philanthropy and Social Responsibility," given on an earlier version of this paper, before the Society for Business Ethics meeting in Boston, MA, on December 28, 1990. How we might determine for which harms corporations are directly or indirectly

causally responsible is not addressed in this paper. Both topics, but especially the latter, raise significant problems.

9. Even if this is not true in any particular case, it is still appropriate to demand such access and forms of redress of present (i.e., democratic or republican) forms of government.

10. Robert H. Bremner, *American Philanthropy* (2nd ed.; Chicago: The University of Chicago Press, 1988), p. 101.

11. This argument allows that other private organizations, such as churches, etc., may legitimately contribute to individuals' welfare needs. The smaller the organization, the more individual the contribution, and the greater the identity of the organization is bound up with promoting the public good, the less there is a problem. On the other hand, some organizations, such as churches, run into problems (e.g., First Amendment issues and attempts to convert others rather than simply aid them) that other private groups do not.

12. Even the park example is not all that simple. There are questions that need to be asked before the park can be built or renovated: what will be the nature and form of the park? Who will maintain it (will anyone?)? Will trash containers be put out and regularly emptied (by whom?)? Is the construction of this park likely to require increased police patrols? Are additional burdens being placed on the city recreational department, trash department, police department? If so, who decides and upon what basis? Admittedly, these questions must be faced whether the city *or* a corporation builds the park. However, the important point is that when corporations aid public welfare many important questions remain to be answered. The city or the public is not suddenly let off the hook.

13. The problem is even more complex since those individuals the corporation addresses in the public forum may themselves primarily hold private values. That is, their vision of themselves and society may have lost any sense of the public. Bellah et al. document the degree to which "Americans . . . are genuinely ambivalent about public life" (Bellah et al., *Habits of the Heart* [Berkeley: University of California Press, 1985], p. 250).

14. Similarly for a host of other projects there are questions which demand social or public decision, which only the public through the government can legitimately give. For example, it might be asked whether it is really so bad for corporations to provide tutors for secondary schools to help with basic reading skills. But are these tutors trained in teach-

ing? Do they serve to justify inadequate teaching staffs? Do they undercut the demands of teachers for adequate social commitment for education? What programs are they trained to teach? Do they constitute an influx of business oriented courses rather than humanity courses, or science courses? These are serious issues which need to be addressed on the social and public level, not simply on the private corporate level.

Likewise, it might be asked whether it is wrong for corporations (e.g., McDonald's) to start drives for houses for relatives of the seriously ill to stay in while at the hospital. But again, supposing that the rest of the community contributes the preponderant amount, why should the community not get the credit for the house? Why doesn't the name of the house reflect public values or ideals?

We need not assume that public answers to all these questions may be easily arrived at. However, if corporations (or other private groups) simply operate on their own standards, the public discussion which may lead to public standards and agreement will be short-circuited. As a result, the public will be impoverished.

15. This claim applies to similar contributions that come from other private groups, e.g., churches, the Audubon Society, etc. When such contributions come from small and numerous groups, there is less reason for concern, since they may counterbalance each other. It is reasonable for a society to encourage such contributions. Nevertheless, society may legitimately review the nature of their contributions, given that their contributions are tax deductible and they enjoy (where applicable) tax-exempt status.

This issue is particularly of concern, however, when such contributions come from large corporations which can bring significant power and resources to bear. Similarly, when churches or other private groups become large and their powers significant, the consideration raised in the text applies as well. In short, when the contributions of private groups are supported by the public through tax deductions and when those contributions may in particular cases have a significant effect on the public, the public may legitimately review the standards according to which the contributions are made.

16. For example, Control Data's program, called "City Venture," which sought to write blueprints for economic rebirth of down-and-out city neighborhoods had to be withdrawn: "A bossy, 'we know what's best' attitude offended prickly independent community groups in Minneapolis and Miami, forcing City Venture to be withdrawn" (Neil R. Peirce, "To Cor-

porate Social Involvement," *The Knoxville Journal,* 1982, p. A4).

17. Robert H. Malott, "Corporate Support of Education: Some Strings Attached," *Harvard Business Review* vol. 56 (1978), pp. 133–38.

18. This is not to say that corporations, or anyone, must (or should) give to causes they believe to be wrong-headed. Rather, if corporations (or other organizations) are given responsibility for public welfare, they may not simply apply their own idiosyncratic standards. This allows, of course, that they could choose, from a range of public welfare needs, to support those compatible with their own views. Since the issue concerns basic deficiencies from which people suffer, this should not be impossible.

19. Similarly Levitt argues: "American capitalism also creates, fosters, and acquiesces in enormous social and economic cancers. Indeed, it fights against the achievement of certain forms of economic and social progress, pouring millions into campaigns against things which people have a right to expect from their government . . ." (Levitt, "The Dangers of Social Responsibility," p. 48).

20. Since corporate social responsibility is, usually, viewed either as charitable or as prudential in nature, corporations can make their own, voluntary choices as to when, what and how much they will do. The alternative is to have the public (the state or the government) take more from them in order to fulfill the public welfare needs. Because this restricts their choices—their freedom (as they would see it)—they argue against state action here. In short, corporate social responsibility is an expression of the liberal view of society. It is also an expression of an individualistic view: "utilitarian individualism" and "expressive individualism" (Bellah et al., *Habits of the Heart,* p. 27ff.). These views contrast with what they call "civic republicanism."

21. Milton Friedman, "The Social Responsibility of Business is to Increase its Profits, in Milton Snoeyenbos, Robert Almeder, James Humber (eds.), *Business Ethics* (Buffalo, New York: Prometheus Books, 1983), p. 78.

22. *Ibid.,* pp. 245, 248.

23. Nancy L. Schwartz, "Distinction Between Public and Private Life." *Political Theory,* vol. 7 (1979), p. 245.

24. Hannah Arendt, *The Human Condition* (Chicago: The University of Chicago Press, 1958), p. 53.

25. Milton Friedman, "The Social Responsibility of Business is to Increase its Profits," in Milton Snoeyenbos, Robert Almeder, James Humber (eds.), *Business Ethics* (Buffalo, New York: Prometheus Books, 1983), p. 79.

26. Friedman, "The Social Responsibility of Business is to Increase its Profits," p. 75.

27. *Ibid.*

28. Cf. John Dewey, *The Public and its Problems* (Chicago: Gateway Books, 1946).

29. Cf. Hannah Arendt. "The public realm, as the common world, gathers us together and yet prevents our falling over each other, so to speak"; *The Human Condition* (Chicago: The University of Chicago Press, 1958), p. 52.

30. Cf. A. John Simmons, *Moral Principles and Political Obligations* (Princeton: Princeton University Press, 1979), pp. 157–90.

31. The following comes from a letter to an editor from a mother of a child in a school adopted by IBM. She was responding to objections that others had raised because children in the school were preparing posters and having assemblies to thank IBM for adopting their school. She argues: "to say that this is taking away from the children's learning time is not true. What better learning experience is there than to teach our children what's going on in their schools and to have them have a special program to thank these companies? . . . I believe it is very important that these adopting companies realize, by way of parents and children, that we are honored and grateful that they are willing to help 'our' children with their education" (Letters to the Editor, *The Knoxville News-Sentinel,* November 28, 1986).

32. Cf. Richard Sennett who complains that as part of the end of public culture "the pursuit of common interests is destroyed in the search for a common identity" (p. 261); *The Fall of Public Man* (New York: Vintage Books, 1976).

33. Cf. Sennett, *Ibid.*

34. IBM, for example, "barred the display of computer-art works designed for the equipment of a major business competitor, Macintosh, in the company's heretofore prestigious IBM Gallery of Science and Art in midtown Manhattan"; Susan Davis, "IBM Nixes Macintosh," *Art in America,* vol. 76 (1990), p. 47. The works barred were part of a touring show organized by the Walker Art Center, IBM, which finances its namesake galleries, "bars its competition 'as a matter of policy'" (*Ibid.,* p. 47).

35. It would not, for example, prohibit linking education and business in various ways. Various courses of study in schools might be coordinated with job opportunities in private business, without corporations providing for those courses or other educational needs. Public and government welfare measures would have to be tied much more closely to local needs and allowed much greater flexibility in resolving those needs.

36. Lodge, *The New American Ideology,* p. 18.

37. Bellah et al., *Habits of the Heart,* p. 256.

38. I am indebted to John Hardwig, W. Michael Hoffman, Larry May, Richard Nunan, and an anonymous referee for their perceptive and helpful comments on earlier versions of this paper.

New Directions in Corporate Social Responsibility

Norman Bowie
Andersen Chair in Corporate Responsibility, University of Minnesota

Among philosophers writing in business ethics, something of a consensus has emerged in the past ten years regarding the social responsibility of business. Although these philosophers were critical of the classical view of Milton Friedman (the purpose of the corporation is to make profits for stockholders), the consensus view had much in common with Friedman, so much so that I referred to my own statement of this position as the neoclassical view of corporate responsibility (Bowie 1982). The heart of the neoclassical view was that the corporation was to make a profit while avoiding inflicting harm. In other formulations the corporation was to make a profit while (1) honoring the moral minimum or (2) respecting individual rights and justice. Tom Donaldson arrived at a similar neoclassical description of the purpose of the corporation by arguing that such a view is derived from the social contract that business has with society (1989).

The stakeholder theory made popular by Ed Freeman does seem to represent a major advance over the classical view (Freeman 1984; Evan and Freeman 1988). It might seem inappropriate to refer to the stakeholder position as neoclassical. Rather than argue that the job of the manager was to maximize profits for stockholders, Freeman argued that the manager's task was to protect and

promote the rights of the various corporate stakeholders. Stakeholders were defined by Freeman as members of groups whose existence was necessary for the survival of the firm—stockholders, employees, customers, suppliers, the local community, and managers themselves.

Despite the vast increase in scope of managerial obligations, a Friedmanite might try to bring stakeholder theory under his or her umbrella. Of course, the managers must worry about the rights and interests of the other corporate stakeholders. If you don't look after them, these other stakeholders will not be as productive and profits will fall. A good manager is concerned with all stakeholders while increasing profits for stockholders. In the Friedmanite view, the stakeholder theorist does not give us an alternative theory of social responsibility; rather, he or she reminds us how an enlightened Friedmanite, as opposed to an unenlightened one, is supposed to manage. The unenlightened Friedmanite exploits stakeholders to increase profits. Although that strategy might succeed in the short run, the morale and hence the productivity of the other stakeholders plummets, and as a result long-run profits fall. To protect long-run profits, the enlightened manager is concerned with the health, safety, and family needs (day care) of employees, a no-question-asked return policy, stable long-term relations with suppliers, and civic activities in the local community. In this way, long-run profitability is protected or even enhanced. In the classical view, the debate between Milton Friedman and Ed Freeman is not a debate about corporate ends, but rather about corporate means to that end.

Moreover, some classicists argue, the neoclassical concern with avoiding harm or honoring the moral minimum does not add anything to Friedman's theory. In *Capitalism and Freedom* (1962) he argues that the manager must obey the law and moral custom. The quotation goes like this:

> In such an economy, there is one and only one social responsibility of business—to use its resources and engage in activities designed to increase its profits so long as it stays within the rules of the game, which is to say, engages in open and free competition, without deception or fraud.

If there really is a social contract that requires business to honor a moral minimum, then a business manager on the Friedmanite model is duty-bound to obey it. To the extent that the moral minimum involves duties to not cause avoidable harm, or to honor individual stakeholder rights, or to adhere to the ordinary canons of justice, then the Friedmanite manager has these duties as well. Even if Friedman didn't emphasize the manager's duties to law and common morality, the existence of the duties are consistent with Friedman's position.

Unfortunately, the compatibility of the classical Friedmanite position with obedience to law and morality is undercut by some of Friedman's most well-known followers. The late Albert Carr (1968) substituted the morality of poker for ordinary morality. Indeed he argued that ordinary morality was inappropriate in business:

> Poker's own brand of ethics is different from the ethical ideals of civilized human relationships. The game calls for distrust of the other fellow. It ignores the claim of friendship. Cunning deception and concealment of one's strength and intentions, not kindness and openheartedness, are vital in poker. No one thinks any the worse of poker on that account. And no one should think the worse of the game of business because its standards of right and wrong differ from the prevailing traditions of morality in our society. . . .

Even more pervasive has been the influence of former *Harvard Business Review* editor Theodore Levitt. He defends various deceptive practices in advertising, which seem to be in violation of ordinary morality, as something consumers really like after all (1970):

> Rather than deny that distortion and exaggeration exist in advertising, in this article I shall argue that embellishment and distortion are among advertising's legitimate and socially desirable purpose: and that illegitimacy in advertising consists only of falsification with larcenous intent. . . . But the consumer suffers from an old dilemma. He wants "truth," but he also wants and needs the alleviating imagery and tantalizing promise of the advertiser and designer.

The writings of these authors give Friedman's theory that "anything for profit" ring that its critics hear. But Friedman need not be interpreted in that way. Many profit-oriented business people do not espouse that interpretation; neither do some academic Friedmanites. What needs to be done is for the Friedmanite school to declare Carr

and Levitt heretics and excommunicate them from the faith. The Friedmanites also need to include as part of their canon some statement of the moral minimum idea so the phrase "rules of the game" in *Capitalism and Freedom* has some flesh and bone.

On one important point the neoclassical theorists and the Friedmanites are already in explicit agreement. Both positions argue that it is *not* the purpose of business to do good. The neoclassicists agree with Levitt that providing for the general welfare is the responsibility of government. A business is not a charitable organization.

> Business will have a much better chance of surviving if there is no nonsense about its goals—that is, if long-run profit maximization is one dominant objective in practice as well as in theory. Business should recognize what government's functions are and let it go at that, stopping only to fight government where government directly intrudes itself into business. It should let government take care of the general welfare so that business can take care of the more material aspects of welfare. (Levitt 1958)

Both the classicists and the neoclassicists have elaborate arguments to support their views. The classicist arguments focus on legitimacy. Corporate boards and managers are not popularly elected. Politicians are. Hence, government officials have a legitimacy in spending tax dollars for public welfare that corporate managers don't. Moreover, the corporate board and managers are agents of the stockholders. Unless the stockholders authorize charitable contributions, the corporate officers have no right to give the stockholders' money away and violate their fiduciary responsibility in doing so.

Levitt (1958) gives the legitimacy argument a final twist. It is the job of the government to provide for the general welfare; but if business starts doing the government's job, the government will take over business. As a result, business and government will coalesce into one powerful group at the expense of our democratic institutions.

Levitt seems to hold the traditional American view, adopted from Montesquieu, that the existence of a democracy requires a balance of competing powers among the main institutions of society. Levitt and Friedman both see the competing institutions as business, government, and labor, each with its distinct and competing interests. If business starts to take on the task of government, the balance of power is upset.

The neoclassical arguments are much more pragmatic. Corporations don't have the resources to solve social problems. Moreover, since the obligation to do good is an open-ended one, society cannot expect corporations to undertake it. A corporation that tries to solve social problems is an institutional Mother Teresa. What it does is good, but its actions, in the language of ethics, are supererogatory.

Some of the neoclassicists add a little sophistication to the argument by showing that competitive pressure will prevent corporations from doing good, even if the competitors all want to. If company X spends more of its money solving social problems than company Y, company Y gains a competitive advantage. Even if company Y wants to contribute to solving social problems, it will try to get company X to contribute even more. Company X has thought this all through; as a result it can't contribute (or contribute as much as it would like). The conclusion is that all competitive companies believe they can't focus on solving social problems even if they want to.

As a result of the arguments, a fairly orthodox position has developed both in theory and in practice. American corporations do not have an obligation to solve social problems. Whatever the notion of corporate responsibility means, it does not mean that. However, the orthodox position does have its critics, and these critics have arguments of their own.

Perhaps the three strongest arguments are based on the duties of gratitude and citizenship and the responsibilities of power. With respect to gratitude, defenders of a duty to help solve social problems argue that society provides tremendous resources to corporations. The local community provides public education that trains workers, a legal system complete with police and courts to enforce corporate contracts, and a huge infrastructure of highways, sewage and garbage disposal, and public health facilities. Corporate taxes are not sufficient payment for the corporations' share of these resources, therefore corporations have a duty out of gratitude to help solve social problems. Moreover,

even if corporate taxes did cover their fair share, corporations are citizens morally similar to individual citizens: as a result, they have a similar obligation to help solve social problems. Thus, corporations have a duty based on citizenship to help solve social problems. Finally, the moral use of power requires that power be used responsibly. The term "stewardship" is often used to describe the responsibilities of those who have great power and resources. Individual corporate leaders make reference to the duties of stewardship when they establish private foundations. Carnegie and Rockefeller are two prominent examples.

In addition to the intellectual arguments on behalf of a duty to help solve social problems, there are many actual cases where corporations have acted on that duty. It is part of the corporate culture in the Twin Cities (Minneapolis and St. Paul). Indeed, it seems to be part of the Minnesota corporate culture. Three chambers of commerce annually compile a list of the corporations who give 2 to 5 percent of their pre-tax profits to charitable organizations. The list contains a number of *Fortune* 500 companies, including General Mills, Honeywell, Pillsbury, and the H. B. Fuller Co. The Minneapolis offices of the accounting firms of Arthur Andersen, Price Waterhouse, Peat Marwick and Mitchell, and Touche Ross and Company are also on the list.

The number of academics who support the view that corporate responsibility involves an obligation to help solve social problems is even smaller than the number of corporations who support the view. Moreover, the corporate culture of the Minnesota business community is considered unique. The orthodox view is that a socially responsible corporation pursues profit while respecting the moral minimum. I have been an adherent of that position, but I now think the position is mistaken. Part of what it means for a corporation to be socially responsible is cooperation with other corporations and with nonprofit social and government agencies to help solve social problems.

SOCIAL RESPONSIBILITY AND THE DUTY TO SOLVE SOCIAL PROBLEMS

I began this section with an argument for a duty to solve social problems. This argument resembles one a Friedmanite could use to defend an obligation on the part of corporate managers to honor the needs and rights of corporate stakeholders. As you recall, a Friedmanite could argue that a concern with the needs and rights of corporate stakeholders is required for long-term profits. Treating one's customers, employees, and suppliers well is a means to profit.

That theme provides a rationale for an instrumental duty of business to solve social problems. The argument I shall make rests on a number of complicated and controversial empirical claims, and I have neither the expertise—nor the space to argue for these empirical claims here. However, these empirical claims constitute something of a conventional wisdom on this subject.

Among the social problems the U.S. faces, most of the more important ones have a severe impact on the quality of the work force. The problem of drug use and other forms of substance abuse, the abysmal quality of public education, the decline in work ethic values, the instability of the family, and the short-term orientation of all corporate stakeholders all affect the firm negatively. The impact is especially acute on employees and suppliers. If the work force is poorly educated, affected with substance abuse, poorly motivated, and short-term oriented, productivity suffers both in quantity and quality.

In future international competition, the quality of the work force is the most important asset a company can have. If capital markets are open, the cost of capital will even out, so any advantage a country might gain through lower costs of capital is short-term. If a country gains an advantage through a technological discovery, highly developed technological competitors will reverse engineer the discovery so the advantage is short-term as well. The one advantage that is relatively long lasting is the quality of one's work force.

In that respect America is at a disadvantage. All the problems pointed out earlier have affected the quality of our work force more severely than in other countries. In addition, racial, religious, and ethnic tensions in our pluralistic work force affect productivity, putting us at a disadvantage against industrial societies with a more homogeneous work force. Thus, if America is to remain compet-

itive, social problems that affect work-force productivity must be addressed.

However, the traditional institutional source for resolving social problems—government—seems to have neither the will nor the power to do so. After all, the costs are high and Americans—as events in the past decade have demonstrated—don't like taxes. In addition to being high, the costs are also immediate. However, the benefits, though higher, are very distant. Politicians have difficulty with a time frame beyond the next election. Therefore, there is little incentive for a politician to pay the costs now. A well worked-out statement of this view can be found in Alan Blinder's *Hard Heads Soft Hearts* (1987).

To make matters worse, our high national debt, the recent war with Iraq, the S&L debacle, and our aging infrastructure will only drain resources from social problems. If international competition requires that such problems be solved, but government is unwilling and perhaps unable to do so, it would seem that business has no choice but to become involved. The long-term competitiveness and hence long-term profitability of business is at stake. If the scenario I have painted is at all accurate, then even a Friedmanite could argue that business should help solve social problems. Business initiative in that area is justified on the grounds that such action is necessary to increase profits.

There certainly is nothing inconsistent with a Friedmanite arguing that business should help solve social problems to increase profit, so long as the dangers from not doing so outweigh the dangers discussed earlier. But I doubt that people like Levitt would ever agree that the increase in profitability would be worth the cost of lost independence now enjoyed by the business community. Even though Friedmanites in theory could support a view of corporate responsibility that included a corporate duty to help solve social problems, in all probability they would not.

On the chance some Friedmanite might support such an expanded concept of social responsibility, let me argue why a Friedmanite approach to an obligation to help solve social problems would probably fail. My argument here is tied up with issues of motivation and intentionality.

Consider what philosophers call "the hedonic paradox": the more people consciously seek happiness the less likely they are to achieve it. The reader is invited to test this assertion by getting up tomorrow and framing his or her activities with a conscious goal of happiness. In other words, do everything to be happy. If you do, almost certainly you will fail to achieve happiness.

To understand the paradox, we must distinguish between the intended end of an action and the feelings we get when we succeed (achieve the goal). If you are thirsty, you seek a glass of water to extinguish the thirst. When you quench your thirst you feel pleasure or contentment. But you didn't get the glass of water to get the contentment that goes with quenching your thirst. And you generally don't act to be happy. You are happy when you succeed in obtaining the goals that constitute the basis of your actions. Happiness is not one of those goals; it is a state one achieves when one successfully gains one's other goals.

What does this have to do with profit? Should profit be a conscious goal of the firm, or the result of achieving other corporate goals? For simplicity's sake let us say there is some relation between providing meaningful work for employees, quality products for customers, and corporate profits. What is the nature of that relationship? Do you achieve meaningful work for employees and quality products for customers by aiming at profits (by making profits your goal), or do you aim at providing meaningful work for employees and quality products for customers (make them your goal) and achieve profits as a result? A Friedmanite is committed to making profits the goal. As we saw in the discussion of stakeholder theory, a Friedmanite will respect the needs and rights of the other stakeholders to increase profits for the stockholders. But for a genuine stakeholder theorist, the needs and rights of the various stakeholders take priority. Management acts in response to those needs: profits are often the happy result.

Both Friedmanites and non-Friedmanites can posit a relationship between profits and meeting stakeholder needs. What divides them is the strength of the causal arrow, a difference over which one should be the conscious objective of management. A Friedmanite argues for profit. A stakeholder theorist argues for the needs and rights of stakeholders. A Friedmanite argues that you treat employees and customers well to make a profit: good treatment is a means to an end. A stakeholder theorist argues that a manager should treat employees and customers well because it is the right thing to do; the needs and rights of the corporate stakeholders are the ends the manager should aim at. Profits are the happy results that usually accompany these ends.

American corporations have thought like Friedmanites even when they speak the language of stakeholder theorists. They introduce quality circles or ESOPS to increase profits. Some of our international competitors have thought like stakeholder theorists even though they have achieved Friedman-like results.

With respect to the duty to help solve social problems, should that duty be taken on because by doing so profits may be increased, or because it is a moral responsibility to do so? To answer that question, I suggest we visit the work of Cornell economist Robert Frank (1988) and consider the spotty success of the introduction of quality circles and other forms of "enlightened" labor management in the U.S.

Frank's point, buttressed by a large amount of empirical evidence from psychology, sociology, and biology, is that an altruistic person (a person who will not behave opportunistically even when he or she can get away with it) is the most desirable person to make a deal with. After all, if you have a contractual relationship with someone, the best person you can deal with is someone you know will honor the terms of the contract even if he or she could get away with not honoring them. An employer wants employees who won't steal or cheat even if they could. A marriage partner wants a spouse who won't cheat even if he or she could. Altruists rather than profit maximizers make the best business partners.

Frank then goes on to make the point Immanuel Kant would make. You can't adopt altruism as a strategy like "honesty is the best policy" and gain the advantages of altruism. After all, if I knew you were being an altruist because it paid, I would conclude that in any case where altruism didn't pay, you would revert to opportunism. My ideal business partner is someone who doesn't merely adopt altruism because it pays but adopts it because he or she is committed to it. She or he is not an opportunist because opportunism is wrong. As Frank says:

> For the model to work, satisfaction from doing the right thing must not be premised on the fact that material gains may later follow; rather it must be *intrinsic* to the act itself. Otherwise a person will lack the necessary motivation to make self-sacrificing choices, and once others sense that, material gains will not, in fact, follow. Under the commitment model, moral sentiments do not lead to material advantage unless they are heartfelt.

Frank's theoretical account of the advantages of committed altruism over reciprocal altruism as the best payoff strategy helps explain the spotty record of "enlightened" employee management techniques. Techniques like quality circles that work very well in Japan and Sweden don't work as well in the U.S. Why? Cultural difference is not a sufficiently specific answer. What cultural differences make the transfer difficult? I hypothesize that since labor/management relations in the U.S. are opportunistically based, labor assumes— probably correctly—that such reforms are motivated not by employer concern for employees but by profit. If that is the motivation, labor reasons, why should labor embrace the reforms? The elements of trust created by genuine concern for employees are missing in the American context. Indeed, both labor and management assume the other will behave opportunistically. Academics assume that too, and agency theory provides a model for the opportunistic framework. Given that cultural and intellectual context, it is no surprise that labor would distrust an employer whose concern with an improved working environment was not genuinely altruistic.

This discussion affects the duty to help solve social problems. If the resolution of these problems would improve America's human capital, that result would be most likely to occur if the investment in human capital were altruistically motivated. The one good thing about corporate efforts to solve so-

cial problems is that it is easy to show that with respect to the individual firm, such efforts must be altruistic. After all, an improved labor force is a classic case of a public good. There is no guarantee that the money spent by an individual firm will benefit that firm. If a firm adopts an inner city elementary school and pours resources into it, there is no reason to think that firm will get its investment back. The reason need not be that many of the students of that elementary school won't work for the supporting firm. After all, it might gain employees from other schools supported by other firms. Rather, the reason is that some firms will ride free off the expenditures of the moral firms. Thus, employees who understand these considerations can be sure that the employers who give money to solve social problems are altruistic.

If this analysis is correct the following conclusions can be drawn:

1. It is in the interest of business to adopt an extended view of corporate social responsibility that includes a duty to help solve social problems.
2. If business adopts that duty because it thinks it will benefit, its actions will be viewed cynically.
3. Moreover, because an improved labor force is a public good for business, the only real reason for an individual firm to help solve social problems is altruistic.
4. Thus, employees and other corporate stakeholders have a good reason to believe that corporate attempts to solve social problems are altruistic.

OBLIGATIONS OF VARIOUS STAKEHOLDERS IN A SOCIALLY RESPONSIBLE CORPORATION

In the previous section I gave an argument to show that everyone has good reason to believe that corporate attempts to solve social problems are genuinely altruistic. What are the implications of this for the various corporate stakeholders, especially customers?

Our ordinary way of speaking is to say the corporation ought to respect stakeholder needs and rights. Thus, we say that the corporation should produce quality products for customers, or that the corporation should not subject its employees to lie detector tests. We speak of the obligation of the firm (firm's management) to employees, customers, and local community. However, this way of speaking tends to give a one-sided emphasis to the moral obligations of the corporation.

My concern is that within the firm conceived of as a moral community, we speak as if all the obligations fall on the firm, or its managers and stockholders. In a previous article, "The Firm as a Moral Community" (Bowie 1991), I argued that Kant's third formulation of the categorical imperative best captures the moral relations that exist among corporate stakeholders. Kant would view a corporation as a moral community in which all of the stakeholders would both create the rules that govern them and be bound to one another by these same rules.

Moral relations are reciprocal. In addition to the obligations of managers, what of the obligations of the employees, customers, or local community to the firm (firm's management)? For example, business ethicists are critical of the so-called employment-at-will doctrine under which employees can be let go for "any reason, no reason, or reason immoral." Such a doctrine is unresponsive to the needs and rights of employees; it permits a manager to ignore both the quality of an employee's work performance and the number of years he or she has been with the firm.

Similarly, business ethicists are critical of the noneconomic layoffs that often accompany a hostile takeover. An example of noneconomic layoffs is when people are fired just because they worked for the old company. The new managers simply want their people in those positions—an understandable view, but one that does not take into account the interests of the employees let go. Those people might have served the target company for 20 years with great loyalty and distinction. Now they find themselves out of work through no fault of their own.

However, these business ethicists seldom criticize employees who leave a corporation on short notice simply to get a better job. Business firms argue that they invest huge amounts of money in training new employees, and losses from turnover

are very high. Sometimes the employee might have been given educational benefits or even paid leave to resolve personal problems such as alcohol and drug abuse. Others may have received company financial support for further education—perhaps even an M.B.A. Yet these employees think nothing of leaving the proven loyal employer for a better job elsewhere. As managers often remind us, loyalty is not a one-way street.

What needs to be decided is the nature of the employment relationship. Because it is among people, it cannot be merely an economic relationship. Although some currently refer to it as such, they are mistaken. All employment relationships have some contractual elements attached to them. A contract represents a kind of promise; even the standard employment relationship is in part moral. Some argue that legally the employment contract is nothing more than an agreement that the employer can let the employee go whenever he or she wants, and the employee can leave whenever he or she wants. There is true reciprocity here, even if the relationship is rather limited morally.

However, in the world of actual business practice one side or the other often behaves in ways that go far beyond the limited legal contractual relationship, thus adding moral capital to the relationship. Loyal employees who may have passed up other jobs are let go; employees leave loyal employers who have invested heavily in their welfare for a slightly better-paying job. Both actions are morally wrong because the duties of reciprocity and gratitude have been breached. Social responsibility under a stakeholder model requires that each stakeholder has reciprocal duties with others. Thus, if an employee has a duty of loyalty to an employer, an employer has a duty of loyalty to an employee.

Let us apply this analysis to a triadic stakeholder relationship—the firm's management, its customers, and the local community. One of the moral problems facing any community is environmental pollution. As with the employment-at-will doctrine, most business ethicists focus on the obligations of the firm. But what of the obligations of the consumers who buy and use the firm's products?

Consider the following instances reported by Alicia Swasy in a recent *Wall Street Journal* article (1988). Wendy's tried to replace foam plates and cups with paper, but customers in the test markets balked.

Procter and Gamble offered Downy fabric softener in a concentrated form that requires less packaging than ready-to-use products. However, the concentrate version is less convenient because it has to be mixed with water. Sales have been poor. Procter and Gamble also manufactures Vizir and Lenor brands of detergents in concentrate form. Europeans will take the trouble; Americans will not.

Kodak tried to eliminate its yellow film boxes but met customer resistance. McDonald's has been testing mini-incinerators that convert trash into energy but often meets opposition from community groups that fear the incinerators will pollute the air. A McDonald's spokesperson points out that the emissions are mostly carbon dioxide and water vapor and are "less offensive than a barbecue."

And Jerry Alder reports in *Newsweek* (1989) that Exxon spent approximately $40,000 each to "save" 230 otters. Otters in captivity cost $800. Fishermen in Alaska are permitted to shoot otters as pests.

Recently environmentalists have pointed out the environmental damage caused by the widespread use of disposable diapers. However, are Americans ready to give up Pampers and go back to cloth diapers and the diaper pail? Most observers think not.

If environmentalists want business to produce products that are more friendly to the environment, they must convince Americans to purchase them. Business will respond to the market. It is the consuming public that has the obligation to make the trade-off between cost and environmental integrity.

Yet another example involves corporate giving. Earlier I cited the Twin Cities, Minnesota business community as providing an example of a local community where many of the firms gave either 2 percent or 5 percent of their pretax profits back to the community. I have never heard anyone argue that on the principle of reciprocity, citizens of the Twin Cities have obligations to these firms. Yet I would argue that these citizens have an obligation to support socially responsible firms over firms that are either socially irresponsible or indifferent to social responsibility. The relation of a local citizen to the companies that do business locally is again not simply economic. Citizens who consider only price in choosing between two department stores are behaving in a socially irresponsible way. If one department store contributes to the local community and the other doesn't, that factor should be taken into account when citizens in that community decide on where to shop. It's more than a matter of price.

The Target department store chain is a branch of the Dayton Hudson Company. It has a special program for hiring the disabled, and even assists these people with up to one-third of their rent. At Christmas it closes its stores to the general public and opens them to the elderly and disabled. These people receive an additional 10 percent discount and free gift wrapping. In many stores 75 percent of the trash generated is recycled. Target is a member of the 5 percent club. The list of its activities that support the community goes on and on. Target's competitors, WalMart and KMart, have nothing comparable. I maintain that Target's superior social performance creates an obligation for members of the community to shop at Target.

All these examples lead to a general point. For too long corporate responsibility has been analyzed simply in terms of the responsibilities of the firm (firm's management) to all other corporate stakeholders except stockholders. I exclude stockholders because the cost of honoring stakeholder obligations comes almost exclusively from their profits. If we are to have a truly comprehensive theory of corporate social responsibility, we must develop a theory for determining the appropriate *reciprocal* duties that exist among corporate stakeholders. If the managers and stockholders have a duty to customers, suppliers, employees, and the local community, then the local community, employees, suppliers, and customers have a duty to managers and stockholders. What these duties are has barely been discussed.

THE COMPLICATIONS OF MORAL PLURALISM

A great complication that exists for any attempt to determine reciprocal stakeholder duties occurs when the existence of moral pluralism is taken into account. For purposes of this paper, moral pluralism is a descriptive term that applies to the widespread disagreement about moral matters that exists among the American people. People disagree as to what is right and wrong. Some consider drug testing to be right. Others think it's wrong. People also disagree about the priorities given to various rights and responsibilities. For example, does the firm's obligation to protect its customers override its obligation to protect the privacy of its employees? And suppose it is decided that the safety of the customers does take priority? Is testing all employees or random testing more fair? The general point is this: If people cannot agree as to what is right and wrong and how to set priorities when our duties conflict, what advice can be given to managers and other corporate stakeholders regarding what their duties are?

The unhappy situation that befell Dayton Hudson in late 1990 illustrates the point exactly. Dayton Hudson has long been a member of the Twin Cities 5 percent club. The funds are distributed through the Dayton Hudson Foundation. For many years Planned Parenthood has been the recipient of relatively small grants of a few thousand dollars. Abortion opponents have charged Planned Parenthood with various degrees of complicity in abortion activities.

In 1990 Dayton Hudson announced that to avoid becoming embroiled in the abortion debate, it would no longer support Planned Parenthood. No decision could have gotten it more embroiled in the debate. Pro-choice forces announced an immediate boycott of Dayton Hudson and its Target stores; hundreds of people cut up their Dayton Hudson credit cards and mailed them back to the company. In a few days Dayton Hudson relented and agreed to provide a grant to Planned Parenthood as it had done in the past. Now the anti-abortion forces were enraged. They organized boycotts and demonstrations that continued into the holiday season.

Dayton Hudson officials were both embarrassed and angry, but they indicated they would not retreat from their position to give 5 percent of their pretax income to charity. Although little was said publicly, the Dayton Hudson public relations disaster gave many executives pause. Perhaps the Friedmanites were right. They were giving away stockholder money for causes deemed inappropriate. Obviously some stockholders would not approve of the company's choices, just as some of Dayton's customers and citizens of the local community didn't.

In addition some executives were rumored to have taken the following position:

1. The money is ours;
2. If people don't like how we spend our money, then we won't spend it on charity at all.

These corporate officials saw Dayton Hudson's protesting customers and citizens in the Twin Cities as ungrateful and unappreciative of the largesse Dayton Hudson had given over the years. These ingrates did not deserve corporate support. Whether corporate support for charities in the Twin Cities will fall off over the next few years remains to be seen.

Should the Dayton Hudson problem become more widespread, a serious impediment toward any corporation's decision to help solve social problems will have arisen. How should such difficulties be resolved? To answer that question we need to return to our model of the firm as a nexus of moral relationships among stakeholders. From that perspective I might suggest some principles that can be used to help resolve the problems created by moral pluralism.

First, if a corporation really has a duty to help solve social problems, we can ask whether the corporation, through its managers, should have sole say as to how the money is to be spent. I think the answer to that question must be "no." A firm as constituted by its stakeholders is not narrowly defined. To let the managers have the sole say is to allow one stakeholder to make the decisions on behalf of all. How can that be justified?

Some argue that legal ownership justifies the decision. On this view the decision should be made by the stockholders, because they are the legal owners. To my knowledge, no corporation decides either the amount of charity or determines those organizations that receive charity by taking a vote of the stockholders. Of course, the matter could be settled in this way, but I have argued elsewhere (Bowie 1990) that the limited short-term view of most stockholders undercuts any moral claim that ownership might have to make the sole decision here.

These arguments, if valid, also count against any view that would justify the manager making this decision as the agent of the stockholder. If the stockholders have no right to make the sole determination in these matters, neither do the stockholders' agents. If no one stakeholder should settle these issues, it seems reasonable to think that all stakeholders should have a voice. How this voice is exercised can be decided in a number of ways.

Some corporations might focus on providing funds to groups that have broad public support, such as the United Way. Agencies like the United Way reflect community decisions concerning which charities are considered worthwhile. Undoubtedly some people in the community will object to the list, and agencies like the United Way have been criticized for leaving out controversial nonprofits that really fight social problems while keeping "middle class" charities such as the Boy Scouts. Despite these objections, deferring to local agencies recognizes the voice of the local community in decisions that are made. Alternatively, a corporation might put community people on its foundation board or community affairs council. I would recommend the first approach. The latter approach runs the risk of filling a board or council with individuals who speak only to narrow interests. Moreover, in line with my argument that moral duties fall on all corporate stakeholders, I would argue that it is the moral responsibility of the community to structure the United Way and other social agencies to meet genuine social needs. It is up to the local community to find a place for unpopular but socially concerned and effective nonprofits. It is up to the local community to solve the problems of representation.

Many corporations have given voice to their employees by matching employee contributions to charity. If an employee gives $100 to his or her college alma mater, the company will kick in $100 as well. Corporations also support charitable organizations in cities and towns where they have plants. They might extend this to cities and towns where their suppliers are located as well. These strategies should be adopted as policy by other corporations unless other defensible ways of giving voice to employees and suppliers can be found.

As for customers, they are part of the local community; unless there are some special circumstances that should be taken into account. I think our analysis will suffice. Customers are given voice the same way the local community is—by supporting local agencies through the United Way or some other similar organization.

Finally, I turn to stockholders. Although I have argued that the amount and type of corporate support given to help solve social problems should not be decided by the stockholders alone, they certainly should have some say in the decisions. Management might poll stockholders to determine their interests or get them to specifically approve the company's program in this area when they cast their annual proxy vote for the election of the board and other matters.

As the tenor of these remarks suggest, we are further along than might have been suspected with regard to giving all stakeholders a voice in corporate decisions. However, we have a way to go, and I have made some suggestions as to the directions we might take.

Let me close by making a point that will seem obvious to philosophers but less obvious to others. In essence I have approached the issues raised by ethical pluralism by process rather than substance. I have not tried to argue that one position on these matters is morally correct and the others morally flawed. Rather, I have tried to elucidate a just process so the various stakeholder voices in these matters can be heard and have some influence on the decision. To put my perspective in Rawls's language (1971), I think the issues presented by ethical pluralism can only be handled by just procedures rather than aiming at just results. In Rawls's language, I am suggesting a system of imperfect procedural justice to address this issue.

REFERENCES

Jerry Alder, "Alaska After Exxon," *Newsweek,* September 18, 1989, pp. 50–62.

Alan S. Blinder, *Hard Heads Soft Hearts* (Reading, Mass.: Addison Wesley, 1987).

Norman Bowie, *Business Ethics* (Englewood Cliffs, N.J.: Prentice Hall Inc., 1982).

Norman Bowie with Ronald Duska, *Business Ethics.* 2nd ed. (Englewood Cliffs, N.J.: Prentice Hall Inc., 1990).

Norman Bowie, "The Firm as a Moral Community," in Richard M. Coughlin, ed., *Perspectives on Socio-Economics* (White Plains, N.Y.: M.E. Sharpe, Inc., 1991).

Albert Carr, "Is Business Bluffing Ethical?" *Harvard Business Review.* January–February 1968, pp. 143–146.

Thomas Donaldson, *The Ethics of International Business* (New York: Oxford University Press, 1989).

William E. Evan and R. Edward Freeman, "A Stakeholder Theory of the Modern Corporation: Kantian Capitalism," in Tom L. Beauchamp and Norman E. Bowie, eds., *Ethical Theory and Business.* 3rd ed. (Englewood Cliffs, N.J.: Prentice Hall, 1998).

Robert Frank, *Passions Within Reason* (New York: W.W. Norton & Co., 1988).

R. Edward Freeman, *Strategic Management: A Stakeholder Approach* (Marshfield, Mass.: Pitman, 1984).

Milton Friedman, *Capitalism & Freedom* (Chicago: University of Chicago Press, 1962).

Milton Friedman, "The Social Responsibility of Business Is to Increase Its Profits," *New York Times Magazine.* September 13, 1970, pp. 32–34, 122–126.

Immanuel Kant, *Foundations of the Metaphysics of Morals* (Lewis White Beck, trans.) (Indianapolis: Bobbs Merrill, 1969).

Theodore Levitt, "The Dangers of Social Responsibility." *Harvard Business Review,* September–October 1958, pp. 41–50.

Theodore Levitt, "The Morality(?) of Advertising," *Harvard Business Review,* July–August 1970, pp. 84–92.

John Rawls, *A Theory of Justice* (Cambridge, Mass.: Harvard University Press, 1971).

Alicia Swasy, "For Consumers, Ecology Comes Second," *Wall Street Journal,* August 23, 1988, p. B1.

QUESTIONS FOR DISCUSSION

1. What do Goodpaster and Matthews mean when they say that the "invisible hand" view and the "hand of government" view of the corporation are "conceptually similar"? How does their proposed "hand of management" view differ?

2. How might Friedman respond to Bowie's view of profit as a byproduct of other corporate goals?

3. Freeman argues that the interest of stakeholders should be balanced by corporate managers. Can you think of any method for doing this that does not favor one group over another? What happens if the interests of different groups are incompatible?

4. Brenkert argues that we should be very wary of corporations participating in the production of public welfare. What are the main points of his argument? Does it imply a reduced role for the interests of some corporate stakeholders (for example, communities)?

CHAPTER 4

Governance and Self-Regulation

Who Rules the Corporation?

Ralph Nader
Founder of Public Citizen, Inc. and Center
for the Study of Responsive Law

Mark Green
Director, The Corporate Accountability Research Group

Joel Seligman
Dean and Ethan A. H. Shepley University Professor, Washington
University School of Law, University of Michigan

All modern state corporation statutes describe a common image of corporate governance, an image pyramidal in form. At the base of the pyramid are the shareholders or owners of the corporation. Their ownership gives them the right to elect representatives to direct the corporation and to approve fundamental corporate actions such as mergers or bylaw amendments. The intermediate level is held by the board of directors, who are required by a provision common to nearly every state corporation law "to manage the business and

---

Excerpted from Ralph Nader, Mark Green, and Joel Seligman, *Taming the Giant Corporation* (New York: W.W. Norton, 1976). Copyright © 1976 by Ralph Nader. Reprinted by permission.

affairs of the corporation." On behalf of the shareholders, the directors are expected to select and dismiss corporate officers; to approve important financial decisions; to distribute profits; and to see that accurate periodic reports are forwarded to the shareholders. Finally, at the apex of the pyramid are the corporate officers. In the eyes of the law, the officers are the employees of the shareholder owners. Their authority is limited to those responsibilities which the directors delegate to them.

In reality, this legal image is virtually a myth. In nearly every large American business corporation, there exists a management autocracy. One man—variously titled the President, or the Chairman of the Board, or the Chief Executive Officer—or a small coterie of men rule the corporation. Far from being chosen by the directors to run the corporation, this chief executive or executive clique chooses the board of directors and, with the acquiescence of the board, controls the corporation.

The common theme of many instances of mismanagement is a failure to restrain the power of these senior executives. A corporate chief executive's decisions to expand, merge, or even violate the law can often be made without accountability to outside scrutiny. There is, for example, the detailed disclosures of the recent bribery cases. Not

189

only do these reports suggest how widespread corporate foreign and domestic criminality has become; they also provide a unique study in the pathology of American corporate management.

At Gulf Corporation, three successive chief executive officers were able to pay out over $12.6 million in foreign and domestic bribes over a 15-year period without the knowledge of "outside" or non-employee directors on the board. At Northrop, chairman Thomas V. Jones and vice president James Allen were able to create and fund the Economic and Development Corporation, a separate Swiss company, and pay $750,000 to Dr. Hubert Weisbrod, a Swiss attorney, to stimulate West German jet sales without the knowledge of the board or, apparently, other senior executives. At 3M, chairman Bert Cross and finances vice president Irwin Hansen ordered the company insurance department to pay out $509,000 for imaginary insurance and the bookkeeper to fraudulently record the payments as a "necessary and proper" business expense for tax purposes. Ashland Oil Corporation's chief executive officer, Orwin E. Atkins, involved at least eight executives in illegally generating and distributing $801,165 in domestic political contributions, also without question.

The legal basis for such a consolidation of power in the hands of the corporation's chief executive is the proxy election. Annually the shareholders of each publicly held corporation are given the opportunity of either attending a meeting to nominate and elect directors or returning proxy cards to management or its challengers signing over their right to vote. Few shareholders personally attend meetings. Sylvan Silver, a Reuters correspondent who covers over 100 Wilmington annual meetings each year, described representative 1974 meetings in an interview: At Cities Service Company, the 77th largest industrial corporation with some 135,000 shareholders, 25 shareholders actually attended the meeting; El Paso Natural Gas with 125,000 shareholders had 50 shareholders; at Coca Cola, the 69th largest corporation with 70,000 shareholders, 25 shareholders attended the annual meeting; at Bristol Meyers with 60,000 shareholders a like 25 shareholders appeared. Even "Campaign GM," the most publicized shareholder challenge of the past two decades, attracted no more than 3,000 of General Motors' 1,400,000 shareholders, or roughly two-tenths of one percent.

Thus, corporate directors are almost invariably chosen by written proxies. Yet management so totally dominates the proxy machinery that corporate elections have come to resemble the Soviet Union's euphemistic "Communist ballot"—that is, a ballot which lists only one slate of candidates. Although federal and state laws require the annual performance of an elaborate series of rituals pretending there is "corporate democracy," in 1973, 99.7 percent of the directorial elections in our largest corporations were uncontested.

THE BEST DEMOCRACY MONEY CAN BUY

The key to management's hegemony is money. Effectively, only incumbent management can nominate directors—because it has a nearly unlimited power to use corporate funds to win board elections while opponents must prepare separate proxies and campaign literature entirely at their own expense.

There is first management's power to print and post written communications to shareholders. In a typical proxy contest, management will "follow up" its initial proxy solicitation with a bombardment of five to ten subsequent mailings. As attorneys Edward Aranow and Herb Einhorn explain in their treatise, *Proxy Contests for Corporate Control:*

> Perhaps the most important aspect of the followup letter is its role in the all-important efforts of a soliciting group to secure the *latest-dated* proxy from a stockholder. It is characteristic of every proxy contest that a large number of stockholders will sign and return proxies to one faction and then change their minds and want to have their stock used for the opposing faction.

The techniques of the Northern States Power Company in 1973 are illustrative. At that time, Northern States Power Company voluntarily employed cumulative voting, which meant that only 7.2 percent of outstanding shares was necessary to elect one director to Northern's 14-person board. Troubled by Northern's record on environmental and consumer issues, a broadly based coalition of public interest groups called the Citizens' Advocate for Public Utility Responsibility (CAPUR) nominated Ms. Alpha Snaby, a former Minnesota state legislator, to run for director. These groups then successfully solicited the votes of over 14 percent of all shareholders, or more than twice the votes necessary to elect her to the board.

Northern States then bought back the election. By soliciting proxies a second, and then a third time, the Power Company was able to persuade (or confuse) the shareholders of 71 percent of the 2.8 million shares cast for Ms. Snaby to change their votes.

Larger, more experienced corporations are usually less heavyhanded. Typically, they will begin a proxy campaign with a series of "buildup" letters preliminary to the first proxy solicitation. In Campaign GM, General Motors elevated this strategy to a new plateau by encasing the Project on Corporate Responsibility's single 100-word proxy solicitation within a 21-page booklet specifically rebutting each of the Project's charges. The Project, of course, could never afford to respond to GM's campaign. The postage costs of soliciting GM's 1,400,000 shareholders alone would have exceeded $100,000. The cost of printing a document comparable to GM's 21-page booklet, mailing it out, accompanied by a proxy statement, a proxy card, and a stamped return envelope to each shareholder might have run as high as $500,000.

Nor is it likely that the Project or any other outside shareholder could match GM's ability to hire "professional" proxy solicitors such as Georgeson & Company, which can deploy up to 100 solicitors throughout the country to personally contact shareholders, give them a campaign speech, and urge them to return their proxies. By daily tabulation of returned proxies, professional solicitors are able to identify on a day-by-day basis the largest blocks of stock outstanding which have yet to return a favorable vote.

THE STATE OF THE BOARD

But does not the board of directors with its sweeping statutory mandate "to manage the business and affairs of every corporation" provide an internal check on the power of corporate executives? No. Long ago the grandiloquent words of the statutes ceased to have any operative meaning. "Directors," William O. Douglas complained in 1934, "do not direct." "[T]here is one thing all boards have in common, regardless of their legal position." Peter Drucker has written. "*They do not function.*" In Robert Townsend's tart analysis. "[M]ost big companies have turned their boards of directors into nonboards. . . . In the years that I've spent on various boards I've never heard a single suggestion from a director (made as a director *at* a board meeting) that produced any result at all."

Recently these views are corroborated by Professor Myles Mace of the Harvard Business School, the nation's leading authority on the performance of boards of directors. In *Directors—Myth and Reality,* Mace summarized the results of hundreds of interviews with corporate officers and directors.

Directors do not establish the basic objectives, corporate strategies or broad policies of large and medium-size corporations, Mace found. Management creates the policies. The board has a right of veto but rarely exercises it. As one executive said, "Nine hundred and ninety-nine times out of a thousand, the board goes along with management. . . ." Or another, "I can't think of a single time when the board has failed to support a proposed policy of management or failed to endorse the recommendation of management."

The board does not select the president or other chief executive officers. "What is perhaps the most common definition of a function of the board of directors—namely, to select the president—was found to be the greatest myth, " reported Mace. "The board of directors in most companies, except in a crisis, does not select the president. The president usually chooses the man who succeeds him to that position, and the board complies with the legal amenities in endorsing and voting his election." A corporate president agreed: "The former company president tapped me to be president, and I assure you that I will select my successor when the time comes." Even seeming exceptions such as RCA's 1975 ouster of Robert Sarnoff frequently turn out to be at the instigation of senior operating executives rather than an aroused board.

The board's role as disciplinarian of the corporation is more apparent than real. As the business-supported Conference Board conceded, "One of the most glaring deficiencies attributed to the corporate board . . . is its failure to monitor and evaluate the performance of the chief executive in a concrete way." To cite a specific example, decisions on executive compensation are made by the president—with perfunctory board approval in most situations. In the vast majority of corporations, Professor Mace found, the compensation committee, and the board which approves the recommendations of the compensation committee, "are not decision-making bodies."

Exceptions to this pattern become news events. In reporting on General Motors' 1971 annual shareholders' meeting, the *Wall Street Journal* noted that, "The meeting's dramatic highlight was an impassioned and unprecedented speech by the Rev. Leon Sullivan, GM's recently appointed Negro director, supporting the Episcopal Church's efforts to get the company out of South Africa. It was the first time that a GM director had ever spoken against management at an annual meeting." Now Rev. Sullivan is an unusual outside director, being General Motor's first black director and only "public interest" director. But what makes Leon Sullivan most extraordinary is that he was the first director in *any* major American corporation to come out publicly against his own corporation when its operations tended to support apartheid.

REVAMPING THE BOARD

The modern corporation is akin to a political state in which all powers are held by a single clique. The senior executives of a large firm are essentially not accountable to any other officials within the firm. These are precisely the circumstances that, in a democratic political state, require a separation of powers into different branches of authority. As James Madison explained in the *Federalist No. 47:*

> The accumulation of all powers, legislative, executive, and judiciary, in the same hands, whether of one, a few or many, and whether hereditary, self-appointed, or elective, may justly be pronounced the

very definition of tyranny. Were the federal constitution, therefore, really chargeable with this accumulation of power, or with a mixture of powers, having a dangerous tendency to such an accumulation, no further arguments would be necessary to inspire a universal reprobation of the system.

A similar concern over the unaccountability of business executives historically led to the elevation of a board of directors to review and check the actions of operating management. As a practical matter, if corporate governance is to be reformed, it must begin by returning the board to this historical role. The board should serve as an internal auditor of the corporations, responsible for constraining executive management from violations of law and breach of trust. Like a rival branch of government, the board's function must be defined as separate from operating management. Rather than pretending directors can "manage" the corporation, the board's role as disciplinarian should be clearly described. Specifically, the board of directors should:

- establish and monitor procedures that assure that operating executives are informed of and obey applicable federal, state, and local laws;
- approve or veto all important executive management business proposals such as corporate bylaws, mergers, or dividend decisions;
- hire and dismiss the chief executive officer and be able to disapprove the hiring and firing of the principal executives of the corporation; and
- report to the public and the shareholders how well the corporation has obeyed the law and protected the shareholders' investment.

It is not enough, however, to specify what the board should do. State corporations statutes have long provided that "the business and affairs of a corporation shall be managed by a board of directors," yet it has been over a century since the boards of the largest corporations have actually performed this role. To reform the corporation, a federal chartering law must also specify the manner in which the board performs its primary duties.

First, to insure that the corporation obeys federal and state laws, the board should designate executives responsible for compliance with these laws and require periodic signed reports describing the effectiveness of compliance procedures. Mechanisms to administer spot checks on compliance with the principal statutes should be created. Similar mechanisms can insure that corporate "whistle blowers" and nonemployee sources may communicate to the board—in private and without fear of retaliation—knowledge of violations of law.

Second, the board should actively review important executive business proposals to determine their full compliance with law, to preclude conflicts of interest, and to assure that executive decisions are rational and informed of all foreseeable risks and costs. But even though the board's responsibility here is limited to approval or veto of executive initiatives, it should proceed in as well-informed a manner as practicable. To demonstrate rational business judgment, the directorate should require management "to prove its case." It should review the studies upon which management relied to make a decision, require management to justify its decision in terms of costs or rebutting dissenting views, and, when necessary, request that outside experts provide an independent business analysis.

Only with respect to two types of business decisions should the board exceed this limited review role. The determination of salary, expense, and benefit schedules inherently possesses such obvious conflicts of interest for executives that only the board should make these decisions. And since the relocation of principal manufacturing facilities tends to have a greater effect on local communities than any other type of business decision, the board should require management to prepare a "community impact statement." This public report would be similar to the environmental impact statements presently required by the National Environmental Policy Act. It would require the corporation to state the purpose of a relocation decision; to compare feasible alternative means; to quantify the costs to the local community; and to consider methods to mitigate these costs. Although it would not prevent a corporation from making a profit-maximizing decision, it would require the corporation to minimize the costs of relocation decisions to local communities.

To accomplish this restructuring of the board requires the institutionalization of a new profession: the full-time "professional" director. Corporate scholars frequently identify William O. Douglas' 1940 proposal for "salaried, professional experts [who] would bring a new responsibility and authority to directorates and a new safety to stockholders" as the origin of the professional director idea. More recently, corporations including Westinghouse and Texas Instruments have established slots on their boards to be filled by full-time directors. Individuals such as Harvard Business School's Myles Mace and former Federal Reserve Board chairman William McChesney Martin consider their own thorough-going approach to boardroom responsibilities to be that of a "professional" director.

To succeed, professional directors must put in the substantial time necessary to get the job done. One cannot monitor the performance of Chrysler's or Gulf's management at a once-a-month meeting; those firms' activities are too sweeping and complicated for such ritual oversight. The obvious minimum here is an adequate salary to attract competent persons to work as full-time directors and to maintain the independence of the board from executive management.

The board must also be sufficiently staffed. A few board members alone cannot oversee the activities of thousands of executives. To be able to appraise operating management, the board needs a trim group of attorneys, economists, and labor and consumer advisors who can analyze complex business proposals, investigate complaints, spot-check accountability, and frame pertinent inquiries.

The board also needs timely access to relevant corporate data. To insure this, the board should be empowered to nominate the corporate financial auditor, select the corporation's counsel, compel the forwarding and preservation of corporate records, require all corporate executives or representatives to answer fully all board questions respecting corporate operations, and dismiss any executive or representative who fails to do so.

This proposed redesign for corporate democracy attempts to make executive management accountable to the law and shareholders without diminishing its operating efficiency. Like a judiciary within the corporation, the board has ultimate powers to judge and sanction. Like a legislature, it oversees executive activity. Yet executive management substantially retains its powers to initiate and administer business operations. The chief executive officer retains control over the organization of the executive hierarchy and the allocation of the corporate budget. The directors are given ultimate control over a narrow jurisdiction: Does the corporation obey the law, avoid exploiting consumers or communities, and protect the shareholders' investment? The executive contingent retains general authority for all corporate operations.

No doubt there will be objections that this structure is too expensive or that it will disturb the "harmony" of executive management. But it is unclear that there would be any increased cost in adopting an effective board. The true cost to the corporation could only be determined by comparing the expense of a fully paid and staffed board with the savings resulting from the elimination of conflicts of interest and corporate waste. In addition, if this should result in a slightly increased corporate expense, the appropriateness must be assessed within a broader social context: should federal and state governments or the corporations themselves bear the primary expense of keeping corporations honest? In our view, this cost should be placed on the corporations as far as reasonably possible.

It is true that an effective board will reduce the "harmony" of executive management in the sense that the power of the chief executive or senior executives will be subject to knowledgeable review. But a board which monitors rather than rubber-stamps management is exactly what is necessary to diminish the unfettered authority of the corporate chief executive or ruling clique. The autocratic power these individuals presently possess has proven unacceptably dangerous: it has led to recurring violations of law, conflicts of interest, productive inefficiency, and pervasive harm to consumers, workers, and the community environment. Under normal circumstances there should be a healthy friction between operating executives and the board to assure that the wisest possible use is made of corporate resources. When corporate

executives are breaking the law, there should be no "harmony" whatsoever.

ELECTION OF THE BOARD

Restructuring the board is hardly likely to succeed if boards remain as homogeneously white, male, and narrowly oriented as they are today. Dissatisfaction with current selection of directors is so intense that analysts of corporate governance, including Harvard Law School's Abram Chayes, Yale political scientist Robert Dahl, and University of Southern California Law School Professor Christopher Stone, have each separately urged that the starting point of corporate reform should be to change the way in which the board is elected.

Professor Chayes, echoing John Locke's principle that no authority is legitimate except that granted "the consent of the governed," argues that employees and other groups substantially affected by corporate operations should have a say in its governance:

> Shareholder democracy, so-called, is misconceived because the shareholders are not the governed of the corporations whose consent must be sought. . . . Their interests are protected if financial information is made available, fraud and overreaching are prevented, and a market is maintained in which their shares may be sold. A priori, there is no reason for them to have any voice, direct or representational, in [corporate decision making]. They are no more affected than nonshareholding neighbors by these decisions. . . .
>
> A more spacious conception of 'membership,' and one closer to the facts of corporate life, would include all those having a relation of sufficient intimacy with the corporation or subject to its powers in a sufficiently specialized way. Their rightful share in decisions and the exercise of corporate power would be exercised through an institutional arrangement appropriately designed to represent the interests of a constituency of members having a significant common relation to the corporation and its power.

Professor Dahl holds a similar view: "[W]hy should people who own shares be given the privileges of citizenship in the government of the firm when citizenship is denied to other people who also make vital contributions to the firm?" he asks rhetorically. "The people I have in mind are, of course, employees and customers, without whom the firm could not exist, and the general public, without whose support for (or acquiescence in) the myriad protections and services of the state the firm would instantly disappear. . . ." Yet Dahl finds proposals for interest group representation less desirable than those for worker self-management. He also suggests consideration of codetermination statutes such as those enacted by West Germany and ten other European and South American countries under which shareholders and employees separately elect designated portions of the board.

From a different perspective, Professor Stone has recommended that a federal agency appoint "general public directors" to serve on the boards of all the largest industrial and financial firms. In certain extreme cases such as where a corporation repeatedly violates the law, Stone recommends that the federal courts appoint "special public directors" to prevent further delinquency.

There are substantial problems with each of those proposals. It seems impossible to design a general "interest group" formula which will assure that all affected constituencies of large industrial corporations will be represented and that all constituencies will be given appropriate weight. Even if such a formula could be designed, however, there is the danger that consumer or community or minority or franchisee representatives would become only special pleaders for their constituents and otherwise lack the loyalty or interest to direct generally. This defect has emerged in West Germany under codetermination. Labor representatives apparently are indifferent to most problems of corporate management that do not directly affect labor. They seem as deferential to operating executive management as present American directors are. Alternatively, federally appointed public directors might be frozen out of critical decision-making by a majority of "privately" elected directors, or the appointing agency itself might be biased.

Nonetheless, the essence of the Chayes-Dahl-Stone argument is well taken. The boards of directors of most major corporations are, as CBS's Dan Rather criticized the original Nixon cabinet,

too much like "twelve grey-haired guys named George." The quiescence of the board has resulted in important public and, for that matter, shareholder concerns being ignored.

An important answer is structural. The homogeneity of the board can only be ended by giving to each director, in addition to a general duty to see that the corporation is profitably administered, a separate oversight responsibility, a separate expertise, and a separate constituency so that each important public concern would be guaranteed at least one informed representative on the board. There might be nine corporate directors, each of whom is elected to a board position with one of the following oversight responsibilities:

1. Employee welfare
2. Consumer protection
3. Environmental protection and community relations
4. Shareholder rights
5. Compliance with law
6. Finances
7. Purchasing and marketing
8. Management efficiency
9. Planning and research

By requiring each director to balance responsibility for representing a particular social concern against responsibility for the overall health of the enterprise, the problem of isolated "public" directors would be avoided. No individual director is likely to be "frozen out" of collegial decision-making because all directors would be of the same character. Each director would spend the greater part of his or her time developing expertise in a different area; each director would have a motivation to insist that a different aspect of a business decision be considered. Yet each would simultaneously be responsible for participating in all board decisions, as directors now are. So the specialized area of each director would supplement but not supplant the director's general duties.

To maintain the independence of the board from the operating management it reviews also requires that each federally chartered corporation shall be directed by a purely "outside" board. No executive, attorney, representative, or agent of a corporation should be allowed to serve simultaneously as a director of that same corporation. Directorial and executive loyalty should be furthered by an absolute prohibition of interlocks. No director, executive, general counsel, or company agent should be allowed to serve more than one corporation subject to the Federal Corporate Chartering Act.

Several objections may be raised. First, how can we be sure that completely outside boards will be competent? Corporate campaign rules should be redesigned to emphasize qualifications. This will allow shareholder voters to make rational decisions based on information clearly presented to them. It is also a fair assumption that shareholders, given an actual choice and role in corporate governance, will want to elect the men and women most likely to safeguard their investments.

A second objection is that once all interlocks are proscribed and a full-time outside board required, there will not be enough qualified directors to staff all major firms. This complaint springs from that corporate mentality which, accustomed to 60-year-old white male bankers and businessmen as directors, makes the norm a virtue. In fact, if we loosen the reins on our imagination, America has a large, rich, and diverse pool of possible directorial talent from academics and public administrators and community leaders to corporate and public interest lawyers.

But directors should be limited to four two-year terms so that boards do not become stale. And no director should be allowed to serve on more than one board at any one time. Although simultaneous service on two or three boards might allow key directors to "pollinize" directorates by comparing their different experiences, this would reduce their loyalty to any one board, jeopardize their ability to fully perform their new directorial responsibilities, and undermine the goal of opening up major boardrooms to as varied a new membership as is reasonable.

The shareholder electoral process should be made more democratic as well. Any shareholder or allied shareholder group which owns .1 percent of the common voting stock in the corporation or comprises 100 or more individuals and does not include a present executive of the corporation, nor

act for a present executive, may nominate up to three persons to serve as directors. This will exclude executive management from the nomination process. It also increases the likelihood of a diverse board by preventing any one or two sources from proposing all nominees. To prevent frivolous use of the nominating power, this proposal establishes a minimum shareownership condition.

Six weeks prior to the shareholders' meeting to elect directors, each shareholder should receive a ballot and a written statement on which each candidate for the board sets forth his or her qualifications to hold office and purposes for seeking office. All campaign costs would be borne by the corporation. These strict campaign and funding rules will assure that all nominees will have an equal opportunity to be judged by the shareholders. By preventing directorates from being bought, these provisions will require board elections to be conducted solely on the merit of the candidates.

Finally, additional provisions will require cumulative voting and forbid "staggered" board elections. Thus any shareholder faction capable of jointly voting approximately 10 percent of the total number of shares cast may elect a director.

A NEW ROLE FOR SHAREHOLDERS

The difficulty with this proposal is the one that troubled Juvenal two millennia ago: *Quis custodiet ipsos custodes,* or Who shall watch the watchmen? Without a full-time body to discipline the board, it would be so easy for the board of directors and executive management to become friends. Active vigilance could become routinized into an uncritical partnership. The same board theoretically elected to protect shareholder equity and internalize law might instead become management's lobbyist.

Relying on shareholders to discipline directors may strike many as a dubious approach. Historically, the record of shareholder participation in corporate governance has been an abysmal one. The monumental indifference of most shareholders is worse than that of sheep; sheep at least have some sense of what manner of ram they follow. But taken together, the earlier proposals—an outside, full-time board, nominated by rival shareholder groups and voted on by beneficial owners—will increase involvement by shareholders. And cumulative voting insures that an aroused minority of shareholders—even one as small as 9 or 10 percent of all shareholders—shall have the opportunity to elect at least one member of the board.

But that alone is hardly sufficient. At a corporation the size of General Motors, an aggregation of 10 percent of all voting stock might require the allied action of over 200,000 individuals—which probably could occur no more than once in a generation. To keep directors responsive to law and legitimate public concerns requires surer and more immediate mechanisms. In a word, it requires arming the victims of corporate abuses with the powers to swiftly respond to them. For only those employees, consumers, racial or sex minorities, and local communities harmed by corporate depredations can be depended upon to speedily complain. By allowing any victim to become a shareholder and by permitting any shareholder to have an effective voice, there will be the greatest likelihood of continuing scrutiny of the corporation's directorate.

Shareholders are not the only ones with an incentive to review decisions of corporate management; nor, as Professors Chayes and Dahl argue, are shareholders the only persons who should be accorded corporate voting rights. The increasing use by American corporations of technologies and materials that pose direct and serious threats to the health of communities surrounding their plants requires the creation of a new form of corporate voting right. When a federally chartered corporation engages, for example, in production or distribution of nuclear fuels or the emissions of toxic air, water, or solid waste pollutants, citizens whose health is endangered should not be left, at best, with receiving money damages after a time-consuming trial to compensate them for damaged property, impaired health, or even death.

Instead, upon finding of a public health hazard by three members of the board of directors or 3 percent of the shareholders, a corporate referendum should be held in the political jurisdiction affected by the health hazard. The referendum would be drafted by the unit triggering it—either the three board members or a designate of the

shareholders. The affected citizens by majority vote will then decide whether the hazardous practice shall be allowed to continue. This form of direct democracy has obvious parallels to the initiative and referendum procedures familiar to many states—except that the election will be paid for by a business corporation and will not necessarily occur at a regular election.

This type of election procedure is necessary to give enduring meaning to the democratic concept of "consent of the governed." To be sure, this proposal goes beyond the traditional assumption that the only affected or relevant constituents of the corporation are the shareholders. But no longer can we accept the Faustian bargain that the continued toleration of corporate destruction of local health and property is the cost to the public of doing business. In an equitable system of governance, the perpetrators should answer to their victims.

Power and Accountability: The Changing Role of the Corporate Board of Directors

Irving S. Shapiro
Former Chairman and CEO, E.I. duPont de Nemours & Company

The proper direction of business corporations in a free society is a topic of intense and often heated discussion. Under the flag of corporate governance there has been a running debate about the performance of business organizations, together with a flood of proposals for changes in the way corporate organizations are controlled.

It has been variously suggested that corporate charters be dispensed by the Federal Government as distinct from those of the states (to tighten the grip on corporate actions); that only outsiders unconnected to an enterprise be allowed to sit on its

Excerpted from a paper presented in the Fairless Lecture Series, Carnegie-Mellon University, Oct. 24, 1979. Reprinted by permission.

board of directors or that, as a minimum, most of the directors should qualify as "independent"; that seats be apportioned to constituent groups (employees, women, consumers and minorities, along with stockholders); that boards be equipped with private staffs, beyond the management's control (to smoke out facts the hired executives might prefer to hide or decorate); and that new disclosure requirements be added to existing ones (to provide additional tools for outside oversight of behavior and performance).

Such proposals have come from the Senate Judiciary Committee's antitrust arm; from regulatory agency spokesmen, most notably the current head of the Securities and Exchange Commission, Harold Williams, and a predecessor there, William Cary; from the professoriat in schools of law and business; from the bench and bar; and from such observers of the American scene as Ralph Nader and Mark Green.[1]

Suggestions for change have sometimes been offered in sympathy and sometimes in anger. They have ranged from general pleas for corporations to behave better, to meticulously detailed reorganization charts. The span in itself suggests part of the problem: "Corporate Governance" (like Social Responsibility before it) is not a subject with a single meaning, but is a shorthand label for an array of social and political as well as economic concerns. One is obliged to look for a way to keep discussion within a reasonable perimeter.

There appears to be one common thread. All of the analyses, premises, and prescriptions seem to derive in one way or another from the question of accountability: Are corporations suitably controlled, and to whom or what are they responsible? This is the central public issue, and the focal point for this paper.

One school of opinion holds that corporations cannot be adequately called to account because there are systemic economic and political failings. In this view, nothing short of a major overhaul will serve. What is envisioned, at least by many in this camp, are new kinds of corporate organizations constructed along the lines of democratic political institutions. The guiding ideology would be communitarian, with the needs and rights of the community emphasized in preference to profit-seeking goals now pursued by corporate leaders (presumably with Darwinian abandon, with natural selection weeding out the weak, and with society left to pick up the external costs).

BOARDS CHANGING FOR BETTER

Other critics take a more temperate view. They regard the present system as sound and its methods of governance as morally defensible. They concede, though, that changes are needed to reflect new conditions. Whether the changes are to be brought about by gentle persuasion, or require the use of a two-by-four to get the mule's attention, is part of the debate.

This paper sides with the gradualists. My position, based on a career in industry and personal observation of corporate boards at work, is that significant improvements have been made in recent years in corporate governance, and that more changes are coming in an orderly way: that with these amendments, corporations are accountable and better monitored than ever before; and that pat formulas or proposals for massive "restructuring" should be suspect. The formula approach often is based on ignorance of what it takes to run a large enterprise, on false premises as to the corporate role in society, or on a philosophy that misreads the American tradition and leaves no room for large enterprises that are both free and efficient.

The draconian proposals would almost certainly yield the worst of all possibilities, a double-negative tradeoff: They would sacrifice the most valuable qualities of the enterprise system to gain the least attractive features of the governmental system. Privately owned enterprises are geared to a primary economic task, that of joining human talents and natural resources in the production and distribution of goods and services. That task is essential, and two centuries of national experience suggest these conclusions: The United States has been uncommonly successful at meeting economic needs through reliance on private initiative; and the competitive marketplace is a better course-correction device than governmental fiat. The enterprise system would have had to have failed miserably before the case could be made for replacing it with governmental dictum.

Why should the public have any interest in the internal affairs of corporations? Who cares who decides? Part of the answer comes from recent news stories noting such special problems as illegal corporate contributions to political campaigns, and tracking the decline and fall of once-stout companies such as Penn Central. Revelations of that kind raise questions about the probity and competence of the people minding the largest stores. There is more to it than this, though. There have always been cases of corporate failures. Small companies have gone under too, at a rate far higher than their larger brethren.[2] Instances of corruption have occurred in institutions of all sizes, whether they be commercial enterprises or some other kind.

Corporate behavior and performance are points of attention, and the issue attaches to size, precisely because people do not see the large private corporation as entirely private. People care about what goes on in the corporate interior because they see themselves as affected parties whether they work in such companies or not.

There is no great mystery as to the source of this challenge to the private character of governance. Three trends account for it. First is the growth of very large corporations. They have come to employ a large portion of the workforce, and have become key factors in the nation's technology, wealth and security. They have generated admiration for their prowess, but also fear of their imputed power.

The second contributing trend is the decline of owner-management. Over time, corporate shares have been dispersed. The owners have hired managers, entrusted them with the power to make decisions, and drifted away from involvement in corporate affairs except to meet statutory requirements (as, for example, to approve a stock split or elect a slate of directors).

That raises obvious practical questions. If the owners are on the sidelines, what is to stop the managers from remaining in power indefinitely, using an inside position to control the selection of their own bosses, the directors? Who is looking over management's shoulder to monitor performance?

The third element here is the rise in social expectations regarding corporations. It is no longer considered enough for a company to make products and provide commercial services. The larger it is, the more it is expected to assume various obligations that once were met by individuals or communities, or were not met at all.

With public expectations ratcheting upward, corporations are under pressure to behave more like governments and embrace a universe of problems. That would mean, of necessity, that private institutions would focus less on problems of their own choice.

If corporations succumbed to that pressure, and in effect declared the public's work to be their own, the next step would be to turn them into institutions accountable to the public in the same way that units of government are accountable.

But the corporation does not parallel the government. The assets in corporate hands are more limited and the constituents have options. There are levels of appeal. While the only accountability in government lies within government itself—the celebrated system of checks and balances among the executive, legislative, and judicial branches—the corporation is in a different situation: It has external and plural accountability, codified in the law and reinforced by social pressure. It must "answer" in one way or another to all levels of government, to competitors in the marketplace who would be happy to have the chance to increase their own market share, to employees who can strike or quit, and to consumers who can keep their wallets in their pockets. The checks are formidable even if one excludes for purposes of argument the corporation's initial point of accountability, its stockholders (many of whom do in fact vote their shares, and do not just use their feet).

The case for major reforms in corporate governance rests heavily on the argument that past governmental regulation of large enterprises has been impotent or ineffectual. This is an altogether remarkable assertion, given the fact that the nation has come through a period in which large corporations have been subjected to an unprecedented flood of new legislation and rule making. Regulation now reaches into every corporate nook and cranny—including what some people suppose (erroneously) to be the sanctuary of the boardroom.

Market competition, so lightly dismissed by some critics as fiction or artifact, is in fact a vigorous force in the affairs of almost all corporations. Size lends no immunity to its relentless pressures. The claim that the largest corporations somehow have set themselves above the play of market forces or, more likely, make those forces play for themselves, is widely believed. Public opinion surveys show that. What is lacking is any evidence that this is so. Here too, the evidence goes the other way. Objective studies of concentrated industries (the auto industry, for instance) show that corporate size does not mean declining competitiveness, nor does it give assurance that the products will sell.

Everyday experience confirms this. Consider the hard times of the Chrysler Corporation today, the disappearance of many once-large companies from the American scene, and the constant rollover in the membership list of the "100 Largest," a churning process that has been going on for years and shows no signs of abating.[3]

If indeed the two most prominent overseers of corporate behavior, government and competition, have failed to provide appropriate checks and balances, and if that is to be cited as evidence that corporations lack accountability, the burden of proof should rest with those who so state.

The basics apply to Sears Roebuck as much as to Sam's appliance shop. Wherever you buy the new toaster, it should work when it is plugged in. Whoever services the washing machine, the repairman should arrive at the appointed time, with tools and parts.

Special expectations are added for the largest firms, however. One is that they apply their resources to tasks that invite economies of scale, providing goods and services that would not otherwise be available, or that could be delivered by smaller units only at considerable loss of efficiency. Another is that, like the elephant, they watch where they put their feet and not stamp on smaller creatures through clumsiness or otherwise.

A second set of requirements can be added, related not to the markets selected by corporations individually, but to the larger economic tasks that must be accomplished in the name of the national interest and security. In concert with others in society, including big government, big corporations are expected to husband scarce resources and develop new ones, and to foster strong and diverse programs of research and development, to the end that practical technological improvements will emerge and the nation will be competitive in the international setting.

Beyond this there are softer but nonetheless important obligations: To operate with respect for the environment and with careful attention to the health and safety of people, to honor and give room to the personal qualities employees bring to their jobs, including their need to make an identifiable mark and to realize as much of their potential as possible; to lend assistance in filling community needs in which corporations have some stake; and to help offset community problems which in some measure corporations have helped to create.

This is not an impossible job, only a difficult one. Admitting that the assignment probably is not going to be carried out perfectly by any organization, the task is unlikely to be done even half well unless some boundary conditions are met. Large corporations cannot fulfill their duties unless they remain both profitable and flexible. They must be able to attract and hold those volunteer owners; which is to say, there must be the promise of present or future gain. Companies must have the wherewithal to reinvest significant amounts to revitalize their own capital plants, year after year in unending fashion. Otherwise, it is inevitable that they will go into decline versus competitors elsewhere, as will the nation.

Flexibility is no less important. The fields of endeavor engaging large business units today are dynamic in nature. Without an in-and-out flow of products and services, without the mobility to adapt to shifts in opportunities and public preferences, corporations would face the fate of the buggywhip makers.

Profitability and flexibility are easy words to say, but in practice they make for hard decisions. A company that would close a plant with no more than a passing thought for those left unemployed would and should be charged with irresponsibility; but a firm that vowed never to close any of its plants would be equally irresponsible, for it might be consigning itself to a pattern of stagnation that could ultimately cost the jobs of the people in all of its plants.

The central requirement is not that large corporations take the pledge and bind themselves to stated actions covering all circumstances, but that they do a thoughtful and informed job of balancing competing (and ever changing) claims on corporate resources, mediating among the conflicting (also changing) desires of various constituencies, and not giving in to any one-dimensional perspective however sincerely felt. It is this that describes responsible corporate governance.

Certainly, corporations do not have the public mandate or the resources to be what Professor George Lodge of the Harvard Business School would have them be, which is nationally chartered community-oriented collectives.[4] Such a mission for corporations would be tolerable to society only if corporations were turned into mini-governments— but that takes us back to the inefficiency problem noted earlier. The one task governments have proven they almost always do badly is to run production and distribution organizations. The only models there are to follow are not attractive. Would anyone seriously argue that the public would be ahead if General Motors were run along the lines of Amtrak, or Du Pont were managed in the manner of the U.S. Postal System?

Once roles are defined, the key to success in running a large corporation is to lay out a suitable division of labor between the board and the management, make that division crystal clear on both sides, and staff the offices with the right people. Perhaps the best way to make that split is to follow the pattern used in the U.S. Constitution, which stipulates the powers of the Federal Government and specifies that everything not covered there is reserved to the states or the people thereof. The board of directors should lay claim to five basic jobs, and leave the rest to the paid managers.

The duties the board should not delegate are these:

1. The determination of the board policies and the general direction the efforts of the enterprise should take.
2. The establishment of performance standards— ethical as well as commercial—against which

the management will be judged, and the communication of these standards to the management in unambiguous terms.
3. The selection of company officers, and attention to the question of succession.
4. The review of top management's performance in following the overall strategy and meeting the board's standards as well as legal requirements.
5. The communication of the organization's goals and standards to those who have a significant stake in its activities (insiders and outsiders both) and of the steps being taken to keep the organization responsive to the needs of those people.

The establishment of corporate strategy and performance standards denotes a philosophy of active stewardship, rather than passive trusteeship. It is the mission of directors to see that corporate resources are put to creative use, and in the bargain subjected to calculated risks rather than simply being tucked into the countinghouse for safekeeping.

That in turn implies certain prerequisites for board members of large corporations which go beyond those required of a school board member, a trustee of a charitable organization, or a director of a small, local business firm. In any such assignments one would look for personal integrity, interest and intelligence, but beyond these there is a dividing line that marks capability and training.

The stakes are likely to be high in the large corporation, and the factors confronting the board and management usually are complex. The elements weighing heavily in decisions are not those with which people become familiar in the ordinary course of day-to-day life, as might be the case with a school board.

Ordinarily the management of a corporation attends to such matters as product introductions, capital expansions, and supply problems. This in no way reduces the need for directors with extensive business background, though. With few exceptions, corporate boards involve themselves in strategic decisions and those involving large capital commitments. Directors thus need at least as much breadth and perspective as the management, if not as much detailed knowledge.

If the directors are to help provide informed and principled oversight of corporate affairs, a good number of them must provide windows to the outside world. That is at least part of the rationale for outside directors, and especially for directors who can bring unique perspective to the group. There is an equally strong case, though, for directors with an intimate knowledge of the company's business, and insiders may be the best qualified to deliver that. What is important is not that a ratio be established, but that the group contain a full range of the competences needed to set courses of action that will largely determine the long-range success of the enterprise.

BOARDS NEED WINDOWS

The directors also have to be able and willing to invest considerable time in their work. In this day and age, with major resources on the line and tens of thousands of employees affected by each large corporation, there should be no seat in the boardroom for people willing only to show up once a month to pour holy water over decisions already made. Corporate boards need windows, not window dressing!

There are two other qualities that may be self-evident from what has been said, but are mentioned for emphasis. Directors must be interested in the job and committed to the overall purpose of the organization. However much they may differ on details of accomplishment, they must be willing to work at the task of working with others on the board. They ought to be able to speak freely in a climate that encourages open discussion, but to recognize the difference between attacking an idea and attacking the person who presents it. No less must they see the difference between compromising tactics to reach consensus and compromising principles.

Structures and procedures, which so often are pushed to the fore in discussions of corporate governance, actually belong last. They are not unimportant, but they are subordinate.

Structure follows purpose, or should, and that is a useful principle for testing some of the proposals for future changes in corporate boards. Today, two-thirds to three-quarters of the directors of most large corporations are outsiders, and it is being proposed that this trend be pushed still farther, with the only insider being the chief executive officer, and with a further stipulation that he not be board chairman.

This idea has surfaced from Harold Williams, and variations on it have come from other sources.

The idea bumps into immediate difficulties. High-quality candidates for boards are not in large supply as it is. Conflicts of interest would prohibit selection of many individuals close enough to an industry to be familiar with its problems. The disqualification of insiders would reduce the selection pool to a still smaller number, and the net result could well be corporate boards whose members were less competent and effective than those now sitting.

Experience would also suggest that such a board would be the most easily manipulated of all. That should be no trick at all for a skillful CEO, for he would be the only person in the room with a close, personal knowledge of the business.

The objective is unassailable: Corporate boards need directors with independence of judgment; but in today's business world, independence is not enough. In coping with such problems as those confronting the electronics corporations beset by heavy foreign competition, or those encountered by international banks which have loans outstanding in countries with shaky governments, boards made up almost entirely of outsiders would not just have trouble evaluating nuances of the management's performance; they might not even be able to read the radar and tell whether the helmsman was steering straight for the rocks.

If inadequately prepared individuals are placed on corporate boards, no amount of sincerity on their part can offset the shortcoming. It is pure illusion to suppose that complex business issues and organizational problems can be overseen by people with little or no experience in dealing with such problems. However intelligent such people might be, the effect of their governance would be to expose the people most affected by the organization—employees, owners, customers, suppliers—to leadership that would be (using the word precisely) incompetent.

It is sometimes suggested that the members of corporate boards ought to come from the constituencies—an employee-director, a consumer-director, an environmentalist-director, etc. This Noah's Ark proposal, which is probably not to be taken seriously, is an extension of the false parallel between corporations and elected governments.

The flaw in the idea is all but self evident: People representing specific interest groups would by definition be committed to the goals of their groups rather than any others; but it is the responsibility of directors (not simply by tradition but as a matter of law as well) to serve the organization as a whole. The two goals are incompatible.

If there were such boards they would move at glacial speed. The internal political maneuvering would be Byzantine, and it is difficult to see how the directors could avoid an obvious challenge of accountability. Stockholder suits would pop up like dandelions in the spring.

One may also question how many people of ability would stand for election under this arrangement. Quotas are an anathema in a free society, and their indulgence here would insult the constituencies themselves—a woman on the board not because she is competent but only because she is female; a black for black's sake; and so on ad nauseam.

A certain amount of constituency pleading is not all bad, as long as it is part of a corporate commitment. There is something to be said for what Harold Williams labels "tension," referring to the divergence in perspective of those concerned primarily with internal matters and those looking more at the broader questions. However, as has been suggested by James Shepley, the president of Time, Inc., "tension" can lead to paralysis, and is likely to do so if boards are packed with groups known to be unsympathetic to the management's problems and business realities.

As Shepley commented, "The chief executive would be out of his mind who would take a risk-laden business proposition to a group of directors who, whatever their other merits, do not really understand the fine points of the business at hand, and whose official purpose is to create 'tension.'"[5]

Students of corporate affairs have an abundance of suggestions for organizing the work of boards, with detailed structures in mind for committees on audit, finance, and other areas; plus prescriptions for membership. The danger here is not that boards will pick the wrong formula—many organization charts could be made to work—but that boards will put too much emphasis on the wrong details.

The idea of utilizing a committee system in which sub-groups have designated duties is far more important than the particulars of their arrangement. When such committees exist, and they are given known and specific oversight duties, it is a signal to the outside world (and to the management) that performance is being monitored in a no-nonsense fashion.

It is this argument that has produced the rule changes covering companies listed on the New York Stock Exchange, calling for audit committees chaired by outside directors, and including no one currently active in management. Most large firms have moved in that direction, and the move makes sense, for an independently minded audit committee is a potent instrument of corporate oversight. Even a rule of that kind, though, has the potential of backfiring.

Suppose some of the directors best qualified to perform the audit function are not outsiders? Are the analytical skills and knowledge of career employees therefore to be bypassed? Are the corporate constituencies well served by such an exclusionary rule, keeping in mind that all directors, insiders or outsiders, are bound by the same legal codes and corporate books are still subject to independent, outside audit? It is scarcely a case of the corporate purse being placed in the hands of the unwatched.

Repeatedly, the question of structure turns on the basics: If corporations have people with competence and commitment on their boards, structure and process fall into line easily; if people with the needed qualities are missing or the performance standards are unclear, corporations are in trouble no matter whose guidebook they follow. Equally, the question drives to alternatives: The present system is surely not perfect, but what is better?

By the analysis presented here the old fundamentals are still sound, no alternative for radical change has been defended with successful argument, and the best course appears to be to stay within the historical and philosophical traditions of American enterprise, working out the remaining problems one by one.

NOTES

1. U.S. Senate, Committee on the Judiciary Subcommittee on Antitrust, Monopoly & Business Rights; Address by Harold M. Williams, *Corporate Accountability,* Fifth

Annual Securities Regulation Institute, San Diego, California (January 18, 1978); W. Cary, *A Proposed Federal Corporate Minimum Standards Act,* 29 Bus. Law. 1101 (1974) and W. Cary, *Federalism & Corporate Law: Reflections Upon Delaware,* 83 Yale L. J., 663 (1974); D. E. Schwartz, *A Case for Federal Chartering of Corporations,* 31 Bus. Law. 1125 (1976); M. A. Eisenberg, *Legal Modes of Management Structure in the Modern Corporation; Officers, Directors & Accountants,* 63 Calif. L. Rev. 375 (1975); A. J. Goldberg, *Debate on Outside Directors, New York Times,* October 29, 1972 (§3, p. 1); Ralph Nader & Mark Green, *Constitutionalizing the Corporation: The Case for Federal Chartering of Giant Corporations* (1976).

2. *See* "Sixty Years of Corporate Ups, Downs & Outs," *Forbes,* September 15, 1977, p. 127 et seq.
3. *See* Dr. Betty Bock's Statement before Hearings on S.600, Small and Independent Business Protection Act of 1979, April 25, 1979.
4. G. Lodge, *The New American Ideology* (1975).
5. Shepley, *The CEO Goes to Washington,* Remarks to Fortune Corporation Communications Seminar, March 28, 1979.

Who Should Control the Corporation?

Henry Mintzberg
Professor of Management Studies, McGill University

Who should control the corporation? How? And for the pursuit of what goals? Historically, the corporation was controlled by its owners—through direct control of the managers if not through direct management—for the pursuit of economic goals. But as shareholding became dispersed, owner control weakened; and as the corporation grew to very large size, its economic actions came to have increasing social consequences. The giant, widely held corporation came increasingly under the implicit control of its managers, and the concept of social responsibility—the voluntary consideration of public social goals alongside the private economic ones—arose to provide a basis of legitimacy for their actions.

To some, including those closest to the managers themselves, this was accepted as a satisfactory arrangement for the large corporation. "Trust it" to the goodwill of the managers was their credo; these people will be able to achieve an appropriate balance between social and economic goals.

But others viewed this basis of control as fundamentally illegitimate. The corporation was too large, too influential, its actions too pervasive to be left free of the direct and concerted influence of outsiders. At the extreme were those who believed that legitimacy could be achieved only by subjecting managerial authority to formal and direct external control. "Nationalize it," said those at one end of the political spectrum, to put ultimate control in the hands of the government so that it will pursue public social goals. No, said those at the other end, "restore it" to direct share holder control, so that it will not waiver from the pursuit of private economic goals.

Other people took less extreme positions. "Democratize it" became the rallying cry for some, to open up the governance of the large, widely held corporation to a variety of affected groups—if not the workers, then the customers, or conservation interests, or minorities. "Regulate it" was also a popular position, with its implicit premise that only by sharing their control with government would the corporation's managers attend to certain social goals. Then there were those who accepted direct management control so long as it was tempered by other, less formal types of influence. "Pressure it," said a generation of social activists, to ensure that social goals are taken into consideration. But others argued that because the corporation is an economic instrument, you must "induce it" by providing economic incentives to encourage the resolution of social problems.

Finally, there were those who argued that this whole debate was unnecessary, that a kind of invisible hand ensures that the economic corporation acts in a socially responsible manner. "Ignore it" was their implicit conclusion.

This article is written to clarify what has become a major debate of our era, *the* major debate revolving around the private sector: Who should control the corporation, specifically the large, widely held corporation, how, and for the pursuit of what goals? The answers that are eventually accepted will determine what kind of society we and our children shall live in. . . .

As implied earlier, the various positions of who should control the corporation, and how, can be laid out along a political spectrum, from nationalization at one end to the restoration of shareholder power at the other. From the managerial perspective, however, those two extremes are not so far apart. Both call for direct control of the corporation's managers by specific outsiders, in one case

the government to ensure the pursuit of social goals, in the other case the shareholders to ensure the pursuit of economic ones. It is the moderate positions—notably, trusting the corporation to the social responsibility of its managers—that are farthest from the extremes. Hence, we can fold our spectrum around so that it takes the shape of a horseshoe.

Figure 1 shows our "conceptual horseshoe," with "nationalize it" and "restore it" at the two ends. "Trust it" is at the center, because it postulates a natural balance of social and economic goals. "Democratize it," "regulate it," and "pressure it" are shown on the left side of the horseshoe, because all seek to temper economic goals with social ones. "Induce it" and "ignore it," both of which favor the

FIGURE 1
The Conceptual Horseshoe

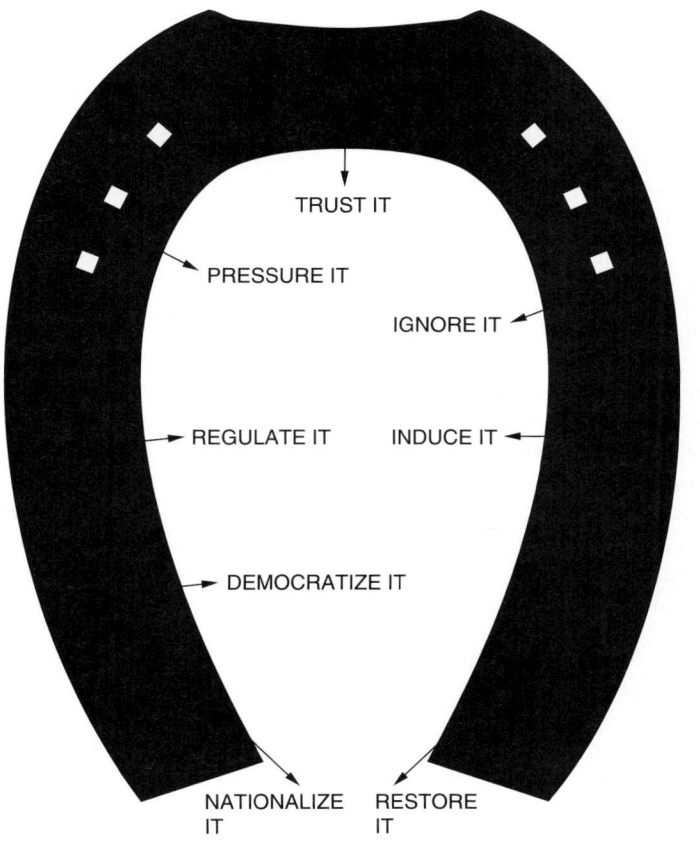

TRUST IT

PRESSURE IT

IGNORE IT

REGULATE IT   INDUCE IT

DEMOCRATIZE IT

NATIONALIZE   RESTORE
IT   IT

exclusive pursuit of economic goals, are shown on the right side.

This conceptual horseshoe provides a basic framework to help clarify the issues in this important debate. We begin by discussing each of these positions in turn, circling the horseshoe from left to right. Finding that each (with one exception) has a logical context, we conclude—in keeping with our managerial perspective—that they should be thought of as forming a portfolio from which society can draw to deal with the issue of who should control the corporation and how.

"NATIONALIZE IT"

Nationalization of the corporation is a taboo subject in the United States—in general, but not in particular. Whenever a major corporation runs into serious difficulty (i.e., faces bankruptcy with possible loss of many jobs), massive government intervention, often including direct nationalization, inevitably comes up as an option. This option has been exercised: U.S. travellers now ride on Amtrak; Tennessee residents have for years been getting their power from a government utility; indeed, the Post Office was once a private enterprise. Other nations have, of course, been much more ambitious in this regard.

From a managerial and organizational perspective, the question is not whether nationalization is legitimate, but whether it works—at least in particular, limited circumstances. As a response to concerns about the social responsibility of large corporations, the answer seems to be no. The evidence suggests that social difficulties arise more from the size of an organization and its degree of bureaucratization than from its form of ownership.[1] On the other hand, contrary to popular belief in the United States, nationalization does not necessarily harm economic efficiency. Over the years, Renault has been one of the most successful automobile companies outside Japan; it was nationalized by the French government shortly after World War II. . . . When people believe that government ownership leads to interference, politicization, and inefficiency, that may be exactly what happens. However, when they believe

that nationalization has to work, then state-owned enterprises may be able to attract the very best talent in the country and thereby work well.

But economic efficiency is no reason to favor nationalization any more than is concern about social responsibility. Nationalization does, however seem to make sense in at least two particular circumstances. The first is when a mission deemed necessary in a society will not be provided adequately by the private sector. That is presumably why America has its Amtrak, and why Canada created its Canadian National. . . . The second is when the activities of an organization must be so intricately tied to government policy that it is best managed as a direct arm of the state. The Canadian government created Petrocan to act as a "window" and a source of expertise on the sensitive oil industry.

Thus, it is not rhetoric but requirement that should determine the role of this position as a solution to who should control the corporation. "Nationalize it" should certainly not be embraced as a panacea, but neither should it be rejected as totally inapplicable.

"DEMOCRATIZE IT"

A less extreme position—at least in the context of the American debate—is one that calls for formal devices to broaden the governance of the corporation. The proponents of this position either accept the legal fiction of shareholder control and argue that the corporation's power base is too narrow, or else they respond to the emergent reality and question the legitimacy of managerial control. Why, they ask, do stockholders or self-selected managers have any greater right to control the profound decisions of these major institutions than do workers or customers or the neighbors downstream.

This stand is not to be confused with what is known as "participative management." The call to "democratize it" is a legal, rather than ethical one and is based on power, not generosity. Management is not asked to share its power voluntarily; rather, that power is to be reallocated constitutionally. That makes this position a fundamental and important one, *especially* in the United States with its strong tradition of pluralist control of its institutions.

The debate over democratization of the corporation has been confusing, in part because many of the proposals have been so vague. We can bring some order to it by considering, in organizational terms, two basic means of democratization and two basic constituencies that can be involved. As shown in Table 1, they suggest four possible forms of corporate democracy. One means is through the election of representatives to the board of directors, which we call *representative democracy*. The other is through formal but direct involvement in internal decision making processes, which we call *participatory democracy*. Either can focus on the workers—either all the employees or just those in operating tasks—or else on a host of outside interest groups, the latter giving rise to a *pluralistic* form of democracy. These are basic forms of corporate democracy in theory. With one exception, they have hardly been approached—let alone achieved—in practice. But they suggest where the "democratize it" debate may be headed. . . .

Critics . . . have pointed out the problems of defining constituencies and finding the means to hold elections. "One-person, one-vote" may be easily applied to electing representatives of the workers, but no such simple rule can be found in the case of the consumer or environmental representatives, let alone ones of the "public interest." Yet it is amazing how quickly things become workable in the United States when Americans decide to put their collective mind to it. Indeed, the one case of public directors that I came across is telling in this regard. According to a Conference Board report, the selection by the Chief Justice of the Supreme Court of New Jersey of 6 of the 24 members of the board of Prudential Insurance as public directors has been found by the company to be "quite workable."[2]

Despite its problems, representative democracy is crystal clear compared with participatory democracy. What the French call "auto-gestion" (as opposed to "co-gestion," or co-determination) seems to describe a kind of bottom-up, grassroots democracy in which the workers participate directly in decision making (instead of overseeing management's decisions from the board of directors) and also elect their own managers (who then become more administrators than bosses). Yet such proposals are inevitably vague, and I have heard of no large mass production or mass service firm—not even one owned by workers or a union—that comes close to this.

What has impeded worker participatory democracy? In my opinion, something rather obvious has stood in its way; namely, the structure required by the very organizations in which the attempts have been made to apply it. Worker participatory democracy—and worker representative democracy

---

TABLE 1

FOUR BASIC FORMS OF CORPORATE DEMOCRACY

		Groups Involved	
		Internal Employees	**External Interest Groups**
Focus of Attention	Board of Directors	Worker Representative Democracy (European style, e.g., "co-determination" or worker ownership)	Pluralistic Representative Democracy (American style, e.g., "public interest" directors)
	Internal Decision-Making Process	Worker Participatory Democracy (e.g., works councils)	Pluralistic Participatory Democracy (e.g., outsiders on new product committees)

too, for that matter—has been attempted primarily in organizations containing large numbers of workers who do highly routine, rather unskilled jobs that are typical of most mass production and service—what I have elsewhere called Machine Bureaucracies.[3] The overriding requirement in Machine Bureaucracy is for tight coordination, the kind that can only be achieved by central administrators. For example, the myriad of decisions associated with producing an automobile at Volvo's Kalmar works in Sweden cannot be made by autonomous groups, each doing as it pleases. The whole car must fit together in a particular way at the end of the assembly process. These decisions require a highly sophisticated system of bureaucratic coordination. That is why automobile companies are structured into rigid hierarchies of authority, not because their managers lust for power (though lust for power some of them no doubt do). . . .

Participatory democracy is approached in other kinds of organizations. These are not the large, mass output corporations, but rather the autonomous professional institutions such as universities and hospitals, which have very different needs for central coordination. . . . But the proponents of democracy in organizations are not lobbying for changes in hospitals or universities. It is the giant mass producers they are after, and unless the operating work in these corporations becomes largely skilled and professional in nature, nothing approaching participative democracy can be expected.

In principal, the pluralistic form of participatory democracy means that a variety of groups external to the corporation can somehow control its decision-making processes directly. In practice, of course, this concept is even more elusive than the worker form of participatory democracy. To fully open up the internal decision-making processes of the corporation to outsiders would mean chaos. Yet certain very limited forms of outside participation would seem to be not only feasible but perhaps even desirable. . . . Imagine telephone company executives resolving rate conflicts with consumer groups in quiet offices instead of having to face them in noisy public hearings.

To conclude, corporate democracy—whether representative or participatory in form—may be an elusive and difficult concept, but it cannot be dismissed. It is not just another social issue, like conservation or equal opportunity, but one that strikes at the most fundamental of values. Ours has become a society of organizations. Democracy will have decreasing meaning to most citizens if it cannot be extended beyond political and judicial processes to those institutions that impinge upon them in their daily lives—as workers, as consumers, as neighbors. This is why we shall be hearing a great deal more of "democratize it."

"REGULATE IT"

In theory, regulating the corporation is about as simple as democratizing it is complex. In practice, it is, of course, another matter. To the proponents of "regulate it," the corporation can be made responsive to social needs by having its actions subjected to the controls of a higher authority—typically government, in the form of a regulatory agency or legislation backed up by the courts. Under regulation, constraints are imposed externally on the corporation while its internal governance is left to its managers. . . .

To some, regulation is a clumsy instrument that should never be relied upon; to others, it is a panacea for the problems of social responsibility. At best, regulation sets minimum and usually crude standards of acceptable behavior; when it works, it does not make any firm socially responsible so much as stop some from being grossly irresponsible. Because it is inflexible, regulation tends to be applied slowly and conservatively, usually lagging public sentiment. Regulation often does not work because of difficulties in enforcement. The problems of the regulatory agencies are legendary—limited resources and information compared with the industries they are supposed to regulate, the cooptation of the regulators by industries, and so on. When applied indiscriminately, regulation either fails dramatically or else succeeds and creates havoc.

Yet there are obvious places for regulation. A prime one is to control tangible "externalities"—costs incurred by corporations that are passed on to the public at large. When, for example, costly pollution or worker health problems can be attributed directly to a corporation, then there seems to be every reason to force it (and its customers) to incur these costs directly, or else to terminate the actions that generate them. Likewise, regulation may have a place where competition encourages the unscrupulous to pull all firms down to a base level of behavior, forcing even the well-intentioned manager to ignore the social consequences of his actions. Indeed, in such cases, the socially responsible behavior is to encourage sensible regulation. "Help us to help ourselves," businessmen should be telling the government.

Although the public has generally been sympathetic to it, "regulate it," even in highly limited form, has hardly been the position of businessmen. . . Most discouraging is Theodore Levitt's revelation some years ago that business has fought every piece of proposed regulatory or social legislation throughout this century, from the Child Labor Act on up. In Levitt's opinion, much of that legislation has been good for business—dissolving the giant trusts, creating a more honest and effective stock market, and so on. Yet, "the computer is programmed to cry wolf."[4] One reason why so much legislation has been excessive and ineffective may be because it has been enacted with the support of the general public but over the obstinate resistance of businessmen.

In summary, regulation is a clumsy instrument but not a useless one. Were the business community to take a more enlightened view of it, regulation could be applied more appropriately, and we would not need these periodic housecleanings to eliminate the excesses.

"PRESSURE IT"

"Pressure it" is designed to do what "regulate it" fails to do: provoke corporations to act beyond some base level of behavior, usually in an area that regulation misses entirely. Here, activists bring ad hoc campaigns of pressure to bear on one or a group of corporations to keep them responsive to the activists' interpretation of social needs. . . .

"Pressure it" is a distinctively American position. While Europeans debate the theories of nationalization and corporate democracy in their cafés, Americans read about the exploits of Ralph Nader et al. in their morning newspapers. Note that "pressure it," unlike "regulate it," implicitly accepts management's right to make the final decisions. Perhaps this is one reason why it is favored in America.

While less radical than the other positions so far discussed, "pressure it" has nevertheless proved far more effective in eliciting behavior sensitive to social needs. . . .

Activist groups have pressured for everything from the dismemberment of diversified corporations to the development of day care centers. Of special note is the class action suit, which has opened up a whole new realm of corporate social issues. But the effective use of the pressure campaign has not been restricted to the traditional activist. President Kennedy used it to roll back U.S. Steel price increases in the early 1960s, and business leaders in Pittsburgh used it in the late 1940s by threatening to take their freight-haulage business elsewhere if the Pennsylvania Railroad did not replace its coal burning locomotives to help clean up their city's air.

"Pressure it" as a means to change corporate behavior is informal, flexible, and focused; hence, it has been highly successful. Yet it is irregular and ad hoc, with different pressure campaigns sometimes making contradictory demands on management. Compared to the positions to its right on the horseshoe, "pressure it," like the other positions to its left, is based on confrontation rather than cooperation.

"TRUST IT"

To a large and vocal contingent, which parades under the banner of "social responsibility," the corporation has no need to act irresponsibly, and therefore there is no reason for it to either be nationalized by the state, democratized by its different constituencies, regulated by the government, or pressured by activists. This contingent believes that the corporation's leaders can be trusted to attend to social goals for their own sake, simply because it is the noble thing to do. (Once this position was known as *noblesse oblige,* literally "nobility obliges.")

We call this position "trust it," or, more exactly, "trust the corporation to the goodwill of its managers," although looking from the outside in, it might just as well be called "socialize it." We place it in the center of our conceptual horseshoe because it alone postulates a natural balance between social and economic goals—a balance which is to be attained in the heads (or perhaps the hearts) of responsible businessmen. And, as a not necessarily incidental consequence, power can be left in the hands of the managers; the corporation can be trusted to those who reconcile social and economic goals.

The attacks on social responsibility, from the right as well as the left, boil down to whether corporate managers should be trusted when they claim to pursue social goals; if so, whether they are capable of pursuing such goals; and finally, whether they have any right to pursue such goals.

The simplest attack is that social responsibility is all rhetoric, no action. E.F. Cheit refers to the "Gospel of Social Responsibility" as "designed to justify the power of managers over an ownerless system. . . .

Others argue that businessmen lack the personal capabilities required to pursue social goals. Levitt claims that the professional manager reaches the top of the hierarchy by dedication to his firm and his industry; as a result, his knowledge of social issues is highly restricted.[5] Others argue that an orientation to efficiency renders business leaders inadept at handling complex social problems (which require flexibility and political finesse, and sometimes involve solutions that are uneconomic). . . .

The most far reaching criticism is that businessmen have no right to pursue social goals. "Who authorized them to do that?", asks Braybrooke, attacking from the left.[6] What business have they—self-selected or at best appointed by shareholders—to impose *their* interpretation of the public good on society. Let the elected politicians, directly responsible to the population, look after the social goals.

But this attack comes from the right, too. Milton Friedman writes that social responsibility amounts to spending other people's money—if not that of shareholders, then of customers or employees. Drawing on all the pejorative terms of right-wing ideology, Friedman concludes that social responsibility is a "fundamentally subversive doctrine," representing "pure and unadulterated socialism," supported by businessmen who are "unwitting puppets of the intellectual forces that have been undermining the basis of a free society these past decades." To Friedman, "there is one and only one social responsibility of business—to use its resources and engage in activities designed to increase its profits so long as it stays within the rules of the game."[7] Let businessmen, in other words, stick to their own business, which is business itself.

The modern corporation has been described as a rational, amoral institution—its professional managers "hired guns" who pursue "efficiently" any goals asked of them. The problem is that efficiency really means measurable efficiency, so that the guns load only with goals that can be quantified. Social goals, unlike economic ones, just don't lend themselves to quantification. As a result, the performance control systems—on which modern corporations so heavily depend—tend to drive out social goals in favor of economic ones. As Robert Ackerman concluded in a study of performance control systems:

> The financial reporting system may actually inhibit social responsiveness. By focusing on economic performance . . . such a system directs energy and resources to achieving results measured in financial terms. It is the only game in town, so to speak, at least the only one with an official scorecard.[8]

In the contemporary large corporation, professional amorality turns into economic morality. When the screws of the performance control systems are turned tight—as they were, for example, in the General Electric price fixing scandal of the early 1960s—economic morality can turn into social immorality. And it happens often: A *Fortune* writer found that "a surprising number of [big companies] have been involved in blatant illegalities" in the 1970s, at least 117 of 1,043 firms studied.[9]

Even when the chief executive is personally committed to social goals, the control systems he must rely upon to manage far flung operations may preclude him from doing anything about them. Thus, while he sings the praises of social responsibility, his employees are forced to march to the tune of economic performance. And then they respond to questionnaires with complaints about having to compromise their ethics.

How, then, is anyone to "trust it"?

The fact is that we have to trust it, for two reasons. First, the strategic decisions of large organizations inevitably involve social as well as economic consequences that are inextricably intertwined. The neat distinction between economic goals in the private sector and social goals in the public sector just doesn't hold up in practice. Every important decision of the large corporation—to introduce a new product line, to close an old plant, whatever—generates all kinds of social consequences. There is no such thing as purely economic decisions in big business. Only a conceptual ostrich, with his head deeply buried in the abstractions of economic theory, could possibly use the distinction between economic and social goals to dismiss social responsibility.

The second reason we have to "trust it" is that there is always some degree of discretion involved in corporate decision making, discretion to thwart social needs or to attend to them. Things could be a lot better in today's corporation, but they could also be an awful lot worse. It is primarily our ethics that keep us where we are. If the performance control systems favored by diversified corporations cut too deeply into our ethical standards, then our choice is clear: to reduce these standards or call into question the whole trend toward diversification.

To dismiss social responsibility is to allow corporate behavior to drop to the lowest level, propped up only by external controls such as regulation and pressure campaigns. Solzhenitsyn, who has experienced the natural conclusion of unrestrained bureaucratization, warns us (in sharp contrast to Friedman) that "a society with no other scale but the legal one is not quite worthy of man . . . A society which is based on the letter of the law and never reaches any higher is scarcely taking advantage of the high level of human possibilities."[10]

This is not to suggest that we must trust it completely. We certainly cannot trust it unconditionally by accepting the claim popular in some quarters that only business can solve the social ills of society. Business has no business using its resources without constraint in the social sphere—whether to support political candidates or to dictate implicitly through donations how non-profit institutions should allocate their efforts. But where business is inherently involved, where its decisions have social consequences, that is where social responsibility has a role to play: where business creates externalities that cannot be measured and attributed to it (in other words, where regulation is ineffective); where regulation would work if only business would cooperate with it; where the corporation can fool its customers, or suppliers, or government through superior knowledge; where useful products can be marketed instead of wasteful or destructive ones. In other words, we have to realize that in many spheres we must trust it, or at least socialize it (and perhaps change it) so that we can trust it. Without responsible and ethical people in important places, our society is not worth very much.

"IGNORE IT"

"Ignore it" differs from the other positions on the horseshoe in that explicitly or implicitly it calls for no change in corporate behavior. It assumes that social needs are met in the course of pursuing economic goals. We include this position in our horseshoe because it is held by many influential people and also because its validity would preempt support for the other positions. We must, therefore, investigate it alongside the others.

It should be noted at the outset that "ignore it" is not the same position as "trust it." In the latter, to be good is the right thing to do; in the present case, "it pays to be good." The distinction is subtle but important, for now it is economics, not ethics, that elicits the desired behavior. One need not strive to be ethical; economic forces will ensure that social needs fall conveniently into place. Here we have moved one notch to the right on our horseshoe, into the realm where the economic goals dominate. . . .

"Ignore it" is sometimes referred to as "enlightened self-interest," although some of its proponents are more enlightened than others. Many a true believer in social responsibility has used the argument that it pays to be good to ward off the attacks from the right that corporations have no business pursuing social goals. Even Milton Friedman must admit that they have every right to do so if it pays them economically. The danger of such arguments, however—and a prime reason "ignore it" differs from "trust it"—is that they tend to support the status quo: corporations need not change their behavior because it already pays to be good.

Sometimes the case for "ignore it" is made in terms of corporations at large, that the whole business community will benefit from socially responsible behavior. Other times the case is made in terms of the individual corporation, that it will benefit directly from its own socially responsible actions. A popular claim in the 1960s, for example, was that satisfied workers lead to greater productivity. "Treat them well, get them involved, and you will make money," we were told by a generation of industrial psychologists. This particular claim has been largely discredited, but many others have taken its place—for example, that companies that are good neighbors by polluting less are more profitable. Others make the case for "ignore it" in "social investment" terms, claiming that socially responsible behavior pays off in a better image for the firm, a more positive relationship with customers, and ultimately a healthier and more stable society in which to do business.

Then, there is what I like to call the "them" argument: "If we're not good, *they* will move in"—"they" being Ralph Nader, the government, whoever. In other words, "Be good or else." The trouble with this argument is that by reducing social responsibility to simply a political tool for sustaining managerial control of the corporation in the face of outside threats, it tends to encourage general pronouncements instead of concrete actions (unless, of course, "they" actually deliver with pressure campaigns). . . .

The "ignore it" position rests on some shaky ground. It seems to encourage average behavior at best; and where the average does not seem to be good enough, it encourages the status quo. In fact, ironically, "ignore it" makes a strong case for "pressure it," since the whole argument collapses in the absence of pressure campaigns. Thus while many influential people take this position, we question whether in the realities of corporate behavior it can really stand alone.

"INDUCE IT"

Continuing around to the right, our next position drops all concern with social responsibility per se and argues, simply, "pay it to be good," or, from the corporation's point of view, "be good only where it pays." Here, the corporation does not actively pursue social goals at all, whether as ends in themselves or as means to economic ends. Rather, it undertakes socially desirable programs only when induced economically to do so—usually through government incentives. If society wishes to clean up urban blight, then let its government provide subsidies for corporations that renovate buildings; if pollution is the problem, then let corporations be rewarded for reducing it.

"Induce it" faces "regulate it" on the opposite side of the horseshoe for good reason. While one penalizes the corporation for what it does do, the other rewards it for doing what it might not otherwise do. Hence these two positions can be direct substitutes: pollution can be alleviated by introducing penalties for the damage done or by offering incentives for the improvements rendered.

Logic would, however, dictate a specific role for each of these positions. Where a corporation is doing society a specific, attributable harm—as in the case of pollution—then paying it to stop hardly seems to make a lot of sense. If society does not wish to outlaw the harmful behavior altogether, then surely it must charge those responsible for it—the corporation and, ultimately, its customers. Offering financial incentives to stop causing harm would be to invite a kind of blackmail—for example, encouraging corporations to pollute so as to get paid to stop. And every citizen would be charged for the harm done by only a few.

On the other hand, where social problems exist which cannot be attributed to specific corporations, yet require the skills of certain corporations for solution, then financial incentives clearly make sense (so long, of course, as solutions can be clearly defined and tied to tangible economic rewards). Here, and not under "trust it," is where the "only business can do it" argument belongs. When it is true that only business can do it (and business has not done it to us in the first place), then business should be encouraged to do it. . . .

"RESTORE IT"

Our last position on the horseshoe tends to be highly ideological, the first since "democratize it" to seek a fundamental change in the governance and the goals of the corporation. Like the proponents of "nationalize it," those of this position believe that managerial control is illegitimate and must be replaced by a more valid form of external control. The corporation should be restored to its former status, that is, returned to its "rightful" owners, the shareholders. The only way to ensure the relentless pursuit of economic goals—and that means the maximization of profit, free of the "subversive doctrine" of social responsibility—is to put control directly into the hands of those to whom profit means the most.

A few years ago this may have seemed to be an obsolete position. But thanks to its patron saint Milton Friedman . . . it has recently come into prominence. . . .

Friedman has written:

> In a free-enterprise, private-property system, a corporate executive is an employee of the owners of the business. He has direct responsibility to his employers. That responsibility is to conduct the business in accordance with their desires, which generally will be to make as much money as possible while conforming to the basic rules of the society, both those embodied in law and those embodied in ethical custom.[11]

Interestingly, what seems to drive Friedman is a belief that the shift over the course of this century from owner to manager control, with its concerns about social responsibility, represents an unstoppable skid around our horseshoe. In the opening chapter of his book *Capitalism and Freedom,* Friedman seems to accept only two possibilities—traditional capitalism and socialism as practiced in Eastern Europe. The absence of the former must inevitably lead to the latter.

The preservation and expansion of freedom are today threatened from two directions. The one threat is obvious and clear. It is the external threat coming from the evil men in the Kremlin who promise to bury us. The other threat is far more subtle. It is the internal threat coming from men of good intentions and good will who wish to reform us.[12]

The problem of who should control the corporation thus reduces to a war between two ideologies—in Friedman's terms, "subversive" socialism and "free" enterprise. In this world of black and white, there can be no middle ground, no moderate position between the black of "nationalize it" and the white of "restore it," none of the grey of "trust it." Either the owners will control the corporation or else the government will. Hence: " 'restore it' or else." Anchor the corporation on the right side of the horseshoe, Friedman seems to be telling us, the only place where "free" enterprise and "freedom" are safe.

All of this, in my view, rests on a series of assumptions—technical, economic, and political—which contain a number of fallacies. First is the fallacy of the technical assumption of shareholder control. Every trend in ownership during this century seems to refute the assumption that small shareholders are either willing or able to control the large, widely held corporation. The one place where free markets clearly still exist is in stock ownership, and that has served to detach ownership from control. When power is widely dispersed—among stockholders no less than workers or customers—those who share it tend to remain passive. It pays no one of them to invest the effort to exercise their power. Hence, even if serious shareholders did control the boards of widely held corporations (and one survey of all the directors of the *Fortune 500* in 1977 found that only 1.6% of them represented significant shareholder interests),[13] the question remains open as to whether they would actually try to control the management.

The economic assumptions of free markets have been discussed at length in the literature. Whether there exists vibrant competition, unlimited entry, open information, consumer sovereignity, and labor mobility is debatable. Less debatable is the conclusion that the larger the corporation, the greater is its ability to interfere with these processes. The issues we are discussing center on the giant corporation. . . .

Those who laid the foundation for conventional economic theory—such as Adam Smith and Alfred Marshall—never dreamed of the massive amounts now spent for advertising campaigns, most of them designed as much for affect as for effect; of the waves of conglomeration that have combined all kinds of diverse businesses into single corporate entities; of chemical complexes that cost more than a billion dollars; and of the intimate relationships that now exist between giant corporations and government, as customer and partner not to mention subsidizer. The concept of arm's length relationships in such conditions is, at best, nostalgic. What happens to consumer sovereignty when Ford knows more about its gas tanks than do its customers? And what does labor mobility mean in the presence of an inflexible pension plan, or commitment to a special skill, or a one-factory town? It is an ironic twist of conventional economic theory that the worker is the one who typically stays put, thus rendering false the assumption of labor mobility, while the shareholder is the mobile one, thus spoiling the case for owner control.

The political assumptions are more ideological in nature, although usually implicit. These assumptions are that the corporation is essentially amoral, society's instrument for producing goods and services, and, more broadly, that a society is "free" and "democratic" so long as its governmental leaders are elected by universal suffrage and do not interfere with the legal activities of businessmen. But many people—a large majority of the general public, if polls are to be believed—seem to subscribe to one or more assumptions that contradict these "free enterprise" assumptions.

One assumption is that the large corporation is a social and political institution as much as an economic instrument. Economic activities, as noted previously, produce all kinds of social consequences. Jobs get created and rivers get polluted, cities get built and workers get injured. These social consequences cannot be factored out of corporate strategic decisions and assigned to government.

Another assumption is that society cannot achieve the necessary balance between social and economic needs so long as the private sector attends only to economic goals. Given the pervasiveness of business in society, the acceptance of Friedman's prescriptions would drive us toward a one-dimensional society—a society that is too utilitarian and too materialistic. Economic morality, as noted earlier, can amount to a social immorality.

Finally, the question is asked: Why the owners? In a democratic society, what justifies owner control of the corporation any more than worker control, or consumer control, or pluralistic control? Ours is not Adam Smith's society of small proprietors and shopkeepers. His butcher, brewer, and baker have become Iowa Beef Packers, Anheuser-Busch, and ITT Continental Baking. What was once a case for individual democracy now becomes a case for oligarchy. . . .

I see Friedman's form of "restore it" as a rather quaint position in a society of giant corporations, managed economies, and dispersed shareholders—a society in which the collective power of corporations is coming under increasing scrutiny and in which the distribution between economic and social goals is being readdressed.

Of course, there are other ways to "restore it." "Divest it" could return the corporation to the business or central theme it knows best, restoring the role of allocating funds between different businesses to capital markets instead of central headquarters. Also, boards could be restored to positions of influence by holding directors legally responsible for their actions and by making them more independent of managers . . . We might even wish to extend use of "reduce it" where possible, to decrease the size of those corporations that have grown excessively large on the basis of market or political power rather than economies of scale, and perhaps to eliminate certain forms of vertical integration. In many cases it may prove advantageous, economically as well as socially, to have the corporation trade with its suppliers and customers instead of being allowed to ingest them indiscriminately.[14]

I personally doubt that these proposals could be any more easily realized in today's society than those of Friedman, even though I believe them to be more desirable. "Restore it" is the nostalgic position on our horseshoe, a return to our fantasies of a glorious past. In this society of giant organizations, it flies in the face of powerful economic and political forces.

CONCLUSION: IF THE SHOE FITS . . .

I believe that today's corporation cannot ride on any one position any more than a horse can ride on part of a shoe. In other words, we need to treat the conceptual horseshoe as a portfolio of positions from which we can draw, depending on circumstances. Exclusive reliance on one position will lead to a narrow and dogmatic society, with an excess concentration of power. We have learned about the dangers of unrestrained government ownership. No less menacing is the unrestrained pursuit of the economic interests of the shareholders, or of the oligarchy of ostensibly "socially responsible" managers. Lord Acton taught us that absolute power corrupts absolutely. In contrast, the use of a variety of positions can encourage the pluralism I believe most of us feel is necessary to sustain democracy. If the shoe fits, then let the corporation wear it.

I do not mean to imply that the eight positions do not represent fundamentally different values and, in some cases, ideologies as well. Clearly they do. But I also believe that anyone who makes an honest assessment of the realities of power in and around today's large corporations must conclude that a variety of positions have to be relied upon. Anyone can tilt to the left, right, or center of our horseshoe, favoring popular, shareholder, or managerial control, along with social or economic goals or both in balance. But even the most devoted adherent of conventional economic theory cannot, for example, dismiss regulation totally, any more than the most flaming radical can deny the place of economic goals in the corporation.

I tilt to the left of center, as has no doubt been obvious in my comments to this point. Let me summarize my own prescriptions as follows, and in the process provide some basis for evaluating the relevant roles of each of the eight positions.

First "Trust It," or at Least "Socialize It." Despite my suspicions about much of the rhetoric that passes for social responsibility and the discouraging evidence about the behavior of large contemporary organizations (not only corporations), I remain firmly convinced that without honest and responsible people in important places, we are in deep trouble. We need to trust it because, no matter how much we rely on the other positions, managers will always retain a great deal of power. And that power necessarily has social no less than economic consequences. The positions on the right side of our horseshoe ignore these social consequences while some of those on the left fail to recognize the difficulties of influencing these consequences in large, hierarchical organizations. Sitting between these two sets of positions, managers can use their discretion to satisfy or to subvert the wishes of the public. Ultimately, what managers do is determined by their sense of responsibility as individual members of society.

Although we must "trust it," we cannot *only* "trust it." As I have argued, there is an appropriate and limited place for social responsibility—essentially to get the corporation's own house in order and to encourage it to act responsibly in its own sphere of operations. Beyond that, social responsibility needs to be tempered by other positions around our horseshoe.

Then "Pressure It," Ceaselessly. As we have seen, too many forces interfere with social responsibility. The best antidote to these forces is the ad hoc pressure campaign, designed to pinpoint unethical behavior and raise social consciousness about issues. . . .

In fact, "pressure it" underlies the success of most of the other positions. Pressure campaigns have brought about necessary new regulations and have highlighted the case for corporate democracy. As we have seen, the "ignore it" position collapses without "pressure it." Indeed, what if not a pressure campaign is the media blitz of Milton Friedman to "restore it."

After That, Try to "Democratize It." A somewhat distant third in my portfolio is "democratize it," a position I view as radical only in terms of the current U.S. debate, not in terms of fundamental American values. Democracy matters most where it affects us directly—in the water we drink, the jobs we perform, the products we consume. How can we call our society democratic when many of its most powerful institutions are closed to governance from the outside and are run as hierarchies of authority from within?

As noted earlier, I have no illusions about having found the means to achieve corporate democracy. But I do know that Americans can be very resourceful when they decide to resolve a problem—and this is a problem that badly needs resolving. Somehow, ways must be found to open the corporation up to the formal influence of the constituencies most affected by it—employees, customers, neighbors, and so on—without weakening it as an economic institution. At stake is nothing less than the maintenance of basic freedoms in our society.

Then, Only Where Specifically Appropriate, "Regulate It" and "Induce It." Facing each other on the horseshoe are two positions that have useful if limited roles to play. Regulation is neither a panacea nor a menace. It belongs where the corporation can abuse the power it has and can be penalized for that abuse—notably where externalities can be identified with specific corporations. Financial inducements belong, not where a corporation has created a problem, but where it has the capability to solve a problem created by someone else.

Occasionally, Selectively, "Nationalize It" and "Restore It," but Not in Friedman's Way. The extreme positions should be reserved for extreme problems. If "pressure it" is a scalpel and "regulate it" a cleaver, then "nationalize it" and "restore it" are guillotines.

Both these positions are implicitly proposed as alternatives to "democratize it." One offers public control, the other "shareholder democracy." The trouble is that control by everyone often turns out to be control by no one, while control by the owners—even if attainable—would remove the corporation even further from the influence of those most influenced by it.

Yet, as noted earlier, nationalization sometimes makes sense—when private enterprise cannot provide a necessary mission, at least in a sufficient or appropriate way, and when the activities of a corporation must be intricately tied in to government policy.

As for "restore it," I believe Friedman's particular proposals will aggravate the problems of political control and social responsibility, strengthening oligarchical tendencies in society and further tilting what I see as the current imbalance between social and economic goals. In response to Friedman's choice between "subversive" socialism and "free" enterprise, I say "a pox on both your houses." Let us concentrate our efforts on the intermediate positions around the horseshoe. . . . I stand with Friedman in wishing to see competitive markets strengthened; it is just that I believe his proposals lead in exactly the opposite direction.

Finally, Above All, Don't "Ignore It." I leave one position out of my portfolio altogether, because it contradicts the others. The one thing we must not do is ignore the large, widely-held corporation. It is too influential a force in our lives. Our challenge is to find ways to distribute the power in and around our large organizations so that they will remain responsive, vital, and effective.

REFERENCES

1. E. M. Epstein, for example, finds the social record of nationalized firms in the U.K. not much better than the private ones, a conclusion reinforced by C. Jenkins, who advocates nationalization. E. M. Epstein, "The Social Role of Business Enterprise in Britain: An American Perspective; Part II," *The Journal of Management Studies* (1977), pp. 281–316; and C. Jenkins, *Power at the Top* (Westport, CT: Greenwood Press, 1976).
2. From J. Bacon and J. K. Brown, *Corporate Directorship Practices: Role, Selection and Legal Status of the Board* (The Conference Board and the American Society of Corporate Secretaries, Inc., 1975), p. 48.
3. See Henry Mintzberg, *Structure in Fives: Designing Effective Organizations* (Englewood Cliffs, NJ: Prentice Hall, 1983).
4. T. Levitt, "Why Business Always Loses," *Harvard Business Review* (March/April 1968), p. 83.
5. Levitt, op. cit.
6. D. Braybrooke, "Skepticism of Wants, and Certain Subversive Effects of Corporations on American Values," in S. Hook, ed., *Human Values and Economic Policy* (New York, NY: New York University Press, 1967), p. 224.

7. Milton Friedman, "A Friedman Doctrine: The Social Responsibility of Business is to Increase its Profits," *The New York Times Magazine,* September 13 1970, pp. 33, 126.
8. Robert W. Ackerman, *The Social Challenge to Business* (Cambridge, MA: Harvard University Press, 1975), p. 56.
9. I. Ross, "How Lawless are the Big Companies?" *Fortune,* December 1, 1980, p. 57.
10. Aleksander Solzhenitsyn, from "Why The West Has Succumbed to Cowardice," *The Montreal Star News and Review,* June 10, 1978, p. B1.
11. Friedman, op. cit., p. 33.
12. Milton Friedman, *Capitalism and Freedom* (Chicago, IL: University of Chicago Press, 1962), p. 20.
13. L. Smith, "The Boardroom Is Becoming a Different Scene," *Fortune,* May 8, 1978, pp. 150–154, 158, 162, 166, 168.
14. A number of these proposals would be worthwhile to pursue in the public and parapublic sectors as well, to divide up overgrown hospitals, school systems, social service agencies, and all kinds of government departments.

What Can We Learn from the U.S. Federal Sentencing Guidelines for Organizational Ethics?

Mark S. Schwartz
Lecturer of Business Ethics, The Wharton School, University of Pennsylvania

Dove Izraeli
Professor of Marketing and Business Ethics, Tel Aviv University

Joseph E. Murphy
Managing Director, Integrity Interactive

INTRODUCTION

In November 1991, unique legal standards were enacted in the United States which had a pro-

Adapted from "What Can We Learn From the U.S. Federal Sentencing Guidelines for Organizational Ethics?" by Dove Izraeli and Mark S. Schwartz, *Journal of Business Ethics,* volume 17, numbers 9–10, July 1998, pp. 1045–1055. Reprinted by permission of Kluwer Academic Publishers.

found effect on corporate America (Izraeli, 1997). The standards, referred to as the U.S. Federal Sentencing Guidelines for Organizations ("Guidelines"), used the 'carrot and stick' approach to create incentives for thousands of corporations to create or modify their compliance or ethics programs (Izraeli, 1994).

The Guidelines were developed by the United States Sentencing Commission, a new governmental body which came into existence in 1984. The Commission was charged with the responsibility for creating uniformity in the sentencing of offenders of federal laws. Following the promulgation of Guidelines in 1987 for sentencing individuals convicted of federal offenses, the Commission proceeded to create Guidelines for organizations which went into effect in 1991 (Kaplan et al., 1993a: 136–137). The Guidelines (discussed in greater detail below) consisted essentially of a manual for judges to apply when determining the appropriate sentence for corporations convicted of a federal crime. Judges were being required for the first time to consider whether the convicted corporation had established an 'effective compliance program' prior to the violation taking place, in other words, whether the corporation had taken appropriate steps to prevent and detect violations of the law.

According to Win Swinsen, the former Deputy General Counsel of the Sentencing Commission, one of the primary reasons for the enactment of sentencing guidelines for organizations was that the U.S. government lacked a clear corporate crime sentencing and enforcement policy. As a result, judges were having great difficulty in finding meaningful ways to sentence corporations. Empirical research conducted by the Sentencing Commission on corporate sentencing practices demonstrated that ". . . corporate sentencing was in disarray . . . nearly identical cases were treated differently." In addition, average fines were found to be ". . . less than the cost corporations had to pay to obey the law" (Sentencing Commission, 1995: 30).

To address these concerns, the Commission eventually came to accept the 'carrot and stick' approach to corporate sentencing. This approach was based on three principal and related objectives: (1) to define a model for good corporate citizenship; (2) to use the model to make corporate sentencing fair by providing objective, defined criteria; and (3) to use the model to create incentives for companies to take crime controlling actions. The final objective was designed to shift from the previous 'speed trap' enforcement policy of the past (i.e., merely lie and wait for corporate offenders and then fine them), to a more interactive approach. By providing financial incentives, the government was inviting companies to undertake effective, crime-controlling actions which in turn would put less pressure on already limited government enforcement resources (U.S. Sentencing Commission, 1995: 34).

Since the enactment of the law, numerous corporations have been prosecuted under the Guidelines, some suffering fines and penalties in the tens and even hundreds of millions of dollars (U.S. Sentencing Commission, 1996). Empirical evidence (discussed below) is now suggesting that the implementation of these programs is raising the level of legal and ethical behavior in corporations. Somewhat surprisingly, despite their impact and apparent success, the Guidelines appear to remain somewhat of a mystery to non-U.S. countries and corporations (Izraeli, 1995).

It may be the case that the time has arrived for countries other than the U.S. to consider the development of legislation similar to the Guidelines, using the Guidelines as a model or framework to follow. To make this argument, this paper will consist of two parts. Part one discusses the Guidelines in general, their purpose, impact, utilization by the U.S. courts, and effectiveness in achieving their objectives. Part two discusses why the time has arrived for other countries to consider the Guidelines due to foreign companies operating in the U.S., the development of a globalized business community, and a changing regulatory environment.

The paper will conclude by suggesting the potential benefits for other countries in adopting legislation similar to the Guidelines, the current limitations of the Guidelines and how they might be addressed, and finally an initial implementation strategy for countries to utilize in designing their own legislation.

(1) WHAT ARE THE GUIDELINES?

According to the Guidelines, any organization is liable to payments of restitution, fines, and periods of probation if convicted for a federal offense connected with price fixing, bid-rigging, copyright and trademark infringement, bribery, fraud, money laundering, extortion, embezzlement, conspiracy, as well as other types of misconduct. The preamble to the Guidelines states that the organization operates only through its agents, usually its managers, and is, therefore, liable for the offenses committed by them. Naturally, the managers are personally responsible and liable for their own behavior. The innovation of the Guidelines lies in the fact that the sentences imposed on the organization and its agents are designed to achieve the following objectives: (a) just punishment; (b) sufficient deterrence; and (c) encourage the development of internal mechanisms to prevent, identify and report on criminal behavior in organizations (i.e., through a 'carrot and stick' approach).

The Guidelines require judges to follow a specific formula in determining fines. The range of potential fines is based on two factors: (1) the seriousness of the federal offense (i.e., the 'base fine'); and (2) the culpability of the organization (i.e., the 'multiplier'). The base fine is the greater of the company's monetary gain, the victim's monetary loss, or a specified amount depending on the type of offense (ranging anywhere from $5,000 to $72,500,000). Once the base fine is determined, federal judges are required to multiply this amount by a 'culpability score.' The culpability score can lead to either a substantial increase or decrease of the base fine, depending on which of several factors are in existence. The culpability score will increase when: (a) a larger sized organization is involved; (b) high-level employees are involved in the offense or have tolerated the offense; (c) the organization has a prior history of engaging in similar misconduct; (d) the organization has violated a court order; or (e) the organization has obstructed justice relative to the offense. As a result of these factors, a company could find itself facing up to hundreds of millions of dollars in fines (the 'stick') (Sentencing Commission, 1995: 9–27).

At the same time, the Guidelines provide organizations with an opportunity to take steps which can substantially mitigate the severity of the base fine (up to 95%). The Guidelines provide that the culpability score can be reduced (i.e., the 'carrot') if the organization engages in: (a) self-reporting; (b) cooperation and acceptance of responsibility; and/or (c) establishing, prior to the offense occurring, an 'effective compliance program' to prevent and detect violations of the law. In addition to potential fines, judges are required to place organizations with 50 or more employees on probation when they are deemed not to have an effective compliance program in place (Sentencing Commission, 1995: 9–27).

To assist corporations in knowing exactly what constitutes an appropriate internal detection and prevention mechanism (i.e., an effective compliance program), the Guidelines list seven minimum 'due diligence' requirements: "(1) compliance standards and procedures must be tailored to the company's particular business and needs [e.g., a code of conduct or ethics]; (2) high-level personnel must be responsible for the program; [e.g., a compliance or ethics officer]; (3) due care must be taken not to give substantial discretionary authority to those who may have a propensity for illegal conduct; (4) compliance standards must be communicated to all employees and other agents in an effective manner [e.g., training or publications]; (5) the company must take steps to actually achieve compliance, e.g., through auditing and monitoring systems and by enabling employees to report suspected violations without fear of retribution; [e.g., an employee 'hotline']; (6) the program must be enforced consistently through a system of discipline; and (7) when violations do occur, steps must be taken to improve the program and report the violations" (Kaplan et al., 1993a: 138–142).

(2) IMPACT OF GUIDELINES

Although the Guidelines have been in existence for less than a decade, they have already had a significant impact on corporate America. As determined by a number of surveys, the primary impact has been the creation or enhancement of compliance or ethics programs by thousands of companies across the United States, and even outside of the U.S.

In some cases, the Guidelines have provided a model for an organization's entire compliance or ethics program. For example, The Bank of Tokyo has made the Guidelines "the focal point of its overall compliance effort" (U.S. Sentencing Commission, 1995: 63). According to the bank, the Guidelines gave them ". . . a clear picture of what a compliance program should look like and a set of instructions on how to construct a program." The bank also found that ". . . virtually every compliance directive we received, regardless of the source, fit comfortably within the structure that is suggested by the [seven elements for compliance]" (U.S. Sentencing Commission, 1995: 65). In addition to The Tokyo Bank, other New York-area banks as well as a Canadian bank, the CIBC, ". . . have begun to use the guidelines as a foundation for their overall compliance efforts" (U.S. Sentencing Commission, 1995: 67).

Other companies, even if they already had some sort of compliance or ethics program in place before 1991, have indicated that the Guidelines were one of the factors which influenced the enhancement of already existing compliance or ethics programs. According to "A National Study of Compliance Practices" which involved 333 corporations representing various sizes and industries, 44 percent of the respondents stated that the Guidelines caused them to add vigor to their compliance programs, while 20 percent added compliance programs because of their awareness of the Guidelines (U.S. Sentencing Commission, 1995: 134). According to Andrew Apel, the author of the study, ". . . certainly, the guidelines are having a significant impact on what organizations are doing to prevent and detect violations of law" (U.S. Sentencing Commission, 1995: 129). Another study by the Council of Ethical Organizations of approximately 750,000 employees from 203 large U.S. companies also found that the Guidelines have had an influence on corporate ethics programs. The survey found that 38 percent of the companies significantly improved their ethics compliance environments following the enactment of the Guidelines (U.S. Sentencing Commission, 1995: 178).

Unfortunately, the studies did not break down the impact of the Guidelines on individual components of ethics programs. Despite this gap, one can assume that the Guidelines have had the greatest impact on four components: (1) ethics training; (2) ethics officers; (3) ethics offices; and (4) ethics hotlines. Each of these components can be related to one of the seven elements of an effective compliance program as stipulated by the Guidelines. It should be noted, however, that one component in particular, a code of ethics, did not come into existence merely as a result of the Guidelines. As several studies have indicated, the vast majority of large U.S. companies (93 percent) already had a code of ethics in place by 1990 (Center For Business Ethics, 1992).

(3) UTILIZATION BY THE COURTS

The Guidelines have clearly had an impact on the establishment or enhancement of corporate ethics programs. One of the reasons for this achievement is that in the case of an offense the size of the fine is conditional on the existence of a compliance or ethics program. But have U.S. courts actually utilized the Guidelines in sentencing corporations?

According to the U.S. Sentencing Commission Annual Report, 218 organizations were sentenced according to the Guidelines during 1998, with 160 organizations subject to the Guidelines' fine provisions. Although this represented a 1 percent decrease from 1997, it represented a 39 percent increase from 1996 (157 sentences), a 96 percent increase from 1995 (111 sentences), and a 153 percent increase from 1994 (86 sentences).

Although three-quarters of the firms sentenced in 1998 had less than 100 employees, one firm employed over 70,000 individuals. The major types of offenses included fraud (32%); environmental waste discharge (21%); tax (11%); money laundering (7%); antitrust (6%); and environmental wildlife violations (4%). In over half of the organizations sentenced pursuant to the fine guidelines, personnel with substantial authority were involved in or tolerated the criminal activity (U.S. Sentencing Commission, 1998).

The Guidelines have had an even more significant impact on probation. Approximately 65 percent of companies sentenced from 1994–1998 were placed on probation, with approximately 12–20 percent of these being ordered to implement compliance programs (U.S. Sentencing Commission, 1998). The Guidelines were to have less of an impact on the courts' consideration of corporate compliance programs when assessing fines. Since 1994, only a handful of the prosecutions involved a direct consideration of the defendant's compliance program by the court. In one case, the fine was reduced on the basis of the company being held to have an effective compliance program (Kaplan, 1995: 1). Somewhat surprisingly, none of the organizations sentenced during 1998 was found to have an effective compliance program to prevent and detect violations of the law (U.S. Sentencing Commission, 1998).

The potential consequences of the failure to implement an effective compliance program have now been well highlighted. In 1996, a Manhattan federal court sentenced Daiwa Bank to pay a fine of $340 million under the Guidelines. The case involved a bank employee who lost $1.1 billion in unauthorized trades. The two main reasons for the fine were the bank's "lack of a meaningful compliance program" and its "consequent failure to report the employee's wrongdoing" (Kaplan, 1996: 1). In May 1998, in what was the largest criminal fine in U.S. history, Hoffman-LaRoche, a large Swiss pharmaceutical company, was fined $500 million under the Guidelines after being convicted of an anti-trust conspiracy. The company, along with two other firms, attempted to control the prices and sales volume of a series of vitamins (Kaplan, 1999: 1).

Another development which has been noted due to the Guidelines is being referred to as 'the shadow effect.' Essentially, the Guidelines are also being considered by courts and government agencies in criminal cases other than those brought under the Guidelines. Companies such as National Medical Enterprises (involving kickbacks), Lucas Aerospace (involving falsifying test data), and C. R. Bard (involving fraud) were all ordered to adopt extensive compliance programs in addition to paying fines. Even defendants in civil cases such as Prudential Securities (involving fraud) or Grumman Corporation (involving kickbacks) were ordered to implement compliance programs, which were much more onerous than if conducted voluntarily (Kaplan, 1995: 2–3). In the 1996 Delaware Chancery Court case In *Re Caremark International Inc.,* the judge essentially relied on the Guidelines in warning that directors themselves can be held personally liable if they have failed to institute an adequate compliance program to prevent illegal acts by employees (Kaplan, 1997:2). In terms of government agencies, the Environmental Protection Agency and the U.S. Department of Health and Human Services have both issued standards for companies based on the Guidelines' compliance criteria (Kaplan, 1993b: ch.20, 8–10.2).

(4) EFFECTIVENESS OF GUIDELINES

It can be seen from the above discussion that the Guidelines have had an impact on the creation and implementation of ethics programs, and have actually been utilized by the courts in assessing fines and placing companies on probation. Despite this impact, one could ask a more fundamental question: "Have the Guidelines helped to achieve their ultimate purpose, the reduction of corporate crime and an improvement in ethical behavior?"

Although it may be some time before we can know the answer to this question with any degree of certainty, a study released by the Ethics Resource Center entitled, "Ethics in American Business: Policies, Programs and Perceptions" provides an initial indication that ethics programs are beneficial in improving organizational ethics. The survey examined employee attitudes and behavior in relation to the existence of three components of an ethics program: (1) codes of conduct, (2) the introduction of ethics into employee and management training, and (3) the establishment of ethics and compliance offices. Over 4,000 U.S. workers were surveyed representing different levels of responsibility, job functions, company size, and industries (Ethics Resource Center, 1994).

The survey indicates that ethics programs appear to improve ethical behavior. The results are summarized as follows:

Corporate ethics programs appear to have a distinctly positive impact on employee behavior and their opinions about the ethics of fellow employees, management, their companies and even themselves. The most positive effects were reported in companies which had all three program components—codes of conduct, ethics training and ethics offices. Striking differences could be seen in the responses of employees in companies with comprehensive ethics programs and the responses of those in companies with no program elements or with only a code of conduct. Indeed, a code of conduct as the sole element of an ethics effort often seemed to have a negative effect on employee perceptions. Ethics initiatives appeared to increase employee awareness of misconduct, employee willingness to report misconduct, and the level of satisfaction with the outcome of their reporting. (Ethics Resource Center, 1994: 6)

Another study by the Council of Ethical Organizations of 750,000 employees from large U.S. corporations found that, "Employees of companies that had implemented or fortified comprehensive ethics compliance programs in response to the guidelines . . . reported that they were less likely to violate laws and policies" (Sentencing Commission, 1995: 178).

There are a few cautionary notes to consider, however, regarding the above noted studies. Although studies have shown that corporations have enhanced their ethics programs because of the Guidelines, and that companies with a comprehensive ethics program appear to have a higher level of ethical behavior, one cannot necessarily make the conclusion that the Guidelines are responsible for improved ethical behavior. One of the weaknesses with the Ethics Resource Center and Council of Ethical Organization's studies as with most business ethics studies is that they only measure self-reported data, as well as perceptions of behavior, as opposed to actual behavior. It should not be forgotten that many companies have implemented compliance or ethics programs irrespective of the Guidelines. In any event, the evidence to date indicates that the Guidelines have had an influence on ethics programs which appear to lead to improved ethical behavior in organizations.

There are numerous reasons to suggest why the time has arrived for countries around the world including Latin American countries to consider adopting legal standards similar to the Guidelines. The rest of the paper will focus on these reasons such as the potential dangers to foreign companies operating in the U.S., the development of a globalized business environment, and a changing regulatory environment around the world.

PART TWO—COULD OTHER COUNTRIES BENEFIT FROM ADOPTING LEGISLATION SIMILAR TO THE GUIDELINES?

There are numerous reasons to suggest why the time has arrived for countries around the world to consider adopting legislation similar to the Guidelines. These reasons include foreign companies operating in the U.S., the development of a globalized business environment, and a changing regulatory environment around the world.

(5) FOREIGN COMPANIES CURRENTLY OPERATING IN THE U.S.

Most large corporations in the world currently conduct business in the U.S. Many of these companies will establish U.S. subsidiaries with branch offices or factories located in the U.S. or obtain U.S. supplied financing and list their shares on American stock exchanges. For these companies, there is a direct and immediate reason to create compliance or ethics programs, regardless of whether their home country has created any legal incentives to do so. Failure to create programs for their U.S. operations can result in financial penalties which could otherwise be avoided. Daiwa Bank and Hoffman-LaRoche, as discussed above, are excellent examples of non-U.S. companies which suffered by not having implemented an appropriate compliance or ethics program.

According to Jeff Kaplan, the Daiwa Bank lesson is especially important for foreign companies doing business in the U.S., ". . . [T]he entire disaster occurred not because the bank was greedy or malevolent, but simply because it failed to accord due weight to U.S. regulatory mandates" (Kaplan, 1996: 11). According to Lori Tansey, president of the International Business Ethics Institute, "With-

out question many foreign companies doing business in the United States fail to understand the requirements of United States law. Most are not aware of the sentencing guidelines or their implications" (Kaplan, 1996: 11). If this is the case, non-U.S. companies will continue to suffer by not taking into consideration the potential impact of the Guidelines.

For those countries with companies operating in the U.S., there is then a direct benefit to adopting legal standards similar to the Guidelines. Non-U.S. corporations would have an automatic incentive to create compliance or ethics programs in their home country, and if the programs are applicable to operations in the U.S., these corporations would gain automatic protection from non-compliance when doing business in the U.S. Unfortunately for some non-U.S. companies, such as Daiwa Bank, they had to learn their lesson the hard way.

(6) CHANGING BUSINESS ENVIRONMENT: GLOBALIZATION

One can point to the changing business environment around the world as a major motivator for countries to consider implementing legal standards similar to the Guidelines. Clearly, the business world is becoming a smaller place. According to Lori Tansey, "the most significant development in today's business world is globalization" (Tansey, 1995: 1). Several world trading blocks have been established, such as NAFTA (North American Free Trade Agreement) and the EU (European Union). International sales by U.S. multinationals were over $1 trillion in 1991 (Tansey, 1995: 1). Other evidence of globalization includes the growth of multinational corporations and international joint ventures. Changing technologies such as the internet, e-mail, fax, and video conferencing continue to make the world a smaller place where communication anywhere around the world is almost instantaneous. As the international corporate world becomes more closely inter-connected, the obligations of multinational corporations to take measures to comply with worldwide legislation increases.

Another development over the years has been the increasing internationalization of ethical standards. According to Richard DeGeorge, "the growth of multinationals and the closer integration of U.S. and non-U.S. firms makes all the more necessary the development of business ethics on an international scale" (DeGeorge, 1987: 209). Several initiatives have demonstrated the need to generate consensus around the world on the issue of ethical standards. For example, Getz (1990) has pointed to several international codes which apply to multinational corporations: (1) the International Chamber of Commerce (ICC); (2) the International Labour Organization (ILO); and (3) the United Nations Commission on Transnational Corporations (UN/CTC). A further example of apparent worldwide consensus on the impropriety of unethical activity is the recent Organisation for Economic Co-operation and Development's (OECD) "Convention on Combating Bribery of Foreign Public Officials in International Business Transactions." The Convention was signed by OECD members as well as several non-member countries in December 1997. The intention of the Convention is that signatories will work towards criminalizing bribery of foreign public officials.

The Caux Principles, created by leaders from the Japanese, European, and U.S. business communities, emphasize the growing importance of international ethical standards:

> The Caux Round Table believes that the world business community should play an important role in improving economic and social conditions. As a statement of aspirations, this document aims to express a world standard against which business behavior can be measured. We seek to begin a process that identifies shared values, reconciles differing values, and thereby develops a shared perspective on business behavior acceptable to and honored by all. (Caux Round Table, 1994: 2)

In addition to international codes, organizations devoted to encouraging international standards of ethical conduct have emerged. Transparency International, based in Berlin, Germany, is an organization which was established to focus on corruption in international business transactions. One of the goals is ". . . practical change, in laws, institutions and policies, that will drastically reduce the incidence of corruption in the future" (Transparency International,

1996: 7). By 1999, the organization had over 100 national chapters established or in progress around the world (Transparency International, 1999).

These developments of globalized business and acceptable international business conduct serve to reinforce the impetus for countries around the world to both individually and collectively work together in creating incentives for corporations to establish compliance or ethics programs designed to reduce corporate crime and unethical activity. Developing legal standards similar to the Guidelines would provide that incentive to the international corporate world.

(7) CHANGING REGULATORY ENVIRONMENT: OTHER COUNTRIES

Is the United States the only country in the world to have developed legal standards which create incentives for corporations to adopt compliance or ethics programs? A survey of three political entities, Europe, Australia, and Canada, indicates that these areas of the world have already developed or are in the process of developing measures which in some respects even go beyond those of the U.S. Sentencing Guidelines.

Europe has already taken steps to create incentives for companies to establish compliance programs. The Commission of the European Union has mitigated the penalties for firms for a number of years when they have been found to have compliance programs with respect to competition law (Tansey, 1995:1). For example, in a case involving Toshiba Europe GMBH, the European Union gave the company credit for developing a program to ensure compliance with the EU's competition law (LeClair et al., 1997: 31).

Australia may be the world leader, at least on paper, in terms of corporate compliance initiatives. Two pieces of legislation are particularly significant. The first is the Australian Trade Practices Act, which regulates such activities as anti-trust or misleading advertising. According to the Act, "an effective compliance program can constitute a corporate defense" and is also a key factor in the assessment of the penalty. Not only sound policies and procedures must be adopted, but the corporation must also actively supervise and enforce these policies (Tansey, 1995: 2). Australia also took a major step by amending its Criminal Code (assented to on March 15, 1995). One of the key provisions of the Code now states that a corporation can be criminally responsible if it is established that "a corporate culture existed within the body corporate that directed, encouraged, tolerated or led to non-compliance with the relevant provision" or by showing that "the body corporate failed to create and maintain a corporate culture that required compliance with the relevant provision." [Criminal Code Bill 1994, Part 2.5, Division 12, Section 12.3(2) (c and d)]. What is substantially different about this legislation is that it relates directly to liability, and not merely the sentencing of corporations as does the U.S. Sentencing Guidelines.

Canada is somewhat behind the U.S., Europe, and Australia, but is catching up quickly. The Canadian government is now beginning to recognize the importance and value of encouraging companies to develop compliance systems. A recent Information Bulletin on Corporate Compliance Programs from the Canadian Competition Bureau, which regulates the Canadian Competition Act (e.g., bid-rigging, price discrimination, misleading advertising), looks remarkably similar to the U.S. Federal Sentencing Guidelines in recommending that companies establish an 'effective compliance program' with respect to the Act. By doing so, the Bulletin suggests that companies may benefit in terms of alternative case resolutions, immunity and sentencing recommendations, and due diligence defences (Industry Canada, 1997). The fact that the program relates not only to sentencing but to actual defences is an aspect which goes beyond the U.S. Guidelines. An 'effective compliance program' is defined as including five components: (1) the involvement and support of senior management; (2) development of relevant policies and procedures; (3) on-going education of management and employees; (4) monitoring and audit mechanisms; and (5) disciplinary mechanisms (Industry Canada, 1997).

All of these countries (and other U.S. agencies) have moved to some degree, and in some respects even beyond the U.S. Sentencing Guidelines. This worldwide trend combined with the increasing globalization of business serve as an impetus for other countries to consider the development of legislation similar to the Guidelines.

(8) BENEFITS OF ADOPTING GUIDELINES

Would the Guidelines serve a purpose in the rest of the world? One does not have to look too far to find evidence of the extent and cost of corporate fraud and corruption around the world. A survey conducted by KPMG International found that "fraud is a significant problem for companies around the world" (KPMG, 1996: 4). The survey included a total of 18 countries representing North America, Asia, Europe, Australia, Africa, and the Middle East. The survey found that 52% of respondents stated that they had experienced fraud in the past year, with 48% believing that fraud is a major problem for their business today and over 50% believing that fraud will continue to increase (KPMG, 1996: 4). Another study found that more than half the employees surveyed had observed conduct within their organizations either occasionally (46 percent) or often (7 percent) over the past year which they thought violated the law or the organizations' standards of ethical business conduct. Of those employees who did observe misconduct, 21 percent said they did not report the misconduct to management or another appropriate person (Society for Human Resources Management/Ethics Resource Center, 1997: 5). One might speculate whether the same situation exists in other countries of the world, suggesting that worldwide corporate misconduct is even more pervasive than current surveys suggest.

There have been several estimates of the total cost of fraud. Some commentators suggest that "while-collar crime is conservatively estimated to cost businesses well in excess of $100 billion per year" (Driscoll et al., 1995: 233). The KPMG survey suggests that ". . . fraud costs corporations worldwide billions of dollars each year" (KPMG, 1996: 10). A similar international study by Ernst & Young found that over one quarter of businesses surveyed had lost over $1 million (U.S.) in total due to fraud (Ernst & Young, 1996: 1).

Assuming that the U.S. Sentencing Guidelines create economic incentives for corporations to adopt measures to reduce corporate crime, fraud and corruption, and to improve ethical behavior, then all stakeholders may benefit. Corporations benefit by reducing the extent of corporate crime and unethical activity, meaning the preservation of corporate assets, and by having illegal or unethical activity reported internally before reaching the court system or the media. Consumers benefit by not being forced to bear the costs of unethical activity by employees. Employees benefit by having the corporation provide the means through compliance and ethics programs by which employees are able to do what they know is right and legal, and not to feel pressured to act otherwise. Governments benefit by creating an economic incentive for corporations to self-regulate themselves, relieving much of the burden from enforcement agencies. Society is the net beneficiary of less corporate crime and unethical activity, as potentially hundreds of billions of dollars in economic benefits are generated as a result, leading to an overall increase in both the global standard of living and the quality of life.

One of the advantages of the Guidelines' approach is that motivation for adopting compliance or ethics programs is not necessarily an issue. Although U.S. courts may consider whether the company has adopted the program as mere window dressing, and is not really enforcing its standards, it really does not matter whether the company is complying only because of the Guidelines, or because it is the right thing to do. It may even be the case that companies which initially adopt programs as a type of insurance policy may eventually come to see that there is an ethical justification for adopting such programs. What is evident is that it is easier to convince senior management to spend money to create a compliance or ethics program when there is an external economic incentive for doing so. Later, after seeing the program in effect, senior management would be in a position to see the intangible benefits of having such a program in place.

Another advantage of the Guidelines is its flexibility in only suggesting a minimum framework for setting up an 'effective compliance program.' Companies can and probably should go beyond the seven elements listed to be sure they meet the Guidelines' 'due diligence' standard. The flexibility of the 'due diligence' approach makes it easily transferable to other countries in the world by enabling governments to develop their own recommended elements. For example, the Canadian government requires only five elements in their list of components of an 'effective compliance program.' What companies have found most helpful about the Guidelines, however, is that at least, they provide a benchmark of what constitutes an acceptable compliance program.

(9) LIMITATIONS OF GUIDELINES

Despite the potential benefits for other countries in adopting something similar to the Guidelines, there are still a number of potential limitations to the Guidelines which must be recognized and addressed. One possible criticism of the Guidelines is that they really only create an incentive for companies to create legal compliance programs. In other words, although the Guidelines are often mentioned in conjunction with 'ethics' programs, companies are really only being required to adopt measures which require employees to follow the law, and not necessarily engage in activity which goes 'beyond the law.' In fact, a review of the Guidelines' text reveals that the word 'ethics' does not exist. A secondary problem is that companies may end up creating codes of ethics which are essentially legal documents, which are more difficult to understand and less accepted by employees (Sentencing Commission, 1995: 177).

It is somewhat understandable that the Guidelines take this approach. To make a pronouncement that companies must create a program which leads to employees acting 'beyond the law' or 'ethically' and will be rewarded for doing so would not necessarily serve a purpose, and may no longer be functional. In addition, several companies are finding that although they might begin with a legal compliance approach, over time they shift the emphasis of their programs to an ethics, values, or integrity approach. For example, Levi Strauss and Co., which began with a lengthy code of ethics, has shifted their emphasis to a one page statement of their values and principles (Raiborn and Payne, 1990: 883). Other companies are finding that a combined legal compliance and ethics approach is the best route to go. In any event, one can argue that a company with a legal or compliance program is better than one without any program.

Another potential limitation or weakness of the Guidelines is that they only relate to compliance with U.S. federal law, of a criminal nature. The Guidelines do not relate to state law or civil litigation. The Guidelines also only relate to sentencing (e.g., restitution, fines, or probation), as opposed to possible defences to liability or actual liability itself. As observed above, other countries such as Australia and Canada may relate compliance or ethics initiatives directly to liability and to possible defences which can be raised. It has also been the case that U.S. state courts and courts considering civil litigation matters are beginning to take direction from the Guidelines. All of this activity provides a certain degree of assurance that other countries, in adopting legal standards similar to the Guidelines, have the ability to determine the range of activity which their standards would cover.

A further potential criticism is that the Guidelines appear to require that at a minimum all seven elements must be demonstrated to some degree by the defendant corporation in order to obtain credit for having an 'effective compliance program.' This seems to render the court's evaluation of whether a company has an effective program an 'all or nothing' evaluation. For example, a convicted company would necessarily be deemed to lack an effective program when it fails to incorporate even one element, such as background checks, despite the other six elements being determined to be of outstanding quality. It may therefore be the case that a greater deal of flexibility should be built into the existence of all seven elements than currently exists.

Another potential problem is that the implementation of one of the seven elements of an effective compliance program, the setting up of a reporting channel (e.g., 'hotline') to report noncompliance, has a danger of being abused. Employees may want to get revenge on a fellow employee, or merely be expressing discontent with one's employment, and take advantage of an anonymous phone line to report illegitimate problems (Trevino and Nelson, 1995: 257). These spurious phone calls can cost the corporation resources, and create problems for innocent employees who must defend themselves against an alleged complaint.

Despite the danger of abuse, one might assume that only a small proportion of phone calls through their hotlines are not legitimate. It can also be argued that the overall benefits of having a hotline, such as keeping problems internal as opposed to reaching external sources, outweigh the potential problems. Corporate experience with hotlines is still relatively recent, and over time and with more experience, problems such as abuse can be dealt with in an appropriate fashion.

An argument may be raised that suggesting that other countries consider the development of legal standards similar to the U.S. Guidelines is just a further continuation of the imposition of U.S. legal/ethical norms or standards upon other jurisdictions, or at least the emulation of such norms or standards. This may be one reason why it has been difficult for other countries in the world to adopt legislation similar to the U.S. Foreign Corrupt Practices Act (although this appears to now be in the process of changing based on the recent OECD Convention on Combating Bribery of Foreign Public Officials in International Business Transactions as discussed above). For many countries, there may be an automatic resistance to following any regulatory model being used by the U.S.

It is helpful to realize that in some respects the model was already in existence for many countries prior to the Guidelines coming into effect in 1991. For example, the Australian Trade Practices Act and the European Commission have been in existence prior to 1991. It must also be recognized that the development by other countries of legal standards similar to the Guidelines would not require non-U.S. corporations to abide by U.S. law (unless they are doing business in the U.S. of course), but merely require these corporations to abide by the laws of their respective home country. It is difficult to imagine that a country's government would not have an interest in having their corporations create programs which lead to less corporate crime or unethical activity, unless government officials are somehow personally benefiting from such activity.

A further limitation to the Guidelines being adopted by other countries is that multinational corporations are going to be faced with a situation involving an even more pronounced conflict of laws or ethical norms. For example, if one of the requirements is to create a code of ethics, how would a company deal with the wide range of laws and ethical norms which exist throughout the world?

This limitation may be less problematic than it appears on its surface. Multinationals are already addressing such concerns by modifying their corporate codes of ethics to adjust to situational contexts. Although many like to argue that ethics vary across the world, others point out that there may be greater consensus on what activity is considered ethical or unethical than is currently accepted. For example, although certain countries of the world are known to be prone to extensive bribery, ". . . there is no country in the world where bribery is either legally or morally acceptable" (Heimann, 1994: 7).

(10) IMPLEMENTATION STRATEGY

The discussion above is designed to provide readers with a basic understanding of the Sentencing Guidelines, their purpose, impact, effectiveness, and arguments to support their adoption by other countries around the world. Clearly, the actual implementation strategy will depend on a number of factors to be considered by the respective governments. The following is a possible checklist of initial considerations in developing an implementation strategy:

- What is the current extent of corporate crime and unethical activity? Are we concerned about these levels and their impact on society?
- What is the current extent of corporate compliance programs in place? Are there any corporate leaders which can act as role models for others?
- What type of political system is in effect? Is there sufficient political support and will for the adoption of this type of legislation? Which government department or departments are best suited to administer this type of legislation?
- How developed is our legal framework (e.g., legislation, court system)? If the legislation is adopted, will it be enforced (i.e., considered by the courts or administrative tribunals)?
- What are the current cultural and religious norms in effect? Should these norms be considered when making recommendations as to what constitutes an 'effective compliance program'?

- What subject areas merit first attention (e.g., environment, consumer protection, worker health and safety, etc.)?

CONCLUSION

All of society stands to benefit from a reduction in corporate crime and unethical activity. The U.S. Federal Sentencing Guidelines provide a model which to date appears to be successful in achieving this goal. Other countries and groups of countries around the world, including Australia, Europe, and Canada, have already adopted or are in the process of adopting similar legal incentives.

Hopefully the success of the Guidelines will encourage other countries to consider developing their own regulatory incentives for corporations to abide by the law and engage in activities to promote the level of ethics in all organizations.

REFERENCES

1. Center for Business Ethics. (1992). "Instilling Ethical Values in Large Corporations," *The Journal of Business Ethics,* Vol. 11, 863–867.
2. De George, R. T. (1987). "The Status of Business Ethics: Past and Future," *Journal of Business Ethics,* Vol. 6, 201–211.
3. Department of Justice Canada and O'Reilly, J. W. (1994). "Toward A New General Part of the Criminal Code of Canada: Details on Reform Options," (Ottawa, Ontario).
4. Driscoll, D. M., Hoffman, W. M., and Petry, E. S. (1995). *The Ethical Edge.* (New York: MasterMedia Limited).
5. Ernst & Young. (1996, May). "International Fraud Survey," (London, England).
6. Ethics Resource Center. (1994). "Ethics in American Business: Policies, Programs and Perceptions," (Washington, D.C.).
7. French, P. (1984). "The Hester Prynne Sanction," *Business and Professional Ethics Journal,* Vol. 4, No. 2, 19–32.
8. Getz, K. A. (1990). "International Codes of Conduct: An Analysis of Ethical Reasoning," *Journal of Business Ethics,* Vol. 9, No. 7, 567–577.
9. Heimann, F. F. (1994, November 8). "Should Foreign Bribery be a Crime?" Paper presented at the Conference on Bribery in International Trade, (Milan, Italy).

10. Industry Canada (1997). *Information Bulletin on Corporate Compliance Programs,* (Hull, Quebec).

11. Izraeli, D. (1994). "The Stick and Carrot Law: Guidelines for Sentencing Organizations" in A. Kfir (ed.), *Excellence in the Public Service* (Hebrew), Haifa University.

12. Izraeli, D. (1995). "Impact of the U.S. Sentencing Guidelines on Organizations," Paper presented at the 3rd International Jerusalem Conference on Ethics in the Public Service, June 25–29, 1995.

13. Izraeli, D. (1997). "Promoting Business Ethics Through Legislation," in D. Izraeli & N. Zohar (eds), *Ethics and Social Responsibility—Israeli Studies* (Hebrew), (Tel-Aviv, Israel: Tscherikover Publishers - Gomeh Scientific Publications.

14. Izraeli, D. and Schwartz, M. S. (1998). "What Can We Learn from the U.S. Federal Sentencing Guildelines for Organizational Ethics?" *Journal of Business Ethics,* Vol. 17, Nos. 9–10, July 1998, pp. 1045–1055.

15. Kaplan, J. M., Dakin, L. S., and Smolin, M. R. (1993a). "Living With the Organizational Sentencing Guidelines," *California Management Review,* Vol. 36, No. 1, 136–146.

16. Kaplan, J. M., Murphy, F. E., and Swenson, W. M. (1993b, 1997). *Compliance Programs and the Corporate Sentencing Guidelines,* (Deerfield, IL: Clark, Boardman, Callaghan).

17. Kaplan, J. M. (1995, July/August). "The Sentencing Guidelines: A 'Still Developing' Picture," Ethikos, Vol. 9, No. 1. 1–3.

18. Kaplan, J. M. (1996, May/June). "Why Daiwa Bank Will Pay $340 Million Under the Sentencing Guidelines," *Ethikos,* Vol. 9, No. 6, 1–3, 11.

19. Kaplan, J. M. (1997). "Follow Sentencing Guidelines' Compliance Measures, Court Tells Directors," *Ethikos,* Vol. 10, No. 4, 1–2, 11.

20. Kaplan, J. M. (1998). "Hoffman-LaRoche Case: A Sentencing Guidelines Milestone," *Ethikos,* Vol. 13, No. 1: 1–3, 10–11.

21. KPMG. (1996, April). International Fraud Report, (Amsterdam, Netherlands).

22. LeClair, D. T., Ferrell, O. C., and Ferrell, L. (1997). "Federal Sentencing Guidelines for Organizations: Legal, Ethical, and Public Policy Issues for International Marketing," *Journal of Public Policy & Marketing,* Vol. 16, No. 1, 26–37.

23. Raiborn, C. A. and Payne, D. (1990). "Corporate Codes of Conduct: A Collective Conscience and Continuum," *Journal of Business Ethics,* 9, 879–889.

24. Schwartz, M. S. (1996). "Corporate Compliance and Ethical Decision Making in Canada," *Corporate Conduct Quarterly,* Vol. 5, No. 1, 1996, 6–7, 17.

25. Society for Human Resources Management/Ethics Resource Center. (1997). "Business Ethics Survey Report" (Washington, D.C.).

26. Tansey, L. (1995). "Corporate Compliance Programs: International Implications," *Corporate Conduct Quarterly,* Vol. 4, No. 2.

27. Transparency International. (1996). *Annual Report* (Berlin, Germany).

28. Transparency International. (1997a). *Corruption Perceptions Index* (Berlin, Germany).

29. Transparency International. (1997b). *Annual Report* (Berlin, Germany).

30. Transparency International. (1999). Website Information, http://www.transparency.de/organisation/chapters/all.html (Berlin, Germany).

31. Trevino, L. K. and Nelson, K. A. (1995). *Managing Business Ethics* (New York: John Wiley and Sons).

32. U.S. Sentencing Commission. (1995, September 7–8). "Corporate Crime in America: Strengthening the 'Good Citizen' Corporation," Proceedings of the Second Symposium on Crime and Punishment in the United States, Washington, D.C.

33. U.S. Sentencing Commission. (1996). *Annual Report* (Washington, D.C.).

34. U.S. Sentencing Commission. (1998). *Annual Report* (Washington, D.C.).

QUESTIONS FOR DISCUSSION

1. Nader, Green, and Seligman quote Peter Drucker's comment "There is one thing all boards have in common, regardless of their legal position. They do not function." What are the traditional functions of the corporate board? According to Nader, Green, Seligman, and Mintzberg, how do boards sometimes fail to fulfill that function? How would Nader, Green, and Seligman like to see the function of the board changed?

2. Mintzberg details a number of ways that corporations might be controlled. Which do you think is most likely to succeed? Why? Is it plausible to suppose, as he does, that all of them (except "ignore it") should and can be used, depending on the circumstances?

3. Schwartz, Izraeli, and Murphy appear to support the use of the U.S Federal Sentencing Guidelines despite its limitations. Are the Guidelines an appropriate way to encourage companies to self-regulate? Can you think of any other approaches that can be taken by government?

Stuart Howser

Stuart Howser works for the U.S. subsidiary of a German company. During lunch break, he notices that a group of people have gathered outside the head office. On the huge open courtyard of the extravagant building, people are marching back and forth, waving their placards with comments such as "We still remember" and "You profited from our grandparents' pain." Stuart goes outside to learn more about the protest. He enters into the following dialogue with one of the protestors:

Stuart: Can you please tell me why are you protesting against the company?

Protestor: Because during World War II this company employed slave labor. It profited from the sweat and pain of my father, a survivor of the Holocaust, and we demand compensation.

Stuart: I understand you're upset, but it wasn't the company's fault. If anyone is to blame, it was the Nazi government of the time, which demanded that companies use slave labor. If what you ask for is compensation for pain and suffering, shouldn't you be asking the current German government?

Protestor: No, I blame the company, they made the decision to use the slave labor, not all German companies did so.

Stuart: But wasn't it because of such work that many avoided dying in the concentration camps?

Protestor: You really think that even if that were true, that this exonerates the company from its moral responsibility?

Stuart: But this took place more than half a century ago. Almost all of the people who were responsible for slave labor are now dead. I don't even think that many of the former shareholders are still alive. Isn't there a point in time at which a company is no longer responsible for previous actions?

Protestor: As long as the company still exists, even if in name only, it is still responsible for its actions of the past.

Stuart: Well, if my father had been a Nazi involved in terrible crimes, would you hold me morally accountable for the past actions of my dead father?

Protestor: No, I would not hold you accountable, other than your obligation to be aware of your father's actions and to help ensure that such things don't happen again. But companies are different. You are not your father, but the company, despite the turnover in employees and shareholders, is the same company.

Stuart: But only in name! The company doesn't even sell many of the same products! And we are merely the U.S. subsidiary!

DISCUSSION QUESTIONS

- Who has the stronger arguments, the protestor or Stuart? Why?
- Are corporations capable of moral responsibility? Or are only human beings responsible?
- Is there a certain point in time at which companies are no longer responsible for actions in the past? If so, what is that point?

Deborah Wilson

Deborah Wilson is the CEO of a small manufacturing firm which specializes in baked goods and specialty sauces. The firm has grown significantly over its first 3 years, and in order to raise funding for further expansion, Deborah decides that it is time for her firm to go public through an IPO. Deborah believes that her firm's success is primarily due to the support she has received from her local community, her local suppliers, and her employees. As a result, she has decided that before going public the firm should officially adopt a number of new policies. One of her policies would be to place a salary limit for any employee of the firm, including herself as CEO, at 10 times the salary of the lowest paid employee. She also wants to dedicate 5 percent of the firm's pre-tax profits to local charities which would be selected each year on the basis of a vote by the firm's employees. She also wants to institute a policy of only using local or state suppliers as long as they meet the firm's quality standards, regardless of whether a cheaper supplier exists out of state. She knows that such policies might have a negative long-term impact on the firm's bottom line, but believes that such policies are in keeping with her own personal views regarding her firm's obligations toward society.

While discussing such policies with the lead investment broker, Deborah is surprised by their reaction. In attempting to resist Deborah's efforts, they argue that such actions will not necessarily produce any short-term or even long-term financial gains for the firm, and that they may detract a number of investors from buying shares during the IPO. Even the employees are raising some concerns about how the policies will affect the financial prosperity of the firm. Deborah must consider whether she must drop or tone down her new policies in order to gain the lead investor's support for the IPO.

DISCUSSION QUESTIONS

- As a public company, is Deborah entitled to use shareholder money in order to implement her new policies?
- Do Deborah's new policies have any ethical justification?
- In what respects might Deborah's policies be good long-term business?

Not a Fool, Not a Saint

Thomas Teal
Reporter for *Fortune Magazine*

At a European trade show in Brussels during the first week of September, Malden Mills of Lawrence, Massachusetts, introduced a broad new line of high-end upholstery fabrics. Buyers snapped up the sleek material, derived from the company's hugely successful line of Polartec and Polarfleece apparel knits. A victory, certainly. And one more step in an uphill comeback by a factory that suffered one of the biggest industrial fires in New England history less than a year ago, a factory whose owner achieved heroic stature by keeping more than 1,000 jobless employees at full pay for several months after the blaze.

Yet Aaron Feuerstein, owner, president, and CEO of Malden Mills, has good reason to feel un-

appreciated. It's true that his work force adores him, that almost every newspaper, TV station, and business magazine in the U.S. has sung his praises, that Bill Clinton invited him to Washington for the State of the Union address, and that columnists, unions, and religious leaders all across the country have declared him a saint. But much of this celebrity is based on the misleading premise that this 70-year-old acted selflessly, against his own best interests, which is another way of saying that he acted the way a saint might act: irrationally.

In fact, it seems pretty clear that some people call Feuerstein a saint because they don't quite have the courage to call him a fool. They don't think he should be rebuilding his mill, at least not in Lawrence. They think he should have pocketed the insurance proceeds, closed the business, and walked away. Or else they think he should have grabbed the chance to move the company to some state or country with lower labor costs.

Some commentators have even accused him of risking the very survival of his business with a lot of grandstanding magnanimity that served no purpose but self-advertisement. There's a suggestion that real businessmen are tougher than Feuerstein, that responsible owners never pay any employee a dime more than they have to, and that no factory owner could possibly have done what Feuerstein has done unless he'd been touched by God or is just touched, period. These people, for instance, argue that Feuerstein certainly could have skipped the grand gesture of paying out some $15 million in wages and benefits to already overpaid workers when they no longer had a place to work. One business school professor has suggested pointedly that not everyone should look to him as a model.

Most of this carping is nonsense. But in a way, so is much of the praise. Why in the world should it be a sign of divinely inspired nuttiness to treat a work force as if it was an asset, to cultivate the loyalty of employees who hold the key to recovery and success, to take risks for the sake of a large future income stream, even to seek positive publicity? These are the things Aaron Feuerstein has done, and most people stand in amazement as if they were witnessing a miracle or a traffic accident.

I was one of them until I discovered that Feuerstein is at heart a hard-nosed businessman. He has some minor eccentricities—a weakness for little bursts of Shakespeare, a tendency to wander off into far corners of the room as he thinks and talks—and his Old Testament intensity and biblical pronouncements can be slightly intimidating, despite his warmth. The two hours I spent with him, however, convinced me that he is as tough-minded as he is righteous, a man entirely up to the job of running a factory for profit.

Take downsizing. Would anyone have guessed that Feuerstein was a devotee? At one point, as he was warming to an attack on the unconscionable Al Dunlap (the man who dismantled Scott Paper and fired a third of its work force), I interrupted to suggest that maybe Scott Paper was overstaffed, and Feuerstein surprised me: "If one-third of the people in that company were wastefully employed, then Dunlap did the right thing." And then the new patron saint of working Americans surprised me some more. "Legitimate downsizing as the result of technological advances or as a result of good industrial engineering? Absolutely, I'm in favor of it. And we do it here all day long . . . We try to do it in such a way as to minimize human suffering, but the down-

sizing must be done." Under the benevolent, angular exterior lurks a businessman—a businessman who understands labor. The trick, he told me, is to keep growing fast enough to give new jobs to the people technology displaces, to weed out unnecessary jobs "without crushing the spirit of the work force." If all you're after is cutting costs, if you "just have a scheme to cut people—that sort of thing is resented by labor, and you're never forgiven." Feuerstein has a union shop, has long invested heavily in technology that eliminates jobs, and has never had a strike—not exactly the hallmarks of a fool.

Or take the insurance question. Feuerstein could certainly have closed the factory, sold the business, pocketed the proceeds, and spent the rest of his days in a hammock. But men in their 70s who still come to work every day for the sheer exhilaration of the job don't turn to hammocks in a crisis. His decision to rebuild seems to have been spontaneous and immediate, made more or less by the light of the flames and without much thought to the insurance proceeds. And still it was a rational decision. Factories are insured for their replacement cost, and if you don't replace them, you may have to settle for the depreciated value of the lost building and machinery, in this case a lot of modern machinery and several antediluvian buildings. You can solve this equation without the higher math. An insurance payoff is likely to be much larger when it's taken as a contribution toward a state-of-the-art manufacturing facility, partly because it has the potential to produce income for your family for two or three generations to come. Last year's pre-fire, pretax profit was $20 million on sales of $400 million. Twenty million times two or three generations comes to an awful lot of money.

Or take self-advertisement. Feuerstein has not been shy with the media. Malden Mills has been featured everywhere from *People* to *Dateline* to the Lands' End catalogue, and it's all been free. What's more, if the insurance settlement should wind up in court—not wildly improbable—will it hurt Feuerstein's chances of winning that half the people in the country worship the ground he walks on? Do insurance companies care about their reputations? You bet.

As for the idea that he might relocate the company somewhere with lower wages, Feuerstein moved the company to Lawrence (from Malden, just outside Boston) in 1956, at a time when New England textile mills thought local labor too expensive and were streaming south like carpetbaggers. A great many of those companies failed anyway, despite the lower wages they spent so much money to find, and Feuerstein is sure he knows why: They gave too much attention to costs and not enough to quality. He responds with contempt to suggestions that Malden Mills should move offshore. (Labor in the South is no longer such a bargain.)

"Why would I go to Thailand to bring the cost lower when I might run the risk of losing the advantage I've got, which is superior quality?" In any case, he goes on, lower wages are a temporary advantage. Quality lasts. At least it *can* last if you focus hard on expertise and the freedom to innovate. But to do that, you have to focus hard on employees. When Feuerstein came to Lawrence, he wasn't looking for cheap labor but for skilled labor—capable, experienced textile designers, engineers, and workers who could give him the edge he needed to compete more effectively.

It's here he has shown his real genius. Any idiot with a strong enough stomach can make quick money, sometimes a lot of it, by slashing costs and milking customers, employees, or a company's reputation. But clearly that's not the way to make a lot of money for a long time. The way to do that is to create so much value that your customers wouldn't dream of looking for another supplier. Indeed, the idea is to build a value creation *system* of superior products, service, teamwork, productivity, and cooperation with the buyer. Reduced to its essence, that means superior technology and superior employees. Reduced still further, as Aaron Feuerstein can tell you, it means superior employees. The correlation between loyal customers and loyal employees is no coincidence.

For Malden Mills, the first test and the breakthrough came in the early 1980s with the total collapse of the market for what was then a company mainstay—artificial furs. It was the R&D and production employees who saved the company over the next few years, using their superior expertise in synthetic fibers, napping, and finishing to create a series of lightweight, thermal, resilient, woollike fabrics under the brand names Polarfleece and Polartec. They look good, feel good, wick well, don't pill, and hold up to repeated washing. Moreover, they're all engineered to order. The retailer wants, say, a fabric for cyclists that's windproof and light but also soft, absorbent, and quick-drying. Malden's ability to satisfy such orders has made Polartec a favorite of upscale retailers like Lands' End, L.L. Bean, Patagonia, the North Face, Eddie Bauer, and a dozen more.

Best of all, these customers are loyal. Customer retention at Malden Mills runs roughly 95%, which is world class. Employee retention runs above 95%, which is prodigious but can hardly come as a surprise to anyone familiar with Feuerstein's approach to personnel. As for productivity, from 1982 to 1995, revenues in constant dollars more than tripled while the work force barely doubled. Compare that with an overall productivity increase for the U.S. of a little better than 1% per year. Thanks to its employees, Malden Mills has risen from at least one five-alarm crisis in the past. No wonder Aaron Feuerstein loves those employees enough to risk $15 million to keep them available and motivated and to help him rise from the literal ashes of last year's catastrophe. This isn't the work of a saint or a fool, it's the considered and historically successful policy of a genial manufacturing genius who might serve as a model for *every* man and woman in business.

Tennessee Coal and Iron (A & B) Condensed

John B. Matthews, Jr.
Former Wilson Professor of Business Administration, Emeritus, Harvard University

In the early 1960s the Tennessee Coal & Iron Division (TCI) of United States Steel Corporation (USS) was one of that corporation's largest divisions. Originally an independent company, TCI became a subsidiary of USS in 1907. It continued to grow, adding quarries, mines, reservoirs, electric power systems, coke, and wire. Many other kinds of plants and steel facilities were attached over the years. By the beginning of World War II, TCI was by far the largest producer of primary steel and many other products in the 11-state southern region that it served. It moved from subsidiary to divisional status in 1953.

TCI's peak employment was in 1942, when a total of 33,000 employees was attained. A number of factors, including the decline in steel demand and a switch to imported ores, reduced the number of TCI employees to about 24,000 in 1955–1957 and to 16,000 in 1964. Nearly 12,000 of these were production and maintenance employees, and about one-third of the 12,000 were blacks. Nearly all of the production and maintenance employees were covered by a contract between USS and the United Steelworkers of America (USW). Despite the decline in its employment rolls, TCI continued to be by far the largest employer in Birmingham and the Jefferson County area of Alabama. Arthur Wiebel, president of TCI, estimated that the next largest employer was about one-third the size of TCI. Birmingham had a civilian male labor force of 78,000 and Jefferson County, of which Birmingham was the center, had a civilian male labor force of about 155,000. The ratio of whites to blacks was about 2 to 1 in Jefferson County, and about 2 to 1 1/3 in Birmingham itself.

TCI'S EMPLOYMENT RECORD AND RACIAL INTEGRATION

In 1963 the nation's attention was focused on racial disturbances in various parts of the South, with some of the most violent occurrences in Birmingham. Bombings of black churches, incidents of personal violence, and threats of all types occurred as the drive toward racial integration kindled or kept alive old racial hatreds.

The movement toward integration was also taking place inside TCI's many plants in and around Birmingham. USS had had, orally since 1902 and in writing since 1918, a policy that employment would be made available without regard to race, color, creed, or national origin. This policy, however, was affected by labor agreements, and a portion of the USS policy manual had, for several years, read as follows: "Application of this policy as it relates to union-represented employees will be in accordance with applicable provisions of labor agreements."

Thus for many years prior to the 1960s, the combined effects of seniority, contracts at individual plant and local union levels, strike threats, and local racial customs had resulted in a high degree of racial segregation within TCI's plants. It was against this backdrop that senior officials of USS, TCI, and the USW had to work to bring about a lessening of racial discrimination within TCI.

Three major events occurred to help these officials in their efforts. (1) A human relations committee was formed in 1960 by 11 major steel producers and the USW as a mechanism for exploring and solving common problems. (2) In March 1961 President John F. Kennedy issued executive order 10925 which was intended to prevent discrimination within companies bidding for or holding government contracts. The order also established the Committee on Equal Employment Opportunity (CEEO) and Vice President Lyndon B. Johnson was appointed its chairman. (3) Finally, there was a continuing decline in demand for TCI's products, which made it more difficult for senior employees to hold their jobs in spite of the more than 1,000 separate and rigid lines of promotion among the production and maintenance workers.

These factors, plus months of hard and laborious work by company and union officials, bore fruit. Lines of promotion were broadened and all claims of racial discrimination brought before the CEEO were closed out by June 1963. As a result of these actions and a new 1962 contract between the USW and the 11 major steel producers that provided for sweeping changes, Hobart Taylor, Jr., executive vice chairman of the CEEO, wrote a letter to USS which included the following paragraph: "May I thank you, too, for the example which U.S. Steel has given the rest of the managers in this country by its courageous move in Birmingham at a time of great social tension in the area. This was an important milestone toward true equal employment opportunity. You have earned the gratitude of those of us who are also working toward this important national goal."

TCI'S ROLE IN THE COMMUNITY

In spite of the major accomplishments toward integration within TCI's plants and mines, however, TCI's role in the community had been an issue for some time and was to become a major one in summer 1963. The remainder of this case concerns that issue.

By summer's end 1963, officials of the United States Steel Corporation and its Tennessee Coal & Iron Division believed that the problems of job integration among TCI's 12,000 white and black production and maintenance workers had been solved in a satisfactory fashion. In addition, the physical violence that had permeated the Birmingham area in the spring and early summer of 1963 had greatly abated.

The tension that had preceded and accompanied the violence, however, continued to exist in the community at large. In discussing the situation, James Reston made the following (excerpted) comments in the *New York Times* on September 22, 1963:

> The point, then, is not that Birmingham is lacking in young leaders, and not that it is lacking in biracial committees, but that the real power structure of the city—the older men who run the industries, banks and insurance companies that in turn influence the stores and big law firms—are not leading the peace effort.
>
> There are about a dozen men in this group, some of whom have worked quietly for a compromise, some of whom have tried and then withdrawn. But at no time have they all worked together.
>
> [The Reston story listed 13 prominent Birmingham businessmen and lawyers, among them "Arthur W. Wieble (sic), president of the Tennessee Coal & Iron Division of United States Steel. . . ."]
>
> There is general agreement here that these men, working together with the leaders of the local clergy of both races, could do more to produce a compromise in a month than Federal troops, Federal offi-

cials and all the national Negro organizations put together could in years.

> The question is who, if anybody, can get them together. They damn "The Kennedys" and concede that Senator Goldwater would carry Alabama against the president tomorrow, but even this prospect only creates a new dilemma.[1]

THE USE OF ECONOMIC INFLUENCE

On October 22, 1963, a *New York Times* reporter met with Wiebel, C. Thomas Spivey (TCI director of personnel services), and Clinton Milstead (TCI director of public relations) in Wiebel's conference room. The meeting lasted from 9:00 a.m. until 2:30 p.m. and was largely concerned with the work of TCI and union officials in bringing about job integration within TCI.

During his visit, the reporter also asked Wiebel whether TCI would use its economic power to speed integration in the community itself. According to Wiebel, the reporter suggested that TCI might put pressure on its suppliers, its bank connections, and some of its customers to aid the cause of Birmingham's blacks.

Both the question and the suggestion came as a surprise to Wiebel and his associates. In the preceding months, TCI officials had held extended conversations with union officers, representatives of the president's Committee on Equal Employment Opportunity, General Royall and Colonel Blaik, and black leaders. No question about the use of economic pressure by TCI had arisen in any discussion with these groups, and no suggestions concerning its use had been made officially, although unofficially USS had been criticized in the press.

Wiebel told the reporter that there were two major reasons why TCI would not resort to economic coercion as the area's largest employer to try to solve Birmingham's racial problems. He pointed out that neither TCI nor USS had sufficient economic power in the area to solve the problem, and that neither had the right to tell people what they ought or ought not to do. He also stated that, if TCI were to do what the reporter suggested, charges would be made that TCI and USS were trying to run Birmingham.

One Media's Interpretation of Events

Three days later, under an October 22 dateline, the *New York Times* carried a two-column story about TCI and racial integration in Birmingham. Much of the story concerned activities within TCI. Only the lead paragraphs, which discussed the issue of the division's economic influence in the community are reproduced below from the *New York Times,* October 25, 1963:

> The United States Steel Corporation, the largest employer in Birmingham, appears to be making significant strides in opening up Negro job opportunities in its Alabama plants.
>
> But the nation's biggest steel maker appears to be making little effort to wield its economic influence to help solve the community's racial problems.
>
> These conclusions emerge from talks with officials of U.S. Steel's Tennessee Coal & Iron Division here, as well as with others in both the North and South familiar with the situation.
>
> Critics have contended that Roger M. Blough, U.S. Steel chairman, could contribute greatly toward stemming the racial strife here by simply instructing local officials to exert their power toward that end.

Progress in Plants

> But the company officials here insist they do not have that much power, and in any event they show no signs of using what power they do have on the community's racial front.[2]

Blough's Response

On October 29, at a press conference called to announce the results of USS operations during the preceding quarter, Roger M. Blough, chairman of the USS board of directors, was asked to comment on USS policies in its TCI operation and, more particularly, on the use of its "economic influence" in the Birmingham area as a means of influencing local opinion. The portion of his response dealing with the latter issue follows below:

> Now, the criticism that U.S. Steel hasn't used what some people refer to as . . . economic influence, which I presume to mean some kind of economic force to bring about some kind of a change, is, I think, an improper matter upon which to criticize either Mr. Wiebel or U.S. Steel. I think I would have to take considerable time to fully explain this point, but very briefly, I'd like to say this—that I do not either believe that it would be a wise thing for U.S. Steel to be other than a good citizen in a community, or to attempt to have its ideas of what is right for the community enforced upon that community by some sort of economic means. This is repugnant to me personally, and I am sure it is repugnant to my fellow officers in U.S. Steel. I doubt very much that this in principle is a good thing for any corporation to follow. When we as individuals are citizens in a community, we can exercise what small influence we may have as citizens, but for a corporation to attempt to exert any kind of economic compulsion to achieve a particular end in the social area seems to me to be quite beyond what a corporation should do, and I will say also, quite beyond what a corporation can do.
>
> . . . we have fulfilled our responsibility in the Birmingham area—whatever responsibility we have as a corporation or as individuals working with a corporation, because, after all, a corporation is nothing but individuals.

Further Public Responses

The October 30 issue of the *New York Times* carried a front-page story devoted primarily to Blough's comments about the Birmingham-TCI situation, and on October 31 the following editorial appeared in the paper:

Corporate Race Relations

> When it comes to speaking out on business matters, Roger Blough, chairman of the United States Steel Corporation, does not mince words. Mr. Blough is a firm believer in freedom of action for corporate management, a position he made clear in his battle with the Administration last year. But he also has put some severe limits on the exercise of corporate responsibility, for he rejects the suggestion that U.S. Steel, the biggest employer in Birmingham, Ala., should use its economic influence to erase racial tensions. Mr. Blough feels that U.S. Steel has fulfilled its responsibilities by following a nondiscriminatory hiring policy in Birmingham, and looks upon any other measures as both "repugnant" and "quite beyond what a corporation should do" to improve conditions.
>
> The hands-off strategy surely underestimates the potential influence of a corporation as big as U.S. Steel, particularly at the local level. It could, without affecting its profit margins adversely or getting itself

directly involved in politics, actively work with those groups in Birmingham trying to better race relations. Steel is not sold on the retail level, so U.S. Steel has not been faced with the economic pressure used against the branches of national chain stores.

Many corporations have belatedly recognized that it is in their own self-interest to promote an improvement in Negro opportunities. As one of the nation's biggest corporations, U.S. Steel and its shareholders have as great a stake in eliminating the economic imbalances associated with racial discrimination as any company. Corporate responsibility is not easy to define or to measure, but in refusing to take a stand in Birmingham, Mr. Blough appears to have a rather narrow, limited concept of his influence.[3]

Also on October 31, the *Congressional Record* contained remarks made by Representative Ryan of the State of New York:

Mr. Speaker, yesterday's *New York Times* carried two stories—one of high corporate indifference, the other of high corporate profits. The statement of Roger Blough, Chairman of the Board of United States Steel Corp., that the corporation should not use its influence to improve racial conditions in strife-torn Birmingham is the epitome of corporate irresponsibility and callousness.

United States Steel willingly accepts all the benefits of our laws and constitution which guarantee the rights of corporations and of private property, but refuses to accept its obligation to support the same laws and constitution which also declare all men equal.

Apparently United States Steel sees its only responsibility as to make profits. Public welfare is not its concern. This callous attitude is a giant step backward by a giant corporation.

It is ironic that, in the same conference, Roger Blough reported a sharp increase in third quarter sales and earnings. Who is responsible for these profits? Roger Blough in his plush New York office did not bring this about by himself. Behind the profits are some 15,000 steelworkers in Birmingham, many of whom are black, who mine the ore, melt the steel, cut it, shape it, and by their hard labor create the product with which the profits are made. These steelworkers and their families live in a town of terror—a town with segregated schools and bigoted police where our citizens are denied their constitutional rights. United States Steel says to these workers, "Give us your labor but do not expect us to be concerned with your lives or the lives of your children."

United States Steel also says to American Society, "We will benefit from the advantages of American Society and its economic system and its laws but do not expect us to share any responsibility for improving human relations in that society."

Even a schoolboy knows that citizenship has obligations as well as privileges. If all citizens, whether private or corporate, insisted on privileges while refusing obligations, our free democratic society would disintegrate.

Mr. Speaker, power without responsibility is tyranny. United States Steel's policy of inaction is in reality a policy of action. Birmingham and other southern cities are permitted to abuse American citizens and deny to them the right to live decently because the so-called respectable and responsible people and organizations remain silent. In the case of United States Steel this unconscionable silence in Birmingham is shocking. As a giant of industry, it has a moral obligation to speak out. In Birmingham, where it is the largest employer, this corporation could use its tremendous influence to bring about substantial and constructive change.

I urge all members and all citizens to raise their voice in protest against this callous irresponsibility and indifference. It is time for United States Steel to put people ahead of profits.

President Kennedy, at a press conference on November 1, was asked to comment on Blough's stand. The question and the president's answer follow below:

Question: The United States Steel Corporation has rejected the idea that it should use economic pressure in an effort to improve race relations in Birmingham, Alabama. Do you have any comment on that position, and do you have any counsel for management and labor in general as to their social responsibility in the areas of tension of this kind?

President Kennedy: Actually, Mr. Blough has been somewhat helpful in one or two cases that I can think of in Birmingham. I don't think he should narrowly interpret his responsibility for the future. That is a very influential company in Birmingham, and he wants to see that city prosper, as do we all. Obviously, the federal government cannot solve this matter. So that business has a responsibility—labor and, of course, every citizen. So I would think that particularly a company which is as influential as United States Steel in Birmingham I would hope would use its influence on the side of comity between the races.

Otherwise, the future of Birmingham, of course, is not as happy as we hoped it would be. In other words, it can't be decided—this matter—in Washington. It has to be decided by citizens everywhere. Mr. Blough is an influential citizen. I am sure he will do the best he can.

On November 4, the Congressional Record carried the following remarks by Representative George Huddleston, Jr., of Alabama:

Mr. Speaker, in recent days, what I consider unjustifiable criticism has been lodged at Mr. Roger M. Blough, chairman of the board of the United States Steel Corp., as a result of comments he made in a press conference held in New York on Tuesday, October 29, in which he discussed the role of business in race relations, with particular reference to the Birmingham situation. Some misunderstanding has arisen as a result of this criticism and I feel that, in all fairness to the United States Steel Corp., Mr. Blough, and the people of Birmingham, the record should be clarified. For this purpose, I insert herewith in the *Congressional Record* a verbatim transcript of Mr. Blough's press conference of October 29.

I want to especially call the attention of the Members of Congress to Mr. Blough's comments regarding whether business should attempt to apply economic sanctions to a community in order to further so-called social or moral reforms. Mr. Blough states that such effort by business is repugnant to him and his company, and I think I speak for the overwhelming majority of the citizens of Birmingham in applauding his firm and forthright stand. For any enterprise, government or private, to attempt to exert economic pressures on the people of any community to bring about social changes is truly repugnant to the American way of life.

We in Birmingham are proud of the contributions that United States Steel's TCI division has over the years made to the economy of our city and look forward to continued cooperation for our mutual benefit in the future.

Blough's Reply

The *New York Times* of November 7 contained a letter from Blough.[4]

To the Editor of the *New York Times*:

From your Oct. 31 editorial "Corporate Race Relations" it would appear that you are under considerable misapprehension as to what I said in my press conference of the previous day concerning the policy and actions of United States Steel in Birmingham. For example, you said:

"Mr. Blough feels that U.S. Steel has fulfilled its responsibilities by following a nondiscriminatory hiring policy in Birmingham, and looks upon any other measures as both 'repugnant' and 'quite beyond what a corporation should' do to improve conditions."

Quite to the contrary, I recounted in some detail the efforts of U.S. Steel management to use its influence in Birmingham to promote better communications and better understanding between the races— not just during the recent crises but over a period of many years.

Unfortunately, the able representatives of the *Times* who attended that press conference made only casual reference to this part of my remarks in their stories. For your information therefore, and for the information of your readers, I should like to summarize the specific statements I made on this point:

The present president of our Tennessee Coal & Iron Division, Arthur Wiebel, has been working since 1946 toward developing understanding and strengthening communications between the races in Birmingham.

In 1949 he became a trustee of the Jefferson County Coordinating Council of Social Forces devoted to civic and social improvement.

In 1951 an interracial committee of this council, with Mr. Wiebel as a member, was formed to improve the lot of the Negroes in many fields: health, sanitation, safety, business, housing and cultural and recreational opportunities. That same year the committee made a formal request that the Birmingham city government employ Negro policemen. That request was denied.

Mr. Wiebel worked, for example, for a Negro upper-middle-class housing project considered as attractive as any in that economic range anywhere in the nation. He helped get Negro insurance companies and investors in Birmingham to make home mortgage money available to Negroes.

From 1953 to 1961 he was a trustee of Tuskegee Institute, an outstanding Negro institution of higher learning.

As a member of the Senior Citizens Committee, last May when serious racial problems occurred in Birmingham he devoted as much time and effort as anyone there in trying to resolve this matter. More recently, he has worked in cooperation with General Royall and Colonel Blaik, and was one of 44 business leaders endorsing a recent public appeal for the employment of qualified Negroes on the Birmingham police force.

Mr. Wiebel has also been active in the United Fund, which supports Negro welfare activities, and in the Red Cross. He is a charter member of the Committee of a Hundred, devoted to bringing new industry to Birmingham, and in more ways than I can recount he has tried to carry out what is our overall U.S. Steel policy of being a good citizen in the community in which we live.

I also said that as individuals we can exercise what influence we may have as citizens, but for a corporation to attempt to exert any kind of economic compulsion to achieve a particular end in the social area seems to me to be quite beyond what a corporation should do and quite beyond what a corporation can do.

To recapitulate, then, let me make our position perfectly clear:

I believe that U.S. Steel in its own plants should provide equal opportunities for all employees, and that it does so in Birmingham, as the *Times* recently reported.

I believe that U.S. Steel management people, as citizens, should use their influence persuasively to help resolve the problems of their communities wherever they may be—and that they are doing so in Birmingham.

I believe that while government—through the proper exercise of its legislative and administrative powers—may seek to compel social reforms, any attempt by a private organization like U.S. Steel to impose its views, its beliefs and its will upon the community by resorting to economic compulsion or coercion would be repugnant to our American constitutional concepts, and that appropriate steps to correct this abuse of corporate power would be universally demanded by public opinion, by Government and by the *New York Times*.

So, even if U.S. Steel possessed such economic power—which it certainly does not—I would be unalterably opposed to its use in this fashion.

We shall, however, continue to use our best efforts in Birmingham to be as helpful as possible.

> Roger Blough
> Chairman, Board of Directors
> United States Steel Corporation
> New York, Nov. 2, 1963

National Media Response to the Issues Raised

The matter of the possible use of economic pressure by business firms to speed the process of racial integration drew considerable attention in newspapers throughout the country. News stories, editorials, and letters from readers took various positions on Blough's stand and on President Kennedy's remarks. Several such comments follow below:

> Somehow Mr. Blough seems to say that the injunction "we are our brother's keepers" does not apply to corporations, or at least not to U.S. Steel. I am sure that even a most casual examination of this proposition will destroy it. Many large enterprises, including U.S. Steel, have made substantial contributions to the welfare of the community or the nation, beyond the necessities of profit and loss.
>
> What I am afraid Mr. Blough means is that in the current effort to eliminate all the remaining vestiges of a servile history he would prefer to be neutral, at least in deed if not in thought. If we cannot be sure as to what is morally correct in this struggle, when ever will we be able to know right from wrong?
>
> If U.S. Steel strong and great as it is, will not exert its strength for justice, what can be expected from lesser mortals? What strength U.S. Steel has in Birmingham is best known to it, but that it should be used, I have no doubt.
>
> Carl Rachlin
> General Counsel, CORE
> New York, Nov. 8, 1963

Big Steel and Civil Rights

What is the extent of the moral responsibilities of the modern, impersonal, publicly owned corporation? The question has been raised in acute fashion in Birmingham, Ala., where the city's largest single employer is the Tennessee Coal & Iron Division of U.S. Steel Corp.

U.S. Steel, and Tennessee president Arthur Wiebel in particular, have been under pressure from civil rights activists to do more to promote the individual rights of Negroes in that embattled city. In response to criticism, the corporation recently disclosed that it has been moving quietly to erase some traditional barriers that have held hundreds of Negroes to low paying jobs. U.S. Steel has merged into one line previously separate lines of promotion for

Negroes and whites in its steel plants. For instance, Negroes in the open hearth shop can now rise along with whites to a job class which pays $3.83 an hour and offers a 40% incentive. Previously they had been limited to a maximum job class offering $2.78 and a 15% incentive. Moreover, in the corporation's Fairfield plant, whites are working under Negroes for the first time. The situation reportedly has caused some discontent among white workers. But U.S. Steel has been strict in the application of its policy. Workers who object are sent home. According to a corporation official, the objectors usually return quickly to the plant. Jobs, after all, are not so easy to get in the steel industry these days.

Beyond taking these forthright steps in its own operations in Birmingham, however, U.S. Steel is inclined to go no further. According to Roger M. Blough, U.S. Steel chairman, the idea that a company should "attempt to have its ideas of what is right for the community enforced upon that community by some sort of economic means" is "clearly repugnant to me personally" and "repugnant to my fellow officers" at U.S. Steel. "We have fulfilled our responsibility in the Birmingham area," Mr. Blough said at the corporation's recent third quarter press conference. For a corporation to attempt to exert any kind of economic compulsion to achieve a particular end in the social area "seems to be quite beyond what a corporation should do, and . . . quite beyond what a corporation can do." But corporate officials who are citizens in a community "can exercise what small influence we may have as citizens," Mr. Blough said. Apparently, U.S. Steel's chairman was referring among other things to Mr. Wiebel's recent support of a move to put Negro policemen on the Birmingham police force.

A careful study of America's industrial past would probably make it difficult for Mr. Blough to support in factual detail the argument that corporations are prevented from achieving particular ends in "the social area." State and local taxes, for instance, clearly play an important social role in the community, and large corporations can wield enormous influence over tax policy. But Birmingham is a unique situation, as puzzling to politicians as it is to businessmen. Even the federal government has been reluctant to apply economic sanctions by withholding federal funds from states which defy Negro rights. Can U.S. Steel be expected to do more?

Indeed Big Steel has left little doubt of its sincerity in advancing civics rights in its own operations. If other businesses . . . and more particularly unions . . . were to follow the corporation's example of on-the-job reforms in the South, the civil rights problems of cities like Birmingham would be a lot closer to solution.

In the realm of morality, one positive example may be worth a dozen damaging sanctions in promoting a worthy end.[5]

The Company in the Community

There are still a lot of people around who remember the old "company town"—those communities so dominated by one business enterprise that the politics, the business and very often even the social customs of the people were ordained in the company boardroom.

Some of these company towns were run badly. But many were actually run very well, the company management having a sincere interest in the well-being of the community. In many places the company out of necessity provided housing, streets, schools, hospitals, recreation centers, churches and a host of other things which the people would otherwise not have had. Often the resulting municipal government was a model of good management.

Yet even in the best run such communities the people always chafed. However high-minded the motives, high-handed power was rightly resented and people found intolerable the economic power that could tell the banker to whom he should lend, the shopkeeper whom he should hire, the town councillors what laws they should pass. Thus today companies make their very considerable contributions to the community in other ways—in good jobs, in gifts to local services and in lending their influence to civic progress—and, like other outmoded institutions, the "company town" has passed without mourning.

Or anyway, so it was until lately. Now in the new context of the civil rights struggle, there are voices demanding that our large corporations use exactly this sort of power to force their desired moral standards on the communities in which they live.

Specifically this has been urged by otherwise thoughtful people in the case of Birmingham. Just the other day Roger Blough of U.S. Steel had to devote the major part of a business press conference to "explaining" why the company did not use its economic power to compel that unhappy city to mend its ways.

The question here was not about U.S. Steel's own practices. Nationwide it follows a practice of nondiscrimination in employment; upwards of 10% of its employees are Negroes, including a number in clerical jobs, supervisory assignments, skilled trades and professional positions. In Birmingham itself, according to Mr. Blough, the U.S. Steel subsidiary has about 30% Negroes among its employees.

Nor, is there any argument here about the duty of a company or its officers to provide moral leadership for what they believe to be right, whether in Birmingham or anywhere else.

In this instance the present president of the U.S. Steel division in Birmingham, Arthur Wiebel, has since 1946 been active in groups working for better race relations; since 1951 he has served on the integration committee formed by local citizens, white and Negro; he is a trustee of Tuskegee Institute, a Negro college; and in the latest difficulties he played an active and prominent role in the quiet citizens' group which has worked hard to improve the situation for Negroes in Birmingham.

Mr. Blough made it quite clear that he approved and encouraged this kind of leadership. But to the voices of impatience this is not enough. It is said by some that companies like U.S. Steel should not merely persuade but coerce the community into adopting the policies they believe to be right.

It is probably true, as these voices say, that a company as large as U.S. Steel could wield powerful weapons against the people of Birmingham. It could, as some clamor that it should, boycott local suppliers who did not act as U.S. Steel thinks they should; it could threaten to take away all or a part of its business if the city authorities didn't do as it wishes; it could even halt its contributions to local civic organizations, from hospitals to recreation facilities, if they did not conduct their affairs in an approved fashion.

Perhaps, although we gravely doubt it, such coercion might win some immediate point for the Negroes of Birmingham. But it would certainly do so at an injury to all the people of Birmingham and most of all at a grievous injury to good government and society everywhere.

Mr. Blough himself put it well: "I do not believe it would be a wise thing for U.S. Steel to be other than a good citizen in a community, or to attempt to have its ideas of what is right for the community enforced upon the community."

As a good citizen, business can use its influence for good, but the old fashioned "company town" is better buried. And no one—least of all those who seek wider democracy—should wish for its resurrection.[6]

NOTES

1. © 1963 by the New York Times Company. Reprinted by permission.
2. Ibid.
3. Ibid.
4. Reprinted by permission of United States Steel Corporation.
5. *American Metal Market,* November 11, 1963. Reprinted with permission.
6. Reprinted by permission of *The Wall Street Journal.* © Dow Jones & Company, Inc. (November 4, 1963). All rights reserved.

Report of the Compensation Committee of the Board of Directors

General Electric Company

COMPENSATION POLICIES FOR EXECUTIVE OFFICERS

The Management Development and Compensation Committee of the Board of Directors (the Committee), consisting entirely of non-employee directors, approves all of the policies under which compensation is paid or awarded to the Company's executive officers. The Company's basic compensation program for executive officers currently consists of the following elements: annual payments of salary and bonuses; annual grants of stock options; and periodic grants of restricted stock units (RSUs) and other contingent long-term financial performance awards. As described more fully below, each element of the Company's executive compensation program has a somewhat different purpose. All stock options, RSU and contingent long-term financial performance awards are made under the share-owner-approved GE 1990

Long-Term Incentive Plan (the Plan), which limits total annual awards to less than 1% of issued shares. In 1997, the share owners approved the material terms of performance goals to be set by the Committee for payments of bonuses. RSUs and long-term performance awards to the Company's executive officers, and approved an amendment to the Plan to establish a limit on the number of stock options that may be awarded to any individual, so that the Company could continue to obtain tax deductions for the full amount of such payments and awards under pertinent tax law.

As in prior years, and in accordance with the material terms of the performance goals approved by the share owners, all of the Committee's judgments during 1998 regarding the appropriate form and level of executive compensation payments and incentive awards were ultimately based upon the Committee's assessment of the Company's executive officers, the increasingly competitive demand for superior executive talent, the Company's overall performance, and GE's future objectives and challenges. Although the Committee did not generally rely solely upon a guideline or formula based on any particular performance measure or single event in 1998, key factors affecting the Committee's judgments included, among other things: strong increases in the earnings of the Company; solid productivity gains in a period of intense competition; development and implementation of aggressive quality initiatives to achieve preeminent leadership in all the Company's product and service offerings; increased revenues generated outside the United States and further improvements in the Company's global competitive position through a number of strategic transactions and joint ventures with partners in developing markets; accelerated growth of the Company's global service offerings; leadership in ensuring compliance with applicable law and Company ethics policies; and continuation of productivity, asset utilization and employee involvement initiatives that, among other things, provided improved cash flow and increased return on share owner equity. The Committee also considered the compensation practices and performances of other major corporations that are most likely to compete with the Company for the services of executive officers. Based upon all factors it deemed relevant, including those noted above and the Company's superior overall long-term performance, the Committee considered it appropriate, and in the best interest of the share owners, to set the overall level of the Company's salary, bonus and other incentive compensation awards above the average of companies in the comparison group in order to enable the Company to continue to attract, retain and motivate the highest level of executive talent possible.

Salary payments in 1998 were made to compensate ongoing performance throughout the year. Bonuses for 1998 were based upon the Committee's determination that the Company's 1998 financial results had exceeded the performance goals previously established by the Committee and upon its judgment regarding the significance of each executive officer's contributions during 1998. Potentially valuable stock options have been granted to the Company's six most highly compensated executive officers. Each stock option permits the holder, generally for a period of ten years, to purchase one share of GE stock from the Company at the market price of GE stock on the date of grant. Stock options normally become exercisable in two installments, the first half after three years and the other half after five years from the date of grant. In most cases, the restrictions on 25% of RSUs lapse three years after grant, an additional 25% lapse in seven years, and the remaining 50% lapse at retirement. RSUs were awarded to four of the Company's six most highly compensated executive officers in 1998. Stock options and RSUs provide strong incentives for continued superior performance because, under the terms of these awards, unexercised stock options and RSUs for which restrictions have not lapsed are forfeited if the executive officers is terminated by the Company for performance or voluntarily leaves the Company before retirement.

The Committee's decisions concerning the specific 1998 compensation elements for individual executive officers, including the Chief Executive Officer, were made within this broad framework and in light of each executive officer's level of responsibility, performance, current salary, prior-year bonus and other compensation awards. As noted above, in all cases the Committee's specific decisions involving 1998 executive officer compensation were ultimately based upon the Committee's judgment about the individual executive officer's performance and potential future contributions, and about whether each particular payment or award would provide an appropriate reward and incentive for the executive to sustain and enhance the Company's long-term superior performance.

BASIS FOR CHIEF EXECUTIVE OFFICER COMPENSATION

For 1998, Mr. Welch received total cash payments of $10,000,000 in salary and bonus. The Committee considered this level of payment appropriate in view of Mr. Welch's leadership of one of the world's top companies in terms of earnings, balance sheet strength, creation of share owner value and management processes. In 1998, the Committee also granted Mr. Welch 500,000 stock options, which will become exercisable upon Mr. Welch's retirement, and 300,000 Restricted Stock Units, for which the restriction will lapse upon Mr. Welch's retirement. The primary basis for the Committee's determination to grant such stock options and RSUs to Mr. Welch in 1998 was to provide a strong incentive for him to continue to increase the value of the Company during the remainder of his employment. As reported in the last two Proxy Statements, the Board of Directors entered into an employment contract with Mr. Welch in 1996, which requires him to serve as the Chairman and Chief Executive Officer of the Company until December 31, 2000, at the pleasure of the Board of Directors on terms no less favorable than his then current conditions of employment. In addition, after that date, the contract requires Mr. Welch, when requested by the Company's then current Chief Executive Officer, to be available for up to 30 days a year for the remainder of his lifetime to provide consulting services or to participate in external events or activities on behalf of the Company. In return for these commitments by Mr. Welch, the Board agreed to pay him, during the term of the consulting agreement, a daily consulting fee for the days he renders services based on

his daily salary rate in the year prior to his retirement, the first five days of which will be paid in advance through an annual retainer, and to provide him continued lifetime access to Company facilities and services comparable to those which are currently made available to him by the Company.

The specific bases for the Committee's determinations regarding Mr. Welch's compensation in 1998 included his aggressive leadership, which drove the Company's outstanding financial results and improved its overall global competitive position; his vision and determination to achieve preeminent quality in all of the Company's products and services; his drive to reinforce a culture of integrity, stretch targets, boundaryless behavior and employee involvement throughout the Company, and his firm commitment to create a leadership team that will continue the Company's success well into the next century. As in prior years, the key judgment the Committee made in determining Mr. Welch's 1998 compensation was its assessment of his ability and dedication to continue increasing the long-term value of the Company for the share owners by continuing to provide the leadership and vision that he has provided throughout his eighteen-year tenure as Chairman and Chief Executive Officer, during which GE's market value has increased by more than $300,000,000,000. This performance is further highlighted by the performance graph as shown in Figure 2, which covers Mr. Welch's tenure as CEO and compares GE stock performance with the stock performance of other companies, as measured by broad market indices.

BROAD-BASED EMPLOYEE STOCK OPTION PROGRAM

Approximately 23,000 individuals below the executive officer level have been awarded one or more stock option grants under a broad-based stock option program initiated in 1989. This program is an increasingly vital element of the Company's drive to identify, develop and motivate the high-potential leadership who will sustain GE's outstanding performance far into the 21st century. It also reinforces in the Company the entrepreneurial environment and spirit of a small company by providing

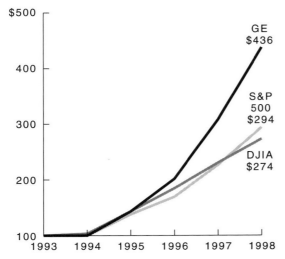

FIGURE 1
FIVE-YEAR PERFORMANCE GRAPH: 1993–1998
Comparison of Five-Year Cumulative Total Return Among
GE, S&P 500 and Dow Jones Industrial Average (DJIA)
The annual changes for the five- and eighteen-year
periods shown in the graphs on this and to the right are
based on the assumption that $100 had been invested in
GE stock and each index on December 31, 1993 (as
required by SEC rules) and 1980, respectively, and that
all quarterly dividends were reinvested at the average of
the closing stock prices at the beginning and end of the
quarter. The total cumulative dollar returns shown on the
graphs represent the value that such investments would
have had on December 31, 1998.

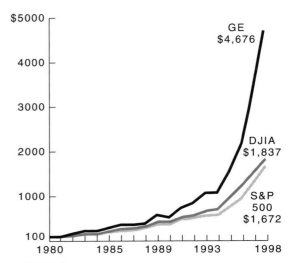

FIGURE 2
EIGHTEEN-YEAR PERFORMANCE GRAPH: 1980–1998
Comparison of Eighteen-Year Cumulative Total Return
Among GE, S&P 500 and Dow Jones Industrial Average
(DJIA)
The graph below shows the cumulative total return to GE
share owners since December 31, 1980, shortly before
Mr. Welch became Chairman and Chief Executive Officer
in April 1981, compared with the same indices shown on
the five-year graph, thus illustrating the relative
performance of the Company during his tenure in that
position. As with the five-year graph, this comparison
assumes that $100 was invested in GE and each index at
the start of the period and that all dividends were
reinvested. The total cumulative dollar returns shown
represent the value that such investments would have
had on December 31, 1998.

real incentives for these employees to sustain and
enhance GE's long-term performance. The Committee believes that the superior performance of
these individuals will contribute significantly to the
Company's future success.

COMPENSATION COMMITTEE INTERLOCKS AND INSIDER PARTICIPATION

The Management Development and Compensation
Committee is composed of the following non-
employee directors: Silas S. Cathcart (Chairman),
Claudio X. Gonzalez, Gertrude G. Michelson, Frank
H. T. Rhodes and Andrew C. Sigler. Mr. Cathcart
was reappointed to the Committee in 1992 and be-

came Chairman in 1993. He served as a member of
the Committee from 1977 to 1987 and as a director
of GE since 1972, except for the period during 1987
to 1989 when he served as Chairman and CEO of
Kidder, Peabody Group Inc., a former operating
subsidiary of the Company.

SHARE OWNER PROPOSAL NO. 4

Franklin Research & Development Corporation, 711
Atlantic Avenue, Boston, MA 02111-2809, and
other filers have notified GE that they intend to present the following proposal at this year's meeting:

"Whereas, increases in CEO compensation continue to dwarf the compensation increases enjoyed by employees. Between 1990 and 1997, CEO cash compensation rose 86% and average total compensation (including stock options) rose 298% to $7,800,000, vastly exceeding a 22% increase in factory wages and a growth of 110% in S&P 500 earnings (Business Week Survey of Executive Compensation: Bureau of Labor Statistics);

"Whereas, in 1997, top US CEOs earned on average 326 times the average factory workers' pay, a dramatic rise from the 42 times reported in 1980;

"Whereas, General Electric's CEO in 1997 was the 11th highest paid US CEO, making $39,894,000, a 44.5% increase from 1996. This represents 5.1 times the pay of the average US CEO, more than 1,400 times the average US factory worker, and 9,571 times the $4,168 average wage for Mexican maquiladora workers, thousands of whom work for General Electric;

"Whereas, General Electric's efforts to cut costs have been disproportionately focused on the factory floor, while ignoring the executive suite. Between 1995 and 1997, a period in which our company laid off thousands of workers, the top five officers enjoyed increases in cash compensation of 46%;

"Whereas, in opposing this resolution last year, General Electric's Board pointed to the 'unique contribution Mr. Welch has made to the creation of more than $225 billion of share owner value during his tenure as Chief Executive Officer.' We believe this value has been created not by one individual, but by hundreds of thousands of current and former General Electric employees who by working together have created tremendous value;

"Whereas, growing research on effective organizations stresses the importance of empowering front-line workers, a goal undermined by compensation policies that reward top executives at the expense of workers closest to the customers and production;

"Whereas, business leaders and thinkers ranging from J.P. Morgan to Peter Drucker have argued against wide pay gaps within enterprises and called for limits on executive pay based on multiples of worker compensation;

"Therefore, be it resolved, that shareholders urge the Board to address the issue of runaway remuneration of CEOs and the widening gap between highest and lowest paid workers by:

1. Establishing a cap on CEO compensation expressed as a multiple of pay of the lowest paid worker at General Electric;
2. Preparing a report for shareholders explaining the determinations used in order to determine the appropriate cap.

"Supporting Statement: Last year this resolution was supported by 6% of General Electric's shareholders. In asking General Electric to establish a cap on executive compensation, we have not sought to impose our own arbitrary cap on executive pay. Instead we have asked our company to wrestle with the issue of the rising wage gap that exists between corporate executives and those they seek to lead. By imposing the financial discipline of a pay cap, we hope our company can help reverse a long standing trend that is neither good for business, nor society. Please vote YES."

YOUR BOARD OF DIRECTORS RECOMMENDS A VOTE AGAINST THIS PROPOSAL

Setting the compensation and incentives for the Chief Executive Officer is a key responsibility of the Board of Directors. As discussed in the report of the Management Development and Compensation Committee of the Board above, your directors consider a number of factors in establishing those incentives and compensation. Based upon its consideration of these factors, your directors believe that Mr. Welch's overall compensation level is appropriate in light of the value that his superior leadership, vision and dedication provided to the share owners during his eighteen-year tenure as Chief Executive Officer. This value is highlighted in the Performance Graph as shown in Figure 2, comparing the value of GE stock with broad market indices. Because of the unique contribution that Mr. Welch has made to the creation of more than $300,000,000,000 of share owner value during his tenure as Chief Executive Officer, your directors do not believe it would be in the best interests of the share owners to establish an arbitrary cap on the compensation paid to the Chief Executive Officer, and therefore recommend a vote against this proposal.

Words of Warning: Ruling Makes Directors Accountable for Compliance

Dominic Bencivenga
Freelance writer based in Babylon, New York

A Delaware Court of Chancery decision released last year amidst very little fanfare has become a rallying point for attorneys who are carrying its message to corporate directors: Take compliance seriously or you could face liability for the consequences.

The ruling issued in September, *In re: Caremark International Inc. Derivative Litigation,* CV-13670, lays the groundwork for expanding directors' obligations and good faith duty of care, shifting their role from passive observer to active guardian of corporate integrity.

Chancellor William T. Allen said in *Caremark* that directors, who traditionally deal with problems as they arise, have an obligation to take an active part in ensuring that a company has adequate compliance and information gathering systems.

"Failure to do so under some circumstances may, in theory at least, render a director liable for losses caused by non-compliance," Chancellor Allen wrote.

WAKE-UP CALL

Prior to *Caremark,* directors' liability was perceived as minimal. But now, those who fail to monitor compliance efforts may find themselves facing enormous liability that could overwhelm director and officer insurance policies, attorneys said.

Caremark "does move the compliance ball quite a distance from where it was 20 years ago," said Professor Harvey J. Goldschmid, of Columbia University School of Law. "Now there is an affirmative obligation. No longer can directors sit back and assume everything is okay. It means they have to set up compliance programs, and meaningful information-gathering programs, and make use of external and internal auditing."

The ruling is the Delaware court's first to articulate a position that many in the corporate compliance bar have been advocating for much of the decade. While the judge's comments came in a ruling approving a shareholder settlement and attorney's fees, attorneys say the *Caremark* holding is likely to have a significant impact on Corporate America. Many of the nation's largest companies are incorporated in Delaware, and the Chancery Court is a leading authority in corporate law on which other states often rely.

"The *Caremark* decision is by far the greatest step forward in compliance program [law] that ever occurred, other than the U.S. Sentencing Guidelines," commented Jeffrey J. Binder, NYNEX Corp. general attorney and chief compliance counsel.

For corporate directors who are just beginning to hear about *Caremark,* "It is a wake-up call," said Jeffrey M. Kaplan, a partner at Arkin Schaffer & Kaplan in New York. "Even companies which have good compliance programs don't do nearly enough in terms of involving the board of directors."

"*Caremark* is only just beginning to penetrate the boardroom consciousness," said Gregory J. Wallance, a partner at Kaye, Scholer, Fierman, Hays & Handler LLP, who is co-charging a seminar on the decision's impact in June. "We will see in the next year or two an acceleration in the trend toward implementing compliance programs."

Compliance came to the fore following the 1991 federal Corporate Sentencing Guidelines, which allow judges to fine companies if their employees commit crimes. Some prominent cases have included a $340 million fine against Daiwa Bank or a $100 million fine for Archer-Daniels-Midland Co.

But judges can levy lesser fines if they determine that the company had tried to prevent wrongdoing by implementing compliance or ethics programs. In order to limit liability, the sentencing guidelines require companies to tailor oversight programs to specific industries, delegate authority, explain the compliance standards to employees, measure the program's effectiveness, and move quickly to discipline employees after learning of wrongdoing.

Some regulated industries, including financial services, telecommunications and defense, typically have well-developed compliance programs, while deregulated industries, such as utilities, have been lax, attorneys said.

Chancellor Allen issued the memorandum opinion after reviewing the fairness of a proposed settlement in a consolidated suit brought by shareholders of Caremark International Inc. In 1994, federal prosecutors charged Caremark, a health care provider, with violating federal laws by paying doctors and hospitals to refer Medicare and Medicaid patients. The company subsequently pleaded guilty to mail fraud and paid $250 million in restitution.

Shareholders began filing civil suits a day after the company was indicted, alleging that the directors had breached their fiduciary duty of care by failing to properly supervise employees.

In approving the settlement, which required the company to improve compliance and pay $869,500 in attorney's fees, Chancellor Allen noted that the Caremark directors had made a good faith effort to protect the company.

But he used the case to hold that directors could be held liable, rejecting a longstanding reading of the 1963 Delaware Supreme Court case, *Graham v. Allis-Chalmers*, Del. Supr 188 A.2d 125, that a board has no responsibility to ensure that management implements compliance and information systems.

GOOD FAITH DEFINED

"There is really a growing perception that compliance has to be as much a business objective as legal," Mr. Wallance said.

Delaware and most states allow companies to eliminate by charter amendment the liability of a director for money damages for breaching the duty of care, except in such cases where directors act "not in good faith." Mr. Goldschmid said. As a result, only in extreme situations could they be liable for money damages.

Caremark is "one of the first times anyone discussed what good faith might mean," he said. Based on the decision, "failure to set up an information or compliance system may indicate the kind of extreme departure from standards of care which would constitute a lack of good faith."

As a result, directors "have to be more accountable for what happens in a company than they have in the past," said Carole Basri, executive director of the New York Chapter of the American Corporate Counsel Association and a consultant at Deloitte & Touche LLP.

Avoiding *Caremark* liability will mean establishing compliance programs that are part of the management structure, run by high-ranking executives who report regularly to the board and have authority to act, attorneys suggested. Directors must oversee compliance programs, including receiving regular reports and an annual review of training efforts, discipline, the results of compliance audits, and sufficient financial information. The annual reports also should identify potential problems and outline ways to prevent or address them.

While *Caremark* makes clear that directors do not have to approve daily business decisions, board involvement is critical in making a program effective, said Joseph E. Murphy, executive vice president of Compliance Systems Legal Group in New Jersey, who has written on compliance. "If all you do is go through the motions and have a code no one reads, you never audit the program and don't discipline anyone, it won't do any good."

At NYNEX, for example, Mr. Binder said that a company officer oversees the overall compliance program and reports to the board. An officer oversees each of 19 risk areas, such as telecommunications regulations, antitrust and insider trading, and employees working in each area receive specific training about the law and proper business procedures.

By addressing liability, Chancellor Allen gave "fair notice to directors," Mr. Kaplan said. "They won't be able to say in the future that they didn't know."

Many corporations insure their officers and directors against liability, but those policies may not protect completely against a Daiwa Bank or ADM-type fine, attorneys said. In cases where the insurance does cover such fines, premiums will likely skyrocket.

Attorneys representing shareholders in lawsuits against companies are likely to rely on *Caremark* in the discovery process.

The ruling will allow plaintiff's attorneys to "take each director through what could be an enormously painful deposition process," Mr. Kaplan said.

Directors who plead ignorance or who did not fulfill their duty "would be so embarrassed" by the prospect of being shown to be derelict under *Caremark* that "they will be begging to settle," he said.

PART THREE

WORK IN THE CORPORATION

In Part Two we examined the notion that business organizations have obligations not only, or even primarily, to their shareholders, but also to other stakeholders in the firm. One of the most important of these groups of stakeholders is the corporation's employees. They provide the productive and decision-making power of the business. In a very real sense, they are the corporation.

What obligations hold between a company and its employees? The traditional view of the relation between employer and employee has been that it is a free agreement or contract between the two parties for their mutual benefit. According to this contract, the primary responsibility of the employer is to pay fair wages. In return, employees owe the company loyalty, obedience, and satisfactory job performance. Either party can terminate the contract at any time, and traditionally, this power to terminate has been thought sufficient to protect the interests of both employers and employees. Like the traditional understanding of the corporation itself, however, this simple model of employer-employee relations has been challenged. Some thinkers argue that the employees' interests are not sufficiently protected by the right to quit. In the past two decades, a strong interest has emerged in securing more extensive rights for employees to protect them from potential abuses of power in the workplace. In Chapter 5, we examine the rights and duties of employees, with a special focus on the employee rights and on issues of worker health and safety and privacy. The rights of free speech and dissent in the workplace have also received increasing attention, as "whistle-blowing" incidents—cases in which employees go above their supervisors or to the public to reveal corporate wrongdoing—have become more and more common. The last two articles in Chapter 5 are devoted to the ethical issues raised by the practice of whistle-blowing.

In Chapter 6 we turn to a variety of other workplace issues, including affirmative action, sexual harassment, business and family, and women in the workplace. These issues have been the subject of much controversy and legislative action, particularly discrimination and sexual harassment. The elimination of harassment and discrimination is essential both to a truly free society and to a truly efficient market. As a major social institution, business has a significant role to play in the termination of harassment and discrimination in U.S. society. But how should business exercise this role? How should corporations regulate interactions between men and women in the workplace? Should they eliminate racial discrimination by adopting a policy of "preferential hiring?" And what policies should business have about family life? How should businesses handle the increasing amount of racial and ethnic diversity in the workplace? All of these issues are examined in our selections.

EMPLOYEE RIGHTS AND DUTIES

Until recently employee rights have been restricted to those specified in the contract between employee and employer. Generally these had to do with wages, job description, hours, pension, and other benefits. If an employee did not like the treatment he or she received at the hands of an employer, did not wish to carry out an order, or disagreed with company policy, he or she could leave the job. Conversely, employers were permitted to fire employees for any reason or for no reason at all. Both parties, then, were free to terminate their contract at any time. But because jobs have usually been harder to find than employees, many felt that employers held the power and that employees were relatively powerless and required protection.

Today corporations are subject to laws governing minimum wages and maximum hours, health and safety standards, and forbidding discrimination in hiring, firing, and promotion. For example, an employer cannot fire an employee for union activity. But what exactly are the additional ethical rights, if any, held by employees? Ronald Duska, in his article "Employee Rights," explores more fully the nature of rights and their application in the workplace. After outlining the various means by which rights can be morally justified, Duska attempts to clarify and delimit the "right to work," and the "right to meaningful work." According to Duska, one would probably only have a right to work in a socialist society, as opposed to a free-market state. In terms of the right to meaningful work, Duska argues that at best, what can be claimed is a right to a job that is made as meaningful as possible. He then discusses the extent to which a number of employee rights are justified. Based on the asymmetries of power in the employer-employee relationship, employees have a right to a safe and healthy work environment. This right would even override the right of shareholders to profit maximization. Although there is no right to job security, employees do have a right of due process regarding the decision to fire or demote the employee. Other employee rights discussed by Duska include the right to privacy, the right to compensation for injury, the right to equal treatment without regard to race or gender, freedom from harassment, and the right to a living wage.

Tibor Machan, in his article "Human Rights, Workers' Rights, and the 'Right' to Occupational Safety," takes a different approach, by arguing that there is no such thing as special workers' rights. Workers do possess rights, but as human beings, not as workers. This implies that there are no special rights that need government protection or duties of employers toward employees that need government enforcement. Would a completely free labor market necessarily lead to exploitations such as child labor or a neglect of health and safety at the workplace? Machan thinks not. He discusses the example of a not so prosperous coal mine advertising for jobs. At the present time, the employer is not equipped to provide completely safe work conditions when compared with its competitors. Should we be concerned? Machan argues that as long as prospective employees are made aware of the safety hazards, taking a more paternalistic approach is inappropriate. Workers have options. They can reject the job, bargain on their own, organize and insist on safer conditions, or pool resources, borrow, and purchase the firm. If employers are required by law to spend the firm's funds to meet safety requirements, fewer funds will be available for additional wages or to purchase additional sites. More importantly, the liberty of the employer-employee relation would have been intruded upon.

One important employee right that is examined by Laura P. Hartman, in her article "The Rights and Wrongs of Workplace Snooping," is that of privacy. Firms are becoming increasingly concerned with the extent of legal liability they are exposed to for their employees' actions. At the same time, with employees spending long hours at the workplace, employers might expect that a certain amount of personal business would be conducted during the day. What should be the appropriate balance between employees' rights of privacy at the workplace, and the right of employers to monitor their actions? Should employers be permitted to conduct surveillance on their employees in the restroom, changing room, lunch room, or parking lot? Can it be continuous, or conducted secretly? Is notification of the monitoring a sufficient defense to the employer? Pincus Hartman addresses the issue by first discussing the extent to which employees are now being monitored, especially through the growth of new technologies such as hidden audio, video, and computer monitoring systems. In discussing the ethical issues related to workplace "snooping," she argues that there is a delicate balance to be achieved between the employer's and the employee's interests. She concludes with a list of guidelines to consider when thinking about monitoring the actions of employees, including always giving advance notice of monitoring and avoiding monitoring private areas such as restrooms.

Another important workplace problem—drug use by employees—has been estimated to cost business millions of dollars in the form of lowered productivity, absenteeism, employee error, and other problems. Drug use also carries the risk of serious physical injury to consumers, the public, or employees themselves. To counter these problems, many companies have instituted programs to test applicants and current employees for drug use. Many Fortune 500 firms, as well as numerous smaller companies, now employ some kind of drug test. Are such programs a threat to employee privacy? Joseph DesJardins and Ronald Duska claim that they are. DesJardins and Duska argue that employers have a right to information that is directly related to job performance. But drug use, they claim, is not directly relevant. People use drugs differently, and drugs can have varied effects. Some drug users will be impaired on the job, but others will not. The commonly used drug tests, moreover, do not give much information about impairment. They show only the presence of the drug's metabolite in the urine and not the kind of drug, the amount that is present, or how long ago the drug was taken. An astute supervisor can spot impairment in the form of absenteeism, carelessness, low productivity, or psychological problems. If these problems do arise, the supervisor may discipline the employee for these reasons alone. There is no need to inquire into the employee's use of drugs. However, if no performance problems show up, there is no impairment—the employee is doing the job. Again, drug testing is not necessary. Thus, DesJardins and Duska conclude, if what the employer is truly interested in is performance, drug test results are either superfluous or irrelevant. Testing is only justified, they argue, in jobs in which drug use poses a "clear and present" danger to others. In a *Wall Street Journal* interview conducted by Michael

Waldholz, two corporate executives debate the acceptability of drug testing, touching on several of the issues raised by Des Jardins and Duska.

In the final two articles in Chapter 5, we consider the dilemma of disclosing corporate wrongdoing or misconduct. For example, occasionally an employee discovers, or is asked to participate in, an activity he or she believes to be unethical or illegal. In such a situation the employee may choose to "blow the whistle" or reveal the activity, either to someone higher up within the corporation (usually called "internal" whistle-blowing) or to the public ("external") whistle-blowing.

Do employees have the right, or perhaps even the obligation, to blow the whistle on corporate wrongdoing? Should they receive legal protection from such retaliations by their employer as firing, blackballing, or attacks on professional integrity? Some, such as Ralph Nader, recommend not only that whistle-blowing receive protection but that it be actively encouraged as a means of improving corporate responsibility. Others are violently opposed to whistle-blowing, feeling that it violates the duties of employees to their employer. James M. Roche, former chairman of General Motors Corporation states:

> Some of the enemies of business now encourage an employee to be disloyal to the enterprise. They want to create suspicion and disharmony and pry into the proprietary interests of the business: However this is labeled—industrial espionage, whistle-blowing, or professional responsibility—it is another tactic for spreading disunity and creating conflict.

Legally, an employee is regarded as the agent of the corporation for which he or she works. Agency law states that employees have a duty to obey the directions of their employers, to act solely in their employers' interests in all matters related to their employment, and to refrain from disclosing confidential information that, if revealed, might harm their employers. The law does not require employees to carry out commands that are illegal or immoral, but neither does it authorize them to reveal such commands to the public or (for the most part) protect them from reprisals if they do so.

In his article, Richard De George argues that because it is a form of disloyalty, and because it can cause harm to the firm, whistle-blowing needs moral justification. De George believes that whistle-blowing is only morally permissible under certain conditions: when serious (physical) harm is threatened and when the employee has already exhausted channels within the corporation in an attempt to correct the problem. De George regards whistle-blowing as a supererogatory, self-sacrificing, or heroic act and believes that employees very rarely have an obligation to blow the whistle. For such an obligation to be present, De George believes, an employee must have documented evidence of serious potential harm and have good reason to believe that blowing the whistle will actually succeed in averting the harm. The best solution to the problem of whistle-blowing in the workplace, claims De George, is to encourage channels of communication and response inside the corporation so that employees are not forced to be "moral heroes."

In response, Gene James believes that De George's criteria are too strict. Harms such as sexual harassment, fraud, or invasion of privacy may also justify blowing the whistle, he believes, even though these do not involve the physical harm that De George finds necessary. James also believes that whistle-blowing is more often obligatory than De George admits. Employees who are aware of the potentially harmful consequences of a corporate act and who fail to blow the whistle, James holds, bear part of the responsibility for those consequences. In these cases, the duty to blow the whistle outweighs both the risk of job loss and the duty of loyalty to the corporation.

It is not always clear that a dissenting employee is being disloyal to the corporation. In many cases, corporations could have saved themselves thousands of dollars in lawsuits and a tarnished public image by responding to dissenting employees. In part, whether a dissenting employee is acting in the interest of the corporation depends upon how broadly we interpret the nature, function, and goals of business. If the function of business is to produce a reliable product and refrain from harming its stakeholders as well as making a profit, then it could be argued that top management—not whistle-blowers—are acting against the interest of their companies.

THE MODERN WORKPLACE: TRANSITION TO EQUALITY AND DIVERSITY

For many years in the United States, work in the corporation was dominated by one group—white males. Middle- and upper-level management were the exclusive preserve of white males. Lower-level jobs were all that women, African Americans, and other minorities could hope for. There was no real possibility of advancement for women and minorities. They were excluded, sometimes subtly, sometimes callously, from full participation in corporate life.

This is gradually changing. As a consequence of legislation and different social realities and attitudes, management is no longer composed solely of white males. This, we hope and anticipate, will continue in the future. However, it brings with it many new problems for corporations and those who run them. Many of these problems are discussed in the articles in Chapter 6.

The first two articles in Chapter 6 discuss the perennially controversial topics of affirmative action and reverse discrimination. Louis Pojman approaches the issue of affirmative action by first defining a number of key terms, such as discrimination, prejudice, bias, equal opportunity, and affirmative action. He then outlines seven arguments on each side of the issue. Arguments supporting affirmative action include, for example, the equal results argument, the compensation argument, and the diversity argument. Some arguments against affirmative action are that it requires discrimination against a different group, that it encourages mediocrity, and that it has not been successful. He concludes that there is a real danger that well-intentioned people, in their attempts to redress the inequities of the past, are engaging in new forms of unjust discrimination.

In "What Is Wrong with Reverse Discrimination?" Edwin Hettinger defends from a utilitarian point of view the hiring of slightly less qualified blacks and women rather than slightly more qualified white males. This is justified, he argues, since the ultimate goal is the elimination of racial and sexual inequality. He identifies two objections to reverse discrimination as troubling: that people are judged on the basis of characteristics over which they have no control; and that white males are not compensated for the burden they bear in achieving an egalitarian society. He concludes that these two objections are relatively minor when weighed against the injustices of racial and sexual inequality. The reader may want to test Hettinger's conclusions against the "Kantian Utilitarian" principle proposed in the last section of the introduction to this text.

Another major issue in the workplace is sexual harassment. For years sexual harassment was dismissed or ignored by corporate management. It was just a fact of work life that women had to deal with as best they could, even though it was clearly a pernicious and ethically repugnant practice. Recently, however, this has begun to change. Legislation has been passed to prohibit sexual harassment, and corporations have at last begun to take action against it. In their article in Chapter 6, Ellen Bravo and Ellen Cassedy offer a commonsense definition of sexual harassment as offering sexual attention to someone who didn't ask for it and doesn't want it. They note that there are two kinds of sexual harassment: quid pro quo harassment in which an employee must submit to keep her job or receive a raise or promotion; and hostile environment harassment in which unwelcome sexual conduct creates an environment in which an employee cannot reasonably be expected to perform her job satisfactorily. By using a number of scenarios and examples, they show how these concepts apply, and they dispel a number of myths about sexual harassment.

Bravo and Cassedy also point out that the "reasonable person" standard so often used by courts to gauge behavior has been replaced by the "reasonable woman" standard as the law has evolved to take account of the perspective of women in the workplace. In their conclusions, however, they argue that despite this, the law and enforcement system still pose formidable obstacles for victims of harassment.

The next article by Domènec Melé, "Organization of Work in the Company and Family Rights of the Employees," addresses the fact that the traditional view of work and family—the man at work and the woman at home—no longer applies. Changing demographics and new attitudes toward work are bringing more and more women into the workplace. But with both parents working, and with the increasing number of single parents in the workforce, dependent care becomes a major issue for workers. Melé argues in his article that this new reality must be reorganized by employers. In other words, employees have legitimate family responsibilities that employers must respect. He provides a list of key family rights, including the right to find the necessary social support to consolidate the unity and stability of the family; the right to socio-economic conditions with respect to raising children; the right to working hours and periods necessary to devote to one's spouse and children and to just being together; the right to a quality of work life allowing for necessary attention to one's family; and the right to sufficient compensation to start and maintain a family. He presents a number of scenarios connected to these rights in which company policy can attack the family's unity and stability.

In the final article in Chapter 6 entitled "Women in the Workplace," Al Gini addresses a range of issues for working women. After discussing the rise of women in the workplace, Gini discusses the question of whether a sense of justice exists for women at the workplace. Are women treated differently at work? Are they evaluated on the basis of merit and ability? Is there a "glass ceiling" preventing women from advancing? Gini points to evidence indicating that few women encounter a level playing field. And not only does Gini point to evidence that women are not equals in the workplace, but that things may even in some respects be getting worse. Do women face similar problems of injustice at the home front? Gini suggests that this also continues to be the case. Despite the rise of women at the workplace, men continue to do significantly less housework than women. He suggests that much more change is required before justice will be achieved by women at home as well as at work.

MINI-CASES AND CASES FOR PART THREE

The mini-cases in Part Three relate to specific issues faced by employees in the workplace. In "Joan Drew," an employee must decide how to handle a case of sexual harassment. Bravo and Cassedy's article can be helpful in dissecting this case. In "Julie Simpson," the employee must decide whether to accept a gift from a vendor, a typical conflict of interest situation faced by many employees.

The cases of Part Three continue to explore issues of work in the corporation. In "Bank-Boston's Layoffs Program: 'Death with Dignity,'" a series of suggestions are provided as to how a firm might engage in downsizing in a more ethically appropriate manner. One might reflect on the articles by Ronald Duska ("Employee Rights") and by Tibor Machan ("Human Rights, Workers' Rights, and the 'Right' to Occupational Safety") in evaluating whether the company is going too far or not far enough in its actions. In "Lanscape," an employee is faced with the dilemma of whether to provide certain software for the purpose of monitoring the computers of other employees to verify if they are using drugs. One might consider the article "The Rights and Wrongs of Workplace Snooping," by Laura Pincus Hartman in determining what is appropriate for the company. In *"United States* v. *General Electric,"* the legal decision is provided for the case of whistle-blower Chester Walsh, in his attempt to claim a portion of the U.S. government's settlement with General Electric under the *False Claims Act.* The company was prosecuted for making illicit payments to an Israeli airforce general in order to secure certain contracts. The arguments raised by Richard De George and Gene James in their whistle-blowing articles can be considered in evaluating the case. In "Texaco: The Jelly Bean Diversity Fiasco," the case of racial discrimination at the company is presented. The company settled for $176 million, the largest sum ever for a discrimination case, following the release of a tape in which black employees are referred to as "black jelly beans." The case can be used to discuss the affirmative action debate between Louis Pojman and Edwin Hettinger. Finally, "The Case of the Mismanaged Ms." addresses the issue of sexual discrimination. In addition to Ellen Bravo and Ellen Cassedy's article, the case brings out points raised in the articles by Domènec Melé and Al Gini.

CHAPTER 5

Employee Rights and Duties

Employee Rights

Ronald Duska
Charles Lamont Post Chair of Ethics and the Professions,
American College, and former Executive Director,
Society of Business Ethics

Does drug testing violate an employee's right to privacy? Should companies be able to fire employees without cause? Is there a right to a safe workplace? All of these questions revolve around the notion of employee rights, one of the most important in business ethics. Much recent legislation has been passed which specifies employees' rights and which regulates working conditions, hiring and firing procedures, harassment and a host of other areas. There has been so much regulation and so many assertions of rights, recently, that some critics bemoan what they see as an unwarranted proliferation of rights. Sometimes, rights seem to be created out of thin air. Opponents of those critics, however, are not concerned about a proliferation of rights, but rather see the articula-

tions of new rights as an inevitable product of a society's concern for preserving and protecting human dignity. Defenders of the expansion of rights follow the lead of Judge Blackstone (1941) who in Book I of his famous *Commentaries on the Law,* asserts that "The principal aim of society is to protect individuals in the enjoyment of those absolute rights, which were vested in them by the immutable laws of nature, but which could not be preserved in peace, without the mutual assistance and intercourse of social communities. The primary end of human laws is to maintain and regulate these absolute rights of individuals."

From Blackstone's perspective, our human laws, rather than proliferating rights arbitrarily, are doing exactly what they are supposed to be doing—identifying and specifying human rights which were never before articulated, particularly in the workplace and particularly for the employee.

The purpose of this essay is to examine the nature of rights and their application in the workplace.

A right can be defined as either a capacity, possession, or condition of existence which entitles either an individual or group to the enjoyment of some object or state of being. For example, the right to free speech is a condition of existence which entitles one to express one's thoughts as one sees fit. Of course, if someone has a right, someone else must have an obligation to respect that right. Hence, a right is a relational entity. In the case of employee rights, there are correlative employer obligations. However, employers have rights too, so that there are also employee duties. However, in this essay we will concentrate on employee rights, rather than the rights of other groups. First, though, we need a clearer idea about what rights are.

Quite simply, rights are entitlements by virtue of which one person justifiably lays claim to an object or state of being against another person, who has an obligation to respect that claim. One respects a claim either by providing the object claimed, assisting in the achievement of the state of being claimed, or, at the very least, not standing in the way of the obtaining of the object or the achieving of the state of being. We add the qualification that the claim is justified, for one could claim a right that was not justified, and, in that case, it would not be a right. Thus, asserting a right carries with it the belief that the entitlement claim is justified. Thus, if an employee has a right to a safe workplace, that employee is justified in claiming that right, and in expecting and demanding that his or her employer meet certain standards in setting up the employee's work area.

Rights are secured either by nature, human laws or societal conventions, including a grant or a purchase. That being so, we can distinguish between three possible types of rights: natural, conventional or civil (legal). Philosophers and jurists split on the issue of whether nature secures any rights. Positivists who deny the existence of natural rights and reduce moral law to the ethos and customs of various societies, necessarily claim that there are only customary (conventional) rights or legal rights, rights which are the result of legislation. Hence, rights apply only to those whom the laws or traditions designate. The difficulty with this positivist position is that, if it were true, every system of rights would be self-legitimating and there could be no claims of natural rights or objective moral rights by which one can evaluate the soundness of the laws or the conventions. Hence, there would be no framework of rights with which to criticize a regime that took away rights from one or another group, e.g. gays, women, Jews.

Those who claim that there are universal rights and that some legal systems such as those which permit slavery are immoral and violate moral rights, must maintain that rights are grounded somehow in the nature of things, or in some sort of objective moral code. Most people implicitly recognize or appeal to such a higher set of rights, called moral rights or natural rights.

But what would those natural rights be grounded in? The most basic grounding would be in the needs of human beings. One is entitled, or has a right, to those things which are necessary for a quality existence. This was the method of philosophically grounding rights in western cultures from the time of Socrates to the modern era, called Natural Law theory. For example, Aquinas, in the thirteenth century, with respect to the right of property asserted that "Whatever is held in superabundance is owed by natural right to those in need." John Locke (1960) in the seventeenth century echoed Aquinas, and argued for the natural rights to life, liberty and property. In line with the theories of Locke, the writers of the American Declaration of Independence claimed basic rights to life, liberty and the pursuit of happiness. For them, as for Locke, these rights were grounded in the fact that our dignity arises from our being children of God. Further, the existence of these rights, and the equality of all men, was thought to be a self-evident truth.

However, Locke added to the right to property argument a consideration of fairness. It is only fair that people be entitled to that for which they work. The notion of a right to property based on need begins to fade with the development of Capitalism, and the later enlightenment figures such as David Hume are skeptical of the self-evidence claim and attempt to ground rights without an appeal to God or Nature. This leads to a more modern approach from either a deontological or utilitarian perspective. Either rights flow from the basic equality and dignity of humans—Immanuel Kant grounds them in the fact that rational beings are ends in themselves—or they flow from the natural needs of humans which must be met to maximize happiness (John Stuart Mill).

Of course, the Utilitarian, Jeremy Bentham (1941) refers to rights as "nonsense on stilts," since from his point of view, the word "right" is just shorthand for securing those actions which will bring about that greatest happiness. From Bentham's perspective one finds rights, not by consulting a catalogue of rights, but by examining whether behavior such as respecting peoples' property leads to more pleasure than pain. His successor, John Stuart Mill grounds rights in the same way. Mill defends the existence of a right to liberty by demonstrating that a society which allows its members to express themselves freely will be a society that is better off (happier) than a society which does not allow such self expression.

Deontologists, following Kant, would maintain that the difficulty with this position is that it makes the rights of individuals susceptible to revocation if they no longer serve the needs of the society. This is incompatible with the notion of inalienable or indefeasible rights, where inalienable means those incapable of being surrendered or transferred, and indefeasible means not capable of being annulled, voided or undone. Of course, Marx, critiquing Kant's individualism maintained that rights are egoistic since they give the individual predominance over the community. Sides of this debate can be seen in contemporaries such as H. L. A. Hart (1955) and Ronald Dworkin (1978).

Whatever the grounding of rights, there are certain other aspects of rights theory that must be mentioned. It is often held that for every right there is a correlative duty. Hence, if I have rights to life and liberty, others have a duty to respect that right and not interfere with my life and liberty.

Since rights is a relational concept, the elucidation of the rights will reflect the view of the relationship. So while in England and Europe, the predominant view of the employer-employee relationship was that of master-servant, with its consequent rights and obligations, in the USA the predominant view of the relationship was as a quasi contractual or implied contractual relationship. Some Pacific Rim countries, of course, have their own cultural version of some sort of quasi familial relationship, with their consequent rights and obligations. Thus, the list of employee rights will vary according to the predominant image of the relationship. For example, if one views the relationship in feudal terms such as lord and serf, then while the serf has few claims to private property and independence, he has large claims to protection and sustenance.

The reciprocity of rights and duties leads to a distinction between positive and negative rights, for if every right has a corresponding duty and rights are based on needs, the question arises who has the duty to provide those goods? Positive rights are rights of recipience. They are claims to entitlement to receive certain goods or services. For example, the right to an education is a positive right. The right to employment is a positive right. Whether such rights exist is a subject of debate, for given the law of reciprocity of rights and duties, if I have a right to education, someone has a correlative obligation to provide the education. If I have a right to employment, someone has the obligation to provide the employment. The last is a difficult kind of claim in a free market society, for how can it be claimed that anyone has an obligation to start a business so that others have employment? If one lays the obligation on the state, then the free market is compromised.

Some argue that it makes sense to claim such rights only when there are facilities to provide the goods available. What sense would it make to claim a right to health care in a society that had no health care delivery systems? It certainly would make sense to claim a need for health care, but that underscores the difference between a right and a need.

Given the above difficulties with the notion of positive rights, some claim that there are only negative rights, for negative rights do not require others to provide the goods or the needs. They are rights that protect those goods or needs. Hence the rights to life, liberty and property are negative rights, for no one has the obligation to provide those goods, only an obligation to respect them which means in essence, not to violate them.

Still, as Stanley I. Benn (1967) says, the positive rights are different, a more modern concept that is the corollary of the equally modern notion of social justice.

Rights of this kind are different in that though they appear to make a very definite claim, the correlative duty seems to rest neither on individuals at large (as with freedoms) nor on anyone in particular. To say, as does the 1948 UN Universal Declaration of Human Rights, that "everyone as a member of society, has the right to social security" (article 22) and "to a standard of living adequate for the health and well-being of himself and his family, including food, clothing, housing" (article 25), is not to say that his government has a duty to provide these things; many who subscribe to this declaration would deny that such services were a government's proper business. Rather, statements of this kind provide, in the words of the Preamble, "a common standard of achievement for all peoples;" that is, they are canons by which social economic, and political arrangements can be criticized. Human rights, in short, are statements of basic needs or interests. They are politically significant as grounds of protest and justification for reforming policies. They differ from appeals to benevolence and charity in that they invoke ideals like justice and equality. A man with a right has no reason to be grateful to benefactors; he has grounds for grievance when it is denied. The concept presupposes a standard below which it is intolerable that a human being should fall—not just in the way that cruelty to an animal is not to be tolerated but, rather, that human deprivations affront some ideal conception of what a human life ought to be like, a conception of human excellence. It is on the face of it unjust that some men enjoy luxuries while others are short of necessities, and to call some interests luxuries and others necessities is implicitly to place them in an order of priorities as claims. Upsetting that order then demands to be justified.

Are rights inalienable? Is not some interference justifiable? The classic case against free speech is that one is not free to shout fire in a crowded theater if there is no fire. Issues of killing in self-defense and in war, and issues of capital punishment, require working out the limits of the indefeasibility. It is helpful to remember that the modern working out of rights was for the purpose of securing a justification for rebelling against governmental authority. Since, one of the primary functions of government was to secure the rights of its citizens. If the government, for no good reason, violated those rights, it failed in its primary task as a government, thereby losing its legitimate authority.

Besides the traditional doctrines on rights, the number of rights articulated have expanded. For example the UN declaration of human rights in article 22, claims that everyone has a right "to a standard of living adequate for the health and well-being of himself and his family, including food, clothing, housing." (This echoes the "right to a living wage" enunciated in the Papal Encyclical *Rerum Novarum,* in 1891.) Others claim rights such as a right to adequate health care. There are contemporary concerns for animal rights. In such contexts, we see clearly that these rights claims are statements of basic needs or interests, either of humans or animals, which rest on criteria for the good life which become a standard by which to judge existing governments and policies.

EMPLOYEE RIGHTS

Given the above we can now sort out various claims about employee rights. Legal rights of employees are simply those that exist through legislation or government regulations. However, claims made about natural rights, or conventional rights of employees will be based on how one views the relationship between employer and employee. The supposed "proliferation of rights" that is taking place in the latter part of the twentieth century, can be best understood as what results from new ways of viewing the employer-employee relationship.

There are philosophers who view employer-employee relationships as reciprocal relationships where moral obligations exist by virtue of those relationships. The primary example of reciprocal relationships are those found in a family. For example, parents are in a relationship with their children where they are obliged to provide for the children's food, shelter, clothing and education. Consequently, the children have rights to receive those things. However, this relationship also gives the parents the right to lay down rules without consultation with the children, a kind of paternalism. Of course, reformers of the nuclear family wish to invest the children with a right to participate in family decisions. Attributing such rights to children, however, alters the view of how the family should operate—and, consequently, what the family is—since, in one sense, a family is described by its nexus and relationships, and the obligations and rights that go with those relationships. Hence, some sets of relationships are in essence moral, since they specify rights and obligations in describing the relationship.

Different views of what the employer-employee relationship is, and ought to be, will yield different claims of rights and obligations on the part of the employer and employee. So, depending on the way the relationship is viewed, different rights will be claimed.

One of the earliest views of the employer-employee relationship was of the master-servant view. That was the successor to the feudal dependency relationship of lord-serf. If we look at the lord-serf relationship, we see that the lord had the obligation to provide for the serf's safety. The serf owed his allegiance and first fruits of his labor to the lord. That means the lord had a right to those first fruits, but the lord, in return, owed to the serf safety and protection. Thus the serf had rights that the lord needed to respect. There were, of course, unscrupulous lords who did not respect those rights, but they are considered evil, or at least some sort of moral slackers. Further, there was a bond of loyalty that was expected. Paternalism was justified and, although there was equality among lords and among serfs, there was no equality between lord and serf. As a matter of fact, it was commonplace for the serf to bow down to the lord in an expression of fealty.

The master-servant relationship, which was an operative paradigm at the beginning of the industrial revolution, was severely critiqued by Marx on the one hand and enlightenment utilitarians on the other. To break the feudal mode, the view of the employer-employee relationship had to be revised away from the master-servant view. It was replaced by the implied contractual view, which simply views the relationship as a contractual relationship of two self-sufficient individuals, agreeing to engage in commerce with one another. One claim against the implied contractual view is that it does not take enough note of the complexity of the relationship between employer and employee.

Since each of these views are analogies to the real situation, the analogies sometimes fit and sometimes do not. A master-servant or slave view is more accurate to the extent that it reflects more the asymmetry of power inherent in some contrac-

tual relationships, particularly involving those employees with no marketable skills. An implied contractual relationship reflects more the equality relationship that is a political desiderata since the enlightenment. Contractual relationships do not carry the baggage of loyalty, which is a virtue, and obligation more in accord with master-servant. Hence, the rights claimed will usually reflect the model of the relationship developed.

The most recent and useful model of the employer-employee relationship in business ethics, superseding the master-slave and implied contract views, that has been developed in recent years is the stakeholder model, according to which the various constituencies of the business are seen as having a stake in the business. In the light of our subject, that means the business will impact on some of the interests of the stakeholders, be they members of the community where the business is located, potential hires, customers, other businesses with whom the company does business, stockholders or employees. If those interests are important, those stakeholder constituencies can make a rights' claim against the business. For example, vendors can claim a right to be paid for their services, but they can do that on the contract view. The consumer movement has claimed that consumers have a right to truthful advertising and a safe, quality product. The government claims a right to taxes. Communities make claims to rights to protection against environmental impurities, and last but not least, employees claim a plethora of rights. Rights expand and multiply as certain things are seen as necessary for a sufficient quality of life, or for the maintenance of one's dignity. We would expect those rights' claims to change as the view of the relationship of employer-employee changes.

Some rights are basic and some are derivative. Some philosophers have claimed that all human rights can be derived from Kant's second Categorical Imperative. "Act so as never to treat another rational being merely as a means to an end." Marx uses this as a moral critique of Capitalism. It reduces the worker to a commodity, a thing. Using someone as a thing is the height of immorality. Note though that Marx had no use for the notion of rights; neither, for that matter, did Jeremy Bentham. Kant's rule requires us to respect other human beings as fellow members of the Kingdom of ends. It is Kant's way of asserting basic human dignity.

Let us look at what specific rights have been claimed for employees in recent times. Such a list, of course, will not be exhaustive; no list of rights is. Nor will this list attempt to order the rights in terms of which are derived from which. To do that would require settling an issue in ethical theory of whether rights are derived from basic necessities for the good life or from the basic requirements necessary to achieve human dignity. In either case, as society changes and life adapts to new circumstances, newly perceived necessities will become candidates for rights. As the employer-employee relationship evolves, new rights will be asserted.

The Right to Work

Clearly, one cannot be an employee unless one is employed, so it seems somewhat odd to talk about the right to work as an employee's right. One can talk of a potential employee's right, but even, in that case, since there is no actual employer, who would have the corresponding obligation to provide a job? However, since having a job is currently an "essential need" or requirement for most people, it can be argued that all able-bodied individuals have a right to a job. So, the right to work would be a right of recipients that leaves it unspecified who has the obligation to provide the work. We cannot require a particular employer to provide a job for a particular individual. What can be claimed is that, if a particular employer has a job to offer, perspective employees, with proper qualifications, have a right to an equal opportunity to attain the job.

Does the person who is "most qualified" have a right to the job? The condition of qualified has force only within the context of a business which has as one of its primary goals, the maximization of productivity. In a family-owned private business, set up for the security of the family, the owner is perfectly within his or her rights to hire any of the children they wish without regard to qualifications, since the owner may have started the business for the specific purpose of providing jobs and financial security for members of the family.

Hence, if there are rights to work, they seem to be delimited by circumstances. It seems the claim that every able-bodied person has a right to work can only make sense if a consequent obligation to provide jobs falls primarily on the state to set up an environment that encourages job creation, and enforces equal opportunity for hiring. This would mean there would seem to be more force to the claim of a right to work within the context of a more socialist state than in a more free market oriented state. Certainly, one of the motivations behind socialism is the feeling of the necessity of providing jobs to the unemployed based on a belief that everyone who is able has a right to a job.

The Right to Meaningful Work

A corollary to the right to work, is the claim of some that there is a right to meaningful work, i.e. a moral claim that tedious, repetitive, and boring work is dehumanizing. As John Ruskin (1968) said, "It is a good and desirable thing, truly, to make many pins in a day; but if we could only see with what crystal sand their points were polished—sand of human soul, much to be magnified before it can be discerned for what it is—we should think there might be some loss in it also." All agree it is a good thing to create jobs that do not alienate or dehumanize, but is the creation of jobs, that have meaning and purpose (whatever that might mean beyond the fact that they provide, through the division of labor a desired good for society), really an obligation of anyone? Is it even possible? There are some jobs that are tedious and distasteful by their very nature. Yet they need to be done.

There is an analogy here with the right to property. Most people want to claim property as their own, as long as it is beneficial for them, but any right to property should carry with it an obligation to protect the rest of society from that property which turns obnoxious. Not all property is beneficial. There is garbage, old cars, junk, and old deserted buildings. Does the right to property entail a right to dispose of it without any obligation, if it is undesirable property? One would think not. There needs to be more attention paid to the downside of property.

Just as there is undesirable property, similarly there are tedious jobs in the world. Society needs someone to do them. The issue of distributive justice must focus on how this burden of the world is to be distributed, as well as the goods of the world. Since some jobs are burdensome, a view that claims a right to meaningful work and equates meaningful work only with jobs that are not burdensome, is seriously flawed in facing reality. At most, what can be claimed is a right of a worker to a job which is made as meaningful as possible. The correlative duty would be for the employers to do what they can to alleviate tediousness, burdensome, and dehumanizing working conditions.

The Rights of the Employee

Once hired, an employee certainly can claim rights such as:

- The right to a safe and healthy work environment
- The right to job security and due process in firing and promoting
- The right to privacy
- The right to compensation for injury
- The right to participation or voice in matters affecting workers
- The right to equal treatment without regard to race or gender
- The right to pension protection
- The rights to collective bargaining such as those established by the National Labor Relations Board
- The right to be free from harassment
- The right to a living wage

We will examine each to see what the claim is based on and to what extent it is justified.

The Right to a Safe and Healthy Work Environment   One can defend the claim that employees have a right to a safe and healthy environment on the grounds that an employer like everyone else is obliged to do no harm. However, such a claim is challenged by some defenders of a free market view which sees the employment relationship as simply a contractual arrangement, wherein both parties are free to accept or reject the terms of the contract. From such a perspective, the worker is seen as free to choose to do the job under whatever circumstances it occurs. If workers desire a safe and healthy environment, then they can refuse to

work under those unsafe conditions. If enough workers refuse, there will be a short supply of workers and the employer will be forced either to develop safer work environments or to pay higher wages to reflect the higher safety risk. Defenders of the right to a safe work environment counter that the employment relationship must be seen in a more realistic light. It is clear that in an urbanized market economy where there are more workers than desirable jobs, there are severe asymmetries of power between employer and employee. Given that fact, the employee is forced to take certain jobs to survive, so that the conditions of a contract—two free and autonomous individuals making an uncoerced choice—are difficult to meet. Consequently, a claim that it is not incumbent on an employer to provide a safe and healthy work environment if the worker chooses to accept a job under such circumstances is disingenuous. Such an attitude justified the sweatshops of the late nineteenth and early twentieth century, but it seems no longer tenable.

Even if the free market contractual approach were tenable, the requirements of the free contract would make it imperative that the prospective employee knows the safety and health risks before going into the situation. So, the perspective employee could claim a right to the knowledge of the *conditions* of the job, as well as a right to some later choice if new and unforeseen health and safety factors come to light. There seems to be no way under either model that an employer can justify withholding such vital information from employees.

Given the realities of the asymmetries of power in the employer-employee relationship, it seems reasonable to assume that there should be a right to a safe and healthy work environment. Further, such a right would necessarily override the right of shareholders to profit maximization. All profit maximization is trumped by other stakeholder rights so the goal of business which is to maximize profits becomes limited to as much profit as possible while respecting the rights of other stakeholders.

The Right to Job Security and the Process in Disciplining, Demoting, Promoting, and Firing   It was long held that the employer had a right to fire employees at will—the core of the doctrine euphemistically named, "employment at will." The arguments were: for the sake of efficiency (a utilitarian argument) and to respect the property rights of owners (a deontological argument), owners were free to fire workers as they wished. The business was the owner's property and the owner had the right to do what he or she willed with that property, including firing employees for whatever reason or no reason.

This view, of course, fails to recognize that the employment relationship is a reciprocal relationship which involves interdependencies between an employer and an employee. Implied or explicit agreements and promises are entered into when a job is offered and accepted. No prospective employees, in their right mind, would *freely* accept a job on the condition that they could be let go on the whim of the employer. The operative word here is *freely*. If one has little or no choice, one accepts to work under conditions that would not otherwise be endured. Reasonable people expect that others have justifiable reasons for what they do. Hence, there is a right to job security which means the person, once hired, has a right to hold that job as long as there are no good reasons for terminating the employment.

Given the right to job security, it is incumbent on the employer to give the employee the right to due process when decisions are made concerning his or her welfare. Such decision involve a renegotiation of the implied understanding. The insistence on due process is made because employers who hold power over the employee is analogous to the US government which holds power over its citizens. Since, to avoid the abuse of power, governments cannot act against its citizens without giving due process and since the employee is in the same subservient relationship to the employer, as the citizen to the government, similar protections need to be given. Hence, there should be right to due process, a right to procedures, including notice and a hearing or process where good reasons for firing or demotion need to be presented. Of course, given that most states in the USA are still employment-at-will states, the right to due process can be no more than a moral right, since it is not recognized as a legal right, except,

of course, where it was negotiated into a contract. However, as we know, provisions in contracts that give power to one or the other party are only negotiated from strength.

The Right to Privacy   The right to privacy is also argued for by drawing an analogy of the employee to the citizen. The right to privacy is not specifically mentioned in the US constitution, but is asserted in the rulings of supreme court justices. Justice Brandeis (1890), one of the first to assert privacy rights, maintained that the right to privacy was "the right to be let alone." The claim to a right to privacy springs from an individualism which asserts that no one has the right to tell another what to do in his or her personal and private life, and also asserts that other people do not have the right to know what goes on in a person's private life if that person does not wish to disclose it. A derivative of the general right to privacy, is of course, the right to freedom in one's off hours, as long as what one does not hurt the employer. Privacy rights, of course, are negative rights. The employer need not do anything except respect an employee's privacy.

There are arguments against privacy rights or, at least, arguments that there are times when those rights can be overridden. Specifically, privacy rights can be overridden when private action *harms* others. That, of course, means the actions are no longer private. Such a stance, however, respects privacy rights much more than an earlier view which held an employer had a right to tell an employee what they could or could not do in his or her private life. Here, we have the question of how much an employer is entitled to demand from an employee which is not job relevant. What are the rights of the employer vis-à-vis the employee?

Defenders of procedures which seem to violate privacy, such as polygraphs and drug testing, defend this invasion of privacy on the grounds that it conflicts with others' rights to a safe workplace. However, that would not be a denial of the right to privacy, only a claim that it conflicts with other rights.

The right to privacy, of course, implies a right to freedom in one's off hours and relates to a different and more controversial rights' claim, the claim that employees have a right to freedom of speech. Now, few contest the right to free expression of opinions, but what if those opinions, possibly gained in working for a company, when publicly expressed, are harmful to that company. The complexity of such issues indicate that a great deal of work needs to be done in resolving the public/private distinction and how it relates to the employer-employee relationship.

The Right to Compensation for Injury   A rather compelling case can be made for a right to compensation for injury, on the basis of economic harm. There are good reasons to believe in compensatory justice. When one person suffers economic harm from another person's activity, the injured party is entitled to compensation. It is the principle that makes parents tell their child to fix or pay for the neighbor's window that the child broke. If I suffer harm in your service, fairness would seem to dictate that you reimburse me for that harm. There is, of course, an exception in the case where the harm was expected and compensation initially took the risk of harm into account, so that the employee was paid more for participating in a high risk job. As in other cases we have seen, the strength of the rights' claim here will rest on the characteristics of the contract or agreement, explicit or implied, between the employer and employee.

The Right to Participation or Voice in Matters Affecting Workers   This is a recently articulated and much more controversial right, but it is a right that flows out of the temper of the times that call for solidarity and total quality control management. As the view of the relationships between owners, managers and employees changes, and as the notion of stakeholder gains ascendancy, the employee is seen as a more and more important player in the corporate culture. Accordingly, in those matters which seriously affect workers, participation in deciding their own fate is seen not so much as a desideratum, but more as a right. The existence of such a right becomes tenable, if one recognizes the asymmetry of power between employer and employee, and how that affects employment agreements. The right is asserted as a foil to ward off the potential abuse of power that can arise from such asymmetry. Existing agreements, to be morally binding, need to be the result of informed mutual consent. If existing implied and explicit contracts or established relationships need to be changed, those affected by the result of the changes ought to have a voice in renegotiating the revisions.

The Right to Equal Treatment without Regard to Race or Gender   Since violations of equal treatment occur in the workplace, it seems obvious that one assert a right to equal treatment without regard to race or gender, where race or gender are irrelevant, as they usually are. This is a general human right, derived from the principle of justice which can be applied to workers specifically.

The Right to Pension Protection   This right is a much more specific right and does not seem too problematic. Given the beliefs in a right to one's own property, or to what one worked for, and granting that the pension is the property of the workers, promised by the employer, it would seem that good stewardship would oblige the companies to protect the pension and not to put it at risk in speculative business projects.

The Right to Organization Bargaining and the Right to Strike   These are, of course, legal rights and established by legislation and regulation in the USA by the NLRB, but there is a moral basis for the NLRB regulations. The US bishops remind us that human nature being what it is, one way to overcome power is to confront it with equal power. In modern industrialized societies with most of the power on the side of corporations, organizations of workers or consumers are indispensable to redress the balance of power. Hence, to gain the power to secure their rights, workers need to be able to organize. To attack the ability to organize is to attack a right essential to human dignity.

The Right to Be Free from Harassment   This right, like the right to equal treatment is a human right, that should not be violated anywhere, let alone in the workplace. Emphasis lately has been on the right to be free from *sexual* harassment, but it is imperative to note that there are other forms of harassment.

The Right to a Living Wage   This is the last employee right we wish to consider. As far back as 1891, Pope Leo XIII, in an encyclical entitled *Rerum Novarum* (Of New Things), articulated a number of employee rights. Among these was the right to a living wage. For him, a living wage was enough to support a family with children, so that the children were adequately cared for. It is debatable how many jobs today pay a living wage. At any rate, the Pope's call for rights was reiterated by the US bishops in 1986. The bishops not only argued for a living wage, they articulated a set of rights. The argument was simple and familiar.

According to the bishops, asymmetry of power presses workers into choosing between an inadequate wage and no wage at all. Justice demands minimum guarantees. "The provision of wages and other benefits sufficient to support a family adequately is a basic necessity to prevent (the) exploitation of workers. The dignity of workers requires adequate health care, security for old age or disability, unemployment compensation, healthful working conditions, weekly rest, periodic holidays for leisure and reasonable security against arbitrary dismissal" (National Council of Catholic Bishops, 1986).

We do not claim that this list is exhaustive, even if it is exhausting. For, if we ground rights on necessity, then as society articulates the new necessities required for living well in a new technologically advanced age, it will also articulate newly discovered goods which will become candidates for rights.

REFERENCES

1. Aquinas, T., *Summa Theologica*. I-II. Q. 66. a.7.
2. Benn, S. I., 1967: Rights. *Encyclopedia of Philosophy*. Vol. 7&8*, 199.
3. Bentham, J. 1941: *Introduction to the Principles of Morals and Legislation*. Blackstone. First published in 1798.
4. Blackstone, W. 1941: *Commentaries on the Law*. Abridged edn. edited by B.C. Gavit. Washington, DC: University of Chicago Press. 26, 68.
5. Brandeis, Justice and Warren, S. 1890. *Harvard Law Review*.
6. Dworkin, R. 1978: *Taking Rights Seriously*. New Impression with a Reply to Critics. London: Duckworth.
7. Hart, H. L. A. 1955: Are there any natural rights? *Philosophical Review*, 64. 212–13.
8. Locke, J. 1960: *Two Treatises of Government*. Cambridge. Edited by P. Laslett. First published in 1690.
9. National Council of Catholic Bishops 1986: Economic justice for all. *Origins*. 16(24). November 27, Washington DC: US Catholic Conference.
10. Ruskin, J. 1968: Stones of Venice. In M. Abrams et al. (eds). *The Norton Anthology of English Literature*, Vol. 2. New York: W. W. Norton, 1295.

Human Rights, Workers' Rights, and the "Right" to Occupational Safety

Tibor R. Machan
Freedom Communications Professor of Free Enterprise and Business Ethics, Argyrus School of Business and Economy, Chapman University

INTRODUCTION

I take the position of the nonbeliever.[1] I do not believe in special workers' rights. I do believe that workers possess rights as human beings, as do publishers, philosophers, disc jockeys, students, and priests. Once fully interpreted, these rights may impose special standards at the workplace, as they may in hospitals, on athletics fields, or in the marketplace.

HUMAN RIGHTS

Our general rights, those we are morally justified to secure by organized force (e.g., government),

---

From *Safety in the Workplace* by Gene O. Norman (and from *Moral Rights in the Workplace,* ed. Gertrude Ezorsky. (Albany: State University of New York Press, 1987)). Reprinted by permission of the author.

are those initially identified by John Locke: life, liberty, and property. [*John Locke* (1632–1704), an English philosopher, was the first systematic theorist of *liberalism*, the view that the state's purpose is to preserve the natural rights of its citizens to life, liberty and property.] That is, we need ask no one's permission to live, to take actions, and to acquire, hold, or use peacefully the productive or creative results of our actions. We may, morally, resist (without undue force) efforts to violate or infringe upon our rights. Our rights are

1. absolute.
2. unalienable, and
3. universal:
   a. in social relations no excuse legitimatizes their violation;
   b. no one can lose these rights, though their exercise may be restricted (e.g., to jail) by what one chooses to do; and
   c. everyone has these rights, whether acknowledged or respected by others or governments or under different descriptions (within less developed conceptual schemes).[2]

I defend this general rights theory elsewhere.[3] Essentially, since adults are rational beings with the moral responsibility to excel as such, a good or suitable community requires these rights as standards. Since this commits one to a virtuously self-governed life, others should respect this as equal members of the community. Willful invasion of these rights—the destruction of (negative) liberty—must be prohibited in human community life.

So-called positive freedom—that is, the enablement to do well in life—presupposes the prior importance of negative freedom. As, what we might call, self-starters, human beings will generally be best off if they are left uninterfered with to take the initiative in their lives.

WORKERS' RIGHTS

What about special workers' rights? There are none. As individuals who intend to hire out their skills for what they will fetch in the marketplace, however, workers have the right to offer these in return for what others, (e.g., employers) will offer

in acceptable compensation. This implies free trade in the labor market.

Any interference with such trade workers (alone or in voluntary cooperation) might want to engage in, with consent by fellow traders, would violate both the workers' and their traders' human rights. Freedom of association would thereby be abridged. (This includes freedom to organize into trade associations, unions, cartels, and so forth.)

Workers' rights advocates view this differently. They hold that the employee-employer relationship involves special duties owed by employers to employees, creating (corollary) rights that governments, given their purpose, should protect, Aside from negative rights, workers are owed respect of their positive rights to be treated with care and consideration.

This, however, is a bad idea. Not to be treated with care and consideration can be open to moral criticism. And lack of safety and health provisions may mean the neglect of crucial values to employees. In many circumstances employers should, morally, provide them.

This is categorically different from the idea of enforcible positive rights. (Later I will touch on unfulfilled reasonable expectations of safety and health provisions on the job!) Adults aren't due such service from free agents whose conduct should be guided by their own judgments and not some alien authority. This kind of moral servitude (abolished after slavery and serfdom) of some by others has been discredited.

Respect for human rights is necessary in a moral society—one needn't thank a person for not murdering, assaulting, or robbing one—whereas being provided with benefits, however crucial to one's well being, is more an act of generosity than a right.

Of course moral responsibilities toward others, even strangers, can arise. When those with plenty know of those with little, help would ordinarily be morally commendable. This can also extend to the employment relationship. Interestingly, however, government "regulation may impede risk-reducing change, freezing us into a hazardous present when a safer future beckons."[4]

My view credits all but the severely incapacitated with the fortitude to be productive and wise when ordering their affairs, workers included. The form of liberation that is then vital to workers is precisely the bourgeois kind: being set free from subjugation to others, including governments. Antibourgeois "liberation" is insultingly paternalistic.[5]

ALLEGING SPECIAL WORKERS' RIGHTS

Is this all gross distortion? Professor Braybrooke tells us, "Most people in our society . . . must look for employment and most (taking them one by one) have no alternative to accepting the working conditions offered by a small set of employers— perhaps one employer in the vicinity."[6] Workers need jobs and cannot afford to quibble. Employers can wait for the most accommodating job prospects.

This in part gives rise to special workers' rights doctrines, to be implemented by government occupational safety, heath and labor-relations regulators, which then "makes it easier for competing firms to heed an important moral obligation and to be, if they wish, humane."[7]

Suppose a disadvantaged worker, seeking a job in a coal mine, asks about safety provision in the mine. Her doing so presupposes that (1) she has other alternatives, and (2) it's morally and legally optional to care about safety at the mine, not due to workers by right. Prior to government's energetic prolabor interventions, safety, health, and related provisions for workers had been lacking. Only legally mandated workers' rights freed workers from their oppressive lot. Thus, workers must by law be provided with safety, health care, job security, retirement, and other vital benefits.

Workers' rights advocates deny that employers have the basic (natural or human) private property rights to give them full authority to set terms of employment. They are seen as nonexclusive stewards of the workplace property, property obtained by way of historical accident, morally indifferent historical necessity, default, or theft. There is no genuine free labor market. There are no jobs to offer since they are not anyone's to give. The picture we should have of the situation is that society should be regarded as a kind of large team or family; the rights of its respective parts (individuals) flow not from their free and independent moral nature, but from the relationship of the needs and usefulness of individuals as regards the purposes of the collective.

By this account, everyone lacks the full authority to enter into exclusive or unilaterally determined and mutual agreements on his or her terms. Such terms—of production, employment, promotion, termination, and so on—would be established, in line with moral propriety, only by the agency (society, God, the party, the democratic assembly) that possesses the full moral authority to set them.

Let us see why the view just stated is ultimately unconvincing. To begin with, the language of rights does not belong within the above framework. That language acknowledges the reality of morally free and independent human beings and includes among them workers, as well as all other adults. Individual human rights assume that within the limits of nature, human beings are all efficacious to varying degrees, frequently depending upon their own choices. Once this individualist viewpoint is rejected, the very foundation for rights language disappears (notwithstanding some contrary contentions).[8]

Some admit that employers are full owners of their property, yet hold that workers, because they are disadvantaged, are owed special duties of care and considerateness, duties which in turn create rights the government should protect. But even if this were right, it is not possible from this position to establish enforcible *public* policy. From the mere existence of *moral* duties employers may have to employees, no enforcible public policy can follow; moral responsibilities require freely chosen fulfillment, not enforced compliance.

Many workers' rights advocates claim that a free labor market will lead to such atrocities as child labor, hazardous and health-impairing working conditions, and so forth. Of course, even if this were true, there is reason to think that OSHA-type regulatory remedies are illusionary. As Peter Huber argues, "regulation of health and safety is not only a major obstacle to technological transformation and innovation but also often aggravates the hazards it is supposed to avoid."[9]

However, it is not certain that a free labor market would lead to child labor and rampant neglect of safety and health at the workplace. Children are, after all, dependents and therefore have rights owed them by their parents. To subject children to hazardous, exploitative work, to deprive them of normal education and health care, could be construed as a violation of their individual rights as young, dependent human beings. Similarly, knowingly or negligently subjecting workers to hazards at the workplace (of which they were not made aware and could not anticipate from reasonable familiarity with the job) constitutes a form of actionable fraud. It comes under the prohibition of the violation of the right to liberty, at times even the right to life. Such conduct is actionable in a court of law and workers, individually or organized into unions, would be morally justified, indeed advised, to challenge it.

A consistent and strict interpretation of the moral (not economic) individualist framework of rights yields results that some advocates of workers' rights are aiming for. The moral force of most attacks on the free labor market framework tends to arise from the fact that some so-called free labor market instances are probably violations of the detailed implications of that approach itself. Why would one be morally concerned with working conditions that are fully agreed to by workers? Such a concern reflects either the belief that there hadn't been any free agreement in the first place, and thus workers are being defrauded, or it reflects a paternalism that, when construed as paternalism proper instead of compassion, no longer carries moral force.

Whatever its motives, paternalism is also insulting and demeaning in its effect. Once it is clear that workers can generate their own (individual and/or collective) response to employers' bargaining power—via labor organizations, insurance, craft associations, and so on—the favorable air of the paternalistic stance diminishes considerably. Instead, workers are seen to be regarded as helpless, inefficacious, inept persons.

THE "RIGHT" TO OCCUPATIONAL SAFETY

Consider an employer who owns and operates a coal mine. (We could have chosen any firm, pri-

vately or "publicly" owned, managed by hired executives with the full consent of the owners, including interested stockholders who have entrusted, by their purchase of stocks, others with the goal of obtaining economic benefits for them.) The firm posts a call for jobs. The mine is in competition with some of the major coal mines in the country and the world. But it is much less prosperous than its competitors. The employer is at present not equipped to run a highly-polished, well-outfitted (e.g., very safe) operation. That may lie in the future, provided the cost of production will not be so high as to make this impossible.

Some of the risks will be higher for workers in this mine than in others. Some of the mineshafts will have badly illuminated stairways, some of the noise will be higher than the levels deemed acceptable by experts, and some of the ventilation equipment will be primitive. The wages, too, will be relatively low in hopes of making the mine eventually more prosperous.

When prospective employees appear and are made aware of the type of job being offered, and its hazards they are at liberty to

a. accept or reject
b. organize into a group and insist on various terms not in the offing,
c. bargain alone or together with others and set terms that include improvements, or
d. pool workers' resources, borrow, and purchase the firm.

To deny that workers could achieve such things is not yet to deny that they are (negatively) free to do so. But to hold that this would be extraordinary for workers (and thus irrelevant in this sort of case) is to

1. assume a historical situation not in force and certainly not necessary,
2. deny workers the capacity for finding a solution to their problems, or
3. deny that workers are capable of initiative.

Now suppose that employers are compelled by law to spend the firm's funds to meet safety requirements deemed desirable by the government regulators. This increased cost of production reduces available funds for additional wages for present and future employees, not to mention available funds for future prospect sites. This is what has happened: The employee-employer relationship has been unjustly intruded upon, to the detriment not only of the mine owners, but also of those who might be employed and of future consumers of energy. The myth of workers' rights is mostly to blame.

CONCLUSION

I have argued that the doctrine of special workers' rights is unsupported and workers, accordingly, possess those rights that all other humans possess, the right to life, liberty, and property. Workers are not a special species of persons to be treated in a paternalistic fashion and, given just treatment in the community, they can achieve their goals as efficiently as any other group of human beings.[10]

NOTES

1. I wish to thank the Earhart, Jon M. Olin, and Reason Foundations for making it possible, in part, for me to work on this project. I also wish to thank Bill Puka and Gertrude Ezorsky for their very valuable criticism of an earlier draft of this essay, despite their very likely disapproval of my views.
2. This observation rests, in part, on epistemological insights available, for example, in Hanna F. Pitkin, *Wittgenstin and Justice* (Berkeley, Calif.: University of California Press, 1972).
3. Tibor R. Machan, "A Reconsideration of Natural Rights Theory," *American Philosophical Quarterly* 19 (January 1980): 61–72.
4. Peter Huber, "Exorcists vs. Gatekeepers in Risk Regulations," *Regulation* (November/December 1983), 23.
5. But see Steven Kelman, "Regulation and Paternalism," *Rights and Regulation,* ed. T. R. Machan and M. B. Johnson (Cambridge, Mass.: Ballinger Publ. Co., 1983), 217–248.
6. David Braybrooke, *Ethics in the World of Business* (Totawa, N.J.: Rowman & Allanheld, 1983), 223.
7. Ibid., 224.
8. For an attempt to forge a collectivist theory of rights, see Tom Campbell, *The Left and Rights* (London and Boston: Routledge & Kegan Paul, 1983).

9. Huber, "Exorcists vs. Gatekeepers," 23.
10. Ibid. Huber observes that "Every insurance company knows that life is growing safer, but the public is firmly convinced that living is becoming ever more hazardous" (p. 23). In general, capitalism's benefits to workers have simply not been acknowledged, especially by moral and political philosophers! It is hardly possible to avoid the simple fact that the workers of the world believe differently, judging by what system they prefer to emigrate to whenever possible.

The Rights and Wrongs of Workplace Snooping

Laura P. Hartman
Assistant Vice President, DePaul University and former Grainger Chair of Business Ethics, University of Wisconsin

Employers have a number of reasons to consider monitoring employee email—more than two million of them, if you ask Chevron Corporation. Recently, the San Francisco-based oil company was required to pay four plaintiffs a total of $2.2 million after their attorneys found email evidence of sexual harassment. The attorneys had found a smoking gun when they located, on Chevron's own email server, an email message that had been sent to a number of people within the company containing a list of jokes about "why beer is better than women." Had Chevron been monitoring its employees' email, it might have seen the problem coming.

Then again, firms have been legally chastised for monitoring employee activities, as well. Recently, the Boston Sheraton settled a law suit brought by its employees for more than $200,000. The employees claimed an invasion of privacy when the hotel had secretly monitored the hotel's employee locker room.

The question of monitoring employee activities is a thorny one, both legally and ethically. Consid-

From *Journal of Business Strategy,* May/June, 1998. © Faulkner & Gray, Inc. Republished with permission.

ering recent increases in employee salaries and corporate liability for employee actions, one might expect employers to be interested, at least, in what their workers are doing.

On the other hand, given the high expectations about employee loyalty and commitment in terms of the number of hours employees spend at their work places, employers can expect that a worker might conduct a bit of personal business during the course of the work day. Achieving balance on this issue is challenging, especially in light of recent advances in technology that allow for intrusions into an employee's personal life in ways never before imagined.

HOW PRIVATE IS THE WORKPLACE?

Today, invasions of privacy in the workplace occur far more frequently than one might expect. In fact, a 1993 study indicated that 30% of 1,000 firms surveyed had searched their employees' computer files, electronic mail, and voicemail, subjecting more than 20 million employees to computer monitoring alone. And a more recent study evidences the explosion of growth in this particular area since the 1993 survey.

A survey conducted and released in May 1997 by the American Management Association revealed that 63% of mid-sized to large firms conduct some form of electronic surveillance. In most cases, the surveillance is relatively benign-video cameras in company lobbies and phone bills that show numbers called from individual extensions. But 35% of the firms the AMA surveyed used more invasive measures for some of their employees, as shown in the table.

A supervisor may have completely justifiable reasons for monitoring employees or for evaluating them based on the results of the monitoring. Having knowledge of employee personal information or emails may be helpful to ensuring compliance with discrimination laws, administering benefits, or placing workers in positions for which they are best suited.

For example, had Chevron monitored email messages, and had its employees known of this practice, employees would have been forewarned that they should send only business-related messages through the system. And had they known email was monitored, it is far less likely that Chevron's email server would have ended up as the repository for a smoking gun.

In addition, the more complicated a task, the more necessary effective work place supervision becomes. Instead of editing a document by using interoffice mail to transmit it from the author to her or his supervisor, the supervisor may choose to save time by simply reading it on the author's computer. On the other hand, workers feel a lack of respect if their bosses are looking over their shoulder at every turn, which may in turn affect productivity or the culture of the workplace.

While some workers believe that they are safe from such intrusions or express no concern about the sharing of their personal information, reports of intrusion horror stories abound. James Russell Wiggins' employer conducted a background check and fired him because the report showed a prior conviction for cocaine possession. Despite Wiggins' protests that the information was patently false, his company refused to rehire him. After it was discovered that his identity had been confused

Electronic Surveillance in the Workplace	
Type of Monitoring	**Percent of Firms**
Videotaping Employee Activities	15.7%
Reviewing Email Messages	14.9%
Reviewing Computer Files	13.7%
Taping Telephone Conversations	10.4%
Taping and Reviewing Voicemail Messages	5.3%

FIGURE 1
Electronic Surveillance in the Workplace
Source: American Management Association, http://www.amanet.org

with that of James Ray Wiggins, a lawsuit ensued, which remains in the courts today. Indeed, according to a Congressional report, half of all credit reports and background checks contain mistakes.

The American worker is becoming more aware of the possibility for intrusions or violation, as well. A survey conducted by Louis Harris & Associates and Dr. Alan Westin showed that 89% of the American public is concerned about threats to their personal privacy, with 55.5% saying that they are "very concerned."

While no related case has yet reached the Supreme Court, these actions have received lower court attention. As early as 1990, Torrance, Calif.-based Epson America survived a lawsuit filed by a terminated employee who had complained about Epson's practice of reading all employee email. The court found in favor of the Epson because the employees were notified that their email may be monitored.

However, relying on court precedent for protection is a double-edged sword. An employee-plaintiff in one federal action won a case against his employer where the employer had monitored the worker's telephone for a period of 24 hours in order to determine whether the worker was planning a robbery. The court held that the company had gone too far and had insufficient evidence to support its claims. In another action, Northern Telecom settled a claim brought by employees who were allegedly secretly monitored over a 13-year period. In this case, the Brampton, Ontario-based telecom company agreed to pay $50,000 to individual plaintiffs and $125,000 for attorneys' fees.

MIRACLES OF MODERN TECHNOLOGY

Undisclosed or disclosed monitoring of employees has reached new proportions with the ease and availability of clandestine monitors. Counter Spy Shop, a division of New York-based CCS Group, has retail outlets in several large cities and specializes in selling high technology gear for monitoring purposes. The firm, which does business on the Internet as well as through a traditional sales force, sells devices that allow companies to conduct covert audio and video surveillance, as well as items that can encrypt or scramble any of the

firm's transmissions (to ward off potential corporate sabateurs).

According to Counter Spy Shop's sales manager Tom Felice, "the more discreet the devices are, the more popular." And Felice says that one-third of the Fortune 500 shops at the Counter Spy Shop. The Counter Spy Shop sells not only traditional monitoring equipment, but also such scientifically questionable devices as one that tells the caller whether the individual on the other end of the line is telling the truth. The device uses voice stress analysis of voice tremors in order to determine whether the individual is lying and costs about $5,000.

Technology has produced other far less traditional methods of monitoring. One product is called the Truth Phone. Manufactured by New York-based Communication Control Systems, it promises to analyze voices during telephone calls in order to detect possible deception. And New Jersey-based Net/Tech sells Hygiene Guard, a product that tracks whether employees are using soap dispensers and washing their hands after they use the restroom. If they fail to do so, the device may beep periodically or flash to alert supervisors. Not surprisingly, few employees are fans of Hygiene Guard: "They're starting with these little badges. The next thing, they're using video cameras. Some people feel violated. It's an insult," claims a union employee. The local union in one case is concerned that the purpose of the badges is not too ensure clean hands, but to protect against workers who linger too long or make too many trips to the restrooms.

COMPUTER MONITORING

Because many employees use personal computers on the job, and because those computers are often linked either to the Internet or, at least, to an internal network, monitoring employees has become simpler. But the reasons employers have for monitoring have become more complex.

For example, assume that ABC Corp. employees repeatedly access specific locations of competitors' web sites looking for competitive information. By tracking those hits, ABC's competitors might learn which of their technology interests ABC's employees, and this may give competitors insight into the direction of ABC's research and development.

Further, firms have reason for concern if employees download program files without compensating the creator or use copywritten information from the Web without giving credit to the original author. These actions can expose the firm to potentially significant copyright infringement liability.

Finally, Internet access makes a company vulnerable not only to unauthorized access by hackers but also to numerous viruses, which employees can inadvertently introduce to company systems by downloading software programs from the Web or even simply exchanging email with others outside the company.

In fact, email raises a host of additional questions. Monitoring these transmissions is becoming more common in corporate America and elementary to even the most basic technician. Employers may monitor email transmission to make sure their trade secrets remain secret or to ensure that email is used only for business purposes. They also may want to maintain consistent quality of everything that goes out under the firm's "letterhead." In other words, when an employee sends an email using a company-provided email server, usually the firm's name is identifiable through the individual's email address. A firm should be just as concerned about what goes out above that email signature as it is about what goes out on its letterhead in order to ensure that inappropriate communications are not considered "employer authorized" in a legal context.

WHAT'S FAIR IN WORK AND MONITORING?

While no one would feel their privacy had been invaded if their manager decided to read over a business letter to a client before the employee mailed the letter, drawing the line between that which is personal and that which is public can be difficult.

Employers argue that monitoring is an effective means to ensure a safe and secure working environment and to protect individuals and the firm's assets or resources. And some employers contend that monitoring may boost efficiency, productivity, and customer service, and allows them to more accurately evaluate performance.

For example, monitoring is considered to be a "real time" aid to performance appraisals. Super-

visors have easy, immediate access to information that will help them in their nurturing and evaluation of their employees. Consider the impact of telephone monitoring on the evaluation of a customer service representative. The supervisor who monitors telephone calls to the service desk can now truly review her or his employees at work.

But critics of monitoring point to research evidencing a link between monitoring and psychological and physical health problems, increased boredom, high tension, extreme anxiety, depression, anger, severe fatigue, and musculoskeletal problems. In his 1992 research, Swiss economist Bruno Frey found evidence that monitoring worsened employee morale and thereby negatively affected performance. Monitored employees tended to believe their employer had low expectations of them (because the firm felt the need to monitor), so they, in essence, lived down to those expectations. In addition, critics of monitoring are concerned with the employee's legitimate expectation of privacy in certain areas of the working environment, and whether the employees are notified of the presence of monitoring.

Under common law, unreasonable intrusions into employees' private affairs are prohibited. An invasion of privacy, called "intrusion into seclusion," is defined as "intentional intrusion upon the solitude or seclusion of another that is highly offensive to a reasonable person." Private sector employees, therefore, have privacy in those areas in which they have a legitimate expectation of privacy—a restroom or changing room, for instance. In *K-Mart v. Trotti*, the court held that the search of an employee's company-owned locker was an unlawful invasion of privacy since the employees used their own locks and therefore had a reasonable expectation of privacy. But the law is murky on this issue; for example, an employer's search of employee lunch buckets was held reasonable by another court.

Employees obviously would have no reasonable expectation of privacy if an employer notifies them that they will be monitored in specific situations during specific times. But notification does not provide complete immunity from charges of invasion of privacy. A Kansas District Court remarked that "a reasonable person could find it highly offensive that an employer records an employee's personal phone calls in the circumstances where the employer did not discourage employees from making personal calls at their desks and did not inform the plaintiff employees that their personal calls would be recorded." When applied to email, this finding suggests that an employee has a reasonable expectation of privacy if an employer issues an employee a password or suggests that email is confidential.

ETHICAL CONSIDERATIONS

That is what the law says. But what is the ethical answer? In the case of employee privacy relating to monitoring, the employer must make a decision about how to handle the need to supervise and to evaluate workers. The first step of the process is to determine the values of the firm. This step may already have been taken if the firm has developed a mission or statement of principles.

Next, the employer must consider whether monitoring satisfies the goals or mission of the firm. Assuming it does (since a negative relationship here would end the discussion and resolve the dilemma), the employer must be accountable to those affected by the decision to monitor by considering their personal interests.

In order to respect employees' privacy rights and their right to make informed decisions about their actions, the employer should give adequate notice of the intent to monitor, including the form of monitoring, its frequency, and the purpose of the monitoring.

In addition, in order to balance the employers interests with those of the work force, the employer should offer a means by which the employee can control the monitoring to create personal boundaries. For example, if the employer is randomly monitoring telephone calls, there should be a notification device such as a beep on the line whenever monitoring is taking place or the employee should have the ability to block any monitoring during personal calls.

If you're thinking of monitoring your employees, Kevin Conlon, district counsel for the Communication Workers of America, suggests that you follow these guidelines:

1. There should be no monitoring in highly private areas, such as restrooms.
2. Monitoring should be limited to the workplace.
3. Employees should have full access to any information gathered through monitoring.
4. Continuous monitoring should be banned.
5. All forms of secret monitoring should be banned. Employees should always be given advance notice of monitoring.
6. Only information relevant to the job should be collected.
7. Monitoring should result in the attainment of some business interest.

A monitoring program developed according to these strictures not only respects the personal autonomy of the individual worker, but also allows the employer to supervise effectively the work done, to protect against misuse of resources, and provides an appropriate mechanism by which to evaluate each worker's performance.

Drug Testing in Employment

Joseph R. DesJardins
Professor and Head, Department of Philosophy,
College of St. Benedict/Saint John's University

Ronald Duska
Charles Lamont Post Chair of Ethics and the Professions,
American College, and former Executive Director,
Society for Business Ethics

According to one survey, nearly one-half of all *Fortune* 500 companies were planning to administer drug tests to employees and prospective employees by the end of 1987.[1] Counter to what

---

Excerpted from "Drug Testing in Employment" by J. R. DesJardins and R. Duska, *Business and Professional Ethics Journal,* volume 6, number 3, Fall 1987, pp. 3–21. Copyright by J. R. DesJardins and R. Duska. Printed by permission of the authors.
[*Author's note:* Versions of this paper were read to the Department of Philosophy at Southern Connecticut State College and to the Society of Business Ethics. The authors would like to thank those people, as well as Robert Baum and Norman Bowie and the editors of *Business and Professional Ethics Journal,* for their many helpful comments.]

seems to be the current trend in favor of drug testing, we will argue that it is rarely legitimate to override an employee's or applicant's right to privacy by using such tests or procedures.[2]

OPENING STIPULATIONS

We take privacy to be an "employee right" by which we mean a presumptive moral entitlement to receive certain goods or be protected from certain harms in the workplace.[3] Such a right creates a *prima facie* obligation on the part of the employer to provide the relevant goods or, as in this case, refrain from the relevant harmful treatment. These rights prevent employees from being placed in the fundamentally coercive position where they must choose between their job and other basic human goods.

Further, we view the employer-employee relationship as essentially contractual. The employer-employee relationship is an economic one and, unlike relationships such as those between a government and its citizens or a parent and a child, exists primarily as a means for satisfying the economic interests of the contracting parties. The obligations that each party incurs are only those that it voluntarily takes on. Given such a contractual relationship, certain areas of the employee's life remain their own private concern and no employer has a right to invade them. On these presumptions we maintain that certain information about an employee is rightfully private, i.e. the employee has a right to privacy.

THE RIGHT TO PRIVACY

According to George Brenkert, a right to privacy involves a three-place relation between a person A, some information X, and another person B. The right to privacy is violated only when B deliberately comes to possess information X about A, and no relationship between A and B exists which would justify B's coming to know X about A.[4] Thus, for example, the relationship one has with a mortgage company would justify that company's coming to know about one's salary, but the relationship one has with a neighbor does not justify the neighbor's coming to know that information.

Hence, an employee's right to privacy is violated whenever personal information is requested, collected and/or used by an employer in a way or for any purpose that is *irrelevant to* or *in violation of* the contractual relationship that exists between employer and employees.

Since drug testing is a means for obtaining information, the information sought must be relevant to the contract in order for the drug testing not to violate privacy. Hence, we must first decide if knowledge of drug use obtained by drug testing is job relevant. In cases where the knowledge of drug use is *not* relevant, there appears to be no justification for subjecting employees to drug tests. In cases where information of drug use is job relevant, we need to consider if, when, and under what conditions using a means such as drug testing to obtain that knowledge is justified.

IS KNOWLEDGE OF DRUG USE JOB RELEVANT INFORMATION?

There seem to be two arguments used to establish that knowledge of drug use is job relevant information. The first argument claims that drug use adversely affects job performance thereby leading to lower productivity, higher costs, and consequently lower profits. Drug testing is seen as a way of avoiding these adverse effects. According to some estimates twenty-five billion ($25,000,000,000) dollars are lost each year in the United States because of drug use.[5] This occurs because of loss in productivity, increase in costs due to theft, increased rates in health and liability insurance, and such. Since employers are contracting with an employee for the performance of specific tasks, employers seem to have a legitimate claim upon whatever personal information is relevant to an employee's ability to do the job.

The second argument claims that drug use has been and can be responsible for considerable harm to the employee him/herself, fellow employees, the employer, and/or third parties, including consumers. In this case drug testing is defended because it is seen as a way of preventing possible harm. Further, since employers can be held liable for harms done both to third parties, e.g. customers, and to the employee or his/her fellow employees, knowledge of employee drug use will allow employers to gain information that can protect themselves from risks such as liability. But how good are these arguments? We turn to examine the arguments more closely.

THE FIRST ARGUMENT: JOB PERFORMANCE AND KNOWLEDGE OF DRUG USE

The first argument holds that drug use leads to lower productivity and consequently implies that a knowledge of drug use obtained through drug testing will allow an employer to increase productivity. It is generally assumed that people using certain drugs have their performances affected by such use. Since enhancing productivity is something any employer desires, any use of drugs that reduces productivity affects the employer in an undesirable way, and that use is, then, job relevant. If such production losses can be eliminated by knowledge of the drug use, then knowledge of that drug use is job relevant information.

On the surface this argument seems reasonable. Obviously some drug use in lowering the level of performance can decrease productivity. Since the employer is entitled to a certain level of performance and drug use adversely affects performance, knowledge of that use seems job relevant.

But this formulation of the argument leaves an important question unanswered. To what level of performance are employers entitled? Optimal performance, or some lower level? If some lower level, what? Employers have a valid claim upon some *certain level* of performance, such that a failure to perform up to this level would give the employer a justification for disciplining, firing or at least finding fault with the employee. But that does not necessarily mean that the employer has a right to a maximum or optimal level of performance, a level above and beyond a certain level of acceptability. It might be nice if the employee gives an employer a maximum effort or optimal performance, but that is above and beyond the call of the employee's duty and the employer can hardly claim a right at all times to the highest level of performance of which an employee is capable.

That there are limits on required levels of performance and productivity becomes clear if we recognize that job performance is person-related. It is person-related because one person's best efforts at a particular task might produce results well below the norm, while another person's minimal efforts might produce results abnormally high when compared to the norm. For example a professional baseball player's performance on a ball field will be much higher than the average person's since the average person is unskilled at baseball. We have all encountered people who work hard with little or no results as well as people who work little with phenomenal results. Drug use by very talented people might diminish their performance or productivity, but that performance would still be better than the performance of the average person or someone totally lacking in the skills required. That being said, the important question now is whether the employer is entitled to an employee's maximum effort and best results, or merely to an effort sufficient to perform the task expected.

If the relevant consideration is whether the employee is producing as expected (according to the normal demands of the position and contract) not whether he/she is producing as much as possible, then knowledge of drug use is irrelevant or unnecessary. Let's see why.

If the person is producing what is expected, knowledge of drug use on the grounds of production is irrelevant since, *ex hypothesi* the production is satisfactory. If, on the other hand, the performance suffers, then, to the extent that it slips below the level justifiably expected, the employer has *prima facie* grounds for warning, disciplining or releasing the employee. But the justification for this is the person's unsatisfactory performance, not the person's use of drugs. Accordingly, drug use information is either unnecessary or irrelevant and consequently there are not sufficient grounds to override the right of privacy. Thus, unless we can argue that an employer is entitled to optimal performance, the argument fails.

This counter-argument should make it clear that the information which is job relevant, and consequently which is not rightfully private, is information about an employee's level of perform-ance and not information about the underlying causes of that level. The fallacy of the argument which promotes drug testing in the name of in-creased productivity is the assumption that each employee is obliged to perform at an optimal, or at least, quite high level. But this is required under few, if any, contracts. What is required contractu-ally is meeting the normally expected levels of production or performing the tasks in the job-description adequately (not optimally). If one can do that under the influence of drugs, then on the grounds of job performance at least, drug use is rightfully private. If one cannot perform the task adequately, then the employee is not fulfilling the contract, and knowledge of the cause of the failure to perform is irrelevant on the contractual model.

Of course, if the employer suspects drug use or abuse as the cause of the unsatisfactory perfor-mance, then she might choose to help the person with counseling or rehabilitation. However, this does not seem to be something morally required of the employer. Rather, in the case of unsatisfactory performance, the employer has a *prima facie* justifi-cation for dismissing or disciplining the employee.

THE SECOND ARGUMENT: HARM AND THE KNOWLEDGE OF DRUG USE TO PREVENT HARM

Even though the performance argument is inade-quate, there is an argument that seems somewhat stronger. This is an argument that takes into ac-count the fact that drug use often leads to harm. Using a type of Millian argument that allows inter-ference with a person's rights in order to prevent harm, we could argue that drug testing might be justified if such testing led to knowledge that would enable an employer to prevent harm.

Drug use certainly can lead to harming others. Consequently, if knowledge of such drug use can prevent harm, then, knowing whether or not one's employee uses drugs might be a legitimate con-cern of an employer in certain circumstances. This second argument claims that knowledge of the employee's drug use is job relevant because em-ployees who are under the influence of drugs can

pose a threat to the health and safety of themselves and others, and an employer who knows of that drug use and the harm it can cause has a responsi-bility to prevent it. Employers have both a general duty to prevent harm and the specific responsibil-ity for harms done by their employees. Such re-sponsibilities are sufficient reason for an employer to claim that information about an employee's drug use is relevant if that knowledge can prevent harm by giving the employer grounds for dismiss-ing the employee or not allowing him/her to per-form potentially harmful tasks. Employers might even claim a right to reduce unreasonable risks, in this case the risks involving legal and economic li-ability for harms caused by employees under the influence of drugs, as further justification for knowing about employee drug use.

But let us examine this more closely. Upon ex-amination, certain problems arise, so that even if there is a possibility of justifying drug testing to prevent harm, some caveats have to be observed and some limits set out.

Jobs with Potential to Cause Harm

In the first place, it is not clear that every job is one with a potential to cause harm, or at least with potential to cause harm sufficient to override a *prima facie* right to privacy. To say that employers can use drug testing where that can prevent harm is not to say that every employer has the right to know about the drug use of every employee. Not every job poses a serious enough threat to justify an employer coming to know this information.

In deciding which jobs pose serious enough threats certain guidelines should be followed. First the potential for harm should be *clear* and *present*. Perhaps all jobs in some extended way pose poten-tial threats to human well-being. We suppose an accountant's error could pose a threat of harm to someone somewhere. But some jobs like those of airline pilots, school bus drivers, public transit drivers and surgeons, are jobs in which unsatisfac-tory performance poses a clear and present danger to others. It would be much harder to make an ar-gument that job performances by auditors, secre-taries, executive vice-presidents for public rela-tions, college teachers, professional athletes, and the like, could cause harm if those performances were carried on under the influence of drugs. They would cause harm only in exceptional cases.[6]

Not Every Person Is to Be Tested

But, even if we can make a case that a particular job involves a clear and present danger for causing harm if performed under the influence of drugs, it is not appropriate to treat everyone holding such a job the same. Not every job-holder is equally threatening. There is less reason to investigate an airline pilot for drug use if that pilot has a twenty-year record of exceptional service than there is to investigate a pilot whose behavior has become erratic and unreliable recently, or than one who reports to work smelling of alcohol and slurring his words. Presuming that every airline pilot is equally threatening is to deny individuals the respect that they deserve as autonomous, rational agents. It is to ignore previous history and significant differences. It is also probably inefficient and leads to the lowering of morale. It is the likelihood of causing harm, and not the fact of being an airline pilot *per se,* that is relevant in deciding which employees in critical jobs to test.

So, even if knowledge of drug use is justifiable to prevent harm, we must be careful to limit this justification to a range of jobs and people where the potential for harm is clear and present. The jobs must be jobs that clearly can cause harm, and the specific employee should not be someone who is reliable with a history of such reliability. Finally, the drugs being tested should be those drugs, the use of which in those jobs is really potentially harmful.

LIMITATIONS ON DRUG TESTING POLICIES

Even when we identify those jobs and individuals where knowledge of drug use would be job relevant information, we still need to examine whether some procedural limitations should not be placed upon the employer's testing for drugs. We have said that in cases where a real threat of harm exists and where evidence exists suggesting that a particular employee poses such a threat, an employer

could be justified in knowing about drug use in order to prevent the potential harm. But we need to recognize that as long as the employer has the discretion for deciding when the potential for harm is clear and present, and for deciding which employees pose the threat of harm, the possibility of abuse is great. Thus, some policy limiting the employer's power is called for.

Just as criminal law places numerous restrictions protecting individual dignity and liberty on the state's pursuit of its goals, so we should expect that some restrictions be placed on an employer in order to protect innocent employees from harm (including loss of job and damage to one's personal and professional reputation). Thus, some system of checks upon an employer's discretion in these matters seems advisable. Workers covered by collective bargaining agreements or individual contracts might be protected by clauses in those agreements that specify which jobs pose a real threat of harm (e.g. pilots but not cabin attendants) and what constitutes a just cause for investigating drug use. Local, state, and federal legislatures might do the same for workers not covered by employment contracts. What needs to be set up is a just employment relationship—one in which an employee's expectations and responsibilities are specified in advance and in which an employer's discretionary authority to discipline or dismiss an employee is limited.

Beyond that, any policy should accord with the nature of the employment relationship. Since that relationship is a contractual one, it should meet the condition of a morally valid contract, which is informed consent. Thus, in general, we would argue that only methods that have received the informed consent of employees can be used in acquiring information about drug use.[7]

A drug-testing policy that requires all employees to submit to a drug test or to jeopardize their job would seem coercive and therefore unacceptable. Being placed in such a fundamentally coercive position of having to choose between one's job and one's privacy does not provide the conditions for a truly free consent. Policies that are unilaterally established by employers would likewise be unacceptable. Working with employees to develop company policy seems the only way to insure that the policy will be fair to both parties. Prior notice of testing would also be required in order to give employees the option of freely refraining from drug use. It is morally preferable to prevent drug use than to punish users after the fact, since this approach treats employees as capable of making rational and informed decisions.

Further procedural limitations seem advisable as well. Employees should be notified of the results of the test, they should be entitled to appeal the results (perhaps through further tests by an independent laboratory) and the information obtained through tests ought to be kept confidential. In summary, limitations upon employer discretion for administering drug tests can be derived from the nature of the employment contract and from the recognition that drug testing is justified by the desire to prevent harm, not the desire to punish wrongdoing.

EFFECTIVENESS OF DRUG TESTING

Having declared that the employer might have a right to test for drug use in order to prevent harm, we still need to examine the second argument a little more closely.

It is important to keep in mind that: (1) if the knowledge doesn't help prevent the harm, the testing is not justified on prevention grounds; (2) if the testing doesn't provide the relevant knowledge it is not justified either; and finally, (3) even if it was justified, it would be undesirable if a more effective means of preventing harm were discovered.

Upon examination, the links between drug testing, knowledge of drug use, and prevention of harm are not as clear as they are presumed to be. As we investigate, it begins to seem that the knowledge of the drug use even though relevant in some instances is not the most effective means to prevent harm.

Let us turn to this last consideration first. Is drug testing the most effective means for preventing harm caused by drug use?

Consider. If someone exhibits obviously drugged or drunken behavior, then this behavior itself is grounds for preventing the person from continuing in the job. Administering urine or blood tests, sending the specimens out for testing and waiting for a response, will not prevent harm in this instance. Such drug testing because of the time lapse involved, is equally superfluous in those cases where an employee is in fact under the influence of drugs, but exhibits no or only subtly impaired behaviour.

Thus, even if one grants that drug testing somehow prevents harm an argument can be made that there might be much more effective methods of preventing potential harm such as administering dexterity tests of the type employed by police in possible drunk-driving cases, or requiring suspect pilots to pass flight simulator tests.[8] Eye-hand coordination, balance, reflexes, and reasoning ability can all be tested with less intrusive, more easily administered, reliable technologies which give instant results. Certainly if an employer has just cause for believing that a specific employee presently poses a real threat of causing harm, such methods are just more effective in all ways than are urinalysis and blood testing.

Even were it possible to refine drug tests so that accurate results were immediately available, that knowledge would only be job relevant if the drug use was clearly the cause of impaired job performance that could harm people. Hence, testing behavior still seems more direct and effective in preventing harm than testing for the presence of drugs *per se*.

In some cases, drug use might be connected with potential harms not by being causally connected to motor-function impairment, but by causing personality disorders (e.g. paranoia, delusions, etc.) that affect judgmental ability. Even though in such cases a *prima facie* justification for urinalysis or blood testing might exist, the same problems of effectiveness persist. How is the knowledge of the drug use attained by urinalysis and/or blood testing supposed to prevent the harm? Only if there is a causal link between the use and the potentially harmful behavior would such knowledge be relevant. Even if we get the results of the test immediately, there is the necessity to have an established causal link between specific drug use and anticipated harmful personality disorders in specific people.

But even when this link is established, it would seem that less intrusive means could be used to detect the potential problems, rather than relying upon the assumption of a causal link. Psychological tests of judgment, perception and memory, for example, would be a less intrusive and more direct means for acquiring the relevant information, which is, after all, the likelihood of causing harm and not the presence of drugs *per se*. In short, drug testing even in these cases doesn't seem to be very effective in preventing harm on the spot.

Still, this does not mean it is not effective at all. Where it is most effective in preventing harm is in its getting people to stop using drugs or in identifying serious drug addiction. Or to put it another way, urinalysis and blood tests for drug use are most effective in preventing potential harm when they serve as a deterrent to drug use *before* it occurs, since it is very difficult to prevent harm by diagnosing drug use *after* it has occurred but before the potentially harmful behavior takes place.

Drug testing can be an effective deterrent when there is regular or random testing of all employees. This will prevent harm by inhibiting (because of the fear of detection) drug use by those who are occasional users and those who do not wish to be detected.

It will probably not inhibit or stop the use by the chronic addicted user, but it will allow an employer to discover the chronic user or addict, assuming that the tests are accurately administered and reliably evaluated. If the chronic user's addiction would probably lead to harmful behavior to others, the harm is prevented by taking that user off the job. Thus regular or random testing will prevent harms done by deterring the occasional user and by detecting the chronic user.

But we have said that testing without probable cause is unacceptable. Any type of regular testing of all employees is unacceptable. We have argued that testing employees without first establishing probable cause is an unjustifiable violation of employee privacy. Given this, and given the expense of general and regular testing of all employees (especially if this is done by responsible laboratories), it is more likely that random testing will be employed as the means of deterrence. But surely testing of randomly selected innocent employees is as intrusive to those tested as is regular testing. The argument that there will be fewer tests is correct on quantitative grounds, but qualitatively the intrusion and unacceptability are the same. The claim that employers should be allowed to sacrifice the well-being of (some few) innocent employees to deter (some equally few) potentially harmful employees seems, on the face of it, unfair. Just as we do not allow the state randomly to tap the telephones of just any citizen in order to prevent crime, so we ought not to allow employers to drug test all employees randomly to prevent harm. To do so is again to treat innocent employees solely as a means to the end of preventing potential harm.

This leaves only the use of regular or random drug testing as a deterrent in those cases where probable cause exists for believing that a particular employee poses a threat of harm. It would seem that in this case, the drug testing is acceptable. In such cases only the question of effectiveness remains: Are the standard techniques of urinalysis and blood testing more effective means for preventing harms than alternatives such as dexterity tests? It seems they are effective in different ways. The dexterity tests show immediately if someone is incapable of performing a task, or will perform one in such a way as to cause harm to others. The urinalysis and blood-testing will prevent harm indirectly by getting the occasional user to curtail their use, and by detecting the habitual or addictive user, which will allow the employer to either give treatment to the addictive personality or remove them from the job. Thus we can conclude that drug testing is effective in a limited way, but aside from inhibiting occasional users because of fear of detection, and discovering habitual users, it seems problematic that it does much to prevent harm that couldn't be achieved by other means.

In summary, then, we have seen that drug use is not always job relevant, and if drug use is not job relevant, information about it is certainly not job relevant. In the case of performance it may be a cause of some decreased performance, but it is the performance itself that is relevant to an employee's position, not what prohibits or enables him to do the job. In the case of potential harm being done by an employee under the influence of drugs, the drug use seems job relevant, and in this case drug testing to prevent harm might be legitimate. But how this is practical is another question. It would seem that standard motor dexterity or mental dexterity tests, immediately prior to job performance, are more efficacious ways of preventing harm, unless one concludes that drug use invariably and necessarily leads to harm. One must trust the individuals in any system in order for that system to work. One cannot police everything. It might work to randomly test people, to find drug users, and to weed out the few to forestall possible future harm, but are the harms prevented sufficient to over-ride the rights of privacy of the people who are innocent and to overcome the possible abuses we have mentioned? It seems not.

Clearly, a better method is to develop safety checks immediately prior to the performance of a job. Have a surgeon or a pilot or a bus driver pass a few reasoning and motor-skill tests before work. The cause of the lack of a skill, which lack might lead to harm, is really a secondary issue.

NOTES

1. *The New Republic,* March 31, 1986.
2. This trend primarily involves screening employees for such drugs as marijuana, cocaine, amphetamines, barbiturates, and opiates (e.g., heroin, methadone and morphine). While alcohol is also a drug that can be abused in the workplace, it seldom is among the drugs mentioned in conjunction with employee testing. We believe that testing which proves justified for controlled substances will, *a fortiori,* be justified for alcohol as well.
3. "A Defense of Employee Rights," Joseph Des Jardins and John McCall, *Journal of Business Ethics* 4, (1985). We should emphasize that our concern is with the *moral* rights of privacy for employees and not with any specific or prospective *legal* rights. Readers interested in pursuing the legal aspects of employee drug testing should consult: "Workplace Privacy Issues and Employer Screening Policies" by Richard Lehr and David Middlebrooks in *Employee Relations Law Journal* (Vol. 11, no. 3), pp. 407–21; and "Screening Workers for Drugs: A Legal and Ethical Framework" by Mark Rothstein, in *Employee Relations Law Journal* (Vol. 11, no. 3), pp. 422–36.
4. "Privacy, Polygraphs, and Work," George Brenkert, *Journal of Business and Professional Ethics* vol. 1, no. 1 (Fall 1981). For a more general discussion of privacy in the workplace see "Privacy in Employment" by Joseph Des Jardins, in *Moral Rights in the Workplace* edited by Gertrude Ezorsky (SUNY Press, 1987). A good resource for philosophical work on privacy can be found in "Recent Work on the Concept of Privacy" by W.A. Parent, in *American Philosophical Quarterly* (Vol. 20, Oct. 1983), pp. 341–56.
5. *U.S. News & World Report* Aug. 1983; *Newsweek* May 1983.
6. Obviously we are speaking here of harms that go beyond the simple economic harm which results from unsatisfactory job performance. These economic harms were discussed in the first argument above. Further, we ignore such "harms" as providing bad role-models for adolescents, harms often used to justify drug tests for professional athletes. We think it unreasonable to hold an individual responsible for the image he/she provides to others.
7. The philosophical literature on informed consent is often concerned with "informed consent" in a medical context. For an interesting discussion of informed consent in the workplace, see Mary Gibson, *Worker's Rights* (Rowman and Allanheld, 1983), especially pp. 13–14 and 74–75.
8. For a reiteration of this point and a concise argument against drug testing see Lewis L. Maltby, "Why Drug Testing Is a Bad Idea," *Inc.* June, 1987, pp. 152–153. "But the fundamental flaw with drug testing is that it tests for the wrong thing. A realistic program to detect workers whose condition puts the company or other people at risk would test for the condition that actually creates the danger. The reason drunk or stoned airline pilots and truck drivers are dangerous is their reflexes, coordination, and timing are deficient. This impairment could come from many situations—drugs, alcohol, emotional problems—the list is almost endless. A serious program would recognize that the real problem is workers' impairment, and test for that. Pilots can be tested in flight simulators. People in other jobs can be tested by a trained technician in about 20 minutes—at the job site." p. 152.

Drug Testing in the Workplace: Whose Rights Take Precedence?

Michael Waldholz
Staff Reporter, *The Wall Street Journal*

Amid growing national concern over substance abuse, drug testing in the workplace has become an explosive issue.

To those who support it, testing, which is commonly done through urinalysis, is often a question of protecting business interests. "For us, it is the financial security of billions of dollars entrusted to us by clients," says Edwin A. Weihenmayer, vice president and director of the human-resources group at Kidder, Peabody & Co. The New York-based investment bank began drug testing this summer as part of a comprehensive drug-prevention program.

Critics, for their part, tend to view such measures as unnecessarily or even unconstitutionally invasive. "For us, it just doesn't make good business sense to police our employees' private lives," says Lewis L. Maltby, vice president of Drexelbrook Engineering Co. The small instrumentation company in Horsham, Pa., has decided against drug tests.

What follows is a debate organized by *The Wall Street Journal* between the two executives.

Mr. Maltby: We've considered testing and totally rejected it. One reason is the accuracy problem. In an often-cited study, the U.S. Centers for Disease Control got false positive results of up to 66% from 13 randomly chosen private labs. The CDC said none of the labs were reliable. That isn't a very strong base to build a program on.

Mr. Weihenmayer: You've hit on the one controversial aspect of drug-prevention programs. Our program consists of policy statements and a lot of communication: manager-awareness training, employee-assistance programs. And, yes, testing—of new hires, and just recently we began unannounced testing of current employees too.

We want to create a workplace mentality where people say, "If I work at Kidder, I don't do drugs." I see our workers accepting that objective, and I believe it's due to an umbrella of programs. It wouldn't be happening just with testing, but testing gives our program teeth.

Testing can be inaccurate if you use lousy labs, fail to monitor movement of the urine specimens, don't do reconfirmation tests. But we've addressed those problems. When an employee provides a sample, it is sealed and signed. Prescription-drug use is noted. Everywhere the sample moves, it's signed. If a test is positive for drugs, we feel we have an obligation to reconfirm. And if that's positive, we go back and give the employee a chance to explain any extenuating circumstance before we act.

Mr. Maltby: Ed is right: If the only test you use is the inexpensive test, which costs $15 or so but which is highly unreliable, you'll have serious problems. But the state-of-the-art test for reconfirmation costs from $75 to $100, which will multiply your costs an order of magnitude or so. Spending that much money isn't cost-justified for most companies. But unless you do, you're going to be firing people who shouldn't be fired.

Mr. Weihenmayer: If it's an important business issue, you'll spend the money. We'll spend over $100,000 this year on our drug program. And that's just direct costs. A lot more cost is involved in dialoguing with our 7,000 employees, explaining why we test, answering all their questions. But I don't think you can put a price tag on the comfort that our clients have with the way we're processing and managing their money.

Mr. Maltby: I think we disagree on the relevance of the information you get from testing. Kidder tests, at least in part, to assure its customers. Our only concern is job performance. But drug testing isn't a job-performance test. For instance, traces of drugs can remain in the system for days. I can't tell, if an employee takes a drug test on Monday, whether he is impaired now, whether he is sober as a judge or whether he had a couple of puffs on a joint Saturday night.

Mr. Weihenmayer: We're concerned about performance. We're concerned about the effects of alcohol, but I can tell from someone's behavior if

---

they come to work drunk. Not so with drugs. About 80% of performance problems from drugs are invisible. I equate our concern with that of the airline industry. When you walk on a plane, you don't want pilots to just appear drug free. You want to be absolutely sure they are.

We're also concerned about the potential pressures that result from drug use, whether it's done at work or not. Drug use can be expensive, and can exert financial demands—temptations—we don't want on employees who are dealing with transactions worth millions of dollars.

Mr. Maltby: I challenge the idea that you can't detect drug-related deterioration in job performance. In my experience, a really good supervisor who's paying attention is the best way to detect a problem. A supervisor should be watching if employees come in late, if they are sick often on Mondays, whether their error rate is up or their attention span is down. A well-tuned-in supervisor is a much better indicator of whether an employee has a problem than some testing program.

I really don't think, as Ed is saying, that for the sake of client perception you can fire someone for what they did on Saturday night if it's not affecting their job performance.

Mr. Weihenmayer: I can tell you there are situations where supervisors were paying attention, where performance seemed fine, but that until an account problem surfaced through computer controls we didn't know we had a drug-related problem. We just aren't prepared to tolerate a problem until it arises, just as the airline industry can't tolerate drug use until a collision makes it visible.

Our program isn't designed to get rid of people. We invest a lot of money to find people and train them. And what we want to do is influence them toward working in our way, which is drug free. We want people to say, "I used marijuana casually, but this job is so important I quit." We can't afford to risk whatever results from that casual use, whether it affects the job or a person's financial integrity. Security in an industry dealing with billions of dollars demands that.

Mr. Maltby: We just don't think you need to test to keep the workplace drug free. After all, drugs are just a symptom of something else. What you really want is a committed, dedicated work force, people who like their jobs and care enough not to come to work stoned. What we do is select and nurture employees that are going to do a good job. We think if we do that, the drug problem takes care of itself.

We're incredibly careful about the people we hire. We do multiple reference checks, even for floor sweepers. And then we take a lot of time and trouble to really know our people. Our supervisors know their people's families; they work to build trust and rapport. If they have problems financial or otherwise, (the supervisors) want to know about it, and we have programs to provide them help. We've found that with that kind of trust people will confide in you when a problem arises, before they feel they must use drugs in a dangerous way. I think the proof is that we believe drug problems affect only about 1% of our work force.

Mr. Weihenmayer: The relationship and concern expressed here is commendable, and everyone should strive for that. But the point is you think your drug incidence is 1%, but you don't know. Even if you do a thorough check, someone's going to get exposed to drugs after they join you.

Mr. Maltby: The implication is that we have employees running around with problems and we don't know it. We produce precision instrumentation for chemical plants and refineries. If we had drug problems at work, it would affect our product and cause life-threatening problems, and we'd be up to our eyeballs in lawsuits.

Mr. Weihenmayer: Our belief, put simply, is that certain industries require this type of assured security—pilots, air-traffic controllers, for instance. I think protecting a person's savings is crucial too. We want people to feel Kidder is doing everything possible to protect their savings. At the same time, we are trying to be very sensitive to the needs of our employees.

Mr. Maltby: You're saying you can have a testing program *and* the kind of employee relations I'm talking about. I say you can't. The two are inimical. Ours is based on a relationship that doesn't just come from a paycheck. When you say to an employee, "You're doing a great job; just the same, I want you to pee in this jar and I'm sending someone to watch you," you've undermined that trust.

Mr. Weihenmayer: I'll grant you it makes it more difficult. It bothers us if they're bothered. That's why we spend so much time explaining our objectives. Also, when we test a department, everyone from top to bottom is tested. For most employees who test positive, we reexplain our policy, ask them to commit themselves to be drug free and to undergo periodic testing. The company makes available, at its expense, help if they feel they need it. But if they test positive again, they are subject to immediate termination.

We've had employees who say in good conscience they can't take the test. We treat that person with respect, but we explain that on this matter we have to call the shots. You may anguish a bit over the damage which is done, but it's extremely important for the program's integrity that everyone take the test.

We don't have watchers. It would make the program more accurate, but we have drawn the line because it would be too embarrassing.

Mr. Maltby: But that's the kind of swamp you get into with testing. Right now, the threat to the program is small. But as people learn how to beat the system, the only way you're going to keep people from monkeying around is to watch them.

Mr. Weihenmayer: I don't think it will be a problem. Who is going to carry a urine sample around 365 days of the year?

Whistle Blowing

Richard T. De George
Distinguished Professor of Philosophy, University of Kansas

We shall restrict our discussion to a specific sort of whistle blowing, namely, *nongovernmental, impersonal, external whistle blowing*. We shall be

Abridged with permission of Macmillan College Publishing Company from *Business Ethics* (2nd edition) by Richard T. De George. Copyright © 1986 by Macmillan College Publishing Company, Inc.

concerned with (1) employees of profit-making firms, who, for moral reasons, in the hope and expectation that a product will be made safe, or a practice changed, (2) make public information about a product or practice of the firm that due to faulty design, the use of inferior materials, or the failure to follow safety or other regular procedures or state of the art standards (3) threatens to produce serious harm to the public in general or to individual users of a product. We shall restrict our analysis to this type of whistle blowing because, in the first place, the conditions that justify whistle blowing vary according to the type of case at issue. Second, financial harm can be considerably different from bodily harm. An immoral practice that increases the cost of a product by a slight margin may do serious harm to no individual, even if the total amount when summed adds up to a large amount, or profit. (Such cases can be handled differently from cases that threaten bodily harm.) Third, both internal and personal whistle blowing cause problems for a firm, which are for the most part restricted to those within the firm. External, impersonal whistle blowing is of concern to the general public, because it is the general public rather than the firm that is threatened with harm.

As a paradigm, we shall take a set of fairly clear-cut cases, namely, those in which serious bodily harm—including possible death—threatens either the users of a product or innocent bystanders because of a firm's practice, the design of its product, or the action of some person or persons within the firm. (Many of the famous whistle-blowing cases are instances of such situations.) We shall assume clear cases where serious, preventable harm will result unless a company makes changes in its product or practice.

Cases that are less clear are probably more numerous, and pose problems that are difficult to solve, for example, how serious is *serious,* and how does one tell whether a given situation is serious? We choose not to resolve such issues, but rather to construct a model embodying a number of distinctions that will enable us to clarify the moral status of whistle blowing, which may, in turn, provide a basis for working out guidelines for more complex cases.

Finally, the only motivation for whistle blowing we shall consider here is moral motivation.

Those who blow the whistle for revenge, and so on, are not our concern in this discussion.

Corporations are complex entities. Sometimes those at the top do not want to know in detail the difficulties encountered by those below them. They wish lower-management to handle these difficulties as best they can. On the other hand, those in lower-management frequently present only good news to those above them, even if those at the top do want to be told about difficulties. Sometimes, lower-management hopes that things will be straightened out without letting their superiors know that anything has gone wrong. For instance, sometimes a production schedule is drawn up, which many employees along the line know cannot be achieved. Each level has cut off a few days of the production time actually needed, to make his projection look good to those above. Because this happens at each level, the final projection is weeks, if not months, off the mark. When difficulties develop in actual production, each level is further squeezed and is tempted to cut corners in order not to fall too far behind the overall schedule. The cuts may be that of not correcting defects in a design, or of allowing a defective part to go through, even though a department head and the workers in that department know that this will cause trouble for the consumer. Sometimes a defective part will be annoying; sometimes it will be dangerous. If dangerous, external whistle blowing may be morally mandatory.

The whistle blower usually fares very poorly at the hands of his company. Most are fired. In some instances, they have been blackballed in the whole industry. If they are not fired, they are frequently shunted aside at promotion time, and treated as pariahs. Those who consider making a firm's wrongdoings public must therefore be aware that they may be fired, ostracized, and condemned by others. They may ruin their chances of future promotion and security; and they also may make themselves a target for revenge. Only rarely have companies praised and promoted such people. This is not surprising, because the whistle blower forces the company to do what it did not want to do, even if, morally, it was the right action. This is scandalous. And it is ironic that those guilty of endangering the lives of others—even of indirectly killing them—frequently get promoted by their companies for increasing profits.

Because the consequences for the whistle blower are often so disastrous, such action is not to be undertaken lightly. Moreover, whistle blowing may, in some cases, be morally justifiable without being morally mandatory. The position we shall develop is a moderate one, and falls between two extreme positions: that defended by those who claim that whistle blowing is always morally justifiable, and that defended by those who say it is never morally justifiable.

WHISTLE BLOWING AS MORALLY PERMITTED

The kind of whistle blowing we are considering involves an employee somehow going public, revealing information or concerns about his or her firm in the hope that the firm will change its product, action, or policy, or whatever it is that the whistle blower feels will harm, or has harmed others, and needs to be rectified. We can assume that when one blows the whistle, it is not with the consent of the firm, but against its wishes. It is thus a form of disloyalty and of disobedience to the corporation. Whistle blowing of this type, we can further assume, does injury to a firm. It results in either adverse publicity or in an investigation of some sort, or both. If we adopt the principle that one ought not to do harm without sufficient reason, then, if the act of whistle blowing is to be morally permissible, some good must be achieved that outweighs the harm that will be done.

There are five conditions, which, if satisfied, change the moral status of whistle blowing. If the first three are satisfied, the act of whistle blowing will be morally justifiable and permissible. If the additional two are satisfied, the act of whistle blowing will be morally obligatory.

Whistle blowing is morally permissible if—

1. The firm, through its product or policy, will do serious and considerable harm to the public, whether in the person of the user of its product, an innocent bystander, or the general public.

Because whistle blowing causes harm to the firm, this harm must be offset by at least an equal amount of good, if the act is to be permissible. We have specified that the potential or actual harm to others must be serious and considerable. That requirement may be considered by some to be both too strong and too vague. Why specify "serious and considerable" instead of saying, "involve more harm than the harm that the whistle blowing will produce for the firm?" Moreover, how serious is "serious?" And how considerable is "considerable?"

There are several reasons for stating that the potential harm must be serious and considerable. First, if the harm is not serious and considerable, if it will do only slight harm to the public, or to the user of a product, the justification for whistle blowing will be at least problematic. We will not have a clear case. To assess the harm done to the firm is difficult; but though the harm may be rather vague, it is also rather sure. If the harm threatened by a product is slight or not certain, it might not be greater than the harm done to the firm. After all, a great many products involve some risk. Even with a well-constructed hammer, one can smash one's finger. There is some risk in operating any automobile, because no automobile is completely safe. There is always a trade-off between safety and cost. It is not immoral not to make the safest automobile possible, for instance, and a great many factors enter into deciding just how safe a car should be. An employee might see that a car can be made slightly safer by modifying a part, and might suggest that modification: but not making the modification is not usually grounds for blowing the whistle. If serious harm is not threatened, then the slight harm that is done, say by the use of a product, can be corrected after the product is marketed (e.g., as a result of customer complaint). Our society has a great many ways of handling minor defects, and these are at least arguably better than resorting to whistle blowing.

To this consideration should be added a second. Whistle blowing is frequently, and appropriately, considered an unusual occurrence, a heroic act. If the practice of blowing the whistle for relatively minor harm were to become a common occurrence, its effectiveness would be diminished. When serious harm is threatened, whistle blowers are listened to by the news media, for instance, because it

is news. But relatively minor harm to the public is not news. If many minor charges or concerns were voiced to the media, the public would soon not react as it is now expected to react to such disclosures. This would also be the case if complaints about all sorts of perceived or anticipated minor harm were reported to government agencies, although most people would expect that government agencies would act first on the serious cases, and only later on claims of relatively minor harm.

There is a third consideration. Every time an employee has a concern about possible harm to the public from a product or practice we cannot assume that he or she makes a correct assessment. Nor can we assume that every claim of harm is morally motivated. To sift out the claims and concerns of the disaffected worker from the genuine claims and concerns of the morally motivated employee is a practical problem. It may be claimed that this problem has nothing to do with the moral permissibility of the act of whistle blowing; but whistle blowing is a practical matter. If viewed as a technique for changing policy or actions, it will be justified only if effective. It can be trivialized. If it is, then one might plausibly claim that little harm is done to the firm, and hence the act is permitted. But if trivialized, it loses its point. If whistle blowing is to be considered a serious act with serious consequences, it should be reserved for disclosing potentially serious harm, and will be morally justifiable in those cases.

Serious is admittedly a vague term. Is an increase in probable automobile deaths, from 2 in 100,000 to 15 in 100,000 over a one-year period, serious? Although there may be legitimate debate on this issue, it is clear that matters that threaten death are *prima facie* serious. If the threatened harm is that a product may cost a few pennies more than otherwise, or if the threatened harm is that a part or product may cause minor inconvenience, the harm—even if multiplied by thousands or millions of instances—does not match the seriousness of death to the user or the innocent bystander.

The harm threatened by unsafe tires, which are sold as premium quality but that blow out at 60 or 70 mph, is serious, for such tires can easily lead to death. The dumping of metal drums of toxic waste into a river, where the drums will rust, leak, and cause cancer or other serious ills to those who drink the river water or otherwise use it, threatens serious harm. The use of substandard concrete in a building, such that it is likely to collapse and kill people, poses a serious threat to people. Failure to x-ray pipe fittings, as required in building a nuclear plant, is a failure that might lead to nuclear leaks; this involves potential serious harm, for it endangers the health and lives of many.

The notion of *serious* harm might be expanded to include serious financial harm, and kinds of harm other than death and serious threats to health and body. But as we noted earlier, we shall restrict ourselves here to products and practices that produce or threaten serious harm or danger to life and health. The difference between producing harm and threatening serious danger is not significant for the kinds of cases we are considering.

> 2. Once an employee identifies a serious threat to the user of a product or to the general public, he or she should report it to his or her immediate superior and make his or her moral concern known. Unless he or she does so, the act of whistle blowing is not clearly justifiable.

Why not? Why is not the weighing of harm sufficient? The answer has already been given in part. Whistle blowing is a practice that, to be effective, cannot be routinely used. There are other reasons as well. First, reporting one's concerns is the most direct, and usually the quickest, way of producing the change the whistle blower desires. The normal assumption is that most firms do not want to cause death or injury, and do not willingly and knowingly set out to harm the users of their products in this way. If there are life-threatening defects, the normal assumption is, and should be, that the firm will be interested in correcting them—if not for moral reasons, at least for prudential reasons, viz., to avoid suits, bad publicity, and adverse consumer reaction. The argument from loyalty also supports the requirement that the firm be given the chance to rectify its action or procedure or policy before it is charged in public. Additionally, because whistle blowing does harm to the firm, harm in general is minimized if the firm is informed of the problem and allowed to correct it. Less harm is done to the firm in this way, and if the harm to the

public or the users is also averted, this procedure produces the least harm, on the whole.

The condition that one report one's concern to one's immediate superior presupposes a hierarchical structure. Although firms are usually so structured, they need not be. In a company of equals, one would report one's concerns internally, as appropriate.

Several objections may be raised to this condition. Suppose one knows that one's immediate superior already knows the defect and the danger. In this case reporting it to him or her would be redundant, and condition two would be satisfied. But one should not presume without good reason that one's superior does know. What may be clear to one individual may not be clear to another. Moreover, the assessment of risk is often a complicated matter. To a person on one level what appears as unacceptable risk may be defensible as legitimate to a person on a higher level, who may see a larger picture, and knows of offsetting compensations, and the like.

However, would not reporting one's concern effectively preclude the possibility of anonymous whistle blowing, and so put one in jeopardy? This might of course be the case; and this is one of the considerations one should weigh before blowing the whistle. We will discuss this matter later on. If the reporting is done tactfully, moreover, the voicing of one's concerns might, if the problem is apparent to others, indicate a desire to operate within the firm, and so make one less likely to be the one assumed to have blown the whistle anonymously.

By reporting one's concern to one's immediate superior or other appropriate person, one preserves and observes the regular practices of firms, which on the whole promote their order and efficiency; this fulfills one's obligation of minimizing harm, and it precludes precipitous whistle blowing.

> 3. If one's immediate superior does nothing effective about the concern or complaint, the employee should exhaust the internal procedures and possibilities within the firm. This usually will involve taking the matter up the managerial ladder, and, if necessary— and possible—to the board of directors.

To exhaust the internal procedures and possibilities is the key requirement here. In a hierarchically structured firm, this means going up the chain of command. But one may do so either with or without the permission of those at each level of the hierarchy. What constitutes exhausting the internal procedures? This is often a matter of judgment. But because going public with one's concern is more serious for both oneself and for the firm, going up the chain of command is the preferable route to take in most circumstances. This third condition is satisfied of course if, for some reason, it is truly impossible to go beyond any particular level.

Several objections may once again be raised. There may not be time enough to follow the bureaucratic procedures of a given firm; the threatened harm may have been done before the procedures are exhausted. If, moreover, one goes up the chain to the top and nothing is done by anyone, then a great deal of time will have been wasted. Once again, prudence and judgment should be used. The internal possibilities may sometimes be exhausted quickly, by a few phone calls or visits. But one should not simply assume that no one at any level within the firm will do anything. If there are truly no possibilities of internal remedy, then the third condition is satisfied.

As we mentioned, the point of the three conditions is essentially that whistle blowing is morally permissible if the harm threatened is serious, and if internal remedies have been attempted in good faith but without a satisfactory result. In these circumstances, one is morally justified in attempting to avert what one sees as serious harm, by means that may be effective, including blowing the whistle.

We can pass over as not immediately germane the questions of whether in nonserious matters one has an obligation to report one's moral concerns to one's superiors, and whether one fulfills one's obligation once one has reported them to the appropriate party.

WHISTLE BLOWING AS MORALLY REQUIRED

To say that whistle blowing is morally permitted does not impose any obligation on an employee. Unless two other conditions are met, the employee does not have a moral obligation to blow the whistle. To blow the whistle when one is not morally required to do so, and if done from moral motives (i.e., concern for one's fellow man) and at risk to oneself, is to commit a supererogatory act. It is an act that deserves moral praise. But failure to so act deserves no moral blame. In such a case, the whistle blower might be considered a moral hero. Sometimes he or she is so considered, sometimes not. If one's claim or concern turns out to be ill-founded, one's subjective moral state may be as praiseworthy as if the claim were well-founded, but one will rarely receive much praise for one's action.

For there to be an obligation to blow the whistle, two conditions must be met, in addition to the foregoing three.

> 4. The whistle blower must have, or have accessible, documented evidence that would convince a reasonable, impartial observer that one's view of the situation is correct, and that the company's product or practice poses a serious and likely danger to the public or to the user of the product.

One does not have an obligation to put oneself at serious risk without some compensating advantage to be gained. Unless one has documented evidence that would convince a reasonable, impartial observer, one's charges or claims, if made public, would be based essentially on one's word. Such grounds may be sufficient for a subjective feeling of certitude about one's charges, but they are not usually sufficient for others to act on one's claims. For instance, a newspaper is unlikely to print a story based simply on someone's undocumented assertion.

Several difficulties emerge. Should it not be the responsibility of the media or the appropriate regulatory agency or government bureau to carry out an investigation based on someone's complaint? It is reasonable for them to do so, providing they have some evidence in support of the complaint or claim. The damage has not yet been done, and the harm will not, in all likelihood, be done to the complaining party. If the action is criminal, then an investigation by a law-enforcing agency is appropriate. But the charges made by whistle blowers are often not criminal charges. And we do not expect newspapers or government agencies to carry out investigations whenever anyone claims that possible harm will be done by a product or practice. Unless harm is imminent, and very serious (e.g., a bomb threat), it is appropriate to act on evidence that substantiates a claim. The usual procedure, once an investigation is started or a complaint followed up, is to contact the party charged.

One does not have a moral obligation to blow the whistle simply because of one's hunch, guess, or personal assessment of possible danger, if supporting evidence and documentation are not available. One may, of course, have the obligation to attempt to get evidence if the harm is serious. But if it is unavailable—or unavailable without using illegal or immoral means—then one does not have the obligation to blow the whistle.

> 5. The employee must have good reason to believe that by going public the necessary changes will be brought about. The chance of being successful must be worth the risk one takes and the danger to which one is exposed.

Even with some documentation and evidence, a potential whistle blower may not be taken seriously, or may not be able to get the media or government agency to take any action. How far should one go, and how much must one try? The more serious the situation, the greater the effort required. But unless one has a reasonable expectation of success, one is not obliged to put oneself at great risk. Before going public, the potential whistle blower should know who (e.g., government agency, newspaper, columnist, TV reporter) will make use of his or her evidence, and how it will be handled. He or she should have good reason to expect that the action taken will result in the kind of change or result that he or she believes is morally appropriate.

The foregoing fourth and fifth conditions may seem too permissive to some and too stringent to others. They are too permissive for those who wish everyone to be ready and willing to blow the whistle whenever there is a chance that the public will be harmed. After all, harm to the public is more serious than harm to the whistle blower, and, in the long run, if everyone saw whistle blowing as obligatory, without satisfying the last two conditions, we would all be better off. If the fourth and fifth conditions must be satisfied, then people will only rarely have the moral obligation to blow the whistle.

If, however, whistle blowing were mandatory whenever the first three conditions were satisfied, and if one had the moral obligation to blow the whistle whenever one had a moral doubt or fear about safety, or whenever one disagreed with one's superiors or colleagues, one would be obliged to go public whenever one did not get one's way on such issues within a firm. But these conditions are much too weak, for the reasons already given. Other, stronger conditions, but weaker than those proposed, might be suggested. But any condition that makes whistle blowing mandatory in large numbers of cases, may possibly reduce the effectiveness of whistle blowing. If this were the result, and the practice were to become widespread, then it is doubtful that we would all be better off.

Finally, the claim that many people very often have the obligation to blow the whistle goes against the common view of the whistle blower as a moral hero, and against the commonly held feeling that whistle blowing is only rarely morally mandatory. This feeling may be misplaced. But a very strong argument is necessary to show that although the general public is morally mistaken in its view, the moral theoretician is correct in his or her assertion.

A consequence of accepting the fourth and fifth conditions stated is that the stringency of the moral obligation of whistle blowing corresponds with the common feeling of most people on this issue. Those in higher positions and those in professional positions in a firm are more likely to have the obligation to change a firm's policy or product—even by whistle blowing, if necessary— than are lower-placed employees. Engineers, for instance, are more likely to have access to data and designs than are assembly-line workers. Managers generally have a broader picture, and more access to evidence, than do nonmanagerial employees. Management has the moral responsibility both to see that the expressed moral concerns of those below them have been adequately considered and that the firm does not knowingly inflict harm on others.

The fourth and fifth conditions will appear too stringent to those who believe that whistle blowing is always a supererogatory act, that it is always

moral heroism, and that it is never morally obligatory. They might argue that, although we are not
permitted to do what is immoral, we have no general moral obligation to prevent all others from
acting immorally. This is what the whistle blower
attempts to do. The counter to that, however, is to
point out that whistle blowing is an act in which
one attempts to prevent harm to a third party. It is
not implausible to claim both that we are morally
obliged to prevent harm to others at relatively little
expense to ourselves, and that we are morally
obliged to prevent great harm to a great many others, even at considerable expense to ourselves.

The five conditions outlined can be used by an
individual to help decide whether he or she is
morally permitted or required to blow the whistle.
Third parties can also use these conditions when attempting to evaluate acts of whistle blowing by others, even though third parties may have difficulty
determining whether the whistle blowing is morally
motivated. It might be possible successfully to blow
the whistle anonymously. But anonymous tips or
stories seldom get much attention. One can confide
in a government agent, or in a reporter, on condition
that one's name not be disclosed. But this approach,
too, is frequently ineffective in achieving the results
required. To be effective, one must usually be willing to be identified, to testify publicly, to produce
verifiable evidence, and to put oneself at risk. As
with civil disobedience, what captures the conscience of others is the willingness of the whistle
blower to suffer harm for the benefit of others, and
for what he or she thinks is right.

PRECLUDING THE NEED FOR WHISTLE BLOWING

The need for moral heroes shows a defective society and defective corporations. It is more important to change the legal and corporate structures
that make whistle blowing necessary than to convince people to be moral heroes.

Because it is easier to change the law than to
change the practices of all corporations, it should
be illegal for any employer to fire an employee, or
to take any punitive measures, at the time or later,
against an employee who satisfies the first three

aforementioned conditions and blows the whistle
on the company. Because satisfying those conditions makes the action morally justifiable, the law
should protect the employee in acting in accordance with what his or her conscience demands. If
the whistle is falsely blown, the company will
have suffered no great harm. If it is appropriately
blown, the company should suffer the consequences of its actions being made public. But to
protect a whistle blower by passing such a law is
no easy matter. Employers can make life difficult
for whistle blowers without firing them. There are
many ways of passing over an employee. One can
be relegated to the back room of the firm, or be
given unpleasant jobs. Employers can find reasons
not to promote one or to give one raises. Not all of
this can be prevented by law, but some of the
more blatant practices can be prohibited.

Second, the law can mandate that the individuals responsible for the decision to proceed with a
faulty product or to engage in a harmful practice
be penalized. The law has been reluctant to interfere with the operations of companies. As a result,
those in the firm who have been guilty of immoral
and illegal practices have gone untouched even
though the corporation was fined for its activity.

A third possibility is that every company of a
certain size be required, by law, to have an inspector general or an internal operational auditor,
whose job it is to uncover immoral and illegal
practices. This person's job would be to listen to
the moral concerns of employees, at every level,
about the firm's practices. He or she should be independent of management, and report to the audit
committee of the board, which, ideally, should be
a committee made up entirely of outside board
members. The inspector or auditor should be
charged with making public those complaints that
should be made public if not changed from within.
Failure on the inspector's part to take proper action with respect to a worker's complaint, such
that the worker is forced to go public, should be
prima facie evidence of an attempt to cover up a
dangerous practice or product, and the inspector
should be subject to criminal charges.

In addition, a company that wishes to be moral,
that does not wish to engage in harmful practices

or to produce harmful products, can take other steps to preclude the necessity of whistle blowing. The company can establish channels whereby those employees who have moral concerns can get a fair hearing without danger to their position or standing in the company. Expressing such concerns, moreover, should be considered a demonstration of company loyalty and should be rewarded appropriately. The company might establish the position of ombudsman, to hear such complaints or moral concerns. Or an independent committee of the board might be established to hear such complaints and concerns. Someone might even be paid by the company to present the position of the would-be whistle blower, who would argue for what the company should do, from a moral point of view, rather than what those interested in meeting a schedule or making a profit would like to do. Such a person's success within the company could depend on his success in precluding whistle blowing, as well as the conditions that lead to it.

Whistle Blowing: Its Moral Justification

Gene G. James
Professor of Philosophy, University of Memphis

Whistle blowing may be defined as the attempt of an employee or former employee of an organization to disclose what he or she believes to be wrongdoing in or by the organization. Like blowing a whistle to call attention to a thief, whistle blowing is an effort to make others aware of practices one considers illegal or immoral. If the wrongdoing is reported to someone higher in the

organization, the whistle blowing may be said to be *internal.* If the wrongdoing is reported to outside individuals or groups, such as reporters, public interest groups, or regulatory agencies, the whistle blowing is *external.* If the harm being reported is primarily harm to the whistle blower alone, such as sexual harassment, the whistle blowing may be said to be *personal.* If it is primarily harm to other people that is being reported, the whistle blowing is *impersonal.* Most whistle blowing is done by people currently employed by the organization on which they are blowing the whistle. However, people who have left an organization may also blow the whistle. The former may be referred to as *current* whistle blowing, the latter as *alumni* whistle blowing. If the whistle blower discloses his or her identity, the whistle blowing may be said to be *open;* if the whistle blower's identity is not disclosed, the whistle blowing is *anonymous.*

Whistle blowers almost always experience retaliation. If they work for private firms and are not protected by unions or professional organizations, they are likely to be fired. They are also likely to receive damaging letters of recommendation and may even be blacklisted so that they cannot find work in their profession. If they are not fired, they are still likely to be transferred, given less interesting work, denied salary increases and promotions, or demoted. Their professional competence is usually attacked. They are said to be unqualified to judge, misinformed, etc. Since their actions may threaten both the organization and their fellow employees, attacks on their personal lives are also frequent. They are called traitors, rat finks, disgruntled, known trouble makers, people who make an issue out of nothing, self-serving, and publicity seekers. Their life-styles, sex lives, and mental stability may be questioned. Physical assaults, abuse of their families, and even murder are not unknown as retaliation for whistle blowing.

WHISTLE BLOWING AND THE LAW[1]

The law does not at present offer whistle blowers very much protection. Agency law, the area of common law which governs relations between employees and employers, imposes a duty on employees to keep confidential any information learned through their employment that might be detrimental to their employers. However, this duty does not hold if the employee has knowledge that the employer either has committed or is about to commit a felony. In this case the employee has a positive obligation to report the offense. Failure to do so is known as misprision and makes one subject to criminal penalties.

One problem with agency law is that it is based on the assumption that unless there are statutes or agreements to the contrary, contracts between employees and employers can be terminated at will by either party. It therefore grants employers the right to discharge employees at any time for any reason or even for no reason at all. The result is that most employees who blow the whistle, even those who report felonies, are fired or suffer other retaliation. One employee of thirty years was even fired the day before his pension became effective for testifying under oath against his employer, without the courts doing anything to aid him.

This situation has begun to change somewhat in recent years. In *Pickering v. Board of Education* in 1968 the Supreme Court ruled that government employees have the right to speak out on policy issues affecting their agencies provided doing so does not seriously disrupt the agency. A number of similar decisions have followed, and the right of government employees to speak out on policy issues now seems firmly established. But employees in private industry cannot criticize company policies without risking being fired. In one case involving both a union and a company doing a substantial portion of its business with the federal government, federal courts did award back pay to an employee fired for criticizing the union and the company but did not reinstate or award him punitive damages.

A few state courts have begun to modify the right of employers to dismiss employees at will. Courts in Oregon and Pennsylvania have awarded damages to employees fired for serving on juries. A New Hampshire court granted damages to a woman fired for refusing to date her foreman. A West Virginia court reinstated a bank employee who reported illegal interest rates. The Illinois Supreme Court upheld the right of an employee to

sue when fired for reporting and testifying about criminal activities of a fellow employee. However, a majority of states still uphold the right of employers to fire employees at will unless there are statutes or agreements to the contrary. To my knowledge only one state, Michigan, has passed a law prohibiting employers from retaliating against employees who report violations of local, state, or federal laws.

A number of federal statutes contain provisions intended to protect whistle blowers. The National Labor Relations Act, Fair Labor Standards Act, Title VII of the 1964 Civil Rights Act, Age Discrimination Act, and the Occupational Safety and Health Act all have sections prohibiting employers from taking retaliatory actions against employees who report or testify about violations of the acts. Although these laws seem to encourage and protect whistle blowers, to be effective they must be enforced. A 1976 study[2] of the Occupational Safety and Health Act showed that only about 20 percent of the 2300 complaints filed in fiscal years 1975 and 1976 were judged valid by OSHA investigators. About half of these were settled out of court. Of the sixty cases taken to court at the time of the study in November 1976, one had been won, eight lost, and the others were still pending. A more recent study[3] showed that of the 3100 violations reported in 1979, only 270 were settled out of court and only sixteen litigated.

Since the National Labor Relations Act guarantees the right of workers to organize and bargain collectively, and most collective bargaining agreements contain a clause requiring employers to have just cause for discharging employees, these agreements would seem to offer some protection for whistle blowers. In fact, however, arbitrators have tended to agree with employers that whistle blowing is an act of disloyalty which disrupts business and injures the employer's reputation. Their attitude seems to be summed up in a 1972 case in which the arbitrator stated that one should not "bite the hand that feeds you and insist on staying for future banquets."[4] One reason for this attitude, pointed out by David Ewing, is that unions are frequently as corrupt as the organizations on which the whistle is being blown. Such unions he says, "are not likely to feed a hawk that comes to prey in their own barnyard."[5] The record of professional societies is not any better. They have generally failed to come to the aid or defense of members who have attempted to live up to their codes of professional ethics by blowing the whistle on corrupt practices.

THE MORAL JUSTIFICATION OF WHISTLE BLOWING

Under what conditions, if any, is whistle blowing morally justified? Some people have argued that whistle blowing is never justified because employees have absolute obligations of confidentiality and loyalty to the organization for which they work. People who argue this way see no difference between employees who reveal trade secrets by selling information to competitors and whistle blowers who disclose activities harmful to others.[6] This position is similar to another held by some business people and economists that the sole obligation of corporate executives is to make a profit for stockholders. If this were true, corporate executives would have no obligations to the public. However, no matter what one's special obligations, one is never exempt from the general obligations we have to our fellow human beings. One of the most fundamental of these obligations is to not cause avoidable harm to others. Corporate executives are no more exempt from this obligation than other people.

Just as the special obligations of corporate executives to stockholders cannot override their more fundamental obligations to others, the special obligations of employees to employers cannot override their more fundamental obligations. In particular, obligations of confidentiality and loyalty cannot take precedence over the fundamental duty to act in ways that prevent unnecessary harm to others. Agreements to keep something secret have no moral standing unless that which is to be kept secret is itself morally justifiable. For example, no one can have an obligation to keep secret a conspiracy to murder someone, because murder is an immoral act. It is for this reason also that employees have a legal obligation to report an employer who has committed or is about to commit a felony. Nor can one justify participation in an illegal or immoral activity by arguing that one was merely following orders. Democratic governments repudiated this type of defense at Nuremberg.

It has also been argued that whistle blowing is always justified because it is an exercise of the right to free speech. However, the right to free speech is not absolute. An example often used to illustrate this is that one does not have the right to shout "Fire" in a crowded theater because that is likely to cause a panic in which people may be injured. Analogously, one may have a right to speak out on a particular subject, in the sense that there are no contractual agreements which prohibit one from doing so, but it nevertheless be the case that it would be morally wrong for one to do so because it would harm innocent people, such as one's fellow workers and stockholders who are not responsible for the wrongdoing being disclosed. The mere fact that one has the right to speak out does not mean that one ought to do so in every case. But this kind of consideration cannot create an absolute prohibition against whistle blowing, because one must weigh the harm to fellow workers and stockholders caused by the disclosure against the harm to others caused by allowing the organizational wrong to continue. Furthermore, the moral principle that one must consider all people's interests equally prohibits giving priority to one's own group. There is, in fact, justification for not giving as much weight to the interests of the stockholders as to those of the public, because stockholders investing in corporate firms do so with the knowledge that they undergo financial risk if management acts in imprudent, illegal, or immoral ways. Similarly, if the employees of a company know that it is engaged in illegal or immoral activities and do not take action, including whistle blowing, to terminate the activities, then they too must bear some of the guilt for the actions. To the extent that these conditions hold, they nullify the principle that one ought to refrain from whistle blowing because speaking out would cause harm to the organization. Unless it can be shown that the harm to fellow workers and stockholders would be *significantly greater* than the harm caused by the organizational wrongdoing, the obligation to avoid unnecessary harm to the public must take precedence. Moreover, as argued above, this is true even when there are specific agreements which prohibit one from speaking out, because such agreements are morally void if the organization is engaged in illegal or immoral activities. In that case one's obligation to the public overrides one's obligation to maintain secrecy.

CRITERIA FOR JUSTIFIABLE WHISTLE BLOWING

The argument in the foregoing section is an attempt to show that unless special circumstances hold, one has a obligation to blow the whistle on illegal or immoral actions—an obligation that is grounded on the fundamental human duty to avoid preventable harm to others. In this section I shall attempt to spell out in greater detail the conditions under which blowing the whistle is morally obligatory. Since Richard De George has previously attempted to do this, I shall proceed by examining the criteria he has suggested.[7]

De George believes there are three conditions that must hold for whistle blowing to be morally permissible and two additional conditions that must hold for it to be morally obligatory. The three conditions that must hold for it to be morally permissible are:

1. The firm, through its product or policy, will do serious and considerable harm to the public, whether in the person of the user of its product, an innocent bystander, or the general public.
2. Once an employee identifies a serious threat to the user of a product or to the general public, he or she should report it to his or her immediate superior and make his or her moral concern known. Unless he or she does so, the act of whistle blowing is not clearly justifiable.
3. If one's immediate superior does nothing effective about the concern or complaint, the employee should exhaust the internal procedures and possibilities within the firm. This usually will involve taking the matter up the managerial ladder, and, if necessary—and possible—to the board of directors.

The two additional conditions which De George thinks must hold for whistle blowing to be morally obligatory are:

4. The whistle blower must have, or have accessible, documented evidence that would convince a reasonable, impartial observer that one's view of the situation is correct and that the company's product or practice poses a serious and likely danger to the public or to the user of the product.
5. The employee must have good reason to believe that by going public the necessary changes will be brought about. The chance of being successful must be worth the risk one takes and the danger to which one is exposed.[8]

De George intends for the proposed criteria to apply to situations in which a firm's policies or products cause physical harm to people. Indeed, the first criterion he proposes is intended to restrict the idea of harm even more narrowly to threats of serious bodily harm or death.

De George apparently believes that situations which involve threats of serious bodily harm or death are so different from those involving other types of harm, that the kind of considerations which justify whistle blowing in the former situations could not possibly justify it in the latter. Thus, he says, referring to the former type of whistle blowing: "As a paradigm, we shall take a set of fairly clear-cut cases, namely, those in which serious bodily harm—including possible death—threatens either the users of a product or innocent bystanders."[9]

One problem in restricting discussion to clear-cut cases of this type, regarding which one can get almost universal agreement that whistle blowing is justifiable, is that it leaves us with no guidance when we are confronted with more usual situations involving other types of harm. Although De George states that his "analysis provides a model for dealing with other kinds of whistle blowing as well,"[10] his criteria in fact provide no help in deciding whether one should blow the whistle in situations involving such wrongs as sexual harassment, violations of privacy, industrial espionage, insider trading, and a variety of other harmful actions.

No doubt, one of the reasons De George re-stricts his treatment the way he does is to avoid having to define harm. This is indeed a problem. For if we fail to put any limitations on the idea of harm, it seems to shade into the merely offensive or distasteful and thus offer little help in resolving moral problems. But, on the other hand, if we re-strict harm to physical injury, as De George does, it then applies to such a limited range of cases that it is of minimal help in most of the moral situa-tions which confront us. One way of dealing with this problem is by correlating harm with violations of fundamental human rights such as the rights to due process, privacy, and property, in addition to the right to freedom from physical harm. Thus, not only situations which involve threats of physical harm, but also those involving actions such as sex-ual harassment which violate the right to privacy and causes psychological harm, compiling unnec-essary records on people, and financial harm due to fraudulent actions, are situations which may justify whistle blowing.

A still greater problem with De George's analy-sis is that even in cases where there is a threat of serious physical harm or death, he believes that this only makes whistle blowing morally permissi-ble, rather than creating a strong *prima facie* obli-gation in favor of whistle blowing. His primary reasons for believing this seem to be those stated in criterion 5. Unless one has reason to believe that the whistle blowing will eliminate the harm, and the cost to oneself is not too great, he does not believe whistle blowing is morally obligatory. He maintains that this is true even when the person in-volved is a professional whose code of ethics re-quires her or him to put the public good ahead of private good. He argued in an earlier article, for example, that:

> The myth that ethics has no place in engineering has . . . at least in some corners of the engineering profession . . . been put to rest. Another myth, how-ever, is emerging to take its place—the myth of the en-gineer as moral hero. . . . The zeal . . . however, has gone too far, piling moral responsibility upon moral responsibility on the shoulders of the engineer. This emphasis . . . is misplaced. Though engineers are members of a profession that holds public safety

paramount, we cannot reasonably expect engineers to be willing to sacrifice their jobs each day for principle and to have a whistle ever at their sides.[11]

He contends that engineers have only the ob-ligation "to do their jobs the best they can."[12] This includes reporting their concerns about the safety of products to management, but does *not* include "the obligation to insist that their percep-tions or . . . standards be accepted. They are not paid to do that, they are not expected to do that, and they have no moral or ethical obliga-tion to do that."[13]

To take a specific case, De George maintains that even though some Ford engineers had grave misgivings about the safety of Pinto gas tanks, and several people had been killed when tanks ex-ploded after rear-end crashes, the engineers did not have an obligation to make their misgivings public. De George's remarks are puzzling because the Pinto case would seem to be exactly the kind of clear-cut situation which he says provides the paradigm for justified whistle blowing. Indeed, if the Ford engineers did not have an obligation to blow the whistle, it is difficult to see what cases could satisfy his criteria. They knew that if Pintos were struck from the rear by vehicles traveling thirty miles per hour or more, their gas tanks were likely to explode, seriously injuring or killing peo-ple. They also knew that if they did not speak out, Ford would continue to market the Pinto. Finally, they were members of a profession whose code of ethics requires them to put public safety above all other obligations.

De George's remarks suggest that the only obli-gation the Ford engineers had was to do what man-agement expected of them by complying with their job descriptions and that so long as they did that no one should find fault with them or hold them ac-countable for what the company did. It is true that when people act within the framework of an orga-nization, it is often difficult to assess individual re-sponsibility. But the fact that one is acting as a member of an organization does not relieve one of moral obligations. The exact opposite is true. Be-cause most of the actions we undertake in organi-zational settings have more far-reaching conse-quences than those we undertake in our personal lives, our moral obligation to make sure that we do not harm others is *increased* when we act as a member of an organization. The amount of moral responsibility one has for any particular organizational action depends on the extent to which: (1) the consequences of the action are foreseeable, and (2) one's own action or failure to act is a cause of those consequences. It is important to include failure to act here, because frequently it is easier to determine what will happen if we do not act than if we do, and because we are morally responsible for not preventing harm as well as for causing it.

De George thinks that the Ford engineers would have had an obligation to blow the whistle only if they believed doing so would have been likely to prevent the harm involved. But we have an obligation to warn others of danger even if we believe they will ignore our warnings. This is especially true if the danger will come about partly because we did not speak out. De George admits that the public has a right to know about dangerous products. If that is true, then those who have knowledge about such products have an obligation to inform the public. This is not usurping the public's right to decide acceptable risk: it is simply supplying people with the information necessary to exercise that right.

De George's comments also seem to imply that in general it is not justifiable to ask people to blow the whistle if it would threaten their jobs. It is true that we would not necessarily be justified in demanding this if it would place them or their families' lives in danger. But this is *not* true if only their jobs are at stake. It is especially not true if the people involved are executives and professionals, who are accorded respect and high salaries, not only because of their specialized knowledge and skills, but also because of the special responsibilities we entrust to them. Frequently, as in the case of engineers, they also subscribe to codes of ethics which require them to put the public good ahead of their own or the organization's good. Given all this, it is difficult to understand why De George does not think the Ford engineers had an obligation to blow the whistle in the Pinto case.

The belief that whistle blowing is an act of disloyalty and disobedience seems to underlie De George's

second and third criteria for justifiable whistle blowing: The whistle blower must have first reported the wrongdoing to his or her immediate superior and, if nothing was done, have taken the complaint as far up the managerial ladder as possible. Some of the problems with adopting these suggestions as general criteria for justified whistle blowing are: (1) It may be one's immediate supervisor who is responsible for the wrongdoing. (2) Organizations differ considerably in both their procedures for reporting, and how they respond to, wrongdoing. (3) Not all wrongdoing is of the same type. If the wrongdoing is of a type that threatens people's health or safety, exhausting channels of protest within the organization may result in unjustified delay in correcting the problem. (4) Exhausting internal channels of protest may give people time to destroy evidence needed to substantiate one's allegations. (5) Finally, it may expose the employee to possible retaliation, against which she or he might have some protection if the wrongdoing were reported to an external agency.

His fourth criterion, that the whistle blower have documented evidence which would convince an impartial observer, is intended to reduce incidences of whistle blowing by curbing those who would blow the whistle on a mere suspicion of wrongdoing. It is true that one should not make claims against an organization based on mere guesses or hunches, because if they turn out to be false one will have illegitimately harmed the organization and innocent people affiliated with it. But, De George also wishes to curb whistle blowing, because he thinks that if it were widespread, that would reduce its effectiveness. De George's fourth and fifth criteria are, therefore, deliberately formulated in such a way that if they are satisfied, "people will only rarely have the moral obligation to blow the whistle."[14]

De George's fear, that unless strict criteria of justification are applied to whistle blowing it might become widespread, is unjustified. If it is true, as he himself claims, that there is a strong tradition in America against "ratting," that most workers consider themselves to have an obligation of loyalty to their organization, and that whistle blowers are commonly looked upon as traitors, then it is unlikely that whistle blowing will ever be a widespread practice. De George believes that if one is unable to document wrongdoing without recourse to illegal or immoral means, this relieves one of the obligation to blow the whistle. He argues:

> One does not have an obligation to blow the whistle simply because of one's hunch, guess, or personal assessment of possible danger, if supporting evidence and documentation are not available. One may, of course, have the obligation to attempt to get evidence if the harm is serious. But if it is unavailable—or unavailable without using illegal or immoral means—then one does not have the obligation to blow the whistle.[15]

I have already indicated above that I do not think one has an obligation to blow the whistle on possible wrongdoing on the basis of a mere guess or hunch because this might harm innocent people. But if one has good reason to believe that wrongdoing is occurring even though one cannot document it without oneself engaging in illegal or immoral actions, this does not relieve one of the obligation to blow the whistle. Indeed, if this were true one would almost never have an obligation to blow the whistle, because employees are rarely in a position to satisfy De George's fourth criterion that the whistle blower "must have, or have accessible, documented evidence that would convince a reasonable, impartial observer that one's view of the situation is correct." Indeed, it is precisely because employees are rarely ever in a position to supply this type of documentation without themselves resorting to illegal or immoral actions, that they have an obligation to inform others who have the authority to investigate the possible wrongdoing. The attempt to secure such evidence on one's own may even thwart the gathering of evidence by the proper authorities. Thus, instead of De George's criterion being a necessary condition for justifiable whistle blowing, the attempt to satisfy it would prevent its occurrence. One has an obligation to gather as much evidence as one can so that authorities will have probable cause for investigation. But, if one is convinced that wrongdoing is occurring, one has an obligation to report it even if one is unable to adequately document it. One will have then done one's duty even if the authorities ignore the report.

The claim that it is usually necessary for the whistle blower to speak out openly for whistle blowing to be morally justified implies that anonymous whistle blowing is rarely, if ever, justified. Is this true? It has been argued that anonymous whistle blowing is never justified because it violates the right of people to face their accusers. But, as Frederick Elliston has pointed out, although people should be protected from false accusations, it is not necessary for the identity of whistle blowers to be known to accomplish this. "It is only necessary that accusations be properly investigated, proven true or false, and the results widely disseminated."[16]

Some people believe that because the whistle blower's motive is not known in anonymous whistle blowing, this suggests that the motive is not praiseworthy and in turn raises questions about the moral justification of anonymous whistle blowing. De George apparently believes this, because in addition to stating that only public whistle blowing by previously loyal employees who display their sincerity by their willingness to suffer is likely to be effective and morally justified, he mentions at several places that he is restricting his attention to whistle blowing for moral reasons. He says, e.g., that "the only motivation for whistle blowing we shall consider . . . is moral motivation."[17] However, in my opinion, concern with the whistle blower's motive is irrelevant to the moral justification of whistle blowing. It is a red herring which takes attention away from the genuine moral issue involved: whether the whistle blower's claim that the organization is doing something harmful to others is true. If the claim is true, then the whistle blowing is justified regardless of the motive. If the whistle blower's motives are not moral, that makes the act less praiseworthy, but this is a totally different issue. As De George states, whistle blowing is a "practical matter." But precisely because this is true, the justification of whistle blowing turns on the truth or falsity of the disclosure, not on the motives of the whistle blower. Anonymous whistle blowing is justified because it can both protect the whistle blower from unjust attacks and prevent those who are accused of wrongdoing from shifting the issue away from their wrongdoing by engaging in an irrelevant *ad hominem* attack on the whistle blower. Preoccupation with the whistle blower's motives facilitates this type of irrelevant diversion. It is only if the accusations prove false or inaccurate that the motives of the whistle blower have any moral relevance. For it is only then, and not before, that the whistle blower rather than the organization should be put on trial.

The view that whistle blowing is *prima facie* wrong because it goes against the tradition that "ratting" is wrong is indefensible because it falsely assumes both that we have a general obligation to not inform others about wrongdoing and that this outweighs our fundamental obligation to prevent harm to others. The belief that whistle blowers should suffer in order to show their moral sincerity, on the other hand, is not only false and irrelevant to the issue of the moral justification of whistle blowing, but is perverse. There are *no* morally justifiable reasons a person who discloses wrongdoing should be put at risk or made to suffer. The contradictory view stated by De George that "one does not have an obligation to put oneself at serious risk without some compensating advantage to be gained,"[18] is also false. Sometimes doing one's duty requires one to undertake certain risks. However, both individuals and society in general should attempt to reduce these risks to the minimum. In the next section I consider some of the actions whistle blowers can take to both make whistle blowing effective and avoid unnecessary risk. In the last section I briefly consider some of the ways society can reduce the need for whistle blowing.

FACTORS TO CONSIDER IN WHISTLE BLOWING

Since whistle blowing usually involves conflicting moral obligations and a wide range of variables and has far-reaching consequences for everyone concerned, the following is not intended as a recipe or how-to-do list. Like all complicated moral actions, whistle blowing cannot be reduced to such a list. Nevertheless, some factors can be stated which whistle blowers should consider in disclosing wrongdoing if they are to also act prudently and effectively.

Make Sure the Situation Is One That Warrants Whistle Blowing

Make sure the situation is one that involves illegal or immoral actions which harm others, rather than one in which you would be disclosing personal matters, trade secrets, customer lists, or similar material. If the disclosure would involve the latter as well, make sure that the harm to be avoided is great enough to offset the harm from the latter.

Examine Your Motives

Although it is not necessary for the whistle blower's motives to be praiseworthy for whistle blowing to be morally justified, examining your motives can help in deciding whether the situation is one that warrants whistle blowing.

Verify and Document Your Information

Try to obtain information that will stand up in regulatory hearings or court. If this is not possible, gather as much information as you can and indicate where and how additional information might be obtained. If the *only* way you could obtain either of these types of information would be through illegal procedures, make sure the situation is one in which the wrongdoing is so great that it warrants this risk. Although morality requires that in general we obey the law, it sometimes requires that we break it. Daniel Ellsberg's release of the Pentagon papers was a situation of this type in my opinion. If you do have to use illegal methods to obtain information, try to find alternative sources for any evidence you uncover so that it will not be challenged in legal hearings. Keep in mind also that if you use illegal methods to obtain information you are opening yourself to *ad hominem* attacks and possible prosecution. In general illegal methods should be avoided unless substantial harm to others is involved.

Determine the Type of Wrongdoing Involved and to Whom It Should Be Reported

Determining the exact nature of the wrongdoing can help you both decide what kind of evidence to obtain and to whom it should be reported. For example, if the wrongdoing consists of illegal actions such as the submission of false test reports to government agencies, bribery of public officials, racial or sexual discrimination, violation of safety, health, or pollution laws, then determining the nature of the law being violated will help indicate which agencies have authority to enforce the law. If, on the other hand, the wrongdoing is not illegal, but is nevertheless harmful to the public, determining this will help you decide whether you have an obligation to publicize the actions and if so how to go about it. The best place to report this type of wrongdoing is usually to a public interest group. Such an organization is more likely than the press to: (1) be concerned about and advise the whistle blower how to avoid retaliation, (2) maintain confidentiality if that is desirable, (3) investigate the allegations to try to substantiate them, rather than sensationalizing them by turning the issue into a "personality dispute." If releasing information to the press is the best way to remedy the wrongdoing, the public interest group can help with or do this.

State Your Allegations in an Appropriate Way

Be as specific as possible without being unintelligible. If you are reporting a violation of law to a government agency, and if possible to do so, include technical data necessary for experts to verify the wrongdoing. If you are disclosing wrongdoing that does not require technical data to substantiate it, still be as specific as possible in stating the type of illegal or harmful activity involved, who is being harmed and how.

Stick to the Facts

Avoid name calling, slander, and being drawn into a mud-slinging contest. As Peter Raven-Hansen wisely points out: "One of the most important points . . . is to focus on the disclosure. . . . This rule applies even when the whistle blower believes that certain individuals are responsible. . . . The disclosure itself usually leaves a trail for others to follow the miscreants."[19] Sticking to the facts also helps the whistle blower minimize retaliation.

Decide Whether the Whistle Blowing Should Be Internal or External

Familiarize yourself with all available internal channels for reporting wrongdoing and obtain as much data as you can both on how people who have used these channels were treated by the organization and what was done about the problems they reported. If people who have reported wrong-

doing in the past have been treated fairly and the problems corrected, use internal channels. If not, find out which external agencies would be the most appropriate to contact. Try to find out also how these agencies have treated whistle blowers, how much aid and protection they have given them, etc.

Decide Whether the Whistle Blowing Should Be Open or Anonymous

If you intend to blow the whistle anonymously, decide whether partial or total anonymity is required. Also document the wrongdoing as thoroughly as possible. Finally, since anonymity may be difficult to preserve, anticipate what you will do if your identity becomes known.

Decide Whether Current or Alumni Whistle Blowing Is Required

Sometimes it is advisable to resign one's position and obtain another before blowing the whistle. This is because alumni whistle blowing helps protect one from being fired, receiving damaging letters of recommendation, or even being blacklisted in one's profession. However, changing jobs should not be thought of as an alternative to whistle blowing. If one is aware of harmful practices, one has a moral obligation to try to do something about them, which cannot be escaped by changing one's job or location. Many times people who think the wrongdoing involved is personal, harming only them, respond to a situation by simply trying to remove themselves from it. They believe that "personal whistle blowing is, in general, morally permitted but not morally required."[20] For example, a female student subjected to sexual harassment, and fearful that she will receive low grades and poor letters of recommendation if she complains, may simply change departments or schools. However, tendencies toward wrongdoing are rarely limited to specific victims. By not blowing the whistle the student allows a situation to exist in which other students are likely to be harassed also.

Make Sure You Follow Proper Guidelines in Reporting the Wrongdoing

If you are not careful to follow any guidelines that have been established by organizations or external agencies for a particular type of whistle blowing, including using the proper forms, meeting deadlines, etc., wrongdoers may escape detection or punishment because of "technicalities."

Consult a Lawyer

Lawyers are advisable at almost every stage of whistle blowing. They can help determine if the wrongdoing violates the law, aid in documenting it, inform you of any laws you might break in documenting it, assist in deciding to whom to report it, make sure reports are filed correctly and promptly, and help protect you from retaliation. If you cannot afford a lawyer, talk with an appropriate public interest group that may be able to help. However, lawyers frequently view problems within a narrow legal framework, and decisions to blow the whistle are moral decisions, so in the final analysis you will have to rely on your own judgment.

Anticipate and Document Retaliation

Although not as certain as Newton's law of motion that for every action there is an equal reaction, whistle blowers whose identities are known can expect retaliation. Furthermore, it may be difficult to keep one's identity secret. Thus whether the whistle blowing is open or anonymous, personal or impersonal, internal or external, current or alumni, one should anticipate retaliation. One should, therefore, protect oneself by documenting every step of the whistle blowing with letters, tape recordings of meetings, etc. Without this documentation, the whistle blower may find that regulatory agencies and the courts are of little help in preventing or redressing retaliation.

BEYOND WHISTLE BLOWING

What can be done to eliminate the wrongdoing which gives rise to whistle blowing? One solution would be to give whistle blowers greater legal protection. Another would be to change the nature of organizations so as to diminish the need for whistle blowing. These solutions are of course not mutually exclusive.

Many people are opposed to legislation to protect whistle blowers because they think that it is unwarranted interference with the right to freedom of contract. However, if the right to freedom of contract is to be consistent with the public interest, it cannot serve as a shield for wrongdoing. It does this when threat of dismissal prevents people from blowing the whistle. The right of employers to dismiss at will has been previously restricted by labor laws which prevent employers from dismissing employees for union activities. It is ironic that we have restricted the right of employers to fire employees who are pursuing their economic self-interest but allowed them to fire employees acting in the public interest. The right of employers to dismiss employees in the interest of efficiency should be balanced against the right of the public to know about illegal, dangerous, and unjust practices of organizations. The most effective way to achieve this goal would be to pass a federal law protecting whistle blowers.

Laws protecting whistle blowers have also been opposed on the grounds that: (1) employees would use them to mask poor performance, (2) they would create an "informer ethos," and (3) they would take away the autonomy of business, strangling it in red tape.

The first objection is illegitimate because only those employees who could show that an act of whistle blowing preceded their being penalized or dismissed, and that their employment records were adequate up to the time of the whistle blowing, could seek relief under the law.

The second objection is more formidable but nevertheless invalid. A society that encourages snooping, suspicion, and mistrust does not conform to most people's idea of the good society. Laws which encourage whistle blowing for self-interested reasons, such as the federal tax law which pays informers part of any money that is collected, could help bring about such a society.[21] However, laws protecting whistle blowers from being penalized or dismissed are quite different. They do not reward the whistle blower; they merely protect him or her from unjust retaliation. It is unlikely that state or federal laws of this type would promote an informer society.

The third objection is also unfounded. Laws protecting whistle blowers would not require any positive duties on the part of organizations—only the negative duty of not retaliating against employees who speak out in the public interest.

However not every act of apparent whistle blowing should be protected. If (1) the whistle blower's accusations turn out to be false and, (2) it can be shown that she or he had no probable reasons for assuming wrongdoing, then the individual should not be shielded from being penalized or dismissed. Both of these conditions should be satisfied before this is allowed to occur. People who can show that they had probable reasons for believing that wrongdoing existed should be protected even if their accusations turn out to be false. If the accusation has not been disproved, the burden of proof should be on the organization to prove that it is false. If it has been investigated and proven false, then the burden of proof should be on the individual to show that she or he had probable reasons for believing wrongdoing existed. If it is shown that the individual did not have probable reasons for believing wrongdoing existed, and the damage to the organization from the false charge is great, it should be allowed to sue or seek other restitution. Since these provisions would impose some risks on potential whistle blowers, they would reduce the possibility of frivolous action. If, on the other hand, it is found that the whistle blower had probable cause for the whistle blowing and the organization has penalized or fired him or her, then that person should be reinstated, awarded damages, or both. If there is further retaliation, additional sizeable damages should be awarded.

What changes could be made in organizations to prevent the need for whistle blowing? Some of the suggestions which have been made are that organizations develop effective internal channels for reporting wrongdoing, reward people with salary increases and promotions for using these channels, and appoint senior executives, board members, ombudspersons, etc., whose primary obligations would be to investigate and eliminate organizational wrongdoing. These changes could be undertaken by organizations on their own or mandated by law. Other changes which might be mandated are requiring that certain kinds of records be kept, assessing larger fines for illegal actions, and making executives and other professionals personally liable for filing false reports, knowingly marketing dangerous products, failing to monitor how policies are being implemented, and so forth. Although these reforms could do much to reduce the need for whistle blowing, given human nature it is highly unlikely that this need can ever be totally eliminated. Therefore, it is important to have laws which protect whistle blowers and for us to state as clearly as we can both the practical problems and moral issues pertaining to whistle blowing.

NOTES

1. For discussion of the legal aspects of whistle blowing see Lawrence E. Blades, "Employment at Will vs. Individual Freedom: On Limiting the Abusive Exercise of Employer Power," *Columbia Law Review,* vol. 67 (1967); Philip Blumberg, "Corporate Responsibility and the Employee's Duty of Loyalty and Obedience: A Preliminary Inquiry," *Oklahoma Law Review,* vol. 24 (1967); Clyde W. Summers, "Individual Protection Against Unjust Dismissal: Time for a Statute," *Virginia Law Review,* vol. 62 (1976); Arthur S. Miller, "Whistle Blowing and the Law," in Ralph Nader, Peter J. Petkas, and Kate Blackwell, *Whistle Blowing,* New York: Grossman Publishers, 1972; Alan F. Westin, *Whistle Blowing!,* New York: McGraw-Hill, 1981. See also vol. 16, no. 2, Winter 1983, *University of Michigan Journal of Law Reform,* special issue, "Individual Rights in the Workplace: The Employment-At-Will Issue."
2. For a discussion of this study which was conducted by Morton Corn see Frank von Hipple, "Professional Freedom and Responsibility: The Role of the Professional Society," *Newsletter on Science, Technology and Human Values,* vol. 22, January 1978.
3. See Westin, *Whistle Blowing!*
4. See Martin H. Marlin, "Protecting the Whistleblower from Retaliatory Discharge," in the special issue of the *University of Michigan Journal of Law Reform.*
5. David W. Ewing, *Freedom inside the Organization,* New York: E. P. Dutton, 1977, pp. 165–166.
6. For a more detailed discussion of this argument see Gene G. James, "Whistle Blowing: Its Nature and Justification," *Philosophy in Context,* vol. 10 (1980).
7. See Richard T. De George, 2d ed., *Business Ethics,* New York: Macmillan, 1986. Earlier versions of De George's criteria can be found in the first edition (1982), and in "Ethical Responsibilities of Engineers in Large Organizations," *Business and Professional Ethics Journal,* vol. 1, no. 1, Fall 1981.
8. De George, *Business Ethics,* pp. 230–234.

9. *Ibid.,* p. 223.
10. *Ibid.,* p. 237.
11. De George, "Ethical Responsibilities of Engineers," p. 1.
12. *Ibid.,* p. 5.
13. *Ibid.*
14. De George, *Business Ethics,* p. 235.
15. *Ibid.,* p. 234.
16. Frederick A. Ellison, "Anonymous Whistleblowing," *Business and Professional Ethics Journal,* vol. 1, no. 2, Winter 1982.
17. De George, *Business Ethics,* p. 223.
18. *Ibid.,* p. 234.
19. Peter Raven-Hansen, "Dos and Don'ts for Whistleblowers: Planning for Trouble," *Technology Review,* May 1980, p. 30. My discussion in this section is heavily indebted to this article.
20. De George, *Business Ethics,* p. 222.
21. People who blow the whistle on tax evaders in fact rarely receive any money because the law leaves payment to the discretion of the Internal Revenue Service.

QUESTIONS FOR DISCUSSION

1. Does Machan's argument that there should be no special workers' rights make sense? What do you think would happen if occupational health and safety legislation did not exist?
2. Some argue that employers are entitled to "job relevant" information about their employees but that acquiring information that is not job relevant violates employees' privacy. What could be meant by "job relevant" information? Why do Des Jardins and Duska argue that the information revealed by drug tests isn't really job relevant?
3. You are director of personnel for a large company that produces insecticides. The president of the company asks for your advice on instituting a drug-testing program. Should one be instituted? If not, why not? If so, what is the fairest possible way to do so? Having read all the readings in this chapter, draft a memo to the president with your answer.
4. Discuss the case "Lanscape" in light of the article by Pincus Hartman. How far should employers be allowed to go in monitoring their employees' actions?
5. "Employees owe their employers loyalty and obedience; therefore, they should never blow the whistle." Make a case for or against this statement, keeping in mind the arguments of De George and James.
6. De George believes that employees are obligated to blow the whistle only if they have documented evidence of a serious harm, and if they have reason to believe that whistle-blowing will be effective in preventing the harm. Why does James think these criteria are too strict? Do you agree with De George or James, and why?

CHAPTER 6

The Modern Workplace: Transition to Equality and Diversity

The Moral Status of Affirmative Action

Louis P. Pojman
Professor of Philosophy, United States Military Academy, West Point

"A ruler who appoints any man to an office, when there is in his dominion another man better qualified for it, sins against God and against the State."

—The *Koran*

"[Affirmative Action] is the meagerest recompense for centuries of unrelieved oppression."

—quoted by Shelby Steele as the justification for Affirmative Action

Hardly a week goes by but that the subject of Affirmative Action does not come up. Whether in the guise of reverse discrimination, preferential hiring, non-traditional casting, quotas, goals and time tables, minority scholarships, or race-norming, the issue confronts us as a terribly perplexing problem. Last summer's Actor's Equity debacle over the casting of the British actor, Jonathan Pryce, as a

From *Public Affairs Quarterly,* Vol. 6, Issue 2 (April 1992), pp. 181–206. Reprinted by permission of *Public Affairs Quarterly.*

Eurasian in Miss Saigon; Assistant Secretary of Education Michael Williams' judgement that Minority Scholarships are unconstitutional; the "Civil Rights Bill of 1991," reversing recent decisions of the Supreme Court which constrain preferential hiring practices; the demand that Harvard Law School hire a black female professor; grade stipends for black students at Pennsylvania State University and other schools; the revelations of race norming in state employment agencies; as well as debates over quotas, underutilization guidelines, and diversity in employment; all testify to the importance of this subject for contemporary society.

There is something salutary as well as terribly tragic inherent in this problem. The salutary aspect is the fact that our society has shown itself committed to eliminating unjust discrimination. Even in the heart of Dixie there is a recognition of the injustice of racial discrimination. Both sides of the affirmative action debate have good will and appeal to moral principles. Both sides are attempting to bring about a better society, one which is color blind, but they differ profoundly on the morally proper means to accomplish that goal.

And this is just the tragedy of the situation: good people on both sides of the issue are ready to tear each other to pieces over a problem that has no easy or obvious solution. And so the voices become shrill and the rhetoric hyperbolic. The same spirit which divides the pro-choice movement from the right to life movement on abortion divides liberal pro-Affirmative Action advocates from liberal anti-Affirmative Action advocates. This problem, more than any other, threatens to destroy the traditional liberal consensus in our society. I have seen family members and close friends who until recently fought on the same side of the barricades against racial injustice divide in enmity over this issue. The anti-affirmative liberals ("liberals who've been mugged") have tended towards a form of neo-conservativism and the pro-affirmative liberals have tended to side with the radical left to form the "politically correct ideology" movement.

In this paper I will confine myself primarily to Affirmative Action policies with regard to race, but much of what I say can be applied to the areas of gender and ethnic minorities.

I. DEFINITIONS

First let me define my terms:

Discrimination is simply judging one thing to differ from another on the basis of some criterion. "Discrimination" is essentially a good quality, having reference to our ability to make distinctions. As rational and moral agents we need to make proper distinctions. To be rational is to discriminate between good and bad arguments, and to think morally is to discriminate between reasons based on valid principles and those based on invalid ones. What needs to be distinguished is the difference between rational and moral discrimination, on the one hand, and irrational and immoral discrimination, on the other hand.

Prejudice is a discrimination based on irrelevant grounds. It may simply be an attitude which never surfaces in action, or it may cause prejudicial actions. A prejudicial discrimination in action is immoral if it denies someone a fair deal. So discrimination on the basis of race or sex where these are not relevant for job performance is unfair. Likewise, one may act prejudicially in applying a relevant criterion on insufficient grounds, as in the case where I apply the criterion of being a hard worker but then assume, on insufficient evidence, that the black man who applies for the job is not a hard worker.

There is a difference between *prejudice* and *bias*. Bias signifies a tendency towards one thing rather than another where the evidence is incomplete or based on non-moral factors. For example, you may have a bias towards blondes and I towards red-heads. But prejudice is an attitude (or action) where unfairness is present—where one *should* know or do better, as in the case where I give people jobs simply because they are red-heads. Bias implies ignorance or incomplete knowledge, whereas prejudice is deeper, involving a moral failure—usually a failure to pay attention to the evidence. But note that calling people racist or sexist without good evidence is also an act of prejudice. I call this form of prejudice "defamism," for it unfairly defames the victim. It is a contemporary version of McCarthyism.

Equal Opportunity is offering everyone a fair chance at the best positions that society has at its disposal. Only native aptitude and effort should be decisive in the outcome, not factors of race, sex or special favors.

Affirmative Action is the effort to rectify the injustice of the past by special policies. Put this way, it is Janus-faced or ambiguous, having both a backward-looking and a forward-looking feature. The backward-looking feature is its attempt to correct and compensate for past injustice. This aspect of Affirmative Action is strictly deontological. The forward-looking feature is its implicit ideal of a society free from prejudice; this is both deontological and utilitarian.

When we look at a social problem from a backward-looking perspective we need to determine who has committed or benefited from a wrongful or prejudicial act and to determine who deserves compensation for that act.

When we look at a social problem from a forward-looking perspective we need to determine what a just society (one free from prejudice) would look like and how to obtain that kind of society. The forward-looking aspect of Affirmative Action is paradoxically race-conscious, since it uses race to bring about a society which is not race-conscious, which is colorblind (in the morally relevant sense of this term).

It is also useful to distinguish two versions of Affirmative Action. *Weak Affirmative Action* involves such measures as the elimination of segregation (namely the idea of "separate but equal"), widespread advertisement to groups not previously represented in certain privileged positions, special scholarships for the disadvantaged classes (e.g., all the poor), using underrepresentation or a history of past discrimination as a tie breaker when candidates are relatively equal, and the like.

Strong Affirmative Action involves more positive steps to eliminate past injustice, such as reverse discrimination, hiring candidates on the basis of race and gender in order to reach equal or near equal results, proportionate representation in each area of society.

II. ARGUMENTS FOR AFFIRMATIVE ACTION

Let us now survey the main arguments typically cited in the debate over Affirmative Action. I will briefly discuss seven arguments on each side of the issue.

1. Need For Role Models

This argument is straightforward. We all have need of role models, and it helps to know that others like us can be successful. We learn and are encouraged to strive for excellence by emulating our heroes and role models.

However, it is doubtful whether role models of one's own racial or sexual type are necessary for success. One of my heroes was Gandhi, an Indian Hindu, another was my grade school science teacher, one Miss DeVoe, and another was Martin Luther King. More important than having role models of one's own type is having genuinely good people, of whatever race or gender, to emulate. Furthermore, even if it is of some help to people with low self-esteem to gain encouragement from seeing others of their particular kind in leadership roles, it is doubtful whether this need is a sufficient condition to justify preferential hiring or reverse discrimination. What good is a role model who is inferior to other professors or business personnel? Excellence will rise to the top in a system of fair opportunity. Natural development of role models will come more slowly and more surely. Proponents of preferential policies simply lack the patience to let history take its own course.

2. The Need of Breaking the Stereotypes

Society may simply need to know that there are talented blacks and women, so that it does not automatically assign them lesser respect or status. We need to have unjustified stereotype beliefs replaced with more accurate ones about the talents of blacks and women. So we need to engage in preferential hiring of qualified minorities even when they are not the most qualified.

Again, the response is that hiring the less qualified is neither fair to those better qualified who are passed over nor an effective way of removing inaccurate stereotypes. If competence is accepted as the criterion for hiring, then it is unjust to override it for purposes of social engineering. Furthermore, if blacks or women are known to hold high positions simply because of reverse discrimination, then they will still lack the respect due to those of their rank. In New York City there is a saying among doctors, "Never go to a black physician under 40," referring to the fact that AA has affected the medical system during the past fifteen years. The police use "Quota Cops" and "Welfare Sergeants" to refer to those hired without passing the standardized tests. (In 1985 180 black and hispanic policemen, who had failed a promotion test, were promoted anyway to the rank of sergeant.) The destruction of false stereotypes will come naturally as qualified blacks rise naturally in fair competition (or if it does not—then the stereotypes may be justified). Reverse discrimination sends the message home that the stereotypes are deserved—otherwise, why do these minorities need so much extra help?

3. Equal Results Argument

Some philosophers and social scientists hold that human nature is roughly identical, so that on a fair playing field the same proportion from every race and gender and ethnic group would attain to the highest positions in every area of endeavor. It would follow that any inequality of results itself is evidence for inequality of opportunity. John Arthur, in discussing an intelligence test, Test 21, puts the case this way.

> History is important when considering governmental rules like Test 21 because low scores by blacks can

be traced in large measure to the legacy of slavery and racism: segregation, poor schooling, exclusion from trade unions, malnutrition, and poverty have all played their roles. Unless one assumes that blacks are naturally less able to pass the test, the conclusion must be that the results are themselves socially and legally constructed, not a mere given for which law and society can claim no responsibility.

The conclusion seems to be that genuine equality eventually requires equal results. Obviously blacks have been treated unequally throughout U.S. history, and just as obviously the economic and psychological effects of that inequality linger to this day, showing up in lower income and poorer performance in school and on tests than whites achieve. Since we have no reason to believe that differences in performance can be explained by factors other than history, equal results are a good benchmark by which to measure progress made toward genuine equality.[1]

The result of a just society should be equal numbers in proportion to each group in the work force.

However, Arthur fails even to consider studies that suggest that there are innate differences between races, sexes, and groups. If there are genetic differences in intelligence and temperament within families, why should we not expect such differences between racial groups and the two genders? Why should the evidence for this be completely discounted?

Perhaps some race or one gender is more intelligent in one way than another. At present we have only limited knowledge about genetic differences, but what we do have suggests some difference besides the obvious physiological traits.[2] The proper use of this evidence is not to promote discriminatory policies but to be *open* to the possibility that innate differences may have led to an over-representation of certain groups in certain areas of endeavor. It seems that on average blacks have genetic endowments favoring them in the development of skills necessary for excellence in basketball.

Furthermore, on Arthur's logic, we should take aggressive AA against Asians and Jews since they are over-represented in science, technology, and medicine. So that each group receives its fair share, we should ensure that 12% of the philosophers in the United States are Black, reduce the percentage of Jews from an estimated 15% to 2%—firing about 1,300 Jewish philosophers. The fact that Asians are producing 50% of Ph.D's in science and math and blacks less than 1% clearly shows, on this reasoning, that we are providing special secret advantages to Asians.

But why does society have to enter into this results game in the first place? Why do we have to decide whether all difference is environmental or genetic? Perhaps we should simply admit that we lack sufficient evidence to pronounce on these issues with any certainty—but if so, should we not be more modest in insisting on equal results? Here is a thought experiment. Take two families of different racial groups, Green and Blue. The Greens decide to have only two children, to spend all their resources on them, to give them the best education. The two Green kids respond well and end up with achievement test scores in the 99th percentile. The Blues fail to practice family planning. They have 15 children. They can only afford 2 children, but lack of ability or whatever prevents them from keeping their family down. Now they need help for their large family. Why does society have to step in and help them? Society did not force them to have 15 children. Suppose that the achievement test scores of the 15 children fall below the 25th percentile. They cannot compete with the Greens. But now enters AA. It says that it is society's fault that the Blue children are not as able as the Greens and that the Greens must pay extra taxes to enable the Blues to compete. No restraints are put on the Blues regarding family size. This seems unfair to the Greens. Should the Green children be made to bear responsibility for the consequences of the Blues' voluntary behavior?

My point is simply that Arthur needs to cast his net wider and recognize that demographics and childbearing and -rearing practices are crucial factors in achievement. People have to take some responsibility for their actions. The equal results argument (or axiom) misses a greater part of the picture.

4. The Compensation Argument

The argument goes like this: blacks have been wronged and severely harmed by whites. Therefore white society should compensate blacks for the injury caused them. Reverse discrimination in terms of preferential hiring, contracts, and scholarships is a fitting way to compensate for the past wrongs.

This argument actually involves a distorted notion of compensation. Normally, we think of compensation as owed by a specific person *A* to another person *B* whom *A* has wronged in a specific way *C*. For example, if I have stolen your car and used it for a period of time to make business profits that would have gone to you, it is not enough that I return your car. I must pay you an amount reflecting your loss and my ability to pay. If I have only made $5,000 and only have $10,000 in assets, it would not be possible for you to collect $20,000 in damages—even though that is the amount of loss you have incurred.

Sometimes compensation is extended to groups of people who have been unjustly harmed by the greater society. For example, the United States government has compensated the Japanese-Americans who were interred during the Second World War, and the West German government has paid reparations to the survivors of Nazi concentration camps. But here a specific people have been identified who were wronged in an identifiable way by the government of the nation in question.

On the face of it the demand by blacks for compensation does not fit the usual pattern. Perhaps Southern States with Jim Crow laws could be accused of unjustly harming blacks, but it is hard to see that the United States government was involved in doing so. Furthermore, it is not clear that all blacks were harmed in the same way or whether some were *unjustly* harmed or harmed more than poor whites and others (e.g., short people). Finally, even if identifiable blacks were harmed by identifiable social practices, it is not clear that most forms of Affirmative Action are appropriate to restore the situation. The usual practice of a financial payment seems more appropriate than giving a high level job to someone unqualified or only minimally qualified, who, speculatively, might have been better qualified had he not been subject to racial discrimination. If John is the star tailback of our college team with a promising professional future, and I accidentally (but culpably) drive my pick-up truck over his legs, and so cripple him, John may be due compensation, but he is not due the tailback spot on the football team.

Still, there may be something intuitively compelling about compensating members of an oppressed group who are minimally qualified. Suppose that the Hatfields and the McCoys are enemy clans and some youths from the Hatfields go over and steal diamonds and gold from the McCoys, distributing it within the Hatfield economy. Even though we do not know which Hatfield youths did the stealing, we would want to restore the wealth, as far as possible, to the McCoys. One way might be to tax the Hatfields, but another might be to give preferential treatment in terms of scholarships and training programs and hiring to the McCoys.[3]

This is perhaps the strongest argument for Affirmative Action, and it may well justify some weak versions of AA, but it is doubtful whether it is sufficient to justify strong versions with quotas and goals and time tables in skilled positions. There are at least two reasons for this. First, we have no way of knowing how many people of group *G* would have been at competence level *L* had the world been different. Secondly, the normal criterion of competence is a strong *prima facie* consideration when the most important positions are at stake. There are two reasons for this: (1) society has given people expectations that if they attain certain levels of excellence they will be awarded appropriately and (2) filling the most important positions with the best qualified is the best way to insure efficiency in job-related areas and in society in general. These reasons are not absolutes. They can be overridden. But there is a strong presumption in their favor so that a burden of proof rests with those who would override them.

At this point we get into the problem of whether innocent non-blacks should have to pay a penalty in terms of preferential hiring of blacks. We turn to that argument.

5. Compensation from Those who Innocently Benefited from Past Injustice

White males as innocent beneficiaries of unjust discrimination of blacks and women have no grounds for complaint when society seeks to rectify the tilted field. White males may be innocent of oppressing blacks and minorities (and women), but they have unjustly benefited from that oppression or discrimination. So it is perfectly proper that less qualified women and blacks be hired before them.

The operative principle is: He who knowingly and willingly benefits from a wrong must help pay for the wrong. Judith Jarvis Thomson puts it this way. "Many [white males] have been direct beneficiaries of policies which have down-graded blacks and women . . . and even those who did not directly benefit . . . had, at any rate, the advantage in the competition which comes of the confidence in one's full membership [in the community], and of one's right being recognized as a matter of course."[4] That is, white males obtain advantages in self respect and self-confidence deriving from a racist system which denies these to blacks and women.

Objection. As I noted in the previous section, compensation is normally individual and specific. If *A* harms *B* regarding *x*, *B* has a right to compensation from *A* in regards to *x*. If *A* steals *B*'s car and wrecks it, *A* has an obligation to compensate *B* for the stolen car, but *A*'s son has no obligation to compensate *B*. Furthermore, if *A* dies or disappears, *B* has no moral right to claim that society compensate him for the stolen car—though if he has insurance, he can make such a claim to the insurance company. Sometimes a wrong cannot be compensated, and we just have to make the best of an imperfect world.

Suppose my parents, divining that I would grow up to have an unsurpassable desire to be a basketball player, bought an expensive growth hormone for me. Unfortunately, a neighbor stole it and gave it to little Lew Alcindor, who gained the extra 18 inches—my 18 inches—and shot up to an enviable 7 feet 2 inches. Alias Kareem Abdul Jabbar, he excelled in basketball, as I would have done had I had my proper dose.

Do I have a right to the millions of dollars that Jabbar made as a professional basketball player—the unjustly innocent beneficiary of my growth hormone? I have a right to something from the neighbor who stole the hormone, and it might be kind of Jabbar to give me free tickets to the Laker basketball games, and perhaps I should be remembered in his will. As far as I can see, however, he does not *owe* me anything, either legally or morally.

Suppose further that Lew Alcindor and I are in high school together and we are both qualified to play basketball, only he is far better than I. Do I

deserve to start in his position because I would have been as good as he is had someone not cheated me as a child? Again, I think not. But if being the lucky beneficiary of wrong-doing does not entail that Alcindor (or the coach) owes me anything in regards to basketball, why should it be a reason to engage in preferential hiring in academic positions or highly coveted jobs? If minimal qualifications are not adequate to override excellence in basketball, even when the minimality is a consequence of wrong-doing, why should they be adequate in other areas?

6. The Diversity Argument

It is important that we learn to live in a pluralistic world, learning to get along with those of other races and cultures, so we should have fully integrated schools and employment situations. Diversity is an important symbol and educative device. Thus preferential treatment is warranted to perform this role in society.

But, again, while we can admit the value of diversity, it hardly seems adequate to override considerations of merit and efficiency. Diversity for diversity's sake is moral promiscuity, since it obfuscates rational distinctions, and unless those hired are highly qualified the diversity factor threatens to become a fetish. At least at the higher levels of business and the professions, competence far outweighs considerations of diversity. I do not care whether the group of surgeons operating on me reflect racial or gender balance, but I do care that they are highly qualified. And likewise with airplane pilots, military leaders, business executives, and, may I say it, teachers and professors. Moreover, there are other ways of learning about other cultures besides engaging in reverse discrimination.

7. Anti-Meritocratic (Desert) Argument to Justify Reverse Discrimination: "No One Deserves His Talents"

According to this argument, the competent do not deserve their intelligence, their superior character, their industriousness, or their discipline; therefore they have no right to the best positions in society; therefore society is not unjust in giving these positions to less (but still minimally) qualified blacks and women. In one form this argument holds that since no one deserves anything, society may use any criteria it pleases to distribute goods. The criterion most often designated is social utility. Versions of this argument are found in the writings of John Arthur, John Rawls, Bernard Boxill, Michael Kinsley, Ronald Dworkin, and Richard Wasserstrom. Rawls writes, "No one deserves his place in the distribution of native endowments, any more than one deserves one's initial starting place in society. The assertion that a man deserves the superior character that enables him to make the effort to cultivate his abilities is equally problematic; for his character depends in large part upon fortunate family and social circumstances for which he can claim no credit. The notion of desert seems not to apply to these cases."[5] Michael Kinsley is even more adamant:

> Opponents of affirmative action are hung up on a distinction that seems more profoundly irrelevant: treating individuals versus treating groups. What is the moral difference between dispensing favors to people on their "merits" as individuals and passing out society's benefits on the basis of group identification?
>
> Group identifications like race and sex are, of course, immutable. They have nothing to do with a person's moral worth. But the same is true of most of what comes under the label "merit." The tools you need for getting ahead in a meritocratic society—not all of them but most: talent, education, instilled cultural values such as ambition—are distributed just as arbitrarily as skin color. They are fate. The notion that people somehow "deserve" the advantages of these characteristics in a way they don't "deserve" the advantage of their race is powerful, but illogical.[6]

It will help to put the argument in outline form.

1. Society may award jobs and positions as it sees fit as long as individuals have no claim to these positions.
2. To have a claim to something means that one has earned it or deserves it.
3. But no one has earned or deserves his intelligence, talent, education or cultural values which produce superior qualifications.
4. If a person does not deserve what produces something, he does not deserve its products.
5. Therefore better qualified people do not deserve their qualifications.

6. Therefore, society may override their qualifications in awarding jobs and positions as it sees fit (for social utility or to compensate for previous wrongs).

So it is permissible if a minimally qualified black or woman is admitted to law or medical school ahead of a white male with excellent credentials or if a less qualified person from an "underutilized" group gets a professorship ahead of a far better qualified white male. Sufficiency and underutilization together outweigh excellence.

Objection. Premise 4 is false. To see this, reflect that just because I do not deserve the money that I have been given as a gift (for instance) does not mean that I am not entitled to what I get with that money. If you and I both get a gift of $100 and I bury mine in the sand for 5 years while you invest yours wisely and double its value at the end of five years, I cannot complain that you should split the increase 50/50 since neither of us deserved the original gift. If we accept the notion of responsibility at all, we must hold that persons deserve the fruits of their labor and conscious choices. Of course, we might want to distinguish moral from legal desert and argue that, morally speaking, effort is more important than outcome, whereas, legally speaking, outcome may be more important. Nevertheless, there are good reasons in terms of efficiency, motivation, and rough justice for holding a strong *prima facie* principle of giving scarce high positions to those most competent.

The attack on moral desert is perhaps the most radical move that egalitarians like Rawls and company have made against meritocracy, but the ramifications of their attack are far reaching. The following are some of its implications. Since I do not deserve my two good eyes or two good kidneys, the social engineers may take one of each from me to give to those needing an eye or a kidney—even if they have damaged their organs by their own voluntary actions. Since no one deserves anything, we do not deserve pay for our labors or praise for a job well done or first prize in the race we win. The notion of moral responsibility vanishes in a system of levelling.

But there is no good reason to accept the argument against desert. We do act freely and, as such, we are responsible for our actions. We deserve the fruits of our labor, reward for our noble feats and punishment for our misbehavior.

We have considered seven arguments for Affirmative Action and have found no compelling case for Strong AA and only one plausible argument (a version of the compensation argument) for Weak AA. We must now turn to the arguments against Affirmative Action to see whether they fare any better.[7]

III. ARGUMENTS AGAINST AFFIRMATIVE ACTION

1. Affirmative Action Requires Discrimination Against a Different Group

Weak Affirmative Action weakly discriminates against new minorities, mostly innocent young white males, and Strong Affirmative Action strongly discriminates against these new minorities. As I argued in II.5, this discrimination is unwarranted, since, even if some compensation to blacks were indicated, it would be unfair to make innocent white males bear the whole brunt of the payments. In fact, it is poor white youth who become the new pariahs on the job market. The children of the wealthy have no trouble getting into the best private grammar schools and, on the basis of superior early education, into the best universities, graduate schools, managerial and professional positions. Affirmative Action simply shifts injustice, setting blacks and women against young white males, especially ethnic and poor white males. It does little to rectify the goal of providing equal opportunity to all. If the goal is a society where everyone has a fair chance, then it would be better to concentrate on support for families and early education and decide the matter of university admissions and job hiring on the basis of traditional standards of competence.

2. Affirmative Action Perpetuates the Victimization Syndrome

Shelby Steele admits that Affirmative Action may seem "the meagerest recompense for centuries of unrelieved oppression" and that it helps promote diversity. At the same time, though, notes Steele, Affirmative Action reinforces the spirit of victimization by telling blacks that they can gain more by emphasizing their suffering, degradation and helplessness than by discipline and work. This message holds the danger of blacks becoming permanently handicapped by a need for special treatment. It also sends to society at large the message that blacks cannot make it on their own.

Leon Wieseltier sums up the problem this way.

> The memory of oppression is a pillar and a strut of the identity of every people oppressed. It is no ordinary marker of difference. It is unusually stiffening. It instructs the individual and the group about what to expect of the world, imparts an isolating sense of aptness. . . . Don't be fooled, it teaches, there is only repetition. For that reason, the collective memory of an oppressed people is not only a treasure but a trap.
>
> In the memory of oppression, oppression outlives itself. The scar does the work of the wound. That is the real tragedy: that injustice retains the power to distort long after it has ceased to be real. It is a posthumous victory for the oppressors, when pain becomes a tradition. And yet the atrocities of the past must never be forgotten. This is the unfairly difficult dilemma of the newly emancipated and the newly enfranchised: an honorable life is not possible if they remember too little and a normal life is not possible if they remember too much.[8]

With the eye of recollection, which does not "remember too much," Steele recommends a policy which offers "educational and economic development of disadvantaged people regardless of race and the eradication from our society—through close monitoring and severe sanctions—of racial and gender discrimination."[9]

3. Affirmative Action Encourages Mediocrity and Incompetence

Last Spring Jesse Jackson joined protesters at Harvard Law School in demanding that the Law School faculty hire black women. Jackson dismissed Dean of the Law School, Robert C. Clark's standard of choosing the best qualified person for the job as "Cultural anemia." "We cannot just define who is qualified in the most narrow vertical academic terms," he said. "Most people in the world are yellow, brown, black, poor, non-Christian and don't speak English, and they can't wait for some White males with archaic rules to appraise them."[10] It might be noted that if Jackson is correct about the depth of cultural decadence at Harvard, blacks might be well advised to form and support their own more vital law schools and leave places like Harvard to their archaism.

At several universities, the administration has forced departments to hire members of minorities even when far superior candidates were available. Shortly after obtaining my Ph.D. in the late 70's I was mistakenly identified as a black philosopher (I had a civil rights record and was once a black studies major) and was flown to a major university, only to be rejected for a more qualified candidate when it was discovered that I was white.

Stories of the bad effects of Affirmative Action abound. The philosopher Sidney Hook writes that "At one Ivy League university, representatives of the Regional HEW demanded an explanation of why there were no women or minority students in the Graduate Department of Religious Studies. They were told that a reading of knowledge of Hebrew and Greek was presupposed. Whereupon the representatives of HEW advised orally: 'Then end those old fashioned programs that require irrelevant languages. And start up programs on relevant things which minority group students can study without learning languages.'"[11]

Nicholas Capaldi notes that the staff of HEW itself was one-half women, three-fifths members of minorities, and one-half black—a clear case of racial over-representation.

In 1972 officials at Stanford University discovered a proposal for the government to monitor curriculum in higher education: the "Summary Statement . . . Sex Discrimination Proposed HEW Regulation to Effectuate Title IX of the Education Amendment of 1972" to "establish and use internal procedure for reviewing curricula, designed both to ensure that they do not reflect discrimination on the basis of sex and to resolve complaints concerning allegations of such discrimination, pursuant to procedural standards to be prescribed by the Director of the office of Civil Rights." Fortu-

nately, Secretary of HEW Caspar Weinberger when alerted to the intrusion, assured Stanford University that he would never approve of it.[12]

Government programs of enforced preferential treatment tend to appeal to the lowest possible common denominator. Witness the 1974 HEW Revised Order No. 14 on Affirmative Action expectations for preferential hiring: "Neither minorities nor female employees should be required to possess higher qualifications than those of the lowest qualified incumbents."

Furthermore, no tests may be given to candidates unless it is *proved* to be relevant to the job.

> No standard or criteria which have, by intent or effect, worked to exclude women or minorities as a class can be utilized, unless the institution can demonstrate the necessity of such standard to the performance of the job in question.
>
> Whenever a validity study is called for . . . the user should include . . . an investigation of suitable alternative selection procedures and suitable alternative methods of using the selection procedure which have as little adverse impact as possible. . . . Whenever the user is shown an alternative selection procedure with evidence of less adverse impact and substantial evidence of validity for the same job in similar circumstances, the user should investigate it to determine the appropriateness of using or validating it in accord with these guidelines.[13]

At the same time Americans are wondering why standards in our country are falling and the Japanese are getting ahead. Affirmative Action with its twin idols, Sufficiency and Diversity, is the enemy of excellence. I will develop this thought below (III.6).

4. Affirmative Action Policies Unjustly Shift the Burden of Proof

Affirmative Action legislation tends to place the burden of proof on the employer who does not have an "adequate" representation of "underutilized" groups in his work force. He is guilty until proven innocent. I have already recounted how in the mid-eighties the Supreme Court shifted the burden of proof back onto the plaintiff, while Congress is now attempting to shift the burden back to the employer. Those in favor of deeming disproportional representation "guilty until proven innocent" argue that it is easy for employers to discriminate against minorities by various subterfuges, and I agree that steps should be taken to monitor against prejudicial treatment. But being prejudiced against employers is not the way to attain a just solution to discrimination. The principle: innocent until proven guilty, applies to employers as well as criminals. Indeed, it is clearly special pleading to reject this basic principle of Anglo-American law in this case of discrimination while adhering to it everywhere else.

5. An Argument from Merit

Traditionally, we have believed that the highest positions in society should be awarded to those who are best qualified—as the Koran states in the quotation at the beginning of this paper. Rewarding excellence both seems just to the individuals in the competition and makes for efficiency. Note that one of the most successful acts of integration, the recruitment of Jackie Robinson in the late 40's, was done in just this way, according to merit. If Robinson had been brought into the major league as a mediocre player or had batted .200 he would have been scorned and sent back to the minors where he belonged.

Merit is not an absolute value. There are times when it may be overridden for social goals, but there is a strong *prima facie* reason for awarding positions on its basis, and it should enjoy a weighty presumption in our social practices.

In a celebrated article Ronald Dworkin says that "Bakke had no case" because society did not owe Bakke anything. That may be, but then why does it owe anyone anything? Dworkin puts the matter in Utility terms, but if that is the case, society may owe Bakke a place at the University of California/Davis, for it seems a reasonable rule-utilitarian principle that achievement should be rewarded in society. We generally want the best to have the best positions, the best qualified candidate to win the political office, the most brilliant and competent scientist to be chosen for the most challenging research project, the best qualified pilots to become commercial pilots, only the best soldiers to become generals. Only when little is at stake do we weaken

the standards and content ourselves with sufficiency (rather than excellence)—there are plenty of jobs where "sufficiency" rather than excellence is required. Perhaps we now feel that medicine or law or university professorships are so routine that they can be performed by minimally qualified people—in which case AA has a place.

But note, no one is calling for quotas or proportional representation of *underutilized* groups in the National Basketball Association where blacks make up 80% of the players. But if merit and merit alone reigns in sports, should it not be valued at least as much in education and industry?

6. The Slippery Slope

Even if Strong AA or Reverse Discrimination could meet the other objections, it would face a tough question: once you embark on this project, how do you limit it? Who should be excluded from reverse discrimination? Asians and Jews are overrepresented, so if we give blacks positive quotas, should we place negative quotas to these other groups? Since white males, "WMs," are a minority which is suffering from reverse discrimination, will we need a New Affirmative Action policy in the 21st century to compensate for the discrimination against WMs in the late 20th century?

Furthermore, Affirmative Action has stigmatized the *young* white male. Assuming that we accept reverse discrimination, the fair way to make sacrifices would be to retire *older* white males who are more likely to have benefited from a favored status. Probably the least guilty of any harm to minority groups is the young white male—usually a liberal who has been required to bear the brunt of ages of past injustice. Justice Brennan's announcement that the Civil Rights Act did not apply to discrimination against white shows how the clearest language can be bent to serve the ideology of the moment.[14]

7. The Mounting Evidence Against the Success of Affirmative Action

Thomas Sowell of the Hoover Institute has shown in his book *Preferential Policies: An International Perspective* that preferential hiring almost never solves social problems. It generally builds in mediocrity or incompetence and causes deep resentment. It is a short term solution which lacks serious grounding in social realities.

For instance, Sowell cites some disturbing statistics on education. Although twice as many blacks as Asian students took the nationwide Scholastic Aptitude Test in 1983, approximately fifteen times as many Asian students scored above 700 (out of a possible 800) on the mathematics half of the SAT. The percentage of Asians who scored above 700 in math was also more than six times higher than the percentage of American Indians and more than ten times higher than that of Mexican Americans—as well as more than double the percentage of whites. As Sowell points out, in all countries studied, "intergroup performance disparities are huge" (108).

> There are dozens of American colleges and universities where the median combined verbal SAT score and mathematics SAT score total 1200 or above. As of 1983 there were less than 600 black students in the entire US with combined SAT scores of 1200. This meant that, despite widespread attempts to get a black student "representation" comparable to the black percentage of the population (about 11%), there were not enough black students in the entire country for the Ivy League alone to have such a "representation" without going beyond this pool—even if the entire pool went to the eight Ivy League colleges.[15]

Often it is claimed that a cultural bias is the cause of the poor performance of blacks on SAT (or IQ tests), but Sowell shows that these test scores are actually a better predictor of college performance for blacks than for Asians and whites. He also shows the harmfulness of the effect on blacks of preferential acceptance. At the University of California, Berkeley, where the freshman class closely reflects the actual ethnic distribution of California high school students, more than 70% of blacks fail to graduate. All 312 black students entering Berkeley in 1987 were admitted under "Affirmative Action" criteria rather than by meeting standard academic criteria. So were 480 out of 507 Hispanic students. In 1986 the median SAT score for blacks at Berkeley was 952, for Mexican Americans 1014, for American Indians 1082 and for Asian Americans 1254. (The average SAT for all students was 1181.)

The result of this mismatching is that blacks who might do well if they went to a second tier or third tier school where their test scores would indicate they belong, actually are harmed by preferential treatment. They cannot compete in the institutions where high abilities are necessary.

Sowell also points out that Affirmative Action policies have mainly assisted the middle class black, those who have suffered least from discrimination. "Black couples in which both husband and wife are college-educated overtook white couples of the same description back in the early 1970's and continued to at least hold their own in the 1980's" (115).

Sowell's conclusion is that similar patterns of results obtained from India to the USA wherever preferential policies exist. "In education, preferential admissions policies have led to high attrition rates and substandard performances for those preferred students . . . who survived to graduate." In all countries the preferred tended to concentrate in less difficult subjects which lead to less remunerative careers. "In the employment market, both blacks and untouchables at the higher levels have advanced substantially while those at the lower levels show no such advancement and even some signs of retrogression. These patterns are also broadly consistent with patterns found in countries in which majorities have created preferences for themselves . . ."(116).

The tendency has been to focus at the high level end of education and employment rather than on the lower level of family structure and early education. But if we really want to help the worst off improve, we need to concentrate on the family and early education. It is foolish to expect equal results when we begin with grossly unequal starting points—and discriminating against young white males is no more just than discriminating against women, blacks or anyone else.

CONCLUSION

Let me sum up. The goal of the Civil Rights movement and of moral people everywhere has been equal opportunity. The question is: how best to get there. Civil Rights legislation removed the legal barriers to equal opportunity, but did not tackle the deeper causes that produced differential results. Weak Affirmative Action aims at encouraging minorities in striving for the highest positions without unduly jeopardizing the rights of majorities, but the problem of Weak Affirmative Action is that it easily slides into Strong Affirmative Action where quotas, "goals," and equal results are forced into groups, thus promoting mediocrity, inefficiency, and resentment. Furthermore, Affirmative Action aims at the higher levels of society—universities and skilled jobs—yet if we want to improve our society, the best way to do it is to concentrate on families, children, early education, and the like. Affirmative Action is, on the one hand, too much, too soon and on the other hand, too little, too late.

Martin Luther said that humanity is like a man mounting a horse who always tends to fall off on the other side of the horse. This seems to be the case with Affirmative Action. Attempting to redress the discriminatory iniquities of our history, our well-intentioned social engineers engage in new forms of discriminatory iniquity and thereby think that they have successfully mounted the horse of racial harmony. They have only fallen off on the other side of the issue.[16]

NOTES

1. John Arthur, *The Unfinished Constitution* (Belmont, CA, 1990), p. 238.
2. See Phillip E. Vernon's excellent summary of the literature in *Intelligence: Heredity and Environment* (New York, 1979) and Yves Christen "Sex Differences in the Human Brain" in Nicholas Davidson (ed.) *Gender Sanity* (Lanham, 1989) and T. Bouchard, *et al.,* "Sources of Human Psychological Differences: The Minnesota Studies of Twins Reared Apart," *Science,* vol. 250 (1990).
3. See Michael Levin, "Is Racial Discrimination Special?" *Policy Review,* Fall issue (1982).
4. Judith Jarvis Thomson, "Preferential Hiring" in Marshall Cohen, Thomas Nagel and Thomas Scanlon (eds.), *Equality and Preferential Treatment* (Princeton, 1977).
5. John Rawls, *A Theory of Justice* (Cambridge, 1971), p. 104; See Richard Wasserstrom "A Defense of Programs of Preferential Treatment," *National Forum* (Phi Kappa Phi Journal), vol. 58 (1978). See also Bernard Boxill, "The Morality of Preferential Hiring," *Philosophy and Public Affairs,* vol. 7 (1978).
6. Michael Kinsley, "Equal Lack of Opportunity," *Harper's,* June issue (1983).
7. There is one other argument which I have omitted. It is one from precedence and has been stated by Judith Jarvis Thomson in the article cited earlier:

   "Suppose two candidates for a civil service job have equally good test scores, but there is only one job available. We could decide between them by coin-tossing. But in fact we do allow for declaring for *A* straightaway, where *A* is a veteran, and *B* is not. It may be that *B* is a non-veteran through no fault of his own . . . Yet the fact is that *B* is not a veteran and *A* is. On the assumption that the veteran has served his country, the country owes him something. And it is plain that giving him preference is not an unjust way in which part of that debt of gratitude can be paid" (p. 379f).

   The two forms of preferential hiring are analogous. Veteran's preference is justified as a way of paying a debt of gratitude; preferential hiring is a way of paying a debt of compensation. In both cases innocent parties bear the burden of the community's debt, but it is justified.

   My response to this argument is that veterans should not be hired in place of better qualified candidates, but that benefits like the GI scholarships are part of the contract with veterans who serve their country in the armed services. The notion of compensation only applies to individuals who have been injured by identifiable entities. So the analogy between veterans and minority groups seems weak.
8. Quoted in Jim Sleeper, *The Closest of Strangers* (New York, 1990), p. 209.
9. Shelby Steele, "A Negative Vote on Affirmative Action," *New York Times,* May 13, 1990 issue.
10. *New York Times,* May 10, 1990 issue.
11. Nicholas Capaldi, *op. cit.,* p. 85.
12. Cited in Capaldi, *op. cit.,* p. 95.
13. *Ibid.*
14. The extreme form of this New Speak is incarnate in the Politically Correct Movement ("PC" ideology) where a new orthodoxy has emerged, condemning white, European culture and seeing African culture as the new savior of us all. Perhaps the clearest example of this is Paula Rothenberg's book *Racism and Sexism* (New York, 1987) which asserts that

there is no such thing as black racism; only whites are capable of racism (p. 6). Ms. Rothenberg's book has been scheduled as required reading for all freshmen at the University of Texas. See Joseph Salemi, "Lone Star Academic Politics," no. 87 (1990).

15. Thomas Sowell, *op. cit.,* p. 108.
16. I am indebted to Jim Landesman, Michael Levin, and Abigail Rosenthal for comments on a previous draft of this paper. I am also indebted to Nicholas Capaldi's *Out of Order* for first making me aware of the extent of the problem of Affirmative Action.

What Is Wrong with Reverse Discrimination?

Edwin C. Hettinger
Professor, Department of Philosophy and Religious Studies, College of Charleston

Many people think it obvious that reverse discrimination is unjust. Calling affirmative action reverse discrimination itself suggests this. This discussion evaluates numerous reasons given for this alleged injustice. Most of these accounts of what is wrong with reverse discrimination are found to be deficient. The explanations for why reverse discrimination is morally troubling show only that it is unjust in a relatively weak sense. This result has an important consequence for the wider issue of the moral justifiability of affirmative action. If social policies which involve minor injustice are permissible (and perhaps required) when they are required in order to overcome much greater injustice, then the mild injustice of reverse discrimination is easily overridden by its contribution to the important social goal of dismantling our sexual and racial caste system.

By 'reverse discrimination' or 'affirmative action' I shall mean hiring or admitting a slightly less well qualified woman or black, rather than a slightly more qualified white male, for the purpose of helping to eradicate sexual and/or racial inequality, or for the purpose of compensating

From *Business & Professional Ethics Journal* (Fall 1987), pp. 39–51. Reprinted by permission of the author.

women and blacks for the burdens and injustices they have suffered due to past and ongoing sexism and racism. There are weaker forms of affirmative action, such as giving preference to minority candidates only when qualifications are equal, or providing special educational opportunities for youths in disadvantaged groups. This paper seeks to defend the more controversial sort of reverse discrimination defined above. I begin by considering several spurious objections to reverse discrimination. In the second part, I identify the ways in which this policy is morally troubling and then assess the significance of these negative features.

SPURIOUS OBJECTIONS

1. Reverse Discrimination as Equivalent to Racism and Sexism

In a discussion on national television, George Will, the conservative news analyst and political philosopher, articulated the most common objection to reverse discrimination. It is unjust, he said, because it is discrimination on the basis of race or sex. Reverse discrimination against white males is the same evil as traditional discrimination against women and blacks. The only difference is that in this case it is the white male who is being discriminated against. Thus if traditional racism and sexism are wrong and unjust, so is reverse discrimination, and for the very same reasons.

But reverse discrimination is not at all like traditional sexism and racism. The motives and intentions behind it are completely different, as are its consequences. Consider some of the motives underlying traditional racial discrimination. Blacks were not hired or allowed into schools because it was felt that contact with them was degrading, and sullied whites. These policies were based on contempt and loathing for blacks, on a feeling that blacks were suitable only for subservient positions and that they should never have positions of authority over whites. Slightly better qualified white males are not being turned down under affirmative action for any of these reasons. No defenders or practitioners of affirmative action (and no significant segment of the general public) think that contact with white males is degrading or sullying, that white males are contemptible and loathsome, or that white males—by their nature—should be subservient to blacks or women.

The consequences of these two policies differ radically as well. Affirmative action does not stigmatize white males; it does not perpetuate unfortunate stereotypes about white males; it is not part of a pattern of discrimination that makes being a white male incredibly burdensome. Nor does it add to a particular group's "already overabundant supply" of power, authority, wealth, and opportunity, as does traditional racial and sexual discrimination. On the contrary, it results in a more egalitarian distribution of these social and economic benefits. If the motives and consequences of reverse discrimination and of traditional racism and sexism are completely different, in what sense could they be morally equivalent acts? If acts are to be individuated (for moral purposes) by including the motives, intentions, and consequences in their description, then clearly these two acts are not identical.

It might be argued that although the motives and consequences are different, the act itself is the same: reverse discrimination is discrimination on the basis of race and sex, and this is wrong in itself independently of its motives or consequences. But discriminating (i.e., making distinctions in how one treats people) on the basis of race or sex is not always wrong, nor is it necessarily unjust. It is not wrong, for example, to discriminate against one's own sex when choosing a spouse. Nor is racial or sexual discrimination in hiring necessarily wrong. This is shown by Peter Singer's example in which a director of a play about ghetto conditions in New York City refuses to consider any white applicants for the actors because she wants the play to be authentic.[1] If I am looking for a representative of the black community, or doing a study about blacks and disease, it is perfectly legitimate to discriminate against all whites. Their whiteness makes them unsuitable for my (legitimate) purposes. Similarly, if I am hiring a wet-nurse, or a person to patrol the women's change rooms in my department store, discriminating against males is perfectly legitimate.

These examples show that racial and sexual discrimination are not wrong in themselves. This is not to say that they are never wrong; most often they clearly are. Whether or not they are wrong, however, depends on the purposes, consequences, and context of such discrimination.

2. Race and Sex as Morally Arbitrary and Irrelevant Characteristics

A typical reason given for the alleged injustice of all racial and sexual discrimination (including affirmative action) is that it is morally arbitrary to consider race or sex when hiring, since these characteristics are not relevant to the decision. But the above examples show that not all uses of race or sex as a criterion in hiring decisions are morally arbitrary or irrelevant. Similarly, when an affirmative action officer takes into account race and sex, use of these characteristics is not morally irrelevant or arbitrary. Since affirmative action aims to help end racial and sexual inequality by providing black and female role models for minorities (and non-minorities), the race and sex of the job candidates are clearly relevant to the decision. There is nothing arbitrary about the affirmative action officer focusing on race and sex. Hence, if reverse discrimination is wrong, it is not wrong for the reason that it uses morally irrelevant and arbitrary characteristics to distinguish between applicants.

3. Reverse Discrimination as Unjustified Stereotyping

It might be argued that reverse discrimination involves judging people by alleged average characteristics of a class to which they belong, instead of judging them on the basis of their individual characteristics, and that such judging on the basis of stereotypes is unjust. But the defense of affirmative action suggested in this paper does not rely on stereotyping. When an employer hires a slightly less well qualified woman or black over a slightly more qualified white male for the purpose of helping to overcome sexual and racial inequality, she judges the applicants on the basis of their individual characteristics. She uses this person's sex or skin color as a mechanism to help achieve the goals of affirmative action. Individual characteristics of the white male (his skin color and sex) prevent him from serving one of the legitimate goals of employment policies, and he is turned down on this basis.

Notice that the objection does have some force against those who defend reverse discrimination on the grounds of compensatory justice. An affirmative action policy whose purpose is to compensate women and blacks for past and current injustices judges that women and blacks on the average are owed greater compensation than are white males. Although this is true, opponents of affirmative action argue that some white males have been more severely and unfairly disadvantaged than some women and blacks. A poor white male from Appalachia may have suffered greater undeserved disadvantages than the upper-middle class woman or black with whom he competes. Although there is a high correlation between being female (or being black) and being especially owed compensation for unfair disadvantages suffered, the correlation is not universal.

Thus defending affirmative action on the grounds of compensatory justice may lead to unjust treatment of white males in individual cases. Despite the fact that certain white males are owed greater compensation than are some women or blacks, it is the latter that receive compensation. This is the result of judging candidates for jobs on the basis of the average characteristics of their class, rather than on the basis of their individual characteristics. Thus compensatory justice defenses of reverse discrimination may involve potentially problematic stereotyping. But this is not the defense of affirmative action considered here.

4. Failing to Hire the Most Qualified Person Is Unjust

One of the major reasons people think reverse discrimination is unjust is because they think that the most qualified person should get the job. But why should the most qualified person be hired?

A. Efficiency One obvious answer to this question is that one should hire the most qualified person because doing so promotes efficiency. If job qualifications are positively correlated with job performance, then the more qualified person will tend to do a better job. Although it is not always true that there is

such a correlation, in general there is, and hence this point is well taken. There are short term efficiency costs of reverse discrimination as defined here.

Note that a weaker version of affirmative action has no such efficiency costs. If one hires a black or woman over a white male only in cases where qualifications are roughly equal, job performance will not be affected. Furthermore, efficiency costs will be a function of the qualifications gap between the black or woman hired, and the white male rejected: the larger the gap, the greater the efficiency costs. The existence of efficiency costs is also a function of the type of work performed. Many of the jobs in our society are ones which any normal person can do (e.g., assembly line worker, janitor, truck driver, etc.). Affirmative action hiring for these positions is unlikely to have significant efficiency costs (assuming whoever is hired is willing to work hard). In general, professional positions are the ones in which people's performance levels will vary significantly, and hence these are the jobs in which reverse discrimination could have significant efficiency costs.

While concern for efficiency gives us a reason for hiring the most qualified person, it in no way explains the alleged injustice suffered by the white male who is passed over due to reverse discrimination. If the affirmative action employer is treating the white male unjustly, it is not because the hiring policy is inefficient. Failing to maximize efficiency does not generally involve acting unjustly. For instance, a person who carries one bag of groceries at a time, rather than two, is acting inefficiently, though not unjustly.

It is arguable that the manager of a business who fails to hire the most qualified person (and thereby sacrifices some efficiency) treats the owners of the company unjustly, for their profits may suffer, and this violates one conception of the manager's fiduciary responsibility to the shareholders. Perhaps the administrator of a hospital who hires a slightly less well qualified black doctor (for the purposes of affirmative action) treats the future patients at that hospital unjustly, for doing so may reduce the level of health care they receive (and it is arguable that they have a legitimate expectation to receive the best health care possible for the money they spend). But neither of these examples of inefficiency leading to injustice concern the white male "victim" of affirmative action, and it is precisely this person who the opponents of reverse discrimination claim is being unfairly treated.

To many people, that a policy is inefficient is a sufficient reason for condemning it. This is especially true in the competitive and profit oriented world of business. However, profit maximization is not the only legitimate goal of business hiring policies (or other business decisions). Businesses have responsibilities to help heal society's ill's, especially those (like racism and sexism) which they in large part helped to create and perpetuate. Unless one takes the implausible position that business' only legitimate goal is profit maximization, the efficiency costs of affirmative action are not an automatic reason for rejecting it. And as we have noted, affirmative action's efficiency costs are of no help in substantiating and explaining its alleged injustice to white males.

B. The Most Qualified Person Has a Right to the Job   One could argue that the most qualified person for the job has a right to be hired in virtue of superior qualifications. On this view, reverse discrimination violates the better qualified white male's right to be hired for the job. But the most qualified applicant holds no such right. If you are the best painter in town, and a person hires her brother to paint her house, instead of you, your rights have not been violated. People do not have rights to be hired for particular jobs (though I think a plausible case can be made for the claim that there is a fundamental human right to employment). If anyone has a right in this matter, it is the employer. This is not to say, of course, that the employer cannot do wrong in her hiring decision; she obviously can. If she hires a white because she loathes blacks, she does wrong. The point is that her wrong does not consist in violating the right some candidate has to her job (though this would violate other rights of the candidate).

C. The Most Qualified Person Deserves the Job   It could be argued that the most qualified person should get the job because she deserves it in

virtue of her superior qualifications. But the assumption that the person most qualified for a job is the one who most deserves it is problematic. Very often people do not deserve their qualifications, and hence they do not deserve anything on the basis of those qualifications. A person's qualifications are a function of at least the following factors: (a) innate abilities, (b) home environment, (c) socio-economic class of parents, (d) quality of the schools attended, (e) luck, and (f) effort or perseverance. A person is only responsible for the last factor on this list, and hence one only deserves one's qualifications to the extent that they are a function of effort.

It is undoubtedly often the case that a person who is less well qualified for a job is more deserving of the job (because she worked harder to achieve those lower qualifications) than is someone with superior qualifications. This is frequently true of women and blacks in the job market: they worked harder to overcome disadvantages most (or all) white males never faced. Hence, affirmative action policies which permit the hiring of slightly less well qualified candidates may often be more in line with considerations of desert than are the standard meritocratic procedures.

The point is not that affirmative action is defensible because it helps insure that more deserving candidates get jobs. Nor is it that desert should be the only or even the most important consideration in hiring decisions. The claim is simply that hiring the most qualified person for a job need not (and quite often does not) involve hiring the most deserving candidate. Hence the intuition that morality requires one to hire the most qualified people cannot be justified on the grounds that these people deserve to be hired.

D. The Most Qualified Person Is Entitled to the Job   One might think that although the most qualified person neither deserves the job nor has a right to the job, still this person is entitled to the job. By 'entitlement' in this context, I mean a natural and legitimate expectation based on a type of social promise. Society has implicitly encouraged the belief that the most qualified candidate will get the job. Society has set up a competition and the prize is a job which is awarded to those applying with the best qualifications. Society thus reneges on an implicit promise it has made to its members when it allows reverse discrimination to occur. It is dashing legitimate expectations it has encouraged. It is violating the very rules of a game it created.

Furthermore, the argument goes, by allowing reverse discrimination, society is breaking an explicit promise (contained in the Civil Rights Act of 1964) that it will not allow race or sex to be used against one of its citizens. Title VII of that Act prohibits discrimination in employment on the basis of race or sex (as well as color, religion, or national origin).

In response to this argument, it should first be noted that the above interpretation of the Civil Rights Act is misleading. In fact, the Supreme Court has interpreted the Act as allowing race and sex to be considered in hiring or admission decisions.[2] More importantly, since affirmative action has been an explicit national policy for the last twenty years (and has been supported in numerous court cases), it is implausible to argue that society has promised its members that it will not allow race or sex to outweigh superior qualifications in hiring decisions. In addition, the objection takes a naive and utopian view of actual hiring decisions. It presents a picture of our society as a pure meritocracy in which hiring decisions are based solely on qualifications. The only exception it sees to these meritocratic procedures is the unfortunate policy of affirmative action. But this picture is dramatically distorted. Elected government officials, political appointees, business managers, and many others clearly do not have their positions solely or even mostly because of their qualifications. Given the widespread acceptance in our society of procedures which are far from meritocratic, claiming that the most qualified person has a socially endorsed entitlement to the job is not believable.

5. Undermining Equal Opportunity for White Males

It has been claimed that the right of white males to an equal chance of employment is violated by affirmative action. Reverse discrimination, it is said, undermines equality of opportunity for white males.

If equality of opportunity requires a social environment in which everyone at birth has roughly the same chance of succeeding through the use of his or her natural talents, then it could well be argued that given the social, cultural, and educational disadvantages placed on women and blacks, preferential treatment of these groups brings us closer to equality of opportunity. White males are full members of the community in a way in which women and blacks are not, and this advantage is diminished by affirmative action. Affirmative action takes away the greater than equal opportunity white males generally have, and thus it brings us closer to a situation in which all members of society have an equal chance of succeeding through the use of their talents.

It should be noted that the goal of affirmative action is to bring about a society in which there is equality of opportunity for women and blacks without preferential treatment of these groups. It is not the purpose of the sort of affirmative action defended here to disadvantage white males in order to take away the advantage a sexist and racist society gives to them. But noticing that this occurs is sufficient to dispel the illusion that affirmative action undermines the equality of opportunity for white males.

LEGITIMATE OBJECTIONS

The following two considerations explain what is morally troubling about reverse discrimination.

1. Judging on the Basis of Involuntary Characteristics

In cases of reverse discrimination, white males are passed over on the basis of membership in a group they were born into. When an affirmative action employer hires a slightly less well qualified black (or woman), rather than a more highly qualified white male, skin color (or sex) is being used as one criterion for determining who gets a very important benefit. Making distinctions in how one treats people on the basis of characteristics they cannot help having (such as skin color or sex) is morally problematic because it reduces individual autonomy. Discriminating between people on the basis of features they can do something about is preferable, since it gives them some control over how others act towards them. They can develop the characteristics others use to give them favorable treatment and avoid those characteristics others use as grounds for unfavorable treatment.

For example, if employers refuse to hire you because you are a member of the American Nazi Party, and if you do not like the fact that you are having a hard time finding a job, you can choose to leave the party. However, if a white male is having trouble finding employment because slightly less well qualified women and blacks are being given jobs to meet affirmative action requirements, there is nothing he can do about this disadvantage, and his autonomy is curtailed.

Discriminating between people on the basis of their involuntary characteristics is morally undesirable, and thus reverse discrimination is also morally undesirable. Of course, that something is morally undesirable does not show that it is unjust, nor that it is morally unjustifiable.

How morally troubling is it to judge people on the basis of involuntary characteristics? Notice that our society frequently uses these sorts of features to distinguish between people. Height and good looks are characteristics one cannot do much about, and yet basketball players and models are ordinarily chosen and rejected on the basis of precisely these features. To a large extent our intelligence is also a feature beyond our control, and yet intelligence is clearly one of the major characteristics our society uses to determine what happens to people.

Of course there are good reasons why we distinguish between people on the basis of these sorts of involuntary characteristics. Given the goals of basketball teams, model agencies, and employers in general, hiring the taller, better looking, or more intelligent person (respectively) makes good sense. It promotes efficiency, since all these people are likely to do a better job. Hiring policies based on these involuntary characteristics serve the legitimate purposes of these businesses (e.g., profit and serving the public), and hence they may be morally justified despite their tendency to reduce the control people have over their own lives.

This argument applies to reverse discrimination as well. The purpose of affirmative action is to help eradicate racial and sexual injustice. If affirmative action policies help bring about this goal, then they can be morally justified despite their tendency to reduce the control white males have over their lives.

In one respect this sort of consequentialist argument is more forceful in the case of affirmative action. Rather than merely promoting the goal of efficiency (which is the justification for businesses hiring naturally brighter, taller, or more attractive individuals), affirmative action promotes the nonutilitarian goal of an egalitarian society. In general, promoting a consideration of justice (such as equality) is more important than is promoting efficiency or utility. Thus in terms of the importance of the objective, this consequentialist argument is stronger in the case of affirmative action. If one can justify reducing individual autonomy on the grounds that it promotes efficiency, one can certainly do so on the grounds that it reduces the injustice of racial and sexual inequality.

2. Burdening White Males without Compensation

Perhaps the strongest moral intuition concerning the wrongness of reverse discrimination is that it is unfair to job seeking white males. It is unfair because they have been given an undeserved disadvantage in the competition for employment; they have been handicapped because of something that is not their fault. Why should white males be made to pay for the sins of others?

It would be a mistake to argue for reverse discrimination on the grounds that white males deserve to be burdened and that therefore we should hire women and blacks even when white males are better qualified. Young white males who are now entering the job market are not more responsible for the evils of racial and sexual inequality than are other members of society. Thus, reverse discrimination is not properly viewed as punishment administered to white males.

The justification for affirmative action supported here claims that bringing about sexual and racial equality necessitates sacrifice on the part of white males who seek employment. An important step in bringing about the desired egalitarian society involves speeding up the process by which women and blacks get into positions of power and authority. This requires that white males find it harder to achieve these same positions. But this is not punishment for deeds done.

Thomas Nagel's helpful analogy is state condemnation of property under the right of eminent domain for the purpose of building a highway. Forcing some in the community to move in order that the community as a whole may benefit is unfair. Why should these individuals suffer rather than others? The answer is: Because they happen to live in a place where it is important to build a road. A similar response should be given to the white male who objects to reverse discrimination with the same "Why me?" question. The answer is: Because job seeking white males happen to be in the way of an important road leading to the desired egalitarian society. Job-seeking white males are being made to bear the brunt of the burden of affirmative action because of accidental considerations, just as are homeowners whose property is condemned in order to build a highway.[3]

This analogy is extremely illuminating and helpful in explaining the nature of reverse discrimination. There is, however, an important dissimilarity that Nagel does not mention. In cases of property condemnation, compensation is paid to the owner. Affirmative action policies, however, do not compensate white males for shouldering this burden of moving toward the desired egalitarian society. So affirmative action is unfair to job seeking white males because they are forced to bear an unduly large share of the burden of achieving racial and sexual equality without being compensated for this sacrifice. Since we have singled out job seeking white males from the larger pool of white males who should also help achieve this goal, it seems that some compensation from the latter to the former is appropriate.

This is a serious objection to affirmative action policies only if the uncompensated burden is substantial. Usually it is not. Most white male "victims" of affirmative action easily find employment. It is highly unlikely that the same white male will repeatedly fail to get hired because of affirmative action. The burdens of affirmative action should be spread as evenly as possible among all the job seeking white males. Furthermore, the burden job seeking white males face—of finding it somewhat more difficult to get employment—is inconsequential when compared to the burdens ongoing discrimination places on women and blacks. Forcing job seeking white males to bear an extra burden is acceptable because this is a necessary step toward achieving a much greater reduction in the unfair burdens our society places on women and blacks. If affirmative action is a necessary mechanism for a timely dismantlement of our racial and sexual caste system, the extra burdens it places on job seeking white males are justified.

Still the question remains: Why isn't compensation paid? When members of society who do not deserve extra burdens are singled out to sacrifice for an important community goal, society owes them compensation. This objection loses some of its force when one realizes that society continually places undeserved burdens on its members without compensating them. For instance, the burden of seeking efficiency is placed on the shoulders of the least naturally talented and intelligent. That one is born less intelligent (or otherwise less talented) does not mean that one deserves to have reduced employment opportunities, and yet our society's meritocratic hiring procedures make it much harder for less naturally talented members to find meaningful employment. These people are not compensated for their sacrifices either.

Of course, pointing out that there are other examples of an allegedly problematic social policy does not justify that policy. Nonetheless, if this analogy is sound, failing to compensate job-seeking white males for the sacrifices placed on them by reverse discrimination is not without precedent. Furthermore, it is no more morally troublesome than is failing to compensate less talented members of society for their undeserved sacrifice of employment opportunities for the sake of efficiency.

CONCLUSION

This article has shown the difficulties in pinpointing what is morally troubling about reverse discrimination. The most commonly heard objections to reverse discrimination fail to make their case. Reverse discrimination is not morally equivalent to traditional racism and sexism since its goals and consequences are entirely different, and the act of treating people differently on the basis of race or sex is not necessarily morally wrong. The race and sex of the candidates are not morally irrelevant in all hiring decisions, and affirmative action hiring is an example where discriminating on the basis of race or sex is not morally arbitrary. Furthermore, affirmative action can be defended on grounds that do not involve stereotyping. Though affirmative action hiring of less well qualified applicants can lead to short run inefficiency, failing to hire the most qualified applicant does not violate this person's rights, entitlements, or deserts. Additionally, affirmative action hiring does not generally undermine equal opportunity for white males.

Reverse discrimination is morally troublesome in that it judges people on the basis of involuntary characteristics and thus reduces the control they have over their lives. It also places a larger than fair share of the burden of achieving an egalitarian society on the shoulders of job seeking white males without compensating them for this sacrifice. But these problems are relatively minor when compared to the grave injustice of racial and sexual inequality, and they are easily outweighed if affirmative action helps alleviate this far greater injustice.

NOTES

I thank Cheshire Calhoun, Beverly Diamond, John Dickerson, Jasper Hunt, Glenn Lesses, Richard Nunan, and Martin Perlmutter for helpful comments.

1. Peter Singer, "Is Racial Discrimination Arbitrary?" *Philosophia,* vol. 8 (November 1978), pp. 185–203.
2. See Justice William Brennan's majority opinion in United Steel Workers and Kaiser Aluminum v. Weber, United States Supreme Court, *443 U.S. 193* (1979). See also Justice Lewis Powell's majority opinion in the University of California v. Bakke, United States Supreme Court, *438 U.S. 265* (1978).
3. Thomas Nagel, "A Defense of Affirmative Action" in *Ethical Theory and Business,* 2nd edition, ed. Tom Beauchamp and Norman Bowie (Englewood Cliffs, NJ: Prentice Hall, 1983), p. 484.

Sexual Harassment in the Workplace

Ellen Bravo
Co-Director, 9 to 5, National Association of Working Women

Ellen Cassedy
A founder of 9 to 5, National Association of Working Women

SECTION 1: WHAT SEXUAL HARASSMENT IS—AND IS NOT

Louette Colombano was one of the first female police officers in her San Francisco district. While listening to the watch commander, she and the other officers stood at attention with their hands behind their backs. The officer behind her unzipped his fly and rubbed his penis against her hands.

Diane, a buyer, was preparing to meet an out-of-town client for dinner when she received a message: her boss had informed the client that she would spend the night with him. Diane sent word that she couldn't make it to dinner. The next day she was fired.

Few people would disagree that these are clear-cut examples of sexual harassment. Touching someone in a deliberately sexual way, demanding that an employee engage in sex or lose her job—such behavior is clearly out of bounds. But in less obvious cases, many people are confused about where to draw the line.

Is all sexual conversation inappropriate at work? Is every kind of touching off limits? Consider the following examples. In your opinion, which, if any, constitute sexual harassment?

- A male manager asks a female subordinate to lunch to discuss a new project.
- A man puts his arm around a woman at work.
- A woman tells an off-color joke.

Reprinted with permission from *The 9 to 5 Guide to Combating Sexual Harassment,* 2nd edition, 9 to 5 Working Women Education Fund, 1999, pp. 11–48.

- These comments are made at the workplace:
  "Your hair looks terrific."
  "That outfit's a knockout."
  "Did you get any last night?"

The answer in each of these cases is, "It depends." Each one *could* be an example of sexual harassment—or it could be acceptable behavior.

Take the case of the manager asking a female subordinate to lunch to discuss a new project. Suppose this manager often has such lunchtime meetings with his employees, male and female. Everyone is aware that he likes to get out of the office environment in order to get to know the associates a little better and to learn how they function—for example, whether they prefer frequent meetings or written reports, detailed instructions or more delegation of responsibility. The female subordinate in this case may feel she's being treated just like other colleagues and be glad to receive the individual attention.

On the other hand, suppose this subordinate has been trying for some time, unsuccessfully, to be assigned to an interesting project. The only woman who does get plum assignments spends a lot of time out of the office with the boss; the two of them are rumored to be sleeping together. The lunch may represent an opportunity to move ahead, but it could mean that the manager expects a physical relationship in return. In this case, an invitation to lunch with the boss is laden with unwelcome sexual overtones.

An arm around the shoulder, an off-color joke, comments about someone's appearance, or even sexual remarks may or may not be offensive. What matters is the relationship between the two parties and how each of them feels.

"Your hair looks terrific," for instance, could be an innocuous compliment if it were tossed off by one coworker to another as they passed in the hall. But imagine this same phrase coming from a male boss bending down next to his secretary's ear and speaking in a suggestive whisper. Suddenly, these innocent-sounding words take on a different meaning. The body language and tone of voice signify something sexual. While the comment itself may not amount to much, the secretary is left to wonder *what else the boss has in mind.*

On the other hand, even words that may seem grossly inappropriate— "Did you get any last night?"—can be harmless in certain work situations. One group of male and female assemblyline workers talked like this all the time. What made it okay? They were friends and equals—no one in the group had power over any of the others. They were all comfortable with the banter. They hadn't drawn up a list specifying which words were acceptable to the group and which were not. But they had worked together for some time and knew one another well. Their remarks were made with affection and accepted as good-natured. No one intended to offend— and no one was offended. The assembly-line area was relatively isolated, so the workers weren't in danger of bothering anyone outside their group. Had a new person joined the group who wasn't comfortable with this kind of talk, the others would have stopped it. They might have thought the new person uptight, they might not have liked the new atmosphere, but they would have respected and honored any request to eliminate the remarks.

This is the essence of combating sexual harassment—creating a workplace that is built on mutual respect.

Try assessing whether each of the following scenarios constitutes sexual harassment. Then consider the analysis that follows.

Scenario 1

Justine works in a predominantly male department. She has tried to fit in, even laughing on occasion at the frequent sexual jokes. The truth is, though, that she gets more irritated by the jokes each day. It is well known in the department that Justine has an out-of-town boyfriend whom she sees most weekends. Nonetheless, Franklin, one of Justine's coworkers, has said he has the "hots" for her and that—boyfriend or not—he's willing to do almost anything to get a date with her. One day, Sarah, another of Justine's coworkers, overheard their boss talking to Franklin in the hallway. "If you can get her to go to bed with you," the boss said, "I'll take you out to dinner. Good luck." They chuckled and went their separate ways. (*From the consulting firm of Jane C. Edmonds & Associates, Inc.,* Boston Globe, *10/24/91.*)

The boss is out of line. True, he probably didn't intend anyone to overhear him. But why was he having this conversation in the hallway? What was he doing having the conversation at all? The boss is responsible for keeping the workplace free of harassment. Instead, he's giving Franklin an incentive to make sexual advances to a coworker and then to brag about it.

The conversation may constitute harassment not only of Justine but also of Sarah, who overheard the conversation. A reasonable woman might easily wonder, "Who's he going to encourage to go after *me?*" Ideally, Sarah should tell the two men she was offended by their remarks. But given that one of them is her boss, it would be understandable if she were reluctant to criticize his behavior.

Franklin isn't just romantically interested in Justine; he "has the hots" for her and is willing to "do almost anything" to get a date with her. Justine could well be interested in a "fling" with Franklin. But she's irritated by the sexual remarks and innuendoes in the workplace. It's unlikely that she would be flattered by attention from one of the men responsible for this atmosphere.

Justine can just say no to Franklin. But she may well object to having to say no over and over. And most women are not pleased to be the brunt of jokes and boasts. Some may argue that whether Franklin and Justine get together is a personal matter between the two of them. The moment it becomes the subject of public boasting, however, Franklin's interest in Justine ceases to be just a private interaction.

The law doesn't say Justine should be tough enough to speak up on her own—it says the company is responsible for providing an environment free of offensive or hostile behavior. As the person in charge, the boss ought to know what kind of remarks are being made in the workplace and whether employees are offended by them. Instead of making Franklin think the way to win favor with him is to pressure a coworker into bed, the manager might want to arrange for some training on sexual harassment.

Scenario 2

Freda has been working for Bruce for three years. He believes they have a good working relationship. Freda has never complained to Bruce about anything and appears to be happy in her job. Bruce regularly compliments Freda on her clothing; in his opinion, she has excellent taste and a good figure. Typically, he'll make a remark like "You sure look good today." Last week, Freda was having a bad day and told Bruce that she was "sick and tired of being treated like a sex object." Bruce was stunned. (*From the consulting firm of Jane C. Edmonds & Associates, Inc.,* Boston Globe, *10/24/91.*)

There's really not enough information to come to any conclusions in this case. The scenario explains how Bruce feels, but not Freda. In the past, when he said, "Hey, you look good today," did Freda usually answer, "So do you"? Or did he murmur, "Mmm, you look go-o-o-o-d," and stare at her chest while she crossed her arms and said, "Thank you, sir"? In addition to complimenting Freda's appearance, did Bruce ever praise her work? Did he compliment other women? Men?

It is plausible that Freda might have been upset earlier. She probably wouldn't say she was tired of being treated like a sex object unless she'd felt that way before. Why didn't she speak up sooner? It's not uncommon for someone in Freda's situation to be reluctant to say anything for fear of looking foolish or appearing to be a "bad sport." Remember, Bruce is her boss.

Bruce states that he was stunned when Freda blew up at him. He needs to consider whether Freda might have given him any signals he ignored. He should ask himself how his compliments fit in with the way he treats other employees. Has he really given Freda an opening to object to his remarks?

The most comfortable solution might be for Bruce and Freda to sit down and talk. Perhaps Freda doesn't really mind the compliments themselves but wants more attention paid to her work. If Freda has been upset about the compliments all along, Bruce is probably guilty only of not paying close attention to her feelings. He should let her know that he values her work *and* her feelings, listen carefully to what she has to say, and encourage her to speak up promptly about issues that may arise in the future.

Scenario 3

Barbara is a receptionist for a printing company. Surrounding her desk are five versions of ads printed by the company for a beer distributor. The posters feature women provocatively posed with a can of beer and the slogan, "What'll you have?" On numerous occasions, male customers have walked in, looked at the posters, and commented, "I'll have you, baby." When Barbara tells her boss she wants the posters removed, he responds by saying they represent the company's work and he's proud to display them. He claims no one but Barbara is bothered by the posters.

The legal standard in this case is not how the boss feels, but whether a "reasonable woman" might object to being surrounded by such posters. The company has other products it could display. Barbara has not insisted that the company refuse this account or exclude these posters from the company portfolio. She has merely said she doesn't want the posters displayed around *her* desk. Barbara's view is substantiated by how she's been treated; the posters seem to give customers license to make suggestive remarks to her.

Scenario 4

Therese tells Andrew, her subordinate, that she needs him to escort her to a party. She says she's selecting him because he's the most handsome guy on her staff. Andrew says he's busy. Therese responds that she expects people on her staff to be team players.

Therese may have wanted Andrew merely to accompany her to the party, not to have a sexual relationship with her. And Andrew might have been willing to go along if he hadn't been busy. Nevertheless, a reasonable employee may worry about what the boss means by such a request, particularly when it's coupled with remarks about personal appearance.

Andrew might not mind that Therese finds him handsome. But most people would object to having their job tied to their willingness to make a social appearance with the boss outside of work. The implicit threat also makes Therese's request unacceptable. The company should prohibit managers from requiring subordinates to escort them to social engagements.

Scenario 5

Darlene invites her coworker Dan for a date. They begin a relationship that lasts several months. Then Darlene decides she is no longer interested and breaks up with Dan. He wants the relationship to continue. During the workday, he frequently calls her on the interoffice phone and stops by her desk to talk. Darlene tries to brush him off, but with no success. She asks her manager to intervene. The manager says he doesn't get involved in personal matters.

Most managers are rightly reluctant to involve themselves in employees' personal relationships. Had Darlene asked for help dealing with Dan outside of work, the manager would have been justified in staying out of it. He could have referred her to the employee assistance program, if the company had one.

Once Dan starts interfering with Darlene's work, however, it's a different story. The company has an obligation to make sure the work environment is free from harassment. If Darlene finds herself less able to do her job or uncomfortable at work because of Dan and if her own efforts have failed, the manager has both the right and the responsibility to step in and tell Dan to back off.

Scenario 6

Susan likes to tell bawdy jokes. Bob objects. Although he doesn't mind when men use such language in the office, he doesn't think it's appropriate for women to do so.

An employee who objects to off-color jokes shouldn't have to listen to them at work, and management should back him up. Bob's problem, however, is restricted to jokes told by women. If he doesn't have the same problem when men tell such jokes, it's his problem—not the company's. Management can't enforce Bob's double standard.

Scenario 7

Janet is wearing a low-cut blouse and short shorts. John, her coworker, says, "Now that I can see it, you gotta let me have some." Janet tells him to buzz off. All day, despite Janet's objections, John continues to make similar remarks. When Janet calls her supervisor over to complain, John says, "Hey, can you blame me?"

The company has a right to expect clothing appropriate to the job. If Janet's clothes are inappropriate, management should tell her so. But Janet's outfit doesn't give John license to say or do whatever he likes. Once she tells him she doesn't like his comments, he should stop—or be made to do so.

Scenario 8

Someone posts a *Hustler* magazine centerfold in the employee men's room. No women use this room.

Some would say that if the women aren't aware of the pinups in the men's room, they can't be offensive. But when men walk out of the restroom with such images in their mind's eye, how do they view their female coworkers? And when the women find out about the pinups—as they will—how will they feel? As the judge ruled in a 1991 Florida case involving nude posters at a shipyard, the presence of such pictures, even if they aren't intended to offend women, "sexualizes the work environment to the detriment of all female employees."

A COMMON-SENSE DEFINITION

Sexual harassment is not complicated to define. To harass someone is to bother him or her. Sexual harassment is bothering someone in a sexual way. The harasser offers sexual attention to someone who didn't ask for it and doesn't welcome it. The unwelcome behavior might or might not involve touching. It could just as well be spoken words, graphics, gestures or even looks (not any look—but the kind of leer or stare that says, "I want to undress you").

Who decides what behavior is offensive at the workplace? The recipient does. As long as the recipient is "reasonable" and not unduly sensitive, sexual conduct that offends him or her should be changed.

That doesn't mean there's a blueprint for defining *sexual harassment.* "Reasonable" people don't always agree. Society celebrates pluralism. Not everyone is expected to have the same standards of morality or the same sense of humor. Still, reasonable people will agree *much of the time* about what constitutes offensive behavior or will recognize that certain behavior or language can be expected to offend some others. Most people make distinctions between how they talk to their best friends, to their children, and to their elderly relatives. Out of respect, they avoid certain behavior in the presence of certain people. The same distinctions must be applied at work.

Sexual harassment is different from the innocent mistake—that is, when someone tells an off-color joke, not realizing the listener will be offended, or gives what is meant as a friendly squeeze of the arm to a coworker who doesn't like to be touched. Such behavior may represent insensitivity, and that may be a serious problem, but it's usually not sexual harassment. In many cases, the person who tells the joke that misfires or who pats an unreceptive arm *knows right away* that he or she has made a mistake. Once aware or made aware, this individual will usually apologize and try not to do it again.

DO THEY MEAN IT?

Some offensive behavior stems from what University of Illinois psychologist Louise Fitzgerald calls "cultural lag." "Many men entered the workplace at a time when sexual teasing and innuendo were commonplace," Fitzgerald told the *New York Times.* "They have no idea there's anything wrong with it." Education will help such men change their behavior.

True harassers, on the other hand, *mean* to offend. Even when they know their talk or action is offensive, they continue. Sexual harassment is defined as behavior that is not only unwelcome but *repeated.* (Some kinds of behavior are *always* inappropriate, however, even if they occur only once. Grabbing someone's breast or crotch, for example, or threatening to fire a subordinate who won't engage in sexual activity does not need repetition to be deemed illegal.)

The true harasser acts not out of insensitivity but precisely because of the knowledge that the behavior will make the recipient uncomfortable. The harasser derives pleasure from the momentary or continuing powerlessness of the other individual. In some cases, the harasser presses the victim to have sex, but sexual pleasure itself is not the goal. Instead, the harasser's point is to dominate, to gain power over another. As University of Washington psychologist John Gottman puts it, "Harassment is a way for a man to make a woman vulnerable."

Some harassers target the people they consider the most likely to be embarrassed and least likely to file a charge. Male harassers are sometimes attempting to put "uppity women" in their place. In certain previously all-male workplaces, a woman who's simply attempting to do her job may be considered uppity. In this instance, the harassment is designed to make the woman feel out of place, if not to pressure her out of the job. Such harassment often takes place in front of an audience or is recounted to others afterwards ("pinch and tell"). . . .

PART OF THE JOB

Some harassers who don't consciously set out to offend are nevertheless unwilling to curb their behavior even after they're told it's offensive. If a woman doesn't like it, they figure that's her problem. And some harassers consider sexual favors from subordinates to be a "perk," as much a part of the job as a big mahogany desk and a private executive bathroom.

Men can be harassed by women, or both harasser and victim can be of the same sex. Overwhelmingly, however, sexual harassment is an injury inflicted on women by men. While the number of hardcore harassers is small, their presence is widely felt. Sexual harassment is ugly. And it's damaging—to the victims, to business, and to society as a whole.

SECTION 2: COUNTERING THE MYTHS ABOUT SEXUAL HARASSMENT

From the Senate chambers to the company mailroom, from the executive suite to the employee lounge, from the locker room to the bedroom, a debate is raging over sexual harassment. No matter what the forum, the same arguments arise. Here are some of the most common myths about harassment rebutted by the facts.

Myth: Sexual harassment doesn't deserve all the attention it's getting. It's a rare disorder unique to a few sick people.

Fact: No exact figures exist, but a large body of research conducted at workplaces and universities suggests that at least 50 percent of women—as well as a smaller percentage of men—have been sexually harassed, either on the job or on campus. Very few people are considered to be "chronic harassers," but most of these are not psychopaths. Many men in the workplace, whether intentionally or not, end up encouraging or condoning harassment.

Myth: Sexual harassment is a fact of life that people might as well get used to. It's so widespread that it's pointless to try to stamp it out.

Fact: To expect men to engage in abusive behavior is insulting. The notion that women should take responsibility for preventing harassers from behaving offensively at the workplace is also a myth. Like other forms of sexual abuse, harassment is usually a means of exerting power, not of expressing a biological urge. Yes, sexual harassment is widespread, but the answer is to stop it, not to accept it.

Myth: Most men accused of harassment don't really intend to offend women.

Fact: A small percentage of men are dead serious about engaging in abusive behavior on the job. They know their behavior makes women uncomfortable; that's why they do it.

Other men are surprised to find that what they intend as innocent teasing isn't received that way. They need to make some simple changes in behavior. After all, beginning in early childhood, most people are taught that different settings require different codes of behavior. Children learn not to use swear words at Grandma's dinner table and not to insult the teacher. At the workplace, it's safest to assume that a coworker *won't* like sexual comments or gestures. If you find out you've offended someone, simply apologize.

Myth: If women want to be treated equally on the job, they can't expect special treatment—whether at the construction site or in the executive boardroom.

Fact: Women don't want special treatment. They want *decent* treatment—the same decent treatment most men want for themselves.

Myth: Many charges of sexual harassment are false—the women are either fantasizing or lying in order to get men in trouble.

Fact: According to a survey of Fortune 500 managers conducted by *Working Woman* magazine (December 1988), false reports are rare. "Every story I hear is very specific and very detailed," said one survey respondent, "too much so to be made up." Said another respondent, "More than 95 percent of our complaints have merit."

There's little incentive for women to come forward with false harassment charges. The real problem is not that reports are fraudulent but that women who *are* suffering severe harassment remain silent for fear of being humiliated and derailing their careers.

Myth: A man's career can be destroyed by an accusation of sexual harassment, while the woman who accuses him suffers no consequences.

Fact: A woman's *life* can be destroyed by sexual harassment, at least for a time. Offensive behavior *should* bring consequences for the perpetrator. But most cases don't result in heavy penalties.

A good corporate policy, however, protects both the accuser and the accused by ensuring confidentiality and a fair hearing. A range of disciplinary action is needed—from warnings and reprimands to suspensions and terminations—depending on the severity of the offense.

As things stand now, it's usually the victim who suffers a career setback. Many harassers receive only a slap on the wrist or no reprisals at all, even for serious offenses.

Myth: You can't blame a guy for looking. Women bring harassment on themselves by the way they dress.

Fact: Truly provocative clothing doesn't belong at the workplace, and management shouldn't allow it. Yet under no circumstances does a woman's appearance give men license to break the law.

Many employers require women to dress in a way that calls attention to their physical appearance. Waitresses, for example, may be required to wear uniforms with short skirts or low necklines. In 1991, Continental Airlines reservation clerk Teresa Fischette was summarily fired when she refused to wear makeup on the job. Only after the *New York Times* publicized her case and she appeared on a television talk show did she win back her position.

Without questioning the importance of being well groomed, many women resent having to conform to a highly specific "look" for the benefit of clients or coworkers. Not only is it expensive and time-consuming, it can lead others to treat them like sex objects at the workplace.

Myth: Women send mixed signals. Half the time when they say no, they really mean yes.

Fact: Men can't assume they're the ones who know best what women "really want." Especially at the workplace, some women can't put up strong resistance to sexual pressure without fear of endangering their jobs. Dr. Michelle Paludi, a psychologist at Hunter College in New York City, finds that "90 percent of women who have been sexually harassed want to leave, but can't because they need their job." Take a no as a no.

Myth: Women who make clear that they don't welcome sexual attention don't get harassed. If a woman doesn't like what's happening, she can say so.

Fact: Most hard-core harassers know their conduct is unwelcome; that's why they continue. Some women do say no again and again and find that their resistance is simply ignored. Others hesitate to speak up because they fear being ridiculed or ostracized.

While women do have a responsibility to communicate when sexual attention is unwelcome, the employer has a prior legal responsibility: to create an environment where no woman is punished for refusing to accept offensive behavior.

Myth: All this attention to harassment will give women ideas, causing them to imagine problems where there are none.

Fact: In the short run, defining *sexual harassment* and providing women with ways to speak up probably *will* lead to an increase in the number of reports filed, most of them concerning legitimate, not imagined, offenses. In the long run, however, public discussion of the issue will cut down on unwelcome sexual attention on the job. The result will be fewer harassment complaints and a more harmonious and productive work world for all.

Myth: Cracking down on sexual harassment will lead to a boring and humorless workplace.

Fact: Antiharassment policies are aimed at repeated, unwelcome sexual attention, not at friendly relations among coworkers. Social interaction that's mutually enjoyable is fine, so long as it doesn't interfere with work or offend others.

The aim of a sexual-harassment policy is to eliminate *offensive* interactions, not *all* interactions. Most encounters defined as sexual harassment have nothing to do with a romantic agenda. They involve an assertion of power, not of affection.

But sex between managers and their subordinates—or between faculty and students—is a different story. Many employers and college administrators recognize that romantic relationships are fraught with danger when one party to the affair has economic or academic power over the other. Even when it seems that both parties have entered freely into the relationship, management is right to worry about the potential for exploitation and adverse effects on the workplace or academic setting.

SECTION 3: WHAT THE LAW SAYS

What words would you use to describe sexual harassment? Participants in workplace training sessions are always full of answers. "Humiliating," they call out. "Unwelcome." "Repeated." "Power abuse." The list goes on. Yet in session after session, at one workplace after another, no one but the instructor states a word that's just as important as all the rest: *illegal.* Sexual harassment is against the law.

It's not surprising that most people are uninformed about the law on sexual harassment. Not until 1977 did a federal court uphold a harassment charge. The Supreme Court did not do so until 1986. Until a short time ago, sexual harassment was a problem without a name or a remedy.

Employees and employers alike can be thankful that sexual harassment is unlawful. Those who use the laws to file charges aren't the only ones who benefit. For *all* employees, simply knowing they have a right to a harassment-free workplace makes it easier to insist on fair treatment. For many potential harassers, the laws are an effective deterrent. And for employers seeking to enforce appropriate workplace behavior, the laws are invaluable. . . .

FEDERAL LAW DEFINES HARASSMENT

Title VII of the Civil Rights Act of 1964 makes it illegal to discriminate against employees on the basis of race, color, religion, sex, or national origin. As enforced by the Equal Employment Opportunity Commission (EEOC), the law gives every employee the right to work in an environment free of intimidation, insult, or ridicule based on race, religion, or sex.

Here's how the EEOC, a Washington-based agency with regional offices, defines *sexual harassment:*

> Unwelcome sexual advances, requests for sexual favors, and other verbal or physical conduct of a sexual nature constitute sexual harassment when
>
> 1. submission to such conduct is made either explicitly or implicitly a term or condition of an individual's employment or academic advancement,
> 2. submission to or rejection of such conduct by an individual is used as the *basis for employment decisions* or academic decisions affecting such individual, or
> 3. such conduct has the purpose or effect of unreasonably *interfering with an individual's work* or academic performance or creating an intimidating, *hostile,* or offensive working or academic *environment.*

Illegal sexual harassment falls into four categories: *quid pro quo,* hostile environment, sexual favoritism, and harassment by nonemployees.

Quid Pro Quo

Quid pro quo means something given in return for something else. In this type of sexual harassment, a supervisor makes unwelcome sexual advances and either states or implies that the victim *must* submit if she wants to keep her job or receive a raise, promotion, or job assignment.

These cases are the most clear-cut. The courts generally hold the employer liable for any such harassment, whether he knew about it or not. That's because anyone who holds a supervisory position, with power over terms of employment, is considered to be an "agent" of the employer, that is, "acting for" the employer.

> *Deborah, an office manager at a small firm, couldn't stop Bill, the sales and marketing manager, from coming by her desk to complain about his unsatisfying sex life with his wife. She insisted again and again that she wasn't interested in hearing about his personal affairs, but nothing she said would deter*

him. Finally, Deborah went to their boss for help. "Put your faith in God," was all he had to say. Deborah did her best to avoid Bill, but then a corporate restructuring took place and he became president of the firm. "I'm on the other side of the desk now," he told Deborah in their first meeting. "Either we engage in a sexual relationship, or I no longer need an office manager." Deborah filed a charge and won.

Hostile Environment

An employee doesn't have to be fired, demoted, or denied a raise or promotion to be "harmed"—and to file a charge. Even if no threat is involved, unwelcome sexual conduct can have the effect of "poisoning" the victim's work environment. Sexually explicit jokes, pinups, graffiti, vulgar statements, abusive language, innuendoes; and overt sexual conduct can create a hostile environment.

In these cases, the employer is considered liable if he knew or should have known of the harassment and did nothing to stop it. If the harassment is out in the open, if everyone except the employer knows all about it, then he *ought* to have known—whether or not anyone brings the matter to his attention.

Where no *quid pro quo* is involved, the courts generally don't rule in favor of the victim unless the incidents of harassment are repeated, pervasive, and harmful to the victim's emotional well-being. A single incident isn't enough to prove the existence of a hostile environment, unless the incident is extreme. An employer can let a vulgar remark or two go by without being found in violation of the law. But if someone intentionally *touches* an employee in a sexual way on the job even once and the employer ignores the behavior, then the EEOC will generally find that harassment has occurred.

Hostile environment cases may leave more room for argument than *quid pro quo* cases.

The victim will strengthen his or her case by complaining or protesting at the time of the harassment, preferably in writing. This kind of documentation will prove that the victim finds the sexual attention unwelcome—and will also help prove that the offensive behavior occurred in the first place, if the employer is inclined to deny it.

But a verbal or written protest is not absolutely necessary to winning a case—the EEOC recognizes that it's not always possible to speak up. Even if the employer claims, as a defense, that there was a grievance procedure and the victim never used it, the EEOC will examine what may have deterred the victim from doing so. How often has the grievance procedure been used? Do all employees know it exists? Have other harassment victims felt comfortable using it?

Carol Zabkowicz, a warehouse worker, was tormented by a group of male coworkers who enjoyed upsetting her by calling out her name and then exposing their genitals or buttocks when she looked up. Carol complained to management, to no avail. "If we didn't see it, it didn't happen" was the company's position. Even when she brought witnesses with her and submitted evidence in the form of obscene cartoons that had been left at her workstation, management did nothing. When the case went to court, the company was found guilty of "malicious, blatant discrimination."

The employer's best defense will be to take the strong preventive and remedial action recommended in the EEOC's guidelines:

The employer should affirmatively raise the subject with all supervisory and nonsupervisory employees, express strong disapproval, and explain the sanctions for harassment. The employer should also have a procedure for resolving sexual harassment complaints. The procedure should be designed to encourage victims of harassment to come forward and should not require a victim to complain first to the offending supervisor. It should ensure confidentiality as much as possible and provide effective remedies and protection of victims and witnesses against retaliation.

If the employer takes strong action immediately upon finding out about a "hostile environment" problem, the EEOC may find that the situation has been resolved satisfactorily and close the case . . .

Sexual Favoritism

In this type of harassment, a supervisor rewards only those employees who submit to sexual demands. The *other* employees, those who are *denied* raises or promotions, can claim that they're penalized by the sexual attention directed at the favored coworkers.

Catherine A. Broderick, an attorney with the federal Securities and Exchange Commission, filed a suit charging that the agency was run "like a brothel." Senior attorneys were having affairs with secretaries and junior attorneys and rewarding them with cash bonuses and promotions. When Broderick complained, she received poor reviews and was threatened with firing. She won her case, receiving $128,000 in back pay and a promotion.

Harassment by Nonemployees

An employer can be held responsible for harassment by people outside the company—such as customers, vendors, or contractors—if the employer has control or could have control over their actions.

The owner of an office building required a female elevator operator to wear a sexy uniform. People riding the elevator made lewd remarks and propositioned her. The operator complained to the owner and said she refused to wear the uniform. For this she was fired. She brought suit against the employer and won.

THE LEGAL HISTORY OF SEXUAL HARASSMENT

The legal history of sexual harassment is surprisingly short. Not until 1964 was sex discrimination itself declared illegal—and only by a fluke. During the debate over the proposed Civil Rights Act at that time, a Southern member of Congress proposed what he considered an absurd amendment, making sex discrimination illegal along with race discrimination. His intent was only to make sure the bill wouldn't pass; to his chagrin, however, the plan backfired. The bill became law with his amendment intact, and discrimination on the basis of sex as well as race was outlawed.

Eight years later, in 1972, Congress passed the Equal Employment Opportunity Act giving enforcement powers to the EEOC. That same year, President Nixon signed the Education Amendments, forbidding discrimination by any education program receiving federal funds. . . .

In the precedent-setting *Barnes v. Costle* case, sexual harassment victims gained a foothold in the courts. The U.S. Court of Appeals for the District of Columbia ruled in 1977 in favor of a woman whose government job was abolished because she wouldn't submit to her boss's demand for sexual favors. "But for her womanhood," the court said, "the woman wouldn't have lost her job." If she'd been a man, in other words, she wouldn't have been treated this way. Therefore, the harassment was not just an isolated instance of supervisory misbehavior; it was illegal sex discrimination. . . .

Hostile Environment: An Uphill Battle

While the concept of *quid pro quo* harassment was accepted by courts in the 1970s, victims of hostile environment harassment fought an uphill battle in the 1980s. . . .

At last, in June 1986, the Supreme Court upheld the concept of *hostile environment harassment*. In *Meritor Savings Bank v. Vinson,* the court affirmed that harassment is illegal even if the victim hasn't lost any job benefits—even if it's not a *quid pro quo* situation. Employees have "the right to work in an environment free from discriminatory intimidation, ridicule, and insult," the Court said.

Mechelle Vinson, a bank teller who worked her way up to a position as an assistant branch manager, claimed that her supervisor repeatedly pressured her to have sex with him. At first she resisted; finally, afraid of losing her job, she gave in to his advances. Over the next several years, he fondled her in front of other employees, followed her into the restroom, and exposed himself at work. He had sex with her 40 or 50 times and raped her on more than one occasion. Finally, she went on leave and was fired. Her employer's defense was that she'd made up the whole story, dressed provocatively, and never used the grievance procedure.

Voluntary?

The lower court found that if there was a sexual relationship between Vinson and her supervisor, it was a voluntary one, and that the employer wasn't liable because Vinson hadn't complained. But the court of appeals disagreed. Even though Vinson had indeed agreed to have sex with the supervisor, said the court, her participation couldn't fairly be called "voluntary" because she was afraid she'd lose her job if she refused. Further, regardless of whether she had lodged a complaint, the bank was liable because a supervisor is an agent of the employer.

The bank appealed to the Supreme Court, which affirmed the court of appeals. The Court said that the question was not whether Vinson had made a voluntary decision to have sex with her supervisor, but whether the sexual relationship was welcome or unwelcome to her.

The Court also asserted that merely having a sexual harassment policy and a grievance procedure didn't automatically excuse the employer from liability. But the Court didn't go so far as to say that employers were always liable for the actions of supervisors. Where no *quid pro quo* threats are made, the Court said, the employer's liability must be determined on a case-by-case basis.

The Case of the Reasonable Woman

It's common practice in the courtroom to examine behavior through the eyes of the hypothetical "reasonable person," the so-called "man in the street." But in 1991, in *Ellison v. Brady,* the U.S. Court of Appeals for the Ninth Circuit created a new standard: the "reasonable woman."

Kerry Ellison, an agent for the Internal Revenue Service in San Mateo, California, charged that a coworker persisted in pressuring her for dates even though she kept refusing him. He sent her bizarre "love letters" that she found frightening. "I know that you are worth knowing with or without sex," said one letter. "I have enjoyed you so much over the past few months. Watching you. Experiencing you from so far away." When Ellison complained to a supervisor, the coworker was transferred. He filed a grievance, however, and won a return to Ellison's office. At this point, Ellison filed a harassment charge.

A district court dismissed the case, calling the coworker's conduct "isolated and genuinely trivial." But the Ninth Circuit of the U.S. Court of Appeals disagreed. The "severe and pervasive" harassment directed at Ellison, the court wrote, had created "an abusive working environment." And while IRS managers told the coworker to stop his illegal harrassment, they didn't subject him to any disciplinary action—no reprimand, no probation, no threat of termination. They even decided

to transfer him back to Ellison's office without consulting her.

In the court's view, the reasonable-person standard could end up simply reinforcing discrimination. After all, if harassment is common and widespread, doesn't it follow that an average, "reasonable" person can engage in harassment? Fairness demands that the law take note of women's unique perspective. The court wrote:

> Conduct that many men consider unobjectionable may offend many women. Because women are disproportionately victims of rape and sexual assault, women have a stronger incentive to be concerned with sexual behavior. Women who are victims of mild forms of sexual harassment may understandably worry whether a harasser's conduct is merely a prelude to a violent sexual assault. Men, who are rarely victims of sexual assault, may view sexual conduct in a vacuum without a full appreciation of the social setting or the underlying threat of violence that a woman may perceive.

Robinson v. Jacksonville Shipyards: Workplace Pornography Banned

Another breakthrough came in 1991. For the first time, a court ruled that pornography at the workplace constituted sex discrimination.

Lois Robinson, a welder, was one of only six women among over 800 skilled craftworkers at a Florida shipyard. When female employees reported demeaning jokes and comments to managers, their complaints were not taken seriously. In addition, pictures of nude women were displayed— sometimes by managers—throughout the workplace. One pinup showed a meat spatula pressed against a woman's pubic area. Another picture featured a nude woman holding a whip. A drawing on the wall featured a nude woman's body with "USDA Choice" stamped across it as if it were a piece of meat. . . .

The district court upheld Robinson's harassment charge, finding that pornography may be far more threatening to women in the workplace than it is outside. "Pornography on an employer's wall or desk communicates a message about the way he views women, a view strikingly at odds with the way women wish to be viewed in the workplace," the court decision declared. Further, "a preexisting atmosphere that deters women from entering or continuing in a profession or job" is as bad as "a sign declaring 'Men Only.'"

The shipyard was ordered to remove the offensive pictures and to implement an antiharassment policy drafted by the National Organization for Women Legal Defense and Education Fund. Two employees were held personally liable for harassment, and the company was ordered to pay Robinson's legal fees, as well as $1 in damages.

An Abridgment of Free Speech?

The employer, with the approval of the American Civil Liberties Union, protested that being forced to remove the posters and graffiti would mean abridging employees' freedom of speech. But many women's groups strongly backed the court's ruling. The messages contained in the pornographic posters would be called sexual harassment—and declared illegal—if they were stated out loud at the workplace. Why should pictures be allowed to convey what workers aren't allowed to say on the job? The "right" of supervisors and male workers to express themselves offensively before a captive audience of female workers must be balanced against other goals, like avoiding discrimination and getting the work done. . . .

Victims Win Right to Collect Damages Under Federal Law

Until the end of 1991, federal law didn't allow harassment victims—or victims of any other form of sex discrimination—to collect much money. All they could win under Title VII were remedies that would make them "whole"—reinstatement if they'd been fired, a promotion if they'd been denied one, back pay, and attorney's fees. There were no remedies for out-of-pocket expenses like medical bills or for emotional pain and suffering. Nor was there any way to assess punitive damages against the employer.

Under the circumstances, many harassment victims saw little reason to sue under Title VII, especially if they didn't want their job back or hadn't been fired in the first place. They couldn't collect a penny, nor would their employer suffer any significant consequences. Victims also found it difficult to interest attorneys in their cases, since there was no chance of collecting damages, even if they won.

In 1991, however, in the wake of Anita Hill's testimony on sexual harassment before the Senate Judiciary Committee, Congress passed legislation strengthening several aspects of civil rights law. The Civil Rights Act of 1991 gives victims of sex, race, and religious discrimination the right to sue for both *compensatory* and *punitive* damages. Victims can sue to collect compensation for the abuse they've suffered, as well as to collect penalties designed to punish the employer. This makes it easier for victims to interest attorneys in taking their cases on a contingent-fee basis. (The lawyer receives little or no payment up front but takes a percentage of the total award, if any, once the case is resolved.) Out-of-pocket medical expenses can now be recovered as well. Further, the law gives the right to trial by jury, and juries are generally acknowledged to be more sympathetic to the victim than judges.

In February 1992, the Supreme Court affirmed that Title IX of the Education Amendments of 1972 gives students the right to recover damages from schools and school officials for sexual harassment and other forms of sex discrimination. . . .

THE LAW EVOLVES

Despite the few big-money settlements that have grabbed headlines and the steady progress in court decisions, both the law and the enforcement system still pose formidable obstacles for the victim of harassment. The burden is on the victim to prove both that harassment took place and that the offender's conduct was unwelcome. Too often, the courtroom inquiry tends to focus not on what the offender did but on how the victim responded—how strongly she resisted, how quickly she protested, how sincere her objections were. Frequently, judges and juries fail to recognize how hard it is to speak up against harassment if the offender is your boss.

As new statutes are passed and new cases decided, sexual harassment law continues to evolve.

In coming years, strides may be made toward more effectively preventing harassment, protecting the victim, and imposing appropriate penalties on harasser and employer.

SECTION 4: WHAT EVERY GOOD EMPLOYER SHOULD DO

After the Clarence Thomas hearings in October 1991 and the passage of the federal Civil Rights Act shortly thereafter, many managers examined their policies on sexual harassment. What they saw ranged from an effective preventive program to no policy at all.

"A THRIVING WORKPLACE DEPENDS ON A HARASSMENT-FREE ENVIRONMENT"

Managers who promote this view are most successful in combating sexual harassment. Smart managers do want to avoid legal liability. But above all, they should root out anything that seriously interferes with employee morale, well-being, and productivity. They should recognize that sexual harassment can happen anywhere and that no matter how careful the hiring and promotion practices, no workplace has a guarantee against insensitivity or misconduct. They should work to prevent harassment from occurring, while dealing with it promptly if it does take place.

Managers in this category will understand that no employee is indispensable. Even if an employee brings in money or prestige, his misconduct should not be tolerated.

Many companies with well-developed policies, such as AT&T and Du Pont, have had them in place for more than a decade. Texas Industries began to develop its policy as soon as it started placing women in traditionally male jobs, such as driving and production engineering. While some companies began devising or reworking policies after the Supreme Court first ruled against harassment in 1986, firms like Merck & Co. said the ruling merely affirmed the policies they had already instituted. . . .

DEVELOPING OR REVISING AN IN-HOUSE POLICY ON SEXUAL HARASSMENT

There's no one model for a good sexual harassment policy. Employers need to develop procedures based on their particular circumstances. But all policies should be designed to send a clear message: "We will not tolerate sexual harassment. We will do everything in our power to prevent it from happening. If you have a complaint, we will listen to it. We will follow the most effective course of action to stop the offensive behavior as speedily and thoroughly as possible."

A good sexual harassment policy should incorporate the following elements:

Employee Involvement

Employees who have been or could be the targets of harassment should have a voice. Men who might otherwise feel defensive should also help to develop the policy. Rather than selecting one or two employee "representatives" at the outset, solicit comments and suggestions companywide. Through a union or professional association, some employees may know of a strong policy elsewhere; encourage them to pass on any information that may be helpful. . . .

Written Policy

A written policy tailored to the company should be included in any employee handbook and orientation materials. The policy should define what harassment is and is not, describe how harassment will be handled within the company, explain how to file a charge with a government agency, and spell out what the law says. But set *higher standards* than the law requires; for example, federal law does not prohibit harassment against homosexuals, but in-house policy should make clear that such harassment will not be tolerated. . . .

Publicity

Publicize the policy by every means used to communicate business goals. "Employers ought constantly to reinforce their commitment to a work force free from sexual harassment, using whatever the usual trusted mechanisms of the company are," says consultant Freada Klein. That could be anything from a newsletter to posters to global voice mail. "Some companies send a statement stapled to employee paychecks," says Klein. "Others send periodic memos about the number of complaints they've had and what the resolution has been."

Support from the Top

It's important to have visible support from top management. After the Thomas hearings, Richard Teerlink, the CEO of Harley-Davidson, gave a ten-minute talk about harassment to the top 150 managers. "He talked very candidly and told us, 'This is serious stuff that goes along with our values of respecting the individual,'" said Margaret Crawford, director of the company's human resources department. "'It's not just an issue of what's legal or illegal, but what's right and wrong and how do you treat people in the workplace. Managers will be held accountable for the environment your workers have to live in.' That ten-minute off-the-cuff presentation did more than anything else could have done. Word was out in the hallways. People came forward with questions, some situations they were uncomfortable about. They saw this as a very strong message that the company will not take harassment lightly."

Prevention

A successful policy depends on *education of all employees.* Training should be *ongoing,* not a one-time session, and presented *on paid time.* The program should aim to help all employees to understand the issues and the seriousness of the problem, ensure that those experiencing harassment know their rights, and inform any hardcore offenders that they won't get away with harassment. . . .

Clearly Defined Procedures that Protect the Complainant—and the Accused

The policy must clearly spell out the complaint procedures, including where to report problems, what steps will follow, timetables, methods of investigation, and follow-up. To maximize options

for the complainant, the policy must allow for *several different channels.* The procedure should not require the complainant to report the problem to her supervisor, since that person may be the harasser. At least one option should be to complain to an employee through an affirmative action committee, women's committee, or other employee committee. If feasible, designate an ombudsperson to counsel victims. Du Pont Company has a sexual harassment hotline with a toll-free number listed in the company's telephone directory. Four staff specially trained in sexual harassment and rape prevention are assigned to the hotline; each carries a beeper.

The policy must state unequivocally that no one will be punished for coming forward and that *every* complaint will be taken seriously. No retaliatory action should be permitted against a complainant. But make clear, too, that false accusations will not be condoned and that *due process* will be followed. . . .

Organization of Work in the Company and Family Rights of the Employees

Domènec Melé
Professor and Head of Business Ethics Department,
IESE—International Graduate School of Management,
University of Navarra, Spain

Businessmen are well aware of the marked relationship between family affairs of employees and their behavior in the company. The organization of work and activities in the company considerably affect family life. Some work set-ups can lead to

From *Journal of Business Ethics,* vol. 8, no. 8 (1989), pp. 647–655. Copyright © 1989 Kluwer Academic Publishers. Reprinted by permission of Kluwer Academic Publishers.

family problems, and family problems, in turn, affect employee performance in the company. This intrinsic relationship between the family and organization of work makes it a subject of great concern to both employees and managers.

In countries such as Spain, where the family is a deep-rooted institution, the family-company relationship arouses considerable concern. According to a survey recently conducted by IESE among two hundred Spanish managers, the study of the family-work relationship came out as one of the four or five most important subjects that must be taught in the business ethics course.[1]

Until now, very little attention has been given to the study of the relationship between the organization of work in the company and the family rights and duties of the employee. However, a number of interesting works are available, albeit focussed only on some particular problems and referring specifically to American society.[2]

Some people consider that the family, by being a part of the employee's personal life, has no bearing on the company. Thus, any interference by the company in the employee's family life, is seen as an intrusion into the personal life of the employee. As such, it must be avoided. But in doing so, companies fail to take into account the importance of the family as the basic unit of society and its corresponding rights.

Others consider that it is sufficient to have flexible agreements between the company and its employees concerning family issues. In this situation, the rights of the family are taken into account only if the negotiating parties are conscious of them. Many times the family duties of the employees are viewed only as interests which are in conflict with the company's interests. They fail to realize, however, that the family is a source of real rights.

It must be pointed out that in the "Universal Declaration of Human Rights" and in the "International Agreement of Civil and Political Rights", it is categorically stated that "the family is the natural and fundamental unit of society and is entitled to the protection of society and the State.[3] Other international texts on human rights are couched in similar terms,[4] showing the existence of a wide international consensus on the intrinsic value of the

family. In addition, a detailed Charter of the Rights of Family[5] was published by the Roman Catholic Church in 1983 and a European Charter of Family Rights is being prepared at the moment.[6]

Nevertheless, some family rights can easily be infringed upon as a result of the organizational work within the company. These rights can be enumerated as follows:

a. The right to find the necessary social support to consolidate the unity and stability of the family so that it may carry out its specific task.
b. The right to socio-economic conditions that enable it to carry out its duties with respect to the procreation and upbringing of children.
c. The right to working hours and periods necessary to devote to the other spouse, the children and to just being together.
d. The right to a quality of work life that does not affect the workers' genetic heritage nor their physical or mental health nor the necessary attention to their respective families.
e. The right to a sufficient compensation to start and maintain a family.

The following discussion deals with some aspects of work organization connected with the above-mentioned family rights illustrated in several scenarios taken from cases that have been published or that the author has direct knowledge of.

BUSINESS AND WORKING ENVIRONMENT MUST FAVOR MARITAL UNITY AND STABILITY

Company policy on work organization may attack the family's unity and stability in a variety of situations such as those illustrated in the following scenarios:

a. Bribery or Extortion Using Extra-marital Sexual Relations

The use of sexual favour is a well known way of bribery or extortion.

Scenario 1
A company invites several managers from client companies to a convention at which its latest products will be presented. The reception includes all

kinds of entertainment, including callgirls, which are supposed to smooth the way for sales to the potential buyers.

b. Sexual Harassment

Sexual harassment within the company is, of course, another form against the unity and stability of marriage. It usually happens with extortion from someone superior.

Scenario 2

A male supervisor sexually harasses a female subordinate. The subordinate is aware of the unfavorable consequences that would result from rejecting the supervisor's advances: loss of promotion, misleading information on her performance to their superiors, effect on salary increases, and perhaps, dismissal in a future restructuring.

c. Situations That Favor Sexual Attraction in the Company

Moreover, some company practices—work arrangement, business trips, etc.—can also lead to immoderate sexual attraction among employees, although, these company practices are not conceived to lead to such consequences.

Scenario 3

A fast-moving finance company specialising in high-risk loans wishes to recruit a recent Harvard MBA graduate. On his first visit to the company, the young MBA realised that most of the women in the office were young and very attractive. In fact, he had never seen so many pretty women in one place before.

Later he learned that the company's vice-president (only him?) usually had some employee accompany him on his business trips, suggesting that they sleep together to "save the firm the price of a second room".

The executives earned a lot of money but if they wanted to get to the top they had to work Saturdays and Sundays. With all this, it is not surprising that the company's divorce rate was somewhat high.[7]

In all these situations, in addition to damaging the family, the business organization itself will suffer adverse consequences: distorted communications, hostile self-interests that go against the company's interest, impairment of the work unit's reputation, greater slowness in decision-taking, etc.

d. Dual Careers and Prolonged Separation of Spouses

In cases where both husband and wife work, a good working opportunity which requires relocation to another city, may come to either of the two. The overall success, however, can only be guaranteed if the other spouse can be permitted to relocate to the same city. Otherwise, the family may suffer temporary separation or the professional life of one may suffer to give in to the other.

A better alternative can be found if firms could take into account the family issues in dual careers.

Scenario 4

A large group of companies has recruited Antonio to turn around one of its ailing companies near Barcelona. Antonio is then asked to do the same in another company in the south of Spain. It is planned that he will spend three to five years in the new company. Antonio may have a very good career before him in this group of companies but he must be prepared to accept all the changes the company requires.

Antonio is married with three children aged less than 14. His wife Montse is an architect and works for the regional government. Her career prospects are also good. Montse also takes an active part in political life and knows a lot of people in the Barcelona area. Their children are happily enrolled in a school in Barcelona. Montse and Antonio also think that such a dramatic cultural change would not be good for the children. Antonio's bosses have pressured him a lot on this change and have made him understand that if he does not accept their demands, he can expect little future in the company. Antonio faces a dilemma and fears that he would not be able to find such a good job in another company.

It is hard to say just how much a company can pressure its employees in defense of its legitimate interests but it is clear that if it does not act with a certain consideration for family circumstances, it will be favoring the breakup of the family. Also, the prolonged separation of spouses gives rise to a lot of problems, especially when this separation is accompanied by frequent dealings with people of the other sex for work or social reasons, which may also undermine the unity and stability of the family.

On this point, the comment made by R. Quinn[8] is interesting in that he states that in 74% of the love affairs that occur at work, the man holds a higher position than the woman and, in almost half of the cases, the woman involved is his secretary.

In all these scenarios, of course, the person involved is free to refuse the proposition of infidelity but the company's policy, the work environment or the behaviour of its managers may significantly influence the preservation of the unity and stability of the marriage.

The company can make it easier to fulfill the duties of marital unity and stability by acting in the following areas:

1. Forbidding its employees to use all forms of bribery including the exploitation of the sexual instincts of potential customers.
2. Penalizing those who take advantage of their power by extorting people in exchange for sexual gratifications.
3. Taking steps to prevent sexual harassment between employees, especially those occurring from the abuse of power. It should be borne in mind that, according to the Merit System Protection Board, sexual harassment has little to do with mutual physical attraction, provocative behaviour or even sex.[9] It is above all an expression of dominance and nonreciprocal behaviour directed by the strongest at the weakest.
4. Acting with care in the design of work organization and avoiding, as much as possible, forms of business activity that may easily result in thoughtless sexual provocation among its employees.
5. Creating an appropiate atmosphere within the company in order to avoid sexual harassment and to encourage managers to exercise care in their relations with the people with whom they work the most.
6. Taking into account the effects of dual careers on the families, avoiding the considerable pressure on the employees resulting in discrimination.
7. Avoiding as much as possible prolonged separations of spouses.

COMPATIBILITY OF WORK WITH THE OBLIGATIONS OF PARENTHOOD

Attention given to the family, and especially to the bringing up of children, can be unacceptably low as a result of the ineffective work organization in the company. The organization itself can hinder, and in some cases, even prevent the parents from freely choosing the type of education their children should receive. Here are a few situations:

a. Moving Employees or Managers to Another City or Country

This may affect the professional or social interests of the concerned spouse or of the rest of the family, as well as affecting the children's education (change of school, educational system or culture).

Scenario 5

A leading leather tanning factory in Valencia (Spain) opened a factory in Indonesia. The factory had to be managed by someone trusted by the company, who knew the tanning process and the leather-tanning trade well. The company management was convinced that this person had to be one of its employees. However, moving the employee with his family not only meant having to live in a different country and culture but also the impossibility of finding a school that would educate his children in accordance with his wishes. In fact, in spite of the promotion and the good pay, there was no-one willing to accept the position and relocate.

The company saw two alternatives: pressure the person concerned in various ways until he was persuaded to move or find alternative solutions that respect the family rights. The final solution was to appoint two managers who would work alternately on three month periods in Indonesia and Valencia.

b. Business Trips That Excessively Shorten the Amount of time Available to the Family

Scenario 6

A Barcelona company is in the turnkey business of building and selling ceramic and earthenware plants. It has projects all over the world. Part of its staff of 1,500 employees work on the assembly and start-up of the new plants and, where necessary, on repairing those already existing.

These travelling workers spend from six months to two years away from their city (normally abroad). Their allowances are not excessive and they are not given more vacation time than their non-travelling colleagues. If necessary, the return from one country is tied up with the departure for an assignment in another country, as a result the worker is hardly able to spend any time with his family. Of course, his employment contract includes the obligation to travel as often as necessary.

On occasions, especially when the stay is going to be long, the workers take their families with them. The educational problems that arise are heightened by the cultural and religious differences in the customer-countries, some of which have communist governments.

The trips abroad are organized without any consideration for the worker's personal situation.

Obviously, moving away is not equally distressing for all employees. Consider the case of a bachelor, or of a man whose children are already grown up or of a man whose children are of school age. It does not seem reasonable to exclude an employee's family situation unless no consideration is made of the personal aspect of work.

A totally liberal approach would argue that business trips and work abroad are within the contractual provisions and previously freely agreed upon. However, such circumstances harm family rights. And because family rights are natural rights, they must obviously come before any other kinds of commitment, including working commitments.

On the other hand, contracts that contain elements of coercion may lead one to question their fairness. This would be the case of a contract that did not respect the worker's family rights if the freedom of choice was reduced, as occurs, for example, in situations of excess supply of labor.

c. Rigidity in Working Hours and the Possibility of Working at Home

It is becoming increasingly common for both wife and husband to work outside the home. In the USA, more than two-fifths of the work force (47 million employees), are composed of spouses in working households.[10] In Europe, the proportion of this kind of people could vary widely according to the country but is important enough to pay attention to.[11]

Rigid working hours adversely affect mothers who wish or need to work out of home, especially when the children are still young. This is perhaps one of the most pressing problems for many young families. The problems that usually arise when both parents work are well known: the care of small children, the mismatch between work and school vacations and working hours, the care of children when they fall ill and above all, the deficiencies in upbringing that usually arise because of lack of time and the parents being too tired to give enough attention to their children.

There seems to be no doubt that the best solution to these problems is to spend more time working at home, especially when the children are very young. However, this is not always possible for a number of reasons.

Some companies have proposed various solutions ranging from locating kindergartens and schools next to companies to flexible working hours. They are solutions that each have their pros and cons and respond rather to a compromise of interest than to a social recognition of the rights and duties of parents, foremost among which is the care and upbringing of their children.

On the other hand, working outside of home with a reasonable degree of flexibility may also provide very suitable solutions.[12]

Nancy R. Pearcy, a writer resident in Canada and a former feminist, advocates work in the house and not just housework. This would be compatible with the mother's important task of bringing up her children. She thinks that women who work at home can have the best of both worlds: earn a living while being able to freely organize their working hours, in accordance with the number and age of their children.[13] The idea is interesting and even feasible in some situations; however, when there is no appropriate labor legislation, there may be companies that take advantage of conscientious and hard-working mothers to exploit them using the well-known practices of the underground economy:

Scenario 7

An imitation jewelry firm contracts out assembly work to homeworkers. Without any employment contract, social security, abnormally low piece rates and tax avoidance, this firm is able to make large profits while the workers—mothers with small children in almost all cases—are able to look after their offspring while working at home but with a ridiculously low pay.

It does not seem fair that labor legislation prevents flexible working schedule or homeworking. Perhaps this justifies some forms of black economy but, in any case, business ethics demands that abuses be avoided and that alternatives be devised to solve this problem which, for many families, has serious effects.

d. Excessive Working Hours and Lack of Vacation Periods Which Hinder Family Life and Especially the Care of Children

Inflexible and prolonged working hours and rigidity at work in general (prohibition of part-time working, vacation periods dictated by the company, etc.) all too often affect family duties, especially those of mothers who work out of home. This situation largely depends on the company management. Even though working hours can be influenced by labor legislation, companies usually still have ample room for maneuver.

Scenario 8

Arturo Garcia, the managing director of a Spanish firm employing 90 people, usually has his lunch outside of the office and, after a long rest, returns to his office at about 5:30. He then starts to work at a feverish pace. He wants his immediate subordinates to extend their working day until very late to help him. One of his secretaries, who is an excellent worker, has stated her desire not to extend her working hours beyond the normal time because she must go to fetch her children from school. This attitude has upset Mr. Garcia who is not prepared to promote that person nor increase her salary beyond that stated in the collective agreement because, according to him, "she can't be counted on."

Arturo Garcia places his convenience and habits before the legitimate rights of his employees. Mr. Garcia could probably organize his work without interfering with the family rights of his employees.

e. Overwork to the Detriment of Family Life

In some occasions, temporary increases in the workload make it necessary to do a lot of overtime work. And this at times becomes a habit and the person is forced to do overtime work on a regular basis. Without guidance, he may lose sight of the fact that work is not an end in itself.

Scenario 9

Juan is a top executive in a Spanish automobile company. He is married and has three children aged 6, 8 and 11. He leaves home at 6:30 A.M. and gets back exhausted at about 10 P.M. when the children are already in bed. He also goes to the office on many weekends or takes work home. His job requires frequent travel. In order to make the best use of time, he often starts his trips on a Sunday.

Juan earns a lot of money which he uses to try to satisfy all his wife's and children's desires. His wife, Maria, often complains that she has everything except a husband. The few times she is with her husband to talk about their children, she tries to explain to him that he cannot delegate to her his part of the children's upbringing. Juan justifies himself by saying that the amount of work he has to do is due to the pace set by the company's president and that he has to work as hard as the president does to maintain his position, earn enough money and maintain the, admittedly high, standard of living of his family.

In the situation of overwork shown in the previous situation, the initial responsibility lies with the employee. Juan should reconsider his scale of values, his duties as father and husband, his behavior towards his family and the organization of his own work. However, the company may also be partly responsible. Could Juan alone change the situation without giving up his job? Perhaps, but the management style imposed by the president no doubt has a significant influence.

WORKING CONDITIONS IN RELATION TO FAMILY DUTIES

Hygiene and safety conditions at work primarily affect the worker. However, working conditions may have effects that go beyond the individual worker, involving his family life.

The following two situations, while not intended to be exhaustive, illustrate two types of inadequate working conditions and their relation to family rights.

a. Physical, Chemical or Psychological Conditions That Affect the Employee's Health

This obviously affects to a greater or lesser extent the real possibilities of carrying out family activities.

Scenario 10

In Spain, as in other countries, in the mid-60's there was no protection against the deafening noise in the cement factory mills. The people who worked there ended up completely deaf. In exchange, the company paid them a bonus for dangerous work. It is not difficult to imagine the problems of oral communication that occur in the family.

Today, this situation has been overcome in most industrialized countries by thick insulating walls and remote control. It is a point that is usually well protected by legislation in industrialized countries. The problem lies in the enforcement of this legislation and, above all, in the working conditions in certain developing nations.

b. Lack of Protection of Fertility and Genetic Heritage or Inadequate Working Conditions for Pregnant Mothers

The protection of the transmission of life derives from the right of the new being already conceived to life or the genetic heritage which may be altered as a result of the action of certain substances present at the place of work. It also derives from the inalienable right of parents to responsibly transmit life, which should not be harmed by working conditions.

Scenario 11

AT&T detected a high rate of miscarriages among the female workers in the chip manufacturing lines. Consequently, in 1986, AT&T decided to transfer those pregnant workers who were working on the semiconductor production lines.[14]

RESPECT OF INDEPENDENCE AND FAMILY PRIVACY

The company, as also the rest of society, should not interfere in family privacy nor in its future prospects. Nor should it pressure or discriminate due to:

a. the status of the spouse and the number of children
b. the type of education or school chosen by the parents
c. the family's moral or religious values.

Scenario 12

In 1978, the American Cyanamid Company in Willow Island (West Virginia) had a dye production plant which used lead chromate, a fetotoxic substance.

Eight women worked in this section. As a result of legislation, the company drew up a series of safety regulations which included removing women from this section unless they could certify they were sterile. In fact, of the eight women employed in the lead dye section, five had themselves surgically sterilized. This drastic decision was probably influenced by the poor economic conditions in the area, the small size of the Willow Island facilities and the non-existence of jobs available for the women in the immediate short term. In subsequent lawsuits, the company argued that it had tried to dissuade the five women from sterilizing themselves and that it had offered them suitable alternatives in the form of jobs of similar rank and pay. If this is true, the offer was either not convincing or the regulations made did not take into account sufficiently the logical consequences in those female workers who destroyed all possibility of having children in order to keep their jobs.[15]

In cases such as this, the organization of work may violate family privacy and one of the most important family rights: the right of responsible procreation. This type of situation shows the inadequacy of a system of ethics that does not take into account the foreseeable consequences.

SUFFICIENT COMPENSATION FOR A DECENT FAMILY LIFE

Paying unjustly low wages is another way of violating family independence. It is well-known that remuneration for work done is the principle means of living for most employees.

If real pay is insufficient to bring up a family, then a basic right is trampled under foot which, to a large extent, conditions all the rest.

Scenario 13

A Spanish company employs 60 workers. Its financial situation is good. Most of the workers hold positions that require little skill or experience. However, wages are scaled above all according to years of service (for historical reasons and union pressure) and to date, very few benefits have been given to workers and their families. Unfortunately, economic protection of the family in Spain is one of the lowest in Europe (an annual allowance of 2000 pesetas per child and tax deduction of 16,000 pesetas per child, in 1987).

Some of the workers in this company with large families are in serious financial difficulties. Others see in the current pay system an effective coercion tool against procreation. Obviously, these problems affect the working atmosphere.

Management is considering restructuring wage rates taking into account not only production but also the worker's family situation.

In several international human rights documents, the need has been stated to provide economic protection for the family.[16] John Paul II, following a long tradition of social teaching by the Roman Catholic Church, insists in the encyclical *Laborem exercens* on the need for a sufficient level of remuneration to enable the employee to lead a decent family life.[17]

The State, mainly through welfare benefits and tax deductions, can provide a certain economic protection for the family. However, the company cannot remain aloof from the economic rights of its employees' families, especially when State aid is insufficient. This consideration gives rise to two statements:

a. The wages paid should not be less than those required by an average family to live a decent life within the context of the time and place concerned.

b. The benefits granted by the company to its workers should cover all members of their families. These benefits should be greater the lesser the protection given by society in general to families. It is not always easy to give these family-weighted benefits. It requires a lot of solidarity not only from the company with respect to its employees but also among the individual employees, taking into consideration the over all financial capability of the firm to grant the benefits.

Efforts should also be made to prevent a particular company from being excessively affected by the size of its workers' families.

Also, those workers with large families may be discriminated against. It therefore seems advisable to create special funds for families from certain groups of companies or economic sectors. Thus, it would be possible to better respect the economic rights of the family without resorting to the State or overburdening individual companies.

CONCLUSION

The narrow attitude towards work which separates the worker from his family life should be dispelled. The worker is not just "labor" but a person who has family duties of crucial importance for himself and for society.

Family duties fall primarily upon the members of the family itself but, by being natural rights of all those who have chosen marriage and family, they should be respected and even promoted by the firm to ensure social justice in employer-employee relations.

It is one of the company's ethical obligations to organize work, taking into account the family duties of its employees and their subsequent compliance.

The idea that the loose agreement between employee and employer is insufficient, and unjust without the explicit consideration of the rights of the family. When the negotiating parties do not have the same power or there exists the need to work, family rights and other rights may be disregarded in the name of freedom of negotiation.

Family rights must be enforced with care and not just as a mere legalism in the organization or work in the firm. By doing so, the efforts to respect family rights will lead to corresponding improvements in labor relations.

Finally, when employees feel hindered to comply with their family duties because of excessive work, they became unmotivated and less efficient. Hence the organization is worse off.

NOTES

1. It will be published.
2. Such as those by Cfr. R. M. Kanter: 1977, 'Work and Family in the United States' (Russell Suge: New York). R. Bailyn: 1978, 'Accommodation of Work to Family' in 'Working Couples' ed. by R. Rapoport and R. N. Rapoport (Harper and Row: New York). J. P. Fernandez: 1986, 'Child Care and Corporation Productivity: Resolving Family/Work Conflicts'. (Lexington Books: Lexington). A. C. Michalos: 1986, 'Job Satisfaction. Marital Satisfaction and the Quality of Life: A Review and a Preview', in 'Research and the Quality of Life', ed. by F. M. Andres (Univerity of Michigan Press: Ann Arbor Michigan), pp. 57–83.
3. U.N.O.: *Universal Declaration of Human Rights,* Art. 16,3 (Paris, 12.10.1948); *International Agreement of Economic, Social and Cultural Rights,* Art. 10,1 and Art. 23,1, adopted by the General Assembly of the UN in its resolution 2200 A (XXI) on 11.16.1966. Came into effect on 12.30.1976.

4. *American Declaration of Human Rights* (1948), Art. 6; *European Social Charter* (1961), Art. 16; *American Convention of Human Rights* (1969), Art. 17,1. Recommendation 2018 (XX) adopted by the General Assembly of the UN on 12.1.1965; *Declaration on social progress and development* proclaimed by the General Assembly of the UN in its resolution 2542 (XXIV) on 12.11.1969.

5. Holy See: 1983, *Charter of the Rights of the Family* (London, Catholic Truth Society). In 1981, Pope John Paul II pointed out some basic family rights and committed the Holy See to prepare a Charter on the Rights of the Family (Exh. Apost. *Familiaris consortio,* n. 46. London, Catholic Truth Society). This Charter has been the first monografic international document on the rights of the family.

6. This European Charter of Family Rights was proposed by Mr. Oreja, the Secretary General of the Council of Europe in his address to the 20th Conference of European Ministries responsible for the family. (Allocution du Secrétaire Général pour la 20e Conférence des Ministers Européen chargés des Affaires familiaires. Brussels, May 19, 1987).

7. C. P. Dredge—V. Sathe. *Mike Miller (A),* Case Study of Harvard Business School, ICCM 9.482.061.

8. R. E. Quinn: March 1977, 'Coping with Cupid: The Formation, Impact and Management of Organizational Romance', in *Administrative Science Quarterly.*

9. Merit System Protection Board: 1981, 'Sexual Harassment in the Federal Workplace', (U.S. Government Printing Office).

10. Conference Board: 1985, 'Corporations and Families: Changing Practices and Perspectives', Report No. 868. (Conference Board, New York).

11. On the employment of women by age group in different European countries: vid. 1986, 'Year Book of Labour Statistics', 406th Issue, pp. 35–42. (International Labour Office, Geneva).

12. K. Ropp: 1987, 'Case studies' in 'Personnel Administrator', *32*, No. 8. pp. 72–79.

13. Cfr. N. R. Pearcey: 1987, 'Why I Am Not a Feminist (Any More)'; *The Human Life Review* New York, March, pp. 80–88.

14. Cfr. *La Actualidad Electrónica,* Barcelona, January, 1987, p. 20.

15. Cfr. J. B. Matthews—K. E. Goodpaster—L. L. Nash: 1985, *Policies and Personas. A casebook in Business ethics.* (McGraw-Hill, New York) pp. 72ff.

16. Cfr. U.N.O. *Universal Declaration of Human Rights,* Art. 23.3; *European Social Charter,* Art. 4.1;

U.N.O. *International Agreement on Human Rights,* Art. 11.1, etc.

17. John Paul II. Enc. *Laborem exercens,* No. 19. (Boston: St. Paul Press, 1981).

Women in the Workplace

Al Gini
Associate Professor, Philosophy Department,
Loyola University of Chicago

The single most important event in the American labor market in the twentieth century has been the unprecedented entry of large numbers of women into the workforce.[1] When Freud cited work and love as the foundations of human behavior, he might as well have used the words *work* and *family.* These are the two major institutions on which any society is based. Work and family are the two primary pillars of human existence, and every society in every age must grapple with the delicate mechanisms and relationships that influence and support these two fundamental phenomenon.[2] As we enter into Bill Clinton's proverbial "bridge into the twenty-first century," the sheer numbers of women who have entered the workforce threaten to irreparably alter and seriously change both the quality and quantity of our work and family lives. And, like it or not, we must be prepared to "adapt, adopt, or modify" some of our most sacred social ideals, icons, and stereotypes about work and the family.

Cultural critic Barbara Ehrenreich once commented that 30 years ago the stereotypical liberated women was a braless radical, hoarse from denouncing the twin evils of capitalism and patriarchy.[3] Today's stereotype is more often a blue-suited executive carrying an attaché case and engaging in leveraged buy-outs—before transmogrifying into a perfect mother, gourmet cook, and seductive lover in the evenings. Neither stereotype is or ever was

From *Business and Society Review,* no. 99, 1998, pp. 3–17. Copyright © 1998, Center for Business Ethics at Bentley College, published by Blackwell Publishers. Reprinted with permission of the Center for Business Ethics.

perfectly true, but they can tell us a great deal about what many women and men would like to believe. What is true, says "Women at Work" columnist Carol Kleiman, is that most workplaces continue to operate, at the level of official organizational policy, as if men (specifically white males) constitute the majority of the workforce and that most women are still at home managing the multiple roles of homemaking and child-rearing. As a result, both male and female employees must cope with the mounting stress of balancing work and family demands.[4] Somewhere between disregard and denial, suggests Kleiman, workplaces have to deal with the inescapable demographic fact that since the mid-1980s, women and minority males have made up the majority of the workforce.[5]

According to Stephanie Coontz in *The Way We Never Were* (1992), women have always been part of the workforce, and working mothers are not simply a new demographic phenomenon of the later-half of the twentieth century.[6] Women, Coontz argues, have never had "free-rider" status in regard to work outside the home, but their active participation in the workforce has always been dependent on need, circumstance, and, to a very large extent, "cultural permission." A classic example of this is the model of "Rosie the Riveter" during World War II who did her bit to once again "make the world safe for democracy." When the GI Joe husbands, brothers, and sons of Rosie marched off to war, Rosie marched into factories across America and took on complicated new jobs, gained new skills, and produced both the necessary domestic goods as well as the military hardware needed to win the war. When the war was won and our GIs came home, many of the women were happy to quit and leave the workplace to the men. Others were unwilling to give up their newly won responsibilities, independence, and income and expressed a desire to continue working. Management, however, says Coontz, went to extraordinary lengths to purge women workers from high-paying and nontraditional jobs. The women who wanted or needed to work were not summarily expelled from the labor force, but were downgraded to lower-paid, "female" jobs. Nevertheless, according to Coontz:

Even at the end of the purge, there were more women working than before the war, and by 1952 there were two million more wives at work than at the peak of wartime production. The jobs available to these women, however, lacked the pay and the challenges that had made war time work so satisfying, encouraging women to define themselves in terms of home and family even when they were working.[7]

During the war, working as Rosie the Riveter was a badge of honor, a mark of distinction, a women's patriotic duty. After the war "cultural permission" once again shifted. *Esquire* magazine called working wives a "menace," and *Life* termed married women's employment a "disease." Being a full-time wife and mother were lauded as a woman's true vocation, the only job that could provide a woman with a "sense of fulfillment, of happiness, of complete pervading contentment."[8]

RISE OF WOMEN IN THE WORKPLACE

Sixty years ago the notion of an unfulfilled homemaker was, for most but certainly not all women, unheard of. Prior to World War II, the maintenance of a house and (often) a large family was a full-time occupation and acknowledged as such. Those women who did venture outside the home in search of full- or part-time employment did so either out of dire financial need or in an attempt to earn a little "pin-money" to subsidize a few household extras. Only in recent years have the everyday tasks of meal-making and house and clothing maintenance become less than full-time jobs. This, and the decrease in family size, left large numbers of women no longer merely bored by housekeeping, but, in the view of many, underemployed and underestimated. However, it wasn't until the late 1950s and early 1960s that women once again received "cultural permission" to enter the workforce in search of jobs, careers, and a new sense of identity. Some of the factors that contributed to this cultural shift included the feminist movement and its impact on social consciousness, technological advances in the information and communications industries, the conversion to a service economy, increased access to education, fair employment and affirmative action legislation, and the ever-increasing costs of a higher standard of living. While contemporary women's grandmothers may or may not have found satisfaction solely employed in their homes, their daughters and granddaughters now find full-time work outside the home not only possible and desirable, but, in many cases, financially necessary.

At the turn of twentieth century, only five million of the 28 million working Americans were women. One quarter of these were teenagers and only a very few were married. As recently as 1947, women accounted for fewer than 17 million of the 59 million employed. Since that time, however, six of every 10 additions to the workforce have been women. Between 1969 and 1979 women took on two thirds of the 20 million newly created jobs,[9] between 1980 and 1992 women accounted for three fifths of the increase in the American workforce.[10] In 1984 the Census Bureau reported that for the first time in history the prototype of American worker—the adult white male—no longer made up the majority of the labor force.[11] Women and minority men now hold approximately 57% of all jobs. In 1995 with a labor force of 124.9 million, 57.5 million of these are women. In 1960, 35.5% of all women and 78.8% of all men worked full time; in 1995, 55.6% of all women and 70.8% of all men work full time.[12] Depending on how you crunch the numbers, women now make up 46%–49% of the entire workforce. Between 1947 and 1995 women's participation in the workforce has increased 17%. Some demographers suggest that employed women may represent a simple majority of the workforce early in the twenty-first century.[13] The Bureau of Labor Statistics more conservatively estimates that women will maintain but not necessarily exceed the present percentage of the workforce. The bureau projects a labor force of 150.5 million workers by the year 2005, of these, 71.8 million will be women.[14]

While single and divorced women have long had relatively high labor force participation rates, fewer than 25% of married women were working full time in 1960. That number today is 33.3 million or 61% of married women. Of these married women, 70.2% have children under 17 years of age.[15] It is estimated that two thirds of all mothers are now in the labor force and that more mothers have paid jobs or are actively looking for a job than are nonworking mothers. Two-job families now make up 58% of married couples with children.[16] One set of statistics indicate that 20% of women in double-income families earns more than their husbands.[17] A more recent survey conducted by the Women's Voice Project, an ongoing study by the Center for Policy Alternatives in Washington, suggests that as many as 55% of all married women earn half or more of their family's income.[18]

According to social commentator John W. Wright, an unmistakable sign of the depth and degree of the social change going on in the workplace is the significant increase in the number of women who go back to work immediately after having a baby. In 1976, said Wright, about 31% of the women who gave birth returned to or entered the labor force: by 1985 the proportion climbed to 48%.[19] In a series of interviews I conducted with human resources specialists, most estimated that at their places of employment 75% of the women who had babies returned to work within 12 weeks of giving birth. Another fundamental social change that has occurred because of this increasing presence of women in the workplace is that women in significant numbers have begun to seek employment outside the occupations traditionally labeled as "women's professions." While nurses, teachers, librarians, and clerical workers are still predominately women, the proportion of female engineers, architects, and public officials—while still small in whole numbers—has more than doubled since 1960.[20] Typically, law and medical school classes are now composed of between 40% and 50% women. According to the Department of Labor special report *Working Women Count,* 30% of working women are engaged in service and sales jobs; 13.1% have factory, craft, construction, and technical jobs or jobs in the transportation industry; 27.6% of working women have professional or executive-level jobs; and of those working in the corporate environment in a professional capacity, 40% of all middle-management positions are held by women.[21] In general, although women are grossly overrepresented at the lower-paying end and in entry levels of all kinds of work, especially in the professions, it is clear that the once absolute distinction between "woman's work" and "man's work" has begun to blur.

What lessons can be drawn from some of these statistics? To begin with, obviously we no longer operate under a gender-based division of labor. The entrance of women into the labor market has changed the composition of the workforce and the workplace as well as the structure of family life. According to *Working Women Count,* it is now expected that 99% of all American women will work for pay sometime during their lives.[22] Nontraditional families are now the majority.[23] The old notion of the 1950s traditional family—dad's at work and mom is home with the kids—no longer often exists. Again, depending on whose figures you are willing to accept, it is estimated that less than 15% of all households fit the 1950s family model.[24] As recently as 1960, 43% of all families conformed to the single-earner model,[25] but in less than 40 years we have become a nation of DINKS (Double-Income-No-Kids) and DISKS (Double-Income-Some-Kids). According to sociologist Uma Sekaran, "The number of two-career families, single-parent families, and unmarried working couples living together is steadily increasing. This population constitutes more than 90% of today's labor force. Organizations are . . . beginning to feel the impact of this new breed of employee."[26]

Second, women are now *demanding* the right to define themselves in the way that men have always defined themselves—through their jobs. Being a wife, a mother, a homemaker has, over the course of the past two or three generations, simply changed until it no longer meets the definition of work to which most people now subscribe. It has been argued that when the first wave of women baby-boomers hit the college campuses in the early 1960s, no matter what they were majoring in, the only degree they were really after was an M.R.S.[27] Not anymore! According to a survey cited by Arlie Russell Hochschild, less than 1% of 200,000 freshmen women surveyed wanted to be a "full-time homemaker." In a 1986 survey of senior college women, 80% thought it was "very important" to have a career.[28] And in 1995, fully 86% of recent women college graduates thought of themselves as "careerist."[29] In this society, who we are is directly tied to what we do. Women now want to be known by their accomplishments and occupations and not merely as "Mrs. John Smith" or "Little Johnny's mommy." When First Lady Barbara Bush gave the commencement speech at Wellesley College in 1991, many of the all-women student body loudly protested her appearance because her only claim to fame was as somebody's wife.[30] Gloria Emerson has pointed out, in her award-winning *Some American Men,* that every 12-year-old boy in America knows what must be done to achieve identity and make it as a man: money must be made—nothing else is as defining or as masculine as this.[31] Rightly or wrongly, women now want to forge their own sense of self-worth and identity by means of paid employment—the principle activity that is classified as work. In the words of demographer Daniel Yankelovich, women now view a paid job as "a badge of membership in the larger society and an almost indispensable symbol of self-worth."[32]

Third, in a very real sense, women's desire for a new work-based sense of self-worth was initially spurred on by the ideas and issues raised by Betty Friedan, Gloria Steinem, and the feminist movement; the "new breed" of women sought to be autonomous agents, able to guide and direct themselves, determining their purpose and role in life by their own choices and actions in their careers. They no longer wanted to be viewed as "second-class citizens," relegated to hearth and home and totally dependent on the will and whim of a man. Perhaps, however, a more prudent analysis of the rush of (especially) married women into the workplace is to suggest that their motivation was both ideological as well as practical. Yes, many women desired a new sense of identity on par with men. Yes, many women no longer wanted to feel emotionally and financially dependent. But at the same time, many of these women sought out jobs/careers as a means of contributing to the ever-increasing costs of middle-class existence: suburban homes, Montessori schools, Suzuki music lessons, good colleges. As recently as 1980, only 19% of working women surveyed by Roper Starch Worldwide said that their incomes were necessary to support their family, while 43% said they worked to bring in extra money.[33]

In 1995, however, 44% of employed women said that they worked out of necessity and only 23% to earn extra cash. The survey concluded that married working women now view their incomes as essential to their family's well being. In part, because of this, only 43% look on their work as a career, while 55% consider their work a necessary job.[34] The new piece of cynical conventional wisdom currently circulating around college campuses today reads something like this: "Guys, look around. Don't just marry the pretty one. Marry the smart one, the one who's got the best chance of landing a good job. Why? Because you're going to need each other to acquire the things and lifestyle that your parents managed to achieve on one salary!" (For example, in 1989, 79% of all homes bought were purchased by two-income households.[35] Some realtors estimate that in the mid-1990s, 85% of all home purchases were made by double-income family units.)[36]

Women may once have entered the workforce out of desire, but today they stay because of need. Not only have they been granted "cultural permission" to seek out work, they have now acquired a "financial imperative" to do so. In the not-too-distant past, women had three choices about employment: don't work at all; work part time; work full time. Now, like men, their options have been reduced to just one—most women must work faithfully all of their lives, without interruption or openly wishing otherwise.

Finally, perhaps the second most stunning demographic statistic of the later half of the twentieth century has been the precipitous rise and continuous high rate of divorce in America; 90% of men and women eventually marry, but 50% of all first marriages end in divorce and an alarming 60% of second marriages also end in divorce.[37] Besides the trauma and pain these divorces have on husbands and wives, the practical and psychological effects of the divorce are equally traumatizing and painful for the children involved. The immediate consequences of a divorce is that almost 60% of all children will live in a single-parent household for a significant period of time before they are 18 years old.[38] Although 70% of divorced adults will re-marry, sometimes again and again, the long-term consequences of divorce on children translates into fully 25% of all children primarily growing up in a one-parent household.[39]

The vast majority of children in a divorce are in the custodial care of the mother. Whatever the causes of the divorce, the practical and financial fallout of the separation is much harder on the women. According to psychologist Lenore Weitzman, in the first year after divorce, women experience a 73% loss in their standard of living, whereas men experience a 42% gain.[40] Even when divorced fathers dutifully comply with child support payments and maintain a high level of emotional involvement with their children, the primary responsibility for both the day-to-day and long-term well-being of the children falls to the mother.

The reality of divorce is now an accepted part of our social tapestry. Another strand of our increasing complex social tapestry is the high proportion of unmarried teenage mothers as well as the growing number of women who choose to have children outside of wedlock, i.e., the "Murphy Brown" phenomenon. Because of all of this, one of the major lessons learned by women, wives, ex-wives, mothers, and young girls alike is that "it is the very rare girl/woman who won't have to worry about her own self-sufficiency." According to Karen Nussbaum, former head of the U. S. Department of Labor's Women's Bureau, "There should be no girl out there (anymore) who thinks someone else is going to take care of me." Life has changed, and the expectations of women must also change. Work for women is now less of an option and more of a brute necessity. "If (today) girls aren't working when they get out of high school," says Nussbaum, "they will be at some point."[41] While for many women work remains a badge of honor and a symbol of self-worth and identity, now, owing to the reconfiguration of family life, added to the equation is the fundamental element of simple survival.

JUSTICE ON THE JOB

Whether propelled by "cultural permission" or compelled by "financial necessity," women have assaulted the door of the corporate citadel and they have gained admission. Women are now being sought after by various industries for entry-level positions more than are men. In this way, corporations can claim, at least *prima facie*, that they are complying with the rules of affirmative action and open employment. As one human resources vice-president told me off the record and in muffled tones, "If you are a black woman, with an Hispanic surname, married to a Jewish man, and have a physical infirmity [handicap]—you are a prize candidate for immediate employment!" The issue for most women nowadays is not getting a job, but rather what happens to them once they are on the job.

It is, of course, wrong to suggest that all women encounter prejudicial behavior from their coworkers and bosses or are forced to endure personal and institutional resistance to their careers and professional advancement. Unfortunately, however, enough anecdotal and statistical evidence exists to suggest that as individuals and as a class or category of workers, women are not evaluated or dealt with solely in terms of merit and ability. According to management scholar Judy B. Rosener, few women encounter a level playing field on the job. Most women are forced to cope with the usually unarticulated but nevertheless pervasive background problem she calls "sexual static." Rosener argues that most male managers and workers, especially these over the age of 40 who grew up in an era when the vast majority of the professional ranks were male dominated, see females in the workplace, first and foremost, as females—not as colleagues. For too many men, says Rosener, their views of females as coworkers is clouded by their inability to see them other than in their "traditional sex roles" as mothers, sisters, daughters, and potential lovers and wives. Sexual static hangs in the air like snow on a television screen, interfering with communications and hampering "normal business conduct" between men and women. What results are mixed signals, misunderstanding, embarrassment, anger, confusion, and fear.[42]

Sexual static, suggests business ethicist Patricia H. Werhane, is not necessarily about a "hostile work environment," but it is about an "uncomfortable work environment," an environment that out of habit or ignorance is "sexually charged," an environment that creates an atmosphere is which "men and women feel uneasy about their professional interrelationships and how these might be misinterpreted as sexual ones."[43] However, sexual static is not the same thing as sexual harassment. It is not about inappropriate sexual comments, unwelcome sexual advances, or requests for sexual favors as a term or condition of an individual's employment, advancement, or success. Sexual static is in some sense the attempt to avoid and defuse even the suggestion of sexual harassment and abuse. It is the attention that occurs when men and women are not sure how to comport themselves in a business or social environment. From the male manager's point of view, very often personal sexual insecurity leads to dysfunctional corporate decision-making. "We have a real bright woman who has what it takes to be a partner," said a senior male attorney at a major West Coast firm, "but I can't bring myself to vote to promote her because she turns me on, and it gets in my way." Fear of gossip is another motivating factor for some men. "Every time I promote a woman," said a 50-year-old male advertising executive, "I worry about people suspecting I have a romantic interest in her. I guess that's why all the women who have been promoted in this company are middle-aged and on a scale of 1 to 10, about a 5."[44] (This assumes, of course, that average or plain-looking middle-aged men and women will not be attracted to each other!)

Whatever the cause or cases of sexual static—antiquated cultural/sexual mores, insecurity/immaturity, or a puritanical attempt to stifle eros in the workplace—sexual static gets in the way of communication in the workplace and restricts the development of good management skills and good managers."[45] Rosener and Werhane agree that although everyone involved losses both personally and professionally, women are the primary victims of sexual static. Sexual static perpetuates stereotypical sex roles, denies women the opportunity to acquire new skills and experiences, too often denies women the support of a senior male mentor who can act as a role model and protector, and, finally, denies the principle of professional objectivity.[46]

In the end, argues Werhane, sexual static negatively impacts on everyone involved both professionally and personally because it denies the principle of professional objectivity. Professional objectivity maintains that there is a body of facts and knowledge that constitutes the discipline of management and that management practices can and should be unbiased and impersonal. The principle of objectivity requires that the most skilled and effective persons be hired and promoted to leadership positions. Unfortunately, concludes Werhane, "we live in a society in which business is conducted in an atmosphere where merit or worthiness is the ideal but not the practice."[47] Not only do we not live in a sex-, gender-, color-, ethnic-, and age-neutral environment, the practice of sexual static intentionally reinforces the divisive notion that men and women are two separate and competitive species loosely connected by sex, children, and financial arrangements!

Even without the tensions of gender relationships, the major organizational problem facing working women is the now proverbial glass-ceiling effect. A majority of American women in the workplace—regardless of race, class, type of job, or job location—feel that the glass ceiling is firmly in place and thereby keeping them in their place. According to the nationally based survey *Working Woman Count,* more than 60% of the women respondents said that they had little or no opportunity for advancement.[48] Unfortunately, the term "glass ceiling" is an elegantly accurate metaphor. If one can picture the climb up the corporate ladder to success, somewhere above the rung that is labeled "middle management" there is an invisible barrier that women can see through to the top, but are unable to pass through. Like Scotty's miraculous molecular transporter device in the *Star Trek* series, only men and a very small percentage of women are able to "beam" their way past this barrier on their journey to the upper echelons of corporate command and control. The glass ceiling is a metaphor that does not just apply to elite knowledge workers making it into the upper echelons of corporate management; the glass ceiling refers to the institutional and personal prejudices that women encounter in every kind of job at every level in the workplace. And, in a larger social context, the glass ceiling symbolizes how we view and value women both on and off the job. Even those women who manage to pass through this transparent barrier often find themselves in jobs that have a "glass floor": that is, jobs where their every move can be seen and scrutinized, jobs where their every misstep or miscalculation causes cracks and fissures, jobs where their first big mistake has them figuratively crashing through to the floor below—or worse.

Even though women now represent 46%–49% of the workforce, in excess of 97% of all senior management is still male. Where women are starting to achieve representation equal with their numbers is in the lower and middle ranks of management. *Business Week* reports that half the entry-level management corps is female, and soon the middle ranks will be, too. Overall, women now occupy an unprecedented 41%–43% of lower- and middle-management positions.[49] However, a report released in October 1996, by Catalyst, Inc., a New York research firm that focuses on women in business, revealed that only 10% of the top jobs at the nation's 500 largest companies are held by women. Alarmingly, some 105 of these 500 companies have no women corporate officers at all, and only 2.4% of all the women employed in these 500 companies have achieved the rank of chairperson, president, CEO, or executive vice-president. Even of the 24 "Best Companies for Women to Work For" featured in a 1990 *Business Week* cover story, in 1996 just four have women in more than 25% of all of their corporate officer posts.[50] In a related but separate report, Catalyst also announced that women present on the boards of directors of Fortune 500 companies have finally exceeded 10%. Women now hold 626 of the total 6123 Fortune 500 board seats, or 10.2%. Altogether, 83% of Fortune 500 companies have at least one woman on their boards. According to Sheila Wellington, Catalyst president, while these numbers are important, they're "absolutely minuscule." "What this shows" says Wellington, "is that people who say 'the gains have been made, so let's move on' are dead wrong. It shows that the number of women who have made it to the apex are still so few. . . . Clearly, there's a lot more work to be done."[51] The absence of women from positions of power in business is also reflected in our political system. In 1995, on the seventy-fifth anniversary of women's suffrage in the United States, the Center for Policy Alternatives reported that across the nation, women represent only 20% of state legislators, 25% of statewide elective executive officers, 10% of U.S. representatives, 8% of U.S. senators, and 2% (one out of 50) of governors.[52] As Katherine Spillar, national coordinator for the Fund for the Feminist Majority, so wryly put it— "at the current rates of increase it will be (only) 475 years before women reach equality in executive suites."[53]

Some critics suggest that those few women who have broken through the glass ceiling to positions of real authority and power in senior management and the executive suite have managed to do so not by using the tactics and strategies of feminism but rather by out-competing and out-performing men on their own terms. These are women, claim Chicago-based consultants Megan Buffington and Jane Neff, who aren't out to revolutionize, feminize, or humanize the workplace. Rather, they are classic careerists who happen to be women, and as women they felt that they couldn't afford to lose at anything they do because they might not get another chance. Like any dedicated careerist they have done their job, made their numbers, and, if and when it was necessary, kicked ass and haven't bothered to take prisoners. In fact, argue Buffington and Neff, some of these successful women are more combative and ruthless than their male counterparts because they feel they have to prove that, despite the fact they are women, they can be rough, tough, and resilient. Buffington and Neff call this phenomenon "The Only Bra in the Room Syndrome" and claim that the model for their clever metaphor is Chicago's first female mayor, Jane Byrne.

By all accounts Jane Byrne may have been a winner and—when the situation required—a "lady"—but, in her heart, she was one of "the boys." A long-time operative in Richard J. Daley's— "Da Mayor"—political machine, Byrne's earned her spurs because she did her job, because she could keep a secret, and because over the years she built up a campaign war chest of favors and funds. When Daley suddenly died, Byrne mustered her forces and utilized her experience and energy to best "the machine's" anointed candidate for mayor, Michael Bilandic, by convincing the electorate that she was Daley's true ideological protege and therefore had more of the "right stuff" than did Bilandic. As one political pundit put it, "It was a campaign that literally reeked of the smell of testosterone!" After she was elected and subsequently lost in her bid for a second term, she reportedly told Pulitzer Prize-winning journalist Ed Rooney that she really hated losing the mayor's job because she had worked so hard at it and had really wanted to be an effective mayor—and because she knew that people saw her mistakes not just as miscalculations or even due to the limits of her character or intelligence, but rather because, in the end she was, after all, just a woman!

According to Buffington and Neff, another characteristic of "the Only Bra in the Room" type of achiever is her lack of empathy for and support of other working women, especially subordinates. Having achieved success by playing hardball and working hard, they expect the same from others they work with. Having neither sought out nor been granted special consideration as a woman, they do not offer support when women claim special consideration. Having made it in spite of the fact that they are women, their focus is on success and not sensitivity. They tend to be intolerant of office schmoozing or the public demonstration of emotion and affection surrounding the celebration of a birthday or an anniversary. They leave their private lives at the office door and they expect others to do so as well. But, worst of all, too many of these successful women do not reach back to mentor other women, either out of a twisted sense of sexist elitism or simple old-fashioned political selfishness. In other words: "I made it without any help and if you're any good so will you" or "Since I'm already here, there's no more room at the table." Because of all of this, suggest Buffington and Neff, many women do not like to work for female bosses. In a recent Gallop poll conducted in 22 countries, women overwhelmingly preferred male to female bosses in all but three countries surveyed: India, where women preferred to work for women, and El Salvador and Honduras, where women were evenly split in their preferences. In the U.S. 45% of men and women surveyed said they would prefer a man as a boss against 20% who would prefer a women. The rest didn't indicate a preference.[54]

In the early 1990s, Chicago's famous satirical ensemble Second City performed a skit, loosely based on a Gary Trudeau *Doonesbury* cartoon strip, that neatly sums up the meaning and message of the "Only Bra in the Room" thesis. In the skit, Barbie Wawa (a.k.a. Barbara Walters) is conducting an in-depth interview with Chairwoman X of an unnamed Fortune 500 firm. "So tell me," asks Ms. Wawa, "how is it that you've been able to manage a successful and influential career while at the same time balancing your commitment to a husband, three children, a social life, athletic interests, and community involvement?"

"It's really quite simple to explain," replies Chairwoman X in a voice and manner that communicates equal parts of destain and boredom. "To begin with, I have a very high I.Q. and I am a workaholic and an insomniac. My husband and I have been legally separated for years. The children are grown and gone and I really only see them on holidays—if then. There is nothing personal about my social life. The only functions and gatherings I attend are those that I deem absolutely necessary for political or business reasons. I exercise daily, not for pleasure, but in an attempt to reduce anxiety and lower my blood pressure and cholesterol level. And, finally, I send checks to local causes, not out of genuine empathy or concern, but in order to keep up appearances and to foster a good reputation!"

Somewhat stunned but still smiling, Ms. Wawa says in a concluding aside to the audience. "Well, Madam Chairwoman, that certainly does explain why you're so successful, and it also explains why so many of your contemporaries think you have got real balls!"

Although the glass ceiling is a mere metaphorical construct and therefore only an imaginary edifice, its ability to impede the professional lives of women is very real. Not only does the glass ceiling prohibit some women from advancing to the highest echelons of corporate management, it denies other women on the shop floor and in the office equal opportunities for training, advancement, and promotion.

Worse still, not only does the glass ceiling cap advancement and promotion, it also has a limiting effect on salaries. According to the Department of Labor, of the 250,000 women who took part in their nationwide in-depth study and survey of women in the workplace, published as *Working Women Count,* the second most commonly heard complaints were about "unequal and unfair pay."[55] Even though it has been 35 years since the passage of the Equal Pay Act (1963), respondents said that unequal pay is a dollar-and-cents workplace reality and that woman are simply not being paid the same as men who do the same job. Although, the discrepancy between men's and women's pay has narrowed significantly, the gap remains significant. In 1993, based on annual earnings of full-time, full-year workers, a woman earned 71 cents for every dollar earned by a man, and in 1996 the International Labor Organization reported that the majority of women in America earn 75 cents for every dollar earned by men doing the same job.[56] Nationwide it is estimated that women with college degrees earn slightly more than men with high school degrees and on average $10,000 less than men with comparable educations. Of the women who took part in the *Working Women Count* survey, 23% had part-time jobs (fewer than 35 hours per week) and 77% had full-time jobs (40 hours or more per week). From the data available, 16.3% reported earning less than $10,000 per year, 39% reported earning between $10,000 and $25,000, 15.8% earned between $25,000 to $35,000, 10.4% earned between $35,000 and $50,000, and 4.8% earned between $50,000 and $75,000. If we break down some of these figures, it is worth noting that 71.1% of these women earned less than $35,000 per year. It is also worth noting that 35% of the sample are the sole support for themselves and their families, and 58% of that group makes less than $25,000 per year.[57] While women may nearly constitute the simple majority of the workforce, it was clear that they are a long way from surpassing men in pay.

Besides the subtle and sometimes subconscious background effects of sexual static, two other major factors contribute to the perpetuation of the glass ceiling as a formidable barrier against women—babies and men. While biology may not be all of destiny, it certainly constitutes a major part. No matter what your particular stance on the debates and controversies surrounding intergender conflicts, there is at least one indisputable gender-based fact—men don't get pregnant, women do. Now, the first child—depending on one's age, job, salary, family support system, marital status, and daycare options—is usually manageable. But the arrivals of two or three babies brings most women to their knees and forces them to reanalyze their commitment to work. Sure, the sit-com actress Phylicia Rashad on the old *Bill Cosby Show* managed wonderfully. She had it all: a law practice, a beautiful house, and four active children. She also had Bill Cosby for a husband, who ostensibly was an obstetrician but in fact spent most of the day taking care of his own children rather than his patient's children. (Let's also remember that we're talking about a TV show and not real life!) The simple fact is that children change the meter, measure, and structure of our lives, but corporations and most places of employment still operate as if all their employees, men and women alike, have no other concerns, responsibilities, or interests once they enter the workplace.

According to the Women's Bureau of the Department of Labor, the single greatest concern of working women is finding a way to balance work, family, and child care. Never has the number of women with young children in the workplace been higher: 67% of women with children under 18 are working or actively seeking employment. This includes 54% of mothers with children under the age of three, 58% of mothers with children under six, and 75% of all mothers with school-age children. These mothers report, almost in one voice, that the juggling act of kids and work results in a constant state of anxiety, fatigue, frustration, and guilt, both on and off the job. As one working woman told me, "I don't even know what I should feel bad

about first! The job? Because I always feel I should be working harder? The kids? Because I miss them so much and I know I'm missing so much. The house? Because it doesn't feel like a home anymore, it's just a place where we live. Or my husband? Good old—what the hell is his name?" Of the mothers surveyed for *Working Women Count,* 56% complained about not being able to find adequate affordable child care services, 49% wanted paid leaves "to care for a newborn and sick relatives," and 35% wanted more "flexible working schedules" in an attempt to balance the day-to-day necessities of work and private life.[58] In some sense, these demands and desires are a direct response and reaction to the one piece of "occupational wisdom" that all working women have been forced to absorb and abide by: "You can take time to baby a client, but you can't take time to baby your own baby."[59]

In 1989, in an attempt to speak to the needs of babies, women, and men, women's advocate and founder of Catalyst Felice N. Schwartz published *Management Women and the New Facts of Life,* which the press dubbed *"The Mommy Track."* Schwartz thought her ideas benign, benevolent, and enlightened and was surprised by the drubbing she took from the press, corporate policy-makers, and working women. Schwartz argued that given the fact that women are now major players in the workplace, given the costs involved in training and developing female employees, given the assumption that experience equals expertise, and given the reality that many women, sooner or later, get pregnant, accommodations have to be made. What Schwartz proposed is that corporations establish a two-tier working venue for female employees: the "career primary track" and the "career and family track". Those who chose the "career primary track" would be considered fully available for any and all work-related tasks, and the "career and family track" women would be considered to be on modified assignment with more limited responsibilities than their "career primary" colleagues. Schwartz suggested that over the course of a woman's employment and depending on the needs of her family that she would be allowed to go back and forth between career tracks. In this way, she suggested, corporations will be able to retain experienced employees and the women involved could pursue their careers without being forced to totally abdicate their responsibilities as mothers and nurturers.[60]

Critics and sister-feminists alike immediately attacked her ideas and relabeled her categories "the achievers" versus "the breeders." Although Schwartz offered her track system as a means of ensuring future generations of successful working women and well-balanced, happy, and healthy children, many commentators saw her proposal not as a reasonable trade off but as a passport to permanent status as a second-class citizen and a one-way ticket to a mediocre career. The "mommy track," they said, ties women to the old-fashioned notion that singles out women rather than men for complete parental responsibility or sacrifice. "The 'mommy track' is not a 'new alternative'; it is, rather, a 'dead end'."

In a 1997 article in *Fortune Magazine,* Betsy Morris argued that the issues raised by Schwartz—balancing careers, babies, and long-term family responsibilities—have neither been resolved nor have they gone away. In fact, Morris claims things have gotten much worse. And for all their politically correct talk, says Morris, most companies don't much care about or like kids:

> Today, in the corridors of business as elsewhere, families are getting more lip service than ever. Being on the right side of work and family issues—having the proper programs, letting Mom and Dad slip out to watch a T-ball game—is very PC. But corporate America harbors a dirty (little) secret. People in human resources know it. So do a lot of CEOs, although they don't dare discuss it. Families are no longer a big plus for a corporation; they are a big problem. An albatross. More and more, the business world seems to regard children not as the future generation of workers but as luxuries you're entitled to after you've won your stripes. It's fine to have kids' pictures on your desk—just don't let them cut into your billable hours.[61]

Companies want all their employees, women and men alike, to clock as much face time as possible. They are interested in results, productivity, and success and not in child care commitments and kindergarten recitals. In the spirt of full disclosure, says Morris, all corporate manuals should carry the following warning:

> Ambitious (especially women) beware. If you want to have children, proceed at your own risk. You must be very talented, or on very solid ground, to overcome the damage a family can do to your career.[62]

JUSTICE AT HOME

The problems, prejudices, and injustices that women face in the workplace are, unfortunately, mirrored in and in fact exaggerated on the home front. In the words of Helen Gurley Brown, author and former editor of *Cosmopolitan* magazine, "Women can have fame and fortune, office affairs, silicon injections, and dazzling designer clothes. But the one thing she can't have, apparently, is a man who shares the work at home."[63] There is a price to pay for having "made it," and, by all accounts, women are being asked to pick up most of the tab.

Arlie Russell Hochschild, in her important 1989 book *The Second Shift,* claims that even though women have won certain rights in the workplace, they have not won many rights at home—in fact, in many cases, women are losing ground. According to Hochschild, women in dual-income families not only carry the burdens and responsibilities of their profession or place of employment, but 80% of most working women also have the task of carrying the burden of the second job—their second shift—the home, the kids, and, yes, the care and maintenance of their husbands.

On average, Hochschild claims, American women in the past two decades have worked an extra 15 hours per week around the house than have men. On a day-to-day basis, that breaks down to women roughly averaging three hours a day on housework while men average 17 minutes, and women spend 50 minutes a day exclusively with their children while men spend 12 minutes. Over a year, this adds up to women putting in an extra month of 24-hour days on household chores. According to Hochschild's computations, 61% of men do little or no housework; 21% attempt, on an irregular basis, to do their share of household chores; and only 18% of men actually share housework equally.[64] In effect, says Hochschild, the second shift means that women put in a double day. They're on duty at work. They're on duty at home. And, the next day, they're on double duty again! As one angry woman put it, "I do my half. I do half of his half. And the rest [just] doesn't get done!"[65]

Although some of Hochschild's findings are unexpected—for example, working-class husbands actually did more around the house than did ostensibly more liberal middle-class professional husbands—most of her conclusions regarding the cultural cause(s) of the second-shift phenomenon are painfully pedestrian, parochial, and paternalistic. To begin with she suggests that most men feel that their work is more important than their wives' jobs. Although their wives' salaries may be necessary, most men, because they earn more and because they have been traditionally seen as the head of the family, view their work as the primary defining ingredient regarding household status and class. Secondly, most men believe that women are natural nurturers and are better suited for child care. Finally, although domestic chores may be aesthetically and hygienically necessary, they are neither creative nor important and therefore are not the concern of the progenitor and main provider of the family. Sadly, suggests Hochschild, what passes for benevolence and understanding from some husbands of wives working a double-shift day sounds something like this: "Hey, I'm not like my dad. I don't need my wife home all the time. I'm a modern guy. If she wants to work and have a family too, that's fine with me—as long as she can manage it!"

Hochschild argues that the sudden surge of women into the marketplace has not been accompanied by a new cultural understanding of both marriage and work that would have made this transition smoother. Families have changed. Women have changed. Work has changed. But most workplaces have remained inflexible in the face of the family demands of their workers. At home, most men have yet to really adapt, in seri-ous lifestyle ways, to the changes in women. Because of this absence of change, said Hochschild, because of the burdens of the second shift, the revolutionary movement of women into the workforce in search of identity, independence, and financial security remains at best a "stalled revolution."[66]

In her most recent book *The Time Bind* (1997) Hochschild suggests that not only is the revolution still "stalled," but the burdens and fallout of the second shift have gotten more complex. Even with men actively contributing to child care and household chores, men and women still find themselves desperately trying to juggle their commitments to family and work. The demands of a workaholic corporate system and the needs of families and children have us rushing from one responsibility to another and have us trapped in a "time bind" of guilt. Unfortunately, says Hochschild, "many working families are both prisoners and architects of the time bind in which they find themselves.[67] They want it all: great jobs, great families, and all the goodies that go along with it. But the more energy and time they pump into work and the more time and energy they pump out of the home, the more emotionally stressful their lives become. Ironically, what Hochschild discovered in her three-year study of a "family-friendly" Fortune 500 firm, is that for a growing number of two-career couples, when work and family compete, work wins. Or, to be more accurate, many workers choose to escape into work because life at home has become a "frantic exercise in beat-the-clock, while work by comparison seems a haven of grown-up sociability, competence, and relative freedom."[68]

According to Hochschild, the worlds of home and work have begun to reverse places. Work has become a form of "home" (a village of associates, peers, coworkers) and home has become "hard work" (a locus of duty, tasks, chores, and demanding personalities). Work is the new "neighborhood," where we spend most of our time, where we talk to friends and develop relationships and expertise. Meanwhile, says Hochschild, home is now the place where we are the least secure and the most harried:

At home the divorce rate has risen, and the emotional demands have become more baffling and complex. In addition to teething, trantrums, and the normal development of growing children, the needs of elderly parents are creating more tasks for the modern family—as are the blending, unblending, reblending of new step-parents, step-children, exes, and former in-laws.[69]

By comparison, work is less chaotic, cleaner, more enriching, and much less personal. As one female worker candidly admitted to Hochschild, "I put in for (overtime). . . . I get home, and the minute I turn the key, my (teenage) daughter is right there. . . . The baby is still up. . . . The dishes are still in the sink. . . . My husband is in the other room hollering at my daughter, 'I don't ever get any time to talk to your mother. . . . you're always monopolizing her time! . . .' They all come at me at once."[70] Is it any wonder, asks Hochschild, that work becomes home and home becomes work? Work is less demanding, a surrogate, a refuge from our troubled private lives. It is also a place where conflicts that originate in the home can be discussed, debated, and subjected to sympathetic scrutiny. In the sanctuary of work, says Hochschild, increasing numbers of women are discovering the "great male secret—work can be an escape from the pressures of home! In the words of a James Thurber character as he leaves for work after a long weekend of kith and kin. "Ah, thank God it's Monday!" Somewhat reluctantly, Hochschild concludes that for more and more women, "the world of 'male' work seems more honorable and valuable than the 'female' world of home and children."[71] The paradoxical result of such a shift, suggests Hochschild, is altogether too clear: that for which we work—families—is that which is most hurt by our work!

In a very real sense what Hochschild is implying is that every dual-career family needs a full-time wife. One National Public Radio (NPR) pundit, in commenting on *The Time Bind,* argued that given Hochschild's findings and insights, perhaps the only way to save the family is to change it:

In the future individuals who want to "have it all" — children and a career—without shortchanging one or the other or both will be required to enter into a communal marriage involving six precertified adults. Two of them will work full time in order to support the family. Two will be in charge of the house and kids. And two of them will be held in ready reserve, to fill in wherever they are needed. Divorce will be forbidden, all property will be owned in joint tenancy, sleeping arrangements are negotiable and sex will be strictly optional. Hey, why not give it a try? Nothing else seems to be working.[72]

WHAT NOW?

Women have changed. The economy has changed. The workplace has changed. Families have changed. Unfortunately, most men have neither privately nor professionally adapted to these changes, nor have the rules of work been sufficiently altered to accommodate these changes. Are women in the workplace to stay? Absolutely. Women report that they both need and want to work. Current research also suggests that no matter how taxing and hectic their lives, women who do paid work feel less depressed, have a higher sense of personal worth, and are happier and more satisfied than women who do not have jobs. Do men need women in the workplace? Yes. Demographic trends regarding birth rates, urban population patterns, and college graduation rates necessitate women's active participation in the workplace. Do men want women in the workplace? Yes and no. For a lot of men, women simply represent another group of individuals that they have to compete with for jobs, salaries, promotions. And for some men there yet remains a sense of social awkwardness about women's roles and men's appropriate response.

For too many men, women's commitment to work and their general dependability remain suspect because of "the one immutable, enduring difference between men and women—maternity."[73] On the job, families and babies are seen as a vulnerability, an impediment rather than as a normal and necessary part of life that we have to accommodate. According to Betsy Morris, in an interesting turn of events, the newly resuscitated "ultimate male status symbol [of the 1990s] is not a fancy car or a fancy second home, or a wife with a fancy career. You're really made it, buddy, if you can afford a wife that doesn't work. She may be a drag on earnings, but she provides a rare modern luxury: peace on the home front."[74]

Finally, will women rise in the ranks and assume power proportional to their numbers in the workplace? No, I don't think so. But the reasons for this are much more straightforward and much less gender specific and sexually biased than some social commentators would have us think.

To begin with, the rules of work are, by and large, still being written by men, and these rules both consciously and unconsciously communicate a certain male indifference to any other concerns in the workplace beyond the job at hand. As both Robert Bly and Gloria Emerson have argued, the primary masculine imperative is to fulfill their role as worker/provider. Consequently, most workplace rules primarily reflect professional and not personal issues. Secondly, although it is true that the predominantly male corporate structure has been unwilling to alter the rules and share the power base, this reluctance is not necessarily misogynistic in its origins. The term *power* comes from the Latin *posse:* "to do, to be able, to change, to influence, to affect." In general, power is about control, the ability to produce intended effects or results. To have power is to possess the capacity to control or direct change. The first maxim of power is self-perpetuation; nobody gladly gives up power. This principle is not testosterone based or predominately/primarily masculine in it origins. It is purely Machiavellian. That is, those who have power (in this case, men) will only reluctantly give it up. The goal of power, said Machiavelli, is not to allow change, because change always leads to the alienation of power and the status quo, and an alternation of the status quo is never in the best interest of those who posses power. Although the issue at hand is the power of the "good-old-boy" network," we are not talking about a cabal of evil men conspiring to keep women in their place. In effect, the motivating principle involved in this and every power struggle is much more visceral than simple *machismo.*

Things are not going to change entirely anytime soon. But change of a fashion is occurring. As singer-actress-director Barbra Streisand said on her 1992 induction into the Women in Film Hall of Fame; "Not so long ago we were referred to as 'dolls,' 'tomatoes,' 'chicks,' 'babes,' 'broads.' We've graduated to being called 'tough cookies,' 'foxes,' 'bitches,' and 'witches.' I guess that's progress."[75]

NOTES

1. "Changing Profile of the U.S. Labor Force," *U.S. News and World Report,* 2 September 1985, 46, 47.
2. Bradley K. Googins, *Work/Family Conflicts* (New York: Auburn House, 1991), 1, 286.
3. Barbara Ehrenreich, "Strategies of Corporate Women," *The New Republic,* 27 January 1987, 28.
4. Carol Kleiman, "On the Job," *Chicago Tribune,* Jobs Section, 1 November 1987, 1.
5. Kathryn M. Borman, "Fathers, Mothers, and Child Care in the 1980s," in *Women in the Workplace: Effects on Families,* ed. Kathryn M. Borman et al. (Norwood: Ablex Publishing, 1984), 73.
6. Stephanie Coontz, *The Way We Never Were* (New York: Basic Books, 1992), 31–41.
7. Coontz, 31.
8. Coontz, 32.
9. Ralph E. Smith (ed.), *The Subtle Revolution: Women at Work* (Washington, DC: The Urban Institute, 1979), 1.
10. "Are Men Becoming the Second Sex?" *Chicago Tribune* WomeNews Section, 9 February 1997, 6.
11. "Sixth Annual Salary Survey," *Working Woman Magazine,* 5 January 1985, 65.
12. "Employment Status of Women," *Statistical Abstract of the United States,* 116th Edition (Maryland: Berwan Press, 1996), 400.
13. Borman, 73.
14. John Schmeltzer, "Daughters Will Face Many of Mom's Barriers at Work," *Chicago Tribune,* Business Section, 28 April 1994, 1.
15. *Statistical Abstract of the United States,* 400.
16. Arlie Russell Hochschild, *The Second Shift* (New York: Viking, 1989), 2.
17. Hochschild, *The Second Shift,* 93–94, Daniel Evan Weiss, *The Great Divide: How Females and Males Really Differ* (New York: Poseidon Press, 1991), 32.
18. Carol Kleiman, "Women's Voices Poll Speaks of Solutions as Well as Questions," *Chicago Tribune,* Business Section, 12 November 1996, 3.
19. John W. Wright, *The American Almanac of Jobs and Salaries* (New York: Avon, 1997), 650, 651.
20. "Sixth Annual Salary Survey," 65.

21. Women's Bureau, *Working Women Count* (Washington, DC: Department of Labor, 1994), 13. Lisa Anderson, "Women Escape Affirmative Action Feud," *Chicago Tribune,* 16 May 1995, 1.
22. Women's Bureau, 10.
23. Coontz, 23.
24. Googins, 95.
25. Googins, 4.
26. Googins, 5.
27. Sara Ann Friedman, *Work Matters* (New York: Viking, 1996), xii.
28. Hochschild, *The Second Shift,* 263.
29. Maureen Brendan, interview by author, Chicago, 8 May 1996.
30. Friedman, xii.
31. Gloria Emerson, *Some American Men* (New York: Simon and Schuster, 1985), 32.
32. Daniel Yankelovich, "The New Psychological Contracts at Work," *Psychology Today,* May 1978, 86.
33. "Annual Report on Salaries," *Working Woman Magazine,* October 1995, 22.
34. "Annual Report on Salaries," 22.
35. Coontz, 266.
36. David R. Koller, interview by author, Chicago, 12 December 1996.
37. Coontz, 3.
38. Googins, 22.
39. Coontz, 3, 15.
40. Hochschild, *The Second Shift,* 249.
41. Schmeltzer, 2.
42. Judith Rosener, "Coping with Sexual Static," *New York Times Magazine,* 7 December 1986, 89ff.
43. Patricia A. Werhane, "Sexual Static and the Ideal of Professional Objectivity," in *It Comes with the Territory,* ed. A. R. Gini and T. J. Sullivan (New York: Random House, 1989), 170.
44. Rosener, 89ff.
45. Rosener, 89ff.
46. Werhane, 173.
47. Werhane, 171.
48. Women's Bureau, 36.
49. Amanda T. Segal and Wendy Zeller, "Corporate Women," *Business Week,* 8 June 1992, 76.
50. "Breaking Through," *Business Week,* 17 February 1997, 64.
51. Barbara Sullivan, "Women Cross 10% Barrier in Presence on Boards," *Chicago Tribune,* Business Section, 12 December 1996, 1, 2.
52. *The State of the States for Women and Politics* (Washington, DC: The Center for Policy Alternatives, n.d.), 2, 3.
53. Segal and Zeller, 74.
54. Mike Dorning, "Poll Details Global Role of Gender Bias," *Chicago Tribune,* 27 March 1996, 1.
55. Women's Bureau, 20.
56. Carol Kleiman, "Equal Pay for Work of Equal Value—A Gender Free Gain," *Chicago Tribune,* Business Section, 17 September 1996, 3.
57. Women's Bureau, 13.
58. Women's Bureau, 31, 32.
59. Hochschild, *The Second Shift,* 96.
60. Felice N. Schwartz, "Management Women and the New Facts of Life," *Harvard Business Review,* January/February 1989, 65–76.
61. Betsy Morris, "Is Your Family Wrecking Your Career?" *Fortune,* 17 March 1998, 71, 72.
62. Morris, 72.
63. Hochschild, *The Second Shift,* 26.
64. Hochschild, *The Second Shift,* 3, 4, 260.
65. Hochschild, *The Second Shift,* 259.
66. Hochschild, *The Second Shift,* 12.
67. Arlie Russell Hochschild, *The Time Bind* (New York: Metropolitan Books, 1997), 249.
68. Laura Shapiro, "The Myth of Quality Time," *Newsweek,* 12 May 1967, 64.
69. Arlie Russell Hochschild, "There's No Place Like Work," *The New York Times Magazine,* 20 April 1997, 53.
70. Hochschild, "There's No Place Like Work," 53.
71. Hochschild, "There's No Place Like Work," 84.
72. Al Gini, "Work, Time, and Hochschild," interview on *Metropolis,* NPR–WBEZ, Chicago, 21 May 1997.
73. Schwartz, 66.
74. Morris, 72.
75. Friedman, 231.

QUESTIONS FOR DISCUSSION

1. Using the guidelines developed by Bravo and Cassedy, decide what you would do in "The Case of the Mismanaged Ms."
2. Discuss "Texaco: The Jelly Bean Diversity Fiasco" in light of the arguments given by Pojman and Hettinger.
3. How do the theories of Rawls, Nozick, and Smart (from Chapter 1) apply to the debate about affirmative action?
4. Should employees have their "family rights" respected to the extent suggested by Melé?

Joan Drew

Joan Drew, an associate in the Assurance and Business Advisory Services (ABAS), has been working on the audit of a long-time client. Last week following a late-night session, the client's chief financial officer asked her to go out for a drink. She was quite surprised, but politely declined and didn't think twice about the incident. A few days later, the CFO again asked her to go out. This time when she declined, the CFO seemed somewhat upset, noting, "You don't know what you're missing."

Since then, the CFO seems to go out of his way to stare at Drew. Today, the CFO intercepted her in the coffee area, commenting, "I don't like to be refused."

Drew now feels that the situation has gotten out of hand, and she is actually somewhat frightened. Since the CFO is the key client contact, she is concerned about what will happen if she reports the situation to the ABAS partner. She is so embarrassed about the whole thing that she hasn't mentioned the problem to anyone else on the team.

What should Drew do?

DISCUSSION QUESTIONS

- What are the legal ramifications in this situation?
- At what point did the CFO's conduct become improper?
- Could the associate have done anything differently to defuse the situation?
- What if the situation had been different, and there was mutual attraction. Could the associate have accepted the invitation?

Julie Simpson

Julie, a secretary in the Purchasing Department, was recently given the responsibility of entering information into a new system the department was implementing. The system is a proprietary software product developed by ABC Systems, Inc., that tracks performance measurements. She was excited to take on this new responsibility, especially since it involved a three-week training program in San Diego at the vendor's training facility.

Julie attended the training session in San Diego and felt confident about her new skills. On the last

day of training, the vendor placed a gift on the seat of each participant in the training class as a congratulatory gesture for completing the course. Along with all her classmates, she was given an electronic calendar. Having recently ordered the same electronic calendar for her supervisor, she knew that the value of the calendar was over $200.

Should Julie accept the gift from the vendor?

DISCUSSION QUESTIONS

- What conflicts of interest exist in this situation, if any?
- What are Julie's responsibilities?
- Does the value of the gift warrant consideration?
- Would the situation be different if Julie were a buyer in the Purchasing Department?

Adapted from Niagara Mohawk Holdings, Inc. training materials. © 1999 Niagara Mohawk Holdings, Inc. Printed with permission.

BankBoston's Layoffs Program: Death with Dignity

Andrew W. Singer
Co-Editor and Publisher, *Ethikos*

A company merges with a local competitor. One result is redundancies in the workforce. Layoffs are required if the company is to realize the merger's promised efficiencies.

But how to conduct those layoffs? That was the question faced by BankBoston, the Boston-based bank holding company, after its merger with Massachusetts-based BayBanks Inc., in 1996. What the company settled on was something that has been called "death with dignity."

Formally, the initiative is called the Transition Assistance Program. The idea was to support laid-off employees through things like education grants and internships at other companies. The bank agreed, for example, to pay part-time salaries of furloughed employees at nonprofit organizations for up to six months.

In releasing first-year results from the "work reduction" program in June, BankBoston Execu-

Reprinted by permission of Ethikos, Inc. (Mamaroneck, NY)

tive Vice President Helen Drinan noted, "No company can guarantee its employees permanent employment, but all companies can pledge resources toward employability. Through our Transition Assistance Program, we sought to provide real opportunities to outgoing employees."

2,000 POSITIONS ELIMINATED

BankBoston announced in December of 1995 that it was buying BayBanks, Inc., a New England institution that employed 8,000 people. BankBoston had 24,000 employees. There was significant overlap on the retail bank side in Massachusetts.

Soon after the merger BankBoston announced that 2,000 positions at the combined companies would be eliminated. How to get to that number? Attrition was one possibility. The company announced a hiring freeze in both banks to begin immediately. This brought down the number of jobs to be eliminated "quite a bit," according to Karen Schwartzman, Director, Media Relations, BankBoston. But after six months, the bank still had to eliminate 1,300 jobs.

So in June 1996, BankBoston announced an "enhanced retirement program" with eligibility determined by an employee's age or years of service. This attracted about half of those eligible—and took care of another 900 positions. But the bank still faced 400 layoffs.

Here the bank's management "sat back and thought," recalls Schwartzman. Clearly, some people now would have to be fired. But the bank asked: "How can we maximize the employability of the people leaving the company?"

CREATING ALTERNATIVES

It developed several options. One was "a stipend to anyone who went to work for a nonprofit organization (NPO)." There are 200 nonprofits in the New England area, says Schwartzman. "We'll pay the person's salary on a part-time basis for six months while they test each other out," the bank said. A stipend of $10 per hour was to be paid for up to 20 hours a week for those using the NPO as "a means to further develop their career paths or simply to support a worthy cause." To further promote this option, the bank mailed out hundreds of letters to community organizations throughout New England. According to the bank, these mailings "brought in dozens of job opportunities—from technical assistance to administrative support."

This was open to all early retirees and laid off employees. It recognized that a 55-year old doesn't always have the same salary needs as he or she might have had in earlier years, so they can work for a United Way, a local hospital, the American Red Cross, or the Girl Scouts.

A second option was for those "interested in a normal competitive salary," recounts Schwartzman. BankBoston offered to pay a salary of $15 an hour for up to 40 hours a week for three months at "any for-profit company that doesn't compete with Bank-Boston." The idea was to pay the bill while the person was undergoing training at the new company.

The bank developed a list of more than 200 internships with non-competing employers, "in disciplines ranging from real estate and law to education and human resources." Among the results, according to the company, "one former Bank-Boston employee is employed by the Boston Center for Rehabilitative & Subacute Care; another, a former mortgage sales and service center supervisor, is a conference planner at International Business Communications."

The bank offered job retraining through educational grants of up to $3,000.

They also offered small business loans for those "willing to start their own business," says Schwartzman. "Very few," however, were prepared to take advantage of this.

Of the 400 who were laid off, 350 "took advantage of something," whether training or going back to school. One hundred of those took "job-related options." Many others took advantage of outplacement and support services that were also offered.

The idea for the program "came from the CEO's office in the course of conversation with Cardinal Law." Archbishop of Boston, says Schwartzman. "It was not Cardinal Law's idea, but he gave it a push."

Why do it? "It makes your employees like you better," explains Schwartzman, "and if they are happy, they will service their customers better." Satisfied customers will bring return business to the company. The bank, adds Schwartzman, is convinced of "the correlation between employee satisfaction and customer service."

Some customers, too, make their choices based on the quality of the company offering a given product. Such a program doesn't hurt the company's image.

Isn't such a program costly? "Of course there are costs, but the behavior of shareholders is the best test. The stock is at an all-time high," she said in late July, observing that shareholders "don't want money spent frivolously." She concludes, "The return must be worth it."

Would such a program work, however, at a company that was laying off 4,000 employees, or 20,000—rather than only 400? "If 20,000 are being laid off, the company probably has more than 100,000 employees. It's a different dynamic."

The point is that "there are definitely things you can do to manage things better without slash and burn."

'DOING THE RIGHT THING'

Is ethics involved here? "Absolutely, ethics is involved here. This is called doing the right thing by your company. The way people leave has a huge impact on the people left behind."

Harvard Business School professor Rosabeth Moss Kanter calls it "enlightened divorce or death with dignity." Programs such as BankBoston's "reassure continuing employees that the company will keep its promises," she wrote in a recent *Wall Street Journal* Op-Ed piece. "The BankBoston people I interviewed said they were grateful their friends and neighbors were getting such help. They expressed optimism about their own future and respect for the bank's leaders; good morale paid off in high productivity during a demanding merger integration."

A certain "guilt factor" exists, too, among those employees who remain with the company, observes Schwartzman, "Why me and not him?" they often ask. Such a program "shows you're a caring employer."

"Ethics is a huge part."

Lanscape

Ernest Kallman
Former Professor of Computer Information Systems, and Research Fellow, Center for Business Ethics, Bentley College

John Grillo
Former Professor of Computer Information Systems, and Research Fellow, Center for Business Ethics, Bentley College

Clare Valerian is a systems analyst at Califon, Inc., a large distributor of electronic equipment. Her primary responsibility is to make certain that the 127 end users in Califon's U.S. headquarters can access data, post to accounts, send and receive e-mail, and perform all other daily activities through their use of the corporate Local Area Network. She describes herself as a facilitator and trouble shooter. She must respond quickly to the users' complaints and needs, even so far as to provide training for novice users. It's a demanding

---

Found in Ernest A. Kallman and John P. Grillo, *Ethical Decision Making and Information Technology: An Introduction with Cases,* pp. 36–38. Copyright © 1993 by McGraw-Hill, Inc. Reproduced by permission of McGraw-Hill, Inc.

and time-consuming job, and until the appearance two weeks ago of the LANSCAPE utility, Clare was spending up to 12 hours a day one-on-one with her users. Much of that time was travel time. She seemed to spend more time on the escalators and elevators, in the stairwells, and riding the interoffice shuttle carts than with her users. The telephone couldn't help, because Clare had to see for herself exactly what the users saw on their terminals. LANSCAPE has changed her workday completely. She now uses the utility program and the telephone at her desk without ever having to go directly to the users' workstations and terminals. The program allows Clare to view and actually take over the activities of network users. Typically, her first task upon arriving at her desk is to check her e-mail messages for trouble spots, print them out, fire up LANSCAPE, and call each user with a problem one at a time.

"John, this is Clare in Systems. You left me a message about a problem with the inventory re-order module. I've got your screen up on my terminal now. Can you get out of the word processor and transfer to the inventory system? . . . Good, I see the main menu . . . now, the re-order module . . . go ahead and repeat the steps that got you into trouble yesterday. OK, . . . fine . . . oops, I see what you did. The system asks for 'ENTER' and you hit 'RETURN.' What kind of keyboard do you have? . . . That's what I thought. For now, remember to hit 'ENTER.' I'll get the maintenance programmer to change the module to accept 'RETURN' too. Sorry about that. . . . Thanks, 'bye."

"Bill, this is Clare in Systems. Your word processor bombed? Why don't you call it up and repeat the . . . Oh, I see the problem. You're working with the buggy Version 2.3. I'll delete it from the system. You'll have to remember to use V2.4 from now on . . . No problem, 'bye."

Clare is delighted with the LANSCAPE utility. She roves electronically from one troubled user to another, seeing on her screen exactly what they see. The amount of time it takes to solve the problems is about the same, but because she can solve them from her desk, she has eliminated the frustrating delays of travel time. She is at her desk when the users call, and they are pleased at the fast response time.

Clare even has time to scan users' activities without their making a request. Her troubleshooting has become more proactive than reactive. She can scan a number of users without their knowledge and when she finds one in trouble she can interrupt and help.

"Harry, this is Clare in Systems. I'm looking at your screen now . . . I know you didn't call, but I thought I'd beat you to the punch . . . You can speed up that multiple posting to a single customer by using the tab key instead of updating the record for each entry . . . Yes, like that . . . Glad to be of service. 'Bye."

Last week, Clare and her boss, the Director of User Support, met with the Vice President of Information Systems Art Betony, to discuss LANSCAPE and the way it has helped to solve several tough technical problems.

Clare said, "Without this program, I'd have to control the activities of every user in every system test, and move from one building to the other to guide their activities. With LANSCAPE, I can watch over their shoulders without being there. LANSCAPE is inexpensive and easy to use. I fully endorse its continued use and recommend we obtain additional copies and make it available to all support personnel."

Both managers are pleased with the results. They have solved the problem of slow and costly user support with the best of all solutions, one that is both more efficient and cost effective. They not only get an increase in user satisfaction but also an increase in productivity.

Yesterday Art was having his usual Tuesday lunch with his boss, the Executive Vice President, Alberta Wilson. They use these meetings to discuss any information systems issues that may be pending. This time, though, Art couldn't stop praising the successful implementation and use of LANSCAPE.

"With your background in human resources and production planning, I know you can appreciate the importance of the productivity gains we've made. And they're truly important. But from the information systems point of view, I am even more pleased that we are able to use the power of the computer itself to help us make it a more effective business tool."

Ms. Wilson seemed especially interested. She asked, "You mean you can tell me any time what people are doing?"

"Not quite," Art answered, "We can only see the screens of the users who are logged in. But of course that's exactly what my people need for their purposes."

"But the people you observe this way . . . they know they're being observed, right?"

"No, not unless I tell them. The LANSCAPE program doesn't change anything on their screens. Of course, that's a necessary feature of the system, because my people have to see exactly what the users see."

"Could you install LANSCAPE on my terminal, in my office?" she asked.

Art replied, "Of course, we could, but what value would that be?"

Alberta leaned forward and whispered, "I shouldn't reveal this outside the Human Resources Department, but I think I will in order to enlist your support. We may have one or more persons at Headquarters dealing in drugs. We have suspects but no proof. Somehow these people are taking orders and making deliveries right on the premises during company time. I suspect that they are using the phone and maybe even the computer to make their deals. We have tried various surveillance methods to no avail. What I want to do is use LANSCAPE to randomly check on what the known suspects are doing. Then if we catch them 'redhanded,' we'll have our evidence and we can prosecute."

Art frowned and said "Gee, I don't know if I should give you that software, Alberta. Let me think about it and get back to you."

United States v. General Electric

United States District Court, Ohio

31 U.S.C. Sec. 3730 and its predecessors sometimes are referred to as the "False Claims Act" or the "Whistleblower Statute." The statute essen-

tially provides for an award to any person who brings to the attention of the United States evidence of fraud . . . This section and its predecessors have had a long history. The original statute was enacted by the Congress of the United States in March 1863, several months before the Battle of Gettysburg. There is historical evidence that a critical position known as Little Roundtop was almost overrun by Confederate troops because of a lack of Union rifles and ammunition. Armament which had been purchased from private suppliers arrived in boxes that contained only sawdust. . . .

Beginning in December 1984, Chester Walsh, an employee of the General Electric Company, was assigned to duties in the State of Israel as the manager of the overseas aircraft operation in Israel. During the period of time that he was so assigned, he learned that funds of money provided by the United States for specific projects sought by the government of Israel in fact were being diverted to other uses. What Mr. Walsh apparently did not know, or did not learn until somewhat later, was that funds not only were diverted, but apparently were also embezzled by an Israeli Air Force Colonel (later an Israeli Air Force General) known as Rami Dotan, and by a high-ranking General Electric official by the name of Herbert Steindler.

Mr. Walsh began accumulating documents indicating the diversion of money to what he assumed to be different projects. In mid 1987, while on a visit to the United States, he consulted counsel. After returning to Israel, he continued to accumulate documents which he ultimately "smuggled" out of Israel to Switzerland, where he had been reassigned, and then to the United States. The documents in this case are quite numerous. The vast bulk of them were produced by Mr. Walsh. In November 1990, General Dotan was arrested; shortly thereafter this action was brought and held under seal. Information thereupon was supplied to the United States Department of Justice as required by the statute. In August 1991, approximately nine months later, the Department of Justice elected to proceed with the lawsuit. In the interim Mr. Walsh had numerous conferences with the FBI. In December 1990, he agreed to wear a body microphone whereby he obtained evidence from three other employees of General Electric.

In the words of Agent Kosky, Mr. Walsh's contribution was substantial. The actual language [from his deposition] is as follows:

Question: As a result of your participation and perceptions, what is your opinion about how substantial Mr. Walsh's contribution was to your investigation and the litigation of this action?

Answer: The government knew absolutely nothing that had gone amiss at General Electric. General Electric had taken substantial measures to cover it up for a space of two years. I have no reason to believe that anyone within General Electric would have ever told us besides Mr. Walsh. Mr. Walsh brought us the only information that we had. We built on it through our own efforts and the fruits of the criminal and civil cases that were settled last summer are a direct result of what Mr. Walsh brought us and would have come from no other source to my knowledge to this day. . . .

The Court notes in passing that this entire transaction actually resulted in a "profit" to the United States. In addition to the $59,500,000 received from General Electric, the United States also recovered $6,158,301 from bank accounts where General Dotan and Mr. Steindler had secreted the money embezzled from the United States. Evidence presented to the Court indicated that the direct losses to the United States totaled $41,656,598. The excess of collection over such losses amounted to $18,627,202. The Court currently is holding $14,875,000, which represents the maximum that may be awarded to Mr. Walsh. The "bottom line" appears to be that the United States of America will realize at least a $4,000,000 "profit."

While funds were improperly taken from a number of different projects, there is one that should be described in more detail. A fund of money was provided for the construction of "Test Cell No. 5" on an Israeli air base. This installation was intended to test GE engines in the field. From time to time progress reports would be issued and money would be authorized accordingly. The reality was that Test Cell No. 5 never existed. Another employee of General Electric by the name of Alaric Fine became suspicious of the progress reports and sought to inquire into the real progress of Test Cell No. 5. He was frustrated in his efforts by representatives of the Israeli Air Force, who denied him access to the air base where the test cell supposedly was located. When he finally reported his suspicions to General Electric, he was removed from his position with the program in Israel and assigned to another area. Whether or not such transfer was a "demotion" is a matter of opinion. . . .

It is the crux of the argument by the United States Department of Justice that Mr. Walsh waited too long; that had he supplied the information available to him when he became aware of the truth, he arguably could have reduced the loss to the United States. Mr. Walsh in response points out what happened to Mr. Fine and also his fear of personal harm by General Dotan. That fear was not irrational. [The court mentions evidence of an indictment against General Dotan for conspiring to kidnap, threaten and injure a person who was to testify.]

General Dotan pleaded guilty to all counts of the indictment including the above, and currently is serving a term in an Israeli prison.

There has never been an assertion in this proceeding that Mr. Walsh personally profited from the fraud. The most that the Department of Justice can assert is that he "should have" revealed this information earlier. . . . It may be that the example of Mr. Fine did not give Mr. Walsh good reason to pause. It may be that Mr. Walsh could have found a better method for smuggling the documents out of Israel at an earlier date. All of the foregoing possible and perhaps might have changed the results. Perhaps.

There is no dispute that Mr. Walsh provided information whereby the United States recovered in excess of seventy million dollars.

There is no dispute that the documents that Mr. Walsh smuggled from Israel detailed the assertions that he was making, and that without them it would have been difficult, if not impossible, to sustain a case against General Electric.

Chester Walsh, as an individual, is of very little importance in this action. Whether he moved as expeditiously as possible, whether he should have shared his information earlier, whether he was disloyal to General Electric, really is not before this Court.

It is instead the very concept of "whistleblowers" that appears to be in issue. The pattern of behavior in these cases by the Department of Justice always has been a mystery. The use of *a qui tam* plaintiff is nothing new. The Internal Revenue Service has for decades offered a monetary reward to anyone who provides information regarding tax evasion. It is a standard practice of law enforcement agencies to pay confidential informants. It is customary in entrapment cases for a jury to be advised that "criminal activity is such that stealth, stratagems and undercover agents are necessary weapons in the arsenal of the police officer." No one likes "snitches," but they can be valuable. In view of their widespread use, it is worthy of note that the Department of Justice has considered such individuals as adversaries rather than allies. This is not the first case where this Court has noted the antagonism of the Justice Department to a whistleblower. The reason continues to be unknown, but the attitude is clear.

Mr. Walsh performed a service to the United States. Whistleblowers in general perform services to the United States. It is at least naive to believe that an appeal to "patriotism" alone will cause disclosures of fraud. The Congress of the United States has determined that whistleblowing should be encouraged by monetary rewards. This case is a classic example. Fraud on the United States was disclosed by Mr. Walsh. The money was returned in full, and even if the relator is awarded the maximum under the statute, the United States still will show a net profit.

Despite the foregoing, the Court is impressed by one argument of the United States. Awards of the full 25 percent fee should be reserved for only those individuals whose conduct in disclosing the fraud is virtually flawless. . . .

In accordance with the foregoing, the Court believes that an appropriate award to this plaintiff is twenty-two and one-half percent (22 1/2 %) of the amount realized by the United States in the civil settlement with General Electric. Mr. Walsh therefore is awarded the sum of Thirteen Million Three Hundred Eighty-seven Thousand Five Hundred Dollars ($13,387,500).

It is so ordered.

Texaco: The Jelly Bean Diversity Fiasco

Marianne M. Jennings
Professor of Legal and Ethical Studies, College of Business,
Arizona State University

In November, 1996, Texaco, Inc., was rocked by the disclosure of tape-recorded conversations among three executives about a racial discrimination suit pending against the company. The suit, seeking $71 million, had been brought by 6 employees, on behalf of 1500 other employees, who alleged the following forms of discrimination:

> I have had KKK printed on my car. I have had my tires slashed and racial slurs written about me on bathroom walls. One co-worker blatantly called me a racial epithet to my face.
>
> Throughout my employment, three supervisors in my department openly discussed their view that African-Americans are ignorant and incompetent, and, specifically, that Thurgood Marshall was the most incompetent person they had ever seen.
>
> Sheryl Joseph, formerly a Texaco secretary in Harvey, Louisiana, was given a cake for her birthday which occurred shortly after she announced that she was pregnant. The cake depicted a black pregnant woman and read. "Happy Birthday, Sheryl. It must have been those watermelon seeds."

The suit also included data on Texaco's workforce:

1989	Minorities as a percentage of Texaco's workforce	15.2%
1994	Minorities as a percentage of Texaco's workforce	19.4%

The acting head of the EEOC wrote in 1995, "Deficiencies in the affirmative-action programs suggest that Texaco is not committed to insuring comprehensive, facility by facility, compliance with the company's affirmative-action responsibilities."

Faced with the lawsuit, Texaco's former treasurer, Robert Ulrich, senior assistant treasurer, J. David

From *Business Ethics: Case Studies and Selected Readings* (3rd ed.), by M. M. Jennings. © 1999. Reprinted with permission of South-Western College Publishing, a division of Thomson Learning.

# of Years to Promotion by Job Classification

Minority Employees	Job	Other Employees
6.1	Accountant	4.6
6.4	Senior Accountant	5.4
12.5	Analyst	6.3
14.2	Financial Analyst	13.9
15.0	Assistant Accounting Supervisor	9.8

Senior Managers

	White	Black
1991	1,887	19
1992	2,001	21
1993	2,000	23
1994	2,029	23

Racial Composition (% of Blacks) by Pay Range

Salary	Texaco	Other Oil Companies
$ 51,100	5.9%	7.2%
$ 56,900	4.7%	6.5%
$ 63,000	4.1%	4.7%
$ 69,900	2.3%	5.1%
$ 77,600	1.8%	3.2%
$ 88,100	1.9%	2.3%
$ 95,600	1.4%	2.6%
$106,100	1.2%	2.3%
$117,600	0.8%	2.3%
$128,800	0.4%	1.8%

(African-Americans make up 12% of the U.S. population)

Keough, and senior coordinator for personnel services, Richard A. Lundwall, met and discussed the suit. A tape transcript follows:

They look through evidence, deciding what to turn over to the plaintiffs.

Lundwall: Here, look at this chart. You know, I'm not really quite sure what it means. This chart is not mentioned in the agency, so it's not important that we even have it in there. . . . They would never know it was here.

Keough: They'll find it when they look through it.
Lundwall: Not if I take it out they won't.

The executives decide to leave out certain pages of a document; they worry that another version will turn up.

Ulrich: We're gonna purge the [expletive deleted] out of these books, though. We're not going to have any damn thing that we don't need to be in them—

Lundwall: As a matter of fact, I just want to be reminded of what we discussed. You take your data and . . .

Keough: You look and make sure it's consistent to what we've given them already for minutes. Two versions with the restricted and that's marked clearly on top—

Ulrich: But I don't want to be caught up in a cover-up. I don't want to be my own Watergate.

Lundwall: We've been doing pretty much two versions, too. This one here, this is strictly my book, your book . . .

Ulrich: Boy, I'll tell you, that one, you would put that and you would have the only copy. Nobody else ought to have copies of that.

Lundwall: O.K.?

Ulrich: You have that someplace and it doesn't exist.

Lundwall: Yeah, O.K.

Ulrich: I just don't want anybody to have a copy of that.

Lundwall: Good. No problem.

Ulrich: You know, there is no point in even keeping the restricted version anymore. All it could do is get us in trouble. That's the way I feel. I would not keep anything.

Lundwall: Let me shred this thing and any other restricted version like it.

Ulrich: Why do we have to keep the minutes of the meeting anymore?

Lundwall: You don't, you don't.

Ulrich: We don't?

Lundwall: Because we don't, no, we don't because it comes back to haunt us like right now—

Ulrich: I mean, the pendulum is swinging the other way, guys.

The executives discuss the minority employees who brought the suit.

Lundwall: They are perpetuating an us/them atmosphere. Last week or last Friday I told . . .

Ulrich: [Inaudible.]

Lundwall: Yeah, that's what I said to you, you want to frag grenade? You know, duck, I'm going to throw one. Well, that's what I was alluding to. But the point is not, that's not bad in itself but it does perpetuate us/them. And if you're trying to get away and get to the we . . . you can't do that kind of stuff.

Ulrich: [Inaudible.] I agree. This diversity thing. You know how black jelly beans agree. . . .

Lundwall: That's funny. All the black jelly beans seem to be glued to the bottom of the bag.

Ulrich: You can't have just we and them. You can't just have black jelly beans and other jelly beans. It doesn't work.

Lundwall: Yeah. But they're perpetuating the black jelly beans.

Ulrich: I'm still having trouble with Hanukkah. Now, we have Kwanza (laughter).

The release of the tape prompted the Reverend Jesse Jackson to call for a nationwide boycott of Texaco. Sales fell 8%, Texaco's stock fell 2%, and several institutional investors were preparing to sell their stock.

Texaco did have a minority recruiting effort in place and the "jelly bean" remark was tied to a diversity trainer the company had hired. The following are excerpts from Texaco's statement of vision and values:

Respect for the Individual

Our employees are our most important resource. Each person deserves to be treated with respect and dignity in appropriate work environments, without regard to race, religion, sex, age, national origin, disability or position in the company. Each employee has the responsibility to demonstrate respect for others.

The company believes that a work environment that reflects a diverse workforce, values diversity, and is free of all forms of discrimination, intimidation, and harassment is essential for a productive and efficient workforce. Accordingly, conduct directed toward any employee that is unwelcome, hostile, offensive, degrading, or abusive is unacceptable and will not be tolerated.

A federal grand jury began an investigation at Texaco to determine whether there had been obstruction of justice in the withholding of documents.

Within days of the release of the tape, Texaco settled its bias suit for $176.1 million, the largest sum ever allowed in a discrimination case. The money will allow a 11% pay raise for blacks and other minorities who joined in the law suit.

Texaco's chairman and CEO, Peter I. Bijur, issued the following statement after agreeing to a settlement:

Texaco is facing a difficult but vital challenge. It's broader than any specific words and larger than any lawsuit. It is one we must and are attacking head-on.

We are a company of 27,000 people worldwide. In any organization of that size, unfortunately, there are bound to be people with unacceptable, biased attitudes toward race, gender and religion.

Our goal, and our responsibility, is to eradicate this kind of thinking wherever and however it is found in our company. And our challenge is to make Texaco a company of limitless opportunity for all men and women.

We are committed to begin meeting this challenge immediately through programs with concrete goals and measurable timetables.

I've already announced certain specific steps, including a redoubling of efforts within Texaco to focus on the paramount value of respect for the individual and a comprehensive review of our diversity programs at every level of our company.

We also want to broaden economic access to Texaco for minority firms and increase the positive impact our investments can have in the minority community. This includes areas such as hiring and promotion; professional services such as advertising, banking, investment management and legal services; and wholesale and retail station ownership.

To assist us, we are reaching out to leaders of minority and religious organizations and others for ideas and perspectives that will help Texaco succeed in our mission of becoming a model of diversity and workplace equality.

It is essential to this urgent mission that Texaco and African-Americans and other minority community leaders work together to help solve the programs we face as a company—which, after all, echo the problems faced in society as a whole.

Discrimination will be extinguished only if we tackle it together, only if we join in a unified, common effort.

Working together, I believe we can take Texaco into the 21st century as a model of diversity. We can make Texaco a company of limitless opportunity. We can make Texaco a leader in according respect to every man and woman.

Even after the announcement, Texaco stock was down $3 per share, a loss of $800 million total, and the boycott was continued. Texaco's proposed merger with Shell Oil began to unravel as Shell's CEO expressed concern about Texaco's integrity. However, after the settlement, additional information about the case began to emerge.

Holman W. Jenkins, Jr. wrote the following piece for the *Wall Street Journal:*

Quietly, corporate America is debating whether Texaco's Peter Bijur did the right thing.

Mr. Bijur gets paid to make the hard calls, and with the airwaves aflame over "nigger" and "black jelly beans," Texaco took a battering in the stock and political markets. He had every reason for wanting to put a stop-loss on the media frenzy. "Once the taped conversations were revealed," he says, settling was "reasonable and honorable." So now Texaco is betting $176 million that paying off minority employees and their lawyers is the quickest way out of the news.

But as the company's own investigation showed, the truly inflammatory comments reported in the media never took place. They were purely a fabrication by opposing lawyers, and trumpeted by a credulous New York Times. And some digging would have shown this problem cropping up before in the career of Mike Hausfeld, lead attorney for the plaintiffs.

In an antitrust case years ago, he presented a secret recording that he claimed showed oil executives conspiring to threaten gasoline dealers. But a check by the same expert who handled the Nixon Watergate tapes showed no such thing. Says Larry Sharp, the Washington antitrust lawyer who opposed Mr. Hausfeld: "To put it generously, he gave himself the benefit of the doubt in making the transcript."

But this time the lie has been rewarded, and the broader public, unschooled in legal cynicism, heads home believing Texaco an admitted racist.

The catechism of corporate crisis management says you can't fight the media. Mr. Bijur had to consider that Jesse Jackson was threatening a boycott if Texaco failed to "regret, repent and seek renewal." Mr. Jackson pointedly added that "any attempt to shift to denial would add insult to injury"—a warning against trying to spread some egg to the faces of those who were fooled by the fake transcript.

There may have been wisdom, if not valor, in Mr. Bijur's decision to run up the white flag. But he also evinced symptoms of Stockholm Syndrome, telling CNN that Texaco was just the "tip of the iceberg" of corporate racism. Ducking this fight so ignominiously may yet prove a penny-wise, pound-foolish strategy. The City of Philadelphia has decided to dump its Texaco holdings anyway, partly out of fear of more litigation.

What else could Texaco have done? It could have apologized for any offense, but stuck up for its former treasurer Bob Ulrich, who was wronged by the phony transcript and stripped of his medical benefits by Texaco. And the company could have vowed to fight the lawsuit like the dickens, arguing that Texaco is not the cause of society's racial troubles but has tried to be part of the solution.

Start with the tapes: A fair listening does not necessarily reveal a "racist" conversation by executives at Texaco, but certainly a candid conversation about the problems of race at Texaco. They spoke of "jelly beans" dividing into camps of "us" and "them," an honest representation of life at many companies, not just in the oil patch.

Mr. Bijur could have made this point, starting with the New York Times, which has been embroiled in its own discrimination lawsuit with Angela Dodson, once its top-ranking black female. In a complaint filed with New York City's Human Rights Commission, she claims the paper was "engaged in gender-based harassment and disability-based discrimination . . . because The Times no longer wanted me, as a black person, to occupy a position as Senior editor."

Her deepest ire is reserved for Times veteran Carolyn Lee, who is white and more accustomed to being lauded as a champion of women and minorities. Ms. Dodson told the Village Voice: "It got to the point that whenever I was in her presence or earshot she made remarks [about other black people] that could only be taken as negative."

This sounds remarkably like the anecdotes filed in the Texaco complaint. All an outsider can safely conclude is that race makes everything more complicated, as sensitivity begets sensitivity. Mr. Bijur would have done more for racial understanding had he used his platform to open up this subject.

Yes, the cartoonist racists are out there, he might have said, but the Times coverage of Texaco only found cartoonist racists. The paper could have looked to its own experience for another story—a story about how garden-variety interpersonal conflict can land even decent people in the snares of racial mistrust.

This is what affirmative action, by throwing people together, was supposed to get us past. And it may be no accident that our most quota-ridden newspaper, USA Today, jumped off the bandwagon on the Texaco tapes, noting the ambiguity of whether the "jelly bean" remarks were meant to be hostile or friendly to blacks.

And McPaper kept on asking intelligent questions, like whether the New York Times had been "used by plaintiffs in the case to promote a faulty but more inflammatory transcript?" ("Not unless the court was used," answered Times Business Editor John Geddes, sounding like a lawyer himself.)

So Mr. Bijur was not facing a uniformly hopeless media torrent. The truth, even a complicated truth, catches up with the headlines eventually.

In time, he might have found surprising allies drifting to his side. The New Republic and the New Yorker have run thoughtful articles arguing that businesses should be allowed to use quotas but shouldn't be subject to harassment litigation if they don't. Right now, we do the opposite: Forbid companies to promote by quota, then sue them under federal "adverse impact" rules when they don't.

In effect, liberal voices are arguing that business could do more for minorities with less conflict if freedom of contract were restored. The world is changing, and companies have their own reasons nowadays for wanting minorities around. They need input from different kinds of people on how to deal with different kinds of people. No doubt this is why McPaper feels free to thumb its nose at the conformity crowd on stories like Texaco and church-burnings. (See September's Harvard Business Review for what business is thinking about diversity now.)

If companies were set free to assemble the work forces most useful to them, they could sweep away a heap of excuses for recrimination. Whites couldn't feel cheated out of jobs. Blacks wouldn't end up at companies that want them only for window-dressing. And the world could go back to feeling OK about being an interesting place. We might even allow that cultural patterns other than racism may explain why so many rednecks, and so few blacks, become petroleum engineers.

Mr. Bijur may have made the best of a bad deal for his shareholders. Whether it was best for America is a different judgment.[1]

Richard Lundwall, the executive who taped the sessions with the other executives was charged with one count of obstruction of justice. Lundwall had turned over the tapes of the conversations to lawyers for the plaintiffs in the discrimination suit on October 25, 1996. Lundwall had been terminated.

Texaco hired attorney Michael Armstrong to investigate the underlying allegations. Mr. Armstrong found the tapes had not been transcribed correctly.

As part of its settlement, Texaco agreed to, at a cost of $55 million, assign a task force to police hiring and promotion as well as requiring mentors for black employees and sensitivity training for white employees.

The following interview with CEO Bijur appeared in *Business Week:*

Q: How did your legal strategy change once the news of the tapes was printed?

A: When I saw [the story], I knew that this lawsuit was pending and moving forward. I made the judgment that we needed to accelerate the settlement process. And those discussions on settlement commenced almost immediately.

Q: It has been reported that you didn't get the board of directors involved with the settlement talks and other issues. Why not?

A: You're drawing conclusions that are erroneous. The board was fully involved throughout the entire process. I talked to numerous directors personally. We had several board and executive committee meetings. The board was fully supportive of our actions.

Q: Have you met with shareholders?

A: Yes, of course. I went down to [New York] and met with the Interfaith Center on Corporate Responsibility, which is a group of religious shareholders. I expressed our position on this and listened carefully to their position and got some good counsel and guidance. But I wanted to provide our side of the issue as well. I have met with [New York State Comptroller] Carl McCall and [New York City Comptroller] Alan Hevesi about concerns that they had, and I will continue to meet with other shareholders as I normally do.

Q: Why do you think the oil industry has such a poor reputation on issues of racial diversity and gender equality? How does Texaco stack up against the others?

A: The percentage of minorities within Texaco is just about average for the petroleum industry. We have made really significant progress in the last several years in improving the percentage. But there are some very interesting points that need to be examined to place in context what may be going on in this industry. I just read a study that showed that in 1995, there were only nine petroleum engineering minority graduates that came out of all engineering schools in the United States—only nine. That's not an excuse. But it is indicative of why it is difficult for this industry to have a lot of people in the pipeline. Now, of course, that does not apply to accountants, finance people, and anybody else. But we are a very technically oriented industry.

Q: Have you personally witnessed discrimination at Texaco?

A: In the nearly 31 years I have been with Texaco, I have never witnessed an incident of racial bias or prejudice. And had I seen it, I would have taken disciplinary action. I've never seen it.

Q: Is there a widespread culture of insensitivity at Texaco?

A: I do not think there is a culture of institutional bias within Texaco. I think we've got a great many very good and decent human beings, but that unfortunately we mirror society. There is bigotry in society. There is prejudice and injustice in society. I am sorry to say that, and I am sorry to say that probably does exist within Texaco. I can't do much about society, but I certainly can do something about Texaco.

Q: What are your views on affirmative action?

A: Texaco's views on affirmative action have not changed a bit. We have supported affirmative action, and we will continue to support affirmative action.

Q: This is your first big trial since taking over. What have you learned?

A: I've learned that as good as our programs are in the company—and they really are quite good, even in this area—there's always more we can do. We've got to really drill down into the programs. We've got to make certain that they're meeting the objectives and goals we've set for them.

Q: Are there other lessons in terms of your style of management?

A: I don't think I would do anything different the next time than what I did this time.

Q: How will you make sure the spirit as well as the letter of the policy is followed at Texaco?

A: We're going to put more and more and more emphasis on it until we get it through everybody's head: Bigotry is not going to be tolerated here.[2]

Robert W. Ulrich was indicted in 1997. Mr. Lundwall entered a "not guilty" plea on July 8, 1997, and J. David Keough has sued Texaco for libel. Texaco named Mary Bush, a financial consultant, as its first black female board member.

As Lundwall's prosecution has proceeded, new discoveries have been made. For example, "purposeful erasures" have been found on the tapes.

In an interim report on its progress toward the settlement goals, Texaco revealed the following:

Polishing the Star

As part of its settlement of a discrimination lawsuit brought by black employees, Texaco has moved on a half-dozen fronts to alter its business practices.

Hiring Asked search firms to identify wider arrays of candidates. Expanded recruiting at historically minority colleges. Gave 50 scholarships and paid internships to minority students seeking engineering or technical degrees.

Career Advancement Wrote objective standards for promotions. Developing training program for new managers. Developing a mentoring program.

Diversity Initiatives Conducted two-day diversity training for more than 8,000 of 20,000 U.S. employees. Tied management bonuses to diversity goals. Developing alternative dispute resolution and ombudsman programs.

Purchasing Nearly doubled purchases from minority- or women-owned businesses. Asking suppliers to report their purchases from such companies.

Financial Services Substantially increased banking, investment management and insurance business with minority- and women-owned firms. A group of such firms underwrote a $150 million public financing.

Retailing Added three black independent retailers, 18 black managers of company-owned service stations, 12 minority or female wholesalers, 13 minority- or women-owned Xpress Lube outlets and 6 minority- or women-owned lubricant distributors.

In May 1998, the Texaco executives were acquitted of all criminal charges.

NOTES

1. Reprinted with permission of *The Wall Street Journal* © 1996 Dow Jones & Company, Inc. All rights reserved.
2. Smart, Tim. "Texaco: Lessons From A Crisis-in-Progress." Reprinted from December 2, 1996, issue of *Business Week* by special permission, © 1997 by McGraw Hill, Inc.

The Case of the Mismanaged Ms.

Sally Seymour
Former Lecturer in Communication, Management Communication, Harvard Business School

It started out as one of those rare quiet mornings when I could count on having the office to myself. The Mets had won the World Series the night before, and most of the people in the office had celebrated late into the night at a bar across the street. I'm a fan too, but they all like to go to one of those bars where the waitresses dress like slave girls and the few women customers have to run a mine field of leers when they go to a ladies' room labeled "Heifers." Instead, I watched the game at home with my husband and escaped a hangover.

So I was feeling pretty good, if a little smug, when Ruth Linsky, a sales manager here at Triton, stormed past my secretary and burst into my office. Before I could say good morning, she demanded to know what business it was of the company who she slept with and why. I didn't know what she was talking about, but I could tell it was serious. In fact, she was practically on the verge of tears, but I knew she wasn't the type to fly off the handle.

Ruth had been with the company for three years, and we all respected her as a sensible and intelligent woman. She had been top in her class at business school and we recruited her hand when she graduated, but she didn't join us for a couple of years. She's since proved to be one of our best people in sales, and I didn't want to lose her. She fumed around the room for a while, not making much sense, until I talked her into sitting down.

"I've had it with this place and the way it treats women!" she shouted.

I allowed her to let off some more steam for a minute or two, and then I tried to calm her down. "Look, Ruth," I said, "I can see you're upset, but I need to know exactly what's going on before I can help you."

"I'm not just upset, Barbara," she said, "I'm damned mad. I came over to Triton because I thought I'd get more chances to advance here, and I just found out that I was passed over for director of the marketing division and Dick Simon got it instead. You know that I've had three outstanding years at the company, and my performance reviews have been excellent. Besides, I was led to believe that I had a pretty good shot at the job."

"What do you mean, 'led to believe'?"

"Steve heard through the grapevine that they were looking for a new marketing director, and he suggested I put in my name," she said. "He knows my work from when we worked together over at Forge Techtronics, and he said he'd write a letter in support. I wouldn't have even known they were looking for someone if Steve hadn't tipped me off."

Steve Baines is vice president of manufacturing. He's certainly a respected senior person in the company and he pulls some weight, but he doesn't have sole control of the marketing position. The hierarchy doesn't work that way, and I tried to get Ruth to see that. "Okay, so Steve wrote a letter for you, but he's only one of five or six VPs who have input in executive hiring decisions. Of course it helps to have his support, but lots of other factors need to be considered as well."

"Come off it, Barbara," Ruth snapped. "You know as well as I do there's only one thing that really matters around here and that's whether you're one of the boys. I've got a meeting this afternoon with my lawyer, and I'm going to file a sexual discrimination suit, a sexual harassment suit, and

whatever other kind of suit she can come up with. I've had it with this old-boy crap. The only reason I'm here is that, as human resources director, you should know what's going on around here."

So the stakes were even higher than I had thought; not only did it look like we might lose Ruth, but we also might have a lawsuit on our hands. And to top it off, with the discrimination issue Ruth might be trying to get back at us for promoting Dick. I felt strongly about the importance of this legal remedy, but I also knew that using it frivolously would only undermine women's credibility in legitimate cases.

"Ruth," I said, "I don't doubt your perceptions, but you're going to need some awfully strong evidence to back them up."

"You want evidence? Here's your evidence. Number one: 20% of the employees in this company are women. Not one is on the board of directors, and not one holds an executive-level position. You and I are the only two in mid-level positions. Number two: there's no way for women to move into the mid-level positions because they never know when they're available. When a vacancy comes up, the VPs—all men, of course—decide among themselves who should fill it. And then, over and over again I hear that some guy who hasn't worked half as hard as most of the women at his level has been given the plum. Number three: there are plenty of subtle and sometimes not-so-subtle messages around here that women are less than equal."

"Ruth, those are still pretty vague accusations," I interrupted. "You're going to have to come up with something more specific than feelings and suppositions."

"Don't worry, Barbara. Just keep listening and maybe you'll learn something about how this company you think so highly of operates. From the day Ed Coulter took over as vice president of marketing and became my boss, he's treated me differently from the male sales managers. Instead of saying good morning, he always has some comment about my looks—my dress is nice, or my hair looks pretty, or the color of my blouse brings out my eyes. I don't want to hear that stuff. Besides, he never comments on a guy's eyes. And then there's that calendar the sales reps have in their back office. Every time I go in there for a sales meeting, I feel like I've walked into a locker room."

So far, this all seemed pretty harmless to me, but I didn't want Ruth to feel I wasn't sympathetic. "To tell you the truth, Ruth, I'm not so sure all women here find compliments like that insulting, but maybe you can give me other examples of discriminatory treatment."

"You bet I can. It's not just in the office that these things happen. It's even worse in the field. Last month Ed and I and Bill, Tom, and Jack went out to Dryden Industries for a big project meeting. I'll admit I was a little nervous because there were some heavy hitters in the room, so I kept my mouth shut most of the morning. But I was a team member and I wanted to contribute.

"So when Ed stumbled at one point, I spoke up. Well, it was like I had committed a sacrilege in church. The Dryden guys just stared at me in surprise, and then they seemed actually angry. They ignored me completely. Later that afternoon, when I asked Ed why I had gotten that reaction, he chuckled a little and explained that since we hadn't been introduced by our specific titles, the Dryden guys had assumed I was a research assistant or a secretary. They thought I was being presumptuous. But when Ed explained who I was, they admitted that I had made an important point.

"But that wasn't all," she went on. "The next day, when we explained to them that I would be interviewing some of the factory foremen for a needs assessment, one of the executives requested that someone else do it because apparently there's a superstition about women on the factory floor bringing bad luck. Have you ever heard of anything so stupid? But that's not the worst of it. Ed actually went along with it. After I'd pulled his bacon out of the fire the day before. And when I nailed him for it, he had the gall to say 'Honey, whatever the client wants, the client gets.'

"Well, we got the contract, and that night we all went out to dinner and everything was hurray for our team. But then, when I figured we'd all go back to the hotel for a nightcap, Ed and the guys just kind of drifted off."

"Drifted off?" I asked.

"Yeah. To a bar. They wanted to watch some basketball game."

"And you weren't invited?"

"I wasn't invited and I wasn't disinvited," she said. "They acted like they didn't know what to say."

By this point Ruth had cooled down quite a bit, and although she still seemed angry, she was forthright in presenting her case. But now her manner changed. She became so agitated that she got up from her chair to stare out the window. After a few minutes, she sort of nodded her head, as if she had come to some private, difficult decision, and then crossed the room to sit down again. Looking at her lap and twisting a paper clip around in her hands, she spoke so softly that I had to lean forward to hear her.

"Barbara," she began, "what I'm going to tell you is, I hope, in confidence. It's not easy for me to talk about this because it's very personal and private, but I trust you and I want you to understand my position. So here goes. When Steve Baines and I were both at Forge, we had a brief affair. I was discreet about it; it never interfered with business, and we ended it shortly after we both came to work here. But we're still very close friends, and occasionally we have dinner or a drink together. But it's always as friends. I think Ed found out about it somehow. The day after I notified the head office that I wanted to be considered for the director position, Ed called me into his office and gave me a rambling lecture about how we have to behave like ladies and gentlemen these days because of lawsuits on sexual harassment.

"At the time, I assumed he was referring somehow to one of our junior sales reps who had gotten drunk at the Christmas party and made a fool of himself with a couple of secretaries; but later I began to think that the cryptic comment was meant for me. What's more, I think Ed used that rumor about my relationship with Steve to block my promotion. And that, Barbara, is pure, sexist, double-standard hypocrisy because I can name you at least five guys at various levels in this company who have had affairs with colleagues and clients, and Ed is at the top of the list."

I couldn't deny the truth of Ruth's last statement, but that wasn't the point, or not yet. First I had to find out which, if any, of her accusations were true. I told her I needed some time and asked if she could give me a week before calling in a lawyer. She said no way. Having taken the first step, she was anxious to take the next, especially since she didn't believe things would change at Triton anyway. We dickered back and forth, but all I could get from her was a promise to hold off for 24 hours. Not much of a concession, but it was better than nothing.

Needless to say, I had a lot to think about and not very much time to do it in. It was curious that this complaint should come shortly after our organization had taken steps to comply with affirmative action policies by issuing a companywide memo stating that we would continue to recruit, employ, train, and promote individuals without regard to race, color, religion, sex, age, national origin, physical or mental handicap, or status as a disabled veteran or veteran of the Vietnam era. And we did this to prevent any problems in the future, not because we'd had trouble in the past. In fact, in my five years as HRM director, I'd never had a sexual discrimination or harassment complaint.

But now I was beginning to wonder whether there had never been grounds for complaint or whether the women here felt it was useless or even dangerous to complain. If it was the latter, how had I contributed to allowing that feeling to exist? And this thought led me to an even more uncomfortable one: Had I been co-opted into ignoring injustices in a system that, after all, did pretty well by me? Was I afraid to slap the hand that buttered my bread?

Questioning one's own motives may be enlightening, but it's also time consuming, and I had more pressing matters to deal with before I could indulge in what would likely be a painful self-analysis. I asked my secretary to find George Drake, CEO of Triton, and get him on the phone. In the meantime, I wrote down as much as I could remember of what Ruth had just told me. When George finally called, I told him I knew his schedule was full but we had an emergency of sorts on our hands and I needed an hour of his time this morning. I also asked that Ed Coulter be called into the meeting. George told me I had the hour.

When I got to George's office, Ed and George were already waiting. They were undoubtedly curious about why I had called this meeting, but as I've seen people do in similar situations, they covered their anxiety with chitchat about ball games and hangovers. I was too impatient for these rituals, so I cut the conversation short and told them that we were going to have a serious lawsuit on our hands in a matter of days if we didn't act very quickly. That got their attention, so I proceeded to tell Ruth's story. When I began, George and Ed seemed more surprised than anything else, but as I built up Ruth's case their surprise turned to concern. When I finished, we all sat in silence for I don't know how long and then George asked Ed for comments.

"Well, George," Ed said, "I don't know what to say. Ruth certainly was a strong contender for the position, and her qualifications nearly equaled Dick's, but it finally came down to the fact that Dick had the seniority and a little more experience in the industrial sector. When you've got two almost equally qualified candidates, you've got to distinguish them somehow. The decision came down to the wire, which in this case was six months seniority and a few more visits to factory sites."

"Were those the only criteria that made a difference in the decision?" George wanted to know.

"Well, not exactly. You know as well as I do that we base hiring decisions on a lot of things. On one hand, we look at what's on paper: years at the company, education, experience, recommendations. But we also rely on intuition, our feel for the situation. Sometimes, you don't know exactly why, but you just feel better about some people than others, and I've learned that those gut reactions are pretty reliable. The other VPs and I all felt good about Dick. There's something about him—he's got the feel of a winner. You know? He's confident—not arrogant—but solid and really sharp. Bruce had him out to the club a couple of times, and I played squash with him all last winter. We got to know him and we liked what we saw; he's a family man, kids in school here, could use the extra money, and is looking to stick around for a while. None of these things mean a lot by themselves, of course, but together they add up.

"Don't get me wrong. I like Ruth too. She's very ambitious and one of our best. On the other hand, I can't say that I or any of the VPs know her as well as we know Dick. Of course, that's not exactly Ruth's fault, but there it is."

I had to be careful with the question I wanted Ed to respond to next because Ruth had asked for my confidence about the affair. I worded it this way: "Ed, did any part of your decision take into account Ruth's relationship with anyone else at the company?"

The question visibly disturbed Ed. He walked across the room and bummed a cigarette from me—he had quit last week—before answering: "Okay, I didn't want to go into this, but since you brought it up. . . . There's a rumor—well it's stronger than a rumor—that Ruth is more than professionally involved with Steve Baines—I mean she's having an, ah, sexual affair with him. Now before you tell me that's none of my business, let me tell you about some homework I did on this stuff. Of course it's real tricky. It turns out there are at least two court cases that found sexual discrimination where an employer involved in a sexual relationship with an employee promoted that person over more qualified candidates.

"So here's what that leaves us with: we've got Steve pushing his girlfriend for the job. You saw the letter he wrote. And we've got Dick with seniority. So if we go with Ruth, what's to keep Dick from charging Steve and the company on two counts of sexual discrimination: sexual favoritism because Ruth is Steve's honey and reverse discrimination because we pass over a better qualified man just to get a woman into an executive position. So we're damned if we do and damned if we don't. We've got lawsuits if we don't advance Dick, and, so you tell me, lawsuits if we don't advance Ruth!"

We let that sink in for a few seconds. Then George spoke up: "What evidence do you have, Ed, that Steve and Ruth are having an affair?" he asked.

"Look, I didn't hire some guy to follow them around with a camera, if that's what you mean," Ed said. "But come on, I wasn't born yesterday; you can't keep that kind of hanky-panky a secret forever. Look at the way she dresses; she obviously enjoys men looking at her, especially Steve. In fact, I saw them having drinks together at Dino's the other night and believe me, they didn't look like they were talking business. All that on top of the rumors, you put two and two together."

Well, that did it for me. I'd been trying to play the objective observer and let Ed and George do all the talking, but Ed's last comment, along with some budding guilt about my own blindness to certain things at Triton that Ruth had pointed out, drove me out in the open. "Come off it, Ed," I said. "That's not evidence, that's gossip."

Now Ed turned on me: "Look," he shouted, "I didn't want to talk about this, but now that you've brought it up, I'll tell you something else. Even if we didn't have to worry about this sexual discrimination business, I still wouldn't back Ruth for the director's job." He calmed down a bit. "No offense, Barbara, but I just don't think women work out as well as men in certain positions. Human resources is one thing. It's real soft, person-to-person stuff. But factories are still a man's world. And I'm not talking about what I want it to be like. I'm talking facts of life.

"You see what happens when we send a woman out on some jobs, especially in the factories. To be any good in marketing you have to know how to relate to your client; that means getting to know him, going out drinking with him, talking sports, hunting, whatever he's interested in. A lot of our clients feel uncomfortable around a woman in business. They know how to relate to their wives, mothers, and girlfriends, but when a woman comes to the office and wants to talk a deal on industrial drills—well, they don't know what to do.

"And then there's the plain fact that you can't depend on a woman the way you can on a guy. She'll get married and her husband will get transferred, or she'll have a baby and want time off and not be able to go on the road as much. I know, Barbara, you probably think I'm a pig, or whatever women's libbers call guys like me these days. But from where I'm sitting, it just made good business sense to choose Dick over Ruth."

"Ed, I don't believe it," I said. "The next thing you'll tell me is that women ought to stay at home, barefoot and pregnant." There was a long silence after that—my guess was that I had hit on exactly what Ed thought. At least he didn't deny it. Ed stared at the rug, and George frowned at his coffee cup. I tried to steer the conversation back to the subject at hand, but it dwindled into another silence. George took a few notes and then told Ed he could go back to work. I assumed I was excused too, but as I started to leave, George called me back.

"Barbara, I'm going to need your help thinking through this mess," he said. "Of course we've got to figure out how we can avoid a lawsuit before the day is out, but I also want to talk about what we can do to avoid more lawsuits in the future. While Ed was talking I took some notes, and I've got maybe four or five points I think we ought to hash out. I'm not saying we're going to come up with all the answers today, but it'll be a start. You ready?"

"Shoot."

"Okay, let's do the big one first," he began. "What should I have done or not done to avoid this situation? I mean, I was just patting myself on the back for being so proactive when I sent out that memo letting everyone know the company policy on discrimination. I wrote it not thinking we had any problem at Triton. But just in case we did, I figured that memo would take care of it."

"Well, it looks like it's not enough just to have a corporate policy if the people in the ranks aren't on board. Obviously it didn't have much of an effect on Ed."

"So what am I supposed to do? Fire Ed?"

Being asked for my honest opinion by my CEO was a new experience for me and I appreciated it, but I wasn't going to touch that last question with a ten-foot pole. Instead I went on to another aspect: "And even if you get your managers behind you, your policy won't work if the people it's supposed to help don't buy it. Ruth was the first woman to complain around here. Are the others afraid to speak up? Or do they feel like Ed about a woman's place, or have husbands who do? Maybe they lack confidence even to try for better jobs, that is, if they knew about them."

"Okay," he said, "I'll admit that our system of having the VPs make recommendations, our 'old-boy network,' as Ruth called it, does seem to end

up excluding women, even though the exclusion isn't intentional. And it's not obvious discrimination, like Ed's claim that Ruth is unqualified for a position because she is a woman. But wouldn't open job posting take away our right to manage as we see fit? Maybe we should concentrate instead on getting more women into the social network, make it an old boys' and old girls' club?"

"To tell you the truth, George, I don't much want to play squash with you," I replied, "but maybe we're getting off the subject. The immediate question seems to be how we're going to get more women into executive positions here, or, more specifically, do we give Ruth the director of marketing position that we just gave Dick?"

"On that score, at least, it seems to me that Ed has a strong argument," George said. "Dick is more qualified. You can't get around that."

I had wanted to challenge Ed on this point when he brought it up earlier, but I wasn't quite sure of myself then. Now that George was asking me for advice and seemed to be taking what I had to say seriously, I began to think that I might have something valuable to offer. So I charged right in. "George, maybe we're cutting too fine a line with this qualifications business. I know a lot of people think affirmative action means promoting the unqualified over the qualified to achieve balance. I think that argument is hogwash at best and a wily diversion tactic at worst. To my mind, Ruth and Dick are equally qualified, or equal enough. And wouldn't it make good business sense to get a diverse set of perspectives—women's, men's, blacks', whites'—in our executive group?"

"But isn't that reverse discrimination—not promoting Dick because he's a man? How would a judge respond to that? That's a question for a lawyer."

George leaned forward. "Let's talk about my last point, the one I think we've both been avoiding. What about this affair between Ruth and Steve? Boy, this is one reason why women in the work force are such trouble—no, just joking, Barbara, sorry about that. Look, I don't like lawsuits any more than anyone else, but I'd do anything to avoid this one. We'd be a laughing stock if it got out that Triton promoted unqualified people because they slept with the boss. I don't know how I'd explain that one to my wife."

"Look, George," I said, "in the first place, Dick's superior qualifications are debatable; in the second place, we have no proof that Ruth and Steve are involved in that way; and in the third place, what if they were once involved but no longer are? Does a past relationship condemn them for life? Isn't there a statute of limitations on that kind of thing, or are we going to make her put a scarlet letter on her briefcase? I thought these discrimination laws were supposed to protect women, but now it looks like a woman can be denied a promotion because someone thinks she's a floozy."

"Wait a second, Barbara. Don't make me look like such a prig," George said. "I realize that when men and women work together sexual issues are bound to crop up. I just don't know what I'm supposed to do about it, if anything. In some cases a woman may welcome a guy coming on to her, but what if it's her boss? And then there's that subtle stuff Ruth brought up—the calendar, dirty jokes, the male employees excluding women by going to bars to watch TV—and other women. And Ruth's treatment at that factory—how can we control our clients? I'm not sure these are things you can set policy on, but I am sure that I can't ignore them any longer."

And there we were. All the issues were on the table, and we had about 21 hours to make our decisions and act on them.

PART FOUR

THE CORPORATION IN SOCIETY

In Part Three we examined some aspects of the relationship of business to one of its most important internal constituencies, its employees. Here we turn attention to the relationship between business and its external constituencies—that is, between business and its environment. In Chapter 7, we examine the relationship between business and consumers by looking at some of the ethical aspects of marketing and sales as well as product safety; Chapter 8 explores some ethical dimensions of the relation of business to the natural environment; Chapter 9 takes up ethical problems raised by multinational business operations.

BUSINESS AND CONSUMERS

Business organizations exist by selling goods and services to consumers. Consumers, therefore, are one of business' most important constituencies, literally essential for its survival. Traditionally, the relationship between business and consumers in U.S. society has been defined by the free market, which links business and consumers in what is intended to be a mutually beneficial relationship. Business is free to make as large a profit as possible on its transactions with consumers; but—the theory goes—business succeeds only by giving consumers what they want. Both consumer and business interests are protected by the "invisible hand" of the market. Presumably an unsatisfactory or undesirable product, or one offered at an unreasonable price, will not sell. In such a system, it is often said that "the consumer is king," and sellers must serve the consumer or go out of business.

This system can work in practice, however, only if two conditions are met: (1) There is no deception, and the consumer receives adequate and accurate information about products on the market to make rational market decisions; and (2) the consumer is free to choose what to buy. Does the real world really meet these conditions, however? This question is the takeoff point for some of the most important debates about business and consumer relations in business ethics.

One business activity that has led thinkers to question the accuracy of the traditional picture of business and consumer relations is advertising or marketing. Advertising of some kind is necessary to convey information to consumers and to make them aware of what products are available. But how much information is really conveyed in such slogans as "Coke is the real thing" or "This Bud's for you"? It is not surprising that many observers of advertising conclude that its main purpose is not to inform but to persuade.

Advertisers have been accused not only of failing to inform the public but of creating needs and desires that the consumer otherwise would not have had. This is the charge made by John Kenneth Galbraith in his article "The Dependence Effect." Galbraith argues that in the United States the manufacture of consumer demands is as important as, if not more important than, the manufacture of products that satisfy those demands. The same companies that satisfy wants, he claims, also create those wants by advertising, establishing a self-perpetuating cycle of desire and satisfaction. If consumers truly wanted all the products on the market, Galbraith claims, such creation of desire would not be necessary. Genuine desires originate with the consumer and do not need to be created from outside. Galbraith might regard the extensive advertising campaign for cigarettes as an example of this want creation.

If Galbraith is correct, consumers are being manipulated into buying things they do not really want or need. The consumer is not the "king" in this picture, but a pawn. Recalling our discussion of Kant in the general introduction, we might say that if Galbraith is correct, then consumers are being treated by producers as means to an end rather than as ends in themselves. For rather than responding to consumer needs, producers are creating needs and looking on the consumer as nothing more than an instrument for making profits. Creation of consumer needs is also bad, according to Galbraith, because it encourages the excessive consumption of private goods that are not really essential, and diverts spending away from public goods like clean air, livable cities, parks, and public transportation. People would get a great deal of satisfaction from such public goods, Galbraith believes, but since there is comparatively little advertising to persuade us to spend our money on public goods, private goods tend to dominate. Galbraith feels that although our society is rich in private goods, it is poor in public goods.

But does advertising really manipulate us in the way that Galbraith claims? F. A. von Hayek does not think so. von Hayek agrees that many of our wants are created by production. Living in a society in which many material goods are available generates wants we would not have if we were raised in a different sort of society. But, he claims, this does not mean these wants are not urgent or important. Most of what we regard as our "highest" desires—for art, literature, education—are instilled in us by our culture. If only internally generated wants or needs were legitimate, we would have to conclude that the only important desires are for food, sex, and shelter. Advertising is only one cultural element that shapes our desires, von Hayek concludes. It cannot, by itself, determine our wants.

In discussing the ethical issues related to marketing, George Brenkert uses the example of Heileman Brewing Company's attempt to market a malt liquor, named PowerMaster, to inner-city blacks. After identifying a series of objections raised against the actions of the company, Brenkert concludes by discussing the issue of associated groups and collective responsibility, in addition to individual and organizational responsibility.

As noted by Galbraith and Brenkert, advertisers and salespeople are often accused of deceiving and manipulating the public through techniques such as "puffery" or exaggeration, failure to tell the whole truth about a product, misleading pricing and packaging, and ap-

more pollution and pay less for products than to have less pollution and pay more. Society may decide differently in the future, but until that day comes, business has no special role to play in environmental protection.

Bowie continues, however, by pointing out that business has often acted improperly with regard to the environment in the political arena. Businesses have lobbied strongly against environmental laws and regulation. This is ethically unacceptable, Bowie claims, because it is unwarranted interference with the public's expression of its preferences. Thus, in a sense, business does have an obligation to the environment. But the obligation is not to interfere in the political arena rather than to exceed the requirements of environmental law and regulation.

W. Michael Hoffman expresses a very different view. He argues that business has obligations to protect the environment that go beyond the law. As he sees it, business should show moral leadership in this area, and not wait for government action. He also explores "ecological homocentrism," which claims that society including business, ought to protect the environment solely because doing so prevents harm to human beings and human interests. He argues that a broader and deeper moral perspective is required, one that goes beyond self-interest and grants moral standing to the environment itself. Not to do so risks loss of the very insight that grounds ethical concern for the environment in the first place.

Larry Ruff's "The Economic Common Sense of Pollution" shifts the discussion from appropriate business obligations in relation to the environment to the best means to help control pollution levels. He suggests that we should strive, not for no pollution, but for an "optimum" level of pollution at which the cost of further pollution abatement exceeds the benefits. The best way to regulate pollution control, Ruff argues, is to place a price on the right to pollute. The price would be set by a public body, and would allow anyone to pollute as long as he or she is willing to pay the price. Ruff argues that this would lead people to regulate their pollution in the most efficient possible way.

In the final article in Chapter 8, Karen Blumenfeld uses a case analysis to discuss ethical issues surrounding internal investigations of situations that go beyond strict compliance with environmental regulations. Her article reflects what could result if Bowie's position is accepted. She argues that in such a case an auditor has a conflict between legitimate moral obligations. On the one hand, he has a duty to protect the public from possible environmental harm. On the other, he has a fiduciary duty to his or her employer not to disclose confidential information. Blumenfeld then proposes six tests to determine the circumstances under which the auditor's obligation to the public outweighs his obligations to his employer. These include the potential environmental harm is significant; the auditor has exhausted all reasonable internal reporting channels; and the hazard is not on a reasonable timetable for remediation.

Determining whether a situation meets all six tests is not simple because environmental risks are open to alternative evaluations. Hence, there is no guarantee that reasonable people using the six tests would all arrive at the same conclusion. Nevertheless, Blumenfeld claims, the six tests offer the best way to judge highly complex ethical situations typical of the kind faced by those in the environmental field.

INTERNATIONAL BUSINESS

Multinational corporations are business organizations that maintain extensive operations in more than one country. Multinational business faces many of the same ethical issues as domestic business, but the fact that multinationals conduct business across national and cultural lines raises special problems. Legal and cultural standards may differ from culture to culture. Practices that are benign in the United States may be inappropriate or even unethical in other contexts. Because they are so large and widely dispersed, multinational corporations do not come under the complete control of any one government, and some fear that their interests diverge from those of both their home and host countries.

Extensive investment by multinational corporations can help the economies of developing nations, but such investment can have harmful effects as well. Multinational investment can lead to extensive dependence on foreign capital and technology, leaving the developing nation powerless and vulnerable. Many multinationals establish foreign operations to get cheap labor or to engage in hazardous production processes without the expense of conforming to U.S. health and safety and environmental regulations. The natural desire of multinational corporations to do business in a secure investment climate sometimes leads them to support authoritarian and repressive regimes. Multinational industry can stifle local enterprise and submerge the characteristic culture of the nations in which the industry operates. Finally, successful private enterprise does not always lead to the satisfaction of the needs of developing countries.

Richard De George suggests that some of the dilemmas that appear to face multinational corporations doing business in the Third World in fact arise from assuming that U.S. standards are universal moral standards. There are important differences in culture and values between First and Third World countries, De George believes, and these should be respected. In spite of these differences, however, De George believes that there are universal moral norms that can be applied across cultures, and he offers seven principles that might serve as guidelines for evaluating the actions of multinational corporations.

Manuel Velasquez questions whether multinational corporations have any moral obligations to contribute to the international common good. He argues that in a restricted but not insignificant portion of international transactions, corporations have no such obligations because doing so will put them at a serious competitive disadvantage. He concludes that this shows the need for an international agency capable of forcing all multinationals to contribute to the global common good.

Thomas Donaldson in his article "Values in Tension: Ethics Away From Home" continues the discussion on what ethical standards should be adhered to when a business operates abroad. He rejects both extreme positions, that of "cultural relativism," or when in Rome do as the Romans do, and that of "ethical imperialism," or doing everywhere what one does at home. He argues for an approach that balances the two extremes, and provides three guiding principles to do so: (1) respect for core human values, which determine the absolute moral threshold for all business activities; (2) respect for local traditions; and (3) the belief that context matters when deciding what is right and wrong.

The next article in Chapter 9 examines a major ethical challenge faced by managers of multinationals abroad: the widespread occurrence of bribery and extortion. In the United States, bribery of foreign officials is illegal and almost universally regarded as unethical. Following the signing of the Organisation for Economic Co-operation and Development's (OECD) "Convention on Combating Bribery of Foreign Public Officials in International Business Transactions" in December 1997, a number of other countries are now working toward criminalizing bribery of foreign public officials. But in many countries, claim U.S. managers, bribery is a way of life, necessary to conducting business. Is it morally permissible to bribe if bribery is a common practice in the culture in which you are doing business? What, really, is wrong with bribery?

Scott Turow explains that the essence of bribery is the attempt to corrupt a public official's impartial judgment, giving the briber an unfair advantage over others. Managers of multinationals who bribe to secure a contract are trying to "buy" the loyalty of foreign officials, loyalty that the officials actually owe to their public. It is easy to see that the practice of bribery is hostile to a free market system. In a free market system, companies compete to offer consumers the best product at the best price. Bribery shifts the terms of competition from quality and price to the size of the sum of money paid to a government official. Widespread bribery would make fair competition impossible. Bribery also injures the consumer, because the selection of an item on any basis other than quality and price often leads to the purchase of an inferior product.

In the final article in Chapter 9, S. Prakash Sethi discusses a number of the issues that arise for global companies in relation to their codes of conduct. Despite his concerns over the current state of code use, Sethi argues that codes are both necessary and desirable, but only if properly developed and implemented. He proceeds to provide his recommendations on developing and implementing a meaningful code of conduct, including the critical aspect of creating an independent monitoring system. He discusses the experience of Mattel, in creating and implementing its "Global Manufacturing Principles."

MINI-CASES AND CASES FOR PART FOUR

The first mini-case in Part Four "Pat Sheritan," addresses the obligation to disclose overbilling to one's customer or client. The dilemma faced in "John Snyder" involves appropriate international ethical standards, as well as environmental ethics. The articles in Chapter 9 dealing with international business and the environment can be useful background for discussing this mini-case.

The cases of Part Four provide an opportunity for greater reflection on ethical issues related to consumers, the environment, and international business. In "The Ford Pinto," the issue of a car company continuing to manufacture a car despite knowledge of a dangerous defect is raised. In which of Velasquez's consumer protection approaches is the company situated? In "The Ethics of Marketing: Nestlé's Infant Formula," the company must address particular marketing issues arising in a Third World environment, as well as its obligations to ensure its product is used properly. Holley's discussion of the morality of sales practices can be used to evaluate Nestlé's actions. In "Toy Wars," the firm must address marketing issues related to military toys. Both cases raise many of the issues presented in the articles by Galbraith and von Hayek. In "Forests of the North Coast: The Owls, the Trees, and the Conflicts," animal activists come head-to-head with the logging community of the Pacific Northwest over the issue of the spotted owl. In "U.S. and Mexico Confront a Toxic Legacy," a series of environmental issues are raised. Both of these cases can be used to reflect upon Bowie, Hoffman, and Ruff's articles. Finally, in "The Project at Moza Island," issues of bribery are confronted in an international context. Readers can use the case to consider the points raised by Donaldson and Turow in their articles.

CHAPTER 7

The Consumer

The Dependence Effect

John Kenneth Galbraith
Paul M. Warburg Professor of Economics,
Emeritus, Harvard University

The theory of consumer demand, as it is now widely accepted, is based on two broad propositions, neither of them quite explicit but both extremely important for the present value system of economists. The first is that the urgency of wants does not diminish appreciably as more of them are satisfied or, to put the matter more precisely, to the extent that this happens it is not demonstrable and not a matter of any interest to economists or for economic policy. When man has satisfied his physical needs, then psychologically grounded desires take over. These can never be satisfied or, in any case, no progress can be proved. The concept of satiation has very little standing in economics. It is neither useful nor scientific to speculate on the comparative cravings of the stomach and the mind.

The second proposition is that wants originate in the personality of the consumer or, in any case that they are given data for the economist. The latter's task is merely to seek their satisfaction. He has no need to inquire how these wants are formed. His function is sufficiently fulfilled by maximizing the goods that supply the wants.

The notion that wants do not become less urgent the more amply the individual is supplied is broadly repugnant to common sense. It is something to be believed only by those who wish to believe. Yet the conventional wisdom must be tackled on its own terrain. Intertemporal comparisons of an individual's state of mind do rest on doubtful grounds. Who can say for sure that the deprivation which afflicts him with hunger is more painful than the deprivation which afflicts him with envy of his neighbour's new car? In the time that has passed since he was poor his soul may have become subject to a new and deeper searing. And where a society is concerned, comparisons between marginal satisfactions when it is poor and those when it is affluent will involve not only the same individual at different times but different individuals at different times. The scholar who wishes to believe that with increasing affluence there is no reduction in the urgency of desires and goods is not without points for debate. However

387

plausible the case against him, it cannot be proved. In the defence of the conventional wisdom this amounts almost to invulnerability.

However, there is a flaw in the case. If the individual's wants are to be urgent they must be original with himself. They cannot be urgent if they must be contrived for him. And above all they must not be contrived by the process of production by which they are satisfied. For this means that the whole case for the urgency of production, based on the urgency of wants, falls to the ground. One cannot defend production as satisfying wants if that production creates the wants.

Were it so that man on arising each morning was assailed by demons which instilled in him a passion sometimes for silk shirts, sometimes for kitchenware, sometimes for chamber-pots, and sometimes for orange squash, there would be every reason to applaud the effort to find the goods, however odd, that quenched this flame. But should it be that his passion was the result of his first having cultivated the demons, and should it also be that his effort to allay it stirred the demons to ever greater and greater effort, there would be question as to how rational was his solution. Unless restrained by conventional attitudes, he might wonder if the solution lay with more goods or fewer demons.

So it is that if production creates the wants it seeks to satisfy, or if the wants emerge *pari passu* with the production, then the urgency of the wants can no longer be used to defend the urgency of the production. Production only fills a void that it has itself created.

The even more direct link between production and wants is provided by the institutions of modern advertising and salesmanship. These cannot be reconciled with the notion of independently determined desires, for their central function is to create desires—to bring into being wants that previously did not exist.[1] This is accomplished by the producer of the goods or at his behest. A broad empirical relationship exists between what is spent on production of consumers' goods and what is spent in synthesizing the desires for that production. A new consumer product must be introduced with a suitable advertising campaign to arouse an

interest in it. The path for an expansion of output must be paved by a suitable expansion in the advertising budget. Outlays for the manufacturing of a product are not more important in the strategy of modern business enterprise than outlays for the manufacturing of demand for the product. None of this is novel. All would be regarded as elementary by the most retarded student in the nation's most primitive school of business administration. The cost of this want formation is formidable. In 1956 total advertising expenditure—though, as noted, not all of it may be assigned to the synthesis of wants—amounted to about ten thousand million dollars. For some years it had been increasing at a rate in excess of a thousand million dollars a year. Obviously, such outlays must be integrated with the theory of consumer demand. They are too big to be ignored.

But such integration means recognizing that wants are dependent on production. It accords to the producer the function both of making the goods and of making the desires for them. It recognizes that production, not only passively through emulation, but actively through advertising and related activities, creates the wants it seeks to satisfy.

The businessman and the lay reader will be puzzled over the emphasis which I give to a seemingly obvious point. The point is indeed obvious. But it is one which, to a singular degree, economists have resisted. They have sensed, as the layman does not, the damage to established ideas which lurks in these relationships. As a result, incredibly, they have closed their eyes (and ears) to the most obtrusive of all economic phenomena, namely modern want creation.

This is not to say that the evidence affirming the dependence of wants on advertising has been entirely ignored. It is one reason why advertising has so long been regarded with such uneasiness by economists. Here is something which cannot be accommodated easily to existing theory. More previous scholars have speculated on the urgency of desires which are so obviously the fruit of such expensively contrived campaigns for popular attention. Is a new breakfast cereal or detergent so much wanted if so much must be spent to compel in the consumer the sense of want? But there has been little tendency to go on to examine the implications of this for the theory of consumer demand and even less for the importance of production and productive efficiency. These have remained sacrosanct. More often the uneasiness has been manifested in a general disapproval of advertising and advertising men, leading to the occasional suggestion that they shouldn't exist. Such suggestions have usually been ill received.

And so the notion of independently determined wants still survives. In the face of all the forces of modern salesmanship it still rules, almost undefiled, in the textbooks. And it still remains the economist's mission—and on few matters is the pedagogy so firm—to seek unquestioningly the means for filling these wants. This being so, production remains of prime urgency. We have here, perhaps, the ultimate triumph of the conventional wisdom in its resistance to the evidence of the eyes. To equal it one must imagine a humanitarian who was long ago persuaded of the grievous shortage of hospital facilities in the town. He continues to importune the passers-by for money for more beds and refuses to notice that the town doctor is deftly knocking over pedestrians with his car to keep up the occupancy.

And in unravelling the complex we should always be careful not to overlook the obvious. The fact that wants can be synthesized by advertising, catalysed by salesmanship, and shaped by the discreet manipulations of the persuaders shows that they are not very urgent. A man who is hungry need never be told of his need for food. If he is inspired by his appetite, he is immune to the influence of Messrs. Batten, Barton, Durstine and Osborn. The latter are effective only with those who are so far removed from physical want that they do not already know what they want. In this state alone men are open to persuasion.

The general conclusion of these pages is of such importance for this essay that it had perhaps best be put with some formality. As a society becomes increasingly affluent, wants are increasingly created by the process by which they are satisfied. This may operate passively. Increases in consumption, the counterpart of increases in production, act by suggestion or emulation to create wants. Or producers may proceed actively to create wants through advertising and salesmanship. Wants thus come to depend on output. In technical terms it can no longer be assumed that welfare is greater at an all-round higher level of production than at a lower one. It may be the same. The higher level of production has, merely, a higher level of want creation necessitating a higher level of want satisfaction. There will be frequent occasion to refer to the way wants depend on the process by which they are satisfied. It will be convenient to call it the Dependence Effect.

The final problem of the productive society is what it produces. This manifests itself in an implacable tendency to provide an opulent supply of some things and a niggardly yield of others. This disparity carries to the point where it is a cause of social discomfort and social unhealth. The line which divides our area of wealth from our area of poverty is roughly that which divides privately produced and marketed goods and services from publicly rendered services. Our wealth in the first is not only in startling contrast with the meagerness of the latter, but our wealth in privately produced goods is, to a marked degree, the cause of crisis in the supply of public services. For we have failed to see the importance, indeed the urgent need, of maintaining a balance between the two.

This disparity between our flow of private and public goods and services is no matter of subjective judgment. On the contrary, it is the source of the most extensive comment which only stops short of the direct contrast being made here. In the years following World War II, the papers of any major city—those of New York were an excellent example—told daily of the shortages and shortcomings in the elementary municipal and metropolitan services. The schools were old and overcrowded. The police force was under strength and underpaid. The parks and playgrounds were insufficient. Streets and empty lots were filthy, and the sanitation staff was under-equipped and in need of men. Access to the city by those who work there was uncertain and painful and becoming more so. Internal transportation was overcrowded, unhealthful, and dirty. So was the air. Parking on the streets had to be prohibited, and there was no space elsewhere. These deficiencies were not in new and novel services but in old and established ones. Cities have long swept their streets, helped their people move around, educated them, kept order, and provided horse rails for vehicles which sought to pause. That their residents should have a non-toxic supply of air suggests no revolutionary dalliance with socialism.

The contrast was and remains evident not alone to those who read. The family which takes its mauve and cerise, air-conditioned, power-steered, and power-braked car out for a tour passes through cities that are badly paved, made hideous by litter, blighted buildings, billboards, and posts for wires that should long since have been put underground. They pass on into a countryside that has been rendered largely invisible by commercial art. (The goods which the latter advertise have an absolute priority in our value system. Such aesthetic considerations as a view of the countryside accordingly come second. On such matters we are consistent.) They picnic on exquisitely packaged food from a portable icebox by a polluted stream and go on to spend the night at a park which is a menace to public health and morals. Just before dozing off on an air-mattress, beneath a nylon tent, amid the stench of decaying refuse, they may reflect vaguely on the curious unevenness of their blessings. Is this, indeed, the American genius?

The case for social balance has, so far, been put negatively. Failure to keep public services in minimal relation to private production and use of goods is a cause of social disorder or impairs economic performance. The matter may now be put affirmatively. By failing to exploit the opportunity to expand public production we are missing opportunities for enjoyment which otherwise we might have had. Presumably a community can be as well rewarded by buying better schools or better parks as by buying bigger cars. By concentrating on the latter rather than the former it is failing to maximize its satisfactions. As with schools in the community, so with public services over the country at large. It is scarcely sensible that we should satisfy our wants in private goods with reckless abundance, while in the case of public goods, on the evidence of the eye, we practice extreme self-denial. So, far from systematically exploiting the opportunities to derive use and pleasure from these services, we do not supply what would keep us out of trouble.

The conventional wisdom holds that the community, large or small, makes a decision as to how much it will devote to its public services. This decision is arrived at by democratic process. Subject to the imperfections and uncertainties of democracy, people decide how much of their private income and goods they will surrender in order to have public services of which they are in greater need. Thus there is a balance, however rough, in the enjoyments to be had from private goods and services and those rendered by public authority.

It will be obvious, however, that this view depends on the notion of independently determined consumer wants. In such a world one could with some reason defend the doctrine that the consumer, as a voter, makes an independent choice between public and private goods. But given the dependence effect—given that consumer wants are created by the process by which they are satisfied— the consumer makes no such choice. He is subject to the forces of advertising and emulation by which production creates its own demand. Advertising operates exclusively, and emulation mainly, on behalf of privately produced goods and services.[2] Since management and emulative effects operate on behalf of private production, public services will have an inherent tendency to lag behind. Car demand which is expensively synthesized will inevitably have a much larger claim on income than parks or public health or even roads where no such influence operates. The engines of mass communication, in their highest state of development, assail the eyes and ears of the community on behalf of more beer but not of more schools. Even in the conventional wisdom it will scarcely be contended that this leads to an equal choice between the two.

The competition is especially unequal for new products and services. Every corner of the public psyche is canvassed by some of the nation's most talented citizens to see if the desire for some merchantable product can be cultivated. No similar process operates on behalf of the nonmerchantable services of the state. Indeed, while we take the cultivation of new private wants for granted we would be measurably shocked to see it applied to public services. The scientist or engineer or advertising man who devotes himself to developing a new carburetor, cleanser, or depilatory for which the public recognizes no need and will feel none until an advertising campaign arouses it, is one of the valued members of our society. A politician or a public servant who dreams up a new public service is a wastrel. Few public offenses are more reprehensible.

So much for the influences which operate on the decision between public and private production. The calm decision between public and private consumption pictured by the conventional wisdom is, in fact, a remarkable example of the error which arises from viewing social behavior out of context. The inherent tendency will always be for public services to fall behind private production. We have here the first of the causes of social imbalance.

NOTES

1. Advertising is not a simple phenomenon. It is also important in competitive strategy and want creation is, ordinarily, a complementary result of efforts to shift the demand curve of the individual firm at the expense of others or (less importantly, I think) to change its shape by increasing the degree of product differentiation. Some of the failure of economists to identify advertising with want creation may be attributed to the undue attention that its use in purely competitive strategy has attracted. It should be noted, however, that the competitive manipulation of consumer desire is only possible, at least on any appreciable scale, when such need is not strongly felt.
2. Emulation does operate between communities. A new school or a new highway in one community does exert pressure on others to remain abreast. However, as compared with the pervasive effects of emulation in extending the demand for privately produced consumers' goods there will be agreement, I think, that this intercommunity effect is probably small.

The *Non Sequitur* of the "Dependence Effect"

F. A. von Hayek
Former Professor Emeritus of Economics,
University of Chicago and University of Freiburg

For well over a hundred years the critics of the free enterprise system have resorted to the argument that if production were only organized rationally, there would be no economic problem. Rather than face the problem which scarcity creates, socialist reformers have tended to deny that scarcity existed. Ever since the Saint-Simonians their contention has been that the problem of production has been solved and only the problem of distribution remains. However absurd this contention must appear to us with respect to the time when it was first advanced, it still has some persuasive power when repeated with reference to the present.

The latest form of this old contention is expounded in *The Affluent Society* by Professor J. K. Galbraith. He attempts to demonstrate that in our affluent society the important private needs are already satisfied and the urgent need is therefore no longer a further expansion of the output of commodities but an increase of those services which are supplied (and presumably can be supplied only) by government. Though this book has been extensively discussed since its publication in 1958, its central thesis still requires some further examination.

I believe the author would agree that his argument turns upon the "Dependence Effect" [p. 389 of this book]. The argument of this chapter starts from the assertion that a great part of the wants which are still unsatisfied in modern society are not wants which would be experienced spontaneously by the individual if left to himself, but are wants which are created by the process by which they are

Excerpted from "The *Non Sequitur* of the 'Dependence Effect'" by F. A. von Hayek, *Southern Economic Journal* (April 1961). Copyright © 1961. Reprinted by permission of the publisher.

satisfied. It is then represented as self-evident that for this reason such wants cannot be urgent or important. This crucial conclusion appears to be a complete *non sequitur* and it would seem that with it the whole argument of the book collapses.

The first part of the argument is of course perfectly true: we would not desire any of the amenities of civilization—or even of the most primitive culture—if we did not live in a society in which others provide them. The innate wants are probably confined to food, shelter, and sex. All the rest we learn to desire because we see others enjoying various things. To say that a desire is not important because it is not innate is to say that the whole cultural achievement of man is not important.

This cultural origin of practically all the needs of civilized life must of course not be confused with the fact that there are some desires which aim, not as a satisfaction derived directly from the use of an object, but only from the status which its consumption is expected to confer. In a passage which Professor Galbraith quotes, Lord Keynes seems to treat the latter sort of Veblenesque conspicuous consumption as the only alternative "to those needs which are absolute in the sense that we feel them whatever the situation of our fellow human beings may be." If the latter phrase is interpreted to exclude all the needs for goods which are felt only because these goods are known to be produced, these two Keynesian classes describe of course only extreme types of wants, but disregard the overwhelming majority of goods on which civilized life rests. Very few needs indeed are "absolute" in the sense that they are independent of social environment or of the example of others, and that their satisfaction is an indispensable condition for the preservation of the individual or of the species. Most needs which make us act are needs for things which only civilization teaches us to exist at all, and these things are wanted by us because they produce feelings or emotions which we would not know if it were not for our cultural inheritance. Are not in this sense probably all our esthetic feelings "acquired tastes"?

How complete a *non sequitur* Professor Galbraith's conclusion represents is seen most clearly if we apply the argument to any product of the arts, be it music, painting, or literature. If the fact that people would not feel the need for something if it were not produced did prove that such products are of small value, all those highest products of human endeavor would be of small value. Professor Galbraith's argument could be easily employed without any change of the essential terms, to demonstrate the worthlessness of literature or any other form of art. Surely an individual's want for literature is not original with himself in the sense that he would experience it if literature were not produced. Does this then mean that the production of literature cannot be defended as satisfying a want because it is only the production which provokes the demand? In this, as in the case of all cultural needs, it is unquestionably, in Professor Galbraith's words, "the process of satisfying the wants that creates the wants." There have never been "independently determined desires for" literature before literature has been produced and books certainly do not serve the "simple mode of enjoyment which requires no previous conditioning of the consumer." Clearly my taste for the novels of Jane Austen or Anthony Trollope or C. P. Snow is not "original with myself." But is it not rather absurd to conclude from this that it is less important than, say, the need for education? Public education indeed seems to regard it as one of its tasks to instill a taste for literature in the young and even employs producers of literature for that purpose. Is this want creation by the producer reprehensible? Or does the fact that some of the pupils may possess a taste for poetry only because of the efforts of their teachers prove that since "it does not arise in spontaneous consumer need and the demand would not exist were it not contrived, its utility or urgency, ex contrivance, is zero?"

The appearance that the conclusions follow from the admitted facts is made possible by an obscurity of the wording of the argument with respect to which it is difficult to know whether the author is himself the victim of a confusion or whether he skillfully uses ambiguous terms to make the conclusion appear plausible. The obscurity concerns the implied assertion that the wants of the consumers are determined by the producers. Professor Galbraith avoids in this connection any terms as crude and definite as "determine." The expressions he employs, such as that wants are "dependent on" or the "fruits of" production, or that "production creates the wants" do, of course, suggest determination but avoid saying so in plain terms. After what has already been said it is of course obvious that the knowledge of what is being produced is one of the many factors on which it depends what people will want. It would scarcely be an exaggeration to say that contemporary man, in all fields where he has not yet formed firm habits, tends to find out what he wants by looking at what his neighbours do and at various displays of goods (physical or in catalogues or advertisements) and then choosing what he likes best.

In this sense the tastes of man, as is also true of his opinions and beliefs and indeed much of his personality, are shaped in a great measure by his cultural environment. But though in some contexts it would perhaps be legitimate to express this by a phrase like "production creates the wants," the circumstances mentioned would clearly not justify the contention that particular producers can deliberately determine the wants of particular consumers. The efforts of all producers will certainly be directed towards that end: but how far any individual producer will succeed will depend not only on what he does but also on what the others do and on a great many other influences operating upon the consumer. The joint but uncoordinated efforts of the producers merely create one element of the environment by which the wants of the consumers are shaped. It is because each individual producer thinks that the consumers can be persuaded to like his products that he endeavours to influence them. But though this effort is part of the influences which shape consumers' tastes, no producer can in any real sense "determine" them. This, however, is clearly implied in such statements as that wants are "both passively and deliberately the fruits of the process by which they are satisfied." If the producer could in fact deliberately determine what the consumers will want, Professor Galbraith's conclusions would have some validity. But though this is skillfully suggested, it is nowhere made credible, and could hardly be made credible because it is not true.

Though the range of choice open to the consumers is the joint result of, among other things, the efforts of all producers who vie with each other in making their respective products appear more attractive than those of their competitors, every particular consumer still has the choice between all those different offers.

A fuller examination of this process would, of course, have to consider how, after the efforts of some producers have actually swayed some consumers, it becomes the example of the various consumers thus persuaded which will influence the remaining consumers. This can be mentioned here only to emphasize that even if each consumer were exposed to pressure of only one producer, the harmful effects which are apprehended from this would soon be offset by the much more powerful example of his fellows. It is of course fashionable to treat this influence of the example of others (or, what comes to the same thing, the learning from the experience made by others) as if it amounted all to an attempt of keeping up with the Joneses and for that reason was to be regarded as detrimental. It seems to me that not only the importance of this factor is usually greatly exaggerated but also that it is not really relevant to Professor Galbraith's main thesis. But it might be worthwhile briefly to ask what, assuming that some expenditure were actually determined solely by a desire of keeping up with the Joneses, that would really prove? At least in Europe we used to be familiar with a type of persons who often denied themselves even enough food in order to maintain an appearance of respectability or gentility in dress and style of life. We may regard this as a misguided effort, but surely it would not prove that the income of such persons was larger than they knew how to use wisely. That the appearance of success, or wealth, may to some people seem more important than many other needs, does in no way prove that the needs they sacrifice to the former are unimportant. In the same way, even though people are often persuaded to spend unwisely, this surely is no evidence that they do not still have important unsatisfied needs.

Professor Galbraith's attempt to give an apparent scientific proof for the contention that the need for the production of more commodities has greatly decreased seems to me to have broken down completely. With it goes the claim to have produced a valid argument which justifies the use of coercion to make people employ their income for those purposes of which he approves. It is not to be denied that there is some originality in this latest version of the old socialist argument. For over a hundred years we have been exhorted to embrace socialism because it would give us more goods. Since it has so lamentably failed to achieve this where it has been tried, we are now urged to adopt it because more goods after all are not important. The aim is still progressively to increase the share of the resources whose use is determined by political authority and the coercion of any dissenting minority. It is not surprising, therefore, that Professor Galbraith's thesis has been most enthusiastically received by the intellectuals of the British Labour Party where his influence bids fair to displace that of the late Lord Keynes. It is more curious that in this country it is not recognized as an outright socialist argument and often seems to appeal to people on the opposite end of the political spectrum. But this is probably only another instance of the familiar fact that on these matters the extremes frequently meet.

Marketing to Inner-City Blacks: PowerMaster and Moral Responsibility

George G. Brenkert

Professor and Director, Connelly Program in Business Ethics, McDonough School of Business, Georgetown University

I. INTRODUCTION

The nature and extent of marketers' moral obligations is a matter of considerable debate. This is particularly the case when those who are targeted

From *Business Ethics Quarterly*, Vol. 8, No. 1, 1998, pp. 1–18.

by marketers live in disadvantaged circumstances and suffer various problems disproportionately with other members of the same society. An interesting opportunity to explore this difficult area of marketing ethics is presented by Heileman Brewing Company's failed effort to market PowerMaster, a malt liquor, to inner-city blacks. The story of PowerMaster is relatively simple and short. Its ethical dimensions are much more complicated.

In the following, I wish to consider the moral aspects of this case within the context of a market society such as the U.S. which permits the forms of advertising it presently does. To do so, I first briefly evaluate three kinds of objections made to the marketing of PowerMaster. I contend that none of these objections taken by itself clearly justifies the criticism leveled at Heileman. Heileman might reasonably claim that it was fulfilling its economic, social and moral responsibilities in the same manner as were other brewers and marketers. Accordingly, I argue that only if we look to the collective effects of all marketers of malt liquor to the inner-city can we identify morally defensible grounds for the complaints against marketing campaigns such as that of PowerMaster. The upshot of this argument is that marketers must recognize not only their individual moral responsibilities to those they target, but also a collective responsibility of all marketers for those market segments they jointly target. It is on this basis that Heileman's marketing of PowerMaster may be faulted. This result is noteworthy in that it introduces a new kind of moral consideration which has rarely been considered in discussions of corporate moral responsibilities.

II. HEILEMAN AND POWERMASTER

G. Heileman Brewing Co. is a Wisconsin brewer which produces a number of beers and malt liquors, including Colt Dry, Colt 45, and Mickey's. In the early 1990s, competition amongst such brewers was increasingly intense. In January 1991, Heileman was facing such economic difficulties that it filed for protection from creditors under Chapter 11 of the U.S. Bankruptcy Code (Horovitz, 1991b, D1). To improve its financial situation, Heileman sought to market, beginning in June 1991, a new malt liquor called "PowerMaster." At that time there was considerable growth in the "up-strength malt liquor category." In fact, "this higher-alcohol segment of the business [had] been growing at an explosive 25% to 30% a year" (Freedman, 1991a: B1). To attempt to capitalize on this market segment, Heileman produced PowerMaster, a malt liquor that contained 5.9% alcohol, 31% more alcohol than Heileman's top-selling Colt 45 (4.5% alcohol). Reportedly, when introduced only one other malt liquor (St. Ides) offered such a powerful malt as PowerMaster (Freedman, 1991a: B1).

Further, since malt liquor had become "the drink of choice among many in the inner city," Heileman focused a significant amount of its marketing efforts on inner-city blacks. Heileman's ad campaign played to this group with posters and billboards using black male models. Advertisements assured consumers that PowerMaster was "Bold Not Harsh." Hugh Nelson, Heileman's marketing director, was reported to have claimed that "the company's research . . . shows that consumers will opt for PowerMaster not on basis of its alcohol content but because of its flavor. The higher alcohol content gives PowerMaster a 'bold not nasty' taste . . ." (Freedman, 1991a: B4).

In response, a wide variety of individuals and groups protested against Heileman's actions. Critics claimed that both advertisements and the name "PowerMaster" suggested the alcoholic strength of the drink and the "buzz" that those who consumed it could get. Surgeon General Antonia Novello criticized the PowerMaster marketing scheme as "insensitive" (Milloy, 1991: B3). Reports in *The Wall Street Journal* spoke of community activists and alcohol critics branding Heileman's marketing campaign as "socially irresponsible" (Freedman, 1991b: B1). "Twenty-one consumer and health groups, including the Center for Science in the Public Interest, also publicly called for Heileman to halt the marketing of PowerMaster and for BATF to limit the alcohol content of malt liquor" (Colford and Teinowitz, 1991: 29). A reporter for the *L.A. Times* wrote that "at issue is growing resentment by blacks and other minorities who feel that they are being

unfairly targeted—if not exploited—by marketers of beer, liquor and tobacco products" (Horovitz, 1991: D6). Another reporter for the same paper claimed that "[a]nti-alcohol activists contend that alcoholic beverage manufacturers are taking advantage of minority groups and exacerbating inner-city problems by targeting them with high-powered blends" (Lacey, 1992: A32). And Reverend Calvin Butts of the Abyssinian Baptist Church in New York's Harlem said that "this [Heileman] is obviously a company that has no sense of moral or social responsibility" (Freedman, 1991a: B1).

Though the Bureau of Alcohol, Tobacco and Firearms (BATF) initially approved the use of "PowerMaster" as the name for the new malt liquor, in light of the above protests it "reacted by enforcing a beer law that prohibits labels 'considered to be statements of alcoholic content' " (Milloy, 1991: B3). It insisted that the word "Power" be removed from the "PowerMaster" name (Freedman, 1991b: B1). As a consequence of the actions of the BATF and the preceding complaints, Heileman decided not to market PowerMaster.

III. THE OBJECTIONS

The PowerMaster marketing campaign evoked three distinct kinds of moral objections:

First, because its advertisements drew upon images and themes related to power and boldness, they were criticized as promoting satisfactions only artificially and distortedly associated with the real needs of those targeted. As such, the PowerMaster marketing campaign was charged with fostering a form of moral illusion.

Second, Heileman was said to lack concern for the harm likely to be caused by its product. Blacks suffer disproportionately from cirrhosis of the liver and other liver diseases brought on by alcohol. In addition, alcohol-related social problems such as violence and crime are also prominent in the inner-city. Accordingly, Heileman was attacked for its lack of moral sensitivity.

Third, Heileman was accused of taking unfair advantage of those in the inner-city whom they had targeted. Inner-city blacks were said to be especially vulnerable, due to their life circumstances, to advertisements and promotions formulated in terms of power, self-assertion and sexual success. Hence, to target them in the manner they did with a product such as PowerMaster was a form of exploitation. In short, questions of justice were raised.

It is important not only for corporations such as Heileman but also for others concerned with such marketing practices to determine whether these objections show that the PowerMaster marketing program was morally unjustified. The economic losses in failed marketing efforts such as Power-Master are considerable. In addition, if the above objections are justified, the moral losses are also significant.

The first objection maintained that by emphasizing power Heileman was, in effect, offering a cruel substitute for a real lack in the lives of inner-city blacks. PowerMaster's slogan, "Bold not Harsh," was said to project an image of potency. "The brewers' shrewd marketing," one critic maintained, "has turned malt liquor into an element of machismo" (Lacey, 1992: A1). George Hacker, Director of the National Coalition to Prevent Impaired Driving, commented that "the real irony of marketing PowerMaster to inner-city blacks is that this population is among the most lacking in power in this society" (Freedman, 1991a, B1).

This kind of criticism has been made against many forms of advertising. The linking of one's product with power, fame, and success not to mention sex is nothing new in advertising. Most all those targeted by marketers lack (or at least want) those goods or values associated with the products being promoted. Further, other malt liquor marketing campaigns had referred to power. For example, another malt liquor, Olde English "800," claimed that "It's the Power." The Schlitz Red Bull was associated with the phrase "The Real Power" (Colford and Tenowitz, 1991: 1). Nevertheless, they were not singled out for attack or boycott as PowerMaster was.

Accordingly, however objectionable it may be for marketers to link a product with something which its potential customers (significantly) lack and which the product can only symbolically or indirectly satisfy, this feature of the PowerMaster marketing campaign does not uniquely explain or justify the complaints that were raised against the marketing of PowerMaster. In short, this objection appears far too general in scope to justify the particular attention given PowerMaster. Heileman could not have reasonably concluded, on its basis, that it was being particularly morally irresponsible. It was simply doing what others had done and for which they had not been boycotted or against which such an outcry had not been raised. It is difficult to see how Heileman could have concluded that it was preparing a marketing program that would generate the social and moral protest it did, simply from an examination of its own plan or the similar individual marketing programs of other brewers.

The second objection was that the marketers of PowerMaster showed an especial lack of sensitivity in that a malt liquor with the potency of Power-Master would likely cause additional harm to inner-city blacks. According to various reports, "alcoholism and other alcohol-related diseases extract a disproportionate toll on blacks. A 1978 study by the National Institute on Alcohol Abuse and Alcoholism found that black men between the ages of 25 and 44 are 10 times more likely than the general population to have cirrhosis of the liver" (*N.Y. Times,* 1991). *Fortune* reported that "The Department of Health and Human Services last spring released figures showing a decline in life expectancy for blacks for the fourth straight year—down to 69.2 years, vs. 75.6 years for whites. Although much of the drop is attributable to homicide and AIDS, blacks also suffer higher instances of . . . alcohol-related illnesses than whites (*Fortune,* 1991: 100). Further, due to the combined use of alcohol and cigarettes, blacks suffer cancer of the esophagus at a disproportional rate than the rest of the population. Similarly, assuming that black women would drink PowerMaster, it is relevant that the impact of alcohol use in the inner-city is also manifested in an increased infant mortality rate and by newborn children with fetal alcohol syndrome (*The Workbook,* 1991: 18). Finally, a malt liquor with a high percentage of alcohol was expected to have additional harmful effects on the levels of social ills, such as violence, crime, and spousal abuse. As such, PowerMaster would be further destructive of the social fabric of the inner-city.

Under these circumstances, the second objection maintained, anyone who marketed a product which would further increase these harms was being morally obtuse to the problems inner-city blacks suffer. Accordingly, Heileman's Power-Master marketing campaign was an instance of such moral insensitivity.

Nevertheless, this objection does not seem clearly applicable when pointed simply at Power-Master. Surely inner-city blacks are adults and should be allowed, as such, to make their own choices, even if those choices harm themselves, so long as they are not deceived or coerced when making those choices and they do not harm others. Since neither deception nor coercion were involved in PowerMaster's marketing campaign, it is an unacceptable form of moral paternalism to deny them what they might otherwise wish to choose.

Further, those who raised the above complaints were not those who would have drunk PowerMaster, but leaders of various associations both within and outside the inner-city concerned with alcohol abuse and consumption. This was not a consumer-led protest. Reports of the outcry over PowerMaster contain no objections from those whom Heileman had targeted. No evidence was presented that these individuals would have found PowerMaster unsatisfactory. Argument is needed, for example, that these individuals had (or should have had) over-riding interests in healthy livers. Obviously there are many people (black as well as white) who claim that their interests are better fulfilled by drinking rather than abstinence.

Finally, argument is also needed to show that this increase in alcoholic content would have any significant effects on the targeted group. It might be that any noteworthy effects would be limited because the increased alcoholic content would prove undesirable to those targeted since they would become intoxicated too quickly. "Overly rapid intoxication undercuts sales volume and annoys consumers," *The Wall Street Journal* reported (Freedman, 1991a: B1). Supposedly this consequence led one malt brewer to lower the alcoholic content of its product (Freedman, 1991a: B1). Furthermore, malt liquor is hardly the strongest alcohol which blacks (or others) drink. Reportedly, "blacks buy more than half the cognac sold in the United States" (*The Workbook,* 1991: 18). Cheap forms of wine and hard liquor are readily available. Thus, it is far from obvious what significant effects PowerMaster alone would have in the inner-city.

One possible response to the preceding replies brings us to the third objection. This response is that, though inner-city blacks might not be deceived or coerced into drinking PowerMaster, they were particularly vulnerable to the marketing campaign which Heileman proposed. Because of this, Heileman's marketing campaign (wittingly or unwittingly) would take unfair advantage of inner-city blacks.

Little, if any attempt, has been made to defend or to explore this charge. I suggest that there are at least three ways in which inner-city blacks—or anyone else, for that matter—might be said to be specially vulnerable.

A person would be cognitively vulnerable if he or she lacked certain levels of ability to cognitively process information or to be aware that certain information was being withheld or manipulated in deceptive ways. Thus, if people were not able to process information about the effects of malt liquor on themselves or on their society in ways in which others could, they would be cognitively vulnerable.

A person would be motivationally vulnerable if he or she could not resist ordinary temptations and/or enticements due to his or her own individual characteristics. Thus, if people were unable, as normal individuals are, to resist various advertisements and marketing ploys, they would be motivationally vulnerable.

And people would be socially vulnerable when their social situation renders them significantly less able than others to resist various enticements. For example, due to the poverty within which they live, they might have developed various needs or attitudes which rendered them less able to resist various marketing programs.

Nevertheless, none of these forms of vulnerability was explored or defended as the basis of the unfair advantage which the PowerMaster marketers were said to seek. And indeed it is difficult to see what account could be given which would explain how the use of the name "PowerMaster," and billboards with a black model, a bottle of

PowerMaster and the slogan "Bold Not Harsh" would be enough to subvert the decision making or motivational capacities of inner-city blacks. To the extent that they are adults and not under the care or protection of other individuals or agencies due to the state of their cognitive or motivational abilities, there is a *prima facie* case that they are not so vulnerable. Accordingly, the vulnerability objection raises the legitimate concern that some form of unjustified moral paternalism lurks behind it.

In short, if we consider simply the individual marketing program of PowerMaster, it is difficult to see that the three preceding objections justified the outcry against Heileman. Heileman was seeking to satisfy its customers. As noted above, none of the reported complaints came from them. Heileman was also seeking to enhance its own bottom line. But in doing so it was not engaged in fraud, deception or coercion. The marketing of Power-Master was not like other morally objectionable individual marketing programs which have used factually deceptive advertisements (e.g., some past shaving commercials), taken advantage of the target group's special vulnerabilities (e.g., certain television advertisements to children who are cognitively vulnerable), or led to unusual harm for the group targeted (e.g., Nestlé's infant formula promotions to Third World Mothers). Black inner-city residents are not obviously cognitively vulnerable and are not, in the use of malt liquor, uniformly faced with a single significant problem such as Third World Mothers are (viz., the care of their infants). As such, it is mistaken to think that PowerMaster's marketing campaign was morally offensive or objectionable in ways in which other such campaigns have been. From this perspective, then, it appears that Heileman could be said to be fulfilling its individual corporate responsibilities.

IV. ASSOCIATED GROUPS AND COLLECTIVE RESPONSIBILITY

So long as we remain simply at the level of the individual marketing campaign of PowerMaster, it is doubtful that we can grasp the basis upon which the complaints against PowerMaster might be justified. To do so, we must look to the social level

and the collection of marketing programs of which PowerMaster was simply one part. By pushing on the bounds within which other marketers had remained, PowerMaster was merely the spark which ignited a great deal of resentment which stemmed more generally from the group of malt liquor marketers coming into the inner-city from outside, aggressively marketing products which disproportionately harmed those in the inner-city (both those who consume the product and others), and creating marketing campaigns that took advantage of their vulnerabilities.

As such, this case might better be understood as one involving the collective responsibility of the group of marketers who target inner-city blacks rather than simply the individual responsibility of this or that marketer. By "collective responsibility" I refer to the responsibility which attaches to a group (or collective), rather than to the individual members of the group, even though it is only through the joint action (or inaction) of group members that a particular collective action or consequence results. The objections of the critics could then more plausibly be recast in the form that the *collection* of the marketer's campaigns was consuming or wasting public health or welfare understood in a twofold sense: first, as the lack of illness, violence, and crime, and, second, as the presence of a sense of individual self that is based on the genuine gratification of real needs. When the individual marketers of a group (e.g., of brewers) engage in their own individual marketing campaigns they may not necessarily cause significant harms—or if they do create harm, the customers may have willingly accepted certain levels of individual risk of harm. However, their efforts may collectively result in significant harms not consciously assumed by anyone.

Similarly, though the individual marketing efforts may not be significant enough to expose the vulnerabilities of individuals composing their market segment, their marketing efforts may collectively create a climate within which the vulnerabilities of those targeted may play a role in the collective effect of those marketing campaigns. Thus, it is not the presence of this or that billboard from PowerMaster which may be objectionable so much as the large total number of billboards in the inner-city which advertise alcohol and to which PowerMaster contributed. For example, it has been reported that "in Baltimore, 76 percent of the billboards located in low-income neighborhoods advertise alcohol and cigarettes; in middle and upper-income neighborhoods it is 20 percent" (*The Workbook,* 1991: 18). This "saturation advertising" may have an effect different from the effect of any single advertisement. Similarly, it is not PowerMaster's presence on the market as such, which raises moral questions. Rather, it is that alcohol marketers particularly target a group which not only buys " . . . more than half the cognac sold in the United States and . . . consume[s] more than one-third of all malt liquor . . ." (*The Workbook,* 1991: 18), but also disproportionately suffers health problems associated with alcohol. The connection between the amount of alcohol consumed and the alcohol related health problems is hardly coincidental. Further, if the level of alcohol consumption is significantly related to conditions of poverty and racism, and the consequent vulnerabilities people living in these conditions may suffer, then targeting such individuals may also be an instance of attempting to take unfair advantage of them.

Now to make this case, it must be allowed that individual persons are not the only ones capable of being responsible for the effects of their actions. A variety of arguments have been given, for example, that corporations can be morally responsible for their actions. These arguments need not be recited here since even if they were successful, as I think some of them are, the marketers who target inner-city blacks do not themselves constitute a corporation. Hence, a different kind of argument is needed.

Can there be subjects of responsibility other than individuals and corporations? Virginia Held has argued that under certain conditions random collections of individuals can be held morally responsible. She has argued that when it would be obvious to the reasonable person what a random collection of individuals ought to do and when the expected outcome of such an action is clearly favorable, then that random collection can be held morally responsible (Held, 1970: 476).

However, again the marketers of malt liquor to inner city blacks do not seem to fit this argument since they are not simply a random collection of individuals. According to Held, a random collection of individuals " . . . is a set of persons distinguishable by some characteristics from the set of all persons, but lacking a decision method for taking action that is distinguishable from such decisions methods, if there are any, as are possessed by all persons" (Held, 1970: 471). The examples she gives, "passengers on a train" and "pedestrians on a sidewalk," fit this definition but are also compatible with a stronger definition of a group of individuals than the one she offers. For example, her definition would include collections of individuals with no temporal, spatial or teleological connection. Clearly marketers of malt liquor to inner-city blacks constitute a group or collection of individuals in a stronger sense than Held's random collection of individuals.

Consequently, I shall speak of a group such as the marketers who target inner-city blacks as an associated group. Such groups are not corporations. Nor are they simply random collections of individuals (in Held's sense). They are groups in a weaker sense than corporations, but a stronger sense than a random collection of individuals. I shall argue that such groups may also be the subject of moral responsibility. This view is based upon the following characteristics of such groups.

First, an associated group is constituted by agents, whether they be corporate or personal, who share certain characteristics related to a common set of activities in which they engage. Thus, the marketers who target inner-city blacks share the characteristic that they (and no one else) target this particular market segment with malt-liquor. They engage in competition with each other to sell their malt-liquor according to the rules of the (relatively) free market. Though they themselves do not occupy some single spatial location, the focus of their activities, the ends they seek, and their temporal relatedness (i.e., marketing to the inner-city in the same time period) are clearly sufficient to constitute them as a group.

Second, though such associated groups do not have a formal decision-making structure which unites them, Stanley Bates has reminded us that "there are other group decision methods, [that] . . . are not formal . . ." (Bates, 1971:345). For example, the brewers presently at issue might engage in various forms of implicit bargaining. These informal and implicit group decision methods may involve unstructured discussions of topics of mutual interest, individual group member monitoring of the expectations and intuitions of other group members, and recognition of mutual understandings that may serve to coordinate the expectations of group members (cf. Schelling, 1963). Further, brewers in the United States have created the Beer Institute, which is their Washington-based trade group, one of whose main purposes is to protect "the market environment allowing for brewers to sell beer profitably, free from what the group views as unfair burdens imposed by government bodies."[1] The Beer Institute provides its members with a forum within which they may meet annually, engage in workshops, discuss issues of mutual concern, agree on which issues will be lobbied before Congress on their behalf and may voluntarily adopt an advertising code to guide their activities. Such informal decision-making methods amongst these brewers and suppliers are means whereby group decisions can be made.

Third, members of associated groups can be said to have other morally relevant characteristics which foster a group "solidarity" and thereby also unify them as a group capable of moral responsibility (cf. Feinberg, 1974: 234). These characteristics take three different forms. a) Members of the group share a community of interests. For example, they all wish to sell their products to inner-city blacks. They all seek to operate with minimal restrictions from the government on their marketing activities within the inner-city. They all are attempting to develop popular malt liquors. They all strive to keep the costs of their operations as low as possible. b) Further, they are joined by bonds of sentiment linked with their valuing of independent action and successfully selling their products. Though they may try to outcompete each other, they may also respect their competitors when they perform well in the marketplace. c) Finally, they can be said to share a common lot in that actions by one brewer that bring public condemnation upon that brewer may also extend public attention and condemnation to the other brewers as well—

as happened in the PowerMaster case. Similarly, regulations imposed on one typically also affect the others. Thus, heavy regulation tends to reduce all their profits, whereas light regulation tends to have the opposite effect.

The unity or solidarity constituted by the preceding characteristics among the various marketers would be openly manifested, for example, if the government were to try to deny them all access to the inner-city market segment. In such a circumstance, they would openly resist, take the government to court, and protest with united voice against the injustice done to them, both individually and as a group. In this sense, there is (at the least) a latent sense of solidarity among such marketers (cf. May, 1987: 37). When they act, then each acts in solidarity with the others and each does those things which accord with the kinds of actions fellow group members are inclined to take. All this may occur without the need for votes being taken or explicit directions given among the various brewers (cf. May, 1987:40).

Fourth, associated groups like inner-city marketers can investigate the harms or benefits that their products and marketing programs jointly do to those who are targeted. They can also study the overall effects of their own individual efforts. They could do so both as individual businesses and as a group. In the latter case, the Beer Institute might undertake such studies. Similarly, these marketers might jointly commission some other organization to study these effects. In short, they are capable both as individual businesses and as a group, of receiving notice as to the effects of their individual and collective actions. In short, communication amongst the group members is possible.

Finally, associated groups can modify their activities. They are not simply inevitably or necessarily trapped into acting certain ways. For example, the inner-city malt liquor marketers might voluntarily reduce the number of billboards they use within the inner-city. They might not advertise in certain settings or in certain forms of media. They might not use certain appeals, e.g., touting the high alcoholic content of their products. As such, they could take actions to prevent the harms or injustices of which they are accused. At present brewers subscribe to an advertising code of ethics which the Beer Institute makes available and has recently updated. The Beer Institute might even lobby the government on behalf of this group for certain limitations on marketing programs so as to eliminate moral objections raised against such marketing programs.

The preceding indicates that this group can act: it has set up the Beer Institute; it may react with unanimity against new regulations; it may defend the actions of its members; it may investigate the effects its group members have on those market segments which they have targeted. It does not act as a group in marketing particular malt liquors. The law prevents such collective actions. However, marketing malt liquor to particular groups is an action which this group may approve or disapprove. The group lobbies Congress on behalf of its members' interests. The group has organized itself such that through development and support of the Beer Institute its interests are protected. There is no reason, then, that such a group may not also be morally responsible for the overall consequences of its members' marketing.

Does the preceding argument suggest that the group of marketers would run afoul of concerns about restraint of trade? The above argument need not imply that inner-city marketers are always a group capable of moral action and responsibility— only that under certain circumstances it could be. Hence, the above argument does not suggest that this group constitutes anything like a cartel. In addition, the above argument does not suggest that marketers agree on pricing formulas, on reserving certain distributional areas for this or that marketer, or similar actions which would constitute classic forms of restraint of trade. Further, the preceding argument leaves open what mechanisms might be legally used whereby these moral responsibilities are discharged. It might be that individual marketers voluntarily agree to such actions as they presently do with their advertising code. On the other hand, they might collectively appeal to the government to approve certain general conditions such that the playing field within which they compete would be altered to alleviate moral objections to their marketing campaigns, but would remain relatively level in comparison with their situations prior to the imposition of such conditions.

If the preceding is correct, then given the assumption that basic items of public welfare (e.g., health, safety, decision-making abilities, etc.) ought not to be harmed, two important conclusions follow regarding the marketing of malt liquor to inner-city blacks.

First, malt liquor marketers have a collective responsibility to monitor the effects of their activities and to ensure that they jointly do not unnecessarily cause harm to those they target or trade on their vulnerabilities. Assuming that malt liquor does harm inner-city blacks and that the marketing programs through which malt liquor is sold to this market segment play some significant causal role in creating this harm, then they have an obligation to alter their marketing to inner-city blacks in such a way that the vulnerabilities of inner-city blacks are not exploited and that unnecessary harm does not come to them.

Second, where the collective consequences of individual marketing efforts create the harms claimed for alcohol among inner-city blacks, and marketers as a group do not discharge the preceding collective responsibility, then there is a need for some agency outside those individual marketers to oversee or regulate their actions. Obviously, one form this may take is that of an industry or professional oversight committee; another form might be that of government intervention.

V. IMPLICATIONS AND CONCLUSION

The implications of this social approach to the PowerMaster case are significant:

First, marketers cannot simply look at their own individual marketing campaigns to judge their moral level. Instead, they must also look at their campaign within the context of all the marketing campaigns which target the market segment at which they are aiming. This accords with Garrett Hardin's suggestion that "the morality of an act is a function of the state of the system at the time it is performed" (Hardin, 1968: 1245; emphasis omitted). It is possible that marketers could fulfill their individual responsibilities but not their collective responsibilities.

Second, when the products targeted at particular market segments cause consumers to suffer disproportionately in comparison with other comparable market segments, marketers must determine the role which their products and marketing programs play in this situation. If they play a contributory role, they should (both individually and as a group) consider measures to reduce the harm produced. One means of doing this is to voluntarily restrict or modify their appeals to that market segment. In the present case, industry organizations such as The Beer Institute might play a leading role in identifying problems and recommending countermeasures. Otherwise when harm occurs disproportionately to a market segment, or members of that segment are especially vulnerable, outside oversight and regulation may be appropriate.

Third, marketers have a joint or collective responsibility to the entire market segment they target, not simply for the effects of their own products and marketing campaigns, but more generally for the effects of the combined marketing which is being done to that segment. The protests against PowerMaster are best understood against the background of this collective responsibility.

Thus, when we think of responsibility in the market we must look beyond simply the responsibility of individual agents (be they personal or corporate). We must look to the responsibility of groups of persons as well as groups of corporations. Such responsibility is not personal or individual, but collective. Examination of the case of PowerMaster helps us to see this.

Accordingly, the preceding analysis helps to explain both why PowerMaster was attacked as it was and also why it seemed simply to be doing what other marketers had previously done. Further, it helps us to understand the circumstances under which the above objections against marketing malt liquor to inner-city blacks might be justified. However, much more analysis of this form of collective harm and the vulnerability which is said to characterize inner-city blacks needs to be undertaken.

Finally, it should be emphasized that this paper advocates recognition of a new subject of moral responsibility in the market. Heretofore, moral responsibility has been attributed to individuals and corporations. Random collections of individuals have little applicability in business ethics. However the concept of associated groups and their collective responsibility has not been previously explored. It adds a new dimension to talk about responsibility within current discussions in business ethics.

NOTE

1. "The Beer Institute," *Encyclopedia of Associations,* Carolyn A. Fischer and Carol A. Schwartz (eds.), vol. 1 (New York: Gale Research Inc., 1995), p. 27.

BIBLIOGRAPHY

Bates, Stanley (1971), "The Responsibility of 'Random Collections'," *Ethics,* 81, 343–349.

Benn, Stanley I. (1967), "Freedom and Persuasion," *The Australasian Journal of Philosophy,* 45, 259–275.

Brown, Jesse W. (1992), "Marketing Exploitation," *Business and Society Review,* Issue 83 (Fall), p. 17.

Colford, Steven W. and Teinowitz, Ira (1991), "Malt liquor 'power' failure," *Advertising Age,* July 1, pp. 1, 29.

Farhi, Paul (1991), "Surgeon General Hits New Malt Liquor's Name, Ads," *Washington Post,* June 26, pp. A1, A4.

Feinberg, Joel (1974), "Collective Responsibility," in *Doing & Deserving.* Princeton: Princeton University Press, pp. 222–251.

Fortune (1991), "Selling Sin to Blacks," October 21, p. 100.

Freedman, Alix (1991a), "Potent, New Heileman Malt is Brewing Fierce Industry and Social Criticism," *Wall Street Journal,* June 17, pp. B1, B4.

———(1991b), "Heileman, Under Pressure, Scuttles PowerMaster Malt," *Wall Street Journal,* July 5, pp. B1, B3.

Hardin, Garrett (1968), "The Tragedy of the Commons," *Science,* 162, 1243–1248.

Held, Virginia (1970), "Can a Random Collection of Individuals Be Morally Responsible?," *The Journal of Philosophy,* 67, 471–481.

Horovitz, Bruce (1991), "Brewer Faces Boycott Over Marketing of Potent Malt Liquor," *L. A. Times,* June 25, pp. D1, D6.

Lacey, Marc (1992), "Marketing of Malt Liquor Fuels Debate," *L. A. Times,* December 15, pp. A32, A34.

May, Larry (1987), *The Morality of Groups*. Notre Dame: University of Notre Dame Press.

Milloy, Courland (1991), "Race, Beer Don't Mix," *The Washington Post*, July 9, p. B3.

New York Times, The (1991), "The Threat of Power-Master," July 1, p. A12.

Schelling, Thomas (1963), *The Strategy of Conflict*. New York: Oxford University Press.

Teinowitz, Ira and Colford, Steven W. (1991), "Targeting Woes in PowerMaster Wake," *Advertising Age*, July 8, 1991, p. 35.

"The Beer Institute," *Encyclopedia of Associations* (1995), Carolyn A. Fischer and Carol A. Schwartz (eds.), vol. 1, New York: Gale Research Inc.

Workbook, The (1991), "Marketing Booze to Blacks," Spring, 16, 18–19.

Zimmerman, Michael J. (1985), "Sharing Responsibility," *American Philosophical Quarterly*, 22, 115–122.

A Moral Evaluation of Sales Practices

David M. Holley
Department of Philosophy and Religion,
University of Southern Mississippi

In this paper I will attempt to develop a framework for evaluating the morality of various sales practices. Although I recognize that much of the salesforce in companies is occupied exclusively or primarily with sales to other businesses, my discussion will focus on sales to the individual consumer. Most of what I say should apply to any type of sales activity, but the moral issues arise most clearly in cases in which a consumer may or may not be very sophisticated in evaluating and responding to a sales presentation.

My approach will be to consider first the context of sales activities, a market system of production and distribution. Since such a system is generally justified on teleological grounds, I describe several conditions for its successful achievement of key goals. Immoral sales practices are analyzed as attempts to undermine these conditions.

I

The primary justification for a market system is that it provides an efficient procedure for meeting people's needs and desires for goods and services.[1] This appeal to economic benefits can be elaborated in great detail, but at root it involves the claim that people will efficiently serve each other's needs if they are allowed to engage in voluntary exchanges.

A crucial feature of this argument is the condition that the exchange be voluntary. Assuming that individuals know best how to benefit themselves and that they will act to achieve such benefits, voluntary exchange can be expected to serve both parties. On the other hand, if the exchanges are not made voluntarily, we have no basis for expecting mutually beneficial results. To the extent that mutual benefit does not occur, the system will lack efficiency as a means for the satisfaction of needs and desires. Hence, this justification presupposes that conditions necessary for the occurrence of voluntary exchange are ordinarily met.

What are these conditions? For simplicity's sake, let us deal only with the kind of exchange involving a payment of money for some product or service. We can call the person providing the product the *seller* and the person making the monetary payment the *buyer*. I suggest that voluntary exchange occurs only if the following conditions are met:

1. Both buyer and seller understand what they are giving up and what they are receiving in return.
2. Neither buyer nor seller is compelled to enter into the exchange as a result of coercion, severely restricted alternatives, or other constraints on the ability to choose.
3. Both buyer and seller are able at the time of the exchange to make rational judgments about its costs and benefits.

Excerpted from "A Moral Evaluation of Sales Practices" by David M. Holley. *Business and Professional Ethics Journal*, Vol: 5, No. 1, circa 1987, pp. 3–21. Copyright © David M. Holley. Reprinted by permission of the author.

I will refer to these three conditions as the knowledge, noncompulsion, and rationality conditions, respectively.[2] If the parties are uninformed, it is possible that an exchange might accidentally turn out to benefit them. But given the lack of information, they would not be in a position to make a rational judgment about their benefit, and we cannot reasonably expect beneficial results as a matter of course in such circumstances. Similarly, if the exchange is made under compulsion, then the judgment of personal benefit is not the basis of the exchange. It is possible for someone to be forced or manipulated into an arrangement that is in fact beneficial. But there is little reason to think that typical or likely.[3]

It should be clear that all three conditions are subject to degrees of fulfillment. For example, the parties may understand certain things about the exchange but not others. Let us posit a theoretical situation in which both parties are fully informed, fully rational, and enter into the exchange entirely of their own volition. I will call this an *ideal exchange.* In actual practice there is virtually always some divergence from the ideal. Knowledge can be more or less adequate. Individuals can be subject to various irrational influences. There can be borderline cases of external constraints. Nevertheless, we can often judge when a particular exchange was adequately informed, rational, and free from compulsion. Even when conditions are not ideal, we may still have an *acceptable exchange.*

With these concepts in mind, let us consider the obligations of sales personnel. I suggest that the primary duty of salespeople to customers is to avoid undermining the conditions of acceptable exchange. It is possible by act or omission to create a situation in which the customer is not sufficiently knowledgeable about what the exchange involves. It is also possible to influence the customer in ways that short-circuit the rational decision-making process. To behave in such ways is to undermine the conditions that are presupposed in teleological justifications of the market system. Of course, an isolated act is not sufficient to destroy the benefits of the system. But the moral acceptability of the system may become questionable if the conditions of acceptable exchange are widely abused. The indi-vidual who attempts to gain personally by undermining these conditions does that which, if commonly practiced, would produce a very different system from the one that supposedly provides moral legitimacy to that individual's activities.

II

If a mutually beneficial exchange is to be expected, the parties involved must be adequately informed about what they are giving up and what they are receiving. In most cases this should create no great problem for the seller,[4] but what about the buyer? How is she to obtain the information needed? One answer is that the buyer is responsible for doing whatever investigation is necessary to acquire the information. The medieval principle of *caveat emptor* encouraged buyers to take responsibility for examining a purchase thoroughly to determine whether it had any hidden flaws. If the buyer failed to find defects, that meant that due caution had not been exercised.

If it were always relatively easy to discover defects by examination, then this principle might be an efficient method of guaranteeing mutual satisfaction. Sometimes, however, even lengthy investigation would not disclose what the buyer wants to know. With products of great complexity, the expertise needed for an adequate examination may be beyond what could reasonably be expected of most consumers. Even relatively simple products can have hidden flaws that most people would not discover until after the purchase, and to have the responsibility for closely examining every purchase would involve a considerable amount of a highly treasured modern commodity, the buyer's time. Furthermore, many exchange situations in our context involve products that cannot be examined in this way—goods that will be delivered at a later time or sent through the mail, for example. Finally, even if we assume that most buyers, by exercising enough caution, can protect their interests, the system of *caveat emptor* would take advantage of those least able to watch out for themselves. It would in effect justify mistreatment of a few for a rather questionable benefit.

In practice the buyer almost always relies on the seller for some information, and if mutually beneficial exchanges are to be expected, the information needs to meet certain standards of both quality and quantity. With regard to quality, the information provided should not be deceptive. This would include not only direct lies but also truths that are intended to mislead the buyer. Consider the following examples:

1. An aluminum siding salesperson tells customers that they will receive "bargain factory prices" for letting their homes be used as models in a new advertising campaign. Prospective customers will be brought to view the houses, and a commission of $100 will be paid for each sale that results. In fact, the price paid is well above market rates, the workmanship and materials are substandard, and no one is ever brought by to see the houses.[5]
2. A used car salesperson turns back the odometer reading on automobiles by an average of 25,000 to 30,000 miles per car. If customers ask whether the reading is correct, the salesperson replies that it is illegal to alter odometer readings.
3. A salesperson at a piano store tells an interested customer that the "special sale" will be good only through that evening. She neglects to mention that another "special sale" will begin the next day.
4. A telephone salesperson tells people who answer the phone that they have been selected to receive a free gift, a brand new freezer. All they have to do is buy a year's subscription to a food plan.
5. A salesperson for a diet system proclaims that under this revolutionary new plan the pounds will melt right off. The system is described as a scientific advance that makes dieting easy. In fact, the system is a low-calorie diet composed of foods and liquids that are packaged under the company name but are no different from standard grocery store items.

The possibilities are endless, and whether or not a lie is involved, each case illustrates a salesperson's attempt to get a customer to believe something that is false in order to make the sale. It might be pointed out that these kinds of practices would not deceive a sophisticated consumer. Per-

haps so, but whether they are always successful deceptions is not the issue. They are attempts to mislead the customer, and given that the consumer must often rely on information furnished by the salesperson, they are attempts to subvert the conditions under which mutually beneficial exchange can be expected. The salesperson attempts to use misinformation as a basis for customer judgment rather than allowing that judgment to be based on accurate beliefs. Furthermore, if these kinds of practices were not successful fairly often, they would probably not be used.

In the aluminum siding case, the customer is led to believe that there will be a discount in exchange for a kind of service, allowing the house to be viewed by prospective customers. This leaves the impression both that the job done will be of high quality and that the price paid will be offset by commissions. The car salesperson alters the product in order to suggest false information about the extent of its use. With such information, the customer is not able to judge accurately the value of the car. The misleading reply to inquiries is not substantially different from a direct lie. The piano salesperson deceives the customer about how long the product will be obtainable at a discount price. In this case the deception occurs through an omission. The telephone solicitor tries to give the impression that there has been a contest of some sort and that the freezer is a prize. In this way, the nature of the exchange is obscured.

The diet-system case raises questions about how to distinguish legitimate "puffery" from deception. Obviously, the matter will depend to some extent on how gullible we conceive the customer to be. As described, the case surely involves an attempt to get the customer to believe that dieting will be easier under this system and that what is being promoted is the result of some new scientific discovery. If there were no prospect that a customer would be likely to believe this, we would probably not think the technique deceptive. But in fact a number of individuals are deceived by claims of this type.

Some writers have defended the use of deceptive practices in business contexts on the grounds that there are specific rules applying to these contexts that differ from the standards appropriate in other contexts. It is argued, for example, that deception is standard practice, understood by all participants as something to be expected and, therefore, harmless, or that it is a means of self-defense justified by pressures of the competitive context.[6] To the extent that claims about widespread practice are true, people who know what is going on may be able to minimize personal losses, but that is hardly a justification of the practice. If I know that many people have installed devices in their cars that can come out and puncture the tires of the car next to them, that may help keep me from falling victim, but it does not make the practice harmless. Even if no one is victimized, it becomes necessary to take extra precautions, introducing a significant disutility into driving conditions. Analogously, widespread deception in business debases the currency of language, making business communication less efficient and more cumbersome.

More importantly, however, people are victimized by deceptive practices, and the fact that some may be shrewd enough to see through clouds of misinformation does not alter the deceptive intent. Whatever may be said with regard to appropriate behavior among people who "know the rules," it is clear that many buyers are not aware of having entered into some special domain where deception is allowed. Even if this is naive, it does not provide a moral justification for subverting those individuals' capacity for making a reasoned choice.

Only a few people would defend the moral justifiability of deceptive sales practices. However, there may be room for much more disagreement with regard to how much information a salesperson is obligated to provide. In rejecting the principle of *caveat emptor,* I have suggested that there are pragmatic reasons for expecting the seller to communicate some information about the product. But how much? When is it morally culpable to withhold information? Consider the following cases:

1. An automobile dealer has bought a number of cars from another state. Although they appear to be new or slightly used, these cars have been involved in a major flood and were sold by the previous dealer at a discount rate. The salesperson knows the history of the cars and does not mention it to customers.

2. A salesperson for an encyclopedia company never mentions the total price of a set unless he has to. Instead he emphasizes the low monthly payment involved.

3. A real estate agent knows that one reason the couple selling a house with her company want to move is that the neighbors often have loud parties and neighborhood children have committed minor acts of vandalism. The agent makes no mention of this to prospective customers.

4. An admissions officer for a private college speaks enthusiastically about the advantages of the school. He does not mention the fact that the school is not accredited.

5. A prospective retirement home resident is under the impression that a particular retirement home is affiliated with a certain church. He makes it known that this is one of the features he finds attractive about the home. Though the belief is false, the recruiters for the home make no attempt to correct the misunderstanding.

In all these cases the prospective buyer lacks some piece of knowledge that might be relevant to the decision to buy. The conditions for ideal exchange are not met. Perhaps, however, there can be an acceptable exchange. Whether or not this is the case depends on whether the buyer has adequate information to decide if the purchase would be beneficial. In the case of the flood-damaged autos, there is information relevant to evaluating the worth of the car that the customer could not be expected to know unless informed by the seller. If this information is not revealed, the buyer will not have adequate knowledge to make a reasonable judgment. Determining exactly how much information needs to be provided is not always clear-cut. We must in general rely on our assessments of what a reasonable person would want to know. As a practical guide, a salesperson might consider, "What would I want to know if I were considering buying this product?"

Surely a reasonable person would want to know the total price of a product. Hence the encyclopedia salesperson who omits this total is not providing adequate information. The salesperson may object that this information could be inferred from other information about the monthly payment, length of term, and interest rate. But if the intention is not to have the customer act without knowing the full price, then why shouldn't it be provided directly? The admissions officer's failure to mention that the school is unaccredited also seems unacceptable when we consider what a reasonable person would want to know. There are some people who would consider this a plus, since they are suspicious about accrediting agencies imposing some alien standards (e.g., standards that conflict with religious views). But regardless of how one evaluates the fact, most people would judge it to be important for making a decision.

The real estate case is more puzzling. Most real estate agents would not reveal the kind of information described, and would not feel they had violated any moral duties in failing to do so. Clearly, many prospective customers would want to be informed about such problems. However, in most cases failing to know these facts would not be of crucial importance. We have a case of borderline information. It would be known by all parties to an ideal exchange, but we can have an acceptable exchange even if the buyer is unaware of it. Failure to inform the customer of these facts is not like failing to inform the customer that the house is on the site of a hazardous waste dump or that a major freeway will soon be adjacent to the property.

It is possible to alter the case in such a way that the information should be revealed or at least the buyer should be directed another way. Suppose the buyer makes it clear that his primary goal is to live in a quiet neighborhood where he will be undisturbed. The "borderline" information now becomes more central to the customer's decision. Notice that thinking in these terms moves us away from the general standard of what a reasonable person would want to know to the more specific standard of what is relevant given the criteria of this individual. In most cases, however, I think that a salesperson would be justified in operating under general "reasonable person" standards until particular deviations become apparent.[7]

The case of the prospective retirement home resident is a good example of how the particular criteria of the customer might assume great importance. If the recruiters, knowing what they know about this man's religious preferences, allow him to make his decision on the basis of a false as-

sumption, they will have failed to support the conditions of acceptable exchange. It doesn't really matter that the misunderstanding was not caused by the salespeople. Their allowing it to be part of the basis for a decision borders on deception. If the misunderstanding was not on a matter of central importance to the individual's evaluation, they might have had no obligation to correct it. But the case described is not of that sort.

Besides providing nondeceptive and relatively complete information, salespeople may be obligated to make sure that their communications are understandable. Sales presentations containing technical information that is likely to be misunderstood are morally questionable. However, it would be unrealistic to expect all presentations to be immune to misunderstanding. The salesperson is probably justified in developing presentations that would be intelligible to the average consumer of the product he or she is selling and making adjustments in cases where it is clear that misunderstanding has occurred.

III

The condition of uncompelled exchange distinguishes business dealings from other kinds of exchanges. In the standard business arrangement, neither party is forced to enter the negotiations. A threat of harm would transform the situation to something other than a purely business arrangement. Coercion is not the only kind of compulsion, however. Suppose I have access to only one producer of food. I arrange to buy food from this producer, but given my great need for food and the absence of alternatives, the seller is able to dictate the terms. In one sense I choose to make the deal, but the voluntariness of my choice is limited by the absence of alternatives.

Ordinarily, the individual salesperson will not have the power to take away the buyer's alternatives. However, a clever salesperson can sometimes make it seem as if options are very limited and can use the customer's ignorance to produce the same effect. For example, imagine an individual who begins to look for a particular item at a local store. The salesperson extolls the line carried by his store, warns of the deficiencies of alternative brands, and warns about the dishonesty of competitors, in contrast to his store's reliability. With a convincing presentation, a customer might easily perceive the options to be very limited. Whether or not the technique is questionable may depend on the accuracy of the perception. If the salesperson is attempting to take away a legitimate alternative, that is an attempt to undermine the customer's voluntary choice.

Another way the condition of uncompelled choice might be subverted is by involving a customer in a purchase without allowing her to notice what is happening. This would include opening techniques that disguise the purpose of the encounter so there can be no immediate refusal. The customer is led to believe that the interview is about a contest or a survey or an opportunity to make money. Not until the end does it become apparent that this is an attempt to sell something, and occasionally if the presentation is smooth enough, some buyers can be virtually unaware that they have bought anything. Obviously, there can be degrees of revelation, and not every approach that involves initial disguise of certain elements that might provoke an immediate rejection is morally questionable. But there are enough clear cases in which the intention is to get around, as much as possible, the voluntary choice of the customer. Consider the following examples:

1. A seller of children's books gains entrance to houses by claiming to be conducting an educational survey. He does indeed ask several "survey" questions, but he uses these to qualify potential customers for his product.
2. A salesperson alludes to recent accidents involving explosions of furnaces and, leaving the impression of having some official government status, offers to do a free safety inspection. She almost always discovers a "major problem" and offers to sell a replacement furnace.
3. A man receives a number of unsolicited books and magazines through the mail. Then he is sent a bill and later letters warning of damage to his credit rating if he does not pay.

These are examples of the many variations on attempts to involve customers in exchanges without letting them know what is happening. The first two cases involve deceptions about the purpose of the encounter. Though they resemble cases discussed earlier that involved deception about the nature or price of a product, here the salesperson uses misinformation as a means of limiting the customer's range of choice. The customer does not consciously choose to listen to a sales presentation but finds that this is what is happening. Some psychological research suggests that when people do something that appears to commit them to a course of action, even without consciously choosing to do so, they will tend to act as if such a choice had been made in order to minimize cognitive dissonance. Hence, if a salesperson successfully involves the customer in considering a purchase, the customer may feel committed to give serious thought to the matter. The third case is an attempt to get the customer to believe that an obligation has been incurred. In variations on this technique, merchandise is mailed to a deceased person to make relatives believe that some payment is owed. In each case, an effort is made to force the consumer to choose from an excessively limited range of options.

IV

How can a salesperson subvert the rationality condition? Perhaps the most common way is to appeal to emotional reactions that cloud an individual's perception of relevant considerations. Consider the following cases:

1. A man's wife has recently died in a tragic accident. The funeral director plays upon the husband's love for his wife and to some extent his guilt about her death to get him to purchase a very expensive funeral.
2. A socially insecure young woman has bought a series of dance lessons from a local studio. During the lessons, an attractive male instructor constantly compliments her on her poise and natural ability and tries to persuade her to sign up for more lessons.[8]
3. A life insurance salesperson emphasizes to a prospect the importance of providing for his family in the event of his death. The salesperson tells several stories about people who put off this kind of preparation.
4. A dress salesperson typically tells customers how fashionable they look in a certain dress.

Her stock comments also include pointing out that a dress is slimming or sexy or "looks great on you."

5. A furniture salesperson regularly tells customers that a piece of furniture is the last one in stock and that another customer recently showed great interest in it. He sometimes adds that it may not be possible to get any more like it from the factory.

These cases remind us that emotions can be important motivators. It is not surprising that salespeople appeal to them in attempting to get the customer to make a purchase. In certain cases the appeal seems perfectly legitimate. When the life insurance salesperson tries to arouse the customer's fear and urges preparation, it may be a legitimate way to get the customer to consider something that is worth considering. Of course, the fact that the fear is aroused by one who sells life insurance may obscure to the customer the range of alternative possibilities in preparing financially for the future. But the fact that an emotion is aroused need not make the appeal morally objectionable.

If the appeal of the dress salesperson seems more questionable, this is probably because we are not as convinced of the objective importance of appearing fashionable, or perhaps because repeated observations of this kind are often insincere. But if we assume that the salesperson is giving an honest opinion about how the dress looks on a customer, it may provide some input for the individual who has a desire to achieve a particular effect. The fact that such remarks appeal to one's vanity or ambition does not in itself make the appeal unacceptable.

The furniture salesperson's warnings are clearly calculated to create some anxiety about the prospect of losing the chance to buy a particular item unless immediate action is taken. If the warnings are factually based, they would not be irrelevant to the decision to buy. Clearly, one might act impulsively or hastily when under the spell of such thoughts, but the salesperson cannot be faulted for pointing out relevant considerations.

The case of the funeral director is somewhat different. Here there is a real question of what

benefit is to be gained by choosing a more expensive funeral package. For most people, minimizing what is spent on the funeral would be a rational choice, but at a time of emotional vulnerability it can be made to look as if this means depriving the loved one or the family of some great benefit. Even if the funeral director makes nothing but true statements, they can be put into a form designed to arouse emotions that will lessen the possibility of a rational decision being reached.

The dance studio case is similar in that a weakness is being played upon. The woman's insecurity makes her vulnerable to flattery and attention, and this creates the kind of situation in which others can take advantage of her. Perhaps the dance lessons fulfill some need, but the appeal to her vanity easily becomes a tool to manipulate her into doing what the instructor wants.

The key to distinguishing between legitimate and illegitimate emotional appeals lies in whether the appeal clouds one's ability to make a decision based on genuine satisfaction of needs and desires. Our judgment about whether this happens in a particular case will depend in part on whether we think the purchase likely to benefit the customer. The more questionable the benefits, the more an emotional appeal looks like manipulation rather than persuasion. When questionable benefits are combined with some special vulnerability on the part of the consumer, the use of the emotional appeal appears even more suspect.

V

I have attempted to provide a framework for evaluating the morality of a number of different types of sales practices. The framework is based on conditions for mutually beneficial exchange and ultimately for an efficient satisfaction of economic needs and desires. An inevitable question is whether this kind of evaluation is of any practical importance.

If we set before ourselves the ideal of a knowledgeable, unforced, and rational decision on the part of a customer, it is not difficult to see how some types of practices would interfere with this process. We must, of course, be careful not to set the standards too high. A customer may be partially but adequately informed to judge a purchase's potential benefits. A decision may be affected by nonrational and even irrational factors and yet still be rational enough in terms of being plausibly related to the individual's desires and needs. There may be borderline cases in which it is not clear whether acting in a particular way would be morally required or simply overscrupulous, but that is not an objection to this approach, only a recognition of a feature of morality itself.[9]

NOTES

1. The classic statement of the argument from economic benefits is found in Adam Smith, *The Wealth of Nations* (1776) (London: Methusen and Co. Ltd., 1930). Modern proponents of this argument include Ludwig von Mises, Friedrich von Hayek, and Milton Friedman.

2. One very clear analysis of voluntariness making use of these conditions may be found in John Hospers' *Human Conduct: Problems of Ethics,* 2nd ed. (New York: Harcourt Brace Jovanovich, 1982), pp. 385–388.

3. I will refer to the three conditions indifferently as conditions for voluntary exchange or conditions for mutually beneficial exchange. By the latter designation I do not mean to suggest that they are either necessary or sufficient conditions for the occurrence of mutual benefit, but that they are conditions for the reasonable expectation of mutual benefit.

4. There are cases, however, in which the buyer knows more about a product than the seller. For example, suppose Cornell has found out that land Fredonia owns contains minerals that make it twice as valuable as Fredonia thinks. The symmetry of my conditions would lead me to conclude that Cornell should give Fredonia the relevant information unless perhaps Fredonia's failure to know was the result of some culpable negligence.

5. This case is described in Warren Magnuson and Jean Carper, *The Dark Side of the Market-Place* (Englewood Cliffs, N.J.: Prentice Hall, 1968). pp. 3–4.

6. Albert Carr, "Is Business Bluffing Ethical?" *Harvard Business Review* 46 (January–February 1968): 143–153. See also Thomas L. Carson, Richard E. Wokutch, and Kent F. Murrmann, "Bluffing in Labor Negotiations: Legal and Ethical Issues," *Journal of Business Ethics* 1 (1982): 13–22.

7. My reference to a reasonable person standard should not be confused with the issue facing the FTC of whether to evaluate advertising by the reasonable consumer or ignorant consumer standard as described in Ivan Preston, "Reasonable Consumer or Ignorant Consumer: How the FTC Decides," *Journal of Consumer Affairs* 8 (Winter 1974): 131–143. There the primary issue is with regard to whom the government should protect from claims that might be misunderstood. My concern here is with determining what amount of information is necessary for informed judgment. In general I suggest that a salesperson should begin with the assumption that information a reasonable consumer would regard as important needs to be revealed and that when special interests and concerns of the consumer come to light they may make further revelations necessary. This approach parallels the one taken by Tom Beauchamp and James Childress regarding the information that a physician needs to provide to obtain informed consent. See their *Principles of Biomedical Ethics,* 2nd ed. (New York: Oxford University Press, 1983), pp. 74–79.

8. This is adapted from a court case quoted in Braybrooke, pp. 68–70.

9. This paper was written during a sabbatical leave from Friends University at the Center for the Study of Values, University of Delaware. I wish to thank Friends University for the leave and Dr. Norman Bowie for his hospitality during my stay at the Center.

The Ethics of Consumer Protection[1]

Manuel Velasquez
The Dirksen Professor of Business Ethics, Management Department, Santa Clara University

INTRODUCTION

Consider the nature of the consumer products discussed below:

In 1996 the Food and Drug Administration reported that tobacco products were killing 400,000 Americans each year, more than acquired immune deficiency syndrome (AIDS), alcohol, car accidents,

---

Source: From *Business Ethics: Concepts and Cases,* 4th ed. by Velasquez, Manuel, © 1993. Reprinted by permission of Prentice-Hall, Inc., Upper Saddle River, NJ.

murders, suicides, illegal drugs, and fires *combined.* As their traditional markets have stopped growing, American cigarette companies—Phillip Morris, R. J. Reynolds, and American Brands—have focused on new populations. In December 1991, the *Journal of the American Medical Association* published studies showing that R. J. Reynold's Joe Camel cartoon cigarette campaign was strongly attracting children and adolescents to smoking.[2] Two other groups have been targeted by tobacco marketing campaigns: minorities and women. Minority groups in inner-city neighborhoods have lower access to health education, are less aware of the risks of smoking, are a rapidly growing population, and are particularly vulnerable and responsive to targeted advertising. Women, with greater independence and purchasing power than ever before, are the fastest growing group of smokers, and among them lung cancer has now overtaken breast cancer as the leading cause of death from cancer.

In October 1996, the Environmental Protection Agency conducted tests of several common lawn herbicides containing toxic chemicals and found that after outdoor spraying on house lawns, the contamination levels inside homes were between ten and one hundred times the levels on the lawn.[3] Brought into the home by foot traffic and pets, the chemicals were quickly and invisibly smeared over floors and carpets. Babies and children playing or crawling on contaminated carpets and floors picked up the chemicals on their hands, clothes, and toys, and transferred them to their mouths.

After reviewing several cases in which BIC Corporation lighters were alleged to have injured children and others, the U.S. Court of Appeals, Third Circuit, ruled in 1992 that "on balance, the high social value placed on the safety of people and property threatened by childplay fires, the high gravity of risk, the considerable probability of risk, and the likelihood of a reasonably available alternative, may outweigh BIC's interest in producing its lighters without child-proofing features." In a related case, a woman, Ethel Smith, flicked on a Bic Corporation lighter to light her cigarette. It exploded in her hands, killing her and severely burning her husband. Earlier, Cynthia Littlejohn suffered severe burns about her torso that required seven painful skin grafts when a Bic lighter in her pocket spontaneously ignited and enveloped her in flames.[4] The company later confessed that its own tests showed that 1.2 percent of its lighters were faulty. Experts claimed that the defects could have been corrected for "a couple of pennies a lighter." Some 200 people a year, half of them children, are killed in lighter-related injuries.[5]

Americans are exposed daily to astonishingly high levels of risk from the use of consumer products. In 1995 more than 19 million people suffered serious accidental injuries and 93,000 were killed, more than half of them in accidents involving consumer products.[6] After declining by more than 20 percent between 1979 and 1992 (when deaths reached a 68-year low of 86,777), accidental deaths rose for three straight years in 1993, 1994, and 1995. The National Safety Council estimated that the total costs of these injuries in 1995 was $435 billion.

But product injuries make up only one category of costs imposed on unwary consumers. Consumers must also bear the costs of deceptive selling practices, of shoddy product construction, of products that immediately break down, and of warranties that are not honored. For example, several years ago, the engine of Martha and George Rose's Chevrolet station wagon began missing and white smoke poured out of the tailpipe as she drove it six miles to work.[7] Two non-Chevrolet mechanics who then checked the car later testified that the radiator and cooling system were "in satisfactory condition," that the radiator "was not boiling over," and that the temperature light on the dashboard "was not burning." Upon taking the engine apart, a mechanic found that a hairline crack in the engine block had allowed water to enter the cylinder head, meaning that the car would need an expensive new engine. The engine was still under a "5-year or 50,000-mile" warranty, so the Roses thought the Chevrolet division of General Motors would bear the large costs of repairing what they concluded was an inherently defective engine block. However, when a Chevrolet service manager examined the dismantled car, he insisted that the problem was that the radiator thermostat had stuck shut so no coolant had reached the engine. Since the thermostat was only under a "12-month or 12,000-miles" warranty that had by then expired, and since, the Chevrolet manager claimed, the faulty thermostat had caused the engine to overheat and the engine block to crack, Chevrolet had no responsibility under the warranty. Moreover, the car had been torn down and worked on by unauthorized mechanics. Although the Roses pointed out that the other mechanics had found no evidence of overheating and that no Chevrolet mechanic had suggested replacing the thermostat at any of their regular maintenance servicings, the General Motors field manager and his superiors, both in New Orleans and in Detroit, refused to honor the warranty. Without the engine, the car that General Motors had sold them was now worth only 10 percent of what they had originally paid for it. Because they could not afford an attorney for a trial they might lose, the Roses could not file suit against General Motors.

The sales practices of Pacific Bell Telephone Company, which serves California telephone customers, provide another illustration of the difficulties that face consumers. On April 23, 1986, the Pacific Utilities Commission of California released a report stating that Pacific Bell service representatives were duping new telephone customers into buying expensive optional features by quoting a fee for new telephone service that included the expensive features, but without telling the new customer that the features were optional, that the consumer was being charged extra for them, and that basic service was available at a much cheaper monthly fee. A sales representative of the telephone company described the way that she approached a new customer calling to get a new telephone hook-up:

> I'm going to tell you that "You will get unlimited local calling, Touchtone service, our four, custom-calling services and a 20 percent discount in the Pacific Bell service area; the central office fee to turn the services on is $37.50 and I have all of these things available and it's only $22.20 a month." Most customers will say, "That's fine." It really isn't a bad deal, but how many people know they don't have to buy all those things, that they can get basic service for $9.95? The company says, "People should be intelligent enough to ask; why should it be PacBell's job to tell them?" People who don't speak English, well, they end up with those services. Sometimes they call back and say, "What is this? I didn't want this." [Pacific Telephone sales representative][8]

According to the Utilities Commission report, 65 percent of Pacific Bell's phone order centers did not quote the basic $9.95 monthly rate that al-

lowed unlimited local calls, but instead quoted only a "standard price" which included extra features (such as a device that tells a customer another call is waiting, automatic forwarding of a call to another phone, equipment for three-way or conference calls, codes that automatically dial a preset number, and extra charges for call discounts at certain times or certain areas) that cost as much as $27.20 a month. The sales representatives pleaded that the company's marketing managers imposed stiff sales quotas on them and would put them on probation if they failed to meet the quotas. In one city, for example, they were expected to sell $197 to $238 worth of services each hour they spent on the telephone with customers. A Utilities Commission staff member remarked that "Marketing management appears to be more concerned about generating revenues than they are about ethical and fair treatment of customers."[9]

Consumers are also bombarded daily by an endless series of advertisements urging them to buy certain products. Although sometimes defended as sources of information, advertisements are also criticized on the grounds that they rarely do more than give the barest indications of the basic function a product is meant to serve and sometimes misrepresent and exaggerate its virtues. Economists argue that advertising expenditures are a waste of resources, while sociologists bemoan the cultural effects of advertising.[10]

This chapter examines the many ethical issues raised by product quality and advertising. The first few sections discuss various approaches to consumer issues and the last sections deal with consumer advertising. We will begin with a focus on what is perhaps the most urgent issue: consumer product injuries and the responsibilities of manufacturers.

MARKETS AND CONSUMER PROTECTION

Consumer advocates point out that in 1992 alone there were more than 585,000 injuries requiring hospital treatment inflicted on youngsters and adults using toys, nursery equipment, and playground equipment; more than 322,000 people were mangled using home workshop equipment; 2,055,000 people needed emergency treatment for injuries involving home furnishings; and 3,467,000 more people required treatment for injuries involving home construction materials.[11] Injuries from auto-related accidents in 1995 averaged 44,200 each week; while deaths averaged 120 per day; financial losses were estimated at $479 million per day.[12]

Many people believe that consumers automatically will be protected from injury by the operations of free and competitive markets, and that neither governments nor businesspeople have to take special steps to deal with these issues. As we have seen, free markets promote an allocation, use, and distribution of goods that is, in a certain sense, just, respectful of rights, and efficiently productive of maximum utility for those who participate in the market. Moreover, in such markets, the consumer is said to be "sovereign." When consumers want and will willingly pay for something, sellers have an incentive to cater to their wishes. If sellers do not provide what consumers want, then sellers will suffer losses. However, when sellers provide what consumers want, they will profit. As the author of a leading textbook on economics writes, "Consumers direct by their innate or learned tastes, as expressed in their dollar votes, the ultimate uses to which society's resources are channeled."[13]

In the "market" approach to consumer protection, consumer safety is seen as a good that is most efficiently provided through the mechanism of the free market whereby sellers must respond to consumer demands. If consumers want products to be safer, then they will indicate this preference in markets by willingly paying more for safer products and by showing a preference for manufacturers of safe products while turning down the goods of manufacturers of unsafe products. Producers will have to respond to this demand by building more safety into their products or they risk losing customers to competitors who cater to the preferences of consumers. Thus, the market ensures that producers respond adequately to consumers' desires for safety. On the other hand, if consumers do not place a high value on safety and demonstrate neither a willingness to pay more for safety

nor a preference for safer products, then it is wrong to push increased levels of safety down their throats through government regulations that force producers to build more safety into their products than consumers demand. Such government interference, as we saw earlier, distorts markets, making them unjust, disrespectful of rights, and inefficient. It is just as wrong for businesspeople to decide on their own that consumers should have more protection than they are demanding, as to force on them costly safety devices that they would not buy on their own. Only consumers can say what value they place on safety, and they should be allowed to register their preferences through their free choices in markets and not be coerced by businesses or governments into paying for safety levels they may not want.

For example, an appliance selling for $100 may indicate that it will overheat if it is used for more than an hour and a half, while one selling for $400 may indicate that it can be run safely all day and night continuously. Some buyers will prefer the cheaper model, willingly trading the somewhat higher risk for the $300 cut in price, while others will prefer the more expensive one. If government regulations forced all appliance makers to make only the safer model, or if manufacturers voluntarily decided to make only the safer model, then consumers who do not feel that the increase in safety is worth $300 extra to them will be out of luck. If they cannot do without the appliance, they will be forced to pay the extra $300 even if they would have preferred spending it on something else that is more valuable to them. They are thus, unjustly forced to pay money for something they do not want, and their resources are inefficiently wasted on something that produces little utility for them.

Critics to this market approach respond, however, that the benefits of free markets obtain with certainty only when markets have the seven characteristics that define them: (1) there are numerous buyers and sellers, (2) everyone can freely enter and exit the market, (3) everyone has full and perfect information, (4) all goods in the market are exactly similar, (5) there are no external costs, (6) all buyers and sellers are rational utility maximizers, and (7) the market is unregulated. Critics of the market approach to consumer issues argue that these characteristics are absent in consumer markets, focusing especially on characteristics (3) and (6).

Markets are efficient, critics point out, only if condition (3) obtains—that is, only if participants have full and perfect information about the goods they are buying. But obviously, consumers are frequently not well informed about the products they buy simply because the sophisticated consumer products on contemporary market shelves are too complex for anyone but an expert to be knowledgeable about them. Not surprisingly, manufacturers, who are knowledgeable about their products, might not voluntarily provide information about the safety levels or defective characteristics of their products to consumers. Since gathering information is expensive, a consumer may not have the resources to acquire the information on his or her own by, for example, testing several competing brands to determine which provides the most safety for the cost.

In theory it would be possible for consumers who want information to turn to organizations such as the Consumers Union that make a business of acquiring and selling product information. That is, market mechanisms should create a market in consumer information if that is what consumers want. However, for two reasons related to the nature of information, it is difficult for such organizations to cover their costs by selling information to consumers. First, as several economists have pointed out, once information is provided to one person who pays for it, it is easily leaked to many others who do not pay, especially in this age of photocopiers.[14] Since people know they can become "free riders" and acquire the information compiled by others without paying for it themselves, the number of people who willingly pay for the information is too small to allow the organization to cover its costs. Second, consumers are often unwilling to pay for information because they do not know what its value to them will be until after they get it and then they no longer need to pay for it since it is already in their possession. For example, a consumer may pay for the information contained in a research report and then find that he or she already knew what was in the report, or that it is about products other than those he or she wants to buy, or that it is irrelevant information about those products. Since consumers cannot know in advance precisely what they are buying when they buy information, they are unwilling to pay the costs organizations must charge to gather the information.[15] Markets alone, then, are not able to support organizations that can provide consumers with the information they need. Instead, such organizations must rely on charitable contributions or on government grants.

A second criticism of the argument that free markets can deal with all consumer issues takes aim at characteristic (6) of free markets: the assumption that the consumer is a "rational utility maximizer." As one author put it, the consumer assumed by such arguments is "a budget-minded, rational individual, relentlessly pushing toward maximizing his satisfaction . . . [who is able] to think well ahead, to 'wait,' to consider. The consumer defined by the theory watches every penny."[16] More precisely, the "rational utility maximizer" that the consumer is assumed to be, is a person who has a well-defined and consistent set of preferences, and who is certain how his or her choices will affect those preferences.

Unfortunately, virtually all consumer choices are based on probability estimates we make concerning the chances that the products we buy will function as we think they will. All the research available shows that we become highly inept, irrational, and inconsistent when we make choices based on probability estimates.[17]

First, as is obvious to any observer, few of us are good at estimating probabilities. We typically underestimate the risks of personal life-threatening activities—such as driving, smoking, eating fried foods—and of being injured by the products we use, and we overestimate the probabilities of unlikely but memorable events such as tornadoes or attacks by grizzly bears in national parks.[18] Studies have shown that our probability judgments go astray for a number of reasons, including the following:

1. Prior probabilities are ignored when new information becomes available, even if the new information is irrelevant.

2. Emphasis on "causation" results in the under-weighing of evidence that is relevant to probability but is not perceived as "causal."
3. Generalizations are made on the basis of small sample findings.
4. Belief is placed in a self-correcting but nonexistent "law of averages."
5. People believe that they exert control over purely chance events.[19]

Second, as a number of researchers have shown, people are irrational and inconsistent when weighing choices based on probability estimates of future costs or payoffs. For example, one set of researchers found that when people are asked to rank probable payoffs, they inconsistently will rank one payoff as being *both* better and worse than another. Another investigator found that when people were asked which of two probable payoffs they preferred, they would often say that they would pay *more* for the payoff that they *least* preferred. Another set of studies found that in many cases, a majority of persons would prefer one probable payoff to another in one context, but reversed their preferences in a different context although the probable payoffs were identical in both contexts.[20]

Finally, as several critics have pointed out, markets often fail to incorporate the most fundamental characteristic of competitive markets; the presence of numerous buyers and sellers. Although buyers or consumers in most markets are numerous, still many, perhaps most, consumer markets are monopolies or oligopolies; that is, they are dominated by one or by a very few large sellers. Sellers in monopoly and oligopoly markets are able to extract abnormally high profits from consumers by ensuring that supply is insufficient to meet demand, thereby creating shortages that put upward pressures on prices.

On balance, then, it does not appear that market forces by themselves can deal with all consumer concerns for safety, freedom from risk, and value. Market failures, characterized by inadequate consumer information, irrationality in the choices of consumers, and concentrated markets, undercut arguments that try to show that markets alone can

provide adequate consumer protection. Instead, consumers must be protected through the legal structures of government and through the voluntary initiatives of responsible businesspeople. We will turn, then, to examining several views about the responsibilities of businesses toward consumers, views that have formed the basis of many of our consumer laws and of increased calls for greater acceptance of responsibility for consumer protection on the part of business.

It is clear, of course, that part of the responsibility for consumer injuries must rest on consumers themselves. Individuals are often careless in their use of products. "Do-it-yourselfers" use power saws without guards attached or inflammable liquids near open flames. People often use tools and instruments that they do not have the skill, the knowledge, or the experience to handle.

Injuries also arise from flaws in product design, in the materials out of which products are made, or in the processes used to construct products. Insofar as manufacturing defects are the source of product-related injuries, consumer advocates claim, the duty of minimizing injuries should lie with the manufacturer. The producer is in the best position to know the hazards raised by a certain product and to eliminate the hazards at the point of manufacture. In addition, the producer's expertise makes the producer knowledgeable about the safest materials and manufacturing methods and enables him to build adequate safeguards into the design of the product. Finally, because the producer is intimately acquainted with the workings of the product, he or she can best inform the consumer on the safest way to use the product and on the precautions to be taken.

Where, then, does the consumer's duty to protect his or her own interests end, and where does the manufacturer's duty to protect consumers' interests begin? Three different theories on the ethical duties of manufacturers have been developed, each one of which strikes a different balance between the consumer's duty to himself or herself and the manufacturer's duty to the consumer; the contract view, the "due care" view, and the social costs view. The contract view would place the greater responsibility on the consumer, while the "due care" and social costs views place the larger measure of responsibility on the manufacturer. We will examine each of these views.

THE CONTRACT VIEW OF BUSINESS'S DUTIES TO CONSUMERS

According to the contract view of the business firm's duties to its customers, the relationship between a business firm and its customers is essentially a contractual relationship, and the firm's moral duties to the customer are those created by this contractual relationship.[21] When a consumer buys a product, this view holds, the consumer voluntarily enters into a "sales contract" with the business firm. The firm freely and knowingly agrees to give the consumer a product with certain characteristics and the consumer in turn freely and knowingly agrees to pay a certain sum of money to the firm for the product. In virtue of having voluntarily entered this agreement, the firm then has a duty to provide a product with those characteristics, and the consumer has a correlative right to get a product with those characteristics.

The contract theory of the business firm's duties to its customers rests on the view that a contract is a free agreement that imposes on the parties the basic duty of complying with the terms of the agreement. We examined this view earlier and noted the two justifications Kant provided for the view: A person has a duty to do what he or she contracts to do, because failure to adhere to the terms of a contract is a practice (1) that cannot be universalized, and (2) that treats the other person as a means and not as an end.[22] Rawls's theory also provides a justification for the view, but one that is based on the idea that our freedom is expanded by the recognition of contractual rights and duties: An enforced system of social rules that requires people to do what they contract to do will provide them with the assurance that contracts will be kept. Only if they have such assurance will people feel able to trust each other's word, and on that basis to secure the benefits of the institution of contracts.[23]

We also noted that traditional moralists have argued that the act of entering into a contract is subject to several secondary moral constraints:

1. Both of the parties to the contract must have full knowledge of the nature of the agreement they are entering.
2. Neither party to a contract must intentionally misrepresent the facts of the contractual situation to the other party.
3. Neither party to a contract must be forced to enter the contract under duress or undue influence.

These secondary constraints can be justified by the same sorts of arguments that Kant and Rawls use to justify the basic duty to perform one's contracts. Kant, for example, easily shows that misrepresentation in the making of a contract cannot be universalized, and Rawls argues that if misrepresentation were not prohibited, fear of deception would make members of a society feel less free to enter contracts. However, these secondary constraints can also be justified on the grounds that a contract cannot exist unless these constraints are fulfilled. For a contract is essentially a *free agreement* struck between two parties. Since an agreement cannot exist unless both parties know what they are agreeing to, contracts require full knowledge and the absence of misrepresentation. Since freedom implies the absence of coercion, contracts must be made without duress or undue influence.

The contractual theory of business's duties to consumers, then, claims that a business has four main moral duties: The basic duty of (1) complying with the terms of the sales contract, and the secondary duties of (2) disclosing the nature of the product, (3) avoiding misrepresentation, and (4) avoiding the use of duress and undue influence. By acting in accordance with these duties, a business respects the right of consumers to be treated as free and equal persons, that is, in accordance with their right to be treated only as they have freely consented to be treated.

The Duty to Comply

The most basic moral duty that a business firm owes its customers, according to the contract view, is the duty to provide consumers with a product that lives up to those claims that the firm expressly made about the product, which led the customer to enter the contract freely, and which formed the customer's understanding concerning what he or she was agreeing to buy. In the early 1970s, for example, Winthrop Laboratories marketed a painkiller that the firm advertised as "nonaddictive." Subsequently, a patient using the painkiller became addicted to it and shortly died from an overdose. A court found Winthrop Laboratories liable for the patient's death because, although it had expressly stated that the drug was nonaddictive, Winthrop Laboratories had failed to live up to its duty to comply with this express contractual claim.[24]

As this example suggests, our legal system has incorporated the moral view that firms have a duty to live up to the express claims they make about their products. The Uniform Commercial Code, for example, states in Section 2-314:

> Any affirmation of fact or promise made by the seller to the buyer that related to the goods and becomes part of the basis of the bargain creates an express warranty that the goods shall conform to the affirmation or promise.

In addition to the duties that result from the *express* claim a seller makes about the product, the contract view also holds that the seller has a duty to carry through on any *implied* claims he or she knowingly makes about the product. The seller, for example, has the moral duty to provide a product that can be used safely for the ordinary and special purposes for which the customer, relying on the seller's judgment, has been led to believe it can be used. The seller is morally bound to do whatever he or she knows the buyer understood the seller was promising, since at the point of sale sellers should have corrected any misunderstandings they were aware of.[25]

This idea of an "implied agreement" has also been incorporated into the law. Section 2-315 of the Uniform Commercial Code, for example, reads:

> Where the seller at the time of contracting has reason to know any particular purpose for which the goods are required and that the buyer is relying on the seller's skill or judgment to select or furnish suitable goods, there is . . . an implied warranty that the goods shall be fit for such purpose.

The express or implied claims that a seller might make about the qualities possessed by the product range over a variety of areas and are affected by a number of factors. Frederick Sturdivant classifies these areas in terms of four variables: "The definition of product quality used here is: the degree to which product performance meets predetermined expectation with respect to (1) reliability, (2) service life, (3) maintainability, and (4) safety."[26]

Reliability   Claims of reliability refer to the probability that a product will function as the consumer is led to expect that it will function. If a product incorporates a number of interdependent components, then the probability that it will function properly is equal to the result of multiplying together each component's probability of proper functioning.[27] As the number of components in a product multiplies, therefore, the manufacturer has a corresponding duty to ensure that each component functions in such a manner that the total product is as reliable as he or she implicitly or expressly claims it will be. This is especially the case when malfunction poses health or safety hazards. The U.S. Consumer Product Safety Commission lists hundreds of examples of hazards from product malfunctions in its periodic announcements.[28]

Service Life   Claims concerning the life of a product refer to the period of time during which the product will function as effectively as the consumer is led to expect it to function. Generally, the consumer implicitly understands that service life will depend on the amount of wear and tear to which one subjects the product. In addition, consumers also base some of their expectations of service life on the explicit guarantees the manufacturer attaches to the product.

A more subtle factor that influences service life is the factor of obsolescence.[29] Technological advances may render some products obsolete when a new product appears that carries out the same functions more efficiently. Or purely stylistic changes may make last year's product appear dated and less desirable. The contract view implies that a seller who knows that a certain product will become obsolete has a duty to correct any mistaken beliefs he or she knows buyers will form concerning the service life they may expect from the product.

Maintainability   Claims of maintainability are claims concerning the case with which the product can be repaired and kept in operating condition. Claims of maintainability are often made in the form of an express warranty. Whirlpool Corporation, for example, appended this express warranty on one of its products:

> During your first year of ownership, all parts of the appliance (except the light bulbs) that we find are defective in materials or workmanship will be repaired or replaced by Whirlpool free of charge, and we will pay all labor charges. During the second year, we will continue to assume the same responsibility as stated above except you pay any labor charges.[30]

But sellers often also imply that a product may be easily repaired even after the expiration date of an express warranty. In fact, however, product repairs may be costly, or even impossible, because of the unavailability of parts.

Product Safety   Implied and express claims of product safety refer to the degree of risk associated with using a product. Since the use of virtually any product involves some degree of risk, questions of safety are essentially questions of *acceptable known* levels of risk. That is, a product is safe if its attendant risks are known and judged to be "acceptable" or "reasonable" by the *buyer* in view of the benefits the buyer expects to derive from using the product. This implies that the seller complies with his or her part of a free agreement if the seller provides a product that involves only those risks he or she says it involves, and the buyer purchases it with the understanding. The National Commission on Product Safety, for example, characterized "reasonable risk" in these terms:

> Risk of bodily harm to users are not unreasonable when consumers understand that risks exist, can appraise their probability and severity, know how to cope with them, and voluntarily accept them to get benefits they could not obtain in less risky ways. When there is a risk of this character, consumers have reasonable opportunity to protect themselves; and public authorities should hesitate to substitute their value judgments about the desirability of the risk for those of the consumers who choose to incur it. But preventable risk is not reasonable (a) when consumers do not know that it exists; or (b) when,

though aware of it, consumers are unable to estimate its frequency and severity; or (c) when consumers do not know how to cope with it, and hence are likely to incur harm unnecessarily; or (d) when risk is unnecessary in that it could be reduced or eliminated at a cost in money or in the performance of the product that consumers would willingly incur if they knew the facts and were given the choice.[31]

Thus, the seller of a product (according to the contractual theory) has a moral duty to provide a product whose use involves *no greater risks* than those the seller *expressly* communicates to the buyer or those the seller *implicitly* communicates by the implicit claims made when marketing the product for a use whose normal risk level is well known. If the label on a bottle, for example, indicates only that the contents are highly toxic ("Danger: Poison"), the product should not include additional risks from flammability. Or, if a firm makes and sells skis, use of the skis should not embody any unexpected additional risks other than the well-known risks which attend skiing (it should not, for example, involve the added possibility of being pierced by splinters should the skis fracture). In short, the seller has a duty to provide a product with a level of risk which is no higher than he or she expressly or implicitly claims it to be, and which the consumer freely and knowingly contracts to assume.

The Duty of Disclosure

An agreement cannot bind unless both parties to the agreement know what they are doing and freely choose to do it. This implies that the seller who intends to enter a contract with a customer has a duty to disclose exactly what the customer is buying and what the terms of the sale are. At a minimum, this means the seller has a duty to inform the buyer of any facts about the product that would affect the customer's decision to purchase the product. For example, if the product the consumer is buying possesses a defect that poses a risk to the user's health or safety, the consumer should be so informed. Some have argued that sellers should also disclose a product's components or ingredients, its performance characteristics, costs of operation, product ratings, and any other applicable standards.[32]

Behind the claim that entry into a sales contract requires full disclosure is the idea that an agreement is free only to the extent that one knows what alternatives are available: Freedom depends on knowledge. The more the buyer knows about the various products available on the market and the more comparisons the buyer is able to make among them, the more one can say that the buyer's agreement is voluntary.[33]

The view that sellers should provide a great deal of information for buyers, however, has been criticized on the grounds that information is costly and, therefore, should itself be treated as a product for which the consumer should either pay or do without. In short, consumers should freely contract to purchase information as they freely contract to purchase goods, and producers should not have to provide it for them.[34] The problem with the criticism is that the information on which a person bases his or her decision to enter a contract is a rather different kind of entity from the product exchanged through the contract. Since a contract must be entered into freely, and since free choice depends on knowledge, contractual transactions must be based on an open exchange of information. If consumers had to bargain for such information, the resulting contract would hardly be free.

The Duty Not to Misrepresent

Misrepresentation, even more than the failure to disclose information, renders freedom of choice impossible. That is, misrepresentation is coercive: The person who is intentionally misled acts as the deceiver wants the person to act and not as the person would freely have chosen to act if he or she had known the truth. Since free choice is an essential ingredient of a binding contract, intentionally misrepresenting the nature of a commodity is wrong.

A seller misrepresents a commodity when he or she represents it in a way deliberately intended to deceive the buyer into thinking something about the product that the seller knows is false. The deception may be created by a verbal lie, as when a used model is described as "new," or it may be created by a gesture, as when an unmarked used model is displayed together with several new models. That is, the deliberate intent to misrepresent by false implication is as wrong as the explicit lie.

The varieties of misrepresentation seem to be limited only by the ingenuity of the greed that creates them.[35] A computer software or hardware manufacturer may market a product it knows contains "bugs" without informing buyers of that fact; a manufacturer may give a product a name that the manufacturer knows consumers will confuse with the brand-name of a higher-quality compelling product; the manufacturer may write "wool" or "silk" on material made wholly or partly of cotton; the manufacturer may mark a fictitious "regular price" on an article that is always sold at a much lower "sale" price; a business may advertise an unusually low price for an object which the business actually intends to sell at a much higher price once the consumer is lured into the store; a store may advertise an object at an unusually low price, intending to "bait and switch" the unwary buyer over to a more expensive product; a producer may solicit paid "testimonials" from professionals who have never really used the product. We shall return to some of these issues when we discuss advertising.

The Duty Not to Coerce

People often act irrationally when under the influence of fear or emotional stress. When a seller takes advantage of a buyers' fear or emotional stress to extract consent to an agreement that the buyer would not make if the buyer were thinking rationally, the seller is using duress or undue influence to coerce. An unscrupulous funeral director, for example, may skillfully induce guilt-ridden and grief-stricken survivors to invest in funeral services they cannot afford. Since entry into a contract requires *freely* given consent, the seller has a duty to refrain from exploiting emotional states that may induce the buyer to act irrationally against his or her own best interests. For similar reasons, the seller also has the duty not to take advantage of gullibility, immaturity, ignorance, or any other factors that reduce or eliminate the buyer's ability to make free rational choices.

Problems with the Contractual Theory

The main objections to the contract theory focus on the unreality of the assumptions on which the theory is based. First, critics argue, the theory unrealistically assumes that manufacturers make direct agreements with consumers. Nothing could be farther from the truth. Normally, a series of wholesalers and retailers stand between the manufacturer and the ultimate consumer. The manufacturer sells the product to the wholesaler, who sells it to the retailer, who finally sells it to the consumer. The manufacturer never enters into any direct contract with the consumer. How then can one say that manufacturers have contractual duties to the consumer?

Advocates of the contract view of manufacturers' duties have tried to respond to this criticism by arguing that manufacturers enter into "indirect" agreements with consumers. Manufacturers promote their products through their own advertising campaigns. These advertisements supply the promises that lead people to purchase products from retailers who merely function as "conduits" for the manufacturer's product. Consequently, through these advertisements, the manufacturer forges an indirect contractual relationship not only with the immediate retailers who purchase the manufacturer's product but also with the ultimate consumers of the product. The most famous application of this doctrine of broadened indirect contractual relationships is to be found in a 1960 court opinion, *Henningsen v. Bloomfield Motors.*[36] Mrs. Henningsen was driving a new Plymouth when it suddenly gave off a loud cracking noise. The steering wheel spun out of her hands, the car lurched to the right and crashed into a brick wall. Mrs. Henningsen sued the manufacturer, Chrysler Corporation. The court opinion read:

> Under modern conditions the ordinary layman, on responding to the importuning of colorful advertising, has neither the opportunity nor the capacity to inspect or to determine the fitness of an automobile for use; he must rely on the manufacturer who has control of its construction, and to some degree on the dealer who, to the limited extent called for by the manufacturer's instructions, inspects and services it before delivery. In such a marketing milieu his remedies and those of persons who properly claim through him should not depend "upon the intricacies of the law of sales. The obligation of the manufacturer should not be based alone on privity of contract [that is, on a direct contractual relationship]. It

should rest, as was once said, upon 'the demands of social justice'." *Mazetti v. Armous & Co. (1913).* "If privity of contract is required," then, under the circumstances of modern merchandising, "privity of contract exists in the consciousness and understanding of all right-thinking persons . . . Accordingly, we hold that under modern marketing conditions, when a manufacturer puts a new automobile in the stream of trade and promotes its purchase by the public, an implied warranty that it is reasonably suitable for use as such accompanies it into the hands of the ultimate purchaser. Absence of agency between the manufacturer and the dealer who makes the ultimate sales is immaterial.

Thus, Chrysler Corporation was found liable for Mrs. Henningsen's injuries on the grounds that its advertising had created a contractual relationship with Mrs. Henningsen and on the grounds that this contract created an "implied warranty" about the car which Chrysler had a duty to fulfill.

A second objection to the contract theory focuses on the fact that a contract is a two-edged sword. If a consumer can freely agree to buy a product *with* certain qualities, the consumer can also freely agree to buy a product *without* those qualities. That is, freedom of contract allows a manufacturer to be released from his or her contractual obligations by explicitly *disclaiming* that the product is reliable, serviceable, safe, and so on. Many manufacturers fix such disclaimers on their products. The Uniform Commercial Code, in fact, stipulates in Section 2-316:

a. Unless the circumstances indicate otherwise, all implied warranties are excluded by expressions like "as is," "with all faults," or other language that in common understanding calls the buyer's attention to the exclusion of warranties and makes plain that there is no warranty, and

b. When the buyer before entering into the contract has examined the goods or the sample or model as fully as he desired, or has refused to examine the goods, there is no implied warranty with regard to defects than on examination ought in the circumstances to have been revealed to him.

The contract view, then, implies that if the consumer has ample opportunity to examine the product and the disclaimers and voluntarily consents to buy it anyway, he or she assumes the responsibility for the defects disclaimed by the manufacturer, as well as for any defects the customer may carelessly have overlooked. Disclaimers can effectively nullify all contractual duties of the manufacturer.

A third objection to the contract theory criticizes the assumption that buyer and seller meet each other as equals in the sales agreement. The contractual theory assumes that buyers and sellers are equally skilled at evaluating the quality of a product and that buyers are able to adequately protect their interests against the seller. This is the assumption built into the requirement that contracts must be freely and knowingly entered into: Both parties must know what they are doing and neither must be coerced into doing it. This equality between buyer and seller that the contractual theory assumes, derives from the laissez-faire ideology that accompanied the historical development of contract theory.[37] Classical laissez-faire ideology held that the economy's markets are competitive and that in competitive markets the consumer's bargaining power is equal to that of the seller. Competition forces the seller to offer the consumer as good or better terms than the consumer could get from other competing sellers, so the consumer has the power to threaten to take his or her business to other sellers. Because of this equality between buyer and seller, it was fair that each be allowed to try to out-bargain the other and unfair to place restrictions on either. In practice, this laissez-faire ideology gave birth to the doctrine of *caveat emptor*: let the buyer take care of himself.

In fact, sellers and buyers do not exhibit the equality these doctrines assume. A consumer who must purchase hundreds of different kinds of commodities cannot hope to be as knowledgeable as a manufacturer who specializes in producing a single product. Consumers have neither the expertise nor the time to acquire and process the information on which they must base their purchase decisions. Consumers, as a consequence, must usually rely on the judgment of the seller in making their purchase decisions, and are particularly vulnerable to being harmed by the seller. Equality, far from being the rules, as the contract theory assumes, is usually the exception.

THE DUE CARE THEORY

The "due care" theory of the manufacturer's duties to consumers is based on the idea that consumers and sellers do not meet as equals and that the consumer's interests are particularly vulnerable to being harmed by the manufacturer who has a knowledge and an expertise that the consumer does not have. Because manufacturers are in a more advantaged position, they have a duty to take special "care" to ensure that consumers' interests are not harmed by the products that they offer them. The doctrine of *caveat emptor* is here replaced with a weak version of the doctrine of "caveat vendor": let the seller take care. A New York court decision neatly described the advantaged position of the manufacturer and the consequent vulnerability of the consumer:

Today as never before the product in the hands of the consumer is often a most sophisticated and even mysterious article. Not only does it usually emerge as a sealed unit with an alluring exterior rather than as a visible assembly of component parts, but its functional validity and usefulness often depend on the application of electronic, chemical, or hydraulic principles far beyond the ken of the average consumer. Advances in the technologies of materials, of processes, of operational means have put it almost entirely out of the reach of the consumer to comprehend why or how the article operates, and thus even farther out of his reach to detect when there may be a defect or a danger present in its design or manufacture. In today's world it is often only the manufacturer who can fairly be said to know and to understand when an article is suitably designed and safely made of its intended purpose. Once floated on the market, many articles in a very real practical sense defy detection of defect, except possibly in the hands of an expert after laborious, and perhaps even destructive, disassembly. By way of direct illustration, how many automobile purchasers or users have any idea how a power steering mechanism operates or is intended to operate, with its "circulating work and piston assembly and its cross shaft splined to the Pitman arm"? We are accordingly persuaded that from the standpoint of justice as regards the operating aspect of today's products, responsibility should be laid on the manufacturer, subject to the limitations we set forth.[38]

The "due care" view holds, then, that because consumers must depend on the greater expertise of the manufacturer, the manufacturer not only has a duty to deliver a product that lives up to the express and implied claims about it, but in addition the manufacturer has a duty to exercise due care to prevent others from being injured by the product, *even if the manufacturer explicitly disclaims such responsibility and the buyer agrees to the disclaimer.* The manufacturer violates this duty and is "negligent" when there is a failure to exercise the care that a reasonable person could have foreseen would be necessary to prevent others from being harmed by use of the product. Due care must enter into the design of the product, into the choice of reliable materials for constructing the product, into the manufacturing processes involved in putting the product together, into the quality control used to test and monitor production, and into the warnings, labels, and instructions attached to the product. In each of these areas, according to the due care view, the manufacturer, in virtue of a greater expertise and knowledge, has a positive duty to take whatever steps are necessary to ensure that when the product leaves the plant it is as safe as possible, and the customer has a right to such assurance. Failure to take such steps is a breach of the moral duty to exercise due care and a violation of the injured person's right to expect such care, a right that rests on the consumer's need to rely on the manufacturer's expertise. Edgar Schein sketched out the basic elements of the "due care" theory several years ago when he wrote:

> [A] professional is someone who knows better what is good for his client than the client himself does. . . . If we accept this definition of professionalism . . . we may speculate that it is the *vulnerability of the client* that has necessitated the development of moral and ethical codes surrounding the relationship. The client must be protected from exploitation in a situation in which he is unable to protect himself because he lacks the relevant knowledge to do so . . . If [a manufacturer] is . . . a professional, who is his client? With respect to whom is he exercising his expert knowledge and skills? Who needs protection against the possible misuse of these skills? . . . Many economists argue persuasively . . . that the consumer has not been in a position to know what he was buying and hence was in fact, in a relatively vulnerable position . . . Clearly, then, one whole area of values deals with the relationship between the [manufacturer] and consumers.[39]

The due care view, of course, rests on the principle that agents have a moral duty not to harm or injure other parties by their acts and that this duty is particularly stringent when those other parties are vulnerable and dependent on the judgment of the agent. This principle can be supported from a variety of different moral perspectives, but it is most clearly implied by the requirements of an ethic of care. The principle follows almost immediately, in fact, from the requirement that one should care for the well-being of those with whom one has a special relationship, particularly a relationship of dependence such as a child has on its mother. Moreover, an ethic of care imposes the requirement that one should carefully examine the particular needs and characteristics of the person with whom one has a special relationship, in order to ensure that one's care for that person is tailored to that person's particular needs and qualities. As we will see, this emphasis on carefully examining the specific needs and characteristics of a vulnerable party, is also an explicit and critically important part of the due care view.

Although the demands of an ethic of care are aligned with the due care principle that manufacturers have a duty to protect vulnerable consumers, the principle has also been defended from other moral perspectives. Rule-utilitarians have defended the principle on the grounds that if the rule is accepted, everyone's welfare will be advanced.[40] The principle has been argued for on the basis of Kant's theory, since it seems to follow from the categorical imperative that people should be treated as ends and not merely as means, that is, that they have a *positive* right to be helped when they cannot help themselves.[41] Rawls has argued that individuals in the "original position" would agree to the principle because it would provide the basis for a secure social environment.[42] The judgment that individual producers have a duty not to harm or injure vulnerable parties, therefore, is solidly based on several ethical perspectives.

The Duty to Exercise Due Care

According to the due theory, manufacturers exercise sufficient care only when they take adequate steps to prevent whatever injurious effects they can foresee that the use of their product may have on consumers after having conducted inquiries into the way the product will be used and after having attempted to anticipate any possible misuses of the product. A manufacturer, then, is *not* morally negligent when others are harmed by a product and the harm was not one that the manufacturer could possibly have foreseen or prevented. Nor is a manufacturer morally negligent after having taken all reasonable steps to protect the consumer and to ensure that the consumer is informed of any irremovable risks that might still attend the use of the product. A car manufacturer, for example, cannot be said to be negligent from a moral point of view when people carelessly misuse the cars the manufacturer produces. A car manufacturer would be morally negligent only if the manufacturer had allowed unreasonable dangers to remain in the design of the car that consumers cannot be expected to know about or that they cannot guard against by taking their own precautionary measures.

What specific responsibilities does the duty to exercise due care impose on the producer? In general, the producer's responsibilities would extend to three areas.[43]

Design The manufacturer should ascertain whether the design of an article conceals any dangers, whether it incorporates all feasible safety devices, and whether it uses materials that are adequate for the purposes the product is intended to serve. The manufacturer is responsible for being thoroughly acquainted with the design of the item, and to conduct research and tests extensive enough to uncover any risks that may be involved in employing the article under various conditions of use. This requires researching consumers and analyzing their behavior, testing the product under different conditions of consumer use, and selecting materials strong enough to stand up to all probable usages. The effects of aging and of wear should also be analyzed and taken into account in designing an article. Engineering staff should acquaint themselves with hazards that might result from prolonged use and wear, and should warn the consumer of any potential dangers. There is a duty

to take the latest technological advances into account in designing a product, especially where advances can provide ways of designing a product that is less liable to harm or injure its users.

Production The production manager should control the manufacturing processes to eliminate any defective items, to identify any weaknesses that become apparent during production, and to ensure that short-cuts, substitution of weaker materials, or other economizing measures are not taken during manufacture that would compromise the safety of the final product. To ensure this, there should be adequate quality controls over materials that are to be used in the manufacture of the product and over the various stages of manufacture.

Information The manufacturer should fix labels, notices, or instructions on the product that will warn the user of all dangers involved in using or misusing the item and that will enable the user to adequately guard himself or herself against harm or injury. These instructions should be clear and simple, and warnings of any hazards involved in using or misusing the product should also be clear, simple, and prominent. In the case of drugs, manufacturers have a duty to warn physicians of any risks or of any dangerous side-effects that research or prolonged use have revealed. It is a breach of the duty not to harm or injure if the manufacturer attempts to conceal or down-play the dangers related to drug usage.

In determining the safeguards that should be built into a product, the manufacturer must also take into consideration the *capacities* of the persons who will use the product. If a manufacturer anticipates that a product will be used by persons who are immature, mentally deficient, or too inexperienced to be aware of the dangers attendant on the use of the product, then the manufacturer owes them a greater degree of care than if the anticipated users were of ordinary intelligence and prudence. Children, for example, cannot be expected to realize the dangers involved in using electrical equipment. Consequently, if a manufacturer anticipates that an electrical item will probably be used by children, steps must be taken to ensure that a person with a child's understanding will not be injured by the product.

If the possible harmful effects of using a product are serious, or if they cannot be adequately understood without expert opinion, then sale of the product should be carefully controlled. A firm should not oppose regulation of the sale of a product when regulation is the only effective means of ensuring that the users of the product are fully aware of the risks its use involves.

Problems with "Due Care"

The basic difficulty raised by the "due care" theory is that there is no clear method for determining when one has exercised enough "due care." That is, there is no hard and fast rule for determining how far a firm must go to ensure the safety of its product. Some authors have proposed the general utilitarian rule that the greater the probability of harm and the larger the population that might be harmed, the more the firm is obligated to do. But this fails to resolve some important issues. Every product involves at least some small risk of injury. If the manufacturer should try to eliminate even low-level risks, this would require that the manufacturer invest so much in each product that the product would be priced out of the reach of most consumers. Moreover, even *attempting* to balance higher risks against added costs involves measurement problems: How does one quantify risks to health and life?

A second difficulty raised by the "due care" theory is that it assumes that the manufacturer can discover the risks that attend the use of a product before the consumer buys and uses it. In fact, in a technologically innovative society new products whose defects cannot emerge until years or decades have passed will continually be introduced into the market. Only years after thousands of people were using and being exposed to asbestos, for example, did a correlation emerge between the incidence of cancer and exposure to asbestos. Although manufacturers may have greater expertise than consumers, their expertise does not make them omniscient. Who, then, is to bear the costs of injuries sustained from products whose defects neither the manufacturer nor the consumer could have uncovered beforehand?

Third, the due care view appears to some to be paternalistic. For it assumes that the *manufacturer* should be the one who makes the important decisions for the consumer, at least with respect to the levels of risks that are proper for consumers to bear. One may wonder whether such decisions should not be left up to the free choice of consumers who can decide for themselves whether or not they want to pay for additional risk reduction.

THE SOCIAL COSTS VIEW OF THE MANUFACTURER'S DUTIES

A third theory on the duties of the manufacturer would extend the manufacturer's duties beyond those imposed by contractual relationships and beyond those imposed by the duty to exercise due care in preventing injury or harm. This third theory holds that a manufacturer should pay the costs of *any* injuries sustained through any defects in the product, *even when the manufacturer exercised all due care in the design and manufacture of the product and has taken all reasonable precautions to warn users of every foreseen danger.* According to this third theory, a manufacturer has a duty to assume the risks of even those injuries that arise out of defects in the product that no one could reasonably have foreseen or eliminated. The theory is a very strong version of the doctrine of "caveat vendor": let the seller take care.

This third theory, which has formed the basis of the legal doctrine of "strict liability," is founded on utilitarian argument.[44] The utilitarian arguments for this third theory hold that the "external" costs of injuries resulting from unavoidable defects in the design of an artifact constitute part of the costs society must pay for producing and using an artifact. By having the manufacturer bear the external costs that result from these injuries as well as the ordinary internal costs of design and manufacture, all costs will be internalized and added on as part of the price of the product. Internalizing all costs in this way, according to proponents of this theory, will lead to a more efficient use of society's resources. First, since the price will reflect *all* the costs of producing and using the artifact, market forces will ensure that the product is not over-produced, and that resources are not wasted on it. (Whereas if some costs were not included in the price, then manufacturers would tend to produce more than is needed.) Second, since manufacturers have to pay the costs of injuries, they will be motivated to exercise greater care and to thereby reduce the number of accidents. Manufacturers will, therefore, strive to cut down the social costs of injuries, and this means a more efficient care for our human resources. In order to produce the maximum benefits possible from our limited resources, therefore, the social costs of injuries from defective products should be internalized by passing them on to the manufacturer, even when the manufacturer has done all that could be done to eliminate such defects. Third, internalizing the costs of injury in this way enables the manufacturer to distribute losses among all the users of a product instead of allowing losses to fall on individuals who may not be able to sustain the loss by themselves.

Underlying this third theory on the duties of the manufacturer are the standard utilitarian assumptions about the values of efficiency. The theory assumes that an efficient use of resources is so important for society that social costs should be allocated in whatever way will lead to a more efficient use and care of our resources. On this basis, the theory argues that a manufacturer should bear the social costs for injuries caused by defects in a product, even when no negligence was involved and no contractual relationship existed between the manufacturer and the user.

Problems with the Social Costs View

The major criticism of the social costs view of the manufacturer's duties is that it is unfair.[45] It is unfair, the critics charge, because it violates the basic canons of compensatory justice. Compensatory justice implies that a person should be forced to compensate an injured party only if the person could foresee and could have prevented the injury. By forcing manufacturers to pay for injuries that they could neither foresee nor prevent, the social costs theory (and the legal theory of "strict liability" that flows from it) treats manufacturers unfairly. Moreover, insofar as the social costs theory encourages passing the costs of injuries on to all consumers (in the form of higher prices), consumers are also being treated unfairly.

A second criticism of the social costs theory attacks the assumption that passing the costs of all injuries on to manufacturers will reduce the number of accidents.[46] On the contrary, critics claim, by relieving consumers of the responsibility of paying for their own injuries, the social costs theory will encourage carelessness in consumers. An increase in consumer carelessness will lead to an increase in consumer injuries.

A third argument against the social costs theory focuses on the financial burdens the theory imposes on manufacturers and insurance carriers. Critics claim that a growing number of consumers successfully sue manufacturers for compensation for any injuries sustained while using a product, even when the manufacturer took all due care to ensure that the product was safe.[47] Not only have the number of "strict liability" suits increased, critics claim, but the amounts awarded to injured consumers have also escalated. Moreover, they continue, the rising costs of the many liability suits that the theory of "strict liability" has created have precipitated a crisis in the insurance industry because insurance companies end up paying the liability suits brought against manufacturers. These high costs have imposed heavy losses on insurance companies and have forced many insurance companies to raise their rates to levels that are so high that many manufacturers can no longer afford insurance. Thus, critics claim, the social costs or "strict liability" theory wreaks havoc with the insurance industry; it forces the costs of insurance to climb to unreasonable heights; and it forces many valuable firms out of business because they can no longer afford liability insurance nor can they afford to pay for the many and expensive liability suits they must now face.

Defenders of the social costs view, however, have replied that in reality the costs of consumer liability suits are not large. Studies have shown that the number of liability suits filed in state courts has increased at a fairly low rate.[48] Less than 1 percent of product-related injuries result in suits and successful suits average payments of only a few thousand dollars.[49] Defenders of the social cost theory also point out that insurance companies and the insurance industry as a whole have remained quite profitable and claim that higher insurance costs are due to factors other than an increase in the amount of liability claims.[50]

The arguments for and against the social costs theory deserve much more discussion than we can give them here. The theory is essentially an attempt to come to grips with the problem of allocating the costs of injuries between two morally innocent parties: The manufacturer who could not foresee or prevent a product-related injury, and the consumer who could not guard himself or herself against the injury because the hazard was unknown. This allocation problem will arise in any society that, like ours, has come to rely on technology whose effects do not become evident until years after the technology is introduced. Unfortunately, it is also a problem that may have no "fair" solution.

NOTES

1. Readers wishing to conduct research on consumer issues through the internet might begin by turning to the Web sites of the following organizations: The National Safety Council (http://www.nsc.org), the Consumer Product Safety Commission (gopher://cpsc.gov); The Consumer Law Page (http://www.alexanderlaw.com); The Federal Trade Commission (http://www.ftc.gov).
2. Indiana Prevention Resource Center, "Alcohol, Tobacco Campaigns Frequently Aim at Women, Children, Minorities," *Prevention Newsline*, Spring 1992; see also "Poll Shows Camel Ads Are Effective with Kids," *Advertising Age*, April 27, 1992, p. 12.
3. CNN news report, October 1996.
4. Frederick D. Sturdivant and Heidi Vernon-Wortzel, *Business and Society: A Managerial Approach*, 4th ed. (Homewood, IL: Irwin, 1990) pp. 310–11.
5. *Ibid*.
6. National Safety Commission, *Accident Facts*, 1996.
7. The facts summarized in this paragraph are drawn from Penny Addis, "The Life History Complaint Case of Martha and George Rose: 'Honoring the Warranty,' " in Laura Nader, ed., *No Access to Law*, (New York: Academic Press, Inc., 1980), pp. 171–89.
8. Quoted in Ed Pope, "PacBell's Sales Quotas," *San Jose Mercury News*, 24 April 1986, p. 1C; see also "PacBell Accused of Sales Abuse," *San Jose Mer-*

cury News, 24 April 1986, p. 1A; "PacBell Offers Refund for Unwanted Services," *San Jose Mercury News*, 17 May 1986, p. 1A.
9. *Ibid*, p. 134.
10. Several of these criticisms are surveyed in Stephen A. Greyser, "Advertising: Attacks and Counters," *Harvard Business Review*, 50 (10 March 1972): 22–28.
11. U.S. Bureau of the Census, *Statistical Abstract of the United States*, 1995, Table 206.
12. National Safety Council, *Accident Facts*, 1996.
13. Paul A. Samuelson and William D. Nordhaus, *Macroeconomics*, 13th ed. (New York: McGraw-Hill Book Company, 1989), p. 41.
14. See Robert N. Mayer, *The Consumer Movement: Guardians of the Marketplace* (Boston: Twayne Publishers, 1989), p. 67; and Peter Asch, *Consumer Safety Regulation* (New York: Oxford University Press, 1988), p. 50.
15. Peter Asch, *Consumer Safety Regulation*, p. 51.
16. Lucy Black Creighton, *Pretenders to the Throne: The Consumer Movement in the United States* (Lexington, MA: Lexington Books, 1976), p. 85.
17. For an overview of the research on irrationality in decision making see Max Bazerman, *Judgment in Managerial Decision Making*, 3rd ed., (New York: John Wiley & Sons, Inc., 1994), pp. 12–76.
18. Peter Asch, *Consumer Safety Regulation*, pp. 74, 76.
19. *Ibid*.
20. For references to these studies see *ibid*, pp. 70–73.
21. See Thomas Garrett and Richard J. Klonoski, *Business Ethics*, 2nd ed. (Englewood Cliffs, New Jersey: Prentice Hall, 1986), p. 88.
22. Immanual Kant, *Groundwork of the Metaphysic of Morals*, H. J. Paton, ed. (New York: Harper & Row, Publishers, Inc., 1964), pp. 90, 97; see also, Alan Donagan, *The Theory of Morality* (Chicago: The University of Chicago Press), 1977, p. 92.
23. John Rawls, *A Theory of Justice* (Cambridge: Harvard University Press, Belknap Press, 1971), pp. 344–50.
24. *Crocker v. Winthrop Laboratories, Division of Sterling Drug, Inc.*, 514 Southwestern 2d 429 (1974).
25. See Donagan, *Theory of Morality*, p. 91.
26. Frederick D. Sturdivant, *Business and Society*, 3rd. ed. (Homewood, IL: Richard D. Irwin, Inc., 1985), p. 392.
27. *Ibid*., p. 393.
28. The U.S. Consumer Products Safety Commissions' notices of dangerous consumer products are accessible on the Commission's Web page at gopher://cpsc.gov.
29. A somewhat dated but still incisive discussion of this issue is found in Vance Packard, *The Wastemakers* (New York: David McKay Co., Inc., 1960).

30. Quoted in address by S. E. Upton (vice-president of Whirlpool Corporation) to the American Marketing Association in Cleveland, OH: 11 December 1969.

31. National Commission on Product Safety, *Final Report,* quoted in William W. Lowrance, *Of Acceptable Risk* (Los Altos, CA: William Kaufmann, Inc., 1976), p. 80.

32. See Louis Stern, "Consumer Protection via Increased Information," *Journal of Marketing,* 31, no. 2 (April 1967).

33. Lawrence E. Hicks, *Coping with Packaging Laws* (New York: AMACOM, 1972), p. 17.

34. See the discussions in Richard Posner, *Economic Analysis of Law,* 2nd ed. (Boston: Little, Brown and Company, 1977), p. 83; and R. Posner, "Strict Liability: A Comment," *Journal of Legal Studies,* 2, no. 1 (January 1973): 21.

35. See, for example, the many cases cited in George J. Alexander, *Honesty and Competition* (Syracuse, NY: Syracuse University Press, 1967).

36. *Henningsen v. Bloomfield Motors, Inc.,* 32 New Jersey 358, 161 Atlantic 2d 69 (1960).

37. See Friedrich Kessler and Malcolm Pitman Sharp, *Contracts* (Boston: Little, Brown and Company, 1953), p. 1–9.

38. *Codling v. Paglia,* 32 New York 2d 330, 298 Northeastern 2d 622, 345 New York Supplement 2d 461 (1973).

39. Edgar H. Schein, "The Problem of Moral Education for the Business Manager," *Industrial Management Review,* 8 (1966): pp. 3–11.

40. See W. D. Ross, *The Right and the Good* (Oxford: The Clarendon Press, 1930), ch. 2.

41. Donagan, *Theory of Morality,* p. 83.

42. Rawls, *Theory of Justice,* pp. 114–17; 333–42.

43. Discussions of the requirements of "due care" may be found in a variety of texts, all of which, however, approach the issues from the point of view of legal liability: Irwin Gray, *Product Liability: A Management Response* (New York: AMACOM, 1975), ch. 6; Eugene R. Carrubba, *Assuring Product Integrity* (Lexington, MA: Lexington Books, 1975); Frank Nixon, *Managing to Achieve Quality and Reliability* (New York: McGraw-Hill Book Co., 1971).

44. See, for example, Michael D. Smith, "The Morality of Strict Liability In Tort," *Business and Professional Ethics,* 3, no. 1 (December 1979): pp. 3–5; for a review of the rich legal literature on this topic, see Richard A. Posner, "Strict Liability: A Comment," *The Journal of Legal Studies,* 2, no. 1 (January 1973): pp. 205–21.

45. George P. Fletcher, "Fairness and Utility in Tort Theory," *Harvard Law Review,* 85, no. 3 (January 1972): pp. 537–73.

46. Posner, *Economic Analysis of Law,* pp. 139–42.

47. See "Unsafe Products: The Great Debate Over Blame and Punishment," *Business Week,* 30 April 1984; Stuart Taylor, "Product Liability: the New Morass," *New York Times,* 10 March 1985; "The Product Liability Debate," *Newsweek,* 10 September 1984.

48. "Sorting Out the Liability Debate," *Newsweek,* 12 May 1986.

49. Ernest F. Hollings, "No Need for Federal Product-Liability Law," *Christian Science Monitor,* 20 September 1984; see also Harvey Rosenfield, "The Plan to Wrong Consumer Rights," *San Jose Mercury News,* 3 October 1984.

50. Irvin Molotsky, "Drive to Limit Product Liability Awards Grows as Consumer Groups Object," *New York Times,* 6 March 1986.

QUESTIONS FOR DISCUSSION

1. The CEO of Consumer Products Unlimited opened the annual meeting with a speech about CPU's commitment to "serving the needs of the consumer." At the same meeting, she announced the introduction of a new bath soap into the company's product line, which already contained eleven soaps. She explained that it had the same formula as three of CPU's other soaps, but it would have a French name, would cost more, and would appeal to a more sophisticated consumer. The marketing division, she said, was already beginning an aggressive ad campaign. Do consumers *need* CPU's new soap? Do they want it? If so, in what sense? If not, why not? Would CPU's ads be deceptive if they claimed that the soap contained "unique European skin-care ingredients"?

2. Galbraith claims that U.S. society is rich in private goods, such as those produced by CPU, but poor in public goods such as clean air, parks, and public transportation. According to Galbraith, does this mean that people want public goods less than they want private goods? Explain. Would it make sense to conduct advertising campaigns for public goods? Why or why not?

3. Evaluate PowerMaster's sale of malt liquor to minority groups as discussed in the article by George Brenkert in light of Holley's discussion of the morality of sales practices.

CHAPTER 8

The Environment

Morality, Money, and Motor Cars

Norman Bowie
Andersen Chair in Corporate Responsibility,
University of Minnesota

Environmentalists frequently argue that business has special obligations to protect the environment. Although I agree with the environmentalists on this point, I do not agree with them as to where the obligations lie. Business does not have an obligation to protect the environment over and above what is required by law; however, it does have a moral obligation to avoid intervening in the political arena in order to defeat or weaken environmental legislation. In developing this thesis, several points are in order. First, many businesses have violated important moral obligations, and the violation has had a severe negative impact on the environment. For example, toxic waste haulers have illegally dumped hazardous material, and the

From *Business, Ethics, and the Environment: The Public Policy Debate*, edited by W. Michael Hoffman, Robert Frederick, and Edward S. Petry, Jr. (Westport, CT: Quorum Books, 1990). Copyright © Center for Business Ethics at Bentley College, Waltham, MA. Reprinted by permission of the Center for Business Ethics.

environment has been harmed as a result. One might argue that those toxic waste haulers who have illegally dumped have violated a special obligation to the environment. Isn't it more accurate to say that these toxic waste haulers have violated their obligation to obey the law and that in this case the law that has been broken is one pertaining to the environment? Businesses have an obligation to obey the law—environmental laws and all others. Since there are many well-publicized cases of business having broken environmental laws, it is easy to think that business has violated some special obligations to the environment. In fact, what business has done is to disobey the law. Environmentalists do not need a special obligation to the environment to protect the environment against illegal business activity; they need only insist that business obey the laws.

Business has broken other obligations beside the obligation to obey the law and has harmed the environment as a result. Consider the grounding of the Exxon oil tanker *Valdez* in Alaska. That grounding was allegedly caused by the fact that an inadequately trained crewman was piloting the tanker while the captain was below deck and had been drinking. What needs to be determined is whether Exxon's policies and procedures were sufficiently lax so that it could be said Exxon was morally at fault. It might be that Exxon is legally responsible for the accident under the doctrine of respondent superior, but Exxon is not thereby morally responsible. Suppose, however, that Exxon's policies were so lax that the company could be characterized as morally negligent. In such a case, the company would violate its moral obligation to use due care and avoid negligence. Although its negligence was disastrous to the environment, Exxon would have violated no special obligation to the environment. It would have been morally negligent.

A similar analysis could be given to the environmentalists' charges that Exxon's cleanup procedures were inadequate. If the charge is true, either Exxon was morally at fault or not. If the procedures had not been implemented properly by Exxon employees, then Exxon is legally culpable, but not morally culpable. On the other hand, if Exxon lied to government officials by saying that its policies were in accord with regulations and/or were ready for emergencies of this type, then Exxon violated its moral obligation to tell the truth. Exxon's immoral conduct would have harmed the environment, but it violated no special obligation to the environment. More important, none is needed. Environmentalists, like government officials, employees, and stockholders expect that business firms and officials have moral obligations to obey the law, avoid negligent behavior, and tell the truth. In sum, although many business decisions have harmed the environment, these decisions violated no environmental moral obligations. If a corporation is negligent in providing for worker safety, we do not say the corporation violated a special obligation to employees; we say that it violated its obligation to avoid negligent behavior.

The crucial issues concerning business obligations to the environment focus on the excess use of natural resources (the dwindling supply of oil and gas, for instance) and the externalities of production (pollution, for instance). The critics of business want to claim that business has some special obligation to mitigate or solve these problems. I believe this claim is largely mistaken. If business does have a special obligation to help solve the environmental crisis, that obligation results from the special knowledge that business firms have. If they have greater expertise than other constituent groups in society, then it can be argued that, other things being equal, business's responsibilities to mitigate the environmental crisis are somewhat greater. Absent this condition, business's responsibility is no greater than and may be less than that of other social groups. What leads me to think that the critics of business are mistaken?

William Frankena distinguished obligations in an ascending order of the difficulty in carrying them out: avoiding harm, preventing harm, and doing good.[1] The most stringent requirement, to avoid harm, insists no one has a right to render harm on another unless there is a compelling, overriding moral reason to do so. Some writers have referred to this obligation as the moral minimum. A corporation's behavior is consistent with the moral minimum if it causes no avoidable harm to others.

Preventing harm is a less stringent obligation, but sometimes the obligation to prevent harm may be nearly as strict as the obligation to avoid harm. Suppose you are the only person passing a 2-foot-deep working pool where a young child is drowning. There is no one else in the vicinity. Don't you have a strong moral obligation to prevent the child's death? Our obligation to prevent harm is not unlimited, however. Under what conditions must we be good samaritans? Some have argued that four conditions must exist before one is obligated to prevent harm: capability, need, proximity, and last resort.[2] These conditions are all met with the case of the drowning child. There is obviously a need that you can meet since you are both in the vicinity and have the resources to prevent the drowning with little effort; you are also the last resort.

The least strict moral obligation is to do good—to make contributions to society or to help solve problems (inadequate primary schooling in the inner cities, for example). Although corporations may have some minimum obligation in this regard based on an argument from corporate citizenship, the obligations of the corporation to do good cannot be expanded without limit. An injunction to assist in solving societal problems makes impossible demands on a corporation because at the practical level, it ignores the impact that such activities have on profit.

It might seem that even if this descending order of strictness of obligations were accepted, obligations toward the environment would fall into the moral minimum category. After all, the depletion of natural resources and pollution surely harm the environment. If so, wouldn't the obligations business has to the environment be among the strictest obligations a business can have?

Suppose, however, that a businessperson argues that the phrase "avoid harm" usually applies to human beings. Polluting a lake is not like injuring a human with a faulty product. Those who coined the phrase *moral minimum* for use in the business context defined harm as "particularly including activities which violate or frustrate the enforcement of rules of domestic or institutional law intended to protect individuals against prevention of health, safety or basic freedom."[3] Even if we do not insist that the violations be violations of a rule of law, polluting a lake would not count as a harm under this definition. The environmentalists would respond that it would. Polluting the lake may be injuring people who might swim in or eat fish from it. Certainly it would be depriving people of the freedom to enjoy the lake. Although the environmentalist is correct, especially if we grant the legitimacy of a human right to a clean environment, the success of this reply is not enough to establish the general argument.

Consider the harm that results from the production of automobiles. We know statistically that about 50,000 persons per year will die and that nearly 250,000 others will be seriously injured in automobile accidents in the United States alone. Such death and injury, which is harmful, is avoidable. If that is the case, doesn't the avoid-harm criterion require that the production of automobiles for profit cease? Not really. What such arguments point out is that some refinement of the moral minimum standard needs to take place. Take the automobile example. The automobile is itself a good-producing instrument. Because of the advantages of automobiles, society accepts the possible risks that go in using them. Society also accepts many other types of avoidable harm. We take certain risks—ride in planes, build bridges, and mine coal—to pursue advantageous goals. It seems that the high benefits of some activities justify the resulting harms. As long as the risks are known, it is not wrong that some avoidable harm be permitted so that other social and individual goals can be achieved. The avoidable-harm criterion needs some sharpening.

Using the automobile as a paradigm, let us consider the necessary refinements for the avoid-harm criterion. It is a fundamental principle of ethics that "ought" implies "can." That expression means that you can be held morally responsible only for events within your power. In the ought-implies-can principle, the overwhelming majority of highway deaths and injuries is not the responsibility of the automaker. Only those deaths and injuries attributable to unsafe automobile design can be attributed to the automaker. The ought-implies-can principle can also be used to absolve the auto companies of responsibility for death and injury from safety defects that the automakers could not reasonably know existed. The company could not be expected to do anything about them.

Does this mean that a company has an obligation to build a car as safe as it knows how? No. The standards for safety must leave the product's cost within the price range of the consumer ("ought implies can" again). Comments about engineering and equipment capability are obvious enough. But for a business, capability is also a function of profitability. A company that builds a maximally safe car at a cost that puts it at a competitive disadvantage and hence threatens its survival is building a safe car that lies beyond the capability of the company.

Critics of the automobile industry will express horror at these remarks, for by making capability a function of profitability, society will continue to have avoidable deaths and injuries; however, the situation is not as dire as the critics imagine. Certainly capability should not be sacrificed completely so that profits can be maximized. The decision to build products that are cheaper in cost but are not maximally safe is a social decision that has widespread support. The arguments occur over the line between safety and cost. What we have is a classical trade-off situation. What is desired is some appropriate mix between engineering safety and consumer demand. To say there must be some mix between engineering safety and consumer demand is not to justify all the decisions made by the automobile companies. Ford Motor Company made a morally incorrect choice in placing Pinto gas tanks where it did. Consumers were uninformed, the record of the Pinto in rear-end collisions was worse than that of competitors, and Ford fought government regulations.

Let us apply the analysis of the automobile industry to the issue before us. That analysis shows that an automobile company does not violate its obligation to avoid harm and hence is not in violation of the moral minimum if the trade-off between potential harm and the utility of the products rests on social consensus and competitive realities.

As long as business obeys the environmental laws and honors other standard moral obligations, most harm done to the environment by business has been accepted by society. Through their decisions in the marketplace, we can see that most consumers are unwilling to pay extra for products that are more environmentally friendly than less friendly competitive products. Nor is there much evidence that consumers are willing to conserve resources, recycle, or tax themselves for environmental causes.

Consider the following instances reported in the *Wall Street Journal*.[4] The restaurant chain Wendy's tried to replace foam plates and cups with paper, but customers in the test markets balked. Procter and Gamble offered Downey fabric softener in concentrated form that requires less packaging than ready-to-use products; however the concentrate version is less convenient because it has to be mixed with water. Sales have been poor. Procter and Gamble manufactures Vizir and Lenor brands of detergents in concentrate form, which the customer mixes at home in reusable bottles. Europeans will take the trouble; Americans will not. Kodak tried to eliminate its yellow film boxes but met customer resistance. McDonald's has been testing mini-incinerators that convert

trash into energy but often meets opposition from community groups that fear the incinerators will pollute the air. A McDonald's spokesperson points out that the emissions are mostly carbon dioxide and water vapor and are "less offensive than a barbecue." Exxon spent approximately $9,200,000 to "save" 230 otters ($40,000 for each otter). Otters in captivity cost $800. Fishermen in Alaska are permitted to shoot otters as pests.[5] Given these facts, doesn't business have every right to assume that public tolerance for environmental damage is quite high, and hence current legal activities by corporations that harm the environment do not violate the avoid-harm criterion?

Recently environmentalists have pointed out the environmental damage caused by the widespread use of disposable diapers. Are Americans ready to give them up and go back to cloth diapers and the diaper pail? Most observers think not. Procter and Gamble is not violating the avoid-harm criterion by manufacturing Pampers. Moreover, if the public wants cloth diapers, business certainly will produce them. If environmentalists want business to produce products that are friendlier to the environment, they must convince Americans to purchase them. Business will respond to the market. It is the consuming public that has the obligation to make the trade-off between cost and environmental integrity.

Data and arguments of the sort described should give environmental critics of business pause. Nonetheless, these critics are not without counter-responses. For example, they might respond that public attitudes are changing. Indeed, they point out, during the Reagan deregulation era, the one area where the public supported government regulations was in the area of environmental law. In addition, *Fortune* predicts environmental integrity as the primary demand of society on business in the 1990s.[6]

More important, they might argue that environmentally friendly products are at a disadvantage in the marketplace because they have public good characteristics. After all, the best situation for the individual is one where most other people use environmentally friendly products but he or she does not, hence reaping the benefit of lower cost and convenience. Since everyone reasons this way, the real demand for environmentally friendly products cannot be registered in the market. Everyone is understating the value of his or her preference for environmentally friendly products. Hence, companies cannot conclude from market behavior that the environmentally unfriendly products are preferred.

Suppose the environmental critics are right that the public goods characteristic of environmentally friendly products creates a market failure. Does that mean the companies are obligated to stop producing these environmentally unfriendly products? I think not, and I propose that we use the four conditions attached to the prevent-harm obligation to show why not. There is a need, and certainly corporations that cause environmental problems are in proximity. However, environmentally clean firms, if there are any, are not in proximity at all, and most business firms are not in proximity with respect to most environmental problems. In other words, the environmental critic must limit his or her argument to the environmental damage a business actually causes. The environmentalist might argue that Procter and Gamble ought to do something about Pampers; I do not see how an environmentalist can use the avoid-harm criterion to argue that Procter and Gamble should do something about acid rain. But even narrowing the obligation to damage actually caused will not be sufficient to establish an obligation to pull a product from the market because it damages the environment or even to go beyond what is legally required to protect the environment. Even for damage actually done, both the high cost of protecting the environment and the competitive pressures of business make further action to protect the environment beyond the capability of business. This conclusion would be more serious if business were the last resort, but it is not.

Traditionally it is the function of the government to correct for market failure. If the market cannot register the true desires of consumers, let them register their preferences in the political arena. Even fairly conservative economic thinkers allow government a legitimate role in correcting market failure. Perhaps the responsibility for energy conservation and pollution control belongs with the government.

Although I think consumers bear a far greater responsibility for preserving and protecting the environment than they have actually exercised, let us assume that the basic responsibility rests with the government. Does that let business off the hook? No. Most of business's unethical conduct regarding the environment occurs in the political arena.

Far too many corporations try to have their cake and eat it too. They argue that it is the job of government to correct for market failure and then use their influence and money to defeat or water down regulations designed to conserve and protect the environment.[7] They argue that consumers should decide how much conservation and protection the environment should have, and then they try to interfere with the exercise of that choice in the political arena. Such behavior is inconsistent and ethically inappropriate. Business has an obligation to avoid intervention in the political process for the purpose of defeating and weakening environmental regulations. Moreover, this is a special obligation to the environment since business does not have a general obligation to avoid pursuing its own parochial interests in the political arena. Business need do nothing wrong when it seeks to influence tariffs, labor policy, or monetary policy. Business does do something wrong when it interferes with the passage of environmental legislation. Why?

First, such a noninterventionist policy is dictated by the logic of the business's argument to avoid a special obligation to protect the environment. Put more formally:

1. Business argues that it escapes special obligations to the environment because it is willing to respond to consumer preferences in this matter.
2. Because of externalities and public goods considerations, consumers cannot express their preferences in the market.
3. The only other viable forum for consumers to express their preferences is in the political arena.
4. Business intervention interferes with the expression of these preferences.
5. Since point 4 is inconsistent with point 1, business should not intervene in the political process.

The importance of this obligation in business is even more important when we see that environmental legislation has special disadvantages in the political arena. Public choice reminds us that the primary interest of politicians is being reelected. Government policy will be skewed in favor of policies that provide benefits to an influential minority as long as the greater costs are widely dispersed. Politicians will also favor projects where benefits are immediate and where costs can be postponed to the future. Such strategies increase the likelihood that a politician will be reelected.

What is frightening about the environmental crisis is that both the conservation of scarce resources and pollution abatement require policies that go contrary to a politician's self-interest. The costs of cleaning up the environment are immediate and huge, yet the benefits are relatively long range (many of them exceedingly long range). Moreover, a situation where the benefits are widely dispersed and the costs are large presents a twofold problem. The costs are large enough so that all voters will likely notice them and in certain cases are catastrophic for individuals (e.g., for those who lose their jobs in a plant shutdown).

Given these facts and the political realities they entail, business opposition to environmental legislation makes a very bad situation much worse. Even if consumers could be persuaded to take environmental issues more seriously, the externalities, opportunities to free ride, and public goods characteristics of the environment make it difficult for even enlightened consumers to express their true preference for the environment in the market. The fact that most environmental legislation trades immediate costs for future benefits makes it difficult for politicians concerned about reelection to support it. Hence it is also difficult for enlightened consumers to have their preferences for a better environment honored in the political arena. Since lack of business intervention seems necessary, and might even be sufficient, for adequate environmental legislation, it seems business has an obligation not to intervene. Nonintervention would prevent the harm of not having the true preferences of consumers for a clean environment revealed. Given business's commitment to satisfying prefer-

ences, opposition to having these preferences expressed seems inconsistent as well.

The extent of this obligation to avoid intervening in the political process needs considerable discussion by ethicists and other interested parties. Businesspeople will surely object that if they are not permitted to play a role, Congress and state legislators will make decisions that will put them at a severe competitive disadvantage. For example, if the United States develops stricter environmental controls than other countries do, foreign imports will have a competitive advantage over domestic products. Shouldn't business be permitted to point that out? Moreover, any legislation that places costs on one industry rather than another confers advantages on other industries. The cost to the electric utilities from regulations designed to reduce the pollution that causes acid rain will give advantages to natural gas and perhaps even solar energy. Shouldn't the electric utility industry be permitted to point that out?

These questions pose difficult questions, and my answer to them should be considered highly tentative. I believe the answer to the first question is "yes" and the answer to the second is "no." Business does have a right to insist that the regulations apply to all those in the industry. Anything else would seem to violate norms of fairness. Such issues of fairness do not arise in the second case. Since natural gas and solar do not contribute to acid rain and since the costs of acid rain cannot be fully captured in the market, government intervention through regulation is simply correcting a market failure. With respect to acid rain, the electric utilities do have an advantage they do not deserve. Hence they have no right to try to protect it.

Legislative bodies and regulatory agencies need to expand their staffs to include technical experts, economists, and engineers so that the political process can be both neutral and highly informed about environmental matters. To gain the respect of business and the public, its performance needs to improve. Much more needs to be said to make any contention that business ought to stay out of the political debate theoretically and practically possible. Perhaps these suggestions point the way for future discussion.

Ironically business might best improve its situation in the political arena by taking on an additional obligation to the environment. Businesspersons often have more knowledge about environmental harms and the costs of cleaning them up. They may often have special knowledge about how to prevent environmental harm in the first place. Perhaps business has a special duty to educate the public and to promote environmentally responsible behavior.

Business has no reticence about leading consumer preferences in other areas. Advertising is a billion-dollar industry. Rather than blaming consumers for not purchasing environmentally friendly products, perhaps some businesses might make a commitment to capture the environmental niche. I have not seen much imagination on the part of business in this area. Far too many advertisements with an environmental message are reactive and public relations driven. Recall those by oil companies showing fish swimming about the legs of oil rigs. An educational campaign that encourages consumers to make environmentally friendly decisions in the marketplace would limit the necessity for business activity in the political arena. Voluntary behavior that is environmentally friendly is morally preferable to coerced behavior. If business took greater responsibility for educating the public, the government's responsibility would be lessened. An educational campaign aimed at consumers would likely enable many businesses to do good while simultaneously doing very well.

Hence business does have obligations to the environment, although these obligations are not found where the critics of business place them. Business has no special obligation to conserve natural resources or to stop polluting over and above its legal obligations. It does have an obligation to avoid intervening in the political arena to oppose environmental regulations, and it has a positive obligation to educate consumers. The benefits of honoring these obligations should not be underestimated.

NOTES

The title for this chapter was suggested by Susan Bernick, a graduate student in the University of Minnesota philosophy department.

1. William Frankena, *Ethics,* 2d ed. (Englewood Cliffs, N.J.: Prentice Hall, 1973), p. 47. Actually Frankena has four principles of *prima facie* duty under the principle of beneficence: one ought not to inflict evil or harm; one ought to prevent evil or harm; one ought to remove evil; and one ought to do or promote good.
2. John G. Simon, Charles W. Powers, and Jon P. Gunneman. *The Ethical Investor: Universities and Corporate Responsibility* (New Haven, Conn.: Yale University Press, 1972), pp. 22–25.
3. Ibid., p. 21.
4. Alicia Swasy, "For Consumers, Ecology Comes Second," *Wall Street Journal,* August 23, 1988, p. B1.
5. Jerry Alder, "Alaska after Exxon," *Newsweek,* September 18, 1989, p. 53.
6. Andrew Kupfer, "Managing Now for the 1990s," *Fortune,* September 26, 1988, pp. 46–47.
7. I owe this point to Gordon Rands, a Ph.D. student in the Carlson School of Management. Indeed the tone of the chapter has shifted considerably as a result of his helpful comments.

Business and Environmental Ethics

W. Michael Hoffman
Executive Director, Center for Business Ethics, Bentley College

The business ethics movement, from my perspective, is still on the march. And the environmental movement, after being somewhat silent for the past twenty years, has once again captured our attention—promising to be a major social force in the 1990s. Much will be written in the next few years trying to tie together these two movements. This is one such effort.

Concern over the environment is not new. Warnings came out of the 1960s in the form of burning rivers, dying lakes, and oil-fouled oceans. Radioactivity was found in our food, DDT in mother's milk, lead and mercury in our water. Every breath of air in the North American hemisphere was reported as contaminated. Some said

From *Business Ethics Quarterly,* Vol. 1, Issue 2, 1991, pp. 169–184. Reprinted by permission of the author.

these were truly warnings from Planet Earth of eco-catastrophe, unless we could find limits to our growth and changes in our lifestyle.

Over the past few years Planet Earth began to speak to us even more loudly than before, and we began to listen more than before. The message was ominous, somewhat akin to God warning Noah. It spoke through droughts, heat waves, and forest fires, raising fears of global warming due to the buildup of carbon dioxide and other gases in the atmosphere. It warned us by raw sewage and medical wastes washing up on our beaches, and by devastating oil spills—one despoiling Prince William Sound and its wildlife to such an extent that it made us weep. It spoke to us through increased skin cancers and discoveries of holes in the ozone layer caused by our use of chlorofluoro-carbons. It drove its message home through the rapid and dangerous cutting and burning of our primitive forests at the rate of one football field a second, leaving us even more vulnerable to green-house gases like carbon dioxide and eliminating scores of irreplaceable species daily. It rained down on us in the form of acid, defoliating our forests and poisoning our lakes and streams. Its warnings were found on barges roaming the seas for places to dump tons of toxic incinerator ash. And its message exploded in our faces at Cher-nobyl and Bhopal, reminding us of past warnings at Three Mile Island and Love Canal.

Senator Albert Gore said in 1988: "The fact that we face an ecological crisis without any precedent in historic times is no longer a matter of any dispute worthy of recognition."[1] The question, he continued, is not whether there is a problem, but how we will address it. This will be the focal point for a public policy debate which requires the full participation of two of its major players—business and government. The debate must clarify such fundamental questions as: (1) What obliga-tion does business have to help with our environ-mental crisis? (2) What is the proper relationship between business and government, especially when faced with a social problem of the magni-tude of the environment crisis? And (3) what ra-tionale should be used for making and justifying decisions to protect the environment? Corpora-

tions, and society in general for that matter, have yet to answer these questions satisfactorily. In the first section of this paper I will briefly address the first two questions. In the final two sections I will say a few things about the third question.

I.

In a 1989 keynote address before the "Business, Ethics and the Environment" conference at the Center for Business Ethics, Norman Bowie of-fered some answers to the first two questions.

> Business does not have an obligation to protect the environment over and above what is required by law; however, it does have a moral obligation to avoid in-tervening in the political arena in order to defeat or weaken environmental legislation.[2]

I disagree with Bowie on both counts.

Bowie's first point is very Friedmanesque.[3] The social responsibility of business is to produce goods and services and to make profit for its share-holders, while playing within the rules of the mar-ket game. These rules, including those to protect the environment, are set by the government and the courts. To do more than is required by these rules is, according to this position, unfair to business. In order to perform its proper function, every business must respond to the market and operate in the same arena as its competitors. As Bowie puts this:

> An injunction to assist in solving societal problems [including depletion of natural resources and pollu-tion] makes impossible demands on a corporation because, at the practical level, it ignores the impact that such activities have on profit.[4]

If, as Bowie claims, consumers are not willing to respond to the cost and use of environmentally friendly products and actions, then it is not the re-sponsibility of business to respond or correct such market failure.

Bowie's second point is a radical departure from this classical position in contending that business should not lobby against the government's process to set environmental regulations. To quote Bowie:

> Far too many corporations try to have their cake and eat it too. They argue that it is the job of government to

correct for market failure and then they use their influence and money to defeat or water down regulations designed to conserve and protect the environment.[5]

Bowie only recommends this abstinence of corporate lobbying in the case of environmental regulations. He is particularly concerned that politicians, ever mindful of their reelection status, are already reluctant to pass environmental legislation which has huge immediate costs and in most cases very long-term benefits. This makes the obligations of business to refrain from opposing such legislation a justified special case.

I can understand why Bowie argues these points. He seems to be responding to two extreme approaches, both of which are inappropriate. Let me illustrate these extremes by the following two stories.

At the Center's First National Conference on Business Ethics, Harvard Business School Professor George Cabot Lodge told of a friend who owned a paper company on the banks of a New England stream. On the first Earth Day in 1970, his friend was converted to the cause of environmental protection. He became determined to stop his company's pollution of the stream, and marched off to put his new-found religion into action. Later, Lodge learned his friend went broke, so he went to investigate. Radiating a kind of ethical purity, the friend told Lodge that he spent millions to stop the pollution and thus could no longer compete with other firms that did not follow his example. So the company went under, 500 people lost their jobs, and the stream remained polluted.

When Lodge asked why his friend hadn't sought help from the state or federal government for stricter standards for everyone, the man replied that was not the American way, that government should not interfere with business activity, and that private enterprise could do the job alone. In fact, he felt it was the social responsibility of business to solve environmental problems, so he was proud that he had set an example for others to follow.

The second story portrays another extreme. A few years ago "Sixty Minutes" interviewed a manager of a chemical company that was discharging effluent into a river in upstate New York. At the time, the dumping was legal, though a bill to pre-vent it was pending in Congress. The manager remarked that he hoped the bill would pass, and that he certainly would support it as a responsible citizen. However, he also said he approved of his company's efforts to defeat the bill and of the firm's policy of dumping wastes in the meantime. After all, isn't the proper role of business to make as much profit as possible within the bounds of law? Making the laws—setting the rules of the game—is the role of government, not business. While wearing his business hat the manager had a job to do, even if it meant doing something that he strongly opposed as a private citizen.

Both stories reveal incorrect answers to the questions posed earlier, the proof of which is found in the fact that neither the New England stream nor the New York river was made any cleaner. Bowie's points are intended to block these two extremes. But to avoid these extremes, as Bowie does, misses the real managerial and ethical failure of the stories. Although the paper company owner and the chemical company manager had radically different views of the ethical responsibilities of business, both saw business and government performing separate roles, and neither felt that business ought to cooperate with government to solve environmental problems.[6]

If the business ethics movement has led us anywhere in the past fifteen years, it is to the position that business has an ethical responsibility to become a more active partner in dealing with social concerns. Business must creatively find ways to become a part of solutions, rather than being a part of problems. Corporations can and must develop a conscience, as Ken Goodpaster and others have argued—and this includes an environmental conscience.[7] Corporations should not isolate themselves from participation in solving our environmental problems, leaving it up to others to find the answers and to tell them what not to do.

Corporations have special knowledge, expertise, and resources which are invaluable in dealing with the environmental crisis. Society needs the ethical vision and cooperation of all its players to solve its most urgent problems, especially one that involves the very survival of the planet itself. Business must work with government to find appropriate solutions. It should lobby for good environmental legislation and lobby against bad legislation, rather than isolating itself from the legislative process as Bowie suggests. It should not be ethically quixotic and try to go it alone, as our paper company owner tried to do, nor should it be ethically inauthentic and fight against what it believes to be environmentally sound policy, as our chemical company manager tried to do. Instead business must develop and demonstrate moral leadership.

There are examples of corporations demonstrating such leadership, even when this has been a risk to their self-interest. In the area of environmental moral leadership one might cite DuPont's discontinuing its Freon products, a $750-million-a-year-business, because of their possible negative effects on the ozone layer, and Proctor and Gamble's manufacture of concentrated fabric softener and detergents which require less packaging. But some might argue, as Bowie does, that the real burden for environmental change lies with consumers, not with corporations. If we as consumers are willing to accept the harm done to the environment by favoring environmentally unfriendly products, corporations have no moral obligation to change so long as they obey environmental law. This is even more the case, so the argument goes, if corporations must take risks or sacrifice profits to do so.

This argument fails to recognize that we quite often act differently when we think of ourselves as *consumers* than when we think of ourselves as *citizens*. Mark Sagoff, concerned about our overreliance on economic solutions, clearly characterizes this dual nature of our decision making.[8] As consumers, we act more often than not for ourselves; as citizens, we take on a broader vision and do what is in the best interests of the community. I often shop for things I don't vote for. I might support recycling referendums, but buy products in nonreturnable bottles. I am not proud of this, but I suspect this is more true of most of us than not. To stake our environmental future on our consumer willingness to pay is surely shortsighted, perhaps even disastrous.

I am not saying that we should not work to be ethically committed citizen consumers, and in-

vestors for that matter. I agree with Bowie that "consumers bear a far greater responsibility for preserving and protecting the environment than they have actually exercised,"[9] but activities which affect the environment should not be left up to what we, acting as consumers, are willing to tolerate or accept. To do this would be to use a market-based method of reasoning to decide on an issue which should be determined instead on the basis of our ethical responsibilities as a member of a social community.

Furthermore, consumers don't make the products, provide the services, or enact the legislation which can be either environmentally friendly or unfriendly. Grass roots boycotts and lobbying efforts are important, but we also need leadership and mutual cooperation from business and government in setting forth ethical environmental policy. Even Bowie admits that perhaps business has a responsibility to educate the public and promote environmentally responsible behavior. But I am suggesting that corporate moral leadership goes far beyond public educational campaigns. It requires moral vision, commitment, and courage, and involves risk and sacrifice. I think business is capable of such a challenge. Some are even engaging in such a challenge. Certainly the business ethics movement should do nothing short of encouraging such leadership. I feel morality demands such leadership.

II.

If business has an ethical responsibility to the environment which goes beyond obeying environmental law, what criterion should be used to guide and justify such action? Many corporations are making environmentally friendly decisions where they see there are profits to be made by doing so. They are wrapping themselves in green where they see a green bottom line as a consequence. This rationale is also being used as a strategy by environmentalists to encourage more businesses to become environmentally conscientious. In December 1989 the highly respected Worldwatch Institute published an article by one of its senior researchers entitled "Doing Well by Doing Good" which gives numerous examples of corporations improving their pocketbooks by improving the environment. It concludes by saying that "fortunately, businesses that work to preserve the environment can also make a buck."[10]

In a recent Public Broadcast Corporation documentary entitled "Profit the Earth," several efforts are depicted of what is called the "new environmentalism" which induces corporations to do things for the environment by appealing to their self-interest. The Environmental Defense Fund is shown encouraging agribusiness in Southern California to irrigate more efficiently and profit by selling the water saved to the city of Los Angeles. This in turn will help save Mono Lake. EDF is also shown lobbying for emissions trading that would allow utility companies which are under their emission allotments to sell their "pollution rights" to those companies which are over their allotments. This is for the purpose of reducing acid rain. Thus the frequent strategy of the new environmentalists is to get business to help solve environmental problems by finding profitable or virtually costless ways for them to participate. They feel that compromise, not confrontation, is the only way to save the earth. By using the tools of the free enterprise system, they are in search of win-win solutions, believing that such solutions are necessary to take us beyond what we have so far been able to achieve.

I am not opposed to these efforts; in most cases I think they should be encouraged. There is certainly nothing wrong with making money while protecting the environment, just as there is nothing wrong with feeling good about doing one's duty. But if business is adopting or being encouraged to adopt the view that good environmentalism is good business, then I think this poses a danger for the environmental ethics movement—a danger which has an analogy in the business ethics movement.

As we all know, the position that good ethics is good business is being used more and more by corporate executives to justify the building of ethics into their companies and by business ethics consultants to gain new clients. For example, the Business Roundtable's *Corporate Ethics* report states:

The corporate community should continue to refine and renew efforts to improve performance and manage change effectively through programs in corporate ethics . . . corporate ethics is a strategic key to survival and profitability in this era of fierce competitiveness in a global economy.[11]

And, for instance, the book *The Power of Ethical Management* by Kenneth Blanchard and Norman Vincent Peale states in big red letters on the cover jacket that "Integrity Pays! You Don't Have to Cheat to Win." The blurb on the inside cover promises that the book "gives hard-hitting, practical, *ethical* strategies that build profits, productivity, and long-term success."[12] Who would have guessed that business ethics could deliver all that! In such ways business ethics gets marketed as the newest cure for what ails corporate America.

Is the rationale that good ethics is good business a proper one for business ethics? I think not. One thing that the study of ethics has taught us over the past 2500 years is that being ethical may on occasion require that we place the interests of others ahead of or at least on par with our own interests. And this implies that the ethical thing to do, the morally right thing to do, may not be in our own self-interest. What happens when the right thing is not the best thing for the business?

Although in most cases good ethics may be good business, it should not be advanced as the only or even the main reason for doing business ethically. When the crunch comes, when ethics conflicts with the firm's interests, any ethics program that has not already faced up to this possibility is doomed to fail because it will undercut the rationale of the program itself. We should promote business ethics, not because good ethics is good business, but because we are morally required to adopt the moral point of view in all our dealings—and business is no exception. In business, as in all other human endeavors, we must be prepared to pay the costs of ethical behavior.

There is a similar danger in the environmental movement with corporations choosing or being wooed to be environmentally friendly on the grounds that it will be in their self-interest. There is the risk of participating in the movement for the wrong reasons. But what does it matter if business cooperates for reasons other than the right reasons, as long as it cooperates? It matters if business believes or is led to believe that it only has a duty to be environmentally conscientious in those cases where such actions either require no sacrifice or actually make a profit. And I am afraid this is exactly what is happening. I suppose it wouldn't matter if the environmental cooperation of business was only needed in those cases where it was also in business' self-interest. But this is surely not the case, unless one begins to really reach and talk about that amorphous concept "long-term" self-interest. Moreover, long-term interests, I suspect, are not what corporations or the new environmentalists have in mind in using self-interest as a reason for environmental action.

I am not saying we should abandon attempts to entice corporations into being ethical, both environmentally and in other ways, by pointing out and providing opportunities where good ethics is good business. And there are many places where such attempts fit well in both the business and environmental ethics movements. But we must be careful not to cast this as the proper guideline for business' ethical responsibility. Because when it is discovered that many ethical actions are not necessarily good for business, at least in the short-run, then the rationale based on self-interest will come up morally short, and both ethical movements will be seen as deceptive and shallow.

III.

What is the proper rationale for responsible business action toward the environment? A minimalist principle is to refrain from causing or prevent the causing of unwarranted harm, because failure to do so would violate certain moral rights not to be harmed. There is, of course, much debate over what harms are indeed unwarranted due to conflict of rights and questions about whether some harms are offset by certain benefits. Norm Bowie, for example, uses the harm principle, but contends that business does not violate it as long as it obeys environmental law. Robert Frederick, on the other hand, convincingly argues that the harm principle morally requires business to find ways to prevent

certain harm it causes even if such harm violates no environmental law.[13]

However, Frederick's analysis of the harm principle is largely cast in terms of harm caused to human beings and the violation of rights of human beings. Even when he hints at the possible moral obligation to protect the environment when no one is caused unwarranted harm, he does so by suggesting that we look to what we, as human beings, value.[14] This is very much in keeping with a humanistic position of environmental ethics which claims that only human beings have rights or moral standing because only human beings have intrinsic value. We may have duties with regard to nonhuman things (penguins, trees, islands, etc.) but only if such duties are derived from duties we have toward human beings. Nonhuman things are valuable only if valued by human beings.

Such a position is in contrast to a naturalistic view of environmental ethics which holds that natural things other than human beings are intrinsically valuable and have, therefore, moral standing. Some naturalistic environmentalists only include other sentient animals in the framework of being deserving of moral consideration; others include all things which are alive or which are an integral part of an ecosystem. This latter view is sometimes called a biocentric environmental ethic as opposed to the homocentric view which sees all moral claims in terms of human beings and their interests. Some characterize these two views as deep *versus* shallow ecology.

The literature on these two positions is vast and the debate is ongoing. The conflict between them goes to the heart of environmental ethics and is crucial to our making of environmental policy and to our perception of moral duties to the environment, including business. I strongly favor the biocentric view. And although this is not the place to try to adequately argue for it, let me unfurl its banner for just a moment.

A version of R. Routley's "last man" example[15] might go something like this: Suppose you were the last surviving human being and were soon to die from nuclear poisoning, as all other human and sentient animals have died before you. Suppose also that it is within your power to destroy all remaining life, or to make it simpler, the last tree which could continue to flourish and propagate if left alone. Furthermore you will not suffer if you do not destroy it. Would you do anything wrong by cutting it down? The deeper ecological view would say yes because you would be destroying something that has value in and of itself, thus making the world a poorer place.

It might be argued that the only reason we may find the tree valuable is because human beings generally find trees of value either practically or aesthetically, rather than the atoms or molecules they might turn into if changed from their present form. The issue is whether the tree has value only in its relation to human beings or whether it has a value deserving of moral consideration inherent in itself in its present form. The biocentric position holds that when we find something wrong with destroying the tree, as we should, we do so because we are responding to an intrinsic value in the natural object, not to a value we give to it. This is a view which argues against a humanistic environmental ethic and which urges us to channel our moral obligations accordingly.

Why should one believe that nonhuman living things or natural objects forming integral parts of ecosystems have intrinsic value? One can respond to this question by pointing out the serious weaknesses and problems of human chauvinism.[16] More complete responses lay out a framework of concepts and beliefs which provides a coherent picture of the biocentric view with human beings as a part of a more holistic value system. But the final answer to the question hinges on what criterion one decides to use for determining moral worth—rationality, sentience, or a deeper biocentric one. Why should we adopt the principle of attributing intrinsic value to all living beings, or even to all natural objects, rather than just to human beings? I suspect Arne Naess gives as good an answer as can be given.

> Faced with the ever returning question of 'Why?,' we have to stop somewhere. Here is a place where we well might stop. We shall admit that the value in itself is something shown in intuition. We attribute intrinsic value to ourselves and our nearest, and the validity of further identification can be contested, and *is* contested by many. The negation may, however, also be attacked through a series of 'whys?' Ultimately, we are in the same human predicament of having to start somewhere, at least for the moment. We must stop somewhere and treat where we then stand as a foundation.[17]

In the final analysis, environmental biocentrism is adopted or not depending on whether it is seen to provide a deeper, richer, and more ethically compelling view of the nature of things.

If this deeper ecological position is correct, then it ought to be reflected in the environmental movement. Unfortunately, for the most part, I do not think this is being done, and there is a price to be paid for not doing so. Moreover, I fear that even those who are of the biocentric persuasion are using homocentric language and strategies to bring business and other major players into the movement because they do not think they will be successful otherwise. They are afraid, and undoubtedly for good reason, that the large part of society, including business, will not be moved by arguments regarding the intrinsic value and rights of natural things. It is difficult enough to get business to recognize and act on their responsibilities to human beings and things of human interest. Hence many environmentalists follow the counsel of Spinoza:

> . . . it is necessary that while we are endeavoring to attain our purpose . . . we are compelled . . . to speak in a manner intelligible to the multitude . . . For we can gain from the multitude no small advantages. . . .[18]

I understand the temptation of environmentalists employing a homocentric strategy, just as I understand business ethicists using the rationale that good ethics is good business. Both want their important work to succeed. But just as with the good ethics is good business tack, there are dangers in being a closet ecocentrist. The ethicists in both cases fail to reveal the deeper moral base of their positions because it's a harder sell. Business ethics gets marketed in terms of self-interest, environmental ethics in terms of human interest.

A major concern in using the homocentric view to formulate policy and law is that nonhuman nature will not receive the moral consideration it deserves. It might be argued, however, that by appealing to the interests and rights of human beings, in most cases nature as a whole will be protected. That is, if we are concerned about a wilderness area, we can argue that its survival is important to future generations who will otherwise be deprived of contact with its unique wildlife. We can also argue that it is important to the aesthetic pleasure of certain individuals or that, if it is destroyed, other recreational areas will become overcrowded. In this way we stand a chance to save the wilderness area without having to refer to our moral obligations to respect the intrinsic value of the spotted owl or of the old-growth forest. This is simply being strategically savvy. To trot out our deeper ecological moral convictions runs the risk of our efforts being ignored, even ridiculed, by business leaders and policy makers. It also runs head-on against a barrage of counter arguments that human interests take precedence over nonhuman interests. In any event it will not be in the best interest of the wilderness area we are trying to protect. Furthermore, all of the above homocentric arguments happen to be true—people will suffer if the wilderness area is destroyed.

In most cases, what is in the best interests of human beings may also be in the best interests of the rest of nature. After all, we are in our present environmental crisis in large part because we have not been ecologically intelligent about what is in our own interest—just as business has encountered much trouble because it has failed to see its interest in being ethically sensitive. But if the environmental movement relies only on arguments based on human interests, then it perpetuates the danger of making environmental policy and law on the basis of our strong inclination to fulfill our immediate self-interests, on the basis of our consumer viewpoints, on the basis of our willingness to pay. There will always be a tendency to allow our short-term interests to eclipse our long-term interests and the long-term interest of humanity itself. Without some grounding in a deeper environmental ethic with obligations to nonhuman natural things, then the temptation to view our own interests in disastrously short-term ways is that much

more encouraged. The biocentric view helps to block this temptation.

Furthermore, there are many cases where what is in human interest is not in the interest of other natural things. Examples range from killing leopards for stylish coats to destroying a forest to build a golf course. I am not convinced that homocentric arguments, even those based on long-term human interests, have much force in protecting the interests of such natural things. Attempts to make these interests coincide might be made, but the point is that from a homocentric point of view the leopard and the forest have no morally relevant interests to consider. It is simply fortuitous if nonhuman natural interests coincide with human interests, and are thereby valued and protected. Let us take an example from the work of Christopher Stone. Suppose a stream has been polluted by a business. From a homocentric point of view, which serves as the basis for our legal system, we can only correct the problem through finding some harm done to human beings who use the stream. Reparation for such harm might involve cessation of the pollution and restoration of the stream, but it is also possible that the business might settle with the people by paying them for their damages and continue to pollute the stream. Homocentrism provides no way for the stream to be made whole again unless it is in the interests of human beings to do so. In short it is possible for human beings to sell out the stream.[19]

I am not saying that human interests cannot take precedence over nonhuman interests when there are conflicts. For this we need to come up with criteria for deciding on interspecific conflicts of interests, just as we do for intraspecific conflicts of interest among human beings.[20] But this is a different problem from holding that nonhuman natural things have no interests or value deserving of moral consideration. There are times when causing harm to natural things is morally unjustifiable when there are no significant human interests involved and even when there are human interests involved. But only a deeper ecological ethic than homocentrism will allow us to defend this.

Finally, perhaps the greatest danger that biocentric environmentalists run in using homocentric strategies to further the movement is the loss of the very insight that grounded their ethical concern in the first place. This is nicely put by Lawrence Tribe:

> What the environmentalist may not perceive is that, by couching his claim in terms of human self-interest—by articulating environmental goals wholly in terms of human needs and preferences—he may be helping to legitimate a system of discourse which so structures human thought and feeling as to erode, over the long run, the very sense of obligation which provided the initial impetus for his own protective efforts.[21]

Business ethicists run a similar risk in couching their claims in terms of business self-interest.

The environmental movement must find ways to incorporate and protect the intrinsic value of animal and plant life and even other natural objects that are integral parts of ecosystems. This must be done without constantly reducing such values to human interests. This will, of course, be difficult, because our conceptual ideology and ethical persuasion is so dominantly homocentric; however, if we are committed to a deeper biocentric ethic, then it is vital that we try to find appropriate ways to promote it. Environmental impact statements should make explicit reference to nonhuman natural values. Legal rights for nonhuman natural things, along the lines of Christopher Stone's proposal, should be sought.[22] And naturalistic ethical guidelines, such as those suggested by Holmes Rolston, should be set forth for business to follow when its activities impact upon ecosystems.[23]

At the heart of the business ethics movement is its reaction to the mistaken belief that business only has responsibilities to a narrow set of its stakeholders, namely its stockholders. Crucial to the environmental ethics movement is its reaction to the mistaken belief that only human beings and human interests are deserving of our moral consideration. I suspect that the beginnings of both movements can be traced to these respective moral insights. Certainly the significance of both movements lies in their search for a broader and deeper moral perspective. If business and environmental ethicists begin to rely solely on promotional strategies of self-interest, such as good ethics is good business, and of human interest, such as homocentrism, then they face the danger of cutting off the very roots of their ethical efforts.

NOTES

This paper was originally presented as the Presidential Address to the *Society for Business Ethics,* August 10, 1990, San Francisco, CA.

1. Albert Gore, "What is Wrong With Us?" *Time* (January 2, 1989), 66.
2. Norman Bowie, "Morality, Money, and Motor Cars," *Business, Ethics, and the Environment: The Public Policy Debate,* edited by W. Michael Hoffman, Robert Frederick, and Edward S. Petry, Jr. (New York: Quorum Books, 1990), p. 89.
3. See Milton Friedman, "The Social Responsibility of Business Is to Increase Its Profits." *The New York Times Magazine* (September 13, 1970).
4. Bowie, p. 91.
5. Bowie, p. 94.
6. Robert Frederick, Assistant Director of the Center for Business Ethics, and I have developed and written these points together. Frederick has also provided me with invaluable assistance on other points in this paper.
7. Kenneth E. Goodpaster, "Can a Corporation have an Environmental Conscience," *The Corporation, Ethics, and the Environment,* edited by W. Michael Hoffman, Robert Frederick, and Edward S. Petry, Jr. (New York: Quorum Books, 1990).
8. Mark Sagoff, "At the Shrine of Our Lady of Fatima, or Why Political Questions Are Not All Economic," found in *Business Ethics: Readings and Cases in Corporate Morality,* 2nd edition, edited by W. Michael Hoffman and Jennifer Mills Moore (New York: McGraw-Hill, 1990). pp. 494–503.
9. Bowie, p. 94.
10. Cynthia Pollock Shea, "Doing Well By Doing Good," *World-Watch* (November/December, 1989), p. 30.
11. *Corporate Ethics: A Prime Business Asset,* a report by The Business Roundtable, February, 1988, p. 4.
12. Kenneth Blanchard, and Norman Vincent Peale. *The Power of Ethical Management* (New York: William Morrow and Company, Inc., 1988).
13. Robert Frederick, "Individual Rights and Environmental Protection," presented at the Annual Society for Business Ethics Conference in San Francisco, August 10 and 11, 1990.
14. Frederick.
15. Richard Routley, and Val Routley, "Human Chauvinism and Environmental Ethics," *Environmental Philosophy,* Monograph Series, No. 2, edited by Don Mannison, Michael McRobbie, and Richard Routley (Australian National University, 1980), pp. 121ff.

16. See Paul W. Taylor, "The Ethics of Respect for Nature," found in *People, Penguins, and Plastic Trees,* edited by Donald VanDeVeer and Christine Pierce (Belmont, California: Wadsworth, 1986), pp. 178–83. Also see R. and V. Routley, "Against the Inevitability of Human Chauvinism," found in *Ethics and the Problems of the 21st Century,* edited by K. E. Goodpaster and K. M. Sayre (Notre Dame: University of Notre Dame Press, 1979), pp. 36–59.
17. Arne Naess, "Identification as a Source of Deep Ecological Attitudes," *Deep Ecology,* edited by Michael Tobias (San Marcos, California: Avant Books, 1988), p. 266.
18. Benedict de Spinoza, "On the Improvement of the Understanding," found in *Philosophy of Benedict de Spinoza,* translated by R. H. M. Elwes (New York: Tudor Publishing Co., 1936), p. 5.
19. Christopher D. Stone, "Should Trees Have Standing?—Toward Legal Rights for Natural Objects," found in *People, Penguins, and Plastic Tress,* pp. 86–87.
20. See Donald VanDeVeer, "Interspecific Justice," *People, Penguins, and Plastic Trees,* pp. 51–66.
21. Lawrence H. Tribe, "Ways Not to Think about Plastic Trees: New Foundations for Environmental Law," found in *People, Penguins, and Plastic Trees,* p. 257.
22. Stone, pp. 83–96.
23. Holmes Rolston, III, *Environmental Ethics* (Philadelphia: Temple University Press, 1988), pp. 301–13.

The Economic Common Sense of Pollution

Larry E. Ruff
Managing Director, Putnam, Hayes, and Bartlett, Inc., Washington, DC

We are going to make very little real progress in solving the problem of pollution until we recognize it for what, primarily, it is: an economic problem, which must be understood in economic

Excerpted from "The Economic Sense of Pollution" by Larry E. Ruff, *The Public Interest,* No. 9 (Spring 1970), pp. 69–85. Copyright © 1970 by National Affairs Inc. Reprinted with permission of the publisher.

terms. Of course, there are *noneconomic* aspects of pollution, as there are with all economic problems, but all too often, such secondary matters dominate discussion. Engineers, for example, are certain that pollution will vanish once they find the magic gadget or power source. Politicians keep trying to find the right kind of bureaucracy; 'and bureaucrats maintain an unending search for the correct set of rules and regulations. Those who are above such vulgar pursuits pin their hopes on a moral regeneration or social revolution, apparently in the belief that saints and socialists have no garbage to dispose of. But as important as technology, politics, law, and ethics are to the pollution question, all such approaches are bound to have disappointing results, for they ignore the primary fact that pollution is an economic problem.'

MARGINALISM

One of the most fundamental economic ideas is that of *marginalism,* which entered economic theory when economists became aware of the differential calculus in the 19th century and used it to formulate economic problems as problems of "maximization." The standard economic problem came to be viewed as that of finding a level of operation of some activity which would maximize the net gain from that activity, where the net gain is the difference between the benefits and the costs of the activity. As the level of activity increases, both benefits and costs will increase; but because of diminishing returns, costs will increase faster than benefits. When a certain level of the activity is reached, any further expansion increases costs more than benefits. At this "optimal" level, "marginal cost"—or the cost of expanding the activity—equals "marginal benefit," or the benefit from expanding the activity. Further expansion would cost more than it is worth, and reduction in the activity would reduce benefits more than it would save costs. The net gain from the activity is said to be maximized at this point.

This principle is so simple that it is almost embarrassing to admit it is the cornerstone of economics. Yet intelligent men often ignore it in discussion of public issues. Educators, for example, often suggest that, if it is better to be literate than illiterate there is no logical stopping point in supporting education. Or scientists have pointed out that the benefits derived from "science" obviously exceed the costs and then have proceeded to infer that their particular project should be supported. The correct comparison, of course, is between *additional* benefits created by the proposed activity and the *additional* costs incurred.

The application of marginalism to questions of pollution is simple enough conceptually. The difficult part lies in estimating the cost and benefits functions, a question to which I shall return. But several important qualitative points can be made immediately. The first is that the choice facing a rational society is *not* between clean air and dirty air, or between clear water and polluted water, but rather between various *levels* of dirt and pollution. The aim must be to find that level of pollution abatement where the costs of further abatement begin to exceed the benefits.

The second point is that the optimal combination of pollution control methods is going to be a very complex affair. Such steps as demanding a 10 percent reduction in pollution from all sources, without considering the relative difficulties and costs of the reduction, will certainly be an inefficient approach. Where it is less costly to reduce pollution, we want a greater reduction, to a point where an additional dollar spent on control anywhere yields the same reduction in pollution levels.

MARKETS, EFFICIENCY, AND EQUITY

A second basic economic concept is the idea—or the ideal—of the self-regulating economic system. Adam Smith illustrated this ideal with the example of bread in London: the uncoordinated, selfish actions of many people—farmer, miller, shipper, baker, grocer—provide bread for the city dweller, without any central control and at the lowest possible cost. Pure self-interest, guided only by the famous "invisible hand" of competition, organizes the economy efficiently.

The logical basis of this rather startling result is that, under certain conditions, competitive prices convey all the information necessary for making the optimal decision. A builder trying to decide whether to use brick or concrete will weigh his requirements and tastes against the prices of the materials. Other users will do the same, with the result that those whose needs and preferences for brick are relatively the strongest will get brick. Further, profit-maximizing producers will weigh relative production costs, reflecting society's productive capabilities, against relative prices, reflecting society's tastes and desires, when deciding how much of each good to produce. The end result is that users get brick and cement in quantities and proportions that reflect their individual tastes and society's production opportunities. No other solution would be better from the standpoint of all the individuals concerned.

This suggests what it is that makes pollution different. The efficiency of competitive markets depends on the identity of *private* costs and *social* costs. As long as the brick-cement producer must compensate somebody for every cost imposed by his production, his profit-maximizing decisions about how much to produce, and how, will also be socially efficient decisions. Thus, if a producer dumps wastes into the air, river, or ocean; if he pays nothing for such dumping; and if the disposed wastes have no noticeable effect on anyone else, living or still unborn; then the private and social costs of disposal are identical and nil, and the producer's private decisions are socially efficient. *But if these wastes do affect others, then the social costs of waste disposal are not zero. Private and social costs diverge, and private profit-maximizing decisions are not socially efficient.* Suppose, for example, that cement production dumps large quantities of dust into the air, which damages neighbors, and that the brick-cement producer pays these neighbors nothing. In the social sense, cement will be over-produced relative to brick and other products because users of the products will make decisions based on market prices which do not reflect true social costs. They will use cement when they should use brick, or when they should not build at all.

This divergence between private and social costs is the fundamental cause of pollution of all types, and it arises in any society where decisions are at all decentralized—which is to say, in any economy of any size which hopes to function at all. Even the socialist manager of the brick-cement plant, told to maximize output given the resources at his disposal, will use the People's Air to dispose of the People's Wastes; to do otherwise would be to violate his instructions. And if instructed to avoid pollution "when possible," he does not know what to do: how can he decide whether more brick or cleaner air is more important for building socialism? The capitalist manager is in exactly the same situation. Without prices to convey the needed information, he does not know what action is in the public interest, and certainly would have no incentive to act correctly even if he did know.

ESTIMATING THE COSTS OF POLLUTION

Both in theory and practice, the most difficult part of an economic approach to pollution is the measurement of the cost and benefits of its abatement. Only a small fraction of the costs of pollution can be estimated straightforwardly. If, for example, smog reduces the life of automobile tires by 10 percent, one component of the cost of smog is 10 percent of tire expenditures. It has been estimated that, in a moderately polluted area of New York City, filthy air imposes extra costs for painting, washing, laundry, etc., of $200 per person per year. Such costs must be included in any calculation of the benefits of pollution abatement, and yet they are only a part of the relevant costs—and often a small part. Accordingly it rarely is possible to justify a measure like river pollution control solely on the basis of costs to individuals or firms of treating water because it usually is cheaper to process only the water that is actually used for industrial or municipal purposes, and to ignore the river itself.

The costs of pollution that cannot be measured so easily are often called "intangible" or "noneconomic," although neither term is particularly appropriate. Many of these costs are as tangible as burning eyes or a dead fish, and all such costs are relevant to a valid economic analysis. Let us therefore call these costs "nonpecuniary."

The only real difference between nonpecuniary costs and the other kind lies in the difficulty of estimating them. If pollution in Los Angeles harbor is reducing marine life, this imposes costs on society. The cost of reducing commercial fishing could be estimated directly: it would be the fixed cost of converting men and equipment from fishing to an alternative occupation, plus the difference between what they earned in fishing and what they earn in the new occupation, plus the loss to consumers who must eat chicken instead of fish. But there are other, less straightforward costs: the loss of recreation opportunities for children and sportsfishermen and of research facilities for marine biologists, etc. Such costs are obviously difficult to measure and may be very large indeed: but just as surely as they are not zero, so too are they not infinite. Those who call for immediate action and damn the cost, merely because the spiney starfish and furry crab populations are shrinking, are putting an infinite marginal value on these creatures. This strikes a disinterested observer as an overestimate.

The above comments may seem crass and insensitive to those who, like one angry letterwriter to the *Los Angeles Times,* want to ask: "If conservation is not for its own sake, then what in the world *is* it for?" Well, what *is* the purpose of pollution control? Is it for its own sake? Of course not. If we answer that it is to make the air and water clean and quiet, then the question arises: what is the purpose of clean air and water? If the answer is, to please the nature gods, then it must be conceded that all pollution must cease immediately because the cost of angering the gods is presumably infinite. But if the answer is that the purpose of clean air and water is to further human enjoyment of life on this planet, then we are faced with the economists' basic question: given the limited alternatives that a niggardly nature allows, how can we best further human enjoyment of life? And the answer is, by making intelligent marginal decisions on the basis of costs and benefits. Pollution control is for lots of things: breathing comfortably, enjoying mountains, swimming in water, for health, beauty, and the general delectation. But so are many other things, like good food and wine, comfortable housing and fast transportation. The question is not which of these desirable things we should have, but rather what combination is most desirable. To determine such a combination, we must know the rate at which individuals are willing to substitute more of one desirable thing for less of another desirable thing. Prices are one way of determining those rates.

But if we cannot directly observe market prices for many of the costs of pollution, we must find another way to proceed. One possibility is to infer the costs from other prices, just as we infer the value of an ocean view from real estate prices. In principle, one could estimate the value people put on clean air and beaches by observing how much more they are willing to pay for property in non-polluted areas. Such information could be obtained; but there is little of it available at present.

Another possible way of estimating the costs of pollution is to ask people how much they would be willing to pay to have pollution reduced. A resident of Pasadena might be willing to pay $100 a year to have smog reduced 10 or 20 per cent. In Barstow, where the marginal cost of smog is much less, a resident might not pay $10 a year to have smog reduced 10 per cent. If we knew how much it was worth to everybody, we could add up these amounts and obtain an estimate of the cost of a marginal amount of pollution. The difficulty, of course, is that there is no way of guaranteeing truthful responses. Your response to the question, how much is pollution costing *you,* obviously will depend on what you think will be done with this information. If you think you will be compensated for these costs, you will make a generous estimate; if you think that you will be charged for the control in proportion to these costs, you will make a small estimate.

Let us assume that, somehow, we have made an estimate of the social cost function for pollution, including the marginal cost associated with various pollution levels. We now need an estimate of the benefits of pollution—or, if you prefer, of the costs of pollution abatement. So we set the Pollution Control Board (PCB) to work on this task.

The PCB has a staff of engineers and technicians, and they begin working on the obvious question; for each pollution source, how much would it cost to reduce pollution by 10 per cent, 20 per cent, and so on. If the PCB has some economists, they will know that the cost of reducing total pollution by 10 per cent is *not* the total cost of reducing each pollution source by 10 per cent. Rather, they will use the equimarginal principle

and find the pattern of control such that an additional dollar spent on control of any pollution source yields the same reduction. This will minimize the cost of achieving any given level of abatement. In this way the PCB can generate a "cost of abatement" function, and the corresponding marginal cost function.

Once cost and benefit functions are known, the PCB should choose a level of abatement that maximizes net gain. This occurs where the marginal cost of further abatement just equals the marginal benefit. If, for example, we could reduce pollution damages by $2 million at a cost of $1 million, we should obviously impose that $1 million cost. But if the damage reduction is only $1/2 million, we should not and in fact should reduce control efforts.

This principle is obvious enough but is often overlooked. One author, for example, has written that the national cost of air pollution is $11 billion a year but that we are spending less than $50 million a year on control; he infers from this that "we could justify a tremendous strengthening of control efforts on purely economic grounds." That *sounds* reasonable, if all you care about are sounds. But what is the logical content of the statement? Does it imply we should spend $11 billion on control just to make things even? Suppose we were spending $11 billion on control and thereby succeeded in reducing pollution costs to $50 million. Would this imply we were spending too *much* on control? Of course not. We must compare the *marginal* decrease in pollution costs to the *marginal* increase in abatement costs.

PUTTING A PRICE ON POLLUTION

Once the optimal pollution level is determined, all that is necessary is for the PCB to enforce the pattern of controls which it has determined to be optimal. But now a new problem arises: how should the controls be enforced?

There is a very simple way to accomplish this. *Put a price on pollution.* A price-based control mechanism would differ from an ordinary market transaction system only in that the PCB would set the prices, instead of their being set by demand supply forces, and that the state would force payment.

Under such a system, anyone could emit any amount of pollution so long as he pays the price which the PCB sets to approximate the marginal social cost of pollution. Under this circumstance, private decisions based on self-interest are efficient. If pollution consists of many components, each with its own social cost, there should be different prices for each component. Thus, extremely dangerous materials must have an extremely high price, perhaps stated in terms of "years in jail" rather than "dollars," although a sufficiently high dollar price is essentially the same thing. In principle, the prices should vary with geographical location, season of the year, direction of the wind, and even day of the week, although the cost of too many variations may preclude such fine distinctions.

Once the prices are set, polluters can adjust to them any way they choose. Because they act on self-interest they will reduce their pollution by every means possible up to the point where further reduction would cost more than the price. Because all face the same price for the same type of pollution, the marginal cost of abatement is the same everywhere. If there are economies of scale in pollution control, as in some types of liquid waste treatment, plants can cooperate in establishing joint treatment facilities. In fact, some enterprising individual could buy these wastes from various plants (at negative price—i.e., they would get paid for carting them off), treat them, and then sell them at a higher price, making a profit in the process. (After all, this is what rubbish removal firms do now.) If economies of scale are so substantial that the provider of such a service becomes a monopolist, then the PCB can operate the facilities itself.

Obviously, such a scheme does not eliminate the need for the PCB. The board must measure the output of pollution from all sources, collect the fees, and so on. But it does not need to know anything about any plant except its total emission of pollution. It does not control, negotiate, threaten, or grant favors. It does not destroy incentive because development of new control methods will reduce pollution payments.

As a test of this price system of control, let us consider how well it would work when applied to automobile pollution, a problem for which direct control is usually considered the only feasible approach. If the price system can work here, it can work anywhere.

Suppose, then, that a price is put on the emissions of automobiles. Obviously, continuous metering of such emissions is impossible. But it should be easy to determine the average output of pollution for cars of different makes, models, and years, having different types of control devices and using different types of fuel. Through graduated registration fees and fuel taxes, each car owner would be assessed roughly the social cost of his car's pollution, adjusted for whatever control devices he has chosen to install and for his driving habits. If the cost of installing a device, driving a different car, or finding alternative means of transportation is less than the price he must pay to continue his pollution, he will presumably take all the necessary steps. But each individual remains free to find the best adjustment to his particular situation. It would be remarkable if everyone decided to install the same devices which some states currently require; and yet that is the effective assumption of such requirements.

Even in the difficult case of auto pollution, the price system has a number of advantages. Why should a person living in the Mojave desert, where pollution has little social cost, take the same pains to reduce air pollution as a person living in Pasadena? Present California law, for example, makes no distinction between such areas; the price system would. And what incentive is there for auto manufacturers to design a less polluting engine? The law says only that they must install a certain device in every car. If GM develops a more efficient engine, the law will eventually be changed to require this engine on all cars, raising costs and reducing sales. But will such development take place? No collusion is needed for manufacturers to decide unanimously that it would be foolish to devote funds to such development. But with a pollution fee paid by the consumer, there is a real advantage for any firm to be first with a better engine, and even a collusive agreement wouldn't last long in the face of such an incentive. The same is true of fuel manufacturers, who now have no real incentive to look for better fuels. Perhaps most important of all, the present situation provides no real way of determining whether it is cheaper to reduce pollution by muzzling cars or industrial plants. The experts say that most smog comes from cars; but *even if true, this does not imply that it is more efficient to control autos rather than other pollution sources.* How can we decide which is more efficient without mountains of information? The answer is, by making drivers and plants pay the same price for the same pollution, and letting self-interest do the job.

In situations where pollution outputs can be measured more or less directly (unlike the automobile pollution case), the price system is clearly superior to direct control. A study of possible control methods in the Delaware estuary, for example, estimated that, compared to a direct control scheme requiring each polluter to reduce his pollution by a fixed percentage, an effluent charge which would achieve the same level of pollution abatement would be only half as costly—a saving of about $150 million. Such a price system would also provide incentive for further improvements, a simple method of handling new plants, and revenue for the control authority.

In general, the price system allocates costs in a manner which is at least superficially fair: those who produce and consume goods which cause pollution, pay the costs. But the superior efficiency in control and apparent fairness are not the only advantages of the price mechanism. Equally important is the ease with which it can be put into operation. It is not necessary to have detailed information about all the techniques of pollution reduction, or estimates of all costs and benefits. Nor is it necessary to determine whom to blame or who should pay. All that is needed is a mechanism for estimating, if only roughly at first, the pollution output of all polluters, together with a means of collecting fees. Then we can simply pick a price—any price—for each category of pollution, and we are in business. The initial price should be chosen on the basis of some estimate of its effects but need not be the optimal one. If the resulting reduction in pollution is not "enough," the price can be raised until there is sufficient reduction. A change in technology, number of plants, or whatever, can be accommodated by a

change in the price, even without detailed knowledge of all the technological and economic data. Further, once the idea is explained, the price system is much more likely to be politically acceptable than some method of direct control. Paying for a service, such as garbage disposal, is a well-established tradition, and is much less objectionable than having a bureaucrat nosing around and giving arbitrary orders. When businessmen, consumers, and politicians understand the alternatives, the price system will seem very attractive indeed.

An important part of this method of control obviously is the mechanism that sets and changes the pollution price. Ideally, the PCB could choose this price on the basis of an estimate of the benefits and costs involved, in effect imitating the impersonal workings of ordinary market forces. But because many of the costs and benefits cannot be measured, a less "objective," more political procedure is needed. This political procedure could take the form of a referendum, in which the PCB would present to the voters alternative schedules of pollution prices, together with the estimated effects of each. The strongest argument for the price system is not found in idle speculation but in the real world, and in particular, in Germany. The Rhine River in Germany is a dirty stream, recently made notorious when an insecticide spilled into the river and killed millions of fish. One tributary of the Rhine, a river called the Ruhr, is the sewer for one of the world's most concentrated industrial areas. The Ruhr River valley contains 40 per cent of German industry, including 80 per cent of coal, iron, steel and heavy chemical capacity. The Ruhr is a small river, with a low flow of less than half the flow on the Potomac near Washington. The volume of wastes is extremely large—actually exceeding the flow of the river itself in the dry season! *Yet people and fish swim in the Ruhr River.*

This amazing situation is the result of over forty years of control of the Ruhr and its tributaries by a hierarchy of regional authorities. These authorities have as their goal the maintenance of the quality of the water in the area at minimum cost, and they have explicitly applied the equimarginal principle to accomplish this. Water quality is formally defined in a technological rather than an economic way; the objective is to "not kill the fish." Laboratory tests are conducted to determine what levels of various types of pollution are lethal to fish, and from these figures an index is constructed which measures the "amount of pollution" from each source in terms of its fish-killing capacity. This index is different for each source, because of differences in amount and composition of the waste, and geographical locale. Although this physical index is not really a very precise measure of the real economic *cost* of the waste, it has the advantage of being easily measured and widely understood. Attempts are made on an *ad hoc* basis to correct the index if necessary—if, for example, a nonlethal pollutant gives fish an unpleasant taste.

Once the index of pollution is constructed, a price is put on the pollution, and each source is free to adjust its operation any way it chooses. Geographical variation in prices, together with some direct advice from the authorities, encourage new plants to locate where pollution is less damaging. For example, one tributary of the Ruhr has been converted to an open sewer; it has been lined with concrete and landscaped, but otherwise no attempt is made to reduce pollution in the river itself. A treatment plant at the mouth of the river processes all these wastes at low cost. Therefore, the price of pollution on this river is set low. This arrangement, by the way, is a rational, if perhaps unconscious, recognition of marginal principles. The loss caused by destruction of *one* tributary is rather small, if the nearby rivers are maintained, while the benefit from having this inexpensive means of waste disposal is very large. However, if *another* river were lost, the cost would be higher and the benefits lower; one open sewer may be the optimal number.

The revenues from the pollution charges are used by the authorities to measure pollution, conduct tests and research, operate dams to regulate stream flow, and operate waste treatment facilities where economies of scale make this desirable. These facilities are located at the mouths of some tributaries, and at several dams in the Ruhr. If the authorities find pollution levels are getting too high, they simply raise the price, which causes polluters to try to reduce their wastes, and pro-

vides increased revenues to use on further treatment. Local governments influence the authorities, which helps to maintain recreation values, at least in certain stretches of the river.

This classic example of water management is obviously not exactly the price system method discussed earlier. There is considerable direct control, and the pollution authorities take a very active role. Price regulation is not used as much as it could be; for example, no attempt is made to vary the price over the season, even though high flow on the Ruhr is more than ten times larger than low flow. If the price of pollution were reduced during high flow periods, plants would have an incentive to regulate their production and/or store their wastes for release during periods when the river can more easily handle them. The difficulty of continuously monitoring wastes means this is not done; as automatic, continuous measurement techniques improve and are made less expensive, the use of variable prices will increase. Though this system is not entirely regulated by the price mechanism, prices are used more here than anywhere else, and the system is much more successful than any other. So, both in theory and in practice, the price system is attractive, and ultimately must be the solution to pollution problems.

Dilemmas of Disclosure: Ethical Issues in Environmental Auditing

Karen Blumenfeld
Former Director, Alliance Technologies Corporation

Environmental auditors occasionally face conflicts between competing moral demands. Situations may arise where an environmental auditor's duty to his or her employer appears to conflict with the

From *The Corporation, Ethics, and the Environment,* edited by W. Michael Hoffman, Robert Frederick, and Edward S. Petry, Jr. (Westport, CT: Quorum Books, 1990).

duty to protect innocent third parties from harm. This chapter explores a fundamental question of environmental auditing ethics: what is an environmental auditor's ethical responsibility when he or she has identified a potentially serious environmental risk and, after reporting the risk through appropriate company channels, feels that the company is failing to take responsible action? Does the auditor have a moral duty to disclose the potential problem to outside representatives (e.g., the government, the plant's neighbors, or the press), or is any public duty superseded by an obligation to protect the employer's confidentiality?

I will argue that an environmental auditor does not have a special professional duty to protect third parties from harm, but the auditor does have an ordinary moral duty to do so. In the situation described, this ordinary moral duty conflicts with the auditor's fiduciary duty to protect the employer's confidentiality.[1] Both duties represent legitimate moral expectations. A principle for their reconciliation must be defined. In the absence of environmental auditing professional standards or codes of ethics, I propose a series of tests for evaluating auditors' ethical obligations when their duty to the public conflicts with their duty to their employer.

The scope of this chapter is limited in two ways. First, it is limited to ethical issues involved in the disclosure dilemma; legal issues are outside its scope. Second, it focuses exclusively on internal environmental auditors. Because special issues of professional responsibility and liability may arise with outside auditing consultants, I chose to limit the paper's scope to internal environmental auditors.

THE SCENARIO

Ed Anderson is a seasoned environmental auditor. He is a chemical engineer by training and has been with the Western Manufacturing Company for nineteen years. Prior to 1985, Anderson held increasingly responsible positions in three different plants. In 1985, while Anderson was manufacturing engineering director at the Alameda plant, he was offered the opportunity to head the new cor-

porate environmental auditing program. Anderson accepted the offer and now heads a group of four drawn from various company operations. As director of the Environmental Audit Department, Ed Anderson reports to the company's vice-president for health, safety, and the environment. He is responsible for planning, managing, participating in and ensuring the proper reporting of periodic environmental audits of company operations.

Western Manufacturing Company established its corporate environmental auditing program in response to a series of small but embarrassing penalties by the Environmental Protection Agency (EPA) for violations of hazardous waste regulations at two plants. In spite of the company's substantially increased investment in environmental controls, the chief executive officer (CEO) did not feel comfortable that he or his senior management team understood the firm's potential environmental exposures. On hearing about the practice of environmental auditing among nearly all his competitors by 1984 and spurred by the Bhopal tragedy, the CEO decided to establish a corporate environmental auditing program. The program would provide top management with independent assurance that company operations are in compliance with applicable environmental laws and regulations. In initiating the program, the CEO made clear to all corporate staff and line managers the company's commitment to protecting the environment and complying with the law. He clearly articulated his intent that compliance problems identified during environmental audits would be remedied. After all, he observed, the company would be foolhardy to identify and document environmental problems if it did not have a serious commitment to fixing them.

Ed Anderson and the vice-president for health, safety, and the environment designed the audit program based on discussions with other environmental professionals and a detailed review of the environmental auditing literature. Figure 1 illustrates the principles of environmental auditing that Anderson and his boss established for the company. Western's environmental auditing program is now running smoothly. The program has virtually full cooperation from plant personnel who

FIGURE 1

WESTERN MANUFACTURING COMPANY ENVIRONMENTAL AUDITING PRINCIPLES

1. *Environmental Audit Definition:* Environmental auditing is a methodical and documented examination of our facilities' operations and practices to evaluate the extent to which they meet environmental laws and regulations.

2. *Environmental Audit Program Objective:* The primary objective of Western Manufacturing Company's environmental audit program is to provide assurance to top management that facility operations are in compliance with environmental laws and regulations, and that reasonable steps are being taken to correct identified environmental problems.

3. *Environmental Audit Program Direction:* Western Manufacturing Company's environmental audit program is sanctioned by the Chief Executive Officer and the Board of Directors. Top management support is demonstrated through our corporate environmental policy statement, which articulates management's desire for Western Manufacturing Company to be in full compliance with environmental requirements and management's commitment to follow-up on audit findings that require corrections.

4. *Environmental Audit Organization:* The environmental audit function is independent of ad line operations being audited. To assure operational independence, the Environmental Audit Department reports to the Vice President for Health, Safety, and the Environment who reports to the CEO through the Executive Vice President for Corporate Affairs.

5. *Environmental Audit Program Staffing:* The Environmental Audit Department is staffed by experienced individuals drawn from company operations. These individuals are drawn both from plant operations

and from plant environmental staff positions. All environmental auditors receive initial training in audit skills, knowledge and techniques, as well as continuing education and training during their tenure as auditors. It is expected that some number of auditors will return full-time to plant operations after 3–5 years in the Environmental Audit Department. In addition to providing an important corporate assurance function, the environmental auditing program is also considered to provide a useful training ground for rising professionals in the corporation.

6. *Environmental Audit Program Design:* Typically, an audit begins with pre-audit planning which involves notifying the plant being audited, arranging trip logistics, and reviewing background information. The on-site audit activities normally are conducted in four steps: (1) understand and evaluate internal environmental management systems; (2) collect relevant information; (3) evaluate information collected; and (4) report audit findings. Following the on-site visit, the audit concludes with formal reporting and ensuring that identified deficiencies are corrected. These steps are codified in a series of written audit protocols. The scope of each audit is determined in advance and may include air pollution control and/or water pollution control and/or hazardous and solid waste management. A system has been established for determining audit frequency, but in no case will any plant be audited less than once every 4 years.

7. *Quality Assurance:* Program quality assurance will be ensured by periodic independent reviews of Western Manufacturing Company's program by an outside consultant.

generally understand that the program is not designed to punish the plants but rather to protect the company and the plants from unreasonable environmental risks and associated liabilities.

THE AUDITOR'S DISCLOSURE DILEMMA

In January 1989 Ed Anderson and two fellow auditors are on a routine audit at the Columbia plant. At the audit close-out meeting with the plant manager and environmental coordinator, Ed Anderson presents the audit team's findings. He notes that the plant

appears to be largely in compliance with applicable laws, regulations, and permit conditions; however, the most serious finding, in his judgment, is a situation that goes beyond compliance. The audit team has observed that the plant has limited preventive maintenance programs and aging physical facilities. Failure of any of several hazardous chemical storage loading and transfer systems could result in contamination of a water supply serving 750,000 people. Ed Anderson is convinced that a major spillage is imminent. He agrees not to document this issue in his audit report since no compliance problem is involved; however, he asks the plant manager to study the problem further to determine the degree of risk posed to the community.

The following week, Ed Anderson prepares the draft audit report and sends it to the Columbia plant manager with copies to the specialty chemicals division manager, the vice-president for health, safety, and the environment, and the office of general counsel. Four weeks later, the Columbia plant manager's response arrives. Follow-up actions have been specified for each of the audit findings with reasonable timetables for their implementation, but no mention is made of the potential spillage risk. While legally the company is not obliged to take action, Anderson feels that from a risk management standpoint, at least a study of the problem should be undertaken. He telephones the plant manager, who disagrees.

Anderson is unable to find support for his position in the company. The cost of corrective action and the company's plan to close the plant in three years have resulted in a management decision to accept the risk that the plant poses, a risk that management believes to be small. "Drop it," Ed Anderson is told. This is the first serious conflict Anderson has faced since joining the corporate staff. He feels strongly that the problem, if not fully addressed, could cause a major spillage, which would almost certainly contaminate the local water supply; however, it is not his job responsibility to fix environmental problems, only to identify and report them truthfully to company management. Plant management is responsible for fixing the problems. Worse, Ed Anderson is not entirely sure of the probability that a spill may occur. A cursory analysis was equivocal; it would take a considerable amount of effort to evaluate the risk fully.

Anderson feels he is in a moral bind. He believes that as an environmental professional he has a public duty to protect human health and the environment. He views the environmental auditor role as, at least in part, an environmental stewardship responsibility. He suspects he should notify the community about the potential danger even at the risk of losing his job. On the other hand, as a

nineteen-year loyal employee of the Western Manufacturing Company, Anderson feels he has a general professional obligation to maintain the confidentiality of information that he obtained during an audit, under the good faith assumption that his findings would be kept confidential. He also wants to be careful not to undermine the audit program, to which the company is firmly committed, and which has important social value.

THE DILEMMA IN ETHICAL TERMS

Underlying Anderson's disclosure dilemma are two legitimate but opposing assumptions. First, he assumes that environmental professionals have a general duty to protect human health and the environment. Second, he assumes that professionals of all kinds have an obligation to protect the confidentiality of their employers. He feels the second obligation keenly in a situation such as his, where, without the assumption of confidentiality, a socially responsible voluntary corporate activity—environmental auditing—would not exist.

Although Ed Anderson is an engineer, not a philosopher, his assumptions each contain two driving principles: one relates to the fundamental duty underlying his actions and the other to the consequences of his actions. The fundamental duty principle assumes that the ethical value of an action is strictly a function of the inherent moral duty from which the action derives. The consequentialist principle assumes that the ethical value of an action is strictly a function of its consequences. Figure 2 illustrates the fundamental duty and consequentialist principles underlying Ed Anderson's dilemma. In practice, these two principles complement and inform each other; however, for the sake of discussion, the two principles are treated separately.

DISCUSSION

This discussion centers on two questions: (1) Is Ed Anderson morally obliged to protect human health and the environment, and if so, on what basis? (2) Is he morally obliged to protect his employer's confidentiality, and on what basis? The discussion

FIGURE 2

THE DILEMMA IN ETHICAL TERMS

Assumption	Underlying Principles	
	Fundamental Duty	**Consequences**
1. Failure to disclose a hazard which could potentially cause serious harm to human health or the environment is unethical.	There exists a fundamental moral duty to protect innocent third parties from harm.	Disclosure of the hazard might prevent significant human health or environmental damage.
2. Failure of an internal auditor to protect the confidentiality of his or her employer is unethical.	The auditor has a fundamental moral obligation not to disclose company information collected on the assumption that it would remain confidential.	Disclosure of confidential information jeopardizes the trust which underlies all current and future audits.

is organized around the fundamental duty and consequentialist principles underlying each question.

Is the Environmental Auditor Morally Obliged to Protect Human Health and the Environment?

The first question has to do with Ed Anderson's obligation to protect human health and the environment. His concern is that failure to disclose a hazard that could potentially cause serious harm to human health or the environment is unethical.

The Duty

Ed Anderson believes he has a basic moral duty, derived from his position as an environmental auditor, to protect human health and the environment. I will argue that he does have such a duty, but it is the same ordinary moral duty held by any individual, not a special duty derived from his position as environmental auditor.

The environmental auditing field is still emerging and is not yet fully professionalized. As a result, environmental auditors do not, in my judgment, currently have a special professional duty to protect the public—analogous, say, to the duties of public accountants.

The ethics literature is rich with descriptions as to what constitutes a profession. Three examples provide a sense of range of definitions:

Succinctly put, all professions seem to possess: (1) systematic theory, (2) authority, (3) community sanction, (4) ethical codes, and (5) a culture. (Ernest Greenwood in Baumrin and Freedman, 1983, p. 21).

[A profession has] three necessary feature. . . . First, a rather extensive training is required to practice a profession. . . . Second, the training involves a significant intellectual component. . . . Third, the trained ability provides an important service in society. . . . Other features are common to most professions although they are not necessary for professional status. Usually a process of certification or licensing exists. . . . Another feature common to professions is an organization of members. . . . A third common feature of the professional is autonomy in his or her work. (Michael Bayles in Callahan, 1988, p. 28).

In general, we can agree that a profession has the following:

1. a clearly defined field of expertise, which distinguishes members of the profession from all other careers;
2. a period of prescribed education or training which precedes entry into membership;
3. a selective process of entry into the profession, restricting its membership to those qualified;
4. a procedure for testing and licensing, generally approved by a state agency under guidance from the profession itself;

5. a dedication of the profession to social service, meeting obligations to the society and performing services other groups are not capable of offering;

6. correlatively, substitution of service for income and wealth as the primary motivation of members, plus high-quality service regardless of fees received;

7. provision of adequate services for the indigent or those in extremis generally with charge;

8. the application of differential fees for the same service to different clients, according to circumstances or ability to pay; and

9. a set of self-governing rules, inculcating a high code of ethics in relationships among members and in behavior toward society, and requiring provision of service at high levels of competence. (Behrman, 1988, p. 97)

By almost any definition, environmental auditing is not yet formally an established profession. It has no professional standards or self-governing rules, no ethical codes, limited community understanding or sanction, no prescribed training or education, no commonly agreed intellectual component, and no certification of licensure (except in California). Unlike public accountants, who have a rigorous and disciplined set of professional principles and practices, environmental auditors lack a commonly understood mission. As a result, the environmental auditor lacks the financial auditor's recognized position of public trust.

In the absence of explicit professional principles and practices, and an explicit, broadly understood covenant with the public, environmental auditors have no more moral obligation to protect the public than does any other individual.[2] But what is the ordinary obligation to protect the public? Let us look at an example.

Suppose an unemployed bricklayer sitting on the subway overhears a conversation in which a man tells a companion he plans to kill his employer because the employer has discriminated against him. Suppose further that the listener has every reason to believe that the speaker genuinely intends to carry out his threat. The listener has an ordinary moral duty to inform someone, say the police, who may be able to protect the man's employer. His obligation is not derived from any professional duty (indeed the listener is unemployed)

but rather from an ordinary moral duty to protect innocent third parties.

One way to derive this ordinary moral duty is to apply a basic test, developed by the philosopher John Rawls, called the "veil of ignorance" test. By situating a person behind a hypothetical veil of ignorance, this test ensures that an individual evaluates various alternatives without regard to how he or she personally would be affected.

The veil of ignorance test is as follows. If one did not know one's position in a matter (e.g., in Ed Anderson's situation, whether one owns Western Manufacturing Company, is one of the 750,000 residents who rely on the local drinking water supply, etc.), what moral rule would one accept? Without knowing one's position in the unemployed bricklayer's case, one would certainly choose a moral rule that required disclosure since, when the veil of ignorance was lifted, one could turn out to be the potential murderer's boss with a gun to her head. Without knowing one's position in Ed Anderson's situation, one would similarly choose a rule that required disclosure since most people would not voluntarily increase their cancer risk by drinking from a contaminated water supply. Because a veil of ignorance test prevents the auditor from knowing whether he will be the auditor, who leaves on the next outbound flight from Columbia, or a local resident who will unknowingly continue to drink from a contaminated water supply, he must choose disclosure.

Suppose the auditor is not certain that a spill is imminent or is not sure that a spill would actually contaminate the local water supply. Is he still obliged to disclose? At this point, the fundamental duty principle and the consequentialist principle overlap, since one can rightfully question whether an auditor has a fundamental moral duty to protect innocent third parties from harm if the harm is insignificant (e.g., the contamination is minuscule and not likely to increase the community's cancer risk). Here we must turn to the consequentialist principle, which complements the fundamental duty principle by adding a significance test.

The Consequences

Ed Anderson believes that if he does not disclose the potential hazard to the public, significant contamination of a water supply could occur, causing harm to the community. From a moral standpoint, the consequentialist principle is persuasive; if his failure to act could cause dire consequences, then not acting is unethical. From a practical standpoint, however, there must be a high threshold for this principle to be adduced.

In a consequentialist analysis, the auditor must consider—in addition to the potential harm that could be prevented by disclosure—the potential harm that disclosure could cause. For example, the costs to the community and company of raising a potential false alarm could be significant. Psychological distress, depressed property values, lost production, and other negative consequences of disclosure need to be balanced against the potential harm that could result if the hazard is not disclosed. Because the costs of disclosure could be quite high, the costs of remaining silent must be even higher in order to justify disclosure.

Viewed another way, the consequentialist argument can be supported by Rawlsian reasoning. Using the veil of ignorance test, one can evaluate the auditor's fundamental duty to disclose in relation to the consequences of the hazard. The reasoning is as follows: An environmental auditor typically is able to make a general judgment as to the type of consequences that might occur if a problem is uncorrected and the general likelihood of its occurrence. He or she is unlikely to know with precision, however, the probability of such an event's occurring or the exact nature of the consequences.

Assuming for the sake of argument that an auditor were able to know, without doubt, the probability and consequences of an environmental event, there are four possible scenarios for the event's occurrence (Figure 3). In my judgment, only the first of the four risks—the high probability–high harm scenario—scenarios clearly justifies the auditor's duty to disclose. In this scenario, the auditor knows with a high degree of certainty that the environmental hazard will cause significant harm to human health and/or the environment. The veil of ignorance test suggests that most people, not knowing whether they were the auditor or a local resident, would prefer to be informed about imminent and severe contamination of their drinking water supply.

In the second risk scenario (low probability–high harm), people might well choose not to be informed of the potential risk, since we face so many of these risk situations in life (e.g., flying in an airplane) that we often feel better off not being confronted with information about every possible risk. Applying the veil of ignorance test to the third and fourth risk scenarios, both of which involve nonsignificant harm to human health and the environment. I would argue that people do not necessarily want to be informed of these low consequence risks. Clearly risks that are defined by scenarios 2–4 must be characterized and

---

FIGURE 3

FOUR ENVIRONMENTAL RISK SCENARIOS

		Severity of Harm to Health or the Environment	
		High	**Low**
Probability of Occurrence	High	High Probability High Harm `1`	High Probability Low Harm `3`
	Low	Low Probability High Harm `2`	Low Probability Low Harm `4`

appropriately managed by a corporation. However, public disclosure of such risks is not necessarily dictated by moral obligation.

Summary

The analysis suggests that Ed Anderson's assumption—that failure to disclose a hazard that could potentially cause serious harm to human health or the environment is unethical—is justified by the fundamental duty principle and possibly by the consequentialist principle. More information is needed about the consequences of disclosure and nondisclosure to determine whether the latter principle can be adduced.

The fundamental duty principle states that an auditor has an ordinary moral duty to protect innocent third parties from harm. This duty does not arise from the auditor's occupation. However, since environmental auditors are likely to be exposed to more opportunities than most other people to exercise this duty and since auditors are better trained to evaluate environmental risks than the general public, it can be argued that auditors at least have greater opportunities than other people to protect human health and the environment from harm. The consequentialist principle adds a significance test to the disclosure decision by stating that the consequences of the identified hazard must be significant to justify the auditor's obligation for public disclosure.

Is the Environmental Auditor Morally Obliged to Protect His or Her Employer's Confidentiality?

The next question has to do with Ed Anderson's obligation to protect Western Manufacturing Company's confidentiality. His concern is that failure to protect the confidentiality of his employer is unethical.

The Duty

Ed Anderson believes he has a basic moral duty to protect Western Manufacturing Company's confidentiality. I will argue that he does have such a duty and that it is fundamental to the internal auditor-employer relationship.

Because environmental auditing is only an emerging profession, we cannot look to environ-

mental auditing standards or codes of ethics to define the auditor's obligations with respect to protecting an employer's confidentiality. On the other hand, when a company empowers an environmental auditor to conduct audits, the company does so on the basis of trust and confidence that the auditor will protect its interests. Indeed, the environmental auditor-employer relationship is fundamentally a fiduciary relationship: "A fiduciary relation[ship is] the relation existing when one person justifiably reposes confidence, faith, and reliance in another whose aid, advice, or protection is sought in some manner" (*Webster's Third New International Dictionary, Unabridged,* 1981).

When a company voluntarily creates an environmental audit function, it does so with a view toward the social good as well as with its financial interests in mind. To preserve the integrity of the audit program, management expects that environmental auditors will protect the confidentiality of information obtained during the course of conducting audits. If management thought otherwise (in the extreme, that auditors would freely disclose confidential information to the outside), audit programs would not voluntarily be undertaken. The purpose of an environmental audit program is to identify and solve problems before they become public threats, and the success of the environmental audit function is predicated on the auditor's ability to elicit sufficient cooperation from plant personnel to be able to identify environmental problems.

How does the presence of a fiduciary relationship govern the environmental auditor's moral behavior? The dictionary offers further guidance: "[In a fiduciary relationship] good conscience requires one to act at all times for the sole benefit and interests of another with loyalty to those interests" (*Webster's Third New International Dictionary, Unabridged,* 1981). Plainly the fiduciary (the environmental auditor) is expected to act at all times in the interests of the beneficiary (the employer). The notion that an auditor should not publicly disclose information obtained during audits is supported by a fundamental moral principle of keeping promises. The company can undertake a self-auditing program only if it trusts its employees to maintain the confidentiality of audit findings. The foundation of a voluntary audit program rests on the principle of keeping promises, with the implicit assumption of reliance and expectation.

With respect to the auditor's fiduciary relationship, the fundamental duty to protect the employer's confidentiality is closely tied to the consequences of breaching that confidentiality. Indeed the fundamental duty and consequentialist principles are almost inseparable.

The Consequences

Ed Anderson believes that if he discloses the hazard to the public, he jeopardizes the trust that underlies all current and future audits. I will argue that he is correct.

A voluntary environmental audit program rests on the trust between auditor and employer. It is difficult to imagine a company that would deliberately ask its employees to identify and document problems and then report those problems to government authorities or the media without the company's permission. It is equally hard to imagine a plant manager or plant environmental staff cooperating with an auditor (by providing the auditor with access to documents, in-plant interviews, and other sources of information) if it was believed that the auditor would publicly reveal potentially embarrassing information collected during the course of the audit.

Since environmental audit programs serve a public good (because they are designed to identify and correct environmental problems before they cause harm to human health or the environment), protection of the trust on which they are based also serves a public good. A breach of this trust would be discreditable to the company and the auditor and could undermine the basic foundation of the audit program, causing management to reconsider whether to continue with the audit program and causing other companies to question their audit programs. This result would serve neither the company's best interest nor the public's.

The obligation to protect the company's confidentiality is based not only on a fundamental moral duty to keep promises but also on a broader notion of protecting the general public interest.

Ironically, the principle of protecting the general public interest (by maintaining the integrity of audit programs) may be in direct conflict with the principle of protecting specific members of the public (e.g., the local community served by the Columbia public water supply). In this respect, the auditor faces an almost insoluble dilemma between protecting the greater public good and protecting a specific public good. Clearly some kind of balancing test is needed.

Before concluding the consequentialist evaluation, the auditor must consider the potential negative consequences of not protecting the company's confidentiality. Here the auditor must balance the harm done by violating the company's confidence (e.g., undermining future audits) against the harm done by remaining silent. One could argue, for example, that protecting the company's confidentiality is not necessarily in the company's best interest when such protection could ultimately result in lawsuits, fines and penalties, or public embarrassment to the company. Depending on the circumstances, either choice (to disclose or not to disclose) could be interpreted as fulfilling the auditor's moral obligation to protect the company's relevant interests.

Summary

The analysis suggests that Ed Anderson's second assumption—that failure to protect the confidentiality of his employer is unethical—is justified by the fundamental duty principle and by the consequentialist principle. The fundamental duty principle states that the auditor, because of his fiduciary relationship to the company, is obliged to protect confidential information obtained during the course of an audit. This obligation is inherent in the nature of the fiduciary relationship. The consequentialist principle adds that public disclosure of the hazard would jeopardize the trust on which all present and future audits are built.

CONCLUSIONS

Ed Anderson plainly has a conflict between legitimate moral obligations. If he exercises his ordinary moral duty to protect human health and the environment, he abrogates his fiduciary responsibility to his employer. If he strictly interprets his fiduciary responsibility to his employer and fails to disclose the potential hazard to the public, he abrogates his duty to protect a segment of the public. It is impossible for him to honor both duties at the same time. A method is needed to resolve conflicts between an environmental auditor's obligations to his or her employer and to others. The approach I suggest offers six proposed tests to evaluate when an auditor's duty to the public outweighs his or her duty to the employer.

I begin by assuming that the auditor's primary obligation is to the employer. I make this assumption for two reasons. First, the auditor has a fiduciary responsibility to the employer. This responsibility grows out of a basic trust that is essential to the integrity of voluntary corporate environmental audit programs. In addition, the fiduciary responsibility serves more than just the employer since audit programs ultimately serve the general public good. Second, because the environmental audit occupation does not hold an explicit position of public trust and because there are no environmental auditing standards or codes of ethics specifying an auditor's obligation to the public, the auditor has no special obligation to protect the public.

The question then arises, under what circumstances does the auditor's ordinary moral obligation to the public outweigh the fiduciary obligation to his or her employer? Six tests can be used to balance these obligations.[3]

1. The potential human health or environmental harm that could result from the hazard is significant.
2. Peer environmental professionals agree that the hazard is potentially significant and is not being adequately addressed by the company.
3. The potential negative consequences of remaining silent outweigh the potential negative consequences of disclosure.
4. The auditor has exhausted all reasonable internal reporting channels.
5. The hazard is not on a reasonable timetable for remediation.
6. The auditor is not primarily motivated by personal gain.

These tests are especially tailored to the environmental auditor. If all six tests are met, the auditor may be justified in making public his or her concerns.

The first test is that the potential human health or environmental harm that could result from the hazard is significant. Granted, reasonable people could disagree about how to define significant (for example, is one death significant, or must multiple deaths occur in order for the consequences to be considered significant?). But the goal here is to determine the potential severity of the problem so the auditor can properly weigh its overall importance.

In Ed Anderson's case, several basic questions must be answered in order to determine the significance of the risk—for example:

- Is Ed Anderson correct in his assessment of imminent (i.e., high probability) spillage?
- Is he right in believing that such spillage would contaminate the local drinking water supply?
- Would the community's excess lifetime cancer risk substantially be increased as a result of the contamination?

In all likelihood, Ed Anderson will not be able to answer these questions alone, nor is it desirable that he do so, since even reasonable people may disagree about probabilities and consequences. This gives rise to the second test: a peer environmental professional must agree that the hazard is potentially significant. Ed Anderson needs to obtain corroboration for his beliefs, as well as supporting data. Ideally he should obtain corroboration from an environmental professional within the company. But if necessary, he should talk to a trusted peer outside the company. This test is to ensure that the auditor is squarely in the midst of a genuine dilemma. No doubt reasonable people could disagree about the seriousness of an environmental hazard or the appropriateness of public disclosure; however, some level of peer corroboration is important for validating the auditor's judgment.

The third test is a balancing test: the potential negative consequences of remaining silent must outweigh the potential negative consequences of disclosure. The auditor has to weigh the negative consequences of disclosure carefully. These may be societal—for example, the costs to the community and the company of a false alarm—or personal—for example, the financial or emotional cost of disagreeing with one's management, jeopardizing a job because of a breach of fiduciary duty to the company, or being harassed or humiliated by people in the company who disagree with the judgment. This test is to ensure that the auditor considers all the consequences of disclosure, not just the potential harm that can be prevented by disclosure.

The fourth test is that the auditor has exhausted all reasonable internal reporting channels. This is critical; the auditor must attempt to give the company every possible opportunity to understand and address the problem. This could mean reporting as high in the company management structure as the company president or even the board of directors. In extreme cases, where an auditor believes that he or she is not being heard by immediate management, the auditor must make every effort to work through the company's internal management before turning to outside authorities. The purpose of this test is to ensure that the auditor has attempted to the fullest extent possible to honor the company's confidentiality while at the same time attempting to ensure correction of the identified hazard.

The fifth test is that the hazard is not adequately being remediated, nor is it on a reasonable timetable for remediation. This is to ensure that the auditor is fully aware of the steps the company is taking (if any) to address the problem.

Finally, the last test is that the auditor not be motivated primarily by personal gain. This test is to ensure that the auditor properly respects his fiduciary obligations and is not acting primarily in a manner to aggrandize himself or herself at the employer's expense.

Determining whether a situation meets the six proposed tests is not simple. In Ed Anderson's case, the most problematic tests are the first two. He does not know with certainty the probability or outcome of a major spill and has not discussed the problem with peer environmental professionals. Ed Anderson would probably elect to disclose the problem publicly if he determined that tests 3–6 were met and that the probability of a major spillage was high, the spill would result in major contamination of the water supply, increasing the community's excess lifetime cancer risk from, say,

10^{-6} to 10^{-5}, and a trusted audit colleague agreed with Ed Anderson's assessment.

In reality, however, environmental risk situations normally are more gray than black and white. Auditors generally do not have the luxury of knowing precisely the probability or outcome of an event. Moreover, there is no guarantee that reasonable people using these tests would draw the same conclusions. The audit practitioner operates in a world of enormous uncertainty. Nevertheless, the six tests offer a way of evaluating a highly complex ethical situation that is quite typical of the kinds of situations faced by environmental auditors.

To elevate the resolution of these dilemmas from the individual to the societal level requires that environmental auditing become more professionalized. Extensive progress already has been made toward environmental audit professionalization. Three environmental audit professional groups exist, and two of them have actively studied the issue of professional standards.[4]

Over the long run, ethical issues will best be addressed through formal professional standards and codes of ethics devoted to environmental auditors. The codes of ethics that exist for engineers, who comprise a large portion of the environmental audit work force, are not quite tailored to environmental auditors' needs because they do not address in depth certain issues unique to the auditor or employer situation, such as the importance of confidentiality to the effectiveness of the audit function. The Institute of Internal Auditors' and Certified Public Accountants' codes of ethics come closer to addressing the special environmental auditor-employer relationship but do not address the substantive issues unique to the environmental audit function, such as the fact that environmental auditors deal with information relevant to human health and welfare. Until professional standards are developed for environmental auditors, tough dilemmas of disclosure will have to be addressed by individual auditors without recourse to written guidance.

NOTES

I am grateful to the following individuals for their thoughtful input to this chapter. Al Alm, Greg Dees,

John Palmisano, Steve Poltorzycki, Ralph Rhodes, Ann Smith, and Bill Yodis. They challenged my thinking and generously offered suggestions for improvement. Any errors, omissions, or misconceptions that remain are solely my responsibility.

1. The environmental auditor's duty to protect the confidentiality of audit findings may be overridden by certain legal circumstances, such as a subpoena requiring the disclosure of such information. However, this chapter assumes no legal obligations to disclose audit findings.
2. Environmental auditors usually have training in a specific field (e.g., chemical engineering, environmental sciences). Because of their training and background, many have professional affiliations with groups that have well-established ethical standards, for example, professional engineers. Membership in such a professional association confers special ethical obligations on an auditor. However, this chapter centers on the auditor's obligations qua auditor. Thus, the auditor's ethical obligations that arise from other affiliations are not dealt with here.
3. In the course of evaluating how an auditor might properly weigh his or her ethical obligations, I arrived at the six tests described. A literature search confirmed that several of these are the types of tests ethicists are likely to apply at a more general level to ethical dilemmas. See, for example, Sissela Bok or Gene G. James in Callahan (1988).

4. Three environmental audit professional groups exist as of this writing: the Environmental Audit Roundtable, the Institute for Environmental Auditing, and the Environmental Audit Forum. The first two groups have addressed the issue of professional standards.

REFERENCES

American Institute of Certified Public Accountants, Inc. 1978. *Ethics in the Accounting Profession.* New York: John Wiley & Sons.

Barry, Vincent E., 1986. *Moral Issues in Business.* Belmont, Calif.: Wadsworth Publishing Company.

Baumrin, Bernard, and Benjamin Freedman, eds. 1983. *Moral Responsibility and the Professions.* New York: Haven Publications.

Bayles, Michael D. 1981. *Professional Ethics.* Belmont, Calif: Wadsworth Publishing Company.

Beauchamp, Tom L., and Norman E. Bowie, eds. 1988. *Ethical Theory and Business.* Englewood Cliffs, N.J.: Prentice Hall.

Behrman, Jack N., 1988. *Essays on Ethics in Business and the Professions.* Englewood Cliffs, N.J.: Prentice Hall.

Bureau of National Affairs., 1986. *Codes of Professional Responsibility.* Washington, D.C.: BNA.

Callahan, Joan C., ed. 1988. *Ethical Issues in Professional Life.* New York: Oxford University Press.

Hoffman, W. Michael, and Jennifer Mills Moore, eds. 1984. *Business Ethics.* New York: McGraw-Hill.

QUESTIONS FOR DISCUSSION

1. Do people have a "right to a livable environment"? If so, is this a barrier right (from the section on rights in the introduction) or a welfare right? Depending on your answer, what would this imply about business' responsibility to the environment?
2. What do you believe to be the main point of disagreement between Bowie and Hoffman? Do you think that most businesspeople would agree with Hoffman's proposal about business' responsibility to the environment? Why or why not?
3. What does Ruff mean by an "optimum" level of pollution? How would he go about determining this level?

CHAPTER 9

International Business

Ethical Dilemmas for Multinational Enterprise: A Philosophical Overview

Richard T. De George
Distinguished Professor of Philosophy, University of Kansas

First World multinational corporations (MNCs) are both the hope of the Third World and the scourge of the Third World. The working out of this paradox poses moral dilemmas for many MNCs. I shall focus on some of the moral dilemmas that many American MNCs face.

Third World countries frequently seek to attract American multinationals for the jobs they provide and for the technological transfers they promise. Yet when American MNCs locate in Third World countries, many Americans condemn them for exploiting the resources and workers of the Third World. While MNCs are a means for improving the standard of living of the underdeveloped coun-

tries, MNCs are blamed for the poverty and starvation such countries suffer. Although MNCs provide jobs in the Third World, many criticize them for transferring these jobs from the United States. American MNCs usually pay at least as high wages as local industries, yet critics blame them for paying the workers in underdeveloped countries less than they pay American workers for comparable work. When American MNCs pay higher than local wages, local companies criticize them for skimming off all the best workers and for creating an internal brain-drain. Multinationals are presently the most effective vehicle available for the development of the Third World. At the same time, critics complain that the MNCs are destroying the local cultures and substituting for them the tinsel of American life and the worst aspects of its culture. American MNCs seek to protect the interests of their shareholders by locating in an environment in which their enterprise will be safe from destruction by revolutions and confiscation by socialist regimes. When they do so, critics complain that the MNCs thrive in countries with strong, often right-wing, governments.[1]

The dilemmas the American MNCs face arise from conflicting demands made from opposing, often ideologically based, points of view. Not all of the demands that lead to these dilemmas are

From *Ethics and the Multinational Enterprise,* edited by W. Michael Hoffman, Ann E. Lange and David A. Fedo (Lanhum, MD: University Press of America, 1986). Copyright © 1986 by the University Press of America. Reprinted by permission of the publisher.

equally justifiable, nor are they all morally mandatory. We can separate the MNCs that behave immorally and reprehensibly from those that do not by clarifying the true moral responsibility of MNCs in the Third World. To help do so, I shall state and briefly defend five theses.

Thesis 1: Many of the moral dilemmas MNCs face are false dilemmas which arise from equating United States standards with morally necessary standards.

Many American critics argue that American multinationals should live up to and implement the same standards abroad that they do in the United States and that United States mandated norms should be followed.[2] This broad claim confuses morally necessary ways of conducting a firm with United States government regulations. The FDA sets high standards that may be admirable. But they are not necessarily morally required. OSHA specifies a large number of rules which in general have as their aim the protection of the worker. However, these should not be equated with morally mandatory rules. United States wages are the highest in the world. These also should not be thought to be the morally necessary norms for the whole world or for United States firms abroad. Morally mandatory standards that no corporation—United States or other—should violate, and moral minima below which no firm can morally go, should not be confused either with standards appropriate to the United States or with standards set by the United States government. Some of the dilemmas of United States multinationals come from critics making such false equations.

This is true with respect to drugs and FDA standards, with respect to hazardous occupations and OSHA standards, with respect to pay, with respect to internalizing the costs of externalities, and with respect to foreign corrupt practices. By using United States standards as moral standards, critics pose false dilemmas for American MNCs. These false dilemmas in turn obfuscate the real moral responsibilities of MNCs.

Thesis 2: Despite differences among nations in culture and values, which should be respected, there are moral norms that can be applied to multinationals.

I shall suggest seven moral guidelines that apply in general to any multinational operating in Third World countries and that can be used in morally evaluating the actions of MNCs. MNCs that respect these moral norms would escape the legitimate criticisms contained in the dilemmas they are said to face.

1. *MNCs should do no intentional direct harm.* This injunction is clearly not peculiar to multinational corporations. Yet it is a basic norm that can be usefully applied in evaluating the conduct of MNCs. Any company that does produce intentional direct harm clearly violates a basic moral norm.

2. *MNCs should produce more good than bad for the host country.* This is an implementation of a general utilitarian principle. But this norm restricts the extent of that principle by the corollary that, in general, more good will be done by helping those in most need, rather than by helping those in less need at the expense of those in greater need. Thus the utilitarian analysis in this case does not consider that more harm than good might justifiably be done to the host country if the harm is offset by greater benefits to others in developed countries. MNCs will do more good only if they help the host country more than they harm it.

3. *MNCs should contribute by their activities to the host country's development.* If the presence of an MNC does not help the host country's development, the MNC can be correctly charged with exploitation, or using the host country for its own purposes at the expense of the host country.

4. *MNCs should respect the human rights of its employees.* MNCs should do so whether or not local companies respect those rights. This injunction will preclude gross exploitation of workers, set minimum standards for pay, and prescribe minimum standards for health and safety measures.

5. *MNCs should pay their fair share of taxes.* Transfer pricing has as its aim taking advantage

of different tax laws in different countries. To the extent that it involves deception, it is itself immoral. To the extent that it is engaged in to avoid legitimate taxes, it exploits the host country, and the MNC does not bear its fair share of the burden of operating in that country.

6. *To the extent that local culture does not violate moral norms, MNCs should respect the local culture and work with it, not against it.* MNCs cannot help but produce some changes in the cultures in which they operate. Yet, rather than simply transferring American ways into other lands, they can consider changes in operating procedures, plant planning, and the like, which take into account local needs and customs.

7. *MNCs should cooperate with the local government in the development and enforcement of just background institutions.* Instead of fighting a tax system that aims at appropriate redistribution of incomes, instead of preventing the organization of labor, and instead of resisting attempts at improving the health and safety standards of the host country, MNCs should be supportive of such measures.

Thesis 3: Wholesale attacks on multinationals are most often overgeneralizations. Valid moral evaluations can be best made by using the above moral criteria for context-and-corporation-specific studies and analysis.

Broadside claims, such that all multinationals exploit underdeveloped countries or destroy their culture, are too vague to determine their accuracy. United States multinationals have in the past engaged—and some continue to engage—in immoral practices. A case by case study is the fairest way to make moral assessments. Yet we can distinguish five types of business operations that raise very different sorts of moral issues: 1) banks and financial institutions; 2) agricultural enterprises; 3) drug companies and hazardous industries; 4) extractive industries; and 5) other manufacturing and service industries.

If we were to apply our seven general criteria in each type of case, we would see some of the differences among them. Financial institutions do not generally employ many people. Their function is to provide loans for various types of development. In the case of South Africa they do not do much—if anything—to undermine apartheid, and by lending to the government they usually strengthen the government's policy of apartheid. In this case, an argument can be made that they do more harm than good—an argument that several banks have seen to be valid, causing them to discontinue their South African operations even before it became financially dangerous to continue lending money to that government. Financial institutions can help and have helped development tremendously. Yet the servicing of debts that many Third World countries face condemns them to impoverishment for the foreseeable future. The role of financial institutions in this situation is crucial and raises special and difficult moral problems, if not dilemmas.

Agricultural enterprises face other demands. If agricultural multinationals buy the best lands and use them for export crops while insufficient arable land is left for the local population to grow enough to feed itself, then MNCs do more harm than good to the host country—a violation of one of the norms I suggested above.

Drug companies and dangerous industries pose different and special problems. I have suggested that FDA standards are not morally mandatory standards. This should not be taken to mean that drug companies are bound only by local laws, for the local laws may require less than morality requires in the way of supplying adequate information and of not producing intentional, direct harm.[3] The same type of observation applies to hazardous industries. While an asbestos company will probably not be morally required to take all the measures mandated by OSHA regulations, it cannot morally leave its workers completely unprotected.[4]

Extractive industries, such as mining, which remove minerals from a country, are correctly open to the charge of exploitation unless they can show that they do more good than harm to the host country and that they do not benefit only either themselves or a repressive elite in the host country.

Other manufacturing industries vary greatly, but as a group they have come in for sustained charges of exploitation of workers and the undermining of the host country's culture. The above guidelines can serve as a means of sifting the valid from the invalid charges.

Thesis 4: On the international level and on the national level in many Third World countries the lack of adequate just background institutions makes the use of clear moral norms all the more necessary.

American multinational corporations operating in Germany and Japan, and German and Japanese multinational corporations operating in the United States, pose no special moral problems. Nor do the operations of Brazilian multinational corporations in the United States or Germany. Yet First World multinationals operating in Third World countries have come in for serious and sustained moral criticism. Why?

A major reason is that in the Third World the First World's MNCs operate without the types of constraints and in societies that do not have the same kinds of redistributive mechanisms as in the developed countries. There is no special difficulty in United States multinationals operating in other First World countries because in general these countries *do* have appropriate background institutions.[5]

More and more Third World countries are developing controls on multinationals that insure the companies do more good for the country than harm.[6] Authoritarian regimes that care more for their own wealth than for the good of their people pose difficult moral conditions under which to operate. In such instances, the guidelines above may prove helpful.

Just as in the nations of the developed, industrial world the labor movement serves as a counter to the dominance of big business, consumerism serves as a watchdog on practices harmful to the consumer, and big government serves as a restraint on each of the vested interest groups, so international structures are necessary to provide the proper background constraints on international corporations.

The existence of MNCs is a step forward in the unification of mankind and in the formation of a global community. They provide the economic base and substructure on which true international cooperation can be built. Because of their special

position and the special opportunities they enjoy, they have a special responsibility to promote the cooperation that only they are able to accomplish in the present world.

Just background institutions would preclude any company's gaining a competitive advantage by engaging in immoral practices. This suggests that MNCs have more to gain than to lose by helping formulate voluntary, UN (such as the code governing infant formulae),[7] and similar codes governing the conduct of all multinationals. A case can also be made that they have the moral obligation to do so.

Thesis 5: The moral burden of MNCs does not exonerate local governments from responsibility for what happens in and to their country. Since responsibility is linked to ownership, governments that insist on part or majority ownership incur part or majority responsibility.

The attempts by many underdeveloped countries to limit multinationals have shown that at least some governments have come to see that they can use multinationals to their own advantage. This may be done by restricting entry to those companies that produce only for local consumption, or that bring desired technology transfers with them. Some countries demand majority control and restrict the export of money from the country. Nonetheless, many MNCs have found it profitable to engage in production under the terms specified by the host country.

What host countries cannot expect is that they can demand control without accepting correlative responsibility. In general, majority control implies majority responsibility. An American MNC, such as Union Carbide, which had majority ownership of its Indian Bhopal plant, should have had primary control of the plant. Union Carbide, Inc. can be held liable for the damage the Bhopal plant caused because Union Carbide, Inc. did have majority ownership.[8] If Union Carbide did not have effective control, it is not relieved of its responsibility. If it could not exercise the control that its responsibility demanded, it should have withdrawn or sold off part of its holdings in that plant. If India had had majority ownership, then it would have had primary responsibility for the safe operation of the plant.

This is compatible with maintaining that if a company builds a hazardous plant, it has an obligation to make sure that the plant is safe and that those who run it are properly trained to run it safely. MNCs cannot simply transfer dangerous technologies without consideration of the people who will run them, the local culture, and similar factors. Unless MNCs can be reasonably sure that the plants they build will be run safely, they cannot morally build them. To do so would be to will intentional, direct harm.

The theses and guidelines that I have proposed are not a panacea. But they suggest how moral norms can be brought to bear on the dilemmas American multinationals face and they suggest ways out of apparent or false dilemmas. If MNCs observed those norms, they could properly avoid the moral sting of their critics' charges, even if their critics continued to level charges against them.

NOTES

1. The literature attacking American MNCs is extensive. Many of the charges mentioned in this paper are found in Richard J. Barnet and Ronald E. Muller, *Global Reach: The Power of the Multinational Corporations,* New York: Simon & Schuster, 1974, and in Pierre Jalee, *The Pillage of the Third World,* translated from the French by Mary Klopper, New York and London: Modern Reader Paperbacks, 1968.
2. The position I advocate does not entail moral relativism, as my third thesis shows. The point is that although moral norms apply uniformly across cultures, U.S. standards are not the same as moral standards, should themselves be morally evaluated, and are relative to American conditions, standard of living, interests, and history.
3. For a fuller discussion of multinational drug companies see Richard T. De George, *Business Ethics,* 2nd ed., New York: Macmillan, 1986, pp. 363–367.
4. For a more detailed analysis of the morality of exporting hazardous industries, see my *Business Ethics,* 367–372.
5. This position is consistent with that developed by John Rawls in his *A Theory of Justice,* Cambridge, Mass.: Harvard University Press, 1971, even though Rawls does not extend his analysis to the international realm. The thesis does not deny that United States, German, or Japanese policies on trade restrictions, tariff levels, and the like can be morally evaluated.
6. See, for example, Theodore H. Moran, "Multinational Corporations: A Survey of Ten Years' Evidence," Georgetown School of Foreign Service, 1984.
7. For a general discussion of UN codes, see Wolfgang Fikentscher, "United Nations Codes of Conduct: New Paths in International Law," *The American Journal of Comparative Law,* 30 (1980), pp. 577–604.
8. The official Indian Government report on the Bhopal tragedy has not yet appeared. The Union Carbide report was partially reprinted in the *New York Times,* March 21, 1985, p. 48. The major *New York Times* reports appeared on December 9, 1984, January 28, 30, and 31, and February 3, 1985.

International Business, Morality, and the Common Good

Manuel Velasquez
The Dirksen Professor of Business Ethics, Management Department, Santa Clara University

During the last few years an increasing number of voices have urged that we pay more attention to ethics in international business, on the grounds that not only are all large corporations now internationally structured and thus engaging in international transactions, but that even the smallest domestic firm is increasingly buffeted by the pressures of international competition.[1] This call for increased attention to international business ethics has been answered by a slowly growing collection of ethicists who have begun to address issues in this field. The most comprehensive work on this subject to date is the recent book *The Ethics of International Business* by Thomas Donaldson.[2]

I want in this article to discuss certain realist objections to bringing ethics to bear on international

From *Business Ethics Quarterly,* Vol. 2, Issue 1 (July 1992), pp. 27–40. Reprinted by permission of the author.

transactions, an issue that, I believe, has not yet been either sufficiently acknowledged nor adequately addressed but that must be resolved if the topic of international business ethics is to proceed on solid foundations. Even so careful a writer as Thomas Donaldson fails to address this issue in its proper complexity. Oddly enough, in the first chapter where one would expect him to argue that, in spite of realist objections, *businesses* have international moral obligations, Donaldson argues only for the less pertinent claim that, in spite of realist objections, *states* have international moral obligations.[3] But international business organizations, I will argue, have special features that render realist objections quite compelling. The question I want to address, here, then, is a particular aspect of the question Donaldson and others have ignored: Can we say that businesses operating in a competitive international environment have any moral obligations to contribute to the international common good, particularly in light of realist objections? Unfortunately, my answer to this question will be in the negative.

My subject, then, is international business and the common good. What I will do is the following. I will begin by explaining what I mean by the common good, and what I mean by international business. Then I will turn directly to the question whether the views of the realist allow us to claim that international businesses have a moral obligation to contribute to the common good. I will first lay out the traditional realist treatment of this question and then revise the traditional realist view so that it can deal with certain shortcomings embedded in the traditional version of realism. I will then bring these revisions to bear on the question of whether international businesses have any obligations toward the common good, a question that I will answer in the negative. My hope is that I have identified some extremely problematic issues that are both critical and disturbing and that, I believe, need to be more widely discussed than they have been because they challenge our easy attribution of moral obligation to international business organizations.

I should note that what follows is quite tentative. I am attempting to work out the implications of certain arguments that have reappeared recently in the literature on morality in international affairs. I am not entirely convinced of the correctness of my conclusions, and offer them here as a way of trying to get clearer about their status. I should also note that although I have elsewhere argued that it is improper to attribute *moral responsibility* to corporate entities, I here set these arguments aside in order to show that even if we ignore the issue of moral responsibility, it is still questionable whether international businesses have obligations toward the common good.

I. THE COMMON GOOD

Let me begin by distinguishing a weak from a strong conception of the common good, so that I might clarify what I have in mind when I refer to the common good.

What I have in mind by a weak conception of the common good is essentially the utilitarian notion of the common good. It is a notion that is quite clearly stated by Jeremy Bentham:

> The interest of the community then is—what? The sum of the interests of the several members who compose it. . . . It is vain to talk of the interest of the community, without understanding what is the interest of the individual. A thing is said to promote the interest or to be for the interest of an individual, when it tends to add to the sum total of his pleasure; or what comes to the same thing, to diminish the sum total of his pains.[4]

On the utilitarian notion of the common good, the common good is nothing more than the sum of the utilities of each individual. The reason why I call this the "weak" conception of the common good will become clear, I believe, once it is contrasted with another, quite different notion of the common good.

Let me describe, therefore, what I will call a strong conception of the common good, the conception on which I want to focus in this essay. It is a conception that has been elaborated in the Catholic tradition, and so I will refer to it as the Catholic conception of the common good. Here is how one writer, William A. Wallace, O.P., characterizes the conception:

A common good is clearly distinct from a *private* good, the latter being the good of one person only, to the exclusion of its being possessed by any other. A common good is distinct also from a *collective* good, which, though possessed by all of a group, is not really participated in by the members of the group; divided up, a collective good becomes respectively the private goods of the members. A true *common* good is universal, not singular or collective, and is distributive in character, being communicable to many without becoming anyone's private good. Moreover, each person participates in the whole common good, not merely in a part of it, nor can any one person possess it wholly.[5]

In the terms used by Wallace, the utilitarian conception of the common good is actually a "collective" good. That is, it is an aggregate of the private goods (the utilities) of the members of a society. The common good in the utilitarian conception is divisible in the sense that the aggregate consists of distinct parts and each part is enjoyable by only one individual. Moreover, the common good in the utilitarian conception is not universal in the sense that not all members of society can enjoy all of the aggregate; instead, each member enjoys only a portion of the aggregate.

By contrast, in the Catholic conception that Wallace is attempting to characterize, the common good consists of those goods that (1) benefit all the members of a society in the sense that all the members of the society have access to each of these goods, and (2) are not divisible in the sense that none of these goods can be divided up and allocated among individuals in such a way that others can be excluded from enjoying what another individual enjoys. The example that Wallace gives of one common good is the "good of peace and order."[6] Other examples are national security, a clean natural environment, public health and safety, a productive economic system to whose benefits all have access, a just legal and political system, and a system of natural and artificial associations in which persons can achieve their personal fulfillment.

It is this strong notion of the common good that the Catholic tradition has had in mind when it has defined the common good as "the sum total of those conditions of social living whereby men are enabled more fully and more readily to achieve their own perfection."[7] It is also the conception that John Rawls has in mind when he writes that "Government is assumed to aim at the common good, that is, at maintaining conditions and achieving objectives that are similarly to everyone's advantage," and "the common good I think of as certain general conditions that are in an appropriate sense equally to everyone's advantage."[8]

The Catholic conception of the common good is the conception that I have in mind in what follows. It is clear from the characterization of the common good laid out above that we can think of the common good on two different levels. We can think of the common good on a national and on an international level. On a national level, the common good is that set of conditions within a certain nation that are necessary for the citizens of that nation to achieve their individual fulfillment and so in which all of the citizens have an interest.

On an international level, we can speak of the global common good as that set of conditions that are necessary for the citizens of all or of most nations to achieve their individual fulfillment, and so those goods in which all the peoples of the world have an interest. In what follows, I will be speaking primarily about the global common good.

Now it is obvious that identifying the global common good is extremely difficult because cultures differ on their views of what conditions are necessary for humans to flourish. These differences are particularly acute between the cultures of the lesser developed third world nations who have demanded a "new economic order," and the cultures of the wealthier first world nations who have resisted this demand. Nevertheless, we can identify at least some elements of the global common good. Maintaining a congenial global climate, for example is certainly part of the global common good. Maintaining safe transportation routes for the international flow of goods is also part of the global common good. Maintaining clean oceans is another aspect of the global common good, as is the avoidance of a global nuclear war. In spite of the difficulties involved in trying to compile a list of the goods that qualify as part of the global common good, then, it is nevertheless possible to identify at least some of the items that belong on the list.

II. INTERNATIONAL BUSINESS

Now let me turn to the other term in my title: international business. When speaking of international business, I have in mind a particular kind of organization: the multinational corporation. Multinational corporations have a number of well known features, but let me briefly summarize a few of them. First, multinational corporations are businesses and as such they are organized primarily to increase their profits within a competitive environment. Virtually all of the activities of a multinational corporation can be explained as more or less rational attempts to achieve this dominant end. Secondly, multinational corporations are bureaucratic organizations. The implication of this is that the identity, the fundamental structure, and the dominant objectives of the corporation endure while the many individual human beings who fill the various offices and positions within the corporation come and go. As a consequence, the particular values and aspirations of individual members of the corporation have a relatively minimal and transitory impact on the organization as a whole. Thirdly, and most characteristically, multinational corporations operate in several nations. This has several implications. First, because the multinational is not confined to a single nation, it can easily escape the reach of the laws of any particular nation by simply moving its resources or operations out of one nation and transferring them to another nation. Second, because the multinational is not confined to a single nation, its interests are not aligned with the interests of any single nation. The ability of the multinational to achieve its profit objectives does not depend upon the ability of any particular nation to achieve its own domestic objectives.

In saying that I want to discuss international business and the common good, I am saying that I want to discuss the relationship between the global common good and multinational corporations, that is, organizations that have the features I have just identified.

The general question I want to discuss is straightforward: I want to ask whether it is possible for us to say that multinational corporations with the features I have just described have an obligation to contribute toward the global common good. But I want to discuss only one particular aspect of this general question. I want to discuss this question in light of the realist objection.

III. THE TRADITIONAL REALIST OBJECTION IN HOBBES

The realist objection, of course, is the standard objection to the view that agents—whether corporations, governments, or individuals—have moral obligations on the international level. Generally, the realist holds that it is a mistake to apply moral concepts to international activities: morality has no place in international affairs. The classical statement of this view, which I am calling the "traditional" version of realism, is generally attributed to Thomas Hobbes. I will assume that this customary attribution is correct; my aim is to identify some of the implications of this traditional version of realism even if it is not quite historically accurate to attribute it to Hobbes.

In its Hobbesian form, as traditionally interpreted, the realist objection holds that moral concepts have no meaning in the absence of an agency powerful enough to guarantee that other agents generally adhere to the tenets of morality. Hobbes held, first, that in the absence of a sovereign power capable of forcing men to behave civilly with each other, men are in "the state of nature," a state he characterizes as a "war . . . of every man, against every man."[9] Secondly, Hobbes claimed, in such a state of war, moral concepts have no meaning:

> To this war of every man against every man, this also is consequent; that nothing can be unjust. The notions of right and wrong, justice and injustice have there no place. Where there is no common power, there is no law: where no law, no injustice.[10]

Moral concepts are meaningless, then, when applied to state of nature situations. And, Hobbes held, the international arena is a state of nature, since there is no international sovereign that can force agents to adhere to the tenets of morality.[11]

The Hobbsian objection to talking about morality in international affairs, then, is based on two premises: (1) an ethical premise about the applicability of moral terms and (2) an apparently empirical premise about how agents behave under certain conditions. The ethical premise, at least in its Hobbsian form, holds that there is a connection between the meaningfulness of moral terms and the extent to which agents adhere to the tenets of morality: If in a given situation agents do not adhere to the tenets of morality, then in that situation moral terms have no meaning. The apparently empirical premise holds that in the absence of a sovereign, agents will not adhere to the tenets of morality: they will be in a state of war. This appears to be an empirical generalization about the extent to which agents adhere to the tenets of morality in the absence of a third-party enforcer. Taken together, the two premises imply that in situations that lack a sovereign authority, such as one finds in many international exchanges, moral terms have no meaning and so moral obligations are nonexistent.

However, there are a number of reasons for thinking that the two Hobbsian premises are deficient as they stand. I want next, therefore, to examine each of these premises more closely and to determine the extent to which they need revision.

IV. REVISING THE REALIST OBJECTION: THE FIRST PREMISE

The ethical premise concerning the meaning of moral terms, is, in its original Hobbsian form, extremely difficult to defend. If one is in a situation in which others do not adhere to any moral restraints, it simply does not logically follow that in that situation one's actions are no longer subject to moral evaluation. At most what follows is that since such an extreme situation is different from the more normal situations in which we usually act, the moral requirements placed on us in such extreme situations are different from the moral requirements that we obtain in more normal circumstances. For example, morality requires that in normal circum-

stances I am not to attack or kill my fellow citizens. But when one of those citizens is attacking me in a dark alley, morality allows me to defend myself by counterattacking or even killing that citizen. It is a truism that what moral principles require in one set of circumstances is different from what they require in other circumstances. And in extreme circumstances, the requirements of morality may become correspondingly extreme. But there is no reason to think that they vanish altogether.

Nevertheless, the realist can relinquish the Hobbsian premise about the meaning of moral terms, replace it with a weaker and more plausible premise, and still retain much of Hobbes' conclusion. The realist or neo-Hobbsian can claim that although moral concepts can be meaningfully applied to situations in which agents do not adhere to the tenets of morality, nevertheless it is not morally wrong for agents in such situations to also fail to adhere to those tenets of morality, particularly when doing so puts one at a significant competitive disadvantage.

The neo-Hobbsian or realist, then, might want to propose this premise: When one is in a situation in which others do not adhere to certain tenets of morality, and when adhering to those tenets of morality will put one at a significant competitive disadvantage, then it is not immoral for one to likewise fail to adhere to them. The realist might want to argue for this claim, first, by pointing out that in a world in which all are competing to secure significant benefits and avoid significant costs, and in which others do not adhere to the ordinary tenets of morality, one risks significant harm to one's interests if one continues to adhere to those tenets of morality. But no one can be morally required to take on major risks of harm to oneself. Consequently, in a competitive world in which others disregard moral constraints and take any means to advance their self-interests, no one can be morally required to take on major risks of injury by adopting the restraints of ordinary morality.

A second argument the realist might want to advance would go as follows. When one is in a situation in which others do not adhere to the ordinary tenets of morality, one is under heavy competitive pressures to do the same. And, when one is under such pressures, one cannot be blamed—i.e., one is excused—for also failing to adhere to the ordinary tenets of morality. One is excused because heavy pressures take away one's ability to control oneself, and thereby diminish one's moral culpability.

Yet a third argument advanced by the realist might go as follows. When one is in a situation in which others do not adhere to the ordinary tenets of morality it is not fair to require one to continue to adhere to those tenets, especially if doing so puts one at a significant competitive disadvantage. It is not fair because then one is laying a burden on one party that the other parties refuse to carry.

Thus, there are a number of arguments that can be given in defense of the revised Hobbsian ethical premise that when others do not adhere to the tenets of morality, it is not immoral for one to do likewise. The ethical premise of the Hobbsian or realist argument, then, can be restated as follows:

> In situations in which other agents do not adhere to certain tenets of morality, it is not immoral for one to do likewise when one would otherwise be putting oneself at a significant competitive disadvantage.

In what follows, I will refer to this restatement as the ethical premise of the argument. I am not altogether convinced that this premise is correct. But it appears to me to have a great deal of plausibility, and it is, I believe, a premise that underlies the feelings of many that in a competitive international environment where others do not embrace the restraints of morality, one is under no obligation to be moral.

V. REVISING THE REALIST OBJECTION: THE SECOND PREMISE

Let us turn, then, to the other premise in the Hobbsian argument, the assertion that in the absence of a sovereign, agents will be in a state of war. As I mentioned, this is an apparently empirical claim about the extent to which agents will adhere to the tenets of morality in the absence of a third-party enforcer.

Hobbes gives a little bit of empirical evidence for this claim. He cites several examples of situations in which there is no third party to enforce civility and where, as a result, individuals are in a "state of war."[12] Generalizing from these few examples, he reaches the conclusion that in the absence of a third-party enforcer, agents will always be in a "condition of war." But the meager evidence Hobbes provides is surely too thin to support his rather large empirical generalization. Numerous empirical counterexamples can be cited of people living in peace in the absence of a third-party enforcer, so it is difficult to accept Hobbes' claim as an empirical generalization.

Recently, the Hobbsian claim, however, has been defended on the basis of some of the theoretical claims of game theory, particularly of the Prisoner's Dilemma. Hobbes' state of nature, the defense goes, is an instance of a Prisoner's Dilemma, and *rational* agents in a Prisoner's Dilemma necessarily would choose not to adhere to a set of moral norms. Rationality is here construed in the sense that is standard in social theory: having a coherent set of preferences among the objects of choice, and selecting the one(s) that has the greatest probability of satisfying more of one's preferences rather than fewer.[13] Or, more simply, always choosing so as to maximize one's interests.

A Prisoner's Dilemma is a situation involving at least two individuals. Each individual is faced with two choices: he can cooperate with the other individual or he can choose not to cooperate. If he cooperates and the other individual also cooperates, then he gets a certain payoff. If, however, he chooses not to cooperate, while the other individual trustingly cooperates, the noncooperator gets a larger payoff while the cooperator suffers a loss. And if both choose not to cooperate, then both get nothing.

It is a commonplace now that in a Prisoner's Dilemma situation, the most rational strategy for a participant is to choose not to cooperate. For the other party will either cooperate or not cooperate. If the other party cooperates, then it is better for one not to cooperate and thereby get the larger payoff. On the other hand, if the other party does not cooperate, then it is also better for one not to cooperate and thereby avoid a loss. In either case, it is better for one to not cooperate.

Now Hobbes' state of nature, the neo-Hobbsian realist can argue, is in fact a Prisoner's Dilemma situation. In Hobbes' state of nature each individual must choose either to cooperate with others by adhering to the rules of morality (like the rule against theft), or to not cooperate by disregarding the rules of morality and attempting to take advantage of those who are adhering to the rules (e.g., by stealing from them). In such a situation it is more rational (in the sense defined above) to choose not to cooperate. For the other party will either cooperate or not cooperate. If the other party does not cooperate, then one puts oneself at a competitive disadvantage if one adheres to morality while the other party does not. On the other hand, if the other party chooses to cooperate, then one can take advantage of the other party by breaking the rules of morality at his expense. In either case, it is more rational to not cooperate.

Thus, the realist can argue that in a state of nature, where there is no one to enforce compliance with the rules of morality, it is more rational from the individual's point of view to choose not to comply with morality than to choose to comply. Assuming—and this is obviously a critical assumption—that agents behave rationally, then we can conclude that agents in a state of nature will choose not to comply with the tenets of ordinary morality. The second premise of the realist argument, then, can, tentatively, be put as follows:

> In the absence of an international sovereign, all rational agents will choose not to comply with the tenets of ordinary morality, when doing so will put one at a serious competitive disadvantage.

This is a striking, and ultimately revealing, defense of the Hobbsian claim that in the absence of a third-party enforcer, individuals will choose not to adhere to the tenets of morality in their relations with each other. It is striking because it correctly identifies, I think, the underlying reason for the Hobbsian claim. The Hobbsian claim is not an empirical claim about how most humans actually behave when they are put at a competitive disadvantage. It is a claim about whether agents that are *rational* (in the sense defined earlier) will adopt certain behaviors when doing otherwise would put

them at a serious competitive disadvantage. For our purposes, this is significant since, as I claimed above, all, most, or at least a significant number of multinationals are rational agents in the required sense: all or most of their activities are rational means for achieving the dominant end of increasing profits. Multinationals, therefore, are precisely the kind of rational agents envisaged by the realist.

But this reading of the realist claim is also significant. I think, because it reveals certain limits inherent in the Hobbsian claim, and requires revising the claim so as to take these limits into account.

As more than one person has pointed out, moral interactions among agents are often quite unlike Prisoner's Dilemmas situations.[14] The most important difference is that a Prisoner's Dilemma is a single meeting between agents who do not meet again, whereas human persons in the real world tend to have repeated dealings with each other. If two people meet each other in a Prisoner's Dilemma situation, and never have anything to do with each other again, then it is rational (in the sense under discussion) from each individual's point of view to choose not to cooperate. However, if individuals meet each other in repeated Prisoner's Dilemma situations, then they are able to punish each other for failures to cooperate, and the cumulative costs of noncooperation can make cooperation the more rational strategy.[15] One can therefore expect that when rational agents know they will have repeated interactions with each other for an indefinite future, they will start to cooperate with each other even in the absence of a third party enforcer. The two cooperating parties in effect are the mutual enforcers of their own cooperative agreements.

The implication is that the realist is wrong in believing that in the absence of a third-party enforcer, rational individuals will always fail to adhere to the tenets of morality, presumably even when doing so would result in serious competitive disadvantage. On the contrary, we can expect that if agents know that they will interact with each other repeatedly in the indefinite future, it is rational for them to behave morally toward each other. In the international arena, then, we can expect that when persons know that they will have repeated interactions with each other, they will tend to adhere to ordinary tenets of morality with each other, assuming that they tend to behave rationally, even when doing so threatens to put them at a competitive disadvantage.

There is a second important way in which the Prisoner's Dilemma is defective as a characterization of real world interactions. Not only do agents repeatedly interact with each other, but, as Robert Frank has recently pointed out, human agents signal to each other the extent to which they can be relied on to behave morally in future interactions.[16] We humans can determine more often than not whether another person can be relied on to be moral by observing the natural visual cues of facial expression and the auditory cues of tone of voice that tend to give us away; by relying on our experience of past dealings with the person; and by relying on the reports of others who have had past dealings with the person. Moreover, based on these appraisals of each other's reliability, we then choose to interact with those who are reliable and choose not to interact with those who are not reliable. That is, we choose to enter Prisoner's Dilemmas situations with those who are reliable, and choose to avoid entering such situations with those who are not reliable. As Robert Frank has shown, given such conditions it is, under quite ordinary circumstances, rational to habitually be reliable since reliable persons tend to have mutually beneficial interactions with other reliable persons, while unreliable persons will tend to have mutually destructive interactions with other unreliable persons.

The implication again is that since signaling makes it rational to habitually cooperate in the rules of morality, even in the absence of a third-party enforcer, we can expect that rational humans, who can send and receive fairly reliable signals between each other, will tend to behave morally even, presumably, when doing so raises the prospect of competitive disadvantage.

These considerations should lead the realist to revise the tentative statement of the second premise of his argument that we laid out above. In its revised form, the second premise would have to read as follows:

In the absence of an international sovereign, all rational agents will choose not to comply with the tenets of ordinary morality, when doing so will put one at a serious competitive disadvantage, provided that interactions are not repeated and that agents are not able to signal their reliability to each other.

This, I believe, is a persuasive and defensible version of the second premise in the Hobbsian argument. It is the one I will exploit in what follows.

VI. REVISED REALISM, MULTINATIONALS, AND THE COMMON GOOD

Now how does this apply to multinationals and the common good? Can we claim that it is clear that multinationals have a moral obligation to pursue the global common good in spite of the objections of the realist?

I do not believe that this claim can be made. We can conclude from the discussion of the realist objection that the Hobbsian claim about the pervasiveness of amorality in the international sphere is false when (1) interactions among international agents are repetitive in such a way that agents can retaliate against those who fail to cooperate, and (2) agents can determine the trustworthiness of other international agents.

But unfortunately, multinational activities often take place in a highly competitive arena in which these two conditions do not obtain. Moreover, these conditions are noticeably absent in the arena of activities that concern the global common good.

First, as I have noted, the common good consists of goods that are indivisible and accessible to all. This means that such goods are susceptible to the free rider problem. Everyone has access to such goods whether or not they do their part in maintaining such goods, so everyone is tempted to free ride on the generosity of others. Now governments can force domestic companies to do their part to maintain the national common good. Indeed, it is one of the functions of government to solve the free rider problem by forcing all to contribute to the domestic common good to which all have access. Moreover, all companies have to interact repeatedly with their host governments, and this leads them to adopt a cooperative stance toward their host government's objective of achieving the domestic common good.

But it is not clear that governments can or will do anything effective to force multinationals to do their part to maintain the global common good. For the governments of individual nations can themselves be free riders, and can join forces with willing multinationals seeking competitive advantages over others. Let me suggest an example. It is clear that a livable global environment is part of the global common good, and it is clear that the manufacture and use of chlorofluorocarbons is destroying that good. Some nations have responded by requiring their domestic companies to cease manufacturing or using chloroflurocarbons. But other nations have refused to do the same, since they will share in any benefits that accrue from the restraint others practice, and they can also reap the benefits of continuing to manufacture and use chloroflurocarbons. Less developed nations, in particular, have advanced the position that since their development depends heavily on exploiting the industrial benefits of chloroflurocarbons, they cannot afford to curtail their use of these substances. Given this situation, it is open to multinationals to shift their operations to those countries that continue to allow the manufacture and use of chloroflurocarbons. For multinationals, too, will reason that they will share in any benefits that accrue from the restraint others practice, and that they can meanwhile reap the profits of continuing to manufacture and use chloroflurocarbons in a world where other companies are forced to use more expensive technologies. Moreover, those nations that practice restraint cannot force all such multinationals to discontinue the manufacture or use of chloroflurocarbons because many multinationals can escape the reach of their laws. An exactly parallel, but perhaps even more compelling, set of considerations can be advanced to show that at least some multinationals will join forces with some developing countries to circumvent any global efforts made to control the global warming trends (the so-called "greenhouse effect") caused by the heavy use of fossil fuels.

The realist will conclude, of course, that in such situations, at least some multinationals will

seek to gain competitive advantages by failing to contribute to the global common good (such as the good of a hospitable global environment). For multinationals are rational agents, i.e., agents bureaucratically structured to take rational means toward achieving their dominant end of increasing their profits. And in a competitive environment, contributing to the common good while others do not, will fail to achieve this dominant end. Joining this conclusion to the ethical premise that when others do not adhere to the requirements of morality it is not immoral for one to do likewise, the realist can conclude that multinationals are not morally obligated to contribute to such global common goods (such as environmental goods).

Moreover, global common goods often create interactions that are not iterated. This is particularly the case where the global environment is concerned. As I have already noted, preservation of a favorable global climate is clearly part of the global common good. Now the failure of the global climate will be a one-time affair. The breakdown of the ozone layer, for example, will happen once, with catastrophic consequences for us all; and the heating up of the global climate as a result of the infusion of carbon dioxide will happen once, with catastrophic consequences for us all. Because these environmental disasters are a one-time affair, they represent a non-iterated Prisoner's Dilemma for multinationals. It is irrational from an individual point of view for a multinational to choose to refrain from polluting the environment in such cases. Either others will refrain, and then one can enjoy the benefits of their refraining; or others will not refrain, and then it will be better to have also not refrained since refraining would have made little difference and would have entailed heavy losses.

Finally, we must also note that although natural persons may signal their reliability to other natural persons, it is not at all obvious that multinationals can do the same. As noted above, multinationals are bureaucratic organizations whose members are continually changing and shifting. The natural persons who make up an organization can signal their reliability to others, but such persons are soon replaced by others, and they in turn are replaced by others. What endures is each organization's single-minded pursuit of increasing its profits in a competitive environment. And an enduring commitment to the pursuit of profit in a competitive environment is not a signal of an enduring commitment to morality.

VII. CONCLUSIONS

The upshot of these considerations is that it is not obvious that we can say that multinationals have an obligation to contribute to the global common good in a competitive environment in the absence of an international authority that can force all agents to contribute to the global common good. Where other rational agents can be expected to shirk the burden of contributing to the common good and where carrying such a burden will put one at a serious competitive disadvantage, the realist argument that it is not immoral for one to also fail to contribute is a powerful argument.

I have not argued, of course, nor do I find it persuasive to claim that competitive pressures automatically relieve agents of their moral obligations, although my arguments here may be wrongly misinterpreted as making that claim. All that I have tried to do is to lay out a justification for the very narrow claim that *certain very special kinds of agents, under certain very limited and very special conditions, seem to have no obligations with respect to certain very special kinds of goods.*

This is not an argument, however, for complete despair. What the argument points to is the need to establish an effective international authority capable of forcing all agents to contribute their part toward the global common good. Perhaps several of the more powerful autonomous governments of the world, for example, will be prompted to establish such an international agency by relinquishing their autonomy and joining together into a coherently unified group that can exert consistent economic, political, or military pressures on any companies or smaller countries that do not contribute to the global common good. Such an international police group, of course, would transform the present world order, and would be much different from present world organizations such as the United Nations. Once such an international force exists, of course, then both Hobbes and the neorealist would say that moral obligations can legitimately be attributed to all affected international organizations.

Of course, it is remotely possible but highly unlikely that multinationals themselves will be the source of such promptings for a transformed world order. For whereas governments are concerned with the well-being of their citizens, multinationals are bureaucratically structured for the rational pursuit of profit in a competitive environment, not the pursuit of citizen well-being. Here and there we occasionally may see one or even several multinationals whose current cadre of leadership is enlightened enough to regularly steer the organization toward the global common good. But given time, that cadre will be replaced and profit objectives will reassert themselves as the enduring end built into the on-going structure of the multinational corporation.

NOTES

1. See for example, the articles collected in W. Michael Hoffman, Ann E. Lange, and David A. Fedo. eds., *Ethics and the Multinational Enterprise* (New York: University Press of America, 1986).
2. Thomas Donaldson, *The Ethics of International Business* (New York: Oxford University Press, 1989).
3. Donaldson discusses the question whether *states* have moral obligations to each other in *op. cit.,* pp. 10–29. The critical question, however, is whether *multinationals,* i.e., profit-driven types of international organizations, have moral obligations. Although Donaldson is able to point out without a great deal of trouble that the realist arguments against morality among nations are mistaken (see pp. 20–23, where Donaldson points out that if the realist were correct, then there would be no cooperation among nations; but since there is cooperation, the realist must be wrong), his points leave untouched the arguments I discuss below which acknowledge that while much cooperation among nations is possible, nevertheless certain crucial forms of cooperation will not obtain among multinationals with respect to the global common good.

4. J. Bentham, *Principles of Morals and Legislation.* 1.4–5.

5. William A. Wallace O.P., *The Elements of Philosophy, A Compendium for Philosophers and Theologians* (New York: Alba House, 1977), pp. 166–67.

6. *Ibid.,* p. 167.

7. "Common Good," *The New Catholic Encyclopedia.*

8. John Rawls, *A Theory of Justice* (Cambridge, MA: Harvard University Press, 1971), pp. 233 and 246.

9. Thomas Hobbes, *Leviathan, Parts I and II,* [1651] (New York: The Bobbs-Merrill Company, Inc., 1958), p. 108.

10. *Ibid.* As noted earlier, I am simply assuming what I take to be the popular interpretation of Hobbes' view on the state of nature. As Professor Philip Kain has pointed out to me, there is some controversy among Hobbes scholars about whether or not Hobbes actually held that moral obligation exists in the state of nature. Among those who hold that moral obligation does not exist in Hobbes' state of nature is M. Oakeshott in "The Moral Life in the Writings of Thomas Hobbes" in his *Hobbes on Civil Association* (Berkeley–Los Angeles: University of California Press, 1975), pp. 95–113; among those who hold that moral obligation does exist in Hobbes' state of nature is A. E. Taylor in "The Ethical Doctrine of Hobbes" in *Hobbes Studies,* ed. K. C. Brown (Cambridge: Harvard, 1965), p. 41ff. Kain suggests that Hobbes simply contradicts himself—holding in some passages that moral obligation does exist in the state of nature and holding in others that it does not— because of his need to use the concept of the state of nature to achieve purposes that required incompatible conceptions of the state of nature; see his "Hobbes, Revolution and the Philosophy of History," in *"Hobbes's 'Science of Natural Justice,'"* ed. C. Walton and P. J. Johnson (Boston: Martinus Nijhoff Publishers, 1987), pp. 203–18. In the present essay I am simply assuming without argument the traditional view that Hobbes made the claim that moral obligation does not exist in the state of nature; my aim is to pursue certain implications of this claim even if I am wrong in assuming that is Hobbes'.

11. See *ibid.,* where Hobbes writes that "yet in all times kings and persons of sovereign authority, because of their independency" are in this state of war.

12. *Ibid.,* pp. 107–8.

13. See Amartya K. Sen, *Collective Choice and Social Welfare* (San Francisco: Holden-Day, Inc., 1970), pp. 2–5.

14. See, for example, Gregory Kavka, "Hobbes' War of All Against All," *Ethics,* 93 (January, 1983), pp. 291–310; a somewhat different approach is that of David Gauthier, *Morals By Agreement* (Oxford: Clarendon Press, 1986) and Russell Hardin, *Morality Within the Limits of Reason* (Chicago: University of Chicago Press, 1988).

15. See Robert Axelrod, *The Evolution of Cooperation* (New York: Basic Books, Inc., 1984), pp. 27–69.

16. Robert Frank, *Passions Within Reason* (New York: W. W. Norton & Company, 1988).

Values in Tension: Ethics Away from Home

Thomas Donaldson

The Mark O. Winkelman Professor, Professor of Legal Studies, and Director, Wharton Ethics Program, The Wharton School, University of Pennsylvania

When we leave home and cross our nation's boundaries, moral clarity often blurs. Without a backdrop of shared attitudes, and without familiar laws and judicial procedures that define standards of ethical conduct, certainty is elusive. Should a company invest in a foreign country where civil and political rights are violated? Should a company go along with a host country's discriminatory employment practices? If companies in developed countries shift facilities to developing nations that lack strict environmental and health regulations, or if those companies choose to fill management and other top-level positions in a host nation with people from the home country, whose standards should prevail?

Even the best-informed, best-intentioned executives must rethink their assumptions about business practice in foreign settings. What works in a company's home country can fail in a country with different standards of ethical conduct. Such difficulties are unavoidable for businesspeople who live and work abroad.

But how can managers resolve the problems? What are the principles that can help them work through the maze of cultural differences and establish codes of conduct for globally ethical business practice? How can companies answer the toughest question in global business ethics: What happens when a host country's ethical standards seem lower than the home country's?

Competing Answers

One answer is as old as philosophical discourse. According to cultural relativism, no culture's ethics are better than any other's; therefore there are no international rights and wrongs. If the people of Indonesia tolerate the bribery of their public officials, so what? Their attitude is no better or worse than that of people in Denmark or Singapore who refuse to offer or accept bribes. Likewise, if Belgians fail to find insider trading morally repugnant, who cares? Not enforcing insider-trading laws is no more or less ethical than enforcing such laws.

The cultural relativist's creed—When in Rome, do as the Romans do—is tempting, especially when failing to do as the locals do means forfeiting business opportunities. The inadequacy of cultural relativism, however, becomes apparent when the practices in question are more damaging than petty bribery or insider trading.

In the late 1980s, some European tanneries and pharmaceutical companies were looking for cheap waste-dumping sites. They approached virtually every country on Africa's west coast from Morocco to the Congo. Nigeria agreed to take highly toxic polychlorinated biphenyls. Unprotected local workers, wearing thongs and shorts, unloaded barrels of PCBs and placed them near a residential area. Neither the residents nor the workers knew that the barrels contained toxic waste.

We may denounce governments that permit such abuses, but many countries are unable to police transnational corporations adequately even if they want to. And in many countries, the combination of ineffective enforcement and inadequate regulations leads to behavior by unscrupulous companies that is clearly wrong. A few years ago, for example, a group of investors became interested in restoring the *SS United States,* once a luxurious ocean liner. Before the actual restoration could begin, the ship had to be stripped of its asbestos lining. A bid from a U.S. company, based on U.S. standards for asbestos removal, priced the job at more than $100 million. A company in the Ukranian city of Sevastopol offered to do the work for less than $2 million. In October 1993, the ship was towed to Sevastopol.

A cultural relativist would have no problem with that outcome, but I do. A country has the right to establish its own health and safety regulations, but in the case described above, the standards and the terms of the contract could not possibly have protected workers in Sevastopol from known health risks. Even if the contract met Ukranian standards, ethical businesspeople must object. Cultural relativism is morally blind. There are fundamental values that cross cultures, and companies must uphold them. (For an economic argument against cultural relativism, see the box "The Culture and Ethics of Software Piracy.")

At the other end of the spectrum from cultural relativism is ethical imperialism, which directs people to do everywhere exactly as they do at home. Again, an understandably appealing approach but one that is clearly inadequate. Consider the large U.S. computer-products company that in 1993 introduced a course on sexual harassment in its Saudi Arabian facility. Under the banner of global consistency, instructors used the same approach to train Saudi Arabian managers that they had used with U.S. managers: the participants were asked to discuss a case in which a manager makes sexually explicit remarks to a new female employee over drinks in a bar. The instructors failed to consider how the exercise would work in a culture with strict conventions governing relationships between men and women. As a result, the training sessions were ludicrous. They baffled and offended the Saudi participants, and the message to avoid coercion and sexual discrimination was lost.

The theory behind ethical imperialism is absolutism, which is based on three problematic principles. Absolutists believe that there is a single list of truths, that they can be expressed only with one set of concepts, and that they call for exactly the same behavior around the world.

THE CULTURE AND ETHICS OF SOFTWARE PIRACY

Before jumping on the cultural relativism bandwagon, stop and consider the potential economic consequences of a when-in-Rome attitude toward business ethics. Take a look at the current statistics on software piracy: In the United States, pirated software is estimated to be 35% of the total software market, and industry losses are estimated at $2.3 billion per year. The piracy rate is 57% in Germany and 80% in Italy and Japan; the rates in most Asian countries are estimated to be nearly 100%.

There are similar laws against software piracy in those countries. What, then, accounts for the differences? Although a country's level of economic development plays a large part, culture, including ethical attitudes, may be a more crucial factor. The 1995 annual report of the Software Publishers Association connects software piracy directly to culture and attitude. It describes Italy and Hong Kong as having " 'first world' per capita incomes, along with 'third world' rates of piracy." When asked whether one should use software without paying for it, most people, including people in Italy and Hong Kong, say no. But people in some countries regard the practice as less unethical than people in other countries do. Confucian culture, for example, stresses that individuals should share what they create with society. That may be, in part, what prompts the Chinese and other Asians to view the concept of intellectual property as a means for the West to monopolize its technological superiority.

What happens if ethical attitudes around the world permit large-scale software piracy? Software companies won't want to invest as much in developing new products, because they cannot expect any return on their investment in certain parts of the world. When ethics fail to support technological creativity, there are consequences that go beyond statistics—jobs are lost and livelihoods jeopardized.

Companies must do more than lobby foreign governments for tougher enforcement of piracy laws. They must cooperate with other companies and with local organizations to help citizens understand the consequences of piracy and to encourage the evolution of a different ethic toward the practice.

The first claim clashes with many people's belief that different cultural traditions must be respected. In some cultures, loyalty to a community—family, organization, or society—is the foundation of all ethical behavior. The Japanese, for example, define business ethics in terms of loyalty to their companies, their business networks, and their nation. Americans place a higher value on liberty than on loyalty; the U.S. tradition of rights emphasizes equality, fairness, and individual freedom. It is hard to conclude that truth lies on one side or the other, but an absolutist would have us select just one.

The second problem with absolutism is the presumption that people must express moral truth using only one set of concepts. For instance, some absolutists insist that the language of basic rights provides the framework for any discussion of ethics. That means, though, that entire cultural traditions must be ignored. The notion of a right evolved with the rise of democracy in post-Renaissance Europe and the United States, but the term is not found in either Confucian or Buddhist traditions. We all learn ethics in the context of our particular cultures, and the power in the principles is deeply tied to the way in which they are expressed. Internationally accepted lists of moral principles, such as the United Nations' Universal Declaration of Human Rights, draw on many cultural and religious traditions. As philosopher Michael Walzer has noted, "There is no Esperanto of global ethics."

The third problem with absolutism is the belief in a global standard of ethical behavior. Context must shape ethical practice. Very low wages, for example, may be considered unethical in rich, advanced countries, but developing nations may be acting ethically if they encourage investment and improve living standards by accepting low wages. Likewise, when people are malnourished or starving, a government may be wise to use more fertilizer in order to improve crop yields, even though that means settling for relatively high levels of thermal water pollution.

When cultures have different standards of ethical behavior—and different ways of handling unethical behavior—a company that takes an absolutist approach may find itself making a disastrous mistake. When a manager at a large U.S. specialty-products company in China caught an employee stealing, she followed the company's practice and turned the employee over to the provincial authorities, who executed him. Managers cannot operate in another culture without being aware of that culture's attitudes toward ethics.

If companies can neither adopt a host country's ethics nor extend the home country's standards, what is the answer? Even the traditional litmus test—What would people think of your actions if they were written up on the front page of the newspaper?—is an unreliable guide, for there is no international consensus on standards of business conduct.

Balancing the Extremes: Three Guiding Principles

Companies must help managers distinguish between practices that are merely different and those that are wrong. For relativists, nothing is sacred and nothing is wrong. For absolutists, many things that are different are wrong. Neither extreme illuminates the real world of business decision making. The answer lies somewhere in between.

When it comes to shaping ethical behavior, companies must be guided by three principles.

- Respect for core human values, which determine the absolute moral threshold for all business activities.
- Respect for local traditions.
- The belief that context matters when deciding what is right and what is wrong.

Consider those principles in action. In Japan, people doing business together often exchange gifts—sometimes expensive ones—in keeping with long-standing Japanese tradition. When U.S. and European companies started doing a lot of business in Japan, many Western business people thought that the practice of gift giving might be wrong rather than simply different. To them, accepting a gift felt like accepting a bribe. As Western companies have become more familiar with Japanese traditions, however, most have come to tolerate the practice and to set different limits on gift giving in Japan than they do elsewhere.

Respecting differences is a crucial ethical practice. Research shows that management ethics differ among cultures; respecting those differences means recognizing that some cultures have obvious weaknesses—as well as hidden strengths. Managers in Hong Kong, for example, have a higher tolerance for some forms of bribery than their Western counterparts, but they have a much lower tolerance for the failure to acknowledge a subordinate's work. In some parts of the Far East, stealing credit from a subordinate is nearly an unpardonable sin.

People often equate respect for local traditions with cultural relativism. That is incorrect. Some practices are clearly wrong. Union Carbide's tragic experience in Bhopal, India, provides one example. The company's executives seriously underestimated how much on-site management involvement was needed at the Bhopal plant to compensate for the country's poor infrastructure and regulatory capabilities. In the aftermath of the disastrous gas leak, the lesson is clear: companies using sophisticated technology in a developing country must evaluate that country's ability to oversee its safe use. Since the incident at Bhopal, Union Carbide has become a leader in advising companies on using hazardous technologies safely in developing countries.

Some activities are wrong no matter where they take place. But some practices that are unethical in one setting may be acceptable in another. For instance, the chemical EDB, a soil fungicide, is banned for use in the United States. In hot climates, however, it quickly becomes harmless through exposure to intense solar radiation and high soil temperatures. As long as the chemical is monitored, companies may be able to use EDB ethically in certain parts of the world.

Defining the Ethical Threshold: Core Values

Few ethical questions are easy for managers to answer. But there are some hard truths that must guide managers' actions, a set of what I call *core human values,* which define minimum ethical standards for all companies.[1] The right to good health and the right to economic advancement and an improved standard of living are two core human values. Another is what Westerners call the Golden Rule, which is recognizable in every major religious and ethical tradition around the world. In Book 15 of his *Analects,* for instance, Confucius counsels people to maintain reciprocity, or not to do to others what they do not want done to themselves.

Although no single list would satisfy every scholar, I believe it is possible to articulate three core values that incorporate the work of scores of theologians and philosophers around the world. To be broadly relevant, these values must include elements found in both Western and non-Western cultural and religious traditions. Consider the examples of values in Figure 1 "What Do These Values Have in Common?"

At first glance, the values expressed in the two lists seem quite different. Nonetheless, in the spirit of what philosopher John Rawls calls *overlapping consensus,* one can see that the seemingly divergent values converge at key points. Despite important differences between Western and non-Western cultural and religious traditions, both express shared attitudes about what it means to be human. First, individuals must not treat others simply as tools; in other words, they must recognize a person's value as a human being. Next, individuals and communities must treat people in ways that respect people's basic rights. Finally, members of a community must

FIGURE 1

WHAT DO THESE VALUES HAVE IN COMMON?

Non-Western	Western
Kyosei (Japanese): Living and working together for the common good.	Individual liberty
Dharma (Hindu): The fulfillment of inherited duty.	Egalitarianism
Santutthi (Buddhist): The importance of limited desires.	Political participation
Zakat (Muslim): The duty to give alms to the Muslim poor.	Human rights

work together to support and improve the institutions on which the community depends. I call those three values *respect for human dignity, respect for basic rights,* and *good citizenship.*

Those values must be the starting point for all companies as they formulate and evaluate standards of ethical conduct at home and abroad. But they are only a starting point. Companies need much more specific guidelines, and the first step to developing those is to translate the core human values into core values for business. What does it mean, for example, for a company to respect human dignity? How can a company be a good citizen?

I believe that companies can respect human dignity by creating and sustaining a corporate culture in which employees, customers, and suppliers are treated not as means to an end but as people whose intrinsic value must be acknowledged; and by producing safe products and services in a safe workplace. Companies can respect basic rights by acting in ways that support and protect the individual rights of employees, customers, and surrounding communities, and by avoiding relationships that violate human beings' rights to health, education, safety, and an adequate standard of living. And companies can be good citizens by supporting essential social institutions, such as the economic system and the education system, and by working with host governments and other organizations to protect the environment.

The core values establish a moral compass for business practice. They can help companies identify practices that are acceptable and those that are intolerable—even if the practices are compatible with a host country's norms and laws. Dumping pollutants near people's homes and accepting inadequate standards for handling hazardous materials are two examples of actions that violate core values.

Similarly, if employing children prevents them from receiving a basic education, the practice is intolerable. Lying about product specifications in the act of selling may not affect human lives directly, but it too is intolerable because it violates the trust that is needed to sustain a corporate culture in which customers are respected.

Sometimes it is not a company's actions but those of a supplier or customer that pose problems.

Take the case of the Tan family, a large supplier for Levi Strauss. The Tans were allegedly forcing 1,200 Chinese and Filipino women to work 74 hours per week in guarded compounds on the Mariana Islands. In 1992, after repeated warnings to the Tans, Levi Strauss broke off business relations with them.

Creating an Ethical Corporate Culture

The core values for business that I have enumerated can help companies begin to exercise ethical judgment and think about how to operate ethically in foreign cultures, but they are not specific enough to guide managers through actual ethical dilemmas. Levi Strauss relied on a written code of conduct when figuring out how to deal with the Tan family. The company's Global Sourcing and Operating Guidelines, formerly called the Business Partner Terms of Engagement, state that Levi Strauss will "seek to identify and utilize business partners who aspire as individuals and in the conduct of all their businesses to a set of ethical standards not incompatible with our own." Whenever intolerable business situations arise, managers should be guided by precise statements that spell out the behavior and operating practices that the company demands.

Ninety percent of all *Fortune 500* companies have codes of conduct, and 70% have statements of vision and values. In Europe and the Far East, the percentages are lower but are increasing rapidly. Does that mean that most companies have what they need? Hardly. Even though most large U.S. companies have both statements of values and codes of conduct, many might be better off if they didn't. Too many companies don't do anything with the documents; they simply paste them on the wall to impress employees, customers, suppliers, and the public. As a result, the senior managers who drafted the statements lose credibility by proclaiming values and not living up to them. Companies such as Johnson & Johnson, Levi Strauss, Motorola, Texas Instruments, and Lockheed Martin, however, do a great deal to make the words meaningful. Johnson & Johnson, for example, has become well known for its Credo Challenge sessions, in which managers discuss ethics in the context of their current business problems and are invited to criticize the company's credo and make suggestions for changes. The participants' ideas are passed on to the company's senior managers. Lockheed Martin has created an innovative site on the World Wide Web and on its local network that gives employees, customers, and suppliers access to the company's ethical code and the chance to voice complaints.

Codes of conduct must provide clear direction about ethical behavior when the temptation to behave unethically is strongest. The pronouncement in a code of conduct that bribery is unacceptable is useless unless accompanied by guidelines for gift giving, payments to get goods through customs, and "requests" from intermediaries who are hired to ask for bribes.

Motorola's values are stated very simply as "How we will always act: [with] constant respect for people [and] uncompromising integrity." The company's code of conduct, however, is explicit about actual business practice. With respect to bribery, for example, the code states that the "funds and assets of Motorola shall not be used, directly or indirectly, for illegal payments of any kind." It is unambiguous about what sort of payment is illegal: "the payment of a bribe to a public official or the kickback of funds to an employee of a customer . . ." The code goes on to prescribe specific procedures for handling commissions to intermediaries, issuing sales invoices, and disclosing confidential information in a sales transaction—all situations in which employees might have an opportunity to accept or offer bribes.

Codes of conduct must be explicit to be useful, but they must also leave room for a manager to use his or her judgment in situations requiring cultural sensitivity. Host-country employees shouldn't be forced to adopt all home-country values and renounce their own. Again, Motorola's code is exemplary. First, it gives clear direction: "Employees of Motorola will respect the laws, customs, and traditions of each country in which they operate, but will, at the same time, engage in no course of conduct which, even if legal, customary, and accepted in any such country, could be deemed to be in violation of the accepted business ethics of Motorola or the laws of the United States relating to business ethics." After laying down such absolutes, Motorola's code then makes clear when individual judgment will be necessary. For example, employees may sometimes accept certain kinds of small gifts "in rare circumstances, where the refusal to accept a gift" would injure Motorola's "legitimate business interests." Under certain circumstances, such gifts "may be accepted so long as the gift inures to the benefit of Motorola" and not "to the benefit of the Motorola employee."

Striking the appropriate balance between providing clear direction and leaving room for individual judgment makes crafting corporate values statements and ethics codes one of the hardest tasks that executives confront. The words are only a start. A company's leaders need to refer often to their organization's credo and code and must themselves be credible, committed, and consistent. If senior managers act as though ethics don't matter, the rest of the company's employees won't think they do, either.

Conflicts of Development and Conflicts of Tradition

Managers living and working abroad who are not prepared to grapple with moral ambiguity and tension should pack their bags and come home. The view that all business practices can be categorized as either ethical or unethical is too simple. As Einstein is reported to have said, "Things should be as simple as possible—but no simpler." Many business practices that are considered unethical in one setting may be ethical in another. Such activities are neither black nor white but exist in what Thomas Dunfee and I have called *moral free space*.[2] In this gray zone, there are no tight prescriptions for a company's behavior. Managers must chart their own courses—as long as they do not violate core human values.

Consider the following example. Some successful Indian companies offer employees the opportunity for one of their children to gain a job with the company once the child has completed a certain level in school. The companies honor this commitment even when other applicants are more qualified than an employee's child. The perk is extremely valuable in a country where jobs are hard to find, and it reflects the Indian culture's belief that the West has gone too far in allowing economic opportunities to break up families. Not surprisingly, the perk is among the most cherished by employees, but in most Western countries, it would be branded unacceptable nepotism. In the United States, for example, the ethical principle of equal opportunity holds that jobs should go to the applicants with the best qualifications. If a U.S. company made such promises to its employees, it would violate regulations established by the Equal Employment Opportunity Commission. Given this difference in ethical attitudes, how should U.S. managers react to Indian nepotism? Should they condemn the Indian companies, refusing to accept them as partners or suppliers until they agree to clean up their act?

Despite the obvious tension between nepotism and principles of equal opportunity, I cannot condemn the practice for Indians. In a country, such as India, that emphasizes clan and family relationships and has catastrophic levels of unemployment, the practice must be viewed in moral free space. The decision to allow a special perk for employees and their children is not necessarily wrong—at least for members of that country.

How can managers discover the limits of moral free space? That is, how can they learn to distinguish a value in tension with their own from one that is intolerable? Helping managers develop good ethical judgment requires companies to be clear about their core values and codes of conduct. But even the most explicit set of guidelines cannot always provide answers. That is especially true in the thorniest ethical dilemmas, in which the host country's ethical standards not only are different but also seem lower than the home country's. Managers must recognize that when countries have different ethical standards, there are two types of conflict that commonly arise. Each type requires its own line of reasoning.

In the first type of conflict, which I call a *conflict of relative development,* ethical standards conflict because of the countries' different levels of economic development. As mentioned before, developing countries may accept wage rates that seem inhumane to more advanced countries in order to attract investment. As economic conditions in a developing country improve, the incidence of that sort of conflict usually decreases. The second type of conflict is a *conflict of cultural tradition.* For example, Saudi Arabia, unlike most other countries, does not allow women to serve as corporate managers. Instead, women may work in only a few professions, such as education and health care. The prohibition stems from strongly held religious and cultural beliefs; any increase in the country's level of economic development, which is already quite high, is not likely to change the rules.

To resolve a conflict of relative development, a manager must ask the following question: Would the practice be acceptable at home if my country were in a similar stage of economic development? Consider the difference between wage and safety standards in the United States and in Angola, where citizens accept lower standards on both counts. If a U.S. oil company is hiring Angolans to work on an offshore Angolan oil rig, can the company pay them lower wages than it pays U.S. workers in the Gulf of Mexico? Reasonable people have to answer yes if the alternative for Angola is the loss of both the foreign investment and the jobs.

Consider, too, differences in regulatory environments. In the 1980s, the government of India fought hard to be able to import Ciba-Geigy's Entero Vioform, a drug known to be enormously effective in fighting dysentery but one that had been banned in the United States because some users experienced side effects. Although dysentery was not a big problem in the United States, in India, poor public sanitation was contributing to epidemic levels of the disease. Was it unethical to make the drug available in India after it had been banned in the United States? On the contrary, rational people should consider it unethical not to do so. Apply our test: Would the United States, at an earlier stage of development, have used this drug despite its side effects? The answer is clearly yes.

But there are many instances when the answer to similar questions is no. Sometimes a host country's standards are inadequate at any level of economic development. If a country's pollution standards are so low that working on an oil rig would considerably increase a person's risk of developing cancer, foreign oil companies must refuse to do business there. Likewise, if the dangerous side effects of a drug treatment outweigh its benefits, managers should not accept health standards that ignore the risks.

When relative economic conditions do not drive tensions, there is a more objective test for resolving ethical problems. Managers should deem a practice permissible only if they can answer no to both of the following questions: Is it possible to conduct business successfully in the host country without undertaking the practice? and Is the practice a violation of a core human value? Japanese gift giving is a perfect example of a conflict of cultural tradition. Most experienced businesspeople, Japanese and non-Japanese alike, would agree that doing business in Japan would be virtually impossible without adopting the practice. Does gift giving violate a core human value? I cannot identify one that it violates. As a result, gift giving may be permissible for foreign companies in Japan even if it conflicts with ethical attitudes at home. In fact, that conclusion is widely accepted, even by companies such as Texas Instruments and IBM, which are outspoken against bribery.

Does it follow that all nonmonetary gifts are acceptable or that bribes are generally acceptable in countries where they are common? Not at all. (See the box "The Problem with Bribery.") What makes the routine practice of gift giving acceptable in Japan are the limits in its scope and intention. When gift giving moves outside those limits, it soon collides with core human values. For example, when Carl Kotchian, president of Lockheed in the 1970s, carried suitcases full of cash to Japanese politicians, he went beyond the norms established by Japanese tradition. That incident galvanized opinion in the United States Congress and helped lead to passage of the Foreign Corrupt Practices Act. Likewise, Roh Tae Woo went beyond the norms established by Korean cultural tradition when he accepted $635.4 million in bribes as president of the Republic of Korea between 1988 and 1993.

Guidelines for Ethical Leadership

Learning to spot intolerable practices and to exercise good judgment when ethical conflicts arise requires practice. Creating a company culture that

---

THE PROBLEM WITH BRIBERY

Bribery is widespread and insidious. Managers in transnational companies routinely confront bribery even though most countries have laws against it. The fact is that officials in many developing countries wink at the practice, and the salaries of local bureaucrats are so low that many consider bribes a form of remuneration. The U.S. Foreign Corrupt Practices Act defines allowable limits on petty bribery in the form of routine payments required to move goods through customs. But demands for bribes often exceed those limits, and there is seldom a good solution.

Bribery disrupts distribution channels when goods languish on docks until local handlers are paid off, and it destroys incentives to compete on quality and cost when purchasing decisions are based on who pays what under the table. Refusing to acquiesce is often tantamount to giving business to unscrupulous companies.

I believe that even routine bribery is intolerable. Bribery undermines market efficiency and predictability, thus ultimately denying people their right to a minimal standard of living. Some degree of ethical commitment—some sense that everyone will play by the rules—is necessary for a sound economy. With-

out an ability to predict outcomes, who would be willing to invest?

There was a U.S. company whose shipping crates were regularly pilfered by handlers on the docks of Rio de Janeiro. The handlers would take about 10% of the contents of the crates, but the company was never sure which 10% it would be. In a partial solution, the company began sending two crates—the first with 90% of the merchandise, the second with 10%. The handlers learned to take the second crate and leave the first untouched. From the company's perspective, at least knowing which goods it would lose was an improvement.

Bribery does more than destroy predictability; it undermines essential social and economic systems. That truth is not lost on businesspeople in countries where the practice is woven into the social fabric. CEOs in India admit that their companies engage constantly in bribery, and they say that they have considerable disgust for the practice. They blame government policies in part, but Indian executives also know that their country's business practices perpetuate corrupt behavior. Anyone walking the streets of Calcutta, where it is clear that even a dramatic redistribution of wealth would still leave most of India's inhabitants in dire poverty, comes face-to-face with the devastating effects of corruption.

---

rewards ethical behavior is essential. The following guidelines for developing a global ethical perspective among managers can help.

Treat corporate values and formal standards of conduct as absolutes. Whatever ethical standards a company chooses, it cannot waver on its principles either at home or abroad. Consider what has become part of company lore at Motorola. Around 1950, a senior executive was negotiating with officials of a South American government on a $10 million sale that would have increased the company's annual net profits by nearly 25%. As the negotiations neared completion, however, the executive walked away from the deal because the officials were asking for $1 million for "fees." CEO Robert Galvin not only supported the executive's decision but also made it clear that Motorola would neither accept the sale on any terms nor do business with those government officials again. Retold over the decades, this story demonstrating Galvin's resolve has helped cement a culture of ethics for thousands of employees at Motorola.

Design and implement conditions of engagement for suppliers and customers. Will your company do business with any customer or supplier? What if a customer or supplier uses child labor? What if it has strong links with organized crime? What if it pressures your company to break a host country's laws? Such issues are best not left for spur-of-the-moment decisions. Some companies have realized that. Sears, for instance, has developed a policy of not contracting production to companies that use prison labor or infringe on workers' rights to health and safety. And BankAmerica has specified as a condition for many of its loans to developing countries that environmental standards and human rights must be observed.

Allow foreign business units to help formulate ethical standards and interpret ethical issues. The French pharmaceutical company Rhone-Poulene Rorer has allowed foreign subsidiaries to augment lists of corporate ethical principles with their own suggestions. Texas Instruments has paid special attention to issues of international business ethics by creating the Global Business Practices Council, which is made up of managers from countries in which the company operates. With the over-arching intent to create a "global ethics strategy, locally deployed," the council's mandate is to provide ethics education and create local processes that will help managers in the company's foreign business units resolve ethical conflicts.

In host countries, support efforts to decrease institutional corruption. Individual managers will not be able to wipe out corruption in a host country, no matter how many bribes they turn down. When a host country's tax system, import and export procedures, and procurement practices favor unethical players, companies must take action.

Many companies have begun to participate in reforming host-country institutions. General Electric, for example, has taken a strong stand in India, using the media to make repeated condemnations of bribery in business and government. General Electric and others have found, however, that a single company usually cannot drive out entrenched corruption. Transparency International, an organization based in Germany, has been effective in helping coalitions of companies, government officials, and others work to reform bribery-ridden bureaucracies in Russia, Bangladesh, and elsewhere.

Exercise moral imagination. Using moral imagination means resolving tensions responsibly and creatively. Coca-Cola, for instance, has consistently turned down requests for bribes from Egyptian officials but has managed to gain political support and public trust by sponsoring a project to plant fruit trees. And take the example of Levi Strauss, which discovered in the early 1990s that two of its suppliers in Bangladesh were employing children under the age of 14—a practice that violated the company's principles but was tolerated in Bangladesh. Forcing the suppliers to fire the children would not have ensured that the children received an education, and it would have caused serious hardship for the families depending on the children's wages. In a creative arrangement, the suppliers agreed to pay the children's regular wages while they attended school and to offer each child a job at age 14. Levi Strauss, in turn, agreed to pay the children's tuition and pro-

vide books and uniforms. That arrangement allowed Levi Strauss to uphold its principles and provide long-term benefits to its host country.

Many people think of values as soft; to some they are usually unspoken. A South Seas island society uses the word *mokita,* which means, "the truth that everybody knows but nobody speaks." However difficult they are to articulate, values affect how we all behave. In a global business environment, values in tension are the rule rather than the exception. Without a company's commitment, statements of values and codes of ethics end up as empty platitudes that provide managers with no foundation for behaving ethically. Employees need and deserve more, and responsible members of the global business community can set examples for others to follow. The dark consequences of incidents such as Union Carbide's disaster in Bhopal remind us how high the stakes can be.

NOTES

1. In other writings, Thomas W. Dunfee and I have used the term *hypernorm* instead of *core human value.*
2. Thomas Donaldson and Thomas W. Dunfee, " Toward a Unified Conception of Business Ethics: Integrative Social Contracts Theory," *Academy of Management Review,* April 1994; and "Integrative Social Contracts Theory: A Communitarian Conception of Economic Ethics," *Economics and Philosophy,* Spring 1995.

What's Wrong with Bribery

Scott Turow
Partner, Sonnenschein Nath & Rosenthal, Chicago, and author of
One L, Presumed Innocent, Burden of Proof, and *Pleading Guilty*

The question on the floor is what is wrong with bribery? I am not a philosopher and thus my answer to that question may be less systematic than others, but it is certainly no less deeply felt. As a

From *Journal of Business Ethics,* Vol. 4, No. 4 (1985), pp. 249–251. Copyright © 1985 by Kluwer Academic Publishers. Reprinted by permission of Kluwer Academic Publishers.

federal prosecutor I have worked for a number of years now in the area of public corruption. Over that course of time, perhaps out of instincts of self-justification, or, so it seems, sharpened moral insights, I have come to develop an abiding belief that bribery is deeply immoral.

We all know that bribery is unlawful and I believe that the legal concepts in this area are in fact grounded in widely accepted moral intuitions. Bribery, as defined by the state of Illinois and construed by the United States Court of Appeals for the Seventh Circuit in the case of *United States v. Isaacs,* in which the former Governor of Illinois, Otto Kerner, was convicted for bribery, may be said to take place in these instances: Bribery occurs when property or personal advantage is offered, without the authority of law, to a public official with the intent that the public official act favorably to the offeror at any time or fashion in execution of the public official's duties.

Under this definition of bribery, the crime consists solely of an unlawful offer, made or accepted with a prohibited state of mind. No particular act need be specified; and the result is immaterial.

This is merely a matter of definition. Oddly the moral underpinnings of bribery are clearer in the context of another statute—the criminal law against mail fraud. Federal law has no bribery statute of general application; it is unlawful of course to bribe federal officials, to engage in a pattern of bribery, or to engage in bribery in certain other specified contexts, e.g., to influence the outcome of a sporting contest. But unlike the states, the Congress, for jurisdictional reasons, has never passed a general bribery statute, criminalizing *all* instances of bribery. Thus, over time the federal mail fraud statute has come to be utilized as the vehicle for some bribery prosecutions. The theory, adopted by the courts, goes to illustrate what lawyers have thought is wrong with bribery.

Mail fraud/bribery is predicated on the theory that someone—the bribee's governmental or private employer—is deprived, by a bribe, of the recipient's undivided loyalties. The bribee comes to serve two masters and as such is an 'unfaithful servant.' This breach of fiduciary duty, when combined with active efforts at concealment becomes actionable under the mail fraud law, assuming certain other jurisdictional requisites are met. Concealment, as noted, is another essential element of the crime. An employee who makes no secret of his dual service cannot be called to task; presumably his employer is thought to have authorized and accepted the divided loyalties. For this reason, the examples of maitre d's accepting payments from customers cannot be regarded as fully analogous to instances of bribery which depend on persons operating under false pretenses, a claimed loyalty that has in truth been undermined.

Some of the stricter outlines of what constitutes bribery, in the legal view, can be demonstrated by example. Among the bribery prosecutions with which I have spent the most time is a series of mail fraud/bribery cases arising out of corruption at the Cook County Board of Appeals. The Board of Appeals is a local administrative agency, vested with the authority to review and revise local real estate property tax assessments. After a lengthy grand jury investigation, it became clear that the Board of Appeals was a virtual cesspool, where it was commonplace for lawyers practicing before the Board to make regular cash payments to some decision-makers. The persons accused of bribery at the Board generally relied on two defenses. Lawyers and tax consultants who made the payments often contended that the payments were, in a fashion, a necessity; the Board was so busy, so overcome by paperwork, and so many other people were paying, that the only way to be sure cases would be examined was to have an 'in' with an official whom payments had made friendly. The first argument also suggests the second: that the payments, whatever their nature, had accomplished nothing untoward, and that any tax reduction petition granted by the bribed official actually deserved the reduction it received.

Neither contention is legally sufficient to remove the payments from the category of bribery. Under the definition above, any effort to cause favorable action constitutes bribery, regardless of the supposedly provocative circumstances. And in practice juries had great difficulty accepting the idea that the lawyers involved had been 'coerced' into making the boxcar incomes—sometimes

$300,000 to $400,000 a year—that many of the bribers earned. Nor is the merits of the cases involved a defense, under the above definitions. Again, in practical terms, juries seemed reluctant to believe that lawyers would be passing the Board's deputy commissioners cash under the table if they were really convinced of their cases' merits. But whatever the accuracy of that observation, it is clear that the law prohibits a payment, even to achieve a deserved result.

The moral rationale for these rules of law seems clear to me. Fundamentally, I believe that any payment to a governmental official for corrupt purposes is immoral. The obligation of government to deal with like cases alike is a principal of procedural fairness which is well recognized. But this principal is more than a matter of procedure; it has a deep moral base. We recognize that the equality of humans, their fundamental dignity as beings, demands that each stand as an equal before the government they have joined to create, that each, as Ronald Dworkin has put, has a claim to government's equal concern and respect. Bribery asks that that principal be violated, that some persons be allowed to stand ahead of others, that like cases not be treated alike, and that some persons be preferred. This I find morally repugnant.

Moreover, for this reason, I cannot accept the idea that bribery, which is wrong here, is somehow more tolerable abroad. Asking foreign officials to act in violation of moral principles must, as an abstract matter, be no less improper than asking that of members of our own government; it even smacks of imperialist attitudes. Furthermore, even dealing with the question on this level assumes that there are societies which unequivocally declare that governmental officials may properly deal with the citizenry in a random and unequal fashion. I doubt, in fact, whether any such sophisticated society exists; more than likely, bribery offends the norms and mores of the foreign country as well.

Not only does bribery violate fundamental notions of equality, but it also endangers the vitality of the institution affected. Most bribery centers on persons in discretionary or decision-making positions. Much as we want to believe that bribery invites gross deviations in duty, a prosecutor's experience is that in many cases there are no objectively correct decisions for the bribed official to make. We discovered that this was the case in the Board of Appeals prosecutions where a variety of competing theories of real estate valuation guaranteed that there was almost always some justification, albeit often thin, for what had been done. But it misses the point to look solely at the ultimate actions of the bribed official. Once the promise of payment is accepted, the public official is no longer the impartial decision-maker he is supposed to be. Whatever claims he might make, it is difficult to conceive of a public official who could convince anyone that he entirely disregarded a secret 'gift' from a person affected by his judgments.

Indeed, part of the evil of bribery inheres in the often indetectable nature of some of its results. Once revealed, the presence of bribery thus robs persons affected of a belief in the integrity of *all* prior decisions. In the absolute case, bribery goes to dissolve the social dependencies that require discretionary decision-making at certain junctions in our social scheme. Bribery, then, is a crime against trust; and to the extent that trust, a belief in the good faith of discretionary decision-makers, is essential to certain bureaucratic and governmental structures, bribery is deeply corrosive.

Because of its costs, the law usually deems bribery to be without acceptable justification. Again, I think this is in line with moral intuitions. Interestingly, the law does not regard extortion and bribery as mutually exclusive; extortion requires an apprehension of harm, bribery desire to influence. Often, in fact, the two are coincident. Morally—and legally, perhaps—it would seem that bribery can be justified only if the bribe-giver is truly without alternatives, including the alternative of refusing payment and going to the authorities. Moreover, the briber should be able to show not merely that it was convenient or profitable to pay the bribe, but that the situation presented a choice of evils in which the bribe somehow avoided a greater peril. The popular example in our discussions has been bribing a Nazi camp guard in order to spare concentration camp internees.

Codes of Conduct for Global Business: Prospects and Challenges of Implementation

S. Prakash Sethi
University Distinguished Professor, and Academic Director-
Executive Program, Zicklin School of Business, Baruch College,
The City University of New York (CUNY)[1]

CORPORATE CODES AND CRITICS

In the United States and Western Europe, corporate codes of conduct have become *de rigueur* for most large corporations. According to recent studies, 60 to 70 percent of major US corporations have issued codes of conduct, and many of the largest foreign multinationals have done so as well. These codes usually attempt to state the company's mission, values, and goals, and to describe its relationship to various stakeholders, both internal and external. Unfortunately, most of these codes suffer from a number of flaws:

- They are presented as public statements of lofty intent and purpose, but lack specific content.
- While they mention the corporation's commitment to its customers, employees, etc., they ignore the *rights* of these key stakeholders in their dealings with the company.
- They make no provisions for internal implementation, and code compliance is not integrated into the organization's procedures and reward structure; hence, managers and employees are often uninformed about the codes and their content, and do not take them seriously.
- They provide no basis or framework for communication with external communities about the efforts and results (success or failure) of the corporation in achieving the codes' objectives.

The inevitable result of these defects is that corporate codes of conduct are often treated with disdain by knowledgeable and influential opinion leaders among various stakeholder groups, as well as by outside analysts and the public at large. To be sure, there are a handful of companies whose codes of conduct are taken more seriously by their constituencies. Notable examples are those of Motorola, Levi Strauss, Texas Instruments, Sara Lee, and Mattel. However, the very smallness of this group reinforces my point. And, with the exception of Mattel, none of these corporations has chosen to make public either the process by which it seeks compliance of its code within its own organization (particularly by its overseas subsidiaries and strategic partners), or the results of its compliance efforts. Nor have the corporations, with the exception of Mattel, subjected their codes or processes to independent outside verification.

The weakness of corporate commitment to code compliance is all too apparent. After thirty years of research and teaching in this field, I can point to only one major corporation that has asked external independent monitors to examine its code compliance and has made the results public. This example is Nestlé, the Swiss-based multinational corporation and one of the world's largest manufacturers of food and related products. Nestlé was confronted with worldwide public boycotts of its products, and demonstrations by advocates of the poor and developing countries for its alleged improper marketing and promotional activities in the sale of infant formula products in these countries. Although inherently safe, these products were too expensive and largely unnecessary in these settings. Poor and uninformed mothers in developing countries were pressured into buying these products through intense promotion. Eventually, the World Health Organization enacted an International Code of Marketing of Breast-Milk Substitutes (Infant Formula Code) which banned most advertising and promotion of such products. Nestlé was strongly opposed to the development of this Code. Nevertheless, after the Code was enacted, Nestlé announced its willingness to abide by the Code and arranged for independent verification and compliance monitoring. The outcome was highly salutory. Within a period of less than four years, Nestlé's reputation was largely restored, and the boycott against the company's products was called off.

[1]The editorial work of Lee E. Preston on this paper is deeply appreciated.
From *Business and Society Review*, Vol. 105, No. 2, (Summer, 2000). © Center for Business Ethics at Bentley College. Published by Blackwell Publishers.

Since that time, only one U.S. multinational corporation has voluntarily promulgated a global code of conduct that committed itself to independent monitoring by an external group of credible and experienced persons charged to make a public report of their findings. That company is Mattel, one of the world's largest producers of children's toys including Barbie, Hot Wheels and Fisher Price products. This experience, and my personal involvement in it, will be further discussed below.

Corporate Response to Criticism

There have, of course, been a few other notable positive responses by major corporations, both individually and collectively, to public criticism. The promulgation of the Sullivan Principles by U.S. firms operating in South Africa is a significant example. For the most part, however, multinational corporations have responded in public pressures in two less-effective ways:

- They claim to abide by all local laws and standards. They also declare that their practices are driven by competitive market forces, low worker productivity, and the extra cost of doing business in different countries. Furthermore, they claim, often with some justification, that wages and working conditions in their own plants are superior to other plants in these areas.
- They promulgate voluntary codes of conduct that appear to address the concerns of their critics. Unfortunately, these weak and haphazard efforts often reveal the *absence* of long-term strategies to deal with underlying issues, as well as inadequate programs of public communication. Very few companies have created codes of conduct or "best practice" by which they can actually guide and evaluate their overseas operations, or the conduct of their local partners and suppliers.

Companies are often seen as being dragged into action only when public pressure becomes too intense to ignore. Alternatively, companies have resisted change by spending incredible amounts of time and effort in discussions about code formulation. This can be seen in the case of the apparel industry's code of conduct. President Clinton announced this initiative with great fanfare in June,

1997, but only after many years of intense public pressure. It then took almost eighteen months for the various parties to come to a specific agreement about what would be audited, who would do the auditing, and what type of report would be published. As a result of these delays and disagreements, the entire process is viewed by the public with great skepticism. As a matter of fact, two of the leading public interest group participants in the negotiations have refused to sign the new accord and have denounced it as too weak. Moreover, if experience to date is any indication, the implementation process is also likely to be subject to intense discussions among the participants, with resultant delays. Thus, it will be quite some time before anyone will have an opportunity to evaluate the importance and effectiveness of this code. The consequence of these failings has been further public antagonism and pressure on the corporations. Thus, rather than gaining public support and recognition for their efforts, the companies involved are being denounced for bad faith. There are also efforts to pursue legislative and regulatory approaches at national and international levels that would compel companies to undertake desired actions.

The Imperative of Global Codes of Conduct

Let me state categorically and unequivocally my belief that corporate codes of conduct are here to stay. Further, they are both necessary and desirable. When properly developed and implemented, codes of conduct can provide the corporation with a voluntary and flexible approach to addressing some of society's concerns, both in general and in the marketplace. Codes can serve both corporate interests and public purposes and can strengthen free market institutions, as well. Effective use of codes can restore public faith in the market economy as the best avenue for enhancing human welfare, advancing regional economic development, and strengthening democratic institutions.

Public sentiment and perspective play a very important role in defining the parameters of discretion that a society will allow the leaders of its various social, political, and economic institutions. In the present instance, as well as in many previous instances involving social issues, the fight for the hearts and minds of the public has invariably been led by corporate critics. Companies, fearing lack of public trust, have refrained from a proactive stance and have instead limited themselves to disputing their critics' charges. This is a losing battle and will always remain so. By yielding the initiative to their critics, companies have allowed their critics to shape the agenda in ways that put business in a perpetually defensive mode, talking about "what they may have done wrong" instead of "what they are doing right."

Codes of conduct offer an invaluable opportunity for responsible corporations to create an individual and highly positive public identity for themselves; that is, a reputation effect that can have a direct result on their bottom line in terms of increased revenues, customer loyalty, expanded markets, a productive work force, and a supportive political and regulatory environment. Furthermore, an increased level of public confidence and trust among important constituencies and stakeholders would lead to greater freedom for management in the running of their business operations, and insulate them from the actions of other, less scrupulous firms in the market-place.

Voluntary codes serve to achieve a larger public purpose in a manner that is flexible and pragmatic and take into account the unique set of problems faced by an industry or by different companies. They also allow the moderate elements among the affected groups to seek reasonable solutions to the issues involved, even before these issues are captured by more radical elements whose primary interest may be in escalating the level of social conflict, rather than fashioning mutually acceptable and feasible solutions. And they avoid the need for further governmental regulation that is invariably more expensive and less efficient (because of political considerations and the need to create regulations that cover all possible situations and contingencies).

CREATING A CODE OF CONDUCT

The remainder of this paper is devoted to a discussion of the development and implementation of a meaningful code of conduct for globally active corporations. This discussion will draw on my

own experience as chair of the Mattel Independent Monitoring Council for Global Manufacturing Principles (MIMCO).

Characteristics of a Viable Code

A corporate code of conduct is in the nature of "private law" or a "promise voluntarily made," whereby an institution makes a public commitment to certain standards of conduct. The fact that issuance of a code is "voluntary" reflects the flexibility of action afforded to a corporation. Commitment to a code affirms that corporations and their critics share a common interest in improving the conditions of their interaction, and in mutually satisfactory resolution of underlying issues.

For a code of conduct to have any reasonable chance of meeting the expectations of all parties involved, the following conditions must be met.

- The code commitments must be economically viable for the corporation, given the dynamics of its technology and competition, and the economic and sociopolitical realities of the environments within which it operates.
- The code must address substantive issues that are of importance to the corporation's various constituencies, particularly employees, communities, and governments.
- The code must be specific about performance standards that can be objectively measured.
- Important constituencies of the corporation must be engaged in the code formulation and implementation process.

Development and Implementation

Development and implementation of a multinational code of conduct is a challenging task because of the differing orientations and concerns of the diverse parties involved; their disparate assumptions about the feasibility of particular goals and benchmarks; and disagreements about the means that are appropriate and feasible to achieve agreed-upon goals. Another major hurdle arises from the organizational ethos and decision-making processes of corporations and other participative and public interest groups. A corporation's primary focus is on the efficiency of processes and the optimization of outcomes. Participative and deliberative processes, e.g., open consultations and procedural norms, are adopted only as means to achieve desired ends and are not seen as values themselves. By contrast, many stakeholder groups place tremendous importance on consultation and information sharing, not only as steps in effective decision-making, but as values themselves. Thus, from their perspective, efficient use of time and resources may take second place to consultation and involvement; and corporate actions that appear to jeopardize participative processes are viewed with distrust.

Assuming that there is adequate commitment to widespread participation and involvement in code development, the next step is to determine the scope of the proposed code. The includes:

- Definition: What aspects of corporate activity and impact are to be included in the code?
- Measurement and Verification: How should corporate performance in these areas be measured, and how should the accuracy of this information be verified?
- Accountability and Reporting: To whom should the corporation be accountable for its performance, and how should this information be made public?

Specificity in all of these matters is critical because an ambiguous code tends either to become meaningless, or to expand into varied meanings as different groups stretch its terms to suit their particular interests. Code requirement must be translated into quantifiable and standardized measurements so that objective and consistent observations can be made by different people, over time. Code compliance must become an element of management routine that is integral, rather than peripheral, to the firm's normal operations. And, most importantly, indicators of code compliance must reflect results rather than intentions; goals met or unmet, not merely actions taken in pursuit of goals.

Two final points on implementations are these:

- The company's top management must be strongly and unequivocally committed to the code, and code compliance must be an element of performance evaluation at all levels of management.

- The company must be willing to expose its record of code compliance to external verification. This last step is particularly important if the firm expects to achieve "reputation effects" and the benefits of stakeholder trust and collaboration, as well as public approval.

Independent Monitoring Systems

One of the most critical aspects of code implementation is the creation of an independent monitoring system. Independent monitoring is necessary for the public to see that companies are indeed doing what they proclaim to be doing. Unfortunately, most companies with codes are extremely reluctant to subject themselves to independent outside monitoring and public dissemination of monitoring results.

This is an area of great disagreement between corporations and their critics, and a major source of public distrust about corporate motives and performance. Reluctance to share information is sometimes justifiably based on the fear that the company will be subjected to inappropriate pressure and harassment, rather than be applauded for the progress it has made. However, inadequate disclosure inevitably suggests that there is something to hide, and suggests a lack of faith in the ability of stakeholders to appreciate and encourage good corporate conduct. It is ironic that corporations expect their financial performance to be publicly reported and audited by independent outsiders for the benefit of investors, but are unwilling to provide other information—often much less sensitive—of comparable concern to other vital constituencies.

Companies have often argued that many indicators of code compliance are internal measures, not conventionally subject to outside review, and that confidentiality makes it easier to take corrective actions though a system of "carrot and stick." This line of argument, however, has not been successful in previous situations involving crises of public confidence and is doomed to failure in the current global socio-political environment. Neither advanced nor developing countries will allow companies to operate any longer under a "veil of secrecy" where issues of human rights and ethical/moral conduct are concerned.

There are currently two approaches to creating and implementing codes of conduct with appropriate performance verification and public reporting processes. One involves industry-wide effort; the other suggests that individual companies should develop their own approaches, based on their unique circumstances. We briefly consider the advantages and disadvantages of each.

Industry-Wide Effort   The case for an industry-wide effort is based on the premise that companies in an industry face similar sets of problems, competitive conditions, and external pressures. Therefore, a combined approach should be feasible, cost effective, and place all companies on the same competitive footing with respect to these issues. An industry-wide approach also gives participating companies a united position with which to respond to their critics and public at large.

There are, however, serious flaws to this logic:

- An industry-wide approach requires consensus before any action can be taken. It therefore plays into the hands of those companies who are least inclined to undertake substantive action, and thus can postpone implementation through endless discussion, procrastination and obfuscation, thereby defeating the purpose of the exercise and inviting public ridicule and distrust.
- It forces industry performance standards to the lowest common denominator; i.e., the company with the weakest record sets the pace for the entire industry.
- It reduces incentives for individual companies to improve their own performance based on their own particular circumstances.
- Since these industry-wide efforts invariably depend on "voluntary compliance" and rarely incorporate monitoring or enforcement measures, poorly performing companies remain undisciplined and taint the record of the entire industry.

I do not believe that, at the present time, an industry-wide approach is either feasible or desirable in most cases. Since very few industries have even a modicum of "commonly accepted" standards or performance criteria in *any* area of public concern, an effort to develop common performance criteria might appear to be—and might actually become—

a form of anti-competitive collusion. Moreover, at the current stage of code development and public acceptance, an industry-wide approach is likely to be very disadvantageous to the companies that are seeking to develop creative, innovative responses to human and social concerns.

Independent Approach   I believe that for a company that is strongly committed to a substantive and effective code of conduct, a "go-it-alone" strategy is preferable at the present time. The direct economic benefits emanating from increased stakeholder trust, cooperation, and loyalty should provide ample incentive; and enhanced public reputation should translate into a more hospitable external socio-political environment over the long term. A go-it-alone company has the flexibility to fashion a code of conduct that takes advantage of its unique capabilities and to develop new systems and procedures of permanent value (and perhaps of market value to other firms as well). Successful individual firm experience may well permit the gradual development of multi-firm approaches.

Monitoring Council

Whatever the specific substantive content of a code of conduct, and whatever its level of sponsorship (division, corporate, or industry), its ultimate success depends upon the verification of its results by independent reviewers. I refer to these individuals as a "Monitoring Council." Such a Council should consist of three to five members with impeccable credentials for independence, knowledge, and, if possible, code formulation and implementation. The Council must have credibility with all constituent groups, including corporate directors and managers, governments, and others stakeholders. I do not believe that it is appropriate to include specific stakeholder representatives as Council members, since the Council's purpose is to determine the extent to which the company is meeting its public commitments, as expressed in its code. (Stakeholder representatives may well be included in consultations concerned with the drafting and revision of a code, which is a different matter.)

The principal task of a Monitoring Council should be oversight, with responsibility for verifying not only the results of field audits but, even more importantly, the company's responses to deficiencies when they are uncovered. Field monitoring of code compliance should be separated from verification and reporting, which should be the sole purview of the Council. The Council should develop a mechanism for receiving information and complaints about corporate performance from both within and outside the company. It should make regular public reports about the company's compliance with its code, and the content of these reports and the manner of their presentation should be the sole responsibility of the Council. The Council should, of course, make every effort to ensure that all facts in its reports are accurate, and that all conclusions are fully justified. Under the best of circumstances, the monitoring function should be viewed as a cooperative effort in which both the monitors and the corporation's field managers strive to ensure compliance. Under the worst of circumstances, where monitors and managers view each other as adversaries, the entire code implementation process will be a failure.

MATTEL EXPERIENCE

Mattel, the world's largest toy manufacturing company, announced the creation of its Global Manufacturing Principles (GMP) in November, 1997. The Code created a set of standards that would apply to all of the company-owned plants as well as those of its more than 300 primary contractor manufacturing facilities around the world. As part of its code formulation and implementation process, the company also committed itself to the establishment of an independent council to monitor its operations to ensure compliance with GMP. It is called the Mattel Independent Monitoring Council for Global Manufacturing Principles (MIMCO). To the best of my knowledge, it was the first time that a major multinational corporation voluntarily committed itself to independent monitoring by outside observers who had complete authority to make their findings available to the public.

In establishing, the Council, Mattel was trying to identify itself as a socially responsible company and good corporate citizen. Mattel believed that it was important that its policies, operational procedures, and performance measures under the GMP

should receive broad public recognition and acceptance. Mattel also considered it extremely important that the relevance and adequacy of the GMP, as applied to the company's overseas operations, particularly in developing countries, be recognized and accepted by its employees and managers worldwide.

The Council currently consists of three members: Dr. S. Prakash Sethi, Distinguished University Professor of Management, Zicklin School of Business, City University of New York; Dr. Murray Weidenbaum, Distinguished University Professor of Economics, Washington University in St. Louis, and a former chairman of the Council of Economics Advisors; and Dr. Paul McCleary, President and CEO of For Children, Inc., and former President and CEO of the Save the Children Foundation.

In accepting their assignments, Council members received a number of important assurances from the company's top management.

- Mattel will ensure that the code meets or exceeds all pertinent host country laws and best industry practices in the areas of its operations.
- The company is committed to the code and will devote the necessary resources to ensure compliance to it by field managers in the company's owned and controlled plants, and will cooperate and assist the company's major vendors to comply with the code.
- The company will create a highly objective, quantifiable, and outcome-oriented set of standards that will add substance and comprehensiveness to the code and ensure the code's implementation in a meaningful manner.
- The company will make every effort to work toward the enhancement of these standards in an evolutionary manner that will enhance the financial and social well-being of its workers, and also contribute to the economic growth of the countries involved.

During its first phase, MIMCO will focus its efforts on auditing those twenty or more plants that are owned or controlled by Mattel. These account for close to 70 percent of Mattel's world-wide production. A very large part of Mattel's production operations are based in the Asia-Pacific Region:

Peoples' Republic of China, Indonesia, and Malaysia. This audit will therefore cover the topics that have been of major public concern in those areas: worker's health and safety, wages, and living conditions. We expect this phase of the audit process to be completed shortly, and our findings will be made public soon thereafter.

An audit is only as good as the questions it asks and the activities and issues it covers. We have spent the last six months developing a highly objective, quantifiable, precise, and statistically rigorous set of instruments that will be used in conducting field audits. These will cover, among other things:

- Worker's environment, health and safety, and working conditions.
- Wages and working hours.
- Living conditions.
- Communications with the management concerning their living and working conditions, new employee orientation methods, and regular training programs.

Mattel has already completed extensive in-house audits to ensure that its own plants, and those of its major suppliers, are in compliance with GMP. Where necessary, it has also worked closely with the company's suppliers to help them improve their operations to meet Mattel's standards—frequently at Mattel's expense. And, in a number of cases, where suppliers have been unable or unwilling to make such an effort, Mattel has discontinued its business relationship with them. Mattel has established a single global task force with members located in its Asian Region headquarters in Hong Kong and in its corporate headquarters in El Segundo, California. This task force has been responsible for generating the necessary databases for Council use in creating audit protocols; these, in turn, will be used by the independent auditors appointed by, and reporting to, the Council.

CONCLUDING THOUGHTS

The emerging global economic order of the 1990s has once again brought capitalism and its principal actor, the multinational corporation, to new levels of prominence and power. Unlike the 1960s, when multinational corporations were seen as a threat to national sovereignty and political freedom, the dominant contemporary view seems to be that the multinational corporation is—or certainly can be—an agent of positive change. However, beneath this veneer of hope and expectation, lies distrust in the unaccountability of the corporate behemoth and the fear of its potential for doing harm whether through misjudgment or abuse of power.

The contemporary tensions between business and society—which will certainly extend into the next millenium—do not arise from obvious conflicts between right and wrong, guilt or innocence. Their more subtle sources are, for example, alternative concepts and combinations of equity and inequity, the distribution of potential social and economic benefits, the virtue of frugality and the sin of undue accumulation, and the morality of principles versus the morality of situations. We realize that we live in an increasingly interdependent, global society where the welfare of the individual human being is deeply, and often unpredictably, embedded in the operation of the entire system. In this complex environment, we cannot pretend to separate moral principles from institutional practices, political power from economic influence, or human and environmental values from material wealth.

The large corporation must become an active agent for social change if it is to make the world safe for itself. Rules of law, democratic institutions, and the ethics of competition and the marketplace are requirements for the continued success of multinational corporations and, indeed, contemporary capitalism. The corporation can no longer pretend to be a reactive participant within the social system, responding (positively or negatively) to pressures and goals arising from other groups. As a dominant institution in society, it must accept responsibility for independent initiative, both with respect to its own goals and the formation of the public agenda. Effective participation requires that the corporation be able to articulate who and what it is from a social perspective, and what role its processes and products play in society. This articulation is, in fact, the ultimate purpose and result of a corporate code of conduct.

QUESTIONS FOR DISCUSSION

1. In your opinion, what are some of the most important ethical problems facing multinational corporations operating in developing countries? Do you think the principles offered by De George might help resolve some of these dilemmas?
2. In your view, exactly what is wrong with bribery? If bribery is a common practice in some countries, why shouldn't U.S. companies be allowed to practice bribery in those countries?
3. Can codes of conduct really make a difference for multinationals as Sethi suggests? What arguments can you make against the use of codes?

Pat Sheritan

Pat Sheritan, a senior associate in Assurance and Business Advisory Services, has recently worked with Financial Advisory Services on a very difficult and highly confidential analysis for the chairman of a medium-size manufacturing company. The chairman had been concerned about certain deals with a new subcontractor that were being promoted by one of the vice presidents.

After some intense research, Sheritan was able to substantiate the chairman's concerns about conflict of interest. As a result, the vice president was fired, and the company avoided what could have been a $5-million loss.

Amid the intense pressure to get bills out promptly, Sheritan inadvertently double-billed the client for some of the analysis. Sheritan realized the error two weeks later. However, by then, the grateful client had already paid the bill.

Sheritan is not sure how to proceed. The amount of the overbilling is relatively small vis-à-vis the total bill, and the total bill was within the range stated in the letter of arrangement. In addition, the summary of time and expenses was never charged for a lot of time that was spent working over several weekends. The client did not require detailed time-charging records to substantiate the amounts billed.

What should Sheritan do?

DISCUSSION QUESTIONS

- How do you decide when to charge and when not to charge time to a client engagement?
- If Sheritan never had to provide the client with substantiating documentation for what she invoiced, has she actually done anything wrong from the client's perspective? After all, she didn't actually reflect all of her time on her time reports.

John Snyder

John Snyder is VP of International Manufacturing for GoodChem USA, and has recently signed a deal to build a major new chemical manufacturing plant in Southeast Asia. He is working through the final details of the proposal with Alex, the appointed Director of the new facility, when a letter arrives from Tang Chen, the VP for International Affairs at GuddoKagaku, the joint venture company that helped GoodChem work through the red-tape which often hampers foreign investors in Southeast Asia.

Tang's letter reminds John once again that neither he nor John were happy with the decision that had been made by the two companies to not install U.S. style scrubbers in the production process. Tang realizes that there was no legal requirement, and that installation of the scrubbers would cost them time and money, which may be critical in securing the competitive edge over the domestic producers—an edge that would make the venture viable. But he still is concerned over the environmental impact this will have on his country. As a side note, he also mentions that he has heard rumors that a powerful and well-connected environmental activist group is preparing to make the actions of GoodChem their next big PR scandal.

Alex is anxious to succeed in the Director's position and points out that that none of the domestic producers has scrubbers in place, and that should the venture not meet the expectations of Senior Management, it would be Alex's career, not John's, on the line. Alex also reminds John that if this project is successful, it will most likely secure John's place in the race for CEO.

But John keeps thinking of Tang's closing remarks that ask John to think of his children before he makes a last decision not to install the scrubbers.

DISCUSSION QUESTIONS

- Would John want his family to live next to a plant without scrubbers?
- What is the short-term cost/long-term risk trade-off in not installing scrubbers?
- In what instances is it acceptable to adhere to host country standards that are less stringent than those of a company's home country?

The Ford Pinto

W. Michael Hoffman
Executive Director, Center for Business Ethics, Bentley College

I

On August 10, 1978, a tragic automobile accident occurred on U.S. Highway 33 near Goshen, Indiana. Sisters Judy and Lynn Ulrich (ages 18 and 16, respectively) and their cousin Donna Ulrich (age 18) were struck from the rear in their 1973 Ford Pinto by a van. The gas tank of the Pinto ruptured, the car burst into flames, and the three teenagers were burned to death.

Subsequently an Elkhart County grand jury returned a criminal homicide charge against Ford, the first ever against an American corporation. During the following twenty-week trial, Judge Harold R. Staffeldt advised the jury that Ford should be convicted of reckless homicide if it were shown that the company had engaged in "plain, conscious and unjustifiable disregard of harm that

might result (from its actions) and the disregard involves a substantial deviation from acceptable standards of conduct."[1]

The key phrase around which the trial hinged, of course, is "acceptable standards." Did Ford knowingly and recklessly choose profit over safety in the design and placement of the Pinto's gas tank? Elkhart County prosecutor Michael A. Cosentino and chief Ford attorney James F. Neal battled dramatically over this issue in a rural Indiana courthouse. Meanwhile, American business anxiously awaited the verdict which could send warning ripples through boardrooms across the nation concerning corporate responsibility and product liability.

II

As a background to this trial some discussion of the Pinto controversy is necessary. In 1977 the magazine *Mother Jones* broke a story by Mark Dowie, general manager of *Mother Jones* business operations, accusing Ford of knowingly putting on the road an unsafe car—the Pinto—in which hundreds of people have needlessly suffered burn deaths and even more have been scarred and disfigured from burns. In his article "Pinto Madness" Dowie charges that:

- Fighting strong competition from Volkswagen for the lucrative small-car market, the Ford Motor Company rushed the Pinto into production in much less than the usual time.
- Ford engineers discovered in preproduction crash tests that rear-end collisions would rupture the Pinto's fuel system extremely easily.
- Because assembly-line machinery was already tooled when engineers found this defect, top Ford officials decided to manufacture the car anyway—exploding gas tank and all—even though Ford owned the patent on a much safer gas tank.
- For more than eight years afterward, Ford successfully lobbied, with extraordinary vigor and some blatant lies, against a key government safety standard that would have forced the company to change the Pinto's fire-prone gas tank.

By conservative estimates Pinto crashes have caused 500 burn deaths to people who would not have been seriously injured if the car had not burst into flames. The figure could be as high as 900. Burning Pintos have become such an embarrassment to Ford that its advertising agency, J. Walter Thompson, dropped a line from the ending of a radio spot that read "Pinto leaves you with that warm feeling."

Ford knows that the Pinto is a firetrap, yet it has paid out millions to settle damage suits out of court, and it is prepared to spend millions more lobbying against safety standards. With a half million cars rolling off the assembly lines each year, Pinto is the biggest-selling subcompact in America, and the company's operating profit on the car is fantastic. Finally, in 1977, new Pinto models have incorporated a few minor alterations necessary to meet that federal standard Ford managed to hold off for eight years. Why did the company delay so long in making these minimal, inexpensive improvements?

- Ford waited eight years because its internal "cost-benefit analysis," which places a dollar value on human life, said it wasn't profitable to make the changes sooner.[2]

Several weeks after Dowie's press conference on the article, which had the support of Ralph Nader and auto safety expert Byron Bloch, Ford issued a news release attributed to Herbert T. Misch, vice president of Environmental and Safety

Engineering, countering points made in the *Mother Jones* article. Their statistical studies conflict significantly with each other. For example, Dowie states that more than 3,000 people were burning to death yearly in auto fires; he claims that, according to a National Highway Traffic Safety Administration (NHTSA) consultant, although Ford makes 24 percent of the cars on American roads, these cars account for 42 percent of the collision-ruptured fuel tanks.[3] Ford, on the other hand, uses statistics from the Fatality Analysis Reporting System (FARS) maintained by the government's NHTSA to defend itself, claiming that in 1975 there were 848 deaths related to fire-associated passenger-car accidents and only 13 of these involved Pintos; in 1976, Pintos accounted for only 22 out of 943. These statistics imply that Pintos were involved in only 1.9 percent of such accidents, and Pintos constitute about 1.9 percent of the total registered passenger cars. Furthermore, fewer than half of those Pintos cited in the FARS study were struck in the rear.[4] Ford concludes from this and other studies that the Pinto was never an unsafe car and has not been involved in some 70 burn deaths annually, as *Mother Jones* claims.

Ford admits that early-model Pintos did not meet rear-impact tests at 20 mph but denies that this implies that they were unsafe compared with other cars of that type and era. In fact, according to Ford, some of its tests were conducted with experimental rubber "bladders" to protect the gas tank, in order to determine how best to have its future cars meet a 20-mph rear-collision standard which Ford itself set as an internal performance goal. The government at that time had no such standard. Ford also points out that in every model year the Pinto met or surpassed the government's own standards, and

it simply is unreasonable and unfair to contend that a car is somehow unsafe if it does not meet standards proposed for future years or embody the technological improvements that are introduced in later model years.[5]

Mother Jones, on the other hand, presents a different view of the situation. If Ford was so concerned about rear-impact safety, why did it delay the federal government's attempts to impose standards? Dowie gives the following answer:

> The particular regulation involved here was Federal Motor Vehicle Safety Standard 301. Ford picked portions of Standard 301 for strong opposition way back in 1968 when the Pinto was still in the blueprint stage. The intent of 301, and the 300 series that followed it, was to protect drivers and passengers after a crash occurs. Without question the worst post-crash hazard is fire. So Standard 301 originally proposed that all cars should be able to withstand a fixed barrier impact of 20 mph (that is, running into a wall at that speed) without losing fuel.
>
> When the standard was proposed, Ford engineers pulled their crash-test results out of their files. The front ends of most cars were no problem—with minor alterations they could stand the impact without losing fuel. "We were already working on the front end," Ford engineer Dick Kimble admitted. "We knew we could meet the test on the front end." But with the Pinto particularly, a 20 mph rear-end standard meant redesigning the entire rear end of the car. With the Pinto scheduled for production in August of 1970, and with $200 million worth of tools in place, adoption of this standard would have created a minor financial disaster. So Standard 301 was targeted for delay, and with some assistance from its industry associates, Ford succeeded beyond its wildest expectations: the standard was not adopted until the 1977 model year.[6]

Ford's tactics were successful, according to Dowie, not only due to their extremely clever lobbying, which became the envy of lobbyists all over Washington, but also because of the proindustry stance of NHTSA itself.

Furthermore, it is not at all clear that the Pinto was as safe as comparable cars with regard to the positioning of its gas tank. Unlike the gas tank in the Capri, which rode over the rear axle, a "saddle-type" fuel tank on which Ford owned the patent, the Pinto tank was placed just behind the rear bumper. According to Dowie,

> Dr. Leslie Ball, the retired safety chief for the NASA manned space program and a founder of the International Society of Reliability Engineers, recently made a careful study of the Pinto. "The release to production of the Pinto was the most reprehensible decision in the history of American engineering," he said. Ball can name more than 40 European and

Japanese models in the Pinto price and weight range with safer gas-tank positioning.

Los Angeles auto safety expert Byron Bloch has made an in-depth study of the Pinto fuel system. "It's a catastrophic blunder," he says. "Ford made an extremely irresponsible decision when they placed such a weak tank in such a ridiculous location in such a soft rear end. It's almost designed to blow up—premeditated."[7]

Although other points could be brought out in the debate between *Mother Jones* and Ford, perhaps the most intriguing and controversial is the cost-benefit analysis study that Ford did entitled "Fatalities Associated with Crash-Induced Fuel Leakage and Fires" released by J. C. Echold, director of automotive safety for Ford. This study apparently convinced Ford and was intended to convince the federal government that a technological improvement costing $11 per car which would have prevented gas tanks from rupturing so easily was not cost effective for society. The costs and benefits are broken down in the following way:

Benefits	
Savings:	180 burn deaths, 180 serious burn injuries, 2,100 burned vehicles
Unit Cost:	$200,000 per death, $67,000 per injury, $700 per vehicle
Total Benefit:	180 × $200,000 + 180 × $67,000 + 2,100 × $700 = *$49.5 million*

Costs	
Sales:	11 million cars, 1.5 million light trucks
Unit Cost:	$11 per car, $11 per truck
Total Cost:	11,000,000 × $11 + 1,500,000 × $11 = *$137 million*

And where did Ford come up with the $200,000 figure as the cost per death? This came from a NHTSA study which broke down the estimated social costs of a death as follows:

Component	1971 Costs
Future productivity losses	
Direct	$132,000
Indirect	41,300
Medical costs	
Hospital	700
Other	425
Property damage	1,500
Insurance administration	4,700
Legal and court	3,000
Employer losses	1,000
Victim's pain and suffering	10,000
Funeral	900
Assets (lost consumption)	5,000
Miscellaneous	200
Total per fatality	$200,725

(Although this analysis was on all Ford vehicles, a breakout of just the Pinto could be done.) *Mother Jones* reports it could not find anybody who could explain how the $10,000 figure for "pain and suffering" had been arrived at.[8]

Although Ford does not mention this point in its news release defense, one might have replied that it was the federal government, not Ford, that set the figure for a burn death. Ford simply carried out a cost-benefit analysis based on that figure. *Mother Jones,* however, in addition to insinuating that there was industry-agency (NHTSA) collusion, argues that the $200,000 figure was arrived at under intense pressure from the auto industry to use cost-benefit analysis in determining regulations. *Mother Jones* also questions Ford's estimate of burn injuries: "All independent experts estimate that for each person who dies by an auto fire, many more are left with charred hands, faces and limbs." Referring to the Northern California Burn Center, which estimates the ratio of burn injuries to deaths at ten to one instead of one to one, Dowie states that "the true ratio obviously throws the company's calculations way off."[9] Finally, *Mother Jones* claims to have obtained "confidential" Ford documents which Ford did not send to Washington, showing that crash fires could largely be prevented by installing a rubber bladder inside the gas tank for only $5.08 per car, considerably less than the $11 per car Ford originally claimed was required to improve crashworthiness.[10]

Instead of making the $11 improvement, installing the $5.08 bladder, or even giving the consumer the right to choose the additional cost for added safety, Ford continued, according to *Mother Jones,* to delay the federal government for eight years in establishing mandatory rear-impact standards. In the meantime, Dowie argues, thousands of people were burning to death and tens of thousands more were being badly burned and disfigured for life, while many of these tragedies could have been prevented for only a slight cost per vehicle. Furthermore, the delay also meant that millions of new unsafe vehicles went on the road, "vehicles that will be crashing, leaking fuel and incinerating people well into the 1980s."[11]

In concluding his article Dowie broadens his attack beyond just Ford and the Pinto.

Unfortunately, the Pinto is not an isolated case of corporate malpractice in the auto industry. Neither is Ford a lone sinner. There probably isn't a car on the road without a safety hazard known to its manufacturer. . . .

Furthermore, cost-valuing human life is not used by Ford alone. Ford was just the only company careless enough to let such an embarrassing calculation slip into public records. The process of willfully trading lives for profits is built into corporate capitalism. Commodore Vanderbilt publicly scorned George Westinghouse and his "foolish" air brakes while people died by the hundreds in accidents on Vanderbilt's railroads.[12]

Ford has paid millions of dollars in Pinto jury trials and out-of-court settlements, especially the latter. *Mother Jones* quotes Al Slechter in Ford's Washington office as saying: "We'll never go to a jury again. Not in a fire case. Juries are just too sentimental. They see those charred remains and forget the evidence. No sir, we'll settle."[13] But apparently Ford thought such settlements would be less costly than the safety improvements. Dowie wonders if Ford would continue to make the same decisions "were Henry Ford II and Lee Iacocca serving twenty-year terms in Leavenworth for consumer homicide."[14]

III

On March 13, 1980, the Elkhart County jury found Ford not guilty of criminal homicide in the Ulrich case. Ford attorney Neal summarized several points in his closing argument before the jury. Ford could have stayed out of the small-car market, which would have been the "easiest way," since Ford would have made more profit by sticking to bigger cars. Instead, Ford built the Pinto "to take on the imports, to save jobs for Americans and to make a profit for its stockholders."[15] The Pinto met every fuel-system standard of any federal, state, or local government, and was comparable to other 1973 subcompacts. The engineers who designed the car thought it was a good, safe car and bought it for themselves and their families. Ford did everything possible to recall the Pinto quickly after NHTSA ordered it to do so. Finally, and more specifically to the case at hand, Highway 33 was a badly designed highway, and the girls were fully stopped when a 4,000-pound van rammed into the rear of their Pinto going at least 50 miles an hour. Given the same circumstances, Neal stated, any car would have suffered the same consequences as the Ulrich's Pinto.[16] As reported in the *New York Times* and *Time,* the verdict brought a "loud cheer" from Ford's board of directors and undoubtedly at least a sigh of relief from other corporations around the nation.

Many thought this case was that of a David against a Goliath because of the small amount of money and volunteer legal help Prosecutor Cosentino had in contrast to the huge resources Ford poured into the trial. In addition, it should be pointed out that Cosentino's case suffered from a ruling by Judge Staffeldt that Ford's own test results on pre-1973 Pintos were inadmissible. These documents confirmed that Ford knew as early as 1971 that the gas tank of the Pinto ruptured at impacts of 20 mph and that the company was aware, because of tests with the Capri, that the over-the-axle position of the gas tank was much safer than mounting it behind the axle. Ford decided to mount it behind the axle in the Pinto to provide more trunk space and to save money. The restrictions of Cosentino's evidence to testimony relating specifically to the 1973 Pinto severely undercut the strength of the prosecutor's case.[17]

Whether this evidence would have changed the minds of the jury will never be known. Some, however, such as business ethicist Richard De George, feel that this evidence shows grounds for charges of recklessness against Ford. Although it is true that there were no federal safety standards in 1973 to which Ford legally had to conform and although Neal seems to have proved that all subcompacts were unsafe when hit at 50 mph by a 4,000-pound van, the fact that the NHTSA ordered a recall of the Pinto and not other subcompacts is, according to De George, "*prima facie* evidence that Ford's Pinto gas tank mounting was substandard."[18] De George argues that these grounds for recklessness are made even stronger by the fact that Ford did not give the consumer a choice to make the Pinto gas tank safer by installing a rubber bladder for a rather modest fee.[19] Giving the consumer such a choice, of course, would have made the Pinto gas tank problem known and therefore probably would have been bad for sales.

Richard A. Epstein, professor of law at the University of Chicago Law School, questions whether Ford should have been brought up on criminal charges of reckless homicide at all. He also points out an interesting historical fact. Before 1966 an injured party in Indiana could not even bring civil charges against an automobile manufacturer solely because of the alleged "uncrashworthiness" of a car; one would have to seek legal relief from the other party involved in the accident, not from the manufacturer. But after *Larson v. General Motors Corp.* in 1968, a new era of crashworthiness suits against automobile manufacturers began. "Reasonable" precautions must now be taken by manufacturers to minimize personal harm in crashes.[20] How to apply criteria of reasonableness in such cases marks the whole nebulous ethical and legal arena of product liability.

If such a civil suit had been brought against Ford, Epstein believes, the corporation might have argued, as it did to a large extent in the criminal suit, that the Pinto conformed to all current applicable safety standards and with common industry practice. (Epstein cites that well over 90 percent of United States standard production cars had their gas tanks in the same position as the Pinto.) But in a civil trial the adequacy of industry standards are ultimately up to the jury, and had civil charges been brought against Ford in this case the plaintiffs might have had a better chance of winning.[21] Epstein feels that a criminal suit, on the other hand, had no chance from the very outset, because the prosecutor would have had to establish criminal intent on the part of Ford. To use an analogy, if a hunter shoots at a deer and wounds an unseen person, he may be held civilly responsible but not criminally responsible because he did not intend to harm. And even though it may be more difficult to determine the mental state of a corporation (or its principal agents), it seems clear to Epstein that the facts of this case do not prove any such criminal intent even though Ford may have known that some burn deaths and injuries could have been avoided by a different placement of its Pinto gas tank and that Ford consciously decided not to spend more money to save lives.[22] Everyone recognizes that there are trade-offs between safety and costs. Ford could have built a "tank" instead of a Pinto, thereby considerably reducing risks, but it would have been relatively unaffordable for most and probably unattractive to all potential consumers.

To have established Ford's reckless homicide it would have been necessary to establish the same of Ford's agents, since a corporation can only act through its agents. Undoubtedly, continues Epstein, the reason why the prosecutor did not try to subject Ford's officers and engineers to fines and imprisonment for their design choices is "the good faith character of their judgment, which was necessarily decisive in Ford's behalf as well."[23] For example, Harold C. MacDonald, Ford's chief engineer on the Pinto, testified that he felt it was important to keep the gas tank as far from the passenger compartment as possible, as it was in the Pinto. And other Ford engineers testified that they used the car for their own families. This is relevant information in a criminal case which must be concerned about the intent of the agents.

Furthermore, even if civil charges had been made in this case, it seems unfair and irrelevant to Epstein to accuse Ford of trading cost for safety. Ford's use of cost-benefit formulas, which must assign monetary values to human life and suffering, is precisely what the law demands in assessing civil liability suits. The court may disagree with the decision, but to blame industry for using such a method would violate the very rules of civil liability. Federal automobile officials (NHTSA) had to make the same calculations in order to discharge their statutory duties. In allowing the Pinto design, are not they too (and in turn their employer, the United States) just as guilty as Ford's agents?[24]

IV

The case of the Ford Pinto raises many questions of ethical importance. Some people conclude that Ford was definitely wrong in designing and marketing the Pinto. The specific accident involving the Ulrich girls, because of the circumstances, was simply not the right one to have attacked Ford on. Other people believe that Ford was neither criminally nor civilly guilty of anything and acted completely responsibly in producing the Pinto. Many others, I suspect, find the case morally perplexing, too complex to make sweeping claims of guilt or innocence.

Was Ford irresponsible in rushing the production of the Pinto? Even though Ford violated no federal safety standards or laws, should it have made the Pinto safer in terms of rear-end collisions, especially regarding the placement of the gas tank? Should Ford have used cost-benefit analysis to make decisions relating to safety, specifically placing dollar values on human life and suffering? Knowing that the Pinto's gas tank could have been made safer by installing a protective bladder for a relatively small cost per consumer, perhaps Ford should have made that option available to the public. If Ford did use heavy lobbying efforts to delay and/or influence federal safety standards, was this ethically proper for a corporation to do? One might ask, if Ford was guilty, whether the engineers, the managers, or both are to blame. If Ford had been found guilty of criminal homicide, was the proposed penalty stiff enough ($10,000 maximum fine for each of the three counts equals $30,000 maximum), or should agents of the corporations such as MacDonald, Iacocca, and Henry Ford II be fined and possibly jailed?

A number of questions concerning safety standards are also relevant to the ethical issues at stake in the Ford trial. Is it just to blame a corporation for not abiding by "acceptable standards" when such standards are not yet determined by society? Should corporations like Ford play a role in setting such standards? Should individual juries be determining such standards state by state, incident by incident? If Ford should be setting safety standards, how does it decide how safe to make its product and still make it affordable and desirable to the public without using cost-benefit analysis?

For that matter, how does anyone decide? Perhaps it is putting Ford, or any corporation, in a catch-22 position to ask it both to set safety standards and to make a competitive profit for its stockholders.

Regardless of how we answer these and other questions it is clear that the Pinto case raises fundamental issues concerning the responsibilities of corporations, how corporations should structure themselves in order to make ethical decisions, and how industry, government, and society in general ought to interrelate to form a framework within which such decisions can properly be made in the future.

NOTES

1. *The Indianapolis Star,* Sunday, Mar. 9, 1980, Section 3, p. 2.
2. Mark Dowie, "Pinto Madness," *Mother Jones,* September–October, 1977, pp. 18, 20. Subsequently Mike Wallace for "Sixty Minutes" and Sylvia Chase for "20-20" came out with similar exposés.
3. *Ibid.,* p. 30.
4. Ford news release (Sept. 9, 1977), pp. 1–3.
5. *Ibid.,* p. 5.
6. Dowie, p. 29.
7. *Ibid.,* pp. 22–23.
8. *Ibid.,* pp. 24, 28.
9. *Ibid.,* p. 28.
10. *Ibid.,* pp. 28–29.
11. *Ibid.,* p. 30.
12. *Ibid.,* p. 32. Dowie might have cited another example which emerged in the private correspondence which transpired almost a half-century ago between Lammot du Pont and Alfred P. Sloan, Jr., then president of GM. Du Pont was trying to convince Sloan to equip GM's lowest-priced cars, Chevrolets, with safety glass. Sloan replied by saying: "It is not my responsibility to sell safety glass. . . . You can say, perhaps, that I am selfish, but business is selfish. We are not a charitable institution—we are trying to make a profit for our stockholders." [Quoted in Morton Mintz and Jerry S. Cohen, *Power,* Inc. (New York: The Viking Press, 1976), p. 110.]
13. *Ibid.,* p. 31.
14. *Ibid.,* p. 32.
15. Transcript of report of proceedings in *State of Indiana v. Ford Motor Company,* Case No. 11-431, Monday, Mar. 10, 1980, pp. 6202–6203. How Neal reconciled his "easiest way" point with his "making more profit for stockholders" point is not clear to this writer.
16. *Ibid.,* pp. 6207–6209.
17. *Chicago Tribune,* Oct. 13, 1979, p. 1, and Section 2, p. 12; *New York Times,* Oct. 14, 1979, p. 26; *The Atlanta Constitution,* Feb. 7, 1980.
18. Richard De George, "Ethical Responsibilities of Engineers in Large Organizations: The Pinto Case," *Business and Professional Ethics Journal,* vol. 1., No. 1 (Fall 1981), p. 4. *The New York Times,* Oct. 26, 1978, p. 103, also points out that during 1976 and 1977 there were thirteen fiery fatal rear-end collisions involving Pintos, more than double that of other United States comparable cars, with VW Rabbits and Toyota Corollas having none.
19. *Ibid.,* p. 5.
20. Richard A. Epstein, "Is Pinto a Criminal?", *Regulation,* March–April, 1980, pp. 16–17.
21. A California jury awarded damages of $127.8 million (reduced later to $6.3 million on appeal) in a Pinto crash in which a youth was burned over 95 percent of his body. See *New York Times,* Feb. 8, 1978, p. 8.
22. Epstein, p. 19.
23. *Ibid.,* pp. 20–21.
24. *Ibid.,* pp. 19–21.

The Ethics of Marketing: Nestlé's Infant Formula

James E. Post
Professor of Management, Boston University

INTRODUCTION

Among the many different types of dilemmas faced by multinational enterprises are those related to its marketing of consumer products. It has now become apparent that the marketing of First World foods in Third World nations poses a special type of concern to the populations and

Excerpted from "Ethical Dilemmas of Multinational Enterprise: An Analysis of Nestlé's Traumatic Experience with the Infant Formula Controversy" by James E. Post, in *Ethics and the Multinational Enterprise* edited by W. Michael Hoffmann, Ann E. Lange, and David A. Fedo (Lanham, MD: University Press of America, 1986). Copyright © 1986 by James E. Post. Reprinted by permission of the author.

governments of host nations, and to the would-be marketers themselves. While there are a number of products that one can cite as illustrative of the generic issue, none has so sharply and clearly defined it as the controversy surrounding the marketing and promotion of infant formula in the developing world.

My perspective on the infant formula controversy, industry, and on Nestlé in particular, is derived from more than a decade of research. In addition to field research on infant formula marketing in Latin America, Africa, and Southern Asia. I have served as a consultant to the World Health Organization (WHO) in the development of the international marketing code, and testified at congressional and United States Senate hearings on these issues. Most recently, it has included about 18 months of service on the Nestlé Infant Formula Audit Commission, which was created to monitor the company's compliance with marketing policies that were drafted for the purpose of implementing the WHO Code.

Rest assured, this is no apologia for Nestlé. I know that some of their managers disagree with my interpretation of the evidence. That troubles me little, for I cannot think of an ethical dilemma that does not breed some disagreement among caring participants. Were it otherwise, I doubt it could be called a dilemma. Among the various types of ethical dilemmas confronting the managers of multinational enterprises (MNEs) are those tied to the introduction of products developed and used in one social environment into a significantly different environment. I prefer to term this the introduction of First World Products in Third World Markets.

The infant formula situation involves a product which is not defective in itself. This distinguishes it from such cases as the dumping of products which are unsafe or deemed unacceptable for sale in the United States, but are accepted for sale in another nation (e.g., Tris-treated sleepwear).

Infant formula is also not harmful to the consumer (user) when used properly under appropriate conditions. This distinguishes it from products such as tobacco, which are, in the view of most health professionals, per se dangerous to all users.

Infant formula is the *definitive* example, however, of a First World product which is safe when used properly, but which is *demanding*. That is, when risk conditions are present, it can be—and is—potentially harmful to users.

The fundamental ethical dilemma for MNE managers, then, is whether such a product can be marketed when it cannot be guaranteed, or reasonably expected, that it will be used by people who meet the minimum conditions necessary for safe use.

EVOLUTION OF A PUBLIC ISSUE

The criticism of the infant formula manufacturers for their aggressive marketing behavior in developing nations became a serious issue in 1970. Prior to that time, individual physicians and health workers had criticized promotional practices, but there was nothing to suggest an organized campaign of criticism. In 1970, however, the Protein-Calorie Advisory Group (PAG) of the United Nations held a meeting in Bogota to discuss the problem of infant malnutrition and disease in developing nations. Participants pointed a finger of blame at the industry, charging that it pushed its products to mothers, many of whom lived in circumstances that made the use of such products a highly risky adventure. First, infant formula must be sold in powdered form in tropical environments, requiring that the mother mix the powder with locally available water. When water supplies are of poor quality, as so often is the case in the developing nations, infants are exposed to disease. Second, since the product must be mixed, preparation instructions are important, and mothers must be able to read. Unfortunately, the rate of illiteracy is very high in many developing nations. Thirdly, since infant formulas are relatively expensive to purchase, there is a temptation to overdilute the powder with water. This effort to "stretch" its uses enables the mother to go a few extra days without buying a new supply. Unfortunately, overdiluted formula preparations provide very poor nutrition to the baby. Thus mothers who came to the health clinics with malnourished babies often reported that a five day supply of formula had been stretched to ten days or more. Having decided to bottlefeed their babies in order to improve their chances for a healthy life. many mothers discovered to their horror that they had actually been starving their little ones. Because corporate advertising by the infant formula companies had promoted the idea that bottlefeeding was better than breastfeeding, a view with which doctors disagreed, there was a sharp condemnation of the industry and its behavior at the Bogota meeting.

Management scholars now understand that public issues often proceed through a predictable series of phases in their evolution. Some refer to this as the "public issue life cycle," modelled after the product life cycle described in marketing research. The public issue life cycle can be thought of as a measure of continuing public concern about an underlying problem.

Phase I of the issue life cycle involved rising awareness and sensitivity to the facts of the issue. In the infant formula controversy, this phase began with the PAG Meeting in 1970 and continued for several years. An important element in the process of rising awareness was the activity of journalist Peter Muller who, with support from the British charity group, War on Want, travelled to Africa in the early 1970s to study allegations of marketing abuses. Muller wrote several articles and a pamphlet which War on Want published in 1974 under the title, *The Baby Killer*. These publications began to draw the attention of a broader public to the problem of sick and dying children, and the connection between commercial practices and this tragedy.

Because Nestlé was, and still is, the industry's largest producer and seller of infant formula products, Muller encountered many examples of Nestlé advertising and promotional practices in Africa. Indeed, Nestlé employees were willing to speak with Muller, while those of other companies were often much less willing. Not surprisingly, then, *The Baby Killer* pamphlet included Nestlé actions as examples of unethical industry behavior. This became very important, because a Swiss public action group, Third World Action Group, reprinted the Muller pamphlet in Switzerland under the new title, *Nestlé Kills Babies!*

Nestlé immediately sued the group for defamation, and in 1975 the case came to trial in Switzer-

land. Because the trial involved several hearings, with experts from developing nations brought in to testify, the media began to show increasing interest in the story. It became quite clear that although the trial involved only Nestlé and the defendants, the entire infant formula industry was being examined and criticized for their actions in the developing nations. Thus, the trial was a turning point in two important ways. First, public interest in the issue expanded greatly as the newspaper stories began to carry the details of what one doctor called "commerciogenic malnutrition"—malnutrition brought about because of corporate commercial practices. Second, the infant formula industry began to respond as an industry, having formed an international association, known as the International Council of Infant Foods Industries (ICIFI). The council, whose existence was announced in Switzerland at the time of the trial, made an immediate effort to develop an international code of marketing which addressed some of the most criticized marketing practices. In this Phase II of the life cycle, both the critics, the media, and the industry recognized that the issue had become an important political matter, as well as a public health concern.

Between 1975 and 1978, the infant formula controversy became increasingly politicized. The media in Europe and the United States paid increasing attention to the conflict. Each newspaper or magazine story brought about more awareness in the general public. The critics highlighted the terrible tragedy of dying and sick children, while the companies, including Nestlé, tried to respond to the criticism individually and through ICIFI. The political pressure mounted against the industry. In 1977, an official consumer boycott of Nestlé and its products was begun in the United States. Interest in the boycott spread quickly, in part because many member churches of the National Council of Churches had been concerned about the problems of world hunger. The Nestlé boycott gave church leaders an opportunity to educate their congregations about the problem of world hunger and suggest a practical course of action that would pressure companies to act responsibly in dealing with the poor and needy of the

Third World. The National Council of Churches had been concerned about many corporate responsibility issues, and had a special research and action unit known as the Interfaith Center on Corporate Responsibility (ICCR). ICCR became actively involved in the boycott campaign, and helped spread the message of consumer action to hundreds of thousands of people in the United States.

The high point of Phase II of the infant formula controversy occurred when boycott sponsors were able to convince the staff of United States Senator Edward Kennedy to hold hearings into the infant formula marketing controversy. These hearings were held in May, 1978 in Washington, DC, and occurred at a time when Senator Kennedy was widely rumored to be considering a campaign for the presidency against incumbent President Jimmy Carter. The media followed Kennedy's every action. On the day of the public hearing, every American television network had cameras in the hearing room, and many famous reporters sat at special tables to hear the testimony of witnesses. The witnesses were heard in three groups. First, people who had worked in developing nations told a tale of human tragedy and marketing abuses by the companies. The second panel consisted of experts in public health (Pan American Health Organization, World Health Organization), medicine, and the author of this paper, who was an expert on the industry. The third panel consisted of the company representatives. Nestlé was represented by the head of its Brazilian operation, and the three American companies were represented by senior executives from their corporate headquarters.

The Kennedy hearings were a landmark in the history of this controversy. They represented the highest level of media attention and political attention that had been achieved in nearly eight years of conflict. Critics had to be pleased with their success. Moreover, Nestlé behaved in a way that actually strengthened the claims of the boycott supporters and organizers. The company's representative charged that the consumer boycott was a conspiracy of church organizations and an indirect attack on the free enterprise system. Senator Kennedy exploded in anger at the charge that the churchmen and health workers were part of a conspiracy to un-

dermine the free enterprise system. The Nestlé statement was a political disaster. Every television program featured the testimony and the reaction from the political leaders in attendance. Nestlé was denounced for its statement and its foolishness.

Phase III of an evolving public issue occurs when some governmental or other formal action begins to develop. In a single nation, this may take the form of a regulatory standard, a piece of legislation, or a government program. In the infant formula controversy, formal action took the form of an international code of marketing conduct which industry and national governments would support. Following the Kennedy hearings, the Director-General of the World Health Organization agreed to convene a meeting of interested parties to lay the groundwork for international action. An important meeting took place in 1979, with delegates calling upon WHO to draft an international marketing code. The code development process took several years, required extensive negotiation, and eventually produced a document that was adopted by the World Health Assembly (the governing body of WHO) in 1981. Throughout this process, Nestlé and other industry members actively participated in the discussions and lobbied for particular terms and provisions. In advance of the World Health Assembly vote, Nestlé was the only company to publicly state that it would follow the code if it was adopted.

Phase IV of a public issue involves the process of implementing the new policy throughout the organizations involved. This is called "institutionalizing" the policy action. Nestlé considered how to implement the WHO Code's provisions following the World Health Assembly's adoption. But there existed a number of very serious obstacles. Many of the Code's terms were imprecise, leaving unanswered questions about the proper interpretations. WHO was reluctant to provide continuing interpretation and reinterpretation of the Code's terms, as this would require a staff of lawyers and a continuing commitment. In addition, the Nestlé boycott continued in both the United States and Europe. Critics continued to pressure the company, and offered alternative interpretations of various code provisions. WHO had no desire to get further drawn into the dispute between the company and its adversaries. Thus, Nestlé was left to negotiate proper interpretations with members of what was now called the International Nestlé Boycott Committee (INBC).

Since 1981, Nestlé has continued to pursue a process of institutionalizing the provisions of the WHO Code by transforming those requirements into policy instructions for its own sales and marketing personnel. A number of innovations have been created to assist this process. These will be discussed below. In early 1984, the international boycott group suspended the Nestlé boycott, following extensive negotiations about such critical issues as product labelling, marketing in health facilities, gifts to medical personnel, and provisions of free supplies to health institutions. By October 1984, the INBC leaders had concluded that Nestlé's commitment to implement the policies had proceeded well enough to permit them to terminate the boycott. Its conclusion was announced at a joint press conference attended by boycott leaders and senior Nestlé managers. Nearly fifteen years after the first formal complaints began, Nestlé had managed to close the controversy over its marketing activities.

ETHICAL ISSUES AND LESSONS

Throughout this long conflict, Nestlé has faced a variety of difficult ethical issues. Some of the broad issues and lessons are summarized below.

All businesses which sell their products in developing nations must consider two basic questions: (1) Is the product an appropriate one for the people in that country? and (2) Are the proposed tactics for marketing the product proper for selling the products but not misleading consumers for whom the product is not appropriate? As Nestlé discovered, both questions are easily overlooked by managers when they are concerned with sales and profits.

Managers should recognize the following points about the appropriateness of products in developing nation markets.

1. Products which are appropriate and acceptable in one social environment may be inappropriate in the social environment of another nation.

Infant formula products are demanding products. There must be pure water with which to prepare them, refrigeration to safely store unused prepared formula, and customers must be able to read instructions and have the income to purchase adequate quantities of the products. The greater the existence of these *risk factors,* the less appropriate the product becomes for marketing. This phenomenon applies to many other consumer products as well.

2. Good products, made without defects, may still be inappropriate because of the inherent riskiness of the environment in which those products are to be used.

Nestlé and its competitors often stated that the market they sought to reach consisted only of those who could safely use the product, and who had adequate income. However, the evidence from many developing nations continuously showed that vast numbers of the population did not meet the necessary requirements for safe use of the product. By selling formula products to such people, managers could know with virtual certainty that there would be overdilution, improper mixing, or contamination with impure water. As Nestlé discovered, many people would denounce and criticize any company that sought to sell its infant formula products under such conditions. When a large part of the population cannot safely use a product, *and* the company cannot effectively segment the market to ensure that only qualified consumers purchase and use it, there may be no choice for the business but to halt sales in that community.

3. Companies may not close their eyes once a product is sold. There is a continuing responsibility to monitor product use, resale, and consumption to determine who is actually using the product, and how. Post-marketing reviews are a necessary step in this process.

Repeatedly, Nestlé and its industry colleagues claimed that they had no desire or intention to see unqualified consumers use their formula products. In 1978 at the United States Senate hearings, representatives from Nestlé, Abbott Laboratories,

American Home Products, and Bristol-Myers were asked whether they conducted any post-marketing research studies to determine who actually used their products. Each company representative answered that his company did no such research and did not know who actually used its products. Naturally, critics attacked the companies for such a careless attitude toward learning the true facts surrounding their products.

4. Products which have been sold to consumers who cannot safely use them must be demarketed. Demarketing may involve withdrawal or recall of products, limitations of the selling of the product, or even a halting of future sales.

The infant formula controversy raised the issue of whether, and when, companies should demarket products which have been commercially successful, but also harmful to innocent consumers. Nestlé and its competitors gradually changed their marketing practices, and recognized that infant formula was not the same "mass market" product that it had once been. The World Health Organization Code specifically indicated that marketing had to be done in ways that guaranteed that the users of formula products had proper information to use the product safely, and to make an intelligent choice about whether or not infant formula was even an appropriate product for them to use. Much of this is to be done by insisting that companies not market directly to mothers, but channel product supplies and advice through health institutions which can ensure that unbiased health information is received by the mother.

5. Marketing strategies must be appropriate to the circumstances of consumers, the social and economic environment in which they live, and to political realities.

Consumer advertising to people for whom product use is highly risky is unacceptable and unethical marketing behavior. Critics of the infant formula industry continued to find evidence of highly aggressive and misleading advertising by companies for many years after the issue became well known. Mass marketing became an unacceptable and inappropriate marketing strategy for infant formula products. The companies, however, had difficulty segmenting their markets and drawing back from the mass market approach. It was only through an industry-wide effort, and then the WHO Code, that managers began to accept that it was more appropriate to focus marketing promotions through the health care system than to consumers directly.

6. Marketing techniques are inappropriate when they exploit a condition of consumer vulnerability.

Many firms in the industry used "milk nurses" during the 1960s and 1970s. These were sales personnel who dressed in nurses' uniforms and visited new mothers in hospitals. They would try to encourage the mother to allow their babies to be fed formula, rather than breastfeed, in order to encourage formula adoptions. Since a mother loses the ability to breastfeed after several days of not doing so, such a decision would then require that the baby continue to be fed from a bottle for the next six months. This would be good for formula sales, if the mother could afford to buy it, but might be bad for the baby if the mother had to find a cheaper substitute product to put in the bottle. In South America, for example, members of my own research team saw mothers feeding a mixture of corn starch and water to babies because they had no money to buy formula. Mothers who have given birth are quite vulnerable, and the use of the milk nurses took advantage of that vulnerability in ways that were unethical and unfair. Actions which exploit consumer vulnerability and result in harm are inappropriate marketing tactics.

7. Marketing strategies should be formulated in such a way as to permit flexibility and adjustment to new circumstances.

In the early 1970s, Nestlé management knew that critics had a legitimate concern for the sales practices of the industry, but were unable to change their marketing activities in response. The company seemed to be "locked in" to a strategy of resistance, denial, and anger at such charges. In retrospect, it seems that Nestlé needed time to change its marketing strategy from a mass-market, consumer-advertising approach, to one which emphasized promotion through the medical and health care system. It took Nestlé much longer to change its marketing strategy than it took many of its competitors. This may have been because of pressures from field managers or from the product marketing staff, which denied the truth of the critics' charges. Whatever the case, the company was injured by its slow response to criticism, and its seeming inability to find an alternative way to continue marketing its products. A company which can only market its products in one way is very vulnerable to public issues and political pressures.

CONCLUSION

Nestlé's traumatic experience with the infant formula controversy has finally come to an end, but the impact is likely to last for many years. The company suffered a major blow to its reputation and to the morale of its people. It is traumatic and difficult for people to be told they are working for a company which "kills babies." Today, Nestlé's senior management is again working to restore the company's economic and cultural fabric. Its future success will depend upon much more than sales and profits. Nestlé has been a successful institution as well as a successful business. Institutions represent a structure of values, and it is this structure which was most sharply affected by the long controversy over infant formula.

If a historian writes the history of Nestlé one hundred years from now, will he or she include a reference to the infant formula controversy? Very likely yes. The conflict continued for more than ten years, cost the company many millions of dollars of revenue, expenses, and profits, and damaged or destroyed the careers of a number of its promising managers. It is impossible to say how long it will take for the company to regain its good name and for the public to once again think of Nestlé as a good corporate citizen.

Multinational corporations must learn to anticipate conflicts of the sort faced by Nestlé, and be prepared to respond in ways that not only justify what the company is doing but also deal with the legitimate concerns of the critics. Union Carbide cannot forget its experience in Bhopal, India: Unilever cannot ignore its experience with Persil in England: Johnson & Johnson cannot forget its experience with Tylenol in the United States: and Nestlé cannot forget its experience with infant formula. Each of these experiences involved a company with a good reputation, successful business strategies, and a major public credibility problem. The resolution of each dilemma required a careful integration of public affairs strategies with the business strategy for the company. And each situation demanded and required that the company's managers recognize the *common interest* that existed between the corporation and the public. In the long run, there is no other way to harmonize the legitimate interests of companies with the legitimate interests of the public.

Toy Wars*

Manuel Velasquez
The Dirksen Professor of Business Ethics, Management Department, Santa Clara University

Early in 1986, Tom Daner, president of the advertising company of Daner Associates, was contacted by Mike Teal, the sales manager of Crako Industries. Crako industries is a family-owned company that manufactures children's toys and had long been a favorite and important client of Daner Associates. The sales manager of Crako Industries explained that the company had just developed a new toy helicopter. The toy was modeled on the military helicopters that had been used in Vietnam and that had appeared in the "Rambo" movies. Mike Teal explained that the toy was developed in response to the craze for military toys that had been sweeping the nation in the wake of the Rambo movies. The family-owned toy company had initially resisted moving into military

---

toys since members of the family objected to the violence associated with such toys. But as segments of the toy market were increasingly taken over by military toys, the family came to feel that entry into the military toy market was crucial for their business. Consequently, they approved development of a line of military toys, hoping that they were not entering the market too late. Mike Teal now wanted Daner Associates to develop a television advertising campaign for the toy.

The toy helicopter Crako designers had developed was about one and one-half feet long, battery-operated, and made of plastic and steel. Mounted to the sides were detachable replicas of machine guns and a detachable stretcher modeled on the stretchers used to lift wounded soldiers from a battlefield. Mike Teal of Crako explained that they were trying to develop a toy that had to be perceived as "more macho" than the top-selling "G.I. Joe" line of toys. If the company were to compete successfully in today's toy market, according to the sales manager, it would have to adopt an advertising approach that was even "meaner and tougher" than what other companies were doing. Consequently, he continued, the advertising clips developed by Daner Associates would have to be "mean and macho." Television advertisements for the toy, he suggested, might show the helicopter swooping over buildings and blowing them up. The more violence and mayhem the ads suggested, the better. Crako Industries was relying heavily on sales from the new toy and some Crako managers felt that the company's future might depend on the success of this toy.

Tom Daner was unwilling to have his company develop television advertisements that would increase what he already felt was too much violence in television aimed at children. In particular he recalled a television ad for a tricycle with a replica machine gun mounted on the handle-bars. The commercial showed the tricycle being pedaled through the woods by a small boy as he chased several other boys fleeing before him over a dirt path. At one point the camera closed in over the shoulder of the boy, focused through the gunsight, and showed the gunsight apparently trying to aim at the backs of the boys as they fled before the tri-

cycle's machine gun. Ads of that sort had disturbed Tom Daner and had led him to think that advertisers should find other ways of promoting these toys. He suggested, therefore, that instead of promoting the Crako helicopter through violence, it should be presented in some other manner. When Teal asked what he had in mind, Tom was forced to reply that he didn't know. But at any rate, Tom pointed out, the three television networks would not accept a violent commercial aimed at children. All three networks adhered to an advertising code that prohibited violent, intense, or unrealistic advertisements aimed at children.

This seemed no real obstacle to Teal, however. Although the networks might turn down children's ads when they were too violent, local television stations were not as squeamish. Local television stations around the country regularly accepted ads aimed at children that the networks had rejected as too violent. The local stations inserted the ads as spots on their non-network programming, thereby circumventing the Advertising Codes of the three national networks. Daner Associates would simply have to place the ads they developed for the Crako helicopter through local television stations around the country. Mike Teal was firm: If Daner Associates would not develop a "mean and tough" ad campaign, the toy company would move their account to an advertiser who would. Reluctantly, Tom Daner agreed to develop the advertising campaign. Crako Industries accounted for $1 million of Daner's total revenues.

Like Crako Industries, Daner Associates was also a family-owned business. Started by his father almost fifty years ago, the advertising firm that Tom Daner now ran had grown dramatically under his leadership. In 1975 the business had grossed $3 million: ten years later it had revenues of $25 million and provided a full line of advertising services. The company was divided into three departments (creative, media, and account executive), each of which had about twelve employees. Tom Daner credited much of the company's success to the many new people he had hired, especially a group with M.B.A.s who had developed new marketing strategies based on more thorough market and consumer analyses. Most decisions, however, were made by a five-person executive committee consisting of Tom Daner, the senior accountant, and the three department heads. As owner-president Tom's views tended to color most decisions, producing what one member of the committee called a "benevolent dictatorship." Tom himself was an enthusiastic, congenial, intelligent and well-read person. During college he had considered becoming a missionary priest but had changed his mind and was now married and the father of three daughters. His personal heroes included Thomas Merton, Albert Schweitzer, and Tom Doley.

When Tom Daner presented the Crako deal to his executive committee he found that they did not share his misgivings. The other committee members felt that Daner Associates should give Crako exactly the kind of ad Crako wanted: one with a heavy content of violence. Moreover, the writers and artists in the creative department were enthused with the prospect of letting their imaginations loose on the project, several feeling that they could easily produce an attention-grabbing ad by "out-violencing" current television programming. The creative department, in fact, quickly produced a copy-script that called for videos showing the helicopter "flying out of the sky with machineguns blazing" at a jungle village below. This kind of ad, they felt, was exactly what they were being asked to produce by their client.

But after viewing the copy, Tom Daner refused to use it. They should produce an ad, he insisted, that would meet their client's needs but that would also meet the guidelines of the national networks. The ad should not glorify violence and war but should somehow support cooperation and family values. Disappointed and somewhat frustrated, the creative department went back to work. A few days later, they presented a second proposal: an ad that would show the toy helicopter flying through the family room of a home as a little boy plays with it: then the scene shifts to show the boy on a rock rising from the floor of the family room: the helicopter swoops down and picks up the boy as though rescuing him from the rock where he had been stranded. Although the creative department was mildly pleased with their attempt, they felt it

was too "tame." Tom liked it, however, and a version of the ad was filmed.

A few weeks later Tom Daner met with Mike Teal and his team and showed them the film. The viewing was not a success. Teal turned down the ad. Referring to the network regulations which other toy advertisements were breaking as frequently as motorists broke the 55-mile-per-hour speed law, he said "That commercial is going only 55 miles an hour when I want one that goes 75." If the next version was not "tougher and meaner," Crako Industries would be forced to look elsewhere.

Disappointed, Tom Daner returned to the people in his creative department and told them to go ahead with designing the kind of ad they had originally wanted: "I don't have any idea what else to do." In a short time the creative department had an ad proposal on his desk that called for scenes showing the helicopter blowing up villages. Shortly afterwards a small set was constructed depicting a jungle village sitting next to a bridge stretching over a river. The ad was filmed using the jungle set as a background.

When Tom saw the result he was not happy. He decided to meet with his creative department and air his feelings. "The issue here," he said, "is basically the issue of violence. Do we really want to present toys as instruments for beating up people? This ad is going to promote aggression and violence. It will glorify dominance and do it with kids who are terrifically impressionable. Do we really want to do this?" The members of the creative department, however, responded that they were merely giving their client what the client wanted. That client, moreover, was an important account. The client wanted an aggressive "macho" ad, and that was what they were providing. The ad might violate the regulations of the television networks, but there were ways to get around the networks. Moreover, they said, every other advertising firm in the business was breaking the limits against violence set by the networks. Tom made one last try: Why not market the toy as an adventure and fantasy toy? Film the ad again, he suggested, using the same jungle backdrop. But instead of showing the helicopter shooting at a burning village, show it flying in to rescue people from the burning village. Create an ad that shows excitement, adventure, and fantasy, but no aggression. "I was trying," he said later, "to figure out a new way of approaching this kind of advertising. We have to follow the market or we can go out of business trying to moralize to the market. But why not try a new approach? Why not promote toys as instruments that expand the child's imagination in a way that is positive and that promotes cooperative values instead of violence and aggression?"

A new film version of the ad was made, now showing the helicopter flying over the jungle set. Quick shots and heightened background music give the impression of excitement and danger. The helicopter flies dramatically through the jungle and over a river and bridge to rescue a boy from a flaming village. As lights flash and shoot haphazardly through the scene the helicopter rises and escapes into the sky. The final ad was clearly exciting and intense. And it promoted the saving of a life instead of violence against life.

It was clear when the final version was shot, however, that it would not clear the network censors. Network guidelines require that sets in children's ads must depict things that are within the reach of most children so that they do not create unrealistic expectations. Clearly the elaborate set (which cost $25,000 to construct) was not within the reach of most children and consequently most children would not be able to recreate the scene of the ad by buying the toy. Moreover, network regulations stipulate that in children's ads, scenes must be filmed with normal lighting that does not create undue intensity. Again, clearly the helicopter ad which created excitement by using quick changes of light and fast cuts did not fall within these guidelines.

After reviewing the film, Tom Daner reflected on some last-minute instructions Crako's sales manager had given him when he had been shown the first version of the ad: The television ad should show things being blown up by the guns of the little helicopter and perhaps even some blood on the fuselage of the toy; the ad had to be violent. Now Tom had to make a decision. Should he risk the account by submitting only the rescue mission ad? Or should he let Teal also see the ad that showed the helicopter shooting up the village, knowing that he

would probably prefer that version if he saw it? And was the rescue mission ad really that much different from the ad that showed the shooting of the village? Did it matter that the rescue mission ad still violated some of the network regulations? What if he offered Teal only the rescue mission ad and Teal accepted the "rescue approach" but demanded he make it more violent: should he give in? And should Tom risk launching an ad campaign that was based on this new untested approach? What if the ad failed to sell the Crako toy? Was it right to experiment with a client's product, especially a product that was so important to the future of the client's business? Tom was unsure what he should do. He wanted to show Teal only the rescue mission commercial but he felt he first had to resolve these questions in his own mind.

Forests of the North Coast: The Owls, the Trees, and the Conflicts

Lisa Newton
Director, Program in Environmental Studies, Fairfield University

Catherine Dillingham
Adjunct Professor, Environmental Ethics, Fairfield University

You may already be familiar with the basic facts of the next case. It addresses the battle between the logging community of the Pacific Northwest and the animal rights advocates who seek to protect the spotted owl population in that same area. Apparently, the two populations can not co-exist. As you read the case, do any alternatives come to mind for resolving this situation? The authors ask whether this case is, as the media contended, basically a class conflict between the blue-collar loggers and the elite, white-collar professional class that typifies the environmental movement.

From *Watersheds: Classic Cases in Environmental Ethics,* 1st edition, by L. H. Newton and C. K. Dillingham, © 1994. Reprinted with permission of Wadsworth, a division of Thomson Learning.

The media have characterized the struggle between the loggers and the environmentalists as essentially a class conflict: the working-class lumbermen against the elite professional class that typifies the environmental movement. How does the United States generally handle white-collar versus blue-collar conflicts? Will the lessons learned elsewhere in that type of conflict help us here?

BACKGROUND: THE TRAGEDY OF TREES

"Save a Life; Kill a Tree?" is an article written by Sallie Tisdale: it describes the most recent "trees vs. people" ammunition, the anticancer drug taxol that is found in the bark of the Pacific Yew of the Northwest old-growth forests. "Save a Logger—Eat a Spotted Owl" is a bumper sticker commonly seen throughout this area. A grocery store in northern California recently displayed boxes of Spotted Owl Helper (a takeoff on Hamburger Helper). A recurring theme in this controversy is that something (usually a tree, but sometimes an owl) has to be killed in order to save something of human value: this gives the whole topic an overtone of tragedy. In tragedy, victory is impossible, and reconciliation comes at terrible cost. Simply because the issue will not yield to politically conscious pragmatism (the peculiarly American version of reason), it invites complications from the political and economic left and right and sanctions violence in defense of endangered values. Our first job, then, is to sort out the complications, so that the intersecting ethical dilemmas can be treated independently. Let us consider the issues:

1. *The owl.* The northern spotted owl is threatened with extinction by logging operations in the Northwest Forest. The owl is protected to some extent by the Endangered Species Act. . . . but the issues involved go beyond the law. Why might we have a moral obligation to save an endangered species? On the other hand, why should we care about insignificant faraway birds, anyway? What good is *biodiversity?* And what should we be willing to do to maintain it?
2. *The trees and the business practices that threaten them.* Ted Gup describes the owl as "a fine bird, yes, but . . . never really the root cause of this great conflict." It is the trees themselves—great groves of Sequoia and other cone-bearing trees, some of them more than 2,000 years old, spontaneously likened to the great cathedrals of Europe by many who have seen them—it is the trees that really fire the imagination. Do we have an obligation to preserve these trees, just as a singular treasure for the world?

   We live with a free-enterprise system that generally serves us well. Do we have an obligation either to protect businesses that operate in environmentally sensitive ways, or to require that all businesses do so? The case of Pacific Lumber Company shows a company that preserved environmental values pitted against hostile financial initiatives that were good for the shareholders but bad for the trees. Does the fiduciary duty of the company extend to the environment? Should the trees have a vote at the annual meeting? Do we have an obligation to protect the workers—the loggers, and their peculiarly specialized way of life?
3. *The varied roles of the government.* . . . . What is the role of the government in protecting owls, trees, business, and ourselves? What do we want the government's role to be? What should government be empowered to do? at what cost?

All these questions turn on one indisputable fact: the Pacific Northwest Rainforests, ecosystems unlike any others in the world, have been logged for a century to the point of threatened extinction, not only of the species housed there but of the forests themselves. These forests are managed and regulated by an incredible mix of national bureaucracies; the actions of these agencies affect the livelihoods of millions of people and the economies of three states. The loggers and lumber companies are in conflict with the environmentalists; both parties are in conflict with the regulators; the politicians are on all sides of the conflict, depending on their constituencies; and everything ends up in court, where the "lawsuits, motions, and appeals . . . [seem to] have increased faster than the owl population."

THE OWL AND ITS TREES

The currents of the Pacific Ocean provide abundant warmth and moisture to the Northwest Coast of the United States. Through millions of years of evolution, these conditions have allowed the appearance, probably 6,000 years ago, of what we now call "old-growth forests." These are forests with some thousand-year-old stands, forests with trees that are 300 feet tall and ten feet in diameter, trees that are at least twice as massive as those found in tropical rainforests, trees that each contain enough lumber to build two houses. These forests extend from the Alaskan panhandle (Sitka Spruce) south through Washington and Oregon (Douglas Fir, Western Hemlock) to northern California (Redwoods, Ponderosa Pine). . . .

The owl is one of those species that requires unique stable conditions to survive; It appears to be totally dependent upon old-growth forest, and hunts there exclusively. To house the owl, the trees must be dense, and some proportion of them must be over 200 years old. Thus, the future of the northern spotted owl is linked with that of the old-growth forest, and the owl is therefore considered an *indicator* species—that is, a species whose condition will indicate the condition of the entire ecosystem (similar to the canary in the coal mine). Not only does the owl require old growth, it requires a lot of it. Studies have shown that, in northern California, each pair ranged among 1,900 acres of old growth; in Oregon, six pairs averaged 2,264 acres as their range; and six pairs studied in Washington had an average range of 3,800 acres.

ENDANGERMENT AND OBLIGATIONS

The northern spotted owl, then, is clearly endangered. To save it, we must save large numbers of the oldest trees. Given that 90 percent of the forest has been cut down already, virtually all the remaining old growth, whether in private or public hands, must be preserved. Should we do this for the sake of the owl?

Do we have an obligation to preserve endangered species? For starters, what does "preservation" mean in this context? If only the genetic material is in question, we can preserve the spotted owl by capturing a sufficient number of breeding pairs (say, 20), putting them in a climate-controlled zoo, and allowing them to produce baby owls to their hearts content—and we can do this without gumming up the logging operations. (If no zoos have room for owls right now, we could freeze owl eggs indefinitely and regenerate the species any time it is convenient to do so.) Or does preservation of a wild species always mean preservation in the wild, living as the species has evolved to live, naturally? If this is preservation, then what cost are we expected to absorb to preserve the habitat? Granted that the owl is worth something to us (we would not wish it extinguished, other things being equal), but what is it worth when it affects these other things: jobs, regional economies, and the evolved lifestyle of the North Coast loggers?

The preservation of a species contributes to the biodiversity of the area—this means, literally, the number and variety of species that are living there. For any ecosystem, we assume that the species have evolved as members of a niche and that the destruction of one species, leaving its niche open and its role unfilled, will have an unfavorable impact on the others. For the sake of *all* species, then, we should preserve *each* species. We cannot predict just which of these species will suddenly prove to be dramatically useful to humans—by, say, providing a cure for cancer. . . . This argument was used, but only hypothetically, until the discovery of taxol, a drug that has recently shown better than expected results in treating ovarian and breast cancer; taxol originates in the bark (and perhaps the needles) of the Pacific Yew, which is indigenous to the old growth. The U.S. Forest Service used to consider the Yew a weed, to be removed from a clear-cut and burned; now, of course, there is pressure from many fronts to harvest these trees for the cancer drug. Would we have ever found out about this use for yew trees if the old groves had all been gone? For the sake of the human species, then, we should protect *any* species, no matter how humble, no matter what measures (within the obvious limits of reason) are required to preserve the conditions that species needs to live.

ACTING TO PRESERVE THE SPECIES

Persuaded by such considerations, Congress passed the Endangered Species Act (ESA) in 1973. According to this bill, the National Marine Fishery Service (Department of Commerce) and the Fish and Wildlife Service (Department of the Interior) are empowered to list marine and land species, respectively, as either threatened or endangered; then, these species can no longer be hunted, collected, injured, or killed. The bill also prohibits any federal agency from carrying out or funding any activity that could threaten or endanger said species *or their habitats.* (This latter provision has caused the most controversy with regard to logging in the old-growth forests, but also other projects, such as dams, highways, and other development receiving federal funding.) Therefore, both the Bureau of Land Management (Department of the Interior) and the Forest Service (Department of Agriculture) must consult with the Fish and Wildlife Service before undertaking any action that might threaten a species such as the owl.

This bill is typical of environmental legislation on several counts: (1) It is informed by the best science available, so it is enlightened, far-reaching, and probably the world's most stringent species-protection legislation. To be in noncompliance with the ESA is a criminal act; both civil and criminal penalties are called for, including imprisonment. (2) This bill is also among those most pitifully funded. Until 1988, the yearly funding amounted to about the cost of 12 Army bulldozers. The 1988 amendments doubled the budget, but legislative environmentalists consider that the bill has nowhere near the support it needs to preserve marine and terrestrial species worldwide. (3) Three cabinet-level departments must work harmoniously together for the act to be implemented.

Implementation presents other problems. According to the 1982 amendment of the act, the economic implications of the protection of a species *may not* be considered in determining its status, whether or not it is endangered; that decision must be based "solely on the basis of the best scientific and commercial data." Economic factors *may* be considered after the listing, during the required preparation of a recovery plan for the listed species. (In practice, because of the complexities involved, few plans have been prepared.) The act also calls for a determination of the species' "critical habitat" but allows a year to elapse after the listing for the determination and acknowledges that, because of complications, the habitat might be indeterminable.

When determining the critical habitat, the Fish and Wildlife Service *must* include economic considerations. On two occasions, court-ordered reconsiderations on the basis of economic impact have impelled the FWS to reduce the acreage required to preserve the owl. Additionally, those who feel that their economic interests are damaged by species protection may appeal to the Endangered Species Committee (the "God Squad"). The bureaucratic hurdles to overcome on the way to actual protection of the owl seem daunting even to the most hardened Washington veterans; nevertheless, it *is* legal protection and, as such, the strongest statement that we can make, as a nation, about the value of our most threatened creatures.

THE TALLEST TREES ON EARTH

. . . Unfortunately for those who hope for the survival of these trees, they are the most commercially valuable trees in the United States. The extent of the original forest and of the remaining acreage is very debatable and probably depends on one's definition of "old growth," which is generally described as the largest old trees, living and dead, standing and fallen, within a multilayered canopy. Estimates of the extent of the original forest range from 20 to 70 million acres (depending on what is considered a large tree); some 70 to 95 percent of this forest has been logged over the last century, and the rate of logging has increased dramatically over the last few decades. Estimates are complicated, too, by the fragmentation of the forest by clear-cutting, leaving some stands isolated in a barren landscape.

From the corporate viewpoint, logging just makes good business sense. The woods, as a popular song would have it, are just trees, and the trees are just wood. Humans have always cut and processed timber for lumber—for houses, boats, fences, furniture—virtually since our beginnings on this planet, and the redwoods are eminently suitable for such harvest. The lumber from redwoods is beautiful, durable, light, strong, has good nail-holding capacity, and is insect- and fire-resistant. Each tree yields an average of 12 or 13 thousand board feet—enough to build two houses. The harvest is very profitable but strictly limited. Once those old-growth trees are logged, there will be no more: The trees will be gone forever. The second growth does not share the characteristics of the old growth in its resistance to insects, disease, fire, and decay, nor is it as dense and massive, of course. We might suppose that the twentieth-century remnants of a 2,000-year-old forest were composed of the best survivors of all attacks: The less-resistant trees will have succumbed centuries ago. The old growth is then an irreplaceable asset: It could be argued that it will become more valuable every year into the indefinite future and that it therefore demands careful husbanding and conservative forestry practices. Wise management would seem to require very sparing cuts of the old growth while encouraging plantations of new trees to satisfy demands for ordinary lumber.

TREES, THE ENVIRONMENT, AND THE LAW

Aristotle and Adam Smith both proved, in very different ways, that private property (specifically, land and all resources for production) was better off, more likely to be taken care of, than public property. We accept as established fact that a private owner is the best caretaker of property. The centrality of the right to private property in John Locke's writing depends on that presumption, as do our standard defenses of the American business system.

Is this presumption now generally false? Pacific Lumber's redwoods are clearly not safe in Hurwitz's hands. Do we have a legal right, then, to take the land away from him? We know that, under the doctrine of eminent domain, we can seize the redwoods for a new national park—but can we seize all that land just to continue a more conservative logging operation? What are the business imperatives of a company that logs redwoods? Is it a sufficient discharge of our obligations to replace 2,000-year-old groves with young growth that can be harvested in 40 to 80 years?

Another environmental effect of the logging, presently unmeasurable, is its contribution to global warming. The old growth is a veritable storehouse of carbon, a fact of increasingly intense interest, for carbon dioxide is the most important of the "greenhouse gases" credited with causing the projected global warming. While these trees are alive they absorb huge amounts of carbon dioxide from the atmosphere in the photosynthetic process. Nature's recycling laws require, of course, that the same amount of gas be returned to the atmosphere, through the trees' respiration and eventual decay, but that happens, as we have noted, over a period of hundreds of years.

When the trees are felled, the photosynthetic carbon dioxide absorption stops and, compounding the crime, when the resulting debris is burned, the stored carbon is abruptly added to the atmosphere as carbon dioxide. The timber industry has claimed that, by cutting old growth and planting young trees with a faster photosynthetic rate, they are actually ameliorating the threat of global warming. To be sure, a rapidly growing tree absorbs more carbon dioxide than a mature tree of the same size, but a small seedling does not approach the chemical activity of the enormous trees in the Northwest Forest, trees that are many times as massive as those found anywhere else in the world. The Northwest old growth "stores more carbon . . . than any other biome—twice as much per unit of area as tropical rainforests."

Incidentally, the claim of the timber companies—that their little plantings are really much better at taking carbon from the air than the mature redwoods—is typical of the self-serving half-truths that tend to harden attitudes in these controversies. This claim, with just enough scientific fact to make it respectable yet clearly in the service of company interests, enrages environmentalists and encourages public cynicism. Should the timber companies be held responsible for global warming—an unintended but predictable, consequence of their operations?

CREATIVE ALTERNATIVES

The strongest indication that the Forest Service and its allied agencies in the federal government might not be the true villains, however, lies in the work they do when the law asks them to think creatively about these forests and their future. Pursuant to the 1960 Multiple Use Sustained Yield Act . . . . the Forest Service, the Bureau of Land Management, and the U.S. Fish and Wildlife Service were asked to describe ways that the owl might be saved and the trees might be put to work for the nation without being cut down. The agencies did a fine job: The combined report of the Forest Service and the BLM, "Actions the Administration May Wish to Consider in Implementing a Conservation Strategy for the Northern Spotted Owl" (May 1, 1990), recommends a drastic cutback in the harvesting of old-growth trees by forbidding export of raw logs, then recommends and describes extensive educational and retraining programs for the loggers who are put out of work by the ban. Technical assistance would make logging and milling more efficient (avoiding the extensive waste entailed by present practices); recreational facilities would make the forests better-known and better-used and create political pressure to conserve the trees. Even more impressive is the FWS report. "Economic Analysis of Designation of Critical Habitat for the Northern Spotted Owl" (August 1991). Going beyond the multiple-use scenario, the report specifically addresses "non-use values," the value to the nation just to have the forests *there:* "Estimates of recreation user demand, benefits of scenic beauty, and benefits of water quality represent only a partial estimate of society's total value for the spotted owl and its associated habitat. The public also is willing to pay for the option of recreation use in the future, the knowledge that the natural ecosystem exists and is protected, and the satisfaction from its bequest to future generations. . . . The average willingness to pay higher taxes and wood product prices reported in a referendum contingent valuation format was $190 per year. The lower limit of the 98 percent confidence range was $117 per household."

These reports place the federal government's environmental services in a new and much better light. Bureaucrats in general, and federal bureaucrats in particular, have been harshly criticized for their role (or lack of same) in the protection of the forests. But these reports on alternate usage of the forests suggest, though, that the idealists who once joined government service to protect the nation's environmental heritage might still be around, waiting only for public opinion to catch up to them. A new agenda for the environment will require a trained corps of experts in science and policy to articulate a national environmental ethic and to frame the plans for implementation. In developing their reports, the Forest Service, the BLM, and the FWS have made an auspicious start.

SUMMARY

The heart of the problem, from an environmental point of view, is the old-growth forest. From the loggers' point of view, the problem is jobs. The owl, the financier, and the government agencies are all bit players in an agonizing twentieth-century drama of loss and conflict. We need not search for villains. Once we all thought that the forests were unlimited. The timber industry's managers watched the old growth disappear before their eyes and did not realize that it could not be restored—that once gone, it would be gone forever; but they were no more ignorant than their regulators, their customers, or their fellow citizens. The environmental movement is not the sole prerogative of Eastern elitists, as the loggers suspect, nor is the timber industry composed of a series of tintypes of Charles Hurwitz, as the environmentalists are convinced.

Protecting the forests will require the abolition of a way of life that has been honored and valued in the immediate past. What, exactly, are we prepared to do to compensate and redirect the people who are stranded by systematic and extensive preservation? On the other hand, are we prepared to spare ourselves that difficult decision by allowing the forests to be destroyed? Once the trees are gone, the industry will die, and the workers will be unemployed anyway, but then it will be *their* problem, not ours. How much are we willing to lose in order to avoid the pain of making this decision now—before it is too late? Our history suggests that we are willing to lose quite a bit.

The most disturbing aspect of our political response to these dilemmas, though, is the hypocrisy of the United States urging Brazil and other Third World countries to halt the cutting of their tropical rainforests to prevent the worsening of global warming, while we cut our forests about twice as fast. To quote an official with the Oregon Natural Resources Council, "It's interesting that we're telling Third World countries, 'don't cut your forests' [while] . . . we're wiping out our fish runs, we're wiping out our biotic diversity, we're sending species to extinction . . . we're not a Third World country. We're not so poor that we have to destroy our ancient forests. And we're not so rich that we can afford to."

U.S. and Mexico Confront a Toxic Legacy

Colum Lynch
Writer and regular contributor to *The Boston Globe*

Here at the Otay Mesa industrial park on the outskirts of Tijuana, subsidiaries of dozens of U.S. corporations sit like a great industrial fortress overlooking Ejido Chilpancingo, a small working-class barrio situated in a valley near the Tijuana River.

Since the industrial park opened over a decade ago, residents of Ejido Chilpancingo say, they have been living in the shadow of a chemical nightmare. Their livestock feed on toxic waste, their air is often blackened by pollutants and their water supply has been fouled by a network of open drainage pipes that poke out over the town from a bluff beneath the industrial park. Its tenants include subsidiaries to such corporate giants as Mobil Oil and Pepsi and to American Optical

The Boston Globe, June 15, 1992. Reprinted by permission.

Corp., a Southbridge, Mass.-based firm that manufactures lenses.

When rain falls upon Ejido Chilpancingo, plant workers release into drainage pipes stockpiled industrial detergents, solvents, heavy metals and petroleum products. The outflow empties into dozens of meandering creeks, rivulets and gulleys before emptying into a river where the town residents bathe.

Ultimately the contaminated waters reach the Rio Tijuana and then flow north back into the United States.

In February, when President George Bush visited Los Angeles and San Antonio to mobilize support for a North American Free Trade Agreement among the United States, Mexico and Canada, he argued that the agreement was the antidote to the environmental problems that afflict communities like Ejido Chilpancingo. By providing benefits to U.S. corporations, he reasoned, the agreement would raise living standards for Mexicans and Americans alike, and "higher standards of living . . . will help people keep the air and water cleaner on both sides of the border."

The agreement has to be ratified by the U.S. Congress, which is unlikely to deal with it until after the November elections.

To deal with the immediate problems, which will cost billions to clean up, Bush has proposed what he called an Integrated Border Plan and asked the U.S. Congress to appropriate $250 million to fund a series of clean-up operations along the U.S. side of the border. (The proposal is now before the House Appropriations Committee.) At the same time, President Carlos Salinas de Gortari promised to commit $460 million over the next three years for environmental clean-up and to improve Mexico's capacity to monitor rampant illegal chemical dumping by foreign corporations along his side of the border.

At Ejido Chilpancingo, where an experiment in free trade has already been going on for over a decade, residents say they can't wait for any benefits from a free trade agreement to trickle down into their community.

U.S., Japanese and Mexican corporations have already transformed their town into an environmental junk yard. From the Otay Mesa industrial park, poisonous plumes of black smoke rise from the industrial waste being illegally burned, emitting an acrid odor of rubber and sulphur. The open-air grounds of a nearby factory are covered with a snowy layer of lead sulphate dust, a compound found in corroded batteries that attacks the central nervous system. Puddles of yellow water collect on the dirt roads of the town square.

Down the road from the square, Jose Juan de Vora, 11, sits wearily on the edge of the single bed in his small one-bedroom home. The boy fell sick months ago. Clumps of his hair have fallen out, a skin infection covered much of his body, and he no longer plays. A rash extends from the top of his ear to his cheekbone.

The boy's mother, Dona Rosa de Vora, 42, says her three granddaughters and many other children of Ejido Chilpancingo have been racked by similar ailments. She says a doctor believes the town's communal water, which often stings the skin upon touch, is responsible for the problems.

The foreign companies that have set up shop at Ejido Chilpancingo over the last 10 years are part of Mexico's *maquiladora* program. The program allows foreign companies to set up *maquiladoras,* or assembly plants, along a 65-mile corridor on the U.S.-Mexico border, and to reap the benefits of low tariffs and cheap Mexican labor. It has drawn hundreds of U.S. firms that manufacture everything from Barbie Dolls to parts for Patriot Missiles. It has also lured hundreds of thousands of Mexican laborers from the interior to take advantage of nearly 100 percent employment, and wages that exceed Mexico's $3 a day minimum.

Under Bush's Free Trade Agreement, towns like Ejido Chilpancingo would sprout up throughout Mexico.

No one is certain what impact the dumping and the fouled waters of Ejido Chilpancingo will ultimately have on the health of residents, but reports of a rare and fatal brain disease among newborns in Brownsville, Tex., which specialists suspect may be linked to pollution, has sent a chill the length of the 2,000-mile U.S.-Mexico border.

A recent study of water samples taken by the Autonomous University of Baja California from one creek in Ejido Chilpancingo found dangerous levels of lead (more than 100 times acceptable levels), zinc, cadmium and chromium (commonly linked to some skin problems) in one stream that runs into the village.

A 1990 government study by Mexico's State Workers Institute of Social Security found that 16.4 percent of the community suffer from skin diseases, and 8.5 percent from respiratory ailments.

"They wouldn't do this in San Diego," thunders Maurilio Pachuca, a crafts merchant who has been organizing residents to stop the toxic dumping in his town. "Well, we're human beings, too!"

But the environmental damage created by industry in Otay Mesa doesn't stop at Ejido Chilpancingo.

On the U.S. side of the border, Jesse Gomez, manager of the Effie May Organic Farm, grows cabbage, beets, carrots, lettuce and broccoli for American consumers on a 130-acre farm along the Rio Tijuana. When heavy rains flood the river, the contaminated water spreads over the land. Business is booming, though he worries that one day his crops will not meet environmental standards if the contamination isn't brought under control.

Gomez says his hopes lie in the construction of a monumental $200 million sewage treatment plant that will process 12 million gallons of raw sewage and toxic soup that run into the United States through the Rio Tijuana. The plant, which would be completed in 1995, is one of the cornerstones of the Bush administration's proposed solution to border pollution.

Some environmentalists say the sewage treatment plant won't solve Gomez's problems. "It's amazing how people in the U.S. could ever feel safe when massive environmental contamination is happening on the other side of an imaginary political line," says Marco Kaltofen, an author of a study for the Boston-based National Toxic Campaign Fund on the impact of the *maquiladora* industry on water pollution along the border.

Kaltofen says sewage treatment plants cannot control the flow of industrial residues like petroleum, heavy metals and pesticides that pollute the Rio Tijuana. "The issue of toxic waste management has to be dealt with in the plants where the chemical waste originates," he says. Otherwise,

"It's out the drain one day, on your dinner table in New York a week later," citing the movement of toxic chemicals from the factories into the food chain through farms along the Rio Tijuana.

The Integrated Environmental Plan, as the scheme is officially called, is designed to erect a line of defense against a number of polluted waterways like the Rio Tijuana that flow into the United States. The plan also includes $75 million to improve drinking water and sewage systems in the hundreds of shanty towns that have sprung up along the U.S. side in the last decade. Another $50 million would finance limited air-pollution management, training for Mexican inspectors, and a system for tracking the movement of raw chemicals imported into Mexico for manufacturing purposes.

Under Mexican law, U.S. manufacturers in Mexico are required to return imported raw chemical waste and solvents used in the manufacturing process in the nation of origin. Only a tiny percentage of the chemical waste, however, finds its way back to the United States. As in the Otay Mesa industrial park, much of it is simply poured down drains, dropped in clandestine garbage dumps or buried in canyons. The estimated cost of cleaning up the border area run as high as $9 billion.

J. Michael McCloskey, chairman of the Sierra Club, calls the plan "short-sighted," because it confronts only the existing problem and fails to provide a long-term strategy for increasing funding as free trade extends throughout Mexico.

He also said the plan lacks an "action-forcing mechanism" to require industry to comply with Mexican or U.S. environmental laws. Mexico has a notoriously poor track record on environmental enforcement. And so far, the U.S. Environmental Protection Agency has only asked manufacturers to take voluntary steps to contain illegal dumping and to reduce the use of toxic materials.

According to Kaltofen, who led the water pollution study, the EPA has refused to sanction U.S. corporate dumpers or even to acknowledge the extent of the U.S. corporations' role in creating a toxic waste disaster zone along the border. The EPA, he says, treats pollution as a "made in Mexico" problem.

EPA spokesman Luke Hester acknowledges that border pollution is a "horrendous problem,"

and he says Mexico is improving its standards daily. Mexico, he says, has doubled the number of border environmental inspectors to 200, and earlier this month the government shut down eight facilities for environmental violations. "We're not going to turn Mexico around overnight," he says, "but there is movement. There's progress."

Environmentalists, meanwhile remain skeptical. Once a free trade agreement is signed, they fear President Bush will lose sight of his vision of a sound environment.

"What assurances," McCloskey asks, "do we have that all of these promises won't be quickly forgotten?"

The Project at Moza Island

John A. Seeger
Professor of Management, Bentley College

Balachandran Manyadath
Deputy General Manager, Voltas International LTD, Abu Dhabi

Sameer had just finished a marathon four-hour meeting with Gulf Sargam's General Manager, Joe Fernandes. The meeting had proved, as expected, inconclusive. In his own matter-of-fact and dry manner, Joe had pointed out the magnitude of the loss on the project. A loss this size would wipe out the limited capital of the firm. It would also adversely affect future relations with Bank of Arabia. Worst of all, it would threaten the very existence of the firm. There was no choice but to negotiate for the release of the impounded funds.

Sameer Mustafa did not blame Joe for thinking the way he did. Nor did he blame his partner,

An Alling Foundation for Ethics Award case. Copyright © 1990 by Columbia University. Printed by permission of the Graduate School of Business, Columbia University.
Events portrayed in this case have been reproduced faithfully, without change. All names and locations have been disguised, with the knowledge and cooperation of the major companies involved.

Nawab, the Director and Chief Executive (D&CE) of Sargam International. (Figure 1 shows the relationships of the firms.) Nawab had called three times during the last 24 hours, urging Sameer to consider the issue carefully in view of the serious long term effects on the joint venture. Sameer Mustafa shared all the apprehensions. Yet he knew that his role demanded that he look at the issue more broadly. And he strongly believed that inherent values were as important to a company as the necessity to conduct business profitably and increase the wealth of the owners.

COMPANY BACKGROUND

Sameer Mustafa was a Palestinian national with a Jordanian passport and a business degree from the University of Texas. He had extensive connections with the government officials and businessmen in the East Arabian Sultanate, and his Gulf Trading Company had formed joint ventures with several leading multinational firms.

In 1948 Sohsee Brothers, Switzerland, and Sorabhjee Group, India, had joined together to form Sargam International Ltd., one of the ten largest multinational corporations in India. The company specialized in building large turn-key construction projects and had successfully completed many contracts in India, Africa, Southeast Asia and the Middle East. It employed 12,000 people, had 115 offices (108 of them in India), and in 1984 had sales revenues of $700 million (U.S.). Sohese Brothers and Sorabhjee Group still owned 40 percent of the shares of the company, the balance being held by the Indian public.

THE JOINT VENTURE

The salient features of the joint-ventures agreement between Gulf Trading Company and Sargam International were simple:

> 51 percent of Gulf Sargam's capital would be contributed by Gulf Trading Company and 49 percent by Sargam International. Total initial capital was Riyal (R)1,200,000.
> Gulf Trading Company would use its good offices to secure contracts from the Government and

private firms in East Arabia. It would also arrange for bank facilities for the execution of large projects. Guarantees against such facilities would be provided by Sameer Mustafa in his capacity as the Owner of Gulf Trading Company (Exhibit 1 defines the nature of the guarantees).

Sargam International would operate the joint venture and it would send one of its managers from India for this purpose. All other technical, administrative and support staff would also be provided by Sargam International.

Gulf Trading Company and Sargam International would share profits in the ratio of 55 percent for Gulf, to 45 percent for Sargam International. Losses, if any, would be equally shared.

ORGANIZATION

Joe Fernandes was the first General Manager of Gulf Sargam. A native of Goa, India (an area once claimed by Portugal), he was an engineer by profession. Joe had joined Sargam International in 1974 and had quickly climbed into middle management ranks. His outstanding performance on several complex construction projects made him the unanimous choice to head the new Middle Eastern joint venture.

At Gulf Sargam, Joe's technical and management staff—all from Sargam International—consisted of five field engineers, one financial analyst, and an administrative officer. All other hiring was done locally. Joe had extensive authority and powers for day-to-day operations of the firm, but he had to get the consent of Sameer Mustafa for "non-routine" decisions.

Four divisions reported to Joe Fernandes in 1986. The largest was Construction, which installed mechanical equipment for heating, ventilating and air conditioning (HVAC) as required by contract specifications. Sargam International held the exclusive area licenses for several world-wide brands of this heavy equipment. A separate Service division provided ongoing maintenance of HVAC equipment and serviced elevators and fire alarm systems. An Electrical division constructed and maintained electrical switchgear, transformers, transmission lines and equipment. A small Finance and Administration division completed the organization. Although total employment fluctuated with contracts, Gulf Sargam typically employed 300 to 400 people.

THE ECONOMIC ENVIRONMENT

The economies of the Middle East countries witnessed unprecedented growth during the oil boom period of the 1970's. But beginning in 1980 most of these countries experienced a glut of oil as demand for petroleum leveled off or declined. Their people realized the good times were far behind them. East Arabia was no exception. With the sharp drop in oil prices and the quota imposed by the Organization of Petroleum Exporting Countries (OPEC), the Government's revenues fell sharply, and its development construction activity dropped to 15 percent of the level sustained in the 1970's. For the few new construction projects that were brought to market for bids, competition was intense. A study undertaken by the Sultanate government during this period indicated that competition and the scarcity of business forced firms to accept contracts with margins as low as five to seven percent. Joe Fernandes reported to Sargam International:

> We have no choice in this matter. With a staff of over 250 people, we need projects to keep our people busy, to cover our overhead expenses, and to at least make a nominal profit for our partners. If we refuse to participate in such projects because of low margins, we would be without work and the cash reserves that we currently possess may carry us through only four months. You may say that this is not a healthy situation but we know that better times are ahead and we have to survive to make substantial profits in the future.

Between 1980 and 1983 Sargam won and completed several projects. Most of them were at very low margins, but through effective control and the dedication of its engineers, it was able to make nominal profits for the two partners. In the summer, 1984, however, the picture changed dramatically.

THE DEVELOPMENT PROJECT AT MOZA ISLAND

In June 1983, the Government decided to modernize the living facilities on Moza, an island 150 miles to the southeast of Abu Sidar, where the country's major liquified petroleum gas (LPG) plants were located. Moza was critically important to the Sultanate's income, but the harsh living conditions there and the primitive state of employee living quarters made it nearly impossible to attract good workers. Modernization was essential.

Moza was a contractor's nightmare. The island could only be accessed by air, flying time from Abu Sidar was one hour. In summer, temperatures averaged around 130°F and relative humidity rarely dropped below 95 percent. The air was severely polluted through minor but constant gas leaks, and reeked of hydrogen sulfide (the smell of rotten eggs). Government regulations therefore specified that the maximum "ON" period on the island for any worker should not exceed 12 weeks. Sandstorms were common during the nine summer months and the combination of temperature, humidity, and gas made the island one of the most difficult places in the world for heavy construction.

The East Arabian Sultanate invited bids from international construction firms in early 1983, and in September the contract for the Moza Island Project was awarded, at a price of R100,000,000, to Al Hasker Contracting Company, a Lebanese organization based in Athens. Hasker, primarily a civil engineering contractor, in turn, awarded various subcontracts to local firms in good standing. In April 1984, Gulf Sargam was awarded the mechanical subcontract at a price of R11,000,000—almost ten times the company's original capital. Joe Fernandes recalled:

> Both Sameer Mustafa and Nawab were unhappy over the low margin—only R1,000,000 estimated profit on the project. Nawab in particular felt that the margin was dangerously low for a project spanning 18 months at a remote location. He saw that a large portion of the contract value involved equipment from European sources, and that exchange rate variations would constitute a potent risk. But I convinced them that it was easier for the Company to execute one large project and earn R1,000,000 than to derive the same benefit from several smaller projects, each of a different type.

To supervise the construction job, the Government employed a prominent consulting firm with offices throughout the Middle East, called Yusuf al Yusuf. This firm in turn appointed Habib Sharif as Engineer-in-Charge and in May 1984, Sharif moved to Moza with his six field engineers. (Yusuf al Yusuf was affiliated with a London consulting firm; several of the supervising engineers were British.)

The contract documents stated that the Engineer-in-Charge was the final authority on every aspect of the project including, but not limited to, approvals of equipment, approval of finished work, approval of variation claims, issue of change orders, interpretation of delays, and grants of extension period. Because the client was the Government of the East Arabian Sultanate, disagreements between contractors and the Engineer-in-Charge could be resolved only by a complex civil arbitration system administered by the government in Abu Sidar.

Joe Fernandes selected Raghu Menon to serve as Moza Island Project Manager for Gulf Sargam. The two men had been associated on several previous projects and Joe knew Raghu as a dedicated, competent, and friendly individual, who got along well with supervising authorities. A good relationship with the Engineer-in-Charge was a necessity on such large projects.

EXECUTION OF THE MOZA ISLAND CONTRACT

From the beginning, Raghu noticed that Habib Sharif often went out of his way to strictly enforce the contract specifications on Gulf Sargam, but not on Al Hasker Construction Company. All construction contracts, by their nature, contain clauses with ambiguous meanings, open to various interpretations; the Moza Island contract was no exception. In normal practice, a contractor would win a favorable interpretation in some of these cases, and would lose in others.

At Moza Island, however, Habib consistently interpreted these clauses to the advantage of the East Arabian Sultanate government, insisting on absolute compliance with the smallest details. Construction drawings, for example, were routinely delayed and then returned for correction of flaws so minute they would not be noticed in normal practice (an example might be a misspelled word like "refrigeration"). In defense, Raghu filed

claims for reimbursement of the additional costs Gulf Sargam was forced to pay.

Raghu's weekly report to his head office during this first three months of the Moza Island project regularly reported Habib's attitude of extreme tolerance with Al Hasker Contracting Company and extreme intolerance with Gulf Sargam. His report on the episode of the X-ray welder provided an example:

> On August 4, 1984, our X-ray welder failed the welding test, even though photographs taken on a sample of 60 welds indicated 100 percent finishes. I was furious but helpless. The contract specifies that the British "Code of Welding Practice" sets our standards, and the Code defines the characteristics of both a perfect weld and a perfect workman. An acceptable workman must have basic communication skills in order to handle emergency situations. Habib argued that our worker lacked communication skills, and shut down the job.
>
> Our man had superb technical skills and was fluent in two languages—Hindi and Malayalam (the native tongue of Kerala province in India)—and he could converse in English too. But not well enough to suit Habib in August. We had to fly in a substitute welder. A month later we put the original man through the test again and he passed.

There was no comment about the welder from Habib Sharif, but in Raghu's eyes, a familiar picture was unfolding. Most construction consultants in the region expected to gain personally from their work, but none would ask an outright bribe. The consultant normally initiated the move with subtle "feelers" and awaited responses from the contractor. If a favorable response did not materialize, stronger signals were sent—each signal causing more disruption to the contractor's work than the earlier one. Raghu had faced this situation in several earlier projects and had, through a combination of diplomacy and skill, survived each situation. Sameer Mustafa had strong feelings on the subject:

> The fact that gratuities are often paid in the Middle East does not make it right to pay them. The practice exists because people—very often foreign corporations—pay when they are asked. There is no law saying you must pay. Taking part in a corrupt system is immoral and it perpetuates the corruption.

Giving in now would set a precedent for all my other operations.

Habib Shamir is playing a game with us. As always, we must make it clear we don't play by those rules. If we hold fast, the man will see we mean it. He will come around.

The game was a nightmare for Raghu. By June 1985, Gulf Sargam had incurred costs on an additional 9,000 man-hours due to delays in approval of drawings and rejection of site work by Yusuf al Yusuf. Gulf Sargam had filed variation claims totalling R1,000,000 but not a single one had been approved.

By early 1986, the game was still in progress. The delays imposed on Gulf Sargam had slowed the entire Moza Island project, but Habib had not wavered. Joe recalled Raghu's 80th progress report from the site, as the project neared conclusion:

We are 6 months behind schedule and the situation is worsening every day. Habib rarely approves our work the first time. Al Hasker Contracting Company's approvals are granted from the office without Habib even visiting the job site. Last evening the space frame (a structure covering an indoor swimming pool, made of lightweight aluminum tubing) erected by Hasker between grids E-H and 21–26 came crashing down. Fortunately, no one was hurt. Habib attributed this mishap to metal fatigue not to Hasker's workmanship.

Last night I met Habib at the club and decided to take him on directly as we must resolve this matter before the end of the project. Habib mentioned to me that Al Hasker Contracting Company has taken "good care" of him and he was accordingly reciprocating their gesture. He expressed surprise that Gulf Sargam had not followed the same policy for the last 12 months, a policy that was common in the Middle East and essential for the smooth execution of a project. But, he said, it was still not too late. He had authority to approve variation claims up to a total of R3,000,000 and Gulf Sargam could still make a profit. The cost of this consideration would be R300,000—10 percent of the claims approved for payment.

Habib Sharif argued that, as Engineer-in-Charge on the job, he had every right to enforce the spirit of the contract agreement on Gulf Sargam. He was only, logically, executing his responsibilities in the fullest sense. The firm had bid on the project on the basis of the specifications. They were given an opportunity to review every single part of the contract prior to acceptance and award of the bid. Gulf Sargam's price to his client was based on full knowledge of the job's terms and conditions, and should have allowed for all nuances; after all, the practice of providing gratuities to consultants was hardly new. If the company now wanted "softer" terms, to increase its profits, it was only reasonable to expect that they part with a small portion of the added reward. The government had budgeted a 20 percent increase in contract value, and to allow for change orders and variation claims from contractors, so the funds were available for disbursement, provided Habib, too, shared in the benefits.

Raghu Menon reported on his response to this argument:

I repeated our company's policy on such financial arrangements, but said I would relay Habib's information to higher authorities. Then I asked how we could be sure he really had the power to deliver. This morning, Habib approved one of my claims—the most dubious one of them all—for R77,000. He has the power.

. . . I am tired and would like to return to India. You cannot match knowledge and expertise with corruption and greed. I suggest that Sameer and you should think over this matter carefully.

CONCLUDING THE MOZA ISLAND PROJECT

On the last day of Ramadam, June 1986, Sameer Mustafa read Joe's internal memo several times. The final scenario was frightening. The Moza Island contract had been completed six months behind schedule, and the firm was exposed to the possibility that Habib could impose the contract's penalty clause. At ten percent of the contract's total value, that would add another R1,100,000 to Gulf Sargam's losses. Even without the penalty, the net loss was R2,138,000 as against an estimated profit of R1,000,000. Variation claims on the client totalled R2,860,000 and only a single one had been approved. Raghu had suffered from

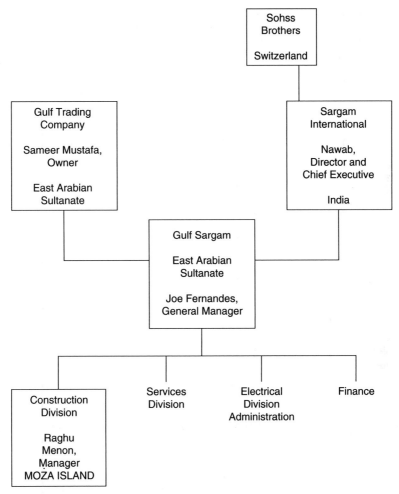

FIGURE 1
Organization of Gulf System

exhaustion and had returned to India a month earlier. His last progress report had been appended to Joe's memo, with a copy marked for Nawab:

> You have to decide on the variation claims before Habib finalizes the contract on June 30. I feel that we are in a hopeless position and we must accede to his request in order to recover our losses. Bear in mind that after this date we can pursue our claims only in the Abu Sidar arbitration committee, and I hope you will appreciate that we would be against the Government. Secondly Habib has, at this stage, every right to impose the penalty clause.

Joe fully endorsed Raghu's views on the matter. He added that as an employee of Sargam International he was obliged to take all possible steps to avoid losses to his parent company and, since all other avenues were exhausted, he believed that Sameer should endorse the payment to Habib. Sameer's partner, the D&CE of Sargam International, also had a point of view. Nawab's telephone calls had pointed out the Indian government's interest in the performance of joint ventures; financial results were monitored regularly, and a loss of this size would be difficult to

EXHIBIT 1

FINANCIAL RESULTS OF OPERATIONS, GULF SARGAM (IN RIYALS[a] 000)

	1980	1981	1982	1983	1984	1985	1986
Sales (Projects)	20	500	1,000	1,400	1,900	12,000[b]	6,000
Sales (Services)	500	600	1,800	2,000	1,800	2000	2,500
Sales (Total)	520	1,100	2,800	3,400	3,700	14,000	8,500
Cost of Sales[c]	320	503	1,643	1,830	2,070	11,470	6,300
Gross Margin	200	597	1,157	1,570	1,630	2,570	2,300
O & A	100	366	800	1,050	1,100	2,000	2,200
Net Profit	100	231	357	520	530	570	100

[a]Exchange rate 3.7 Riyals per U.S. dollar.
[b]Includes Rys 11,000,000 revenue from the Moza Island Project—Booked in 1985 with the concurrence of the auditors for Gulf Trading Co. and Gulf Sargam (a "Big Eight" CPA firm).
[c]Includes cost of goods sold for both projects and services.

Note: Personal Financial Guarantees Given by Sameer Mustafa (in Riyals)
1. Bank overdraft facilities
        (open line of credit)   3,000,000
2. Letter of credit
        (guarantees payment for goods received)   2,000,000
3. Tender guarantees
        (bid bond, forfeited if job not completed)   3,000,000

explain. While Sameer was a single owner, answering to no one, Nawab had important shareholders who would insist on knowing the details of Gulf Sargam's performance.

Sameer paused and shook his head. The decision was made. He picked up the telephone to summon Joe back to his office.

THE PROJECT AT MOZA ISLAND (B)

Sameer Mustafa held firm. The principle was clear, he said. If he succumbed to the pressure of a blackmailer at Moza Island, which was a relatively small part of his holdings in Gulf Trading Company, then the precedent would be set for all his divisions, and for all his managers. He might say it was "just this once," but every employee who ever faced a similar situation in the future would know he had given in once, and so might do it again.

Gulf Sargam closed its 1987 books with a loss of R2,233,000 on the Moza Island project. Habib Shamir invoked the penalty clause, but Gulf Sargam fought it successfully through the Abu Sidar arbitration procedure. Gulf Sargam also filed claims against the client for R2,300,000, for excess costs on work carried out under duress, beyond the contract's terms. The East Arabian arbitrator allowed R220,000 as reasonable, after a long and costly legal battle. The rest of the claims were dismissed as unsupported.

Gulf Sargam never fully recovered, but continued in business through 1990, earning enough to pay the interest on funds it borrowed to replenish its working capital after the loss. Relations between Sameer Mustafa and his partner Nawab were strained, however, and in mid-1988 Sameer sold Gulf Trading Company to a prominent East Arabian citizen and emigrated to Jordan. Raghu resigned to start a small consulting firm with some close associates. In July 1989, Joe Fernandes tendered his resignation from Gulf Sargam, feeling his future with the firm was limited. Nawab, however, refused to accept the resignation.

THE FUTURE
CORPORATE ETHOS

In Part Five we conclude the text with two important subjects. We begin in Chapter 10 with a discussion of emerging ethical issues in business. In Chapter 11, we conclude with a series of articles that challenge and reflect upon the moral corporation, including what insights and measures might be used to develop such an entity, and whether there might be limits to ethics and social responsibility. Both subjects constitute the "Future Corporate Ethos."

EMERGING ETHICAL ISSUES

In business ethics new issues are continually arising. The issues can develop due to the growth of new sectors, new pressures, or new technologies. The following section addresses several of these emerging ethical issues in business, although one could argue that the origins of these issues have been around for some time. As well, one could identify a much longer list of emerging issues; however, we have attempted to identify and select emerging ethical issues in business that we believe to be most significant and/or relevant at the present time. No doubt the importance of such issues and the ways in which they are addressed will change over time. The issues we have selected include ethical concerns over individual investors, the use of financial statements, ethical issues in the health care industry, ethics in relation to the information age, and issues arising in relation to competitive intelligence.

The first emerging issue involves the individual investor. A number of recent media stories have highlighted the potential exploitation of individual investors by brokers. Do individual investors require any additional protections from abuse? Would such additional protections or restrictions be unnecessarily paternalistic? Robert Frederick and W. Michael Hoffman in their article "The Individual Investor in Securities Markets: An Ethical Analysis" take the position that although the "at risk investor" is entitled to participate in the marketplace, there can be circumstances under which attempts to restrict access are justified. These circumstances would have to relate directly to the protection of the investor. They then provide some suggestions about how this might be achieved.

Although not necessarily new, one issue which is receiving greater exposure is the concern that individuals in corporations are collectively involved in accounting fraud, that of "cooking the books." In some cases the fraud may not be exposed for a number of years, but by the time it is discovered, shareholders might be out-of-pocket hundreds of millions of dollars. Lawsuits, government action, and jail time can follow. In discussing the phenomenon, Carl J. Loomis in his article "Lies, Damned Lies, and Managed Earnings" discusses some of the possible motivations that lead to such actions. The activity is often initially portrayed as merely "managed earnings." Whether the activity involves overstating revenues, or understating expenses, the devastating outcome can be the same. Loomis provides a number of examples of the fraud, and discusses how the U.S. government intends to crack down on such activity.

Another sector receiving greater ethical scrutiny is that of health care. With the explosive growth of for-profit managed care organizations, many people are beginning to raise serious concerns over how such organizations are ethically managed. Leonard Friedman and Grant Savage in their article "Can Ethical Management and Managed Care Coexist?" ask whether the principles of business ethics and biomedical ethics can be integrated into for-profit health care organizations. They discuss the conflict in terms of the adequacy and quality of health care for patients in managed care plans versus other plans. They conclude by proposing a model that seeks to consolidate both profit and nonprofit approaches.

Along with the arrival of the new millennium and the information age comes the arrival of new technologies. With new technologies come new ethical issues in business. Richard De George in his article "Business Ethics and the Information Age" first discusses his concern over what he sees as business essentially ignoring new issues arising from the use of information technology, and in particular commerce over the Internet. De George then identifies a number of ethical issues related to technology, including customer service, privacy, truthfulness and accuracy of information, and the protection of intellectual property.

The final article in Chapter 10 deals with the issue of competitive intelligence. Although not a new phenomenon, the growth of methods and means by which competitive intelligence can take place generates important issues over the ethical limits a firm can use to extract information about its competitors. In "Corporate Policy and Ethics of Competitor Intelligence Gathering," Lynn Sharp Paine outlines three of the most prevalent methods of questionable intelligence gathering: (1) those involving deceit or some form of misrepresentation; (2) those involving attempts to influence the judgment of persons entrusted with confidential information; and (3) those involving covert or unconsented to surveillance.

THE MORAL CORPORATION: REFLECTIONS AND CHALLENGES

In earlier parts of the text we explored some of the most important dilemmas faced by American business today. In the final chapter we reflect on some of the issues raised, and look toward the future of the American corporation. In particular, we wish to ask how the business organization of the future will meet the ethical challenges posed to it by society. Its ability to meet these challenges could prove crucial for business' very survival.

Observers of business sometimes speak as if business had no normative role to play in society, but this view is misleading. The legitimacy of business—the public's acceptance of its right to exist and its belief in the rightness of business as an institution—has always rested on business' connection with our highest social values and on its perceived contribution to what we view as the good life or the good society. While business has been essentially a profit-making institution, society has encouraged business to strive for profits in the belief that its doing so would promote the general welfare. Maximizing profits, then, has been the way in which business has discharged its social responsibilities. The invisible hand of the market system, it has been assumed, would function automatically to harmonize self-interest and bring about the good of society as a whole. And indeed business has made enormous contributions to American society. It has supported fundamental social values such as freedom of opportunity, productivity, growth, efficiency, and material well-being. It has encouraged enterprise and creativity. No society has a higher standard of living or such an abundance of goods and services.

The legitimacy of business still rests on public confidence in its contribution to a good society. In the past two decades, however, this confidence has eroded, and our conception of a good society has undergone some transformation. Observers of the American scene have concluded that business could be facing a genuine crisis in legitimacy.

Increasingly, people are challenging the belief that economic well-being is identical with social well-being, or that the former leads automatically to the latter. On the contrary, many now feel that some of the same values that contributed to our economic success—growth, productivity, consumption, the profit motive—have led to unacceptably high social costs, such as environmental damage. Many Americans have lost confidence in the ability of the market system automatically to bring about the general welfare. Rather than encouraging business in the single-minded pursuit of profit and waiting for social well-being to follow, the public is demanding that business broaden the scope of its concerns and assume a more active role in solving social problems and in working for a good society. The social responsibility of business today, the American public seems to be saying, no longer ends with its economic responsibility.

The view that business should assume social as well as economic responsibilities and take an active role in working toward social goals represents a challenge to the traditional understanding of the nature and functions of business. As we have worked through this text, we have seen the impact of this challenge in nearly every aspect of business activity. Traditionally, business organizations have been understood to be the private property of their shareholders. Managers were viewed as agents of the shareholders, bound by an agreement to serve their interests as the shareholders themselves would serve them—which, presumably, was to make a profit. As we have seen, however, the increasing separation of ownership and control and the decreasing confidence in the market system to contribute to public welfare have undermined the idea that management's sole responsibility is to shareholders.

Business is now expected to exercise responsibility toward a range of "stakeholders," including consumers, employees, and the public at large. For example, society now expects corporations not only to supply goods to consumers, but also to exercise care and foresight to make sure that the product is safe for consumer use. Manufacturers' liability for defective products has been extended to include even situations in which manufacturers could not have foreseen and prevented accidents. Society now demands that business avoid undue pollution and depletion of natural resources, and that it operate as much as possible in harmony with the natural environment. Business has been asked not simply to invest where it is most profitable, but to be sensitive to the social consequences of investment and to use its economic power to alleviate social injustice. It is expected not merely to provide jobs for members of the community, but also to offer a safe, healthy, and fulfilling work environment. Many thinkers have called for restrictions on the corporation's freedom to hire and fire, and on the obedience and loyalty it demands from its employees. Increasingly, business organizations are being asked to adopt hiring policies that help solve problems of racism and sexism. As the duties of business organizations are broadened to include social responsibilities, employees who resist or reveal illegal or unethical acts on the part of their employers may in fact be acting in the best interests of the corporation.

Many of the responsibilities corporations are being asked to assume are duties that, until now, have been associated with government. Traditionally, it has been government's job to promote social welfare. The job of business was to make money. Ironically, the government has also been expected to keep its interference with business at a minimum, passing only those regulations necessary to preserve freedom of competition. As public dissatisfaction with business performance has increased, however, the relationship between business and government has shifted. Business is now subject to a multiplicity of social regulations, many of which it feels are unfair and unnecessary. The restrictions placed on business by these regulations constitute a powerful argument for complying voluntarily with society's new demands.

How is business to respond effectively to public expectations, however, when institutional attitudes and forces encourage corporate managers to place profits first? Often today's manager is rewarded with success and esteem not for cutting down on the pollution of a local river or for improving employee satisfaction, but for maximizing profits. Indeed, as we have seen in many of the cases included in the text, pressures to sacrifice ethical concerns to profits are often severe. The corporation can create a closed context in which behavior that might be condemned elsewhere is found acceptable.

However, this need not be the case. Corporations can take steps to encourage ethical behavior by individuals and enhance an ethical corporate culture. In the first article in Chapter 11, "Gaining the Ethical Edge: Procedures for Delivering Values-driven Management," Dawn-Marie Driscoll and W. Michael Hoffman discuss some of these steps. They argue that corporations should address issues of institutional integrity as well as individual integrity. They point out that individuals do not operate in a vacuum: They gain purpose, meaning and direction from the organizations to which they belong. The social and ethical culture of a corporation can have a profound influence on persons who work for the corporation. Consequently, Driscoll and Hoffman argue that ethical people can be corrupted by bad organizations, just as people with questionable integrity can be uplifted by good ones.

So what exactly can corporations do to improve the ethical corporate culture? Driscoll and Hoffman provide a program involving the following steps: self-assessment; commitment from the top; codes of business conduct; training; resources for assistance; organizational ownership; consistent response and enforcement; audits and measurements; and finally, revision and refinements.

If a corporation follows the advice of Driscoll and Hoffman, then it will invest a great deal of time and energy in building an ethical corporate culture. Is it possible for a company to spend too much time and effort on ethics? Can the effort to be ethical have bad consequences? This is one of the questions Andrew Singer investigates in his article "Can a Company Be Too Ethical?" Singer notes that there is a narrower and broader sense of "ethics" as it applies to corporations. The narrower sense covers issues such as bribe taking, theft, and sexual harassment—all of which are clearly prohibited by most people's idea of ethics. In a broader sense, ethics includes issues such as affirmative action, empowering workers, and hiring the hardcore unemployed. It is this sense of "ethics," Singer says, that some corporate executives find problematic. The reason, these executives argue, is that such practices are more harmful to business than helpful. Often they have direct or indirect costs that detract from profits. The best place to be, some claim, is in the middle somewhere—neither too unethical nor too ethical.

An example of a company that may have been too ethical, according to Singer, is Control Data Corporation. Some analysts feel that Control Data devoted too many resources to socially responsible projects, and that this was a major factor in the declining fortunes of the company. There is, according to some of the people quoted in Singer's article, an ethical side of business and a profit side, and the two have to be balanced. If this is correct, however, it seems that becoming ethical is a business decision like any other—one is ethical as long as it is to one's benefit. When being ethical ceases to be beneficial, then ethics are discarded. Driscoll and Hoffman would not find this view congenial.

In a similar vein to Singer's article, Jon Entine raises serious concerns over companies engaging in the practice of "ethical marketing" in his article "Rain-forest Chic." The two companies he focuses on include Ben & Jerry's and The Body Shop, two companies known for their progressive activities. After critically examining a number of their so-called "socially responsible" practices, Entine provides additional insight into the accuracy of such claims. Some of the practices he examines include the "Save the Rain Forest" efforts of Ben & Jerry's through its rain forest crunch ice cream, and the "Trade Not Aid" program of The Body Shop. His article demonstrates that one must be careful before necessarily accepting all of the claims made by such progressive companies, as well as the dangers of setting high standards for assessment once such claims are made.

In her article "Feminist Morality and Competitive Reality: A Role for an Ethics of Care?" Jeanne M. Liedtka discusses whether there is any function that an "ethics of care" can play in enhancing the moral quality or effectiveness of organizations in the future. After providing some background to the ethics of care, she asks the question, "Can organizations care?" Such a question raises similar issues as the article "Can a Corporation Have a Conscience? by Goodpaster and Matthews in Chapter 3. She argues that for an organization to care, such caring must be focused entirely on persons, undertaken as an end in itself, essentially personal, and growth-enhancing for the cared-for. She argues that a caring organization holds a competitive advantage over others in relation to a variety of stakeholders.

In the final article of our text, we conclude with Joanne Ciulla's "The Importance of Leadership in Shaping Business Values." As one of the most important factors in setting an ethical tone for business, Ciulla talks about how leaders can translate values into action and how such values can endure within the organization. She discusses leadership theories and what they say or don't say about values. She concludes by focusing on a particular case study, that of P. Roy Vagelos, CEO of Merck & Company. In this case, Vagelos makes the decision to develop and give away a drug used to cure river blindness for millions around the world, despite the lack of any direct financial benefit to the company.

MINI-CASES AND CASES IN PART FIVE

The first mini-case in Part Five, "Andrew Ames," involves the dilemma of John who has received a sexually explicit joke via e-mail from Andrew. One can consider De George's article on ethics in the information age while discussing this mini-case. The last mini-case, "Bert Tanui," involves the dilemma of what to do when handed a competitor's proposal. The article by Paine on competitive intelligence can be instructive for this mini-case.

The cases in Part Five attempt to draw together many of the articles in previous chapters, as well as those in Chapters 10 and 11. In "From Volumes to Three Words: Texas Instruments," the company describes its own unique journey in the development of its code of ethics. The case provides a concrete example of some of the issues raised by Driscoll and Hoffman in their article. In "Levi Strauss & Co. and China," the company must address the issue of whether or not to pull out of China in order to comply with its own "global sourcing guidelines." Has the company acted appropriately according to the arguments raised by De George, Velasquez, and Donaldson in Chapter 9? What about the concerns raised by Sethi in his article regarding codes of conduct? Might Singer, based on his article, suggest that the company has gone too far? How might Entine, based on his article, evaluate the actions of Levi Strauss? In our final case, "The Case of the Contested Firearms," the ethical issues related to marketing and distributing a potentially dangerous product are presented. The case provides one final opportunity to critically examine the question of a company's social responsibilities.

CHAPTER 10

Emerging Ethical Issues

The Individual Investor in Securities Markets: An Ethical Analysis

Robert E. Frederick
Research Scholar, Center for Business Ethics, and Chair,
Department of Philosophy, Bentley College

W. Michael Hoffman
Executive Director, Center for Business Ethics, Bentley College

Securities markets are full of pitfalls for individual investors. Examples of fraud and regulatory violations in the markets are common. For instance, a recent *Business Week* cover story reports that investors are being duped out of hundreds of millions a years in penny stock scams in spite of SEC regulations.[1] A report in *The Wall Street Journal* on the Chicago futures trading fraud highlights the "danger of being ripped off in futures markets" by unscrupulous floor brokers filling customers'

"market orders"—a type of order that "individual investors should avoid using."[2]

But securities markets present risks to individual investors that go beyond clear violations of regulations and fraud. The above *Wall Street Journal* story, for example, also issued a more general warning to investors,

> Futures are fast moving, risky investment vehicles that are unsuitable for anyone who can't afford to lose and who doesn't have time to pay close attention to trading positions.[3]

Furthermore, it is not only the high risk futures and commodities markets that are perilous for investors. For example, the North American Securities Administration reports that "the securities industry isn't responding well to the problems of small investors in the wake of the stock market crash," problems such as poor execution of trades and being misled by brokers.[4] Even the bond markets, which in the past at least gave the outside appearance of stability, are in increasing turmoil. For instance, the SEC is now investigating the possibility that securities firms dumped billions of dollars of risky municipal bonds on individual investors because they were unable to sell them to institutions.[5] And MetLife is suing RJR-Nabisco on the grounds that individual investors were unjustifiably harmed when the A rated corporate bonds they purchased lost millions in value due to the junk bond financing of the RJR-Nabisco leveraged buyout.[6]

In light of these and many other examples that could be given, suppose the SEC announced that individual investors, for their own protection, no longer have access to securities markets. They are no longer permitted to buy stocks, bonds, or commodities or futures options. If this were to happen there surely would be a public outcry of protest, even moral outrage. The reasons for such outrage probably would revolve around the belief that some fundamental right had been violated, perhaps the presumed right that markets should be free and open so that everyone has an opportunity to better his or her position and enjoy the goods and services of society.

A quick look, however, reveals that not all markets have unrestricted access. Nor is there a generally accepted belief that any rights are being unjustifiably violated in such cases. In consumer markets, for example, individuals under a certain age are prohibited from voting, buying alcoholic beverages, and seeing certain movies. Regardless of age, not just anyone can buy a fully automatic rifle or order a few dozen hand grenades. In fact, not just anyone can drive a car, one must pass a test and be licensed to do that. Furthermore, even after being allowed to drive, this privilege can be revoked if it is abused. And, of course, none of our citizens is legally permitted to participate in certain drug markets, such as cocaine.

But it will be argued that there is good reason for these and other such restrictions. We are attempting to prevent people, the argument goes, from harming themselves or causing harm to others. This is what makes it morally permissible, or even obligatory, to restrict access to certain kinds of consumer products. The ethical principle here is that, when possible, persons ought to be protected from undue harm. Hence, the restrictions in question are justified.

Yet might not this be exactly the rationale behind a possible SEC ban against individual investors entering securities markets? Just as unre-stricted access to some drugs is thought to present unacceptable risks to consumers, trading in today's securities markets may present unacceptable risks to many investors, resulting in great financial rather than physical harm. And since we feel justified in prohibiting consumers from buying what we take to be highly dangerous drugs or other consumer products, shouldn't we, by analogy, be justified in prohibiting certain investors from buying highly risky financial instruments?

This question raises a number of issues. They include:

1. Exactly what kind of investor are we talking about?
2. Do all investors have a right to invest in the securities markets? If so, what kind of right do they have?
3. What sort of justification might be offered for restricting access to the securities markets for some classes of investors? Would it, for example, be a justification based on paternalism?
4. If some investors are restricted, how should it be done?

Although we cannot fully examine all these questions within the scope of this paper, we will briefly discuss each of them. At a later date we hope to give a more complete review of the issues affecting investors in securities markets.

(1) EXACTLY WHAT KIND OF INVESTOR ARE WE TALKING ABOUT?

One sort of investor frequently mentioned in discussions of possible harm is the "small investor." Although this is a very loosely defined notion as far as we can determine, there are several ways it could be made more precise. For example, a small investor could be defined as (a) an investor with assets of no more than X, or (b) an investor with a net worth of no more than X, or (c) someone with no more than X invested in the market, or (d) someone with no more than X% of their assets or net worth invested in the market. The advantage of these characterizations is that they are relatively straightforward. It should be possible to identify the members of these classes without too much trouble, and this would make it much easier to devise appropriate laws and regulations to protect them. They do not, however, delimit the particular class of investors we will be mainly concerned with in this essay. The amount of money that someone has in the market or the percentage of their assets they have invested is not, in our view, the central point at issue. It is, instead, whether some investors ought to be protected from the complexities and vicissitudes of the market despite the size of their portfolios.

Consequently, the type of investor we will be concerned with, and the type we take to be the most likely candidate for the SEC prohibition mentioned earlier, is one that (a) is at relatively *high risk,* where risk is a function of the probability of a certain market event occurring and the degree of harm the investor would suffer were the event to occur, and (b) an investor who is relatively *unsophisticated* about the functioning of the market and hence unappreciative of the degree of risk they face. For example, suppose Jones invests his life savings in high yield bonds issued to finance a LBO, and suppose a few months later the company that issued the bonds suddenly announces that it is going into Chapter 11 bankruptcy. The value of the bonds drops precipitously and for all practical purposes in a matter of hours Jones' savings are wiped out. If Jones did not realize that the high return he was initially receiving was a reflection of the risky nature of the bonds, then he would fall within the category of investors with which we are concerned even assuming he had several million dollars invested.

Although we have no firm data, it is our impression that the number of investors like Jones, which for lack of a better term we will call "at risk investors," is significant. This is due both to the sheer number of investors and to the increasing complexity of securities markets. Still, even if the number is not particularly large, the question remains whether at risk investors ought to be protected.

(2) DO AT RISK INVESTORS HAVE A RIGHT TO PARTICIPATE IN SECURITIES MARKETS?

Obviously at risk investors are legally permitted to invest in securities markets, but do they have a right to do so? And if they do, what kind of right is it? These questions are important since how they are answered will determine in large part what kind of justification will be required to restrict or suspend investments by at risk investors, or whether a justification is possible at all.

Since the word "right" is used in many different senses, we will give rough definitions of the sense in which we will use "right" and associated terms. A "claim right," as we will understand it, is a right established within a system of rules. To have such a right is to have a valid or justified claim for action or forbearance against some person or institution. The notion of a "liberty" is weaker than that of a right. To have a liberty is not to have a duty or obligation to act toward a person or institution in a certain way. Rights imply liberties, but one may have a liberty without an associated right. A still weaker notion is that of a "privilege." To have a privilege is to have revocable permission to act in a certain way.[7]

Claim rights, liberties, and privileges can be either legal or moral depending on whether the rules in question are established by legislative action or follow from a system of morality. It is important to see that legal rights and moral rights need not be the same. A moral right may not be recognized by law, and one may have a legal right to engage in an immoral action.

If at risk investors have claim rights to invest in the market, then the government has a corresponding duty not to interfere with their activity. On the other hand, if they have a liberty to invest, they have no duty not to invest. If they have a privilege, then they are permitted to invest but such permission can be withdrawn. Now, if at risk investors have a claim right to invest, as opposed to a weaker liberty or an even weaker privilege to invest, then the justification required for infringing on that right will be very different from that required if they have a liberty or privilege. Hence it is important to decide, as best we can, exactly which they have.

We believe a strong case can be made that at risk investors have a moral claim right to invest in the market, and that this right follows from the classic "right to freedom" that is so much a part of the American tradition. Donald VanDeVeer expresses the right as follows:

> Each competent person has an equal right to direct the course of his or her own life by choosing any alternative within the sphere of acts not wronging others.[8]

It is a consequence of this right that persons have the right to invest their money as they please in any legal financial instrument, provided that in doing so they do not wrongfully harm other persons. Put another way, it follows from the right to freedom that it is morally permissible for persons to choose to invest in any way they deem appropriate within the bounds of law and a proper regard for the wrongful effects their actions may have on the lives of others.

If this is correct, then any interference with this right, whether by some individual or government agency, is *prima facie* unjustified. There are, however, several objections that could be raised. One of them is that persons simply have no such moral right because they have no rights at all other than those granted by law. Thus, no moral right is violated if the legal right to invest is altered or eliminated. Another is that although persons have moral rights, they do not have the right to freedom that we have attributed to them. We will briefly consider each of these objections.

It is undeniable that there are legal rights grounded in the Constitution, the actions of legislative and regulatory bodies, case law, and so on. But are there rights independent of law? To deny that there are is to deny that persons can have valid claims for action or forbearance on the part of others not sanctioned by law. Therefore, though someone may appeal or request that other persons behave toward them in certain ways, they have no right to expect such behavior in the absence of legal requirement. If other persons do not do as we request, then we may be disappointed or chagrined, but we cannot complain that our rights have been violated, nor that we have been treated unjustly. If they do act as we request, then the proper attitude would seem to be gratitude, and not that we have received what is our just and rightful due.

However, to deny there are moral rights disregards two important points. The first is that legal rights are not always determined by strict appeals to law. There are many examples of case law where decisions appeal to morality and moral rights.[9] Also, documents like the Constitution establish the law, and are not derived from it. They depend on some moral conception of what the law ought to be.

The second point is that if all rights are legal, then there can be no basis for criticizing a legislative action as an unjust violation of right. Suppose, for example, that in a constitutional convention an amendment is passed prohibiting individuals from investing in securities markets. If we believe that this is not only an unfortunate error in judgment, but also that it is unjust and morally unacceptable, then we are appealing to some notion of rights that is outside the bounds of law.

Neither of these points conclusively show that persons have moral rights. They only point out the consequences of denying that there are such rights. For a more positive account of rights, we will turn to the second objection.

The second objection is that although persons may have moral rights, they do not have the right to freedom we proposed, either because they have rights other than the right to freedom or because they do not have the particular right to freedom we suggested. The first alternative has been defended by Ronald Dworkin, who argues that persons have a right to equality instead of a right to freedom.[10] We will not consider Dworkin's argument since we believe that the right to equality also implies investment rights for at risk investors. The second alternative can take two forms. The first is that not all persons have an *equal* right to freedom, and the second is that the right to freedom does not imply that persons may choose *any* alternative within the sphere of actions not wronging others. If some persons do not have a right to freedom, then it is no violation of their moral rights to deny them the opportunity to invest. And if the right to freedom does not imply the right to choose any alternative not harmful to others, then it may not imply the right to invest.

Do all competent persons have an equal right to freedom? The skeptic might deny they do since the only persons that have the right are those that deserve it because of their character, accomplishments, or abilities. We think the skeptic is mistaken, not because all persons are equally deserving in the skeptic's sense, but because all persons have an equal intrinsic value that is worthy of equal respect. And respect for the value of competent persons implies, at a minimum, respect for the choices they make as autonomous moral agents provided those choices do not wrongfully interfere with the choices of others. To do otherwise, to restrict their free choices in the service of some alleged good or end that they do not accept, is to accord them less than the respect they are rightfully due. It is to think of them as unworthy of the opportunity to direct their lives and achieve goals as best they can. It is to deny them the right, if we may so put it, to enjoy their mistakes as well as their successes.

An objection to our argument is that we have pointed to no universally shared property or characteristic in virtue of which all persons have equal value, and hence have provided no "proof" that they do. We grant the first part of the objection, but deny that the sort of proof demanded is necessary. There is no property of persons from which it logically follows that they have intrinsic value that is worthy of respect. The value of persons is "ultimate" or "foundational," as is the fact that such value is worthy of respect. Joel Feinberg puts it this way,

> "Human worth" itself is best understood to name no property in the way that "strength" names strength and "redness" redness. In attributing human worth to every one we may be ascribing no property or set of qualities, but rather expressing an attitude—the attitude of respect—toward the humanity in each man's person. That attitude follows naturally from regarding everyone from the "human point of view," but it is not grounded on anything more ultimate than itself, and is not demonstrably justifiable.[11]

Some may be tempted to conclude that since there is no proof that persons have value that is worthy of respect the only plausible position re-

maining is skepticism about the value of persons. But if there is no proof that persons have such value, neither is there proof that they lack it. It is unfortunate, but true, that neither we nor the skeptic can proceed without begging the question against the other side. Yet attributing worth to persons has one thing to recommend it that skepticism does not, namely, that it is a part of common moral experience that persons are considered worthy of respect. They are regarded as having valid claims for action or forbearance on the part of others, and as deserving the opportunity to accomplish their projects and achieve what they take to be valuable. If persons have intrinsic worth or value, then this part of our common experience has an explanation. If they do not, then at best it is difficult to understand.

There is one other objection to the right of freedom that we proposed. It is that even if all competent persons have an equal right to freedom, it still does not follow that they have the right to make any choice within the sphere of choices that do not wrongfully harm others. It does not follow, for example, that they have the right to make choices that seriously harm themselves. Intervention in such cases may be justified to prevent harm.

But is it? In order to decide, we must consider the possible justifications for interfering with the choices of others.

(3) WHAT SORT OF JUSTIFICATION MIGHT BE OFFERED FOR RESTRICTING THE INVESTMENTS OF AT RISK INVESTORS?

One kind of justification that might be proposed is paternalistic. By paternalism we roughly mean interfering with a person's actions or preferences by restricting their freedom of action or the range of choices normally available to them for the reason that such a restriction promotes or preserves their good, welfare, happiness, or interests. A paternalistic justification for restricting at risk investors would be that exposure to risk for many investors is too great to permit them to continue without some sort of protection that reduces the risk to an acceptable degree. For certain investors an acceptable degree may be no risk at all. For others some risk may be permissible. In either case, the argument goes, as long the intent of intervention is to protect or promote the good of at risk investors, and as long as it does not wrong other persons, then intervention is at least permissible and may be obligatory. It is only in this way that harm to many investors can be prevented.

The standard objection to paternalistic justifications is something like this: If people choose to run the risk to gain what they believe will be the rewards, who are we to interfere? From where do we derive a special dispensation to overrule their choices and interfere with their lives?

Although there is a kernel of truth in this objection, it is much too facile. Some paternalistic acts are clearly justified. Paternalistic reasoning is commonly used to justify restricting the choices of children and people judged incompetent or otherwise unable rationally to consider the consequences of their acts. Moreover, paternalistic justifications are not obviously unreasonable even in cases where the competence of the person is not in question. It is at least initially credible that some consumer products, such as prescription drugs, are not in unrestricted circulation precisely because of paternalistic reasons.

Let us confine our discussion to those persons ordinarily taken to be competent and rational. We still do not believe that paternalism *per se* justifies restricting at risk investors that fall within this category. One reason is that it may be impossible to find out just what the good or welfare of an individual investor is. Not only is there the thorny problem of trying to reach a common and precise understanding of the vague idea of the "good" of a person, there are immense practical difficulties in discovering whether a certain individual's good is served by restricting his or her access to the market. There may be situations where an individual's good is not served, and intervention in those cases would be a wrongful violation of his or her rights.

But suppose regulators do know the good of some individuals. Would paternalism then justify intervening to preserve or promote their good? We believe not in cases where regulators and the person in question have differing conceptions of that person's good. Even if regulators happen to know a person's "true" good better than he or she does themselves, imposing on that person a conception of his or her good they do not accept is not justified. Regulators may attempt to persuade at risk investors to take a different course or provide them with information that they need to make an informed decision, but it is not permissible to deny them the right to direct their lives. VanDeVeer expresses this point so well that it is worth quoting him at length.

> To treat competent persons as beings with relevant wants and needs, like ourselves, is an advance over treating them as inanimate objects, as "mere things," to be used as a natural resource. However, to treat them *as if* they lack what we have and expect to pursue, namely a conception of the good, is to deny them a certain *moral equality*. For if, as paternalistically inclined agents we invasively interfere with nonconsenting competent persons when they wrong no others, we act on our own conception of the good while subverting the efforts of others to act in a like manner. If we believe their vision myopic, their conception defective, as we might and for good reasons, there is no good reason why we may do more than engage in fair, open, attempts to dissuade. . . . To act in a contrary way is to act as if others are clay to be sculpted and not, as we regard ourselves, active sculptors of unique lives.[12]

Although paternalism as characterized thus far does not justify interference with the choices of at risk investors, there are circumstances in which intervention is justified. This can best be explained by using an example not related to investing. Suppose Jones mistakenly believes the food he is about to eat is wholesome but we have good reason to think it is contaminated with botulism. As he raises the fork to his mouth we only have time to strike it away. At first he is angry, but after we explain the reason for our action he is grateful. The act of striking the fork away is an example of paternalistic intervention since it is done for Jones' good but against his wishes. It seems obvious, however, that we acted properly. Intervention in this case is justified since if Jones were fully aware of the circumstances he would act differently or would agree to have us intervene on his behalf. He would consent to our action. Hence, intervention here respects his right to freedom since it is compatible with his goals and does not force upon him some version of his good he would not accept.

Note that it is not merely our superior knowledge of the situation that justifies interference, but also our judgment that Jones would agree that our actions preserve or promote his good. The case would be different were Jones attempting suicide instead of trying to have a decent meal. Paternalistic intervention may not be justified when a person voluntarily undertakes an action harmful to him or herself, provided that person has a reasonably complete understanding of his or her circumstances and the consequences of the action. But it is at least *prima facie* justified, we suggest, when an action is based on incomplete information and thus is, in one sense, less than fully voluntary.[13]

Now suppose there are compelling grounds to believe that some otherwise competent investors are unappreciative of the high degree of risk they face, and that if they were presented with information about those risks they would act either to reduce or eliminate them, or would consent to having restrictions placed on the kinds of investments they could make. Since they would consent to intervention or act differently were they fully aware of the circumstances, intervention on their behalf is justified just as it was justified for Jones. Their rights are not violated since nothing is imposed on them that they would not consent to were they fully aware of the dangers they faced.

A major difference between the Jones case and at risk investors is that we dealt with Jones as an individual, but a regulatory or legislative body would have to deal with at risk investors as a group. There simply is no way to reach them all individually. Furthermore, although such bodies may be able to make reasonable assumptions about the kinds of risks acceptable to most at risk investors, and about the kinds of restrictions to which most of them would agree, it seems inevitable that there will be some investors that would not consent to restrictions because, for example, they have an unusual conception of their good or welfare, or because they find the restrictions highly offensive. For these people restrictions on investing will impose a foreign conception of their good on them and thus is not compatible with their right to direct their lives.

It may seem natural at this point to use utilitarian reasoning to justify preserving the good of many at risk investors at the cost of infringing on the rights of a few. We will try to show that this move does not justify intervention.

Utilitarianism is roughly the view that a morally right action is one that achieves the greatest balance of good over harm for all those affected by the action. Classic utilitarianism defined "good" as pleasure and "harm" as pain. Other definitions have been proposed, but the basic idea behind all forms of utilitarianism is that there is some goal, whether it be pleasure or something else, that all our actions should promote as much as possible. Stated in this unsophisticated form utilitarianism does not justify restrictions on at risk investors. As Ronald Dworkin argued in another context,

> The prospect of utilitarian gains cannot justify preventing a man from doing what he has a right to do. . . . There would be no point in the boast that we respect individual rights unless that involved some sacrifice, and the sacrifice in question must be that we give up whatever marginal benefits . . . [we] . . . would receive from overriding these rights when they proved inconvenient. So the general benefit cannot be a good ground for abridging rights. . . .[14]

Simple utilitarianism focuses only on promoting the good of a certain group considered as a whole. If the rights of individuals must be sacrificed for the sake of the good, then so be it. But we believe, with Dworkin, that rights—justified claims—cannot be overridden for the general good, for that would be to ignore the fact that those claims *are* justified, that there is a moral duty to respect them. It seems to us morally inconsistent to admit, on the one hand, that persons do have justified claims, and then on the other to bypass those claims in the service of some thing else.

Of course, advocates of more sophisticated forms of utilitarianism have responses to our argument. They might claim, for example, that protecting the rights of individuals does promote the long term good of the group, or that in some cases the good of the group overrides the rights of individuals. Unfortunately we cannot analyze these more sophisticated versions of utilitarianism without turning this paper into a book. Thus in the paragraphs to follow we will assume only the simple version described above, with the proviso that our arguments are incomplete and may have to be modified.

To return to the main question, we have argued that paternalistic intervention is justified for one class of at risk investors, but not for another class, since it preserves the rights of the first class but not the second. If this is correct, then intervention both preserves the rights of some investors and promotes their good at the cost of infringing on the rights of other investors. Now, recall that in our initial description of paternalism we said that paternalistic intervention might be justified provided no one is wrongfully harmed. In this case, however, some persons would be wrongfully harmed. Therefore, although the motivation for intervening may be paternalistic, strictly speaking this is not an example of justified paternalism. But leaving that aside, is intervention justified anyway?

If the *reason* given for intervening is promoting the good of at risk investors as a group, then, as we have tried to argue, it is not justified. Suppose, however, the reason is not only that the good of some investors is promoted, but that there is a duty to intervene to protect certain *rights,* in particular, the right of investors not to be harmed. The argument would go something like this: There is good reason to believe that some at risk investors would consent to having restrictions placed on them to protect their financial position and prevent them from suffering financial harm. Since it is a basic function of government to protect its citizens from harm, there is a duty to protect these investors. Hence, placing restrictions on their investment activities is justified even though such restrictions may violate the right of other investors to direct their lives as they see fit.

If this argument is plausible, then there is a conflict of rights between two groups of at risk investors. This is a genuine moral dilemma that can only be resolved by deciding whose rights are to prevail. We believe it should be the right not to be

harmed. An analogy with prescription drugs may be helpful here. One reason there are restrictions on access to drugs is to prevent harm to persons who do not know how to use them correctly. These restrictions are justified, in our view, even supposing there are some individuals willing to take the risk. The right to freedom of this latter group should be and should remain a serious consideration in devising restrictions on drugs, but it does not override the right of others not to be exposed to excessive risk and possible serious harm.

The same holds true of at risk investors. The right of some of them not to be exposed to excessive risk and possible serious financial harm overrides the right of others to invest without restrictions. We emphasize, however, that the right to freedom cannot be lightly dismissed, and must be given due consideration when formulating policies and regulations governing the markets. We will suggest some ways this might be done in the next section.

There are other justifications for restricting at risk investors that we have yet to mention. For example, restrictions might be imposed since losses incurred by at risk investors are likely to cause hardships on family members. Or there might be restrictions on at risk investors to prevent their being wrongfully harmed at the hands of others. Each of these alleged justifications deserves a full discussion. However, if successful they would apply to a much broader class of investors than at risk investors, so we will postpone discussing them until another occasion.

Before moving to the next section we must consider an objection to our argument. The objection is that we have proved too much. We argued that restrictions are justified since some investors' right not to be harmed takes precedence over the right to freedom of other investors. But this argument, in a more general form, applies to many high risk activities other than investing. It would cover everything from skydiving to scuba diving, and hence could be used to place excessive restraints on free choice. Moreover, what we seem to have forgotten in our argument is that not all risk is undesirable, nor is all risk unavoidable. Investing in securities markets is just one of many activities that are risky by their very nature. If risk were eliminated, the very nature of investing and of the markets would be irrevocably changed, and the consequences of such a change could be disastrous for everyone.

We agree that not all risk can or should be eliminated from the securities markets, not even for at risk investors. We also concede that our argument applies to activities other than investing. But there may be a way to modify the argument to take account of the objection. Let us say that a risk associated with a certain activity A is a *reasonable* risk provided that it cannot be eliminated without changing the very nature of the activity itself; otherwise it is unreasonable. For example, a reasonable risk associated with skydiving is riding in an airplane. An unreasonable risk is jumping out of the plane with an improperly packed parachute. But to say that a risk is reasonable does not imply that it should be permitted. Personal injury may be a reasonable risk of gang warfare, but such activities are not permissible. So let us say that a *socially permissible activity* is one that (a) does not impose undue risk of harm on those not participating in the acitivity and, (b) is such that eliminating the activity altogether would place excessive limits on personal freedom, and (c) is such that there are procedures in place for controlling and minimizing unreasonable risks associated with the activity. Now an *acceptable* risk can be defined as a reasonable risk associated with a socially permissible activity; otherwise the risk is unacceptable.

These definitions need clarification and elaboration, but we hope that the basic idea is moderately clear. What we suggest concerning the securities markets is not that all risks be eliminated for at risk investors, but that all unacceptable risks be eliminated. Assuming this would not change the nature of the markets, and since this standard of eliminating risk can be applied to other socially permissible activities, we believe it blunts the force of the objection levelled above.

(4) IF SOME INVESTORS ARE RESTRICTED, HOW SHOULD IT BE DONE?

Since we are not experts in the regulation of securities markets, the best we can do here is make a few suggestions that seem to us worthy of additional investigation. It is a basic premise, essential for any just system of regulation and law, that relevantly different classes of persons be treated in relevantly different ways. Hence, it clearly would be unjust to restrict the activities of all investors to protect some of them. It also follows from this basic premise that distinctions must be drawn within the class of at risk investors. It may turn out in the end that there is no workable method of protecting some at risk investors while preserving the rights of all of them, but it would be a mistake to begin with this assumption.

In light of this it might be suggested that the only plausible course of action is to make sure that at risk investors have all the information they need to make investment decisions. This has at least three advantages. The first is that providing information does not seriously infringe any rights. And establishing stringent policies to ensure that the information is received also may be reasonable. For example, suppose that to demonstrate a minimum level of competence persons must pass an examination before investing, just as they have to pass a driving exam before driving. Different kinds of exams could be given for different kinds of investments. Would such a procedure violate any rights? It certainly would be costly and inconvenient, but we doubt that it is an inordinate restriction on the right to freedom.

A second advantage is that providing information is already one function of the Securities and Exchange Commission. According to the Commission's pamphlet "Consumers' Financial Guide" the three main responsibilities of the Commission are:

1. To require that companies that offer their securities for sale in "interstate commerce" register with the Commission and make available to investors complete and accurate information.
2. To protect investors against misrepresentation and fraud in the issuance and sale of securities.
3. To oversee the securities markets to ensure they operate in a fair and orderly manner.

Although the pamphlet goes on to advise investors that "whatever the choice of investment, make sure that you have complete and accurate information before investing to ensure that you use your funds wisely," it also emphasizes that the SEC does not see itself as the guarantor of investments:

> Registration . . . does not insure investors against loss of their investments, but serves rather to provide information upon which investors may base an informed and realistic evaluation of the worth of a security.

Thus providing information to at risk investors is consistent with the mission of the SEC and would not require massive restructuring of the Commission.

The third advantage is that providing information would be the most direct way to discover whether investors would consent to restrictions. Earlier we argued that restrictions on some at risk investors are justified because they would consent to intervention if they were fully aware of the risk they faced. But instead of imposing regulations based on what investors *would* do were they to have all the relevant information, it is preferable to give them the information whenever possible and see what they *actually* do. This would avoid the danger of imposing on them a conception of their good that they do not accept.

We agree that providing information to at risk investors is a good idea, and propose that methods be initiated that ensure that investors receive the information, rather than just having it available for those that seek it out. However, this may not be enough to eliminate unacceptable risks for at risk investors. Consider the prescription drug market again, and assume that the FDA made strenuous efforts to provide consumers with complete information about drugs. Supposing for a moment that it is legally permissible for consumers to buy drugs, as it is in some countries, this might be enough to eliminate unacceptable risk of harm from drugs for the few that had the time, energy, and expertise to use the information. But for most people it would be an overwhelming blizzard of paper that would be of no real use. As Steven Kelman has argued, the cost of organizing and understanding the information may be so high that the most sensible course of action for most people would be to assign their right to select drugs to some individual or institution with special exper-

tise, provided the choice was made with their best interests in mind.[15] Merely providing information about drugs does not protect persons from harm unless the information is understood. When it appears unlikely that a large class of people will devote the time needed to understand it, then it is appropriate, we believe, to place legal restrictions on their choices. This protects them from harm, but is not an intolerable limitation of freedom.

The same reasoning applies in the securities markets. So much information is available and it is so complex that for many investors beyond a certain point it would be too costly to make the investment in time required to assimilate it all. Having "complete and accurate information," as the SEC suggests, is not enough. Leaving aside the issue of how one determines whether it is complete and accurate (note that not even the SEC does that), there remains the problem of understanding it well enough to make a wise investment decision. Perhaps it could be done, but would it be done by most at risk investors? We are inclined to think not. So we suggest that, just as with prescription drugs, at risk investors be required by law to engage the services of an expert. This would go a long way toward eliminating unacceptable risks for them, and given the significant possibility of harm many investors face, we do not feel it would be an excessive restriction on their freedom. Exceptions would have to be made for those investors willing to become expert in the markets (since they would no longer meet the definition of an at risk investor), and some system of qualifications would need to be established to identify investment counselors capable of advising the other investors.[16]

None of this would be easy. A sophisticated and fine grained system of regulation would be required to classify different types of investors, and often the relationship between investors and investment counselors would change significantly. For example, if in the best judgment of a counselor a certain type of investment is inappropriate for a particular at risk investor, then it would not be permissible for the counselor to make the investment even if the investor insisted. The whole point is to reduce unacceptable risk, and if the investor could override the counselor's advice the system would be subverted.

The counselor could present a range of choices to the investor, some of them more risky than others, but the counselor would have the power to rule out some possibilities. The association between investor and counselor thus would be much more like that between patient and doctor than it is presently.

It is easy to imagine problems, perhaps insuperable problems, with our proposal. It would be expensive, time consuming, and complicated. No doubt there would be considerable public and political opposition. But this proposal, or some version of it, may be one way to accommodate the diverse interests of investors.

There are other ways one might try to reduce unacceptable risks for at risk investors. We will mention only one of them. In recent years strict product liability has become common in consumer markets. Suppose an analogous system were established in financial markets; that is, suppose that for some classes of investors, and possibly only for some types of financial instruments, strict financial product liability applied. This would protect investors, but it also might change the nature of the markets. Whether for better or worse is something it would be imprudent for us to speculate on.

To end, we have outlined some arguments in favor of protecting at risk investors by restricting their investments, and have suggested ways additional protection might be implemented. It is plain that much more work needs to be done on both topics. Moreover, there are many issues we have not discussed, for example, whether protecting at risk investors would place an unreasonable burden on other investors, or whether a more effective way to protect at risk investors would be to place additional restrictions on those who sell securities. The best we can hope for, at this stage of our investigation, is that what we have done thus far will serve as a springboard for further discussion and analysis.

NOTES

1. 'The Penny Stock Scandal', *Business Week* 23 Jan. 1989, pp. 74–82.
2. 'Investors Can Take a Bite Out of Fraud', *The Wall Street Journal* 24 Jan. 1989, p. C1.
3. *The Wall Street Journal* 24 Jan. 1989, p. C1.
4. 'Many Crash Complaints Unresolved', *The Wall Street Journal* 10 Oct. 1988, p. C1. (For additional information on problems faced by individual investors, see John L. Casey, *Ethics in the Financial Marketplace,* Scudder, Stevens & Clark, New York, 1988.)
5. 'SEC Studies Municipals In Trusts', *The Wall Street Journal* 11 Oct. 1988, p. C1.
6. 'Bondholders are Mad as Hell—And No Wonder', *Business Week* 5 Dec. 1988, p. 28.
7. Joel Feinberg, *Social Philosophy* (Prentice-Hall, Inc. Englewood Cliffs, 1973), pp. 55–6. These definitions are based on the ones given by Feinberg.
8. Donald VanDeVeer, *Paternalistic Intervention* (Princeton Univ. Press, Princeton, 1986), p. 59.
9. For examples see Norman Bowie, 'Fair Markets', *Journal of Business Ethics* 7, No. 1 and 2 (1988), pp. 89–98.
10. Ronald Dworkin, *Taking Rights Seriously* (Harvard Univ. Press, Cambridge, 1978), see chapter 12.
11. Feinberg, *Social Philosophy* p. 94.
12. VanDeVeer, *Paternalistic Intervention* p. 113.
13. Our argument here follows that given by VanDeVeer.
14. Ronald Dworkin, 'Taking Rights Seriously' in *Rights,* ed. David Lyons (Wadsworth Publishing Co., Belmont, CA, 1979), p. 100.
15. Steven Kelman, 'Regulation and Paternalism', in *Ethical Theory and Business* eds. T. L. Beauchamp and N. E. Bowie (Prentice Hall Inc., Englewood Cliffs, 1988), p. 153.
16. W. Michael Hoffman and Ralph J. McQuade, 'A Matter of Ethics', *Financial Strategies & Concepts* 4, No. 2 (1986), pp. 47–9.

Lies, Damned Lies, and Managed Earnings

Carol J. Loomis
Reporter, *Fortune Magazine*

Someplace right now, in the layers of a *Fortune* 500 Company, an employee—probably high up and probably helped by people who work for him—is perpetrating an accounting fraud. Down the road that crime will come to light and cost the company's shareholders hundreds of millions of dollars.

Typically, the employee will not have set out to be dishonest, only to dodge a few rules. His fraud, small at first, will build, because the exit he thought just around the corner never appears. In time, some subordinate may say, "Whoa!" But he won't muster the courage to blow the whistle, and the fraud will go on.

Until it's uncovered. The company's stock will drop then, by a big percent. Class-action lawyers will leap. The Securities and Exchange Commission will file unpleasant enforcement actions, levy fines, and leave the bad guys looking for another line of work.

Eventually someone may go to jail.

And the fundamental reason, very often, will be that the company or one of its divisions was "managing earnings"—trying to meet Wall Street expectations or those of the boss, trying also to pretend that the course of business is smooth and predictable when in reality it is not.

Jail? This is not a spot that CEOs and other high-placed executives see themselves checking into, for any reason. *Jail for managing earnings?* Many corporate chiefs would find that preposterous, having come to believe that "making their numbers" is just what executives do. Okay, so the pressure might lead some of them to do dumb (but legal) things—like making off-price deals at the end of a quarter that simply steal from full-priced business down the road. Who cares? Others might even be driven to make hash of the rules that publicly owned companies are required to abide by, Generally Accepted Accounting Principles, known as GAAP. Sure, that might mean crossing a legal line, but so what?

Well, the "so what" is Arthur Levitt, chairman of the SEC and the grand enforcer when it comes to GAAP. Last year, with his attorneys and accountants digging into Bankers Trust and Cendant and W.R. Grace and Livent and Oxford Health Plans and Sunbeam and Waste Management—and who knows what other big companies the SEC isn't talking about—Levitt finally reached the gag point. He simply declared war on bad financial reporting.

The opening shots came in a New York speech, "The Numbers Game," that Levitt gave last September to CPAs, lawyers, and academics. Lynn Turner, chief accountant of the SEC (and formerly a partner of Coopers & Lybrand), recalls that as Levitt started to speak, waiters whipped around serving salads, and people began to eat. "Then," says Turner, "two amazing things happened. First, people put down their forks and started listening very hard. Then—and this just never happens—they pulled out notepads."

What they heard was the SEC chairman committing his agency in no uncertain terms to a serious, high-priority attack on earnings management. Since then several SEC officials have gone out of their way to state that there are many managements doing their accounting honestly, but that night the chairman spared no one. He roundly criticized a business community that greeted "accounting hocus-pocus" with nothing more than "nods and winks." Among the accounting tactics he blasted were improper revenue recognition, unjustified restructuring charges, and the artifices called "cookie-jar reserves." Accountants know all of these (and more) as "accounting irregularities"—*intentional* misstatements in financial reports, which Levitt and his team regard as very often the equivalent of fraud.

In a recent conversation with *Fortune,* Levitt left no doubt that he intends to keep the heat on. What's at stake, he says, is nothing less than the credibility of the U.S. financial-reporting system, traditionally thought to be the best in the world. It will not now, he vowed, be undermined by managements obsessed with making their numbers. "It's a basic cultural change we're asking for," he said, "nothing short of that."

For those who can't get with the program, the punishment increasingly could be criminal prosecution. The SEC does not itself have the ability to bring criminal actions, so the chairman has been out jawboning people who do, like Attorney General Janet Reno and various U.S. Attorneys. Levitt would particularly like to see these folk nail brokers who cheat investors, but there are accounting-fraud cases in which he wants indictments as well.

One U.S. Attorney in tune with the SEC's tough new line is Mary Jo White, of New York's Southern District. White has brought a string of accounting-fraud actions and says she still has "a lot" in the pipeline. Her district has two bigtime criminal cases even now—Livent and Bankers Trust, both stemming from managed earnings. However, as White points out, "On the criminal side, we don't use that polite a term; we call it accounting fraud or 'cooking the books.' " White has also prosecuted smaller cases that she prizes for their deterrence value. Object lessons don't work in most areas of the law, she says, but "significant jail time" for a white-collar executive is apt to give others of his ilk severe shakes.

What qualifies as significant? In March, Donald Ferrarini, the 71-year-old former CEO of a New York insurance brokerage, Underwriters Financial Group (UFG), got 12 years. (He is appealing.) Ferrarini had cooked the most basic recipes in the book: He overstated revenues and understated expenses, a combo that magically converted UFG from a loser into a moneymaker. The scam, uncovered in 1995, cost shareholders, policyholders, and premium finance companies close to $30 million.

One reason Ferrarini faces such a long stretch in jail is that sentencing guidelines treat $30 million as a lot of money. And so they should, considering that there really isn't much difference between $30 million lost in an accounting fraud and the same amount lifted in a bank robbery. But that sum is peanuts compared with the vast sums lost over the past couple of years as one big accounting scandal after another reeled out. The toll doesn't suggest that the next execs to be sentenced for accounting crimes should expect much in the way of leniency.

Whether all this is enough to change the culture at the top of U.S. business remains to be seen. In taking on earnings management, Levitt is threatening a practice many CEOs regard as part of their bill of rights. The former communications director of a prominent *Fortune* 500 company remembers the blast his CEO once let loose at the financial managers and lawyers trying to tell him that the quarterly earnings he proposed to announce weren't accurate. Roared the CEO: "Stop fooling around with my numbers! The No. 1 job of management is to smooth out earnings."

Or take this anecdote out of General Electric's recent history. In 1994 the *Wall Street Journal* ran a long, front-page story detailing the many ways that Jack Welch and his team smoothed earnings at GE. Among them were the careful timing of capital gains (which is a permissible way of managing earnings, says the SEC) and the creative use of restructuring charges and reserves (which sometimes is not). Immediately, so a GE staff member told a *Fortune* writer, GE people got calls from other corporations—specifically, according to the account, AIG, Champion International, and Cigna—saying, "Well, this is what companies do. Why is this a front-page story?"

One would have hoped the answer was obvious. The fundamental problem with the earnings-management culture—especially when it leads companies to cross the line in accounting— is that it obscures facts investors ought to know, leaving them in the dark about the true value of a business. That's bad enough when times are good, like now. Let business go south, and abusive financial reporting can veil huge amounts of deterioration.

The cult of consistent earnings imposes opportunity costs as well. To start with, even the least offensive kinds of earnings management take time, mainly because executives have to decide which of several maneuvers to go for. Then there are the related tasks, especially the need to talk extensively to analysts and massage their earnings-per-share expectations. Custom says those expectations must not be disappointed by even a penny, since a management's inability to come up with a measly cent, when so many opportunities to manipulate earnings exist, will often be interpreted as a stark sign of failure and a reason to bomb the stock.

One well-regarded *Fortune* 500 CEO said recently that he probably spends 35% of his time talking to analysts and big shareholders, and otherwise worrying about the concerns of the Street. Would his company's bottom line be better off if he devoted that time to the business? "Of course," he answered. But there is always the stock price to think about—and naturally the CEO's compensation is structured to make sure he thinks about it a lot. The television show *Fantasy Island* had a line, "The plane! The plane!" In the world of fantasy earnings, the rationale is always "The stock! The stock!"

What has sparked Chairman Levitt's war on falsified earnings reports, however, isn't the occasional distracted CEO. It's the continual eruption of accounting frauds. The accumulation of cases, in fact, keeps suggesting that beneath corporate America's uncannily disciplined march of profits during this decade lie great expanses of accounting rot, just waiting to be revealed.

Right now, among big cookers of books, the grand prize for rot is shared by the two caught up in criminal proceedings, Livent and Bankers Trust. Livent, for its part, vaporized close to $150 million in market value last August when new controlling shareholders (among them Hollywood bigwig Michael Ovitz) asserted that Livent's books had been cooked for years. Prosecutors went on to charge the company's former CEO, *Ragtime* and *Fosse* producer Garth Drabinsky, with creating another showpiece, in which Livent starred as a thriving operation when in reality it was crumbling. Indeed, Livent kept looking presentable only because financial facts were being whisked around like props in a stage set. Drabinsky was indicted in January and even earlier had exited from the U.S., stage north: He is holed up in his homeland, Canada, where he has denied wrongdoing and has said he will fight extradition proceedings. He has also sued both Livent and its auditors, KPMG.

At Bankers Trust, prosecutors say that employees working in the securities-processing business in the mid-1990s met top management's call for good results by misappropriating money that belonged to security holders but hadn't been claimed (and that was required to be escheated to the state). The funds were used to cover the department's general expenses, a procedure that increased profits. The evidence has already caused Bankers Trust to plead guilty and agree to a $63 million fine. In addition, at least three former BT managers, including B.J. Kingdon, the boss of the division that included securities processing, are reported to have been issued "target letters" that signal they may be indicted.

Kingdon, through his lawyer, neither confirms nor denies the existence of a target letter. The lawyer says Kingdon has reacted to reports about this matter with "astonishment" and "outrage." Kingdon, says the lawyer, was not aware that anything unlawful was being done. The lawyer also says that "whatever took place, took place in daylight, with the appropriate levels of the bank monitoring the activity."

That comment raises a question already begging for an answer: whether executives up the line at Bankers Trust, like former CEO Charles Sanford, will be pulled into this affair. The SEC's attempts to curb accounting fraud have always emphasized "tone at the top," and Bankers Trust's management has given a great impression of being tone-deaf. A few years ago the company got into deep trouble for unprincipled selling of derivatives, and even now, in the midst of its securities-processing mess, it has the SEC on its neck because of possible problems with its loan-loss reserves.

A case alleging still another horrific fraud could soon come out of Newark. There, in what one knowledgeable person describes as "conference rooms jammed with lawyers," the office of the U.S. Attorney for New Jersey is boring in on the celebrated case of Cendant. Or, put more precisely, what's under the microscope are the flagrant accounting violations (of which more later) at CUC International, which merged with HFS Inc. in 1997 to form Cendant. The subsequent news of chicanery at CUC clobbered Cendant's stock by more than $14 billion in a single day.

For its part, the SEC has a "formal investigation" in progress on Cendant—that's its term for "you're in trouble"—and the same thing going on at Sunbeam and Waste Management and, down the line in size, Mercury Finance and telecommunications company Telxon. These all are companies that in recent times made major restatements of earnings, usually the first sign of serious accounting problems. Another restater is Oxford Health Plans, which is the subject of a lesser SEC investigation called an "informal inquiry." The big question about Oxford is whether its books got out of control simply because of the well-publicized chaos in its computer systems or because of irregularities as well.

Never fear that the SEC will run out of accounting cases to examine and perhaps move in on, because seldom does a month pass that those ugly words "restatement of earnings" do not fasten themselves to a new company. Joining the crowd recently from the FORTUNE 1,000 were drugstore chain Rite Aid, holding company MCN Energy Group, and drug wholesaler McKesson

HBOC. Ironically, this is McKesson's second brush with accounting infamy this century (see box, "McKesson Again").

Like any good general Arthur Levitt has a strategy for going after this enemy called managed earnings. In his September speech, in fact, he unveiled a list of five accounting problems that would get the unremitting attention of the SEC. They were "big bath" restructuring charges, acquisition accounting, "cookie-jar reserves," the abuse of "materiality," and revenue recognition.

Of these, that last item—the wrongful booking of sales—seems the closest to outright fraud. GAAP includes some firm rules for recognizing revenue, and most don't leave a lot of room for playing around. That hasn't stopped the bad guys. A recent study done for the Committee of Sponsoring Organizations of the Treadway Commission (called COSO), which is supported by various accounting and financial bodies, studied 200 alleged frauds carried out by publicly owned companies in the 11 years ended in 1997. Roughly 50% had a revenue-recognition component. Many of the cases involved small companies, which for that matter pack the list when it comes to fraud of any kind.

Even so, some of the biggest accounting scandals of the past few years (and now McKesson's to boot) have also featured revenue-recognition schemes. Executives at Sensormatic held the books open at the end of quarters so that they could get

---

THE CEO AS FELON

This sampler of CEOs nailed for accounting fraud in the past five years recalls what still another jailed boss, Barry Minkow, of ZZZZ Best, said when sentenced in 1989: "Today is a great day for this country. The system works. They got the right guy."

The CEO	What he did	Conviction/Plea	The outcome
Donald Ferrarini, 71 UNDERWRITERS FINANCIAL GROUP	Reported nonexistent revenues: made losing company look like profit maker.	Convicted, 2/99.	Sentenced to 12 years, one month. He is appealing.
Richard Rubin, 57 DONNKENNY	Concocted false invoices and revenues to meet earnings goals.	Pleaded guilty, 2/99.	Sentence pending; faces maximum of five years.
Chan Desaigoudar, 61 CALIFORNIA MICRO DEVICES	Led staff to record sales for products not shipped—or even manufactured.	Convicted, 7/98.	Serving sentence of 36 months.
Clifford Hotte, 51 HEALTH MANAGEMENT	Altered books well after 1995 year ended to get nearer Street estimates.	Convicted, 5/98.	Sentence of nine years is on appeal.
Paul Safronchik, 35 HOME THEATER PRODUCTS INTL.	Invented customers and sales; showed profits when red ink was the reality.	Pleaded guilty, 12/96.	Serving sentence of 37 months.
Earl Brian, 57 FNN	Spun companies he controlled into elaborate plot that inflated FNN's sales.	Convicted, 10/96.	Serving sentence of five years.
Eddie Antar, 51 CRAZY EDDIE	Fabricated inventory data, overstated income, got PR firms to issue lies.	Pleaded guilty, 5/96.	Serving sentence of six years, ten months.
Steven Hoffenberg, 54 TOWERS FINANCIAL	Ran Ponzi scheme that defrauded Towers investors of $450 million.	Pleaded guilty, 4/95.	Serving sentence of 20 years.
Q. T. Wiles, 79 MINISCRIBE	Falsified books to "make numbers"; shipped bricks instead of disk drives.	Convicted, 7/94.	Served 30-month sentence; released this year.

MCKESSON AGAIN

The accounting scam that rocked the company in 1938 was a doozy. So's the new one.

Before it merged with McKesson-Robbins early this year, software supplier HBO & Co. was known on Wall Street as "a consensus beater," the sort that never disappointed analysts' expectations. Maybe we now know why. In April and again in May, the new company called McKesson HBOC announced major restatements of earnings, and in June it said that seven top executives had either resigned or been fired, including CEO Mark Pulido and CFO Richard Hawkins (who both resigned). The reason for all this? "Sales" at HBO & Co. that didn't deserve the name. Okay, said the market, down with the stock—and $9 billion in value disappeared in a day.

The fact that a McKesson division should today be caught cooking the books is bizarrely ironic. Sixty years ago the company then called McKesson & Robbins was the center of perhaps the most famous accounting-fraud case in history. That swindle occurred because auditing firms were not in those days obliged to confirm the existence of inventory physically. As a result, McKesson's CEO, Donald Coster, conned his outside auditor, Price Waterhouse, into believing that the company had about $10 million of "crude drugs" it didn't have, stored in Canadian warehouses that didn't exist.

The discovery of the fraud in 1938 and the companion revelation that Coster was really Philip Musica, a man who had twice served time (once for bribing customs officials, later for grand larceny), sent McKesson into bankruptcy and rocked the business world. The crisis also produced both a rule that auditors had to henceforth physically check inventory and a famous story about Goldman Sachs' Sidney Weinberg, a McKesson director who was sitting in an emergency board meeting when the news came that Coster/Musica had committed suicide. Unfazed, Weinberg said, "Let's fire him for his sins anyway." Added one wag about the late con man: "Obviously, he couldn't face the Musica."

enough sales in the door to meet their earnings targets. Richard Rubin, former CEO of apparel company Donnkenny, is awaiting sentence for creating false invoices that he used to book sales. And Al Dunlap, who was fired as CEO of Sunbeam by its board, is alleged to have carried out (among other things) a "bill and hold" scam. In other words, Sunbeam recorded the sale of goods but simply held them in its own warehouse, a forbidden combo unless a customer has taken bona fide ownership of the goods and requested they be stored. (Dunlap, says his lawyer, relied on Arthur Andersen's assurances that Sunbeam was conforming to GAAP.) Walter Schuetze, chief accountant of the SEC's Division of Enforcement, sees in these scandals a simple theme: "When it comes to cooking the books, revenue recognition is the recipe of choice."

Lately, though, the other earnings-management techniques on Levitt's list have been coming on like a new cuisine, suddenly and sweepingly popular. Take, first, the charges that hit earnings when a company restructures on its own or as the result of an acquisition. Say that a company commits itself at these junctures to exit a business or close a factory in the near future. Under GAAP, it must today, in what we'll call year one, estimate the costs it will eventually incur in the restructuring—for severance payments, plant closings, and the like—and charge them off, even though many of the expenses won't actually be paid until, say, year two or three. These charges, which end up in a liability called a reserve, tend to put craters in year one's profits. But analysts generally ignore the bottom-line damage these write-offs do, focusing instead on operating earnings. In fact, all too often analysts cheer these charges, figuring that they clear the decks for good results in the future.

Earnings often *do* shine in the wake of a restructuring—but not necessarily because business has improved. Maybe all that happened was that the restructuring change was a "big bath," deliberately made larger than the monies to be paid out, which allows the excess to be channeled back into earnings in year two or year three. Abracadabra!—higher profits than would otherwise have materialized.

Or maybe the company made the restructuring charge a kitchen disposal, using it to gobble up all kinds of costs that by rights should be hitting this year's operating earnings or next. Schuetze recently ticked off some of the impermissible costs the SEC has found in restructuring charges: services to be provided in some future period by lawyers, accountants, and investment bankers; special bonuses for officers; expenses for retraining people. "Even," he said sorrowfully, as if not quite believing this level of deceit, "expenses for training people not yet hired."

Since Levitt's speech, the SEC has sent a letter to about 150 companies that took large restructuring charges last year. The letter warned that their annual reports might be selected for review. It also reminded the companies that they are required to make disclosures about the status of their restructuring reserves—how many dollars paid out so far, how many employees terminated vs. the original plan, and so forth. The implication was that the SEC would be looking to see that the companies were adhering to their restructuring plans and not emerging with reserves that could be popped into earnings at a propitious moment. The disclosure requirements had been there for years but were often ignored. Not anymore.

That's especially true because the SEC has followed through with tough reviews, both of annual reports and registration statements. One SEC target was Rite Aid, which took a large restructuring charge in fiscal 1999 (a year that ended in February) in anticipation of closing 379 stores. The SEC later compelled the company to reduce the size of its restructuring charge (from $290 million to $233 million), add major expenses to its operating costs, and restate its profits from the unaudited figure of $158 million it had reported in March—a figure even then far below "analysts' expectations"—to $144 million. This year, to date, Rite Aid has lost close to $7 billion in market cap, and class-action lawyers are all over its case.

In a second assault on acquisition accounting, the SEC attacked a dearly loved perquisite of tech companies: the write-offs that purchasers in a merger make for an asset called in-process research and development (IPR&D). As merger accounting works, a purchaser must assign values to all the assets it has bought and then, for the most part, capitalize them and write them off in future years—but IPR&D assets—ah, there's a beauty. The value assigned to these must be written off immediately, which means their cost doesn't hang around to clip earnings in future years.

And what are these things anyway? GAAP's definition of IPR&D assets are those "to be used" in R&D—this might be a gleam-in-the-eye technology, for example—as opposed to those "resulting from" R&D, like a proven technology. You can see that these definitions cry out for judgments, and there's the problem. It is the SEC's view that acquirers have done their utmost to assign maximum amounts of their purchase price to IPR&D so that they can ditch these costs immediately. The commission therefore got militant on this issue last year, forcing restatements of earnings when it concluded too much value had been assigned to IPR&D. A publication called the *Analyst's Accounting Observer* counts at least 60 tech companies that have been forced to restate. Among them was Motorola. Its accounting penalty was $99 million, which was the amount of IPR&D "costs" it tried to write off all at once in 1998 and which it will now instead be writing off gradually as the years go by.

Let us dip now, if you will pardon the expression, into another item on Levitt's list, cookie-jar reserves. GAAP, of course, is too stiffly worded to include a term like that. But not even the accounting-challenged have trouble visualizing that these are earnings held back from the period in which they should have been recognized and kept instead for a rainy day. Maybe the husbander is truly worried about bad weather hitting its business (as many banks, for example, claim to be), or maybe it just wants to manage earnings. It doesn't matter: GAAP says companies cannot establish reserves for "contingencies," because such costs can't be estimated. They should hit income statements when they actually arrive.

Beyond that, cookie jars are innately a problem because investors usually can't detect that they exist. Even outside directors, said one recently, typically wouldn't be told that managers had hidden cookies away. That makes it difficult for anyone to fairly value a company, says Harvey Goldschmid, general counsel of the SEC. A second problem, he says, is that managements will often use reserves to "dim the signals" going to both the public and their boards when business turns down.

The SEC says it is looking at a number of companies suspected of harboring improper reserves. In fact, in late June mighty Microsoft admitted that it was getting the eye. The SEC's most elaborate reserve case, however, is the one it launched last

December against W.R. Grace, not just attacking cookie jars but also roping in another item on Levitt's list, "materiality." This term acknowledges that the preparation of financial statements is a complex job and that neither managements nor their outside auditors, however well intentioned, can testify that the figures are accurate down to the penny. Auditors deal with this uncertainty by attesting that a company's statements are accurate "in all material respects." Unfortunately, auditors also lean on materiality when they are trying to convince themselves it's okay for managers to slip intentional misstatements into their financial reports.

The SEC is right now busy drawing a line in the sand about materiality. In the past it has sometimes permitted managements to get by with irregularities in their financial reports just as long as the deliberate misstatements could be classed, often by some ad hoc mathematical logic, as immaterial. But it is now preparing to say—in a staff bulletin soon to appear—that intentional errors made for the purpose of managing earnings just won't be tolerated.

In the W.R. Grace case, moreover, it went after intentional errors made several years back. It seems that in the early 1990s a division of that company, National Medical Care (NMC), made more in profits than it had expected. So NMC, according to the SEC, deliberately underreported its earnings (thereby creating an "irregularity"), stuffing the excess into a cookie-jar reserve that in time got to be $60 million in size. Then in 1993, when profits needed a sugar fix, NMC started feeding the reserve into earnings (thereby compounding the irregularities). Meanwhile, Grace's auditors, Price Waterhouse, went along with these contortions on the grounds that they weren't material.

The SEC, launching its case, objected to the entire goings-on. By June it had exacted cease-and-desist consents from two PricewaterhouseCoopers partners and from Grace itself, which agreed as well to set up a $1 million educational fund to further awareness of GAAP. The commission has also filed cease-and-desist proceedings against seven former Grace officers (among them CEO J.P. Bolduc), of whom three get special attention. These three, who include Grace's former chief financial officer, Brian Smith, are licensed CPAs whom the SEC views as

having engaged in "inappropriate professional conduct." So the commission wants an administrative judge to bar them from practicing before the SEC. That means they could not play *any* part in preparing the financial statements of publicly owned companies or any other SEC registrant.

Smith's lawyer, Wallace Timmeny, once an SEC staffer himself and now at Dechert Price & Rhoads, plans to lean on the materiality argument in defending his client. But he also argues in essence that it would be bitterly unfair for Smith and a couple of other unlucky parishioners to get excommunicated for sins rampant in the rest of the congregation. "If you think what my client did constitutes fraud," he protested to the SEC before the charges came, "then every company in the *Fortune* 500 is engaged in fraud."

The Grace case is important to Levitt's initiative because it sends such a strong message to other companies, some of which should be thinking, "There but for the god of Grace go I." In an entirely different way, the Cendant case demands attention because it displays such gross behavior. The misdeeds are fully documented as well, in a remarkable and unsparing 146-page report done for the audit committee of Cendant's board by the law firm of Willkie Farr & Gallagher and auditors imported for the project, Arthur Andersen. Here are some of the report's findings:

- In the three years 1995–97, CUC's operating income before taxes was improperly inflated by $500 million, which was more than one-third of its reported pretax income for those years.
- Though many of the improprieties occurred in CUC's biggest subsidiary, Comp-U-Card, they reached to 16 others as well. No fewer than 20 employees participated in the wrongdoing.
- Several CUC employees who were interviewed said they understood that the purpose of inflating earnings was to meet "analysts' expectations."
- In the first three quarters of each of the infected years, CUC put out unaudited financial statements that headquarters deliberately falsified, mostly by "adjusting" Comp-U-Card's revenues upward and its expenses downward. These favorable "adjustments" grew: They

PUT BITE INTO AUDIT COMMITTEES

Warren Buffett says boards should make auditors state their real opinion.

Eager for boards to have better audit committees than they do, Arthur Levitt got a special panel to make recommendations for improvement and now wants them adopted. But when the New York Stock Exchange asked its listed companies to comment on the recommendations, back came bullets.

The companies especially disliked a proposal that would have required audit committees to do their homework and then attest in annual reports that the financial statements therein conformed to GAAP. Some protesters thought such a rule would invite lawsuits against audit committee members. Others saw role confusion. Attesting, said one letter, "is what the external auditor is hired to do."

A related objection came from Warren Buffett, chairman of Berkshire Hathaway, who, up to the minute he put up his hand on this one, had publicly and warmly applauded Levitt's campaign against earnings management. Here, though, Buffett disputed the thought that an audit committee, meeting for a few hours a year, could attest to anything meaningful about a company's financial statements. Instead, he said, the committee needs to learn what the outside auditors know—something that "frequently does not occur, even (perhaps especially) when major shortcomings exist."

Buffett said the committee should require the auditors to give detailed answers to three questions:

1. If the auditor were solely responsible for preparation of the company's financial statements, would they have been done differently, in either material or nonmaterial ways? If "differently," the auditor should explain both management's argument and his own.

2. If the auditor were an investor, would he have received the information essential to understanding the company's financial performance during the reporting period?
3. Is the company following the same internal audit procedure the auditor would if he himself were CEO? If not, what are the differences and why?

Buffett then said—in italics—that the auditors' answers should be spelled out in the minutes of the meeting. The point, he said, is to hang "monetary liability" on the auditors, that being the only thing that will drive them to truly do their job instead of becoming subservient to management.

FORTUNE asked Olivia Kirtley, chair of the American Institute of Certified Public Accountants and also chief financial officer of Vermont American Corp., for her opinion about Buffett's ideas. He'd "boiled down" his questions, she said, but they were "in the spirit" of what the AICPA's own audit committee asks of its outside auditors.

Whether her auditing-firm constituency would like a plan that seeks to get them either to do their job well or to accept monetary responsibility for failure is doubtful. Auditors have eased their legal troubles in the past decade, managing to establish that financial statements are the responsibility of management, and also getting help from new laws and a friendly Supreme Court decision. As a result, the number of suits auditors are having to defend is sharply down.

Of course, it is also during this decade that managements have learned all the subterranean routes for meeting "expectations." Is that simply coincidence or has the slimming of monetary consequences made auditors less diligent and more compliant than was once the case? That question is unanswerable. Buffett's three are not.

were $31 million in 1995, $87 million in 1976, and $176 million in 1997.

- At the end of each year, before its outside auditors, Ernst & Young, came in to make their annual review, CUC undid those improprieties (which would almost certainly have been discovered in the audit process) and instead created the earnings it needed mainly by plucking them from cookie-jar reserves.
- In most cases, the explanations that CUC gave Ernst & Young for these reserve infusions satisfied the accounting firm, which in general did

not display impressive detective skills. On one occasion, however, E&Y could not find justification for $25 million transferred helpfully from a reserve—and this it let pass as "immaterial." (Cendant has sued E&Y, which has responded that it was the victim of deception and is "outraged" to be blamed for Cendant's own fraud.)

- In one particularly colorful incident, CUC used a merger reserve it had established in 1997 to swallow up $597,000 of private airplane expenses that its CEO, Walter Forbes, had paid in 1995 and 1996, and for which he had requested reimbursement. Had these expenses not been allocated to the reserve, they would have turned up where they should have: in operating costs.

Naturally, Willkie Farr questioned Forbes about his knowledge of CUC's wrongdoing. He denied knowing anything about it. After the lawyers' report was completed, Forbes also issued a statement saying, in part, "Any suggestion that I 'should have known' about the fraud is completely unfounded."

At a minimum, his obliviousness is odd, since one businessman who spent several hours with Forbes a couple of years ago remembers him as "a walking encyclopedia about his company, given to unusual specificity about numbers and details." But if Forbes truly did not know, at least one reader of the report—this writer—thinks Forbes was a pathetically uninformed CEO and probably one of the worst ever to head a major company. Forbes left Cendant in July 1998 and today, says a spokeswoman, is pursuing startup investments internationally, especially in Europe.

Michael Young, a Willkie Farr litigator and a student of accounting frauds, says they tend to follow a predictable trajectory. The Cendant case was no exception. It started small and grew out of control. It also dragged in employees who were troubled by what they were asked to do but did it anyway. Young remembers one case in which he was about to interview a woman implicated in a fraud. She suddenly burst into tears and said the totally unexpected: "I'm so glad to have someone to talk to about this."

Levitt understands well that the SEC is facing an enormous challenge in trying to get the cultural change it wants. Wall Street itself is an obstacle: It wants consistent earnings, however attained. Speaking at a recent investor-relations conference, one stock analyst, Gary Balter of DLJ, baldly urged that companies consider "hiding earnings" for future use. "If you don't play the game," he said, "you're going to get hurt."

On a second front, the SEC has already run into roadblocks on certain new rules it would like to impose on audit committees (see box). Levitt himself has grown used to visits from business leaders not happy at all with accounting changes disturbing their lives. Even some feds are up in arms. The SEC, bran-

dishing GAAP, is arguing that certain banks have overstated their reserves; banking regulators, perfectly happy with a little conservatism, have risen in protest.

Another issue is whether really egregious cases can be made criminal actions. For a U.S. Attorney, whose alternatives include going after drug dealing, espionage, and bank robbery, it is no easy decision to take on a white-collar case stuffed with the arcana of accounting. According to Levitt's chief policeman, director of enforcement Richard Walker, the cases that ought to wind up in criminal court are those in which a company or executive has exhibited a high level of what lawyers call *scienter*—that is, knowing and willful conduct—and acted "to violate the law, misapply accounting standards, and affect financial reporting." Prosecutors may also weigh aggravating factors such as lies told to auditors or profitable trades made by an executive as he paints a false picture of his company's financial health. Walker, who has been at the SEC for eight years, thinks Levitt's message is in any event getting through. "I'm seeing more acceptance of these cases by U.S. Attorneys today than in all the time I've been here."

Some skeptics point out that Levitt is hardly the first SEC chairman to bear down on cooked books. Abraham Briloff, the crusty accounting professor from Baruch College, has reminded SEC chief accountant Lynn Turner that many another cleanup effort has been tried and has opined that this one, too, will probably fail. Other businessmen think political reality will force Levitt himself to limit his goals. Says one East Coast CEO deeply experienced in finance: "When he goes after GE, I'll know he's serious."

Meanwhile, some corporations continue to behave in ways that make you question whether they've even heard of Levitt. Companies are not in the least required to make forecasts about earnings. Yet this spring, as McKesson was conceding that it had no real handle on the profits of its accounting-troubled unit, HBOC, it was still saying it was comfortable with projections that it could make $2.50 a share for its fiscal year ending next February. McKesson's nervy statement supports the opinion of class-action lawyer William Lerach that it is always good to allow time for the actors in frauds, especially CEOs, to make the self-destructive public statements they almost always do.

If tales like McKesson's confirm the challenge that Levitt faces, there is another that puts a slightly different complexion on things. The SEC's Turner says he knows a largish FORTUNE 500 company that in a recent reporting period ended up with earnings well beyond Street expectations. The boss said to the CFO: "Let's hold some of those back." "Wait a minute," objected the CFO, "don't even go there. Don't you know what the SEC is doing to people?" And the boss looked at the CFO, told him he was in "career limiting" territory, and once again ordered the earnings hid.

And what happened then? Turner's answer: "The CFO, the auditors, and the audit committee got together and managed to convince the boss he was wrong."

That's just one time, at one company. But at least it's a start.

Can Ethical Management and Managed Care Coexist?

Leonard H. Friedman
Assistant Professor, Department of Public Health,
Oregon State University

Grant T. Savage
Associate Professor and Director of MBA Program, College
of Business Administration, Texas Tech University

Oxymorons are words or phrases that have a precise dictionary meaning but may be interpreted as meaning exactly the opposite of what is intended.

Reprinted with permission from L. H. Friedman and G. T. Savage, "Can Ethical Management and Managed Care Coexist?" from *Health Care Management Review,* Spring, vol. 23, issue 2, pp. 56–62, 1998. © 1998 Aspen Publishers, Inc.

Some common oxymorons are "jumbo shrimp," "military intelligence," "smart bombs," and organizational "rightsizing." One final oxymoron is the derisive term "business ethics." After all, everyone knows that the only ethical principle that businesses hold to is their desire to achieve the highest level of profit regardless of cost. While ethics is a part of the curriculum of virtually every business school in the United States and articles regularly appear on ethics and social responsibility, the prevailing sentiment is that businesses exist to make money and everything else is secondary.

While many people will chuckle at these and other examples, there is no humor to be found when we move into the ethical uncertainty created when health service organizations migrate into for-profit, investor-owned status. The trends in this area are both clear and unequivocal. The number of publicly traded health care companies has grown from 33 in 1992 to 144 in 1996 with a corresponding increase in market capitalization over the same time period from $36 billion to $140 billion.[1] In 1985, California was home to 11 nonprofit and 5 small for-profit health maintenance organizations (HMOs). By 1995, there had been almost a complete reversal as evidenced by three very small nonprofit HMOs and the Kaiser-Permanente System competing against seven large, well-organized investor-owned HMOs.[2] For-profit, investor-owned physician management companies that manage and administer the business side of a physician's practice have grown from 3 in 1990 to 27 in 1996.[1]

The hospital industry, which has a long history with for-profit ownership, has seen Columbia/HCA move to the front as perhaps the most aggressive and opportunistic company of all. In 1996, Columbia/ HCA owned or operated 343 hospitals, 136 surgical centers, and 550 home health agencies with total revenue of just under $20 billion.[3] Annual revenue growth of 19 percent since 1992 far exceeded the benchmark Standard and Poors 500 rate of 5 percent for the same time period. Put another way, the value of a $100 investment in Columbia/HCA on

December 31, 1990 would be worth in excess of $400 on December 31, 1995.[4]

The point of this discussion is to help frame the context under which health care organizations are now operating. While there remains a large number of community-based nonprofits with a strong mission statement underscoring their historical support of the people they serve, more and more organizations operate on the premise of giving the highest return possible to their shareholders. Indeed, the rapid transformation of nonprofits into for-profit systems is less than 20 years old.[5] A question that arises from this observation is whether it is antithetical for health care organizations to function under a for-profit, investor-owned model. One possible answer is that health care and profits have no historical or practical purpose being mentioned together. For example, the role of the hospital as a charitable institution in the United States is well documented.[6] Since the mid-1960s, federal and state governments have created programs to fund health insurance for the elderly, disabled, and poor in the forms of Medicare and Medicaid. As early as the 1950s, incentives were provided so that employers could help provide private health insurance for their employees as a nontaxable benefit. These programs and incentives have served to create a perception that healthcare is a basic right of all people and should not be treated as a commodity to be bought and sold on the open market but rather provided as a community good.

However, there is an equally compelling argument for the creation and growth of for-profit health care organizations. Physicians have historically functioned as small businesses with the intent of creating enough revenue to both cover the overhead of the business as well as pay themselves a salary or percentage of any residual funds remaining. As long as the public perceived that physicians were acting in the patients' best interests and patient satisfaction remained high, few if anyone complained about physician incomes. In the same sense, physicians owned and operated hospitals as for-profit enterprises with little if any negative feedback from their communities. In fact, around the turn of the 20th century, over one-half of the nation's hospitals were run as for profit enterprises.[5]

As interesting as the idea of physicians as business people might be, there is an even more important driver in the move toward for-profit health care. During the era of fee-for-service medicine, there were essentially no economic incentives for providers to conduct their business affairs in a cost-efficient or effective manner. All costs could be passed through to the payer or the patient with almost virtual certainty that the bill would be paid in full. Rising expenses such as salaries, new technology, additional services, or other capital improvements could easily be shifted to the payers. Costs for uncompensated care, charity, or bad debt were also passed on to the paying customers. Since insurance or the government paid the majority of the bills, these charges were transparent to the patient. The occasional voice would be raised in protest when, after examining a hospital bill, someone might notice a charge for a $5.00 aspirin tablet, but those complaints were generally pushed aside.

A second economic variable working to promote for-profit health care was the scarcity of physicians and hospitals immediately following World War II. Policies were almost immediately enacted by the federal government in order to create financial incentives for medical schools to increase the size of their entering classes. The Hill-Burton Hospital Survey and Construction Act of 1946 helped fund the construction of hundreds of new hospitals. Measures of economy and efficiency were pushed aside given the simultaneous desires to increase the nation's health care capacity, and at the same time provide employer-sponsored, tax-free health insurance.

Despite the efforts of the federal and state governments to control the rapidly rising costs of health care in the 1970s, the same economic incentives as before continued to motivate providers despite the growth of the multihospital systems that began during this time. It was not until 1983, when a real turning point was reached in the form of the Tax Equity and Fiscal Responsibility Act (TEFRA) that created the Health Care Financing Administration (HCFA) and with it, a new form of paying hospital bills for Medicare patients. Diagnosis related groups (DRGs) were the opening salvo of what has turned out to be nothing less than a total transformation of our health care delivery system. The arrival of DRGs and other methods of prospective payment including capitation, contracting, per diems, and global budgeting have effectively transferred the financial risk of health care from the payer to the provider. A countervailing argument has been made that although the government tried to control health care costs via prospective payment, it was the revolt of the employers that resulted in the burgeoning of managed care.[7] Irrespective of the source of change, the net effect is the same.

In the marketplace, this later reality has been the fundamental basis under which for-profit businesses have always operated. Risk and reward are well-known concepts in business. Successful businesses are the ones that are able to control their overhead costs yet at the same time produce a product or service of sufficient quality so that consumers will be willing to purchase what the business has to sell. The trick has always been trying to juggle cost, quality, and price in a world of other competitors and fickle consumers. Health care organizations (which produce services consumed by patients and typically purchased by employers and the government) are only recently beginning to realize what businesses have known for years. Managed care plans, capitation, and selective contracting are forcing health care providers to reduce their overhead and begin to think in terms of efficiency and effectiveness. For example, in the scenario just described, hospitals are no longer thought of as revenue centers and, instead, have become cost centers.

It should come as no surprise that, given the frame-breaking shift in health care reimbursement occurring over the past two decades, for-profit companies should be entering the world of hospitals and medical practice as never before. For-profits long ago discovered the tools and techniques necessary to survive and thrive in the environment currently surrounding health care organizations. While health policy experts, politicians, and consumers debate the merits and shortcomings of a market-oriented health care delivery system, the reality is that this type of system represents the here and now.[8] At the heart of this new system of for-profit health care organizations is the concept of managed care. In a

managed care plan, patient care is managed in such a way as to attain the best possible medical outcome at the lowest possible cost. There is general agreement that managed care exists along a continuum of increasing cost and quality control with managed indemnity insurance plans at one end and closed panel HMOs at the other extreme.[9] At the present time, there are over 30 million persons enrolled in HMOs, the majority of which are run as for-profits.

The point of this discussion has been to demonstrate the fundamental move of health care delivery from not-for-profit to for-profit status if not actually in ownership, then at least to a change in management perspective. It is at this point that we briefly examine the principles under which for-profit businesses operate in an attempt to understand whether or not an intersection exists between business ethics and biomedical ethics.

BUSINESS ETHICS

At least four models can be used to explain the relationship between business and ethics. The first, which we will call the "principal-agent model," reasons that since executive level managers are agents of the shareholders, then the exclusive job of management is to increase shareholder wealth by increasing the present value of the organization. From this perspective, ethics is simply one more tool to increase shareholder value.[10] While managers might act in a morally proper manner to merge legal, ethical, and social concerns into business practice, any such actions are taken with the intent of adding wealth to the firm. This vision of business ethics is essentially amoral and arguably ought to be rejected.[11]

A second model advocates that managers employ a process of principled moral reasoning as a basis for making decisions. In this instance, morality is viewed as intrinsically good and should be seen as an end in itself, not just as a method for increasing shareholder wealth.[12] In a conflict between moral principles and wealth, morality should always win. However, what is lacking from this viewpoint is a definition of morality.

The third model uses a noninstrumental approach wherein ethics has a binding moral veto over the imperatives of increasing shareholder wealth and seeking profit. By definition, businesses have no special rules that override the moral obligations that managers hold as humans.[13] Students of philosophy will recognize this concept as grounded in the theories of deontological ethics in which moral rightness is not solely dependent on outcomes or results. This viewpoint was first put forth by Immanual Kant who suggests that the four principles common to the general morality of humans include not harming others, respecting authority, avoiding lying, and honoring agreements.[14] The difficulty with noninstrumental ethics in a business environment is that there is precious little, if any, moral certainty in the majority of decisions. In a business environment concerned with meeting the needs of customers, managers are faced with potentially high levels of moral ambiguity when customer requests conflict with these ethical absolutes. In contrast, managers of health service organizations are constantly faced with resolving difficult moral dilemmas as is witnessed in the growth of biomedical ethics committees found in most large hospital settings.

The fourth model for business ethics is expressed in a recent article by Quinn and Jones[12] who posit an agent-morality perspective. They suggest that while noninstrumental ethics are logically sound, they conflict markedly with the principal-agent model that appears to be the dominant ethical platform in U.S. businesses. The authors attempt to frame noninstrumental ethics in such a way that it becomes acceptable to businesses by arguing that moral principles are antecedent to the contract between the principal and agent and cannot be suspended by agreement between them. Only after basic moral duties have been met should shareholder wealth considerations be made a priority.[12]

BIOMEDICAL ETHICS

Persons employed as health care providers or working in health care organizations have traditionally been faced with a graver set of ethical concerns than have persons who work in other service or manufacturing industries. Four philosophical tenets serve as the basis for persons employed in management roles in health care facilities, including respect for others, beneficence, nonmaleficence, and justice.[15,16]

Briefly stated, respect for others consists of respecting individual autonomy, truth telling, and maintaining confidentiality and fidelity.

Beneficence involves providing benefits to persons while at the same time balancing benefit and harm. According to the principle of beneficence, organizations (and their agents) are required to do all they can to aid patients.

Nonmaleficence is often thought to mean "first do no harm." There is an implicit balancing act between providing benefit yet at the same time doing no harm. An example of this conflict can be seen when staff are put at risk when treating trauma patients in the absence of universal precautions.

Standards of justice deal with the equitable distribution of benefits and costs among individuals, groups, and organizations.[17] Distributive justice focuses on the principle of impartiality, holding that all people should be treated the same unless there are relevant differences among them. Procedural justice focuses on the principle of fairness. This form of justice is based on the notion of a social contract between an organization and its primary stakeholders. Provision of services to medically indigent persons presents health care administrators with the clearest example of this ethical standard.

In addition to the ethical principles just described, most professional societies have a code of ethics that apply to all of their members. Examples of such codes include those written by the American College of Healthcare Executives, Medical Group Management Association, and American College of Health Care Administrators.

ETHICAL CONFLICTS IN FOR-PROFIT MANAGED CARE

Persons occupying management and administrative roles in managed care organizations are faced with the complexities of balancing their role as the agent for the shareholders of the firm with the needs of the patients and physicians. A number of conflicts are immediately apparent in this setting and can be classified according to the matrix in the box that follows.

The first conflict revolves around distribution of resources. Managed care organizations explicitly operate under the assumption that resources are limited to that which the insurer pays on the basis of a contractual agreement, capitation rate,

```
+------------------------------------------------+
|      Ethical Conflicts in Managed Care         |
|                                                |
| Resources  Physicians are provided             |
|            financial incentives to             |
|            minimize resource                   |
|            consumption and see as many         |
|            patients as possible in a given     |
|            period of time.                     |
| Wealth     By denying access to tests and      |
|            procedures, are costs               |
|            controlled even though the          |
|            patient will likely benefit from    |
|            the test or procedure?              |
| Equity     Recent studies suggest that the     |
|            poor and elderly have worse         |
|            outcomes in managed care            |
|            than in traditional                 |
|            fee-for-service arrangements.       |
+------------------------------------------------+
```

or other prospective payment mechanism. Physicians are at the heart of this concern in that they are the persons with the sole responsibility of ordering tests, procedures, or hospitalizations. Variable health costs move up or down depending on what the physician orders. In most managed care, funds for referrals to specialists and hospital care reside in what is known as a "risk pool." The size of the risk pool is estimated at the start of the fiscal year and is drawn down as required. At the end of the year, any funds remaining are returned to the primary care physicians as a bonus. The chance that the risk pool will shrink is directly proportional to the tendency of physicians (who have assumed the risk) to mismanage resources. Therefore, an incentive is created that couples practice behavior with financial gain (or loss).

The second conflict centers around wealth and is at least indirectly related to the resource question. In virtually all managed care plans, there exists a mechanism whereby any costly test or hospital admission must be preapproved. In the best case scenario, this form of utilization review is conducted in order to assure the payer that the patient is receiving the most appropriate form of diagnosis or treatment for the particular disease or condition. The quest to obtain information on medical outcomes resides at the heart of this process. In most instances, managed care plans will not pay for experimental or unproved treatments. However, for many managed care plans, anecdotal reports suggest that the necessity to obtain clear approval be-

fore paying for a test or procedure has been twisted to delay or deny payment for costly medically necessary services simply as a way of holding down expenses.[18] There have also been media reports of managed care plans denying payment for bone marrow transplants for severely ill leukemia patients claiming that the treatment was experimental despite significant evidence to the contrary.[19]

The final conflict deals with the issue of equity. From the ethical standpoint of justice, patients in managed care plans with the same insurance ought to be treated equally with respect to access to services, tests, and treatments. In multiple studies comparing the medical outcomes of patients enrolled in managed care plans and traditional fee-for-service programs, no significant difference could be found. This finding supports the contention by managed care organizations that quality is not being sacrificed when costs are reduced. However, a recent study published in the *Journal of the American Medical Association*[20] reports that the elderly and poor do much worse in HMOs than in traditional insurance programs. While there has been criticism of the study,[21] serious questions are raised as to whether health services in HMOs and managed care are provided to consumers in a fair and equitable manner.

A PROPOSED MODEL FOR ETHICAL MANAGEMENT OF MANAGED CARE

Managers and administrators of organizations that provide health services based on a managed care model are by definition torn between two conflicting but equally compelling values. They include the simultaneous needs to provide an appropriate level of health services to the patients whose lives are covered by the organization, yet work to keep expenses as low as possible in order to maximize revenue and profit. From the perspective of a practicing manager, there is tremendous difficulty in achieving these goals due to control of the former by physicians and the shifting of responsibility for the latter from managed care organizations. Treatment decisions, diagnostic tests, drug therapies, and other clinical matters are exclusively in the hands of physicians who have been trained to do whatever is medically necessary for their patients—not what is most clinically- and cost-effective. While administrators can and do advise physicians about the costs of their decisions as well as provide data on utilization, the clinician is the person empowered to control the resources used in patient care. The highly publicized actions of HMOs who deny certain clinical services to patient members have resulted in a public outcry against "bureaucrats," insurance executives, and other nonphysicians making medical resource decisions.

At the same time that administrators in managed care organizations find themselves unable to effectively control the resource utilization decisions of their physician providers, they are also required to act as the fiduciary agents for the owners of the firm. In that capacity, administrators are compelled to put the short-term financial interests of the owners ahead of the medical needs of patients and clinical wishes of the physicians. In the vernacular of managed care organizations, this control issue is most clearly seen by the presence of withholds whereby a certain percentage of the primary care capitation payment is withheld every month and used to pay for cost overruns in referral or institutional services.[22]

Fortunately, there is an ethical solution to this seemingly unsolvable dilemma. The key might lie in an augmented version of the agent-morality perspective. To reiterate, agent-morality theory as set forth by Quinn and Jones suggests that the moral principles of avoiding harm, respecting authority, honoring agreements, and avoiding lying have a higher priority than firm profits.[12] They suggest that because of the nature of managers as agents for the owners of the organization, they are bound to these principles, hence the term agent-morality. However, there needs to be a more persuasive element if this concept is to be applied to managed care in particular and health care organizations in general. Nowhere in their thesis is the concept of fairness, justice, or a level playing field mentioned. In a pure market orientation as envisioned by Adam Smith and other classical economists, while elements of the social contract and moral order were assumed, subsidization for goods or services did not exist.

The public and private subsidy of health services creates the strong perception that health care is a right of all persons as opposed to a commodity bought and sold on the open market. Social policy in the form of Medicare and Medicaid exists to ensure that the elderly, disabled, and poor receive health services. Employer-sponsored health insurance is currently treated as a tax-free benefit. In 1993–1994, President Clinton attempted to reform the United States health care system so that the 40 million plus uninsured could begin to receive a minimum level of health care benefits. As further evidence of the contention that health care is a right, federal legislation was created prohibiting the practice of patient dumping where indigent patients are turned away from hospital emergency departments. The Internal Revenue Service, in granting a 501-C-3 tax exempt status to nonprofit health care organizations, requires them to provide a high level of community benefit that is typically construed to mean charity or uncompensated care.

Given the unique status of health services, managers and administrators should take into account the moral principles of equity and fairness when they make business decisions in combination with the four principles described earlier as part of agent-morality theory. Incorporating the moral principles of equity and fairness is not just a good ethical decision but also makes good business sense for managed care organizations. One example might be providing evening and weekend appointments as well as walk-in clinics for patients who, for whatever reason, might not be able to access services during regular business hours. Another example would be low- or no-charge immunization clinics for school-aged children or the elderly. A shuttle bus sponsored by the medical group could be used to bring elderly, disabled, or otherwise isolated patients to the clinics so that they could keep their appointments. One final thought involves the provision of health promotion and health education classes and programs to all patients. In every one of these examples, there is an initial investment of capital that yields significant returns in either additional revenue or cost savings. The example of the off-hours appointment and walk-in clinic is a tremendous marketing advantage that can effectively be used to attract working families (and their associated employer-paid health insurance dollars). The immunization clinic helps reduce the likelihood that patients will experience preventable communicable diseases and the costs that the managed care plan have to absorb treating those diseases. The shuttle bus service (while initially costly) reduces the downstream expenses associated with patients missing scheduled appointments. Finally, an investment in health promotion and education in a variety of areas including prenatal classes, stop smoking programs, stress reduction, and various support groups has been demonstrated to result in a significant reduction of long-term health costs. Even in for-profit managed care settings, it is not only possible but profitable to include equity and fairness into the calculus of difficult business decisions.

The rapid expansion of managed care as the primary health delivery mechanism in the United States has been primarily driven by for-profit and investor-owned entities. Given the importance of for-profits and the free market in this type of arrangement, business scholars have attempted to provide an ethical framework in order to counteract the principal-agent view that suggested the only role for managers was to maximize the present value of the firm. While some cynics might suggest that for-profit health care organizations operate from this principal-agent perspective, ethical standards already present for clinicians and administrators tend to require different moral standards of performance than in non-health care settings.

Notwithstanding the pervasive cynicism about the state of business ethics, multiple frameworks have been developed that attempt to guide the moral and ethical practice of business management. One of the most persuasive theories is that of an agent-morality perspective. This viewpoint posits that the values of truth telling, avoiding harm, respecting authority, and honoring agreements have a higher institutional priority than earning short-term profits. In the for-profit world of managed care, the values of social equity and fairness should be added given the unique status of health care in our society.

There is no doubt that managed care is here to stay (at least in the short run) as payers of health services attempt to control their expenses yet provide consumers with the highest and most effective quality of health care possible. The onus for control of this equation will lie in the hands of those who manage hospitals, clinics, and other provider groups that participate in managed care plans. While it may be a challenge to remember that patients must be put ahead of profits, it is both possible and desirable to optimize the health of the patient and the organization simultaneously.

REFERENCES

1. The Advisory Board Committee. *The Rising Tide.* Washington, DC: Author, 1996.
2. Health Care Information Associates (HCIA). "Guide to the Managed Care Industry, 1996." *The Rising Tide.* Washington, DC: Author, 1996.
3. Columbia/HCA. *Annual Report.* Nashville, TN: Author, 1996.
4. Columbia/HCA. *Proxy Statement.* Nashville, TN: Author, 1996.
5. Haugland, L., and Dowling, W.L. "The Hospital." In *Introduction to Health Services* (4th ed.), edited by S.J. Williams and P.R. Torrens. Albany, NY: Delmar Publishers, 1993.
6. Friedman, L.H., and Mullins, L.A. "Acute Care Hospitals: Past, Present, and Future." In *Handbook of Health Administration,* edited by A.O. Kilpatrick and J.A. Johnson. New York: Marcel Decker, in press.
7. Wolper, L.F. *Health Care Administration: Principles, Practices, Structure, and Delivery.* Gaithersburg, MD: Aspen Publishers: 1995.
8. Blair, J.D., Fottler, M., Paolino, A., and Rotarius, T. *Medical Group Practices Face the Uncertain Future: Challenges, Opportunities, and Strategies.* Englewood, CO: Center for Research in Ambulatory Health Care Administration, 1995.
9. Wagner, E. "Types of Managed Care Organizations." In *The Managed Health Care Handbook* (3rd ed.), edited by P. Kongstvedt. Gaithersburg, MD: Aspen Publishers, 1996.
10. Goodpaster, K. "Business Ethics and Stakeholder Analysis." *Business Ethics Quarterly* 1, no. 3 (1991): pp. 53–73.
11. Carrol, A. "The Pyramid of Corporate Social Responsibility: Toward the Moral Management of Organizational Stakeholders." *Business Horizons* 34, no. 4 (1991): pp. 39–48.

12. Quinn, D., and Jones, T. "An Agent-Morality View of Business Policy." *Academy of Management Review* 1, no. 1 (1995): pp. 22–42.

13. Goldman, A. *The Moral Foundation of Professional Ethics.* London: Rowman & Littlefield, 1980.

14. Kant, I. *Lectures on Ethics.* New York: Harper and Row, 1963.

15. Garrett, T., Baillie, H., and Garrett, R. *Health Care Ethics: Principles and Problems.* Englewood Cliffs, NJ: Prentice Hall, 1993.

16. Rakich, J., Longest, B., and Darr, K. *Managing Health Services Organizations* (3rd ed.). Baltimore, MD: Health Professions Press, 1992.

17. Greenberg, J. "A Taxonomy of Organizational Justice Theories" *Academy of Management Review* 12, no. 1 (1987): pp. 9–22.

18. Lampros, A. "PERS, HealthNet Join to Study HMO Providers." *The Sacramento Bee* (1 July 1997): A 1.

19. Larson, E. "The Soul of an HMO." *Time Magazine* 174 (22 January 1996): 4.

20. Ware, J.E., Bayliss, M., Rogers, W., Kosinski, M., and Tarlov, A. "Differences in 4-Year Health Outcomes for Elderly and Poor, Chronically Ill Patients Treated in HMO and Fee-for-Service Systems." *Journal of the American Medical Association* 276 (2 October 1996): pp. 1,039–47.

21. Olmos, D. "Ill Elderly and Poor Fare Worse in HMOs, Study Says." *Los Angeles Times* (2 October 1996): A1.

22. Kongstvedt, P. *Essentials of Managed Care* (2nd ed). Gaithersburg, MD: Aspen Publishers, 1997.

Business Ethics and the Information Age

Richard T. De George
Distinguished Professor of Philosophy, University of Kansas

It is an honor to have been chosen the first Bell Atlantic Visiting Professor in Business Ethics and Information Technology, and a pleasure to be here to

From *Business and Society Review,* Vol. 104, No. 3, Fall, 1999. Copyright © 1999, Center for Business Ethics at Bentley College. Published by Blackwell Publishers. Reprinted by permission of the Center for Business Ethics at Bentley College.

inaugurate the professorship. Bentley College has always been in the forefront of business ethics. The college's Center for Business Ethics was one of the first established in the world. As the home of the Ethics Officer Association, the center continues its pioneering work. And it is now leading us into the new millennium as signified by this new professorship. Where business ethics is heading—what the next stage of business ethics should be—is the topic of my remarks today.

The fact that we are entering the information age is a truism, yet exactly what that means is understood differently by different people. The extent to which we have entered the Information age is hinted at by the Y2K phenomenon. Correcting the Y2K problem will cost more than $600 billion dollars worldwide. This shows the extent to which business has integrated and become dependent on computer technology. We shall come to realize on January 1, 2000, all the little places where dare-sensitive information has entered our lives in ways that we have forgotten.

As we enter this new age, we will face new ethical and business issues. I shall briefly present some thoughts about these issues in seven theses that I hope we can pursue in questions and comments from you in the interactive portion of this presentation.

THESIS I

The IT head-in-the-sand syndrome: Many businesses either fail to realize that we have entered the information age or fail to appreciate its importance.

The move of business to the information age raises many ethical issues, but has received little ethical attention, either from business or from business ethicists. Uncovering the ethical issues that grow out of information technology, facing them, and providing ethical guidelines is the major challenge for business and business ethics at the start of the new millennium.

The rise of the Internet as a locus of business is changing marketing, for instance. It makes possible one-on-one marketing by tracking the customer, recording his or her preferences and proclivities, and presenting the customer with products that he or she is likely to want to buy.

Department stores and discount stores, just like TV ads, have to rely on generalizations and average wants and desires. The Internet makes possible an individual fit. As Internet sales climb, they will continue to encroach on, if not yet threaten, department stores and other stores and retail outlets. Many businesses seem not to care or worry, or else do not know how to respond effectively.

Wal-Mart is one of the few traditional firms that realizes it exists in the information age. In a real sense, Wal-Mart is not primarily in the retail business, but in the information business. It's very much like Amazon.com, except that Wal-Mart also owns its own outlets. Like Amazon.com, Wal-Mart has a database that is probably its most important asset. Because of its database, Wal-Mart can customize each of its stores to suit local shoppers and order product to point-of-delivery exactly when each store needs it—saving storage and other costs, and changing the way product is manufactured and delivered.

The effect of such time pressure on factories and workers in the plants that supply Wal-Mart, however, is uncharted territory for the business ethicist. The changes are real. But their ethical impact has yet to be assessed. The security of Internet transactions, the return of goods with which customers are dissatisfied, and the delivery of goods ordered all raise issues to be examined, and carry with them ethical implications. Similarly, how, where, and whether to tax online sellers and buyers is an unresolved question that has been temporarily put on hold by legislation. But the tax base of many cities and local communities relies on local sales taxes, which may well diminish considerably as new ways of buying goods develop in the information age. Business via the Internet changes the relevance of location, geography, times during which businesses are open and employees work, how employees are used, and so on.

In area after area, businesses have not yet started to sort out the implications. And society has not decided whose laws should apply; what rules and regulations should be adopted; who is to decide; and who is responsible for enforcement. The pirating of software, music, books and anything that can be put in digital form is symptomatic of a growing nest of problems.

The failure of business to recognize the move into the information age is demonstrated by its procrastination in facing up to the Y2K problem. That information technology and computer people could not get the attention of management long before the approach of the year 2000, to fix a problem the technicians knew existed and would have to be faced sooner or later, is a sad reflection on business managers. Undoubtedly, many did not understand the problem or its scope, and many who did were unwilling to spend the millions of dollars it would take to fix their systems before they had to, even though the delay added to the cost. Companies are now backing into the information age or being pulled by a technology they do not completely understand, even as they become more and more dependent on it. One result is the focus of my second thesis.

THESIS II

The abdication of IT ethical responsibility: The "Myth of Amoral Computing and Information Technology" permeates the public as well as the business mind, implicitly accepts the technological imperative, and undermines the ethical responsibility of business.

The lack of awareness of the ethical implications of the information age is what I call the "myth of amoral computing and information technology." The myth says that computers are not good or bad, information systems are not good or bad—they simply have a logic and rationale of their own. To speak of ethics with respect to them is to make a category mistake. Hence, when the computer is down, that is no one's fault. When programs malfunction or software has bugs, that is no one's fault. In general, anything that has to do with computers and information technology has a life of its own and is not susceptible to moral evaluation or blame or censure.

This myth is understandable in part because so few people in or out of business truly understand computing and information technology. They are tools that we non-techies like to have and use. But we do not take ethical responsibility for them, and because of our ignorance, we do not expect anyone else to take ethical responsibility for them. The result is a failure both to accept and to assign responsibility.

In businesses in the more developed countries, management for the most part still tends to think of information systems and information technology as something that is not central to the organization. Most managers do not understand them, and tend to ignore them. IS and IT offices are not typically center stage at corporate headquarters, and the typical manager is not a computer techie. The disconnect between corporate leaders and their technical divisions, which often are still off in a back set of rooms and considered part of the support structure and not part of the core business, is the clearest indication that firms have not moved consciously into the information age. Yet if we are truly in a developing information age, then IS and IT need to be at the center of things, and management has to both understand them and take responsibility for them.

The phenomenon of the Y2K problem to which I referred is symptomatic of the myth of amoral computing and information technology. We all know about the Y2K problem. And we know that law firms throughout the U.S., probably throughout the world, are gearing up to handle suits and defend companies against suits for damages as a result of companies failing to solve their Y2K problems in time. Yet amidst all the publicity, there is scarcely any mention of moral blame or discussion of the moral dimensions of the problem. It's as if computer programmers are not responsible for failing to fix programs earlier; managers are not responsible for making sure their products are Y2K compliant; or firms are not responsible for addressing their Y2K problems before they reached crisis proportions. The failure of any moral discussion is almost unbelievable, considering the general concern with business ethics in so many other areas.

THESIS III

Where are the business ethicists when you need them? The task of the business ethicist in the present period of transition—and a task in which few are engaged—is to help anticipate the developments and ease the transition by not losing sight of the effects on people.

The transition is from the industrial age to the information age. The ethical issues in business of the industrial age are those with which we are familiar. The development of the information age came about without conscious direction. As technology developed, the transition came along as a handmaiden. One consequence is that businesses and society as a whole are following the technological imperative—what can be developed is developed and implemented. Because the transition to the information age is currently taking place, many of the ethical issues have not clearly jelled. The task of the business ethicist in this instance is to at least keep up with the technological and social developments and identify problems and potential problems before they cause great harm, and before they became embedded ways of doing business that are difficult to change.

Business ethicists and society in general could wait for ethical problems and injustices of the information age to arise, and do analysis after the fact. Far preferable, however, is to anticipate injustice, prevent it from appearing, and form structures that are ethically justifiable, rather than having to undo and attempt to reform structures that are unfair, socially disruptive, and harmful to some of the parties. We of course cannot anticipate all the ethical issues that will arise. Experience and the empirical approach are also necessary. But we can anticipate more than we might expect, and I suggest that now is the time to start this analysis as we enter the information age. We do not need a new ethics framework, but we have to apply and possibly revise our ethical concepts and norms to fit the new environment. We need an imaginative analysis of the potential harms to people—be they in the realm of privacy, property, the new surveillance sweatshops, or other areas.

THESIS IV

Surmounting the Information nexus: In order to lay out the ethical issues of the information age in business, we must give careful attention to an analysis of the concept of information and the related concepts with which it forms a whole.

We can start by a simple analysis of information to see the virtues and the vices basic to it. A second step is to superimpose the analysis of information upon the analysis of industrialization to see how it changes production, exchange, advertising, conditions of employment, ownership rights, and so on. Each of these is transformed in the information age and the transformation requires new thinking about its effect on people.

If by "information" we mean not simply data but *useful* data, we see immediately that what we are interested in is useful information. Information, as generally used, stands for true knowledge in some area. Its opposites are disinformation, misinformation, and falsehood. Information is not simply data, but data that represents reality. It's true and not false.

Two virtues appear immediately. One is truth (and so truthfulness), the other is accuracy. It follows that the virtues necessary for the information age are not necessarily the same virtues as are or were necessary for the industrial age. In the latter, efficiency became paramount. As opposed to an agricultural age, punctuality became important and time took on critical importance. In the information age, truthfulness and accuracy take on special importance. For if the information is not accurate or truthful or correct, it is worse than useless. It's dysfunctional. It is ironic that truthfulness no longer seems to hold a place of honor in our society. We find people, including high government officials, lying. Truthfulness takes on more importance than ever.

False information is injurious to a system built on information. So we have truth as a necessary virtue and a presupposition, and distortion of the truth, lying, the spreading of false information, as vices to be guarded against. It is not only necessary for people not to lie or deceive or mislead; it's also necessary to represent reality as accurately as possible.

The enemy of accuracy is inaccuracy, which also leads to disinformation and error. These two virtues or values are basic to any system of information if it is to be socially useful and economically valuable for business, as well as for societies and the individuals within them.

Questions that immediately arise are: information of what or whom and for what or whom? Information about the world, or scientific information, is one kind of information. Information about societies, or social information, is another kind. Information about people and corporations is another kind. Important to all of them in an information age is ownership. Together with ownership goes power, and with it the dangers of control and manipulation. Truth leads to the concepts of enlightenment, education, and the potential freeing of individuals and of society. As individuals learn the truth, they are also in a position of empowerment. Politically, this makes enslavement difficult and it promotes self-rule or democracy. Nonetheless, there remains the possibility of the domination of citizens by government and of employees by employers, as well as of one society by another —for instance, through the domination of the communication resources.

Ethics is about people and their relations, and it is with this aspect of information that we can also get some inkling of problems and potential pitfalls of which we should be wary. The computer, so prominent in the information age, has the capacity to change our concept of ourselves and others—our concept of what it is to be human. Computers as tools can free human beings to be truly human. Or, if computers become the models against which we measure humanity, they can dominate our thinking and lead us to see ourselves as computers: as storers and manipulators of information, as thinking machines or robots, devoid of dignity and freedom.

Information about individuals clearly raises the issue of privacy, and information about corporations leads to the comparable problems associated with trade secrecy and espionage. As information becomes a central marketing tool, we are forced to face the harm that we can do to ourselves, society, and social relations through abuses that technology makes possible. As information becomes more and more central, we will also realize the vulnerability of networks. Unfortunately, sabotaging a corporate or national information network is easier than sabotaging the industrial network. The links are more fragile, and the interdependence greater. The need for safeguards against industrial and national information espionage and sabotage are profound and pressing.

To mention or raise these issues is not to solve them. But we can develop the analyses and begin better to understand the nature of the information age and its promises and pitfalls for individuals and for society. This is the beginning of an ethical analysis of the information age.

THESIS V

Confronting the communication complex: Information without communication is useless, and communication without information is empty. The ethics of communication shares the podium with the ethics of information in the new information age.

Information is not useful, even if truthful and accurate, unless it is used. Hence, it needs to be communicated. The communication process, which is developing at an exponential rate, is central to the information age. The virtues of truthfulness and accuracy carry over into communication. But there are elements of communication that pose their own ethical issues: communication of what, to whom, in what form?

In the information age, the communication explosion has resulted in information overload. There is more information than any individual can absorb. The instantaneous communication made possible by computers and the Internet opens the lines of communication to all, in an environment in which anyone can say or publish anything. There is no peer review or editorial overview before something gets published on the Web. And anonymity makes possible irresponsibility. In the name of the freedom of speech that we so cherish, more and more is posted on the World Wide Web under the guise of information. The result is that it is difficult to know what to believe and what to trust as reliable. The function that was previously filled by peer review, editors, and the cost of publication has been eradicated in web publishing. We need some comparable authenticators, which I shall call authentication centers.

In the industrial world, *Consumer Reports* and similar independent groups could test and give impartial judgments about products. Similar independent authenticators are needed with respect to information on the Web. For instance, which web sites that carry medical information are reliable

and authoritative, and which are not? The need for centers of this type in all areas of information is crucial if people are to benefit from the information available, and if they are to be kept from being harmed by the available misinformation and falsehoods, whether deliberate or unintended.

The same is true with respect to business, both for consumers and for suppliers of information. The lines between information and advertising, between information and brainwashing or manipulation, between information and self-interest are crucial. Two examples illustrate the point.

One is the review of books that people see upon going to Amazon.com. The only way such reviews will carry weight with viewers is if they can be sure the reviews are not simply paid for by the book publisher, and that Amazon.com is not paid to promote the book. If either is the cases then the review should be identified as an advertisement, as advertisements are identified in newspapers. The function of authenticator and of advertiser must be kept separate.

The second example is search engines that bring up businesses or organizations as the first few entries in any search. These businesses or organizations pay to have their sites mentioned first. If search engines are to be trusted, they should give the web sites closest to what one requests in a search, not the site that pays the most. If the latter is the standard, then that should be clearly stated, lest once again the distinction between authenticator and advertiser become blurred.

In this brief discussion, I have mentioned a number of other virtues besides truthfulness and accuracy—namely, trust or trustworthiness, and reliability. The four go together and form the basis for a smooth-functioning information processing system. The application of these four key virtues to business is part of the task for the business ethicist.

THESIS VI

The American information privacy schizophrenia: The U.S. is schizophrenic about information privacy, wanting it in theory and giving it away in practice.

Information must be communicated, but it must also be about something. Information about people has become much more important than it was previously because of the great opportunity for a revolution in marketing in which manufacturers can target potential customers in ways not previously possible.

A commonly heard issue that arises in the information age is the question of privacy—a question about which there is great confusion and about which Americans in particular may be said to be schizophrenic. The privacy that many complain is being eroded is not being taken from us. Most of us are giving it away. This privacy, which I shall call personal information privacy, is information about ourselves. Some individuals and some privacy and other groups, such as the Computer Professionals for Social Responsibility, argue in favor of legislation protecting personal information privacy and claim that everyone has a right to such privacy. But it is difficult to defend any strong sense of a right to such privacy when so many people blithely give the information away. Sometimes they do so for no return; sometimes for minimal return, such as the possibility of being notified about products they may be interested in purchasing; and sometimes for more substantial gain.

The importance of personal information to business, and one American response to privacy, is illustrated by the extraordinary offer made by the small company Free-PC.com. In February, the company offered 10,000 (eventually to go to a million) Compaq personal computers free to those willing to provide a variety of information about themselves (including their age, interests, income and hobbies) to receive ads on the Internet, and to have their Internet activities tracked. That information is obviously worth more to the company than the price of a 333 MHz computer with a 4 GB hard drive. The computer is free. It's the information about the users that is valuable. Whether giving up a large area of personal privacy is worth a computer might be a matter of debate and of personal choice. But it is difficult to defend any strong right to personal information privacy when so many value it so cheaply.

Rather than a right to personal information privacy, what most people seem to want is protection from harm as a result of the misuse of personal information. They fear identity theft, or credit card theft, or some harm—psychological, financial or physical—as a result of information about them-

selves being widely and easily available. It is not their privacy that is violated, but their sense of security. Yet the two issues are often confused and the arguments, similarly confused.

The information age is changing the nature of privacy. Nonetheless, as a society we have had almost no debate about what the legitimate limits or privacy are, why they are important, or what violates those limits. Since business is one of the two potential abusers of information—the other being government—this is a clear issue for business ethics. But it is one that has generated very little attention in the literature, and one that most businesses still do not include anything about in their codes.

THESIS VII

Mickey Mouse isn't a program: Information is very different from machines and tangible products, and so requires a new conception of property and property protection applicable to it.

Until fairly recently, a copyright granted protection to the expression of ideas in books and similar forms for 28 years (renewable for another 28 years): The protected period was then changed to the life of the author plus 50 years and to 75 years for a corporate author. In 1998, Congress extended the already-extended period, to the life of the author plus 70 years and to 95 years for a corporate author. The change came just in time to save Mickey Mouse from falling into the public domain, much to the pleasure of the Walt Disney Company.

On the other hand, when faced with the Y2K problem, many computer software companies claimed that their products did not have to be year 2000 compliant until 1996. Some even argued that the deadline should be 1998, because the life of a program was at best two or four years before it became obsolete. Nonetheless, computer programs are covered by copyright for the same 95 years that Mickey Mouse or the latest novel is covered. Does 95 years of protection make sense when the industry claims its products are obsolete after four years or less?

We can share information without depriving ourselves of its full use. It can be stolen from us without depriving us of its use. It is intellectual property. But just as we have not adequately discussed the changing nature of privacy, we as a society have not adequately discussed the changing nature of property applicable in the information age. We have sought to use traditional laws about copyright and patents, and have in the process caused a great deal of confusion. Instead of rethinking intellectual property in the information age, we have tried to make do with concepts and legal doctrines that were not constructed with thought of the kind of intellectual property that is emerging and that does not fit the old mold. What is fair and what is not are issues that form an important part of business ethics for the information age; these are issues that too few in the field presently address.

CONCLUSION

The upshot is that business ethicists have a whole range of issues to which they have scarcely turned their attention.

Cartoonists make fun of the lack of computer literacy and savvy among the older generation, and indirectly praise the ease and expertise with which the younger generation takes to the technology of the information age. They often hit the nail on the head. My hope is that you who are presently students, and who grew up with computers and information technology, will carry out the marriage of business ethics and information technology that we so urgently need in the emerging information age.

Corporate Policy and Ethics of Competitor Intelligence Gathering

Lynn Sharp Paine
John G. McLean Professor of Business Administration,
Harvard Graduate School of Business

. . . The purpose of this paper is to highlight the need for management to address the ethics of competitor intelligence gathering. Recent developments

From *Journal of Business Ethics*, Vol. 10, No. 6 (1991), pp. 423–436. Copyright © 1991 Kluwer Academic Publishers. Reprinted by permission of Kluwer Academic Publishers.

in the business environment have generated increasing interest in competitor intelligence, information that helps managers understand their competitors. Although information about rival firms has always been a valued and sought after commodity, competitor intelligence gathering has only recently begun to be systematized and legitimated as a business function. While understanding the competition is an important part of running a business, there are ethical limits on the types of competitor information that may be acquired; on the methods that may be employed to acquire it: and on the purposes for which it may be used. To date, however, few managers or management educators have addressed the ethics of intelligence gathering.

This paper will focus primarily on methods of acquiring competitor information. Separating legitimate from illegitimate approaches to information acquisition is in practice, the central ethical issue for intelligence-gathering specialists. . . .

GROWTH OF COMPETITOR INTELLIGENCE GATHERING

Evidence of the growth of interest in competitor intelligence is abundant. A 1985 study which looked at the intelligence-gathering budgets of twenty-five Fortune 500 companies found that all had increased substantially over the preceding five-year period.[1] Five years earlier, one-third of the companies had not had intelligence-gathering departments at all. Respondents to a 1986 study of 50 firms anticipated a dramatic increase in their intelligence-gathering budgets and almost all foresaw rapid growth in the staff assigned to intelligence gathering over the succeeding five-year period.[2] The findings of a recent Conference Board study of more than 300 U.S. firms were similar. Nearly all respondents said that monitoring competitors' activities is important and more than two-thirds expect their monitoring efforts to increase.[3] . . .

THE DARKER SIDE

There is, however, a darker side to the growth of intelligence gathering. It is reflected in the use of ethically questionable techniques for collecting information, the increase in trade secret litigation and information crimes, and increase in the resources devoted to corporate security. One expert on trade secret law estimates that court rulings on theft and misappropriation of information have increased four-fold over the past decade to more than 200 a year and that the actual problem of information misappropriation is at least ten times as large.[4] Another reports a surge in information crimes.[5] The American Society for Industrial Security, which includes both outside consultants and in-house security groups, was reported in 1986 to have 24,000 members and to be gaining 5000 new members a year.[6] . . .

The increase in information litigation cannot be explained solely by increasingly complex and costly technology. The increase also reflects the growing use of questionable techniques to gain access to ordinary business information generated by or about competing firms. The use of these techniques may evidence a general decline in ethical standards or a decline in resourcefulness and creativity. It may also be a by-product of increased competition and the competitor orientation of current thinking about business strategy. . . .

QUESTIONABLE METHODS OF ACQUIRING INTELLIGENCE

While surveys have examined people's willingness to engage in specific questionable practices, and at least one author has provided a list of ethical and unethical intelligence-gathering techniques, the ethical principles at issue in this area have not generally been made explicit. However, a review of studies of questionable practices, judicial opinions, news reports, popular articles, and the writings of intelligence-gathering experts, reveals that the most prevalent methods of questionable intelligence gathering full into three broad ethical categories:

1. those involving deceit or some form of misrepresentation:
2. those involving attempts to influence the judgment of persons entrusted with confidential information, particularly the offering of inducements to reveal informations: and
3. those involving covert or unconsented-to surveillance.

Norms prohibiting practices in these categories appear to be weaker than norms prohibiting theft of documents and other tangible property, a fourth category of ethically problematic intelligence gathering.

In contrast to intelligence gathering which relies on information that firms have disclosed to public authorities or to the general public or which is available through open and above-board inquiry, questionable techniques are generally employed to obtain information which the firm has not disclosed, is not obligated to disclose, and probably would not be willing to disclose publicity. But most of these techniques would be objectionable—whatever type of information they elicited—because they offend common standards of morality calling for honesty, respect for relationship of trust and confidence, and respect for privacy. While stating these principles does not resolve difficult and disputed questions concerning their interpretation and application, some of which are discussed below, understanding the principles can contribute to clearer thinking about the factors distinguishing legitimate from illegitimate practice.

Several indicators point to the use of techniques that violate or call into question these principles.

Misrepresentation

Opinion research indicates that many employees say their companies condone and they themselves approve of the use of various forms of misrepresentation to gather competitor intelligence.[7] For example, 45.9% of the respondents to a questionnaire administered to 451 participants in seminars on intelligence gathering approved of getting information by posing as a graduate student working on a thesis.[8] A striking 85.6% of the respondents believe their competitors would use this method of intelligence gathering. . . .

The use of misrepresentation can take many forms: conducting phony job interviews,[9] hiring students to gather intelligence under the guise of doing academic work, posing as a potential joint venturer, supplier or customer. The prevalence of phony interviews has led at least one marketing manager to remind his people that "a job interview may be a total sham, a way to get intelligence."[10] The victims of deceit may be rival firms, themselves, their suppliers and customers, or other parties with access to valuable information.

In a recently litigated case, a marketing manager and his firm were found liable for damages incurred by a competitor that had revealed confidential information to the manager and another employee when they posed as a potential customer.[11] The marketing manager, whose branch office was failing to meet his own quotas, arranged to have a new hire who had not yet joined the firm pose as a potential customer for the competitor's software. The manager attended the software presentation as a friend and consultant of the supposed customer, but without identifying himself or his employer. As a result of the misrepresentation, the pair were given a detailed demonstration of the software, in-depth answers to their questions, and access to the competitor's sales manual. They made unauthorized copies of critical information in the manual and successfully developed a competitive software program within a short period of time. In testimony reported in the court's opinion, the marketing manager referred to himself as a "scoundrel," but explained that market pressures had led him to this tactic.

Improper Influence

A second category of questionable techniques centers on attempting to influence potential informants in ways that undermine their judgment or sense of obligation to protect confidentiality or to act in their employer's best interests. Frequently, the attempt involves offering inducements or the possibility of certain advantages to those who may be able to provide valuable information. In its crudest form, this technique is bribery, the offering of something of value in exchange for the breach of a fiduciary duty. In the recent Pentagon scandals, consultants to defense contractors offered large sums of money to government officials in exchange for revealing information they were as fiduciaries legally obliged to protect. In more subtle cases not involving legal obligations of confidentiality, the inducement may work to compromise the potential informant's judgment. The source may decide to reveal information which is not strictly speaking,

confidential, but whose revelation is contrary to the employer's interests.

The inducement to disclose need not be cash: it may be a better job. The hiring of a rival's employee to gain access to confidential information appears to be a widely used and approved intelligence-gathering technique. Surveys conducted in 1974, 1976, and 1988 all found that many executives would use the practice.[12] Fifty-one percent of the smaller companies and 37% of the larger ones surveyed in 1974 said they expected employees hired from competitors to contribute all they knew to the new job, including the competitor's trade secrets.[13] And the Conference Board found that nearly half the respondents to its 1988 survey regard former employees of competitors as a very or fairly important source of information.[14] About half the executives responding to the 1976 study said they would try to hire a rival's employee to learn about an important scientific discovery that could substantially reduce profits during the coming year.[15]

In 1988, *Advertising Age* asked its readers whether it was ethical to hire an account supervisor from a competitor in order to gain information about the competitor's client. Seventy-three percent of the 157 professionals responding—advertisers, agency personnel, media people, consultants, and "others"—said the practice was ethical.[16] The Center for Communications posed the same hypothetical to professors and students of marketing. Fifty-nine percent of the 626 students responding said the practice was ethical, and 70% said they would do it.[17]

The hiring of employees with access to valuable competitor information has been the subject of numerous recent lawsuits and threatened lawsuits. When Wendy's International decided to substitute Coke products for Pepsi products in its restaurants, Pepsi threatened to sue Coke for pirating executives to gain information about Pepsi's contract and programs with Wendy's and for tampering with contractual relationships.[18] Similar issues have arisen in litigation between Johns-Manville and Guardian Industries,[19] Avis and Hertz,[20] and AT&T and MCI.[21] . . .

These techniques are ethically problematic because they involve attempts to undermine relationships of trust and confidence. In many cases, the information-seeker deliberately creates a conflict of interest in the hope that self-interest will overcome the potential informant's sense of obligation to protect his employer's confidential information or to act on his behalf. One must assume that the offering of valuable inducements reflects the fact, or at least the information-seeker's belief, that the information is not publicly available and can only be acquired, or can be acquired more cheaply, by attempting to induce a breach of confidence or to otherwise influence the judgment of those acting on behalf of the rival firm.

Part of the effectiveness of these inducements is explained by employees' uncertainty about what information may and may not be disclosed. While most firms treat some information as freely available to the public and other information as strictly confidential, there is a great deal of information that could be quite valuable to a competitor and whose confidentiality status is ambiguous in the minds of many employees, suppliers, and customers. For example, a firm may regard certain information shared with a supplier as confidential while the supplier sees it as public knowledge. The annals of trade secret litigation contain many examples of this sort of discrepancy. Indeed, there may be in-house discrepancies about what information is confidential and what may be revealed. The use of disclosure incentives in these cases may be the decisive influence tipping the potential informant's judgment in the direction of disclosure.

Ethical judgments about particular intelligence-gathering practices in this category are complicated by these same uncertainties. Still, legitimate questions about the scope of employees' obligations of confidentiality do not remove the moral difficulty that attaches to offering inducements deliberately intended to undermine a person's judgment or sense of obligation.

Covert Surveillance

Covert surveillance, another category of ethically problematic intelligence gathering, includes electronic espionage as well as other unconsented-to forms of observation such as eavesdropping and aerial photography. This category, perhaps the most difficult to define, raises questions about the legitimate scope of corporate privacy. When covert surveillance involves trespass or theft of tangible property, there is a convenient legal label for condemning it. But when it involves eavesdropping in public places or observation from afar using sophisticated technology, the wrong is most readily described as a violation of corporate privacy. Although the prevailing view is that corporations have no legal right to privacy, the idea persists that businesses and their employees should be able to assume they will not be observed or listened to in certain situations.

The techniques of covert surveillance are varied. They range from planting a spy in a competitor's operation—a technique which also involves deception and perhaps inducing actual employees to violate duties of confidentiality—to strategic eavesdropping in the bar and grill favored by a competitor's employees.[22] A widely discussed case of covert surveillance which resulted in an award of damages for the target company involved aerial photography of an unfinished manufacturing plant.[23] Clever gadgets of various types are available to assist covert observation: binoculars that hear conversations up to five blocks away, a spray that exposes the content of envelopes, a gadget that can read computer screens some two blocks away by picking up radio waves emitted by the machine.[24] Inspecting the competition's trash is another type of unconsented-to surveillance that has received attention in the press and has been litigated in at least one case.[25]

Covert observation, like misrepresentation and improper influence, is yet another way to obtain information which a rival does not wish to divulge. Ethical assessments of various forms of undisclosed observation may be controversial since privacy expectations are quite variable, as are judgments about the legitimacy of those expectations.

Covert observation in or from public places is especially problematic. For example, it may be possible to ascertain the volume of product that competitors are shipping by observing from public property the number of tractor-trailers leaving the plant's loading bays and by noting the size of the product in relation to the size of the trailers.[26] Opinions vary about the legitimacy of this practice. One might say that the firm has consented to observation by not putting a fence around the property.

And yet, just as it is unseemly to peer through an open window into the neighbors living room while walking down the sidewalk, we may think observation an invasion of the firm's privacy. . . .

Unsolicited Intelligence

The questions raised by covert surveillance are closely related to those raised by the receipt of unsolicited information. Disgruntled former employees of rival firms have been known to offer highly confidential technical information as well as more general information to competitors. Two recently litigated cases involved disputes about valuable information acquired as a result of a rival's mistake. In one case, a coded customer list was inadvertently left in the memory of a computer which was purchased at an auction by a competitor. The rival gained access to the codeword from an unwitting computer operator.[27] In another case, a dealer list was accidentally left in the store of a dealer who later became a competitor.[28]

There is no question of deceit or improper influence in these cases. The ethical question centers on whether unsolicited or inadvertently revealed information should be respected as private to the competitor. If intelligence gathering is governed by respect for the competitor's voluntary disclosure decisions, then information acquired through accident or mistake, or a former employee's breach of fiduciary duty, should not be examined and utilized. Indeed, this is the view reflected in the Uniform Trade Secrets Act.[29] Some courts and commentators, however, have taken the position that privacy is forfeited if information is accidentally revealed.[30]

The forfeiture view has some plausibility when disclosure is the result of a rival firm's carelessness. It is not unreasonable to expect a firm to suffer some loss if it acts carelessly. The view has less merit, however, when a third party such as supplier, inadvertently discloses a rival's valuable information. Still, in a survey discussed earlier, nearly half the marketing professionals questioned said it would be ethical to use information acquired as a result of a supplier's mistake.[31] In the survey vignette, a marketing professional is accidentally given slides prepared for direct competitor's final presentation in a competition in which both are participating. Having examined the slides before returning them to the embarrassed employee of the slide supply house, the marketer must decide whether to use the information to alter his presentation to attack the competitor's recommended strategy. . . .

THE DEARTH OF CORPORATE GUIDANCE

Despite the growing importance of intelligence gathering and the occurrence of unethical and questionable practices, top management has not yet faced the issue squarely. Only a handful of corporations offer employees practical guidance on intelligence gathering in their codes of conduct or ethics policies. While codes of conduct are not the only or even the most important, index of a corporation's ethical standards, they do provide some indication of ethical issues though; by the code's author to merit attention. . . .

As a practical matter, the risks of litigation and legal liability can best be minimized by avoiding intelligence-gathering activities in the ethically problematic categories discussed above; or misrepresentation, improper influence, unconsented-to surveillance, and theft. Admittedly, the threat of legal reprisal for engaging in these practices may be minimal in certain situations. Victims of unethical practices may not know they are being targeted, or they may lack evidence to prove their case in a court of law. Moreover, the law does not provide a remedy for every violation of ethics. If the victim of misrepresentation is not individually harmed, for example, he will have no legal recourse against the intelligence gatherer. And even if substantially harmed, the victim may have no remedy if the information acquired does not qualify as a trade secret or if the target firm has not taken adequate steps to protect the information in question.

From a management perspective, however, it is quite impractical to instruct employees to fine-tune their use of questionable practices on the basis of the legal risk in particular situations. Not only is it difficult to undertake an objective assessment of legal risk when under everyday performance pressures, but the legal risk of using unethical practices depends on consequences which are difficult, if not impossible, to anticipate in advance; the kind of information that will be obtained, the use to which it will be put, the harm that the target will suffer, the adequacy of the target's security measures, the likelihood of discovery, and the evidentiary strength of the target's case. What is not known in advance is that certain types of practices, namely, those involving misrepresentation, theft, improper influence, and covert surveillance, can provide the necessary foundation for legal liability. Even from the narrow perspective of legal costs, there is a good case for instructing employees to avoid questionable practices altogether rather than attempt to assess the fine points of legal risk.

INCREASING SECURITY NEEDS

More costly, perhaps, than the litigation and liability risks involved in the use of questionable practices are the increased security needs these practices generate over the long term. Every user of unethical practices must recognize his contribution to a general climate of distrust and suspicion. Insofar as individuals are more likely to engage in unethical conduct when they believe their rivals are doing so, unethical intelligence gathering contributes further to the general deterioration of ethical expectations. As the recent growth of interest in information security illustrates, declining ethical expectations translate into intensified programs for self-protection.

Firms that expect to be subjected to intelligence gathering through covert surveillance, deceit, and various forms of improper influence—especially when legal recourse is unavailable or uncertain—will take steps to protect themselves. They will tighten information security by building walls, installing security systems, purchasing sophisticated counter-intelligence technology, and instituting management techniques to reduce the risks of information leakage. Although some degree of self-protection is necessary and desirable, security can become a dominant consideration and a drain on resources.

Besides their out-of-pocket cost, security activities often introduce operational inefficiences and

stifle creativity. Avoiding the use of the telephone and restricting access to information to employees who demonstrate a "need to know" impose obvious impediments to the exchange of information vital to cooperation within the firm. When researchers, for instance, are denied information about the projects they are working on and about how their work relates to the work of others, they are cut off from stimuli to creativity and useful innovation.

Employee morale and public confidence may also be at stake. Information systems designed to insure that employees do not know enough to hurt the firm if they depart, like the dissemination of information on a "need to know" basis, proceed from a premise of distrust which can undermine employee morale. Even more clearly, information protection programs encourage an attitude of distrust toward outsiders. Employees are trained to be suspicious of public inquiries and to be wary of talking to or cooperating with outsiders who do not have security clearances. Over-restrictions on public access to information and excessive corporate secrecy generate public suspicion and hostility.

Although questionable intelligence-gathering practices may offer short-term advantages, they contribute, over the longer term, to a climate of distrust and the need for costly expenditures to tighten information security. These expenditures represent a diversion of management resources from more productive activities. Moreover, it is doubtful that firms can effectively protect their own valuable information if they encourage or tolerate loose ethical standards in acquiring competitor information. As the 1985 Hallcrest Report on private security in America concluded from studies of employee theft. "[E]ffective proprietary security programs . . . must emanate from a . . . strong sense of organizational ethics in all levels of the organization.[32] . . .

CONCLUSION

Managers who remain silent or fail to incorporate their "official" ethics policies into day-to-day management practice run the risk that they, their employees, and their firms will be involved in costly litigation over questionable intelligence-gathering tactics.

More important, they jeopardize their own information security and run the risk of contributing further to the increasing demand for information protection. This demand represents a costly diversion of resources from the positive and creative aspects of doing business, a drag on innovation, and an impediment to good public relations. By supporting a competitive system which respects the principles of common morality and the right of rivals not to divulge certain information, management supports its own vitality and the vitality of the competitive system.

NOTES

1. Information Data Search, Inc.: 1986, *Corporate Intelligence Gathering, 1985 and 1986 Surveys* (Cambridge, Massachusetts), p. 24.
2. *Id.,* at p. 6.
3. Sutton, H.: 1988, *Competitive Intelligence,* Conference Board Report No. 913 (The Conference Board, Inc., New York), pp. 6–7.
4. Roger Milgrim, author of 12 *Business Organizations,* Milgrim on Trade Secrets (1988), quoted in "Information Thieves Are Now Corporate Enemy No. 1," *Business Week* (May 5, 1986), p. 120.
5. The surge in information crimes is noted by Donn B. Parker of SRI International as reported in "Information Thieves," *Ibid.*
6. Haas, A. D.: 1986, "Corporate Cloak and Dagger," *Amtrak Express* (October/November), pp. 19–20.
7. Cohen, W., and Czepiec, H.: 1988, "The Role of Ethics in Gathering Corporate Intelligence," *Journal of Business Ethics* 7, pp. 199–203.
8. *Id.* at 200–201.
9. Flax, S.: 1984, "How To Snoop On Your Competitors," *Fortune* (May 14), p. 31.
10. Sutton, *Competitive Intelligence,* at p. 15.
11. *Continental Data Systems, Inc. v. Exxon Corporation,* 638 F. Supp. 432 (E.D. Pa. 1986).
12. Wall, "What the Competition is Doing," at pp. 32–34; Brenner, S. N., and Molander, A.: 1977 "Is the Ethics of Business Changing?" *Harvard Business Review* (January–February), p. 57; Industry Ethics Are Alive," *Advertising Age* (April 18, 1988), p. 88.
13. Wall, "What the Competition is Doing," at p. 38.
14. Sutton, *Competitive Intelligence,* at p. 19.
15. Brenner and Molander, "Is the Ethics of Business Changing?' at p. 57.
16. "Industry Ethics Are Alive."
17. The results noted here are available from the Center for Communications, a nonprofit educational organization located in New York, New York.
18. "Pepsi to Sue Coke Over Wendy's," *Washington Post* (November 13, 1986), p. E1.
19. *Johns-Manville Corp. v. Guardian Industries Corp.,* 586 F. Supp. 1034, 1075 (E.D. Mich. 1983), aff'd 770 F.2d 178 (Fed. Cir. 1985).
20. Lewin, "Putting a Lid on Corporate Secrets."
21. "Information Thieves," at pp. 122–123.
22. Both practices are described in Flax, "How to Snoop on Your Competitors," at pp. 28, 32.
23. *E.I. duPont deNemours v. Christopher,* 431 F. 2d. 1012 (5th Cir. 1970), cert. denied, 400 U.S. 1024 (1971).
24. "New Ways to Battle Corporate Spooks," *Fortune* (November 7, 1988), p. 72.
25. *Tennant Co. v. Advance Machine Co.,* 355 N.W. 2d 720.
26. Discussed in Flax, "How to Snoop on Your Competitors," at p. 33.
27. *Defiance Button Mach. Co. v. C & C Metal Products,* 759 F. 2d 1053 (2d Cir. 1985).
28. *Fisher Stoves, Inc. v. All Nighter Stove Works,* 626 F. 2d 193 (1st Cir. 1980).
29. *Uniform Trade Secrets Act With 1985 Amendments,* sec. 1 (2) (ii) (c), in Uniform Laws Annotated, vol. 14 (1980 with 1988 Pocket Part).
30. *Fisher Stoves; Defiance Button, See also Kewanee Oil Co. v. Bicron Corp.,* 416 U.S. 470, 476 (1973).
31. "Industry Ethics Are Alive."
32. Cunningham, W. C. and H. Taylor: 1985 *Private Security and Police in America,* The Hallcrest Report (Portland, Oregon: The Chancellor Press), p. 41.

QUESTIONS FOR DISCUSSION

1. Do individual investors really need additional protection under certain circumstances as Frederick and Hoffman suggest?
2. Has De George captured the full range of ethical issues that have arisen in the information age?
3. Should employers be entitled to monitor all of their employees' activities while on company premises if employees are warned beforehand?

CHAPTER 11

The Moral Corporation: Reflections and Challenges

Gaining the Ethical Edge: Procedures for Delivering Values-driven Management

Dawn-Marie Driscoll
Executive Fellow, Center for Business Ethics, Bentley College, and President, Driscoll Associates

W. Michael Hoffman
Executive Director, Center for Business Ethics, Bentley College

NOT JUST ROTTEN APPLES

Ethics and values are no longer merely personal issues. They are organizational issues as well, as Lynn Sharp Paine has emphasized in arguing that managers need to institute systems that encourage ethical conduct.[1] Such systems or procedures will not prevent all illegalities or improprieties but they can influence the character of an organization and its employees.

It is not that business people are inherently less ethical than others. But these procedures are critical

Reprinted from *Long Range Planning*, Vol. 32, No. 2, 1999, pp. 179–189, with permission from Elsevier Science.

if business organizations seek to develop a moral corporate culture within which individuals can act ethically. We have found that the root of unethical behavior is quite often systemic and not simply the result of rotten apples in the corporate barrel. Ethical people can be brought down by serving in a bad organization, just as people with questionable integrity can be uplifted, or at least neutralized, by serving in an organization with clear values. For that reason managers should carefully examine their organizational cultures to see if the structures and procedures, which systematically bind and move their employees, encourage or inhibit ethical behavior. If they do not, they must then take certain steps to change or supplement them.

One cautionary note must be emphasized, however. Adding values to an organization implies a culture change. However, mere policies and procedures alone will not bring about the change. Just as the individual ingredients of a cake do not constitute an edible dessert, policies and procedures that are devoid of vision will not achieve the desired outcome.

WHERE ARE WE NOW?

The fact that global managers are now exchanging ideas about values programs, rather than just compliance programs, did not happen overnight. The awareness process has been slow to develop, but is now accelerated by global communications that make a business scandal in one country headline news in another. Prescient organizations today realize that many of the world's best companies have made a commitment to ethical business conduct. Others do not want to be left behind, particularly if they want to become customers, suppliers or strategic partners with these global leaders.

In the United States, four factors have brought us to where we are today.[2]

The first was the adoption in 1991 of the Federal Sentencing Guidelines for Organizations,[3] which imposed a mandatory system of heavy fines and rigorous probation conditions for organizations convicted of federal crimes. These guidelines might have gone relatively unnoticed except that regulators were increasingly using financial penalties and even jail time for executives to punish all types of corporate wrongdoing.

While these guidelines represented a hard stick, they also showed an inviting carrot. A company was allowed to reduce its penalties dramatically if it had in place an effective system to prevent and detect violations *before* the offense occurred. Companies could reduce fines, avoid prosecution and use the establishment of such ethics and compliance programs as a defense in civil charges. The guidelines included the elements of what might be considered an effective system, but diligent companies quickly improved upon them in designing their own programs.

While the Sentencing Guidelines may have caught the attention of company lawyers, the Caremark case,[4] decided in 1996, caught the attention of senior managers and boards of directors. The Caremark opinion, written by Delaware's influential chancery court, long a leader in the development of corporate law, was a case of 'good news/bad news'.

Caremark, a medical services company, had been subjected to government investigations and eventually paid $250 million in fines, reimbursements and penalties. Shareholders alleged that the board of directors breached its fiduciary duty of care to Caremark by failing to supervise employees. The good news was that the court exonerated the board of directors, finding that the company had established ethics and compliance reporting systems before the problems began. The bad news was that the court issued a stern warning to other boards, stressing that directors could, at least in theory, face liability for failure to have such a program if improprieties later developed.

Nothing catches the attention of directors more than the word 'liable'. With the development of the Sentencing Guidelines (acting as a quasi-best practices model) and the Caremark edict, directors are now affirmatively required to probe, ask questions and establish procedures that will allow them to find out what is going on in the company.

Third, with the spotlights of the financial press, activist shareholders, regulators and the public shining on corporate misdeeds, many industry groups have decided to take the lead in designing programs of ethical behavior, believing that a model crafted by industry would be preferable to government regulation.

One of the first major efforts came in the mid 1980s when major companies in the defense industry united in response to the Packard Commission Report which investigated high-profile instances of fraud, waste and abuse in the defense industry. The resulting 1986 industry initiative, called the Defense Industry Initiative on Business Ethics and Conduct (DII), contained six principles that provided guidance for companies seeking to develop a comprehensive ethics program.[5]

The DII model of industry cooperation has been followed to a certain degree by other companies. For example, in the wake of allegations of personal trading by mutual fund portfolio managers, the Investment Company Institute convened a special task force to study the issue, rather than wait for the Securities and Exchange Commission to promulgate regulations. The panel recommended a series of clear and vigorous steps all fund companies should take to implement more stringent fund codes of ethics and compliance; two years later, a majority of fund complexes reported they had implemented the panel's recommendations.[6]

Further examples emerge as new crises appear. We expect that industry-wide initiatives will continue as companies come together to set their own values and ethical standards. This development reminds us of the old story about the owner of a paper company, one of the first converts to the cause of environmental protection. He spent millions to prevent his paper mill from polluting nearby rivers and by doing so, could no longer compete with the firms that did not follow his example. The company closed, 500 workers lost their jobs and the river remained polluted. But the business owner still believed that government regulation of paper mills was not the answer. He preferred that government not intervene in business activity. It's too bad he didn't consider an industry-wide conference of his fellow paper mill owners and convince them of the need for voluntary standards they would all pledge to follow.

While industry-wide ethics initiatives are particularly helpful in addressing specific problems, many companies and organizations are not waiting for their peers to 'get religion'. A fourth major factor that has hastened the implementation of comprehensive ethics programs is the growth of the business ethics movement in general, and the creation of the new position of ethics officers in particular. As a result of the DII effort, several large corporations appointed individuals to oversee their compliance efforts. In 1991, the Center for Business Ethics (CBE)[7] at Bentley College hosted a gathering of approximately forty ethics and compliance managers to share information and common concerns. This meeting led to the formation of the national Ethics Officer Association (EOA) in 1992. By 1998 its membership had grown to over 500 professionals who serve as managers of internal ethics and compliance programs. The EOA sponsors two national conferences a year and, in partnership with the CBE, offers executive education and certification programs for ethics officers. Most importantly, the EOA operates as a forum for members to exchange and review hundreds of corporate ethics materials, to attend skills enhancement seminars, to share problems via the EOA's website and to keep current with new developments in the field.

Other associations have also formed to help ethics professionals, including The Ombuds Association, the Healthcare Compliance Association

and the Office of Government Ethics (OGE), which oversees hundreds of ethics and compliance directors within government agencies. The networking and sharing that takes place in such organizations will help ensure that best practices in the business ethics field continue to be promulgated to anyone who is interested in learning about them.

HOW DO WE GO BEYOND WHERE WE ARE NOW? A TEN POINT PROGRAM

Corporate strategists make assumptions and suggest scenarios, analyze internal and external factors and lay out a road map for achieving organizational goals. Leaders articulate a vision and motivate their employees. But at some point, managers must execute the game plan which requires specific action points. What are the elements that will turn values into action? Here is a ten point program that we believe is the minimum required to establish an ethical infrastructure in an organization and to ensure that the institutional memory survives personnel and market upheavals.

Self-assessment

You can't plot a course without knowing where you're starting from. Therefore a self-assessment, or liability inventory,[8] is a necessary first step to determine what procedures are needed to address organizational risks and concerns.

Managers can conduct this in-depth examination themselves, although many prefer to have outside consultants perform the survey and analyze the results, much like an auditor's report and letter of recommendation. A comprehensive risk assessment will consider what ethical issues have faced competitors and partners, as well as where the company itself has had problems. Employee surveys and focus groups will determine how employees view management and the company, what situations, dilemmas and questions they face, and what might be the underlying cause of future problems. This is sometimes referred to as an ethical climate assessment.

The professional services firm of Coopers & Lybrand recently conducted focus group interviews with over 200 employees to identify issues that impacted them and reviewed all existing policies before crafting a new policy statement and publishing its code of conduct book, *The Way We Do Business.* According to Harry Britt, Global Manager of Ethics and Business Conduct, extensive risk assessment is essential before rolling out a new ethics initiative.[9]

Commitment from the Top

No ethics or values initiative should begin without the most senior levels of management making an explicit commitment to long-term success.

Let's start with the board of directors. Directors should specifically authorize ethics and values programs and formally appoint a senior officer to oversee them. Many boards require this officer to report to them regularly, usually through the board's audit committee, regarding the progress in implementing the program. Some boards have established a separate ethics committee of, and for, the board in addition to its audit committee.

Furthermore, some boards of directors, such as the Michigan Physicians Mutual Liability Company, use board meeting or retreat time to undergo their own customized ethics training, focusing on ethical issues at the board level. Consensus about standards of business ethics is critical at the board level, one director explained, and must be discussed well before a crisis hits.[10]

Why is a 'senior officer' appointed by the board to direct its business conduct program? While adhering to company standards and values is every employee's responsibility, this does not mean than an overseer is unnecessary. Here there is an apt analogy to a company's internal auditing function. Every employee in a company is responsible for financial integrity, but a separate internal auditing group is needed to give this focus and direction and to serve as a check on the process. So too, ethics managers serve a similar purpose.

According to Graydon Wood, formerly the ethics officer of Nynex's award-winning ethics program, the ideal qualifications for an ethics officer are that he or she:

- holds a high level position within the company;
- operates with unrestricted access to the chief executive officer and the board of directors, or a committee of the board;

- maintains a high degree of trust and respect among members of the senior management team;
- can assemble resources for effecting internal procedural changes and carrying out investigations;
- has access to information and support mechanisms that provide monitoring, measuring, early warning and detection;
- offers incentives and rewards for productively carrying out the compliance role;
- has the skills to operate effectively with the media, public forums and the legal process.[11]

While some companies have appointed full-time ethics officers, other companies underscore the importance of ethical values by giving its top executive the responsibility. Some do both. For example, at USAA, the diversified financial services company, Chief Executive Officer Robert T. Herres is the Chief Ethics Officer and Elizabeth Gusich, who oversees the program, is the Ethics Program Coordinator. At Bell Atlantic, a telecommunications company with 140,000 employees and 22 million customers, the chief compliance officer is the Chief Executive Officer, who reports directly to the board of directors. The Vice President of Ethics, Compliance, Diversity and Organizational Development also reports to the board of directors' audit committee, as well as the management audit committee and the CEO.

Codes of Business Conduct

A blueprint for building a moral culture within a corporation must include a written ethics code. These corporate codes of ethics vary in quality and substance. Some consist only of a set of specific rules, a list of do's and don'ts (usually corresponding to clearly illegal or unethical actions such as bribery, price-fixing, conflicts of interest, improper accounting practices and acceptance of gifts). Other codes consist largely of general statements that put forth corporate goals and responsibilities, a kind of credo expressing the company's philosophy and values. The more substantive codes consist of both. Rules of conduct without a general values statement lack a framework of meaning and purpose; credos without rules of conduct lack specific content.

In addition, codes of conduct should not imply that whatever has not been strictly prohibited is thereby allowed. There is no way that all ethical or unethical conduct can be exhaustively listed and mandated through a code, nor ought there be. Business ethics, like all areas of ethics, has grey areas that require individual discretion and thought. A good corporate code of values and conduct should include certain managerial and employee guidelines for making ethical decisions, including the principles and factors that one ought to consider before arriving at a decision.[12] Comprehensive codes might also include sources both inside and outside the corporation through which advice and counsel could be offered, as well as cases based on the company's history or industry that might clarify a future ethical dilemma. Whatever these guidelines include, they should make a person aware that there may well be difficult ethical judgments to make based on the values inherent in the code, rather than from the letter of the law. The employee should also know that he or she will be accountable for their behavior. This will place a greater sense of personal ethical responsibility on employees and send a clear message that corporate integrity is dependent on individual integrity.

Here are some guidelines for writing an ethics or conduct code:

- Be clear about the objectives that the code is intended to accomplish.
- Try to get support and ideas from the code from all levels of the organization.
- Be aware of the latest developments in the laws and regulations affecting your industry.
- Write as simply and clearly as possible. Avoid legal jargon.[13]

While most organizations begin an ethics initiative with written codes, they also know that many employees don't read these codes—even when the document is put in front of them. Francis J. Daly, Corporate Director for Ethics and Business Conduct at Northrop Grumman, has a good suggestion: "Codes of conduct should be policies that are easy to read and easily understood by people who don't like to read, can't read or respond much better to visual information. Take creative license in the presentation".[14]

Some companies with mature ethics programs have reduced voluminous codes of conduct to just a few key values, trusting that their employees will do the right thing when confronted with a situation that poses no easy answers. For example, the Sears employee booklet, "Freedoms and Obligations", combines both: the folder contains two inserts, "My Code of Business Conduct" and "My Leadership Principles".

Ivan Seidenberg, Chief Executive Officer of Bell Atlantic, recalled that several years ago company executives thought they should update the code of conduct. Rather than add more rules and regulations, however, they focused on the value of 'responsibility', implying that the company and its employees know how to behave. Each employee now has the responsibility to do the right thing.

Communication Vehicles

The best values program in the world is worth little if it is not communicated well, in various forms and as often as possible. Fortunately, communication in most organizations has evolved from pedantic lectures to the sophisticated uses of high technology and employee interaction.

The values mission of the organization cannot be overemphasized, by talk or by walk. Vincent O'Reilly, former Vice Chairman at Coopers & Lybrand, stresses that all language, every decision, every meeting should contain reference to the basic standards of business conduct of the worldwide accounting firm.

BellSouth, the telecommunications company, uses a variety of communication vehicles to enhance its ethics initiative, "A Commitment to Our Personal Responsibility". F. Duane Ackerman, the President and Chief Executive Officer, introduced the program by sending a letter to every employee. Each also received an attractive 40-page booklet containing BellSouth's Code of Conduct, information on over twenty different subjects (including the law, BellSouth's policies and sample questions and answers), and a resource guide for further questions. Employees were given a wallet-sized card with the toll-free telephone number of the ethics line. All supervisors were given a leader's guide to assist them in conducting meetings with employees to discuss ethical concerns. At the conclusion of the training, every employee signed an affirmative statement indicating they had read and understood the information provided.

But the communication was not a one-time event. BellSouth employees can submit questions anonymously to the ethics office via its website or through their own company e-mail address. They are encouraged to call the company's human resources department, the legal department, the security department, the auditing department or the ethics office if they need information and guidance. The website has the Commitment booklet on-line, frequently asked questions and answers and ordering information for the four-part "Ethics at BellSouth" video series that has a number of dramatizations of ethical dilemmas for use in discussing ethical issues.

BellSouth's ethics officer, Jerry Guthrie, constantly communicates the values and ethics message of the company, inviting himself to departmental meetings, gatherings of company lawyers, human resource managers and even conferences of the company's international managers. Finding new and effective ways to communicate the values directive of the company is one of his top priorities.

Training

Even the most expansive and effective communication mechanisms are not sufficient to instill values into action. Few employees instinctively know how to make an ethical decision or even to think through the process of evaluating potential courses of action and their consequences. Therefore, ethics training seminars are critical. Such seminars allow employees to exchange views with each other about the importance of ethics and about issues that specifically relate to their daily work.

As with codes of conduct, some seminars are better than others. Many are not long enough to accomplish anything significant; many do not adequately prepare the participants in advance of the session: and many are not considered in the larger context of an overall corporate ethics development effort.

Here are some suggested objectives for a training seminar in business ethics:

- to clarify the ethical values and enhance the ethical awareness of employees;
- to uncover and investigate ethical issues and concerns that directly relate to the organization;

- to discuss criteria for ethical decision making within the organization;
- to examine and enrich the structures, strategies, resources, policies and goals which shape the ethical environment and guide the ethical activities of the organization.

The most effective training seminars must be individually designed according to the business issues of the industry and the organization, as well as its particular culture and mission. While the content of such seminars may depend as well on the length of time and the objectives set for the training session, the most effective programs contain these common elements:

- opening remarks by a senior executive;
- an introduction by the trainer;
- a discussion of general ethical principles and business ethics in particular;
- an overview of how companies and organizations are integrating ethical considerations into their operations;
- a discussion of the framework and guidelines for ethical decision making;
- response to various common situations, concerns and myths about business ethics;
- dramatization of ethical dilemmas;
- discussion of the dilemmas, including identification of the ethical issues, application of values and ethical principles and consideration of alternative plans of action;
- design or critique of ethics initiatives at the company or organization, such as its code of conduct and its guidance system for reporting problems or seeking help.[15]

An ethics training seminar should help the participants see or recognize ethical issues, especially those that are not self-evident. An effective seminar should fit the participants with 'moral lenses' through which they will see their world from an ethical point of view. But *ethical awareness* is not the only objective.

Such training seminars should also provide participants with tools for rational ethical analysis and decision making. And further, there should be assistance in how to transfer such *ethical reasoning* into *ethical action* within the corporate context. Finally such seminars should stress the importance of *ethical leadership* and role modelling. There are leaders at all levels of the organization—from the mailroom to the executive suite—and at any one time an employee might seek out a fellow co-worker for ethical advice.[16] The characteristics of a community are shaped out of the dynamics of such role modelling, and a company's ethical character is no exception.

A successful ethics training program should pertain to all levels of the organization, not just upper and middle management. Finally, ethics workshops should occasionally mix different levels of the organization, from hourly workers to executive officers, and even members of the board of directors, in order to promote better understanding and communication among all members of the organization with regard to the company's ethical problems and value commitments. This would help build a stronger and more unified ethical corporate culture.

Resources for Assistance

In the early stages of the business ethics movement, companies instituted reporting hotlines, toll-free telephone numbers promoted as a way for employees to report wrongdoing. But as the calls came in, managers realized that employees would not limit their calls to reporting actual illegalities, since, in some cases, not even lawyers can discern whether a particular set of facts constitutes a violation of law. Managers also saw value in changing the label of the telephone line to a 'helpline' or 'guideline', to serve as a source of advice and counsel on ethical and compliance issues. Today, many ethics officers report that over 40% of their calls on helplines concern internal human resource issues and incidents.

Not all companies install toll-free telephone lines, thinking an 'open door' policy and a clear code of conduct will suffice. But most employees are skeptical about open door systems that require a subordinate to directly confront a boss or a bosses' boss. Rather, they prefer anonymous calls. While some companies staff hotlines with their own personnel, a significant number have turned to outside professional services, which provide 24-hour-a-day, 365-days-a-year coverage.

These helplines have not become vehicles for cynical or revengeful whistleblowers with false in-formation, as some companies feared. Companies such as Lockheed-Martin have implemented procedures that reduce the number of false accusations without impairing the efficacy of the ethics hotline. Callers are asked to state their name, but this information is not included in any further documentation. In most cases, the caller's identity is known only to the ethics officer, as a form of corporate 'witness protection'. At BellSouth, callers are not required to give their name and ethics managers assign a coded number to the call to track the investigation. If callers choose to give their name, they can ask that it not be released.

To protect the rights of those who are being investigated, other companies have a requirement that the accused be notified immediately, except when there are extenuating circumstances. This places the burden of proof on the investigators to explain why notification should not occur. In cases where notification would clearly hamper the investigation, however, the option to withhold notification remains open.

At Northrop Grumman, "When to Challenge" guidelines are an important part of its value statement. Employees are told that if they are ever asked to do something which they believe is either unethical or not in Northrop Grumman's best interest, or if they become aware of any such activities, it is their right and their responsibility to express their concerns. The advantage of a clear statement and guideline like Northrop Grumman's is that it answers perhaps the most difficult ethical questions for an employee; is whistleblowing morally obligatory? Must we take action to prevent harm as well as not cause it ourselves?

Companies with extensive resources for assistance, from telephone lines to websites to ethics offices and e-mail, make it easy for their employees to make difficult ethical choices according to the company's values.[17]

Organizational Ownership

No ethics officer is an island and no program to put values into action will be successful without the full involvement of managers across the organization. For that reason, multidepartmental committees have become an effective supporting structure to any ethics initiative. With senior managers drawn from diverse departments across the company (human resources, security, legal and auditing being key), the ethics officer has a 'kitchen cabinet' to serve as a sounding board and to drive ownership of the program throughout all areas of the business. The committee also helps bring to bear the resources available in participating departments.

At USAA, for example, the Ethics Program Coordinator is part of the office of the General Counsel and works closely with USAA's Ethics Council, a group of senior level executives who review issues of major significance and take appropriate action. The Council is comprised of the Senior Vice President and Chief Financial Officer, who chairs the group; the Senior Vice President, General Counsel and Corporate Secretary; the President of the USAA Alliance Services Company, and the President of the USAA Life Insurance Company.

One risk of a corporate-directed ethics initiative is that it will not take hold in the outlying areas and locations. To prevent this possibility, some companies have deputized specific managers in the field to be responsible for implementing ethics initiatives in their area. Depending on the industry, some companies have assigned responsibility for coverage for discrete risk areas, so that employees have a subject matter expert to turn to when they have questions. These 'responsible officers' for each subject area develop an expertise in certain high-risk areas, such as environmental compliance, and may work in teams with a lawyer or manager for responsibility in the area.[18]

Consistent Response and Enforcement

The most effective way to undermine an ethics program is to discipline a low level employee or one who is not well liked while ignoring similar wrongdoings by a senior executive or star performer. Yet some ethics officers have confidentially stated that ensuring consistent enforcement and response to ethical issues is one of their toughest challenges. It is easy to understand why consistency is a formidable task, particularly in organizations with thousands of employees located at many sites. That is why careful coordination with human resource personnel or an ethics coordinating committee that can review or hear appeals of disciplinary actions are useful tools for ethics officers and managers.

Not all ethical dilemmas involve misconduct, however. Consider the following scenario and stated organizational values of 'care', 'respect' and 'responsibility'. Company X has a general policy of prohibiting employee solicitations in the workplace. This is a way to guarantee that workers do not feel pressured to contribute money or join organizations and to respect their privacy. A well-liked manager's son was involved in a serious automobile accident and his supervisor and co-workers wanted to plan an event to raise money for the son's continuing care and use company resources to inform all employees. The supervisor approached the ethics committee to ask if this would be permitted. The committee, encouraging employees to take responsibility for their own decisions at the local level, stressed considerations such as the pressure on co-workers to participate and contribute money, the precedent such an event might set, the use of company resources for this cause but not another, and obligations to other needy employees, but left the decision to the supervisor. The supervisor went ahead with plans for the event, much to the consternation of the ethics committee, which in hindsight thought it should simply have denied the request. Now it was left with the problem of uneven enforcement of company policies.

Consistent response to ethical issues involves more than wrongdoing. Some organizations have built-in incentives, evaluations and rewards for ethical character, understanding that an employee can diligently follow all procedures but still be viewed as a person with questionable values. Shirley Peterson, former corporate vice president of organization development and ethics at Northrop Grumman, helped the company implement its Leadership Inventory, a checklist of behavioral characteristics tied directly to Northrop values. Each manager receives a summary of how others evaluated him or her and identifies behavioral patterns they need to address.[19] Through this process, Northrop Grumman ensures that its performance appraisal systems are well integrated with its values mission and that both positive and negative behavior exhibited by managers are treated uniformly.

Audits and Measurements

Managers should not establish ethics initiatives, training programs and other infrastructure without constantly measuring their effectiveness. On the process side, audits should reveal whether communication vehicles such as helplines or websites are working, whether employees have acknowledged receiving training and whether employees are even aware of resources available to them. Substantive audits should include detailed investigations into potential violations of law or regulation.

Many companies already perform compliance audits and monitoring, by listening to the way telephone representatives impart information or by reviewing advertisements, offering documents or bid processes. Auditing how employees adhere to an organization's values is a bit more difficult, but many companies are finding effective ways to judge whether the program is working. They use employee, customer and supplier satisfaction surveys, focus groups, and detailed exit interviews, often performed by outside consultants to glean unbiased feedback.

Revision and Refinements

Finally, a program to instill value's into an organization must be more than a precise model of ten points that sits on a shelf. It must be a living instrument. Every month, every year, circumstances and situations change that require managers to reevaluate the goals and contents of even the best values programs. At Motorola, for example, the ethics initiative is called "Motorola Ethics Renewal Process". In an attempt to be flexible and meaningful for the company's 150,000 employees, 60% of whom work outside the United States, the emphasis is on the word 'process'. Rather than a formal program or a detailed audit, Motorola managers have determined that to meet their goal of being the most trusted company in the world, its employees needed a process by which to discuss tough issues.[20]

Glenn Coleman, manager of Ethics Communications and Education at Texas Instruments, explains why TI recently revisited its former code of ethics. "It is time to focus on the values, not just the rules. We've had a written code since 1961, and five years ago, I would have described it as one of the best around. But typically, the Ten Commandments had grown to ten thousand laws, so it was time to try something different to empower our employees, who have to make good decisions on the fly without referring to the rule book". "An international TI team looked at our values within the scope of our company's culture and business objective, and settled on three: Integrity, Innovation and Commitment. We wrapped these words around some modern graphics, published it in a booklet form, translated it into twelve languages, and passed it out to our 45,000 employees around the world. Our booklet is on-line, and cross-referenced by subject matter, with resources, examples and information on more than one hundred subjects".

Coleman believes that the best ethics and values programs are reactive and dynamic. "This is the most interesting time to be working at TI", he said, "as we take this giant step into the future, carrying our ethics program to an even higher plateau. But we see ethics and values waving through everything we do in the company. Everything jives together. We don't feel that the Ethics Office is having to drive ethics anymore; we're being pulled along by the day-to-day operations and decisions of our company and our employees."[21]

HOW WILL WE KNOW WHEN WE GET TO WHERE WE WANT TO BE?

We won't. The task of putting values into action is never finished, which is how it should be. Like the three most important words in selecting real estate (location, location, location) the most important words to remember in maintaining a values-based culture are diligence, diligence, diligence.

But there are clues to indicate whether or not the program is working.

Employees Are Motivated

Loyal, capable employees are so critical to most enterprises today that we've come to call them human assets, intellectual capital or even investors, who are as entitled to tangible rewards as shareholders (who, after all, only invest their money, not their time and effort).[22]

The focus on the behavior and satisfaction level of individual employees may seem misplaced in a discussion of an organization's culture, but an essential dynamic occurs between individuals and organizations. Individuals do not operate in a vacuum. Just as organizations are made up of individuals, individuals are dependent on organizations. Individuals gain meaning, direction and purpose by belonging to and acting out of organizations, social cultures that are formed around common goals, shared beliefs and collective duties. Corporations, like other social organizations, can and do influence individual decisions and action. A values-based program can have a positive influence on employee motivation and performance.

The importance of such a program to individual workers is not to be underestimated. A range of recent surveys demonstrates the significance of ethics initiatives in helping employees sort out conflicting priorities and deal with pressure. An April 1997 study by the Ethics Officer Association and the American Society of Chartered Life Underwriters and Chartered Financial Consultants found that 56% of workers feel pressure to act unethically or illegally on the job, and 48% admitted they had engaged in such actions. These transgressions ranged from deceiving customers to cutting corners on quality.[23]

Even human resource managers, who should know better, aren't immune from pressure.[24] A recent study of human resource professionals found that more than half had observed workplace conduct that violated the law or the organization's standards of ethical business conduct. Nearly half felt pressured to compromise such standards to achieve business objectives.[25]

While such surveys may only report the bad news, ethics officers and other professionals share information about the good news: employees are significantly aided by clear values statements that give them a ready defense against pressure to act unethically, and by resource mechanisms to quickly answer their questions, no matter how insignificant.[26] A company that cares enough about its employees to pay attention to their concerns and realities will ultimately be rewarded by a loyal and satisfied workforce.

Ethical Behavior Pays

Managers oriented to the bottom-line may find this a difficult standard to prove. The corollary may be a better test: unethical behavior can be costly. A person needs only to read the headlines in the business sections of newspapers to understand that the price of misconduct is rising:

- Texaco. $176 million racial discrimination settlement after tape recordings of improper conversations among its top executives were released (1996).
- Archer-Daniels-Midland. $100 million antitrust fine for price-fixing (1996).
- Louisiana-Pacific Corporation. $37 million fine for customer and environmental fraud, including lying to inspectors (1998).
- Laboratory Corporation of America. $187 million in fines and penalties for health care billing fraud (1996).
- Mitsubishi Motor Corporation. $34 million to settle a government investigation of pervasive sexual harassment (1998).
- Royal Caribbean Cruises, Ltd. $9 million fine for deliberately dumping waste off the coast of Florida (1998).

These are examples of real costs, but can you measure savings? One ethics officer confidentially shared his frustration in reporting to his board of directors about the company's ethics and business conduct program. One director asked him how he could statistically measure the program's success. He had to explain that one can't always measure preventive medicine, but that increased employee use of the confidential helpline, employee satisfaction surveys and the prompt resolution of festering problems were distinct benefits that may ensure that the company would not become a newspaper headline in the future.

Being Ahead of the Curve

Most managers prefer a checklist approach to implementing a program; they think through the vision and can then measure the roll-out by seeing if all the 'action items' or programmatic steps have been achieved. If all ten (or twenty or thirty) have been finished, they are satisfied.

Unfortunately, even if you compare your efforts today to the best practices models available, you can't be confident that your work is completed. You don't achieve 'ethics' or 'values'. It's a total way of behaving, not a one-time effort. The best you can strive for is to be ahead of the curve, always striving to be one of the most ethical organizations while knowing that, like sainthood, perfection will never be attained in this lifetime.

We like to use the analogy of affirmative action. An organization can have an impassioned mission statement about diversity as well as a myriad of procedures, efforts and measurements to recruit and retain and promote minorities in the workforce. In truth, with all these endeavors the climate for integrating minorities into the employee pool may be no better than before. But if affirmation action—or putting values into action—is an important goal, you will never stop asking. "How can we do this better than we are?" This is what 'revision and refinement' is all about.

We do have some candidates for Excellence in Ethics and Values, with the caveat that excellence is a moving target. A benchmark comparison of your efforts against the work of these companies—in many cases motivated to excellence by an ethical crisis—is a good starting point.

- General Electric (despite problems with bond trading losses and supervision at its Kidder Peabody subsidiary);
- Sears (despite problems in its automotive repair shops and credit collection departments);
- Northrop Grumman (despite problems in its Pomona testing labs);
- Nynex, now Bell Atlantic (despite problems with employee and vendor improprieties);
- PricewaterhouseCoopers (despite problems with some partner actions in Arizona and Los Angeles).

The goal is to not be discouraged by missteps or problems along the way. Rather, it is to continue to surpass today's professional leaders in business ethics.

CONCLUSION

When Peter Drucker, the legendary management guru, was thirteen, a teacher asked him what he wanted to be remembered for. Drucker, still prolific in his 80's, is still asking himself that ques-

tion, "because it pushes you to see yourself as a different person—the person you can *become*".[27]

So too with our quest for the ethical edge. Managers should not want to be lauded for the good procedures they set in motion, but rather for the values these procedures deliver, ones that create a management culture that is always striving for excellence.

REFERENCES

1. L. Sharp Paine, Managing for organizational integrity, *Harvard Business Review* March–April, 106–117 (1994).
2. For a further discussion see D.M. Driscoll, W.M. Hoffman and J.E. Murphy, Business ethics and compliance: What management is doing and why, *Business and Society Review* 99, July, pp. 35–51 (1998).
3. United States Sentencing Guidelines. Chap. 8. Sentencing of Organizations. Washington, DC (1991).
4. In *Re Caremark International Inc. Derivative Litigation.* 1996 WL 549894 (Del. Chancery C.A. 13670, Sept. 15, 1996).
5. The six principles were (1) provide a written code of business ethics and conduct; (2) train employees concerning their responsibilities; (3) provide a free and open atmosphere; (4) adopt procedures for voluntary disclosure; (5) be responsible to other companies in the industry and (6) have public accountability.
6. Investment Company Institute, *Report of the Advisory Group on Personal Investing,* Washington, DC (1994). Two environmental examples: All members of the Chemical Manufacturers Association have adopted a code of environmental management practice called the Responsible Care Initiative; the International Organization for Standardization's (ISO) 14000 standards attempt to provide a global standard for environmental management.
7. Founded in 1976, the Center for Business Ethics at Bentley College in Waltham, Massachusetts, is one of the oldest and most internationally recognized institutes for the study and exchange of ideas in business ethics among the worlds of academe, business, government, labor and public interests.
8. J. Kaplan, J. Murphy and W. Swenson, *Compliance Programs and the Corporate Sentencing Guidelines,* Clark Boardman Callaghan, Deerfield, IL (1993).
9. In 1998, Coopers & Lybrand merged with Price-Waterhouse to create the firm of PricewaterhouseCoopers, which is now developing a network of ethics programs for its entire global organization.

10. See D.M. Driscoll and W.M. Hoffman, Doing the right thing: business ethics and boards of directors, *Director's Monthly* 18, November, 1–7 (1994) and D.M. Driscoll and W.M. Hoffman, Hark corporate director: tis the call of ethical leadership, *Ethics Today* 3. Winter, 5 (1998).

11. D.M. Driscoll, W.M. Hoffman and E.S. Petry, *The Ethical Edge: Tales of Organizations That Have Faced Moral Crises,* pp. 107–108. MasterMedia Ltd, New York (1995).

12. These factors need not be complex. "What would I advise my child to do?" "How would this look in the newspaper?" "If my decision were to set a precedent, what would be the result?" are examples of mini-tests of an ethical course of action.

13. W.M. Hoffman, Developing the ethical corporation, *Bell Atlantic Quarterly,* 3(1), (1986).

14. Author interview, 15 February (1998).

15. D.M. Driscoll, W.M. Hoffman and E. S. Petry, *The Ethical Edge: Tales of Organizations That Have Faced Moral Crises,* pp. 187–188, MasterMedia Ltd, New York (1995).

16. See D.M. Driscoll and W.M. Hoffman, Spot the red flags in your organization, *Workforce,* June, 135–136 (1997).

17. See D.M. Driscoll, The hazards of blowing the whistle, *Boston Business Journal,* 5–11 July, 8 (1996).

18. J. Kaplan, Sundstrand's 'Responsible Executive' program, *Corporate Conduct Quarterly* 4, 33 (1996).

19. Examples of these behaviors include 'Confronts and deals with integrity issues', 'Leads by example', 'Shows respect for suppliers as team members' and 'Stands up for what he/she believes in'. Source: D.M. Driscoll, W.M. Hoffman and E.S. Petry, *The Ethical Edge: Tales of Organizations That Have Faced Moral Crises,* pp. 153–157, MasterMedia Ltd., New York (1995).

20. K. Purdy, Who's doing what?—A look at industries and companies, *Ethical Management* 7(11), 5–6(1998).

21. Author interview. 3 March (1998).

22. See T.A. Stewart, *Intellectual Capital: The New Wealth of Organizations,* Doubleday, New York (1997).

23. American Society of Chartered Life Underwriters and Chartered Financial Consultants. *Sources and Consequences of Workplace Pressure* (1997).

24. See D.M. Driscoll and W.M. Hoffman, HR plays a central role in ethics programs, *Workforce,* April, 151–152 (1998).

25. The Society for Human Resource Management, *The Society for Human Resource Management/Ethics Resource Center Business Ethics Survey* (1997).

26. One in six employees recently surveyed agrees with the statement that the traditional standards of right and wrong are no longer relevant and one-third either agreed or are ambivalent. But employees are receptive to corporate solutions which outline policies proscribing conduct and encourage employees to police themselves (American Society of Chartered Life Underwriters and Chartered Financial Consultants and Ethics Officer Association, *Technology and Ethics in the Workplace: The Ethical Impact of New Technologies on Workers* (1988)). See also D.M. Driscoll and W.M. Hoffman, Allow employees to speak out on company practices, *Workforce,* November, 73–76 (1997).

27. J. Beatty, *The World According to Peter Drucker,* p. 10. The Free Press, New York (1998).

Can a Company Be Too Ethical?

Andrew W. Singer
Co-editor and Publisher, *Ethikos*

"A couple of years ago, we were competing on a government contract," recalls Norman Augustine, chairman and CEO of Martin Marietta Corp. "The low bid would win. Two days before we were to submit the bid, we got a brown paper bag with our competitor's bid in it."

Martin Marietta didn't "spend 10 minutes" debating what to do with this information, Augustine remembers. The company turned the price sheet over to the U.S. government. Martin Marietta also told its competitor what it had received.

"And we did not change our bid."

What happened? "We lost the contract," recalls Augustine. "As a result, some of our employees lost jobs. And our shareholders lost money."

Is this a case of a company being too ethical?

No, answers Augustine. The outcome was only unfavorable in the short term. "We helped estab-

From *Across the Board* (April 1993). Reprinted by permission of *Across the Board* and the author.

lish a reputation that, in the long run, will draw us business." This he accepts as a matter of faith.

"To me, the subject of ethics deals with principles," explains Augustine, "what you believe to be right or wrong." And insofar as ethics deals with principles, it is not possible to be too ethical. "You can't have too much principle."

But not all agree.

"You can spend too much time, too much effort, on almost anything," says Edward Bowman, Reginald Jones Professor of Corporate Management at The Wharton School at the University of Pennsylvania. "It doesn't mean you shouldn't be ethical." But it does suggest that there are limits.

What happens to a company in a highly competitive industry where "sharp" practices are the norm? If it behaves too nobly, might not other corporations succeed in cutting it off at the knees? Or what about companies that pour heaps of money into safety or environmental compliance—above and beyond what is mandated by law? Won't that hurt the bottom line?

A company, too, can pay so much attention to "doing good" that its traditional business suffers. This was a criticism made against Control Data Corp. (now Ceridian Corp.) under William C. Norris in the 1980s. The company ignored its core business at the expense of so-called humanitarian projects, said critics (more on this shortly).

The question—Can a company be too ethical?—admits of no quick or simple answers. In fact. it is difficult even to arrive at a common definition of what one means by ethical. Strictly speaking, ethics is a discipline for dealing with questions of good or bad, right and wrong—but there is also a broader definition, at least in the minds of many executives and ethicists, that embraces issues of so-called social responsibility. (Supererogatory duties, philosophers might call these.) Issues of bribe-taking, the stealing of competitive information, and sexual harassment clearly accord with most people's notion of ethics, but others, such as affirmative action, investing in South Africa, empowering workers, and hiring the hard-core unemployed can be addressed only if one accepts an expanded concept.

Nonetheless, asking the question sheds some light on how business leaders view ethics and the business enterprise. (For the purposes of this inquiry, we examine business ethics in both the strict and expanded senses of the word.)

Thomas Donaldson, John F. Connelly Professor of Business Ethics at Georgetown University, observes that what is understood as business ethics among executives has undergone a sea change in recent decades. In the '60s, for instance, "business executives tended to identify corporate ethics with philanthropy and social-oriented programs, like hiring the hard-core unemployed.

"Now it has to do more with *how one approaches business objectives.*" Is one being attentive to all one's constituencies, or "stakeholders," including employees, customers, suppliers, and the community in which one operates?

Some people say a company can be too ethical if "it pays its employees like kings," notes Donaldson. They reason that it costs money to pay employees so handsomely, and a company's profit margin may deteriorate, which ultimately hurts shareholders and overall business health. In that case, a serious question arises if the company is behaving toward its shareholders, and others, in a less-than-ethical manner.

THE PRICE OF ETHICS

Most will agree that ethics sometimes exacts a price in the short run. "You know that old definition of a pioneer: He's the one with the arrows in his butt," says Tom Stephens, chairman, president, and CEO of the Manville Corp. (formerly Johns-Manville, of asbestos notoriety).

Manville emerged from bankruptcy in 1988. Today, Stephens feels an obligation for his company to be more ethical than average—given its past and the fact that it was offered a second chance by the courts. (The company, once one of the world's largest manufacturers of asbestos, was subject to 150,000 lawsuits on behalf of individuals whose health was allegedly ruined from asbestos exposure.) Yet this stance has its perils from a short-term profit standpoint.

Take the issue of product labeling. In the late '80s and early '90s, Manville went beyond what the law required in terms of warning labels on its fiberglass products. After the International Agency for Research on Cancer suggested in 1987 that fiberglass was a "possible carcinogen," the company promptly affixed prominent cancer-warning labels to all its fiberglass products. (The company disputes the claim that fiberglass may be a carcinogen, however.)

This in itself is not so unusual: U.S. companies are expected to respond this way in accordance with the Occupational Safety and Health Administration's (OSHA) Hazard Communication Standard. But Manville went further: It put the warning labels on fiberglass products that it shipped to Japan, and translated those warnings into Japanese. Not only was this not required by law, but the Japanese government advised against it.

Government officials there warned "against using the 'C' word," recalls Stephens. (The Japanese have a particular dread of cancer—a legacy of Hiroshima.) They were afraid of frightening the public. Manville's business customers, in turn, were fearful of scaring their workers. Architects worried about alarming lawyers by specifying a possibly carcinogenic building material.

The Japanese said, "We'll tell them what the risks are," according to Stephens. No need to alarm people by affixing such a label.

"But a human being in Japan is no different from a human being in the U.S.," Stephens says. "We told them we had a policy. We had to have a label."

The Japanese response? "The Japanese trade minister said, 'You are very brave.' "

And it *did* have an impact on the company's Japanese sales. (Twenty-five percent of Manville's revenues are derived from outside the United States.) The company lost 40 percent of sales to Japan in one year.

Stephens, Augustine, and others who recount such stories usually add that their business losses are only in the short term. Manville, for instance, was later able to rebuild all of its Japanese business. But do some managers believe that a business can be too ethical—period—and not just in the short term?

Few are likely to say so publicly. "If you ask people directly, they're likely to give you the most socially responsible answer," observes John Delaney,

professor of management at the University of Iowa. But Delaney, who has collected dozens of ethical dilemmas submitted by business executives (including those from a study he conducted of Columbia University business-school graduates), suspects that some executives privately believe a company can, in fact, be too ethical.

He offers this case, which was reported by a corporate auditor at a large, well-known pharmaceutical company:

"The FDA was reviewing our application to place a new drug on the market," the auditor told Delaney. The persistent questioning of the FDA reviewer regarding the application, however, made the auditor uneasy, so he asked to review his company's research-and-development records.

Photocopies of the data provided evidence of "double books." "One set of raw data, completely fabricated, had been provided to me to present to the FDA, while another set of raw data, showing failing results, were the true data," the auditor recalled to Delaney.

The auditor reported his findings, in accordance with corporate procedure, to the international legal department. Eventually, he was asked to testify before the company's board of directors.

"The corporation, as a consequence of the hearing, made me a 'deal.' They would give me all the resources possible to get the drug approval by the FDA. But they promised they would never market the drug. They did not want the embarrassment of the fraud uncovered. . . . I cooperated in the deal, and the company cooperated in its part. Ten years later, the drug is still not on the market."

Subsequent to this "deal," however, the company rewrote the auditor's job description. Its aim seemed to be to make it more unlikely that improprieties of this sort would be uncovered in the future. The new corporate policy prohibited "surprise" audits, for instance. And corporate audit policy was placed directly in the hands of the CEO.

According to Delaney, this suggests that the pharmaceutical concern saw real "costs" in being too ethical. It didn't want to be blatantly unethical—foisting a flawed drug on the public (nor did it fire or demote the whistle-blowing auditor)—but by the same token, it wasn't too keen about uncovering any more episodes of this sort. Hence, it curtailed the audit function. The company seemed to be saying, "Whoa, we don't want to be too ethical. That could lead to real trouble!"

Nor is this stance entirely without financial justification. Back in 1975, the Wharton School's Bowman co-authored "A Strategic Posture Toward Corporate Social Responsibility," a study of 100 companies in the food-processing industry that sought to establish if there was a connection between corporate social responsibility and profits. (Bowman acknowledges that social responsibility is not the same thing as ethics but suggests that the two are related.)

Did the link exist? "If you plot the relationship, the association is curvilinear," says Bowman. That is, as one moves from companies that exhibit little or no social responsibility to those that demonstrate a modest degree, profitability rises. It peaks somewhere in the middle.

(What constituted a socially responsible company? Such factors as concern for the environment and eagerness to hire minorities. An unusually responsible corporation might be one that granted employees paid leaves of absence to work in the local community, for instance.)

"But over on the far right [i.e., among the *most* socially responsible firms], profitability drops off." It is a matter of diminishing marginal returns.

"You can spend too much money on advertising, on computers, on research and development," says Bowman. "Can a company concerned with its overall health spend too much on social responsibility? The answer is yes."

Nonetheless, as a matter of record, "The number of firms that have gotten in trouble for being too ethical is very small," observes David Vogel, professor of business and public policy at the Haas School of Business at the University of California at Berkeley.

While acknowledging that ethics and profits are not always compatible, and a company facing constraints could in theory be too ethical for its own good—such as failing to lay off workers when its sales plummet—in point of fact, "few firms, when faced with that tension, don't give in to the economic constraints," says Vogel.

THE LEGACY OF CONTROL DATA

One of the few examples in which a company might have been harmed by being too good, Vogel acknowledges, is Control Data, which may have sapped its resources with humanitarian programs in the early and mid-'80s.

Indeed, the name of Control Data comes up again and again when one asks if a company can be too ethical. (Rightly or wrongly, people seem to accept a broader definition of ethics here: one that goes beyond questions of right and wrong, and encompasses social responsibility.) The computer company has become a paradigm in the minds of some of a company that faltered for being too good.

Under Norris, its visionary founder, Control Data built factories in riot-torn inner cities in the late 1960s and 1970s. It saw this as doing its part to ameliorate the social situation. "You can't do business in a society that is burning," Norris said at the time. The company had an exemplary record of hiring minority men and women with little formal education and few qualifications, and allowing them to rise through the ranks and become foremen and plant managers.

The company also spent $900 million between 1963 and 1980 trying to develop computer-based education programs for schools. The basic idea was that through computer-based instruction, students could learn at their own rate—unlike a classroom, where everyone must adapt to the teacher's pace. Control Data developed programs for everything from third-grade arithmetic to Farsi and Japanese.

While the company remained profitable, it garnered accolades. In 1983, a poll of Wall Street analysts and corporate directors rated Control Data one of the most admired corporations in the United States.

But then the company's core business began to flounder under the onslaught of intense Japanese competition, particularly in the computer-peripherals business. The corporation lost $568 million in 1985. That year, a new Wall Street poll showed Control Data to be among the country's *least* admired companies.

Norris, who resigned as chairman in 1986, has long disputed the view that he was too attached to socially responsible programs. Control Data was not engaged in sundry humanitarian projects, he insists, but rather in "addressing unmet social needs as business opportunities." Although the computer-based education program proved economically untenable, for example, there is no denying that the market for education and training was—and is— potentially enormous.

"I never felt that criticism was appropriate," Norris tells *Across the Board*. The company devoted no more than 5 percent of its resources to these nontraditional projects, he says. But they were in high-profile areas and were dependent on the cooperation of the public sector, such as local and state governments.

Might he have dedicated too much of his own time and energy, if not the company's resources, to such projects, to the detriment of the company's core business?

"The problem that plagued Control Data was a problem that plagued a lot of companies, but it hit us first," says Norris. "We were moving to a world economy. We didn't recognize it as fast as I would have hoped."

Max DePree, chairman of Herman Miller Inc., the furniture manufacturer, knew Norris "a little bit, and admired him greatly." DePree confirms in an interview that he, too, gained an impression that Norris may have devoted too many resources to socially responsible projects. But that isn't the same thing as saying the company was too ethical, even if that is the idea that has taken hold in the public mind.

"If Control Data had problems [in the mid-1980s], it was probably for the same reasons we all did: We underestimated the competition and we didn't stay focused on what we do," DePree says.

Control Data's socially responsible projects may have diminished Norris' focus, DePree acknowledges—but then the answer would have been to appoint a CEO to handle the core business, something that Norris may have resisted doing.

In any event, "I can't accept that Control Data failed because it was too ethical," DePree says.

Interestingly, Norris himself believes that "there are instances where a company can be too ethical." (And here we are back to a strict definition of ethics.) "But it's often a matter of failing to use common sense.

"One example when I was at Control Data occurred in Mexico. Bribes were commonplace at that time. In fact, government officials were expected to make part of their income through bribes. We had a situation where we shipped an expensive computer there. It was sitting on the dock, and the local official said we had to pay $500 if we wanted to move it out.

"Well, common sense says that you better pay that $500" even if the company has a policy against such payments. "The computer could get stolen; it could rain." Control Data made the payment.

THE MORALITY OF MANAGEMENT

Many view the way a corporation treats its employees as an ethical issue. Does the company treat its workers with dignity, as "ends" in themselves? Or are employees simply a "means" toward greater corporate profits? Companies that have sought to "empower" their workers by giving them a greater say in design and production matters, for instance, often view these actions as having an ethical—as well as a business—component. One is reaffirming employees as "ends" in themselves. But can a company take this notion too far?

Consultant Verne E. Henderson, while supporting worker empowerment generally, believes such a danger exists. In his book *What's Ethical in Business?* (McGraw-Hill, 1992), Henderson looks at People Express Airlines, the discount-fare carrier of the early 1980s.

The company's founder, Donald Burr, "was considered a motivational genius," writes Henderson. "His management style was unique. Employees were called managers, no matter how insignificant their assignment. Productivity, job satisfaction, and initial customer enthusiasm reached new heights for an airline company. Every employee became a shareholder with stock value that grew in most cases to equal one's annual salary in less than four years. His achievement was remarkable, considering the kind of change he introduced. Employees didn't own the company, but they owned the work."

People Express faltered, however, and it was eventually taken over by Frank Lorenzo's Texas Air. The

PHILOSOPHY MEETS FISCAL REALITY

The notion that a company or individual cannot be too ethical reflects a view of ethics and the world that ultimately can be traced back to Aristotle.

Aristotle, it may be recalled, defined virtue as the mean between two blameworthy extremes. Courage, a virtue, represents the mean between cowardice and recklessness. Friendliness, a virtue, is the mean between the extremes of obsequiousness (the desire to please too much) and irascibility (the desire to please too little).

In business, an Aristotelian might see ethics as a sort of balancing act. One has to take into account the demands and needs of various constituencies, or "stakeholders": shareholders, employees, customers, suppliers, and the larger community. No single group can dominate at the expense of any other.

"If one deals with one stakeholder group in an imbalanced way, you do that at the expense of other stakeholders," Guiseppe Bassani, NCR Corp.'s vice president of stakeholder relations, told *ethikos* in September 1991. "In the short term, you can do that. But in the long term, it will kill the company.

"Many times, expectations are not reasonable," he said. A customer may want the company's products for little or nothing. The customer has to be told, "We can't do this. If we do, we'll go out business.

"For me, business ethics is telling people what we can do and what we can't do," Bassani added.

The ethical challenge for Aristotelians is finding that balance, that virtuous mean. A company that refuses to close a failing plant or lay off redundant workers—and subsequently goes bankrupt—is not too ethical, according to this view, but insufficiently ethical. It has slighted one of its key constituencies (shareholders) and probably a second (the remaining workers) at the expense of a third constituency (redundant workers). By failing to achieve that proper balance, management is found lacking in ethical skill.

"Aristotle tells us that ethics is more like building a house than it is like physics," says Georgetown University's Thomas Donaldson. "You learn to build a house by building houses. You learn to be an ethical manager by managing," not by reading textbooks on philosophy.

Professional philosophers sometimes view the practice of business ethics as a theoretical pursuit, continues Donaldson. "It's not. It is an art. It can't be reduced to a science."

For an Aristotelian, it's impossible for a company to be too ethical.

"It is like the question, 'Can a person be too rich, or too thin?'" says Donaldson. In the broadest sense, "a company cannot be too ethical."

But Aristotle's isn't the only perspective on the question. There is another position, one that might be referred to as the Kantian view.

Immanuel Kant, perhaps the most influential moral philosopher of the modern era, viewed moral conduct as something of a struggle. One performs one's moral duty often *in spite* of one's inclinations, or even one's interest. And things don't always work out so well in the end. (Kant's famous example of the individual who refuses to lie, even to save another person's life, is perhaps an extreme illustration of this.)

Many of us would clearly recognize situations in which a person acts ethically and suffers, and not just in the short term. A small-businessman refuses to pay "protection" money, and the mob puts him out of business. Can we really say he was insufficiently ethical for not taking into account stakeholders' interests? Or is it more the case that he was really too ethical—too high-minded—for an imperfect world?

Or consider the struggling entrepreneur who insists on paying his creditors 100 cents on the dollar—even though he could probably force them to accept less—because "a debt is an implied promise, and promises are meant to be kept." He depletes precious working capital and the business fails. Might he not have been more successful if he had fewer scruples?

Can a company be too ethical? "I think if you just take the question at face value, the answer is yes, you can be too ethical," says The Wharton School's Edward Bowman. "But you have to be awfully careful by what you mean by ethical."—**A.S.**

company may have been a victim, at least in some part, of its own good intentions, suggests Henderson in an interview. "The company tried so hard to impart dignity to individual workers and managers that it led to attitudes that were not viable over the long term."

People Express told its employees to do what's right—"even when no one is there to help you. They invited people to be entrepreneurs in an in-dustry where it didn't really work. If the captain has a problem with the airplane, he doesn't call a meeting of the passengers to discuss it." Something of the sort occurred at the company, he suggests.

But a case such as People Express may be the exception, not the rule. "If you listed all the companies that failed, you won't find too many like People Express that failed for doing the right thing," DePree tells *Across the Board.* There are many popular misconceptions about what is meant by a "participative environment," adds DePree, who as chairman of Herman Miller has been credited with forging strong bonds between employees and managers.

"We never talk about everyone voting," he continues. Rather, the company seeks decision-making at its most competent level, "and you can't limit that to the talents of the people at the top." In other words, empowerment doesn't mean that everyone votes on every issue. But it does require more input from a wider range of people than is found at most traditional, command-and-control-type companies.

Asking whether a company can be too ethical "is a bit of a conundrum," says DePree. "I can't imagine where we could be too ethical."

According to Martin Marietta CEO Augustine, it is naive to equate good ethics with profits, at least in the short run.

Martin Marietta is a large NASA contractor. It launches spacecraft for the government, and it earns a substantial incentive bonus when those vehicles are launched successfully.

As an illustration of how a company can lose money in the short term by hewing to its principles, Augustine offers this example:

"One day, our insurance department heard about an insurance policy that would insure our launch bonus, for a low premium. For one nickel on the dollar, we could guarantee the dollar."

On the face of it, such an insurance policy looked like a win-win situation. If the company launched the spacecraft successfully, it would get the bonus from the government. If the launch failed, the insurance company would pay the bonus.

But the deal raised some troubling questions. Why was the customer—the U.S. government, in this instance—providing the company with the incentive? Obviously, it was to make sure that the company did everything in its power, to ensure a successful launch. Wouldn't an insurance policy of the sort described undermine the government's *intent* in offering the launch bonus?

"Our engineers said: 'It would not make a difference,' " recalls Augustine. They would put forth the same 100 percent effort in any case. "And I believed them," he adds. The company's lawyers raised questions of fiduciary responsibility: Didn't the corporation have an obligation to its shareholders to take the insurance policy? There was, notes Augustine, "big money" at stake.

What to do? Augustine's answer was to call the customer—in this case, a general in the U.S. Air Force.

After explaining the insurance matter, "I said: 'Would you care?' " Augustine explained that it was still *his* decision to make, and not the general's, but he would weigh seriously what the general said in making that decision.

"He said he hadn't heard of such a thing, and wondered if others might already be doing it," recalls Augustine. "But he also said he wanted a couple of days to think it over."

Several days later, he called back. The general, upon reflection, reported that "they 'cared' a lot."

"We finally decided not to buy the insurance. And we subsequently had a loss."

In the final analysis, Augustine believes, matters of principle are not for compromise. One behaves as one does because it is right, he suggests (even if determining what is right sometimes takes some doing, such as consulting with the Air Force general). The so-called bad outcomes are only in the short term. "It always pays off in the long term."

But that is unlikely to convince realpolitikers like Henderson. "If a company is too ethical, it can go out of business," he observes. "There's an ethical side and a profit side of the enterprise, and they have to be balanced."

Rain-forest *Chic*

Jon Entine
Author of business journal column, "The Ethical Edge," former TV-news producer and part-time lecturer at NYU

"The church used to be the dominant force in our lives."

The burly, rumpled speaker with wild hair sounds almost professorial as he builds a case for the

From *Report on Business Magazine,* Toronto, Ontario, October 1995, pp. 41–45. © 1995 Jon Entine, runjonrun @earthlink.net, http://www.jonentine.com

coming New Age of profits with principles. "Then came the nation-states, where we looked to government for support and guidance. That era is ending."

Who would have thought that this ruby-faced college dropout would one day hold an audience spellbound with his version of intellectual history. "Today," says Ben Cohen, sounding now like an earnest Republican at a Rotary Club luncheon, "we are in the era of business. Business is our new universal community. We are the leaders who can turn business into a positive social force."

The crowd breaks into applause. The affection, and indeed the adulation, can be felt by everyone in the room. It is a June celebration to open the Los Angeles chapter of Business for Social Responsibility, a trade group that promotes itself as environmentally and socially progressive, and the audience has come to hear its hero. Ben Cohen, 43, and his high-school buddy, Jerry Greenfield, started mixing up batches of ice cream 16 years ago at an abandoned gas station in Burlington, Vt. Today, Chunky Monkey, Cherry Garcia and Rainforest Crunch are staples for fortysomethings everywhere. Although he no longer runs the company day to day, Cohen remains the chairman and lovable, eccentric corporate symbol of Ben & Jerry's Homemade Inc., which has seven Canadian outlets and worldwide sales of about $200 million (U.S.).

The soul of Ben & Jerry's is natural, artery-clogging ice cream and a quixotic social philosophy. It is one of the best known of a growing list of "progressive" firms such as skin-and-hair-care franchisor The Body Shop International PLC (BSI), eco-friendly apparel makers Patagonia and Esprit de Corp, and Tom's of Maine, which sells natural toothpaste and personal-care products.

Cohen's company has set an impressive standard of ethical innovation. It publishes a state-of-the-art social audit of its operations, gives an astonishing 7.5% of pretax profits to charity, buys only local dairy products to help preserve the family farm, and refuses to back down from its support of peace and social-justice causes even if that means alienating some potential customers.

Ben Cohen is more the rule than the exception among successful, New Age entrepreneurs. Many grew up in the sixties, their values shaped by civil-rights activism, Vietnam protests, free love, drugs and an unremitting belief in the moral and cultural ascendancy of the baby-boom generation. Many now run public companies that have ridden the green wave into the hearts, minds and pocketbooks of eco-consumers. Cohen and the founders of other successful eco-businesses, who in many cases are worth millions and even hundreds of millions of dollars in company stock, now jet around the world spreading the New Age gospel of anticapitalist business.

Cohen rails on to his audience about the greedy, soulless character of Corporate America, and then boasts of how a corporation has made a difference in helping save the rain forest. "The success of our Rainforest Crunch," says Cohen, "shows that harvesting Brazil nuts is a profitable alternative for Amazon natives who have seen their lands ravaged to create grazing areas or for mining." The crowd is on its feet. It is an inspiring moment.

Yet Ben & Jerry's own 1995 annual report, released just days before, carries the not-so-socially responsible details of what some anthropologists are calling the "rain-forest fiasco." While the label of Rainforest Crunch, one of Ben & Jerry's flagship products, suggests that buying the ice cream helps preserve the Amazon's endangered rain forests, the documented social benefits of its Third World microproject are ambiguous at best.

The popular fascination for social marketers—who have built an image as a leading force of social change—obscures a far more complex reality. Consumers with a high tolerance for pricy goods—most New Age products command a hefty premium over ordinary brands—play a modest role in raising awareness of social problems. At worst, though, cause-related marketing can be little more than baby-boom agitprop, masking serious lapses at socially conscious firms.

The small companies in the vanguard of the movement are learning that "social responsibility" is a margin game: When profits are rolling in, as they were in the 1980s, progressive gestures are painless. But now, as they face growing pains and intense worldwide competition, many of these enlightened firms are firing workers, closing inner-city stores, cutting back on charity projects, and making their products in overseas sweatshops. In other words, they are acting like most businesses when confronted with difficult bottom-line challenges.

This not-so-pristine reality has been largely absent from the coverage of New Age entrepreneurs because the journalists who have so slavishly chronicled their prior success share with the firms some common cultural values. Many have convinced themselves that growing up protesting Vietnam and environmental degradation forever marks them as progressives, even though they now drive BMWs instead of VWs, and their closest brush with social responsibility is a Ben & Jerry's Peace Pop.

Ironically, the social and environmental contributions of New Age business pale when compared with the substantial reforms taking place in major corporations. Selling quality products, treating employees, vendors and franchisees with integrity, and upgrading their environmental practices are improvements, they have discovered, that go straight to the bottom line. And given their massive financial resources, many familiar blue-chip firms are in a better position than New Age entrepreneurs to effect social change as they quietly, but determinedly, adopt higher standards of affirmative hiring, pollution abatement and community involvement practices. "Even a tiny, 1% improvement in the environmental standards of a DuPont or a Monsanto," says corporate ethics guru Paul Hawken author of *The Ecology of Commerce,* "will have a more meaningful impact than creating a hundred new Patagonias."

We'll look at some unheralded examples of progress on the corporate social responsibility front. But first, a sobering behind-the-gloss look at some firms that have gotten rich and famous by "having a heart" and wearing it on their sleeves.

Efforts to "save the rain forest" have brought together two popular movements: the environmentalists' struggle to protect the forest against clear-cutting and the romantic quest to preserve indigenous cultures. Capitalism-on-the-Amazon as popularized by Ben & Jerry's and The Body Shop has an almost serendipitous history. In 1988, after a Grateful Dead rainforest fundraising concert, Cohen found himself at a party where a Cambridge, Mass. anthropologist explained his pet project of saving the rain forest. The anthropologist convinced Cohen that Amazon natives could achieve self-sufficiency by selling fruits and nuts instead of selling mining and logging rights. A few days later, Cohen was mixing up batches of Brazil-nut brittle ice cream in his Vermont kitchen. Simultaneously, Rainforest Crunch and the rain-forest harvest were born.

The eco-capitalism movement got a big boost the following spring when Sting, The Body Shop founder Anita Roddick and other celebrities turned that year's Amazon peoples' conference in Altamira, Brazil, into an international media event. Within months, BSI was selling rain-forest hair rinse and bath beads while Ben & Jerry's launched Rainforest Crunch. Both companies promoted their rain-forest products as eco-friendly solutions to mining and clear-cutting.

"Money from these nuts," read the label for Rainforest Crunch ice cream when it was launched in 1990, "helps to show that rain forests are more profitable when . . . cultivated for traditional harvest than when their trees are cut and burned for short-term gain." The product was an overwhelming, overnight success—at least for Ben & Jerry's, which reaped millions of dollars' worth of free publicity for showing how profits and principles can go hand in hand.

The view from Amazonia was quite different. Amazon peoples' groups and anthropologists feared opening up this fragile area even to supposedly friendly capitalists. There also is no evidence to support the central premise of the harvest—that nuts could ever approximate the income that natives collect by selling off land rights to miners and foresters.

The anticipated source for Ben & Jerry's nuts—the Xapuri co-operative in the Amazon—never produced the necessary quality or quantity to meet exploding demand. And the description of the Xapuri co-operative as "forest peoples" was odd: The co-op is largely run by ethnic European and mixed-blood rubber tappers who arrived as contract workers at the turn of the century during an earlier wave of rain-forest exploitation.

The harvest soon proved a windfall for the landowners who have long controlled trade in this region. To meet demand, the agency purchasing nuts on Ben & Jerry's behalf, in which Cohen was a partner, was forced to buy from the commercial markets supplied by some of the most notorious, antilabour agribusinesses in Latin America, including the Mutran family, which has been linked in Brazilian press reports with the killings of labour organizers. By the spring of 1994, the Xapuri had cut off all supplies, saying their own harvesting efforts were hopelessly uneconomic. The project has run in the red for the past three years, generating none of the promised charitable contributions to the Amazonians that were to have flowed from sales of Rainforest Crunch. And there is no evidence that the harvest has provided an incentive for forest natives to curtail their auctioning of land, mining and timber rights. "It's really a disingenuous marketing strategy to say if you spend $2.99, you'll help save the rain forest," says Michelle McKinley, executive director of Cultural Survival, which used to run the project for Ben & Jerry's. "We rushed into this project recklessly. We created a fad market overnight and the hard-sell promotions have contributed to a lot of confusion. The harvest just didn't work."

Even Ben & Jerry's latest annual report takes the company to task. "It is a legitimate question," writes environmentalist Paul Hawken, who conducted the audit, "whether representations made on Ben & Jerry's Rainforest Crunch package give an accurate impression to the customer." Hawken quotes sharp criticism from Amazon civil-rights groups, then concludes: "There have been . . . undesirable consequences which some say were predictable and unavoidable." In the five years since Ben & Jerry's launched Rainforest Crunch, traditional commercial suppliers have provided about 95% of the Brazilian nuts used in making the product.

Like many eco-entrepreneurial firms, Ben & Jerry's is a reflection of its hard-driving, frequently myopic leadership, which sometimes admits to major mistakes without correcting them, and turns eager apologies over minor gaffes into yet another marketing promotion. The label on the firm's most famous product was altered in the spring. It no longer tells the story of how purchasers of Rainforest Crunch ice cream are helping aboriginal nut harvesters, but sustainable harvesting in the rain forest is still mentioned. Cohen publicly disputes Hawken's analysis, saying Ben & Jerry's at least meant well, and lamely credits his firm with "creating demand" for rain-forest products.

Ben Cohen often talks about his kinship with Anita Roddick, charismatic founder of U.K.-based The Body Shop International PLC. Cohen and Roddick, 53, are regarded as the king and queen of progressive business.

In 1976, Roddick opened a tiny shop in the faded English resort town of Brighton. It offered "one-stop ear piercing" and sold beauty products with natural-sounding names in refillable plastic bottles. It soon developed a cult following and expanded dramatically through franchising. Today, Anita Roddick and her husband, Gordon, oversee a $1-billion (sales) chain of 1,290 mostly franchised Body Shop outlets in 45 countries. Canada, with 113 stores—all of them franchises—is BSI's third-largest market.

Roddick is arguably the most successful self-made businesswoman in the world. For years, no competitor could match her two-for-one sale: Buy a bottle of non-tested-on-animals Brazil-nut hair rinse and get social justice for free. Roddick became a favourite of affluent baby boomers, a New Age feminist heroine weaned on can-do chutzpah and do-right values. "Anita," Ralph Nader told *People* magazine, "is the most progressive businessperson I know."

BSI, Ben & Jerry's and other eco-marketers have cleverly used cause-related marketing to brand what are essentially commodity products—in this case ice cream and cosmetics—and to fuel a booming niche market in so-called "green" products. They also pad their bottom lines by spending very little, if anything, on conventional advertising. Instead, they benefit from free and largely favourable media coverage of their "new way of doing business." Roddick has long understood the power of the press. As she was preparing to open her first store, a couple of local undertakers started squawking about her use of the name The Body Shop. She went to the local paper, the *Evening Argus,* and landed her first story—a lesson in free media she wouldn't forget. By its own calculation, BSI has racked up as many as 10,000 press mentions in a single year.

Despite glowing press, BSI has long been held in mixed regard in the corporate social responsibility movement. Roddick is almost universally admired for stirring debate on important issues: environmental degradation, the use of animal testing on cosmetics and other products, the role of corporations as model community citizens. But the firm is also known for exaggerating its progressive practices.

The Body Shop is more difficult to read than a Ouija board. Its good works, and its reported problems, can be as much a product of head office as its far-flung franchisees in Australia, Japan or Saudi Arabia. Undeniably, though, BSI draws its spirit from its rags-to-riches-to-Robin Hood model, Anita Roddick.

Roddick is a study in contradictions. She is perhaps best known for her relentless campaign for a total ban on animal testing. The company does aggressively enforce its limited ban by refusing to use ingredients tested within the last five years. The practical impact of the ban is limited, however, given that most ingredients in widespread use today were once animal tested; and many of the new ones are developed first for medicinal use, which BSI says puts them outside its rule. In any event, BSI is hardly unique among the scores of major world cosmetics makers that have adopted similar bans on ingredients recently tested on animals. This reality is reflected in BSI's 1989 decision to back down from its testing-related product claims, and change its product labels to replace the slogan NOT TESTED ON ANIMALS with the vague AGAINST ANIMAL TESTING.

At the International Chamber of Commerce Conference in Cancún in 1993, Roddick lambasted the distinguished business and government leaders in the audience for trading with what she called the "torturers" and "despots" in China's political regime, who allow sweatshops to churn out cheap goods for greedy, "nomadic" capitalists who put low labour costs above ethics. Her admonition: Just say no to trading in Chinese goods. The behind-the-rhetoric reality: BSI for years had bought its popular baskets in China, and they continued to be on sale at Roddick's stores even as she spoke.

BSI has earned a reputation as the premier "natural" cosmetic company. But BSI uses mostly off-the-shelf industrial recipes that employ artifi-

cial colours, synthetic fragrances and chemical preservatives as base ingredients. Its products don't always fare well in comparison tests. *Consumer Reports* magazine rated its Dewberry fragrance last out of 66 products it tested; and in 1993, the German magazine *Öko-Test* (*Green Test*) found formaldehyde residue in a few BSI products. BSI has been vigorously responding to the quality issues, investing in new-product development and striving to prevent bacteria problems.

While BSI was claiming it was giving away "an inordinately high percentage of pretax profits to often controversial charitable campaigns," and Roddick was saying, "What else do I do with the money than give it away?", there are no records that show BSI gave any money to charity prior to becoming a publicly traded company in 1984. And until 1994, BSI donated less than the U.S. corporate average of 1.5% of pretax profits. In the past two years, as criticism mounted, BSI donated an impressive 3% of pretax profits in 1994 and 2.3% in 1995. Roddick touts her "Trade Not Aid" program as a progressive substitute for handouts and claims she pays. "First World wages for Third World goods." In fact, BSI pays going wages and in 1994 paid only about 0.3% of worldwide sales to its Trade Not Aid producers. University of Chicago anthropologist Terence Turner, who has visited BSI's trade project with the Kayapo tribe in Brazil, calls its programs "Aid Not Trade," a play on The Body Shop slogan. "Indigenous cultures give these companies free aid in the form of their green image," Turner says, "with almost no trade in return." Stung by a growing chorus of critics, the company has revamped its ethical trading department and pledges to increase its Third World purchases.

BSI has also suffered its share of franchise problems. The small-business committee of the U.S. House of Representatives has received many complaints from BSI franchisees around the world. "[BSI] is a company that promotes itself as operating on a higher ethical plane than others," says Dean Sagar, an economist with the committee, which recommends changes to franchise legislation. "In their franchising they are not worse than anyone else, but they certainly don't appear to be any better."

In 1993, the U.S. Federal Trade Commission launched an investigation of alleged BSI violations of the Federal Trade Commission Act in the sale of products and franchises, subpoenaing former franchisees and requesting internal documents and videotapes from BSI. The FTC, which seldom resorts to formal charges in its efforts to reform practices, issued a letter in March saying that "no further action is warranted by the Commission at this time," and that the end of the investigation should not be taken as a sign that a violation had or had not occurred.

Finally, many BSI fans are surprised to learn that BSI shares its name, many of its early products and its vaunted refilling philosophy with an earlier pioneer of socially progressive cosmetics, The Body Shop of Berkeley, Calif., which opened its doors in 1970. The founders of the tiny U.S. Body Shop chain sold the rights to its name to the Roddicks in 1987 for $3.5 million (U.S.).

Without question, it was Roddick who conquered the world with her version of the concept, but critics are put off by her image as having more or less exclusively invented the idea of progressive cosmetic marketing.

Despite its problems, BSI still has many loyal supporters. "The Body Shop is a leader in socially responsible corporate participation in Canadian society," says Beverley Wybrow, executive director of The Canadian Women's Foundation. She notes that The Body Shop Canada has used promotional campaigns to generate more than $140,000 in funds for domestic-violence prevention programs in which CWF is a partner.

BSI itself suggests that its performance is being judged against unrealistically high standards. "We *all* admit that we are retailers, pure and simple," says Margot Franssen, president of The Body Shop Canada. "We aren't exactly out to change the world, but instead to make our communities a little bit better." The company operates a state-of-the-art production facility, and it is the rare Canadian firm to offer subsidized on-site day care at its head office.

Depending on one's perspective, Roddick is either a visionary crucified for excessive enthusiasm or an exploiter of idealistic followers. The biggest problem for The Body Shop now is not performance—it has made dramatic strides in al-most every area of its operations in the past two years—but credibility.

It's a rare company, of course, whose history isn't blemished by occasional inconsistencies between the founder's vision and the way that vision is played out. What's rare in this case is Roddick's strident assertion that she occupies a high moral plane shared only with some of her peers in the New Age fraternity. "Over the past decade, while many businesses have pursued what I call business as usual, I have been part of a different, smaller business movement, one that has tried to put idealism back on the agenda," Roddick told the Mexican conclave of big-business leaders, urging them to follow BSI's example. "We are creating new markets of informed and morally motivated consumers. We are succeeding and thriving as businesses and as moral forces."

Even if they lived up to their reputation as models of a new type of "virtuous capitalism," relatively small, faddish firms have little impact on the economy. In that sense, can they be regarded as being a more powerful force for good than such multibillion-dollar firms as drugmaker Merck & Co. and computer giant Hewlett-Packard Co., which for decades have quietly but conscientiously made large charitable contributions, involved themselves in the communities in which they operate, opened their corporate practices to public scrutiny, and pioneered in management practices that create intensely loyal workforces?

The urge to demonize Big Business and idolize eco-entrepreneurs caricatures the complexity of business. Most companies resemble dysfunctional families. Even the best of them make mistakes or compromise their ideals under bottom-line pressure. "Some of the best environmental programs are the creation of some of the worst polluters," notes Paul Hawken. "Innovative solutions are not the exclusive province of so-called progressive companies. We have to keep an open mind and look for solutions wherever they may be."

Many of those solutions originate with Big Business. At a time when affirmative hiring is a popular target of politicians and right-wing talk-show hosts, companies such as Polaroid Corp., Texaco Inc. and Dow Chemical Co. are more determined than ever to promote women and minorities into higher levels of management, and have done so far more aggressively than most New Age companies.

Even before the Bhopal tragedy, chemical companies were a frequent target of environmentalists. Yet the industry's Responsible Care program of scrupulous controls on the manufacture and use of toxic chemicals, largely designed in Canada and adopted by most major North American chemical producers, is an important initiative that other industries are under pressure to emulate.

Big Oil and Canada's Big Five banks are perennial lightning rods for critics in the ecology and consumer-rights movements, and with some justification. But it's two firms drawn from the ranks of Big Oil and banking, Imperial Oil Ltd. and the Royal Bank of Canada, that are spearheading the Imagine campaign to prod all Canadian corporations, which lag U.S. firms in giving, to raise their donations to at least 1% of pretax profits. Imperial gave about $5 million to 600 groups last year alone; the Royal Bank donated $15 million. By comparison, charitable giving during BSI's entire history as a public company totals less than $6 million.

Just as industries long held in poor regard deserve credit for their efforts to improve, high-profile "cause-related" marketers should be viewed with caution. For "socially responsible" business, whether practiced by New Age firms or hulking multinationals, is a land of contradictions.

- Apparel giants Esprit de Corp, Levi Strauss & Co. and The Gap Inc. lavish their employees with progressive benefits, while some of their clothing is manufactured by suppliers that operate sweatshops in countries where human-rights violations are a common occurrence.
- Reebok International Ltd., frequently cited as a progressive employer, has made hopscotch its sourcing credo, moving its manufacturing operations from South Korea and Taiwan to China, Indonesia and Thailand in search of the lowest wages. It also recently paid $12.3 million to settle price-fixing charges in the United States.

Baby boomers now seem less interested in sixties ideals of changing the world than "shopping for a better world"—the title of a popular "green" buying guide. But the inconvenient reality is that it's difficult for consumers to identify the "good guys" even with a scorecard. For instance, which companies are more "ethical" in dealing with the following two controversial issues:

- Gillette Co. and Procter & Gamble Co., which spend millions of dollars on safety-testing of their products and have pioneered in research and development into alternative cosmetics, but perform government-required animal tests; or The Body Shop, which has stimulated a useful public debate but relies on tested-on-animals ingredients and has been attacked by former allies in the animal-rights movement for oversimplifying this complex issue for commercial gain.
- Monsanto Co. and DuPont, which have innovative pollution-control practices, yet have been guilty of environmental violations; or Ben & Jerry's, which publishes an annual audit of its corporate conduct, but sometimes ignores its most important conclusions.

There are no icons in the business world. At best we can identify firms that acknowledge their daily struggle to improve product quality, environmental practices, and worker and community relations, and which open their practices to outside scrutiny. "We are entering a new era in the world of socially responsible managing and investing," says Joan Bavaria, president of Franklin Research & Development Corp., a Boston-based social-investment firm. "It is not a black-and-white world with neat lines of demarcation. This is the real world of complex systems and internal contradictions."

A constructive response to these inevitable contradictions is to confront them. Bavaria is one of the founders of CERES, the Coalition for Environmentally Responsible Economies, which was set up by a group of social and environmental activists and public-pension-fund trustees to develop environmental standards and accounting guidelines in partnership with business. CERES has 54 members pledged to conducting internal audits of their environmental records, including Polaroid, General Motors Corp. and oil producer Sun Co., as well as Ben & Jerry's and The Body Shop. In recruiting new members, CERES looks for larger, "messier" companies that are struggling with problems, but are committed to transparency in disclosing and remedying problems. Even modest changes in the business practices of traditional manufacturing and resource firms—and in Canada that's more than 40% of the GDP—will have far more sweeping economic impact than a handful of

firms claiming no bottom-line instincts but which operate at the fringes of the economy.

Acting responsibly means being responsive to criticism. "I talked with both Ben and Jerry," says business student Ritu Kalra, who was present at a recent speech by Cohen and co-founder Jerry

---

IN SEARCH OF SAINTLY STOCK PICKS

"Ethical" Mutual Funds Have a Devilish Time Keeping Pure

We won't invest in companies that sell tobacco products, or utility and mining firms that use nuclear power," explains David Shuttleworth, vice-president, marketing and sales, for the Ethical Funds, Canada's largest family of "green" mutual funds. Shuttleworth invests only in companies that can pass through ethical "screens" that award high marks for harmonious labour relations and generous charitable giving, and rejects firms engaged in manufacturing tobacco products and nuclear power.

According to the Toronto-based Social Investment Organization, assets in Canadian ethical funds top $1.2 billion. The oldest Canadian fund, started in 1986 by Vancouver City Savings Credit Union, has $410 million in assets. Today it's one of some 20 ethical funds designed to tap affluent boomers seeking guilt-free investments.

But funds can't easily avoid, say, natural resource stocks, which are rejected by many U.S. funds on environmental grounds. "You just can't do that in Canada," says an almost apologetic Michael Jantzi, who heads a firm that researches the ethical track records of publicly traded companies. "Resource companies make up more than 40% of the Toronto Stock Exchange. If you eliminate these sectors, you don't have diversification. And if your fund isn't diversified, its performance is volatile and you will drive out investors." Jantzi's solution? "We screen for 'best in sector.' " That is, he sometimes has to settle for the least-bad actors.

No matter how well intentioned, though, a strategy of investing in "good" companies makes sense only if you suspend some rules of logic. For instance, ethical funds typically favour stocks in the financial-services industry, which is regarded as non-polluting. But it's the rare bank that doesn't have loans to natural-resource firms and defence contractors on its books. Or take "sin" stocks: Naturally Shuttleworth avoids cigarette manufacturers. But what about a firm that makes packaging for them? "Well, yes," he says, "if less than 20% of its business is making tobacco packaging, I guess we would invest." Why 20%? "Well, that's just the cutoff point we set."

The information on which such decisions are made is sometimes suspect. Researchers who advise funds

on stock selection scan data banks for environmental irregularities, but for the most part they depend on information provided by the companies under scrutiny. That's how researchers who gave The Body Shop International PLC (BSI) high ratings chronically failed to detect that the firm's stated goals and achievements didn't always jibe with actual practice. "We used public-domain articles and questionnaires," says senior analyst Simon Billenness at Boston's Franklin Research, which gave BSI its highest ratings, before dumping its 46,000 shares last year. "We learned a hard lesson: This is not a science but an art."

The practice of ethical investing is at its most artistic in the devising of screens that are supposed to distinguish "ethical firms" from others. Says William Martello, assistant professor of policy and environment at the University of Calgary: "Funds make subjective distinctions between defensive weapons and offensive weapons. It doesn't make sense. These are idiosyncratic ideological filters, not ethical screens."

How do the ethical funds perform for investors? Recent studies suggest that the funds track the market. There are some dogs, but also some stars, such as the U.S. growth fund Parnassus, which has an environmental tilt, and boasts a 20%, five-year return.

The more relevant question is: Are the funds helping to make the world a better place? Jantzi think so. "Companies respond to negative publicity," he says. "If we help publicize environmental or ethical inconsistencies, it affects corporate behaviour."

But John Bishop, professor of business ethics at Trent University in Peterborough, Ont., disagrees: "Ethical funds might make investors feel good. But ethical investing accounts for less than 1% of the market. The impact is negligible, like taking a bucket of water out of the shallow end of a swimming pool and emptying it into the deep end."

Tempering idealism with pragmatism, Shuttleworth pleas for patience. "We have our ethical guidelines," he says, but funds have to produce decent returns or even ethical investors will take flight. "The bottom line is still money," Shuttleworth says. "We have to make a profit for our investors."

Greenfield at the University of Pennsylvania's Wharton business school. "Neither of them knew much about the harvest. When it came down to it, they didn't want to comment and didn't feel responsible for misleading labelling or telling half-truths."

The recent revelations about the rain-forest fiasco have hardly slowed Ben & Jerry's ice cream tour. Even though the company has ditched its references to helping aboriginal nut harvesters, not many consumers realize how few of their eco-dollars go toward helping distant Amazonian natives.

At the Los Angeles New Age business meeting, Cohen relentlessly hawks his most famous ice-cream flavour. "We *have* made a difference in the rain forest," he declares. After the speech, dozens of people crowd around Cohen as he signs napkins and dishes out bowls of Rainforest Crunch ice cream. "It's so inspiring," says a fellow entrepreneur, licking her spoon, "to know that business can make money and still do so much good."

Feminist Morality and Competitive Reality: A Role for an Ethic of Care?

Jeanne M. Liedtka
Associate Professor of Business Administration, Darden
Graduate School of Business, University of Virginia

INTRODUCTION

The skit proved to be among the most memorable in the history of *Saturday Night Live.* In it, Lily Tomlin portrayed Ernestine, a Bell System telephone operator. Gleefully, she danced around a well-equipped computer control center flipping switches and chortling, "There goes Peoria!" as she plunged each city into a communications blackout. The scene closed with the corporate motto: "We don't care because we don't have to—we're your phone company."

From *Business Ethics Quarterly,* Vol. 6, Issue 2, 1996, pp. 179–200. Copyright © 1996 *Business Ethics Quarterly.* Reprinted by permission.

How times have changed. No one, it seems these days, cares so much about us as our myriad of phone companies. AT&T is, after all, "our" phone company. Sprint reminds us that the "big guys" can't really care about us the way they do. MCI even cares about our "family and friends". Why? Because they have to—because the new realities of their marketplace award competitive advantage to those whose customers feel cared for.

Nor is this phenomenon limited to the telecommunications industry. A language of care and relationship-building has appeared with prominence in the business lexicon, across industries and geography. Corporate CEOs speak of "nurturing" their employees; in autonomous work teams and strategic alliances across the globe, individuals are "empowered" to build networks of collaborative relationships; everywhere, caring for the customer has become the new corporate mantra.

Ironically, after decades of work by ethicists striving to humanize the work of market mechanisms, the market itself may be offering us an opportunity to use it to drive organizations to care. As Thomas White (1992) has pointed out, many forces seem to be driving business practice into ever-closer alignment with much of the thinking underlying Carol Gilligan's (1982) notions of an "ethic of care" and its attention to relationships and connectedness as central. The avowed willingness to care for *customers,* at least, seems to be all around us. And can employee caring for customers be sustained if they are not cared for by their organization, in turn? Yet, can organizations care?

A decade of writing in feminist morality has focussed on the concept of an ethic of care; it seems timely to ask what relevance this body of work has for today's business context. Is the idea of creating organizations that "care" just another management fad that subverts the essential integrity of concepts of ethical caring? Conversely, are these concepts capable of beginning an important dialogue that may help us to see new possibilities for simultaneously enhancing *both* the effectiveness and the moral quality of organizations in the future? In this paper, I propose to address four questions that I see as central to these issues:

1. Is it possible for organizations to "care," in the sense of the term as used by scholars in the ethics area over the past decade?
2. What are the particular advantages such caring organizations might possess in the marketplace?
3. How might we translate these concepts into the kinds of attributes that would distinguish a caring organization in practice?
4. What are the problematic issues and unresolved questions associated with the concept of caring organizations?

By drawing upon both the academic literature and practitioner discussions of each of these issues in turn, I hope to initiate a conversation that I believe holds promise for bridging the gap between philosophical theorizing and business practice.

Placing Care in Context

The ethic of care focuses on the self as connected to others, with an emphasis on the care-giver's responsibility to the "other" to maintain that connection (Gilligan, 1982). It takes as its distinctive elements an attention to particular others in actual contexts (Held, 1987), a focus on the needs versus the interests of those particular others (Tronto, 1993a), and a commitment to dialogue as the primary means of moral deliberation (Benhabib, 1992). Care is "not a system of principles, but a mode of responsiveness" (Cole and Coultrap-McQuin, 1992).

Care is often compared with the stereotypical masculine ethic of justice. While the latter focuses on defining the self as separate and uses rights to protect boundaries between the self and other, care moves from its view of the connected self to an emphasis on relationships and the responsibilities that they entail. Gilligan's metaphor of the web to represent feminine thinking, has been juxtaposed against the use of hierarchy to represent masculine thinking (White, 1992).

The ethic of care, while it departs from the focus on personal liberty and social contract which underlie the justice tradition, has both theoretical precedents and linkages. Tronto (1993b) situates it within the contextual ethics tradition of Aristotle, Adam Smith, and Alistair McIntyre; Benhabib (1992) links it with the discourse ethics of Habermas. Kittay and Meyers (1987) note:

"The interest in alternatives to a deductive, calculative approach to moral decision-making, with its strong emphasis on individual autonomy, may be traced back to Aristotle and Hume and finds expression in a number of contemporary moral philosophers who stress the importance of virtue, rather than justice, in moral life . . . For Aristotle, moral judgment springs from a moral character attuned to circumstantial and contextual features. It is not a product of an abstract concept of the Good. Moreover, Aristotle stresses the social embeddedness of the human being, a political animal by nature. In a related vein, Hume's ethics are grounded in emotion and personal concern. Hume argued that reason itself could not move us to act morally, but that our ethical life is guided by moral sentiments. Again, attention to relationships is prominent in this view. Alistair McIntyre and Bernard Williams are among the contemporary moral philosophers who call for a return to the notions of virtue, of moral character, and of a personal point of view to counteract the excessive formalism, the calculative ratiocination, and the impersonal perspective of the dominant moral traditions of Kant, on the one hand, and utilitarianism, on the other." (p. 8)

Other linkages exist as well. Though care theorists depart from Kant's focus on universalism, disagreeing with his belief that all rational individuals would construe morality the same way, they share what Rawls attributes to Kant—his premise of a socially constructed view of morality. Similarly, an ethic of care is clearly consistent with the 2nd formulation of the Categorical Imperative to always treat persons as ends, and not merely means. Interpreting this within an ethic of care, however, would require that we recognize and treat each person as a concrete, rather than a generalized other (Benhabib, 1992), and give attention to the particular self-defined ends that each aspires too. Care also has obvious linkages with Kant's duties of benevolence and mutual aid. Where Kant made these imperfect duties, care would render them obligatory, within bounds.

Since the publication, in 1982, of Gilligan's seminal work explicating the ethic of care, *In a Different Voice,* much care-related writing within the philosophy field has focussed on elaborating upon, analyzing, and evaluating the differences between the perspectives of Kohlberg, based on a Rawlsian theory of justice, and those of care. It is not my intention here either to explore this issue in detail,[1] to argue for the superiority of a care ethic, or to trace its place in philosophical tradition. Instead, my interest is in considering specifically whether and how the inclusion of an ethic of care might contribute to enhancing both the effectiveness and the moral quality of the institutions in which we lead our work lives.

In this regard, the literature in business ethics has, until very recently, devoted little attention to any discussion of the ethic of care (White, 1992). This is surprising given the potential relevance of a relationship-based ethic to business, viewed (by some at least) as a relationship-based activity. It is also surprising, given the significant impact that stakeholder theory (Freeman, 1984) has had in this same literature, and the powerful linkages between stakeholder theory and the ethic of care (Wicks, Gilbert, and Freeman, 1994).

The Ethic of Care and Stakeholder Theory

Stakeholder theory, like the ethic of care, is built upon a recognition of interdependence. As Wicks, Gilbert, and Freeman (1994) note:

> "The corporation is constituted by the network of relationships which it is involved in with employees, customers, suppliers, communities, businesses and other groups who interact with and give meaning and definition to the corporation." (p. 12)

Thus, for stakeholder theorists, the interdependence is between groups; for care theorists, it is between and among the individuals who comprise those groups. Care theorists might, in fact, be uncomfortable with the categorization of individuals into groups defined by others. Instead, they would look toward self-defined and possibly multiple identities that narrowly defined, mutually exclusive definitions of stakeholders might ignore. Despite these differences, both views stand in stark contrast to a view of business as a series of one-time arms-length transactions, a topic which we will shortly pursue at greater length.

Within this view of business as a web of on-going connections, care and stakeholder theories act as activity-framing, rather than decision-making, theories. Both offer a perspective and guiding ethos for the moral agent, situated within the on-going

daily activities which characterize the operation of business. Neither theory offers a set of abstract principles to be used as decision heuristics in resolving particular moral dilemmas, arguing that the complexity of concrete circumstances make a priori solutions impossible. Both theories need an ethic of justice to deal with completing claims and inadequate resources.

Both care and stakeholder theories see dialogue-based processes, rather than individual deliberation, as the foundation for the living of a moral life (Benhabib, 1992; Wicks et al, 1994). In stakeholder theory, these processes are driven by a consideration of the impact of actions on the projects of stakeholder groups. In the ethic of care, the focus is the concrete needs of particular individuals. Within care, in particular, it is the conduct of daily life, lived for the most part with long intervals in between the kind of moral dilemmas that have dominated business ethics discussions, that is the focus. In doing so, it places less emphasis on the exercise of free will and choice, and more on recognizing the moral demands ever-present imposed upon us (Scaltsas, 1992). Though this lack of interest in prescribing moral solutions has raised questions as to the adequacy of care as a moral theory (Koehn, 1995), it suits well the realities of corporate life, which is often about that which is required, rather than that which is chosen.

Thus, though care may not, in the absence of considerations of justice, provide a fully self-sufficient theory for moral business conduct (a point to which we will later return), its apparent saliency makes it a candidate worthy of careful attention. In addition, in empirical studies of ethical work climate (Victor and Cullen, 1988), caring has emerged as one of the dominant dimensions of such climates.[2] From both normative and descriptive viewpoints, then, the role of caring in the business context warrants serious attention.

CAN ORGANIZATIONS CARE?

Now we turn to the question of whether the expressions of care prevalent in today's business lexicon are consistent with notion of ethical caring. Furthermore, is it even possible to take Gilligan's essentially individual level theory and extend it to the level of an organization, without subverting it in the process? Only by exploring the particulars of feminist theorists' arguments in detail can these questions be answered.

Defining Care

Central to our inquiry is Noddings' (1984) distinction between "caring for" and "caring about". Ethical caring, she argues, only applies to those *persons* that we care *for*. She uses the term, "aesthetical caring" for objects and things that we care *about,* and is concerned about the extent to which our caring for things subverts our caring for people, by encouraging us to use them instrumentally to achieve other ends. The caring about versus caring for distinction is also made in relation to human beings. If it is people that we care *about,* versus *for,* Noddings views this as representing only a "verbal commitment to the possibility of care" (p. 18). We cannot, she argues, care "for" those who are beyond our reach. Caring represents a personal investment that must always remain at the level of "I"; caring at the more abstract level of "We" is an illusion. This quality of particularity is essential—caring lives in the relationship between me, an individual, and you, another individual. Without this particularity the caring connection is lost and we must re-label the new process: no longer "caring", it becomes "problem-solving", in Nodding's terminology.

The significance of the differentiation between caring and problem-solving goes far beyond semantics. The process of defining generalized "problems" and decoupling these from the lived experiences of individuals who we see ourselves as having relationships with, risks two outcomes antithetical to care. The first is the loss of particularity and resulting dehumanizing of the individuals in need. Cornel West (1993), in discussing race in America, examines what it means to be identified as a "problem":

> The common denominator of these views of race is that each still sees black people as a "problem people," in the words of Dorothy I. Height, president of the National Council of Negro Women, rather than

as fellow American citizens with problems. Her words echo the poignant "unasked question" of W.E.B. DuBois, who, in *The Souls of Black Folk* (1903), wrote:

> 'They approach me in a half-hesitant sort of way, eye me curiously or compassionately, and then instead of saying directly, How does it feel to be a problem? they say, I know an excellent colored man in my town . . . Do not these Southern outrages make your blood boil? At these I smile, or am interested, or reduce the boiling to a simmer, as the occasion may require. To the real question, How does it feel to be a problem? I answer seldom a word.'

> Nearly a century later, we confine discussions about race in America to the "problems" black people pose for whites, rather than consider what this way of viewing black people reveals about us as a nation. This paralyzing framework encourages liberals to relieve their guilty consciences by supporting public funds directed at the "problems." (pp. 5–6)

Thus, instead of care-giving, we assign the role of "care-taking" to bureaucratic systems that are intended to provide care. In this process, however, Noddings' second concern with the problem-solving focus comes into play. Care-takers almost inevitably come to impose their own solutions, without dialogue, on those in need. West, again, illustrates how this phenomenon plays out in dealing with the problems of poor people in America. Conservatives, he argues, have shifted the definition of the problem of poverty from poverty itself to that of the "welfare state."

Tronto (1993a) acknowledges Noddings' distinction between caring for and caring about and uses it to lay out four stages in the caring process. Rather than excluding caring about persons from ethical caring, she views it as a precondition (necessary, but insufficient) for fully realized care. Care begins with "caring about" (stage 1), identifying a need as one that ought to be met. Care progresses to "taking care of" (stage 2), assuming the responsibility for meeting the need. It moves to "care-giving", directly meeting the need (analogous to Noddings' "caring for"), in stage 3. The process culminates with care receiving in stage 4, as the recipient of care responds. Here, too, the personal nature of care ultimately remains fundamental—as it must, for as long as we care "about" the other, they remain generalized rather than concrete. As Benhabib (1992) points out, it is only in the process of personally engaging with the particular other that we gain the specialized knowledge of their context, history, and needs that permits us to fully care for them on *their* terms, rather than ours.

The Practice of Care

In describing care as a *practice,* Tronto (1993a) emphasizes its concern with both thought and action, directed towards some end, and dependent upon the resources of time, skill, and material goods. Along with other scholars (Held, 1993; Ruddick, 1989), Noddings has used the relationship between a mother and her child to illustrate, at its deepest level, her notion of what it means to care. Thus, the essence of caring becomes a focus on acceptance of the other, both in his or her current state, *and* as one capable of growth. Nurturing the development of the one cared for is the critical activity in caring relationships. Contrary to a stereotypical view of caring as fostering dependence, it's aim is the opposite —to care means to respect the other's autonomy and to work to enhance the cared-for's ability to make his or her own choices well. This recognition of the importance of the need, for all humans, to realize their capacities goes back to Aristotle. As Herman (1993) has noted in her exploration of Kant's duties for benevolence and mutual aid, the focus here, as there, is not on pursuing one's ends *for* them, it is on enhancing their capability to pursue their own ends. If, as Flanagan (1982) states, the "motor of cognitive development is contradiction," caring may well be comprised more of "tough love" than of indulgence. Anthropologist and Biographer Mary Catherine Bateson observes (1990):

> "The best care-taker offers a combination of challenge and support . . . To be nurturant is not always to concur and comfort, to stroke and flatter and appease; often, it requires offering a caring version of the truth, grounded in reality. Self-care should include the cold shower as well as the scented tub. Real caring requires setting priorities and limits. Even the hard choices of triage have their own tenderness." (p. 155)

Another aspect of developing an enhanced ability to choose well, is the recognition that choices are made within the context of a "community of mutual aid" (Herman, 1993). Learning to care is essential to my ability to take my place in the community. The community, in insisting that its members develop a capacity to care, helps both the individuals and the larger community in the process. The existence of a transcending mutual purpose that seeks to accommodate and respect, yet, of necessity sometimes bound, the personal projects of individuals within the community's goals, is critical. Without this combination of shared purpose and personal project, caring risks becoming the process of self-sacrifice and denial of self that some feminists fear (Scaltsas, 1992), seeing in it a continuation of women's history of accepting oppression in the name of caring. Self-care, Gilligan argues, is a precondition for giving morally mature care to others. Similarly, bereft of a strong regard for particularity, communities can smother difference and subjugate those in need of care.

In caring, the focus on the other is complete— that is, I focus on them within the context of their world view, and not mine. Caring always involves "feeling with"—receiving the other, rather than projecting one's own view onto the other. Thus, the development process evolves out of the aspirations and capabilities of the cared for, rather than being driven by the needs and goals of the caregiver. This quality, more than any other, plays upon the mother/child imagery so central to work in feminist morality.

Thus, in order for an organization to "care" in the sense that feminist ethicists have used the term, such caring would need to be:

a. focused entirely on *persons,* not "quality," "profits," or any of the other kinds of ideas that much of today's "care-talk" seems to revolve around,

b. undertaken as an *end* in and of itself, and not merely a means toward achieving quality, profits, etc.,

c. essentially *personal,* in that it ultimately involves particular individuals engrossed, at a subjective level, in caring for other particular individuals.

d. *growth-enhancing* for the cared-for, in that it moves them towards the use and development of their full capacities, within the context of their self-defined needs and aspirations.

Care in the Business Context: The Market Mechanism at Work

The previous conditions make clear that much of the potential "caring" that organizations engage in constitutes "problem-solving" in Noddings' vocabulary. It is impersonal, instrumental, and object-focussed. Organizations often use their resources, including employees and suppliers, as means to solve problems in pursuit of the only end of significance—profits. In this view, organizations ordinarily represent a defined set of solutions in search of an appropriate set of problems. To the extent that customers come attached to these problems, firms are forced to engage them in a process in which customers come to believe that the firm's solutions will solve their problems. The term "caring for customers" has been used to describe this process. In this same vein, firms contract with employees and suppliers who have problems of their own, for which they also have solutions. In neither case are the needs of the "other" of interest to the firm, except in so far as they represent a potential source of profitability. This is the market mechanism at work, and it is difficult not to agree with Noddings that "caring" has little role in its functioning. Nor would caring's inclusion appear to offer much in enhancing its effectiveness, if we leave its basic assumptions of arms-length transactions among independent entities pursuing their own projects intact. Relationships here have relevance only so long as they are profitable, in a literal sense. In such a system, caring is likely to foreclose options, make the dissolution of unprofitable relationships more difficult, and increase costs.

The underlying premise here is that of the abstract other—one customer is as good as another, any employee is replaceable, each represents only today's point of intersection between supply and demand—tomorrow may well bring a different set. Taken to its extreme, this becomes the world of the prisoner's dilemma played once, in which self-interest leads to survival, and must, therefore, domi-

nate all decision-making in a rational system. In the absence of a stake in a shared future, cooperation cannot be sustained, because the self-interested "rogues" will drive the benevolent "saints" out of existence in short order (Axelrod, 1984). The predominance of this view of business, and the self-sustaining loop of short-term-oriented, narrowly self-interested behavior that it fosters, accounts for the persistence of non-caring organizations.

Business as Relationships: An Alternative View

I would assert that the leaders of few successful organizations today would characterize their world as that of the prisoner's dilemma played once. Recent research (Collins and Porras, 1994) asserts that visionary companies, those with a strong set of non-financial values and a long-term perspective, both outperform and outlast their less visionary counterparts. Consider the words of George Merck, son of the founder of Merck & Co. and former chairman (Business Enterprise Trust, 1991):

> "We try never to forget that medicine is for the people, it is not for the profits. The profits follow, and if we have remembered that, they have never failed to appear. The better we have remembered it, the larger they have been." (p. 3)

If such views, echoed by other corporate leaders over time, support an alternative conception of business as based on on-going relationships where outcomes other than only profits can be important, how might ethical caring be different in practice than the market mechanisms described above? What does it mean to care for these others—whether they be customers, employees, suppliers, or other stakeholders?

To say that I care about my customers or my employees would place them as particular others and the capabilities that they represent at the center of my attention, and to work with them to realize those capabilities. The customer, for instance, is seen here as having a set of needs and possibilities to which, as a care-giver, I must attend.[3] It is these needs, rather than the organization's prepackaged solutions, that drive my response in a process that is part of an on-going relationship, rather than a transaction.

From Individual to Organizational Caring

Does, then, an assembly of appropriately caring individuals constitute a "caring" organization? Considerable precedent exists, of course, for such anthropomorphizing—we speak of organizations that have values, that learn, that reward. Yet, it would certainly be possible for a subgroup of caring individuals to exist within an organization that worked to subvert their efforts. Thus, I would argue that a caring organization, in addition to being composed of individuals who met the conditions, would need to actively support their efforts through its goals, systems, strategies, and values. This is important for three reasons: (1) it is the organization which determines the reach of each individual, as it defines their roles, responsibilities, and decision-making scope, (2) it is the organization that must provide the resources that allow individual care-givers to successfully care within their reach, (3) it is the organization that must create the system in which care is self-sustaining, in which the reward systems support care-givers and discourage the rogues.

Individual caring is only sustainable, in the long term, within caring systems (Kahn, 1993): "To be cared for is essential for the capacity to be caring" (Gaylin, 1976). The personal investment required to care is substantial and the risks of "burnout" are ever-present, as countless studies of the traditional care-giving professions have demonstrated. In reviewing these studies, however, researchers (Scott, Aiken, Mechanic, and Moravcsik, 1995) found burnout not to be associated with the direct care-giving activities themselves (e.g., caring for AIDS and Cancer patients). Instead, it was linked to the organizational context, in the form of lack of influence in decision-making, dealing with bureaucratic inconveniences, and the lack of opportunities for creativity. Avoiding burnout, these authors argue, requires decentralized decision-making, adequate resources, opportunities for development, and a collaborative environment. Caring, then, though a particular relationship between individuals, is situated within the context of a community, derives its shared focus from the needs of that community, and is only sustainable with the support of that community; care becomes self-reinforcing within

that context. Thus, both because it derives its meaning within the context of community, and because of the personal investment required to care, organizations that support individual caring, that create self-reinforcing systems of caring, are essential if caring is to persist at all.

MARKET-BASED ADVANTAGES OF CARE

If the idea of a caring organization exists as a possibility, albeit unrealized in much of today's "care-talk", what kinds of enhanced competitive advantages might these organizations enjoy? Let me begin to address this question by playing out in more detail (in an obviously oversimplified way) the distinctions that we have already raised between the attitudes and behaviors embedded in the transactional focus of the market mechanisms versus the relationship-based processes of care (see table on next page).

Under what situations might these two very different types of organizations enjoy competitive advantage? Addressing this question requires that we move from discussions of philosophy to business strategy.

Sources of Competitive Advantage

The strategy literature, within the past decade, has shifted dramatically, away from a focus on firms' assets and industry structure as a source of competitive advantage towards a belief that competitive advantage lies with the extent to which an organization is able to build a set of capabilities that allows it serve its customers uniquely well within the demands of their marketplace (Rumelt, Schendel, and Teece, 1991). Building on Day's (1994) definition, these capabilities consist of "complex bundles of skills and accumulated knowledge, exercised through organizational processes, and within organizational contexts, that enable firms to coordinate activities and make use of their assets."

Stalk, Evans, and Shulman (1992) argue that four principles underlie capability-based competition:

1. The building blocks of corporate strategy are not products and markets but business processes.
2. Competitive success depends upon transforming a company's key processes into strategic

Role	Business as market transaction	Business as caring relationship
Customer	Ancillary: Process is driven by organization's need to sell its solutions to some identified set of problems. These come with customers attached.	Primary: Process is driven by the organization's desire to attend carefully to customer's self-defined needs and aspirations and facilitate their achievement.
Employees	Expendable/Replaceable: Their labor is purchased at market rates in order to produce and sell organization's solutions.	Primary: Developing members of a community of mutual purpose and linchpin that creates the organizational capability set and connects it with customer needs.
Suppliers	Interchangeable: Interested in selling their solutions as input into the production of next downstream product. As their customers, our firm is ancillary to their purpose.	Primary: As partners in the process of attending to the end user in the value chain that we share, they attend to us and make possible our customer focus.
Organization and Senior Management	Primary: To plan, supervise, control, and monitor the processes of production and selling to ensure quality and efficiency.	Supporting: To create a caring context and systems which provide resources and decentralized authority that enables employees to care for customers.
Shareholders	Primary: As owners of the business, their interests, in the form of profits earned, dominate decision-making.	Supporting: As members of the workplace community, they provide capital that facilitates the process of meeting the needs of other stakeholders. Their needs are met as the project succeeds.

capabilities that consistently provide superior value to customers.

3. Companies create these capabilities by making strategic investments in a support infrastructure that links together and transcends traditional functions.

4. Capability-based strategies, because they cross functions, must be championed by senior leadership.

Furthermore, Day (1994) argues that the strategic value of any particular capabilities set is determined by three "tests:"

1. Whether it makes a disproportionate contribution to the provision of customer value
2. Whether it can be readily matched by rivals
3. Whether it speeds the firm's adaptation to environmental change

Taken together, a number of themes emerge as common across these perspectives. Perhaps the most obvious is the central role of the customer and the focus on creating value for that customer. This is a very different focus than that of product/market selection, the key strategic task that had long dominated the strategy field. In the past, the customer was a generalized other, the replaceable element—it was the product that had salience and permanence. In the new thinking, today's product is no more than a temporary attempt to create value for a particular customer. Since "value" is obviously in the eye of the beholder, success belongs to those who can move with the customer as his or her needs, and therefore definition of value, changes. Thus, it is the relationship with the customer that has permanence, and today's product which is temporary.

A second theme that emerges concerns the centrality of employees to this process of value creation. If competitive advantage lies in maintaining relationships with customers, then it is the employees who deal directly with these customers who ultimately determine the firm's success or failure. The rest of the organization, including senior management, exists to support and respond to, rather than control and monitor, these front-line workers. In fact, control by senior managers, far removed from customer contact, would appear to increase the risk of losing touch with changing customer needs. In addition, if the source of advantage lies in "bundles of skills and accumulated knowledge," these too reside in employees—not the traditional asset categories of property, plant, and equipment. Rather than viewing these knowledgeable workers as replaceable, sustaining advantage requires that they remain as members of the firm's community—not competitors'. It also requires that flexibility and adaptability be encouraged, so that the need for new capabilities can be anticipated.

The final theme that emerges is a concern that traditional structural categories, like function and hierarchy, can impede, rather than facilitate, success. What is called for are pathways—infrastructure—that encourage coordination and cooperation across units and companies, that support, link, and create processes. This stands in contrast to the scalar chain of command and turf protection mentalities prevalent today.

The Capabilities Created by Transaction vs. Care Orientations

Returning to our question of a role for an ethic of care, we need to ask what kinds of different capabilities the market transaction-based and the caring relationship-based firms might possess, and what implications these might have for competitive success.

Our transactions-oriented firm ought, I argue, to excel at the creation of standardized products and services for identified needs—producing them efficiently and consistently, and marketing them aggressively. To the extent that they know their customer well, their products will be perceived as a good value, and their employees and suppliers will comply with the "day's work for a day's pay" contract that they have created with them. Their chief vulnerability lies with changes in their marketplace. Though they may "know" their customer today, they do not have a ready mechanism for

learning should that customer change. The employees who deal with that customer are: (1) likely focussed on getting the job done as specified, rather than attending to customer voices and (2) even having heard a change in the voices, are far removed from the centers of influence, in terms of decision-making. Mistakes in this carefully orchestrated system are expensive, and so middle managers are risk-averse, as well. If competitors respond more quickly to the changes, customers will merely take their transactions elsewhere, having little to lose by doing so.

Contrast this with the different set of capabilities potential in a care-based organization. Because of its shared purpose around and attention to customers' self-defined needs, both current and future, and empowered employee and supplier community, its strengths would lie in its responsiveness and flexibility. Those who dealt with customers would have ownership of that relationship and the resources and decision-making scope to respond quickly. Rather than being constrained by the narrow limits of organizationally-defined roles, employees would be more likely to adopt the "supra-role" citizenship behaviors (Schnake, 1991) conducive to smooth organization functioning. The vulnerability here would appear to be the potential, from a senior management perspective, of a system "out of control".

If we believe the enormous volume of business writing today, in both practitioner and academic circles, the world of business is no longer characterized by stability and predictability. If this is true, we can assert that the most successful organizations of the future will be flatter, quicker, and more intelligent at every level (Pinchot and Pinchot, 1993; Quinn, 1992). They will need to listen, to inquire, and to experiment. They will be collaborative enterprises (Gray, 1989), which value the diversity of their workforce, and who work in partnership with their suppliers and in the communities in which they reside. They will need to have a strong sense of purpose and employees who care. As Bartlett and Ghoshal have argued:

> "Traditionally, top-level managers have tried to engage employees intellectually through the persuasive logic of strategic analyses. But clinically framed and

contractually based relationships do not inspire the extraordinary effort and sustained commitment required to deliver consistently superior performance. For that, companies need employees who care, who have a strong emotional link with the organization." (p. 81)

Few topics in the practitioner literature have so captured the interest of managers as Peter Senge's (1990) concept of learning organizations. In a world of constant change, the ability to learn may prove to be the only source of competitive advantage in the long-term (Senge, 1990). Senge defines learning as increases in the capacity for effective action, and the similarities between Senge's description of the properties of learning organizations and those we have attributed to organizations centered on an ethic of care are striking. Learning, he asserts, occurs within communities that share a sense of purpose that connects each member to each other, and to the community at large. Learning organizations are characterized by an ability to maintain an open dialogue among members, that seeks first to understand, rather than evaluate, the perspectives of each. Finally, a learning organization looks to the whole of a process, rather than its pieces. Learning organizations exhibit the kind of "constructed knowing" (Belensky, Clinchy, Goldberger, and Tarule, 1986) that connects reason and emotion, intuition and rationality, and that thrives on complexity and ambiguity, rather than simplicity and certainty. Care-based organizations would seem ideally suited for such processes.

The degree of improvement in the moral quality of such organizations. relative to transaction-based firms, would also be substantial. Employees, customers, and suppliers would be treated as ends in themselves, and not merely means to a far greater extent than the instrumentalism of today's market allows. The development of their capacities as community members would occupy a more central role. Embedded within the web of support, trust, and open inquiry, the climate in the workplace would be attentive to the dignity of all, and more welcoming of difference. Such an environment, as Benhabib (1992) has noted, would enhance not only our ability to see the other's perspective, but our commitment to act on that knowledge, to use it to care, as well.

Yet, the challenges of transforming today's organizations into caring organizations are staggering. One has to be troubled that, amid all of the talk about the organization of the future, it remains questionable whether much is really changing *within* organizations today. Far from becoming more caring, many organizations appear to be moving in quite the opposite way. Prahalad and Hamel (1994), leading thinkers in the strategy field, have argued that the organizational appetite for cost-cutting and downsizing constitutes a business version of anorexia:

". . . the United States and Britain have produced an entire generation of denominator managers. They can downsize, declutter, delayer, and divest better than any managers in the world. . . . One of the inevitable results of downsizing is plummeting employee morale. Employees have a hard time squaring all the talk about the importance of human capital with seemingly indiscriminate cutting. . . . And no wonder so few first-level and mid-level employees bring their full emotional and intellectual energies to the task of restructuring. . . . Downsizing belatedly attempts to correct the mistakes of the past; it is not about creating the markets of the future. The simple point is that getting smaller is not enough. Downsizing, the equivalent of corporate anorexia, can make a company thinner; it doesn't necessarily make it healthier." (pp. 9–11)

Creating these new organizations requires more than coining new words to describe them—it requires new organizational structures, systems and processes, and new managerial skills and mindsets. Caring, in its ethical sense, cannot be grafted onto business as usual. Caring is difficult in today's traditional rule-based hierarchies because they are not designed to foster care.

THE ATTRIBUTES OF CARING ORGANIZATIONS

If the idea of a caring organization exists as a possibility, and if that organization might possess significant market-based advantage, it is important to explore what an organization *designed* to care would look like in practice. Unfortunately, there has been little attention given to this subject in the literature.

The Architecture of Care

Perhaps the clearest point emerging from the discussions to-date concern what caring organizations would *not* look like. They are not bureaucracies. Scholars have argued for decades that personal and professional values are difficult to honor in a bureaucratic environment; Ferguson (1984) has argued persuasively that bureaucracy is antithetical to the ability to care. The rules in a bureaucracy become, over time, the ends rather than the means. Thus, caring, even for the customer or client, is subordinated to perpetuation of the organization in its current state. All behavior takes on a political motive, as the superior becomes internalized as the only "other" worthy of concern. Similarly, the divorcing of planning from performing tasks puts even those we deal with directly "out of our reach," since reach is determined as much by sphere of influence as it is by proximity. Finally, Ferguson asserts that openness, which is central to caring, is impossible to sustain in a bureaucracy, as it threatens the status quo that the structure lives to protect.

If caring organizations cannot be bureaucracies, how could they be structured? Because the concept of reach, so fundamental to caring, is partially a function of decision-making scope, the architecture of the organization would need to be highly decentralized to give each individual the "reach" necessary to carry out the caring work on a daily basis, in an autonomous way. It would entail the creation of a web, or network, of connections, where the focus was on the relationships between individuals, rather than the position of "boxes" in a hierarchy.

This would need to be coupled with the provision of the resources necessary to enable successful care-taking—whether those be information, expertise, or budget. Thus, the infrastructure to support care would be as important as the organizational structure. Advances in information technology add importantly to the ability of those who deal with customers to provide individualized care. The image of the front-line service person, equipped with all of the expertise that the firm has to offer available on-line to better serve the customer, fits well the image of a caring organization.

De-Alienating the Workforce

The relationship of the individual to the organization would be characterized by engagement and focus. Iannello (1992) has reported on similar efforts at "de-alienating the workforce," by putting "meaning and values back in jobs." Engagement, based on Kahn's work (1990), is itself the product of meaningful work, a safe environment and the availability of resources. A focus on meaningful work cycles us back to individual decision-making autonomy, coupled with purposefulness. The concept of purposefulness is increasingly prominent in the management literature and occurs when the goals and values of the organization arise from, and are shared with, the individuals in the firm (Senge, 1990; Solomon, 1993). A purposeful firm strategy focuses on excellence in meeting its goals, not beating the competition (Solomon, 1993), and is consistent with such influential theories as Deming's Quality Principles and Prahalad and Hamel's "Strategic Intent." In this world, organizational members at every level need to be strategic thinkers, who understand the organization's purpose and its capabilities, as they respond to ever-changing opportunities to better meet customers' needs. Members must also collectively be given a voice in the setting of strategic direction (Iannello, 1992).

A safe environment offers support and the opportunity to fully involve one's self without fear of consequences (Kahn, 1990). Because a willingness to care places the care-giver at risk (for rejection and for burn-out), a sense of safety is critical to a willingness to be engaged. Similarly, there must be clear boundaries around each individual's and each organization's responsibility to care. Such focus is necessary to avoid overwhelming the care-giver with responsibilities that exceed his or her emotional, intellectual, and physical capacity to care. This is where the creation of trusted collaborative networks can be essential in supporting and extending the capacity of individual care-givers (Handy, 1994).

Internal organizational processes would be characterized by communication, constructive conflict, shared expertise, and continual redefinition and renewal. Communication would reflect the kind of balance between inquiry and advocacy that Senge (1990) describes. Belensky et al (1986) draw a similar distinction between didactic and "real" talk. The first goal of communication in inquiry or "real" talk mode is to achieve an understanding of the assumptions and values underlying the position of the "other," rather than the selling of one's own solution. Questions would be as valued as answers; listening as important as speaking.

Tension will be ever-present. There will always be conflict among stakeholders and more needs than can be met; the caring organization will not be free of conflict. On the contrary, it will acknowledge and work with conflict, rather than suppressing and ignoring it, by using dissent constructively to forge solutions that better serve the needs of the cared-for. Pascal (1990) argues for a dialectical, rather than a trade-off, approach to decision-making, asserting that contention, properly handled through dialogue rather than debate, enhances creativity and personal growth.

Expertise will be shared and individuals will be teachers of some things and learners of others simultaneously, as individuals are constantly stretched to develop their talents. Contrary to the image of sentimentality often attached to the notion of care, "tough love," as noted previously, may be a more apt description. Caring organizations will need to be as tough-minded and results-oriented as any other organization. It will be their methods and aspirations that distinguish them, not their lack of attention to outcomes. The values of mutual respect, honesty, and patience will be its foundation.

QUESTIONS CONCERNING THE CARING PERSPECTIVE

In the decade since the ethic of care was introduced, a significant volume of literature critical of the adequacy of care as a moral theory has been produced. The most visible concerns raised in the literature relate to questions about the use the mother/child dyad, so prevalent in feminist moral writings, as a model for non-familial relationships, issues around freedom and fairness that a more rights-focused perspective offers, and the question

of how one sets the boundaries of care. I address each in turn.

Concerns about Matriarchy

The "mothering" image of caring that is so powerful also raises significant concerns. One of these relates to the issue of power. Is the power differential between parent and child one that we want to embrace as a model for relationships at work? Do we want to replace patriarchy with matriarchy? Held (1993) is not disturbed by these concerns. In proposing her "post-patriarchal" model, she notes that disparity in power is a given in our society and cannot be avoided. Yet, traditional notions of power are useless in the mothering context. Mothers, she argues, do not "wield" power. Instead, "the power of a mothering person is to empower others—to foster transformational growth" through *influence* (p. 209). Iannello (1992) agrees, also advocating a shift in our thinking from power to empowerment. She observes that our current societal context associates power with domination. Yet, power also implies the ability, strength, and energy to get things done. Using the latter conception of power, she argues, allows us to differentiate between power as controlling others and empowerment as controlling oneself.

Ferguson (1984) believes otherwise, asserting that both the presence of inequality and "natural love" inherent in mothering make it unsuitable for generalization outside the bounds of the family. Instead, she offers the model of citizenship, and uses the town meeting with its decentralization, public decision-making, and openness to conflicting views as a guide for care-based organizations. Her view is strikingly similar to that contained in Charles Handy's (1994) recent call for "federated structures," which contain local and separate activities served by a common center. Such structures, he believes, led by the center and managed by the parts, "combine the benefits of scale and autonomy, while retaining a sense of meaning that connects people to purpose" (p. 110).

Questions of Justice

But how are concerns related to fairness and equality addressed within a care-based ethic? Again, Held

(1993) argues that our definitions need reframing. Equality no longer corresponds with equal rights or equal treatment; rather, it requires that we view each member as worthy of equal respect and consideration, and respond to the unique needs they bring with them. In a similar vein, Ferguson asserts that freedom is essential. But rather than viewing freedom as "an arena of privacy surrounding each individual, (where) community is a secondary arrangement among already autonomous beings; freedom must be located in relations among others . . . caring for others by caring for their freedom."

Thus, the issues of freedom, fairness, and power, these theorists argue, can be reconciled within the framework of a care-based organization. Gilligan, in fact, believes that rights are an essential, though not dominant, component of caring. Without rights, "the injunction to care is paralyzing, rights allow us to appropriately value self-interest . . . to act responsively towards self *and* others and thus to sustain connection" (p. 149). Despite the attention given in the literature to characterizations of care *versus* justice, a majority of feminist philosophers would embed care within an ethic of justice. As Tronto (1993a) explains, "the point is not to undermine current moral premises, but to show that they are incomplete." We need justice, she argues, to determine which needs should be met, given limited capacity and resources.

Flanagan and Adler (1983), suggest that such a reconciliation, a "tense synthesis" as Gilligan defines it, though desirable, may prove difficult in practice, if not in theory. They note:

> "We set our overall theme by pointing to the tension in morality between impartiality and particularity . . . Whereas morality comes with pressure toward impartiality, it also comes with an essential connection to our own particularity . . . In fact, it is by no means obvious that there is any way to completely integrate the good (associated with the Ethic of Care's particularity) with the right (associated with the Ethic of Justice's impartiality), as opposed to deciding an issue in terms of one or the other. Each perspective is inadequate without the other, and yet each to some extent excludes the other." (pp. 577, 594)

Lamenting the inability of traditional moral theories to incorporate these issues, Flanagan and Adler argue that "the requisite moral complexity can be appreciated only by sustained reflection on the way morals figure in real life," reminding us of Aristotle's admonition that "precision is not to be sought alike for all discussions, anymore than in all products of the crafts."

Setting the Boundaries of Care

If we accept a premise of care as theoretically embedded within justice, however complex this may prove to be to practice, the issue of how we set the boundaries of care still requires serious attention. Without such attention it is difficult to make an operationally meaningful translation to the business environment, which remains a competitive one, as Daryl Koehn has noted (1995). Do we, for instance, need to care about competitors? Do all customers or employees have an equal claim on our care-giving resources? What are the defenses against the "rogues" inevitable in such environments? A host of questions like these must be answered before we can implement concepts of care in organizational life.

Though it is beyond the scope of this paper to seriously address these boundary issues, some general guidelines could be offered, based on our discussions to-date. Clearly, one's responsibility to care, in its fullest sense that incorporates all four of Tronto's stages, is bounded by one's reach. Reach, in turn, is determined by one's resources of time, skill, and goods, as well as by actual contact. The focus of care is also upon needs, rather than interests. Self-care is also important, so that I do not have a responsibility to give care where to do so would be of significant harm to me. Thus, the business organization, conceived of as a "community of mutual care," would have a responsibility to care for those in proximity to them who have needs that they are especially well-suited, by their capability base, to fulfill, where giving such care does not act against their own needs. Such care should be growth-enhancing for its recipients. The circle of care, as drawn here, would place competitors within the justice realm, employees within the realm of care. It would place small towns in which they had facilities in the realm of care, it would place large cities in which they did not in the realm of justice. It would place potential customers who could be profitably served in the realm of care. Since to give away products on a significant scale would be harmful, it would place potential customers who could not pay in the realm of justice. An exception here would be in an instance where the organization was uniquely suited to meet an important need, and could do so without harming itself. Merck's donation of the cure for river blindness would fall into this category, and be seen as an appropriate act of responsible caring, not extraordinary largesse. Caring's dual focus on the needs and development of the cared for would also bound the types of products and services offered, I believe. It would be difficult to argue that a caring organization could produce cigarettes, or market expensive sneakers aggressively to poor teenagers.

The Question of Organizational Size

A final question, not discussed in the literature but critical to arguing for the relevance of care to businesses on a large scale, is the question of size. How large could a caring organization be? Iannello's work on consensus-based organizations (1992) suggests that they must remain small enough for the collective, as a group, to participate together in strategic decision-making. Hierarchy impedes care; yet, hierarchy is the only well-developed model that we have today to organize large institutions. Can we create new organizational forms that combine the necessary decentralized reach, with an ability to marshall a collective voice in strategic decisions, and achieve the advantages of economies of scale on a centralized basis? Addressing this issue, in particular, requires an interdisciplinary approach that spans the fields of ethics, organizational theory, and strategy.

CONCLUSION

The above discussion makes clear, I hope, the extent to which the potential inherent in organizations centered around an ethic of care is significant, for reasons relating to both the marketplace and the moral realm. I have endeavored here to begin a conversation. Many questions remain to be answered; much work remains to be done. Fieldwork directed at examining these ideas within the context of practicing organizations is essential. To return to the question posed at this paper's outset, the concept of a caring organization *does* offer new possibilities for simultaneously enhancing both the effectiveness and the moral quality of organizations. The realization of that possibility will require enormous change in the way today's organizations operate—changes that we, as scholars, can help to initiate and foster. The current business environment offers unprecedented opportunities to do so.

NOTES

The author would like to thank Pat Werhane, Ed Freeman, Bill Frederick, Norm Bowie, and two anonymous reviewers for their helpful comments.

1. Readers interested in doing so are referred to Lyons (1983), the journals *Ethics,* April 1982 issue, and *Social Research,* Autumn 1983 issue, and the edited volumes *Women and Moral Theory,* edited by Kittay and Meyers (1987), *Explorations in Feminist Ethics,* edited by Cole and Coultrap-McQuin (1992), and *An Ethic of Care: Feminist and Interdisciplinary Perspectives,* edited by Larrabee (1993).
2. The other four dominant dimensions that emerged were independence, rules, instrumental, and law and code.
3. It is important to reinforce here the difference between our notion of care and the generic usage of the term. We do not imply, by caring, that one smothers the customer with unwanted personal attention. A customer in a supermarket line, for instance, may desire quick and efficient service, rather than the exchange of pleasantries. To care for him or her would be to provide such service. Similarly, caring for employees does not necessarily imply delving into their private lives.

BIBLIOGRAPHY

Axelrod, R. (1984). *The Evolution of Cooperation.* New York: Basic Books.

Bartlett, C. and S. Ghoshal (1994). "Changing the Role of Top Management: Beyond Strategy to Purpose," *Harvard Business Review,* November/December; pp. 79–88.

Bateson, M. (1989). *Composing a Life*. New York: Penguin Books.

Belensky, M., Clinchy, G., Goldberger, N., and Tarule, J. (1986). *Women's Ways of Knowing*. New York: Basic Books.

Benhabib, S. (1992). *Situating the Self: Gender, Community, and Postmodernism in Contemporary Ethics*. New York: Routledge.

Business Enterprise Trust (1991). *Merck & Co., Inc. (A)*. Stanford, CA:Business Enterprise Trust.

Cole, E. and S. Coultrap-McQuin (1992). *Explorations in Feminist Ethics*. Bloomington: Indiana University Press.

Collins, J. and J. Porras (1994). *Built to Last*. New York: Harper Business.

Day, G. (1994). "The Capabilities of Market-Driven Organizations," *Journal of Marketing,* 58 (October), pp. 37–52.

Ferguson, K. (1984). *The Feminist Case Against Bureaucracy*. Philadelphia: Temple University Press.

Flanagan, O. (1982). "Virtue, Sex, and Gender: Some Philosophical Reflections on the Moral Psychology Debate," *Ethics,* April, pp. 499–512.

Flanagan, O. and J. Adler (1983). "Impartiality and Particularity," *Social Research,* 50 (3): 576–596.

Freeman, R. E. (1984). *Strategic Management: A Stakeholder Approach*. Boston: Pitman.

Gaylin, W. (1976). *Caring*. New York: Knopf.

Gilligan, C. (1982). *In a Different Voice*. Cambridge, MA: Harvard University Press.

Gray, B. (1989). *Collaborating: Finding Common Ground For Multiparty Problems*. San Francisco: Jossey-Bass.

Hamel, G. and C. Prahalad (1994). *Competing for the Future*. Boston: Harvard Business School Press.

Handy, C. (1994). *The Age of Paradox*. Boston: Harvard Business School Press.

Held, V. (1993). *Feminist Morality: Transforming Culture, Society, and Politics*. Chicago: University of Chicago Press.

Herman, B. (1993). *The Practice of Moral Judgement*. Cambridge, MA: Harvard University Press.

Iannello, K. (1992). *Decisions Without Hierarchy*. New York: Routledge.

Kahn, W. (1990). "Psychological Conditions of Personal Engagement and Disengagement at Work," *Academy of Management Journal,* 33(4): pp. 692–724.

Kahn, W. (1993). "Caring for the Caregivers: Patterns of Organizational Caregiving," *Administrative Science Quarterly,* 38: pp. 539–563.

Kittay, E. and D. Meyers (1987). *Women and Moral Theory*. Totowa, NJ: Rowman & Littlefield.

Koehn, D. (1995). "How Relevant are 'Female Ethics' of Trust and Care to Business Ethics?" presented at the 1995 Annual Meeting of the Society for Business Ethics, Vancouver, B.C.

Larrabee, M. (1993). *An Ethic of Care: Feminist and Interdisciplinary Perspectives*. New York: Routledge.

Lyons, N. (1983). "Two Perspectives: On Self, Relationships, and Morality," *Harvard Educational Review,* 53(2): pp. 125–145.

Noddings, N. (1984). *Caring: A Feminine Approach to Ethics and Moral Education*. Berkeley, CA: University of California Press.

Pascal, R. (1990). *Managing On The Edge*. New York: Simon and Schuster.

Pinchot, G. and E. Pinchot (1994). *The End of Bureaucracy and the Rise of the Intelligent Organization*. San Francisco: Berrett-Koehler Publishers.

Quinn, J. (1992). *Intelligent Enterprise*. New York: The Free Press.

Ruddick, S. (1989). *Maternal Thinking*. Boston: Beacon Press.

Rumelt, R., Schendel, D. and D. Teece (1991). "Strategic Management and Economics," *Strategic Management Journal,* 12 (Winter), pp. 5–30.

Scaltsas, P. (1992). "Do Feminist Ethics Counter Feminist Aims?" in E. Cole and S. Coultrap-McQuin, Eds., *Explorations in Feminist Ethics*. Bloomington: Indiana University Press, pp. 15–26.

Schnake, M. (1991). "Organizational Citizenship: A Review, Proposed Model, and Research Agenda," *Human Relations,* 44(7): pp. 735–59.

Scott, R., Aiken, L., Mechanic, D. and S. Moravcsik (1995). "Organizational Aspects of Caring," *Milbank Quarterly,* 73 (1):77–95.

Senge, P. (1990). *The Fifth Discipline*. New York: Doubleday.

Solomon, R. (1992). *Ethics and Excellence*. New York: Oxford University Press.

Stalk, G., Evans, P. and L. Shulman (1992). "Competing on Capabilities: The New Rules of Corporate Strategy," *Harvard Business Review,* 70 (March/April), pp. 57–69.

Tronto, J. (1993a). *Moral Boundaries: A Political Argument for An Ethic of Care*. New York: Routledge.

Tronto, J. (1993b). "Beyond Gender Difference to a Theory of Care", in M. Larrabee. Ed., *An Ethic of Care: Feminist and Interdisciplinary Perspectives*. New York: Routledge pp. 240–257.

Victor, B. and J. Cullen (1988). "The Organizational Bases of Ethical Work Climates," *Administrative Science Quarterly,* 33: 101–125.

Walker, M. (1992). "Moral Understandings: Alternative Epistemology for a Feminist Ethics," in E. Cole and

S. Coultrap-McQuin, eds., *Explorations in Feminist Ethics.* Bloomington: Indiana University Press, pp. 165–175.

West, C. (1993) *Race Matters.* New York: Vintage Books.

Wicks, A., Gilbert, D., and R. E. Freeman (1994). "A Feminist Reinterpretation of the Stakeholder Concept," *Business Ethics Quarterly,* 4 (4): 475–498.

White, T. (1992). "Business, Ethics, and Carol Gilligan's 'Two Voices'," *Business Ethics Quarterly,* 2(1): pp 51–59.

The Importance of Leadership in Shaping Business Values

Joanne B. Ciulla
Professor and Coston Family Chair in Leadership and Ethics, University of Richmond

Few doubt that leaders play a role, either as founders or promoters of values in organizations. So the more important question is not 'Whose values?' but 'What values?' Just because a leader has values doesn't mean that they are good ones. Furthermore, the question is not so much about what a leader values, but what a leader actually does to demonstrate his or her values. This paper is about how leaders translate values into action and actions into enduring organizational values. I first examine how we have come to think about the values of business leaders and success. I also reflect on what theories of leadership say about how leaders influence followers. Then I argue that the language of *having values* is often inadequate for understanding individual and organizational ethics. Lastly, I look at the leadership of P. Roy Vagelos of Merck & Company to illustrate how the values of founders and current leaders shape the values of their own organizations, and can shape the values of the industries in which they operate.

Reprinted from *Long Range Planning,* Vol. 32. No. 2, 1999, pp. 166–172, with permission from Elsevier Science.

OLD ASSUMPTIONS ABOUT THE VALUES AND VIRTUES OF BUSINESS LEADERS

Some of our attitudes towards the values of business leaders can be traced to the Protestant work ethic, which included the belief that accumulation of wealth was a sign that one was among God's chosen. One of the Calvinists' favorite Biblical passages was "Seest thou a man diligent in his business? He shall stand before kings" (Proverbs xxii 29). This equation of business success and salvation seemed to stick even in the secular world. In the 18th century, Benjamin Franklin tempered the Protestant work ethic with enlightenment ideals. He believed that business leaders should strive for wealth so that they can use it in a humane way to help society. Franklin thought good character was necessary for success. In his autobiography he listed eleven virtues needed for success in business and in life: temperance, silence, order, resolution, sincerity, justice, moderation, cleanliness, tranquility, chastity, and humility. Virtues tell us what we should be like and what we have to do to be that way. Values are what we believe to be important or morally worthy. We usually assume that values motivate us to act, but this isn't always the case. Some are satisfied to have a value and not act on it. This is not possible with a virtue. A person may value courage, but never do anything brave or heroic. Whereas one cannot possess the virtue of courage unless he or she has done something courageous.

America is somewhat distinct in its history of celebrating the values and character of business leaders. For example, in the 19th century. William Makepeace Thayer specialized in biographies of chief executive officers. His books focused on how the values leaders formed early in life contributed to their success. Thayer summed up the moral path to success this way: "Man deviseth his own way, but the Lord directeth his steps".[1] As the number of business journalists grew in America, some dedicated themselves to lionizing business leaders. The Scottish immigrant Bertie Charles (B.C.) Forbes elevated the moral adulation of business leaders into an enduring art form, imitated by business publications throughout the world. When he started

Forbes magazine in 1916, Forbes described it as "a publication that would strive to inject more humanity, more joy, and more satisfaction into business and into life in general".[2] His goal was to convey Franklin's message that work, virtue, and wealth lead to happiness and social benefit.

The 18th and 19th century advocates of the work ethic preached that strong moral character was the key to wealth. By early 20th century the emphasis on moral character shifted to an emphasis on personality. In Dale Carnegie's 1936 classic *How to Win Friends and Influence People,* psychology, not morality, was the key to success in business. This was true in leadership theory as well. Scholars were more interested in studying the personality traits of leaders than their values. This is in part because through most of the 20th century many prominent leadership scholars were psychologists.

The mythologies of business leaders remain popular, even though many of them are not great philanthropists or particularly morally virtuous or advocates of enlightened self-interest.[3] Today business leaders are more likely to be celebrated in the first person than in the third. Consider, for example, the popularity of autobiographies by Al Dunlap, Donald Trump, and Bill Gates, all of whom enjoy touting their own virtues and values to the public.

Recent books such as *Business as a Calling,* by Michael Novak, draw the traditional Protestant connection between success in business and God's favor.[4] Novak, who is a Catholic, argues that successful business people are more religious than other professionals. He cites two studies to back up his view. The first looked at church attendance by elites from the news media, business, politics, labor unions, the military, and religion. It found that groups with the highest proportion of weekly church attendance after religious professionals, were the military at 49% and then business at 35%. The second study, a Conference Board survey of senior executives at Fortune 500 companies, reported that 65% of the respondents said they worshipped at churches or synagogues regularly.[5] Novak infers that church going affects business values. However, we need more evidence

than church attendance to connect religious values with the values a leader brings to work. After all, for some going to Church is nothing more than *going to Church.*

LEADERSHIP THEORIES AND VALUES

The legacy of the Protestant work ethic and its attitudes toward business present a paradox. Are business leaders successful because of their virtues? or Are they virtuous because they are successful? In the literature of leadership studies both seem to be true, depending on how one defines leadership.

Leadership scholars have spent way too much time worrying about the definition of leadership. Some believe that if they could agree on a common definition of leadership, they would be better able to understand it. Joseph Rost gathered together 221 definitions of leadership. After reviewing all of his definitions, one discovers that the definition problem was not really about definitions *per se.* All 221 definitions say basically the same thing—leadership is about one person getting other people to do something. Where the definitions differ was in how leaders got other followers to act and how leaders came up with the something that was to be done. For example, one definition from the 1920s said, "[Leadership is] the ability to impress the will of the leader on those led and induce obedience, respect, loyalty, and cooperation."[6] Another definition from the 1990s said, "Leadership is an influence relationship between leaders and followers who intend real changes that reflect their mutual purposes".[7] We all can think of leaders who fit both of these descriptions. Some use their power to force people to do what they want, others work with their followers to do what everyone agrees is best for them. The difference between the definitions rests on a normative question: "How should leaders treat followers?"

The scholars who worry about constructing the ultimate definition of leadership are asking the wrong question, but inadvertently trying to answer the right one. The ultimate question about leadership is not "What is the definition of leadership?" The whole point of studying leadership is, "What is good leadership?" The use of word *good* here has two senses, morally good and technically good or effective. If a good leader means *good* in both senses, then the two should form a logical conjunction. In other words, in order for the statement "She is a good leader" to be true, it must be true that she is effective *and* she is ethical.

The question, "What constitutes a good leader?" lies at the heart of many public debates about leadership today. We want our leaders to be good in both ways. Nonetheless, we are often more likely to say leaders are good if they are effective, but not moral, than if they are moral, but not effective. Leaders face a paradox. They have to stay in business or get reelected in order to be leaders. If they are not minimally effective at doing these things, their morality as leaders is usually irrelevant, because they are no longer leaders. In leadership, effectiveness sometimes must take priority over ethics. What we hope for are leaders who know when ethics should and when ethics shouldn't take a back seat to effectiveness. History tends to dismiss as irrelevant the morally good leaders who are unsuccessful. President Jimmy Carter was a man of great personal integrity, but during his presidency, he was ineffective and generally considered a poor leader. The conflict between ethics and effectiveness and the definition problem are apparent in what I have called, "the Hitler problem".[8] The answer to the question "Was Hitler a good leader?" is yes, if a leader is defined as someone who is effective or gets the job they set out to do done. The answer is no, if the leader gets the job done, but the job itself is immoral, and it is done in an immoral way. In other words leadership is about more than being effective at getting followers to do things. The quality of leadership also depends on the means and the ends of a leader's actions. The same is true for Robin Hood. While in myth some admire him, he still steals from the rich to give to the poor. His purpose is morally worthy, but the way that he does it is not. Most of us would prefer leaders who do the right thing, the right way for the right reasons.

The way that we assess the impact of a leader's values on an organization also depends on one's theory of leadership. Many still carry with them the "Great Man" theory—leaders are born and not

made. Personality traits, not values catapult leaders to greatness. This theory has been articulated in different ways. Thomas Carlyle wrote about the traits of heroes such as Napoleon. Niccolo Machiavelli described the strategic cunning of his 'Prince'. Frederich Neitszche extolled the will to power of his 'superman'. While the innate qualities of leaders are primary factors in these theories, it is not always clear what makes people want to follow great men.

Charismatic leadership is a close relative to the Great Man Theory. Charismatic leaders have powerful personalities. However the distinguishing feature of charismatic leadership is the emotional relationship that charismatic leaders establish with followers. Charismatic leaders range from a John F. Kennedy, who inspired a generation to try and make the world better, to the cult leader Jim Jones, who lead his followers into suicide. The values of charismatic leaders shape the organization, but in some cases these values do not live on when the charismatic leader is gone.

Other theories of leadership focus on the situation or context of leadership. They emphasize the nature of the task that needs to be done, the external environment, which includes historical, economic, and cultural factors, and the characteristics of followers. Lee Iacocca was the right leader for Chrysler when it went bankrupt, but we don't know if he would be the right leader at some other phase of the firm's history. Ross Perot was a good business man, but many doubted his ability to be effective as a political leader. Situational theories don't explicitly say anything about values, but one might surmise that in some situations a person with particularly strong moral values must emerge as a leader. For example, Nelson Mandela and Václav Havel seemed to have been the right men at the right time. They both offered the powerful kind of moral leadership required for peaceful revolutions in South Africa and the Czech Republic.

A third group of scholars combine trait theories with situational models and focus on the interaction between leaders and followers. The leader's role is to guide the organization along paths that are rewarding to everyone involved. Here values are sure to play an important role, but again it matters what the values are and what they mean to others in the organization. The Ohio studies and the Michigan studies both measured leadership effectiveness in terms of how leaders treated subordinates and how they got the job done. The Ohio Studies looked at leadership effectiveness in terms of 'consideration' or the degree to which leaders act in a friendly and supportive manner, and 'initiating structure' or the way that leaders structure their own role and the role of subordinates in order to obtain group goals.[9] The Michigan Studies measured leaders on the basis of task orientation and relationship orientation.[10] Implicit in these theories and studies is an ethical question. Are leaders more effective when they are kind to people, or are leaders more effective when they use certain techniques for structuring and ordering tasks? Is leadership about moral relationships or techniques?—probably both.[11]

Transforming Leadership and Servant Leadership are normative theories of leadership. Both emphasize the relationship of leaders and followers to each other and the importance values in the process of leadership. James MacGregor Burns' theory of transforming leadership rests on a set of moral assumptions about the relationship between leaders and followers.[12] Burns argues that leaders have to operate at higher need and value levels than those of followers. Charismatic leaders can be transforming leaders, however, unlike many charismatic leaders, the transforming leader engages followers in a dialogue about the tension and conflict within their own value systems. Transforming leaders have very strong values, but they do not force them on others.[13] Ultimately, the transforming leader develops followers so that they can lead themselves.

Burns' theory addresses two pressing moral questions. The morality of means (and this also includes the moral use of power) and the morality of ends. Burns' distinction between transforming and transactional leadership, and modal and end-values offers a way to think about the question "What is a good leader?" both in terms of the relationship of leaders to followers and the means and ends of actions. Transactional leadership rests on the values found in the means of an act. These are called modal values which are things like, responsibility,

fairness, honesty and promise-keeping. Transactional leadership helps leaders and followers reach their own goals by supplying lower level wants and needs so that they can move up to higher needs. Transforming leadership is concerned with end-values, such as liberty, justice, and equality.

Servant leadership has not gotten as much attention as transformational leadership in the literature, but in recent years interest in it by the business community has grown. Servant leaders lead because they want to serve others. In *Servant Leadership,* Robert K. Greenleaf says people follow servant leaders freely because they trust them. Like the transforming leader, the servant leader also tries to morally elevate followers. Greenleaf says servant leadership must pass this test: "Do those served grow as persons? Do they *while being served* become healthier, wiser, freer, more autonomous, more likely themselves to become servants?" He goes on and adds a Rawlsian proviso, "*And,* what is the effect on the least privileged in society?"[14] In both transforming leadership and servant leadership, leaders not only have values, but they help followers develop their own values, which will hopefully overlap or be compatible with those of the organization.

THE PROBLEM ONLY *HAVING* VALUES

Social scientists like to talk about values because they are descriptors. When a poll asks voters if they prefer better schools or lower taxes, we assume that if the majority pick better schools, it means most respondents value education. Ask people about their values and they will tell you what they think is important. Different types of moral statements and concepts *do* different things. For example the statement 'you ought not to kill' prescribes, 'Do not kill' commands, 'Killing is wrong' evaluates, and 'Killing is wrong because I value life' explains, and 'Killing is against my values, which include the value of human life' describes. Values are static concepts. You have to make a lot of assumptions to make a value *do* something. You have to assume that because people value something they act accordingly, but we know this isn't the case. While values change all the time, having a value does not mean that one has or will do something about it.

Since values themselves do not have agency, the main way that a leader influences the organization is through his or her words and actions. One way to understand a leaders values is through their vision. The CEO who says his or her vision is to double market share by the year 2000 has a goal, not a vision. All businesses want to make profits. Visions must have an implicit or explicit moral component to them.[15] Often the moral component has to do with improving the quality of life, particularly in the case of making a product safer, environmentally friendly, or more affordable to those who need it. A leader's vision should tell us where we want to go, why it's good to go there, and the right way for us to get there.

The only way to understand if a business leader's values have an impact is to look at how his or her values connect with actions. Hypocrisy is the most extreme form of values not meeting up with actions. Hypocrites express strong moral values that they do not hold and then act against them. For example, a company that advertises its commitment to green products while continuing to sell products that don't meet it's own espoused green standards is hypocritical.[16] What is most odd about some hypocrites is that they are not always complete liars. Some know they should live up to the values they talk about, but simply do not or will not.

Another problem with values and actions is what Frederick B. Bird calls 'moral silence'. Moral silence is the opposite of hypocrisy. Morally silent leaders act and speak as if they do not hold certain moral values, when they actually do. The company president who cuts 1000 jobs from the payroll may publicly state that he cut jobs to fill what he considers his most important obligation to protect shareholder value. When in fact he is guilt ridden because he really believes that his greatest moral obligation is to his employees. Leaders sometimes lack the ability or the moral courage to act on their values. Similarly, there are some who have values, but are either too busy, distracted, or lazy to act on those values. Consider the case of a female corporate executive who has strong convictions about giving women opportunities for career advancement, but does not go out of her way or take advantage of opportunities to ensure that women in her company have these opportunities.

Often leaders don't realize that the values they hold are in practice contradictory or inconsistent. Once a colleague and I conducted an ethics seminar for the presidents of a large conglomerate. The CEO of the corporation was an enthusiastic participant. During the seminar he expressed his feelings about the importance of honesty and integrity in business. However, as the participants discussed our case studies, it became clear that there were a number of situations in which protecting the company's integrity meant losing business or money. The CEO actively agreed with these conclusions. However, the others in the seminar pointed out to him that quarterly sales determined the compensation for each business unit. The CEO set profit targets for each business unit and used a formula to determine compensation. When it came to performance, he valued the numbers more than anything else. What the CEO failed to realize was that he was espousing the value of integrity, but in effect saying that employees would be punished if they did not act with integrity (with firing) *and* punished if they did act with integrity (with reduced compensation). Some thought that if the CEO really valued integrity, he should make some adjustment to the incentive system to take into account business lost for ethical reasons. One brave man wondered out loud if the CEO didn't really value profits over integrity.

Often companies write codes of ethics or mission statements but don't think through what the values in the statement mean in terms of how they manage their businesses. In 1983 the Harvard Business School wrote a glowing case study of how CEO Jim Beré developed the Borg-Warner code of ethics.[17] Borg-Warner is a conglomerate of automotive, financial services, and security service businesses. Its code began with the statement. "We believe in the dignity of the individual", and "We believe in the commonwealth of Borg-Warner and its people". An elegant framed copy of the code was hung in offices and factories of

Borg-Warner's various businesses. Their ethics code also said, "we must heed the voice of our natural concern for others" and "grant others the same respect, cooperation, and decency we seek for ourselves".[18]

Warner Gear, a division of Borg-Warner, manufactured gears for cars and boats. In 1984 it made a text book turn around in labor relations and productivity. After years of losing money and engaging in endless labor disputes, the union and management finally agreed to cooperate. They formed effective quality circles that saved the company millions of dollars in waste and inefficiency. Company profits soared in 1985.[19] However, in July of that year, with no warning to the managers or employees who implemented the turnaround, Borg-Warner announced it was shipping part of Warner Gear to Kenfig, Wales to save on labor costs. This meant that the factory would lose 300 jobs. While the business decision may have been warranted, the way that it was implemented did not show decency and respect for those who had worked so hard to make the firm successful. All the energy, good will, and commitment of the employees didn't matter, and neither did the grand values that hung on the wall.

Lastly, there are cases where a business leader acts on values that he has never made any concerted effort to express in words to employees. On 11 December 1995 Malden Mills, a textile factory in Massachusetts, burnt down. The owner, Aaron Feuerstein, immediately decided to give out Christmas bonuses and pay his employees full salaries until the factory was repaired. In the midst of massive corporate downsizings this story of kindness captured the public imagination. Feuerstein was a quiet man running a family business. The business itself was known for treating workers fairly, but Feuerstein had never been one to publicly articulate his own values. Given the publicity of his actions after the fire, he was asked by the press to talk about his values. He then explained that his business values came from his Jewish faith and the teachings of the Talmud. Yet for most employees, *where* he got his values didn't matter as much as *what* he did with them.

The point of these examples is to show that a leaders values do indeed shape the values of the firm when they are paired with policies and actions that breathe life into them. The way in which founders influence the values of the company is by setting out their mission, what they want to do, and how they want to do it. But most importantly, their actions write the story of the organization's values. The story can be a morally good one or an evil one. Either way, the role of leaders who come after the founder is to tell and add to the story of the company and its values. This includes ethical lessons learned from its mistakes as well as its moral triumphs.

Howard Garner believes that great leaders are also great story tellers. He says leadership is a process in the minds of individuals who live in a culture. Some stories tend to become more predominant in this process, such as stories that provide an adequate and timely sense of identity for individuals.[20] The story of the fire at Malden Mills will become part of the company's mythology. It not only conveys a message of moral commitment to employees, but it sets a moral standard for those who will take Feuerstein's place.

Leaders' values matter when they are repeatedly reflected in their actions. However, a leader's values and his or her will to act on them are also shaped by the history and the culture of the organization itself. As I pointed out earlier, we sometimes mythologize business leaders because they are successful or imagine that their lone values are responsible for doing some heroic action. But as we saw earlier, there can be a gap between having values and acting on them. This gap is often narrowed or widened by the values already present in the story of the organization.

One of the more dramatic illustrations of business leadership and values is the case of P. Roy Vagelos, CEO of Merck & Co., Inc.[21] Prior to becoming CEO, Vagelos was director of Merck Sharp & Dohme's research laboratories. In 1979 a researcher named William Campbell had a hunch that an antiparasite drug he was working on called Ivermectin might work on the parasite that caused river blindness, a disease that threatens the eyesight and lives of 85 million people in 35 developing countries. He asked Vagelos if he could have the resources to pursue his research. Despite the fact that the market for this drug was essentially the poorest people in the world, Vagelos gave Campbell the go ahead. While the decision was Vagelos', it was also reinforced by the Merck's axiom 'health precedes wealth'.

Campbell's hunch about Ivermectin proved to be right and he developed a drug called 'Mectizan', which was approved for use by the government in 1987. By this time Vagelos had become the CEO of Merck. Now that the drug was approved he sought public underwriting to produce Mectizan. Vagelos hired Henry Kissenger to help open doors for Merck. They approached several sources including the US Agency for International Development and the World Health Organization, but couldn't raise money for the drug. Merck was left with a drug that was only useful to people who couldn't buy it. Vagelos recalled, "We faced the possibility that we had a miraculous drug that would sit on a shelf".[22] After reviewing the company's options, Vagelos and his directors announced that they would give Mectizan away for free, forever, on 21 October 1987. A decade later the drug give-away cost Merck over $200 million. By 1996 Mectizan had reached 19 million people. In Nigeria alone it saved 6 million people from blindness.

Few business leaders ever have the opportunity to do what Vagelos did. His values guided his decisions in this case, but so did the values of the founder. George C. Merck, son of the company's American founder. said that from the very beginning Merck's founders asserted that medicine was for people not profits. However, he quickly added that they also believed that if medicine is for people, profits will follow.[23]

Like many corporate mission statements Merck's says its mission "is to provide society with superior products and services". The statement goes on to assert, "We are in the business of preserving and improving human life". "All of our actions must be measured by our success at achieving this goal". It concludes that "We expect profits from work that satisfies customer needs and that benefits humanity".[24] The values in Merck's mission statement are as grand as the ones in Borg-Warner's. However, the corporate

leaders prior to Vagelos acted on and hence reinforced these values long before Vagelos donated Mectizan. After WWII tuberculosis thrived in Japan. Most Japanese couldn't afford to buy Merck's powerful drug, Streptomycin, to fight it. Merck gave away a large supply of the drug to the Japanese public. The Japanese did not forget. In 1983 the Japanese government allowed Merck to purchase 50.02% of Banyu Pharmaceutical. At the time this was the largest foreign investment in a Japanese company. Merck is currently the largest American pharmaceutical company in Japan. The story makes Merck's mission statement come alive. It is the kind of story that employees learn and internalize when they come to work there.

Vagelos' moral leadership in this case extended beyond his organization into the industry. As Michael Useem points out, Merck has become the benchmark by which the moral behavior of other pharmaceutical companies are judged. Sometimes the moral actions of one CEO or company set the bar higher for others. Useem observes that the message hit home at Glaxo. In comparing Glaxo to Merck, a business writer once called Glaxo "a hollow enterprise lacking purpose and lacking soul".[25] Merck's values seemed to inspire Glaxo's new CEO Richard Sykes. In 1993 Glaxo invested in developing a drug to combat a form of tuberculosis connected to Aids and found mostly among the poor. In 1996 Glaxo donated a potent new product for malaria. Similarly, Dupont is now giving away nylon to filter guinea worms out of drinking water in poor countries and American Cyanamid is donating a larvacide to control them.

A cynic might regard Merck's donation of Streptomycin and Mectizan as nothing more than public relations stunts. But what is most interesting about the actions of Merck's leaders is that while they believed that "by doing good they would do well", at the time that they acted it was unclear exactly when and how the company would benefit. Neither the Japanese after the war nor the poor people of the world who are threatened by river blindness looked likely to return the favor in the near future. While this wasn't an altruistic act, it was not a purely self-interested one either. Since it was unclear if, when, and how Merck would benefit. it is reasonable to assume that Merck's leaders and the values upon which they acted were authentic. They intentionally acted on their values. Any future benefits required a leap of faith on their part.

Business leaders' values matter to the organization only if they act on them. In business ethics and in life we always hope that doing the right thing, while costly and sometimes painful in the short run, will pay off in the long run.

REFERENCES

1. R. M. Huber, *The American Idea of Success,* p. 53, McGraw-Hill, New York (1971).
2. B. C. Forbes, Fact and comment, *Forbes* 60 (1 October), 10 (1947).
3. See "The challenge for America's rich" and "Philanthropy in America", *The Economist* 30 May, 17, 23–25 (1998).
4. M. Novak, *Business as a Calling.* The Free Press, New York (1996).
5. "God Gets Down to Business", Across the board, *The Conference Board* 14(5), 11–12 (1988).
6. B. V. Moore, The May Conference on leadership, *Personnel Journal* 6, 124 (1927).
7. J. Rost, *Leadership for the Twenty-First Century,* p. 102, Praeger, New York (1991).
8. J. B. Ciulla, Leadership ethics: mapping the territory, *Business Ethics Quarterly,* January (1995).
9. E. A. Fleishman, The description of supervisory behavior, *Personnel Psychology* 37, 1–6 (1953).
10. Results from the earlier and later Michigan Studies are discussed in R. Leikert, *New Patterns of Management,* McGraw-Hill, New York (1961), and *The Human Organization: Its Management and Value,* McGraw-Hill, New York (1967).
11. G. Yukl, *Leadership in Organizations,* 2nd ed., Prentice Hall, Englewood Cliffs, NJ (1989), p 96.
12. Burns uses the terms *transforming* and *transformational* in his book. However, he prefers to refer to his theory as *transforming* leadership.
13. J. MacGregor Burns, *Leadership,* pp. 42–43, Harper & Row, New York (1978).
14. R. Greenleaf, *Servant Leadership,* p. 23, Paulist Press, New York (1977).
15. B. Nanus, *Visionary Leadership,* Jossey-Bass, San Francisco (1992).
16. F. B. Bird, *The Muted Conscience,* p. 4, Quorum Books, Westport, CT (1996).
17. K. E. Goodpaster, The beliefs of Borg-Warner, Harvard Business School case 9–383–091, The President and Fellows of Harvard College (1983).
18. P. E. Murphy, *80 Exemplary Ethics Statements,* p. 27, University of Notre Dame Press, Notre Dame, IN (1998).
19. J. B. Ciulla, and K. E. Goodpaster, Building trust at Warner Gear, Harvard Business School Case Services 0-386-0011, p. 11, The President and Fellows of Harvard College (1985).
20. H. Gardner, *Leading Minds,* p. 22, Basic Books, New York (1995).
21. The information about this case is from M. Useem, *The Leadership Moment,* Chap. 1 Times Business Books, New York (1998).
22. *Ibid.,* p. 23.
23. *Ibid.,* p. 29.
24. p. 29.
25. p. 31.

QUESTIONS FOR DISCUSSION

1. Driscoll and Hoffman detail a number of steps a corporation can take to develop an ethical corporate culture. Can you think of any additional steps that might be needed? Do their recommendations make any sense for smaller firms?
2. In your judgment, can corporations be too ethical? If there is a conflict between ethics and profits, what should be done?
3. Should we care about the motivations of companies like Ben & Jerry's and The Body Shop when they engage in social marketing activities? If their only objective is the bottom line, should it matter?

Andrew Ames

Andrew has worked for the company for 23 years and has made lots of friends in that time. There are several guys that he is particularly close with and, outside of work, they go to ball games and golf together regularly in the same league. Over the years they have spent a good deal of time together, and have gotten to know each other very well.

Andrew's brother sent him a sexually explicit joke that was in the form of a cartoon and told him the address on the Internet where it could be found. Andrew went to the site and found a number of very graphic pictures and jokes. On his lunch hour, Andrew downloaded them to his PC and then attached them to an e-mail to his buddies. Since he knew the guys so well, he knew for sure they would not be offended if his humor was not "politically correct."

The next day John opened up his e-mail and saw the one from Andrew. He got a good laugh and wanted to send it to another friend in his department.

What should John do?

DISCUSSION QUESTIONS

- Should John wait till break time or lunchtime to send the e-mail to his friend?
- Is this e-mail OK since it was between friends? Why?
- Would the answer be different if the joke was not of a sexual nature? If there were not pictures/cartoons?
- Is the e-mail Andrew sent to John private?

Bert Tanui

Bert Tanui is a principal consultant in Management Consulting Services. After a difficult price negotiation, he has finally landed a contract with a large electronics firm for the development of a complex inventory management system. Since he knows that there were two other finalists, he is particularly pleased.

This is Tanui's first meeting with the client since the contract award. His objective is to clarify the parameters of the research phase and to identify the people he will be working with during the engagement.

In response to Tanui's opening comments about the scope of the effort, the client reaches into a file and hands him a competitor's proposal.

"Take a look at this. It does a good job of spelling out the requirements."

What should Tanui do?

DISCUSSION QUESTION

- When is it acceptable to look at competitor information (if ever)?

From Volumes to Three Words: Texas Instruments

Dawn-Marie Driscoll
Executive Fellow, Center for Business Ethics, Bentley College, and President, Driscoll Associates

W. Michael Hoffman
Executive Director, Center for Business Ethics, Bentley College

Some companies start with a mission statement and a few core values, and as the company grows, add detailed policies and procedures. Texas Instruments, the global semiconductor company, followed that pattern but then did an astounding thing. It reexamined what it stood for and ended up with just three words. How it discovered its contemporary values is a story of corporate leadership and soul-searching.

TEXAS ORIGINS, TEXAS PRINCIPLES

The "old" Texas Instruments began in the 1930s with a smarter way to find oil deposits in the boom

---

From *Ethics Matters: How to Implement Values-Driven Management* by Dawn-Marie Driscoll and W. Michael Hoffman (Waltham, MA: Center for Business Ethics at Bentley College, 2000). Copyright © 2000 Center for Business Ethics at Bentley College. Reprinted by permission.

towns of East Texas. As Geophysical Services Inc., the company was built on its founders' principles of honesty, integrity and service.

As the company expanded into the world of advanced electronics, it won U.S. Navy contracts during wartime. After the war it developed a range of technological firsts, including the integrated circuit. As the company grew and the modern world became more complex, TI published in 1961 *Ethics in the Business of TI,* its first formal code of ethics, codifying what had been the company's long time legacy of integrity.

BUSINESS ETHICS LEADERSHIP

Throughout the 1970s and 80s, TI became a global powerhouse, with employees operating in more than 30 countries on five continents. Along with TI's growth came more laws, more regulations, and more oversight. TI, an early leader in the business ethics movement, established its ethics office in 1987. In 1991 the company won the David C. Lincoln Ethics and Excellence in Business Award and in 1994 won the American Business Ethics Award and the Bentley College Center for Business Ethics Award.

TI's ethics apparatus was far-reaching and sophisticated. Led by Carl Skooglund, the TI Ethics Director, the office updated *Ethics in the Business of TI* and created several supplemental communication resources—the "Cornerstone" series, a set of glossy publications that featured real questions on ethics from TI employees worldwide, concentrating on specific subjects; more than 400 weekly electronic news articles on current subjects of interest, which were compiled into a resource library called "Instant Experience"; and ethics helplines comprising a secure message system, toll-free phone lines and a U.S post office box separate from the TI internal mail system. The office produced handy pocket guides, informative posters, training materials and an on-line, menu-driven web site linked to all TI Ethics Office materials and resources.

So what was wrong? According to Glenn Coleman, former TI Manager of Ethics Communication and Education, the material was beginning to look like the United States tax code. Too much, too confusing. Not only that, but Texas Instruments was suddenly jolted by a series of events that forced it to become a "new company."

CHANGE HAPPENS FAST

First, in 1996, its popular chairman, Jerry Junkins, died suddenly of a heart attack while traveling in Europe. Revered by all, his death brought into focus other major organizational and policy changes that actually had been in the works prior to the sad event. But now there was a sense of urgency on the part of the new leadership to complete Junkins' plans for reformulating the global semiconductor company into a fast-paced, focused designer and supplier of digital signal processing solutions.

TI sold its defense business to Raytheon, the largest of nearly twenty divestitures and acquisitions over a two-year period. It competed aggressively for the most talented people, dramatically changing its benefits and compensation policies to provide more individual choice and flexibility. The Dallas-based company was shedding its paternalistic, command-and-control ways and emerging into a global leader providing products to serve a networked society. For the first time, TI had more employees outside the United States than inside.

The new Chairman, President and Chief Executive Officer, Tom Engibous, was determined that TI reward its shareholders by increasing its value as a market leader. To do this, they would provide stable financial performance and grow in markets with potential. He placed a strong emphasis on quality strategies, improved profit margins and insisted that every employee define a personal plan for individual development.

Engibous's favorite phrase became "a passion for winning." He wanted TIers to be fast, creative and collaborative, and this superb communicator lost little time in repeating the message to everyone.

Skooglund was concerned. "TI had a long history of ethical emphasis right from its founders," he said. "It was ingrained in the culture and made my job easier.

"But I wasn't sure how ethics would fit in this new TI, with its passion for winning. The heightened emphasis on financial results could have been interpreted to mean doing whatever it takes to get the job done. That could have been a recipe for disaster if we didn't clearly explain how ethics and values were a part of it."

Skooglund met with Engibous to discuss these concerns to develop a plan to assure that the company would not lose its focus on integrity in the face of increased pressure for performance.

NEW MODEL, NEW APPROACH TO ETHICS

Engibous was clear. He was proud of the ethical history of TI and insisted that ethics be a foundation of the new TI. But he was also clear that the company must operate on a values and principles approach, rather than a rules-based approach. Engibous did not want to lose the transformation from TI's old hierarchical model to a new one of empowerment and responsibility.

Skooglund wanted to make sure that he understood. "If we're successful, what's the end state going to look like?" he asked.

Engibous's response couldn't have been clearer. The TI core values would be understood and owned worldwide. TIers' behavior would be consistent with the core values, which would give the company a competitive advantage. Decisions would be made according to the company values, not its rules. Bureaucracy would be minimal, as would barriers to productivity, innovation and collaboration. Policies would be few, simple and easy to understand. TIers would have the flexibility to manage their work and their personal lives. They would be trusted and responsible.

Skooglund understood. Now he just had to translate the marching orders into action. He participated on a cross-functional team to examine all the human resource policies of the company to see which of them could be eliminated.

THE PROCESS OF CHANGE

"We challenged each policy by asking five questions," Skooglund recalled. "Why do we have it? What is the business reason for having it? Is it a legal requirement? What is the worst thing that can happen if we don't have it? Should it be local or corporate?

"We started off with 46 policies. We scrapped 9, recognized that 24 were actually how-tos, or procedures, and we kept 13. The ones we kept we rewrote and significantly shortened. That process took us over a year."

As the process of eliminating policies and other barriers continued, the importance of reassessing the company's basic values took on increased urgency. Skooglund recalled, "We realized that we were taking away a security blanket from many who had become very comfortable in referring day-to-day decisions to the policy book. We were asking TIers to face a future defined by enormous changes, increased complexity and intense competition. The only way we could expect them to make good decisions and choices, and to do it quickly in that environment, was to provide value-based resources and to put them in everyone's hands. Those values had to be crystal clear, directly aligned with TI's business objectives and relevant to every employee worldwide. We launched a year-long process to define those values."

A task force set out to define the TI values in a single document. The first draft was three pages, single-spaced and contained fourteen values. Three

drafts and several international reviews later, the feedback was consistent: shorter is better! Keep them simple, concise and easy to remember.

Skooglund admitted they were rewriting the Constitution when their constituents only wanted soundbites. By the summer of 1997, all the company's human resource directors had reviewed a new draft. It was time to try it out on 19 separate worldwide employee focus groups.

"At that point we knew what we wanted to say," Skooglund said, "but we needed to know what employees were hearing. As a result of the focus groups, the draft changed quite a bit."

JUST THREE WORDS

The three core TI values in the draft were integrity, innovation and commitment. Each value was illustrated by two descriptive phrases, which could be called principles. For example, integrity was linked with "respect and value people" and "be honest."

Skooglund admits that the definitions of values and principles are imprecise and to make matters worse, the final document booklet was entitled "The values *and ethics* of TI."

"Several of our operations, particularly those in Asia, wanted to know precisely why we used these words. What did "values" mean? What did "principles" mean? Is "innovation" really a value? What's the difference between principles and ethics? In hindsight, perhaps we didn't need all those words, but to me, values are deeply seated universal concepts that give us guidance. Principles are more prescriptive and directed towards conduct."

While it is interesting to see the final three words that TI settled on to represent its corporate values, it is more interesting to learn what words and concepts did not make the final document.

The TI Mission Statement, "Leadership in Digital Solutions for the Networked Society," was highlighted in the initial draft. Following the focus group discussions it was left on the cutting room floor. While inspiring, many felt that it had no place in a values document.

Engibous's favorite phrase, "a passion for winning" was interpreted by many focus groups to mean, do whatever it takes, a perspective that surprised and concerned Engibous. "It became clear," Skooglund said, "that we had to put that objective in ethical perspective. But at the same time, Tom and the rest of the leadership team were adamant that a commitment to making TI a winner had to remain an essential principle."

The original draft contained a concept that work should be fun. Asian employees reacted strongly. In their view, the concept of setting fun and humor as a workplace objective was weird. Business is business and should remain so.

The notion that TIers would "respect local customs" was also eliminated, after Europeans complained that the concept was too vague and would open up potential justification for abuses.

One word that Skooglund thought was appropriate evoked a sharp negative reaction, particularly in Europe. The drafters had extolled the virtue of collaboration and teamwork. To some employees, however, collaboration meant collusion. Combine "collaboration" with "world leadership" and "passion for winning" and you have a recipe for world war.

Well if you can't collaborate, how about "nurture informal relationships," in order to reinforce candor and communications? No. Informal doesn't work everywhere, particularly in places where formal relationships indicate respect for one's superiors.

Early drafts frequently contained the words "do not," or "never." Focus groups in Asia thought those words were too negative and suggested that drafters minimize their use, writing the same message but in a positive way. "Bureaucracy" was viewed as a negative and unclear word that didn't make the final draft.

Skooglund was surprised by two concepts that engendered negative responses. "In past documents, we had stressed that TI has an open door process, meaning that any employee could take a concern up the ladder to anyone in the company. But our employee focus groups thought we should leave it out. While some had good experiences with the open door process, evidently enough employees felt they had been burned by it that the concept had taken on a negative aura. We were told that it might create a credibility issue. So we didn't repeat it.

"We also had drafted a principle stating that because one's activities and behavior outside of work could have an impact on the company's reputation, we could have a legitimate reason to take corrective action. While we understood this in the United States, Europeans did not like this idea, believing that one's work and personal life should be kept quite separate. So we left it out."

Through this entire process there was a constant drumbeat of criticism and advice regarding the document, too many words, people won't read it. Keep it simple and straightforward.

All these subtractions made a better document in the end, as each reviewing group urged brevity and clarity. The basic values should be so clear and distinct that employees could keep them in their heads.

After the drafting group reviewed the input from the focus groups, it met with the four top human resource directors, who then met with their regional business teams to approve a final draft.

But the process still wasn't complete. The drafters met individually with the top 9 executives in the company (the Strategy Leadership Team) to review the final draft. In October 1997 the SLT together approved it.

One more step remained. The Stockholder Relations and Public Policy Committee of the Board of Directors approved the final version, and in December 1997 it was officially introduced at the annual TI Leadership Conference.

The fourteen-page booklet was striking in design, its graphics and typeface reflecting a fast-paced global technology company. Those looking for rules would not find any, but the last page contained a list of information resources, including TI's values web site, where specific information could be obtained.

If employees agreed with the notion of decision-making through values, rather than rules, they'd find that TI's new booklet worked. Illustrative bullet sentences under each value and principle help lead to the right decision.

DID IT WORK?

We decided to test TI's new approach to see if we could find the answer to a common ethical dilemma by referencing TI's values. Using the example of employees' use of company computers to access web sites and e-mail, one might first look under Integrity. The value of Integrity is paired with two principles, one of which is "Treat others as we want to be treated." Illustrative bullet points include:

- Recognize and avoid behaviors that others may find offensive, including the manner in which we speak and relate to one another and the material we bring in to the workplace, both printed and electronically.
- Understand that even though TI has the obligation to monitor its business information systems activity, we will respect privacy by prohibiting random searches of individual TIer's communications.

Under the value Commitment, and the principle that TIers "take responsibility," bullet points include:

- Use company assets for personal purposes strictly on an infrequent basis with negligible expense to TI.

Curious employees like us now understand the answer. We shouldn't use their computers to download pornography, but if we want to check the net asset value on our mutual funds or tomorrow's weather, or perhaps send personal e-mails, the company probably wouldn't mind. And if we're unclear about whether such a use of the computer adds expense to TI, we have places to ask. If we're still in doubt, we could take the TI Ethics Quick Test in the back of the booklet.

SUGGESTIONS FOR NEXT TIME

Skooglund, now retired from TI, is happy with the process and the final product that resulted in the three TI values. He admits, however, that with the benefit of hindsight his team would have done a few things differently.

"We drafted the document in English and then translated it into 12 languages. To make sure we translated it right, we retranslated the translation back into English. We wanted to make sure that the document read in a conversational manner. That step proved to be very important but extremely challenging.

"The process worked all right, but what we should have done was postpone the final printing in English until we had finished all the translations, because there were words and phrases we would have changed, based on the feedback from the other parts of the world. We would have been more sensitive to the fact that every word has meaning.

"For example, we have a phrase in the document that insures that every employee can resolve ethics questions without "retribution and retaliation." The Japanese wanted to know what's the difference between retribution on the one hand and retaliation on the other. Well the answer is that there's not a big difference, and when that was brought to our attention, we might have changed the English version if we had the time."

Skooglund would also have orchestrated the timing of the booklet's release a little more precisely. "We wanted to get it out early, so we put it out in a bit of a naked fashion, without really explaining where it fits into the scheme of the new TI and our business objectives. Our web site, which was our primary resource link for more prescriptive information, was late. We conducted company-wide training in values and decision-making, but that didn't happen until later. It would have been better had all pieces been coordinated together."

If that's the worst criticism that Skooglund can muster about a mammoth process on behalf of a global $9 billion company of 44,000 employees, that's not too bad. He and his team deserve a great deal of credit for continuing to be the pioneers that TI has always been in the business ethics movement.

TI may have boiled its volumes of rules and regulations into just three words: *integrity, innovation, commitment,* but the reason remains the same as it has been since the company's founding. Chairman Tom Engibous said it well in his introductory letter to the new TI values document:

"If TIers are going to continue to be successful in this highly competitive global marketplace, we must be creative, fast to act, and we must work together effectively. We must make our choices in an informed manner—in the field and on the factory and office floor. We cannot do this by referring every decision to a book of rules or policies, but rather from having an understanding of an appreciation for the company's values and principles."[1]

Levi Strauss & Co. and China

Timothy Perkins
Colleen O'Connell
Carin Orosco
Mark Rickey
Matthew Scoble
Senior project team of students in the Financial Services Honors Program, School of Economics and Business Administration, St. Mary's College of California; under supervision of Dean Edwin M. Epstein

PART A

The market that is the People's Republic of China consists of more than 1 billion consumers and offers low production costs, but its human rights violations have long been condemned by international bodies. In 1993, Levi Strauss & Co. (LS&Co.) faced one of its more difficult decisions in a long corporate history. Would it continue to conduct business in this enormously promising market or honor its relatively high ethical standards and withdraw?

Levi Strauss: History and Ethical Stance

Founded in the United States in 1873, LS&Co. enjoyed consistent domestic growth for generations and began overseas operations during the 1940s. The company became the world's largest clothing manufacturer in 1977 and achieved $2 billion in sales by the end of the decade. Having offered stock to the public during the 1970s to raise needed capital, management decided fourteen years later to reprivatize in a $2 billion

leveraged buyout, the largest such transaction to date. Management's reasons included its heightened ability to "focus attention on long-term interests (and) . . . to ensure that the company continues to respect and implement its important values and traditions."[1] By 1993, LS&Co. produced merchandise in 24 countries and sold in 60.

LS&Co. has been a leader among U.S.-based corporations in recognizing the importance of business ethics and community relationships. Two 1987 documents developed by management summarize the unique values operating at LS&Co. The Mission Statement . . . affirms the importance of ethics and social responsibility, while the Aspirations Statement . . . lists the values intended to guide both individual and corporate decisions.

CEO Robert Haas frequently explains the importance of the Aspirations Statement as a way employees can realize the company Mission Statement and otherwise address factors that did not receive adequate consideration in the past. Efforts to take the values seriously have led to specific changes in human resources policies and practices. For instance, LS&Co. extends liberal domestic partner benefits, offers flexible-work programs, and has established child-care voucher programs. A series of classes for senior managers focuses on the Aspirations Statement. The company has also earned a reputation as an industry leader in facing controversial social issues. It was one of the first companies to establish programs to support AIDS victims.

In 1990, the company closed a Docker's plant in San Antonio, Texas, transferring production to private contractors in Latin America where wages were more competitive. LS&Co. provided a generous severance package for the laid-off workers that included 90-day notice of the plant closing and extended medical insurance benefits. LS&Co. also contributed $100,000 to local support agencies and $340,000 to the city for extra services to the laid-off workers.[2] Despite these efforts, the company received serious criticism for relocating the plant.

---

[1]Tom Engibous, The Values and Ethics of TI, Texas Instruments, 1998.
From the Council for Ethics in Economics series Current Issues in Business Ethics, No. 5. Copyright © 1995 Council for Ethics in Economics. Reprinted by permission.

Ethical Standards
for International Business

In early 1992, LS&Co. established a set of global sourcing guidelines to help ensure that its worldwide contractors' standards mesh with the company values. A group of 10 employees from different areas of the company spent nine months developing the guidelines. The group used an ethical decision-making model that ranked and prioritized all stakeholders to help design the guidelines. The model examines the consequences of each action and suggests a decision based on a balance between ethics and profits.

The ensuing guidelines, "Business Partner Terms of Engagement" . . . cover environmental requirements, ethical standards, worker health and safety, legal requirements, employment practices, and community betterment. Contractors must: provide safe and healthy work conditions, pay employees no less than prevailing local wages, allow LS&Co. inspectors to visit unannounced, limit foreign laborers' work weeks to a maximum of 60 hours, and preclude the use of child and prison labor.[3]

In addition, the company established "Guidelines for Country Selection" . . . These guidelines cover issues beyond the control of one particular business partner. Challenges such as brand image, worker health and safety, human rights, legal requirements, and political or social stability are considered on a national basis. The company will not source in countries failing to meet these guidelines.

The question would soon be raised: Does China meet these guidelines?

Human Rights and Labor Practices
in China

China is ranked among the world's gravest violators of human rights, although Chinese officials do not regard their actions as such. The U.S. State Department says that China's human rights record falls "far short of internationally accepted norms."[4] Two more-egregious violations include arbitrary arrest and detention (with torture that sometimes results in death). Despite laws prohibiting arbitrary arrest and providing limits on detention, a commonly referenced clause states that family notification and timely charging are not re-

quired if such actions would "hinder the investigation."[5] Judicial verdicts are believed by many observers to be predetermined.

Chinese prison conditions are deplorable, and a long-standing practice holds that all prisoners, including political, must work. Chinese officials say that the fruits of prison-labor are used primarily within the prison system or for domestic sale.

Personal privacy is severely limited in China. Telephone conversations are monitored, mail is often opened and examined, and people and premises are frequently subjected to search without the necessary warrants. China has also engaged in forced family planning, with monitoring of a woman's pregnancy occurring at her place of employment.[6] Official rights to free speech and assembly are extremely restricted, as the world witnessed during the Tiananmen Square massacre in 1989.

Regarding labor conditions, China's leaders have refused to ratify the 10 guidelines prohibiting use of forced labor for commercial purposes established by the International Labor Organization Convention. Although China has regulations prohibiting the employment of children who have not completed nine compulsory years of education, child labor is widespread, especially in rural areas. Surveys show a recent increase in the dropout rate among southern Chinese lower-secondary schools, presumably because the booming local economy lures 12 to 16-year-olds away. At the time of LS&Co.'s deliberations regarding China, no minimum wage existed and safety conditions were found to be "very poor."

LS&Co. in China

This combination of government practices and labor conditions increased pressure within LS&Co. to rethink its decision to operate in China. 1992 operations in the country generated some 10 percent of the company's total Asian contracting and 2 percent of worldwide contracting. Its Chinese operations produced approximately one million pants and shirts in 1993 and operated directly or indirectly through some 30 Chinese contractors. Over one-half the goods produced in China were shipped to Hong Kong to be refined for sale in other countries. These contracts were estimated to be worth $40 million.

LS&Co. is only one of thousands of foreign firms operating in China. The other companies, especially prominent *Fortune 500* companies with factories or manufacturing contracts in China, are cognizant of the human rights and labor conditions. Most of these companies lobbied President Clinton to renew China's Most Favored Nation (MFN) trading status, arguing that the continuing presence of U.S. companies would have a positive influence on reform. According to this viewpoint, investments made by companies such as LS&Co. could transform working conditions and thereby accelerate movement toward the social, economic, and political standards favored by the United States and other western countries.

Should Levi Strauss Stay or Leave?

In assessing the objectionable conditions in China, LS&Co. management felt it could not improve the situation because the violations were well beyond what could be remedied strictly through company communication and cooperation with contractors. At issue were practices that had to be addressed on a larger, national scale.

Leaving the country would expose LS&Co. to the high opportunity cost of foregoing business in a large emerging market. Some managers and employees felt the company would be supporting a repressive regime if it remained in China, while others argued that LS&Co. is a profit-making business enterprise, not a human rights agency. This latter group saw as positive management's acknowledged responsibility to society, but it felt the company also needed to consider its responsibilities to shareholders and employees. Some employees argued that staying in China would enable LS&Co. to improve conditions for Chinese citizens. But other stakeholders countered that remaining in China would violate the company's own guidelines about where it would and would not conduct business.

Important issues that complicated the decision include: the possibility that China might not accept LS&Co. back if the company left until conditions improved. If the company ceased production in China, it might be difficult for it to sell product there due to high tariffs imposed on imported apparel. But, some voices argued, continuing to manufacture in China would have a damaging impact on Levi's reputation, possibly putting at risk its valuable brand image.

PART B

To address the many issues regarding LS&Co.'s continued operations in China, the company organized a China Policy Group (CPG). Composed of 12 employees who together devoted approximately 2,000 hours to reviewing the China situation, the CPG consulted human rights activists, scholars, and executives in its attempt to fully address the critical issues.

The group examined all the issues highlighted in Part A and found itself divided on the question. In March 1993, the CPG delivered a report to LS&Co.'s Executive Management Committee. On April 27, after a half-day of deliberation, this most-senior management group remained undecided over what to do.

Robert Haas Acts

Confronted by the indecision of the Executive Management Committee, LS&Co.'s CEO and Chairman, Robert Haas, ended the stalemate by recommending the company forgo direct investment in China and end existing contracts over a period of three years due to "pervasive violations of basic human rights."[7] He maintained that the company had more to gain by remaining true to its ideals than by continuing to produce in China.

Reactions to the Decision

LS&Co. did not publicly announce its decision, but the news hit the airwaves with a speed and volume that surprised all involved. John Onoda, LS&Co.'s vice president of corporate communications, explained: "We never intended to get in the spotlight. . . . It was leaked and got out in 20 minutes."

Many people were highly skeptical of the company's stated intentions. Some asserted it was only a public relations ploy engineered to make the company look good. "I don't see broad support of it," claimed Richard Brecher, director of business services at the U.S.-China Business Council. "[It] would be regarded much more seriously if Levi's had made a direct investment in China."

In one respect, Brecher is right. The company did not directly invest in China; it produced its merchandise through Chinese contractors. In fact, on the sales side, LS&Co. jeans continue to sell in China through Jardine Marketing Services. Moving production contracts to other countries in Asia raised costs between four and ten percent, depending on which location was chosen. LS&Co. recognized this cost and considers it the price it must pay to uphold its integrity and protect its corporate and brand images.

Vice President Bob Dunn explained, "There's the matter of protecting our brand identity. Increasingly, consumers are sensitive to goods being made under conditions that are not consistent with U.S. values and fairness."[8] Linda Butler, director of corporate communications for LS&Co., iterated this sentiment when she affirmed that it was "better for us to honor our company's values."[9] Some even believe that the decision may ultimately prove profitable to the company. As one person claimed, "In many ways, it strengthens the brand. . . . This is a brand that thinks for itself, and these are values which people who buy the brand want for themselves. They're a badge product for youth who want to say 'I'm different.' "[10]

Impact in China

China's leadership showed no interest in the company's decision. One Chinese foreign ministry official was quoted, "At present there are tens of thousands of foreign companies investing in China. If one or two want to withdraw, please do."[11] Coincidentally, the LS&Co. decision-making process occurred as the United States considered extending China's MFN status. U.S. Trade Representative Mickey Kantor voiced his support for LS&Co. by stating, "As far as what Levi Strauss has done, we can only applaud it; we encourage American companies to be the leader in protecting worker rights and worker safety and human rights wherever they operate."[12]

More recently President Clinton renewed China's MFN trading status without requiring steps to improve human rights.[13] Clinton explained, "I believe the question . . . is not whether we continue to support human rights in China, but how we can best support human rights in China and advance our other very significant issues and interests. I believe we can do it by engaging the Chinese."[14]

The position of the Clinton administration is that the United States should continue trading with China and hope that economic involvement will contribute to improvement in the conditions of Chinese citizens. As one might surmise from the case, LS&Co. takes a different position.

ENDNOTES

1. *San Francisco Chronicle,* July 16, 1985, p. 51.
2. *The 100 Best Companies to Work for in America,* p. 502.
3. *Across the Board,* May 1994, p. 12.
4. *Far Eastern Economic Review,* April 14, 1994. p. 60.
5. *U.S. News & World Report,* August 2, 1993. p. 49.
6. Levi Strauss & Co. executive John Onoda, interview, February 1, 1995.
7. The CPG defined "pervasive human rights violations" as meaning when "the greater majority of the population are denied virtually all human rights. Most human rights violations are severe. Government has taken few or no actions to improve human rights climate and positive change is unlikely or, at best, uncertain."
8. *Wall Street Journal,* May 5, 1994, p. A18.
9. *Far Eastern Economic Review,* April 14, 1994. p. 60.
10. *Wall Street Journal,* May 5, 1994, p. A18.
11. *Far Eastern Economic Review,* April 14, 1994. p. 60.
12. *The New Republic,* June 14, 1993, p. 8.
13. *U.S. Department of State Dispatch,* May 30, 1994, p. 345.
14. Across the Board, May 1994, p. 12.

The Case of the Contested Firearms

George Brenkert
Professor and Director, Connelly Program in Business Ethics, McDonough School of Business, Georgetown University

"Our lawyers are handling the current case," said Bob Graham, CEO of Magnum Industries, a major gun manufacturer doing business across the United States. "I want you to come up with some overall plan as to where we should be going. Start

From *Business and Society Review,* Vol. 104, No. 4 (Winter, 1999); pp. 347–354. Copyright © 1999 Center for Business Ethics at Bentley College. Published by Blackwell. Reprinted with permission.

with a clean slate. What should we be doing with regard to manufacturing and marketing in our handgun division? Should we try to defend our current practices? What about altering them? In what ways? What are our responsibilities and to whom?" Those were the marching orders given to John Diller, Senior VP for Marketing. Diller had been recently hired by Graham in the hope that he could help the beleaguered firm find a way out of its current difficulties. These difficulties had been brought upon them by increasing numbers of law suits filed against them and public charges which accused them of everything from crass indifference to moral culpability in the deaths and injuries of those caused by handguns.

Magnum had been very successful in recent years in the development and marketing of new firearms. Though Magnum offered a full range of firearms, including hunting rifles and target pistols, this market had leveled off. In response, several years ago, it had introduced two other models that had attracted special attention. One was a small, semi-automatic pistol, the Defender, which had a barrel length of only 2.75 inches and an overall length of 5 inches. It was easily concealable, lightweight, and powerful. The other was a special model, the Wildfire, which they advertised as "the gritty answer to tough problems." With a 40 round detachable magazine, a combat-style trigger guard, and surfaces specially treated to resist fingerprints, it had captured the imagination of movie makers, gun magazines and chat rooms on the Internet. There was no doubt that these two models had helped shore up their sales in recent years. But it was these two models that were under attack by the anti-gun lobby and their lawyers. These attacks had not been numerous and had been dismissed by most gun makers as unlikely of success until lately. Now the situation seemed to be changing.

THE LEGAL AND MORAL COMPLAINTS

What had particularly caught the attention of Magnum (and that of all other gun manufacturers) was the verdict of a federal jury in New York City that had found nine gun makers collectively liable for several shootings, even though plaintiff lawyers could not prove what brand of gun had been used in any of the cases. The jury had determined that the manufacturers were liable because of their negligent marketing and distribution of handguns. Even though the manufacturers were ordered to pay only 13% of the full amount, one of the plaintiffs was awarded an eye-popping $3.95 million.[1]

The jury found that manufacturers had over-supplied their products in states with weak gun laws, leading to illegal sales in those with strict regulations, like New York.[2] Elisa Barnes, the plaintiff's chief lawyer in this case, claimed that "the gun makers made no attempts to keep their products from falling into criminal hands, like requiring wholesalers not to supply dealers suspected of selling the weapons to questionable buyers." "They don't care" asserted Michael Feldberg, attorney for one of the plaintiffs.[3] In describing the overall situation, Ms. Barnes said: "This huge pool (of handguns) is like toxic waste. It's been sent down the river by different companies."[4]

Now Chicago, New Orleans, Miami, Atlanta, Newark, N.J., Cleveland, Ohio and Bridgeport, Connecticut had filed similar suits; Philadelphia, Baltimore, and Los Angeles also had lawsuits under consideration. Chicago's action sought $433 million in damages, claiming that gun manufacturers have created a public nuisance and burdened the city with extra costs for public hospitals as well as extra police and fire protection.[5]

No one was denying that most large cities continue to be faced with high levels of violent crime. Many of these crimes are committed with firearms that are possessed and used illegally. Firearms were used to commit 69% of all homicides in 1995 and 68% in 1996. In 1995, there were 35,957 deaths attributable to firearms.[6] The high level of gun violence has had a particularly drastic impact on young persons; homicide is the second leading cause of death for youths aged 15–19.

In 1997, in Chicago alone, there were 8,866 robberies, 4,390 aggravated batteries and 3,963 aggravated assaults in which handguns were used. That same year, only 147 robberies were committed in the city with a firearm other than a handgun. Overall, approximately 87% of firearms used in all crimes in Chicago are handguns. A recent survey showed that 45% of persons arrested in the city obtained their guns in the illegal firearms market. Although most major cities faced the same general set of problems, they approached the legal issues in different ways.

The New Orleans suit, for example, raised a number of relatively straightforward but disturbing issues. It claimed that gun manufacturers, by failing to incorporate appropriate safety devices to prevent use by children and other unauthorized persons, had failed to "personalize" handguns. The suit claimed that at least 30 patents for personalized guns have been granted since 1976. Designs such as combination locks, magnetic locks, radio frequency locks, and encoded chip locks are among the devices patented in attempts to limit the unauthorized use of handguns. Under the Louisiana product liability statute, a manufacturer can be held liable for damage caused by a product that is unreasonably dangerous in design. Under this doctrine, just as car manufacturers have been held liable for failing to install seat belts and air bags, gun makers should be liable for failing to install feasible safety systems.[7] The New Orleans suit alleges that guns that fail to incorporate safety systems to prevent their use by children and other unauthorized users are unreasonably dangerous in design. As a result, the United States leads the world in the number of children who are killed or injured by handguns, with "an average of more than four accidental shootings of children under 15 occur[ring] each day, one of whom dies every other day."[8]

Other cities, such as Chicago (and New York), have taken a more aggressive and less traditional approach to litigation, arguing that gun manufacturers oversupply guns in nearby suburban communities. These guns then end up in Chicago, a city with one of the strictest gun control laws in the nation. This is a result, the City of Chicago contends, of the sales practices of dealers in surrounding communities as well as the manufacturing and marketing practices of the gun manufacturers.

Many of the firearms illegally possessed in Chicago were purchased in a way that should have put the defendant dealers on reasonable notice that the buyer was not obtaining firearms for his own lawful use. For example, Stanley Malone, a resident of Bellwood, Illinois, purchased fourteen pistols from Bell's Gun & Sport Shop and from Suburban Sporting Goods between August, 1994 and June, 1996. He purchased the majority of these firearms to resell to gang members, making a profit of about $60 per firearm ("a straw purchase").[9] Other individuals made similar multiple purchases of handguns over similar periods of time. Sales clerks often made recommendations to undercover police officers regarding means of purchasing the guns to avoid investigation by the Bureau of Alcohol, Tobacco, and Firearms and other authorities. Clerks frequently disregarded comments about how these "buyers" wanted to settle scores with someone. In short, the City of Chicago claims that the practices of dealers in the surrounding communities have caused a large underground market for illegal firearms to flourish within its city limits, making it easy for Chicago residents to obtain firearms in clear violation of the "spirit" of the law.

The role of manufacturers and distributors in this process, the City of Chicago claims, is to knowingly oversupply or "saturate" the market with handguns in areas where gun control laws are less restrictive, knowing that they will be resold in jurisdictions where they cannot be sold legally. By shipping large numbers of firearms to these jurisdictions, the gun manufacturers enhance their profits while disclaiming any knowledge of or responsibility for where their products end up or how they are used. They also distribute substantial quantities of firearms through low-end retailers such as pawn shops and gun stores known to be frequented by criminals and gang members. They choose not to supervise, regulate or standardize their network of distributors and dealers because such practices would limit sales in one of their most lucrative markets.

In addition, gun manufacturers are alleged to design and advertise their products to appeal to illicit buyers (both directly and indirectly), including those who wish to use them for criminal purposes. Among the design features of these handguns are

1) surfaces that offer "resistance to fingerprints"; 2) short barrel lengths and overall lengths; 3) lightweight, detachable magazines; and 4) semiautomatics that can be easily modified to fully automatic. Some models tout the fact that they do not have a hammer, meaning that they are easier to withdraw from a pocket (for quick firing) without snagging on clothing. Advertisements include descriptions of guns as "assault-type pistols" that "deliver more gutsy performance and reliability than any other gun on the market." Another is advertised as being "[c]onsidered the ultimate hideaway, undercover, backup gun available anywhere." The manufacturer, the S. W. Daniels Corporation, marketed this 9-millimeter semiautomatic pistol as the "weapon of choice of the drug lords of the 80s."[10] Another manufacturer called one of its products the "Streetsweeper."[11]

THE GUN INDUSTRY AND THE NATIONAL RIFLE ASSOCIATION

Although they rarely dispute the magnitude of crime problems in major cities, the "pro-gun" sector takes issue with the legal and moral claims made against gun makers. To most gun manufacturers the legal reasoning and arguments above have seemed sophistical and dangerous. The National Rifle Association has held that "this is the beginning [of an attempt] to accomplish . . . through the backdoor . . . what could not be accomplished through the legislative front door— the elimination of private gun ownership in America."[12]

The attempt to control the misuse of guns in this manner is fraught with other problems as well, according to the pro-gun group. "What's next," Wayne Lapierre, spokesman and CEO of the NRA asked, "blaming car manufacturers instead of drunk drivers. . . . Under this theory of law you could eliminate virtually every manufactured product in America."[13] Ralph Boyd, a lawyer who advises gun industries agreed. "The auto industry makes vehicles that exceed . . . the lawful speed limit in any jurisdiction. What would stop someone from using this type of legal theory from saying, 'Hey, you know those commercials that show cars speeding across the countryside, making tight turns on mountains, zipping around pylons on race courses? Why isn't that negligent marketing? Why isn't the auto industry responsible for all the accidents resulting from excessive speed?"[14]

Of course the gun industry has sought innovation in style, weight, size, capacity and speed so as to boost its sales.[15] It is merely responding to the increased competition it faces and the softening of its markets. In general, it feels that its responsibility ends once its products are sold to licensed distributors. "The job of policing gun runners should be left to the Bureau of Alcohol, Tobacco and Firearms, which has never required manufacturers to track their products to the street."[16] Since it considers these lawsuits to pose significant dangers to legitimate rights, the NRA has introduced legislation in at least 20 states that would preclude local governments from suing gun manufacturers and distributors. The latest bill, proposed in Florida, is the toughest, making it a felony for any local official to file a lawsuit of this type.[17]

Besides, gun makers argue, someone ought to raise some questions about the ethics of the lawyers and cities who have brought legal suits against them. Outside of the case in New York, they have little reason, based on the present and past record, to believe that these suits will succeed. Indeed, they have with remarkable consistency been rejected. Instead, they are using these suits to apply financial pressure, or coercion, against the gun makers to pay the cities what amounts to extortion. And yet there have been few complaints raised against such moral tactics. Defenders of the gun makers see this as simply another example of individuals failing to take responsibility for their own behavior and seeking Big Brother, or rather some big law firm, to do for them what people will not do for themselves. It is the morals and lawful behavior of individuals which needs to be addressed in our society, not that of the gun makers.

DILLER'S DILEMMA

In light of all these charges and countercharges and with significant legal threats in clear view, Magnum needed a coherent plan regarding both its response to the suits and the operation of its business in this new environment. John wondered what he should recommend. The theories of public nuisance, of product liability and of collective liability advanced in the lawsuits seemed to extend well beyond their past applications. Besides this was not simply a legal challenge to gun makers. Strong moral charges against the gun manufacturers were also part of the situation they faced. Magnum had to be prepared for all these charges. John wondered whether society and the gun manufacturers had responsibilities for the actions of other adults. How far back up the commercial path should responsibility be pushed and under what conditions? Should Magnum alter its design or marketing of the Defender or the Wildfire? John worried that he would have to have some idea how to answer these questions when he made his recommendation to Graham regarding both their immediate response to this legal situation and their long run approach to producing and marketing firearms.[18]

ENDNOTES

1. Chris Hawke, "Jury Finds Gun Maker Negligence Responsible for Shooting," *Agence France Presse,* Feb. 12, 1999. The case was that of *Hamilton v. Accu-Tek,* No. 95- 0049.
2. Joseph P. Fried, "9 Gun Makers Called Liable for Shootings," *New York Times,* Feb. 12, 1999.
3. *Ibid.*
4. Tom Hays, "AP-Guns-on-Trail," AP Online Feb. 12, 1999.
5. Resa King, "Firepower for the Antigun Lobby," *Business Week,* Feb. 1, 1999.
6. David Kairys, "Legal claims of Cities Against the Manufacturers of Handguns," *Temple Law Review,* vol. 71, no. 1 (Spring, 1998), p. 2.
7. "Background Information on New Orleans Lawsuit Against Gun Industry," Web page, Hand Gun Control, Feb. 19, 1999.
8. Kairys, p. 2.
9. Cf. *City of Chicago and County of Cook v. Beretta et al.*
10. Daniel Wise, *New York Law Journal,* January 7, 1999.
11. Kairys, p. 4.
12. Chris Hawke, "NRA Concerned About Gun Suit Verdict," United Press International, February 12, 1999.
13. *Ibid.*
14. Laura Mansnerus, "Cities' Suits Against Gun Makers Raise Complicated Legal Issues," *Star Tribune* (Minneapolis, MN), February 14, 1999.
15. Cf. King.
16. Cf. Hays.
17. Sharon Walsh, "NRA Pushing to Block Gun Suits," *Washington Post,* Feb. 26, 1999.
18. Thomas M. Jones gave me insightful help in preparing this case.

Bibliography

Action, H.B. *The Morals of Markets: An Ethical Exploration.* London: Longman Group Limited, 1971.

Arthur, John, and William H. Shaw, eds. *Justice and Economic Distribution.* Englewood Cliffs, N.J.: Prentice Hall, 1978.

Attfield, Robin. *The Ethics of Environmental Concern.* New York: Columbia University Press, 1983.

Barry, Vincent, ed. *Moral Issues in Business.* Belmont, Calif.: Wadsworth Publishing Company, 1979, 1983, 1986.

Beauchamp, Tom, and Norman Bowie, eds. *Ethical Theory and Business.* Englewood Cliffs, N.J.: Prentice Hall, 1979, 1983, 1988, 1993.

Becker, Lawrence C., and Charlotte B. Becker, eds. *Encyclopedia of Ethics.* vols. 1–2. New York & London: Garland Publishing, Inc., 1992.

Blackstone, William T., ed. *Philosophy and the Environment Crisis.* Athens. Ga.: University of Georgia Press, 1974.

Blackstone, William T., and Robert D. Heslep, eds. *Social Justice and Preferential Treatment.* Athens: University of Georgia Press, 1977.

Blanchard, Kenneth, and Norman Vincent Peale. *The Power of Ethical Management.* New York: William Morrow and Company, 1988.

Boatright, John R. *Ethics and the Conduct of Business.* Englewood Cliffs, N.J.: Prentice Hall, 1993.

Bok, Sissela. *Secrets.* New York: Pantheon Books, 1983.

Bond, Kenneth M. *Bibliography of Business Ethics and Business Moral Values,* 4th ed., April, 1992. Published by Humboldt State University, Arcata, Calif.

and also distributed by the Center for Business Ethics, Bentley College, Waltham, Mass.

Buchanan, Allen E. *Ethics, Efficiency and the Market.* Totowa, N.J.: Rowman & Allenheld, 1985.

Buchholz, Rogene A. *Essentials of Public Policy for Management.* Englewood Cliffs, N.J.: Prentice Hall, 1985.

Buchholz, Rogene A. *Principles of Environmental Management: The Greening of Business.* Englewood Cliffs, N.J.: Prentice Hall, 1993.

Buchholz, Rogene, A. *Fundamental Concepts and Problems in Business Ethics.* Englewood Cliffs, N.J.: Prentice Hall, 1989.

Buono, Anthony F., and Larry Nichols. *Corporate Policy, Values and Social Responsibility.* New York: Praeger, 1985.

Cairncross, Frances. *Costing the Earth.* Boston, Mass.: Harvard Business School Press, 1992, 1993.

Cavanagh, Gerald F. *American Business Values,* 2d ed. Englewood Cliffs, N.J.: Prentice Hall, 1984.

Cavanagh, Gerald F., and Arthur F. McGovern. *Ethical Dilemmas in the Modern Corporation.* Englewood Cliffs, N.J.: Prentice Hall, 1988.

Cohen, Marshall, Thomas Nagel, and Thomas Scanlon, eds. *Equality and Preferential Treatment.* Princeton, N.J.: Princeton University Press, 1977.

Commons, Dorman L. *Tender Offer: The Sneak Attack in Corporate Takeovers.* University of California Press, 1985.

Corporate Ethics. New York: The Conference Board. Research Report No. 900, 1987.

Corporate Ethics: A Prime Business Asset. A Report on Policy and Practice in Company Conduct. New York: The Business Roundtable, 1988.

Daniels, Norman, ed. *Reading Rawls: Critical Studies of a Theory of Justice.* New York Basic Books, 1976.

De George, Richard T. *Business Ethics.* New York: Macmillan, 1982. 1986.

De George, Richard T. *Competing with Integrity in International Business.* New York: Oxford University Press, 1993.

Des Jardins, Joseph R., and John J. McCall, *Contemporary Issues in Business.* Belmont, Calif.: Wadsworth, 1985.

Des Jardins, Joseph R. *Environmental Ethics: an Introduction to Environmental Philosophy.* Belmont, Calif.: Wadsworth, 1993.

Dickie, Robert B., and Leroy S. Rouner, eds. *Corporations and the Common Good.* Notre Dame, Ind.: University of Notre Dame Press, 1986.

Donaldson, Thomas. *Corporations and Morality.* Englewood Cliffs, N.J.: Prentice Hall, 1982.

Donaldson, Thomas. ed. *Case Studies in Business Ethics.* Englewood Cliffs, N.J.: Prentice Hall, 1984.

Donaldson, Thomas, and Patricia H. Werhane, eds. *Ethical Issues in Business: A Philosophical Approach.* Englewood Cliffs, N.J.: Prentice Hall, 1979, 1983, 1988.

Donaldson, Thomas. *The Ethics of International Business.* New York: Oxford University Press, 1989.

Dworkin, Gerald, Gordon Bermanto, and Peter G. Brown, eds. *Markets and Morals.* Washington, D.C.: Hemisphere Publishing, 1977.

Elliot, Robert, and Arran Gare, eds. *Environmental Philosophy.* University Park, Penn.: The Pennsylvania State University Press, 1983.

Elliston, Frederick, et al. *Whistleblowing: Managing Dissent in the Workplace.* New York: Praeger, 1985.

Ezorsky, Gertrude. *Moral Rights in the Workplace.* Albany: SUNY Press, 1987.

Fairfield, Roy P., ed. *Humanizing the Workplace.* New York: Prometheus Books, 1974.

Freeman, R. Edward. *Strategic Management: A Stakeholder Approach.* Boston: Pitman, 1984.

Freeman, R. Edward, and Daniel R. Gilbert, Jr. *Corporate Strategy and the Search for Ethics.* Englewood Cliffs, N.J.: Prentice Hall, 1988.

French, Peter. *Collective and Corporate Responsibility.* New York: Columbia University Press, 1984.

Friedman, Milton. *Capitalism and Freedom.* Chicago: University of Chicago Press, 1962.

Fullinwider, Robert K. *The Reverse Discrimination Controversy.* Totowa, N.J.: Rowman and Littlefield, 1980.

Fullinwider, Robert K., and Claudia Mills, eds. *The Moral Foundations of Civil Rights.* Totowa, N.J.: Rowman and Littlefield, 1986.

Galbraith, John Kenneth. *The Affluent Society.* Boston: Houghton Mifflin, 1958.

Gauthier, David. *Morals By Agreement.* New York: Oxford University Press, 1986.

Gert, Bernard. *Morality: A New Justification of the Moral Rules.* New York: Oxford University Press, 1966, 1967, 1970, 1973, 1988.

Goodpaster, K.E., and K. M. Sayre. *Ethics and Problems of the 21st Century.* Notre Dame, Ind.: University of Notre Dame, 1979.

Gross, Barry R., ed. *Reverse Discrimination.* Buffalo, N.Y.: Prometheus Books, 1977.

Hayek, F.A. *Law, Legislation and Liberty,* vols. 1–3. Chicago, Ill.: University of Chicago Press, 1976.

Held, Virginia. *Property, Profits and Economic Justice.* Belmont, Calif.: Wadsworth Publishing, 1980.

Hoffman, W. Michael, et al., eds. *Corporate Governance and Institutionalizing Ethics.* Lexington, Mass.: Lexington Books, 1983.

Hoffman, W. Michael, et al., eds. *Business Ethics and the Environment: The Public Policy Debate.* New York: Quorum Books, 1990.

Hoffman, W. Michael, et al., eds. *The Corporation, Ethics and the Environment.* New York: Quorum Books, 1990.

Jackall, Robert. *Moral Mazes.* New York: Random House, 1986.

Jones, Donald G., ed. *Doing Ethics in Business.* Cambridge, Mass.: Oelgeschlager, Gunn & Hain, 1982.

Kipnis, Kenneth, and Diana T. Meyers. *Economic Justice.* Totowa, N.J.: Rowman & Allenheld, 1985.

Ladd, John. "Morality and the Ideal of Rationality in Formal Organizations." *Monist,* vol. 54, 1970, pp. 489–499.

Levitt, Theodore. "The Dangers of Corporate Social Responsibility." *Harvard Business Review,* September–October, 1958, pp. 41–50.

Linowes, David F. *The Corporate Conscience.* New York: Hawthorne Books, 1974.

Lodge, George C. *The New American Ideology.* New York: Alfred A. Knopf, 1979.

Lowrance, William W. *Of Acceptable Risk.* Los Altos, Calif.: William Kaufman, Inc. 1976.

MacIntyre, Alasdair. *After Virtue: A Study in Moral Theory.* Notre Dame, Ind.: University of Notre Dame Press, 1981.

May, Larry. *The Morality of Groups.* Notre Dame, Ind.: University of Notre Dame Press, 1987.

Mishan, E. J. *The Economic Growth Debate.* London: George Allen & Unwin, 1977.

Nader, Ralph, Mark Green, and Joel Seligman. *Taming the Giant Corporation.* New York: W.W. Norton, 1976.

Nelkin, Dorothy, and Michael S. Brown. *Workers at Risk: Voices from the Workplace.* Chicago: University of Chicago Press, 1984.

Novak, Michael. *The Spirit of Democratic Capitalism.* New York: Simon & Schuster, 1982.

Nozick, Robert. *Anarchy, State and Utopia.* New York: Basic Books, 1974.

Pastin, Mark. *The Hard Problems of Management: Gaining the Ethics Edge.* San Francisco: Jossey-Bass, 1986.

Paul, Jeffrey, ed. *Reading Nozick: Essays on Anarchy, State and Utopia.* Totowa, N.J.: Rowman & Allenheld, 1981.

Peters, Thomas J., and Robert H. Waterman, Jr. *In Search of Excellence: Lessons from America's Best-Run Companies.* New York: Harper and Row, 1982.

Phelps, E. S. *Altruism, Morality and Economic Theory.* New York: Russell Sage, 1975.

Posner, Richard A. *The Economics of Justice,* 2d ed. Cambridge, Mass.: Harvard University Press, 1983.

Preston, Ivan L. *The Great American Blow-Up: Puffery in Advertising and Selling.* Madison, Wisc.: The University of Wisconsin Press, 1975.

Rachels, James. *The Elements of Moral Philosophy.* New York: McGraw-Hill, 1986.

Rawls, John. *A Theory of Justice.* New York: Bobbs-Merrill, 1966.

Regan, Tom, ed. *Earthbound: New Introductory Essays in Environmental Ethics.* New York: Random House, 1984.

Sagoff, Mark. *The Economy of the Earth.* London: Cambridge University Press, 1988.

Scherer, Donald, and Thomas Attig, eds. *Ethics and the Environment.* Englewood Cliffs, N.J.: Prentice Hall, 1983.

Schudson, Michael. *Advertising, the Uneasy Persuasion.* New York: Basic Books, 1984.

Schwartz, Barry. *The Battle for Human Nature.* New York: W.W. Norton & Company, 1986.

Singer, Peter, ed. *A Companion to Ethics.* London: Blackwell, 1991.

Stone, Christopher D. *Should Trees Have Standing?* Los Altos, Calif.: William Kaufman, Inc., 1972.

Stone, Christopher D. *Where the Law Ends: The Social Control of Corporate Behavior.* New York: Harper & Row, 1975.

Tavis, Lee, ed. *Multinational Managers and Poverty in the Third World.* Notre Dame, Ind.: Notre Dame University Press, 1982.

Terkel, Studs. *Working.* New York: Pantheon Books, 1974.

Tuleja, Tad. *Beyond the Bottom Line.* New York: Penguin Books, 1985.

VanDeVeer, Donald, and Christine Pierce, eds. *People, Penguins, and Plastic Trees: Basic Issues in Environmental Ethics.* Belmont, Calif.: Wadsworth, 1986.

Walzer, Michael. *Spheres of Justice: A Defense of Pluralism and Equality.* New York: Basic Books, 1983.

Weidenbaum, Murray. *Strengthening the Corporate Board.* St. Louis: Washington University, Center for Study of American Business, 1985.

White, Thomas I. *Business Ethics.* New York: Macmillan, 1993.

Zimmerman, Michael E., et al., eds. *Environmental Philosophy: From Animal Rights to Radical Ecology.* Englewood Cliffs, N.J.: Prentice Hall, 1993.